MW01232252

ADVANCED CRIMINAL PROCEDURE

CASES, COMMENTS, AND QUESTIONS

Fifteenth Edition

■ ■ ■

Yale Kamisar
Clarence Darrow Distinguished University Professor Emeritus of Law, University of Michigan
Professor Emeritus of Law, University of San Diego

Wayne R. LaFave
David C. Baum Professor Emeritus of Law and Center for Advanced Study Professor Emeritus University of Illinois

Jerold H. Israel
Alene and Allan F. Smith Professor Emeritus University of Michigan
Emeritus Ed Rood Eminent Scholar in Trial Advocacy and Procedure, University of Florida, Fredric G. Levin College of Law

Nancy J. King
Lee S. & Charles A. Speir Professor of Law Vanderbilt University Law School

Orin S. Kerr
Frances R. & John J. Duggan Distinguished Professor, University of Southern Califonria Gould School of Law

Eve Brensike Primus
Professor of Law
University of Michigan

AMERICAN CASEBOOK SERIES®

444 Cedar Street, Suite 700
St. Paul, MN 55101
1-877-888-1330

Printed in the United States of America

ISBN: 978-1-68328-990-6

UNITED STATES SUPREME COURT CHART

UNITED STATES SUPREME COURT
1940–1985

1940 1945 1950 1955 1960 1965 1970 1975 1980 1985

Hughes 1930	Stone	Vinson	Warren	Burger
Frankfurter 1939	Goldberg	Fortas	Blackmun	
Black 1937	Powell			
McReynolds 1914	By-rnes	Rutledge	Minton	Brennan
Douglas 1939	Stevens			
Murphy 1940	Clark	Marshall		
Reed 1938	Whittaker	White		
Stone 1925	Jackson	Harlan	Rehnquist	Scalia
Roberts 1930	Burton	Stewart	O'Connor	

1985–PRESENT

1985 1990 1995 2000 2005 2010 2015 2020

Burger	Rehnquist	ROBERTS
Blackmun	BREYER	
Powell	Kennedy	KAVANAUGH
Brennan	Souter	SOTOMAYOR
Stevens	KAGAN	
Marshall	THOMAS	
White	GINSBURG	
Scalia	GORSUCH	
O'Connor	ALITO	

The publishers wish to acknowledge that the above chart was developed from a suggestion by Dean Joe E. Covington of the University of Missouri Law School.

PREFACE TO THE FIFTEENTH EDITION

Advanced Criminal Procedure is one of two "spin-off" volumes reprinting portions of our larger "casebook," *Modern Criminal Procedure* (the other spin-off being *Basic Criminal Procedure*). While *Modern* covers the entirety of the criminal justice process, *Advanced* covers only those topics potentially included in the second of a two-semester combination of courses on criminal procedure. The terms "Basic" and "Advanced" in the two titles do not refer to the character of the subject matter, but simply to the typical sequence of the two course offerings, with *Basic* designed for the first offering and *Advanced* for the second. The two spin-offs provide smaller, soft-bound volumes for use by students who may not take both courses or simply value the convenience of such volumes.

Several eventful Supreme Court terms, numerous legislative changes and lower court rulings, and much significant academic commentary have occurred since the publication of the last edition of *Advanced*. Because of the need to integrate all of this new material, strenuous efforts were made to tighten the editing in the older cases and in the Notes and Questions. As a result, we are pleased to report, this edition is significantly shorter than the previous edition.

Advanced remains, however, a large book, not designed to be taught cover to cover. Our preference is to "include more," affording the instructor maximum freedom to shape his or her course, rather than to strive for a lean presentation that largely dictates the shape of the course. That preference is reflected in our approach to both the breadth of the topics included in *Advanced* and the depth of the treatment of particular topics.

Various steps have been taken to facilitate exploring major topics in depth. Initially, the caselaw presentation is more comprehensive than in the typical casebook. We have taken pains to set forth the views of *all* the Justices in the principal Supreme Court cases (and most major Note cases). We have retained certain older cases which contribute significantly to an understanding of new trends and developments. Additionally, we have covered significant non-constitutional sources of regulation where these sources add substantially to the totality of the regulation of a particular procedure. In doing so, we have looked to the law governing both the state and federal criminal justice systems, and have sought to account for major variations in state law. Finally, at many places, we have sought to enrich the case material with editors' Notes and Questions or extracts from illuminating and stimulating books, reports, articles, studies of administrative practice, model codes, and proposed standards.

The second course in a two-course criminal procedure package typically focuses on the post-investigation stages of the process, starting with the decision to charge. The course titles vary somewhat (with "Bail-to-Jail" a common nickname), but the coverage varies even more. We have included in *Advanced* all of the chapters contained in Parts Three and Four of *Modern*. This includes the charging decision and almost every major step in the process that follows, continuing through post-conviction review. We do not include the motion to suppress as that topic commonly is considered in the course that focuses on police investigations. The appointment of counsel and challenges to the performance of counsel are covered, but in Part One of *Modern* (and Part One of

Advanced). Part One considers topics that are often divided between the two criminal procedure courses, but sometimes are taught entirely in the "Bail-to-Jail" course (especially where students often take only that course or take that course before the course on police practices and investigations).

The post-investigation steps in the process are presented largely in chronological order. The appointment of counsel is an exception, but that chapter can readily be placed alongside the Part Three chapters. So too, the chapter on challenges to counsel's performance can be considered alongside the Part Four chapters. The bail chapter is placed ahead of the charging decision chapter (although the prosecutor's charging review often comes before the first appearance), so that the chapters on the charging decision and its review follow one after another.

As noted above, the subjects considered in Part One are often considered in the other criminal procedure course. Some of the topics considered in parts Three and Four also may be considered in other courses (e.g., Evidence, Trial Practice, Federal Courts (Chapter 29) and Media Law (Chapter 23)). Some of the topics may be omitted because they are similar to topics covered in Civil Procedure and others may be omitted because they are presented infrequently in the every-day administration of the process. Here too, we favor "including more" to provide flexibility, facilitating the instructor's ability to shape the topics covered to the instructor's own sense of priorities and the coverage of other courses offered in the particular school.

One or more of the authors has been fortunate enough to participate actively in four major criminal procedure projects: The American Bar Association's *Standards for Criminal Justice;* The American Law Institute's *Model Code of Pre-Arraignment Procedure;* The National Conference of Commissioners on Uniform State Laws' *Uniform Rules of Criminal Procedure;* and the ongoing revision of the *Federal Rules of Criminal Procedure*. We are indebted to the members of the various committees with whom we have worked for providing us with many leads and insights. We are also indebted to the many users of this book who have offered helpful suggestions on content as to this edition and previous editions. That list, like the list of our student research assistants over the years, has now grown far too long to mention each person individually.

We are especially appreciative of the outstanding secretarial assistance provided on the fifteenth edition, too often under great stress, by Cheri Fidh and Quenna Stewart. We are also indebted to Jordan Anderson, Jordan Bunn, Melissa Cassel, Mitchell Galloway, Sarah Grimsdale, Philip Hammersley, and Salvatore Mancina for their valuable research assistance.

In the past, certain matters of form were often discussed in the preface, but we have more recently added a new feature, *A Guide for Readers,* which discusses those matters (and more). It follows this preface.

And, Finally, a Dedication

In the array of names appearing on the spine and cover of this book, the first listed is that of our dear friend and able collaborator, the inestimable* Yale Kamisar. And

* We use the word "inestimable" advisedly, aware that on a prior occasion a collection of 14 individuals, including four of the undersigned "newcomers," *attempted* an estimate of Kamisar running over one hundred pages. See Tributes, 102 Mich.L.Rev. 1673–1775 (2004).

rightly so, we hasten to add, for Yale is a "founding father" of *Modern Criminal Procedure*: he is the only current author who goes all the way back to the first edition in 1965, he has at one time or another assumed individual responsibility for nearly half of the chapters in the book, and it is at his invitation that the rest of us (the "newcomers," who came aboard between the 3rd and 13th editions) became a part of this enterprise.

While Yale has not played an active role in the preparation of the 15th edition of *Modern* and its "spin-offs", it is fair to say that his influence is very much a part of the current version of this casebook. For one thing, a significant number of the cases and secondary materials that he selected and edited for the book over the years have survived the test of time and thus reappear—to the students' benefit—in the 15th edition. For another, as a consequence of working with Yale on past editions, we "newcomers" have gained a better understanding of how best to select and edit individual items so that they will collectively present the students with a challenging yet meaningful array of material on this complex subject. The guidance that Yale provided to us in prior editions has thus been carried forward into this edition!

As an expression of our appreciation for Yale's friendship, commitment, and longstanding (and continuing) influence on *Modern Criminal Procedure* and its two "spin-offs", the undersigned "newcomers" collectively dedicate this 15th edition to him. Mazel tov!

WAYNE R. LAFAVE
JEROLD H. ISRAEL
NANCY J. KING
ORIN S. KERR
EVE BRENSIKE PRIMUS

May 2019

A GUIDE FOR READERS: OF FORM AND SUBSTANCE

Please read

1. ***Principal cases.*** All of the principal cases "reproduced" in *Advanced Criminal Procedure* are edited versions of the original. Minor deletions (e.g., deleting case citations and footnotes) are made without so specifying. Other deletions, which omit several words, several sentences, or even, on occasion, several paragraphs, generally are indicated either by asterisks or by the use of brackets for the first letter or the first word in a sentence. Brackets within a sentence indicate new text substituted or added by the editors. The editing always seeks to retain the basic reasoning of the opinion edited, and, in most instances, the "flavor" of the opinion as well.

2. ***Major Note cases.*** You will note that for many of the cases described in the Notes, the case name is presented in capital letters. These "ALL-CAPS" cases are especially significant Supreme Court rulings, which are described at some length, often with quotations from the majority opinion. To facilitate promptly locating the most significant cases in a very large collection of citations, both principal cases, and ALL-CAPS Note cases are set forth in bold type in the Table of Cases.

3. ***Footnotes.*** Numbered footnotes are from the cases or articles being quoted. Since most footnotes are deleted, the footnotes included will not be consecutively numbered. Letter footnotes are editor's footnotes, both where attached to cases and to the Notes and Questions following cases. The lettering begins anew with each section.

Notwithstanding the aversion of several Justices of the modern era to more than occasional use of footnotes (most notably, Justices Breyer and O'Connor), frequent footnoting is ubiquitous in the opinions of this era. In many instances, these footnotes have significant substantive content. They may constitute an important element in defining the Court's ruling (e.g., in identifying issues that remain open for further resolution) or explaining the Court's reasons (e.g., in providing the primary response to the analysis of the dissenters). Readers are forewarned that where an edited opinion retains a particular footnote, the editor typically viewed that footnote as providing such important substantive content.

4. ***Abbreviations.*** Standard abbreviations are used throughout. This applies not only to citations but also to references to entities such as the A.B.A. (American Bar Association) or DOJ (U.S. Department of Justice).[1] When a book or article is used so frequently in a chapter as to call for a shorter citation, that shorter citation is noted in the first reference to the article or book in that same chapter (following the full citation). There are, however, two exceptions, both involving treatises cited throughout this book. Both treatises are available on WESTLAW and we have used as the short citation the WESTLAW database for the treatise. These are: Wayne R. LaFave, *Search and Seizure:*

---

[1] Although the DOJ, in September 2018, changed the title of the manual listing its internal regulations from the United States Attorneys' Manual to the Justice Manual, we continue to use the U.S.A.M. citation since major online sources (e.g., Westlaw) continue to use a USAM database in providing access to those regulations. All DOJ publications (including the Manual) are available at https://www.justice.gov.

A Treatise on the Fourth Amendment (5th ed., 2012 and annually updated) cited as SEARCHSZR; Wayne R. LaFave, Jerold H. Israel, Nancy J. King, & Orin S. Kerr, *Criminal Procedure,* (4th ed. 2015 and annually updated) cited as CRIMPROC.

5. ***Cross-references.*** Where an opinion or Note refers to a case or doctrine discussed more fully elsewhere in *Advanced*, we have included in brackets a cross-reference to that discussion. Use of a cross-reference is not intended to suggest that the discussion in the opinion or Note must be supplemented by the cross-referenced material. Rather, that material should be viewed as optional reading, available for the reader who would find helpful a more extensive description of the cited case or doctrine. In some instances, the cross-reference will be to a discussion in the same chapter and will serve to link related discussions. As noted in the preface, *Advanced* consists of Parts I, III, and IV of the larger "casebook," *Modern Criminal Procedure.* Keeping *Advanced*'s pagination identical to Parts I, III, and IV of *Modern* precluded removing cross-references in *Modern* that cited discussions in chapters not included in *Advanced.* Thus, occasional cross-references will be to the deleted *Modern* pages 208–841. Here, the reader who would like to further explore the cross-referenced case will have to look to the original opinion (or possibly exam your library's copy of *Modern*).

6. ***The Index.*** Our index is unusually detailed. It is designed to allow the reader to do all of the following: (1) find the page location for some bit of information that you recall reading at some uncertain location in a previous chapter; (2) find under a single heading all discussions of a particular concept or right that bears upon multiple stages in the process (e.g., "waiver" or "self-incrimination"); (3) find under a single heading the discussion of all practices that raise a particular legal issue (e.g., all investigative practices that present the question of what areas and interests fall within the protection of the Fourth Amendment); and (4) find under a single heading the discussions of the various issues likely to arise in dealing with a particular step in the process (e.g., the preliminary hearing). The second function supplements the numerous cross-references in the Notes and Questions in identifying the interrelationship of various aspects of the process, and the third and fourth functions provide useful checklists in reviewing the subject matter. Indeed, many students have found these index functions quite helpful in preparing for the course examination.

7. ***The annual supplement.*** This book is accompanied by an annual supplement. That supplement serves as both an "updating" supplement and a "statutory" supplement. Initially, the supplement adds cases and other materials published after the cut-off date for inclusion in the fifteenth edition. For Supreme Court cases, that cut-off date was the end of the 2017–2018 term.

The supplement also contains: (1) selected provisions of the United States Constitution; (2) selected federal statutory provisions; (3) the Federal Rules of Criminal Procedure; and (4) any pending amendments to the Federal Rules. Judicial opinions often refer to a Federal Rule without quoting the provision. At other times, the provision will be quoted in an opinion's footnote and that footnote will have been deleted in editing. The Federal Rules portion of the supplement enables the reader to examine the precise wording of the provision being applied. The statutory portion of the supplement similarly provides an essential source where an opinion or Note discusses a particular statutory provision.

In other instances, examining the statutory portion or Federal Rules portion may be needed in order to place the provision being interpreted within the framework of the totality of the statute or the Federal Rules. Thus, the statutory supplement includes as to each statute various sections beyond those cited in opinions and all of the Federal Rules. This breadth of coverage also allows for assignments that go beyond the issues raised in the materials that discuss the particular statute.

ACKNOWLEDGMENTS

Excerpts from the following books and articles appear with the kind permission of the copyright holders.

Bayley, David H., Law Enforcement and the Rule of Law: Is There a Tradeoff?, 2 Criminology and Public Policy 133 (2002). Copyright © 2002 by the American Society of Criminology. Reprinted by permission.

Beale, Sara Sun, Reconsidering Supervisory Power in Criminal Cases: Constitutional and Statutory Limits on the Authority of the Federal Courts, 84 Colum.L.Rev. 1433 (1984). Copyright © 1984 by the Columbia Law Review Association. Reprinted by permission.

Davies, Sharon, Profiling Terror, 1 Ohio St.J.Crim.L. 45 (2003). Copyright © by the Ohio State Journal of Criminal Law. Reprinted with permission.

Garrett, Brandon L., Convicting the Innocent: When Criminal Prosecutions Go Wrong (2011). Harvard University Press. Copyright © 2011 by the President and Fellows of Harvard College. Reprinted by permission.

Harmon, Rachel A., Legal Remedies for Police Misconduct, in Academy for Justice, A Report on Scholarship and Criminal Justice Reform (Erik Luna, ed. 2017). Copyright © 2017 Academy for Justice. Reprinted by permission.

Kennedy, Randall L., Race, Crime, and the Law (1997). Copyright © 1997 by Randall L. Kennedy. Reprinted by permission.

LaFave, Wayne R., Israel, Jerold H., King, Nancy J. & Kerr, Orin S., Criminal Procedure Treatise (4th ed. 2015). Copyright © 2015 by Thomson Reuters. Reprinted by permission.

Maclin, Tracey, "Black and Blue Encounters"—Some Preliminary Thoughts about Fourth Amendment Seizures: Should Race Matter?, 26 Val. U.L.Rev. 243 (1991). Copyright © by the Valparaiso Law Review. Reprinted by permission.

Tonry, Michael, Sentencing in America, 1975–2025, in 42 Crime and Justice 141 (2013). Copyright © 2013 by the University of Chicago Press. Reprinted by permission.

Whitebread, Charles, and Slobogin, Christopher, Criminal Procedure (5th ed. 2008). Copyright © by the Foundation Press, Inc. Reprinted by Permission.

ACKNOWLEDGMENTS

SUMMARY OF CONTENTS

PART 4. THE ADVERSARY SYSTEM AND THE DETERMINATION OF GUILT OR INNOCENCE

TABLE OF CONTENTS

TABLE OF CASES

The names of principal cases and major Note cases (see *A Guide for Readers*) are in bold type. For Commonwealth v. ____, People v. ___, State v. ___, and United States v. ___, see the name of the other party. For "ex. rel" (including cases starting with the name of a government), "Ex parte," and "In re," see the name following that introductory procedural phrase.

This table includes only pages on which the discussion of the case is accompanied by a full citation to the case (both case name and reporter) or a partial citation (typically the case name followed by a page cross-reference to the primary discussion).

Table of Authorities

Bold type is used in this Table to indicate that an excerpt from the cited source appears at the specified location as a main entry in the casebook.

ADVANCED CRIMINAL PROCEDURE

CASES, COMMENTS, AND QUESTIONS

Fifteenth Edition

PART 1

INTRODUCTION

■ ■ ■

CHAPTER 1

ON STUDYING THE LEGAL REGULATION OF THE CRIMINAL JUSTICE PROCESS

■ ■ ■

§ 1. THE CHAPTER'S OBJECTIVES

This Chapter provides the introduction for three different books—*Modern Criminal Procedure*, *Basic Criminal Procedure* (containing Chapters 1–12 of *Modern*), and *Advanced Criminal Procedure* (containing Chapters 1–5 and 13–29 of *Modern*). All three books are designed for use in courses on the legal regulation of the "criminal justice process"—that is, the process through which the substantive criminal law is enforced. That process starts with the investigation of possible criminality and the apprehension of the suspected criminal, the primary subjects considered in *Basic Criminal Procedure* and in Part Two of *Modern Criminal Procedure*. The process then progresses through the charging decision, a variety of pre-adjudication proceedings, the adjudication of the charge, the imposition of sentence upon a defendant found guilty, and any subsequent challenges to the conviction and sentence. These subjects are considered in *Advanced Criminal Procedure* and in Parts Three–Five of *Modern Criminal Procedure*.

Single courses on the criminal justice process typically concentrate on only a portion of the process. Thus, a course may cover the investigative stages (as in a "police practices" course) or concentrate on the post-investigative stages of the process (as in the course commonly described as "the adversary process" or the "bail to jail" course), or it may treat selective parts of both the investigative and post-investigative stages of the process (as in the courses that concentrate on the various constitutional provisions regulating the process). Though the course you are taking deals only with limited portions of the process, a general understanding of the framework of the totality of the process often will contribute substantially to your analysis of the topics covered in that course. For the legal standards and administrative decision-making as to any particular stage in the process is likely to be influenced by the interplay of the procedures applied at that stage with the procedures applied at one or more earlier or later stages in the process. Section two of this Chapter provides the foundation for developing that understanding by providing an overview of the various steps that constitute the totality of the process. The overview also should be helpful in understanding those portions of opinions that set forth the procedural history of the particular case. Many of the terms commonly used in describing procedural history are defined in section two.

The section two overview takes account, at several points, of the differences among states in the types of procedures made applicable to a particular stage in the process. That, however, is only one aspect of the divergence in the legal regulation of the criminal justice process from one jurisdiction to another. Variations also are found in the regulation of identical procedures by different states (and sometimes even in a single state's regulation of a particular procedure as applied to different types of offenses). Section three of this Chapter provides a brief introduction to the division of lawmaking authority that produces this diversity in legal regulation, and explains how that diversity is treated in our descriptions of major patterns of legal regulation in later chapters.

Even greater diversity is found in the administration of the criminal justice process. Legal regulations typically are accompanied by broad grants of discretion, often producing striking variations in the administration of the process from one local agency to another in the same state, although those agencies are operating within the same legal structure. Section four of this Chapter provides a brief summary of the factors that contribute to this diversity in the administration of the process.

Each of the sections that follow in this chapter hopefully will assist you in placing in context the materials presented in the remaining chapters. At times, those materials will explicitly direct your attention to one of the three features of the criminal justice process discussed in this Chapter—i.e., (1) the relationship of any particular procedure to the overall structure of the process, (2) the potential for diversity in legal regulation from one jurisdiction to another, and (3) the potential for substantial administrative diversity, even within a single jurisdiction. These three features should be kept in mind, however, even when not explicitly cited, as they almost always bear upon the likely administrative impact of the particular legal standards under discussion.

§ 2. THE STEPS IN THE PROCESS

A. PROCESS VARIATIONS

This section presents an overview of the procedural steps that carry the process from start to finish in an individual case. The basic objectives of the overview are to position each step within a "typical" progression of the process, to introduce the relevant terminology, and to briefly describe what occurs at each step. The chapters that follow discuss the legal standards that apply to many but not all these procedural steps. The focus there is on the procedures that commonly are the subject of litigation. This overview, in contrast, encompasses procedures that are rarely, if ever, seen as presenting legal difficulties, but nonetheless are important elements in the overall structure of the process.

There is no "standard" set of procedures that are potentially applicable to all cases in all jurisdictions. What the overview describes is the "typical" procedural steps in the progression of a "typical felony case" in a "typical" jurisdiction. That objective incorporates several important limitations, which should be kept in mind.

Initially, the overview concentrates on the procedural steps adopted in a substantial majority of our fifty-two lawmaking jurisdictions (i.e., the fifty states, the District of Columbia, and the federal system, see Note 1, p. 18). Where the jurisdictions are fairly evenly divided, that division will be noted, but where only a small group of states depart from the majority position, that minority position will not be noted. In addition, the overview describes the majority position by reference only to the basic components of a procedure; it ignores variations in other aspects of the procedure. Thus, it lumps together all states requiring grand jury issuance of a charging instrument, ignoring state variations in such matters as the composition of the grand jury and the evidentiary standard applied by the grand jury in deciding to charge.

As discussed in Note 6, p. 21, jurisdictions often draw substantial distinctions in the procedures applied to "minor" and "major" offenses, with most using the distinction between misdemeanors and felonies.[a] Our overview is limited to the processes applied to non-capital felony

[a] All but a handful of jurisdictions utilize one of two seemingly distinct standards to distinguish between felonies and misdemeanors. The federal system and roughly half of the states classify as felonies all crimes punishable by a term of incarceration of more than one year; crimes not punishable by incarceration, or punishable by incarceration for a maximum term of one year or less, are misdemeanors. Most of the remaining states look to the location of the possible sentence of incarceration. If the offense is punishable by incarceration in a penitentiary, it is a felony; offenses punishable by incarceration only in a jail are misdemeanors. States using this distinction, however, commonly also provide for possible incarceration in a penitentiary only if the offense of conviction carries

cases. It thus encompasses almost all basic procedures for serious crimes (special procedures for capital offenses are omitted, but capital offense prosecutions are relatively few in number). It does not, however, consider the sometimes quite different procedures applicable in misdemeanor cases, which far outnumber felonies (see fn. m, p. 17).

As discussed in Section Four, the exercise of discretion determines in part which procedures are applied in a particular case. A procedure may be authorized under the law of a particular jurisdiction, but not required, making its use dependent upon the discretionary choice of an enforcement official (police or prosecutor), a judicial official (magistrate or trial judge), or a defendant. Our overview, in large part, looks only to whether a procedure is authorized. Where, however, available statistics indicate that a widely authorized procedure is rarely utilized in practice in a substantial group of states, the overview will take note of that pattern of discretionary choice.

In describing the administrative functions of the police, prosecutors, magistrates, and trial courts, the overview concentrates on the basic authority common to the particular group, ignoring the institutional differences that bear upon the exercise of that authority. Thus, where the overview speaks of "police officers," it encompasses a wide array of personnel, in a variety of government agencies, who are assigned to the task of enforcing part or all of the criminal law and given the authority that distinguishes "sworn officers" from "civilian" personnel (basically, the authority to make arrests and to carry weapons).[b] It focuses on the general role of such officers, ignoring, for example, the distinctions that may exist in the jurisdictional reach and specific responsibilities of such different types of officers as the detective in a city police department and the park ranger. Similarly, the overview speaks generally of "prosecutors," a term encompassing government attorneys of several different types of agencies to which a state may grant the authority to initiate and present criminal prosecutions.[c] The overview's references to

---

a maximum term of incarceration exceeding one year. Thus, both standards, in practice, will classify as felonies all offenses punishable by a term of imprisonment of more than one year.

[b] In the state criminal justice systems, agencies employing "police officers," using this traditional definition, include: municipal police departments; county sheriffs' offices; state police departments (e.g., the state highway patrol); special-unit enforcement agencies (e.g., campus police departments, conservation departments); and regulatory agencies enforcing a limited class of criminal prohibitions (e.g., crimes relating to businesses selling liquor). The 50 states combined have almost 18,000 agencies employing police officers, with even a small state likely to have close to 100 different police agencies. Within an agency having general policing functions (e.g., a municipal police department), a variety of different employees can be involved in investigative procedures, including patrol officers, detectives, special-unit officers (e.g., vice), and evidence technicians. See CRIMPROC § 1.4(b), (c), (d).

The federal criminal justice system has over 50 agencies employing police officers. However, a half dozen agencies, located either in the Department of Justice (DOJ) or Homeland Security (HS), account for the vast majority of federal prosecutions. Those agencies are: the Federal Bureau of Investigation (DOJ); Customs and Border Protection (HS) (by far the largest federal police agency); the Drug Enforcement Agency (DOJ); the Bureau of Alcohol, Tobacco, Firearms, and Explosives (DOJ); the Secret Service (HS); Immigration and Customs Enforcement (HS); and the United States Marshalls Service (DOJ).

[c] In all but a few states, the dominant prosecuting agency is the office of an elected county or multi-county official (titles include "county prosecutor," "district attorney," and "state's attorney"). There are roughly 2,300 such local prosecuting agencies in these states. Most often, their prosecuting authority is not exclusive. The Attorney General will have an independent authority to initiate prosecution. Even where the Attorney General's authority is quite broad, however, tradition and staffing limitations will restrict its use to a limited group of offenses (often crimes having a statewide impact). Also, in many states, prosecutions for ordinance violations that are essentially misdemeanors may be brought by city attorneys as well as local prosecutors. In the few states that do not utilize local prosecutors, a state agency has authority over all criminal prosecutions, but that agency typically will operate through local offices. See CRIMPPROC § 1.4(e).

In the federal system, all criminal prosecutions are brought by attorneys who are part of the Department of Justice. The vast majority of prosecutions are brought by the United States Attorney assigned to an individual federal judicial district. The United States Attorneys are subordinate to the Attorney General, although traditionally given considerable independence. Federal prosecutions for certain limited groups of offenses (e.g., antitrust or civil rights) are brought by specialized divisions within the Department of Justice ("Main Justice"). See CRIMPROC § 1.4(e).

"magistrates" likewise encompasses judges of a variety of different courts, the common denominator being their assignment to the initial portions of the processing of felony cases and their lack of trial jurisdiction in felony cases.[d] The overview's references to "trial courts" encompasses judges of a less varied group of courts (typically the jurisdiction's basic court of general jurisdiction) having trial authority over felony charges.[e]

Finally, our overview will not take account of variations in chronology. It will assume the chronology that occurs in the majority of felony cases, although many felony cases do not follow that chronology. Similarly, the overview discusses each step as occupying a specific place in the progression of a case, but that is not true of all procedures. While some steps have a definite starting and ending point, others are continuing and overlap other steps in the process. For example, the decision on pretrial release, though it comes initially at the first appearance, is subject to possible reconsideration at several points as the case progresses.

B. STEPS IN THE PROCESS

Step 1: Pre-arrest investigation. Investigation, by the police or prosecutor, is the initial administrative step in the processing of what eventually will become a felony prosecution. Investigation is an ongoing process that continues after the second step noted below (the arrest), and sometimes beyond the filing of charges (see steps 6 and 11) as well. Because the arrest facilitates certain investigative techniques that are not earlier employed, we treat separately pre-arrest and post-arrest investigations (see step 4). However, many of the investigative procedures described as part of pre-arrest investigations (e.g., interviewing witnesses) will also be included in post-arrest investigations.

The vast majority of pre-arrest investigations are undertaken entirely by the police. Various characteristics distinguish different police investigative procedures. One of the most significant, though not formally recognized in the law governing investigations, is the distinction between "reactive" and "proactive" investigations. A reactive investigation is aimed at solving a past crime, while a proactive investigation is aimed at placing the police in a position to respond to an unknown but anticipated ongoing or future crime. The discussion that follows treats separately the investigative procedures most commonly associated with reactive and proactive aspects of

---

[d] These judges are commonly described as "magistrates" because they perform functions that were assigned to magistrates in the English common law system. In most state systems, magistrates are judges of courts of limited jurisdiction (in particular, their trial jurisdiction in criminal cases is limited to some or all misdemeanors). Magistrate courts have a variety of different titles, including "municipal courts," "county courts," "justice of the peace courts," and "district courts." Many states have more than one type of magistrate court, with different courts of limited jurisdiction operating in different parts of the states (e.g., a municipal court in urban areas and a "j.p. court" in rural areas). In some of these states, judges in certain courts of limited jurisdiction need not be lawyers.

In other states, magistrates are judges of a consolidated trial court that combines the authority of courts of limited jurisdiction and courts of general jurisdiction. Here, a separate magistrate division of that single court is assigned to trial jurisdiction over minor crimes and to the processing of the preliminary stages of felony cases.

In the federal system, United States magistrate judges are a part of the federal district court. They often are given considerably broader authority over the preliminary processing of felony cases than state magistrates. Thus, federal magistrate judges may be authorized to hold hearings and make rulings (subject to review by the district court trial judge) as to various issues described in this overview as considered by the state trial court after the felony prosecution reaches that court (see e.g., step 13 infra). See generally CRIMPROC § 1.4(g).

[e] In the state systems, these courts are commonly described as "superior courts," "circuit courts," or "district courts" (where that title is not used for courts of limited jurisdiction). Variations exist, in particular, as to whether their criminal trial jurisdiction includes some types of misdemeanors as well as felonies, and as to the character of their appellate jurisdiction with respect to rulings of the magistrate courts. In the federal system, the 94 United States District Courts are the felony trial courts. See CRIMPROC § 1.4(h).

The "Court Structure Charts" link at www.courtstatistics.org identifies the courts at each level (and each court's jurisdiction) for all 50 states, the District of Columbia, and Puerto Rico.

investigation.[f] It also considers separately the special investigative tools within the exclusive authority of prosecutors.

Reactive Investigations. General purpose police agencies (e.g., local police departments), who employ over 85% of the police officers in this country, traditionally have devoted the vast majority of their investigative efforts to reactive investigations. This is an "incident driven" or "complaint-responsive" style of policing, flowing from various aspects of local policing, including the neighborhood patrol and the 911 emergency telephone link. The police receive a citizen report of a crime (typically from the victim or an eyewitness), or they discover physical evidence indicating that a crime has been committed, and they then proceed to initiate an investigation responsive to that "known crime." Depending upon the type of information that initially identifies the crime, the pre-arrest investigative activity will have one or more of the following objectives: (1) determining that the crime actually was committed; (2) determining who committed the crime; (3) collecting evidence sufficient to support the arrest of the offender (and if readily available, additional evidence that will be sufficient to support a trial conviction); and (4) locating the offender so that he may be arrested. A wide variety of investigative activities may be utilized to achieve these objectives. Those activities include: (1) the interviewing of victims; (2) the interviewing of other witnesses present when the officer arrives at the crime scene; (3) canvassing the neighborhood for (and interviewing) still other persons with relevant information; (4) the interviewing of suspects, which may require a physical stopping of the suspect on the street and a frisking of the suspect (i.e., pat-down of the outer clothing) for possible weapons; (5) examining the crime scene and collecting physical evidence (including possible forensic evidence) found there (and where the offenses involved physical contact with the victim, also collecting possible forensic evidence from the person of the victim); (6) submitting forensic evidence for a possible identification match through the use of one of the national databases (CODIS for DNA, AFIS for fingerprints, and NIDIN for ballistics); (7) checking departmental records and computer files; (8) seeking information from informants; (9) searching for physical evidence of the crime (e.g., stolen property or weapons) in places accessible to the suspect (e.g., his home or automobile) and seizing any evidence found there; (10) surveillance of a suspect (including electronic surveillance) aimed at obtaining leads to evidence or accomplices; and (11) using undercover operatives to gain information from the suspect.

While the variation among investigations is far too great to characterize any single combination of investigative procedures as "typical," it is clear that prearrest investigations rarely take on the characteristics of popular depictions of the crime solving process. In general, investigations less frequently involve the use of scientific methods of investigation, violent confrontations with crafty criminals, or reliance upon informants. Indeed, many of the commonly depicted prearrest investigative procedures are used infrequently. Perhaps the most extreme example is the use of court-ordered electronic surveillance through court-ordered wiretaps and "bugs," a common feature of television dramas, but actually utilized in less than 3,500 of the millions of felony investigations conducted annually throughout the United States.

So too, while pre-arrest investigations obviously include those procedures cited above that are subject to significant legal regulation (e.g., searches), the central role of such procedures in the legal materials discussed in later chapters does not warrant assuming that they similarly are central to pre-arrest felony investigations generally. Indeed, the best available studies indicate

[f] Also relevant to investigations are police strategies that have a primary focus on goals other than investigation (e.g., crime deterrence), but nonetheless strongly influence the investigative process. Community policing, for example, may promote citizen-cooperation in investigations. So too, increased patrol presence at "hot spots" within high-crime neighborhoods, while aimed at deterring crime, will place officers in a better position to promptly respond to crime when it does occur, and thus increase the potential for on-scene arrests. "Hot spot" policing where it is combined with aggressive patrol tactics, as discussed below, is viewed as a component of proactive investigative policing.

that most felony arrests are the product of two elements of pre-arrest investigation that are not subject to significant legal restraints—a patrol officer observing a crime or evidence of a recently committed crime in the course of standard patrol activities and making an on-scene arrest, or an arrest being made in a public place after the victim both identifies the offender by name and directs the officer to the location at which the offender is found. The significance of these two scenarios reflects in large part the difficulties presented in identifying the offender when neither police observation nor victim identification does that.

Proactive Investigations. Although general purpose police agencies traditionally have concentrated their investigative efforts on solving known crimes, those agencies also have regularly used, in a limited fashion, proactive investigations. Indeed, in recent years, many local police departments in large communities have sharply increased their utilization of proactive investigative procedures. Also, many special-function police agencies (such as the federal Drug Enforcement Administration) traditionally have devoted a quite substantial portion of their resources to proactive investigations.

Proactive investigations are aimed at uncovering criminal activity that is not specifically known to the police. The investigation may be aimed at placing the police in a position where they can observe ongoing criminal activity that otherwise would both be hidden from public view and not reported (as typically is the case with offenses that prohibit the possession of contraband or proscribe transactions between willing participants). It may be aimed at inducing persons who have committed crimes of a certain type, including many unknown to the police, to reveal themselves (as in a "fencing sting"). Proactive investigations also often are aimed at anticipating future criminality and placing police in a position to intercept when the crime is attempted. This approach is facilitated by computer programs which use data-mining to identify high crime areas that are particularity troublesome ("hot spots") and the characteristics of both repeat victims and high-rate offenders.

A variety of different procedures may be used in a proactive investigation, with the choice of procedure largely tied to the specific objective of the police agency. Deception is a common element of many proactive procedures. In traditional undercover operations, the police assume a false identity and present themselves as willing to participate in criminal activities (as where undercover agents "set up" fencing operations or narcotics transactions). So too, deception is the key to a "decoy tactic" of providing what appears to be an easy target for victimization (e.g., a drunk with an exposed wallet or a business of the type that is readily subject to extortion). Deception commonly also is critical to the effective use of informants. Where police utilize as informants persons whose activities expose them to a criminal milieu, they are counting on the criminals associating with those persons being deceived by a belief that those persons will not take what they have learned to the police (usually because the persons are themselves engaged in criminal activity, gain their livelihood in part from criminals, or have social ties to the criminals). Surveillance through stakeouts, covert patrols, and electronic monitoring also rests on deception by hiding the surveillance.

Other proactive techniques rely on intrusive confrontations designed to place police in a position where they can observe what otherwise would be hidden or to elicit nervous or unthinking incriminatory responses that will provide a legal grounding for taking further investigative action (e.g., an arrest for a minor offense or stop). Thus, police following an aggressive motorized patrol strategy will fully utilize traffic laws to maximize stops of motorists, thereby gaining greater opportunity to peer into car windows, to ask questions, and to request consent to a search of the vehicle. They also will arrest persons for public disorder offenses (e.g., public consumption of alcohol) in part so that they can then search the arrestee and discover any contraband or weapons that he might be carrying. Similarly, under a practice of heavy field interrogation, police will frequently approach pedestrians and initiate questions to determine who they are and what they are doing. Such intrusive confrontations are most often used on a selective basis, with police concentrating their efforts on those characteristics of the social environment that suggest to them possible criminality (e.g., high-crime neighborhood, suspicious class of persons, unusual behavior). In general, such proactive investigative procedures are more resource intensive, more intrusive, arguably more likely to foster community opposition, and clearly pose more legal problems than typical reactive investigative procedures.

Prosecutorial Investigations. Not all prearrest investigations are conducted by police. For certain types of crimes, the best investigatory tool is the subpoena—a court order directing a person to appear in a particular proceeding for the purpose of testifying and presenting specified physical evidence (e.g., documents) within his possession. The subpoena authority typically is available for the general investigation of crime only through the grand jury, although many jurisdictions also grant a limited subpoena authority to enforcement agencies charged with regulating particular types of potentially criminal activities. The grand jury, although it tends to be known more for its screening function in reviewing the prosecution's decision to charge (see step 10), also has authority to conduct investigations into the possible commission of crimes within the judicial district in which it sits. In carrying out this function, the grand jurors, being a group of laypersons with no special expertise in investigation, quite naturally rely heavily on the direction provided by their legal advisor, who is the prosecutor. Thus, grand jury investigations become, for all practical purposes, investigations by the prosecutor.

Grand jury investigations tend to be used where (1) witnesses will not cooperate with the police (they can be compelled by subpoena to testify before the grand jury and given immunity to replace their self-incrimination privilege should they refuse to testify on that ground); (2) the critical evidence of the crime is likely to be a "paper trail" (or "digital trail") buried in voluminous records of business dealings (as the subpoena can be used to require production of such records where the police lack the necessary probable cause predicate for obtaining those documents through a search); or (3) the area of investigation is especially sensitive, reflecting a strong need to keep the ongoing investigation from the public gaze (an objective facilitated by grand jury secrecy requirements) or to ensure public confidence in the integrity of the investigation (an objective facilitated by the participation of the lay grand jurors). Criminal investigations presenting such special needs tend to deal with crimes of public corruption (e.g., bribery), misuse of economic power (e.g., price-fixing), or widespread distribution of illegal services or goods (e.g., organized crime operations).

Step 2: Arrest. Once a police officer has obtained sufficient information to justify arresting a suspect (i.e., probable cause to believe the person has committed a crime), the arrest ordinarily becomes the next step in the criminal justice process. The term "arrest" is defined differently for different purposes. We refer here only to the act of taking a person into custody for the purpose of charging him with a crime (the standard commonly used in the reporting of arrest statistics). This involves the detention of the suspect (by force if necessary) for the purpose of first transporting him to a police facility and then requesting that charges be filed against him. As an alternative to such a "full custody" arrest, many jurisdictions authorize the officer in certain situations to briefly detain the suspect and then release him upon issuance of an official document (commonly titled a "citation," "summons" or "appearance ticket") which directs the suspect to appear in court on a set date to respond to the charge specified in the document. In most communities, this release-on-citation alternative is only infrequently used (if at all) for felonies (in contrast to misdemeanors, where its use is fairly common).

Where there is no immediate need to arrest a suspect, an officer may seek to obtain an arrest warrant (a court order authorizing the arrest) prior to taking the person into custody. Arrest warrants in most jurisdictions are issued by magistrates. To obtain a warrant, the police must establish, to the satisfaction of the magistrate, that there exists probable cause to believe that the prospective arrestee committed the crime for which he will be arrested. The showing of probable cause may be made by affidavits or live testimony of either the investigating officer or a witness (usually the victim). The vast majority of arrests for felonies are made without first seeking a warrant (and are therefore described as "warrantless arrests").

While the arrest is part of the charging process, it contributes to the investigation. Initially, it provides an opportunity for the investigative practices that depend on the suspect's custody (see step 4 below). It also can provide significant evidence through what is described as the "search incident to the arrest." Contemporaneously with the arrest, the arresting officer usually will search the arrestee's person and remove any weapons, contraband, or evidence relating to a crime (although some police agencies encourage use of only a frisk for weapons, rather than a full search, in certain arrest situations). Under appropriate circumstances, this searching authority may be extended beyond the person of the arrestee to include a contemporaneous search of: certain types of containers being carried by the arrestee (e.g., a purse or package); the passenger compartment of a vehicle, for evidence related to arrest offense, while the arrested driver continues to have access to that area; and that portion of a room that is within the reaching distance of the arrestee where the arrest is made within a structure (e.g., a residence or office).

Step 3: Booking. After the arrestee has been secured and the contemporaneous search incident to the arrest completed, the arrestee will be transported, by the arresting officer or other officers called to the scene, to a police station or similar "holding" facility. It is at this facility that the arrestee will be taken through a process known as "booking". Initially, the arrestee's name, the time of his arrival and the offense for which he was arrested are noted in the police "blotter" or "log". This is strictly a clerical procedure, and does not control whether the arrestee will be charged or what charge may be brought. If it is determined that the arrestee is a juvenile, however, the arrestee will be transferred at this point to a juvenile facility and thereafter processed through the juvenile process (absent a subsequent decision to treat the juvenile as an adult), where that option is available under state law). Felony arrestees ordinarily also will be photographed and fingerprinted (and in many states, an appropriate sample for DNA testing will also be taken from all or a subset of felony arrestees).

Once the booking process is complete, the arrestee ordinarily will be allowed one telephone call. After that, the arrestee will be placed in a "lockup" (usually some kind of cell) pending his subsequent presentation at a first appearance (step 8). Before entering the lockup, the arrestee will be subjected to another search, often more thorough than that conducted incident to the arrest, with his personal belongings removed and inventoried. In some communities, persons arrested on lower-level felonies can gain release from the lockup by meeting the prerequisites of a "stationhouse bail program" (i.e., making a cash deposit, in an amount specified by a judicially approved "bail schedule," and agreeing to certain conduct-restrictions/requirements, including appearance in court on a specified date).

Step 4: Post-arrest investigation. One critical source made available by the arrest itself is the person of the arrestee. That source allows police, for example, to obtain eyewitness identification by placing the arrestee in a lineup, having a witness view the arrestee individually (in a showup), or taking the arrestee's picture and showing it to witnesses (usually with photographs of other persons in a "photographic lineup"). Similarly, the police may obtain from the arrestee identification exemplars, such as handwriting or hair samples, that can be compared with evidence found at the scene of the crime. As the arrestee is now in police custody, police questioning of the arrestee also is greatly facilitated (although custodial interrogation does require that the arrestee be advised of certain rights, including the right not to respond, and that he agree to forego those rights). Other post arrest investigative procedures will be similar to the procedures employed in pre-arrest investigations (e.g., witness interviews), but they will build upon information collected in the course of the arrest and the custodial investigative procedures.

Step 5: The decision to charge. For the vast majority of felony cases, the initial decision to charge a suspect with a crime is made when a police officer makes a warrantless arrest of the suspect. That decision may be reversed on internal review within the police department, typically by a "booking officer." Police departments vary in their willingness to utilize this authority. Some will decide against charging (and immediately release the arrestee) only where the arrest clearly is in error; some will more fully assess the sufficiency of the available evidence; and some will decide against charging even where the evidence is sufficient if the reviewing officer concludes that the offense can more appropriately be handled by a "stationhouse adjustment" (e.g., reconciliation with a family-member victim, or the arrestee's willingness to become an informant). Even where the police agency is willing to exercise such broad review authority, only a very small percentage of felony arrests will be rejected within the police department (although a somewhat larger percentage of felony arrestees are likely to have their booking charge reduced to a misdemeanor).

The ultimate authority over charging rests with the prosecutor, rather than the police. The prosecutor is engaged in an ongoing evaluation of the charge throughout the criminal justice process, but a prosecutor's decision not to go forward on a charge requires a different processing action depending upon whether that decision is made: (1) prior to the filing of complaint (step 6); (2) after the complaint is filed, and prior to the filing of an indictment or information (step 11); or (3) after the filing of the indictment or information. A decision not to proceed at the first stage simply results in the complaint not being filed (leading to the common description of that decision as a "no-paper decision"), and the release of the arrestee from police custody without any involvement of the judiciary. A decision not to proceed at the second stage commonly occurs in connection with the prosecutor's review of the case against the defendant prior to presenting it to a magistrate at a preliminary hearing (step 9) or to a grand jury (step 10). This decision commonly is formalized in a prosecution motion before the magistrate to withdraw the complaint (although, where grand jury review is being used, the prosecutor can ask the grand jury to vote against indicting, which similarly terminates the prosecution). A decision not to proceed further at the third stage (i.e., following the filing of an indictment or information) requires a prosecutor's *nolle prosequi* motion, which must be approved by the trial court.

Prosecutorial review of the police charging decision prior to the filing of the complaint must occur in a short time span, as the arrested defendant must be brought before the magistrate within 24 or 48 hours (see step 8), and the complaint must have been filed at that point. Not surprisingly, there is considerable variation among prosecutors' offices as to the scope of their review at this stage, with some largely leaving the decision to file the complaint to the police, and delaying their initial review of the charge in most felony cases until the second stage noted above.

Where a prosecutor decides against proceeding in the prosecutor's initial screening of the police department's charging decision (whether before or after the filing of the complaint), that conclusion most often will have been based upon anticipated difficulties of proof (e.g., the evidence is insufficient to convict, the victim is reluctant to testify, or key evidence was obtained illegally and therefore will not be admissible). However, the prosecutor also may decide against prosecution, even though the evidence clearly is sufficient, because there exists an adequate alternative to prosecution (e.g., the arrestee is willing to participate in a diversion program,[g] or

[g] A diversion program offers the arrestee the opportunity to avoid conviction if he or she is willing to perform prescribed "rehabilitative steps" (e.g., making restitution to the victim, undertaking a treatment program). The diversion agreement operates, in effect, to place the arrestee on a probationary status without conviction. In many prosecutorial districts, this is achieved by the prosecutor promising not to file charges if the arrestee complies with the prescribed conditions. In others, charges initially are filed with the court, then held in abeyance for the period during which the arrestee is to meet the prescribed conditions, and dismissed with prejudice once the arrestee meets those conditions. Some states have a statewide diversion program (often called a "deferred adjudication" program) operating under judicial supervision. If the arrestee fails to successfully complete the diversion program, the prosecution against the arrestee proceeds (with the charges then filed, if that had not been done previously).

the arrestee is on probation and can be proceeded against more expeditiously by revoking his probation), or special circumstances render prosecution not "in the interest of justice". A decision not to proceed made on reexamination of an earlier decision to prosecute (the typical situation where the prosecutor decides to drop charges at the third stage) is most likely to be the product of a change in circumstances that has either eliminated the need for prosecution (e.g., the defendant has been convicted on other charges) or substantially reduced the likelihood of success (e.g., a critical witness is no longer available).

Where the prosecutor in the initial screening process decides in favor of criminal prosecution, other decisions also must be made. Initially, the prosecutor must determine whether the proposed charge is set at the correct level, or whether there is a need to reduce or raise the offense-level recommended by the police. In many instances, the prosecutor must also consider the potential for charging multiple separate offenses (as where the arrested person allegedly committed several separate crimes in a single criminal transaction or engaged in more than one criminal transaction). Here the prosecutor must determine whether the charging instrument should allege all offenses or simply some of the offenses (e.g., only the most serious, or only those easiest to prove). Where the prosecutor chooses to proceed on more than one charge, the law may give to the prosecutor another choice—whether to bring the charges in a single prosecution or in multiple, separate prosecutions. A similar choice must be made where several people have been arrested for participating in the same crime, as each can be proceeded against separately or the group can be prosecuted jointly through a single charging instrument naming multiple defendants.

Step 6: Filing the complaint. Assuming that the police decide to charge and that decision is not overturned in a pre-filing prosecutorial review, the next step is the filing of charges with the magistrate court, which must be done prior to the arrestee's scheduled first appearance (see step 8). The initial charging instrument commonly is called a "complaint". For most offenses, the complaint will be a fairly brief document. Its basic function is to set forth concisely the allegation that the accused, at a particular time and place, committed specified acts constituting a violation of a particular criminal statute. The complaint will be signed by a "complainant," a person who swears under oath that he or she believes the factual allegations of the complaint to be true. The complainant usually will be either the victim or the investigating officer. When an officer-complainant did not observe the offense being committed, but relies on information received from the victim or other witnesses, the officer ordinarily will note that the allegations in the complaint are based on "information and belief." With the filing of the complaint, the arrestee officially becomes a "defendant" in a criminal prosecution.

Step 7: Magistrate review of the arrest. Following the filing of the complaint and prior to or at the start of the first appearance (see step 8), the magistrate must undertake what is often described as the "*Gerstein* review." As prescribed by the Supreme Court's decision in *Gerstein v. Pugh,*[h] if the accused was arrested without a warrant and remains in custody (or is subject to restraints on his liberty as a condition of stationhouse bail), the magistrate must determine that there exists probable cause for the offense charged in the complaint. This ordinarily is an *ex parte* determination, similar to that made in the issuance of an arrest warrant and based on the same sources of information (see step 2). If the magistrate finds that probable cause has not been established, she will direct the prosecution to promptly produce more information or release the arrested person. Such instances are exceedingly rare, however. Since a judicial probable cause determination already has been made where an arrest warrant was issued, a *Gerstein* review is not required in such cases (or in cases in which the arrestee was indicted by a grand jury prior to his arrest).

Step 8: The first appearance. An arrestee who is held in custody, or who otherwise remains subject to custodial restraints (as where released on stationhouse bail), must be presented before

[h] Discussed at Note 8, p. 328 of *Modern* and *Basic*, and Note 1, p. 918 of *Modern* and *Advanced*.

the magistrate court within a time period typically specified as either 24 or 48 hours. Since the arrestee is now a defendant (the complaint having been filed), and this is his initial appearance in that capacity, this proceeding before the magistrate is described in many jurisdictions as the "first appearance," (although other jurisdictions use "initial presentment," "preliminary arraignment," or "arraignment on the complaint"). Where the accused person was not arrested by the police, but issued a citation (see step 2), the 24 or 48 hour timing requirement does not apply and the first appearance may be scheduled a week or more after the issuance of the citation.

The first appearance in a felony case commonly is a quite brief proceeding. Initially, the magistrate will inform the defendant of the charge in the complaint, of various rights possessed by the defendant, and of the nature of further proceedings. The range of rights and proceedings mentioned will vary from one jurisdiction to another. Commonly, the magistrate will inform the defendant of his right to remain silent, and warn him that anything he says to the court or the police may be used against him at trial. The defendant always will be informed of at least the very next proceeding in the process, which usually will be a preliminary hearing. The magistrate also will set a date for the preliminary hearing unless the defendant at that point waives his right to that hearing.

Where the felony defendant is not represented by counsel at the first appearance, the magistrate's responsibilities include making certain that the defendant is aware of his right to be represented by counsel, including the right to counsel funded by the state if the defendant is indigent. In some jurisdictions the indigency determination is made at the first appearance, and the magistrate initiates the appointment of state-funded counsel on a finding of indigency. In others, the indigency determination will be made prior to the first appearance, by a court administrator or public defender, and the counsel assigned to the indigent defendant will be present at the first appearance.

One of the most important first-appearance functions of the magistrate is to fix the terms under which the defendant can obtain his release from custody pending the disposition of the charges against him. This process is still described as "setting bail," although release today often is conditioned on non-financial requirements (e.g., a promise to appear and a restriction on travel) rather than traditional "bail" (i.e., the posting of a security, such as cash or a bond). As discussed in Chapter 13, setting bail requires consideration of information relating to both the alleged offense and the defendant. This information may be collected prior to the first appearance (typically by a pretrial services agency) or at the first appearance itself. Many jurisdictions have a "preventive detention" exception to the setting of bail for certain types of felonies. Here, upon a necessary finding of danger or likely flight, the magistrate does not set release terms, but instead orders that the defendant continue to be held in custody pending final disposition of the charges. A 2009 study of the processing of felony defendants in large urban counties (see fn. q, p. 18) found that 38% of the felony defendants were detained until the final case disposition (typically because they failed to meet financial conditions for release, rather than application of a preventive detention provision).

Step 9: Preliminary hearing. Following the first appearance, the next scheduled step in a felony case generally is the preliminary hearing (sometimes called a preliminary "examination"). All but a handful of our fifty-two jurisdictions grant the felony defendant a right to a preliminary hearing, to be held within a specified period (typically, within a week or two if the defendant does not gain pretrial release and within a few weeks if released). However, the actual use of the preliminary hearing varies considerably from one state to another (and sometimes from one judicial district to another in the same state). The right to a preliminary hearing is "mooted" if a grand jury issues an indictment (thereby establishing probable cause) prior to the scheduled hearing. Prosecutors in indictment jurisdictions (see step 10 infra), in particular, often use this authority to preclude some or most preliminary hearings. Several states allow for a similar mooting practice by "direct filing" of a particular form of information. Finally, in some jurisdictions, defendants who intend to plead guilty commonly waive the hearing and move directly to the trial court. The end result is that, notwithstanding almost all jurisdictions recognizing preliminary hearings, the hearings are held in almost all felony prosecutions in some states, in a substantial majority in others, in a significant minority in still others, and almost never in a smaller grouping.

Where the preliminary hearing is held, it will provide, like grand jury review, a screening of the decision to charge by a neutral body. In the preliminary hearing, that neutral body is the magistrate, who must determine whether, on the evidence presented, there is sufficient evidence to send the case forward. Ordinarily, a magistrate will already have determined that probable cause exists as part of the *ex parte* screening of the complaint (see step 7). The preliminary hearing, however, provides screening in an adversary proceeding in which both sides are represented by counsel. Typically, the prosecution will present its key witnesses and the defense will limit its response to the cross-examination of those witnesses (although the defense has the right to present its own witnesses and may occasionally do so).

If the magistrate concludes that the evidence presented is sufficient for the prosecution to move forward (usually that it establishes probable cause), she will "bind the case over" to the next stage in the proceedings. In an indictment jurisdiction (see step 10), the case is bound over to the grand jury, and in a jurisdiction that permits the prosecution by information (see step 11), the case is bound over directly to the general trial court. If the magistrate finds that the evidence supports only a lesser charge (e.g., a misdemeanor), the charge will be reduced. If the magistrate finds that the evidence is insufficient to support any charge, the prosecution will be terminated.

Step 10: Grand jury review. Although almost all fifty-two jurisdictions still have provisions authorizing grand jury screening of felony charges, such screening is mandatory only in those jurisdictions requiring felony prosecutions to be instituted by an indictment, a charging instrument issued by the grand jury. In a majority of the states, the prosecution is now allowed to proceed either by grand jury indictment or by information at its option. Because prosecutors in these states commonly choose to prosecute by information, the states providing this option commonly are referred to as "information" states. Eighteen states, the federal system, and the District of Columbia currently require grand jury indictments for all felony prosecutions. These jurisdictions commonly are described as "indictment" jurisdictions. Four additional states are "limited indictment" jurisdictions, requiring prosecution by indictment only for their most severely punished offenses (capital, life imprisonment, or both).

The grand jury is selected randomly from the same pool of prospective jurors (the "venire") as the trial jury. Unlike the trial jury, however, it sits not for a single case, but for a term that may range from one to several months. As in the case of the magistrate at the preliminary hearing, the primary function of the grand jury is to determine whether there is sufficient evidence to justify a trial on the charge sought by the prosecution. The grand jury, however, participates in a screening process quite different from the preliminary hearing. It meets in a closed session and hears only the evidence presented by the prosecution. The defendant has no right to be present or to offer his own evidence.

If a sufficient number of grand jurors (typically a majority) conclude that the prosecution's evidence is sufficient, the grand jury will issue the indictment requested by the prosecutor. The indictment will set forth a brief description of the offense charged, and the grand jury's approval of that charge will be indicated by its designation of the indictment as a "true bill." If the grand jury refuses to approve the proposed indictment, the charges against the defendant will be dismissed.

Step 11: The filing of the indictment or information. If an indictment is issued, it will be filed with the general trial court and will replace the complaint as the accusatory instrument in the case. Where a grand jury indictment either is not required under the law of the jurisdiction, or has been waived, an information will be filed with the trial court. Like the indictment, the information is a charging instrument which replaces the complaint, but it is issued by the prosecutor rather than the grand jury.

Step 12: Arraignment on the information or indictment. After the indictment or information has been filed, the defendant is arraigned—i.e., he is brought before the trial court, informed of the charges against him, and asked to enter a plea of guilty, not guilty, or, as is permitted under some circumstances, *nolo contendere* (a plea in which the defendant accepts a judgment of conviction, but does not admit guilt). In the end, most of those felony defendants whose cases reach the trial court will plead guilty. At the arraignment, however, they are likely to enter a plea of not guilty. Where there has not been a preliminary hearing, defense counsel probably will not be fully apprized of the strength of the prosecution's case at this point in the proceedings. Also, the vast majority of guilty pleas in felony cases are the product of plea negotiations with the prosecution, and in many places, that process does not start until after the arraignment. When the defendant enters a plea of not guilty at the arraignment, the judge will set a trial date, but the expectation generally is that the trial will not be held.

Step 13: Pretrial motions. In most jurisdictions, a broad range of objections must be raised by a pretrial motion. Those motions commonly present challenges to the institution of the prosecution (e.g., claims regarding the grand jury indictment process), attacks upon the sufficiency of the charging instrument, challenges to the scope, location, and timing of the prosecution (claiming improper joinder of charges or parties, improper venue, or violation of speedy trial requirements), requests for discovery when there is a dispute over what is discoverable,[i] and requests for the suppression of evidence allegedly obtained through a constitutional violation. While some pretrial motions are made only by defendants who intend to go to trial, other motions (e.g., for discovery) may benefit as well defendants who expect in the end to plead guilty. Nevertheless, pretrial motions are likely to be made in only a small portion of the felony cases that reach the trial court. Their use tends to vary with the nature of the case. In narcotics cases, for example, motions to suppress are quite common. In the typical forgery case, on the other hand, pretrial motions of any type are quite rare.

Step 14: Guilty plea negotiation and acceptance. Guilty pleas in felony cases most often are the product of a plea agreement under which the prosecution offers certain concessions in return for the defendant's plea. The offering of concessions lies in the discretion of the prosecutor, and as discussed in Chapter 22, there is considerable variation among prosecutors' offices as to what types of concessions will be offered to defendants charged with particular offenses. There also is considerable variation as to the negotiation process itself (e.g., whether the prosecutor will actually "bargain," or simply present a "take-it-or leave-it offer"). Where a plea is entered as result of an agreement with the prosecutor, that agreement must be set forth on the record before the trial court. The trial judge will review the agreement to ensure that its terms are within the law, but cannot second-guess its soundness as a matter of criminal justice policy.

The trial judge's primary responsibility in accepting a guilty plea is to ensure that the defendant understands both the legal consequences of entering a guilty plea and the terms of the plea agreement. If that understanding is present, and there exists a factual basis for the plea

[i] Discovery is a process whereby the prosecution discloses to the defense some or all of the evidence it intends to use at trial and certain other evidence within its possession or control that may be useful to the defense. Jurisdictions vary considerably as to the range of discovery that the prosecution must provide. They generally require the defense to reciprocate by providing somewhat narrower discovery to the prosecution. This may lead to pretrial prosecution motions challenging the defense's failure to provide discovery.

(typically provided by the defendant admitting in court the acts constituting the offense), the plea will be accepted and a date set for sentencing.

Step 15: The trial. Assuming that there has not been a dismissal and the defendant has not entered a guilty plea (or a *nolo contendere* plea), the next step in the criminal process is the trial. In most respects, the criminal trial resembles the civil trial. There are, however, several distinguishing features that are either unique to criminal trials or of special importance in such trials. These include: (1) the presumption of defendant's innocence; (2) the requirement of proof beyond a reasonable doubt; (3) the right of the defendant not to take the stand; (4) the exclusion of evidence obtained by the state in an illegal manner; and (5) the more frequent use (by the prosecution) of incriminating statements previously made by the defendant (often to police).

In felony cases, the defendant is entitled to a trial by jury, but in many jurisdictions, for certain types of offenses, defendants commonly will waive the jury, in favor of bench trial. Where the trial is to a jury, the verdict, whether for acquittal or conviction, in all but a few states, must be unanimous. Where the jury cannot reach agreement, it is commonly described as a "hung jury". Such a jury is discharged without reaching a verdict, and the case may be retried.

The median time frame from the arrest of the defendant to the start of the felony trial can exceed a year in judicial districts with slow moving dockets, but for most judicial districts, it is likely to fall within the range of 5–8 months. The median will be influenced, in particular, by the mix of jury and bench trials, as the time frame tends to be considerably longer for jury trials. While most jurisdictions have speedy trial requirements that impose time limits of 6 months or less, there are various excludable time periods (for factors such as witness unavailability and the processing of motions) which commonly extend the time limit by at least a few months.

In state courts, most jury trials will be completed within 2–3 days. A key variable in setting the length of the trial is the case type, as certain types of offenses (most notably capital homicides) produce trials substantially longer than the typical felony. Thus, the special character of the federal docket (in particular, the complex conspiracy and white collar offenses) explains in large part why trials lasting a week or more are so common in the federal courts. In general, trials to the bench are considerably shorter, and in state courts, unlikely to last more than a day.

Step 16: Sentencing. Following conviction, the next step in the process is the determination of the sentence. In all but a handful of jurisdictions (which allow for jury sentencing, even apart from capital punishment), the sentence determination is the function of the court. Basically three different types of sentences may be used: financial sanctions (e.g., fines, restitution orders); some form of release into the community (e.g., probation, unsupervised release, house arrest); and incarceration in a jail (for lesser sentences) or prison (for longer sentences). Legislatures will place limits on the length of incarceration and the amount of the fine. Quite often, sentencing law further restricts the available options by prohibiting community release and requiring a mandatory minimum for incarceration. Where options exist, states vary considerably in shaping the court's authority in choosing among options, particularly those relating to incarceration. The most common approaches are: (1) allowing the sentencing judge almost open-ended discretion in choosing between options, (2) channeling discretion through the use of sentencing guidelines, directing the judge to weigh specified offender and offense characteristics, and (3) creating a presumptive sentence, with the judge having discretion to depart from that presumption upon concluding that special circumstances so dictate. When the legislation prohibits the imposition of a certain term of incarceration without first finding an aggravating circumstance, that finding becomes a jury issue rather than an aspect of discretionary judicial sentencing.

The process utilized in felony sentencing varies to some extent according to whether judicial discretion is broad or is channeled by guidelines or legislative presumptions. In all jurisdictions, the process is designed to obtain for the court information beyond that which will have come to its attention in the course of trial or in the acceptance of a guilty plea. That information is provided primarily through a presentence report prepared by the probation department, although the prosecution and defense commonly will be allowed to present additional information and to challenge the information contained in the presentence report. The presentation of this information is not subject to the rules governing the presentation of information at trial. The rules of evidence do not apply, and neither the prosecution nor the defense has a right to call witnesses or to cross-examine the sources of adverse information presented in the presentence report or in any additional documentation presented by the opposing side. However, where the sentencing authority of the judge is channeled by reference to weighing specific factors, a judge commonly is required to make a preponderance-of-the-evidence finding as to those factors. Here, if relevant facts are in dispute, the court commonly will find it necessary to hold an evidentiary hearing and to utilize trial-type procedures to resolve that dispute.

Step 17: Appeals.[j] The federal system and over 3/4ths of the states have both an intermediate appellate court (IAP) and a high court (commonly titled "supreme court"), which functions as the "court of last resort" (COLR). Here, defendants convicted in the general trial court ordinarily may obtain appellate review as of right in the IAC, and further review in the COLR at the discretion of that court. In states with only a COLR, appellate review in that court commonly is granted as of right. Where the convicted defendant entered a guilty plea, the cognizable claims on appeal are limited by waivers occurring in the entry of the plea (with several states also making appellate review discretionary). As to sentencing, cognizable claims on appeal include all procedural errors, but review as to the substance of the sentence varies among the jurisdictions, with many considering only a very narrow class of challenges. Even where review is of right and includes significant sentencing review, only a small percentage of conviced defendants will seek review (see fn. p, p. 18).

Step 18: Collateral remedies. After the appellate process is exhausted, imprisoned defendants may be able to use postconviction procedures to challenge their conviction, although the grounds for challenge tend to be limited (e.g., to constitutional violations). Since these procedures are separate from the basic criminal justice process (indeed, some are viewed as civil in nature), they are described as a group as "collateral remedies." Perhaps the most prominent of these collateral remedies is the federal writ of habeas corpus (discussed in Chapter 29), which Congress has expanded to allow state prisoners to raise federal constitutional challenges to their state convictions in federal courts.

C. AN EMPIRICAL PICTURE[k]

The 1967 Report of President Lyndon Johnson's Commission on Law Enforcement and Administration of Justice included the most prominent attempt to present an empirical picture of the criminal justice process as it operates in the 50 states and the District of Columbia. The Commission did that with a flow chart, which did not include numbers, but did indicate through the "differing weights [i.e., width] of line * * * the relative volume of cases disposed of at various points in the system." The introduction to the flow chart warned that its representation was "only suggestive since no nationwide data of this sort exists." Notwithstanding the subsequent increase in police agency participation in the FBI's Uniform Crime Report (UCR) program, the creation of the Bureau of Justice Statistics (BJS) within DOJ (with a Congressional directive to give emphasis in its collection of statistics to "the problems of state and local justice systems"), and the creation

[j] The focus here is on defense appeals from a conviction. The prosecution may appeal from certain types of dismissals, but may not appeal from an acquittal. Since the percentage of dismissals over the objection of the prosecution is low, and prosecutors do not regularly appeal such rulings (even when they could do so), prosecution appeals are infrequent as compared to defense appeals.

[k] CRIMPROC § 1.11 ("Criminal Justice Statistics") cites the sources of the data described in this subsection as well as other sources that contribute to an empirical picture of the process.

of Statistical Analysis Centers in a substantial majority of the states, "national" totals (even allowing for the use of extrapolation to account for non-reporting jurisdictions) are available only as to a few major steps in the criminal justice process. Indeed, even at the individual state level, where coverage is broader, the additional processing statistics relate primarily to the judicial portion of the process, and a majority of the states fail there to provide comprehensive coverage of various key judicial dispositions.

Post-2010 national statistics are largely limited to arrests, prosecutions, and correctional populations. The FBI's UCR provides a national total for "arrests" (encompassing persons "processed by arrest, citation, or summons") for all non-traffic offenses and DUI (but not other motor vehicle violations constituting crimes under state law).[l] In 2017, the UCR national arrest estimate was roughly 10.5 million arrests, reflecting a 26% decrease from the 2007 total.

A national total for criminal prosecutions can be estimated based on state caseload statistics reported by the National Center for State Courts' Court Statistics Project (CSP), and the caseload statistics for the federal courts (less than 2% of the national total). The CSP caseload estimate for the 50 states, the District of Columbia, and Puerto Rico treats separately the criminal caseloads of the magistrate courts and the trial courts of general jurisdiction. Where the state court system is not "consolidated," the potential exists for double counting of felony prosecutions as they are part of the caseload of both court tiers. However, the CSP's 2015 Court Caseload Report identified the double-counting states, allowing for the deduction of the double counted prosecutions from the combined total for all courts. This produced a combined estimate for the CSP jurisdictions and the federal system of roughly 16.7 million. That estimate is supported by a study combining CSP and state reports, which estimated that 13.2 million misdemeanor cases were filed in 2016.[m]

The BJS provides an annual estimate on correctional population as of a particular day in the year. For 2016, that population was roughly 6,600,000, divided between probation (3,673,000), parole (874,800), prison (1,505,400) and local jail (740,700, with 35% sentenced and 65% awaiting court action on a current charge).[n] An earlier survey of state courts provided additional national data relating to sentencing. It reported 1,132,290 felony convictions of adults in 2006, with 41%

---

[l] The exclusion of arrests for other motor vehicle violations has statistical significance. In states where many motor vehicle prohibitions remain criminal, most of those crimes are processed apart from traditional misdemeanors (often in an administrative fashion). However in those states and in states that have largely decriminalized motor vehicle violations, a small group of motor vehicle crimes (e.g., driving without a license or with a revoked or suspended license) have penalties similar to DUI (including, in some instances, mandatory jail sentences) and are treated procedurally in the same fashion. The DUI category typically accounts for roughly 10% of the UCR's arrest total. Data from states that have otherwise decriminalized motor vehicle offenses indicate that arrests and prosecutions for other criminal motor vehicle offenses outnumber DUI, sometimes severalfold.

The UCR's arrest table utilizes 28 crime categories, including a catchall "all other offenses." Apart from that category, only "other assaults" (assaults not in the UCR's "aggravated assault" category) and "drug abuse violations" exceeded the DUI category in 2017, with the drug category accounting for roughly 15% of all arrests. Because various categories include both felonies and misdemeanors, the UCR's total is not readily divided into misdemeanor and felony arrests. Both the UCR and the BJS arrest report also provide a breakdown by age, gender, race and "ethnicity" (Hispanic/Latino). However, those breakdowns are not based on all the arrests reported in the national total, but on the reports received from a somewhat smaller group of participating police agencies.

[m] The ratio of misdemeanor prosecutions to felony prosecutions varies considerably from one state to another (with the reported felony portion as high as 50% in one state and as low as 7% in another). However, a misdemeanor/felony ratio ranging between 3:1 and 4:1 probably describes a majority of the states.

[n] The 2016 total marked a continuation of the decrease in the proportion of the adult population in correctional control. That decrease began in 2007 and stood at 2,640 per 100,000 adult residents in 2016. The imprisonment rate had increased roughly 500% from the mid-1970s to 2007, producing a condition commonly described as a uniquely American state of "mass incarceration."

The prison incarceration total reflects considerable turnover within the year. In 2016, the prison total was roughly 1,500,000, with roughly 600,000 inmates having been admitted that year (71% on new-sentence commitments and 29% on post-custody supervisory violations). Over the year, slightly under 625,000 inmates had been released, with an average time served of 2.6 years and a median time served of 1.3 years. Slightly under 5% of the first-released prisoners had served more than 10 years.

sentenced to prison, 28% sentenced to jail (term of less than one year), 27% placed on probation (i.e., probation only, not jail plus probation), and 4% in a catchall "other" category. Of course, the percentages varied with offense (with prison incarceration at 93% for "murder/nonnegligent manslaughter," and 32% for "fraud/forgery"), as did the lengths of the incarceration sentences (although the median for all prison-incarceration sentences was 36 months). The same survey reported on method of conviction—94% guilty plea, 4% jury trial, and 2% bench trial.[o]

As of 2016, as many as 20 states can be described as providing "comprehensive data" on the disposition of felony cases, at least with respect to dispositions before the trial court of general jurisdiction. Their caseload reports provide data on both outcomes and mode of disposition. Looking only to final dispositions (e.g., excluding transferred cases), the state conviction rates fall between 54% (in a state making heavy use of diversions) and 89%.[p] The primary mode of disposition is the guilty plea (ranging from 56% to 84%), followed by a category labeled "dismissal" (including both dismissals on the motion of the prosecutor and dismissals in response to a defense objection).[q] Where the state does not use a separate category for diversions, the dismissals account for almost all of the non-convictions. As noted in both the state disposition charts and a separate survey by CSP, most states have jury trial rates of 2.2% or less and bench trial rates of 1% or less, and a substantial majority of those trials end in convictions rather than acquittals.[r]

Slightly more than a dozen states (including a few of the largest states) also track the disposition of at least non-traffic misdemeanor prosecutions. Here, non-conviction rates tend to be much higher in light of the heavy use of diversion and dismissals. Most of the reporting states have conviction rates of less than 60%. Convictions are almost exclusively the product of guilty pleas. As noted in both the state reports and a CSP study, misdemeanor trial rates (combining bench and jury) tend to be below 2%, although occasional outlier states will have a slightly higher rate of bench trials (e.g., 4%). Still, considering the number of misdemeanors, even a 1% trial rate is likely to produce more misdemeanor trials than felony trials and a combined total of over 200,000 criminal trials annually.

§ 3. DIVERSITY IN LEGAL REGULATION

1. ***Fifty-two lawmaking jurisdictions.*** Under the United States' version of federalism, each of the fifty state governments retains the authority to enact its own criminal code. Each state

---

[o] Consideralso the BJS report on a 2007 survey of state prosecutors offices. The prosecutors reported 2,176,723 convictions (at any level) in "felony cases" closed that year, with 73,274 "felony jury trial verdicts." As to jury trials, note also the lower percentages discussed in the text at note r infra.

[p] Appellate review will alter the results in less than 1% of the trial court convictions. Less than 5% of the convicted defendants will seek appellate review and their success rate (counting any favorable outcome) will not exceed 20% in the vast majority of states. Thus, for 2016, state IAC and COLR appellate courts resolved under 70,000 appeals, with 12% of those resolutions producing either a reversal, remand, or modification of conviction or sentence.

[q] While the criminal justice system is often described as a "system of guilty pleas," with reference made to guilty plea rates in excess of 95%, that percentage and emphasis focuses on convictions. When non-convictions are taken into account, the guilty plea still dominates, but not so completely. The percentages quoted above come from disposition charts that refer only to trial court dispositions. The percentage of dismissals does not include dismissals before the magistrate. The BJS Urban County Study, focusing on the nation's 75 largest counties (accounting for more that 1/3 of the population), tracks dispositions from the filing of the "felony arrest charge (typically the complaint filed before the magistrate). The latest report, for 2009, listed the following percentages—53% guilty plea to a felony; 11% guilty plea to a misdemeanor; 2% conviction by trial; 1% acquittal at trial; 25% dismissal; and 9% "other outcomes" (defined as including "diversion and deferred adjudication"). By far the highest trial rate (30%) was for murder. Conviction rates varied from 84% for "driver related" felony charges to 56% for felony assault charges.

Data from the federal system reflects a greater dominance of guilty pleas for all dispositions in the district court (with a 90% felony caseload). For 2016, those dispositions were: 86% guilty pleas; 9% dismissals; 0.4% bench trials (with 0.3% bench trial convictions); 2.1% jury trials (with 1.8% jury trial convictions).

[r] The CSP study of 23 states for jury trials and 23 for bench trials did note several outlier states, with felony jury trial rates in the range of 7–10% or felony bench trial rates in the range of 5–9%.

also retains the power to provide for the enforcement of that criminal code through agencies and procedures that it creates. That authority has been used in each state to establish what is basically a single, general criminal justice process applicable throughout the state (although that process may vary with the level of the offense, as discussed in Note 6 infra). Congress has added to these fifty state criminal justice processes its two distinct federal criminal justice processes. First, it has created a separate criminal justice process for the District of Columbia, used to enforce a separate criminal code that applies only in the District. Second, it has created a criminal justice process for the enforcement of the general federal criminal code, which applies throughout the country. This process utilizes the national law enforcement agencies and relies on prosecutions brought in the federal district courts, and is commonly described as "the federal system."

In many fields in which both state and federal governments exercise regulatory authority, the enforcement of federal law by federal officials so clearly dominates the field that law school courses focus almost exclusively on the federal enforcement system. A similar focus would be most inappropriate in the field of criminal procedure. While the federal system may be the most prominent of the nation's fifty-two criminal justice systems, the traditional statistical measures of criminal justice systems rank it simply as one of the larger, but hardly the largest, of our fifty-two systems. Moreover, when the federal system is compared to the state systems as a group, the combined state systems clearly dominate, as they account for the vast bulk of the nation's criminal justice workload (roughly 96% of all felony prosecutions and 98.5% of all criminal prosecutions). Thus, to understand the criminal justice process in its everyday operation, one must take account of the laws regulating the fifty state criminal justice processes, as well as the two federal processes.

2. ***The unifying role of federal constitutional regulation.*** Taking account of fifty-two different criminal justice systems would be a less daunting task if the fifty-two jurisdictions were subject to a single source of law that mandated an exclusive, comprehensive regulation of the process in all fifty-two jurisdictions. But there is no such law. The regulation provided by the federal constitution (as interpreted by the Supreme Court) does, however, provide a common foundation that shapes major portions of the process in all fifty-two jurisdictions.

The Bill of Rights of the Federal Constitution includes a large number of guarantees dealing specifically with the criminal justice process—all the guarantees of the Fourth, Sixth, and Eighth Amendments, and with the inclusion of the Fifth Amendment's due process clause (which clearly applies to criminal proceedings, although extending also to certain non-criminal proceedings), all but one of the guarantees (the just compensation guarantee) of the Fifth Amendment. As discussed in Chapter Two, these provisions bear upon the state criminal justice processes as well as the federal. Applying a "selective incorporation" reading of the Fourteenth Amendment's due process clause (which explicitly governs state governmental activities), the Court has concluded that almost all of these criminal-process Bill of Rights guarantees are fully applicable to the state criminal justice processes. The Supreme Court also has held that the due process clauses of the Fifth and Fourteenth Amendment have an independent content, extending beyond the guarantees specifically directed at the criminal process, and imposing further constitutional limitations upon the state and federal criminal justice processes.

In light of their scope and their applicability to all fifty-two jurisdictions, the applicable federal constitutional guarantees constitute the traditional starting point for describing the law regulating the criminal justice processes of the United States. All fifty-two jurisdictions must, at a minimum, meet the requirements of these constitutional guarantees (as interpreted by the Supreme Court). Constitutional regulation, however, is neither comprehensive nor exclusive. Initially, constitutional regulation does not govern all aspects of the criminal justice process. As to many steps in the process, constitutional regulation is limited to only a few aspects of the applicable procedures. Secondly, even where the constitutional regulation is comprehensive, the states remain free to go beyond the constitutionally mandated minimum and impose more rigorous safeguards.

The significance of federal constitutional regulation varies with the different steps in the criminal justice process. Three models provide a rough picture of that variation. First, as to some procedures (e.g., the preliminary hearing), the Constitution says very little. Here, legal regulation comes primarily from the laws of the individual jurisdiction. Second, as to other procedures, such as searches, the constitutional regulation is so comprehensive as to rival the Internal Revenue Code in its detail and complexity. Here, constitutional standards tend to dominate. Some jurisdictions may add more rigorous standards, and many may add their own requirements as to minor aspects of administration, but the constitutional standards provide the critical legal standards for the vast majority of the fifty-two jurisdictions in regulating the particular procedure. Third, for still other elements of the process (e.g., a trial by jury), the federal constitution provides a substantial set of regulations, but those regulations are not comprehensive in their scope and are not dominant in shaping major aspects of state law. Here, a fairly large group of states will impose under their own laws standards more rigorous than the constitutional prerequisites, and almost all states will seek in their state law to regulate other aspects of the particular step that are not treated by the constitutional standard.

Our discussion of a particular step in the process will always start by considering applicable federal constitutional requirements (if any). When our coverage concentrates entirely on the constitutional standards, as set forth by the Supreme Court, it can be assumed that the second model prevails, i.e., the number of jurisdictions that add substantial requirements of their own is fairly small, and for the vast majority of the fifty-two jurisdictions, the federal constitutional standards provide the basic legal regulation. Where the constitution provides very little direction, or many jurisdictions establish standards more rigorous than the constitutional standard, our discussion will go beyond the constitutional standards and consider the general patterns of regulation under the laws of the fifty-two jurisdictions (as discussed in Note 4 infra).[a]

3. ***Natural divergence.*** With each jurisdiction regulating through its own laws, some degree of diversity is almost inevitable. The English common law provided a common starting point for the criminal justice systems of the original states and the federal system, and continues to provide an element of commonality even to this day. However, as the common law concepts have been adjusted to accommodate new developments in the administrative structure of the process (such as the creation of police departments), and as the process has been reshaped to accommodate new concerns, various factors have led the different jurisdictions to take diverse approaches on common issues. Four factors, in particular, point toward different states adopting somewhat different legal regulations: (1) criminal procedure is not one of those areas of lawmaking in which a need for reciprocity or the interaction of transactions forces the states to seek uniformity; a lack of uniformity in the criminal justice processes of adjoining states is not likely to be a deterrent to the free flow of goods, services, or persons between the states or to restrain economic development within the state; (2) the criminal justice process must be shaped in light of the state's administrative environment, including the demography of the population, the resources available to the process, and the structure of the institutions responsible for the administration of the process (particularly police, prosecutor, and judiciary); states vary considerably as to that

[a] While federal statutes regulating criminal procedure generally apply only to the federal system, Congress in a few instances has utilized its regulatory authority (e.g., its authority over interstate commerce) to prescribe criminal process standards that govern in both the federal and state systems. The prime example is the federal law governing wiretapping and other forms of electronic surveillance.

Federal treaties (particularly multinational conventions) also present the potential for regulating state criminal procedure. However, current treaties that deal with the subject of criminal justice have been construed as not having that effect, either because they are not self-executing, do not create judicially enforceable private remedies, or are subject to a U.S. reservation that limits the treaty's reach to rights also protected by the federal constitution. See CRIMPROC § 1.7(c).

administrative environment, particularly in the division between states that are largely urban and largely rural; (3) criminal process issues tend to be issues of high visibility and, often, high emotional content, leading to lawmaking decisions (at least legislative lawmaking decisions) that are influenced more by symbolic politics (which tend to vary with the ideological assumptions of the local constituency) than the views of those with presumed technical expertise; and (4) the integrated components of the criminal justice process means that a divergence between states in their laws governing one part of the process most likely will necessitate further differences at other stages of the process.

4. ***Describing common patterns.*** The laws of the fifty-two jurisdictions are most likely to vary where (1) federal constitutional regulation is not comprehensive and detailed, and (2) the particular procedure was either unknown at common law or its common law form has been substantially modified as a result of institutional and process changes not anticipated by the common law. Even here, however, if the focus is on the basic structure of the regulation, and not upon administrative refinements, the legal regulations applicable in the vast majority of the fifty-two jurisdictions usually can be characterized as following one or the other of two or three alternative approaches. We will not attempt in this single volume to go beyond describing these basic patterns that differentiate one major grouping from another. It should be kept in mind, however, that there will almost always be a few jurisdictions that take an entirely different approach. So too, jurisdictions described as following the same general approach commonly will present some variation in their implementation of that approach; our description of that approach as applied in a particular jurisdiction cannot be carried over in its entirety to all other jurisdictions adopting the same basic approach.

5. ***Models.*** Very often a basic pattern followed by a substantial grouping of jurisdiction is the product of states emulating reforms adopted in a particular jurisdiction. The federal law of criminal procedure is undoubtedly the most important model in this regard. Notwithstanding significant distinctions in the role and administrative institutions of the federal criminal justice system, as to almost every basic element of that system, a substantial group of states, ranging from a significant minority to an overwhelming majority, have copied in large part the standards of the relevant federal statutes (see Appendix B of the Supplement) or the Federal Rules of Criminal Procedure (see Appendix C of the Supplement). Thus, the discussion in later chapters of the nonconstitutional federal law of criminal procedure is presented not only because of its significant role in regulating the federal criminal justice system, but because it usually reflects also the governing state law in a substantial group of states.

The American Bar Association's *Standards for Criminal Justice* provide another important model. Now in their fourth edition, the *A.B.A. Standards* have been cited thousands of times by appellate courts and have been followed by numerous states in formulating their court rules and statutes. Unlike the Federal Rules, however, the *A.B.A. Standards* have been incorporated into state law on a piecemeal basis, with the state reforms typically looking either to an individual standard or a grouping of standards dealing with a particular aspect of the process (e.g., pretrial discovery). Accordingly, the Standards are not included in Appendix B, but are cited (and quoted) in the text discussion of those topics on which they have been especially influential.

6. ***Procedural subsets.*** Even within a single jurisdiction the law governing the criminal justice process will not be the same for each and every case. All fifty-two jurisdictions utilize at least a few lines of division that produce procedural subsets (i.e., different classes of cases governed by different procedural standards). The most common is the line drawn between felonies and misdemeanors (see fn. a, p. 3). All jurisdictions distinguish between felonies and misdemeanors as to some procedures. In some jurisdictions, judicial procedures vary between the court of general trial jurisdiction and the magistrate court. Very often, this leads to a distinction in the procedure applied to felonies and certain higher-level misdemeanors (triable in the court of general

jurisdiction) and lower level misdemeanors (triable by magistrate). Some lower-level misdemeanors also have been placed in a separate category: though not decriminalized, they are not subject to incarceration upon conviction. These offenses, commonly described as "infractions" or "violations," often are treated differently as to both police authority and judicial processing within the magistrate court. Municipal ordinances often create offenses that are similar to state misdemeanors (carrying a possible penalty of limited incarceration) or infractions (punishable only by fine). In many states, prosecutions under those ordinances (typically by the municipal attorney) are treated in the same manner as state law offenses, but some states apply different procedures for certain steps in adjudication (such as governmental appeals).

We will always take note of differences in constitutional regulation which apply to different classes of crime. State law distinctions, however, will be noted only as to the most significant procedures applicable exclusively to felonies, as our primary focus is on felony prosecutions.

A similar approach will be taken as to state laws creating another procedural subset based on penalty—the distinction drawn, as to various procedures, between felonies subject to capital punishment (limited to certain types of murder) and all other felonies. Our focus will be on the processing of the non-capital case, although here again, distinctions drawn in constitutional regulation between capital and non-capital prosecutions will always be noted.

§ 4. DIVERSITY IN ADMINISTRATION

1. ***Significance of discretion.*** Commentators commonly speak of the immense gap existing between the law of criminal procedure "on the books" and the law of criminal procedure "in action." Part of that gap is attributable to administrative deviance—that is, the failure of public administrators (particularly police, but also prosecutors, magistrates, and trial court judges) to adhere to the law in administering the process. The larger part of the gap, however, is a product of a narrow view of the "governing law," a view which fails to take account of discretion. As commonly defined, discretion flows from the authorization, explicit or implicit, of the law. Discretion exists where the law fails to prescribe standards and thereby either explicitly or implicitly leaves the administrator to his or her own standards. When commentators, in describing "the law," refer only to the various procedures recognized in constitutional provisions, statutes, court rules, and legal decisions, disregarding the discretionary options that are given to administrators as to the use of those procedures, they tend to characterize every failure to utilize a procedure as a departure from the "law on the books." What they are describing, however, is only a departure from the expectation that the law will mandate procedures, rather than simply authorize procedures to be used at the discretion of different participants in the process. The law of criminal procedure frequently departs from that expectation of mandated procedures.

Discretion is a common component of almost all aspects of the criminal justice process. The law grants enforcement officials (police and prosecutor) the authority to institute certain procedures under specified conditions, but typically also grants those officials the discretion not to exercise that authority even when these conditions exist. The law authorizes, for example, the search of the arrested person incident to his arrest, but the police officer has discretion not to exercise that authority if he so chooses. On occasion, the law even grants to the enforcement official the discretion to control the procedural rights made available to a suspect or defendant (as where the prosecutor may determine whether the charges against the defendant are screened by a magistrate at a preliminary hearing or by a grand jury, see § 2, step 9).

The defendant's rights are also subject to the defendant's authority to relinquish those rights. Thus, there is no true gap between the "law" and the "practice" when most prosecutions are resolved without a trial. The law gives the defendant not only a right to a trial, but a right also to waive the trial and plead guilty. Also, the law does not prohibit the government from offering certain types of incentives to encourage such waivers.

2. ***Discretion and administrative diversity.*** When there exists a legal normlessness or a legal norm so broad as to allow reference to personal values, diversity in the exercise of authority is inevitable, as it can hardly be expected that all actors performing the same function will look to the same values in exercising their discretion. Numerous studies suggest, however, that to considerable extent, the values of the individual administrator are shaped and confined by a combination of institutional influences, producing what is commonly described as the "dominant administrative culture," and it is this culture that more often than not guides the exercise of discretion. In the state systems, that culture tends to vary from one community to another since the primary administrative units (police agencies, prosecutors' offices, and magistrate and trial courts) are either a part of local government or organized as local units of a statewide agency.

With the administrative culture varying from one community to another (and where more than one agency performs the same role, varying as well within the community, depending on which agency is involved), it is not surprising that the criminal justice process, as applied, will differ in many respects even where the same legal standards govern. For example, in five different communities in a single state, the standard police response to otherwise similarly situated first offenders caught shoplifting, may be quite different: (1) in one community, the shoplifter may be sent on his way with a "warning"; (2) in another the shoplifter will be proceeded against, but released on a summons; (3) in another, the shoplifter will be taken into custody and transported to the police station, but without being frisked or searched; (4) in another, the shoplifter will be frisked when taken into custody; and (5) in another, the shoplifter taken into custody will be subjected to a complete search. Moreover, the differences in approach are not likely to be limited to this initial police response. Where the shoplifter is proceeded against, further variations are likely to be found as to such matters as the availability of diversion, the use of plea bargains, the defense waiver of jury trial in cases that go to trial, and the exercise of sentencing discretion. In addition, while certain approaches on these issues may be "standard" for the particular community, the potential always exists for individual participants to exercise their discretion in a manner that deviates from that "standard."

Where the exercise of discretion plays a major rule in the application of a particular step in the criminal justice process, our commentary usually will offer illustrations of some alternative modes of exercising that discretion. Those illustrations come from studies which focus on the exercise of discretion in particular localities. Ordinarily, it can be assumed that something close to the same administrative environment can be found in many other communities and the same style of discretionary decisionmaking probably prevails there as well. But it also must be kept in mind that the illustrations hardly cover the full range of possibilities, and that there are many communities in which a quite different administrative environment and quite different exercise of discretion will prevail.

CHAPTER 2

SOURCES OF CRIMINAL PROCEDURE LAW

■ ■ ■

The law of criminal procedure has a number of sources. Foremost is the Constitution of the United States, and specifically various provisions of the Bill of Rights (such as the Fourth, Fifth, and Sixth Amendments) as well as the Due Process Clause of the Fourteenth Amendment. In federal cases the federal court's supervisory power over the administration of the federal criminal justice system provides an additional source of authority. In state cases, state constitutional provisions that (as interpreted by the state courts) furnish an individual more protection than does the U.S. Constitution (as interpreted by the U.S. Supreme Court) can also be important.

§ 1. THE INCORPORATION DOCTRINE

For most of United States history, the constitutional protections found in the first ten amendments to the federal constitution—what we often call the "Bill of Rights"—applied only to the federal government. *See Barron v. Baltimore*, 32 U.S. 243 (1833). The Bill of Rights did not apply to state governments or state officials. Because the overwhelming majority of criminal investigations occurred at the state level, the constitutional criminal procedure protections such as the Fourth Amendment, Fifth Amendment, and Sixth Amendment did not apply to most investigations.

Following the Civil War, the 1868 ratification of the Fourteenth Amendment raised the possibility that the Bill of Rights might begin to apply to the states. The text of the Fourteenth Amendment is directly addressed to the states: "No State shall make or enforce any law which shall abridge the privileges or immunities of citizens of the United States; nor shall any State deprive any person of life, liberty, or property, without due process of law." Initially, however, the Supreme Court ruled that the Fourteenth Amendment did not change the traditional understanding that the Bill of Rights applied only to the federal government. *See Twining v. New Jersey*, 211 U.S. 78 (1908). (Although the Due Process Clause of the Fourteenth Amendment imposed on the states some of the same prohibitions that strands of the Fourth, Fifth, and Sixth Amendments imposed on the federal system, the contours of the due process tests were different. *See infra* Section 2.)

In the middle of the Twentieth Century, the Supreme Court changed direction. In a long string of cases, the Court ruled that most but not all of the protections in the Bill of Rights applied to the states in addition to the federal government. These cases are based what has been called the "incorporation" doctrine. Under the incorporation doctrine, the Due Process Clause of the Fourteenth Amendment is understood to incorporate protections of the Bill of Rights and apply them to the states when they are sufficiently important to be fundamental to the American scheme of ordered liberty. *See, e.g., Mapp v. Ohio*, 367 U.S. 643 (1961) (incorporating the Fourth Amendment); *Malloy v. Hogan*, 378 U.S. 1 (1964) (incorporating the Fifth Amendment privilege against self-incrimination); *Gideon v. Wainwright*, 372 U.S. 335 (1963) (incorporating the Sixth Amendment right to counsel).

A recent incorporation case arose in the context of the Second Amendment's right to keep and bear arms. In *District of Columbia v. Heller*, 554 U.S.570 (2008), the Court held that the Second Amendment protects the right to keep and bear arms for the purpose of self-defense. Thus, the Court struck down a District of Columbia law that banned the possession of handguns in the home.

After *Heller* was decided, petitioners filed a federal suit against the City of Chicago, maintaining that the City's handgun ban violated the Second and Fourteenth Amendments. In McDONALD v. CITY OF CHICAGO, 561 U.S. 742 (2010), a 5–4 majority agreed.

Justice Alito announced the judgment of the Court and delivered the opinion of the Court with respect to Parts I, II-A, II-B, II-D, III-A, and III-B, in which the Chief Justice, Justices Scalia, Kennedy and Thomas joined, and an opinion with respect to Parts II-C, IV, and V, in which the Chief Justice and Justices Scalia and Kennedy joined.

Justice Thomas agreed that the Second Amendment is "fully applicable to the States," "fundamental" to the American "scheme of ordered liberty" and "deeply rooted in the Nation's history and tradition." However, he could not agree that the Second Amendment is enforceable against the States through a clause that speaks only to "process." Instead, he viewed the right to keep and bear arms as a privilege of American citizenship applicable to the States through the Fourteenth Amendment's Privileges or Immunities Clause.

In Part II-D of his opinion, speaking for a majority of the Court at this point, Justice Alito looked back on various cases dealing with the relationship between the Bill of Rights and Fourteenth Amendment Due Process:

"[During an earlier era], even when a right set out in the Bill of Rights was held to fall within the conception of due process, the protection or remedies afforded against state infringement sometimes differed from the protection or remedies provided against abridgement by the Federal Government. To give an example, in *Betts v. Brady*, 316 U.S. 455 (1942), the Court held that, although the Sixth Amendment required the appointment of counsel in all federal criminal cases in which the defendant was unable to retain an attorney, the Due Process Clause required appointment of counsel in state criminal proceedings only where 'want of counsel in [the] particular [case] resulted in a conviction lacking [in] fundamental fairness.' Similarly, in *Wolf v. Colorado*, 338 U.S. 25 (1949), the Court held that the 'core of the Fourth Amendment' was implicit in the concept of ordered liberty and thus 'enforceable against the States through the Due Process Clause,' but that the exclusionary rule, which applied in federal cases, did not apply to the States.

"An alternative theory regarding the relationship between the Bill of Rights and § 1 of the Fourteenth Amendment was championed by Justice Black. This theory held that § 1 of the Fourteenth Amendment totally incorporated all of the provisions of the Bill of Rights. [As] Justice Black noted, the chief congressional proponents of the Fourteenth Amendment espoused the view that the Amendment made the Bill of Rights applicable to the States * * *. Nonetheless, the Court never has embraced Justice Black's 'total incorporation' theory.

"While Justice Black's theory was never adopted, the Court eventually moved in that direction by initiating what has been called a process of 'selective incorporation,' i.e., the Court began to hold that the Due Process Clause fully incorporates particular rights contained in the first eight Amendments. See, e.g., *Gideon v. Wainwright*, 372 U.S. 335 (1963); *Malloy v. Hogan*, 378 U.S. 1 (1964); *Duncan v. Louisiana*, 391 U.S. 145 (1968).

"The decisions during this time abandoned three of the previously noted characteristics of the earlier period. The Court made it clear that the governing standard is not whether *any* 'civilized system [can] be imagined that would not accord the particular protection.' *Duncan*. Instead, the Court inquired whether a particular Bill of Rights guarantee is fundamental to *our* scheme of ordered liberty and system of justice. * * *

"The Court also shed any reluctance to hold that rights guaranteed by the Bill of Rights met the requirements for protection under the Due Process Clause. The Court eventually incorporated almost all of the provisions of the Bill of Rights. Only a handful of the Bill of Rights protections remain unincorporated.[13]

"Finally, the Court abandoned the 'notion that the Fourteenth Amendment applies to the States only a watered-down, subjective version of the individual guarantees of the Bill of Rights,' stating that it would be 'incongruous' to apply different standards 'depending on whether the claim was asserted in a state or federal court.' *Malloy*. Instead, the court decisively held that incorporated Bill of Rights protections 'are all to be enforced against the States under the Fourteenth Amendment according to the same standards that protect those personal rights against federal encroachment.' Id. See also *Mapp v. Ohio* [p. 211].[14]

"Employing this approach, the Court overruled earlier decisions in which it had held that particular Bill of Rights guarantees or remedies did not apply to the States. See, e.g., *Mapp*; *Gideon*; and *Malloy*."

§ 2. THE PROBLEM OF BODILY EXTRACTIONS: ANOTHER LOOK AT THE "DUE PROCESS" AND "SELECTIVE INCORPORATION" APPROACHES

In *Betts v. Brady*, 316 U.S. 455, 461–62 (1942), the Supreme Court explained its view of the difference between applying a due process framework to adjudicate a state defendant's claims and relying on a specific provision in the Bill of Rights: "Due process of law * * * formulates a concept less rigid and more fluid that those envisaged in other specific and particular provisions of the Bill of Rights. Its application is less a matter of rule. Asserted denial is to be tested by an appraisal of the totality of facts in a given case." That might be true enough for certain specific Bill of Rights protections that involve the application of clear rules, but much of the language in the Bill of Rights is rather vague and general (for example, the right to be free from "unreasonable searches and seizures"). In such cases, does dwelling on the literal language simply *shift the focus of broad judicial inquiry* from "due process" to, for example, "freedom of speech," "establishment of religion," "unreasonable searches and seizures," "excessive bail," "cruel and unusual punishments," and "the assistance of counsel"? See Donald A. Dripps, *At the Borders of the Fourth Amendment: Why A Real Due Process Test Should Replace the Outrageous Government Conduct Defense*, 1993 U.Ill.L.Rev. 261 (defending, "as both more faithful to conventional sources of constitutional law and more consonant with the political values of a free society, a revitalized due process test"); John E. Nowak, *Due Process Methodology in the Postincorporation World*, 70 J.

---

[13] In addition to the right to keep and bear arms (and the Sixth Amendment right to a unanimous jury verdict), the only rights not fully incorporated are (1) the Third Amendment's protection against quartering of soldiers; (2) the Fifth Amendment's grand jury indictment requirement; (3) the Seventh Amendment right to a jury trial in civil cases; and (4) the Eighth Amendment's prohibition on excessive fines [though the Supreme Court recently granted certiorari to consider whether to incorporate the excessive fines clause, *see Timbs v. Indiana*, No. 17–1091]. * * *

We never have decided whether the Third Amendment or the Eighth Amendment's prohibition of excessive fines applies to the States through the Due Process Clause. * * * Our governing decisions regarding the Grand Jury Clause of the Fifth Amendment and the Seventh Amendment's civil jury requirement long predate the era of selective incorporation.

[14] There is one exception to this general rule. The Court has held that although the Sixth Amendment right to trial by jury requires a unanimous jury verdict in federal criminal trials, it does not require a unanimous jury verdict in state criminal trials. See *Apodaca v. Oregon*, 406 U.S. 404 (1972). But that ruling was the result of an unusual division among the Justices, not an endorsement of the two-track approach to incorporation. In *Apodaca*, eight Justices agreed that the Sixth Amendment applies identically to both the Federal Government and the States. Nonetheless, among those eight, four Justices took the view that the Sixth Amendment does not require unanimous jury verdicts in federal and state criminal trials. Justice Powell's concurrence in the judgment broke the tie, and he concluded that the Sixth Amendment requires juror unanimity in federal, but not state, cases. *Apodaca*, therefore, does not undermine the well-established rule that incorporated Bill of Rights protections apply identically to the States and Federal Government. * * *

Crim. L. & C. 397, 400–01 (1979) (arguing that decisions based on specific guarantees tend to rely on definitional analysis and fail to explore the interest at stake). *See also* Henry J. Friendly, *The Bill of Rights as a Code of Criminal Procedure,* 53 Calif.L.Rev. 929, 937 (1965); Sanford H. Kadish, *Methodology and Criteria in Due Process Adjudication—A Survey and Criticism,* 66 Yale L.J. 319 (1957); Yale Kamisar, *How Much Does It Really Matter Whether Courts Work Within the "Clearly Marked" Provisions of the Bill of Rights or With the "Generalities" of the Fourteenth Amendment?,* 18 J.Contemp. Legal Issues 513 (2009).

To turn to another cluster of problems—which form the basis for this section—in considering whether, and under what conditions, the police may direct the "pumping" of a person's stomach to uncover incriminating evidence, or the taking of a blood sample from him, without his consent, do the "specific guarantees" in the Bill of Rights against "unreasonable searches and seizures" and against compelling a person to be "a witness against himself" free the Court from the demands of appraising and judging involved in answering these questions by interpreting the "due process" clause?

ROCHIN v. CALIFORNIA, 342 U.S. 165 (1952), arose as follows: Having "some information" that Rochin was selling narcotics, three deputy sheriffs "forced open the door of [his] room and found him sitting partly dressed on the side of the bed, upon which his wife was lying. On a 'night stand' beside the bed the deputies spied two capsules. When asked 'Whose stuff is this?' Rochin seized the capsules and put them in his mouth. A struggle ensued in the course of which the three officers 'jumped upon him' and [unsuccessfully] attempted to extract the capsules. [Rochin] was handcuffed and taken to a hospital. At the direction of one of the officers, a doctor forced an emetic solution through a tube into Rochin's stomach against his will. This 'stomach pumping' produced vomiting. In the vomited matter were found two capsules which proved to contain morphine. [Rochin was convicted of possessing morphine] and sentenced to sixty days' imprisonment. The chief evidence against him was the two capsules."

The Court, per Frankfurter, J., concluded that the police conduct violated Fourteenth Amendment Due Process: "This is conduct that shocks the conscience. Illegally breaking into the privacy of the petitioner, the struggle to open his mouth and remove what was there, the forcible extraction of his stomach's contents—this course of proceeding by agents of government to obtain evidence is bound to offend even hardened sensibilities. They are methods too close to the rack and the screw to permit of constitutional differentiation.

"It has long since ceased to be true that due process of law is heedless of the means by which otherwise relevant and credible evidence is obtained. [The confession] decisions [are] only instances of the general requirement that States in their prosecutions respect certain decencies of civilized conduct. Due process of law, as a historic and generative principle, precludes defining, and thereby confining, these standards of conduct more precisely than to say that convictions cannot be brought about by methods that offend 'a sense of justice.' It would be a stultification of the responsibility which the course of constitutional history has cast upon this Court to hold that in order to convict a man the police cannot extract by force what is in his mind but can extract what is in his stomach.

"[E]ven though statements contained in them may be independently established as true, [c]oerced confessions offend the community's sense of fair play and decency. So here, to sanction the brutal conduct which naturally enough was condemned by the court whose judgment is before us, would be to afford brutality the cloak of law. Nothing would be more calculated to discredit law and thereby to brutalize the temper of a society."

Concurring Justice Black reasoned that the Fifth Amendment's protection against compelled self-incrimination applied to the states and that "a person is compelled to be a witness against himself not only when he is compelled to testify, but also when as here, incriminating evidence is forcibly taken from him by a contrivance of modern science." He maintained that "faithful adherence to the specific guarantees in the Bill of Rights insures a more permanent protection of individual liberty than that which can be afforded by the nebulous [Fourteenth Amendment due process] standards stated by the majority."

In a separate concurring opinion, Justice Douglas also criticized the majority's approach. He contended that the privilege against self-incrimination applied to the states as well as the federal government and because of the privilege "words taken from [an accused's] lips, capsules taken from his stomach, blood taken from his veins are all inadmissible provided they are taken from him without his consent. [This] is an unequivocal, definite and workable rule of evidence for state and federal courts. But we cannot in fairness free the state courts from the [restraints of the Fifth Amendment privilege against self-incrimination] and yet excoriate them for flouting the 'decencies of civilized conduct' when they admit the evidence. This is to make the rule turn not on the Constitution but on the idiosyncracies of the judges who sit here."

Irvine v. California, 347 U.S. 128 (1954), limited *Rochin* to situations involving coercion, violence or brutality to the person.[a] BREITHAUPT v. ABRAM, 352 U.S. 432 (1957), illustrated that under the *Rochin* test state police had considerable leeway even when the body of the accused was "invaded." In *Breithaupt,* the police took a blood sample from an unconscious person who had been involved in a fatal automobile collision. A majority, per Clark, J., affirmed a manslaughter conviction based on the blood sample (which showed intoxication), stressing that the sample was "taken under the protective eye of a physician" and that "the blood test procedure has become routine in our everyday life." "[T]he interests of society in the scientific determination of intoxication, one of the great causes of the mortal hazards of the road," outweighed "so slight an intrusion" of a person's body.

Dissenting Chief Justice Warren, joined by Black and Douglas, JJ., deemed *Rochin* controlling and argued that police efforts to curb the narcotics traffic, involved in *Rochin,* "is surely a state interest of at least as great magnitude as the interest in highway law enforcement. * * * Only personal reaction to the stomach pump and the blood test can distinguish the [two cases]."

Justice Douglas, joined by Black, J., also wrote a separate dissent, maintaining that "if the decencies of a civilized state are the test, it is repulsive to me for the police to insert needles into an unconscious person in order to get the evidence necessary to convict him, whether they find the person unconscious, give him a pill which puts him to sleep, or use force to subdue him."

---

[a] In *Irvine* the police made repeated illegal entries into petitioner's home, first to install a secret microphone and then to move it to the bedroom, in order to listen to the conversations of the occupants—for over a month.

Jackson, J., who announced the judgment of the Court and wrote the principal opinion, recognized that "few police measures have come to our attention that more flagrantly, deliberately, and persistently violated the fundamental principle declared by the Fourth Amendment as a restriction on the Federal Government," but adhered to the holding in *Wolf v. Colorado* (1949), p. 209, that the exclusionary rule in federal search and seizure cases is not binding on the states. (*Wolf* was overruled in *Mapp v. Ohio* (1961), p. 211.) Nor did Justice Jackson deem *Rochin* applicable: "However obnoxious are the facts in the case before us, they do not involve coercion, violence or brutality to the person [as did *Rochin*], but rather a trespass to property, plus eavesdropping."

Because of the "aggravating" and "repulsive" police misconduct in *Irvine,* Frankfurter, J., joined by Burton, J., dissented, maintaining that *Rochin* was controlling, not *Wolf.* (He had written the majority opinions in both cases.) Black, J., joined by Douglas, J., dissented separately, arguing that petitioner had been convicted on the basis of evidence "extorted" from him in violation of the Fifth Amendment's privilege against compelled self-incrimination, which he considered applicable to the states. Douglas, J., dissenting separately, protested against the use in state prosecutions of evidence seized in violation of the Fourth Amendment.

Speaking for himself and Chief Justice Warren, Justice Jackson suggested that copies of the Court's opinion and the record in the case be sent to the U.S. Attorney General for possible federal prosecution. The FBI did conduct an investigation which revealed that the officers who placed the microphone in Irvine's home were acting under orders of the Chief of Police and with the full knowledge of the local prosecutor. Thus, concluded the Department of Justice, "it would be both useless and inadvisable to present [the] matter to the Federal grand jury." See Comment, 7 Stan.L.Rev. 76, 94, fn. 75 (1954).

Nine years later, even though in the meantime the Court had held in *Mapp* that the federal exclusionary rule in search and seizure cases was binding on the states and in *Malloy v. Hogan,* supra, that the Fifth Amendment's protection against compelled self-incrimination was likewise applicable to the states, the Court still upheld the taking by a physician, at police direction, of a blood sample from an injured person, over his objection. SCHMERBER v. CALIFORNIA, 384 U.S. 757 (1966). In affirming the conviction for operating a vehicle while under the influence of intoxicating liquor, a 5–4 majority, per Brennan, J., ruled: (1) that the extraction of blood from petitioner under the aforementioned circumstances "did not offend 'that "sense of justice" ' of which we spoke in *Rochin,*" thus reaffirming *Breithaupt*; (2) that the privilege against self-incrimination, now binding on the states, "protects an accused only from being compelled to testify against himself, or otherwise provide the State with evidence of a testimonial or communicative nature and that the withdrawal of blood and use of the analysis in question did not involve compulsion to these ends";[b] and (3) that the protection against unreasonable search and seizure, now binding on the states, was satisfied because (a) "there was plainly probable cause" to arrest and charge petitioner and to suggest "the required relevance and likely success of a test of petitioner's blood for alcohol"; (b) the officer "might reasonably have believed that he was confronted with an emergency, in which the delay necessary to obtain a warrant, under the circumstances, threatened 'the destruction of evidence' "; and (c) "the test chosen to measure petitioner's blood-alcohol level was a reasonable one * * * performed in a reasonable manner."

Dissenting Justice Black, joined by Justice Douglas, expressed amazement at the majority's "conclusion that compelling a person to give his blood to help the State to convict him is not equivalent to compelling him to be a witness against himself." "It is a strange hierarchy of values that allows the State to extract a human being's blood to convict him of a crime because of the blood's content but proscribes compelled production of his lifeless papers."[c]

NOTES AND QUESTIONS

1. ***The clarity (or lack thereof) of Due Process regulation:*** In light of *Rochin, Breithaupt* and *Schmerber,* when courts decide constitutional questions by "looking to" the Bill of Rights, to what extent do they proceed, as Justice Black expressed it in *Adamson v. California,* 332 U.S. 46 (1947), "within clearly marked constitutional boundaries"? To what extent does resort to these "particular standards" enable courts to avoid substituting their "own concepts of decency and fundamental justice" for the language of the Constitution?

2. ***Does incorporation of the specific amendments add much clarity?*** Did *Mapp* and *Malloy,* decided in the interim between *Breithaupt* and *Schmerber,* affect any Justice's vote? Did the applicability of the "particular standards" of the Fourth and Fifth Amendments inhibit Justices Black, Douglas or Brennan from employing their own concepts of "decency" and "justice" in *Schmerber?* After *Schmerber,* how much force is there in Justice Black's view, concurring in *Rochin,* that "faithful adherence to the specific guarantees in the Bill of Rights assures a more permanent protection of individual liberty than that which can be afforded by the nebulous standards stated by the majority"?

---

[b] In fn. 7 to its opinion, the Court compared "Wigmore's view, 'that the privilege is limited to testimonial disclosure. It was directed at the employment of legal process *to extract from the person's own lips* an admission of guilt, which would thus take the place of other evidence.' 8 Wigmore, *Evidence* § 2263 (McNaughton rev. 1961)." "Our holding today," noted the Court, "is not to be understood as adopting the Wigmore formulation." But see Note 6, p. 689.

[c] Warren, C.J., and Douglas, J., dissented in separate opinions, each adhering to his dissenting views in *Breithaupt.* In a third dissenting opinion, Fortas, J., maintained that "petitioner's privilege against self-incrimination applies" and, moreover, "under the Due Process Clause, the State, in its role as prosecutor, has no right to extract blood from an accused or anyone else, over his protest."

3. ***The relationship between Due Process and specific rights in a post-incorporation world:*** Applying the "shocks-the-conscience" test first articulated in the *Rochin* case, COUNTY OF SACRAMENTO v. LEWIS, 523 U.S. 833 (1998), held, per SOUTER, J., that a police officer did not violate substantive due process by causing death through "reckless indifference" to, or "reckless disregard" for, a person's life in a high-speed automobile chase of a speeding motorcyclist. (The chase resulted in the death of the motorcyclist's passenger when the police car skidded into the passenger after the cycle had tipped over). In such circumstances, concluded the Court, "only a purpose to cause harm unrelated to the legitimate object of arrest will satisfy the element of arbitrary conduct shocking to the conscience, necessary for a due process violation [and for police liability under 42 U.S.C. § 1983]." Regardless of whether the officer's behavior "offended the reasonableness held up by tort law on the balance struck in law enforcement's own codes of practice, it does not shock the conscience."

The Court recalled that it had held in *Graham v. Connor*, 490 U.S. 386 (1989), that "where a particular amendment provides an explicit textual source of constitutional protection against a particular sort of government behavior, that Amendment, not the more generalized notion of substantive due process, must be the guide for analyzing [claims of substantive due process violations]." But the "more-specific-provision" rule of *Graham* did not bar respondents' lawsuit because neither the high-speed chase of the motorcycle nor the accidental killing of the motorcycle passenger constituted a Fourth Amendment "seizure."[d]

4. ***"Free-standing" procedural Due Process claims.*** Whereas *County of Sacramento* addresses the continued vitality of free-standing *substantive* due process claims (and asks whether the state's behavior was "conscience-shocking"), the tests for addressing free-standing *procedural* due process claims are different. The traditional test for addressing questions of procedural due process comes from *Mathews v. Eldridge*, 424 U.S. 319 (1976). Under the *Mathews* balancing test, a court evaluates (a) the private interest affected; (b) the risk of erroneous deprivation of that interest through the procedures used; and (c) the governmental interest at stake in order to determine if the procedures in question are constitutionally sufficient. In *Medina v. California*, 505 U.S. 427 (1992), however, the Supreme Court adopted a different procedural due process test for "assessing the validity of state procedural rules [that] are part of the criminal process." In cases involving challenges to procedural rules about the burden of proof, the admissibility of evidence, or other aspects of state criminal process, *Medina* asks whether the state practice "offends some principle of justice so rooted in the traditions and conscience of our people to be ranked as fundamental." *See, e.g., District Attorney's Office v. Osborne*, 557 U.S. 52 (2009) (using the *Medina* standard to reject the claim of a convicted defendant that state law violated due process in the prerequisites it imposed for granting him access to biological evidence for the purpose of applying DNA testing more sophisticated than what was available at the time of his conviction).

For a recent case that raises questions about whether *Mathews* or *Medina* provides the right framework, see *Nelson v. Colorado*, 137 S.Ct. 1249 (2017) (holding that a state is obligated to refund fees, court costs, and restitution taken from a defendant after that defendant's criminal conviction is invalidated by a reviewing court and no retrial occurs). Justice Ginsburg, writing for the majority, used the *Mathews* balancing approach to strike down Colorado's procedural scheme

---

[d] Concurring in the judgment, Scalia, J., joined by Thomas, J., would not have decided the case by applying the "shocks-the-conscience" test but "on the ground that respondents offer no textual or historical support for their alleged due process right." The concurring Justices maintained that in *Washington v. Glucksberg*, 521 U.S. 702 (1997) (upholding a criminal prohibition against physician-assisted suicide), "the Court specifically rejected the method of substantive-due-process analysis employed by Justice Souter in that case, which is the very same method employed by Justice Souter in his opinion for the Court today."

Justice Kennedy, joined by O'Connor, J., joined the opinion of the Court, but also wrote separately. They "share[d] Justice Scalia's concerns about using the phrase 'shocks the conscience' in a manner suggesting that it is a self-defining test." The phrase, they observed, "has the unfortunate connotation of a standard laden with subjective assessments. In that respect, it must be viewed with considerable skepticism."

for violating defendants' due process rights. The majority believed that this was a case about the continuing deprivation of the defendants' property rather than a case involving state criminal procedures. In contrast, Justice Alito, concurring, would have reached a similar result using the *Medina* standard. He believed that the presumption of innocence was at issue—a core feature of criminal procedure law that necessitated application of the *Medina* standard.

5. ***Continued application of "free-standing" Due Process.*** Jerold Israel, *Free-Standing Due Process and Criminal Procedure: The Supreme Court's Search for Interpretive Guidelines*, 45 St. Louis U.L.J. 303 (2001), reviewed the Court's application of the *Medina* standard in the post-incorporation decades. The article concludes that while the Court has set forth various guidelines for determining the independent content of due process, it has not been consistent in applying those guidelines. The Court has noted that "beyond the specific guarantees enumerated in the Bill of Rights, the Due Process Clause has limited operation" and will be "construed very narrowly." *Dowling v. United States*, 493 U.S. 342 (1990). This position rests on the ground that, since the "Bill of Rights speaks in explicit terms to many aspects of criminal procedure," the expansion of constitutional regulation under the "open-ended rubric of the Due Process Clause * * * invite[s] undue interference with both considered legislative judgments and the careful balance that the constitution strikes between liberty and order." *Medina v. California*, supra.

Notwithstanding such statements, free-standing due process has emerged as: (1) the dominant source of constitutional regulation of the pre-trial and post-trial stages of the process (most notable as to guilty pleas and sentencing); (2) a major source of constitutional regulation of the trial; (3) a lesser, but still significant source of regulation of police practices (see e.g., ch. 10, § 3). So too, while the Court has repeatedly stressed that the historical acceptance of a practice is a strong indicator that the practice does not offend fundamental fairness, it has on various occasions relied on deductive reasoning (often tied to the character of a "fair hearing") to hold unconstitutional practices that were entirely consistent with the common law (typically without discussing historical acceptance). Most often, the Court has described free-standing due process as looking to the circumstances of the particular case and resting, at least in part, on fact-sensitive determinations (particularly as to a likelihood of prejudicial impact), but in several areas, the Court has relied on free-standing due process to formulate per se prohibitions and automatically presume prejudice. The Court at times has advanced a procedural due process counterpart of *Graham v. Connor*, but at other times has turned to free-standing due process without first considering the possible application of a specific guarantee (indeed, even announcing a preference for relying on free-standing due process in *Pennsylvania v. Ritchie*, 480 U.S. 39 (1987).

§ 3. THE FEDERAL COURTS' "SUPERVISORY POWER" OVER THE ADMINISTRATION OF FEDERAL CRIMINAL JUSTICE

As the Court, per FRANKFURTER, J., observed in McNABB v. UNITED STATES, 318 U.S. 332 (1943), "while the power of this Court to undo convictions in *state* courts is limited to the enforcement of those 'fundamental principles of liberty and justice' secured by [fourteenth amendment due process]" (emphasis added), the standards of *federal* criminal justice "are not satisfied merely by observance of those minimal historic safeguards." Rather, "[i]n the exercise of its supervisory authority over the administration of criminal justice in the federal courts, [this Court has] formulated rules of evidence to be applied in federal criminal prosecutions." Thus, in *McNabb,* the Court held incriminating statements obtained during prolonged and hence unlawful detention (i.e., while the suspect was held in violation of federal statutory requirements that he be promptly taken before a committing magistrate) inadmissible in federal courts "[q]uite apart from the Constitution."

For a long, hard look at *McNabb* itself and the federal "supervisory power" generally, see Sara Sun Beale, *Reconsidering Supervisory Power in Criminal Cases: Constitutional and Statutory Limits on the Authority of the Federal Courts,* 84 Colum.L.Rev. 1433 (1984). Professor Beale maintains, inter alia, that "the supervisory power has blurred the constitutional and statutory limitations on the authority of the federal courts [and] fostered the erroneous view that the federal courts exercise general supervision over federal prosecutors and investigators"; and that "there is no statutory or constitutional source of authority broad enough to encompass all of the supervisory power decisions." Id. at 1434–35.

"In cases not involving questions of judicial procedure or a statutory violation," concludes Beale, id. at 1521–22, the federal courts lack the authority "to exclude evidence or to dismiss a prosecution unless the government's conduct violated the Constitution. This analysis requires the federal courts to decide some constitutional issues they are now able to avoid—or at least defer—by grounding their rulings on supervisory power. [Requiring the federal courts to ground decisions on a constitutional basis] would be likely to result in eliminating some restrictions on federal investigators and prosecutors that have been grounded solely on supervisory power. This is as it should be.

"But this approach need not straitjacket the courts. Where there has been a legislative grant of authority, such as the rules enabling legislation, the power of the courts is extensive. Amendments to the Federal Rules of Criminal Procedure may properly regulate some matters that have been the subject of highly questionable supervisory power rulings. * * * But the concept of separation of powers dictates that federal prosecutors and investigators, like their state counterparts, should perform their duties subject only to the requirements imposed by the federal Constitution and statutes, not subject to the federal judiciary's preference for particular policies and practices."

In *United States v. Russell* (1973) (discussed at p. 474, in the course of rejecting respondent's argument that he had been "entrapped" because there had been an intolerable degree of government involvement in the criminal enterprise, the Court, per Rehnquist, J., observed:

"[Several lower federal court decisions] have undoubtedly gone beyond this Court's [precedents] in order to bar prosecutions because of what they [considered] 'overzealous law enforcement.' But the [entrapment defense] was not intended to give the federal judiciary a 'chancellor's foot' veto over law enforcement practices of which it does not disapprove. The execution of the federal laws under our Constitution is confined primarily to the Executive Branch of the Government, subject to applicable constitutional and statutory limitations and to judicially fashioned rules to enforce those limitations."

When a three-justice plurality (Rehnquist, J., joined by the Chief Justice and White, J.,) quoted the "chancellor's foot" passage with approval in another entrapment case, *Hampton v. United States*, 425 U.S. 484 (1976), concurring Justice Powell, joined by Blackmun, J., observed:

"The plurality's use of the 'chancellor's foot' passage from *Russell* may suggest that it also would foreclose reliance on our supervisory power to bar conviction of [a defendant predisposed to commit the crime] because of outrageous police conduct. * * * I do not understand *Russell* to have gone so far. There we indicated only that we should be extremely reluctant to invoke the supervisory power in cases of this kind because that power does not give the 'federal judiciary a 'chancellor's foot' veto over law enforcement practices of which it [does] not approve.' * * * I therefore am unwilling to join the plurality in concluding that, no matter what the circumstances, neither due process principles nor our supervisory power could support a bar to conviction in any case where the Government is able to prove predisposition [to commit the crime]."[a]

[a] Dissenting Justice Brennan, joined by Stewart and Marshall, JJ., agreed with Justices Powell and Blackmun that "*Russell* does not foreclose imposition of a bar to conviction—based upon our supervisory power or due process

Whatever the implications of the "chancellor's foot" passage, both in *Payner,* infra, and in *Hasting,* infra, the Court left no doubt that it took a dim view of the federal courts' exercise of their "supervisory power."

UNITED STATES v. PAYNER, 447 U.S. 727 (1980), arose as follows: An IRS investigation into the financial activities of American citizens in the Bahamas focused on a certain Bahamian bank. When an official of that bank visited the United States, IRS agents stole his briefcase for a time, removed hundreds of documents from the briefcase and photographed them. As a result of this "briefcase caper," defendant Payner was convicted of federal income tax violations. Because Payner lacked "standing" to challenge the "briefcase caper" under the Court's Fourth Amendment precedents (see Ch. 11, § 1), the federal district court invoked its supervisory power to exclude the tainted evidence. The district court found, and these findings were undisturbed by the higher courts, that "the Government counsels its agents that the Fourth Amendment standing limitation permits them to purposefully conduct an unconstitutional search and seizure of one individual in order to obtain evidence against third parties who are the real targets of the government intrusion" and that IRS agents "transacted the 'briefcase caper' with a purposeful, bad faith hostility toward the Fourth Amendment rights of [the bank official] in order to obtain evidence against persons like Payner." But a 6–3 majority, per Powell, J., held that the supervisory power "does not authorize a federal court" to exclude evidence that did not violate the defendant's Fourth Amendment rights:

"[T]he interest in deterring illegal searches does not justify the exclusion of tainted evidence at the instance of a party who was not the victim of the challenged practices. The values assigned to the competing interests do not change because a court has elected to analyze the question under the supervisory power instead of the Fourth Amendment. In either case, the need to deter the underlying conduct and the detrimental impact of excluding the evidence remain precisely the same. [The] district court's reasoning, which the [Sixth Circuit] affirmed, amounts to a substitution of individual judgment for the controlling decisions of this Court. Were we to accept this use of the supervisory power, we would confer on the judiciary discretionary power to disregard the considered limitations of the law it is charged with enforcing."

Dissenting Justice Marshall, joined by Brennan and Blackmun, JJ., maintained that the Court's holding "effectively turns the standing rules created by this Court for assertions of Fourth Amendment violations into a sword to be used by the Government to permit it deliberately to invade one person's Fourth Amendment rights in order to obtain evidence against another person. Unlike the Court, I do not believe that the federal courts are unable to protect the integrity of the judicial system from such gross government misconduct." Continued the dissent:

"The Court's decision to engraft the standing limitations of the Fourth Amendment onto the exercise of supervisory powers is puzzling not only because it runs contrary to the major purpose behind the exercise of the supervisory powers—to protect the integrity of the court—but also because it appears to render the supervisory powers superfluous. In order to establish that suppression of evidence under the supervisory powers would be proper, the Court would also require Payner to establish a violation of his Fourth or Fifth Amendment rights, in which case suppression would flow directly from the Constitution. This approach is totally unfaithful to our prior supervisory power cases, which, contrary to the Court's suggestion, are not constitutional cases in disguise."

UNITED STATES v. HASTING, 461 U.S. 499 (1983), arose as follows: Five defendants were convicted of kidnapping and transporting women across state lines for immoral purposes. Concluding that the prosecutor had violated *Griffin v. California* (p. 1322) by, in effect,

---

principles—where the conduct of law enforcement authorities is sufficiently offensive, even though the individuals entitled to invoke such a defense might be 'predisposed.' "

commenting on the failure of any defendant to take the stand in his own defense, the U.S. Court of Appeals for the Seventh Circuit reversed. The Seventh Circuit was motivated at least in part by what it perceived to be continuing violations of *Griffin* by the prosecutors within its jurisdiction. Although impermissible comment on a defendant's failure to take the stand is subject to a "harmless error" doctrine (see p. 1416), the Seventh Circuit declined to apply that doctrine, stating that its application "would impermissibly compromise the clear constitutional violation of the defendants' Fifth Amendment rights." The Court, per Burger, C.J., reversed:

"[W]e proceed on the assumption that, without so stating, the court was exercising its supervisory powers to discipline the prosecutors of its jurisdiction. * * * We hold that the [harmless error doctrine] may not be avoided by an assertion of supervisory power, simply to justify a reversal of these criminal convictions.

"[I]n the exercise of supervisory powers, federal courts may, within limits, formulate procedural rules not specifically required by the Constitution or the Congress. The purposes underlying use of the supervisory powers are threefold: to implement a remedy for violation of recognized rights; to preserve judicial integrity by ensuring that a conviction rests on appropriate considerations validly before the jury; and finally, as a remedy designed to deter illegal conduct.

"[These goals] are not, however, significant in the context of this case if, as the Court of Appeals plainly implied, the errors alleged are harmless. Supervisory power to reverse a conviction is not needed as a remedy when the error to which it is addressed is harmless since by definition, the conviction would have been obtained notwithstanding the asserted error. Further, in this context, the integrity of the process carries less weight, for it is the essence of the harmless error doctrine that a judgment may stand only when there is no 'reasonable possibility that the [practice] complained of might have contributed to the conviction.' Finally, deterrence is an inappropriate basis for reversal where, as here, the prosecutor's remark is at most an attenuated violation of *Griffin* and where means more narrowly tailored to deter objectionable prosecutorial conduct are available."[5]

Justice Brennan, joined by Marshall, J., concurred in part and dissented in part, observing:

"[Various cases] indicate that the policy considerations supporting the harmless error rule and those supporting the existence of an appellate court's supervisory powers are not in irreconcilable conflict. Both the harmless error rule and the exercise of supervisory powers advance the important judicial and public interest in the orderly and efficient administration of justice. [If] Government prosecutors have engaged in a pattern and practice of intentionally violating defendants' constitutional rights, a court of appeals certainly might be justified in reversing a conviction, even if the error at issue is harmless, in an effort to deter future violations. If effective as a deterrent, the reversal could avert further damage to judicial integrity. * * * Convictions are important, but they should not be protected at any cost."

NOTES AND QUESTIONS

1. ***Federal supervisory power vs. constitutional interpretation.*** Under the *Massiah* doctrine (p. 1416, an indicted defendant has a Sixth Amendment right to counsel as well as his *Miranda* safeguards. Stressing that the "strict standard" governing waiver of counsel at trial should apply to an alleged waiver of the *Massiah* right to counsel as well, in *United States v.*

[5] Here, for example, the court could have dealt with the offending argument by directing the District Court to order the prosecutor to show cause why he should not be disciplined, or by asking the Department of Justice to initiate a disciplinary proceeding against him. The Government informs us that in the last three years, the Department of Justice's Office of Professional Responsibility has investigated 28 complaints of unethical conduct and that one assistant United States attorney resigned in the face of an investigation that he made improper arguments to a grand jury. The Court also could have publicly chastised the prosecutor by identifying him in its opinion.

Mohabir, 624 F.2d 1140 (2d Cir.1980), the court invoked its federal supervisory power to hold that a "valid waiver of the Sixth Amendment right to have counsel present during post-indictment interrogation must be preceded by a federal judicial officer's explanation of the content and significance of this right." However, in *Patterson v. Illinois* (1988) (p. 635, the Supreme Court specifically rejected *Mohabir*'s holding that warnings in addition to the *Miranda* warnings are required to effectuate a waiver of the *Massiah* right (see fn. 8 in *Patterson*), without mentioning that *Mohabir* was an exercise of the Second Circuit's federal supervisory power.

2. ***What can federal courts do under the federal supervisory power?*** The *Hasting* Court noted that, within limits, federal courts may exercise their "supervisory power [to] formulate procedural rules not specifically required by the Constitution or the Congress." After *Payner* and *Hasting, what* procedural rules? Consider *United States v. Williams*, p. 965 (exercise of federal supervisory power over grand juries). After *Payner* and *Hasting,* may the federal courts still *exclude evidence* or reverse a conviction based in part on inadmissible evidence if such exclusion or reversal is not required by the Constitution or the Congress? Cf. *Bank of Nova Scotia v. United States*, 487 U.S. 250 (1988) (Note 2, at p. 977).

3. ***Resistance to federal supervisory power.*** Why has the effort to impose "extraconstitutional" standards on federal law enforcement officials, best illustrated by *McNabb* and its progeny, fared so badly in recent decades? Consider Bennett Gershman, *The New Prosecutors,* 53 U.Pitt.L.Rev. 393, 432 (1992): "First, [the supervisory power] required judges to impose on government officials their own notions of 'good policy.' The judiciary has resisted this invitation. Second, supervisory power increasingly has been viewed as an unwarranted judicial intrusion into the exclusive domain of a coordinate branch of the government. Finally, once supervisory power became subservient to the harmless error rule, it became largely irrelevant."

§ 4. TRENDS AND COUNTERTRENDS IN THE STATE COURTS: THE "NEW FEDERALISM IN CRIMINAL PROCEDURE" AND NEW LIMITATIONS ON STATE RIGHTS PROTECTIONS[a]

When the Warren Court's "criminal procedure revolution" came to a halt, a number of state courts "greeted the Burger Court's retreat from activism not with submission, but with a stubborn independence that displays a determination to keep alive the Warren Court's philosophical commitment to protection of the criminal suspect." Donald E. Wilkes, *More on the New Federalism in Criminal Procedure,* 63 Ky.L.J. 873 (1975) . The most influential article on the subject of state constitutional rights is Justice William Brennan's *State Constitutions and the Protection of Individual Rights,* 90 Harv.L.Rev. 489 (1977), one of the most frequently cited law review articles of modern times. See, too, Justice Brennan's updated views in *The Bill of Rights and the States: The Revival of State Constitutions as Guardians of Individual Rights*, 61 N.Y.U.L.Rev. 535 (1986). See also Hans Linde, *First Things First: Rediscovering the States' Bill of Rights*, 9 U.Balt.L.Rev. 379 (1980).

A state supreme court bent on providing the accused with greater protection than that said to be required by the federal constitution must be careful to make it clear that it is resting its ruling on an independent state ground. As the Court, per O'Connor, observed in MICHIGAN v. LONG, 463 U.S. 1032 (1983), "when the adequacy and independence of any possible state law ground is not clear from the face of the opinion, we will accept as the most reasonable explanation that the state court decided the case the way it did because it believed that federal law required

[a] The phrase "new federalism in criminal procedure" was coined by Professor Donald E. Wilkes, Jr., in his 1974 article, *The New Federalism in Criminal Procedure: State Court Evasion of the Burger Court*, 62 Ky.L.J. 421.

it to do so." Thus, in order to insulate its decision from U.S. Supreme Court review, the state court, to quote *Long* again, must indicate "clearly and expressly" that its ruling is based on "separate, adequate and independent" state grounds.

Justice Brennan and Marshall, who often found themselves in a dissenting role in the 1970's, frequently pointed to—and approved and encouraged—the practice of some state courts (a distinct minority) to interpret state procedural rights more expansively than does the current U.S. Supreme Court. See especially Justice Brennan's dissenting opinion in *Michigan v. Mosley* (p. 590. Justice Brennan also forcefully stated his views on this matter in his 1977 law review article, supra, emphasizing that "the decisions of the [U.S. Supreme] Court are not, and should not be, dispositive of questions regarding rights guaranteed by counterpart provisions of state law. [A]lthough in the past it might have been safe for counsel to raise only federal constitutional issues in state courts, plainly it would be most unwise these days not also to raise the state constitutional questions."

Justice Brennan's advice has not gone unheeded. A dozen years after Brennan wrote his first article on state constitutional rights, Washington Supreme Court Justice Robert Utter, *State Constitutional Law, the United States Supreme Court, and Democratic Accountability,* 64 Wash.L.Rev. 19, 27 (1989), reported that "more than 450 published state court opinions [had interpreted] state constitutions as going beyond federal constitutional guarantees."

Consider Charles H. Whitebread & Christopher Slobogin, Criminal Procedure § 34.02(c) (5th ed. 2008):

"State court reaction against the Supreme Court has been particularly energetic with respect to search and seizure, perhaps because the post-1970 Supreme Court has been especially antagonistic to the Fourth Amendment. Indeed, the first Supreme Court criminal procedure decision to encounter significant state court resistance involved a search and seizure issue. In *United States v. Robinson*, 414 U.S. 218 (1973), the Supreme Court held that a full search is permissible after a lawful custodial arrest, regardless of the crime giving rise to the arrest. Within four years of *Robinson*, four different state courts had held, based on state constitutional language, that the nature of the offense is relevant to whether a full search is justified. Similarly, the courts of at least four states refused to follow *United States v. White*, 401 U.S. 745 (1971), on state law grounds. [At] least three states' courts, again relying on their constitutions, have declined to adopt the Supreme Court's totality of the circumstances approach to the probable cause inquiry established in *Illinois v. Gates*, 462 U.S. 213 (1983).[b]

"* * * A factor that could severely curtail the New Federalism, however, is the hostile reaction of state citizens to their courts' activism. Chief Justice Burger, for one, sought to encourage this reaction while he was on the Court. [He pointed out] that 'when state courts interpret state law to require more than the Federal Constitution requires, the citizens of the state must be aware that they have the power to amend state law to ensure rational law enforcement.' [In] at least two states [California and Florida] the electorate has exercised this power."[c]

[b] For a detailed listing of state constitutional rulings that have declined to adopt the Supreme Court's positions under the Fourth, Fifth, and Sixth Amendments, see 2 Jennifer Friesen, *State Constitutional Law: Litigating Individual Rights, Claims and Defense* (4th ed. 2006 & Supp. 2012).

[c] See also Donald E. Wilkes, *The New Federalism in 1984: Death of the Phoenix?*, in DEVELOPMENTS IN STATE CONSTITUTIONAL LAW 166, 169 (B. McGraw ed. 1985).

CHAPTER 3

SOME GENERAL REFLECTIONS ON THE CONSTITUTIONALIZATION OF CRIMINAL PROCEDURE

■ ■ ■

In the early 20th Century, civil rights abuses of African-Americans—brought to light in criminal prosecutions against them in the South—led the U.S. Supreme Court to assume a more active role in the regulation of the criminal justice system. This involvement in the rights of the accused reached its peak during the Warren Court era, especially in the 1960s. After the 1960s, the High Court's involvement in constitutional-criminal procedure reduced significantly. The constitutionalization of criminal procedure raises a number of important questions addressed in this chapter: (1) Is constitutionalizing criminal procedure the best way to address government abuse or are other branches of government equally or better-suited to redress these problems? (2) Should the law of criminal procedure address racial injustice? If so, how? (3) How should we think about the problem of innocent people being convicted and how prevalent is the problem? (4) Is the system designed for felony prosecutions and, if so, how are misdemeanor prosecutions different? (5) What remedies exist to redress government overreach aside from excluding evidence in criminal cases? (6) How are police officers hired and trained and what can be done locally to address abuses of power?

§ 1. INSTITUTIONAL COMPETENCE

DONALD A. DRIPPS—CONSTITUTIONAL THEORY FOR CRIMINAL PROCEDURE: DICKERSON, MIRANDA, AND THE CONTINUING QUEST FOR BROAD-BUT-SHALLOW

43 Wm. & Mary L.Rev. 1, 45–46 (2001).

American legislatures consistently have failed to address defects in the criminal process, even when they rise to crisis-level proportions. * * * Legislatures across the United States have found billions of dollars for prisons, but the support for indigent defense is shamefully inadequate. * * * Legislatures have not filled the voids created by contemporary pro-government criminal procedure rulings. They have not, for instance, adopted statutory regulations of undercover operations, even though the Court has left such operations unregulated by the Fourth Amendment. They have not adopted statutory requirements for judicial warrants, or the preservation of exculpatory evidence, or plugged holes in the exclusionary rule, let alone delivered the effective tort remedy exclusionary rule critics have advocated for decades.

The record is not an accident, but the product of rational political incentives. Almost everyone has an interest in controlling crime. Only young men, disproportionately black, are at significant risk of erroneous prosecution for garden-variety felonies. Abuses of police search and seizure or interrogation powers rarely fall upon middle-aged, middle-class citizens. When powerful interest groups are subject to the exercise of police powers that pale in comparison to what is visited on young black men luckless enough to reside in a "high crime area," things are different. [But] so long as the vast bulk of police and prosecutorial power targets the relatively powerless (and when will that ever be otherwise?), criminal procedure rules that limit public power will come from the courts or they will come from nowhere.

WILLIAM J. STUNTZ—THE UNEASY RELATIONSHIP BETWEEN CRIMINAL PROCEDURE AND CRIMINAL JUSTICE

107 Yale L.J. 1, 3–12, 72–76 (1997).

[The] criminal justice system is dominated by a trio of forces: crime rates, the definition of crime (which of course partly determines crime rates), and funding decisions—how much money to spend on police, prosecutors, defense attorneys, judges, and prisons. These forces determine the ratio of crimes to prosecutors and the ratio of prosecutions to public defenders, and those ratios in turn go far toward determining what the system does and how the system does it. But the law that defines what the criminal process looks like, the law that defines defendants' rights, is made by judges and Justices who have little information about crime rates and funding decisions, and whose incentives to take account of those factors may be perverse. High crime rates make it easy for prosecutors to substitute cases without strong procedural claims for cases with such claims. Underfunding of criminal defense counsel limits the number of procedural claims that can be pressed. Both phenomena make criminal procedure doctrines seem inexpensive to the appellate judges who define those doctrines. Unsurprisingly, given that regulating the criminal justice system has seemed cheap, the courts have done a lot of regulating—more, one suspects, than they would have done in a world where defendants could afford to litigate more often and more aggressively, or where prosecutors could not so easily substitute some cases for others. Criminal procedure is thus distorted by forces its authors probably do not understand.

The distortion runs both ways. As courts have raised the cost of criminal investigation and prosecution, legislatures have sought out devices to reduce those costs. Severe limits on defense funding are the most obvious example, but not the only one. Expanded criminal liability makes it easier for the government to induce guilty pleas, as do high mandatory sentences that serve as useful threats against recalcitrant defendants. And guilty pleas avoid most of the potentially costly requirements that criminal procedure imposes. These strategies would no doubt be politically attractive anyway, but the law of criminal procedure makes them more so. Predictably, underfunding, overcriminalization, and oversentencing have increased as criminal procedure has expanded.

Nor are the law's perverse effects limited to courts and legislatures. Constitutional criminal procedure raises the cost of prosecuting wealthier defendants by giving those defendants more issues to litigate. The result, at the margin, is to steer prosecutors away from such defendants and toward poorer ones. By giving defendants other, cheaper claims to raise, constitutional criminal procedure also raises the cost to defense counsel of investigating and litigating factual claims, claims that bear directly on their clients' innocence or guilt. The result is to steer defense counsel, again at the margin, away from those sorts of claims and toward constitutional issues. More Fourth, Fifth, and Sixth Amendment claims probably mean fewer self-defense claims and mens rea arguments. This turns the standard conservative criticism of the law of criminal procedure on its head. Ever since the 1960s, the right has argued that criminal procedure frees too many of the guilty. The better criticism may be that it helps to imprison too many of the innocent.

* * * In a world where trivial crimes stay on the books, or one where routine traffic offenses count as crimes, the requirement of probable cause to arrest may mean almost nothing. Officers can arrest for a minor offense—everyone violates the traffic rules—in order to search or question a suspect on a major one. This allows arrests and searches of suspected drug dealers without any ex ante support for the suspicion, the very thing the probable cause standard is supposed to forbid. In a world where sodomy laws remain valid long after their enforcement has ceased, prosecutors

can induce guilty pleas in some problematic sexual assault cases—the need to prove nonconsent disappears, and with it (again, in some cases) the ability to mount a plausible defense. This amounts to convicting defendants of sexual assault without proving the crime, by pointing to another crime that serves as the excuse for punishment, but not the reason.

[Legislatures] fund the system. Legislatures decide how many police officers, prosecutors, and judges to have, and how much to pay them. They also decide how generously to fund criminal defense counsel in those cases (the majority) in which the court appoints counsel. * * *

Over the course of the past couple of decades, legislatures have exercised this funding power to expand substantially the resources devoted to law enforcement, though the budget increases appear less substantial in light of parallel increases in crime. * * * [N]otwithstanding nominal budget increases, spending on indigent defendants in constant dollars per case appears to have declined significantly * * *. The predictable result is public defenders' offices with very large ratios of cases to lawyers.

[There] are a great many constitutional rules, most of which are highly contestable. The rules are produced by a court system that acts quite independently of legislative preference, at least in this area. (*Mapp v. Ohio* and *Miranda v. Arizona* were hardly examples of majoritarian lawmaking.) Perhaps more so than anywhere else in constitutional law, in criminal procedure the broad exercise of judicial power tends to be justified precisely by legislators' unwillingness to protect constitutional interests. Yet these judge-made rules are enforced through the efforts of criminal defense counsel who, in most cases, are paid by the state—the same state whose preferences the rules purport to trump. By buying less criminal defense, the state can buy less enforcement of constitutional criminal procedure. It can, to some degree, trump the trump. Of course, if it does so it necessarily also buys less of whatever else criminal defense counsel do.

* * * Constitutional law has focused relentlessly on the sorts of issues that are susceptible to legal analysis—how to select juries, when to require warrants, which mistrials permit retrial and which ones mean the defendant must go free. These are classic lawyers' issues; they give rise to classic lawyers' arguments. But courts' decisions on those issues are embedded in a system shaped by more open-ended—and more flagrantly political—judgments: How bad should something be before we call it a crime? How much money should we spend on criminal defense? Perhaps courts would do a sufficiently poor job of making these open-ended political judgments that we are better off leaving them to other actors. That is the system's current premise, and the premise is entirely plausible. But if that premise is right, those other actors—chiefly legislators and prosecutors—are able to defeat courts' work on courts' own turf: All those judge-made procedural rules are likely not to work the way they are supposed to. In the criminal justice system's three-legged stool—procedure, substance, and money—procedure is the least stable leg, the one that most depends on the others for support.

So criminal procedure may be no more than an instance of courts properly recognizing the need to intervene in a system that imposes terrible costs on large numbers of people, and then doing what comes naturally, regulating the kinds of things courts are used to regulating. That includes avoiding a kind of decision-making that, for courts, seems unnatural. All of which might be fine if the judicially regulated sphere could be isolated from the rest of the system. Sadly, it cannot. * * *

[The law of criminal procedure prevents some serious wrongs and produces other benefits, some of which are quite familiar.] Yet there are substantial tradeoffs, and the tradeoffs are not so familiar. The criminal process is much harder to control than courts suppose; it is driven by forces the courts do not, and perhaps cannot, direct. When courts do act, their actions are shaped by those forces in ways the courts themselves may not understand, ways that are at best ambiguous and at worst bad. Some part of what the Fourth, Fifth, and Sixth Amendments protect has probably come at the cost of a criminal justice system that is less focused on the merits and hence more likely to convict innocents, a system that disproportionately targets the poor, and a system that convicts for "crimes" that cover vastly more than anyone would wish to punish. The merits of this bargain are at least open to question. * * *

[For] the past thirty-five years, the legal system's discussion of criminal defendants' rights has suffered from an air of unreality, a sense that all goals can be satisfied and all values honored—that we can, for example, have the jury selection process we want at no cost to anything else we might want. * * *

That should change. It is time to acknowledge the tradeoffs, to take seriously the nature of the system the law of criminal procedure regulates and the ways in which that system can evade or undermine the regulation. In a regime like ours, countermajoritarian restraints on the criminal process can succeed only at a cost, the cost is probably substantial, and it is disproportionately imposed on those who least deserve to bear it. Leaving more of the process to majoritarian institutions might be better, not least for some of the defendants the process is designed to protect.

That need not mean leaving defendants to the mercies of state legislatures and local prosecutors. If constitutional law's response to criminal justice has failed, it has failed not just from too much intervention but from too little as well. Making [the right to counsel] a formal right only, without any ancillary funding requirements, has produced a criminal process that is, for poor defendants, a scandal. Courts' reluctance to police legislatures' criminalization and sentencing decisions—coupled with the way those legislative decisions can be used in a system that gives prosecutors blanket authority to choose whom to go after and for what—has produced its own scandals. Defendants' interests might best be protected by less procedure, coupled with a much more activist judicial posture toward funding, the definition of crime, and sentencing—all areas where judges have been loath to take dramatic stands.

The judicial reticence seems to have been motivated by a desire not to trench on the prerogatives of the politicians, a desire to stick to the more law-like and presumably less contentious ground of process. That the 1960s produced a revolution in criminal *procedure* may testify to the underrated conservatism of Warren Court constitutional thought, to that radical Court's willingness to confine its intervention to conventional categories. If so, in this area these conservative instincts may have been misplaced—as, perhaps, was the Court's reformist (procedural) zeal. The system might be better off today had Warren and his colleagues worried less about criminal procedure, and more about criminal justice.

§ 2. RACIAL INJUSTICE

TRACEY MACLIN—"BLACK AND BLUE ENCOUNTERS"—SOME PRELIMINARY THOUGHTS ABOUT FOURTH AMENDMENT SEIZURES: SHOULD RACE MATTER?

26 Valparaiso U.L.Rev. 243, 250, 252–61, 265–70 (1991).

* * * I submit that the dynamics surrounding an encounter between a police officer and a black male are quite different from those that surround an encounter between an officer and the so-called average, reasonable person. My tentative proposal is that the Court should disregard the notion that there is an average, hypothetical, reasonable person out there by which to judge the constitutionality of police encounters. When assessing the coercive nature of an encounter, the Court should consider the race of the person confronted by the police, and how that person's race might have influenced his attitude toward the encounter.

* * * [The] Supreme Court has said over and over that *all citizens*—not just rich, white men from the suburbs—are free to ignore a police officer who accosts them. In *Florida v. Royer* [p. 419, Justice White explained that: "The person approached . . . need not answer any question put to him; indeed, he may decline to listen to the questions at all and may go on his way. He may not be detained even momentarily without reasonable, objective grounds for doing so; and his refusal to listen or answer does not, without more, furnish those grounds."[43]

This is what the law is supposed to be; black men, however, know that a different "law" exists on the street. Black men know they are liable to be stopped at anytime, and that when they question the authority of the police, the response from the cops is often swift and violent. This applies to black men of all economic strata, regardless of their level of education, and whatever their job status or place in the community.

* * * Black males learn at an early age that confrontations with the police should be avoided; black teenagers are advised never to challenge a police officer, even when the officer is wrong. Even if a police officer has arguable grounds for stopping a black male, such an encounter often engenders distinct feelings for the black man. Those feelings are fear of possible violence or humiliation.

To be sure, when whites are stopped by the police, they too feel uneasy and often experience fear. [But] I wonder whether the average white person worries that an otherwise routine police encounter may lead to a violent confrontation. When they are stopped by the police, do whites contemplate the possibility that they will be physically abused for questioning why an officer has stopped them? White teenagers who walk the streets or hang-out in the local mall, do they worry about being strip-searched by the police? Does the average white person ever see himself experiencing what Rodney King or Don Jackson went through during their encounters with the police?

Police officers have shown [that] they will not hesitate to "teach a lesson" to any black male who, even in the slightest way challenges his authority. For example, in Los Angeles, even before [the Rodney King beating], blacks knew not to argue with the police unless they wanted to risk death in a police choke-hold that seemed to be applied more frequently in the case of black males than other citizens.[56]

In addition to fear, distrust is another component that swirls around encounters between black males and the police. Over the years, black males have learned that police officers have little regard for their Fourth Amendment rights. Two years ago in Boston, for instance, a city learned what can happen when a police department is encouraged to ignore the constitutional rights of a targeted class of individuals—black males. In the aftermath of a tragic shooting of a white couple and the declaration of a "war" against teenage gangs and their associates, black males were subjected to what one state judge called "martial law"[57] tactics by a police department that offered no apologies for its disregard of constitutional liberties.[58] * * *

---

[43] *Florida v. Royer* [p. 419], (1983) (plurality opinion) * * *.

[56] See City of Los Angeles v. Lyons, 461 U.S. 95, 116 n. 3 (1983) (Marshall, J., dissenting) ("[S]ince 1975 no less than sixteen persons have died following use of a chokehold by an LAPD police officer. Twelve have been Negro males. [Thus] in a city where Negro males constitute nine per cent of the population, they have accounted for seventy-five per cent of the deaths resulting from the use of chokehold."). * * *

[57] Commonwealth v. Phillips and Woody, No. 080275–6, Memorandum and Order, at 3 (Suffolk Sup.Ct. Sept. 17, 1989) (Judge Cortland Mathers found that a police order that all known gang members and their associates would be searched on sight was "a proclamation of martial law in Roxbury for a narrow class of people, young blacks, suspected of membership in a gang or perceived by the police to be in the company of someone thought to be a member."). * * *

[58] Boston Police Deputy Superintendent William Celester had been quoted as saying: " 'People are going to say we're violating their [gang members'] constitutional rights, but we're not too concerned about that. . . . If we have to violate their rights, if that's what it takes, then that's what we're going to do." * * *

* * * [B]eing black constitutes a "double-brand" in the mind of the police. Black men are associated with "crimes against the person, with bodily harm to police officers, and with a general lack of support for the police."[67] Also, because of their race, black males "are bound to appear discordant to policemen in most of the environment of a middle-class white society. For this reason, black males doubly draw the attention of police officers."[68] In essence, the police officer "identif[ies] the black man with danger."[69]

From the perspective of the black man, however, these police attitudes only reinforce the view that " '[t]he police system is a dictatorship toward the black people.' "[70] * * * Black men are considered suspicious and targeted for questioning not because of any objective or empirical evidence that they are involved in criminality, but because of police bias and societal indifference to the plight of black males who are on the receiving-end of aggressive police tactics. In effect, black men are accorded "sub-citizen" status for Fourth Amendment purposes.

* * * Currently, the Court assesses the coercive nature of a police encounter by considering the *totality of the circumstances* surrounding the confrontation. All I want the Court to do is to consider the role race might play, along with the other factors it considers, when judging the constitutionality of the encounter. * * *

NOTES AND QUESTIONS

1. ***Considering race in a reasonable suspicion analysis.*** A few courts have taken Professor Maclin's suggestion and now consider race in reasonable suspicion analyses. For a recent example, consider the Supreme Judicial Court of Massachusetts's statements about flight in *Commonwealth v. Warren*, 58 N.E.3d 333 (Mass. 2016): "[W]here the suspect is a black male stopped by the police on the streets of Boston, the analysis of flight as a factor in the reasonable suspicion calculus cannot be divorced from the findings in a recent Boston Police Department (department) report documenting a pattern of racial profiling of black males in the city of Boston * * * . We do not eliminate flight as a factor in the reasonable suspicion analysis whenever a black male is the subject of an investigatory stop. However, in such circumstances, flight is not necessarily probative of a suspect's state of mind or consciousness of guilt. * * * Such an individual, when approached by the police, might just as easily be motivated by the desire to avoid the recurring indignity of being racially profiled as by the desire to hide criminal activity. Given this reality for black males in the city of Boston, a judge should, in appropriate cases, consider the report's findings in weighing flight as a factor in the reasonable suspicion calculus."

2. ***Implicit bias.*** In *United States v. Mateo-Medina*, 845 F.3d 546 (3d Cir. 2017), the Third Circuit held that a federal district court had erred in considering the defendant's bare record of prior arrests that did not lead to conviction when imposing a sentence. Chief Judge McKee, writing for the court, noted:

> "In 2013, The Sentencing Project released a shadow report to the United Nations Human Rights Committee, *Regarding Racial Disparities in the United States Criminal Justice System* (Sentencing Project Report).[31] The Sentencing Project Report pointed to a

---

[67] D. Bagley & H. Mendelsohn, *Minorities and the Police* 107 (1969).

[68] Id.

[69] J. Skolnick, *Justice Without Trial* 49 (1966).

[70] B. Blauner, *Black Lives, White Lives* 110 (1989).

[31] The Sentencing Project, *Report of The Sentencing Project to the United Nations Human Rights Committee Regarding Racial Disparities in the United States Criminal Justice System* (August 2013), *available at* http://sentencingproject.org/wp-content/uploads/2015/12/Race-and-Justice-Shadow-Report-ICCPR.pdf (hereinafter Sentencing Project Report).

wide body of scholarship indicating that socioeconomic factors influenced disparities in arrest rates.

"The Sentencing Project Report also remarked on recent research indicating that police are more likely to stop, and arrest, people of color due to implicit bias. Implicit bias, or stereotyping, consists of the unconscious assumptions that humans make about individuals, particularly in situations that require rapid decision-making, such as police encounters. 'Extensive research has shown that in such situations the vast majority of Americans of all races implicitly associate black Americans with adjectives such as "dangerous," "aggressive," "violent," and "criminal." '

"In addition, a recent empirical study analyzed thirteen years' worth of data on race, socioeconomic factors, drug use, and drug arrests.[35] The study found that African-Americans, Hispanics, and whites used drugs in roughly the same percentages, and in roughly the same ways. The study controlled for variables such as whether the participant lived in high-crime, gang-controlled areas. Despite those controls, the study concluded that 'in early adulthood, race disparities in drug arrest[s] grew substantially; as early as age 22, African-Americans had 83% greater odds of a drug arrest than whites and at age 27 this disparity was 235%.' With respect to Hispanics, the study found that socioeconomic factors such as residing in an inner-city neighborhood accounted for much of the disparity in drug arrest rates."

3. ***State legislation.*** Roughly a dozen states have adopted legislation that prohibits racial profiling, which some states define as action taken "solely on the basis of race" while others exclude consideration of race except where race is part of a description of a "specific suspect." *See* CRIMPROC § 1.5(j) (collecting statutes). The Department of Justice has adopted a similar approach for federal law enforcement agencies:

THE JUSTICE DEPARTMENT'S POLICY GUIDANCE REGARDING RACIAL PROFILING (DECEMBER 2014)

* * * Biased practices, as the Federal government has long recognized, are unfair, promote mistrust of law enforcement, and perpetuate negative and harmful stereotypes. Moreover—and vitally important—biased practices are ineffective. As Attorney General Eric Holder has stated, such practices are "simply not good law enforcement." * * *

This new Guidance applies to Federal law enforcement officers performing Federal law enforcement activities, including those related to national security and intelligence, and defines not only the circumstances in which Federal law enforcement officers may take into account a person's race and ethnicity * * * but also when gender, national origin, religion, sexual orientation, or gender identity may be taken into account. This new Guidance also applies to state and local law enforcement officers while participating in Federal law enforcement task forces. Finally, this Guidance promotes training and accountability, to ensure that its contents are understood and implemented appropriately. * * *

A. *Routine or Spontaneous Activities in Domestic Law Enforcement*

* * * Law enforcement agencies and officers sometimes engage in law enforcement activities, such as traffic and foot patrols, that generally do not involve either the ongoing investigation of specific criminal activities or the prevention of catastrophic events or harm to national or homeland security. Rather, their activities are typified by spontaneous action in response to the activities of individuals whom they happen to encounter in the course of their patrols and about

[35] Ojmarrh Mitchell & Michael S. Caudy, *Examining Racial Disparities in Drug Arrests*, JUSTICE QUARTERLY (Jan. 2013), *available at* http://dx.doi.org/10.1080/07418825.2012.761721.

whom they have no information other than their observations. These general enforcement responsibilities should be carried out without any consideration of race, ethnicity, gender, national origin, religion, sexual orientation, or gender identity.

• **Example:** While parked by the side of the George Washington Parkway, a Park Police Officer notices that nearly all vehicles on the road are exceeding the posted speed limit. Although each such vehicle is committing an infraction that would legally justify a stop, the officer may not use a listed characteristic as a factor in deciding which motorists to pull over. Likewise, the officer may not use a listed characteristic in deciding which detained motorists to ask to consent to a search of their vehicles.

* * * Profiling by law enforcement based on a listed characteristic is morally wrong and inconsistent with our core values and principles of fairness and justice. Even if there were overall statistical evidence of differential rates of commission of certain offenses among individuals possessing particular characteristics, the affirmative use of such generalized notions by law enforcement officers in routine, spontaneous law enforcement activities is tantamount to stereotyping. It casts a pall of suspicion over every member of certain groups without regard to the specific circumstances of a particular law enforcement activity, and it offends the dignity of the individual improperly targeted. Whatever the motivation, it is patently unacceptable and thus prohibited under this Guidance for law enforcement officers to act on the belief that possession of a listed characteristic signals a higher risk of criminality. This is the core of invidious profiling, and it must not occur.

The situation is different when an officer has specific information, based on trustworthy sources, to "be on the lookout" for specific individuals identified at least in part by a specific listed characteristic. In such circumstances, the officer is not acting based on a generalized assumption about individuals possessing certain characteristics; rather, the officer is helping locate specific individuals previously identified as involved in crime.

• **Example:** While parked by the side of the George Washington Parkway, a Park Police Officer receives an "All Points Bulletin" to be on the lookout for a fleeing bank robbery suspect, a man of a particular race and particular hair color in his 30s driving a blue automobile. The officer may use this description, including the race and gender of the particular suspect, in deciding which speeding motorists to pull over.

B. *All Activities Other than Routine or Spontaneous Law Enforcement Activities*

In conducting all activities other than routine or spontaneous law enforcement activities, Federal law enforcement officers may consider race, ethnicity, gender, national origin, religion, sexual orientation, or gender identity only to the extent that there is trustworthy information, relevant to the locality or time frame, that links persons possessing a particular listed characteristic to an identified criminal incident, scheme, or organization, a threat to national or homeland security, a violation of Federal immigration law, or an authorized intelligence activity. In order to rely on a listed characteristic, law enforcement officers must also reasonably believe that the law enforcement, security, or intelligence activity to be undertaken is merited under the totality of the circumstances, such as any temporal exigency and the nature of any potential harm to be averted. This standard applies even where the use of a listed characteristic might otherwise be lawful. * * *

Because law enforcement and intelligence actions are necessarily context-specific, in applying each of these factors, law enforcement officers may properly account for relevant facts and circumstances, such as any temporal exigency and the nature of any potential harm to be averted. However, in all cases, law enforcement officers must reasonably believe that the law enforcement or intelligence activity to be undertaken is merited under the totality of the circumstances. * * *

[When] a law enforcement officer relies on a listed characteristic in undertaking an action, that officer must have a reasonable belief that the action is merited under the totality of the circumstances. This standard ensures that, under the circumstances, the officer is acting in good faith when he or she relies in part on a listed characteristic to take action.

- **Example:** A law enforcement officer who is working as part of a federal task force has received a reliable tip that an individual intends to detonate a homemade bomb in a train station during rush hour, but the tip does not provide any more information. The officer harbors stereotypical views about religion and therefore decides that investigators should focus on individuals of a particular faith. Doing so would be impermissible because a law enforcement officer's stereotypical beliefs never provide a reasonable basis to undertake a law enforcement or intelligence action.

Note that these standards allow the use of reliable identifying information about planned future crimes, attacks, or other violations of Federal law. Where officers receive a credible tip from a reliable informant regarding a planned crime or attack that has not yet occurred, the officers may use this information under the same restrictions applying to information obtained regarding a past incident. A prohibition on the use of reliable prospective information would severely hamper law enforcement efforts by essentially compelling law enforcement officers to wait for incidents to occur, instead of taking pro-active measures to prevent them from happening.

- **Example:** While investigating a specific drug trafficking operation, DEA special agents learn that a particular methamphetamine distribution ring is manufacturing the drug in California, and plans to have couriers pick up shipments at the Sacramento, California, airport and drive the drugs back to Oklahoma for distribution. The agents also receive trustworthy information that the distribution ring has specifically chosen to hire older women of a particular race to act as the couriers. DEA agents may properly target older women of that particular race driving vehicles with indicia such as Oklahoma plates near the Sacramento airport. * * *

National security, homeland security, and intelligence activities often are national in scope and focused on prevention of attacks by both known and unknown actors, not just prosecution. For example, terrorist organizations might aim to engage in acts of catastrophic violence in any part of the country (indeed, in multiple places simultaneously, if possible).

These facts do not change the applicability of the Guidance, however. In order to undertake an action based on a listed characteristic, a law enforcement officer must have trustworthy information, relevant to the locality or time frame, linking persons possessing that characteristic to a threat to national security, homeland security, or intelligence activity, and the actions to be taken must be reasonable under the totality of the circumstances.

- **Example:** The FBI receives reliable information that persons affiliated with a foreign ethnic insurgent group intend to use suicide bombers to assassinate that country's president and his entire entourage during an official visit to the United States. Agents may appropriately focus investigative attention on identifying members of that ethnic insurgent group who may be present and active in the United States and who, based on other available information, might be involved in planning some such attack during the state visit. * * *

JUSTICE SONIA SOTOMAYOR—DISSENTING IN UTAH V. STRIEFF

___ U.S. ___, 136 S.Ct. 2056, 195 L.Ed.2d 400 (2016).

[Edward Joseph Strieff, Jr. was stopped by a Utah police officer without reasonable suspicion to justify the stop. As part of that illegal stop, the officer discovered an outstanding traffic warrant and arrested Strieff, finding methamphetamine incident to that arrest. The question presented was whether the Fourth Amendment's exclusionary rule required suppression of the evidence, because it was obtained as a result of an unconstitutional seizure or whether the discovery of the outstanding warrant was a sufficient intervening circumstance to break the causal chain between the unlawful stop and the subsequent arrest/search and render the discovery of the evidence sufficiently attenuated from the initial illegality to permit its use in a subsequent criminal trial. A 5–3 majority of the Supreme Court held that the evidence was admissible. Justices Ginsburg, Sotomayor, and Kagan dissented. Extracts from Justice Sotomayor's separate dissent are below.]

* * * Writing only for myself, and drawing on my professional experiences, I would add that unlawful "stops" have severe consequences much greater than the inconvenience suggested by the name. This Court has given officers an array of instruments to probe and examine you. When we condone officers' use of these devices without adequate cause, we give them reason to target pedestrians in an arbitrary manner. We also risk treating members of our communities as second-class citizens.

Although many Americans have been stopped for speeding or jaywalking, few may realize how degrading a stop can be when the officer is looking for more. This Court has allowed an officer to stop you for whatever reason he wants—so long as he can point to a pretextual justification after the fact. *Whren v. United States*, 517 U.S. 806, 813 (1996). That justification must provide specific reasons why the officer suspected you were breaking the law, *Terry*, 392 U.S., at 21, but it may factor in your ethnicity, *United States v. Brignoni-Ponce*, 422 U.S. 873, 886–887 (1975), where you live, *Adams v. Williams*, 407 U.S. 143, 147 (1972), what you were wearing, *United States v. Sokolow*, 490 U.S. 1, 4–5 (1989), and how you behaved, *Illinois v. Wardlow*, 528 U.S. 119, 124–125 (2000). The officer does not even need to know which law you might have broken so long as he can later point to any possible infraction—even one that is minor, unrelated, or ambiguous. *Devenpeck v. Alford*, 543 U.S. 146, 154–155 (2004); *Heien v. North Carolina*, 574 U.S. ___ (2014).

The indignity of the stop is not limited to an officer telling you that you look like a criminal. The officer may next ask for your "consent" to inspect your bag or purse without telling you that you can decline. See *Florida v. Bostick*, 501 U.S. 429, 438 (1991). Regardless of your answer, he may order you to stand "helpless, perhaps facing a wall with [your] hands raised." *Terry*, 392 U.S., at 17. If the officer thinks you might be dangerous, he may then "frisk" you for weapons. This involves more than just a pat down. As onlookers pass by, the officer may " 'feel with sensitive fingers every portion of [your] body. A thorough search [may] be made of [your] arms and armpits, waistline and back, the groin and area about the testicles, and entire surface of the legs down to the feet.' " *Id.*, at 17, n. 13.

The officer's control over you does not end with the stop. If the officer chooses, he may handcuff you and take you to jail for doing nothing more than speeding, jaywalking, or "driving [your] pickup truck . . . with [your] 3-year-old son and 5-year-old daughter . . . without [your] seatbelt fastened." *Atwater v. Lago Vista*, 532 U.S. 318, 323–324 (2001). At the jail, he can fingerprint you, swab DNA from the inside of your mouth, and force you to "shower with a delousing agent" while you "lift [your] tongue, hold out [your] arms, turn around, and lift [your] genitals." *Florence v. Board of Chosen Freeholders of County of Burlington*, 566 U.S. ___, ___–___ (2012) (slip op., at 2–3); *Maryland v. King*, 569 U.S. ___, ___ (2013) (slip op., at 28). Even if you are innocent, you will now join the 65 million Americans with an arrest record and experience the "civil death" of discrimination by employers, landlords, and whoever else conducts a background check. Chin, The New Civil Death, 160 U.Pa.L.Rev. 1789, 1805 (2012). And, of course, if you fail to pay bail or appear for court, a judge will issue a warrant to render you "arrestable on sight" in the future.

This case involves a *suspicionless* stop, one in which the officer initiated this chain of events without justification. As the Justice Department notes, many innocent people are subjected to the humiliations of these unconstitutional searches. The white defendant in this case shows that anyone's dignity can be violated in this manner. But it is no secret that people of color are disproportionate victims of this type of scrutiny. See M. Alexander, The New Jim Crow 95–136 (2010). For generations, black and brown parents have given their children "the talk"—instructing them never to run down the street; always keep your hands where they can be seen; do not even think of talking back to a stranger—all out of fear of how an officer with a gun will react to them. See, e.g., W. E. B. Du Bois, The Souls of Black Folk (1903); J. Baldwin, The Fire Next Time (1963); T. Coates, Between the World and Me (2015).

By legitimizing the conduct that produces this double consciousness, this case tells everyone, white and black, guilty and innocent, that an officer can verify your legal status at any time. It says that your body is subject to invasion while courts excuse the violation of your rights. It implies that you are not a citizen of a democracy but the subject of a carceral state, just waiting to be cataloged. We must not pretend that the countless people who are routinely targeted by police are "isolated." They are the canaries in the coal mine whose deaths, civil and literal, warn us that no one can breathe in this atmosphere. See L. Guinier & G. Torres, The Miner's Canary 274–283 (2002). They are the ones who recognize that unlawful police stops corrode all our civil liberties and threaten all our lives. Until their voices matter too, our justice system will continue to be anything but.

RANDALL L. KENNEDY—RACE, CRIME, AND THE LAW

158–60 (1997).

When a Mexican-American motorist is selected for questioning in part on the basis of his perceived ancestry, he is undoubtedly being burdened more heavily at that moment on account of his race than his white Anglo counterpart. He is being made to pay a type of racial tax for the campaign against illegal immigration that whites, blacks, and Asians escape. Similarly, a young black man selected for questioning by police as he alights from an airplane or drives a car is being made to pay a type of racial tax for the war against drugs that whites and other groups escape. The tax is the cost of being subjected to greater scrutiny than others. But is that tax illegitimate?

One defense of it is that, under the circumstances, people of other races are simply not in a position to pay the tax effectively. In contrast to apparent Mexican ancestry, neither apparent white nor black nor Asian ancestry appreciably raises the risk that a person near the Mexican border is illegally resident in the United States. Similarly, the argument would run that in contrast to the young black man, the young white man is not as likely to be courier for illicit drugs. The defense could go on to say that, in this context, race is *not* being used invidiously. It is not being used as a marker to identify people to harm through enslavement, or exclusion, or segregation. Rather, race is being used merely as a signal that facilitates efficient law enforcement. In this context, apparent Mexican ancestry or blackness is being used for unobjectionable ends in the same way that whiteness is used in the affirmative action context: as a marker that has the effect, though not the purpose, of burdening a given racial group. Whereas whites are made to pay a racial tax for the purpose of opening up opportunities for people of color in education and employment, Mexican-Americans and blacks are made to pay a racial tax for the purpose of more efficient law enforcement.

We need to pause here to consider the tremendous controversy that has surrounded affirmative action policies aimed at helping racial minorities. Many of the same arguments against race-based affirmative action are applicable as well in the context of race-based police stops. With affirmative action, many whites claim that they are victims of racial discrimination. With race-based police stops, many people of color complain that they are victims of racial discrimination. With affirmative action, many adversely affected whites claim that they are *innocent* victims of a policy that penalizes them for the misconduct of others who also happened to have been white.

With race-based police stops, many adversely affected people of color maintain that they are *innocent* victims of a policy that penalizes them for the misconduct of others who also happen to be colored. Many whites claim that a major drawback of affirmative action which makes it more costly than valuable is the fact of their intense resentment against such programs. Many people of color claim that one of the drawbacks of race-based police stops that makes it more costly than valuable is their resentment against such policies.

There exist, however, a remarkable difference in reactions to these racial policies, both of which involve race-dependent decisionmaking. While affirmative action is under tremendous pressure politically and legally, racial policing is not. * * *

STUART TAYLOR, JR.—POLITICALLY INCORRECT PROFILING: A MATTER OF LIFE OR DEATH

National Law Journal, March 3, 2001, p. 3406.

What would happen if another 19 well-trained al Qaeda terrorists, this time with 19 bombs in their bags, tried to board 19 airliners over the next 19 months? Many would probably succeed, blowing up lots of planes and thousands of people if the forces of head-in-the-sand political correctness prevail—as they did before Sept. 11—in blocking use of national origin as a factor in deciding which passengers' bags to search with extra care.

But a well-designed profiling system might well catch all 19. Such a system would not be race-based; indeed, most Arab-Americans would not fit the profile. It would factor in suspicious behavior, along with national origin, gender, and age. It would spread the burden by selecting at least one white (or black, or Asian) passenger to be searched for every Middle Easterner so selected. And it should be done politely and respectfully.

We have no good alternative. For the foreseeable future, the shortage of high-tech bomb-detection machines and the long delays required to search luggage by hand will make it impossible to effectively screen more than a small percentage of checked bags. The only real protection is to make national origin a key factor in choosing those bags. Otherwise, federalizing airport security and confiscating toenail clippers will be futile gestures.

I revisit this issue in part because research since my Sept. 22 column reinforces my conviction that national-origin profiling may be the only way (in the short term) to avoid hundreds or thousands of deaths.[a] At the same time, critics have persuaded me that the "racial" profiling of

---

[a] In his September 22nd column, *The Case for Racial Profiling at Airports*, National Law Journal p. 2877, Mr. Taylor contrasted racial profiling of people boarding airlines with the racial profiling that occurs when highway police pull over African-Americans in hugely disproportionate numbers to search for drugs. He thought racial profiling of that kind "should be deemed unconstitutional even where there is a statistically valid basis for believing that it will help catch more drug dealers or violent criminals." Taylor continued:

> Such racial profiling is hard to distinguish from—and sometimes involves—plain old racial harassment. It subjects thousands of innocent people to the kind of humiliation that characterizes police states. It hurts law enforcement by fomenting fear and distrust among potential witnesses, tipsters, and jurors. It is rarely justified by any risk of imminent violence. And it makes a mockery of conservative preachings that the Constitution is colorblind.
>
> Stopping hijacking is different. First, preventing mass murder is infinitely more important than finding illegal drugs or guns. Second, 100 percent of the people who have hijacked airplanes to mass-murder Americans have been Arab men. Third, a virulent perversion of Islam is the only mass movement in the world so committed to mass-murdering Americans that its fanatics are willing to kill themselves in the process. Fourth, this movement includes people who have lived legally in America for years—some of whom may be citizens—so the risk of weapons being smuggled onto airplanes cannot be eliminated by giving special scrutiny only to foreign nationals.
>
> In short, the mathematical probability that a randomly chosen Arab passenger might attempt a mass-murder-suicide hijacking—while tiny—is considerably higher than the probability that a randomly chosen white, black, Hispanic, or Asian passenger might. In constitutional law parlance, while racial profiling may

"Arab-looking" people that I previously advocated would be less effective than profiling based on apparent origin in any of the nations known to be exporters of anti-American terrorism—not only nations in the Arab world, but also most, or all, of the nations in the Muslim world. Millions of Arab-Americans would not fit the profile because their American roots would be apparent—from their accents and speech patterns—to trained security screeners.

We have heard a great deal about the dismay of Middle Eastern passengers who have been searched and (in some cases) rudely treated on flights or unjustifiably ejected from airliners. We have heard far less about the dangers of not searching. The reason is that "large and important parts of the American news media practice a virulent form of political correctness that is indistinguishable from censorship," in the words of Richard Cohen, the mostly liberal *Washington Post* columnist.

Opponents of national-origin profiling claim it would be more effective to focus solely on suspicious behavior. They are wrong. Competent terrorists know how to avoid the suspicious-behavior trap. They are not likely to buy one-way tickets the next time. Or to pay in cash. Or to fly from Afghanistan to Pakistan to New York. Or to hang around airport security checkpoints with video cameras. These people are not stupid.

The hardest thing to hide if you are an Islamic terrorist is your Islamic-world origin, as evinced by speech patterns, facial characteristics, skin color, or (to a lesser extent) dress and travel documents. Sure, there is always the risk that the next attack will come from another homegrown Timothy McVeigh, or a Swedish Girl Scout, or (more likely) a mush-headed leftist French coed recruited by al Qaeda. But there are a lot more Islamic terrorists than there are Timothy McVeighs. And not many people from outside the Islamic world appear eager to volunteer for suicide missions. Many Arab-Americans—if not their purported leaders—now seem to understand this. In a *Detroit Free Press* poll of 527 local Arab-Americans, 61 percent supported extra scrutiny of people with Middle Eastern features or accents. * * *

It's unclear whether national-origin profiling would have prevented the hijackings, in part because FAA rules did not bar small knives—although some airlines have suggested that they would have confiscated any box cutters they detected. But politically correct profiling virtually guaranteed that the hijackers' weapons would go undetected.

The Bush administration's profiling policy * * * is cloaked in politically cowardly and dangerous ambiguity. The FAA and Attorney General John Ashcroft have implied opposition to national-origin profiling, even as Ashcroft's subordinates have detained with minimal explanation more than 1,000 people, most Middle-Easterners against whom there appears to be scant evidence of terrorist activity. The administration should have the courage to preach what it practices. * * *

[I]f considered unblinkingly, [national-origin profiling] is not a close call. It has nothing to do with prejudice. It is a matter of life or death.

SHARON L. DAVIES—PROFILING TERROR

1 Ohio St. J. Crim. Law 45, 46–48, 51–53, 85, 99–100 (2003).

Following the attack on the World Trade Center on September 11, 2001, the nation's debate over racial profiling turned an abrupt corner. [The] public's view of racial profiling lurched from dramatically against the practice to decidedly in its favor. * * *

be presumptively unconstitutional, that presumption is overcome in the case of airline passengers, because the government has a compelling interest in preventing mass-murder-suicide hijacking, and because close scrutiny of Arab-looking people is narrowly tailored to protect that interest.

Even as it became apparent that ethnicity figured more heavily into the government's post-9/11 investigation than it first cared to admit, one popular reaction was: so what? After all, nineteen of the 9/11 suicide hijackers were nationals of Middle Eastern states. Didn't simple common sense mandate that government investigators of the events factor the shared ethnicity of additional suspects into their decisions of whom to question, detain, arrest or search? Post 9/11 polls showed that many believed the answer was yes. * * *

This Article rejects the suggestion that Arab or Middle Eastern heritage provides an appropriate basis of suspicion of individuals in the aftermath of the September 11 attacks. In a nation that claims upwards of 3.5 million persons of Arab ancestry, the ethnic characteristics of Arab descent, standing alone, possesses no useful predictive power for separating the September 11 terrorists' accomplices and other terrorist wannabees from innocent Americans.[b] It is a variable that is incapable of sufficiently narrowing what I call the "circle of suspicion" to warrant the kind of reliance pro-profiling arguments would place upon it. * * *

[Even] were we to assume that Middle Eastern origin had some value for distinguishing terrorists from non-terrorists, that ethnic fact would have no value for distinguishing between law-abiding and non-law-abiding persons of Middle Eastern descent. Put slightly differently, even if it had some minimal value for excluding certain people from the "circle of suspicion" (a point this Article contests), it would have no value for moving individual Middle Easterners inside that circle. * * *

A public convinced of its vulnerability might well be willing to endure greater police intrusions in exchange for greater security, even in the absence of hard evidence that the privacy-impairing measures it contemplates will actually deliver that security. But surely public acceptance cannot by itself supply the justification for a law enforcement policy that subscribes to racially-biased policing. The public "consented" to the forced relocation of over 100,000 persons of Japanese ancestry during World War II, but no thoughtful scholar today would defend the government's internment decisions on the basis of that consensus.

[Some have concluded that the Department of Justice's campaign to interview thousands of Middle Eastern men after 9/11] was *not* profiling "to the extent that the agents [were] pursuing case-specific information about the September 11 attacks, albeit in a dragnet fashion." This suggests that whenever an investigative effort derives in some (even remote) sense from an actual crime in which specific information about the racial or ethnic identity of the perpetrator (or perpetrators) is available, it will not technically be profiling, even if the police "dragnet" entire communities of persons with the same racial or ethnic characteristic in an effort to nab those not responsible.

---

[b] See also Frank H. Wu, *Profiling in the Wake of September 11: The Precedent of the Japanese American Internment*, Criminal Justice, Summer 2002, pp. 52, 58: "[I]t may well be that respective probabilities that a random older, white, Protestant American woman and the probability that a younger, Arab Muslim immigrant male are wrongdoers are not the same. But even were there a thousand sleeper agents of Arab descent or Muslim faith, ready to rise up in arms against democracy, they would constitute far less than a fraction of one-tenth of 1 percent of the Arab and Muslim populations of the United States. It is worth disputing whether the disparity in the chances are great enough to offset the tremendous cost to not just Arab Americans and Muslims but all of us if we relinquish our principle of individualism and presumption of innocence." Consider, too, David A. Harris, *Racial Profiling Revisited: "Just Common Sense" in the Fight Against Terrorism?*, Criminal Justice, Summer 2002, pp. 36, 40–41: "[If] we are to avoid attacks in the future by al-Qaeda operatives based on our own soil, we need to do much better in the intelligence arena than we did before September 11. * * * It stands to reason, then, that what we need most right now are good, solid relations with the Arab and Muslim communities in the United States. Profiling that focuses on Arab and Muslim heritage will effectively communicate to these very same communities that we regard all their members not as our partners in law enforcement and terror prevention, but just the opposite: as potential terrorists. * * * [It] is not hard to imagine the result: alienation and anger toward the authorities at a time when we can least afford it."

Yet this argument surely excuses too much. [This] type of over-reliance on racial and ethnic information is extremely unlikely in a diverse society to yield those responsible for crimes. Even where such racial information is logically relevant to a criminal investigation, its value is largely limited to excluding groups of individuals from the circle of suspicion rather than moving any particular individual possessing that racial or ethnic characteristic inside that circle. Once we lose sight of this point, the door to using racial and ethnic information is opened far too wide: the police officer who has arrested a Latino male for involvement in a drug conspiracy can use this as a reason to stop other Latinos anywhere and everywhere.

VERA INSTITUTE STUDY

According to the two-year study conducted by the Vera Institute of Justice, in the aftermath of September 11, Arab-Americans have a greater fear of racial profiling and immigration enforcement than of falling victim to hate crimes. Moreover, post-9/11 measures threaten to destroy decades of work by police departments to build trust in Arab-American communities. *See* Andrea Elliot, *After 9/11, Arab-Americans Fear Police Acts, Study Finds*, N.Y. Times, June 12, 2006, p. A15. About 100 Arab-Americans and more than 100 law enforcement personnel (both police officers and FBI agents) took part in the study, which was conducted from 2003–05. (Approximately two-thirds of Arab-Americans are Christians.) The study was paid for by the National Institute of Justice, a research agency of the Justice Department.

New York Times reporter Elliot summed up the study's findings as follows: "Arab-Americans reported an increasing sense of victimization, suspicion of government and law enforcement, and concerns about protecting their civil liberties." Post 9/11 law enforcement tactics "have sown the deepest fear among Arab-Americans, including unease about the USA Patriot Act, voluntary interviews of thousands of Arab-Americans by federal agents, and an initiative known as Special Registration, in which more than 80,000 immigrant men were fingerprinted, photographed, and questioned by authorities."

§ 3. INNOCENCE

BRANDON L. GARRETT—CONVICTING THE INNOCENT

Pp. 5–12; 262–64 (2011).

Since DNA testing became available in the late 1980s, more than 250 innocent people have been exonerated by postconviction DNA testing.

Who were these innocent people? The first 250 DNA exonerees were convicted chiefly of rape, in 68% of the cases (171), with 9% convicted of murder (22), 21% of both murder and rape (52) and 2% convicted of other crimes like robbery (5). Seventeen were sentenced to death. Eighty were sentenced to life in prison. They served an average of thirteen years in prison. These people were typically in their twenties when they were convicted. Twenty-four were juveniles. All but four were male. At least eighteen were mentally disabled. Far more DNA exonerees were minorities (70%) than is typical among the already racially skewed populations of rape and murder convictions. Of the 250 exonerees, 155 were black, 20 Latino, 74 white and 1 Asian.

Before the invention of DNA testing, the problem of convicting the innocent remained largely out of sight. Many doubted that a wrongful conviction could ever occur. Justice Sandra Day O'Connor touted how "our society has a high degree of confidence in its criminal trials, in no small part because the Constitution offers unparalleled protections against convicting the innocent." Judge Learned Hand famously called "the ghost of the innocent man convicted" an "unreal dream."

Prosecutors have from time to time claimed infallibility, announcing, "Innocent men are never convicted."

* * * [C]elebrated constitutional rights, such as the requirement that jurors find guilt beyond a reasonable doubt and that indigent defendants receive lawyers, provide crucial bulwarks against miscarriages of justice. But those rights and a welter of others the Court has recognized, like the *Miranda* warnings, the exclusionary rule, and the right to confront witnesses, are procedural rules that the State must follow to prevent a conviction from being overturned. Few rules, however, regulate accuracy rather than procedures. Such matters are typically committed to the discretion of the trial judge. * * *

Why didn't appeals or habeas corpus review set innocent people free? * * * One might expect that judges would look for serious mistakes like the ones in these exonerees' cases. However, judges only reluctantly review the evidence after a conviction. After all, most constitutional rights relate to procedure and not accuracy. Most exonerees did not try to challenge flawed trial evidence, and when they did they almost always failed. Judges typically refused to grant a new trial, and some were so sure that these people were guilty that they called the evidence of guilt "overwhelming."

* * * These 250 exonerees are just the tip of the iceberg. The submerged bulk of that iceberg lurks ominously out of view. The most crucial question about these exonerations cannot be answered. We do not know and we cannot know how many other innocent people languish in our prisons. They remain invisible. One of the most haunting features of these exonerations is that so many were discovered by chance. Most convicts who seek postconviction DNA testing cannot get it. Some jurisdictions still deny convicts access to DNA testing that could prove innocence. In our fragmented criminal justice system, exonerations hinge on cooperation of local police, prosecutors, and judges. * * *

Some hardened souls will remain untroubled by DNA exonerations. For example, Justice Scalia has suggested that known wrongful convictions are an inconsequential percentage, an error rate of ".027 percent—or, to put it another way, a success rate of 99.973 percent," if one divides exonerations by the fifteen million felony convictions during the same time period.[82] But should we really be so reassured by the numbers?

If you eat at a fine restaurant and complain of a large bug in your soup, you are not reassured if the waiter tells you, "Don't worry, it will not happen again too often. There have only been a few hundred reported cases of bugs in soup in the United States. While human error is inevitable, with millions of bowls of soup served every year, we have an unparalleled sanitary soup rate." The waiter adds, before turning away with a flourish, "Because we found the bug in your soup, the system worked."

You had better ask to talk to the manager. The restaurant did not find that bug—you did. The system did not work. What system was there? * * *

DNA testing is done chiefly in rape cases, and rape convictions that result in prison sentences make up less than 2% of felony convictions. However, the right comparison group for DNA exonerees is even smaller. Exonerees were almost all convicted of rapes involving a stranger-perpetrator, in which there was a real question about who committed the crime. They received long sentences; on average they served thirteen years before DNA exonerated them. There is no good data on rape convictions in the 1980s. We do know that only a quarter of rape prosecutions involve stranger-perpetrators, and rape convicts overwhelmingly pleaded guilty and received much shorter prison sentences than these exonerees did. So the right control group for the exonerees would be stranger-rape cases from the 1980s in which the defendant took his case to

---

[82] *Kansas v. Marsh*, 548 U.S. 163, 194–195 (2006) (Scalia, J., concurring).

trial. The number of these cases is much, much lower than the fifteen million total felonies cited by Justice Scalia, most likely in the low tens of thousands, making the number of exonerations quite troubling.

§ 4. MISDEMEANORS

ALEXANDRA NATAPOFF—MISDEMEANORS

11 Ann. Rev. L. & Soc. Sci. 255, 255–57 (2015).[a]

* * * Although misdemeanors have always profoundly shaped the criminal justice culture, their influence has been obscured in both practice and theory. Courts and policy makers typically treat misdemeanors as unimportant relative to felonies. The petty offense process is underregulated and largely invisible; criminal law scholarship has long privileged serious offenses and federal practice to the exclusion of petty crimes.

But this felony-centric view is misplaced. In reality, most American crimes are minor. The system files approximately two to three million felony cases every year, compared to approximately ten million misdemeanor cases. Eighty percent of state dockets are misdemeanors; most Americans encounter the criminal system through the petty offense process. It turns out that the lowly misdemeanor—not homicide or rape—is the paradigmatic American crime and the paradigmatic product of the American criminal system.

The misdemeanor perspective opens up new ways of understanding the criminal process as a whole. In particular, it reveals a system that is neither uniform nor consistent. If we conceptualize the criminal system as a pyramid, the lion's share of attention goes to a small but highly visible and relatively functional top. This is the world of serious offenses, federal crimes, and wealthy defendants. Cases are typically well-litigated, law and evidence matter, and due process commitments are at their height. Although the top has its own distinct dysfunctions—astronomical sentences, prosecutorial hegemony—the players tend to follow the conventional rules of the adversarial process.

Because the top of the pyramid is high profile and relatively transparent, it is often treated as representative of the system as a whole. But it is not. As we move down the pyramid, offenses get pettier and more numerous, defendants get poorer, public defenders get more overwhelmed, and courts are less attuned to careful litigation and rule-of-law ideals. At the very bottom we find misdemeanors, a massive sloppy arena dominated by police arrest practices and assembly-line processing. Compared with the top, this world embraces a very different culture, one typically lacking in counsel and due process and overtly driven by class and racial inequalities. Counterintuitively, this problematic bottom is more representative of the American system as a whole, producing the average defendant experience and most of the system's cases and convictions. It is this world of impoverished misdemeanants, crowded jails, and slipshod processes that must be excavated before we can claim to understand what sort of criminal system we actually have.

The misdemeanor perspective raises four interrelated conceptual challenges. The first challenge is to reevaluate the validity of the criminal justice institution itself. Because the petty offense process often deviates wildly from standard requirements of due process, evidence, and the adversarial process, it raises new questions about the legitimacy of the legal arrangements that formally convert millions of people into criminals every year.

---

[a] For a more extensive analysis of the role of misdemeanors in our criminal justice system, see Alexandra Natapoff, *Punishment Without Crime: How our Massive Misdemeanor System Traps the Innocent and Makes America More Unequal* (Basic Books 2018).

Second, the misdemeanor system has a massive wrongful conviction problem that dwarfs the felony innocence docket. It stems not from forensic failures but from the slapdash and coercive nature of the plea bargaining process, in which innocent people routinely plead guilty to avoid further pretrial incarceration or the burdens of misdemeanor court. This wrongful conviction problem has been largely absent from the national innocence debate and its focus on serious cases and DNA exonerations.

Misdemeanors also challenge us to rethink what we mean by punishment. Because misdemeanors typically do not trigger jail time, they are often conceptualized as a species of leniency—a gentler alternative to felony convictions and prison. But petty offenses impose deep and lasting burdens on offenders in ways that have been obscured by the punitive shadow of mass incarceration. These burdens—including criminal records, fines, supervision, and a wide range of formal and informal stigmas—drive much of the inegalitarian and racialized quality of the system as a whole.

Finally, petty offenses highlight the extent to which the criminal system functions not so much as a way of identifying wrongdoers—its classic asserted purpose—but as a form of social management and control. The misdemeanor process has become the primary vehicle for tracking young men of color and marking them with criminal records that follow them for a lifetime. It also manages and marks other disadvantaged groups, such the homeless, the mentally ill, or those with substance abuse problems. In ways that the felony-centric model obscures, the misdemeanor perspective reveals how the criminal process is often marginally concerned with guilt and heavily invested in managing risky and disadvantaged populations.

Ultimately, an appreciation of the petty offense process unsettles answers to basic questions that appear settled in the felony context. For example, what process is "due" to defendants faced with minor charges for which they will not be incarcerated but that may nevertheless affect the rest of their lives? Do all wrongful convictions matter or only serious ones? What constitutes and justifies punishment outside the framework of incarceration, and what is proportionality in that realm? And finally, what is our criminal system actually for?

§ 5. REMEDIES FOR GOVERNMENT MISCONDUCT

RACHEL A. HARMON—LEGAL REMEDIES FOR POLICE MISCONDUCT, IN ACADEMY FOR JUSTICE, A REPORT ON SCHOLARSHIP AND CRIMINAL JUSTICE REFORM

(Erik Luna, ed. 2017)

* * * A variety of legal remedies for constitutional violations by police officers, including the exclusionary rule, civil suits for damages or reform, and criminal prosecution, exist to ensure that officers follow the law and to provide redress when they do not. In recent years, commentators have increasingly complained that police officers violate the law with impunity because these legal means for controlling their behavior are too weak. Over several decades, federal courts have left legal remedies for constitutional violations in place, but cut away at them so that, although they are frequently invoked, they are often not effective at remedying or deterring constitutional violations. The consequence is that policing has a lot of law and little remedy. Police officers are surrounded by potential legal review for every act, even legitimate ones, making them feel constantly scrutinized and overregulated. And yet, the law only infrequently holds officers and departments accountable for constitutional violations, leaving victims of police misconduct and their communities deeply dissatisfied. Both police and citizens feel wronged by the present system. * * *

II. Civil Suits for Damages

The Civil Rights Act of 1871—codified at 42 U.S.C. § 1983 and often known simply as Section 1983—provides a statutory basis for civil suits against police conduct that violates the U.S. Constitution or federal law as a means to deter unconstitutional conduct, vindicate constitutional rights, and provide compensation for victims of constitutional violations. This long-standing statute gained new traction in the late 1970s after the Supreme Court clarified the circumstances in which the suits were available to plaintiffs and Congress passed 42 U.S.C. § 1988, which permitted prevailing parties in Section 1983 cases to recover reasonable attorney's fees.

Although Section 1983 suits are far less common than motions to suppress evidence under the exclusionary rule, Section 1983 authorizes a remedy in circumstances in which the exclusionary rule does not. [For example, damages actions provide a remedy for] violations the exclusionary rule does not address, such as constitutionally excessive force—which produces no evidence—and Fourth Amendment violations against those who are never charged with a crime.

Despite the potential scope of Section 1983, plaintiffs face many practical barriers to bringing lawsuits. There may not be independent witnesses to an event, making misconduct difficult to prove. Victims of police misconduct often have criminal records or other qualities that may make them unappealing to juries, who are, in any case, reluctant to second-guess police decision-making, given the risks officers face on the street. In addition, because of uncertain outcomes and legal obstacles to recovery, potential plaintiffs cannot always find willing, effective, and experienced attorneys to represent them.

Beyond these practical hurdles, there are often overwhelming legal obstacles to Section 1983 actions. Most importantly, according to the Supreme Court's interpretation of the statute, individual officers are entitled to "qualified immunity" from civil damages for violating a person's constitutional rights unless the right at issue was "clearly established" at the time of the alleged conduct. In recent years, the Supreme Court has required increasingly specific and robust precedent to establish a constitutional right clearly, noting that "existing precedent must have placed the statutory or constitutional question beyond debate," with the result that qualified immunity protects all but the "plainly incompetent" officer.

* * * A city (or its department) is only liable under Section 1983 for constitutional violations that it causes through its policies or customs. To establish liability against a city, a plaintiff must show that there was a constitutional violation, that the city caused the violation, and that the violation is attributable to a city policy, formal or informal.[21] Usually, proving these elements requires evidence that city actors knew of and permitted a pattern of similar constitutional violations, as well as evidence that the constitutional violation was actually caused by and was closely related to the policy deficiency. In many cases, proving municipal liability is therefore not only difficult, but requires extensive, expensive discovery.

Even when plaintiffs win civil suits for damages or settle them favorably against individuals or departments, damages actions may not influence police conduct going forward. Individual officers are almost always indemnified by their departments for judgments against them. This means that judgments against individuals are paid for by departments and cities rather than by individual officers. In theory, paying out money should lead departments and cities to seek to prevent constitutional violations by officers to avoid future payments. But in practice, cities sometimes use financial arrangements to pay settlements and judgments that do not penalize police departments, and therefore do not create strong incentives to avoid additional violations. As a consequence, though Section 1983 damages actions can result in considerable costs to cities, they often do little to deter misconduct.

---

[21] *See* Monell v. Dep't of Soc. Servs., 436 U.S. 658, 690–92 (1978).

III. Civil Suits for Equitable Relief by Private Actors

Under federal law, when compensatory damages are an inadequate remedy for a constitutional violation, especially a future harm, private plaintiffs, individually or in aggregate, may seek alternative remedies, known as "equitable relief." This relief usually takes the form of a court's declaration of the rights of the parties or an injunction—a court order requiring or prohibiting certain actions. Equitable relief can be simple and prohibitory or can involve complex mandates for changing government behavior, and private plaintiffs sometimes sue municipalities seeking an order requiring government agencies to engage in substantial departmental reforms. These reforms do not act—like damages or the exclusionary rule—to deter constitutional violations indirectly. Instead, they are intended to cure the systemic conditions that cause constitutional violations.

Lawsuits for complex reforms, often known as structural reform litigation, developed in the 1950s and expanded through the mid-1970s. This litigation was not then and is not now limited to police departments. In fact, structural reform litigation has been more often and more famously used for other purposes, such as to desegregate schools, to improve prison conditions, and to fight housing discrimination by local and state agencies. Nevertheless, both simple and complex forms of equitable relief are often sought in suits against police departments.

Scholars and commentators have long been divided over the value and legitimacy of suits for equitable relief. By the mid-1970s, the U.S. Supreme Court sided with skeptics and imposed some significant limits on private efforts to obtain declaratory relief and injunctions. For plaintiffs challenging policing practices, the most important of these limits is the Court's application of constitutional standing requirements. In *City of Los Angeles v. Lyons*, the Court held that the plaintiff, Lyons, who had been choked to unconsciousness by police officers during a traffic stop, had not demonstrated a "real and immediate" threat of future injury sufficient to establish Article III standing for injunctive relief.[26] Even if the Los Angeles Police Department used illegal chokeholds, as Lyons alleged, the Court held that "it is no more than speculation to assert either that Lyons himself will again be involved in one of those unfortunate instances or that he will be arrested in the future and provoke the use of a chokehold by resisting arrest, attempting to escape, or threatening deadly force or serious bodily injury."[27] Therefore, he could not sue for injunctive relief. * * *

[C]ourts are more likely to find standing and allow equitable challenges under *Lyons* when a policy targets relatively innocent or common conduct, when the department engages in the challenged conduct frequently, when some plaintiffs have suffered harm more than once, and when the department directs the challenged conduct against a visible subpopulation of which the plaintiff is part. Each of these conditions raises the probability that a particular plaintiff will experience future constitutional injury. Some police practices are far more likely than others to meet these conditions. For example, plaintiffs challenging racial profiling, or the illegal, widespread use of enforcement strategies such as stops, frisks, and arrests against minor conduct, will more easily satisfy the requirements of *Lyons* than plaintiffs attempting to change strip-search practices at jails or uses of excessive force. In this way, and others, court-imposed limits on suits for equitable relief have made such suits a powerful but infrequent tool for challenging and changing unconstitutional conduct by law enforcement.

IV. Civil Suits for Equitable Relief by Public Actors

* * * In 1994, Congress gave the Department of Justice the power to bring suits for equitable relief against police departments in the Violent Crime Control and Law Enforcement Act.[30] Using

---

26 461 U.S. 95, 105 (1983).

27 Id. at 108.

30 42 U.S.C. § 14141.

this authority, the Department of Justice has developed a program of investigating and suing police departments engaged in a "pattern or practice" of constitutional violations and negotiating settlements that impose significant changes on those departments. As of the beginning of 2017, the Department of Justice had engaged in substantial investigations of 69 departments and had entered into 40 reform agreements.

* * * [P]attern or practice investigations and litigation by the Department of Justice has varied in volume and aggressiveness during the three presidential administrations that have had the power to enforce the law. Despite this variation, there are some notable constants in pattern-and-practice suits brought by the Department of Justice so far. First, the investigations and suits have focused heavily on the use of excessive force; illegal stops, searches, and arrests; and discriminatory policing by departments. Second, in most cases, when the Department of Justice has found a pattern or practice of constitutional violations by a police department, it has entered into an enforceable agreement with the municipality in which the city agrees to make substantial and specific reforms to the police department. Most of these agreements have been in the form of court-enforceable consent decrees. Third, implementation of the consent decrees has been monitored by independent teams who report to the federal courts supervising the decrees. Finally, although the reforms sought by the Civil Rights Division have evolved over time, they have consistently emphasized reducing discrimination, clarifying the policies that officers follow, improving training and supervision, strengthening data collection and transparency, and reforming citizen complaint and internal accountability systems within police departments.

Legal scholars and other commentators have long viewed pattern-and-practice suits as a powerful tool for improving policing, and the program is largely considered successful in reforming departments that have substantial ongoing problems. Still, these suits raise some concerns. Pattern-and-practice suits are resource intensive for both the federal government and the cities that are sued, and they can represent a substantial federal intrusion in local government. In addition, the limited empirical research studying the effects of pattern-and-practice suits so far has found that, though reforms adopted seemed to improve internal processes and reduce unconstitutional policing, they also tended to alienate line officers. Finally, reforms imposed by consent decree may not be self-sustaining once ongoing monitoring by the Department of Justice and the federal court ends.

In recent years, the Department of Justice has sought to refine its pattern-and-practice program to address some of these concerns. It has also supplemented this program with an alternative: voluntary technical assistance for departments struggling to prevent constitutional violations through the COPS Collaborative Reform program. * * *

V. Criminal Prosecution

Police officers may be prosecuted for constitutional violations under both federal and state law. Under federal law, 18 U.S.C. § 242 makes it a crime to willfully deprive any person of his or her constitutional rights. * * * Criminally prosecuting police officers is harder than suing them civilly. As in all criminal cases, prosecutors are required to prove elements of a crime beyond a reasonable doubt, and Section 242 has elements that can be especially difficult to prove. A federal prosecutor must establish not only that the officer violated the Constitution, but also that the officer did so "willfully," that is, that the officer had the specific intent to do what the law forbids. * * * Not surprisingly, fewer than 100 federal prosecutions are brought against law enforcement officials for constitutional violations each year. * * *

Criminal prosecutions against police officers are likely to be inevitably too rare to deter much misconduct. Nevertheless, they remain of substantial symbolic and normative importance. No other form of remedy so clearly expresses the government's condemnation of specific police violations of law, and none shows as much respect for the victims of police misconduct, especially with respect to police violence.

VI. State Decertification

* * * In most states, the commissions that provide for the training and certification of officers, or other state boards, also have the power to deprive an officer of his license or certification to punish serious misconduct. While the threat of decertification may discourage bad acts, decertification also has a more direct effect: It prevents future violations of the public trust by stopping officers who have committed serious misconduct from continuing to serve as sworn officers in the state. Decertifying officers can also help reassure the public about the state's commitment to law-abiding law enforcement and demonstrate law enforcement's commitment to professional norms. Presently, decertification is inconsistently used, and police departments do not have reliable access to information about decertifications in other states. More systematic use of this tool and an improved system for communicating decertification actions between states, could improve its capacity to reduce police misconduct. * * *

VII. Departmental and Municipal Remedies

Some of the most effective means of preventing police misconduct are within the control of police departments and municipalities. There is wide agreement that hiring well-qualified officers, providing them with extensive and ongoing training, setting forth specific and realistic policies to guide their work, and supervising them well are all critical to ensuring that officers comply with the law. In addition to these management practices, however, departments and municipalities also respond to specific incidents of misconduct in ways that can affect future officer behavior. Most importantly, departments and cities receive citizen complaints about officer conduct, and they investigate and impose discipline for violations of law and departmental policies. This process is important both for deterring misconduct and for communicating a commitment to lawful policing. Since disciplinary mechanisms can be used for misconduct that violates departmental policies as well as law, these mechanisms have far greater potential impact on policing than legal remedies that merely enforce constitutional law.

In most cities, citizen complaints about officer misconduct are investigated and resolved by units of the police department itself, often know as internal affairs units, and discipline, if appropriate, is imposed by command staff. Like legal remedies, internal affairs units often impose scrutiny and burdens that officers resent, and yet rarely vindicate the interests of individuals who feel mistreated by the police. Scholars and other commentators widely criticize internal complaint, investigation, and disciplinary systems in police departments for their ineffectiveness, bias, and lack of transparency. The Department of Justice has leveled similar criticisms in its pattern-and-practice investigations. In many cities, communities distrust the police in part because they believe that internal disciplinary mechanisms do not work. * * *

VIII. Looking Beyond Constitutional Remedies

* * * Although constitutional rights provide an important floor below which police action cannot go, they do a poor job of balancing competing interests when the police enforce the law and individuals are harmed. Because rights are held by individuals, they often do not limit policing practices that impose substantial aggregate harm to communities. Because they are defined categorically and in advance, they must be more permissive toward law enforcement than a careful weighing of the interests at stake would warrant in order to permit discretion in extreme cases. And because they are defined and applied in the context of court rulings, they are formulated based on considerations, such as the ease of judicial administration, that have nothing to do with whether the police practices in question are overly harmful. * * *

This is not to say that constitutional and other legal remedies for policing are no longer important. As the above descriptions suggest, constitutional remedies serve functions other than shaping police action. Criminal prosecutions of officers remain a principal way to declare conduct culpable and to show societal respect for victims. Civil damages compensate injured plaintiffs. And structural reform litigation mitigates systemic problems in policing. Thus, reformers may want to push to strengthen these remedies in the courts; to support pattern-and-practice suits and criminal prosecutions by the Department of Justice; and to promote stronger state tort remedies and criminal prosecutions. Nevertheless, those interested in reform would be wise to look beyond expanding constitutional and statutory remedies to consider alternative means of spurring changes in departments.

§ 6. POLICE DEPARTMENT HIRING AND TRAINING

U.S. DEPT. OF JUSTICE, BUREAU OF JUSTICE STATISTICS, LOCAL POLICE DEPARTMENTS, 2013: PERSONNEL, POLICIES, AND PRACTICES

By Brian A. Reaves, Ph.D., BJS Statistician

(*available at* http://www.bjs.gov/content/pub/pdf/lpd13ppp.pdf)

As of January 1, 2013, more than 12,000 local police departments in the United States employed an estimated 605,000 persons on a full-time basis. This total included about 477,000 sworn officers (those with general arrest powers) and about 128,000 nonsworn employees.

Highlights

- About half (48%) of departments employed fewer than 10 officers.
- More than half (54%) of local police officers were employed in jurisdictions with 100,000 or more residents.
- About 1 in 8 local police officers were female, including about 1 in 10 first-line supervisors.
- About 27% of local police officers were members of a racial or ethnic minority, compared to 15% in 1987.

The overall average starting salary for entry-level local police officers in 2013 was $44,400. * * * In 2013, the average base starting salary for entry-level local police officers was at least $45,000 in all population categories of 25,000 or more. The average starting salary was highest in jurisdictions with 100,000 to 249,999 residents ($50,700) and lowest in jurisdictions with fewer than 2,500 residents ($30,900).

In 2013, about 23% of officers were employed by a department that required new entry-level officers to have a 2-year degree, compared to 7% in 2003. In 2013, all local police departments serving a population of 100,000 or more, and nearly all departments in smaller jurisdictions, had a minimum education requirement for new officers. The most common requirement (84% of departments) was a high school diploma. An estimated 15% of departments had some type of college requirement, including 10% that required a 2-year degree and 1% that required a 4-year degree. An estimated 54% of departments with a degree requirement considered military service as an alternative. Departments serving a population of 1 million or more (29%) were most likely to require a degree. In smaller population categories, the percentage of departments with a degree requirement ranged from 9% in jurisdictions with fewer than 2,500 residents to 20% in jurisdictions with 25,000 to 49,999 residents.

U.S. DEPT. OF JUSTICE, BUREAU OF JUSTICE STATISTICS SPECIAL REPORT: STATE AND LOCAL LAW ENFORCEMENT TRAINING ACADEMIES, 2006 (REVISED 4/14/2009)

By Brian A. Reaves, Ph.D., BJS Statistician
(*available at* http://www.bjs.gov/content/pub/pdf/slleta06.pdf)

Overall, an estimated 57,000 recruits entered basic training programs during 2005. On average, these programs included 761 hours of classroom training. A third of academies had an additional mandatory field training component with an average length of 453 hours. * * *

Just over two-thirds (68%) of training academies required their full-time instructors to have a minimum number of years of law enforcement experience. Among academies with a minimum experience requirement, the average was about 4 years. * * *

Overall, 19% of the academies required their full-time instructors to have a college degree. Slightly more academies required a 4-year degree (11%) than required a 2-year degree (8%). * * *

Eighty-nine percent of academies required full-time trainers to have a state-level certification, and 62% required certification as a subject-matter expert. A less common requirement was certification by the academy (25%). * * *

Basic training included a median 60 hours of firearms instruction and 51 hours of self-defense instruction. Recruits spent the most time learning firearms skills (median instruction time of 60 hours) and self-defense skills (51 hours). The next highest median was for health and fitness training (46 hours). Nearly all academies also trained recruits in procedures related to patrol, investigations, and emergency vehicle operations with a median instruction time of 40 hours each.

Basic first aid (24 hours) and report writing (20 hours) were also included in the basic training program of nearly all academies. Recruits also received a median of 8 hours training on the use of computers and information systems, although such training was limited to 58% of academies.

Legal training was included in all basic training programs with a median of 36 hours of instruction in criminal law and 12 hours in constitutional law. Nearly all academies provided instruction on cultural diversity (a median of 11 hours), community policing strategies (8 hours), and mediation skills/conflict management (8 hours). Special topics covered by basic training programs included domestic violence (a median of 14 hours), juveniles (8 hours), domestic preparedness (8 hours), and hate crimes (4 hours). * * *

[L]ess than half of academies in 2006 provided community policing training on assessing the effectiveness of problem-solving responses (45%), creating problem-solving teams (43%), analyzing crime/calls for service data (38%), using crime mapping to analyze community problems (36%), or applying research methods to study crime and disorder (35%). * * *

A majority of recruits were trained in academies more oriented toward a stress-based military model than a non-stress academic model. The more traditional stress-based model of training is based on the military model and typically includes paramilitary drills, intensive physical demands, public disciplinary measures, immediate reaction to infractions, daily inspections, value inculcation, and withholding of privileges. Proponents of this approach believe it promotes self-discipline in recruits resulting in a commitment to follow departmental policies, better time management, and completion of duties even when undesirable.

The non-stress model emphasizes academic achievement, physical training, administrative disciplinary procedures, and an instructor-trainee relationship that is more relaxed and supportive. Proponents of this approach believe it produces officers better able to interact in a cooperative manner with citizens and community organizations, and therefore more suited to the problem-solving approaches of community-oriented policing. * * *

By type of academy, 43% of state police academies reported their training environment was predominantly stress-based. The next highest percentages were for academies operated by county police (26%) or sheriffs' offices (25%). More than three-fifths of academies operated by county police (89%), state police (75%), sheriffs' offices (71%), or municipal police (66%) had training environments they described as either predominantly stress or more stress than non-stress. * * *

State POST (16%) and college and university academies (13%) were most likely to report using a predominantly non-stress training environment. A majority of state POST (64%) and college and university (60%) academies had training environments that were more non-stress than stress or predominantly non-stress compared to less than half of other academies. * * *

In academies with a training environment described as predominantly non-stress, female and male recruits both had a completion rate of 89%, but as the stress orientation of the training environment increased, completion rates dropped more for female recruits than for male recruits.

In academies with a training environment that was more stress-oriented than non-stress, completion rates for female recruits dropped to 79% compared to 88% for male recruits. In academies with a training environment that was predominantly stress, the difference in completion rates between female (68%) and male (81%) recruits was even greater.

DAVID H. BAYLEY—LAW ENFORCEMENT AND THE RULE OF LAW: IS THERE A TRADEOFF?

2 Criminology & Public Policy 133–35, 146–48 (2002).

The public in every society worries about the integrity of its police. Some have better reasons for this than do others. But everywhere regardless of the objective incidence of misbehavior, people become easily concerned that the police do not abide by the law and misuse their power. At the same time, it is my experience that the police in every society believe that they must occasionally cut legal corners in order to provide effective protection to that very same public. Among police there is a nearly universal mindset that abiding by the rule-of-law and adhering to recognized standards of human rights is sometimes too restrictive, preventing victims from obtaining justice, allowing criminals to go unpunished, and placing society at unacceptable risk.

This mindset of the police and the behavior it engenders, shows up in a number of ways. Police complain almost everywhere about the uncertainties of criminal justice processing—slipshod prosecutions, inept and venal judges, unwilling witnesses, cumbersome procedures, and laws loaded in favor of suspects. Police are regularly accused, even in countries with human rights records that are good by world standards, of engaging in unjustified stops and seizures. They have been found to fabricate evidence and testify falsely in order to gain convictions. So common did these practices seem to be in New York City recently that the Mollen Commissions coined a new word to describe them—"testilying" (1994). Complaints of excessive use of force ostensibly to control crime are also common around the world, whether to obtain confessions from unwilling suspects or to intimidate would-be criminals. Intimidation is especially disturbing when it is directed at whole classes of individuals, as when police say that "those people only understand force" or "people like that" have to be taught respect for the law.

Although the public is most concerned about dramatic infringements of the rule-of-law, such as brutality, planting false evidence, and lying in courts, most of the liberties taken by police are more mundane, routinized, and difficult to detect. For example, a Texas police officer told me how he had developed a challenge-proof method for stopping motorists on suspicion, without a shred of probable cause. After stopping a car, he would thump the left rear fender with his hand as he walked up to it. If the driver asked why the officer had stopped him, the officer would say that the left rear taillight was not working. If the driver checked for himself, which was unusual, the officer would say that his thump must have restored the connection and he would advise the driver, in the interest of safety, to get it checked at a service station. Thus, an illegal stop could be disguised as helpful assistance.

The usual explanation for such behavior is that the police do not understand what is right and wrong; that the values of the police need changing to emphasize more scrupulous adherence to law and to human rights. It follows, then, that the solution is to raise the normative consciousness of the police, to convince them that they have a duty both to uphold the rule-of-law and to provide public safety. I think this diagnosis is mistaken. The problem is not normative, but cognitive. The police generally know what behaviors are right and wrong. The problem is that they believe that the violation of law and of human rights is sometimes required for effective law enforcement. * * *

If my thesis is correct, police must be shown that the costs to them of violating the rule-of-law are greater than are the benefits, that doing right is not only commendable normatively, but also furthers their own collective self-interest. Moral exhortation alone is unpersuasive because it does not address the tradeoffs that police are convinced they face. This explains why, in my experience, lecturing to the police about human rights is met with palpable lack of interest—eyelids droop, note-taking stops, and faces become wooden. The police act as if they know all that, which in many cases is true. The problem is that lectures on human rights are a necessary but not sufficient corrective to the dilemma police officers face. What is needed instead is an evidence-based demonstration that rectitude is useful to the police in fulfilling their mission of preventing and controlling crime. This sort of argument will get their attention. * * *

[Professor Bayley then discusses several arguments that can be made that violating the rule-of-law does not serve the interests of the police: (1) it produces very small, if any, gains in reducing criminality; (2) it impairs crime control by alienating the public; (3) it weakens the authority of the law; (4) it "scapegoats" the police, *i.e.*, it not only causes the police not to "take responsibility for crime onto themselves," but to "deflect attention to themselves and away from the negligence of others;" (5) it jeopardizes criminal prosecutions and wastes community resources; and (6) it places police officers "at risk for the presumed sake of public safety."]

If my assumption is correct that police often violate the rule-of-law because they believe it improves their ability to control and prevent crime, then gathering additional evidence that it does not is an important undertaking. But it is clearly not a sufficient response to the problem. The information must be used so that it changes behavior. How is this to be done?

One possibility would be to broaden the approach to the teaching of law and ethics to police recruits. In addition to instructing them in the requirements of due process and the value of the rule-of-law in democratic societies, they would be presented with the utilitarian arguments made in this paper. In effect, the tradeoff problem would be met head on with police officers at the very beginning of their careers.

At the same time, I am doubtful whether changing the cognitive understanding of police officers individually will be sufficient to offset the occupational culture within which they work. It is unrealistic to expect individual police officers, no matter how well instructed in the arguments made in this essay, to stand against the crime-control understandings and expectations of their colleagues, the public, and their senior officers. The more effective strategy, then, for changing the mindset of police officers is to convince the leaders of police agencies that violating the rule-of-law is not a sound law enforcement strategy, so that they will then be emboldened to change the moral tone, disciplinary mechanisms, management priorities, and career incentives within the organization. Research has shown time and again that organizations are the most powerful determinants of the behavior of the people within them. Cognitive instruction of the kind suggested here should be focused initially and repeatedly on senior police executives. If they can be convinced that violating the rule-of-law is not useful in achieving the goals of police organizations, they will find the means to convince the rank-and-file.

The conclusion of this essay, then, supported by current social science research, is that violating the rule-of-law in order to control crime is mistaken and that the best place to start in reorienting police practices is with the managers of police agencies.

FINAL REPORT OF THE PRESIDENT'S TASK FORCE ON 21ST CENTURY POLICING

1–4 & 10 (2015).

Trust between law enforcement agencies and the people they protect and serve is essential in a democracy. It is key to the stability of our communities, the integrity of our criminal justice system, and the safe and effective delivery of policing services. * * *

Decades of research and practice support the premise that people are more likely to obey the law when they believe that those who are enforcing it have authority that is perceived as legitimate by those subject to the authority. The public confers legitimacy only on those whom they believe are acting in procedurally just ways. In addition, law enforcement cannot build community trust if it is seen as an occupying force coming in from outside to impose control on the community. * * *

Law enforcement culture should embrace a guardian—rather than a warrior—mindset to build trust and legitimacy both within agencies and with the public. Toward that end, law enforcement agencies should adopt procedural justice as the guiding principle for internal and external policies and practices to guide their interactions with rank and file officers and with the citizens they serve. * * *

Procedurally just behavior is based on four central principles: 1. Treating people with dignity and respect 2. Giving individuals "voice" during encounters 3. Being neutral and transparent in decision making 4. Conveying trustworthy motives. Research demonstrates that these principles lead to relationships in which the community trusts that officers are honest, unbiased, benevolent, and lawful. The community therefore feels obligated to follow the law and the dictates of legal authorities and is more willing to cooperate with and engage those authorities because it believes that it shares a common set of interests and values with the police. * * * Law enforcement agencies should also establish a culture of transparency and accountability to build public trust and legitimacy. This is critical to ensuring decision making is understood and in accord with stated policy. * * *

Today's line officers and leaders must be trained and capable to address a wide variety of challenges including international terrorism, evolving technologies, rising immigration, changing laws, new cultural mores, and a growing mental health crisis. * * *

One specific method of increasing the quality of training would be to ensure that Peace Officer and Standards Training (POST) boards include mandatory Crisis Intervention Training (CIT), which equips officers to deal with individuals in crisis or living with mental disabilities, as part of both basic recruit and in-service officer training—as well as instruction in disease of addiction, implicit bias and cultural responsiveness, policing in a democratic society, procedural justice, and effective social interaction and tactical skills. * * *

CHAPTER 4

THE RIGHT TO COUNSEL

■ ■ ■

"Of all the rights that an accused person has, the right to be represented by counsel is by far the most pervasive, for it affects his ability to assert any other rights he may have. [Procedural rules] are designed for those who know [them], and they can become a source of entrapment for those who do not. Substantive criminal law also presents difficulties to the uninitiated."

—Justice Walter V. Schaefer of the Supreme Court of Illinois, *Federalism and State Criminal Procedure*, 70 Harv.L.Rev. 1, 8 (1956).

"Ours is an adversarial system of justice—it requires lawyers on both sides who effectively represent their client's interests, whether it's the government or the accused. When defense counsel are handicapped by lack of training, time, and resources—or when they're just not there when they should be—we rightfully begin to doubt the process and we start to question the results. We start to wonder: Is justice being done? Is justice being served?"

—Eric Holder, U.S. Att'y Gen., Remarks at the Brennan Legacy Awards Dinner, Brennan Center for Justice (Nov. 17, 2009).

The right to counsel is relatively simple for the defendant who has the money to pay for an attorney. But what about the many defendants—indeed, the majority of defendants—who do not? Justice Black once said that "[t]here can be no equal justice where the kind of trial a man gets depends on the amount of money he has." *Griffin v. Illinois*, 351 U.S. 12 (1956). But how far does this principle carry?

Does it apply to misdemeanor cases as well as felony cases? Does it apply to appeals as well as trials? Should we provide indigent defendants with counsel all the way up to, and including, the U.S. Supreme Court? Should a probationer or parolee at a revocation hearing be provided with counsel? What about an indigent parent facing the loss of custody of her child in a parental status termination proceeding? For those individuals who are provided counsel, when are they entitled to counsels' assistance? Are they entitled to counsel of their own choosing? And what if they do not want to be represented by counsel? Under what circumstances can a defendant waive the right to counsel?

These questions and others are addressed in this chapter.

§ 1. THE RIGHT TO APPOINTED COUNSEL AND RELATED PROBLEMS

A. THE RIGHT TO APPOINTED COUNSEL IN CRIMINAL PROCEEDINGS

INTRODUCTION

A look at early English law reveals that the right to counsel had "surprisingly modest beginnings." James Tomkovicz, *The Right to the Assistance of Counsel* 1 (2002). Originally only those accused of minor offenses could be represented by counsel. (Evidently the monarch believed that permitting representation by defense counsel generally would prevent the successful prosecution of serious cases.) However, against a background of a decade of false treason charges against the Whigs, the Treason Act of 1695 provided that those prosecuted for high treason should be allowed to defend themselves by "counsel learned in the law." Thus, at the time of the adoption of the U.S. Constitution, England recognized a right to *retain* counsel to argue matters of fact only for those accused of misdemeanors or high treason.[a]

From the earliest times, the general practice in serious criminal cases in the American colonies was self-representation, not representation by counsel. But by the time the nation was about to ratify the Constitution, most states had granted criminal defendants the right to be represented by a lawyer. No state, however, guaranteed the right to *appointed* counsel. As Professor Tomkovicz has observed, "[i]t seems highly probable that the Sixth Amendment was designed to grant a legal representative of one's own choosing [thereby rejecting the restricted British approach], but no right to have counsel provided by the government."

One hundred and fifty-one years after the ratification of the Sixth Amendment and some sixty years after the adoption of the Fourteenth, the Supreme Court handed down its first significant opinion concerning the right to counsel—*Powell v. Alabama*, 287 U.S. 45 (1932). Although the *Powell* opinion contains sweeping, much-quoted language (such as "the right to be heard would be in many cases of little avail if it did not comprehend the right to be heard by counsel") the Court dwelt on the special circumstances—"above all that [the defendants] stood in peril of their lives." In a case *such as this* the Court told us, "the failure of the trial court to give [the defendants] reasonable time and opportunity to secure counsel was a clear denial of due process." *And in a case with these facts*, "the right to have counsel appointed [is] *a logical corollary of the constitutional right to be heard by counsel.*" (Emphasis added.)

Powell, of course, was a state case. Six years later, in *Johnson v. Zerbst*, 304 U.S. 458 (1938), the Court held, without discussing the likely intent of the Sixth Amendment, that the Amendment guaranteed indigent *federal* defendants (at least all felony defendants) a right to *appointed* counsel. But it would take another twenty-five years before the Court would conclude that the Constitution guaranteed *state* defendants the same unqualified right.

---

[a] At some point in the development of the right to counsel in England, retained counsel could appear on behalf of a felony defendant to argue, but only to argue, matters of law. "When it came to presenting evidence and arguing as to the strength of the evidence, the felony defendant was on his own." CRIMPROC § 1.6(b). However, the distinction between matters of fact and matters of law was hazy and by the middle of the nineteenth century "questions of law" seem to have been extended to include both direct examination and cross-examination. See id.

BETTS V. BRADY

316 U.S. 455, 62 S.Ct. 1252, 86 L.Ed. 1595 (1942).

JUSTICE ROBERTS delivered the opinion of the Court.

Petitioner, an indigent, was indicted for robbery. His request for counsel was denied because local practice permitted appointment only in rape and murder prosecutions. Petitioner then pled not guilty and elected to be tried without a jury. At the trial he chose not to take the stand. He was convicted and sentenced to eight years imprisonment.

[The] due process clause of the Fourteenth Amendment does not incorporate, as such, the specific guarantees found in the Sixth Amendment although a denial by a state of rights or privileges specifically embodied in that and others of the first eight amendments may, in certain circumstances, [deprive] a litigant of due process of law in violation of the Fourteenth. [Due process] formulates a concept less rigid and more fluid than those envisaged in other specific and particular provisions of the Bill of Rights. Its application is less a matter of rule. Asserted denial is to be tested by an appraisal of the totality of facts in a given case.

[Petitioner] says the rule to be deduced from our former decisions is that, in every case, whatever the circumstances, one charged with crime, who is unable to obtain counsel, must be furnished counsel by the state. Expressions in the opinions of this court lend color to the argument, but, as the petitioner admits, none of our decisions squarely adjudicates the question now presented.

In *Powell v. Alabama,* 287 U.S. 45 [1932], ignorant and friendless negro youths, strangers in the community, without friends or means to obtain counsel, were hurried to trial for a capital offense without effective appointment of counsel on whom the burden of preparation and trial would rest, and without adequate opportunity to consult even the counsel casually appointed to represent them. [This] court held the resulting convictions were without due process of law. It said that, in the light of all the facts, the failure of the trial court to afford the defendants reasonable time and opportunity to secure counsel was a clear denial of due process. The court stated further that "under the circumstances [the] necessity of counsel was so vital and imperative that the failure of the trial court to make an effective appointment of counsel was likewise a denial of due process," but added: "whether this would be so in other criminal prosecutions, or under other circumstances, we need not determine. All that it is necessary now to decide, as we do decide, is that in a capital case, where the defendant is unable to employ counsel, and is incapable adequately of making his own defense because of ignorance, feeblemindedness, illiteracy, or the like, it is the duty of the court, whether requested or not, to assign counsel for him as a necessary requisite of due process of law."

[We] have construed the [Sixth Amendment] to require appointment of counsel in all [federal] cases where a defendant is unable to procure the services of an attorney, and where the right has not been intentionally and competently waived. [*Johnson v. Zerbst,* 304 U.S. 458 (1938)].[b] Though [the] amendment lays down no rule for the conduct of the states, the question recurs whether the constraint laid by the amendment upon the national courts expresses a rule so fundamental and essential to a fair trial, and so, to due process of law, that it is made obligatory upon the states by the Fourteenth Amendment. Relevant data on the subject are afforded by constitutional and statutory provisions subsisting in the colonies and the states prior to the inclusion of the Bill of

[b] In holding that the Sixth Amendment required appointment of counsel, the Court, per Black, J., had reasoned: "The Sixth Amendment stands as a constant admonition that if the constitutional safeguards it provides be lost, justice will not 'still be done.' It embodies a realistic recognition of the obvious truth that the average defendant does not have the professional legal skill to protect himself when brought before a tribunal with power to take his life or liberty, wherein the prosecution is presented by experienced and learned counsel. [The] Sixth Amendment withholds from federal courts, in all criminal proceedings, the power and authority to deprive an accused of his life or liberty unless he has or waives the assistance of counsel."

Rights in the national Constitution, and in the constitutional, legislative, and judicial history of the states to the present date.

[I]n the great majority of the states, it has been the considered judgment of the people, their representatives and their courts that appointment of counsel is not a fundamental right, essential to a fair trial. On the contrary, the matter has generally been deemed one of legislative policy.

[In] this case there was no question of the commission of a robbery. The State's case consisted of evidence identifying the petitioner as the perpetrator. The defense was an alibi. Petitioner called and examined witnesses to prove that he was at another place at the time of the commission of the offense. The simple issue was the veracity of the testimony for the State and that for the defendant. As Judge Bond [the author of the state court opinion below] says, the accused was not helpless, but was a man forty-three years old, of ordinary intelligence and ability to take care of his own interests on the trial of that narrow issue. He had once before been in a criminal court, pleaded guilty to larceny and served a sentence and was not wholly unfamiliar with criminal procedure. It is quite clear that in Maryland, if the situation had been otherwise and it had appeared that the petitioner was, for any reason, at a serious disadvantage by reason of the lack of counsel, a refusal to appoint would have resulted in the reversal of a judgment of conviction.

[To] deduce from the due process clause a rule binding upon the states in this matter would be to impose upon them, as Judge Bond points out, a requirement without distinction between criminal charges of different magnitude or in respect of courts of varying jurisdiction. As he says: "Charges of small crimes tried before justices of the peace and capital charges tried in the higher courts would equally require the appointment of counsel. Presumably it would be argued that trials in the Traffic Court would require it."

[While] want of counsel in a particular case may result in a conviction lacking [in] such fundamental fairness, we cannot say that the [Fourteenth Amendment] embodies an inexorable command that no trial for any offense, or in any court, can be fairly conducted and justice accorded a defendant who is not represented by counsel.

The judgment is affirmed.

JUSTICE BLACK, dissenting, with whom JUSTICE DOUGLAS and JUSTICE MURPHY concur.

[The] petitioner [was] a farm hand, out of a job and on relief. [The] court below found that [he] had "at least an ordinary amount of intelligence." It is clear from his examination of witnesses that he was a man of little education.

If this case had come to us from a federal court, it is clear we should have to reverse it, because the Sixth Amendment makes the right to counsel in criminal cases inviolable by the federal government. I believe that the Fourteenth Amendment made the sixth applicable to the states. But this view [has] never been accepted by a majority of this Court and is not accepted today. [I] believe, however, that under the prevailing view of due process, as reflected in the opinion just announced, a view which gives this Court such vast supervisory powers that I am not prepared to accept it without grave doubts, the judgment below should be reversed.

[The] right to counsel in a criminal proceeding is "fundamental." *Powell v. Alabama.* [A] practice cannot be reconciled with "common and fundamental ideas of fairness and right" which subjects innocent men to increased dangers of conviction merely because of their poverty. Whether a man is innocent cannot be determined from a trial in which as here, denial of counsel has made it impossible to conclude, with any satisfactory degree of certainty, that the defendant's case was adequately presented.

NOTES AND QUESTIONS

1. ***Was* Betts *"prejudiced"?*** When the Court reviewed Betts's case, he had appellate counsel, but his lawyer was confident—too confident—that the Court would apply the full measure of the Sixth Amendment right to counsel to the states. Thus he did not make any analysis of the trial and present any specific examples of how Betts might have been prejudiced by the absence of counsel. For the view that a number of such examples could have been shown and that competent trial counsel could have raised many more issues than "the simple issue [of] the veracity of the testimony for the State and that for the defendant," see Yale Kamisar, *The Right to Counsel and the Fourteenth Amendment,* 30 U.Chi.L.Rev. 1, 42–56 (1962).

2. ***The "flat" requirement of counsel in capital cases.*** In *Bute v. Illinois,* 333 U.S. 640 (1948), and subsequent noncapital cases, the Court suggested that there was a "flat" requirement of counsel in capital cases. In *Hamilton v. Alabama,* 368 U.S. 52 (1961), holding that arraignment is so critical a stage in Alabama procedure that denial of counsel at that stage in a capital case violates due process, a unanimous Court declared, per Douglas, J., that "when one pleads to a capital charge without benefit of counsel, we do not stop to determine whether prejudice resulted. [T]he degree of prejudice can never be known." For an explanation and criticism of the Court's distinction between capital and noncapital cases, see Francis A. Allen, *The Supreme Court, Federalism, and State Systems of Criminal Justice,* 8 DePaul L.Rev. 213, 230–31 (1959).

3. ***The absolute right to retained counsel.*** During the *Betts* reign, the Court made it clear that denying a defendant the assistance of *his own lawyer* on *any* issue in the trial of *any* case, constituted a per se violation of "fundamental fairness." Thus, in *Chandler v. Fretag,* 348 U.S. 3 (1954), the Court stamped the right of petitioner "to be heard through his own counsel" as "unqualified." And *Ferguson v. Georgia,* 365 U.S. 570 (1961), held, in effect, that a state may not deny a criminal defendant the right to have his own counsel guide him on direct examination. More recently, the Supreme Court emphasized in *United States v. Gonzalez-Lopez,* 548 U.S. 140 (2006), that "the Sixth Amendment right to counsel of choice . . . commands, not that a trial be fair, but that a particular guarantee of fairness be provided—to wit, that the accused be defended by the counsel he believes to be best." For a discussion of the limits on the right to retained counsel of one's choosing, see infra Section 5.

GIDEON V. WAINWRIGHT

372 U.S. 335, 83 S.Ct. 792, 9 L.Ed.2d 799 (1963).

JUSTICE BLACK delivered the opinion of the Court.

Petitioner was charged in a Florida state court with having broken and entered a poolroom with intent to commit a misdemeanor. This offense is a felony under Florida law. Appearing in court without funds and without a lawyer, petitioner asked the court to appoint counsel for him, whereupon the following colloquy took place:

"The Court: Mr. Gideon, I am sorry, but I cannot appoint Counsel to represent you in this case. Under the laws of the State of Florida, the only time the Court can appoint Counsel to represent a Defendant is when that person is charged with a capital offense. * * *

"The Defendant: The United States Supreme Court says I am entitled to be represented by Counsel."

Put to trial before a jury, Gideon conducted his defense about as well as could be expected from a layman. He made an opening statement to the jury, cross-examined the State's witnesses, presented witnesses in his own defense, declined to testify himself, and made a short argument "emphasizing his innocence to the charge contained in the Information filed in this case." The jury returned a verdict of guilty, and petitioner was sentenced to serve five years in the state prison.

[Since] 1942, when *Betts v. Brady* was decided by a divided Court, the problem of a defendant's federal constitutional right to counsel in a state court has been a continuing source of controversy and litigation in both state and federal courts. To give this problem another review here, we granted certiorari [and] appointed counsel to represent [petitioner].

We accept *Betts*'s assumption, based as it was on our prior cases, that a provision of the Bill of Rights which is "fundamental and essential to a fair trial" is made obligatory upon the States by the Fourteenth Amendment. We think the Court in *Betts* was wrong, however, in concluding that the Sixth Amendment's guarantee of counsel is not one of these fundamental rights. Ten years before *Betts,* this Court, after full consideration of all the historical data examined in *Betts,* had unequivocally declared that "the right to the aid of counsel is of this fundamental character." *Powell.* While the Court at the close of its *Powell* opinion did by its language, as this Court frequently does, limit its holding to the particular facts and circumstances of that case, its conclusions about the fundamental nature of the right to counsel are unmistakable.

[The] fact is that in deciding as it did—that "appointment of counsel is not a fundamental right, essential to a fair trial"—the [*Betts* Court] made an abrupt break with its own well-considered precedents. In returning to these old precedents, sounder we believe than the new, we but restore constitutional principles established to achieve a fair system of justice. Not only these precedents but also reason and reflection require us to recognize that in our adversary system of criminal justice, any person haled into court, who is too poor to hire a lawyer, cannot be assured a fair trial unless counsel is provided for him. This seems to us to be an obvious truth. Governments, both state and federal, quite properly spend vast sums of money to establish machinery to try defendants accused of crime. Lawyers to prosecute are everywhere deemed essential to protect the public's interest in an orderly society. Similarly, there are few defendants charged with crime, few indeed, who fail to hire the best lawyers they can get to prepare and present their defenses. That government hires lawyers to prosecute and defendants who have the money hire lawyers to defend are the strongest indications of the widespread belief that lawyers in criminal courts are necessities, not luxuries. The right of one charged with crime to counsel may not be deemed fundamental and essential to fair trials in some countries, but it is in ours. From the very beginning, our state and national constitutions and laws have laid great emphasis on procedural and substantive safeguards designed to assure fair trials before impartial tribunals in which every defendant stands equal before the law. This noble ideal cannot be realized if the poor man charged with crime has to face his accusers without a lawyer to assist him.

[The] Court in *Betts* departed from the sound wisdom upon which the Court's holding in *Powell* rested. Florida, supported by two other States, has asked that *Betts v. Brady* be left intact. Twenty-two States, as friends of the Court, argue that *Betts* was "an anachronism when handed down" and that it should now be overruled. We agree.

JUSTICE CLARK, concurring in the result.

[T]he Constitution makes no distinction between capital and noncapital cases. The Fourteenth Amendment requires due process of law for the deprival of "liberty" just as for deprival of "life," and there cannot constitutionally be a difference in the quality of the process based merely upon a supposed difference in the sanction involved. How can the Fourteenth Amendment tolerate a procedure which it condemns in capital cases on the ground that deprival of liberty may be less onerous than deprival of life—a value judgment not universally accepted—or that only the latter deprival is irrevocable?

JUSTICE HARLAN, concurring.

I agree that *Betts* should be overruled, but consider it entitled to a more respectful burial than has been accorded, at least on the part of those of us who were not on the Court when that case was decided. I cannot subscribe to the view that *Betts* represented "an abrupt break with its own well-considered precedents." [In *Powell*] this Court declared that under the particular facts there presented—"the ignorance and illiteracy of the defendants, their youth, the circumstances of public hostility [and] above all that they stood in deadly peril of their lives"—the state court had a duty to assign counsel for the trial as a necessary requisite of due process of law. It is evident that these limiting facts were not added to the opinion as an afterthought; they were repeatedly emphasized [and] were clearly regarded as important to the result.

Thus when this Court, a decade later, decided *Betts,* it did no more than to admit of the possible existence of special circumstances in noncapital as well as capital trials, while at the same time to insist that such circumstances be shown in order to establish a denial of due process. The right to appointed counsel had been recognized as being considerably broader in federal prosecutions, see *Johnson v. Zerbst,* but to have imposed these requirements on the States would indeed have been "an abrupt break" with the almost immediate past. The declaration that the right to appointed counsel in state prosecutions, as established in *Powell,* was not limited to capital cases was in truth not a departure from, but an extension of, existing precedent.

The principles declared in *Powell* and in *Betts,* however, had a troubled journey throughout the years that have followed first the one case and then the other.

[In] noncapital cases, the "special circumstances" rule has continued to exist in form while its substance has been substantially and steadily eroded. In the first decade after *Betts,* there were cases in which the Court found special circumstances to be lacking, but usually by a sharply divided vote. However, no such decision has been cited to us, and I have found none, [after] 1950. At the same time, there have been not a few cases in which special circumstances were found in little or nothing more than the "complexity" of the legal questions presented, although those questions were often of only routine difficulty. The Court has come to recognize, in other words, that the mere existence of a serious criminal charge constituted in itself special circumstances requiring the services of counsel at trial. In truth the *Betts* rule is no longer a reality.

This evolution, however, appears not to have been fully recognized by many state courts, in this instance charged with the front-line responsibility for the enforcement of constitutional rights. To continue a rule which is honored by this Court only with lip service is not a healthy thing and in the long run will do disservice to the federal system.

The special circumstances rule has been formally abandoned in capital cases, and the time has now come when it should be similarly abandoned in noncapital cases, at least as to offenses which, as the one involved here, carry the possibility of a substantial prison sentence. (Whether the rule should extend to *all* criminal cases need not now be decided.)[c]

NOTES AND QUESTIONS

1. ***Alternative techniques of overruling available in* Gideon.** Among the traditional arts of overruling are the arguments that (a) the old precedent has not withstood the "lessons of experience" and (b) that its rejection is required by later "inconsistent precedents." See e.g., *Mapp v. Ohio,* p. 211 Were these arguments available in *Gideon?* As to (b) reconsider, for example, the *Chandler* and *Ferguson* cases, establishing the unqualified right to the assistance of counsel *one can hire;* and the post-*Betts* development of the "automatic right" to appointed counsel in capital

[c] Bruce Jacob, now Dean Emeritus and Professor at the Stetson University College of Law, was almost fresh out of law school when he argued the *Gideon* case for the State of Florida. Abe Fortas, later a Supreme Court Justice, argued the case for Gideon. After the Supreme Court reversed his case, Gideon was retried, this time with appointed counsel, and acquitted. See Anthony Lewis, *Gideon's Trumpet* 223–38 (1964). For an interesting look back on the *Gideon* case and what has happened to the *Gideon* principle, see Bruce R. Jacob, *Memories of and Reflections About Gideon v. Wainwright,* 33 Stetson L.Rev. 181 (2003). For another look back at *Gideon,* see Yale Kamisar, Abe Krash, Anthony Lewis & Ellen Podgor, *Gideon at 40: Facing the Crisis, Fulfilling the Promise,* 41 Am.Crim.L.Rev. 131 (2004).

cases and its implicit admission of the unsoundness of the "fair trial" rule. As to (a), consider how, in the two decades since *Betts,* the assumption that a lawyerless defendant would usually be able to defend himself had fared in light of the constant expansion of the "special circumstances" concept; and how the assumption that a "special circumstances" test was more consistent with the "obligations of federalism" than an "absolute rule" had stood up in the face of the proliferation of federal habeas corpus cases produced by the *Betts* rule and the resulting friction between state and federal courts. See generally Jerold H. Israel, *Gideon v. Wainwright: The "Art" of Overruling,* 1963 Supreme Court Rev. 211, 242–69.

2. *Federal delivery systems after* Gideon. In 1964, Congress enacted the Criminal Justice Act, 18 U.S.C.A. § 3006A, requiring federal district courts to adopt a local plan for furnishing counsel to indigent defendants. The Act mandated that the plans include the appointment of "private attorneys," but also allowed almost all districts to add an alternative delivery system of a Federal Public Defender Organization (a governmental entity established within the judicial branch) or a Community Defender Organization (a private non-profit organization, established by the local legal aid society or local bar association). All but a handful of the 94 federal judicial districts have used this alternative (with a substantial majority opting for a public defender organization). The Criminal Justice Act precludes, however, utilizing the public or community defender organization as the exclusive or almost-exclusive provider of government-funded representation, as it requires that "private attorneys shall be appointed in a substantial portion of the cases." Those private attorneys (commonly described as "panel attorneys," because they are selected from a court-approved panel of "qualified attorneys") typically are used in a "substantial minority" of the indigent-defense cases. They usually are assigned to the individual case by the clerk of the court or the defender organization, rather than by a judge. See CRIMPROC § 1.4(f).

3. *State delivery systems after* Gideon. State structures used to provide government-funded counsel tend to vary in several respects from the structure of the Criminal Justice Act. Initially, the choice of delivery system commonly is made by the governmental unit providing the funding, rather than the local court. That governmental entity traditionally has been the county, but over the past few decades, many states have shifted to primary or exclusive state funding.[d] The three most common delivery systems are: (1) individually appointed private attorneys, (2) public defender offices, and (3) contract-attorney organizations (typically a private law firm or a non-profit entity, sponsored by the local bar association or legal aid society, which contracts to provide representation for a large group of cases).

Public defender agencies have long been favored in metropolitan areas. A survey of the 100 most populous counties found that 90 percent had public defender programs. Where states provide the funding, they commonly establish a statewide program, with regional offices (and, in some instances, a separate appellate agency). Other public defender offices are local agencies. The staff of larger offices commonly includes investigators and social workers as well as lawyers and paralegals. Systems using defender offices typically assign to those offices almost all indigent-defense cases, with the primary exceptions being (1) cases in which a potential conflict of interest precludes defender representation [see Note 3, p. 180], and (2) "overflow cases" (where additional cases would exceed an agency-imposed caseload limit). Representation in these non-defender cases typically is provided through individual appointments, although some jurisdictions use a contract attorney program for such cases.

---

[d] As of 2013, 28 states and the District of Columbia had state-administered indigent defense programs. See Suzanne M. Strong, U.S. Dep't of Justice Bureau of Justice Statistics, NCJ 250249, State-Administered Indigent Defense Systems (May, 2017). However, only 23 states completely fund their indigent-defense systems at the state level. In 19 states, counties shoulder the burden for more than half of the funding. See Eve Brensike Primus, *Defense Counsel and Public Defense, in* Academy for Justice, A Report on Scholarship and Criminal Justice Reform (Erik Luna ed., 2017).

A substantial number of mid-size counties and many smaller counties do not have public defender offices. Here, indigent defense needs traditionally have been filled through individual appointments. In some judicial districts, appointment is made by the court, with the judge either exercising discretion in choosing counsel or relying upon a "neutral rotation system." In other districts, the court is removed from the appointment process, with a rotation system administered by an independent official. In recent years, a growing number of mid-sized and small counties have moved to the contract system, with the contract firm agreeing to cover almost the entire indigent-defense docket, or a specific number of cases, for a flat fee or an hourly fee with caps (the typical fee system for individually appointed counsel).

Although commentators have expressed diverse viewpoints as to whether one appointment system or another is more likely to provide better representation, see CRIMPROC § 1.4(f), studies suggest that defendants represented by assigned counsel are more likely to be convicted and are more likely to receive longer sentences than those represented by public defenders. See, e.g., Thomas H. Cohen, *Who's Better at Defending Criminals? Does Type of Defense Attorney Matter in Terms of Producing Favorable Case Outcomes* 25 Crim. Just. Pol'y Rev. 54 (2014); James M. Anderson & Paul Heaton, *How Much Difference Does the Lawyer Make? The Effect of Defense Counsel on Murder Case Outcomes*, 122 Yale L.J. 154 (2012). Anderson & Heaton supra offers some possible reasons for this observed difference: "We find that, in general, appointed counsel have comparatively few resources, face more difficult incentives, and are more isolated than public defenders. The extremely low pay reduces the pool of attorneys willing to take the appointments and makes doing preparation uneconomical."

4. ***Counsel of choice.*** One county in Texas permits indigent defendants to choose their own attorneys from a list of qualified attorneys. Data collected after the first year of this program suggests that the client-choice program participants pled guilty to lesser charges or proceeded to trial more often than their peers. See M. Elaine Nugent-Borakove & Franklin Cruz, *The Power of Choice: The Implications of a System Where Indigent Defendants Choose Their Own Counsel*, p. iii (March 2017), *available at* http://www.tidc.texas.gov/media/55476/the-power-of-choice.pdf. For a discussion of the theory behind the counsel of choice program, see Stephen J. Schulhofer, *Client Choice for Indigent Criminal Defendants: Theory and Implementation*, 12 Ohio St.J.Crim.L. 505 (2015).

5. ***To what extent has the dream of* Gideon *been realized?*** Consider the conclusion reached by the American Bar Association's Standing Committee on Legal Aid and Indigent Defendants after a series of public hearings involving testimony from 32 expert witnesses familiar with the delivery of indigent defense services throughout the states: "Forty years after *Gideon v. Wainwright*, indigent defense remains in a state of crisis, resulting in a system that lacks fundamental fairness and places poor persons at constant risk of wrongful conviction. [T]housands of persons are processed through America's courts every year either with no lawyer at all or with a lawyer who does not have the time, resources, or in some cases the inclination to provide effective representation. All too often, defendants plead guilty, even if they are innocent, without really understanding their legal rights or what is occurring. Sometimes the proceedings reflect little or no recognition that the accused is mentally ill or does not adequately understand English. The fundamental right to a lawyer that Americans assume appl[ies] to everyone accused of criminal conduct effectively does not exist in practice for countless people across the United States." *Gideon's Broken Promise: America's Continuing Quest for Equal Justice*, Exec. Summary at iv–v (2004).[e]

[e] For additional reflections on *Gideon* fifty years later, see articles in the following symposia: *The Gideon Effect: Rights, Justice, and Lawyers Fifty Years After Gideon v. Wainwright*, 122 Yale L.J. 2106 et seq. (2013); *Gideon at 50: Reassessing the Right to Counsel*, 70 Wash. & Lee L. Rev. 835 et seq. (2013); 25 Fed. Sent'g Rep. 87 et seq. (2012).

Commentators agree that "the adequacy of the time and resources at defense counsel's disposal" is a critical factor related to the quality of defense representation, see CRIMPROC § 1.4(f), and that state defense delivery systems are inadequately funded and overwhelmed with unmanageable caseloads. See Prospective Challenges to Delivery System Deficiencies, infra p. 170. In recent years, a growing number of states have created state oversight commissions to prescribe standards for all types of delivery systems within the state. While these commissions vary in their authority, some have mandated qualifications for appointed counsel, caseload limits for defender offices, and attorney training requirements for all government-funded defense counsel. In jurisdictions with capital sentences, states commonly impose, by court rule or commission directive, special standards for death penalty representation (e.g., appointment of two attorneys, with specified experience requirements). For a discussion of the current problems with indigent defense delivery systems and a canvassing of proposed solutions, see Eve Brensike Primus, *Defense Counsel and Public Defense*, *in* Academy for Justice, A Report on Scholarship and Criminal Justice Reform (Erik Luna ed., 2017).

6. ***Data collection and the possibility of evidence-based standards for indigent defense delivery systems.*** Many scholars have called for more data collection about public defender practices and have advocated for the development of evidence-based standards (based on a combination of expert opinion, empirical research/data, and client/defender input) for indigent defense delivery systems. *See, e.g.*, Pamela Metzger & Andrew Guthrie Ferguson, *Defending Data*, 88 S. Cal. L. Rev. 1057 (2015). Others caution that quality data about best practices in public defender offices is difficult to collect and involves normative judgments about what is good public defender work; that a focus on data collection might divert limited resources away from skills training for public defenders; and that there is a risk that the data collected could cause perverse or unintended effects either because it is insufficiently granular and therefore fails to validate worthy indigent defense programs or because it may demonstrate that increased funding will lead to marginal benefits in outcomes. *See, e.g.*, Jennifer E. Laurin, Gideon *by the Numbers: The Emergence of Evidence-Based Practice in Indigent Defense*, 12 Ohio St.J.Crim.L. 325 (2015).

7. ***Indigency standards.*** The Supreme Court did not explain in *Gideon* when a defendant is "indigent" and therefore entitled to appointed counsel. Most jurisdictions have legislation, court rules, or administrative regulations that set forth (often in considerable detail) the standards to be used in determining whether a defendant is financially eligible to receive government-funded counsel. See CRIMPROC § 11.2(g). Many states rely heavily on presumptive eligibility criteria (e.g., income below 125% of the current federal HHS poverty guideline), while others simply direct attention to a series of relevant factors (e.g., possible complexity of the case, family responsibilities, liquidity of assets). While the final say remains with the court, many jurisdictions assign the initial (and typically uncontested) determination to a public defender office, court clerk, or social service agency. Notwithstanding the variations in procedures and standards, the end results from state to state are fairly consistent for demographically similar communities. Thus, a study of defense representation in felony prosecutions in the 75 largest counties found a roughly standard rate of government-funded counsel, in the neighborhood of 82% (as contrasted to 66% for federal felony defendants in the same counties). See CRIMPROC § 1.4(f).

8. ***When must indigent defendants reimburse the government?*** *Rinaldi v. Yeager,* 384 U.S. 305 (1966), invalidated a New Jersey statute which required only those indigent defendants who were sentenced to prison to reimburse the state for the cost of a transcript on appeal, finding an "invidious discrimination" between those convicted defendants and others sentenced only to pay fines or subject only to a suspended sentence or to probation. *James v. Strange,* 407 U.S. 128 (1972), held that a Kansas recoupment statute (which applied whether or not the indigent defendant was convicted) violated equal protection because the indigent defendant could not avail himself of restrictions on wage garnishments and other protective exemptions afforded to other civil judgment debtors.

Fuller v. Oregon, 417 U.S. 40 (1974), however, upheld an Oregon recoupment statute which, under certain circumstances, authorized repayment to the state of the costs of a free legal defense as a condition of probation. A 7–2 majority, per Stewart, J., stressed that "the recoupment statute is quite clearly directed only at those convicted defendants who are indigent at the time of the criminal proceedings against them but who subsequently gain the ability to pay the expenses of legal representation. Defendants with no likelihood of having the means to repay are not put under even a conditional obligation to do so, and those upon whom a conditional obligation is imposed are not subjected to collection procedures until their indigency has ended and no 'manifest hardship' [to defendant or his immediate family] will result."

Dissenting Justice Marshall, joined by Brennan, J., protested that "the important fact which the majority ignores" is that because the repayment of the indigent defendant's debt to the state can be made a condition of his probation, as it was in this case, "[p]etitioner's failure to pay his debt can result in his being sent to prison. In this respect the indigent defendant in Oregon, like [his counterpart in *James*], is treated quite differently from other civil judgment debtors."

Notwithstanding the *Fuller* case, *A.B.A. Standards* § 5–7.2 (3d. ed. commentary) "recommends that defendants be ordered to [make reimbursement] for their defense only in instances where they have made fraudulent representations for purposes of being found eligible for counsel. [The] offer of free legal assistance is rendered hollow if defendants are required to make payments for counsel for several years following conviction. Reimbursement requirements also may serve to discourage defendants from exercising their right to counsel * * *."

EXTENDING *GIDEON* TO MISDEMEANOR CASES

In ARGERSINGER v. HAMLIN, 407 U.S. 25 (1972), the Court, per Douglas, J., struck down a Florida rule (following the line marked out in the jury trial cases) requiring that counsel be appointed only "for nonpetty offenses punishable by more than six months imprisonment," and held that "absent a knowing and intelligent waiver, no person may be *imprisoned* for any offense, whether classified as petty, misdemeanor, or felony unless he was represented by counsel" (emphasis added):

"While there is historical support for limiting the [right] to trial by jury [to] 'serious criminal cases,' there is no such support for a similar limitation on the right to assistance of counsel. [Thus,] we reject [the] premise that since prosecutions for crimes punishable by imprisonment for less than six months may be tried without a jury, they may always be tried without a lawyer. [The] requirement of counsel may well be necessary for a fair trial even in a petty offense prosecution. We are by no means convinced that legal and constitutional questions involved in a case that actually leads to imprisonment even for a brief period are any less complex than when a person can be sent off for six months or more. * * *

"We must conclude, therefore, that the problems associated with misdemeanor and petty offenses often require the presence of counsel to insure the accused a fair trial. [In his concurring opinion,] Mr. Justice Powell suggests that these problems are raised even in situations where there is no prospect of imprisonment. We need not consider the requirements of the Sixth Amendment as regards the right to counsel where loss of liberty is not involved, however, for here, petitioner was in fact sentenced to jail * * *.

"Under the rule we announce today, every judge will know when the trial of a misdemeanor starts that no imprisonment may be imposed, even though local law permits it, unless the accused is represented by counsel. He will have a measure of the seriousness and gravity of the offense and therefore know when to name a lawyer to represent the accused before the trial starts."

Analyzing the problem in terms of general due process rather than the sixth amendment right to counsel, concurring Justice Powell, joined by Rehnquist, J., concluded that "there is a middle course, between the extremes of Florida's six month rule and the Court's rule, which comports with the requirements of the Fourteenth Amendment"—"fundamental fairness" requires that a defendant have the assistance of counsel in petty cases when, but only when, "necessary to assure a fair trial":

"[The] rule adopted today [is] limited to petty offense cases in which the sentence is some imprisonment. The thrust of the Court's position indicates, however, that when the decision must be made, the rule will be extended to all petty offense cases except perhaps the most minor traffic violations. If the Court rejects on constitutional grounds, as it has today, the exercise of any judicial discretion as to need for counsel if a jail sentence is imposed, one must assume a similar rejection of discretion in other petty offense cases. * * *

"I would hold that the right to counsel in petty offense cases is not absolute but is one to be determined by the trial courts exercising a judicial discretion on a case-by-case basis. * * * [T]hree general factors should be weighed. First, the court should consider the complexity of the offense charged. Second, the court should consider the probable sentence that will follow if a conviction is obtained. The more serious the likely consequences, the greater is the probability that a lawyer should be appointed. Third, the court should consider the individual factors peculiar to each case. These, of course, would be the most difficult to anticipate. One relevant factor would be the competency of the individual defendant to present his own case. The attitude of the community toward a particular defendant or particular incident would be another consideration. * * *

"Such a rule is similar in certain respects to the special circumstances rule applied to felony cases in *Betts,* which this Court overruled in *Gideon.* One of the reasons for seeking a more definitive standard in felony cases was the failure of many state courts to live up to their responsibilities in determining on a case-by-case basis whether counsel should be appointed. But this Court should not assume that the past insensitivity of some state courts to the rights of defendants will continue. Certainly if the Court follows the course of reading rigid rules into the Constitution, so that the state courts will be unable to exercise judicial discretion within the limits of fundamental fairness, there is little reason to think that insensitivity will abate."

Petitioner, an indigent, was charged with shoplifting merchandise valued at less than $150, punishable by as much as a $500 fine, or one year in jail, or both. He was not provided counsel. After a bench trial he was convicted of the offense and fined $50. The Supreme Court of Illinois declined to "extend *Argersinger*" to a case where one is charged with an offense for which imprisonment upon conviction is authorized but not actually imposed. A 5–4 majority of the Supreme Court, per Rehnquist, J., agreed, SCOTT v. ILLINOIS, 440 U.S. 367 (1979):

"[W]e believe that the central premise of *Argersinger*—that actual imprisonment is a penalty different in kind from fines or the mere threat of imprisonment—is eminently sound and warrants adoption of actual imprisonment as the line defining the constitutional right to appointment of counsel. * * * We therefore hold that the Sixth and Fourteenth Amendments [require] only that no indigent criminal defendant be sentenced to a term of imprisonment unless the State has afforded him the right to assistance of appointed counsel in his defense."

Concurring Justice Powell noted that "the drawing of a line based on whether there is imprisonment (even for overnight) can have the practical effect of precluding provision of counsel in other types of cases in which conviction can have more serious consequences." He also thought that an "actual imprisonment" rule "tends to impair the proper functioning of the criminal justice system in that trial judges, in advance of hearing any evidence and before knowing anything about the case except the charge, all too often will be compelled to forego the legislatively granted option to impose a sentence of imprisonment upon conviction." Nevertheless, Justice Powell joined the opinion of the Court because "[i]t is important that this Court provide clear guidance to the hundreds of courts across the country that confront this problem daily." He hoped, however, "that in due time a majority will recognize that a more flexible rule is consistent with due process and will better serve the cause of justice."

Justice Brennan, joined by Marshall and Stevens, JJ., dissented:

"[*Argersinger*] established a 'two dimensional' test for the right to counsel: the right attaches to any 'non-petty' offense punishable by more than six months in jail and in addition to any offense where actual incarceration is likely regardless of the maximum authorized penalty. See Steven B. Duke, *The Right to Appointed Counsel: Argersinger and Beyond,* 12 Am.Crim.L.Rev. 601 (1975) .

"The offense of 'theft' with which Scott was charged is certainly not a 'petty' one. It is punishable by a sentence of up to one year in jail. Unlike many traffic or other 'regulatory' offenses, it carries the moral stigma associated with common-law crimes traditionally recognized as indicative of moral depravity. The State indicated at oral argument that the services of a professional prosecutor were considered essential to the prosecution of this offense. Likewise, nonindigent defendants charged with this offense would be well advised to hire the 'best lawyers they can get.' Scott's right to the assistance of appointed counsel is thus plainly mandated by the logic of the Court's prior cases, including *Argersinger* itself.

"Perhaps the strongest refutation of respondent's alarmist prophecies that an authorized imprisonment standard would wreak havoc on the States is that the standard has not produced that result in the substantial number of States that already provide counsel in all cases where imprisonment is authorized—States that include a large majority of the country's population and a great diversity of urban and rural environments. * * * It may well be that adoption by this Court of an authorized imprisonment standard would lead state and local governments to re-examine their criminal statutes. A state legislature or local government might determine that it no longer desired to authorize incarceration for certain minor offenses in light of the expense of meeting the requirements of the Constitution. In my view this re-examination is long overdue. In any event, the Court's actual imprisonment standard must inevitably lead the courts to make this re-examination, which plainly should more properly be a legislative responsibility."

In a separate dissent, Justice Blackmun maintained that the right to counsel "extends at least as far as the right to jury trial" and thus that "an indigent defendant in a state criminal case must be afforded appointed counsel whenever the defendant is prosecuted for a nonpetty criminal offense, that is, one punishable by more than six months' imprisonment, *or* whenever the defendant is actually subjected to a term of imprisonment."

NOTES AND QUESTIONS

1. ***How important are misdemeanor cases when no imprisonment is actually imposed?*** Consider Bruce R. Jacob, *Memories of and Reflections about Gideon v. Wainwright*, 33 Stetson L.Rev. 181, 284 (2003) (writing forty years after he had argued the losing side in Gideon): "The stigma of any criminal conviction, including a misdemeanor conviction that results in a fine, is significant. Any misdemeanor conviction in a person's past, except for a minor traffic offense, makes it difficult for that person to gain entry into medical school or law school, to obtain certain jobs, or to enter the military service. Imposing a fine is a taking of property under [Fourteenth Amendment Due Process]. [Now] that the right to counsel has been incorporated into the Fourteenth Amendment, an indigent defendant in a misdemeanor case, facing a possible fine as punishment, should be entitled to the appointment of counsel."

2. ***Potential judicial prejudice.*** Are unrepresented defendants likely to waive their right to a jury trial, hoping that a judge who sits as factfinder will be able to provide assistance? If so, how in a *non-jury* case, can a judge *properly* make an intelligent pre-trial determination as

to whether the sentence is likely to include incarceration, at least where he will hear the case? Isn't a considerable amount of potentially prejudicial information likely to be injected into the factfinding process? If an indigent defendant charged with an offense usually punished only by a fine is appointed counsel, would a *different* judge hearing the case assume that a colleague had found that the defendant had a "bad record" or had committed the minor offense in an egregious manner? See Commentary to Unif.R.Crim.P. 321(b).

3. ***Judicial reluctance.*** May the problems raised in Note 2 never be reached because of judicial reluctance to conduct pretrial inquiries about the likely sentence? Consider Note, 93 Harv.L.Rev. 82, 87 (1979): "It seems far more likely that, due to the sheer volume of misdemeanor cases, judges simply will not appoint counsel, thereby relinquishing their discretion to impose the penalty of imprisonment." If so, would this constitute improper judicial interference with the legislature's judgment concerning the appropriate range of penalties? See id.

4. ***State practices.*** A number of states need not apply the *Scott* standard, because they provide counsel to any indigent defendant charged with an offense that carries a potential jail sentence. However, at least half the states use the *Scott* "actual imprisonment" standard when determining whether to appoint counsel for at least some category of misdemeanors. For a breakdown of how different states approach this issue, see CRIMPROC § 11.2(a).

5. **Gideon *revisited—and criticized.*** Although he recognizes that "probably no decision in the field of constitutional criminal procedure enjoys anything like the unqualified and unanimous approval" that *Gideon* has received, Professor Dripps criticizes the case for focusing on the language of the Sixth Amendment rather than taking a more general due process approach. Donald A. *Dripps, About Guilt or Innocence* 117 (2003):

"[*Gideon*] took a Procrustean approach to the Sixth Amendment. Where the amendment says the defendant may appear through counsel, *Gideon* stretches the amendment to cover subsidizing counsel for the poor. Where the amendment says ['in *all* criminal prosecutions'], *Gideon* reduces the amendment to covering [felony cases and only those misdemeanor cases leading to incarceration]. Would the Court now or ever uphold a federal statute that forbade a misdemeanor defendant from appearing through privately-retained counsel? If not, how can 'all' mean 'all' when the issue is prohibiting appearance through counsel, but mean 'some' when the issue is providing indigent defense? * * * [By] relying on the Sixth Amendment (albeit in a distorted fashion) the Warren Court deflected attention from instrumental reliability in favor of a formalistic focus on the textually-referenced 'assistance of counsel.' The incorporation approach necessarily failed to describe Gideon's constitutional right with appropriate generality. There is nothing *intrinsically* valuable about lawyers; that is why subsequent cases have developed the idea, if not the reality, that defense counsel's assistance must be *effective.* * * * Gideon's right was not to a lawyer, but to a trial that ran no more than some practically irreducible risk of falsely convicting him."

For an interesting argument that equal protection and due process principles should be interpreted to guarantee indigent misdemeanants a right to counsel even when the Sixth Amendment does not, see Brandon Buskey & Lauren Sudeall Lucas, *Keeping* Gideon*'s Promise: Using Equal Protection to Address the Denial of Counsel in Misdemeanor Cases*, 85 Fordham L. Rev. 2299 (2017).

6. ***Can an uncounseled misdemeanor conviction still be used to enhance a prison sentence when, after being given counsel, a defendant is convicted of a second crime?*** Overruling an earlier decision (*Baldasar v. Illinois*, 446 U.S. 222 (1980)), the Court, per Rehnquist, C.J., held in NICHOLS v. UNITED STATES, 511 U.S. 738 (1994), that a "logical consequence" of *Scott* is that "an uncounseled conviction valid under *Scott* [because no prison term was imposed] may be relied upon to enhance the sentence for a subsequent offense, even though that sentence entails imprisonment. Enhancement statutes, whether in the nature of criminal history provisions

such as those contained in the Sentencing Guidelines, or recidivist statutes that are commonplace in state criminal laws, do not change the penalty imposed for the earlier conviction." (Seven years earlier, when not represented by counsel, Nichols had pled nolo contendere to a state misdemeanor (DUI) and paid a $250 fine. This misdemeanor conviction was used to enhance his sentence when he was subsequently convicted of a federal drug offense.)

The Chief Justice pointed out: "[Nichols] could have been sentenced more severely based simply on evidence of the underlying conduct that gave rise to the previous DUI offense. And the state need prove such conduct only by a preponderance of the evidence. Surely, then, it must be constitutionally permissible to consider a prior uncounseled conviction based on the same conduct where that conduct must be proved beyond a reasonable doubt."

Blackmun, J., joined by Stevens and Ginsburg, JJ., dissented: "It is more logical, and more consistent with the reasoning in *Scott,* to hold that a conviction that is invalid for imposing a sentence for the offense remains invalid for increasing the term of imprisonment imposed for a subsequent conviction. [That] the sentence in *Scott* was imposed in the first instance and the sentence here was the result of an enhancement statute is a distinction without a constitutional difference. * * *"

7. ***If an indigent defendant is not provided counsel, can he be given a suspended sentence or placed on probation?*** Consider ALABAMA v. SHELTON, 535 U.S. 654 (2002), which arose as follows: After being convicted of a misdemeanor, third-degree assault, Shelton, an indigent defendant who had not been afforded counsel, was sentenced to a jail term of 30 days, which the trial court immediately suspended. Shelton was then placed on two years unsupervised probation. The Supreme Court of Alabama took the position that a suspended sentence constitutes a "term of imprisonment" within the meaning of *Argersinger* and *Scott* even though incarceration is not immediate or inevitable. Accordingly, the court affirmed Shelton's conviction and the monetary portion of his punishment, but invalidated "that aspect of his sentence imposing 30 days of suspended jail time." By reversing Shelton's suspended sentence, the court also vacated the two-year term of probation. A 5–4 majority, per GINSBURG, J., affirmed:

"A suspended sentence is a prison term imposed for the offense of conviction. Once the prison term is triggered, the defendant is incarcerated not for the probation violation, but for the underlying offense. The uncounseled conviction at that point 'result[s] in imprisonment'; it 'ends up in the actual deprivation of a person's liberty.' This is precisely what the Sixth Amendment as interpreted in *Argersinger* and *Scott* does not allow.

"[On the basis of figures suggesting that conditional sentences are commonly imposed but rarely activated,] *amicus* argues that a rule requiring appointed counsel in every case involving a suspended sentence would unduly hamper the States' attempts to impose effective probationary punishment. A more 'workable solution,' he contends, would permit imposition of a suspended sentence on an uncounseled defendant and require appointment of counsel, if at all, only at the probation revocation stage, when incarceration is imminent. * * *

"*Amicus* does not describe the contours of the hearing that, he suggests, might precede revocation of a term of probation imposed on an uncounseled defendant. * * * In Alabama, however, the character of the probation revocation hearing currently afforded is not in doubt. The proceeding is an 'informal' one at which the defendant has no right to counsel, and the court no obligation to observe customary rules of evidence. More significant, the sole issue at the hearing—apart from determinations about the necessity of confinement—is whether the defendant breached the terms of probation. * * * The validity or reliability of the underlying conviction is beyond attack. * * *

"We think it plain that a hearing so timed and structured cannot compensate for the absence of trial counsel, for it does not even address the key Sixth Amendment inquiry: whether the adjudication of guilt corresponding to the prison sentence is sufficiently reliable to permit incarceration. Deprived of counsel when tried, convicted, and sentenced, and unable to challenge the original judgment at a subsequent probation revocation hearing, a defendant in Shelton's circumstances faces incarceration on a conviction that has never been subjected to 'the crucible of meaningful adversarial testing.' "

Justice SCALIA, joined by the Chief Justice and Justices Kennedy and Thomas, dissented:

"[What procedures the Alabama courts will adopt if Shelton someday violates the terms of probation and the state decides to deprive him of his liberty] is not the [question] before us, and the Court has no business offering an advisory opinion on its answer. We are asked to decide whether 'imposition of a suspended or conditional sentence in a misdemeanor case invoke[s] a defendant's Sixth Amendment right to counsel.' Since *imposition* of a suspended sentence does not deprive a defendant of his personal liberty, the answer to *that* question is plainly no. In the future, *if and when* the State of Alabama seeks to imprison respondent on the previously suspended sentence, we can ask whether the procedural safeguards attending the imposition of that sentence comply with the Constitution. But that question is *not* before us now. * * *

"Surely the procedures attending reimposition of a suspended sentence would be adequate if they required, upon the defendant's request, complete retrial of the misdemeanor violation with assistance of counsel. By what right does the Court deprive the State of that option? It may well be a sensible option, since most defendants will be induced to comply with the terms of their probation by the mere threat of a retrial that could send them to jail, and since the expense of those rare, counseled retrials may be much less than the expense of providing counsel initially in all misdemeanor cases that bear a possible sentence of imprisonment. And it may well be that, in some cases, even procedures short of complete retrial will suffice."

8. ***Shrinking* Gideon.** Consider Stephanos Bibas, *Shrinking Gideon and Expanding Alternatives to Lawyers*, 70 Wash. & Lee L. Rev. 1287, 1290 (2013):

"*Gideon*'s problems are deep, structural ones. We have been spreading resources too thin, in the process slighting the core cases such as capital and other serious felonies that are the most complex and need the most time and money. A perfunctory chat with a lawyer is little better than no lawyer at all.

"[W]e must shrink the universe of cases covered by *Gideon* to preserve its core. That would mean excluding nonjury misdemeanors and perhaps probationary sentences from its ambit, for example, and thinking harder up front about which cases need to be charged and pursued as felonies.

"Especially in bench trials, there are other ways to simplify cases to make lawyers less necessary. In particular, civil procedure could learn from inquisitorial systems, in which judicial officers are more active and the parties and their lawyers need do less. Magistrates could lead investigations, discovery, and witness examinations, relying less on the parties to proactively frame and pursue their claims. Inquisitorial procedure sounds like a strange transplant from civil-law countries. But it already has parallels in administrative systems for claiming government benefits, in which claimants commonly pursue their claims without lawyers.

"There may also be ways to loosen the bar's stranglehold so that paralegals, social workers, and others can automate delivery of legal services for routine cases. That change would resemble what we see in health care, as nurse practitioners and physician assistants are providing care in routine medical cases.

"In short, *Gideon* can work in the real world only if lawyers drop their grandest ambitions for lawyerizing the world and instead step back to make lawyers less necessary in the first place. The goal should be to concentrate lawyers' efforts on providing quality legal services in the highest-stakes cases where they are needed most. Quality and support matter more than quantity alone."

See also Donald A. Dripps, *Up From* Gideon, 45 Tex. Tech. L. Rev. 113 (2012) (proposing a number of reforms including (1) exempting some self-representing felony defendants, like their misdemeanor counterparts, from sentences of incarceration if convicted; (2) giving counsel for indigent defendants discretion to decline unpromising appeals; (3) permitting lay representation of juvenile and misdemeanor defendants; and (4) recognizing indigent defense as a separate career track from the general practice of law).

B. THE "BEGINNINGS" OF THE RIGHT TO COUNSEL: "CRIMINAL PROSECUTIONS" AND "CRITICAL STAGES"

ROTHGERY V. GILLESPIE COUNTY

554 U.S. 191, 128 S.Ct. 2578, 171 L.Ed.2d 366 (2008).

JUSTICE SOUTER delivered the opinion of the Court.

[Relying on erroneous information that petitioner Rothgery had a previous felony conviction, Texas police arrested him and brought him before a magistrate judge for what is sometimes called an "article 15.17 hearing." At this hearing the Fourth Amendment probable-cause determination is made, bail is set and the defendant is apprised of the accusation against him. In Rothgery's case the magistrate judge concluded that probable cause existed and bail was set at $5,000. Rothgery was committed to jail, from which he was released after posting a security bond. Rothgery had no money for a lawyer and made several unheeded requests for appointed counsel.

[Approximately six months later, Rothgery was indicted by a Texas grand jury for unlawful possession of a firearm by a felon, resulting in his rearrest the next day. When bail was increased to $15,000, Rothgery could not post it. As a result, he was placed in jail and remained there for three weeks.

[Shortly thereafter, Rothgery was finally assigned a lawyer. The lawyer's work led to the dismissal of the indictment. Rothgery then brought this 42 U.S.C. § 1983 action, claiming that if the county had provided him a lawyer within a reasonable time after the hearing, he would not have been indicted, rearrested, or jailed. He maintained that the county's unwritten policy of denying appointed counsel to indigent defendants out on bail until an indictment is entered violated his Sixth Amendment right to counsel. The Court of Appeals concluded, however, that the Sixth Amendment right to counsel did not attach at the Article 15.17 hearing because "the relevant prosecutors were not aware or involved in Rothgery's arrest or appearance" and there was "no indication" that the police alone "had any power to commit the state to prosecute."]

The Sixth Amendment right of the "accused" to assistance of counsel in "all criminal prosecutions" is limited by its terms: "it does not attach until a prosecution is commenced." We have, for purposes of the right to counsel, pegged commencement to "the initiation of adversary judicial criminal proceedings—whether by way of formal charge, preliminary hearing, indictment, information, or arraignment," *United States v. Gouveia*, 467 U.S. 180 (1984). [The] rule is [a] recognition of the point at which "the government has committed itself to prosecute" [and] the accused "finds himself faced with the prosecutorial forces of organized society, and immersed in the intricacies of substantive and procedural criminal law." *Kirby v. Illinois*, 406 U.S. 682 [1972]. The issue is whether Texas's article 15.17 hearing marks that point, with the consequent state obligation to appoint counsel within a reasonable time once a request for assistance is made. * * *

[W]e have twice held that the right to counsel attaches at the initial appearance before a judicial officer, see *Michigan v. Jackson*, 475 U.S. 625 [1986]; *Brewer v. Williams*, 430 U.S. 387

[1977]. This first time before a court, also known as a "preliminary arraignment" or "arraignment on the complaint," is generally the hearing at which "the magistrate informs the defendant of the charge in the complaint and of various rights in further proceedings," and "determine[s] the conditions for pretrial release." Texas's article 15.17 hearing is an initial appearance. * * * *Brewer* and *Jackson* control. * * *

[The *Jackson* case] flatly rejected the distinction between initial arraignment and arraignment on the indictment. [Our] conclusion was driven by the same considerations the Court has endorsed in *Brewer*: by the time a defendant is brought before a judicial officer, is informed of a formally lodged accusation, and has restrictions imposed on his liberty in aid of the prosecution, the State's relationship with the defendant has become solidly adversarial. And that is just as true when the proceeding comes before the indictment (in the case of the initial arraignment on a formal complaint) as when it comes after it (at an arraignment on an indictment). * * *

[T]he overwhelming consensus practice conforms to the rule that the first formal proceedings is the point of attachment. We are advised without contradiction that not only the Federal Government, including the District of Columbia, but 43 States take the first step toward appointing counsel "before, at, or just after initial appearance." [To] the extent [that 7 States] have been denying appointed counsel on the heels of the first appearance, they are a distinct minority. * * *

Neither *Brewer* nor *Jackson* said a word about the prosecutor's involvement as a relevant fact, much less a controlling one. [An] attachment rule that turned on determining the moment of a prosecutor's first involvement would be "wholly unworkable and impossible to administer." * * * And it would have the practical effect of resting attachment on such absurd distinctions as the day of the month an arrest is made or "the sophistication or lack thereof, of a jurisdiction's computer intake system." * * *

[W]hat counts as a commitment to prosecute is an issue of federal law unaffected by allocations of power among state officials under a State's law, and under the federal standard, an accusation filed with a judicial officer is sufficiently formal, and the government's commitment to prosecute it sufficiently concrete, when the accusation prompts arraignment and restrictions on the accused's liberty to facilitate the prosecution. * * *

The County [argues] that in considering the significance of the initial appearance, we must ignore prejudice to a defendant's pretrial liberty, reasoning that it is the concern, not of the right to counsel, but of the speedy-trial right and the Fourth Amendment. We think the County's reliance on [*United States v.*] *Gouveia* is misplaced, and its argument mistaken.

The defendants in *Gouveia* were prison inmates, suspected of murder, who had been placed in an administrative detention unit and denied counsel up until an indictment was filed. [They] argued that their administrative detention should be treated as an accusation for purposes of the right to counsel because the government was actively investigating the crimes. * * * We [saw] no basis for "depart[ing] from our traditional interpretation of the Sixth Amendment right to counsel in order to provide additional protections for [the inmates]."

Gouveia's holding that the Sixth Amendment right to counsel had not attached has no application here. * * * [S]ince we are not asked to extend the right to counsel to a point earlier than formal judicial proceedings (as in *Gouveia*), but to defer it to those proceedings in which a prosecutor is involved, *Gouveia* does not speak to the question before us. * * *

[A]ccording to the County, our cases (*Brewer* and *Jackson* aside) actually establish a "general rule that the right to counsel attaches at the point that [what the County calls] formal charges are filed," with exceptions allowed only in the case of "a very limited set of specific preindictment situations." The County suggests that the latter category should be limited to those appearances at which the aid of counsel is urgent and "the dangers to the accused of proceeding without counsel" are great. Texas's article 15.17 hearing should not count as one of those situations, the County says, because it is not of critical significance, since it "allows no presentation of witness testimony and provides no opportunity to expose weaknesses in the government's evidence, create a basis for later impeachment, or even engage in basic discovery."

We think the County is wrong. * * * Attachment occurs when the government has used the judicial machinery to signal a commitment to prosecute as spelled out in *Brewer* and *Jackson*. Once attachment occurs, the accused at least is entitled to the presence of appointed counsel during any "critical stage" of the postattachment proceedings; what makes a stage critical is what shows the need for counsel's presence. Thus, counsel must be appointed within a reasonable time after attachment to allow for adequate representation at any critical stage before trial, as well as trial itself.

The County thus makes an analytical mistake in its assumption that attachment necessarily requires the occurrence or imminence of a critical stage. On the contrary, it is irrelevant to attachment that the presence of counsel at an article 15.17 hearing, say, may not be critical, just as it is irrelevant that counsel's presence may not be critical when a prosecutor walks over to the trial court to file an information. * * *

Our holding is narrow. We do not decide whether the 6-month delay in appointment of counsel resulted in prejudice to Rothgery's Sixth Amendment rights, and have no occasion to consider what standards should apply in deciding this. We merely affirm what we have held before and what an overwhelming majority of American jurisdictions understand in practice: a criminal defendant's initial appearance before a judicial officer, where he learns the charge against him and his liberty is subject to restriction, marks the start of adversary judicial proceedings that trigger attachment of the Sixth Amendment right to counsel. * * *

CHIEF JUSTICE ROBERTS, with whom JUSTICE SCALIA joins, concurring.

Justice Thomas's analysis of the present issue is compelling, but I believe the result here is controlled by *Brewer v. Williams* and *Michigan v. Jackson*. A sufficient case has not been made for revisiting those precedents, and accordingly I join the Court's opinion.

I also join Justice Alito's concurrence, which correctly distinguishes between the time the right to counsel attaches and the circumstances under which counsel must be provided.

JUSTICE ALITO, with whom THE CHIEF JUSTICE and JUSTICE SCALIA join, concurring.

I join the Court's opinion because I do not understand it to hold that a defendant is entitled to the assistance of appointed counsel as soon as his Sixth Amendment right attaches. As I interpret our precedents, the term "attachment" signifies nothing more than the beginning of the defendant's prosecution. It does not mark the beginning of a substantive entitlement to the assistance of counsel. * * *

[W]e have previously held that "arraignments" that were functionally indistinguishable from the Texas magistration marked the point at which the Sixth Amendment right to counsel "attached." It does not follow, however, and I do not understand the Court to hold, that the county had an obligation to appoint an attorney to represent petitioner within some specified period after his magistration. To so hold, the Court would need to do more than conclude that petitioner's criminal prosecution had begun. It would also need to conclude that the assistance of counsel in the wake of a Texas magistration is part of the substantive guarantee of the Sixth Amendment. That question lies beyond our reach, petitioner having never sought our review of it. * * *

We have [r]ejected the argument that the Sixth Amendment entitles the criminal defendant to the assistance of appointed counsel at a probable cause hearing. See *Gerstein v. Pugh* (1975) [p. 328. * * * At the same time, we have recognized that certain pretrial events may so prejudice the outcome of the defendant's prosecution that, as a practical matter, the defendant must be represented at those events in order to enjoy genuinely effective assistance at trial [referring to the lineup cases at p. 683. * * * We have also held that the assistance of counsel is guaranteed at a pretrial lineup, since "the confrontation compelled by the State between the accused and the victim or witnesses to a crime to elicit identification evidence is peculiarly riddled with innumerable dangers and variable factors which might seriously, even crucially, derogate from a fair trial." Other "critical stages" of the prosecution include pretrial interrogation, a pretrial psychiatric exam, and certain kinds of arraignments. * * *

I interpret the Sixth Amendment to require the appointment of counsel only after the defendant's prosecution has begun, and then only as necessary to guarantee the defendant effective assistance at trial. [Texas] counties need only appoint counsel as far in advance of trial, and as far in advance of any pretrial "critical stage," as necessary to guarantee effective assistance at trial. * * *

The Court expresses no opinion on whether Gillespie County satisfied that obligation in this case. Petitioner has asked us to decide only the limited question whether his magistration marked the beginning of his "criminal prosecutio[n]" within the meaning of the Sixth Amendment. Because I agree with the Court's resolution of that limited question, I join its opinion in full.

JUSTICE THOMAS, dissenting.

* * * Because the Court's holding is not supported by the original meaning of the Sixth Amendment or any reasonable interpretation of our precedents, I respectfully dissent.

[After examining the historical background of the term, Justice Thomas concludes that history furnishes] strong evidence that the term "criminal prosecutio[n]" in the Sixth Amendment refers to the commencement of a criminal suit by filing formal charges in a court with jurisdiction to try and punish the defendant. And on this understanding of the Sixth Amendment, it is clear that petitioner's initial appearance before the magistrate did not commence a "criminal prosecutio[n]." No formal charges had been filed. The only document submitted to the magistrate was the arresting officer's affidavit of probable cause. * * *

As the Court notes, our cases have "pegged commencement" of a criminal prosecution to "the initiation of adversary judicial criminal proceedings—whether by way of formal charge, preliminary hearing, indictment, information, or arraignment," *Kirby v. Illinois* (plurality opinion). The Court has repeated this formulation in virtually every right-to-counsel case decided since *Kirby*. * * *

[Rothgery's] initial appearance was not what *Kirby* described as an "arraignment." An arraignment, in its traditional and usual sense, is a postindictment proceeding at which the defendant enters a plea. Although the word "arraignment" is sometimes used to describe an initial appearance before a magistrate, that is not what *Kirby* meant when it said that the right to counsel attaches at an "arraignment." Rather, it meant the traditional, postindictment arraignment where the defendant enters a plea. * * *

Neither petitioner nor the Court identifies any way in which petitioner's ability to receive a fair trial was undermined by the absence of counsel during the period between his initial appearance and his indictment. Nothing during that period exposed petitioner to the risk that he would be convicted as the result of ignorance of his rights. Instead, the gravamen of petitioner's complaint is that if counsel had been appointed earlier, he would have been able to stave off indictment by convincing the prosecutor that petitioner was not guilty of the crime alleged. But the Sixth Amendment protects against the risk of erroneous *conviction*, not the risk of unwarranted *prosecution*. See *Gouveia* (rejecting the notion that the "purpose of the right to counsel is to provide a defendant with a preindictment private investigator"). * * *

[W]e have never suggested that the accused's right to the assistance of counsel "for his defence" entails a right to use counsel as a sword to contest pretrial detention. To the contrary, we have flatly rejected that notion, reasoning that a defendant's liberty interests are protected by other constitutional guarantees.

NOTES AND QUESTIONS

1. ***Triggering the right to counsel vs. requiring the presence of counsel.*** A defendant is not entitled to the assistance of counsel under the Sixth Amendment unless two conditions exist. First, there must be a "criminal prosecution" as defined by *Rothgery*—meaning that adversarial judicial criminal proceedings must have been commenced through a first formal hearing, a formal charge, a preliminary hearing, an indictment, an information, or an arraignment (whichever comes first). At that point, a defendant's Sixth Amendment right to counsel *attaches*, but that does not mean that the defendant is necessarily entitled to a lawyer's assistance at that very moment. Rather, counsel must be appointed "within a reasonable time after attachment" and the defendant is only entitled to the assistance of that counsel at "critical stages" in the criminal proceeding.

2. ***What is a reasonable time?*** The *Rothgery* Court notes that "counsel must be appointed within a reasonable time after attachment to allow for adequate representation at any critical stage before trial, as well as trial itself," but what is a reasonable time? Rothgery had to wait six months before he got his lawyer. Is that reasonable? What about the 50-year-old woman who was charged with shoplifting in Mississippi who spent 11 months in jail waiting for a lawyer to be appointed? Or the woman charged with stealing $200 from a slot machine who spent 8 months in jail waiting for a lawyer? See Report of the National Right to Counsel Committee, *Justice Denied: America's Continuing Neglect of Our Constitutional Right to Counsel* 86–87 (April 2009) (describing these and other cases). According to more recent reports, in some states defendants routinely remain in pretrial detention for weeks or even months before counsel is appointed. See Douglas L. Colbert, *Prosecution Without Representation*, 59 Buff. L. Rev. 333, 410 & 428–53 (2011) (documenting state delays).

The *Rothgery* Court did not address what, if any, remedy these defendants would have if they were able to demonstrate an unreasonable delay in the provision of counsel. The Court did suggest in dicta, however, that the defendant would have to show prejudice to his Sixth Amendment rights. How would one show prejudice? Would the defendant have to point to specific evidence that was lost due to the delay? Should a defendant's later guilty plea be vacated if there was unreasonable delay in appointing counsel? Consider Colbert at 387–88: "A lawyer's * * * early investigation, and evaluation of the State's case allow a detainee to believe in an assigned counsel's dedication to the case and to consider a trial option. In contrast, the longer the delay before counsel appears * * * , the greater the client's reasonable anxiety about the assigned lawyer's competence and commitment to defend. Many defendants, particularly those in custody, ultimately lose the will to fight and opt to plead guilty because they lack confidence in the late arriving, appointed lawyer."

3. ***What makes a stage critical?*** A criminal defendant's trial is obviously the most critical stage of a criminal prosecution, but the Supreme Court has also held that plea negotiations (*Missouri v. Frye*, 566 U.S. 134 (2012); *Lafler v. Cooper*, 566 U.S. 156 (2012)), pretrial corporeal identifications (*United States v. Wade*, 388 U.S. 218 (1967)), police questioning (*Brewer v. Williams*, 430 U.S. 387 (1977)), and certain kinds of arraignments and preliminary hearings (*Coleman v. Alabama*, 399 U.S. 1 (1970); *White v. Maryland*, 373 U.S. 59 (1963)) are critical stages that require the presence of counsel. At times, the Court has used broad language to describe what constitutes a critical stage. For example, in *Wade*, Justice Brennan, writing for the Court, explained that the Sixth Amendment ensures that the accused "need not stand alone against the State at any stage of the prosecution, formal or informal, in court or out, where counsel's absence might derogate from the accused's right to a fair trial." *Wade*, 388 U.S. at 226–27. At the same

time, however, the Court has held that probable cause hearings (*Gerstein v. Pugh*, 420 U.S. 103 (1975)) and pretrial photographic identification procedures (*United States v. Ash*, 413 U.S. 300 (1973)) are not critical stages requiring the presence of counsel. In refusing to recognize photographic identifications as "critical stages," the Supreme Court, per Justice Blackmun, observed that the right to counsel has always been limited to "trial-like confrontations" between prosecuting authorities and the accused where the lawyer acts as "a spokesman for, or advisor to the accused." Concurring Justice Stewart emphasized that "a photographic identification is quite different from a corporeal lineup, for there are substantially fewer possibilities of impermissible suggestion when photographs are used, and those unfair influences can be readily constructed at trial."

Do you think that the Texas magistration hearing is a "critical stage" at which Rothgery should be entitled to the presence of a lawyer? The majority in *Rothgery* suggests (and Justice Alito's concurrence explicitly claims) that it is not. Why not?

4. ***Bail hearings as critical stages.*** Only ten states guarantee counsel to defendants at the initial bail review hearing. Another ten states deny counsel at bail review hearings while the practices in the remaining thirty states vary by county. The Supreme Court has yet to decide whether a bail review hearing is a "critical stage" in a criminal prosecution. What do you think? For a strong argument that it should be deemed critical, see Colbert supra Note 2.

5. ***Pre-trial psychiatric examinations as critical stages.*** In *Estelle v. Smith*, 451 U.S. 454 (1981), the Supreme Court held that the Sixth Amendment guarantees defendants the opportunity to consult with counsel before deciding whether to submit to a pretrial psychiatric examination. The Court avoided the question whether the defendant would have a Sixth Amendment right to have counsel *present* during the psychiatric examination and, in dicta, suggested that it might be disruptive. See id. at 471 n.14. The lower courts are divided regarding whether a pretrial psychiatric examination is a "critical stage" that entitles defendants to the presence of counsel. Consider the statements of then-judge Scalia in *United States v. Byers*, 740 F.2d 1104, 1118–19 (D.C. Cir. 1984):

"[For an encounter to be considered a 'critical stage,'] the defendant must be confronted *either* with the need to make a decision requiring distinctively legal advice—which may occur even in a context in which the prosecutor or his agents are not present—*or* with the need to defend himself against the direct onslaught of the prosecutor—which may require some skills that are not distinctively legal, such as the quality mentioned in *Wade,* of being 'schooled in the detection of suggestive influences.' * * *

"It is obvious that neither condition exists here. [A]t the psychiatric interview itself, [the defendant] was not confronted by the procedural system; he had no decisions in the nature of legal strategy or tactics to make. [The] only conceivable role for counsel at the examination would have been to observe."

But see Judge Bazelon's response in dissent:

"A court-ordered clinical interview is clearly a 'confrontation' in the sense that the accused is present and is the object of the inquiry. * * * The psychiatrists and other behavioral experts who conduct court-ordered clinical interviews are clearly professional adversaries. They are experts employed by the government. They meet with the accused after he has been charged with a crime and while he is in criminal custody. Their reports are transmitted to the government and may be used by it to help prove the defendant's guilt. They routinely testify on behalf of the government.

"A typical psychiatric or other clinical interview is a complex event, in which the accused exhibits a host of subtle but important behaviors. [T]he expert cannot be a completely objective and reliable informant even with respect to the bare 'facts' of the interview. The same intellectual presuppositions and personal and institutional biases that affect his or her evaluation of the data also affect his or her conscious or unconscious decisions regarding what sort of behavior to notice, remember, and record. And what is left out in that process may—in the minds of other equally competent behavioral scientists—cast serious doubt on the validity of the interviewer's conclusions."

Who is right? For a more recent discussion of the split in the lower courts and the policy arguments involved, see Maxwell C. Smith, *Quiet Eyes: The Need for Defense Counsel's Presence at Court-Ordered Psychiatric Evaluations*, 16 Cap. Def. J. 421 (2004) .

6. ***The period between arraignment and trial as a critical stage.*** Consider *Hurrell-Harring v. State of New York*, 904 N.Y.S.2d 296, 930 N.E.2d 217, 224 (N.Y. 2010): "Also 'critical' for Sixth Amendment purposes is the period between arraignment and trial when a case must be factually developed and researched, decisions respecting grand jury testimony made, plea negotiations conducted, and pretrial motions filed. Indeed, it is clear that 'to deprive a person of counsel during the period prior to trial may be more damaging than denial of counsel during the trial itself.' * * * This complaint contains numerous plain allegations that in specific cases counsel simply was not provided at critical stages of the proceedings. * * * These allegations state a claim [for] basic denial of the right to counsel under *Gideon.*" *See also Kuren v. Luzerne County*, 146 A.3d 715, 743–44 (Pa. 2016) (noting that, without an avenue to pursue the harms that flow from "prolonged pretrial detention, potentially meritorious motions that go unfiled, and inadequate or nonexistent factual investigation, . . . the Sixth Amendment right to counsel would erode into a right without a remedy"); Prospective Challenges to Delivery System Deficiencies, infra p. 170.

7. ***Pre-indictment plea bargaining.*** Is a criminal suspect who has been offered a plea agreement that requires pre-indictment acceptance an "accused" who is entitled to the assistance of counsel under the Sixth Amendment? Most lower courts say "no," citing the Supreme Court's language in *Gouveia* that the right does not attach until "the initiation of adversary judicial criminal proceedings—whether by way of formal charge, preliminary hearing, indictment, information, or arraignment." *See, e.g., Turner v. United States*, 885 F.3d 949, 952 (6th Cir. 2018) (en banc). Some judges disagree, noting that, under *Rothgery*, the Supreme Court's attachment rule is not "a mechanical, indictment-based rule." *Id.* at 980 (Stranch, J., dissenting). Rather, courts should scrutinize any confrontation, "evaluating both the relationship of the state to the accused and the potential consequences for the accused." *See id.*; *see also id.* at 955 (Bush, J., concurring *dubitante*) (arguing that the original public meaning of the Sixth Amendment supports earlier attachment of the right).

§ 2. THE RIGHT TO APPOINTED COUNSEL IN PROCEEDINGS OTHER THAN CRIMINAL PROSECUTIONS: THE CONTINUED VITALITY OF THE *BETTS VS. BRADY* APPROACH

A. PROBATION AND PAROLE REVOCATION HEARINGS: JUVENILE COURT PROCEEDINGS; PARENTAL STATUS TERMINATION PROCEEDINGS; CONTEMPT HEARINGS

GAGNON v. SCARPELLI, 411 U.S. 778 (1973), arose as follows: After pleading guilty to armed robbery, Scarpelli was sentenced to 15 years imprisonment. However, his sentence was suspended and he was placed on probation. A month later, he and a "known criminal" were apprehended while burglarizing a house. Probation was revoked without a hearing on the stated grounds that (a) Scarpelli had associated with known criminals in violation of probation conditions and (b) while associating with a known criminal he had been involved in a burglary. The Court held, per POWELL, J., that an indigent probationer or parolee has no unqualified due process right to be represented by counsel at revocation hearings:[a]

"In *Mempa v. Rhay*, 389 U.S. 128, 88 S.Ct. 254, 19 L.Ed.2d 336 (1967), the Court held a probationer is entitled to be represented by appointed counsel at a combined revocation and sentencing hearing.[b] Reasoning that counsel is required 'at every stage of a criminal proceeding where substantial rights of a criminal accused may be affected,' and that sentencing is one such stage, the Court concluded that counsel must be provided an indigent at sentencing even when it is accomplished as part of a subsequent, probation revocation proceeding. But this line of reasoning does not require a hearing or counsel at the time of probation revocation in a case such as the present one, where the probationer was sentenced at the time of that trial. * * *

"The introduction of counsel into a revocation proceeding will alter significantly the nature of the proceeding. If counsel is provided for the probationer or parolee, the State in turn will normally provide its own counsel; lawyers, by training and disposition, are advocates and bound by professional duty to present all available evidence and arguments in support of their clients' positions and to contest with vigor all adverse evidence and views. The role of the hearing body itself, aptly described in *Morrissey* as being 'predictive and discretionary' as well as fact-finding, may become more akin to that of a judge at a trial, and less attuned to the rehabilitative needs of the individual probationer or parolee. In the greater self-consciousness of its quasi-judicial role, the hearing body may be less tolerant of marginal deviant behavior and feel more pressure to reincarcerate rather than continue nonpunitive rehabilitation. Certainly, the decision-making process will be prolonged, and the financial cost to the State—for appointed counsel, counsel for the State, a longer record, and the possibility of judicial review—will not be insubstantial.

"In some cases, these modifications in the nature of the revocation hearing must be endured and the costs borne because [the] probationer's or parolee's version of a disputed issue can fairly be represented only by a trained advocate. But due process is not so rigid as to require that the significant interests in informality, flexibility, and economy must always be sacrificed.

"In so concluding, we are of course aware that the case-by-case approach to the right to counsel in felony prosecutions adopted in *Betts* [was] later rejected in favor of a *per se* rule. [But we do not] draw from *Gideon* and *Argersinger* the conclusion that a case-by-case approach to furnishing counsel is necessarily inadequate to protect constitutional rights asserted in varying types of proceedings: there are critical differences between criminal trials and probation or parole revocation hearings, and both society and the probationer or parolee have stakes in preserving these differences.

"In a criminal trial, the State is represented by a prosecutor; formal rules of evidence are in force; a defendant enjoys a number of procedural rights which may be lost if not timely raised; and, in a jury trial, a defendant must make a presentation understandable to untrained jurors. In short, a criminal trial under our system is an adversary proceeding with its own unique characteristics. In a revocation hearing, on the other hand, the State is represented not by a prosecutor but by a parole officer with the orientation described above; formal procedures and rules of evidence are not employed; and the members of the hearing body are familiar with the problems and practice of probation or parole. The need for counsel at revocation hearings derives not from the invariable attributes of those hearings but rather from the peculiarities of particular cases. * * *

---

[a] Since Scarpelli did not attempt to *retain* counsel, the Court reserved judgment on "whether a probationer or parolee has a right to be represented at a revocation hearing by retained counsel in situations other than those where the State would be obliged to furnish counsel for an indigent."

[b] Initially, the petitioners' sentencing was deferred subject to probation. The prosecutor subsequently moved to have their probation revoked on the ground that they had committed other crimes. At the hearings, petitioners' probation was revoked and they were sentenced to a term of imprisonment on their original convictions.

"We [find] no justification for a new inflexible constitutional rule with respect to the requirement of counsel. We think, rather, that the decision as to the need for counsel must be made on a case-by-case basis in the exercise of a sound discretion by the state authority charged with responsibility for administering the probation and parole system. * * * Presumptively, it may be said that counsel should be provided in cases where, after being informed of his right to request counsel, the probationer or parolee makes such a request, based on a timely and colorable claim (i) that he has not committed the alleged violation of the conditions upon which he is at liberty; or (ii) [that] there are substantial reasons which justified or mitigated the violation and make revocation inappropriate and that the reasons are complex or otherwise difficult to develop or present. In passing on a request for the appointment of counsel, the responsible agency also should consider, especially in doubtful cases, whether the probationer appears to be capable of speaking effectively for himself. * * *

"We return to the facts of the present case. Because respondent was not afforded either a preliminary hearing or a final hearing, the revocation of his probation did not meet the standards of due process prescribed in *Morrissey*.[c] [Accordingly,] respondent was entitled to a writ of habeas corpus. [Because of respondent's assertions regarding his confession to the crime] we conclude that the failure [to] provide [him] with the assistance of counsel should be reexamined in light of this opinion."

NOTES AND QUESTIONS

1. ***Are probationers better off without lawyers?*** The Court seemed to suggest so in *Gagnon* when it noted that judges might be "less tolerant" and "feel more pressure to reincarcerate" defendants if counsel were introduced in probation revocation hearings. This is not the first time that it has been suggested that defendants would be better off without lawyers. The Assistant Attorney General of Alabama made exactly that argument when he argued against a categorical right to counsel in *Gideon*. See Oral Arg. Tr. ("[A]n indigent appearing without aid of counsel really [stands] a better chance of getting a lighter sentence or even an outright acquittal than one who does have an attorney. . . . [G]enerally speaking indigents charged with crime are not as unfortunately situated as the critics of *Betts* versus *Brady* would have us believe."). Do you think that is true? Consider Erica J. Hashimoto, *Defending the Right of Self-Representation: An Empirical Look at the Pro Se Felony Defendant*, 85 N.C.L.Rev. 423 (2007) (also discussed infra p. 103) (finding that pro se felony defendants don't obtain worse outcomes than represented defendants). If that is true, what does it say about the role of lawyers and the behavior of judges in our criminal justice system?

2. **Betts, Gideon *and* Gagnon *compared.*** How likely is it that a probationer or parolee will be able to convince a court, *without* the benefit of counsel, on the basis of a record made *without* the assistance of counsel, that there are "substantial reasons which justified or mitigated the violation" or that "the reasons are complex or otherwise difficult to develop or present"? How many probationers or parolees will know *what* to point to or look for and *why?* How intelligent a decision can be made as to whether "the probationer appears to be capable of speaking effectively for himself" without knowing what justifications or mitigations a competent lawyer might have raised or developed? Can *Gagnon* escape the criticism of *Betts?* Consider *ABA Standards* § 18–7.5 (commentary); Yale Kamisar, *The Right to Counsel and the Fourteenth Amendment: A Dialogue on "the Most Pervasive Right" of an Accused,* 30 U.Chi.L.Rev. 1, 53, 65 (1962).

3. ***Juvenile court proceedings.*** The *Gagnon* Court talked about "the rehabilitative needs of the individual probationer or parolee" and viewed the probation or parole officer's function "not

[c] *Morrissey v. Brewer*, 408 U.S. 471 (1972), held that even though the revocation of parole is not a part of the criminal prosecution, the loss of liberty involved is a serious deprivation requiring that the parolee be accorded due process. That means a preliminary and a final revocation hearing under the conditions specified in *Morrissey*.

so much to compel conformance to a strict code of behavior as to supervise a course of rehabilitation." But compare *In re Gault,* 387 U.S. 1 (1967), holding that, in respect to juvenile delinquency proceedings that may result in loss of the juvenile's freedom, fourteenth amendment due process requires that "the child and his parent [be] notified of the child's right to be represented by [retained counsel] or, if they are unable to afford counsel that counsel will be appointed to represent the child." The Court stressed the need for counsel to assure a fair hearing in a proceeding "comparable in seriousness to a felony prosecution." It rejected the state's suggestion that the probation officers, parents, and judge might be relied on to "represent the child," finding "no material difference in this respect between adult and juvenile proceedings of the sort involved here."

Gault was hailed as demonstrating the Court's reluctance to be "hemmed in by such artificial labels as 'criminal,' 'civil', or 'quasi-administrative,' " and for taking the position that "a desire to help—the rehabilitation ideal—no longer will serve as the incantation before which procedural safeguards must succumb." Fred Cohen, *Sentencing, Probation, and the Rehabilitative Ideal,* 47 Texas L.Rev. 1, 2 (1968). For a close look at the legacy of *Gault*, see *Symposium, In re Gault: A 40 Year Retrospective on Children's Rights*, 44 Crim.L.Bull. 302 (2008).

4. ***Summary courts-martial.*** In *Middendorf v. Henry,* 425 U.S. 25 (1976), a 7–2 majority held there is no right to appointed counsel at summary courts-martial, even though the officer conducting these proceedings can impose a maximum punishment of 30 days confinement at hard labor. In rejecting even the view that counsel must be provided in "special circumstances," the Court, per Rehnquist, J., observed:

"[E]ven were the Sixth Amendment to be held applicable to court-martial proceedings, the summary court-martial provided for in these cases was not a 'criminal prosecution' within the meaning of that Amendment. [T]he fact that the outcome of a proceeding may result in loss of liberty does not by itself, even in civilian life, mean that the Sixth Amendment's guarantee of counsel is applicable. In *Gagnon,* the respondent faced the prospect of being sent to prison as a result of the revocation of his probation, but we held that the revocation proceeding was nonetheless not a 'criminal proceeding.' [In *Gault*] the juvenile faced possible initial confinement as a result of the proceeding in question, but the Court nevertheless based its conclusion that counsel was required on [Fourteenth Amendment due process], rather than on any determination that the hearing was a 'criminal prosecution' within the meaning of the Sixth Amendment."

5. ***Parental status termination proceedings.*** Over the dissenters' protest that "the unique importance of a parent's interest in the care and custody of his or her child cannot constitutionally be extinguished through formal judicial proceedings without the benefit of counsel" and the dissenters' charge that the Court was "reviv[ing] an ad hoc approach thoroughly discredited nearly 20 years ago in *Gideon,*" in *Lassiter v. Department of Social Services,* 452 U.S. 18 (1981), a 5–4 majority, per Stewart, J., rejected the view that due process requires the appointment of counsel in every parental status termination proceeding involving indigent parents. Thus, the Court left the appointment of counsel in such proceedings to be determined by the state courts on a case-by-case basis.

"The pre-eminent generalization that emerges from the Court's precedents on an indigent's right to appointed counsel," observed the Court, "is that such a right has been recognized to exist only where the litigant may lose his physical liberty if he loses the litigation. * * * Significantly, as a litigant's interest in personal liberty diminishes, so does his right to appointed counsel. [Thus, *Gagnon*] declined to hold that indigent probationers have, *per se*, a right to counsel at revocation hearings, and instead left the decision whether counsel should be appointed to be made on a case-by-case basis."

The Court then examined the termination hearing and found it to be fundamentally fair. "In light of the unpursued avenues of defense, and of the experiences petitioner underwent at this hearing," the dissenters found the Court's conclusion "virtually incredible." Consider Bruce R. Jacob, *Memories of and Reflections about Gideon v. Wainwright*, 33 Stetson L.Rev. 181, 287 (2003): "[Whether counsel is to be appointed in cases involving the termination of parental rights] is to be made on a case-by-case basis, in the same way decisions such as this were made under the *Betts* rule. The rule of *Betts* was considered unworkable by the Court. That was one of the main reasons for the decision in *Gideon*. [If] *Betts* was not workable in 1963, why is it workable now?"

6. ***Where to draw the line?*** Was the *Lassiter* Court's greatest concern where to draw the line? If the state must provide indigents counsel in parental termination proceedings, why not in a child custody fight growing out of a divorce action when one parent is indigent? Why not in an eviction proceeding, when an indigent is about to lose his place of residence? Is there a stronger case for providing counsel in parental termination proceedings than in these other proceedings? Why (not)? See Yale Kamisar, *Gideon v. Wainwright A Quarter-Century Later,* 10 Pace L.Rev. 343, 357–59 (1990).

7. ***Should* Gideon *apply to civil cases?*** In 2006, the American Bar Association adopted a resolution urging federal and state governments to create a right to counsel in civil cases where "basic human needs are at stake." Although a number of states have taken steps to provide limited civil representation, in 2009 California became the first state to enact sweeping legislation recognizing a civil right to counsel and establishing funding for a pilot project designed to provide poor individuals with lawyers in an array of civil cases including child custody, housing, and domestic abuse cases as well as cases involving claims of neglect of the elderly and disabled. While many celebrated California's law, others were deeply skeptical of it. Consider Lawrence J. Siskind, *Civil Gideon: An Idea Whose Time Should Not Come*, American Thinker (August 6, 2011):

"Considering the sorry state of Criminal Gideon, one would expect proponents of a government entitlement program for poor civil litigants to have chosen a different title from 'Civil Gideon.' It's a badly tarnished brand.

"Providing criminal counsel at public expense has ensured that deserving cases are lost in the sea of undeserving ones. The same will happen in the civil sphere if Civil Gideon proponents have their way, and the screening function now provided by legal aid societies is removed.

"Apart from a lack of screening, a government entitlement program is also a bad idea because of plain economics. Economists may not agree on much, but they do agree on one basic idea. If you price a good or service below the market rate, people will want more of it. If civil litigation is free, there will be more of it. And that's not necessarily good for the litigants themselves, or for society as a whole. [Making] counsel available for free, to any party below a certain income level, ensures that many ordinary disputes, once settled by discussions, will become clogs in an increasingly overloaded justice system.

"Finally, Civil Gideon is a bad idea today because the states cannot afford it. [In] 2007, the California State Bar's 2007 Commission on Access to Justice Report found a $394-million gap in unfunded civil legal services. Ironically, that figure is about the same size as the recent budget cut. If California cannot afford its current legal budget, where is it going to find the money for a new legal entitlement program?"

Do you agree? Given the states' financial inability to adequately fund counsel in criminal cases, why should we think that they can adequately fund access in civil cases? Which is more important or is there another way (other than the civil versus criminal divide) to decide which individuals should be entitled to publicly-funded assistance of counsel?

For additional discussion of the pros and cons of recognizing a "civil *Gideon*," see articles in the following symposia: *Toward a Civil Gideon: The Future of American Legal Service*, 7 Harv. L.

& Pol'y Rev. 1 et seq. (2013) and *The Gideon Effect: Rights, Justice, and Lawyers Fifty Years After Gideon v. Wainwright*, 122 Yale L.J. 2106 et seq. (2013).

8. ***Civil contempt hearings.*** When a State enforces its child support orders by threatening with incarceration for civil contempt those who are (1) subject to such an order, (2) able to comply with it, but (3) fail to do so, is the State required to provide counsel at a civil contempt hearing for an *indigent* person potentially faced with such incarceration? The Court addressed this issue in TURNER v. ROGERS, 564 U.S. 431 (2011), a case where the noncustodial parent (Turner) was found in civil contempt of court for failing to make child support payments and sentenced to (and served) 12 months in prison. Neither Turner nor the child's mother was represented by counsel at his brief civil contempt hearing. The judge who sentenced Turner to prison failed to make any finding as to his ability to pay or to indicate on the contempt order form whether he was able to make child support payments.

A 5–4 majority, per Justice Breyer, concluded that "where as here the custodial parent [the one entitled to receive the support] is unrepresented by counsel, the State need not provide counsel to the noncustodial parent." However, the Court "attach[ed] an important caveat, namely, that the State must nevertheless have in place alternative procedures that assure a fundamentally fair determination of the incarceration-related question, whether the supporting parent is able to comply with the support order."

In the Court's view, "a categorical right to counsel in proceedings of [this kind] would carry with it disadvantages (in the form of unfairness and delay) that, in terms of ultimate fairness, would deprive it of significant superiority over the alternatives that we have mentioned. We consequently hold that the Due Process Clause does not *automatically* require the provision of counsel at civil contempt proceedings to an indigent individual who is subject to a child support order, even if that individual faces incarceration (for up to a year)." This is especially so "where the opposing parent or other custodian (to whom support funds are owed) is not represented by counsel and the State provides alternative procedural safeguards equivalent to those we have mentioned (adequate notice of the importance of ability to pay, fair opportunity to present, and to dispute, relevant information and court findings)."

However, "[the] record indicates that Turner received neither counsel nor the benefit of alternative procedures like those we have described. [The] court nonetheless found Turner in contempt and ordered him incarcerated. Under these circumstances Turner's incarceration violated the Due Process Clause."

Dissenting Justice Thomas (joined by Roberts, C.J., and Scalia and Alito, JJ.) protested that although the Court recognizes that appointed counsel was not required in this case, "it nevertheless vacates the judgment of the [state supreme court] on a different ground, which the parties have never raised. Solely at the invitation of the United States as amicus curiae, the majority decides that Turner's contempt proceedings violated due process because it did not include 'alternative procedural safeguards.'" He noted that "[e]ven when the defendant's liberty is at stake, the Court has not concluded that fundamental fairness requires that counsel also be appointed if the proceeding is not criminal," citing *Gagnon v. Scarpelli* and *Middendorf v. Henry*.

The balancing test utilized by the majority, maintained Justice Thomas, "weighs an individual's interest against that of the Government itself," but fails to "account for the interests of the child and custodial parent, who is usually the child's mother. But their interests are the very reason for the child support obligation and the civil contempt proceedings that enforce it."

Thomas observed that "[the] interests of children and mothers who depend on child support are notoriously difficult to protect. [That] some fathers subject to a child support agreement report little or no income 'does not mean they do not have the ability to pay any child support.' [Rather,] many 'deadbeat dads' opt to work in the underground economy to 'shield their earnings from child support enforcement efforts.' [The] States that use civil contempt with the threat of detention find it a 'highly effective' tool for collecting child support when nothing else works."

B. COLLATERAL ATTACK PROCEEDINGS

As is discussed more extensively elsewhere (infra ch. 29, § 1, Note 6), the Supreme Court has held that an indigent prisoner typically has no federal constitutional right to assigned counsel in collateral review proceedings. See *Pennsylvania v. Finley*, 481 U.S. 551 (1987). A 5–4 majority held in *Murray v. Giarratano*, 492 U.S. 1 (1989) that this rule applies no differently in capital cases than in noncapital cases. The Supreme Court has left open the possibility of modifying this general rule for "initial review collateral proceedings," defined as postconviction proceedings that provide the first occasion for a prisoner to raise a constitutional claim (such as a claim of ineffective assistance of trial counsel). See *Coleman v. Thompson*, 501 U.S. 722, 755 (1991) (leaving open the question of whether indigent prisoners have a constitutional right to assigned counsel for initial review collateral proceedings); see also *Martinez v. Ryan*, 566 U.S. 1, 8 (2012) (reiterating that this remains an open question). For a discussion of other aspects of *Martinez v. Ryan*, see infra p. 1439.

§ 3. THE *GRIFFIN-DOUGLAS* "EQUALITY" PRINCIPLE

GRIFFIN V. ILLINOIS: "THERE CAN BE NO EQUAL JUSTICE WHERE THE KIND OF TRIAL A MAN GETS DEPENDS ON THE AMOUNT OF MONEY HE HAS"

Prior to GRIFFIN v. ILLINOIS, 351 U.S. 12 (1956), full direct appellate review could only be had in Illinois by furnishing the appellate court with a bill of exceptions or report of the trial proceedings, certified by the trial judge. Preparation of these documents was sometimes impossible without a stenographic transcript of the trial proceedings, but such a transcript was furnished free only to indigent defendants sentenced to death. *Griffin* upheld by a 5–4 vote the contention that the due process and equal protection clauses of the fourteenth amendment require that *all* indigent defendants be furnished a transcript, at least where allegations that manifest errors occurred at the trial are not denied. See generally Francis A. Allen, *Griffin v. Illinois: Antecedents and Aftermath,* 25 U.Chi.L.Rev. 151, 152 (1957).

There was no opinion of the Court in *Griffin*. Justice Black announced the Court's judgment in a four-justice opinion; Justice Frankfurter concurred specially. In the course of his opinion, Justice Black observed:

"In criminal trials a State can no more discriminate on account of poverty than on account of religion, race, or color. Plainly the ability to pay costs in advance bears no rational relationship to a defendant's guilt or innocence and could not be used as an excuse to deprive a defendant of a fair trial. [It] is true that a State is not required by the federal constitution to provide appellate courts or a right to appellate review at all. [But] that is not to say that a State that does grant appellate review can do so in a way that discriminates against some convicted defendants on account of their poverty. * * *

"All of the States now provide some method of appeal from criminal convictions, recognizing the importance of appellate review to a correct adjudication of guilt or innocence. Statistics show that a substantial proportion of criminal convictions are reversed by state appellate courts. Thus to deny adequate review to the poor means that many of them may lose their life, liberty or property because of unjust convictions which appellate courts would set aside. Many States have recognized this and provided aid for convicted defendants who have a right to appeal and need a transcript but are unable to pay for it. A few have not. Such a denial is a misfit in a country dedicated to affording equal justice to all and special privileges to none in the administration of its criminal law. There can be no equal justice where the kind of trial a man gets depends on the amount of money he has. Destitute defendants must be afforded as adequate appellate review as defendants who have money enough to buy transcripts."

A. APPLICATION (OR EXTENSION) OF *GRIFFIN*

In the decade and a half following *Griffin,* its underlying principle was broadly applied. See *Burns v. Ohio,* 360 U.S. 252 (1959) (state cannot require indigent defendant to pay filing fee before permitting him to appeal); *Smith v. Bennett,* 365 U.S. 708 (1961) (extending ban on filing fees to state post-conviction proceedings); *Long v. District Court of Iowa,* 385 U.S. 192 (1966) (indigent must be furnished a free transcript of a state habeas corpus hearing for use on appeal from a denial of habeas corpus, although availability of transcript not a sine qua non to access to the appellate court); *Roberts v. LaVallee,* 389 U.S. 40 (1967) (indigent defendant entitled to free transcript of preliminary hearing for use at trial, even though both defendant and his counsel attended preliminary hearing and no indication of use to which preliminary hearing transcript could be put—points stressed by dissenting Justice Harlan); *Britt v. North Carolina,* 404 U.S. 226 (1971) (recognition that under ordinary circumstances indigent would be entitled to free transcript of previous trial ending with a hung jury because such a transcript would be "valuable to the defendant" as a discovery device and "as a tool at the [second] trial itself for the impeachment of prosecution witnesses").

In *Mayer v. Chicago,* 404 U.S. 189 (1971), a unanimous Court, per Brennan, J., carried the *Griffin* principle further than it ever has the *Gideon* principle by holding that an indigent appellant "cannot be denied a 'record of sufficient completeness' to permit proper consideration of his claims" because he was convicted of ordinance violations punishable by fine only. "The size of the defendant's pocketbook bears no more relationship to his guilt or innocence in a non-felony than in a felony case." Nor was the Court impressed with the argument that appellant's interest in a transcript in a case where he is not subject to imprisonment is outweighed by the State's fiscal and other interests in not burdening the appellate process:

"*Griffin* does not represent a balance between the needs of the accused and the interests of society; its principle is a flat prohibition against pricing indigent defendants out of as effective an appeal as would be available to others able to pay their own way. The invidiousness of the discrimination that exists when criminal procedures are made available only to those who can pay is not erased by any differences in the sentences that may be imposed. The State's fiscal interest is, therefore, irrelevant.

"We add that even approaching the problem in the terms the city suggests hardly yields the answer the city tenders. The practical effects of conviction of even petty offenses of the kind involved here are not to be minimized. A fine may bear as heavily on an indigent accused as forced confinement.[a] The collateral consequences of conviction may be even more serious, as when (as was apparently a possibility in this case) the impecunious medical student finds himself barred from the practice of medicine because of a conviction he is unable to appeal for lack of funds."[b]

---

[a] But cf. *Argersinger v. Hamlin*, p. 74; *Scott v. Illinois*, p. 75.

[b] Chief Justice Burger joined the Court's opinion, but in a separate opinion emphasized that "there are alternatives in the majority of cases to a full verbatim transcript of an entire trial."

B. THE IMPACT OF THE "EQUALITY" PRINCIPLE ON THOSE WHO CANNOT AFFORD COUNSEL OR OTHER FORMS OF ASSISTANCE

Prior to *Gideon,* the *Griffin* case posed a challenge to *Betts:* How could the *Betts* line of cases be reconciled with the language, if not the holding, of *Griffin?* Since there was an unqualified right to have one's own paid counsel of his choosing at state trial, capital or not, did *Griffin* not imply that an indigent also has this unqualified right? By requiring *special circumstances* to exist before the indigent was entitled to appointed counsel in non-capital state cases, was the indigent not denied equal protection of the law? When the Supreme Court finally overruled the *Betts* case, somewhat surprisingly, it did not rely on *Griffin* at all, but *Douglas v. California,* infra, decided the same day, is another story.

DOUGLAS v. CALIFORNIA, 372 U.S. 353 (1963), arose as follows: Indigent defendants requested, and were denied, the assistance of counsel on appeal. In accordance with a California rule of criminal procedure, the California District Court of Appeals stated that it had "gone through" the record and had come to the conclusion that "no good whatever could be served by appointment of counsel." Under the California procedure, appellate courts had to appoint counsel only if in their opinion it would be helpful to the defendant or the court. A 6–3 majority, per Justice Douglas, viewed the denial of counsel on appeal to an indigent under these circumstances "a discrimination at least as invidious as that condemned in [*Griffin*]:"

"[Whether the issue is a transcript on appeal or the assistance of counsel on appeal] the evil is the same: discrimination against the indigent. For there can be no equal justice where the kind of an appeal a man enjoys 'depends on the amount of money he has.' * * *

"When an indigent is forced to run this gantlet of a preliminary showing of merit, the right to appeal does not comport with fair procedure. [T]he discrimination is not between 'possibly good and obviously bad cases,' but between cases where the rich man can require the court to listen to argument of counsel before deciding on the merits, but a poor man cannot. There is lacking that equality demanded by the Fourteenth Amendment where the rich man, who appeals as of right, enjoys the benefit of counsel's examination into the record, research of the law, and marshalling of arguments on his behalf, while the indigent, already burdened by a preliminary determination that his case is without merit, is forced to shift for himself. The indigent, where the record is unclear or the errors are hidden, has only the right to a meaningless ritual, while the rich man has a meaningful appeal."[c]

Justice Harlan, whom Stewart, J., joined, dissented,[d] maintaining that "the Equal Protection Clause is not apposite, and its application to cases like the present one can lead only to mischievous results." He thought the case "should be judged solely under the Due Process Clause" and that the California procedure did not violate that provision. In rejecting the equal protection argument, Harlan observed:

"Laws such as these do not deny equal protection to the less fortunate for one essential reason: the Equal Protection Clause does not impose on the States 'an affirmative duty to lift the handicaps flowing from differences in economic circumstances.' To so construe it would be to read into the Constitution a philosophy of leveling that would be foreign to many of our basic concepts of the proper relations between government and society. The State may have a moral obligation to eliminate the evils of poverty, but it is not required by the Equal Protection Clause to give to some whatever others can afford.

---

[c] The Court pointed out it was dealing "only with the first appeal, granted as a matter of right," not deciding whether a state had to provide counsel for an indigent seeking discretionary review.

[d] Justice Clark wrote a separate dissenting opinion.

"[I]t should be noted that if the present problem may be viewed as one of equal protection, so may the question of the right to appointed counsel at trial, and the Court's analysis of that right in *Gideon* [is] wholly unnecessary. The short way to dispose of *Gideon,* in other words, would be simply to say that the State deprives the indigent of equal protection whenever it fails to furnish him with legal services, and perhaps with other services as well, equivalent to those that the affluent defendant can obtain."[e]

ROSS V. MOFFITT

417 U.S. 600, 94 S.Ct. 2437, 41 L.Ed.2d 341 (1974).

JUSTICE REHNQUIST delivered the opinion of the Court.

[Like many other states, the North Carolina appellate system is multitiered, providing for both an intermediate Court of Appeals and a Supreme Court. North Carolina authorizes appointment of counsel for a convicted defendant appealing to the intermediate court of appeals, but not for a defendant who seeks either discretionary review in the state supreme court or a writ of certiorari in the U.S. Supreme Court. In one case, the Mecklenburg County forgery conviction, respondent sought appointed counsel for discretionary review in the state supreme court. In another case, the Guilford County forgery conviction, respondent was represented by the public defender in the state supreme court, but sought court-appointed counsel to prepare a writ of certiorari to the U.S. Supreme Court. On federal habeas corpus, a unanimous panel of the U.S. Court of Appeals for the Fourth Circuit, per Haynsworth, C.J., held that the *Douglas* rationale required appointment of counsel in both instances.]

[*Griffin* and succeeding cases, such as *Burns v. Ohio* and *Smith v. Bennett* (the filing fee cases summarized at p. 93),] stand for the proposition that a State cannot arbitrarily cut off appeal rights for indigents while leaving open avenues of appeal for more affluent persons. In *Douglas,* however, [the] Court departed somewhat from the limited doctrine of [these] cases [and] held that the State must go further and provide counsel for the indigent on his first appeal as of right. It is this decision we are asked to extend today. * * *

The precise rationale for the *Griffin* and *Douglas* lines of cases has never been explicitly stated, some support being derived from the Equal Protection Clause of the Fourteenth Amendment, and some from the Due Process Clause of that Amendment. Neither clause by itself provides an entirely satisfactory basis for the result reached, each depending on a different inquiry which emphasizes different factors. "Due process" emphasizes fairness between the State and the individual dealing with the State, regardless of how other individuals in the same situation may be treated. "Equal protection," on the other hand, emphasizes disparity in treatment by a State between classes of individuals whose situations are arguably indistinguishable. We will address these issues separately in the succeeding sections.

Recognition of the due process rationale in *Douglas* is found both in the Court's opinion and in the dissenting opinion of Mr. Justice Harlan. [Indeed,] Mr. Justice Harlan thought that the due process issue in *Douglas* was the only one worthy of extended consideration. * * *

We do not believe that the Due Process Clause requires North Carolina to provide respondent with counsel on his discretionary appeal to the State Supreme Court. At the trial stage of a criminal proceeding, the right of an indigent defendant to counsel [is] fundamental and binding upon the States by virtue of the Sixth and Fourteenth Amendments. But there are significant

[e] One may ask, too, why the Court failed even to discuss the applicability of the *Griffin-Douglas* "equality" principle to the issue raised in *Scott v. Illinois,* p. 75. Since it is plain that one charged with an offense *punishable* by incarceration may *retain* counsel for his defense, does not the "equality" principle suggest that the "actual imprisonment" standard, even if it defensibly defines the Sixth Amendment right to appointed counsel, is unsatisfactory under the equal protection clause?

differences between the trial and appellate stages of a criminal proceeding. The purpose of the trial stage from the State's point of view is to convert a criminal defendant from a person presumed innocent to one found guilty beyond a reasonable doubt. * * *

By contrast, it is ordinarily the defendant, rather than the State, who initiates the appellate process, seeking not to fend off the efforts of the State's prosecutor but rather to overturn a finding of guilt made by a judge or jury below. The defendant needs an attorney on appeal not as a shield to protect him against being "haled into court" by the State and stripped of his presumption of innocence, but rather as a sword to upset the prior determination of guilt. This difference is significant for, while no one would agree that the State may simply dispense with the trial stage of proceedings without a criminal defendant's consent, it is clear that the State need not provide any appeal at all. *McKane v. Durston*. The fact that an appeal *has* been provided does not automatically mean that a State then acts unfairly by refusing to provide counsel to indigent defendants at every stage of the way. Unfairness results only if indigents are singled out by the State and denied meaningful access to that system because of their poverty. That question is more profitably considered under an equal protection analysis. * * *

The Fourteenth Amendment "does not require absolute equality or precisely equal advantages," nor does it require the State to "equalize economic conditions." *Griffin* (Frankfurter, J., concurring). It does require [that] indigents have an adequate opportunity to present their claims fairly within the adversarial system. * * * The question is not one of absolutes, but one of degrees. In this case we do not believe that the Equal Protection Clause [requires] North Carolina to provide free counsel for indigent defendants seeking to take discretionary appeals to the North Carolina Supreme Court, or to file petitions for certiorari in this Court. * * *

The facts show that respondent, in connection with his Mecklenburg County conviction, received the benefit of counsel in examining the record of his trial and in preparing an appellate brief on his behalf for the state Court of Appeals. Thus, prior to his seeking discretionary review in the State Supreme Court, his claims "had once been presented by a lawyer and passed upon by an appellate court." *Douglas*. We do not believe that it can be said, therefore, that a defendant in respondent's circumstances is denied meaningful access to the North Carolina Supreme Court simply because the State does not appoint counsel to aid him in seeking review in that court. At that stage he will have, at the very least, a transcript or other record of trial proceedings, a brief on his behalf in the Court of Appeals setting forth his claims of error, and in many cases an opinion by the Court of Appeals disposing of his case. These materials, supplemented by whatever submission respondent may make *pro se*, would appear to provide the Supreme Court of North Carolina with an adequate basis on which to base its decision to grant or deny review.

We are fortified in this conclusion by our understanding of the function served by discretionary review in the North Carolina Supreme Court. The critical issue in that court, as we perceive it, is not whether there has been "a correct adjudication of guilt" in every individual case, but rather whether "the subject matter of the appeal has significant public interest," whether "the cause involves legal principles of major significance to the jurisprudence of the state," or whether the decision below is in probable conflict with a decision of the Supreme Court. The Supreme Court may deny certiorari even though it believes that the decision of the Court of Appeals was incorrect, since a decision which appears incorrect may nevertheless fail to satisfy any of the criteria discussed above. Once a defendant's claims of error are organized and presented in a lawyer-like fashion to the Court of Appeals, the justices of the Supreme Court of North Carolina who make the decision to grant or deny discretionary review should be able to ascertain whether his case satisfies the standards established by the legislature for such review.

This is not to say, of course, that a skilled lawyer, particularly one trained in the somewhat arcane art of preparing petitions for discretionary review, would not prove helpful to any litigant able to employ him. An indigent defendant seeking review in the Supreme Court of North Carolina is therefore somewhat handicapped in comparison with a wealthy defendant who has counsel assisting him in every conceivable manner at every stage in the proceeding. But both the opportunity to have counsel prepare an initial brief in the Court of Appeals and the nature of discretionary review in the Supreme Court of North Carolina make this relative handicap far less than the handicap borne by the indigent defendant denied counsel on his initial appeal as of right in *Douglas*. And the fact that a particular service might be of benefit to an indigent defendant does not mean that the service is constitutionally required. The duty of the State under our cases is not to duplicate the legal arsenal that may be privately retained by a criminal defendant in a continuing effort to reverse his conviction, but only to assure the indigent defendant an adequate opportunity to present his claims fairly in the context of the State's appellate process. We think respondent was given that opportunity under the existing North Carolina system.

Much of the discussion in the preceding section is equally relevant to the question of whether a State must provide counsel for a defendant seeking review of his conviction in this Court. North Carolina will have provided counsel for a convicted defendant's only appeal as of right, and the brief prepared by that counsel together with one and perhaps two North Carolina appellate opinions will be available to this Court in order that it may decide whether or not to grant certiorari. This Court's review, much like that of the Supreme Court of North Carolina, is discretionary and depends on numerous factors other than the perceived correctness of the judgment we are asked to review. * * *

JUSTICE DOUGLAS, with whom JUSTICE BRENNAN and JUSTICE MARSHALL concur, dissenting.

[In his opinion below] Chief Judge Haynsworth could find "no logical basis for differentiation between appeals of right and permissive review procedures in the context of the Constitution and the right to counsel." More familiar with the functioning of the North Carolina criminal justice system than are we, he concluded that "in the context of constitutional questions arising in criminal prosecutions, permissive review in the state's highest court may be predictably the most meaningful review the conviction will receive." The North Carolina Court of Appeals, for example, will be constrained in diverging from an earlier opinion of the State Supreme Court, even if subsequent developments have rendered the earlier Supreme Court decision suspect. "[T]he state's highest court remains the ultimate arbiter of the rights of its citizens."

Chief Judge Haynsworth also correctly observed that the indigent defendant proceeding without counsel is at a substantial disadvantage relative to wealthy defendants represented by counsel when he is forced to fend for himself in seeking discretionary review from the State Supreme Court or from this Court. It may well not be enough to allege error in the courts below in layman's terms; a more sophisticated approach may be demanded:

"An indigent defendant is as much in need of the assistance of a lawyer in preparing and filing a petition for certiorari as he is in the handling of an appeal as of right. In many appeals, an articulate defendant could file an effective brief by telling his story in simple language without legalisms, but the technical requirement for applications for writs of certiorari are hazards which one untrained in the law could hardly be expected to negotiate. * * * "

NOTES AND QUESTIONS

1. ***Effects of* Ross.** Is *Mayer v. Chicago* (p. 93) "good law" after *Ross?* Are *Long v. District Court*, *Roberts v. LaVallee,* and *Britt v. North Carolina* (all summarized at p. 93) "good law" after *Ross?* Does the *Long* line of cases (never mentioned by the *Ross* Court) constitute a significant "departure" from what the *Ross* Court calls the "limited doctrine" of *Griffin* and succeeding cases?

2. ***Minimal access vs. equal protection.*** Consider Laurence H. Tribe, *American Constitutional Law* 1647 (2d ed. 1988): "[The *Ross* Court] disengaged *Griffin* from *Douglas,* deftly

rewove the *Griffin* transcript and filing fee decisions together as minimal access cases rather than equal protection cases, and neatly severed *Douglas* from this newly created body of law."

3. ***Does the* Ross *opinion's "equal protection analysis" closely resemble a "due process analysis"?*** Indeed, now that *Ross* is on the books, does the "equality" principle *add anything* to what the indigent defendant or prisoner already has in his arsenal? Consider Yale Kamisar, *Poverty, Equality, and Criminal Procedure*, in National College of District Attorneys, *Constitutional Law Deskbook* 1–101 to 1–108 (1977):

"[The *Ross* 'equal protection analysis'] seems to put to one side the admitted fact that an indigent seeking discretionary review is 'somewhat handicapped in comparison with a wealthy defendant who has counsel assisting him' and focuses instead on whether an indigent seeking discretionary review without counsel has a '*meaningful* opportunity' (emphasis added) to present his claims in the state supreme court—to provide the court 'with an *adequate* basis for its decision to grant or deny review' (emphasis added)—*regardless* of whether a wealthy defendant who has counsel at this stage has a *significantly better* opportunity to present his claims.

"[What *Ross*] really seems to be asking, and deciding, is whether an indigent in respondent's circumstances has a *fair chance,* a *fighting chance* (or the requisite *minimum* chance), to get the attention of the state supreme court. [This] is 'due process,' not 'equal protection' reasoning. * * *

"So long as the indigent defendant's 'brand of justice' satisfies certain minimal standards—passes government inspection, one might say—[*Ross* tells us that] *it need not be* the same brand of justice or the same 'choice' or 'prime' grade of justice as the wealthy man's. [In some phases of the criminal process an indigent will not have 'meaningful access' to the hearing body or an 'adequate opportunity' to present his claim], but in [such] cases 'fundamental fairness'—'due process'—will require the state to furnish counsel. In those cases where due process *does not* impose a duty on the state to provide counsel, *neither,* it seems, *will 'equal protection.'* "

4. ***Is there a right to appointed counsel on discretionary appeal from a plea of guilty?*** When appointed counsel is not provided for indigent defendants seeking first-tier discretionary appellate review of guilty pleas or *nolo contendere* pleas, which case governs, *Ross* or *Douglas*? The *Douglas* case does, a 6–3 majority of the Court told us in HALBERT v. MICHIGAN, 545 U.S. 605 (2005).

Under Michigan law, the intermediate Court of Appeals adjudicated appeals from criminal convictions as of right *except* that those convicted on guilty or *nolo contendere* pleas had to apply for leave to appeal. The Michigan Supreme Court held that nothing in the Constitution required that counsel be appointed for plea-convicted defendants seeking review in the Court of Appeals. The Court, per Ginsburg, J., disagreed:

"Halbert's case is framed by two prior decisions of this Court concerning state-funded appellate counsel, *Douglas* and *Ross.* * * * With which of those decisions should the instant case be aligned? We hold that *Douglas* provides the controlling instruction. Two aspects of the Michigan Court of Appeals' process following plea-based convictions lead us to that conclusion. First, in determining how to dispose of an application for leave to appeal, Michigan's intermediate appellate court looks to the merits of the claims made in the application. Second, indigent defendants pursuing first-tier review in the Court of Appeals are generally ill equipped to represent themselves.

"[As] *Ross* emphasized, a defendant seeking State Supreme Court review following a first-tier appeal as of right earlier had the assistance of appellate counsel. [A] first-tier review applicant, forced to act *pro se*, will face a record unreviewed by appellate counsel, and will be equipped with no attorney's brief prepared for, or reasoned opinion by, a court of review. * * *

"Navigating the appellate process without a lawyer's assistance is a perilous endeavor for a layperson, and well beyond the competence of individuals, like Halbert, who have little education, learning disabilities, and mental impairments.

"While the State has a legitimate interest in reducing the workload of its judiciary, providing indigents with appellate counsel will yield applications easier to comprehend. Michigan's Court of Appeals would still have recourse to summary denials of leave applications in cases not warranting further review. And when a defendant's case presents no genuinely arguable issue, appointed counsel may so inform the court. See *Anders v. California*, 386 U.S. 738 (1967)."

Justice Thomas, joined by Scalia, J., and Rehnquist, C.J., dissented:

"[The majority] finds that all plea-convicted indigent defendants have the right to appellate counsel when seeking leave to appeal. The majority does not say where in the Constitution that right is located—the Due Process Clause, the Equal Protection Clause, or some purported confluence of the two. * * *

"Instead, the majority pins its hopes on a single case: *Douglas v. California*. *Douglas*, however, does not support extending the right to counsel to any form of discretionary review, as *Ross* and later cases make clear. Moreover, Michigan has not engaged in the sort of invidious discrimination against indigent defendants that *Douglas* condemns. Michigan has done no more than recognize the undeniable difference between defendants who plead guilty and those who maintain their innocence, in an attempt to divert resources from largely frivolous appeals to more meritorious ones. The majority substitutes its own policy preference for that of Michigan voters, and it does so based on an untenable reading of *Douglas*. * * *

"Far from being an 'arbitrary' or 'unreasoned' distinction, Michigan's differentiation between defendants convicted at trial and defendants convicted by plea is sensible. [T]he danger of wrongful convictions is less significant than in *Douglas*. In *Douglas*, California preliminarily denied counsel to all indigent defendants, regardless of whether they maintained their innocence at trial or conceded their guilt by plea. Here, Michigan preliminarily denies paid counsel only to indigent defendants who admit or do not contest their guilt. * * *

"Lacking support in this Court's cases, the majority effects a not-so subtle shift from whether the record is adequate to enable discretionary review to whether plea-convicted defendants are generally able to '[n]aviga[te] the appellate process without a lawyer's assistance.' This rationale lacks any stopping point. *Pro se* defendants may have difficulty navigating discretionary direct appeals and collateral proceedings, but this Court has never extended the right to counsel beyond first appeals as of right. The majority does not demonstrate that *pro se* defendants have any more difficulty filing leave applications before the Michigan courts than, say, filing petitions for certiorari before this Court."

§ 4. WAIVER OF THE RIGHT TO COUNSEL: THE RIGHT TO PROCEED *PRO SE*

FARETTA V. CALIFORNIA

422 U.S. 806, 95 S.Ct. 2525, 45 L.Ed.2d 562 (1975).

JUSTICE STEWART delivered the opinion of the Court.

[Well before the date of his trial, Faretta, charged with grand theft, requested that he be allowed to represent himself. Questioning by the trial judge revealed that Faretta had once before represented himself in a criminal prosecution, that he had a high school education, and that he did not want to be represented by the public defender because he thought that office had too heavy a caseload. The trial judge subsequently held a hearing to inquire into Faretta's ability to conduct his own defense. In the course of that hearing, the judge questioned Faretta as to his knowledge of the hearsay rule and the law governing the challenge of jurors. Taking account of Faretta's answers, the judge ruled that Faretta had not made an intelligent and knowing waiver of his right to counsel. The judge also ruled that Faretta had no constitutional right to conduct his own defense. The judge then appointed the public defender to represent Faretta. Throughout the subsequent trial, the judge required that Faretta's defense be conducted only through the appointed lawyer. Faretta was found guilty as charged and sentenced to prison. The appellate court affirmed his conviction.]

The right of self-representation finds support in the structure of the Sixth Amendment, as well as in the English and colonial experience from which the Amendment emerged. * * *

The Sixth Amendment does not provide merely that a defense shall be made for the accused; it grants to the accused personally the right to make his defense. It is the accused, not counsel, who must be "informed of the nature and cause of the accusation," who must be "confronted with witnesses against him," and who must be accorded "compulsory process for obtaining witnesses in his favor." [T]he right to self-representation—to make one's defense personally—is thus necessarily implied by the structure of the Amendment. The right to defend is given directly to the accused; for it is he who suffers the consequences if the defense fails.

The counsel provision supplements this design. It speaks of the "assistance" of counsel, and an assistant, however expert, is still an assistant. The language and spirit of the Sixth Amendment contemplate that counsel, like the other defense tools guaranteed by the Amendment, shall be an aid to a willing defendant—not an organ of the State interposed between an unwilling defendant and his right to defend himself personally. To thrust counsel upon the accused, against his considered wish, thus violates the logic of the Amendment. [It] is true that when a defendant chooses to have a lawyer manage and present his case, law and tradition may allocate to the counsel the power to make binding decisions of trial strategy in many areas. This allocation can only be justified, however, by the defendant's consent, at the outset, to accept counsel as his representative. An unwanted counsel "represents" the defendant only through a tenuous and unacceptable legal fiction. Unless the accused has acquiesced in such representation, the defense presented is not the defense guaranteed by the Constitution, for, in a very real sense, it is not *his* defense.

The Sixth Amendment, when naturally read, thus implies a right of self-representation. This reading is reinforced by the Amendment's roots in English legal history. [After an extensive discussion of the right of self-representation in England and the American colonies, the Court concluded:]

In sum, there is no evidence that the colonists and the Framers ever doubted the right of self-representation, or imagined that this right might be considered inferior to the right of assistance of counsel. To the contrary, [they], as well as their English ancestors, always conceived of the right to counsel as an "assistance" for the accused, to be used at his option, in defending himself. The Framers selected in the Sixth Amendment a form of words that necessarily implies the right of self-representation. That conclusion is supported by centuries of history.

There can be no blinking the fact that the right of an accused to conduct his own defense seems to cut against the grain of this Court's decisions holding that the Constitution requires that no accused can be convicted and imprisoned unless he has been accorded the right to the assistance of counsel. For it is surely true that the basic thesis of those decisions is that the help of a lawyer is essential to assure the defendant a fair trial. And a strong argument can surely be made that the whole thrust of those decisions must inevitably lead to the conclusion that a State may constitutionally impose a lawyer upon even an unwilling defendant.

But it is one thing to hold that every [accused] has the right to the assistance of counsel, and quite another to say that a State may compel a defendant to accept a lawyer he does not want. The value of state-appointed counsel was not unappreciated by the Founders, yet the notion of compulsory counsel was utterly foreign to them. [To] force a lawyer on a defendant can only lead him to believe that the law contrives against him. Moreover, it is not inconceivable that in some rare instances, the defendant might in fact present his case more effectively by conducting his own defense. Personal liberties are not rooted in the law of averages. The right to defend is personal. The defendant, and not his lawyer or the State, will bear the personal consequences of a conviction. It is the defendant, therefore, who must be free personally to decide whether in his particular case counsel is to his advantage. And although he may conduct his own defense ultimately to his own detriment, his choice must be honored out of "that respect for the individual which is the lifeblood of the law."[46]

When an accused manages his own defense, he relinquishes, as a purely factual matter, many of the traditional benefits associated with the right to counsel. For this reason, in order to represent himself, the accused must "knowingly and intelligently" forego those relinquished benefits. *Johnson v. Zerbst*, 304 U.S. 458 (1938). Although a defendant need not himself have the skill and experience of a lawyer in order competently and intelligently to choose self-representation, he should be made aware of the dangers and disadvantages of self-representation, so that the record will establish that "he knows what he is doing and his choice is made with eyes open." *Adams v. United States ex rel. McCann*, 317 U.S. 269 (1942).

Here, weeks before trial, Faretta clearly and unequivocally declared [that] he wanted to represent himself and did not want counsel. The record affirmatively shows that [defendant] was literate, competent, and understanding, and that he was voluntarily exercising his informed free will. The trial judge had warned [defendant] that he thought it was a mistake not to accept the assistance of counsel and that [defendant] would be required to follow all the "ground rules" of trial procedure. We need make no assessment of how well or poorly [defendant] had mastered the intricacies of the hearsay rule and the California code provisions that govern challenges of potential jurors on *voir dire* [matters about which the trial judge specifically questioned defendant before ruling that he had not made an intelligent and knowing waiver of his right to the assistance of counsel]. For [defendant's] technical legal knowledge, as such, was not relevant to an assessment of his knowing exercise of the right to defend himself.

CHIEF JUSTICE BURGER, with whom JUSTICE BLACKMUN and JUSTICE REHNQUIST join, dissenting.

[The goal of achieving justice] is ill-served, and the integrity of and public confidence in the system are undermined, when an easy conviction is obtained due to the defendant's ill-advised decision to waive counsel. [The criminal justice system] should not be available as an instrument of self-destruction. [B]oth the "spirit and the logic" of the Sixth Amendment are that every person accused of crime shall receive the fullest possible defense; in the vast majority of cases this command can be honored only by means of the expressly-guaranteed right to counsel, and the trial judge is in the best position to determine whether the accused is capable of conducting his defense.

---

[46] We are told that many criminal defendants representing themselves may use the courtroom for deliberate disruption of their trials. But the right of self-representation has been recognized from our beginnings by federal law and by most of the States, and no such result has thereby occurred. Moreover, the trial judge may terminate self-representation by a defendant who deliberately engages in serious and obstructionist misconduct. Of course, a State may—even over objection by the accused—appoint a "standby counsel" to aid the accused if and when the accused requests help, and to be available to represent the accused in the event that termination of the defendant's self-representation is necessary.

The right of self-representation is not a license to abuse the dignity of the courtroom. Neither is it a license not to comply with relevant rules of procedural and substantive law. Thus, whatever else may or may not be open to him on appeal, a defendant who elects to represent himself cannot thereafter complain that the quality of his own defense amounted to a denial of "effective assistance of counsel."

True freedom of choice and society's interest in seeing that justice is achieved can be vindicated only if the trial court retains discretion to reject any attempted waiver of counsel and insist that the accused be tried according to the Constitution. This discretion is as critical an element of basic fairness as a trial judge's discretion to decline to accept a plea of guilty.

JUSTICE BLACKMUN, with whom THE CHIEF JUSTICE and JUSTICE REHNQUIST join, dissenting.

I cannot agree that there is anything in the [Constitution] that requires the States to subordinate the solemn business of conducting a criminal prosecution to the whimsical—albeit voluntary—caprice of every accused who wishes to use his trial as a vehicle for personal or political self-gratification. * * * I do not believe that any amount of *pro se* pleading can cure the injury to society of an unjust result, but I do believe that a just result should prove to be an effective balm for almost any frustrated *pro se* defendant. * * *

I note briefly the procedural problems that, I suspect, today's decision will visit upon trial courts in the future. * * * Must every defendant be advised of his right to proceed *pro se?* If so, when must that notice be given? Since the right to the assistance of counsel and the right to self-representation are mutually exclusive, how is the waiver of each right to be measured? If a defendant has elected to exercise his right to proceed *pro se,* does he still have a constitutional right to assistance of standby counsel? How soon in the criminal proceeding must a defendant decide between proceeding by counsel or *pro se?* Must he be allowed to switch in mid-trial? May a violation of the right to self-representation ever be harmless error? Must the trial court treat the *pro se* defendant differently than it would professional counsel? * * * The procedural problems spawned by an absolute right to self-representation will far outweigh whatever tactical advantage the defendant may feel he has gained by electing to represent himself.

NOTES AND QUESTIONS

1. *Questioning and reaffirming* Faretta. Twenty-five years after *Faretta* was decided, Justice Stevens expressed doubts about the merits of the decision. In MARTINEZ v. COURT OF APPEAL OF CALIFORNIA, 528 U.S. 152 (2000) (discussed Note 3 infra), he wrote:

"The historical evidence relied upon by *Faretta* as identifying a right of self-representation is not always useful because it pertained to times when lawyers were scarce, often mistrusted, and not readily available to the average person accused of crime. For one who could not obtain a lawyer, self-representation was the only feasible alternative to asserting no defense at all. [But] an individual's decision to represent himself is no longer compelled by the necessity of choosing self-representation over incompetent or nonexistent representation. [Therefore,] while *Faretta* is correct in concluding that there is abundant support for the proposition that a right to self-representation has been recognized for centuries, the original reasons for protecting that right do not have the same force when the availability of competent counsel for every indigent defendant has displaced the need—although not always the desire—for self-representation. [No] one, including [the] *Faretta* majority, attempts to argue that as a rule *pro se* representation is wise, desirable or efficient. * * * Our experience has taught us that a 'pro se defense is usually a bad defense, particularly when compared to a defense provided by an experienced criminal defense attorney.' "

Justice Scalia, however, did not share his colleague's "apparent skepticism:"

"I have no doubt that the Framers of our Constitution, who were suspicious enough of governmental power—including judicial power—that they insisted upon a citizen's right to be judged by an independent jury of private citizens, would not have found acceptable the compulsory assignment of counsel *by the government* to plead a criminal defendant's case. [While] I might have rested the [*Faretta*] decision upon the Due Process Clause rather than the Sixth Amendment, I believe it was correct. [That] asserting the right of self-representation may often, or even usually, work to the defendant's disadvantage is no more remarkable—and no more a basis for withdrawing the right—than is the fact that proceeding without counsel in custodial interrogation, or confessing to the crime, usually works to the defendant's disadvantage. Our system of laws generally presumes that the criminal defendant, after being fully informed, knows his own best interests and does not need them dictated by the State. Any other approach is unworthy of a free people."

Justice Breyer wrote separately to express his concern "that judges closer to the firing line have sometimes expressed dismay about the practical consequences" of *Faretta*. However, he added "without some strong factual basis for believing that *Faretta's* holding has proved counterproductive in practice, we are not in a position to reconsider the constitutional assumptions that underlie that case."

A subsequent empirical study examined the outcomes for *pro se* felony defendants in federal and states cases and found that those outcomes "were at least as good as, and perhaps even better than the outcomes for their represented counterparts." Erica J. Hashimoto, *Defending The Right of Self-Representation: An Empirical Look at the Pro Se Felony Defendant*, 85 N.C.L.Rev. 423 (2007). While the sample of *pro se* defendants going to trial was quite small (23 cases), the percentage of acquittals was identical to that for represented defendants, and *pro se* defendants had a higher percentage of jury convictions that were limited to lesser-included misdemeanors. In the federal sample, while the percentage of trial acquittals was lower, the author noted that, as to overall outcomes, "*pro se* felony defendants do not appear to have done significantly worse than federal court defendants who were represented by counsel." Id. Relying in part on this study, the Supreme Court, per Justice Breyer, declined a recent invitation to overrule *Faretta*. See *Indiana v. Edwards*, 554 U.S. 164 (2008), other aspects of which are discussed infra Note 1, p. 109.

2. ***Harmless error.*** Nine years after *Faretta*, the Supreme Court answered one of Justice Blackmun's questions when it emphasized that a violation of the right to self-representation could never be harmless error. See *McKaskle v. Wiggins*, 465 U.S. 168, 178 n.8 (1984) ("Since the right of self-representation is a right that when exercised usually increases the likelihood of a trial outcome unfavorable to the defendant, its denial is not amenable to 'harmless error' analysis. The right is either respected or denied; its deprivation cannot be harmless.").

3. ***Does the principle of self-representation apply to appeals as well?*** In MARTINEZ v. COURT OF APPEAL OF CALIFORNIA, 528 U.S. 152 (2000), defendant (who described himself as a self-taught paralegal with 25 years experience) was convicted of embezzlement after representing himself at trial. He sought to represent himself on appeal as well, but was rebuffed by the state appellate courts. The Supreme Court, per Stevens, J., held, without a dissent, that "neither the holding nor the reasoning in *Faretta* requires [a state] to recognize a constitutional right to self-representation on direct appeal from a criminal conviction." Justice Stevens reasoned:

"Appeals as of right in federal courts were nonexistent for the first century of our Nation, and appellate review of any sort was 'rarely allowed.' * * * Thus, unlike the inquiry in *Faretta*, the historical evidence does not provide any support for an affirmative constitutional right to appellate self-representation. * * * The *Faretta* majority's reliance on the structure of the Sixth Amendment is also not relevant. The Sixth Amendment identifies the basic rights that the accused shall enjoy in 'all criminal prosecutions.' * * * The Sixth Amendment does not include any right to appeal. * * * It necessarily follows that the Amendment itself does not provide any basis for finding a right to self-representation on appeal."

As for a right to self-representation based on a respect for individual autonomy grounded in the Due Process Clause, Justice Stevens noted:

"[W]e are entirely unpersuaded that the risk of either [counsel] disloyalty or suspicion of disloyalty is a sufficient concern to conclude that a constitutional right of self-representation is a necessary component of a fair appellate proceeding. * * * As the *Faretta* opinion recognized, the right to self-representation is not absolute. * * * Even at the trial level, therefore, the government's interest in ensuring the integrity and efficiency of the trial at times outweighs the defendant's interest in acting as his own lawyer. In the appellate context, the balance between the two competing interests surely tips in favor of the State. The status of the accused defendant, who retains a presumption of innocence throughout the trial process, changes dramatically when a jury returns a guilty verdict. * * * Considering the change in position from defendant to appellant, the autonomy interests that survive a felony conviction are less compelling than those motivating the decision in *Faretta*. Yet the overriding state interest in the fair and efficient administration of justice remains as strong as at the trial level."

4. ***"Standby counsel."*** McKASKLE v. WIGGINS, 465 U.S. 168 (1984), made explicit "what is already implicit in *Faretta:* a defendant's Sixth Amendment rights are not violated when a trial judge appoints standby counsel—even over the defendant's objection[a]—to relieve the judge of the need to explain and enforce basic rules of courtroom protocol or to assist the defendant in overcoming routine obstacles that stand in the way of the defendant's achievement of his own clearly indicated goals." In describing the role of stand-by counsel, Justice O'Connor, writing for the Court noted:

"[T]he right to speak for oneself entails more than the opportunity to add one's voice to a cacophony of others. [Thus,] the *Faretta* right must impose some limits on the extent of standby counsel's unsolicited participation.

"First, the *pro se* defendant is entitled to preserve actual control over the case he chooses to present to the jury. This is the core of the *Faretta* right. If standby counsel's participation over the defendant's objection effectively allows counsel to make or substantially interfere with any significant tactical decisions, or to control the questioning of witnesses, or to speak *instead* of the defendant on any matter of importance, the *Faretta* right is eroded.

"Second, participation by standby counsel without the defendant's consent should not be allowed to destroy the jury's perception that the defendant is representing himself. The defendant's appearance in the status of one conducting his own defense is important in a criminal trial, since the right to appear *pro se* exists to affirm the accused's individual dignity and autonomy. * * *

"Participation by standby counsel outside the presence of the jury engages only the first of these two limitations. [T]he appearance of a *pro se* defendant's self-representation will not be unacceptably undermined by counsel's participation outside the presence of the jury. * * * Thus, *Faretta* rights are adequately vindicated in proceedings outside the presence of the jury if the *pro se* defendant is allowed to address the court freely on his own behalf and if disagreements between counsel and the *pro se* defendant are resolved in the defendant's favor whenever the matter is one that would normally be left to the discretion of counsel. * * *

"Participation by standby counsel in the presence of the jury is more problematic. It is here that the defendant may legitimately claim that excessive involvement by counsel will destroy the appearance that the defendant is acting *pro se*. * * * Nonetheless, we believe that a categorical bar on participation by standby counsel in the presence of the jury is unnecessary. * * *

"If a defendant is given the opportunity and elects to have counsel appear before the court or jury, his complaints concerning counsel's subsequent unsolicited participation lose much of their force. A defendant does not have a constitutional right to choreograph special appearances by counsel. Once a *pro se* defendant invites or agrees to any substantial participation by counsel,

[a] Who should compensate the standby counsel in this situation? See Poulin, infra Note 5 ("no court has directly addressed how to compensate standby counsel forced upon a nonindigent defendant").

subsequent appearances by counsel must be presumed to be with the defendant's acquiescence, at least until the defendant expressly and unambiguously renews his request that standby counsel be silenced."

Dissenting Justice White, joined by Brennan and Marshall, JJ., protested:

"Under the Court's new test, it is necessary to determine whether the *pro se* defendant retained 'actual control over the case he [chose] to present to the jury' and whether standby counsel's participation 'destroy[ed] the jury's perception that the defendant [was] representing himself.' Although this test purports to protect all of the values underlying our holding in *Faretta,* it is unclear whether it can achieve this result.

"As long as the *pro se* defendant is allowed his say, the first prong of the Court's test accords standby counsel at a bench trial or any proceeding outside the presence of a jury virtually untrammeled discretion to present any factual or legal argument to which the defendant does not object. The limits placed on counsel's participation in this context by the 'actual control' test are more apparent than real. * * *

"Although the Court is more solicitous of a *pro se* defendant's interests when standby counsel intervenes before a jury, the test's second prong suffers from similar shortcomings. To the extent that trial and appellate courts can discern the point at which counsel's unsolicited participation substantially undermines a *pro se* defendant's appearance before the jury, a matter about which I harbor substantial doubts, their decisions will, to a certain extent, 'affirm the accused's individual dignity and autonomy.' But they will do so incompletely, for in focusing on how the jury views the defendant, the majority opinion ignores *Faretta's* emphasis on the defendant's own perception of the criminal justice [system.]"

5. ***Lower courts and standby counsel.*** Anne Bowen Poulin, *The Role of Standby Counsel in Criminal Cases: In the Twilight Zone of The Criminal Justice System*, 76 N.Y.U. L. Rev. 676 (2000), notes that "judicial decisions addressing *pro se* defendants' complaints," reveal several "troubling patterns" in current practice. These include:

(1) Some courts are "actually hostile" to *pro se* defendants' request for standby counsel, as reflected by an appellate court suggestion that "the defendant be given the stark choice of self-representation (with no standby counsel) or the assistance of counsel"—thereby ensuring that the decision to proceed *pro se* will not be made "with the comforting knowledge" that a back-up is always available.

(2) A common scenario leading to *pro se* representation involves: (1) an indigent defendant seeks replacement of appointed counsel, (2) the trial judge determines that the defendant's complaints against counsel do not present the extreme situation needed for mandatory replacement (see Note 3, p. 194); (3) the defendant is told that he must choose between continued representation by appointed counsel or proceeding *pro se*; (4) the defendant chooses to proceed *pro se*; and (5) the court then appoints as standby counsel the "very attorney whose representation precipitated the defendant's complaint."

(3) "In cases where the defendant is not irretrievably estranged from standby counsel," defendants quite naturally will drift towards asking counsel to make presentations as "defendants often assume that standby counsel is not merely a resource but also someone available to act for the defendant." However, in such a situation, some courts refuse to allow standby counsel to assume this "larger role" (particularly at trial), insisting that the defendant choose between waiving his "*Faretta* rights" or utilizing counsel strictly as an advisor.

(4) Many standby counsel will not (a) take it upon themselves to explore "factual investigations and legal options that the defendant might overlook" and then bring their findings to the attention of the defendant, (b) raise legal objections on their own initiative, or (c) present

mitigating evidence at sentencing on their own initiative—all actions advocated by the author. This failure to initiate assistance arguably is a product in part of various lower court opinions that characterize the role of standby counsel as simply "an observer, an attorney who attends the trial or other proceeding and who may offer advice, but who does not speak for the defendant or bear responsibility for his defense." *United States v. Taylor*, 933 F.2d 307 (5th Cir.1991).

To what extent does the acceptance of such practices follow from a "judicial perception that standby counsel serves the court's purpose rather than the defendant's"? Poulin, supra. Did the Court in *McKaskle* approve of an "active role" for standby counsel, in which counsel acts as "part of the defense team," subject to the "defendant's right to actual control of the case and to the appearance of control in the presence of the factfinder"? Id.

6. ***Ineffective assistance of standby counsel.*** Lower courts generally have rejected claims of ineffective assistance by standby counsel. They note that the *pro se* defendant cannot complain of his own ineffective performance, (see *Faretta*, fn.46) and the final decisions are being made by the defendant. They also note that ineffective assistance claims are tied to a constitutional right to counsel's assistance, and the defendant has no constitutional right to the assistance of standby counsel. See Poulin, supra. However, "some courts" have held that *pro se* defendants may claim ineffective assistance of standby counsel as to erroneous "legal advice." Id.

7. ***Timing of an assertion.*** In *Faretta*, the Court stressed that the defendant made his request to represent himself "well before the date of trial." Lower courts have held that the defendant's right to self-representation is conditioned on a timely assertion of that right, which ordinarily is satisfied by a request made before the scheduled trial date (provided the defendant does not insist upon a continuance as a condition of proceeding *pro se*). The trial court has "broad discretion to reject as untimely a request made during the course of trial." See CRIMPROC § 11.5(d).

8. ***Notice of the right to self-representation.*** The lower courts have uniformly held that, in the absence of a clear indication on the defendant's part that he wants to consider representing himself, the court has no constitutional obligation to inform the defendant of his right to proceed *pro se*. Notification of the right to proceed *pro se*, these courts emphasize, might undermine the "overriding constitutional policy" favoring the provision of counsel by suggesting that counsel is not needed. See CRIMPROC § 11.5(b) (collecting cases). As one circuit put it, "because the right to self-representation does not implicate constitutional fair trial considerations to the same extent as does an accused's right to counsel, it requires neither notice of the right's existence prior to legal proceedings nor a knowing and intelligent waiver." *Munkus v. Furlong*, 170 F.3d 980, 983 (10th Cir. 1999) (internal quotation omitted). But wouldn't notice of the right to self-representation solve some of the timing problems discussed supra Note 7?

Do you agree that the right to self-representation should be subordinate to the right to counsel? Could you imagine a system wherein the court would have to advise a defendant that he has the right to either represent himself or to proceed through counsel and then require the defendant to choose one and waive the other? What is wrong with that system? Should there be a preference for counsel given the empirical data discussed supra Note 1?

NOTES AND QUESTIONS ON WARNING REQUIREMENTS AND THE WAIVER OF THE RIGHT TO COUNSEL

The *Faretta* Court held that, before a defendant would be permitted to proceed *pro se*, he would have to "knowingly and intelligently" waive his right to counsel. See *Johnson v. Zerbst*, 304 U.S. 458 (1938). As part of that waiver process, the Court noted, "he should be made aware of the dangers and disadvantages of self-representation, so that the record will establish that 'he knows what he is doing and his choice is made with eyes open.' " What do these statements mean? Are certain, specific warnings required before an individual can waive the right to counsel? How extensive must the colloquy be? And how searching must the waiver inquiry be?

1. ***State and federal practices after* Faretta.** Relying on the above-quoted statements, several lower courts after *Faretta* concluded that the Sixth Amendment requires reference to "specific disadvantages" of proceeding without counsel rather than a "vague, general admonishment." These courts have suggested that defendants should be informed "(1) that 'presenting a defense is not a simple matter of telling one's story,' but requires adherence to various 'technical' rules governing the conduct of a trial; (2) that a lawyer has substantial experience and training in trial procedure and that the prosecution will be represented by an experienced lawyer; (3) that a person unfamiliar with legal procedures may allow the prosecutor an advantage by failing to make objections to inadmissible evidence, may not make effective use of such rights as the *voir dire* of jurors, and may make tactical decisions that produce unintended consequences; (4) that there may be possible defenses and other rights of which counsel would be aware and if those are not timely asserted, they may be lost permanently; (5) that a defendant proceeding *pro se* will not be allowed to complain on appeal about the competency of his representation; and (6) 'that the effectiveness of his defense may well be diminished by his dual role as attorney and accused.'" CRIMPROC. § 11.5(c). According to these courts, once these warnings are given, the waiver inquiry should be "realistically 'designed to reveal [defendants'] understanding.'" The trial court should determine through a penetrating inquiry (which goes beyond requiring "yes" and "no" answers) that the defendant understands and appreciates those disadvantages and consequences. See id.

Other courts, however, "take the position that *Faretta* requires only that the defendant have been aware of the disadvantages of proceeding *pro se*, and that awareness can be established without regard to any admonitions or colloquies." See id. (collecting cases). Consider, for example, Judge Easterbrook's statements for the court in *United States v. Hill*, 252 F.3d 919 (7th Cir. 2001):

"Waiver does not depend on astute (or even rudimentary) understanding of how rights can be employed to best advantage. Defendants routinely plead guilty, waiving oodles of constitutional rights, in proceedings where rights are named but not explained. For example, the judge will tell the defendant that the plea waives the right to jury trial but will not describe how juries work, when they are apt to find a prosecutor's case insufficient, why the process of formulating and giving jury instructions creates issues for appeal, and so on. [The] contention that 'knowing and intelligent' means something different when a defendant elects self-representation than when the same defendant elects a bench trial (or waives another constitutional right) has its genesis in *Faretta*. [But] *Faretta* adopted the waiver standard of *Johnson v. Zerbst*, which noted that the determination 'whether there has been an intelligent waiver of the right to counsel must depend, in each case, upon the particular facts and circumstances surrounding the case, including the background, experience, and conduct of the accused.' That standard can be met without a demonstration that the accused has a deep understanding of how counsel could assist him."

2. ***The Supreme Court's response.*** In IOWA v. TOVAR, 541 U.S. 77 (2004), the Supreme Court rejected one state's interpretation of the Sixth Amendment as requiring specific warnings regarding the usefulness of an attorney before a *pro se* defendant could plead guilty. The two warnings at issue included a warning that "waiving the assistance of counsel in deciding whether to plead guilty [entails] the risk that a viable defense will be overlooked" and the warning "that by waiving his right to an attorney he will lose the opportunity to obtain an independent opinion on whether, under the facts and applicable law, it is wise to plead guilty." This "rigid and detailed admonishment," the Supreme Court held, is not mandated by the Sixth Amendment. Rather, "[t]he constitutional requirement is satisfied when the trial court informs the accused of the nature of the charges against him, of his right to be counseled regarding his plea, and of the range of

allowable punishments attendant upon the entry of a guilty plea." Justice Ginsburg, writing for the Court, explained:

"We have described a waiver of counsel as intelligent when the defendant 'knows what he is doing and his choice is made with eyes open.' We have not, however, prescribed any formula or script to be read to a defendant who states that he elects to proceed without counsel. The information a defendant must possess in order to make an intelligent election, our decisions indicate, will depend on a range of case-specific factors, including the defendant's education or sophistication, the complex or easily grasped nature of the charge, and the stage of the proceeding. See *Johnson*. [Similarly,] the information a defendant must have to waive counsel intelligently will 'depend, in each case, upon the particular facts and circumstances surrounding that case.'

"[The] States are free to adopt by statute, rule, or decision any guides to the acceptance of an uncounseled plea they deem useful. See, e.g., Alaska Rule Crim. Proc. 39(a) (2003); Fla. Rule Crim. Proc. 3.111(d) (2003); Md. Ct. Rule 4–215 (2002); Minn. Rule Crim. Proc. 5.02 (2003); Pa. Rule Crim. Proc. 121, comment (2003). We hold only that the two admonitions the Iowa Supreme Court ordered are not required by the Federal Constitution."

Does *Tovar* hold open the possibility that, under some circumstances, the judge accepting a waiver of counsel in connection with the entry of a guilty plea must advise the defendant of the possible benefits of counsel's assistance in considering whether to plead guilty? If so, what circumstances might require such advice? Would such advice be required where an element of the offense charged called for an arguably subjective jury determination (e.g., what constitutes negligence) and the facts presented in establishing a factual basis for the guilty plea were sufficient to convince a jury on that element, but not overwhelmingly so?

3. ***The importance of the stage of the proceeding.*** Notice that the *Tovar* Court included "the stage of the proceeding" in its list of relevant factors that inform what warnings are required in a case. Justice Ginsburg elaborated on this factor later in her opinion for the Court:

"As to waiver of trial counsel, we have said that before a defendant may be allowed to proceed *pro se,* he must be warned specifically of the hazards ahead. *Faretta v. California*. [Later,] in *Patterson v. Illinois*, 487 U.S. 285 (1988), we elaborated on 'the dangers and disadvantages of self-representation' to which *Faretta* referred. '[A]t trial,' we observed, 'counsel is required to help even the most gifted layman adhere to the rules of procedure and evidence, comprehend the subtleties of *voir dire,* examine and cross-examine witnesses effectively[,] object to improper prosecution questions, and much more.' Warnings of the pitfalls of proceeding to trial without counsel, we therefore said, must be 'rigorous[ly]' conveyed. We clarified, however, that at earlier stages of the criminal process, a less searching or formal colloquy may suffice. *Patterson* concerned postindictment questioning by police and prosecutor. At that stage of the case, we held, the warnings required by *Miranda v. Arizona* adequately informed the defendant not only of his Fifth Amendment rights, but of his Sixth Amendment right to counsel as well. [*Patterson*] describes a 'pragmatic approach to the waiver question,' one that asks 'what purposes a lawyer can serve at the particular stage of the proceedings in question, and what assistance he could provide to an accused at that stage,' in order 'to determine the scope of the Sixth Amendment right to counsel, and the type of warnings and procedures that should be required before a waiver of that right will be recognized.' We require less rigorous warnings pretrial, *Patterson* explained, not because pretrial proceedings are 'less important' than trial, but because, at that stage, 'the full dangers and disadvantages of self-representation [are] less substantial and more obvious to an accused than they are at trial.' "

Does this mean that a court could give even fewer warnings than the Court deemed necessary in *Tovar* before obtaining a waiver of the right to counsel at an earlier stage than the guilty plea, where the consequences were less serious (e.g., waiver of counsel in connection with the waiver of a preliminary hearing)? What, if anything, does this dicta suggest about what warnings are required before a defendant is permitted to proceed *pro se* at trial?

4. ***State law requirements.*** As noted in *Tovar*, states often require more extensive advisements for the waiver of counsel as a matter of state law. Such state provisions commonly require, in addition to an explanation of the advantages that come with representation by counsel, the prerequisites set forth in Justice Black's opinion (for a four justice plurality) in *Von Moltke v. Gillies*, 332 U.S. 708 (1948): "To be valid such a waiver must be made with an apprehension of the nature of the charges, the statutory offenses included within them, the range of allowable punishments thereunder, possible defenses to the charges and circumstances in mitigation thereof and all other facts essential to a broad understanding of the whole matter." *Von Moltke*, like *Tovar*, involved a defendant who waived counsel in connection with the entry of a guilty plea.

5. ***The competency standard and the standard for waiving the right to counsel.*** In order to be deemed competent to stand trial, a criminal defendant must have "sufficient present ability to consult with his lawyer with a reasonable degree of rational understanding" and "a rational as well as factual understanding of the proceedings against him." *Dusky v. United States*, 362 U.S. 402 (1960). In GODINEZ v. MORAN, 509 U.S. 389 (1993) (a case in which a capital defendant discharged his attorneys, pled guilty, and was ultimately sentenced to death), a 7–2 majority rejected the notion that competency to plead guilty or to waive the right to counsel must be measured by a higher or different standard than the competency standard for standing trial. On the relationship between the competency standard and the standard for waiver of the right to counsel, Justice Thomas, writing for the Court, explained:

"[T]here is no reason to believe that the decision to waive counsel requires an appreciably higher level of mental functioning than the decision to waive other constitutional rights. [The defendant] suggests that a higher competency standard is necessary because a defendant who represents himself ' "must have greater powers of comprehension, judgment, and reason than would be necessary to stand trial with the aid of an attorney." ' But this argument has a flawed premise; the competence that is required of a defendant seeking to waive his right to counsel is the competence to *waive the right,* not the competence to represent himself. [A] criminal defendant's ability to represent himself has no bearing upon his competence to *choose* self-representation."

The majority also warned, however, that a finding of competency to stand trial would not in itself establish the understanding needed for pleading guilty or waiving the right to counsel: "[A] trial court must satisfy itself that the waiver [of] constitutional rights is knowing and voluntary. In this sense, there is a 'heightened' standard for pleading guilty and for waiving the right to counsel, but it is not a heightened standard of *competence.*" The purpose of a competency inquiry, explained the Court, is to determine whether a defendant "has the *ability* to understand the proceedings," but "the purpose of the 'knowing and voluntary' inquiry [is] to determine whether the defendant actually *does* understand the significance and consequences of a particular decision and whether the decision is uncoerced."

NOTES AND QUESTIONS ON THE LIMITS OF THE RIGHT TO SELF-REPRESENTATION

1. ***Denying the right of self-representation to mentally ill defendants.*** In INDIANA v. EDWARDS, 554 U.S. 164 (2008), the Supreme Court held that a state has the authority to permit its trial courts to deny self-representation to mentally ill defendants when those defendants "suffer from severe mental illness to the point where they are not competent to conduct trial proceedings by themselves." Justice BREYER, writing for the majority, explained:

"We assume that a criminal defendant has sufficient mental competence to stand trial (i.e., the defendant meets Dusky's standard) and that the defendant insists on representing himself during that trial. We ask whether the Constitution permits a State to limit that defendant's self-representation right by insisting upon representation by counsel at trial—on the ground that the defendant lacks the mental capacity to conduct his trial defense unless represented.

"Several considerations taken together lead us to conclude that the answer to this question is yes. First, the Court's precedent, while not answering the question, points slightly in the direction of our affirmative answer. Godinez [simply] leaves the question open. But the Court's 'mental competency' cases set forth a standard that focuses directly upon a defendant's 'present ability to consult with his lawyer,' Dusky. [They] assume representation by counsel and emphasize the importance of counsel. They thus suggest (though do not hold) that an instance in which a defendant who would choose to forgo counsel at trial presents a very different set of circumstances, which in our view, calls for a different standard.

"At the same time *Faretta*, the foundational self-representation case, rested its conclusion in part upon preexisting state law set forth in cases all of which are consistent with, and at least two of which expressly adopt, a competency limitation on the self-representation right. See 422 U.S. at 813, and n. 9 (citing 16 state-court decisions and two secondary sources). * * *

"Second, the nature of the problem before us cautions against the use of a single mental competency standard for deciding both (1) whether a defendant who is represented by counsel can proceed to trial and (2) whether a defendant who goes to trial must be permitted to represent himself. Mental illness itself is not a unitary concept. It varies in degree. It can vary over time. It interferes with an individual's functioning at different times in different ways. * * * In certain instances an individual may well be able to satisfy *Dusky's* mental competence standard, for he will be able to work with counsel at trial, yet at the same time he may be unable to carry out the basic tasks needed to present his own defense without the help of counsel. * * *

"The American Psychiatric Association (APA) tells us [that] '[d]isorganized thinking, deficits in sustaining attention and concentration, impaired expressive abilities, anxiety, and other common symptoms of severe mental illnesses can impair the defendant's ability to play the significantly expanded role required for self-representation even if he can play the lesser role of represented defendant.' * * *

"Third, in our view, a right of self-representation at trial will not 'affirm the dignity' of a defendant who lacks the mental capacity to conduct his defense without the assistance of counsel. *McKaskle*. * * * To the contrary, given that defendant's uncertain mental state, the spectacle that could well result from his self-representation at trial is at least as likely to prove humiliating as ennobling. Moreover, insofar as a defendant's lack of capacity threatens an improper conviction or sentence, self-representation in that exceptional context undercuts the most basic of the Constitution's criminal law objectives, providing a fair trial.

"[Fourth,] proceedings must not only be fair, they must 'appear fair to all who observe them.' An *amicus* brief reports one psychiatrist's reaction to having observed a patient (a patient who had satisfied *Dusky*) try to conduct his own defense: '[H]ow in the world can our legal system allow an insane man to defend himself?' The application of *Dusky's* basic mental competence standard can help in part to avoid this result. But given the different capacities needed to proceed to trial without counsel, there is little reason to believe that *Dusky* alone is sufficient. At the same time, the trial judge, particularly one such as the trial judge in this case, who presided over one of Edwards' competency hearings and his two trials, will often prove best able to make more fine-tuned mental capacity decisions, tailored to the individualized circumstances of a particular defendant.

"We consequently conclude that the Constitution permits judges to take realistic account of the particular defendant's mental capacities by asking whether a defendant who seeks to conduct his own defense at trial is mentally competent to do so. That is to say, the Constitution permits States to insist upon representation by counsel for those competent enough to stand trial under *Dusky* but who still suffer from severe mental illness to the point where they are not competent to conduct trial proceedings by themselves.

"Indiana has also asked us to adopt, as a measure of a defendant's ability to conduct a trial, a more specific standard that would 'deny a criminal defendant the right to represent himself at trial where the defendant cannot communicate coherently with the court or a jury.' We are sufficiently uncertain, however, as to how that particular standard would work in practice to refrain from endorsing it as a federal constitutional standard here. We need not now, and we do not, adopt it."

Justice SCALIA (joined by Justice THOMAS) dissented from the Court's decision:

"The Court is correct that this case presents a variation on *Godinez:* It presents the question not whether another constitutional requirement (in *Godinez,* the proposed higher degree of competence required for a waiver) limits a defendant's constitutional right to elect self-representation, but whether a State's view of fairness (or of other values) permits it to strip the defendant of this right. But that makes the question before us an easier one. While one constitutional requirement must yield to another in case of conflict, nothing permits a State, because of *its* view of what is fair, to deny a constitutional protection. * * *

"While there is little doubt that preserving individual "dignity" (to which the Court refers) [is] paramount among [the] purposes [of the right to self-representation], there is equally little doubt that the loss of 'dignity' the right is designed to prevent is *not* the defendant's making a fool of himself by presenting an amateurish or even incoherent defense. Rather, the dignity at issue is the supreme human dignity of being master of one's fate rather than a ward of the State—the dignity of individual choice.

"A further purpose that the Court finds is advanced by denial of the right of self-representation is the purpose of assuring that trials 'appear fair to all who observe them.' To my knowledge we have never denied a defendant a right simply on the ground that it would make his trial appear less 'fair' to outside observers, and I would not inaugurate that principle here. But were I to do so, I would not apply it to deny a defendant the right to represent himself when he knowingly and voluntarily waives counsel. * * *

"In singling out mentally ill defendants for this treatment, the Court's opinion does not even have the questionable virtue of being politically correct. At a time when all society is trying to mainstream the mentally impaired, the Court permits them to be deprived of a basic constitutional right—for their own good.

"Today's holding is extraordinarily vague. The Court does not accept Indiana's position that self-representation can be denied ' "where the defendant cannot communicate coherently with the court or a jury." ' * * * It holds only that lack of mental competence can under some circumstances form a basis for denying the right to proceed *pro se.* We will presumably give some meaning to this holding in the future, but the indeterminacy makes a bad holding worse. Once the right of self-representation for the mentally ill is a sometime thing, trial judges will have every incentive to make their lives easier [by] appointing knowledgeable and literate counsel."

2. *A cynical view of* Godinez *and* Edwards. One commentator has suggested that, taken together, *Godinez* and *Edwards* effectively mean that mentally ill defendants who are nonetheless competent to stand trial should be allowed to plead without counsel, but those same defendants should not be permitted to go to trial without counsel. On this understanding, "[o]ne would not be churlish in concluding that the overriding objective of *Godinez* and *Edwards* is to ensure that the state can proceed as efficiently as possible in dealing with mentally ill people." See Christopher Slobogin, *Mental Illness and Self-Representation: Faretta, Godinez, and Edwards*, 7 Ohio St.J.Crim.L. 391 (2009) . Do you agree?

3. ***The need to preserve a fair trial.*** The majority's focus in *Edwards* on the "appearance of fairness" and the potential for an "unfair trial" could have consequences that go far beyond denying mentally ill defendants a right to self-representation. Even before *Edwards*, some lower courts viewed *Faretta* as leaving open the possibility of denying self-representation, notwithstanding a waiver of the right to counsel that is both knowing and voluntary, where the trial court views representation by counsel as absolutely necessary to ensure a fair trial—in particular, where a physical disability (e.g., a speech impediment) or educational deficiency "may significantly affect [defendant's] ability to communicate a possible defense to the jury." *Pickens v. State*, 292 N.W.2d 601 (Wis.1980); see CRIMPROC § 11.5(d) (collecting cases). What standard should lower courts use to determine whether a defendant is capable of representing himself at trial? When should the state's interest in ensuring a fair trial trump the defendant's autonomy interest in self-representation?

4. ***Reconciling the state's interest in fair proceedings and the defendant's autonomy interest.*** Consider Slobogin, supra: "First, the [*Edwards*] Court could have reaffirmed, rather than ignored, *Godinez*'s (and *Faretta*'s) holding that the key issue is competency to choose, not competency to represent oneself. Second, contra to *Godinez*, it could have recognized that one needs greater capacity to choose to waive counsel than to surrender other rights, which would have better protected both the defendant's autonomy interest and the state's interest in fair proceedings. Third, it could have further protected those interests by requiring an inquiry that *Godinez* did not consider: an investigation of the reasons the defendant wants to proceed *pro se*. If those reasons are delusional or non-existent, then the autonomy that gives rise to a right to self-representation does not exist. But otherwise the defendant who understands the risks of waiving the right to counsel should be allowed to represent himself; no competency-to-represent-oneself test, a la *Edwards*, should be required. [These] prescriptions more properly balance the interests identified in *Faretta*, *Godinez* and *Edwards*. They also achieve another goal [—namely,] the de-stigmatization and dignification of people with mental illness."

5. ***Forfeiture of the right to counsel.*** A series of lower court cases have held that misconduct by the defendant can produce a forfeiture of the right to assistance of counsel, requiring defendant thereafter to proceed *pro se*. Two settings have most frequently led to findings of forfeiture: (1) defendant assaulted or threatened counsel, who then asked to withdraw; (2) defendant was given ample time to obtain counsel, and after assuring the court that he would obtain counsel by the date of the trial, appeared on that date without counsel and without a reasonable excuse for failing to have obtained counsel. See CRIMPROC §§ 11.3(c), 11.4(d). Other courts have refused to accept the concept of forfeiture in such situations, but will force the defendant to proceed *pro se* on the basis of a "waiver by conduct." They require that the defendant previously has been made aware that the misconduct at issue would result in the loss of his right to counsel. Id. But see *State v. Carruthers*, 35 S.W.3d 516 (Tenn.2000) (reviewing the cases that have "attempted" to distinguish the concepts of "implicit waiver by conduct" and "forfeiture," finding the distinction "slight," and concluding that the right to counsel may be forfeited by interactions with counsel (here threats) that seek to "manipulate, delay, or disrupt trial proceedings").

§ 5. THE RIGHT TO "COUNSEL OF CHOICE"

Although the Supreme Court has recognized that "the right to select and be represented by one's preferred attorney is comprehended by the Sixth Amendment," *Wheat v. United States*, 486 U.S. 153 (1988) [p. 189], it has also emphasized that "the essential aim of the Amendment is to guarantee an effective advocate for each criminal defendant rather than to ensure that a defendant will inexorably be represented by the lawyer whom he prefers." Id. As a result, "[t]he Sixth Amendment right to choose one's own counsel is circumscribed in several important respects. Regardless of his persuasive powers, an advocate who is not a member of the bar may not represent clients (other than himself) in court. Similarly, a defendant may not insist on representation by an attorney he cannot afford or who for other reasons declines to represent the defendant. Nor may a defendant insist on the counsel of an attorney who has a previous or ongoing relationship with an opposing party, even when the opposing party is the Government. [Finally,] where a court justifiably finds an actual conflict of interest, [it may] insist that defendants be separately represented." Id.

If one of the above-listed limitations on the right to counsel of choice does not exist, what is a defendant's remedy if his right to counsel of choice is violated? The Supreme Court addressed that question in the case that follows.

UNITED STATES V. GONZALEZ-LOPEZ

548 U.S. 140, 126 S.Ct. 2557, 165 L.Ed.2d 409 (2006).

JUSTICE SCALIA delivered the opinion of the Court.

We must decide whether a trial court's erroneous deprivation of a criminal defendant's choice of counsel entitles him to reversal of his conviction.

Respondent Cuauhtemoc Gonzalez-Lopez was charged in the Eastern District of Missouri with conspiracy to distribute more than 100 kilograms of marijuana. His family hired attorney John Fahle to represent him. After the arraignment, respondent called a California attorney, Joseph Low, to discuss whether Low would represent him, either in addition to or instead of Fahle. Low flew from California to meet with respondent, who hired him.

The following week, respondent informed Fahle that he wanted Low to be his only attorney. Low then filed an application for admission *pro hac vice*. The District Court denied his application without comment. A month later, Low filed a second application, which the District Court again denied without explanation.

The case proceeded to trial, and Dickhaus represented respondent. Low again moved for admission and was again denied. The court also denied Dickhaus's request to have Low at counsel table with him and ordered Low to sit in the audience and to have no contact with Dickhaus during the proceedings. [Respondent] was unable to meet with Low throughout the trial, except for once on the last night. The jury found respondent guilty.

Respondent appealed, and the Eighth Circuit vacated the conviction. The Court [held] that the District Court erred in [denying Low's] motions [and] violated respondent's Sixth Amendment right to paid counsel of his choosing. The [Eighth Circuit] then concluded that this Sixth Amendment violation was not subject to harmless-error review. We granted certiorari.

The Government here agrees, as it has previously, that the Sixth Amendment guarantees the defendant the right to be represented by an otherwise qualified attorney whom that defendant can afford to hire, or who is willing to represent the defendant even though he is without funds. To be sure, the right to counsel of choice "is circumscribed in several important respects." *Wheat.* But the Government does not dispute the Eighth Circuit's conclusion in this case that the District Court erroneously deprived respondent of his counsel of choice.

The Government contends, however, that the Sixth Amendment violation is not "complete" unless the defendant can show that substitute counsel was ineffective within the meaning of *Strickland v. Washington*—i.e., that substitute counsel's performance was deficient and the defendant was prejudiced by it. In the alternative, the Government contends that the defendant must at least demonstrate that his counsel of choice would have pursued a different strategy that would have created a "reasonable probability that [the] result of the proceedings would have been different,"—in other words, that he was prejudiced within the meaning of *Strickland* by the denial of his counsel of choice even if substitute counsel's performance was not constitutionally deficient.[1] To support these propositions, the Government points to our prior cases, which note that the right to counsel "has been [accorded] not for its own sake, but because of the effect it has on the ability of the accused to receive a fair trial." *Mickens v. Taylor* [Note 2, p. 184]. A trial is not unfair and thus the Sixth Amendment is not violated, the Government reasons, unless a defendant has been prejudiced.

Stated as broadly as this, the Government's argument in effect reads the Sixth Amendment as a more detailed version of the Due Process Clause—and then proceeds to give no effect to the details. It is true enough that the purpose of the rights set forth in that Amendment is to ensure a fair trial; but it does not follow that the rights can be disregarded so long as the trial is, on the whole, fair.

[T]he Sixth Amendment right to counsel of choice [commands,] not that a trial be fair, but that a particular guarantee of fairness be provided-to wit, that the accused be defended by the counsel he believes to be best. "The Constitution guarantees a fair trial through the Due Process Clauses, but it defines the basic elements of a fair trial largely through the several provisions of the Sixth Amendment, including the Counsel Clause." *Strickland*. In sum, the right at stake here is the right to counsel of choice, not the right to a fair trial; and that right was violated because the deprivation of counsel was erroneous. No additional showing of prejudice is required to make the violation complete.

The cases the Government relies on involve the right to the effective assistance of counsel, the violation of which generally requires a defendant to establish prejudice. The earliest case generally cited for the proposition that "the right to counsel is the right to the effective assistance of counsel," was based on the Due Process Clause rather than on the Sixth Amendment, see *Powell* [*v. Alabama*, p. 65]. And even our recognition of the right to effective counsel within the Sixth Amendment was a consequence of our perception that representation by counsel "is critical to the ability of the adversarial system to produce just results." *Strickland*. Having derived the right to effective representation from the purpose of ensuring a fair trial, we have, logically enough, also derived the limits of that right from that same purpose. The requirement that a defendant show prejudice in effective representation cases arises from the very nature of the specific element of the right to counsel at issue there—*effective* (not mistake-free) representation. Counsel cannot be "ineffective" unless his mistakes have harmed the defense (or, at least, unless it is reasonably likely that they have). Thus, a violation of the Sixth Amendment right to *effective* representation is not "complete" until the defendant is prejudiced.

The right to select counsel of one's choice, by contrast, has never been derived from the Sixth Amendment's purpose of ensuring a fair trial.[3] It has been regarded as the root meaning of the

---

1 The dissent proposes yet a third standard-viz., that the defendant must show "an identifiable difference in the quality of representation between the disqualified counsel and the attorney who represents the defendant at trial." That proposal suffers from the same infirmities (outlined later in text) that beset the Government's positions. In addition, however, it greatly impairs the clarity of the law. How is a lower-court judge to know what an identifiable difference consists of? Whereas the Government at least appeals to *Strickland* and the case law under it, the most the dissent can claim by way of precedential support for its rule is that it is consistent with cases that never discussed the issue of prejudice.

3 In *Wheat v. United States*, 486 U.S. 153 (1988) [p. 189], where we formulated the right to counsel of choice and discussed some of the limitations upon it, we took note of the overarching purpose of fair trial in holding that the trial court has discretion to disallow a first choice of counsel that would create serious risk of conflict of interest. * * * It is one thing to conclude that the right to counsel of choice may be limited by the need for fair trial, but quite another to say that the right does not exist unless its denial renders the trial unfair.

constitutional guarantee. Where the right to be assisted by counsel of one's choice is wrongly denied, therefore, it is unnecessary to conduct an ineffectiveness or prejudice inquiry to establish a Sixth Amendment violation. Deprivation of the right is "complete" when the defendant is erroneously prevented from being represented by the lawyer he wants, regardless of the quality of the representation he received. To argue otherwise is to confuse the right to counsel of choice—which is the right to a particular lawyer regardless of comparative effectiveness—with the right to effective counsel—which imposes a baseline requirement of competence on whatever lawyer is chosen or appointed.

Having concluded, in light of the Government's concession of erroneous deprivation, that the trial court violated respondent's Sixth Amendment right to counsel of choice, we must consider whether this error is subject to review for harmlessness. In *Arizona v. Fulminante,* 499 U.S. 279 (1991) [p. 665, we divided constitutional errors into two classes. The first we called "trial error," because the errors "occurred during presentation of the case to the jury" and their effect may "be quantitatively assessed in the context of other evidence presented in order to determine whether [they were] harmless beyond a reasonable doubt." These include "most constitutional errors." The second class of constitutional error we called "structural defects." These "defy analysis by 'harmless-error' standards" because they "affec[t] the framework within which the trial proceeds," and are not "simply an error in the trial process itself." Such errors include the denial of counsel, *Gideon* [p. 68] [and] the denial of the right of self-representation, *McKaskle v. Wiggins* [Note 2, p. 103].

We have little trouble concluding that erroneous deprivation of the right to counsel of choice, "with consequences that are necessarily unquantifiable and indeterminate, unquestionably qualifies as 'structural error.' " Different attorneys will pursue different strategies with regard to investigation and discovery, development of the theory of defense, selection of the jury, presentation of the witnesses, and style of witness examination and jury argument. And the choice of attorney will affect whether and on what terms the defendant cooperates with the prosecution, plea bargains, or decides instead to go to trial. In light of these myriad aspects of representation, the erroneous denial of counsel bears directly on the "framework within which the trial proceeds," *Fulminante*—or indeed on whether it proceeds at all. It is impossible to know what different choices the rejected counsel would have made, and then to quantify the impact of those different choices on the outcome of the proceedings. Many counseled decisions, including those involving plea bargains and cooperation with the government, do not even concern the conduct of the trial at all. Harmless-error analysis in such a context would be a speculative inquiry into what might have occurred in an alternate universe.

The Government acknowledges that the deprivation of choice of counsel pervades the entire trial, but points out that counsel's ineffectiveness may also do so and yet we do not allow reversal of a conviction for that reason without a showing of prejudice. But the requirement of showing prejudice in ineffectiveness claims stems from the very definition of the right at issue; it is not a matter of showing that the violation was harmless, but of showing that a violation of the right to effective representation *occurred.* A choice-of-counsel violation occurs *whenever* the defendant's choice is wrongfully denied. Moreover, if and when counsel's ineffectiveness "pervades" a trial, it does so (to the extent we can detect it) through identifiable mistakes. We can assess how those mistakes affected the outcome. To determine the effect of wrongful denial of choice of counsel, however, we would not be looking for mistakes committed by the actual counsel, but for differences in the defense that would have been made by the rejected counsel—in matters ranging from questions asked on *voir dire* and cross-examination to such intangibles as argument style and relationship with the prosecutors. We would have to speculate upon what matters the rejected counsel would have handled differently—or indeed, would have handled the same but with the benefit of a more jury-pleasing courtroom style or a longstanding relationship of trust with the prosecutors. And then we would have to speculate upon what effect those different choices or different intangibles might have had. The difficulties of conducting the two assessments of prejudice are not remotely comparable.

Nothing we have said today casts any doubt or places any qualification upon our previous holdings that limit the right to counsel of choice and recognize the authority of trial courts to establish criteria for admitting lawyers to argue before them. As the dissent too discusses, the right to counsel of choice does not extend to defendants who require counsel to be appointed for them. Nor may a defendant insist on representation by a person who is not a member of the bar, or demand that a court honor his waiver of conflict-free representation. See *Wheat* [fn.3]. We have recognized a trial court's wide latitude in balancing the right to counsel of choice against the needs of fairness, *Wheat*, and against the demands of its calendar. The court has, moreover, an "independent interest in ensuring that criminal trials are conducted within the ethical standards of the profession and that legal proceedings appear fair to all who observe them." *Wheat*. None of these limitations on the right to choose one's counsel is relevant here. This is not a case about a court's power to enforce rules or adhere to practices that determine which attorneys may appear before it, or to make scheduling and other decisions that effectively exclude a defendant's first choice of counsel. However broad a court's discretion may be, the Government has conceded that the District Court here erred when it denied respondent his choice of counsel. Accepting that premise, we hold that the error violated respondent's Sixth Amendment right to counsel of choice and that this violation is not subject to harmless-error analysis.

JUSTICE ALITO, with whom THE CHIEF JUSTICE, JUSTICE KENNEDY, and JUSTICE THOMAS join, dissenting.

I disagree with the Court's conclusion that a criminal conviction must automatically be reversed whenever a trial court errs in applying its rules regarding *pro hac vice* admissions and as a result prevents a defendant from being represented at trial by the defendant's first-choice attorney. Instead, a defendant should be required to make at least *some* showing that the trial court's erroneous ruling adversely affected the quality of assistance that the defendant received. In my view, the majority's contrary holding is based on an incorrect interpretation of the Sixth Amendment and a misapplication of harmless-error principles. I respectfully dissent.

The majority makes a subtle but important mistake at the outset in its characterization of what the Sixth Amendment guarantees. The majority states that the Sixth Amendment protects "the right of a defendant who does not require appointed counsel to choose who will represent him." What the Sixth Amendment actually protects, however, is the right to have *the assistance* that the defendant's counsel of choice is able to provide. It follows that if the erroneous disqualification of a defendant's counsel of choice does not impair the assistance that a defendant receives at trial, there is no violation of the Sixth Amendment.

The language of the Sixth Amendment supports this interpretation. The Assistance of Counsel Clause focuses on what a defendant is entitled to receive ("Assistance"), rather than on the identity of the provider. The background of the adoption of the Sixth Amendment points in the same direction. The specific evil against which the Assistance of Counsel Clause was aimed was the English common-law rule severely limiting a felony defendant's ability to be assisted by counsel.

There is no doubt, of course, that the right "to have the Assistance of Counsel" carries with it a limited right to be represented by counsel of choice. At the time of the adoption of the Bill of Rights, when the availability of appointed counsel was generally limited, that is how the right inevitably played out: A defendant's right to have the assistance of counsel necessarily meant the right to have the assistance of whatever counsel the defendant was able to secure. But from the beginning, the right to counsel of choice has been circumscribed.

For one thing, a defendant's choice of counsel has always been restricted by the rules governing admission to practice before the court in question.

The right to counsel of choice is also limited by conflict-of-interest rules.

Similarly, the right to be represented by counsel of choice can be limited by mundane case-management considerations. If a trial judge schedules a trial to begin on a particular date and defendant's counsel of choice is already committed for other trials until some time thereafter, the trial judge has discretion under appropriate circumstances to refuse to postpone the trial date and thereby, in effect, to force the defendant to forgo counsel of choice.

These limitations on the right to counsel of choice are tolerable because the focus of the right is the quality of the representation that the defendant receives, not the identity of the attorney who provides the representation. Limiting a defendant to those attorneys who are willing, available, and eligible to represent the defendant still leaves a defendant with a pool of attorneys to choose from-and, in most jurisdictions today, a large and diverse pool. Thus, these restrictions generally have no adverse effect on a defendant's ability to secure the best assistance that the defendant's circumstances permit.

Because the Sixth Amendment focuses on the quality of the assistance that counsel of choice would have provided, I would hold that the erroneous disqualification of counsel does not violate the Sixth Amendment unless the ruling diminishes the quality of assistance that the defendant would have otherwise received. This would not require a defendant to show that the second-choice attorney was constitutionally ineffective within the meaning of *Strickland v. Washington*. Rather, the defendant would be entitled to a new trial if the defendant could show "an identifiable difference in the quality of representation between the disqualified counsel and the attorney who represents the defendant at trial."

But even accepting, as the majority holds, that the erroneous disqualification of counsel of choice always violates the Sixth Amendment, it still would not follow that reversal is required in all cases. * * * [In *Neder v. United States*, 527 U.S. 1 (1999) [p. 1420], the Court applied harmless error analysis after rejecting] the argument that the omission of an element of a crime in a jury instruction "necessarily render[s] a criminal trial fundamentally unfair or an unreliable vehicle for determining guilt or innocence." In fact, in that case, "quite the opposite [was] true: Neder was tried before an impartial judge, under the correct standard of proof and with the assistance of counsel; a fairly selected, impartial jury was instructed to consider all of the evidence and argument in respect to Neder's defense. . . ." *Id.*

Neder's situation—with an impartial judge, the correct standard of proof, assistance of counsel, and a fair jury—is much like respondent's. Fundamental unfairness does not inexorably follow from the denial of first-choice counsel. The "decision to retain a particular lawyer" is "often uninformed;" a defendant's second-choice lawyer may thus turn out to be better than the defendant's first-choice lawyer. More often, a defendant's first-and second-choice lawyers may be simply indistinguishable. These possibilities would not justify violating the right to choice of counsel, but they do make me hard put to characterize the violation as "*always* render[ing] a trial unfair."

Either of the two courses outlined above—requiring at least some showing of prejudice, or engaging in harmless-error review—would avoid the anomalous and unjustifiable consequences that follow from the majority's two-part rule of error without prejudice followed by automatic reversal.

Under the majority's holding, a defendant who is erroneously required to go to trial with a second-choice attorney is automatically entitled to a new trial even if this attorney performed brilliantly.

Under the majority's holding, a trial court may adopt rules severely restricting *pro hac vice* admissions, but if it adopts a generous rule and then errs in interpreting or applying it, the error automatically requires reversal of any conviction, regardless of whether the erroneous ruling had any effect on the defendant.

Under the majority's holding, some defendants will be awarded new trials even though it is clear that the erroneous disqualification of their first-choice counsel did not prejudice them in the least. Suppose, for example, that a defendant is initially represented by an attorney who previously represented the defendant in civil matters and who has little criminal experience. Suppose that this attorney is erroneously disqualified and that the defendant is then able to secure the services of a nationally acclaimed and highly experienced criminal defense attorney who secures a surprisingly favorable result at trial—for instance, acquittal on most but not all counts. Under the majority's holding, the trial court's erroneous ruling automatically means that the Sixth Amendment was violated—even if the defendant makes no attempt to argue that the disqualified attorney would have done a better job. In fact, the defendant would still be entitled to a new trial on the counts of conviction even if the defendant publicly proclaimed after the verdict that the second attorney had provided better representation than any other attorney in the country could have possibly done.

NOTES AND QUESTIONS

1. ***Admission pro hac vice.*** The Supreme Court has not ruled on the extent to which a defendant's right to representation by "counsel of choice" restricts a trial court's authority to deny admission *pro hac vice* when that attorney is licensed in another jurisdiction.[a] Lower courts have suggested that a "court cannot peremptorily refuse to permit representation by out-of-state counsel[, but] it can insist upon special prerequisites to ensure 'ethical and orderly administration of justice,' taking account of possible scheduling difficulties, ease of exchanges between opposing counsel, and past behavior of counsel suggesting a lack of responsibility." CRIMPROC § 11.4(c).

2. ***Scheduling considerations.*** As the *Gonzalez-Lopez* majority notes, a trial court is given "wide latitude in balancing the right to counsel of choice [against] the demands of [the court's] calendar." See also the dissent ("[T]he right to be represented by counsel of choice can be limited by mundane case-management considerations."). Appellate decisions reviewing trial court denials of scheduling accommodations sought by defendants to facilitate representation by counsel of choice typically involve requests for continuances in order to replace current counsel with new counsel. Those decisions agree that trial courts cannot give scheduling concerns per se priority in that situation, but must engage in case-by case balancing. The leading Supreme Court ruling on the subject noted: "The matter of a continuance is traditionally within the trial court's discretion. . . . There are no mechanical tests for deciding when a denial of a continuance is so arbitrary as to violate [defendant's constitutional right]. The answer must be found in the circumstances present in every case, particularly the reasons presented to the trial judge at the time the request is denied." *Ungar v. Sarafite*, 376 U.S. 575 (1964).

As noted in CRIMPROC. § 11.4(c), "[w]hile appellate courts note that they will give considerable leeway to the trial court in its determination not to grant a continuance, a substantial

[a] In *Leis v. Flynt*, 439 U.S. 438 (1979), the Court majority rejected the claim of out-of-state attorneys that the state court's refusal to permit them to represent the defendant in an obscenity prosecution violated the attorneys' constitutional rights. The Court held that the interest of an out-of-state attorney in being allowed to appear *pro hac vice* did not rise to the level of a "cognizable property or liberty interest within the terms of the Fourteenth Amendment." The Court noted that it was not ruling on whether the constitutional rights of the defendant might be violated since that claim was not before it. Three dissenting justices rejected "the notion that a state trial judge has arbitrary and unlimited power to refuse a nonresident lawyer permission to appear in his courtroom," noting that "the client's interest in representation by out-of-state counsel [surely] is entitled to some measure of constitutional protection."

body of cases have found abuses of discretion resulting in a denial of defendants' constitutional rights." Among the factors weighed are whether the request came at a point sufficiently in advance of trial to permit the trial court to readily adjust its calendar, whether the continuance would carry the trial beyond the period specified in the speedy trial act, whether the continuance would inconvenience witnesses, and whether the defendant had some legitimate cause for dissatisfaction with counsel, even though it fell short of the "good cause" that automatically justifies replacement.

3. ***Replacing appointed counsel.*** As both the *Gonzalez-Lopez* majority and dissent note, "the right to counsel of choice does not extend to defendants who require counsel to be appointed for them." Thus, even where the state's practice is to appoint private attorneys to represent indigent defendants, the court has no constitutional obligation to give any weight to a defendant's request for a particular attorney who is both qualified and willing to accept appointment. But see CRIMPROC § 11.4(a) (noting that "[a]t least two states have departed from [this] traditional position," and require the appointing court to weigh any special factors supporting defendant's preference against countervailing administrative considerations); Janet Moore, *The Antidemocratic Sixth Amendment*, 91 Wash. L. Rev. 1705 (2016) (arguing that indigent defendants should have a constitutional right to counsel of choice).

Relatedly, indigent defendants have no right to replace appointed counsel with an alternate counsel who is available and willing to accept appointment apart from certain extreme situations that produce "good cause" for replacing counsel. See infra Note 2, p. 205. Does it follow that the court can replace appointed counsel, notwithstanding defendant's preference to stay with that counsel, even where retention of current counsel requires only a relatively minor disruption in the court's schedule? Consider, in this connection, the situation presented in MORRIS v. SLAPPY, 461 U.S. 1 (1983).

In *Slappy*, the public defender initially assigned to defendant had represented defendant at the preliminary hearing (where defendant was bound over on charges of rape, robbery, and burglary), and had conducted an extensive investigation, before he was hospitalized for emergency surgery shortly before trial. An experienced attorney in the same office was assigned as a replacement, and six days later the trial started as scheduled. After the trial was under way, defendant Slappy, on his own initiative, asked for a continuance, arguing that the replacement attorney had insufficient time to prepare. After the attorney assured the trial court that he was "ready," the continuance was denied. On the third day of trial, Slappy again asked for a continuance, stating that he wanted to be represented by his original attorney and viewed himself as currently unrepresented. When that motion was denied, Slappy announced that he would no longer cooperate with the replacement attorney or participate in the trial. The trial continued and Slappy was convicted on several counts.

On subsequent federal habeas review, the Ninth Circuit overturned the convictions, concluding that the trial court had violated the Sixth Amendment when it failed to take into consideration defendant's interest in continued representation by the original attorney (it had not even inquired into the probable length of that attorney's absence). In reaching this conclusion, the Ninth Circuit noted that the Sixth Amendment "would be without substance if it did not include the right to a meaningful attorney-client relationship," and stated that the trial court had erred in ignoring Slappy's right to a "meaningful attorney-client relationship."

The Supreme Court, per Burger, C.J., overturned the Ninth Circuit ruling. The Court initially found no merit in the claim that a continuance had been needed to allow the replacement counsel to prepare for trial. It also concluded that Slappy's motion on the third day of trial, for a continuance and a return to representation by original counsel, had been untimely. Chief Justice Burger also rejected the Ninth Circuit's vision of the Sixth Amendment:

"The Court of Appeals' conclusion that the Sixth Amendment right to counsel 'would be without substance if it did not include the right to a *meaningful attorney-client relationship*' (emphasis added) is without basis in the law. [No] court could possibly guarantee that a defendant will develop the kind of rapport with his attorney—privately retained or provided by the public—that the Court of Appeals thought part of the Sixth Amendment guarantee of counsel. Accordingly, we reject the claim that the Sixth Amendment guarantees a 'meaningful relationship' between an accused and his counsel."

Although he concurred in the result (because he agreed with the Court that Slappy did not make a timely motion for a continuance based on the original attorney's unavailability), Justice Brennan, joined by Marshall, J., disagreed with the thrust of the Court's reasoning. He noted:

"In light of the importance of a defendant's relationship with his attorney to his Sixth Amendment right to counsel, recognizing a qualified right to continue that relationship is eminently sensible. The Court of Appeals simply held that where a defendant expresses a desire to continue to be represented by counsel who already has been appointed for him by moving for a continuance until that attorney again will be available, the trial judge has an obligation to inquire into the length of counsel's expected unavailability and to balance the defendant's interest against the public's interest in the efficient and expeditious administration of criminal justice. Contrary to the Court's suggestion, this does not require a trial court 'to guarantee' attorney-defendant 'rapport.' * * * The defendant's interest in preserving his relationship with a particular attorney is not afforded absolute protection. If the attorney is likely to be unavailable for an extended period, or if other factors exist that tip the balance in favor of proceeding in spite of a particular attorney's absence, the defendant's motion for a continuance clearly may be denied. Such denials would be subject to review under the traditional 'abuse of discretion' standard. As the Court of Appeals suggested, however, the balancing is critical. In the absence of a balancing inquiry a trial court cannot discharge its 'duty to preserve the fundamental rights of an accused.' "

4. ***Is there a right to counsel of choice on appeal?*** Given that a defendant has no right to proceed *pro se* on appeal and thus can be forced to accept counsel against his will, see *Martinez v. Court of Appeal of California* (discussed supra § 4, Note 3, p. 103), at least one lower court has held that there is no Sixth Amendment right to counsel of choice on appeal. See, e.g., *Tamalini v. Stewart*, 249 F.3d 895 (9th Cir. 2001). But see *State v. Peterson*, 757 N.W.2d 834 (Wis. 2008) (suggesting that there is a limited constitutional right to counsel of choice at a postconviction hearing). Even if such a right exists in theory, some lower courts have recognized that there is a potential conflict of interest in having the same lawyer at trial and on appeal, because defendants often raise the ineffectiveness of their trial counsel as a claim for relief on appeal, and an attorney cannot be expected to raise his or her own ineffectiveness. See, e.g., Adam Liptak, *Longtime Death Case Lawyer Appeals Ouster*, N.Y. Times (Mar. 24, 2003) (describing one such case); see also Eve Brensike Primus, *Structural Reform in Criminal Defense: Relocating Ineffective Assistance of Counsel Claims*, 92 Cornell L. Rev. 679, 724–27 (2007) (arguing that new counsel should be required for all criminal defendants on appeal for this reason) (discussed infra Chapter 5, § 1, Note 4, p. 125).

5. ***Forfeiture statutes and the right to counsel of choice.*** In CAPLIN & DRYSDALE, CHARTERED v. UNITED STATES, 491 U.S. 617 (1989), a law firm sued the United States government to recover legal fees that it did not receive after defending Charles Reckmeyer on charges of running an illegal drug operation. The law firm had not received its fees, because the government had seized Reckmeyer's funds in accordance with a federal statute providing that a person convicted of specified drug violations forfeits all property "constituting or derived from" the proceeds of those violations. This federal statute, the law firm argued, effectively denies defendants convicted of the qualifying drug offenses of their Sixth Amendment rights to counsel of choice. The Supreme Court, in a 5–4 decision written by Justice White, disagreed, noting that

a "defendant has no Sixth Amendment right to spend another person's money for services rendered by an attorney, even if those funds are the only way that defendant will be able to retain the counsel of his choice." The majority also noted that "there is a strong governmental interest in obtaining full recovery of all forfeitable assets, an interest that overrides any Sixth Amendment interest in permitting criminals to use assets adjudged forfeitable to pay for their defense." That governmental interest, according to Justice White, includes (1) an interest in "recovering all forfeitable assets, for such assets are deposited in a Fund that supports law-enforcement efforts in a variety of important and useful ways;" (2) an interest in "returning property, in full, to those wrongfully deprived or defrauded of it;" and (3) an interest in "lessen[ing] the economic power of organized crime and drug enterprises."

In a companion case, *United States v. Monsanto*, 491 U.S. 600 (1989), the Supreme Court extended its holding in *Caplin & Drysdale* to permit statutorily-authorized *pre-trial* seizure of assets accumulated as a result of alleged narcotics trafficking. Justice White again wrote for the 5–4 majority: "[I]f the Government may, post-trial, forbid the use of forfeited assets to pay an attorney, then surely no constitutional violation occurs when, after probable cause is adequately established, the Government obtains an order barring a defendant from frustrating that end by dissipating his assets prior to trial."

The Supreme Court limited the scope of *Caplin & Drysdale* and *Monsanto* in LUIS v. UNITED STATES, 136 S.Ct. 1083 (2016), when it drew a sharp distinction between, on the one hand, assets obtained as a result of the crime or property that is traceable to the crime and, on the other hand, property that is untainted by the defendant's alleged criminal activities. According to five members of the Court, "the pretrial restraint of legitimate, untainted assets needed to retain counsel of choice violates the Sixth Amendment." Justice Breyer, writing for a plurality, distinguished *Caplin & Drysdale* and *Monsanto*, noting that, in those cases, the property was " 'tainted,' and that title to the property therefore had passed from the defendant to the Government before the court issued its order freezing (or otherwise disposing of) the assets." When the property is untainted, however, it remains the property of the defendant and the Government has no "equivalent governmental interest in that property." The plurality then balanced the government's interest in restraining defendant's use of her property against her Sixth Amendment right to retain counsel, and noted that "a Sixth Amendment right to assistance of counsel . . . is a fundamental constituent of due process of law," whereas the Government's contingent interest in securing criminal forfeiture and the victims' interest in securing restitution "would seem to lie somewhat further from the heart of a fair, effective criminal justice system." Justice Thomas disagreed with this balancing approach, but agreed that a pretrial freeze of untainted assets violates the Sixth Amendment right to counsel of choice, because "history" and "the common law drew a clear line between tainted and untainted assets."

Justice Kennedy, writing for himself and Justice Alito, dissented noting that the majority's decision is inconsistent with precedent and "rewards criminals who hurry to spend, conceal, or launder stolen property by assuring them that they may use their own funds to pay for an attorney after they have dissipated the proceeds of their crime." Justice Kagan wrote a separate dissent questioning the wisdom of the Court's decision in *Monsanto*, but noting that the result in this case should be dictated by that precedent. Do you agree with the majority or the dissent? Do you think drawing a line between tainted and untainted assets is workable?

CHAPTER 5

THE PERFORMANCE OF COUNSEL

■ ■ ■

§ 1. THE INEFFECTIVE ASSISTANCE OF COUNSEL (IAC) CLAIM: BASIC FEATURES

1. ***Supreme Court recognition.*** The Supreme Court's seminal ruling in *Powell v. Alabama* (1932) is known primarily as being the first Supreme Court ruling to establish a constitutional right to the appointment of counsel to assist an indigent defendant (see p. 65). *Powell*, however, also laid the foundation for the IAC claim. *Powell* noted that "the state's [due process] duty [to provide appointed counsel] is not discharged by an appointment at such time or under such circumstances as to preclude the giving of effective aid in preparation of the trial of the case," and it concluded that the appointment in the case before it suffered from that flaw (see Note 2, p. 168). Between *Powell* and the *Gideon* ruling in 1963 (holding the Sixth Amendment right to counsel applicable to the states, see p. 68), the Court acknowledged in various contexts that the right to appointed counsel, under either the due process clause (in state cases) or the Sixth Amendment (in federal cases), encompassed an element of adequate performance by that appointed counsel. A failure in the "representation rendered," the Court noted, could "convert the appointment of counsel * * * [into a] sham." Only one case, *Glasser v. United States,* Note 1, p. 179, found a Sixth Amendment violation, and that was based on the trial court having taken action that prevented defendant's counsel from providing the "effective assistance of counsel." It was not until several years after *Gideon* that the Court began to refer to a defense right to challenge a conviction based solely on counsel's inadequate performance—described as an "ineffective assistance of counsel claim" (a description today commonly shortened in commentary and judicial opinions to the "IAC claim"). That claim was said to have its roots in the earliest Supreme Court discussions of the constitutional right to counsel's assistance, starting with *Powell.*

2. ***The prerequisite constitutional right.*** The IAC claim does not distinguish between appointed and retained counsel. See *Cuyler v. Sullivan*, 446 U.S. 335 (1980) (rejecting the contention that a less rigorous standard should apply to retained counsel since the defendant chose that counsel). However, the IAC claim only applies where there is a constitutional right to the assistance of counsel that extends to both appointed and retained counsel. It has been argued that, in some additional settings, there is a separate constitutionally protected right to utilize the assistance of retained counsel, recognizing the individual's interest in "defending himself in whatever manner he deems best, using every legitimate resource at his command." *People v. Crovedi*, 417 P.2d 868 (Cal. 1966). Consider also fn. a at p. 87. *Wainwright v. Torna*, 455 U.S. 586 (1982), flatly rejected extending the IAC claim to one such possible situation. There, respondent Torna's felony convictions had been affirmed by an intermediate state appellate court. His subsequent application for a writ of certiorari was dismissed by the state supreme court because it had not been filed timely. Respondent contended that he had been denied the effective assistance of counsel by the failure of his retained counsel to file that application in time. Summarily reversing a federal habeas ruling that had sustained respondent's contention, the Court majority (per curiam) held that respondent had no constitutional right to retain counsel's effective assistance. It noted: "*Ross v. Moffitt* [p. 95] held that a criminal defendant does not have a constitutional right to counsel to pursue discretionary state appeals or applications for review in this Court. [Since] respondent had no constitutional right to counsel, he could not be deprived of

the effective assistance of counsel by his retained counsel's failure to file the application timely." *Torna's* reference to the absence of a "constitutional right to counsel" centered on a constitutional right that guarantees representation by retained or appointed counsel, based on a need to ensure fairness in the proceeding. That was the character of the proposed right to counsel rejected in *Ross v. Moffit*. *Torna* is not read as suggesting that the state constitutionally could have precluded Torna's reliance on retained counsel in filing an application for review, but simply as holding that, at that stage, the client must "bear the consequences of his unwise choice of counsel." CRIMPROC § 11.7a.[a]

3. ***The adversarial process benchmark.*** It was not until 1984, in the companion rulings of *United States v. Cronic* and *Strickland v. Washington*, that the Court "articulat[ed] a comprehensive conception of ineffective assistance of counsel." CRIMPROC § 11.7(c). As *Strickland* noted, previous rulings largely had involved judicial restrictions upon counsel's performance and the Court had no occasion "to elaborate on the meaning of the constitutional requirement of effective assistance * * * in cases presenting claims of 'actual ineffectiveness' "—i.e., where "counsel * * * deprive[d] a defendant of the right to effective assistance * * * simply by failing to render 'adequate legal assistance.' " In both *Cronic* and *Strickland*, the Court stressed that the actual performance of counsel was to be evaluated in light of the underlying purpose of the constitutional right to counsel—providing what *Strickland* described as an adversarial process "benchmark" (p. 128). See also Note 2, p. 135 (discussing commentator criticism of the grounding for that benchmark, as it was explained in *Cronic* (below) and *Strickland*).

UNITED STATES v. CRONIC, 466 U.S. 648 (1984), the first announced of the two cases, did not require the Court to apply its performance benchmark. As discussed in Note 2, p. 167, the lower court there had concluded that the circumstances faced by appointed counsel justified presuming that counsel's performance had been constitutionally deficient. A unanimous Supreme Court rejected that reasoning, and remanded for consideration of the adequacy of counsel's actual performance. The function of the counsel guarantee, it reasoned, required looking to counsel's actual performance, rather than presuming inadequacy, absent special situations that were not present in this case. The Court (per Stevens, J.) offered the following description, of that function and its shaping of the IAC claim.

"The substance of the Constitution's guarantee of the effective-assistance of counsel is illuminated by reference to its underlying purpose. '[T]ruth,' Lord Eldon said, 'is best discovered by powerful statements on both sides of the question.' * * * The very premise of our adversary system of criminal justice is that partisan advocacy on both sides of a case will best promote the ultimate objective that the guilty be convicted and the innocent go free. * * * Unless the accused receives the effective assistance of counsel, a serious risk of injustice infects the trial itself. * * * Thus, the adversarial process protected by the Sixth Amendment requires that the accused have, 'counsel acting in the role of an advocate'. The right to the effective assistance of counsel is * * * the right of the accused to require the prosecution's case to survive the crucible of meaningful adversarial testing. When a true adversarial criminal trial has been conducted—even if defense counsel may have made demonstrable errors—the kind of testing envisioned by the Sixth Amendment has occurred. But if the process loses its character as a confrontation between adversaries, the constitutional guarantee is violated.

[a] Many states provide assigned counsel for the indigent defendants in one or more settings (e.g., collateral proceedings) in which the constitution does not require such appointment. See Pt. B, p. 92, and Note 6(b), p. 1428. Some of those states read the statutory provision requiring those appointments as allowing a challenge to the performance of that counsel under a state IAC claim, which may or may not apply the same performance standard as the federal constitutional claim. The IAC standards of the federal constitutional claim are also utilized in some contexts in determining whether objections can be raised for the first time in a federal habeas proceeding. See Note 1(b), p. 1438, and Note 1(d), p. 1439.

"The Court of Appeals * * * [here] did not indicated that there had been an actual breakdown of the adversarial process during the trial of this case, * * * [but] instead * * * [adopted] an inference that counsel was unable to discharge his duties. In our evaluation of this conclusion, we begin by recognizing that the right to effective counsel is recognized not for its own sake, but because of the effect it has on the ability of the accused to receive a fair trial. Absent some effect of challenged conduct on the reliability of the trial process, the Sixth Amendment guarantee is generally not implicated."

4. ***Raising an ineffectiveness claim.*** Three major obstacles restrict raising an IAC claim on direct appeal from a conviction: (1) very often, the attorney on appeal is the trial counsel or an appellate specialist in the same office, and those attorneys not only are unlikely to look to their own (or their colleague's) ineptitude in developing grounds for appeal, but if they do look there, they face the ethical restrictions imposed on an attorney challenging his own (or his colleague's) representation; (2) many IAC claims are based on actions or omissions that are not revealed in the trial court record (e.g., a failure to investigate); and (3) even where the claim is based on an action by counsel reflected in the trial record, and the trial record suggests no explanation for that action other than incompetence, an off-record explanation could cast that action in an entirely different light, providing a reasonable strategic justification for the action. Because of these obstacles, most jurisdictions prefer that IAC claims be presented on collateral attack (where both sides have the opportunity to present evidence that goes beyond the trial record and the defendant can raise the claim *pro se* or with a different attorney).

Some jurisdictions have concluded that so few IAC claims can be resolved on the trial record that all claims must be presented on collateral attack; they find greater benefit in ensuring that all aspects of potentially ineffective assistance are considered together than in allowing the few exceptions to be raised on direct appeal. Other jurisdictions allow IAC claims to be raised on appeal where the grounding for the claim arguably appears in the trial court record. They warn the defendant, however, that the limitations of that record may impact review of the claim. As noted in *United States v. Taglia*, 922 F.2d 413 (7th Cir.1991): "When the only record on which a claim of ineffective assistance is based is the trial record, every indulgence will be given to the possibility that a seeming lapse or error by defense counsel was in fact a tactical move flawed only in hindsight." Thus, the defendant must establish that there could be no explanation for counsel's performance other than counsel's ineptitude, and if the defendant fails to make that showing on the trial record, there will be no possibility of expanding the record on collateral attack, as rejection of a claim on appeal ordinarily precludes reconsideration on collateral attack. Still other jurisdictions seek to distinguish between claims depending upon whether they can be presented fully on appeal; where that condition can be met, and new counsel represents the defendant on appeal, the claim must be raised on appeal (a failure to do so results in forfeiture of the claim).

Some commentators and courts have argued against the above approaches. They view deferring all (or most) IAC claims to collateral attack as having serious drawbacks for both the judiciary and the defendant. The state judiciary can readily be subjected to the wasteful use of limited resources: (1) in having bifurcated review of a single conviction (the initial appellate review and the subsequent postconviction proceeding on the IAC claim, with another appeal possible from that proceeding); (2) in dealing with borderline frivolous appeals by appointed appellate counsel who face a trial record devoid of any significant direct-appeal issues because of the trial counsel's incompetence; and (3) where trial counsel failed to object to possible trial errors apparent on the record, requiring the appellate court to first address whether those errors should be reviewable, notwithstanding the lack of objection, under the "plain error" doctrine, even though a court on collateral attack will subsequently consider whether that lack of objection establishes the ineffective assistance of counsel. The drawbacks for the defendant stem primarily from delay and procedural obstacles that accompany collateral review in many states. State postconviction proceedings are available only after the exhaustion of appellate review, which typically will take at least a few years (and in some jurisdictions as much as 4 or 5 years). At that point, the time gap makes investigation more difficult, both in establishing what trial counsel failed to do and what would have been uncovered if counsel had done more. The delay also may operate to preclude collateral-attack IAC claims by the many defendants who have served their prison sentences or completed their probationary terms, as many jurisdictions allow collateral attacks only by convicted persons who remain in custody. Another procedural obstacle in many jurisdictions is the absence of a right to appointed counsel on collateral attack. See Notes 6(b), p. 1428, 1(d), p. 1439.

These drawbacks have led commentators to urge that the challenge procedure be restructured to facilitate raising IAC claims at the trial court level, prior to pursuing an appeal, rather than on collateral attack. See Eve Brensike Primus, *Structural Reform in Criminal Defense: Relocating Ineffective Assistance of Counsel Claims*, 92 Cornell L.Rev. 679 (2007) (presenting the most complete restructuring proposal, which would include: (1) requiring, as to appointed and retained counsel, that appellate counsel be different from trial counsel; (2) giving appellate counsel at least six months to investigate the possibility that trial counsel was ineffective; (3) extending time limits for new trial motions to cover this period and thereby allow the new counsel to supplement the record and raise an IAC claim in the trial court.) A small group of states have moved partially in this direction. Thus, several states allow appellate counsel to request a remand to the trial court to pursue an evidentiary hearing on an IAC claim. However, such procedures often impose "unrealistic time limits," do not guarantee an opportunity for an evidentiary hearing, and do not provide for new appellate counsel. See Primus, supra. No state has adopted a critical prerequisite for requiring all defendants to seek an appellate remand when they desire to raise an IAC claim—prohibiting retained trial counsel from also representing the defendant on appeal. See Note 4, p. 120. But consider *Frazier v. State*, 303 S.W.3d 674 (Tenn. 2010) (retained postconviction counsel who was also retained trial counsel had an inherent conflict of interest as to a possible ineffective-assistance claim, requiring disqualification or a valid waiver by the client).

5. ***Counsel's testimony.*** When an ineffective assistance claim is presented on collateral attack or a new trial motion, an evidentiary hearing permits the defendant to establish what occurred in counsel's pretrial preparation, what communications occurred between defendant and counsel, and what might have occurred if counsel had taken other actions (e.g., what further investigation would have revealed). In this connection, the defendant (or the prosecution) may require the trial counsel to testify. Moreover, that testimony may reveal conversations between the client and the lawyer, as the challenge to counsel's performance constitutes an implicit waiver of the lawyer-client privilege. Courts are divided as to whether the waiver extends to subsequent use of counsel's testimony against the defendant in another proceeding and whether the waiver extends to the prosecution's examination of the attorney's entire trial file (which may provide a better picture of the attorney's overall performance). See CRIMPROC § 11.7(e). See also Notes 2–4, pp. 159–160 (addressing the treatment of counsel's testimony).

§ 2. THE *STRICKLAND* STANDARDS

1. ***Pre-*Strickland.** Prior to the Supreme Court's ruling in *Strickland*, infra, lower courts had divided on several aspects of the IAC claim. Initially, there was division in their description of the level of performance that would be so deficient as to constitute ineffective assistance. For many years, the prevailing test had been whether counsel's performance was so poor "as to reduce the trial to a 'farce' or render it a mockery of justice." Courts varied in their interpretation of this vague standard, but some clearly required lawyering so inept as to fail completely to challenge the prosecution's case. However, many courts had moved to a standard that asked whether counsel's performance reflected the skills and diligence generally expected from criminal defense attorneys. In applying that performance standard, most courts looked to the totality of the performance under the circumstances of the particular case—an approach commonly characterized as "judgmental."

See *United States v. Decoster*, 624 F.2d 196 (D.C.Cir.1976) (Leventhal, J.). However, several lower court judges had called for adoption of a "categorical approach," which measured performance against a checklist of minimum duties owed to the client (typically duties noted in the *ABA Standards Relating to the Defense Function*). See e.g., *United States v. Decoster*, supra (Bazelon, J. dissenting).

Lower courts also were divided on the needed showing as to the impact of counsel's deficient performance. Opinions promoting a categorical approach argued that no such showing should be necessary, but all but a few courts concluded that some showing of "prejudice" was needed to establish the ineffective assistance of counsel. There was considerable variation, however, in the description of that showing. Some courts focused simply on whether there would otherwise have been a substantial difference in the thrust of the representation, while others looked to the likelihood of a difference in the outcome of the prosecution (with those courts then differing as to the needed degree of likelihood).

In *Strickland*, the en banc Court of Appeals had referred to these divisions, and was itself divided both on the use of a quasi-categorical approach and the appropriate standard of prejudice. The Supreme Court opinion in *Strickland* responded not only to the specific rulings below, but to the various divisions among lower courts in their basic conception of the IAC claim.

STRICKLAND V. WASHINGTON

466 U.S. 668, 104 S.Ct. 2052, 80 L.Ed.2d 674 (1984).

JUSTICE O'CONNOR delivered the opinion of the Court. * * *

During a 10-day period * * *, respondent [Washington] planned and committed three groups of crimes, which included three brutal stabbing murders, torture, kidnaping, severe assaults, attempted murders, attempted extortion, and theft. After his two accomplices were arrested, respondent surrendered to police and voluntarily gave a lengthy statement confessing to the third of the criminal episodes. [He was indicted and the state court] * * * appointed an experienced criminal lawyer to represent him.

Counsel actively pursued pretrial motions and discovery. He cut his efforts short, however, and he experienced a sense of hopelessness about the case, when he learned that, against his specific advice, respondent had also confessed to the first two murders. By the date set for trial, respondent was subject to indictment for three counts of first-degree murder and multiple counts of robbery, kidnaping for ransom, breaking and entering and assault, attempted murder, and conspiracy to commit robbery. Respondent waived his right to a jury trial, again acting against counsel's advice, and pleaded guilty to all charges, including the three capital murder charges.

In the plea colloquy, respondent told the trial judge that, although he had committed a string of burglaries, he had no significant prior criminal record and that at the time of his criminal spree he was under extreme stress caused by his inability to support his family. He also stated, however, that he accepted responsibility for the crimes. The trial judge told respondent that he had "a great deal of respect for people who are willing to step forward and admit their responsibility" but that he was making no statement at all about his likely sentencing decision. * * * Counsel advised respondent to invoke his right under Florida law to an advisory jury at his capital sentencing hearing. Respondent rejected the advice and waived the right. He chose instead to be sentenced by the trial judge without a jury recommendation.

In preparing for the sentencing hearing, counsel spoke with respondent about his background. He also spoke on the telephone with respondent's wife and mother, though he did not follow up on the one unsuccessful effort to meet with them. He did not otherwise seek out character witnesses for respondent. Nor did he request a psychiatric examination, since his conversations with his client gave no indication that respondent had psychological problems. * * * [Counsel's decision] not to present and hence not to look further for evidence concerning respondent's character and emotional state * * * reflected counsel's sense of hopelessness about overcoming the evidentiary effect of respondent's confessions to the gruesome crimes. It also reflected the judgment that it was advisable to rely on the plea colloquy for evidence about respondent's background and about his claim of emotional stress: the plea colloquy communicated sufficient information about these subjects, and by forgoing the opportunity to present new evidence on these subjects, counsel prevented the State from cross-examining respondent on his claim and from putting on psychiatric evidence of its own.

Counsel also excluded from the sentencing hearing other evidence he thought was potentially damaging. He successfully moved to exclude respondent's "rap sheet." Because he judged that a presentence report might prove more detrimental than helpful, as it would have included respondent's criminal history and thereby would have undermined the claim of no significant history of criminal activity, he did not request that one be prepared.

At the sentencing hearing, counsel's strategy was based primarily on the trial judge's remarks at the plea colloquy as well as on his reputation as a sentencing judge who thought it important for a convicted defendant to own up to his crime. Counsel argued that respondent's remorse and acceptance of responsibility justified sparing him from the death penalty. Counsel also argued that respondent had no history of criminal activity and that respondent committed the crimes under extreme mental or emotional disturbance, thus coming within the statutory list of mitigating circumstances. He further argued that respondent should be spared death because he had surrendered, confessed, and offered to testify against a codefendant and because respondent was fundamentally a good person who had briefly gone badly wrong in extremely stressful circumstances. The State put on evidence and witnesses largely for the purpose of describing the details of the crimes. * * *

[T]he trial judge found numerous aggravating circumstances and no (or a single comparatively insignificant) mitigating circumstance. With respect to each of the three convictions for capital murder, the trial judge concluded: "A careful consideration of all matters presented to the court impels the conclusion that there are insufficient mitigating circumstances . . . to outweigh the aggravating circumstances." He therefore sentenced respondent to death on each of the three counts of murder and to prison terms for the other crimes. The Florida Supreme Court upheld the convictions and sentences on direct appeal. * * *

[Washington subsequently sought collateral relief in state court. In support of his claim of ineffective assistance of counsel, Washington submitted 14 affidavits from "friends, neighbors, and relatives" stating that they would have provided favorable character evidence if asked. He also submitted "one psychiatric report and one psychological report stating that respondent, though not under the influence of extreme emotional disturbance, was 'chronically frustrated and depressed because of his economic dilemma.' " In denying the ineffectiveness claim, the state court noted that counsel could reasonably have decided not to seek psychiatric reports, as a previous psychiatric examination, conducted by state order soon after Washington's arraignment, had stated that there was no indication of major medical illness, and the two reports now submitted by Washington similarly failed to establish the extreme mental or emotional disturbance that constituted a mitigating circumstance. Relying on the plea colloquy and thereby cutting off the state's use of psychiatric rebuttal testimony was a reasonable strategy. The state court also concluded that, "in any event, the aggravating circumstances were so overwhelming that no substantial prejudice resulted from the absence at sentencing of the psychiatric evidence offered in the collateral attack." It then "rejected the challenge to counsel's failure to develop and to present character evidence for much the same reasons."

[Washington subsequently sought federal habeas relief, claiming ineffective assistance on essentially the same grounds presented in the state collateral proceedings. Although conducting an evidentiary hearing, the district court "disputed none of the state court's factual findings concerning trial counsel's assistance and made findings of its own that [were] consistent with the state court findings." The district court "concluded that, although trial counsel made errors in judgment in failing to investigate nonstatutory mitigating evidence further * * *, no prejudice resulted." On review, the Court of Appeals, sitting en banc, developed a special "framework" for analyzing ineffective assistance claims based on the failure to investigate, and remanded the case "for new factfinding under the newly announced standards." The Court of Appeals majority drew a distinction between a failure to investigate where "there is only one plausible line of defense" and "where there is more than one plausible line," the former requiring substantial investigation and the latter allowing counsel at some point to make a strategic decision not to pursue (and hence not to further investigate) a certain line of defense. As to both situations, the en banc majority outlined in some detail the factors to be considered in determining whether counsel fulfilled the duty to investigate. The majority also concluded that, as to prejudice, it was sufficient to show that counsel's violation of that duty "resulted in actual and substantial disadvantage"; it "expressly rejected the prejudice standard articulated * * * in [the] plurality opinion in * * * *Decoster* [Note 1, p. 126] * * * requir[ing] a showing that specified deficient conduct of counsel was likely to have affected the outcome of the proceeding."]

* * * [This] Court has recognized that "the right to counsel is the right to the effective assistance of counsel." *McMann v. Richardson*, 397 U.S. 759 (1970). Government violates the right to effective counsel when it interferes in certain ways with the ability of counsel to make independent decisions about how to conduct the defense [citing the cases discussed in Note 5, p. 170]. Counsel, however, can also deprive a defendant of the right to effective legal assistance, simply by failing to render "adequate legal assistance" * * *. The Court has not elaborated on the meaning of the constitutional requirement of effective assistance in the latter class of cases—that is, those presenting claims of "actual ineffectiveness." In giving meaning to the requirement, however, we must take its purpose—to ensure a fair trial—as the guide. The benchmark for judging any claim of ineffectiveness must be whether counsel's conduct so undermined the proper functioning of the adversarial process that the trial cannot be relied on as having produced a just result.

The same principle applies to a capital sentencing proceeding such as that provided by Florida law. We need not consider the role of counsel in an ordinary sentencing, which may involve informal proceedings and standardless discretion in the sentencer, and hence may require a different approach to the definition of constitutionally effective assistance. A capital sentencing proceeding like the one involved in this case, however, is sufficiently like a trial in its adversarial format and in the existence of standards for decision that counsel's role in the proceeding is comparable to counsel's role at trial—to ensure that the adversarial testing process works to produce a just result under the standards governing decision. For purposes of describing counsel's duties, therefore, Florida's capital sentencing proceeding need not be distinguished from an ordinary trial.

A convicted defendant's claim that counsel's assistance was so defective as to require reversal of a conviction or death sentence has two components. First, the defendant must show that counsel's performance was deficient. This requires showing that counsel made errors so serious that counsel was not functioning as the "counsel" guaranteed the defendant by the Sixth Amendment. Second, the defendant must show that the deficient performance prejudiced the defense. This requires showing that counsel's errors were so serious as to deprive the defendant of a fair trial, a trial whose result is reliable. Unless a defendant makes both showings, it cannot be said that the conviction or death sentence resulted from a breakdown in the adversary process that renders the result unreliable.

As all the Federal Courts of Appeals have now held, the proper standard for attorney performance is that of reasonably effective assistance. The Court indirectly recognized as much when it stated in *McMann,* supra, that a guilty plea cannot be attacked as based on inadequate legal advice unless counsel was not "a reasonably competent attorney" and the advice was not "within the range of competence demanded of attorneys in criminal cases." When a convicted defendant complains of the ineffectiveness of counsel's assistance, the defendant must show that counsel's representation fell below an objective standard of reasonableness.

More specific guidelines are not appropriate. The Sixth Amendment refers simply to "counsel," not specifying particular requirements of effective assistance. It relies instead on the legal profession's maintenance of standards sufficient to justify the law's presumption that counsel will fulfill the role in the adversary process that the Amendment envisions. The proper measure of attorney performance remains simply reasonableness under prevailing professional norms.

Representation of a criminal defendant entails certain basic duties. Counsel's function is to assist the defendant, and hence counsel owes the client a duty of loyalty, a duty to avoid conflicts of interest. From counsel's function as assistant to the defendant derive the overarching duty to advocate the defendant's cause and the more particular duties to consult with the defendant on important decisions and to keep the defendant informed of important developments in the course of the prosecution. Counsel also has a duty to bring to bear such skill and knowledge as will render the trial a reliable adversarial testing process.

These basic duties neither exhaustively define the obligations of counsel nor form a checklist for judicial evaluation of attorney performance. In any case presenting an ineffectiveness claim, the performance inquiry must be whether counsel's assistance was reasonable considering all the circumstances. Prevailing norms of practice as reflected in American Bar Association standards and the like are guides to determining what is reasonable, but they are only guides. No particular set of detailed rules for counsel's conduct can satisfactorily take account of the variety of circumstances faced by defense counsel or the range of legitimate decisions regarding how best to represent a criminal defendant. Any such set of rules would interfere with the constitutionally protected independence of counsel and restrict the wide latitude counsel must have in making tactical decisions. See *United States v. Decoster* [Note 1, p. 126]. Indeed, the existence of detailed guidelines for representation could distract counsel from the overriding mission of vigorous advocacy of the defendant's cause. Moreover, the purpose of the effective assistance guarantee of the Sixth Amendment is not to improve the quality of legal representation, although that is a goal of considerable importance to the legal system. The purpose is simply to ensure that criminal defendants receive a fair trial.

Judicial scrutiny of counsel's performance must be highly deferential. It is all too tempting for a defendant to second-guess counsel's assistance after conviction or adverse sentence, and it is all too easy for a court, examining counsel's defense after it has proved unsuccessful, to conclude that a particular act or omission of counsel was unreasonable. A fair assessment of attorney performance requires that every effort be made to eliminate the distorting effects of hindsight, to reconstruct the circumstances of counsel's challenged conduct, and to evaluate the conduct from counsel's perspective at the time. Because of the difficulties inherent in making the evaluation, a court must indulge a strong presumption that counsel's conduct falls within the wide range of reasonable professional assistance; that is, the defendant must overcome the presumption that, under the circumstances, the challenged action "might be considered sound trial strategy." There are countless ways to provide effective assistance in any given case. Even the best criminal defense attorneys would not defend a particular client in the same way.

The availability of intrusive post-trial inquiry into attorney performance or of detailed guidelines for its evaluation would encourage the proliferation of ineffectiveness challenges. Criminal trials resolved unfavorably to the defendant would increasingly come to be followed by a second trial, this one of counsel's unsuccessful defense. Counsel's performance and even willingness to serve could be adversely affected. * * *

Thus, a court deciding an actual ineffectiveness claim must judge the reasonableness of counsel's challenged conduct on the facts of the particular case, viewed as of the time of counsel's conduct. A convicted defendant making a claim of ineffective assistance must identify the acts or omissions of counsel that are alleged not to have been the result of reasonable professional judgment. The court must then determine whether, in light of all the circumstances, the identified acts or omissions were outside the wide range of professionally competent assistance. In making that determination, the court should keep in mind that counsel's function, as elaborated in prevailing professional norms, is to make the adversarial testing process work in the particular case. At the same time, the court should recognize that counsel is strongly presumed to have rendered adequate assistance and made all significant decisions in the exercise of reasonable professional judgment.

These standards require no special amplification in order to define counsel's duty to investigate, the duty at issue in this case. As the Court of Appeals concluded, strategic choices made after thorough investigation of law and facts relevant to plausible options are virtually unchallengeable; and strategic choices made after less than complete investigation are reasonable precisely to the extent that reasonable professional judgments support the limitations on investigation. In other words, counsel has a duty to make a reasonable investigation or to make a reasonable decision that makes particular investigations unnecessary. In any ineffectiveness case, a particular decision not to investigate must be directly assessed for reasonableness in all the circumstances, applying a heavy measure of deference to counsel's judgments.

The reasonableness of counsel's actions may be determined or substantially influenced by the defendant's own statements or actions. Counsel's actions are usually based, quite properly, on informed strategic choices made by the defendant and on information supplied by the defendant. In particular, what investigation decisions are reasonable depends critically on such information. For example, when the facts that support a certain potential line of defense are generally known to counsel because of what the defendant has said, the need for further investigation may be considerably diminished or eliminated altogether. And when a defendant has given counsel reason to believe that pursuing certain investigations would be fruitless or even harmful, counsel's failure to pursue those investigations may not later be challenged as unreasonable. In short, inquiry into counsel's conversations with the defendant may be critical to a proper assessment of counsel's investigation decisions, just as it may be critical to a proper assessment of counsel's other litigation decisions.

An error by counsel, even if professionally unreasonable, does not warrant setting aside the judgment of a criminal proceeding if the error had no effect on the judgment. The purpose of the Sixth Amendment guarantee of counsel is to ensure that a defendant has the assistance necessary to justify reliance on the outcome of the proceeding. Accordingly, any deficiencies in counsel's performance must be prejudicial to the defense in order to constitute ineffective assistance under the Constitution.

In certain Sixth Amendment contexts, prejudice is presumed. Actual or constructive denial of the assistance of counsel altogether is legally presumed to result in prejudice. So are various kinds of state interference with counsel's assistance. *United States v. Cronic*, fn. 25 [see p. 168]. Prejudice in these circumstances is so likely that case by case inquiry into prejudice is not worth the cost. Moreover, such circumstances involve impairments of the Sixth Amendment right that are easy to identify and, for that reason and because the prosecution is directly responsible, easy for the government to prevent.

One type of actual ineffectiveness claim warrants a similar, though more limited, presumption of prejudice. In *Cuyler v. Sullivan* [Note 6, p. 182], the Court held that prejudice is presumed when counsel is burdened by an actual conflict of interest. In those circumstances, counsel breaches the duty of loyalty, perhaps the most basic of counsel's duties. Moreover, it is difficult to measure the precise effect on the defense of representation corrupted by conflicting interest. Given the obligation of counsel to avoid conflicts of interest and the ability of trial courts to make early inquiry in certain situations likely to give rise to conflicts, see e.g., Fed.R.Crim.P. 44(c), it is reasonable for the criminal justice system to maintain a fairly rigid rule of presumed prejudice for conflicts of interest. Even so, the rule is not quite the *per se* rule of prejudice that exists for the Sixth Amendment claims mentioned above. Prejudice is presumed only if the defendant demonstrates that counsel "actively represented conflicting interests" and "that an actual conflict of interest adversely affected his lawyer's performance." *Cuyler v. Sullivan.*

Conflict of interest claims aside, actual ineffectiveness claims alleging a deficiency in attorney performance are subject to a general requirement that the defendant affirmatively prove prejudice. The government is not responsible for, and hence not able to prevent, attorney errors that will result in reversal of a conviction or sentence. Attorney errors cannot be classified according to likelihood of causing prejudice. Nor can they be defined with sufficient precision to inform defense attorneys correctly just what conduct to avoid. Representation is an art, and an act or omission that is unprofessional in one case may be sound or even brilliant in another. Even if a defendant shows that particular errors of counsel were unreasonable, therefore, the defendant must show that they actually had an adverse effect on the defense.

It is not enough for the defendant to show that the errors had some conceivable effect on the outcome of the proceeding. Virtually every act or omission of counsel would meet that test, and not every error that conceivably could have influenced the outcome undermines the reliability of the result of the proceeding. Respondent suggests requiring a showing that the errors "impaired the presentation of the defense." That standard, however, provides no workable principle. Since any error, if it is indeed an error, "impairs" the presentation of the defense, the proposed standard [provides] no way of deciding what impairments are sufficiently serious to warrant setting aside the outcome of the proceeding.

On the other hand, we believe that a defendant need not show that counsel's deficient conduct more likely than not altered the outcome in the case. * * * [While this standard] * * * is widely used for assessing motions for new trial based on newly discovered evidence * * *, it is not quite appropriate. * * * The high standard for newly discovered evidence claims presupposes that all essential elements of a presumptively accurate and fair proceeding were present in the proceeding whose result is challenged. An ineffective assistance claim asserts the absence of one of the crucial assurances * * *, so finality concerns are somewhat weaker and the appropriate standard of prejudice should be somewhat lower. * * * Accordingly, the appropriate test for prejudice finds its roots in the test for materiality of exculpatory information not disclosed to the defense by the prosecution, *United States v. Agurs*, 427 U.S. 97 (1976), and in the test for materiality of testimony made unavailable to the defense by Government deportation of a witness, *United States v. Valenzuela-Bernal*, 458 U.S. 858 (1982). The defendant must show that there is a reasonable probability that, but for counsel's unprofessional errors, the result of the proceeding would have been different. A reasonable probability is a probability sufficient to undermine confidence in the outcome.

In making [this] determination, * * * a court should presume, absent challenge to the judgment on grounds of evidentiary insufficiency, that the judge or jury acted according to law. An assessment of the likelihood of a result more favorable to the defendant must exclude the possibility of arbitrariness, whimsy, caprice, "nullification," and the like. A defendant has no entitlement to the luck of a lawless decisionmaker, even if a lawless decision cannot be reviewed.

The assessment of prejudice should proceed on the assumption that the decisionmaker is reasonably, conscientiously, and impartially applying the standards that govern the decision. It should not depend on the idiosyncracies of the particular decisionmaker, such as unusual propensities toward harshness or leniency. Although these factors may actually have entered into counsel's selection of strategies and, to that limited extent, may thus affect the performance inquiry, they are irrelevant to the prejudice inquiry. Thus, evidence about the actual process of decision, if not part of the record of the proceeding under review, and evidence about, for example, a particular judge's sentencing practices, should not be considered in the prejudice determination.

The governing legal standard plays a critical role in defining the question to be asked in assessing the prejudice from counsel's errors. When a defendant challenges a conviction, the question is whether there is a reasonable probability that, absent the errors, the factfinder would have had a reasonable doubt respecting guilt. When a defendant challenges a death sentence such as the one at issue in this case, the question is whether there is a reasonable probability that, absent the errors, the sentencer—including an appellate court, to the extent it independently reweighs the evidence—would have concluded that the balance of aggravating and mitigating circumstances did not warrant death.

In making this determination, a court hearing an ineffectiveness claim must consider the totality of the evidence before the judge or jury. Some of the factual findings will have been unaffected by the errors, and factual findings that were affected will have been affected in different ways. Some errors will have had a pervasive effect on the inferences to be drawn from the evidence, altering the entire evidentiary picture, and some will have had an isolated, trivial effect. Moreover, a verdict or conclusion only weakly supported by the record is more likely to have been affected by errors than one with overwhelming record support. Taking the unaffected findings as given, and taking due account of the effect of the errors on the remaining findings, a court making the prejudice inquiry must ask if the defendant has met the burden of showing that the decision reached would reasonably likely have been different absent the errors.

A number of practical considerations are important for the application of the standards we have outlined. Most important, in adjudicating a claim of actual ineffectiveness of counsel, a court should keep in mind that the principles we have stated do not establish mechanical rules. Although those principles should guide the process of decision, the ultimate focus of inquiry must be on the fundamental fairness of the proceeding whose result is being challenged. In every case the court should be concerned with whether, despite the strong presumption of reliability, the result of the particular proceeding is unreliable because of a breakdown in the adversarial process that our system counts on to produce just results.

To the extent that this has already been the guiding inquiry in the lower courts, the standards articulated today do not require reconsideration of ineffectiveness claims rejected under different standards. Cf. *Trapnell v. United States,* 725 F.2d 149 (2d Cir.1983) (in several years of applying "farce and mockery" standard along with "reasonable competence" standard, court "never found that the result of a case hinged on the choice of a particular standard"). In particular, the minor differences in the lower courts' precise formulations of the performance standard are insignificant: the different formulations are mere variations of the overarching reasonableness standard. With regard to the prejudice inquiry, only the strict outcome-determinative test, among the standards articulated in the lower courts, imposes a heavier burden on defendants than the tests laid down today. The difference, however, should alter the merit of an ineffectiveness claim only in the rarest case.

Although we have discussed the performance component of an ineffectiveness claim prior to the prejudice component, there is no reason for a court deciding an ineffective assistance claim to approach the inquiry in the same order or even to address both components of the inquiry if the defendant makes an insufficient showing on one. In particular, a court need not determine whether counsel's performance was deficient before examining the prejudice suffered by the defendant as a result of the alleged deficiencies. The object of an ineffectiveness claim is not to grade counsel's performance. If it is easier to dispose of an ineffectiveness claim on the ground of lack of sufficient prejudice, which we expect will often be so, that course should be followed. Courts should strive to ensure that ineffectiveness claims not become so burdensome to defense counsel that the entire criminal justice system suffers as a result. * * *

Having articulated general standards for judging ineffectiveness claims, we think it useful to apply those standards to the facts of this case in order to illustrate the meaning of the general principles. The record makes it possible to do so. * * * The facts make clear that the conduct of respondent's counsel at and before respondent's sentencing proceeding cannot be found unreasonable. They also make clear that, even assuming the challenged conduct of counsel was unreasonable, respondent suffered insufficient prejudice to warrant setting aside his death sentence.

With respect to the performance component, the record shows that respondent's counsel made a strategic choice to argue for the extreme emotional distress mitigating circumstance and to rely as fully as possible on respondent's acceptance of responsibility for his crimes. Although counsel understandably felt hopeless about respondent's prospects, nothing in the record indicates [that] counsel's sense of hopelessness distorted his professional judgment. Counsel's strategy choice was well within the range of professionally reasonable judgments, and the decision not to seek more character or psychological evidence than was already in hand was likewise reasonable.

The trial judge's views on the importance of owning up to one's crimes were well known to counsel. The aggravating circumstances were utterly overwhelming. Trial counsel could reasonably surmise from his conversations with respondent that character and psychological evidence would be of little help. Respondent had already been able to mention at the plea colloquy the substance of what there was to know about his financial and emotional troubles. Restricting testimony on respondent's character to what had come in at the plea colloquy ensured that contrary character and psychological evidence and respondent's criminal history, which counsel has successfully moved to exclude, would not come in. On these facts, there can be little question, even without application of the presumption of adequate performance, that trial counsel's defense, though unsuccessful, was the result of reasonable professional judgment.

With respect to the prejudice component, the lack of merit of respondent's claim is even more stark. The evidence that respondent says his trial counsel should have offered at the sentencing hearing would barely have altered the sentencing profile presented to the sentencing judge. As the state courts and District Court found, at most this evidence shows that numerous people who knew respondent thought he was generally a good person and that a psychiatrist and a psychologist believed he was under considerable emotional stress that did not rise to the level of extreme disturbance. Given the overwhelming aggravating factors, there is no reasonable probability that the omitted evidence would have changed the conclusion that the aggravating circumstances outweighed the mitigating circumstances and, hence, the sentence imposed. * * *

Failure to make the required showing of either deficient performance or sufficient prejudice defeats the ineffectiveness claim. Here there is a double failure. More generally, respondent has made no showing that the justice of his sentence was rendered unreliable by a breakdown in the adversary process caused by deficiencies in counsel's assistance. * * * We conclude, therefore, that the District Court properly declined to issue a writ of habeas corpus. * * *[a]

---

[a] Justice Brennan's separate opinion, concurring in part and dissenting in part, is omitted. Justice Brennan dissented from the judgment based on his view that capital punishment was unconstitutional. He joined the Court's opinion as to the IAC claim, but added that "the standards announced today can and should be applied with concern for the special considerations that must attend counsel's performance in a capital sentencing proceeding."

JUSTICE MARSHALL, dissenting.

[The] opinion of the Court revolves around two holdings. First, the majority ties the constitutional minima of attorney performance to a simple "standard of reasonableness." Second, the majority holds that only an error of counsel that has sufficient impact on a trial to "undermine confidence in the outcome" is grounds for overturning a conviction. I disagree with both of these rulings.

My objection to the performance standard adopted by the Court is that it is so malleable that, in practice, it will either have no grip at all or will yield excessive variation in the manner in which the Sixth Amendment is interpreted and applied by different courts. To tell lawyers and the lower courts that counsel for a criminal defendant must behave "reasonably" and must act like "a reasonably competent attorney" is to tell them almost nothing. * * * The debilitating ambiguity of an "objective standard of reasonableness" in this context is illustrated by the majority's failure to address important issues concerning the quality of representation mandated by the Constitution. * * * Is a "reasonably competent attorney" a reasonably competent adequately paid retained lawyer or a reasonably competent appointed attorney? It is also a fact that the quality of representation available to ordinary defendants in different parts of the country varies significantly. Should the standard of performance mandated by the Sixth Amendment vary by locale? The majority offers no clues as to the proper responses to these questions.

* * * I agree that counsel must be afforded "wide latitude" when making "tactical decisions" regarding trial strategy, but many aspects of the job of a criminal defense attorney are more amenable to judicial oversight [than the majority indicates]. For example, much of the work involved in preparing for a trial, applying for bail, conferring with one's client, making timely objections to significant, arguably erroneous rulings of the trial judge, and filing a notice of appeal if there are colorable grounds therefor could profitably be made the subject of uniform standards. * * * The opinion of the Court of Appeals in this case represents one sound attempt to develop particularized standards designed to ensure that all defendants receive effective legal assistance. For other generally consistent efforts, see [citing several lower court decisions, and adding in a footnote reference that "many of these rely heavily on the standards developed by the American Bar Association"] * * *. By refusing to address the merits of these proposals, and indeed suggesting that no such effort is worthwhile, the opinion of the Court, I fear, will stunt the development of the constitutional doctrine in this area.

I object to the prejudice standard adopted by the Court for two independent reasons. First, it is often very difficult to tell whether a defendant convicted after a trial in which he was ineffectively represented would have fared better if his lawyer had been competent. Seemingly impregnable cases can sometimes be dismantled by good defense counsel. On the basis of a cold record, it may be impossible for a reviewing court confidently to ascertain how the government's evidence and arguments would have stood up against rebuttal and cross-examination by a shrewd, well prepared lawyer. The difficulties of estimating prejudice after the fact are exacerbated by the possibility that evidence of injury to the defendant may be missing from the record precisely because of the incompetence of defense counsel. In view of all these impediments to a fair evaluation of the probability that the outcome of a trial was affected by ineffectiveness of counsel, it seems to me senseless to impose on a defendant whose lawyer has been shown to have been incompetent the burden of demonstrating prejudice.

Second and more fundamentally, the assumption on which the Court's holding rests is that the only purpose of the constitutional guarantee of effective assistance of counsel is to reduce the chance that innocent persons will be convicted. In my view, the guarantee also functions to ensure that convictions are obtained only through fundamentally fair procedures. * * * A proceeding in which the defendant does not receive meaningful assistance in meeting the forces of the state does not, in my opinion, constitute due process. * * * We [have held] * * * that certain constitutional rights are "so basic to a fair trial that their infraction can never be treated as harmless error." Among these rights is the right to counsel. In my view, the right to *effective* assistance of counsel is entailed by the right to counsel, and abridgment of the former is equivalent to abridgment of the latter. I would thus hold that a showing that the performance of a defendant's lawyer departed from constitutionally prescribed standards requires a new trial regardless of whether the defendant suffered demonstrable prejudice thereby. * * *

[The] majority suggests that, "[f]or purposes of describing counsel's duties," a capital sentencing proceeding "need not be distinguished from an ordinary trial." I cannot agree. The Court has repeatedly acknowledged that the Constitution requires stricter adherence to procedural safeguards in a capital case than in other cases. * * *

The [above] views * * * oblige me to dissent from the majority's disposition of the case before us. It is undisputed that respondent's trial counsel made virtually no investigation of the possibility of obtaining testimony from respondent's relatives, friends, or former employers pertaining to respondent's character or background. Had counsel done so, he would have found several persons willing and able to testify that, in their experience, respondent was a responsible, nonviolent man, devoted to his family, and active in the affairs of his church. Respondent contends that his lawyer could have and should have used that testimony to "humanize" respondent, to counteract the impression conveyed by the trial that he was little more than a cold-blooded killer. Had this evidence been admitted, respondent argues, his chances of obtaining a life sentence would have been significantly better.

Measured against the standards outlined above, respondent's contentions are substantial. Experienced members of the death-penalty bar have long recognized the crucial importance of adducing evidence at a sentencing proceeding that establishes the defendant's social and familial connections. * * * The State makes a colorable—though in my view not compelling—argument that defense counsel in this case might have made a reasonable "strategic" decision not to present such evidence at the sentencing hearing on the assumption that an unadorned acknowledgment of respondent's responsibility for his crimes would be more likely to appeal to the trial judge, who was reputed to respect persons who accepted responsibility for their actions. But however justifiable such a choice might have been after counsel had fairly assessed the potential strength of the mitigating evidence available to him, counsel's failure to make any significant effort to find out what evidence might be garnered from respondent's relatives and acquaintances surely cannot be described as "reasonable." Counsel's failure to investigate is particularly suspicious in light of his candid admission that respondent's confession and conduct in the course of the trial gave him a feeling of "hopelessness" regarding the possibility of saving respondent's life. * * *

NOTES AND QUESTIONS

1. **Strickland *in other settings.*** As discussed in *Strickland* (p. 130) and in §§ 4–6, infra, certain types of claims relating to performance are not governed by the two-pronged *Strickland* test. *Strickland* does provide, however, the basic standards for assessing incompetent performance claims in most settings. In *Smith v. Murray*, 477 U.S. 527 (1986), the Court held that the "test of *Strickland v. Washington*" was not limited to trial counsel, but also applied to the alleged ineffective assistance of appellate counsel on a first appeal of right. *Hill v. Lockhart*, 474 U.S. 52 (1985), concluded that past precedent on counsel's ineffective assistance in a guilty plea case converted into the application of the *Strickland* standards. Lower courts have held *Strickland* to apply to counsel's performance not only in capital sentencing, but in sentencing generally.

2. ***Continuous criticism and continuous adherence.*** From the outset, academic commentators almost unanimously criticized *Strickland*. In large part, the criticism followed Justice Marshall's analysis, with heavy emphasis on the court's willingness to accept the limitation of a deferential ex ante judicial review of counsel's performance. The subsequent lower

court application of *Strickland* over several decades is viewed as bolstering that criticism. Commentators note, in particular, that various institutional deficiencies in state indigent-defense delivery systems (see Note 5, p. 72) make it self-evident that incompetent performance is widespread, yet various studies show that only a "notoriously low" percentage of IAC claims are successful (CRIMPROC § 11.10(a), 4–8% in state courts), as the "lax" standards of *Strickland* present an "open invitation" to limit conviction reversals to the most extreme cases. Commentators have suggested that the Court must start anew, or at least withdraw from the elements of the *Strickland* opinion that promote such laxness, but the Court has not been convinced.

The Court has sometimes been sharply divided over the application of *Strickland*, and arguably has added content somewhat different from what might have been anticipated immediately after *Strickland*, but it has continuously stressed the controlling role of the *Strickland* opinion. Its own analysis of IAC claims has always looked first for guidance in what *Strickland* might have said about the particular type of alleged incompetence (e.g., the failure to investigate). Perhaps more significantly, as noted in CRIMPROC § 11.10(b): "Subsequent Supreme Court rulings, in advising lower courts, have repeatedly emphasized the need to interpret 'the *Strickland* standard' in light of the guiding considerations set forth in the *Strickland* opinion. * * * [Indeed, those rulings have] referred to institutional concerns that furnish additional support for emphasizing those guiding considerations, in particular procedural settings, and have demanded, in general, 'strict adherence' to the 'high bar' *Strickland* imposes for a finding of a Sixth Amendment violation [*Richter*, p. 154]. Thus, it has insisted that the assessment of counsel's conduct be viewed 'as of the time of counsel's conduct,' taking into account the legal standards, scientific knowledge, investigatory tools, and conventional wisdom on a particular tactic prevailing at that time, * * * [thereby precluding use of the IAC claim] to avoid limitations on the retroactive application of legal changes, and [it similarly has warned against allowing the IAC claim] to function as a ready means of avoiding forfeiture rules [*Richter*, p. 154]."

3. *Reasonableness and attorney practice patterns.* Apart from Justice Marshall's queries, *Strickland* has not been read as suggesting that "reasonableness is to be judged by reference to any empirical survey of attorney practices." CRIMPROC § 11.10(b). The Court did refer to "prevailing norms of practice" (p. 129), but that reference was to standards of professionalism (see Note 4, infra), which do not necessarily reflect the full range of practice patterns, and the Court added that those norms are only "guides." *Strickland*, lower courts have noted, described the performance standard in terms that ultimately require reference to the function of the counsel guarantee. The Court spoke of the "competence demanded of attorneys in criminal cases" and the requirement that counsel "bring to bear such skill and knowledge as will render the trial a reliable adversarial testing process." Such language "clearly rejected a measurement based solely on a comparison of counsel with his or her peers." CRIMPROC § 11.7(c). Cf. *Rogers v. Zant*, 13 F.3d 384 (11th Cir.1994) ("Even if many reasonable lawyers would have not have done as defense counsel did at trial, no relief can be granted on ineffectiveness grounds unless it is shown that no reasonable lawyer in the circumstances would have done so.") Consider also *Harrington v. Richter*, p. 155 ("The question is whether an attorney's representation amounted to incompetence under prevailing professional norms, not whether it deviates from best practices or *most common custom*") (emphasis added).

While attorney practice patterns do not define the expected level of counsel performance, that does not necessarily render those patterns irrelevant. In two of its post-*Strickland* rulings, the Court did refer to the standard practice of defense lawyers at the time of representation in the state of defendant's conviction. In *Wiggins v. Smith*, Note 2, p. 162, the Court noted that the defense counsel's failure to obtain a social history report for use in capital sentencing was "contrary to standard practice in Maryland * * * at the time" (where the Public Defender Office provided funding for such a report). In *Cullen v. Pinholster*, Note 4, p. 166, the Court noted that the family mitigation defense that defense counsel had employed as an alternative to a standard mitigation defense was "known to the defense Bar in California at the time and had been used by other attorneys." The Court added that the dissent did not contest this characterization and had "cit[ed] no evidence that such an approach would have been inconsistent with the standard of professional competence in capital cases that prevailed in Los Angeles in 1984."

Wiggins and *Pinholster* have been described as giving weight to practice patterns in a relatively narrow context—considering local practice as it relates to a unique practice environment created by local law (in *Pinholster*) or local logistical considerations (the state funding in *Wiggins*). Are significant limitations also attached to the Court's reference to a national practice pattern in *Padilla v. Kentucky*, Note 4, infra? The Court there concluded that the "weight of professional norms" requires counsel to advise the defendant of the "deportation risk" of conviction. The sources cited as establishing that professional norm included not only standards issued by professional organizations (as well as professional guidance in treatises and law review articles), but also the common practice of defender organizations nationally.

4. ***The guidance of ABA Standards.*** *Strickland* notes that the "prevailing norms of practice as reflected in American Bar Association Standards and the like" can be used only as "guides to determining what is reasonable" (p. 129). In several of the Court's rulings considering counsel's failure to fully investigate possible mitigating circumstances in capital cases (e.g., *Wiggins v. Smith*, Note 2, p. 162, and *Rompilla v. Beard*, Note 3, p. 163), the Court's finding of ineffective assistance relied in part on counsel having failed to fulfill an obligation prescribed in the ABA Standards. Those rulings led some lower courts to treat the ABA Standards as a critical evaluative measure of competent performance, although other courts discounted the Standards as too often prescribing the kind of particularized requirements that *Strickland* had warned against. *Bobby v. Van Hook* responded to the former position, and *Padilla v. Kentucky* arguably responded to the latter. Commentators have suggested, however, that the message these cases sent, as to the appropriate treatment of the Standards, was not entirely consistent.

In BOBBY v. VAN HOOK, 558 U.S. 4 (2009), a unanimous Court held that the Sixth Circuit had erred in finding that counsel provided ineffective assistance when he failed to further investigate and present potential mitigating evidence in a capital sentencing proceeding. The Sixth Circuit reasoned that counsel's investigation fell short of the directives of the ABA Guidelines for the Appointment and Performance of Defense Counsel in Death Penalty Cases (compliance in this case would have required contacting a much broader range of relatives as well as a psychiatrist who was familiar with defendant's childhood experiences). That conclusion, the Court noted, ignored *Strickland's* warning that professional standards could be useful " 'guides' as to what reasonableness entails * * * only to the extent they describe the professional norms prevailing when the professional representation took place." The ABA Guidelines on Death Penalty Cases had been "announced 18 years after Van Hook went to trial," were far more detailed than the ABA Standards in effect in 1985, and were erroneously treated by the Sixth Circuit as "inexorable commands with which all capital defense counsel 'must fully comply'." The Court's *per curiam* opinion added in a footnote: "The narrow grounds for our opinion should not be regarded as accepting the legitimacy of a less categorical use of the [Death Penalty] Guidelines to evaluate post-2003 representation. For that to be proper, the Guidelines must reflect '[p]revailing norms of practice,' *Strickland*, and 'standard practice,' *Wiggins*, and must not be so detailed that they would 'interfere with the constitutionally protected independence of counsel and restrict the wide latitude counsel must have in making tactical decisions,' *Strickland*. We express no views on whether the 2003 Guidelines meet these criteria."

Justice Alito, concurring, added: "I join the Court's *per curiam* opinion but emphasize my understanding that the opinion in no way suggests that the American Bar Association's Guidelines for the Appointment and Performance of Defense Counsel in Death Penalty Cases * * * have special relevance in determining whether an attorney's performance meets the standard required by the Sixth Amendment. * * * The views of the association's members, not to mention the views of the members of the advisory committee that formulated the 2003 Guidelines, do not necessarily reflect the views of the American bar as a whole. It is the responsibility of the courts to determine the nature of the work that a defense attorney must do in a capital case in order to meet the obligations imposed by the Constitution, and I see no reason why the ABA Guidelines should be given a privileged position in making that determination."

In PADILLA v. KENTUCKY, 559 U.S. 356 (2010), the Court majority described two sets of ABA Standards (along with other sources, see Note 3, supra) as reflecting "prevailing professional norms" that established a very specific responsibility of defense counsel—informing a non-citizen client of the risk of deportation on entry of a guilty plea (see Note 12, p. 1201). After citing the discussion of the ABA standards in both *Strickland* and *Bobby v. Van Hook*, the Court majority stated that such professional standards (here also including National Legal Aid & Defender Office standards) "may be valuable measures of the prevailing professional norms of effective representation, especially as those standards have been adapted to deal with the intersection of modern criminal prosecutions and immigration laws." However, in ascertaining those norms, the Court also looked to descriptions of actual practice (see Note 3, supra), and in assessing what *Strickland*'s performance prong required, it looked to additional factors relating to the functions of counsel in advising on a guilty plea.

Justice Alito's concurring opinion in *Padilla* advanced an advice-obligation more limited than that required by the majority. See fn. f, p. 1202. In this connection, he questioned both the majority's analysis and its reliance upon "professional norms". He noted: (1) while prevailing professional norms are a "relevant consideration," "ascertaining the level of professional competence required by the Sixth Amendment is ultimately the task for the courts"; (2) "we must recognize [also] that such standards [as the ABA standards] may represent only the aspirations of a bar group rather than an empirical assessment of actual practice"; and (3) "it is hard to see how [the] norms [cited by the majority] can support the duty the Court today imposes on defense counsel * * * [as] many criminal defense attorneys have little understanding of immigration law * * * [and] the Court's opinion [goes beyond] * * * just requir[ing] defense counsel to warn the client of a general risk of removal."

5. ***Prejudice and "just results."*** *Strickland* advises lower courts, in applying the *Strickland* standards, to ask whether "the result of the particular proceeding is unreliable because of a breakdown in the adversarial process that our system counts on to produce just results." See p. 132. *Cronic* describes that adversarial process as designed to achieve accuracy of verdict—that the "guilty be convicted and the innocent go free" (see Note 3, p. 123). In *Kimmelman v. Morrison,* 477 U.S. 365 (1986), Justice Powell suggested that the prejudice prong has to be read in light of these objectives and not simply by reference to the probability of a different outcome.

Justice Brennan's opinion for the Court in *Kimmelman* concluded that counsel's failure to make a timely motion to suppress constituted deficient performance. Although the Supreme Court had held in *Stone v. Powell*, p. 1430, that motions to suppress were not cognizable on federal habeas review, that ruling did not control as to an IAC claim presented on habeas review, notwithstanding that the claim was based on incompetence in failing to seek suppression. The Court noted that the ruling barring habeas review of suppression motions had emphasized that the suppression motion excluded evidence "typically reliable and often the most probative information bearing on guilt or innocence." The Sixth Amendment right to counsel, in contrast, had an objective that went beyond reliable factfinding, as evidenced by its availability to "the innocent and guilty alike." "Consequently," the opinion noted, "we decline to hold either that the guarantee of effective assistance of counsel belongs solely to the innocent or that it attaches only to matters affecting the determination of actual guilt."

Justice Brennan's opinion remanded to the lower court for a determination as to whether the impact of the lack of suppression was sufficient to meet the prejudice component. That led to a concurring opinion by Justice Powell (joined by Burger, C.J., and Rehnquist, J.). Justice Powell noted that the state had not raised the question of whether "the admission of illegally seized but reliable evidence can ever constitute 'prejudice' under *Strickland*." The reasoning of *Strickland*, he added, "strongly suggests that only errors that call into question the basic justice of the defendant's conviction suffice to establish prejudice." The "question * * * must be whether the particular harm suffered * * * due to counsel's incompetence rendered the defendant's trial fundamentally unfair." Where the defendant has been denied the exclusion of "illegally seized, but reliable evidence, the harm suffered * * * is not the denial of a fair and reliable adjudication of * * * [guilt], but rather the absence of a windfall." The function of the adversary system is "to promote the truth," and the "right to effective assistance flows logically from that premise." Accordingly, "it would shake that right loose from its constitutional moorings to hold that the Sixth Amendment protects criminal defendants against errors that merely deny those defendants a windfall."

6. Although Justice Brennan's opinion for the Court did not respond specifically to Justice Powell's concurring opinion, numerous lower courts have concluded that Justice Brennan's reasoning in rejecting the state's reliance on *Stone* implicitly rejected Justice Powell's reading of *Strickland*'s prejudice prong. In *Lockhart v. Fretwell*, 506 U.S. 364 (1993), the Court majority agreed that the reference to a "just result" required more than simply looking to whether, but for counsel's deficient performance, a different result would have been reached. In *Lockhart*, the ineffective assistance claim rested on counsel's failure to object to the capital sentence being based on an aggravating factor that duplicated an element of an underlying felony. At the time, an Eighth Circuit ruling prohibited use of such an aggravating factor, but that Eighth Circuit ruling had subsequently been overruled, and use of that aggravating factor would have been permissible at the time that defendant's federal habeas claim was decided.

The *Lockhart* majority (per Rehnquist, C.J.) reasoned that *Strickland* "focuses on the question of whether a counsel's deficient performance renders the result of the trial unreliable or the proceeding fundamentally unfair." Here "the result of the sentencing proceeding is neither unfair nor unreliable" as the ineffectiveness "does not deprive the defendant of any substantive or procedural right to which the law entitles him." *Strickland* had noted that "a defendant has no entitlement to the luck of a lawless decisionmaker." Building on that point, the Court in *Nix v. Whiteside*, 475 U.S. 157 (1986), had held that defendant could not be prejudiced by claimed incompetence (through counsel's allegedly improper threat of withdrawal) where that incompetence operated only to preclude the use of perjured testimony that might have produced a different verdict. Here also, as in *Nix,* the *Lockhart* majority reasoned, prejudice could not be based on counsel error that would have "grant[ed] the defendant a windfall to which the law does not entitle him."

Subsequently, in *Williams (Terry) v. Taylor*, 529 U.S. 362 (2000), the Court overturned a state ruling that read *Lockhart's* discussion of unfairness as extending broadly beyond the unusual *Lockhart* fact situation. The state court there had found that incompetency in a capital sentencing proceeding did not meet the prejudice requirement where, notwithstanding the requisite probability of a different outcome, the reviewing court could not also say that the sentencing proceeding was so lacking as to produce "fundamental unfairness."

7. In LAFLER v. COOPER, 566 U.S. 156 (2012), the Court was sharply divided as to the appropriate reading of the above cases and the character of *Strickland's* prejudice requirement. The state there conceded that defense counsel had violated the performance prong of *Strickland* by providing deficient advice that led to the defendant's rejection of a prosecution offer to accept a guilty plea to a single count, with a prosecution recommendation of a sentence of 51–85 months.

The state argued, however, that the prejudice prong was not established even though defendant was convicted at trial on all three charged counts and received a sentence of 185–360 months.[b] Rejecting that contention, Justice Kennedy's opinion for the 5–4 majority reasoned:

"The question for this Court is how to apply *Strickland*'s prejudice test where ineffective assistance results in a rejection of the plea offer and the defendant is convicted at the ensuing trial. To establish *Strickland* prejudice a defendant must 'show that there is a reasonable probability that, but for counsel's unprofessional errors, the result of the proceeding would have been different.' In the context of pleas a defendant must show the outcome of the plea process would have been different with competent advice. * * * In *Hill v. Lockhart*, 474 U.S. 52 (1985), when evaluating the petitioner's claim that ineffective assistance led to the improvident acceptance of a guilty plea, the Court required the petitioner to show 'that there is a reasonable probability that, but for counsel's errors, [the defendant] would not have pleaded guilty and would have insisted on going to trial.' * * * In contrast to *Hill,* here the ineffective advice led not to an offer's acceptance but to its rejection. Having to stand trial, not choosing to waive it, is the prejudice alleged. In these circumstances a defendant must show that but for the ineffective advice of counsel there is a reasonable probability that the plea offer would have been presented to the court (*i.e.,* that the defendant would have accepted the plea and the prosecution would not have withdrawn it in light of intervening circumstances), that the court would have accepted its terms, and that the conviction or sentence, or both, under the offer's terms would have been less severe than under the judgment and sentence that in fact were imposed. * * *

"Petitioner [the state warden] and the Solicitor General [amicus curiae] propose a different, far more narrow, view of the Sixth Amendment. They contend there can be no finding of *Strickland* prejudice arising from plea bargaining if the defendant is later convicted at a fair trial. The three reasons petitioner and the Solicitor General offer for their approach are unpersuasive.

"First, petitioner and the Solicitor General claim that the sole purpose of the Sixth Amendment is to protect the right to a fair trial. Errors before trial, they argue, are not cognizable under the Sixth Amendment unless they affect the fairness of the trial itself. * * * The Sixth Amendment, however, is not so narrow in its reach. The Sixth Amendment requires effective assistance of counsel at critical stages of a criminal proceeding. Its protections are not designed simply to protect the trial, even though 'counsel's absence [in these stages] may derogate from the accused's right to a fair trial.' *United States v. Wade,* [p. 683. The constitutional guarantee applies to pretrial critical stages that are part of the whole course of a criminal proceeding, a proceeding in which defendants cannot be presumed to make critical decisions without counsel's advice. This is consistent, too, with the rule that defendants have a right to effective assistance of counsel on appeal, even though that cannot in any way be characterized as part of the trial. * * * The precedents also establish that there exists a right to counsel during sentencing in both noncapital and capital cases. Even though sentencing does not concern the defendant's guilt or innocence, ineffective assistance of counsel during a sentencing hearing can result in *Strickland* prejudice because 'any amount of [additional] jail time has Sixth Amendment significance.' *Glover v. United States*, [531 U.S. 198 (2001)]. * * *

"Second, petitioner claims this Court refined *Strickland*'s prejudice analysis in *Lockhart v. Fretwell*, to add an additional requirement that the defendant show that ineffective assistance of counsel led to his being denied a substantive or procedural right. The Court has rejected the argument that *Fretwell* modified *Strickland* before and does so again now. See *Williams v. Taylor*, * * * . [*Fretwell*] presented the 'unusual circumstance where the defendant attempts to

[b] The state also argued that (1) the AEDPA standard of review precluded reversal because the state court ruling was not clearly contrary to past Supreme Court precedent, and (2) the federal habeas court erred in fashioning a remedy (assuming a violation of *Strickland*). The Court's responses on these issues are discussed at Note 7, p. 1459 and at p. 1192.

demonstrate prejudice based on considerations that, as a matter of law, ought not inform the inquiry.' Ibid. (O'Connor, J., concurring). * * * It is for this same reason a defendant cannot show prejudice based on counsel's refusal to present perjured testimony, even if such testimony might have affected the outcome of the case. See *Nix v. Whiteside* * * *.

"It is, of course, true that defendants have 'no right to be offered a plea . . . nor a federal right that the judge accept it.' *Missouri v. Frye*, [p. 1190]. In the circumstances here, that is beside the point. If no plea offer is made, or a plea deal is accepted by the defendant but rejected by the judge, the issue raised here simply does not arise. Much the same reasoning guides cases that find criminal defendants have a right to effective assistance of counsel in direct appeals even though the Constitution does not require States to provide a system of appellate review at all. As in those cases, '[w]hen a State opts to act in a field where its action has significant discretionary elements, it must nonetheless act in accord with the dictates of the Constitution.' * * *

"Third, petitioner seeks to preserve the conviction obtained by the State by arguing that the purpose of the Sixth Amendment is to ensure 'the reliability of [a] conviction following trial.' This argument, too, fails to comprehend the full scope of the Sixth Amendment's protections; and it is refuted by precedent. *Strickland* recognized '[t]he benchmark for judging any claim of ineffectiveness must be whether counsel's conduct so undermined the proper functioning of the adversarial process that the trial cannot be relied on as having produced a just result.' The goal of a just result is not divorced from the reliability of a conviction * * *; but here the question is not the fairness or reliability of the trial but the fairness and regularity of the processes that preceded it, which caused the defendant to lose benefits he would have received in the ordinary course but for counsel's ineffective assistance.

"There are instances, furthermore, where a reliable trial does not foreclose relief when counsel has failed to assert rights that may have altered the outcome. In *Kimmelman v. Morrison,* the Court held that an attorney's failure to timely move to suppress evidence during trial could be grounds for federal habeas relief. The Court rejected the suggestion that the 'failure to make a timely request for the exclusion of illegally seized evidence' could not be the basis for a Sixth Amendment violation because the evidence 'is typically reliable and often the most probative information bearing on the guilt or innocence of the defendant.' 'The constitutional rights of criminal defendants,' the Court observed, 'are granted to the innocent and the guilty alike. Consequently, we decline to hold either that the guarantee of effective assistance of counsel belongs solely to the innocent or that it attaches only to matters affecting the determination of actual guilt.' The same logic applies here. The fact that respondent is guilty does not mean he was not entitled by the Sixth Amendment to effective assistance or that he suffered no prejudice from his attorney's deficient performance during plea bargaining.

"In the end, petitioner's three arguments amount to one general contention: A fair trial wipes clean any deficient performance by defense counsel during plea bargaining. That position ignores the reality that criminal justice today is for the most part a system of pleas, not a system of trials. Ninety-seven percent of federal convictions and ninety-four percent of state convictions are the result of guilty pleas. See *Frye*. As explained in *Frye*, the right to adequate assistance of counsel cannot be defined or enforced without taking account of the central role plea bargaining plays in securing convictions and determining sentences."

Part I of Justice Scalia's dissent, joined by Chief Justice Roberts and Justice Thomas, responded to the majority's reasoning. Justice Alito, in a separate dissent, agreed that, "for the reasons set forth in Par[t] I * * * of Justice Scalia's dissent, the Court's holding * * * misapplies our ineffective-assistance-of-counsel case law." Justice Scalia reasoned in Part I:

"This case and its companion, *Missouri v. Frye*, raise relatively straightforward questions about the scope of the right to effective assistance of counsel. Our case law originally derived that right from the Due Process Clause, and its guarantee of a fair trial, *United States v. Gonzalez-Lopez* [p. 114], but the seminal case of *Strickland v. Washington* located the right within the Sixth Amendment. As the Court notes, the right to counsel does not begin at trial. It extends to 'any stage of the prosecution, formal or informal, in court or out, where counsel's absence might derogate from the accused's right to a fair trial.' * * * And it follows from this that *acceptance* of a plea offer is a critical stage. That, and nothing more, is the point of the Court's observation in *Padilla v. Kentucky* [Note 12, p. 1201] that 'the negotiation of a plea bargain is a critical phase of litigation for purposes of the Sixth Amendment right to effective assistance of counsel.' The defendant in *Padilla* had accepted the plea bargain and pleaded guilty, abandoning his right to a fair trial; he was entitled to advice of competent counsel before he did so. The Court has never held that the rule articulated in [cases like] *Padilla* * * * extends to all aspects of plea negotiations, requiring not just advice of competent counsel before the defendant accepts a plea bargain and pleads guilty, but also the advice of competent counsel before the defendant rejects a plea bargain and stands on his constitutional right to a fair trial. The latter is a vast departure from our past cases, protecting not just the constitutionally prescribed right to a fair adjudication of guilt and punishment, but a judicially invented right to effective plea bargaining.

"It is also apparent from *Strickland* that bad plea bargaining has nothing to do with ineffective assistance of counsel in the constitutional sense. *Strickland* explained that '[i]n giving meaning to the requirement [of effective assistance], . . . we must take its purpose—to ensure a fair trial—as the guide.' Since 'the right to the effective assistance of counsel is recognized not for its own sake, but because of the effect it has on the ability of the accused to receive a fair trial,' *United States v. Cronic*, the 'benchmark' inquiry in evaluating any claim of ineffective assistance is whether counsel's performance 'so undermined the proper functioning of the adversarial process' that it failed to produce a reliably 'just result.' *Strickland*. That is what *Strickland*'s requirement of 'prejudice' consists of: Because the right to effective assistance has as its purpose the assurance of a fair trial, the right is not infringed unless counsel's mistakes call into question the basic justice of a defendant's conviction or sentence.

"To be sure, *Strickland* stated a rule of thumb for measuring prejudice which, applied blindly and out of context, could support the Court's holding today: 'The defendant must show that there is a reasonable probability that, but for counsel's unprofessional errors, the result of the proceeding would have been different.' *Strickland* itself cautioned, however, that its test was not to be applied in a mechanical fashion, and that courts were not to divert their 'ultimate focus' from 'the fundamental fairness of the proceeding whose result is being challenged.' And until today we have followed that course.

"In *Lockhart v. Fretwell,* * * * [we] determined that a prejudice analysis 'focusing solely on mere outcome determination, without attention to whether the result of the proceeding was fundamentally unfair or unreliable,' would be defective. Because counsel's error did not 'deprive the defendant of any substantive or procedural right to which the law entitles him,' the defendant's sentencing proceeding was fair and its result was reliable, even though counsel's error may have affected its outcome.[2] * * * As the Court itself observes, a criminal defendant has no right to a plea

[2] *Kimmelman v. Morrison,* cited by the Court, does not contradict this principle. That case * * * considered whether our holding that Fourth Amendment claims fully litigated in state court cannot be raised in federal habeas "should be extended to Sixth Amendment claims of ineffective assistance of counsel where the principal allegation and manifestations of inadequate representation is counsel's failure to file a timely motion to suppress evidence allegedly obtained in violation of the Fourth Amendment." Our negative answer to that question had nothing to do with the issue here. The parties in *Kimmelman* had not raised the question "whether the admission of illegally seized but reliable evidence can ever constitute 'prejudice' under *Strickland*"—a question similar to the one presented her—and the Court therefore did not address it. Id. (Powell, J., concurring in judgment). *Kimmelman* made clear, however, how the answer to that question is to be determined: "The essence of an ineffective-assistance claim is that counsel's unprofessional errors so upset the adversarial balance between defense and prosecution *that the trial was rendered unfair and the verdict rendered suspect*," Id. (emphasis added). "Only those habeas petitioners who can prove under

bargain. * * * Counsel's mistakes in this case thus did not 'deprive the defendant of a substantive or procedural right to which the law entitles him.' Far from being 'beside the point,' *Ante* [p. 141], that is critical to correct application of our precedents. Like *Fretwell,* this case 'concerns the unusual circumstance where the defendant attempts to demonstrate prejudice based on considerations that, as a matter of law, ought not inform the inquiry.' * * *"

8. ***Prejudice and "fundamental unfairness."***

WEAVER V. MASSACHUSETTS

___ U.S. ___, 137 S.Ct. 1899, 198 L.Ed.2d 420 (2017).

JUSTICE KENNEDY delivered the opinion of the Court. * * *

In 2003, a 15-year-old boy was shot and killed in Boston. A witness saw a young man fleeing the scene of the crime and saw him pull out a pistol. A baseball hat fell off of his head. The police recovered the hat, which featured a distinctive airbrushed Detroit Tigers logo on either side. The hat's distinctive markings linked it to 16-year-old Kentel Weaver. He is the petitioner here. DNA obtained from the hat matched petitioner's DNA. * * * Petitioner was [later] indicted in Massachusetts state court for first-degree murder and the unlicensed possession of a handgun. He pleaded not guilty and proceeded to trial.

The pool of potential jury members was large, some 60 to 100 people. The assigned courtroom could accommodate only 50 or 60 in the courtroom seating. As a result, the trial judge brought all potential jurors into the courtroom so that he could introduce the case and ask certain preliminary questions of the entire venire panel. Many of the potential jurors did not have seats and had to stand in the courtroom. After the preliminary questions, the potential jurors who had been standing were moved outside the courtroom to wait during the individual questioning of the other potential jurors. * * * As all of the seats in the courtroom were occupied by the venire panel, an officer of the court excluded from the courtroom any member of the public who was not a potential juror. So when petitioner's mother and her minister came to the courtroom to observe the two days of jury selection, they were turned away.

All this occurred before the Court's [2012] decision in *Presley v. Georgia* [p. 1332] made it clear that the public-trial right extends to jury selection as well as to other portions of the trial. Before *Presley,* Massachusetts courts would often close courtrooms to the public during jury selection, in particular during murder trials. * * * In this case petitioner's mother told defense counsel about the closure at some point during jury selection. But counsel "believed that a courtroom closure for [jury selection] was constitutional." As a result, he "did not discuss the matter" with petitioner, or tell him "that his right to a public trial included the [jury *voir dire*]," or object to the closure.

During the ensuing trial, the government presented strong evidence of petitioner's guilt. Its case consisted of the incriminating details outlined above, including petitioner's confession to the police. The jury convicted petitioner on both counts. The court sentenced him to life in prison on the murder charge. * * * Five years later, petitioner filed a motion for a new trial in Massachusetts state court. As relevant here, he argued that his attorney had provided ineffective assistance by failing to object to the courtroom closure. After an evidentiary hearing, the trial court recognized a violation of the right to a public trial based on the following findings: The courtroom had been closed; the closure was neither *de minimis* nor trivial; the closure was unjustified; and the closure was full rather than partial (meaning that all members of the public, rather than only some of them, had been excluded from the courtroom). The trial court further determined that defense

---

Strickland that they have been denied a fair trial . . . will be granted the writ," Id. (emphasis added). In short, *Kimmelman's* only relevance is to prove the Court's opinion wrong.

counsel failed to object because of "serious incompetency, inefficiency, or inattention." On the other hand, petitioner had not "offered any evidence or legal argument establishing prejudice." For that reason, the court held that petitioner was not entitled to relief.

Petitioner appealed the denial of the motion for a new trial to the Massachusetts Supreme Judicial Court. The court consolidated that appeal with petitioner's direct appeal. As noted, there had been no objection to the closure at trial; and the issue was not raised in the direct appeal. The Supreme Judicial Court then affirmed in relevant part. Although it recognized that "[a] violation of the Sixth Amendment right to a public trial constitutes structural error," the court stated that petitioner had "failed to show that trial counsel's conduct caused prejudice warranting a new trial." * * * There is disagreement among the Federal Courts of Appeals and some state courts of last resort about whether a defendant must demonstrate prejudice in a case like this one—in which a structural error is neither preserved nor raised on direct review but is raised later via a claim alleging ineffective assistance of counsel. * * * This Court granted certiorari to resolve that disagreement. The Court does so specifically and only in the context of trial counsel's failure to object to the closure of the courtroom during jury selection. * * *

II

This case requires a discussion, and the proper application, of two doctrines: structural error and ineffective assistance of counsel. The two doctrines are intertwined; for the reasons an error is deemed structural may influence the proper standard used to evaluate an ineffective-assistance claim premised on the failure to object to that error.

The concept of structural error can be discussed first. In *Chapman v. California* [p. 1417], this Court "adopted the general rule that a constitutional error does not automatically require reversal of a conviction." If the government can show "beyond a reasonable doubt that the error complained of did not contribute to the verdict obtained," the Court held, then the error is deemed harmless and the defendant is not entitled to reversal. The Court recognized, however, that some errors should not be deemed harmless beyond a reasonable doubt. These errors came to be known as structural errors. The purpose of the structural error doctrine is to ensure insistence on certain basic, constitutional guarantees that should define the framework of any criminal trial. Thus, the defining feature of a structural error is that it "affect[s] the framework within which the trial proceeds," rather than being "simply an error in the trial process itself." For the same reason, a structural error "def[ies] analysis by harmless error standards." *Arizona v. Fulminante*, 499 U.S. 279 (1991). The precise reason why a particular error is not amenable to that kind of analysis—and thus the precise reason why the Court has deemed it structural—varies in a significant way from error to error. There appear to be at least three broad rationales.

First, an error has been deemed structural in some instances if the right at issue is not designed to protect the defendant from erroneous conviction but instead protects some other interest. This is true of the defendant's right to conduct his own defense, which, when exercised, "usually increases the likelihood of a trial outcome unfavorable to the defendant." *McKaskle v. Wiggins,* [Note 2, p. 103]. That right is based on the fundamental legal principle that a defendant must be allowed to make his own choices about the proper way to protect his own liberty. See *Faretta v. California,* [p. 99]. Because harm is irrelevant to the basis underlying the right, the Court has deemed a violation of that right structural error. See *United States v. Gonzalez-Lopez* [p. 113].

Second, an error has been deemed structural if the effects of the error are simply too hard to measure. For example, when a defendant is denied the right to select his or her own attorney, the precise "effect of the violation cannot be ascertained." *Gonzalez-Lopez*, supra. Because the government will, as a result, find it almost impossible to show that the error was "harmless beyond a reasonable doubt," *Chapman*, the efficiency costs of letting the government try to make the showing are unjustified.

Third, an error has been deemed structural if the error always results in fundamental unfairness. For example, if an indigent defendant is denied an attorney or if the judge fails to give a reasonable-doubt instruction, the resulting trial is always a fundamentally unfair one. * * * It therefore would be futile for the government to try to show harmlessness.

These categories are not rigid. In a particular case, more than one of these rationales may be part of the explanation for why an error is deemed to be structural. For these purposes, however, one point is critical: An error can count as structural even if the error does not lead to fundamental unfairness in every case. See *Gonzalez-Lopez,* supra at n.4 (rejecting as "inconsistent with the reasoning of our precedents" the idea that structural errors "always or necessarily render a trial fundamentally unfair and unreliable").

As noted above, a violation of the right to a public trial is a structural error. It is relevant to determine why that is so. In particular, the question is whether a public-trial violation counts as structural because it always leads to fundamental unfairness or for some other reason. * * * [*Waller v. Georgia* [Note 2, p. 1295] and *Pressley*, supra, address the scope of the public trial guarantee.] These opinions teach that courtroom closure is to be avoided, but that there are some circumstances when it is justified. The problems that may be encountered by trial courts in deciding whether some closures are necessary, or even in deciding which members of the public should be admitted when seats are scarce, are difficult ones. For example, there are often preliminary instructions that a judge may want to give to the venire as a whole, rather than repeating those instructions (perhaps with unintentional differences) to several groups of potential jurors. On the other hand, various constituencies of the public—the family of the accused, the family of the victim, members of the press, and other persons—all have their own interests in observing the selection of jurors. How best to manage these problems is not a topic discussed at length in any decision or commentary the Court has found.

So although the public-trial right is structural, it is subject to exceptions. * * * Though these cases [of justified closure] should be rare, a judge may deprive a defendant of his right to an open courtroom by making proper factual findings in support of the decision to do so. The fact that the public-trial right is subject to these exceptions suggests that not every public-trial violation results in fundamental unfairness.

A public-trial violation can occur, moreover, as it did in *Presley,* simply because the trial court omits to make the proper findings before closing the courtroom, even if those findings might have been fully supported by the evidence. It would be unconvincing to deem a trial fundamentally unfair just because a judge omitted to announce factual findings before making an otherwise valid decision to order the courtroom temporarily closed. As a result, it would be likewise unconvincing if the Court had said that a public-trial violation always leads to a fundamentally unfair trial. Indeed * * * in the two cases in which the Court has discussed the reasons for classifying a public-trial violation as structural error, the Court has said that a public-trial violation is structural for a different reason: because of the "difficulty of assessing the effect of the error." *Gonzalez-Lopez,* supra at n. 4; see also *Waller,* supra at n. 9.

The public-trial right also protects some interests that do not belong to the defendant. After all, the right to an open courtroom protects the rights of the public at large, and the press, as well as the rights of the accused. * * * *Press-Enterprise II* [Note 3, p. 1295]. So one other factor leading to the classification of structural error is that the public-trial right furthers interests other than protecting the defendant against unjust conviction. These precepts confirm the conclusion the Court now reaches that, while the public-trial right is important for fundamental reasons, in some cases an unlawful closure might take place and yet the trial still will be fundamentally fair from the defendant's standpoint. * * *

III

The Court now turns to the proper remedy for addressing the violation of a structural right, and in particular the right to a public trial. Despite its name, the term "structural error" carries with it no talismanic significance as a doctrinal matter. It means only that the government is not entitled to deprive the defendant of a new trial by showing that the error was "harmless beyond a reasonable doubt." *Chapman*. Thus, in the case of a structural error where there is an objection at trial and the issue is raised on direct appeal, the defendant generally is entitled to "automatic reversal" regardless of the error's actual "effect on the outcome." *Neder v. United States* [p. 1420]. * * * The question then becomes what showing is necessary when the defendant does not preserve a structural error on direct review but raises it later in the context of an ineffective-assistance-of-counsel claim. To obtain relief on the basis of ineffective assistance of counsel, the defendant as a general rule bears the burden to meet two standards: * * * deficient performance * * * [and] prejudice. *Strickland*.

The prejudice showing is in most cases a necessary part of a *Strickland* claim. * * * That said, the concept of prejudice is defined in different ways depending on the context in which it appears. In the ordinary *Strickland* case, prejudice means "a reasonable probability that, but for counsel's unprofessional errors, the result of the proceeding would have been different." But the *Strickland* Court cautioned that the prejudice inquiry is not meant to be applied in a "mechanical" fashion. *Strickland*. For when a court is evaluating an ineffective-assistance claim, the ultimate inquiry must concentrate on "the fundamental fairness of the proceeding." Ibid. Petitioner therefore argues that under a proper interpretation of *Strickland,* even if there is no showing of a reasonable probability of a different outcome, relief still must be granted if the convicted person shows that attorney errors rendered the trial fundamentally unfair. For the analytical purposes of this case, the Court will assume that petitioner's interpretation of *Strickland* is the correct one. In light of the Court's ultimate holding, however, the Court need not decide that question here.

As explained above, not every public-trial violation will in fact lead to a fundamentally unfair trial. Nor can it be said that the failure to object to a public-trial violation always deprives the defendant of a reasonable probability of a different outcome. Thus, when a defendant raises a public-trial violation via an ineffective-assistance-of-counsel claim, *Strickland* prejudice is not shown automatically. Instead, the burden is on the defendant to show either a reasonable probability of a different outcome in his or her case or, as the Court has assumed for these purposes, to show that the particular public-trial violation was so serious as to render his or her trial fundamentally unfair.

Neither the reasoning nor the holding here calls into question the Court's precedents determining that certain errors are deemed structural and require reversal because they cause fundamental unfairness, either to the defendant in the specific case or by pervasive undermining of the systemic requirements of a fair and open judicial process. See Murray, A Contextual Approach to Harmless Error Review, 130 Harv.L.Rev. 1791, 1813, 1822 (2017) (noting that the "eclectic normative objectives of criminal procedure" go beyond protecting a defendant from erroneous conviction and include ensuring " 'that the administration of justice should reasonably appear to be disinterested' "). Those precedents include *Sullivan v. Louisiana*, 508 U.S. 275 (1993) (failure to give a reasonable-doubt instruction); *Tumey v. Ohio,* 273 U.S. 510 (1927) (biased judge); and *Vasquez v. Hillery* [Note 7, p. 955] (exclusion of grand jurors on the basis of race). This Court, in addition, has granted automatic relief to defendants who prevailed on claims alleging race or gender discrimination in the selection of the petit jury, see *Batson v. Kentucky* [p. 1251], * * * though the Court has yet to label those errors structural in express terms. * * * The errors in those cases necessitated automatic reversal after they were preserved and then raised on direct appeal.

And this opinion does not address whether the result should be any different if the errors were raised instead in an ineffective-assistance claim on collateral review.

The reason for placing the burden on the petitioner in this case, however, derives both from the nature of the error and the difference between a public-trial violation preserved and then raised on direct review and a public-trial violation raised as an ineffective-assistance-of-counsel claim. As explained above, when a defendant objects to a courtroom closure, the trial court can either order the courtroom opened or explain the reasons for keeping it closed. When a defendant first raises the closure in an ineffective-assistance claim, however, the trial court is deprived of the chance to cure the violation either by opening the courtroom or by explaining the reasons for closure.

Furthermore, when state or federal courts adjudicate errors objected to during trial and then raised on direct review, the systemic costs of remedying the error are diminished to some extent. That is because, if a new trial is ordered on direct review, there may be a reasonable chance that not too much time will have elapsed for witness memories still to be accurate and physical evidence not to be lost. There are also advantages of direct judicial supervision. Reviewing courts, in the regular course of the appellate process, can give instruction to the trial courts in a familiar context that allows for elaboration of the relevant principles based on review of an adequate record. For instance, in this case, the factors and circumstances that might justify a temporary closure are best considered in the regular appellate process and not in the context of a later proceeding, with its added time delays.

When an ineffective-assistance-of-counsel claim is raised in postconviction proceedings, the costs and uncertainties of a new trial are greater because more time will have elapsed in most cases. The finality interest is more at risk, see *Strickland* (noting the "profound importance of finality in criminal proceedings"), and direct review often has given at least one opportunity for an appellate review of trial proceedings. These differences justify a different standard for evaluating a structural error depending on whether it is raised on direct review or raised instead in a claim alleging ineffective assistance of counsel. * * * In sum, "[a]n ineffective-assistance claim can function as a way to escape rules of waiver and forfeiture and raise issues not presented at trial," thus undermining the finality of jury verdicts. *Harrington v. Richter,* [p. 154]. For this reason, the rules governing ineffective assistance claims "must be applied with scrupulous care."

IV

The final inquiry concerns the ineffective-assistance claim in this case. Although the case comes on the assumption that petitioner has shown deficient performance by counsel, he has not shown prejudice in the ordinary sense, *i.e.,* a reasonable probability that the jury would not have convicted him if his attorney had objected to the closure. * * * It is of course possible that potential jurors might have behaved differently if petitioner's family had been present. And it is true that the presence of the public might have had some bearing on juror reaction. But here petitioner offered no "evidence or legal argument establishing prejudice" in the sense of a reasonable probability of a different outcome but for counsel's failure to object. * * * In other circumstances a different result might obtain. If, for instance, defense counsel errs in failing to object when the government's main witness testifies in secret, then the defendant might be able to show prejudice with little more detail. Even in those circumstances, however, the burden would remain on the defendant to make the prejudice showing, because a public-trial violation does not always lead to a fundamentally unfair trial.

In light of the above assumption that prejudice can be shown by a demonstration of fundamental unfairness, the remaining question is whether petitioner has shown that counsel's failure to object rendered the trial fundamentally unfair. The Court concludes that petitioner has not made the showing. Although petitioner's mother and her minister were indeed excluded from the courtroom for two days during jury selection, petitioner's trial was not conducted in secret or in a remote place. * * * The closure was limited to the jury *voir dire*; the courtroom remained open during the evidentiary phase of the trial; the closure decision apparently was made by court officers rather than the judge; there were many members of the venire who did not become jurors but who did observe the proceedings; and there was a record made of the proceedings that does not indicate any basis for concern, other than the closure itself.

There has been no showing, furthermore, that the potential harms flowing from a courtroom closure came to pass in this case. For example, there is no suggestion that any juror lied during *voir dire*; no suggestion of misbehavior by the prosecutor, judge, or any other party; and no suggestion that any of the participants failed to approach their duties with the neutrality and serious purpose that our system demands.

* * *

In the criminal justice system, the constant, indeed unending, duty of the judiciary is to seek and to find the proper balance between the necessity for fair and just trials and the importance of finality of judgments. When a structural error is preserved and raised on direct review, the balance is in the defendant's favor, and a new trial generally will be granted as a matter of right. When a structural error is raised in the context of an ineffective-assistance claim, however, finality concerns are far more pronounced. For this reason, and in light of the other circumstances present in this case, petitioner must show prejudice in order to obtain a new trial.

JUSTICE THOMAS, with whom JUSTICE GORSUCH joins, concurring.

I write separately with two observations about the scope of the Court's holding. First, this case comes to us on the parties' "assumption[s]" that the closure of the courtroom during jury selection "was a Sixth Amendment violation" and that "defense counsel provided ineffective assistance" by "failing to object" to it. The Court previously held in a *per curiam* opinion—issued without the benefit of merits briefing or argument—that the Sixth Amendment right to a public trial extends to jury selection. See *Presley v. Georgia,* (Thomas, J., dissenting). I have some doubts about whether that holding is consistent with the original understanding of the right to a public trial, and I would be open to reconsidering it in a case in which we are asked to do so.

Second, the Court "assume[s]," for the "analytical purposes of this case," that a defendant may establish prejudice under *Strickland* by demonstrating that his attorney's error led to a fundamentally unfair trial. * * * *Strickland* did not hold, as the Court assumes, that a defendant may establish prejudice by showing that his counsel's errors "rendered the trial fundamentally unfair." Because the Court concludes that the closure during petitioner's jury selection did not lead to fundamental unfairness in any event, no part of the discussion about fundamental unfairness is necessary to its result.

In light of these observations, I do not read the opinion of the Court to preclude the approach set forth in Justice Alito's opinion, which correctly applies our precedents.[c]

---

[c] But consider, Primus & Murray, Redefining *Strickland* Prejudice after *Weaver v. Massachusetts*, Harv.L.Rev. Blog (May 22, 2018), reviewing the first year of judicial responses to *Weaver* and concluding that "state and lower federal courts have already begun embracing *Weaver*'s dicta about fundamental unfairness as justification for enlarging *Strickland*'s conception of prejudice." Those courts have looked to the grounding of the structural violation that counsel failed to challenge, assuming that per se prejudice will be established if the violation has been categorized as structural because it invariably produces fundamental unfairness in the judicial process. Most of the cases addressed IAC claims based on the failure to challenge a public trial violation, with the courts ruling that the closure at issue was partial and thus similar to that presented in *Weaver*. Several cases addressed deficient counsel performance related to the right to a jury trial, and in finding the fundamental-unfairness grounding inapplicable, stressed that the error fell short of any outright denial of the right to jury trial (as would be presented if the defendant was never offered the opportunity to select a jury trial and counsel failed to object). The fundamental-unfairness grounding was held to apply where counsel failed to object to an unconstitutional reasonable doubt instruction (a structural defect so identified in *Weaver*) and where counsel failed to challenge an asset freeze that inhibited

JUSTICE ALITO, with whom JUSTICE GORSUCH joins, concurring in the judgment.

This case calls for a straightforward application of the familiar standard for evaluating ineffective assistance of counsel claims. *Strickland v. Washington.* * * * The [*Strickland*] prejudice requirement—which is the one at issue in this case—"arises from the very nature" of the right to effective representation: Counsel simply "cannot be 'ineffective' unless his mistakes have harmed the defense (or, at least, unless it is reasonably likely that they have)," *Gonzalez-Lopez* [p. 114]. In other words, "a violation of the Sixth Amendment right to *effective* representation is not 'complete' until the defendant is prejudiced." Ibid. * * *

Weaver makes much of the *Strickland* Court's statement that "the ultimate focus of inquiry must be on the fundamental fairness of the proceeding." *Strickland* [p. 132]. But the very next sentence clarifies what the Court had in mind, namely, the reliability of the proceeding. In that sentence, the Court explains that the proper concern—"[i]n every case"—is "whether, despite the strong presumption of reliability, the result of the particular proceeding is unreliable." Ibid. In other words, the focus on reliability is consistent throughout the *Strickland* opinion. * * * [T]here are two ways of meeting the *Strickland* prejudice requirement. A defendant must demonstrate either that the error at issue was prejudicial or that it belongs to the narrow class of attorney errors that are tantamount to a denial of counsel, for which an individualized showing of prejudice is unnecessary [*Cronic,* Note 2, p. 167].

Weaver attempts to escape this framework by stressing that the deprivation of the right to a public trial has been described as a "structural" error, but this is irrelevant under *Strickland.* The concept of "structural error" comes into play when it is established that an error occurred at the trial level and it must be decided whether the error was harmless. * * * The prejudice prong of *Strickland* is entirely different. It does not ask whether an error was harmless but whether there was an error at all, for unless counsel's deficient performance prejudiced the defense, there was no Sixth Amendment violation in the first place. See *Gonzalez-Lopez* (even where an attorney's deficient performance "pervades the entire trial," "we do not allow reversal of a conviction for that reason without a showing of prejudice" because "the requirement of showing prejudice in ineffectiveness claims stems from the very definition of the right at issue") [p. 115]. Weaver's theory conflicts with *Strickland* because it implies that an attorney's error can be prejudicial even if it "had no effect," or only "some conceivable effect," on the outcome of his trial. That is precisely what *Strickland* rules out. * * *

JUSTICE BREYER, with whom JUSTICE KAGAN joins, dissenting.

The Court notes that *Strickland's* "prejudice inquiry is not meant to be applied in a 'mechanical' fashion," and I agree. But, in my view, it follows from this principle that a defendant who shows that his attorney's constitutionally deficient performance produced a structural error should not face the additional—and often insurmountable—*Strickland* hurdle of demonstrating that the error changed the outcome of his proceeding. * * *

The Court has recognized that structural errors' distinctive attributes make them "defy analysis by 'harmless-error' standards." It has therefore *categorically* exempted structural errors from the case-by-case harmlessness review to which trial errors are subjected. Our precedent does not try to parse which structural errors are the truly egregious ones. It simply views *all* structural errors as "intrinsically harmful" and holds that *any* structural error warrants "automatic reversal" on direct appeal "without regard to [its] effect on the outcome" of a trial. *Neder v. United States* [p. 1420].

defendant's right to select counsel of choice and restricted the preparation of the defense. See also CRIMPROC § 11.10(d).

The majority here does not take this approach. It assumes that *some* structural errors—those that "lead to fundamental unfairness"—but not others, can warrant relief without a showing of actual prejudice under *Strickland*. While I agree that a showing of fundamental unfairness is sufficient to satisfy *Strickland,* I would not try to draw this distinction. * * * Even if some structural errors do not create fundamental unfairness, *all* structural errors nonetheless have features that make them "defy analysis by 'harmless-error' standards." *Fulminante* [p. 144]. This is why *all* structural errors—not just the "fundamental unfairness" ones—are exempt from harmlessness inquiry and warrant automatic reversal on direct review. Those same features mean that *all* structural errors defy an actual-prejudice analysis under *Strickland*. * * *

The problem is evident with regard to public-trial violations. This Court has recognized that "the benefits of a public trial are frequently intangible, difficult to prove, or a matter of chance." *Waller v. Georgia*. As a result, "a requirement that prejudice be shown 'would in most cases deprive [the defendant] of the [public-trial] guarantee, for it would be difficult to envisage a case in which he would have evidence available of specific injury.' " Ibid. In order to establish actual prejudice from an attorney's failure to object to a public-trial violation, a defendant would face the nearly impossible burden of establishing how his trial might have gone differently had it been open to the public.

I do not see how we can read *Strickland* as requiring defendants to prove what this Court has held cannot be proved. If courts do not presume prejudice when counsel's deficient performance leads to a structural error, then defendants may well be unable to obtain relief for incompetence that deprived them "of basic protections without which a criminal trial cannot reliably serve its function as a vehicle for determination n of guilt or innocence." *Neder*. This would be precisely the sort of "mechanical" application that *Strickland* tells us to avoid. * * *

§ 3. *STRICKLAND* APPLIED

1. ***An immense body of precedent.*** Apart from one or two search-and-seizure issues, no criminal process issue has more often been addressed in appellate opinions than the question of what constitutes ineffective assistance of counsel under the *Strickland* standards. Such rulings cover almost every action that could be taken by defense counsel, with the challenges sometimes based on what counsel failed to do and sometimes based on what counsel actually did. The body of precedent is immense, with hundreds of opinion added each year. As might be expected with such a large body of precedent, "the rulings are hardly consistent in their treatment of even roughly similar fact situations." CRIMPROC § 11.10.

The number of issues considered in this immense body of precedent is far too great to permit review here, even in a summary fashion. Indeed the post-*Strickland* Supreme Court rulings on IAC claims (over two dozen rulings) cover more issues that can be treated here. Apart from the paragraphs setting forth the two prongs of the *Strickland* standard, perhaps the most frequently discussed paragraphs in *Strickland* are those discussing strategic choices and their relationship to counsel's investigation (see p. 130). The cases included in this section focus on the Court's subsequent application of the principles stated there, read in light of other aspects of the *Strickland* opinion. The section considers only performance relating to a trial or sentencing proceeding. As for the application of *Strickland* to the defendant's consideration of a guilty plea, see Ch. 22, §§ 3 and 5.

2. ***Federal habeas review of state claims.*** Although the Supreme Court occasionally considers a state defendant's IAC claim on a direct review of a state court ruling affirming defendant's conviction, IAC claims usually are considered by the Court on review of a federal

habeas corpus challenge to the defendant's state conviction.[a] Prior to 1996, where a state court rejected an ineffective assistance claim and the defendant subsequently presented that claim in a federal habeas challenge, federal courts treated the issue as involving a mixed question of law and fact and therefore subject to de novo review. Thus, *Strickland* noted that its two-pronged test, and the principles governing application of that test, were applicable on federal habeas review of a state court rejection of an IAC claim, just as they were in the initial state court consideration of the IAC claim, notwithstanding that the "presumption of finality * * * is at its strongest on collateral attacks." In 1996, however, Congress adopted the Antiterrorism and Effective Death Penalty Act (AEDPA), which adopted a special review standard for federal habeas cases where the state court had considered and rejected on the merits the constitutional claim at issue. The review standard was no longer whether the state court had correctly interpreted federal constitutional law in rejecting the claim, but whether the state court's application of governing Supreme Court precedent was "objectively unreasonable." See § 2254(d)(1) (also allowing habeas relief where the state court ruling is "contrary to" that federal precedent, a review standard that typically would apply to an IAC claim only where the state court applied a test "contrary to" *Strickland*).

The bearing of this § 2254(d)(1) standard is discussed in *Harrington v. Richter,* infra. See also Ch. 29, § 6 (which includes a portion of the *Richter* opinion, not reproduced below, discussing the function of § 2254(d) as it relates to habeas review generally). Not all of the post 1996 Supreme Court rulings have involved application of the AEDPA standard. De novo review was applied where the habeas petition had been filed pre-AEDPA, and for post-AEDPA petitions, where the state court had not ruled on the particular prong of the *Strickland* test (e.g., where the state court had rejected the claim on a failure to show prejudice and had not considered the performance prong).

HARRINGTON V. RICHTER

562 U.S. 86, 131 S.Ct. 770, 178 L.Ed.2d 624 (2011).

JUSTICE KENNEDY delivered the opinion of the Court.

* * * It is necessary to begin by discussing the details of a crime committed more than a decade and a half ago. * * * Sometime after midnight on December 20, 1994, sheriff's deputies in Sacramento County, California, arrived at the home of a drug dealer named Joshua Johnson. Hours before, Johnson had been smoking marijuana in the company of Richter and two other men, Christian Branscombe and Patrick Klein. When the deputies arrived, however, they found only Johnson and Klein. Johnson was hysterical and covered in blood. Klein was lying on a couch in Johnson's living room, unconscious and bleeding. Klein and Johnson each had been shot twice. Johnson recovered; Klein died of his wounds.

Johnson gave investigators this account: After falling asleep, he awoke to find Richter and Branscombe in his bedroom, at which point Branscombe shot him. Johnson heard more gunfire in the living room and the sound of his assailants leaving. He got up, found Klein bleeding on the living room couch, and called 911. A gun safe, a pistol, and $6,000 cash, all of which had been in the bedroom, were missing. * * * Evidence at the scene corroborated Johnson's account. Investigators found spent shell casings in the bedroom (where Johnson said he had been shot) and in the living room (where Johnson indicated Klein had been shot). In the living room there were two casings, a .32 caliber and a .22 caliber. One of the bullets recovered from Klein's body was a

[a] IAC claims were a mainstay of almost 20,000 state-prisoner federal habeas petitions filed annually in 2003–2004. Roughly 50% of the petitions in non-capital habeas cases and 80% in capital cases included IAC claims. See King, et. al, Note 3, p. 1426, at 51–52, 89. The percentage of successful IAC claims in non-capital cases was less than one percent. Ibid. (Table 4), although not all rejections were based on the merits, as a substantial portion of petitions failed on such grounds as failure to exhaust state remedies and procedural default in state cases. See Ch. 29, § 1. As to the much higher success ratio in capital cases, see fn. e, p. 162.

.32 and the other was a .22. In the bedroom there were two more casings, both .32 caliber. In addition detectives found blood spatter near the living room couch and bloodstains in the bedroom. Pools of blood had collected in the kitchen and the doorway to Johnson's bedroom. Investigators took only a few blood samples from the crime scene. One was from a blood splash on the wall near the bedroom doorway, but no sample was taken from the doorway blood pool itself.

Investigators searched Richter's residence and found Johnson's gun safe, two boxes of .22-caliber ammunition, and a gun magazine loaded with cartridges of the same brand and type as the boxes. A ballistics expert later concluded the .22-caliber bullet that struck Klein and the .22-caliber shell found in the living room matched the ammunition found in Richter's home and bore markings consistent with the model of gun for which the magazine was designed.

Richter and Branscombe were arrested. At first Richter denied involvement. He would later admit taking Johnson's pistol and disposing of it and of the .32-caliber weapon Branscombe used to shoot Johnson and Klein. Richter's counsel produced Johnson's missing pistol, but neither of the guns used to shoot Johnson and Klein was found.

Branscombe and Richter were tried together on charges of murder, attempted murder, burglary, and robbery. Only Richter's case is presented here. * * * The prosecution built its case on Johnson's testimony and on circumstantial evidence. Its opening statement took note of the shell casings found at the crime scene and the ammunition and gun safe found at Richter's residence. Defense counsel offered explanations for the circumstantial evidence and derided Johnson as a drug dealer, a paranoid, and a trigger-happy gun fanatic who had drawn a pistol on Branscombe and Richter the last time he had seen them. And there were inconsistencies in Johnson's story. In his 911 call, for instance, Johnson first said there were four or five men who had broken into his house, not two; and in the call he did not identify Richter and Branscombe among the intruders.

Blood evidence does not appear to have been part of the prosecution's planned case prior to trial, and investigators had not analyzed the few blood samples taken from the crime scene. But the opening statement from the defense led the prosecution to alter its approach. Richter's attorney outlined the theory that Branscombe had fired on Johnson in self-defense and that Klein had been killed not on the living room couch but in the crossfire in the bedroom doorway. Defense counsel stressed deficiencies in the investigation, including the absence of forensic support for the prosecution's version of events.

The prosecution took steps to adjust to the counterattack now disclosed. Without advance notice and over the objection of Richter's attorney, one of the detectives who investigated the shootings testified for the prosecution as an expert in blood pattern evidence. He concluded it was unlikely Klein had been shot outside the living room and then moved to the couch, given the patterns of blood on Klein's face, as well as other evidence including "high velocity" blood spatter near the couch consistent with the location of a shooting. The prosecution also offered testimony from a serologist. She testified the blood sample taken near the pool by the bedroom door could be Johnson's but not Klein's.

Defense counsel's cross-examination probed weaknesses in the testimony of these two witnesses. The detective who testified on blood patterns acknowledged that his inferences were imprecise, that it was unlikely Klein had been lying down on the couch when shot, and that he could not say the blood in the living room was from either of Klein's wounds. Defense counsel elicited from the serologist a concession that she had not tested the bedroom blood sample for cross-contamination. She said that if the year-old sample had degraded, it would be difficult to tell whether blood of Klein's type was also present in the sample.

For the defense, Richter's attorney called seven witnesses. Prominent among these was Richter himself. Richter testified he and Branscombe returned to Johnson's house just before the shootings in order to deliver something to one of Johnson's roommates. By Richter's account, Branscombe entered the house alone while Richter waited in the driveway; but after hearing screams and gunshots, Richter followed inside. There he saw Klein lying not on the couch but in the bedroom doorway, with Johnson on the bed and Branscombe standing in the middle of the room. According to Richter, Branscombe said he shot at Johnson and Klein after they attacked him. Other defense witnesses provided some corroboration for Richter's story. His former girlfriend, for instance, said she saw the gun safe at Richter's house shortly before the shootings.

The jury returned a verdict of guilty on all charges. Richter was sentenced to life without parole. On appeal, his conviction was affirmed [by the California Court of Appeals]. * * * The California Supreme Court denied a petition for review, and Richter did not file a petition for certiorari with this Court. His conviction became final.

Richter later petitioned the California Supreme Court for a writ of habeas corpus.[b] He asserted a number of grounds for relief, including ineffective assistance of counsel. As relevant here, he claimed his counsel was deficient for failing to present expert testimony on serology, pathology, and blood spatter patterns, testimony that, he argued, would disclose the source of the blood pool in the bedroom doorway. This, he contended, would bolster his theory that Johnson had moved Klein to the couch. * * * He offered affidavits from three types of forensic experts. First, he provided statements from two blood serologists who said there was a possibility Klein's blood was intermixed with blood of Johnson's type in the sample taken from near the pool in the bedroom doorway. Second, he provided a statement from a pathologist who said the blood pool was too large to have come from Johnson given the nature of his wounds and his own account of his actions while waiting for the police. Third, he provided a statement from an expert in bloodstain analysis who said the absence of "a large number of satellite droplets" in photographs of the area around the blood in the bedroom doorway was inconsistent with the blood pool coming from Johnson as he stood in the doorway. Richter argued this evidence established the possibility that the blood in the bedroom doorway came from Klein, not Johnson. If that were true, he argued, it would confirm his account, not Johnson's.

The California Supreme Court denied Richter's petition in a one-sentence summary order. * * * Richter [then] filed a petition for habeas corpus in United States District Court. He reasserted the claims in his state petition. The District Court denied his petition, and a three-judge panel of the Court of Appeals for the Ninth Circuit affirmed. [However], the Court of Appeals [then] granted rehearing en banc and reversed the District Court's decision. * * * As a preliminary matter, the Court of Appeals questioned whether 28 U.S.C. § 2254(d) [Note 2, supra] was applicable to Richter's petition, since the California Supreme Court issued only a summary denial when it rejected his *Strickland* claims; but it determined the California decision was unreasonable in any event and that Richter was entitled to relief. The court held Richter's trial counsel was deficient for failing to consult experts on blood evidence in determining and pursuing a trial strategy and in preparing to rebut expert evidence the prosecution might—and later did—offer. Four judges dissented from the en banc decision. * * *

The statutory authority of federal courts to issue habeas corpus relief for persons in state custody is provided by 28 U.S.C. § 2254, as amended by the Antiterrorism and Effective Death Penalty Act of 1996 (AEDPA). * * * As an initial matter, it is necessary to decide whether § 2254(d) applies when a state court's order is unaccompanied by an opinion explaining the reasons relief

[b] California allows the state habeas petitioner to bypass lower courts and file directly with the California Supreme Court. The petition must state fully and particularly the facts establishing the grounds for relief, supported by "available documentary evidence * * * including trial transcripts and affidavits or declarations." If a prima facie case is established and the state's response establishes a factual dispute, an evidentiary hearing by a lower court will be ordered. However, if a prima facie case in not established (reading against the defendant all gaps, ambiguities, and inconsistencies in the alleged facts and accompanying documentary evidence), the petition is denied, typically in a summary ruling. See CRIMPROC § 11.10(a).

has been denied. [The Court here examined and rejected various arguments advanced by Richter for viewing § 2254(d) as implicitly excluding summary rulings, or viewing the summary order here as resting on grounds other than the merits. See pp. 1453–1455]. * * * [Since] Richter has failed to show that the California Supreme Court's decision did not involve a determination of the merits of his claim. Section 2254(d) applies to his petition.

Federal habeas relief may not be granted for claims subject to § 2254(d) unless it is shown that the earlier state court's decision "was contrary to" federal law then clearly established in the holdings of this Court, § 2254(d)(1); or that it "involved an unreasonable application of" such law, § 2254(d)(1); or that it "was based on an unreasonable determination of the facts" in light of the record before the state court, § 2254(d)(2). The Court of Appeals relied on the second of these exceptions to § 2254(d)'s relitigation bar, the exception in § 2254(d)(1) permitting relitigation where the earlier state decision resulted from an "unreasonable application of" clearly established federal law. In the view of the Court of Appeals, the California Supreme Court's decision on Richter's ineffective-assistance claim unreasonably applied the holding in *Strickland*. The Court of Appeals' lengthy opinion, however, discloses an improper understanding of § 2254(d)'s unreasonableness standard and of its operation in the context of a *Strickland* claim.

The pivotal question is whether the state court's application of the *Strickland* standard was unreasonable. This is different from asking whether defense counsel's performance fell below *Strickland*'s standard. Were that the inquiry, the analysis would be no different than if, for example, this Court were adjudicating a *Strickland* claim on direct review of a criminal conviction in a United States district court. Under AEDPA, though, it is a necessary premise that the two questions are different. For purposes of § 2254(d)(1), "an *unreasonable* application of federal law is different from an *incorrect* application of federal law." * * * A state court must be granted a deference and latitude that are not in operation when the case involves review under the *Strickland* standard itself. * * * A state court's determination that a claim lacks merit precludes federal habeas relief so long as "fairminded jurists could disagree" on the correctness of the state court's decision. * * *. [Also,] as this Court has explained, "[E]valuating whether a rule application was unreasonable requires considering the rule's specificity. The more general the rule, the more leeway courts have in reaching outcomes in case-by-case determinations." "[I]t is not an unreasonable application of clearly established Federal law for a state court to decline to apply a specific legal rule that has not been squarely established by this Court." *Knowles v. Mirzayance,* 556 U.S. 111 (2009).

Here it is not apparent how the Court of Appeals' analysis would have been any different without AEDPA. The court explicitly conducted a *de novo* review; and after finding a *Strickland* violation, it declared, without further explanation, that the "state court's decision to the contrary constituted an unreasonable application of *Strickland*." AEDPA demands more. Under § 2254(d), a habeas court must determine what arguments or theories supported or, as here, could have supported, the state court's decision; and then it must ask whether it is possible fairminded jurists could disagree that those arguments or theories are inconsistent with the holding in a prior decision of this Court. The opinion of the Court of Appeals all but ignored * * * [this] question* * *. Because [it] had little doubt that Richter's *Strickland* claim had merit, the Court of Appeals concluded the state court must have been unreasonable in rejecting it. * * *

The conclusion of the Court of Appeals that Richter demonstrated an unreasonable application by the state court of the *Strickland* standard now must be discussed. * * * "Surmounting *Strickland*'s high bar is never an easy task." *Padilla v. Kentucky* [Note 12, p. 1201]. An ineffective-assistance claim can function as a way to escape rules of waiver and forfeiture and raise issues not presented at trial, and so the *Strickland* standard must be applied with scrupulous care, lest "intrusive post-trial inquiry" threaten the integrity of the very adversary process the right to counsel is meant to serve. *Strickland.* Even under *de novo* review, the standard for judging counsel's representation is a most deferential one. Unlike a later reviewing court, the attorney observed the relevant proceedings, knew of materials outside the record, and interacted with the client, with opposing counsel, and with the judge. It is "all too tempting" to "second-guess counsel's assistance after conviction or adverse sentence." Ibid. * * * The question is whether an attorney's representation amounted to incompetence under 'prevailing professional norms,' not whether it deviated from best practices or most common custom.

Establishing that a state court's application of *Strickland* was unreasonable under § 2254(d) is all the more difficult. The standards created by *Strickland* and § 2254(d) are both "highly deferential," and when the two apply in tandem, review is "doubly" so, *Knowles*. The *Strickland* standard is a general one, so the range of reasonable applications is substantial. Federal habeas courts must guard against the danger of equating unreasonableness under *Strickland* with unreasonableness under § 2254(d). When § 2254(d) applies, the question is not whether counsel's actions were reasonable. The question is whether there is any reasonable argument that counsel satisfied *Strickland*'s deferential standard. * * *

The Court of Appeals first held that Richter's attorney rendered constitutionally deficient service because he did not consult blood evidence experts in developing the basic strategy for Richter's defense or offer their testimony as part of the principal case for the defense. *Strickland,* however, permits counsel to "make a reasonable decision that makes particular investigations unnecessary." It was at least arguable that a reasonable attorney could decide to forgo inquiry into the blood evidence in the circumstances here.

Criminal cases will arise where the only reasonable and available defense strategy requires consultation with experts or introduction of expert evidence, whether pretrial, at trial, or both. There are, however, "countless ways to provide effective assistance in any given case. Even the best criminal defense attorneys would not defend a particular client in the same way." *Strickland.* Rare are the situations in which the "wide latitude counsel must have in making tactical decisions" will be limited to any one technique or approach. Ibid. It can be assumed that in some cases counsel would be deemed ineffective for failing to consult or rely on experts, but even that formulation is sufficiently general that state courts would have wide latitude in applying it. Here it would be well within the bounds of a reasonable judicial determination for the state court to conclude that defense counsel could follow a strategy that did not require the use of experts regarding the pool in the doorway to Johnson's bedroom.

From the perspective of Richter's defense counsel when he was preparing Richter's defense, there were any number of hypothetical experts—specialists in psychiatry, psychology, ballistics, fingerprints, tire treads, physiology, or numerous other disciplines and subdisciplines—whose insight might possibly have been useful. An attorney can avoid activities that appear "distractive from more important duties." *Bobby v. Van Hook,* [Note 4, p. 137]. Counsel was entitled to formulate a strategy that was reasonable at the time and to balance limited resources in accord with effective trial tactics and strategies. * * *

In concluding otherwise the Court of Appeals failed to "reconstruct the circumstances of counsel's challenged conduct" and "evaluate the conduct from counsel's perspective at the time." *Strickland.* In its view Klein's location was "the single most critical issue in the case" given the differing theories of the prosecution and the defense, and the source of the blood in the doorway was therefore of central concern. But it was far from a necessary conclusion that this was evident at the time of the trial. There were many factual differences between prosecution and defense versions of the events on the night of the shootings. It is only because forensic evidence has emerged concerning the source of the blood pool that the issue could with any plausibility be said to stand apart. Reliance on "the harsh light of hindsight" to cast doubt on a trial that took place now more than 15 years ago is precisely what *Strickland* and AEDPA seek to prevent. * * *

Even if it had been apparent that expert blood testimony could support Richter's defense, it would be reasonable to conclude that a competent attorney might elect not to use it. The Court of Appeals opinion for the en banc majority rests in large part on a hypothesis that reasonably could have been rejected. The hypothesis is that without jeopardizing Richter's defense, an expert could have testified that the blood in Johnson's doorway could not have come from Johnson and could have come from Klein, thus suggesting that Richter's version of the shooting was correct and Johnson's a fabrication. This theory overlooks the fact that concentrating on the blood pool carried its own serious risks. If serological analysis or other forensic evidence demonstrated that the blood came from Johnson alone, Richter's story would be exposed as an invention. An attorney need not pursue an investigation that would be fruitless, much less one that might be harmful to the defense. Here Richter's attorney had reason to question the truth of his client's account, given, for instance, Richter's initial denial of involvement and the subsequent production of Johnson's missing pistol.

It would have been altogether reasonable to conclude that this concern justified the course Richter's counsel pursued. Indeed, the Court of Appeals recognized this risk insofar as it pertained to the suggestion that counsel should have had the blood evidence tested. 578 F.3d, at 956, n. 9.[c] But the court failed to recognize that making a central issue out of blood evidence would have increased the likelihood of the prosecution's producing its own evidence on the blood pool's origins and composition; and once matters proceeded on this course, there was a serious risk that expert evidence could destroy Richter's case. Even apart from this danger, there was the possibility that expert testimony could shift attention to esoteric matters of forensic science, distract the jury from whether Johnson was telling the truth, or transform the case into a battle of the experts. * * * True, it appears that defense counsel's opening statement itself inspired the prosecution to introduce expert forensic evidence. But the prosecution's evidence may well have been weakened by the fact that it was assembled late in the process; and in any event the prosecution's response shows merely that the defense strategy did not work out as well as counsel had hoped, not that counsel was incompetent.

To support a defense argument that the prosecution has not proved its case it sometimes is better to try to cast pervasive suspicion of doubt than to strive to prove a certainty that exonerates. All that happened here is that counsel pursued a course that conformed to the first option. If this case presented a *de novo* review of *Strickland,* the foregoing might well suffice to reject the claim of inadequate counsel, but that is an unnecessary step. The Court of Appeals must be reversed if there was a reasonable justification for the state court's decision. In light of the record here there was no basis to rule that the state court's determination was unreasonable.

---

[c] In the cited footnote, the Ninth Circuit majority reasoned: "We agree with the dissent that counsel's decision not to ask the prosecution to *test* the blood sample before trial in order to determine blood type was not unreasonable, as such a test might have eliminated existing ambiguities that were useful to the defense and instead have produced definitive results that were damaging. However, there could have been no negative consequence to *consulting* a blood spatter expert or a serology expert prior to trial. An adequate pretrial investigation would not have alerted the State to counsel's strategy, or somehow 'cooked his own client.' Dissent at 969. Had counsel consulted a blood spatter expert, the State would have been unaware that he had done so until the point at which counsel presented expert testimony at trial, and then only if he made an informed decision that doing so would be helpful to the defense. Had counsel consulted a serology expert, the State would similarly have been unaware of such pretrial consultations unless and until counsel made an informed decision to ask the expert to test the blood type, or until he presented the expert as a witness to counter the testimony of the State's serology expert. Such consultations would not, therefore, have posed any risk."

The Ninth Circuit dissent responded that an investigatory consultation at best would have led to testing and "very well could have (and in this case would have) aided the State in producing inculpatory evidence against his client." Counsel could assume that the defense was better off without testing, and "if the state decided independently to test the blood samples and found potentially exculpatory evidence it was required by law to disclose the result to defense counsel. *Brady v. Maryland* [p. 1130]." Consider also fn. b, p. 178.

The Court of Appeals erred in dismissing strategic considerations like these as an inaccurate account of counsel's actual thinking. Although courts may not indulge "*post hoc* rationalization" for counsel's decisionmaking that contradicts the available evidence of counsel's actions, *Wiggins v. Smith* [Note 2, p. 162], neither may they insist counsel confirm every aspect of the strategic basis for his or her actions.[d] There is a "strong presumption" that counsel's attention to certain issues to the exclusion of others reflects trial tactics rather than "sheer neglect." *Yarborough v. Gentry,* 540 U.S. 1, 8 (2003). After an adverse verdict at trial even the most experienced counsel may find it difficult to resist asking whether a different strategy might have been better, and, in the course of that reflection, to magnify their own responsibility for an unfavorable outcome. *Strickland,* however, calls for an inquiry into the objective reasonableness of counsel's performance, not counsel's subjective state of mind.

The Court of Appeals also found that Richter's attorney was constitutionally deficient because he had not expected the prosecution to offer expert testimony and therefore was unable to offer expert testimony of his own in response. * * * The Court of Appeals erred in suggesting counsel had to be prepared for "any contingency." *Strickland* does not guarantee perfect representation, only a " 'reasonably competent attorney.' " * * * Representation is constitutionally ineffective only if it "so undermined the proper functioning of the adversarial process" that the defendant was denied a fair trial. *Strickland.* Just as there is no expectation that competent counsel will be a flawless strategist or tactician, an attorney may not be faulted for a reasonable miscalculation or lack of foresight or for failing to prepare for what appear to be remote possibilities.

Here, Richter's attorney was mistaken in thinking the prosecution would not present forensic testimony. But the prosecution itself did not expect to make that presentation and had made no preparations for doing so on the eve of trial. For this reason alone, it is at least debatable whether counsel's error was so fundamental as to call the fairness of the trial into doubt.

Even if counsel should have foreseen that the prosecution would offer expert evidence, Richter would still need to show it was indisputable that *Strickland* required his attorney to act upon that knowledge. Attempting to establish this, the Court of Appeals held that defense counsel should have offered expert testimony to rebut the evidence from the prosecution. But *Strickland* does not enact Newton's third law for the presentation of evidence, requiring for every prosecution expert an equal and opposite expert from the defense.

In many instances cross-examination will be sufficient to expose defects in an expert's presentation. When defense counsel does not have a solid case, the best strategy can be to say that there is too much doubt about the State's theory for a jury to convict. And while in some instances "even an isolated error" can support an ineffective-assistance claim if it is "sufficiently egregious and prejudicial," *Murray v. Carrier,* 477 U.S. 478 (1986), it is difficult to establish ineffective assistance when counsel's overall performance indicates active and capable advocacy. Here Richter's attorney represented him with vigor and conducted a skillful cross-examination. As noted, defense counsel elicited concessions from the State's experts and was able to draw attention to weaknesses in their conclusions stemming from the fact that their analyses were conducted long after investigators had left the crime scene. For all of these reasons, it would have been reasonable to find that Richter had not shown his attorney was deficient under *Strickland.*

---

[d] The Ninth Circuit majority concluded that the defense strategy posed by the Ninth Circuit dissenters (basically that set forth in the Supreme Court's opinion) was nothing more than a "post hoc rationalization," as evidenced by counsel's deposition (which was part of the record before the federal habeas court). In that deposition, the Ninth Circuit majority noted: "Counsel was unable to provide any reasoned explanation for failing to consult forensic experts or to seek expert testimony in order to corroborate his client's testimony or prepare to rebut the prosecution's case," as his explanation was simply that his strategy "was to pit his client's credibility against Johnson and to attack the evidentiary gaps in the police investigation of the crime scene." Indeed, "counsel acknowledged that he missed crucial information when conducting his cross-examination" and that with the assistance of experts, "you don't make those mistakes like I made."

The Court of Appeals further concluded that Richter had established prejudice under *Strickland* given the expert evidence his attorney could have introduced. It held that the California Supreme Court would have been unreasonable in concluding otherwise. This too was error. * * * In assessing prejudice under *Strickland,* the question is not whether a court can be certain counsel's performance had no effect on the outcome or whether it is possible a reasonable doubt might have been established if counsel acted differently. * * * Instead, *Strickland* asks whether it is "reasonably likely" the result would have been different. This does not require a showing that counsel's actions "more likely than not altered the outcome," but the difference between *Strickland*'s prejudice standard and a more-probable-than-not standard is slight and matters "only in the rarest case." Id. The likelihood of a different result must be substantial, not just conceivable.

It would not have been unreasonable for the California Supreme Court to conclude Richter's evidence of prejudice fell short of this standard. His expert serology evidence established nothing more than a theoretical possibility that, in addition to blood of Johnson's type, Klein's blood may also have been present in a blood sample taken near the bedroom doorway pool. At trial, defense counsel extracted a concession along these lines from the prosecution's expert. The pathology expert's claim about the size of the blood pool could be taken to suggest only that the wounded and hysterical Johnson erred in his assessment of time or that he bled more profusely than estimated. And the analysis of the purported blood pattern expert indicated no more than that Johnson was not standing up when the blood pool formed.

It was also reasonable to find Richter had not established prejudice given that he offered no evidence directly challenging other conclusions reached by the prosecution's experts. For example, there was no dispute that the blood sample taken near the doorway pool matched Johnson's blood type. * * * Nor did Richter provide any direct refutation of the State's expert testimony describing how blood spatter near the couch suggested a shooting in the living room and how the blood patterns on Klein's face were inconsistent with Richter's theory that Klein had been killed in the bedroom doorway and moved to the couch.

There was, furthermore, sufficient conventional circumstantial evidence pointing to Richter's guilt. It included the gun safe and ammunition found at his home; his flight from the crime scene; his disposal of the .32-caliber gun and of Johnson's pistol; his shifting story concerning his involvement; the disappearance prior to the arrival of the law enforcement officers of the .22-caliber weapon that killed Klein; the improbability of Branscombe's not being wounded in the shootout that resulted in a combined four bullet wounds to Johnson and Klein; and the difficulties the intoxicated and twice-shot Johnson would have had in carrying the body of a dying man from bedroom doorway to living room couch, not to mention the lack of any obvious reason for him to do so. There was ample basis for the California Supreme Court to think any real possibility of Richter's being acquitted was eclipsed by the remaining evidence pointing to guilt. * * *

The California Supreme Court's decision on the merits of Richter's *Strickland* claim required more deference than it received. Richter was not entitled to the relief ordered by the Court of Appeals. The judgment is reversed, and the case is remanded for further proceedings consistent with this opinion.

JUSTICE KAGAN took no part in the consideration or decision of this case.

JUSTICE GINSBURG, concurring in the judgment.

In failing even to consult blood experts in preparation for the murder trial, Richter's counsel, I agree with the Court of Appeals, "was not functioning as the 'counsel' guaranteed the defendant by the Sixth Amendment." *Strickland v. Washington.* The strong force of the prosecution's case, however, was not significantly reduced by the affidavits offered in support of Richter's habeas petition. I would therefore not rank counsel's lapse "so serious as to deprive [Richter] of a fair trial, a trial whose result is reliable." Ibid. For that reason, I concur in the Court's judgment.

NOTES AND QUESTIONS

1. ***Section 2254(d)(1) deference.*** CRIMPROC § 11.10(a) notes that, between 2003–2011, the Supreme Court reversed (often without dissent) seven Ninth Circuit IAC rulings, finding in each that the Ninth Circuit erred in concluding that a state court had unreasonably applied *Strickland* in its rejection of an IAC claim. CRIMPROC adds that, while these Supreme Court decisions were based on § 2254(d)(1) and its "additional layer of deference," they may, in some respects, be viewed as binding precedent for state courts in their interpretation of *Strickland.* That is because "the Court often has pointed to flaws in the Ninth Circuit analysis that seemingly also would be flaws in a de novo application of *Strickland.*" *Harrington v. Richter* is offered as an illustration of such a ruling in its treatment of "several Ninth Circuit errors." But consider *State v. Denz,* 306 P.3d 98 (Ariz.App. 2013) ("*Harrington's* * * * persuasive value must be evaluated in light of its procedural posture * * * under the AEDPA's * * * highly deferential [review], whereas we review de novo the trial court's ultimate conclusion here"; also noting that the failure to consult a medical expert in the case before it was "factually distinguishable").

2. ***Establishing "counsel's actual thinking."*** In its rejection of the Court of Appeals conclusion as to "counsel's actual thinking" (p. 157), the Supreme Court addressed a recurring issue in lower court IAC rulings—what weight should be given to what defense counsel does or does not say in the collateral attack proceedings raising the IAC claim? As discussed in Note 5, p. 125, the raising of the claim allows counsel to testify, and very often either the defense or the prosecution will require that counsel testify and produce any supporting documentary evidence in the case file as to counsel's efforts and reasoning. The Ninth Circuit, in a pre-*Strickland* ruling, warned against courts in habeas proceedings insisting on counsel's testimony and thereby placing counsel "in the unenviable position where, if he can recall his reasons, and they are good, he is hurting his former client, and if he can't recall his reasons or they are bad, or not very good, he is impugning his professional competence." *Kuhl v. United States,* 370 F.2d 20 (9th Cir. 1966). However, courts considering IAC claims in postconviction proceedings have since become accustomed to hearing counsel's testimony and weighing such considerations in evaluating that testimony.

3. ***Supreme Court consideration of counsel's explanation.*** *Harrington v. Richter* was not the first Supreme Court ruling to address the weight given to counsel's explanation. In *Burger v. Kemp*, as discussed in Note 5, p. 187, the Court majority stressed that the habeas court had heard counsel's testimony and accepted his explanation as to his strategic thinking, and that finding had been "twice sustained by the Court of Appeals." In *Wiggins v. Smith,* discussed in Note 2, p. 162, one of the defense counsel had testified that both counsel had decided to focus their sentencing hearing presentation on "disputing Wiggins direct responsibility for the murder," but the Court majority concluded that the "record of the actual sentencing proceeding" indicated that counsel "had never abandoned the strategy of presenting a mitigation offence" (indeed, they had presented "a half hearted mitigation case"). Thus, it appeared that their failure to investigate more thoroughly and seek a social history report "resulted from inattention." In describing counsel's inaction as the product of a "reasoned strategic judgment," the state court had relied on a "*post hoc* rationalization." See also fn. g, p. 165.

In another case decided during the same term as *Richter*, *Cullen v. Pinholster*, Note 4, p. 166, the Court again rejected a Ninth Circuit conclusion that a particular strategy was no more than a "*post hoc* rationalization" Here, the question was whether the state court could reasonably have found that counsel gave serious consideration to presenting a traditional mitigation defense in capital sentencing, but concluded that the better strategy was to rely on a more limited "family sympathy mitigation defense." The issue arose in a procedural setting identical to *Harrington* (on a summary denial by the California Supreme Court), and the Supreme Court was divided 5–3 as to whether the record would have allowed the state court reasonably to conclude that counsel had actually explored the possibility of a traditional mitigation defense. The dissenters, like the Ninth Circuit, relied heavily on a statement that defense counsel had made to the trial court, supplemented, in particular, by an affidavit of one of defendant's co-counsel. Defense counsel had moved to preclude the state from presenting aggravation witnesses, arguing that the required notice had not been provided, and stating that they accordingly "had not prepared any evidence by way of mitigation." The dissent viewed this as "the best available evidence" of counsel's treatment of mitigation, but the majority concluded that this statement was simply designed to reinforce the claim as to lack of notice. Other evidence in the record would support a conclusion that defense counsel expected all along that their notice objection might fail and had spent "considerable time and effort investigating mitigation." The dissent noted that the one counsel had stated in his affidavit that he could not recall any extensive exploration of mitigation issues, but the majority noted that the affidavit also acknowledged that the other counsel (now deceased) was primarily responsible for that area and the affidavit was made seven years after trial.

In rejecting the Ninth Circuit's conclusion as to "*post hoc* rationalizations," neither *Harrington* nor *Pinholster* referred to the limitations imposed by § 2254(d)(2), which authorizes the habeas court to grant relief on a claim adjudicated on the merits in state court proceedings where that adjudication "was based on an unreasonable determination of facts in light of the evidence presented in the state court proceeding." *Wood v. Allen*, 558 U.S. 290 (2010), held that a finding that defense counsel made a strategic determination not to pursue a particular action was a factual determination subject to § 2254(d)(2) (or possibly the "even more deferential" § 2254(e)(1)). Was the Court thereby indicating in these cases that the state court's reasonable application of *Strickland* was not necessarily tied to whether counsel actually considered the particular strategy supporting her actions? Consider Note 4, infra.

4. ***Counsel's "actual thought" and "objective reasonableness."*** The *Richter* opinion notes that "*Strickland* * * * calls for an inquiry into the objective reasonableness of counsel's performance, not counsel's subjective state of mind." That point was also made in *Pinholster* in connection with Court majority's discussion of the Ninth Circuit's *post hoc* rationalization analysis. Does the objective reasonableness standard thus support the reasoning in *Hammond v. Hall,* 586 F.3d 1289 (11th Cir. 2009)? Defense counsel there obtained a jury instruction to disregard the prosecutor's comments after the prosecutor made an inappropriate reference to the defendant's parole eligibility. At a postconviction hearing on defendant's IAC claim, defense counsel acknowledged that he did not consider a mistrial because he did not recognize that state law entitled defendant to an automatic mistrial. Rejecting the IAC claim, the Court of Appeals reasoned that "the question is not why Hammond's counsel failed to move for a mistrial * * *, but whether a competent attorney could have decided not to move for one." Competency of performance under *Strickland* was to be determined by asking whether "a hypothetical competent counsel reasonably could have taken action at trial identical to actual trial counsel." That standard sustained counsel's performance here as there were substantial strategic reasons for preferring a curative instruction over a mistrial.

5. ***The isolated error.*** As *Richter* notes (p. 157), findings of incompetent performance typically are based on counsel's overall performance, but an "isolated error" may be sufficient. Numerous cases have been based on such errors, with commentators noting that this is an area in which the separate prongs of *Strickland* tend to merge. See e.g., CRIMPROC § 11.10(c) ("The potential prejudicial impact of the subject dealt with by counsel reaches over into the competency determination, as that impact obviously relates to the care and effort expected from a competent adversary"). The Eleventh Circuit has suggested that where a performance challenge is based on counsel's failure to object to a trial error, that failure must "at least" relate to an error so serious

that, if raised for the first time on appeal, it would "satisfy the standard of prejudice we employ for plain error." *Gordon v. United States*, 518 F.3d 1291 (11th Cir. 2008). Plain error, as discussed in Ch. 28, § 4, requires a defense showing that (1) the error "affects the outcome" (i.e., would not be a harmless error) and (2) results in a "miscarriage of justice." (i.e., "seriously affects" the "fairness, integrity, or public reputation of judicial proceedings").

Consider also Easterbrook, J., commenting on an IAC analysis that focused on two alleged deficiencies in counsel's performance: "When analyzing the performance element of *Strickland*, the court asks only whether counsel may have erred by not interviewing and calling two potential witnesses. That's the way Carter framed the issue. It is the wrong question to ask. *Strickland* directs a court to examine the totality of counsel's performance, not to concentrate on a supposed error while losing sight of what the lawyer *did* for his client. * * * As happens too often, however, lawyers for the state have gone along with the petitioner's (understandable) desire to focus attention on what trial counsel arguably omitted, rather than the full course of representation. But this does not imply that it is right to ignore what Carter's lawyers did and focus only on what arguably did not occur." *Carter v. Duncan*, 619 F.3d 931 (7th Cir. 2016) (Easterbrook, J., concurring).

6. ***The limits of tactical decision making.*** Apart from requiring that the tactical decision be based on adequate investigation of the law and facts, what other limits apply to the "wide latitude counsel must have in making tactical decisions" (p. 155)? Consider *State v. Davis*, 872 So.2d 250 (Fla. 2004). There, defense counsel, representing an African-American defendant accused of murdering a white woman, informed the jury on voir dire that he did not like black people, that he was ashamed of his prejudice, but it sometimes did make him "mad towards black people because they're black." He urged the jury, which was entirely white, to live up to its word not to let race become a factor, stressing the need, as he well knew, to be especially vigilant against some feelings they may have "deep down," as he did.

On direct appeal from defendant's conviction, the Florida Supreme Court held that counsel's remarks to the jury brought his assistance below the level required by *Strickland*. The court reasoned that counsel's statements as to his own racial prejudice simply was not a "legitimate tactical approach," for "whether or not counsel is in fact a racist, his expressions of prejudice against African-Americans cannot be tolerated." The "manner in which counsel approached the subject [of racial prejudice] unnecessarily tended either to alienate jurors who did not share his animus against African-Americans * * *, or to legitimizing racial prejudice without accomplishing counsel's stated objective of bringing latent bias out into the open."

Mitigating Evidence and Capital Sentencing

1. ***Investigation in capital cases.*** Since *Strickland,* the Supreme Court has returned to the issue presented there—application of the *Strickland* standards to defense counsel's investigation and presentation of mitigating evidence in a capital sentencing hearing—in a long line of cases. See CRIMPROC § 11.10(c) (citing eleven post-*Strickland* rulings). All involved habeas review of state convictions and most of the Court's rulings reversed Court of Appeals decisions as having erroneously either sustained or rejected state court rulings that denied IAC claims. In some, the IAC claim was reviewed de novo, and in others, § 2254(d)(1) applied.

Where the Court concluded that the IAC claim should have been sustained, it did so by distinguishing its earlier rulings that had rejected IAC claims (including *Strickland* itself). Nonetheless, many commentators and several lower courts have viewed those decisions finding IAC violations, particularly *Wiggins v. Smith* and *Rompilla v. Beard* (described below), as having moved to a more rigorous scrutiny of counsel's performance in capital sentencing investigations, and to a less stringent view of the showing needed to establish prejudice.[e] Others derive a quite different lesson from these rulings, particularly when considered along with later rulings, such as *Cullen v. Pinholster* (described below). They maintain that the capital sentencing cases that have produced sharp divisions in the Court simply indicate that there is sufficiently flexibility in the governing law for differences in judicial perspective to govern the outcome—either through different readings of the record or differences in assessing application of *Strickland* principles at the edges. Still, they argue, the guiding principles remain the same and their basic content remains stable, as evidence by unanimous or near-unanimous Supreme Court rulings reversing federal circuits that appeared to disregard those principles in rejecting or sustaining IAC claims. See CRIMPROC § 11.10(c) (noting the variation among the circuits in their application of *Strickland* in capital sentencing cases, and the Court's response in per curiam reversals). Although the differing characterizations are based upon an analysis of the total body of the Court's capital sentencing rulings, the three cases described below clearly have attracted the most attention.

2. In WIGGINS v. SMITH, 539 U.S. 510 (2003), a 7–2 majority, per O'Connor, J., held that a state prisoner was entitled to federal habeas relief, as the state court had rendered an "unreasonable application of *Strickland*" in rejecting the defendant's claim of ineffective assistance at a capital sentencing hearing. After the trial court rejected a defense motion to bifurcate the sentencing hearing and thereby separate the issue of defendant's direct responsibility for the murder from the issue of mitigation, defense counsel (two experienced public defenders), apart from an opening statement reference to defendant's "difficult life" and "clean record," concentrated entirely on the direct responsibility issue. The state court concluded that counsel had made a reasonable strategic decision not to present any evidence of defendant's personal history. The Supreme Court majority found that determination unreasonable in light of the inadequacy of the investigation that led to counsels' decision. As the Supreme Court majority read the state court's decision (in contrast to the reading of dissenting Justices Scalia and Thomas), defense counsel were deemed to have satisfied their investigative responsibilities when they first examined two sources (a presentence investigative report [PSI] and Department of Social Service [DSS] records) that provided "rudimentary knowledge" of the harsh circumstances of the defendant's youth, and then decided (as they later testified) to focus their presentation entirely on disputing the defendant's direct responsibility for the killing. Rejecting that determination, the Court majority noted both that the trial court record strongly suggested that counsels' "failure to investigate thoroughly [defendant's personal history] resulted from inattention, not reasoned strategic judgment" (see Note 3, p. 159), and that "counsels' decision not to expand their investigation beyond the PSI and the DSS records fell short of the professional standards that prevailed in Maryland [at the time of the trial]." In support of the latter determination, the majority noted that: (1) the two sources examined by counsel suggested a significant potential for mitigation in defendant's personal history; (2) those sources did not suggest offsetting aggravating

[e] Commentators point to several factors that may have influenced that shift, apart from a partial change in the Court's composition. First, studies of federal habeas cases show a much higher success rate in capital cases, with a prime factor being successful IAC challenges to representation at capital sentencing hearings. See King, et. al., Note 3, p. 1426 (noting an earlier study reporting a 40% reversal rate and finding a 15% reversal rate in post AEDPA petitions). Second, there had been "a steady stream of highly publicized DNA exonerations in capital cases," with ineffective counsel often cited as contributing to the erroneous conviction. Third, the American Bar Association urged capital punishment states to adopt a death penalty moratorium until the state was able to achieve various reforms (including upgrading representation) that had produced a system flawed in both litigation of guilt and assignment of capital sentences. Fourth, various justices had taken note of the special bearing of the quality of representation upon the assignment of the death penalty. An Associated Press Report, Death Moratorium Backed, April 10, 2001, quoted Justice Ginsberg as having stated: "I have yet to see a death case among the dozens coming to the Supreme Court on eve-of-execution stay applications in which the defendant was well represented at trial. . . . People who are well represented do not get the death penalty." Justice Blackmun, dissenting from a denial of certiorari in *McFarland v. Scott,* 512 U.S. 1256 (1994), denounced key capital punishment states for failing to appoint qualified attorneys in death cases. Justice O'Connor in a 2001 speech noted that, "perhaps, it is time to look at minimum standards for appointed counsel in death cases." Lack of Lawyers Hinders Appeals in Death Cases, N.Y. Times, July 5, 2001.

factors, and thus did not present "the double edge we found to justify limited investigations in other cases, cf. *Burger v. Kemp,* 483 U.S. 776 (1987)"[f]; (3) "standard practice in Maryland in capital cases at the time * * * included the preparation of a social history report" (a step also required by the ABA Guidelines for death penalty representation); and (4) Public Defender funding had been available to obtain such a report.

3. In ROMPILLA v. BEARD, 545 U.S. 374 (2005), Rompilla's "evidence in mitigation consisted of relatively brief testimony: five of his family members argued in effect for residual doubt, and beseeched the jury for mercy" and Rompilla's 14 year-old-son "testified that he loved his father and would visit him in prison." However, state postconviction counsel produced significant mitigating evidence that trial counsel had failed to uncover relating to Rompilla's childhood, mental capacity, health, and alcoholism. The state court rejected the IAC claim, and the Third Circuit majority, applying the AEDPA, concluded that the state court's application of *Strickland* had been reasonable, "given defense counsel's efforts to uncover mitigation material, which included interviewing Rompilla and certain family members, as well as consultation with three mental health experts." A dissenting judge found otherwise, "concluding that counsels' failure to obtain relevant records on Rompilla's background was owing to the lawyers' unreasonable reliance on family members and medical experts to tell them what records might be useful." The Court majority (per Souter, J.) did not resolve this issue, finding ineffective representation based on a different failure in counsels' investigation. It noted:

"Counsel knew that the Commonwealth intended to seek the death penalty by proving Rompilla had a significant history of felony convictions indicating the use or threat of violence, an aggravator under state law. Counsel further knew that the Commonwealth would attempt to establish this history by proving Rompilla's prior conviction for rape and assault, and would emphasize his violent character by introducing a transcript of the rape victim's testimony given in that earlier trial. * * * It is clear, however, that defense counsel did not look at any part of that file, including the transcript, until warned by the prosecution a second time, [in] a colloquy the day before the evidentiary sentencing phase began, [that] the prosecutor * * * would present the transcript of the victim's testimony to establish the prior conviction. * * * [C]rucially, even after obtaining the transcript of the victim's testimony on the eve of the sentencing hearing, counsel apparently examined none of the other material in the file.

"With every effort to view the facts as a defense lawyer would have done at the time, it is difficult to see how counsel could have failed to realize that without examining the readily available file they were seriously compromising their opportunity to respond to a case for aggravation. * * * Without making reasonable efforts to review the file, defense counsel could have had no hope of knowing whether the prosecution was quoting selectively from the transcript, or whether there were circumstances extenuating the behavior described by the victim. The obligation to get the file was particularly pressing here owing to the similarity of the violent prior offense to the crime charged and Rompilla's sentencing strategy stressing residual doubt.

"The notion that defense counsel must obtain information that the State has and will use against the defendant is not simply a matter of common sense. As the District Court points out, the American Bar Association Standards for Criminal Justice in circulation at the time of

---

[f] In *Burger*, the Court majority, in a 5–4 decision, concluded that while counsel "could well have made a more thorough investigation" as to mitigating background evidence, the decision to limit that investigation and focus on other issues reflected a "reasonable professional judgment," taking account of the substantial drawbacks suggested by the initial investigation. Counsel had expressed concern that: (1) evidence of defendant's unhappy childhood would come primarily from defendant's mother, but her testimony also would reveal that the defendant "had committed at least one petty offense" (while, "as the record [otherwise] stood, there was absolutely no evidence that petitioner had any prior criminal record of any kind"); (2) the psychologist's testimony would suggest that petitioner "never expressed any remorse about his crime"; and (3) the psychologist's report indicated that placing the defendant on the stand was risky as defendant "might even have bragged about [the] crime."

Rompilla's trial describes the obligation in terms no one could misunderstand in the circumstances of a case like this one:

> 'It is the duty of the lawyer to conduct a prompt investigation of the circumstances of the case and to explore all avenues leading to facts relevant to the merits of the case and the penalty in the event of conviction. The investigation should always include efforts to secure information in the possession of the prosecution and law enforcement authorities. The duty to investigate exists regardless of the accused's admissions or statements to the lawyer of facts constituting guilt or the accused's stated desire to plead guilty.' 1 *ABA Standards for Criminal Justice* 4–4.1 (2d ed. 1982 Supp.). * * *

[W]e long have referred [to these ABA Standards] as 'guides to determining what is reasonable.' *Wiggins v. Smith*, (quoting *Strickland v. Washington*), and the Commonwealth has come up with no reason to think the quoted standard impertinent here.

"The dissent thinks [our] analysis creates a 'rigid, *per se*' rule that requires defense counsel to do a complete review of the file on any prior conviction introduced; but that is a mistake. Counsel fell short here because they failed to make reasonable efforts to review the prior conviction file, despite knowing that the prosecution intended to introduce Rompilla's prior conviction not merely by entering a notice of conviction into evidence but by quoting damaging testimony of the rape victim in that case. The unreasonableness of attempting no more than they did was heightened by the easy availability of the file at the trial courthouse, and the great risk that testimony about a similar violent crime would hamstring counsel's chosen defense of residual doubt. It is owing to these circumstances that the state courts were objectively unreasonable in concluding that counsel could reasonably decline to make any effort to review the file. Other situations, where a defense lawyer is not charged with knowledge that the prosecutor intends to use a prior conviction in this way, might well warrant a different assessment.

"Since counsel's failure to look at the file fell below the line of reasonable practice, there is a further question about prejudice, that is, whether 'there is a reasonable probability that, but for counsel's unprofessional errors, the result of the proceeding would have been different.' *Strickland*. * * * If the defense lawyers had looked in the file on Rompilla's prior conviction, it is uncontested they would have found a range of mitigation leads that no other source had opened up. In the same file with the transcript of the prior trial were the records of Rompilla's imprisonment on the earlier conviction, which defense counsel testified she had never seen. The prison files pictured Rompilla's childhood and mental health very differently from anything defense counsel had seen or heard. An evaluation by a corrections counselor states that Rompilla was 'reared in the slum environment of Allentown, Pa. vicinity. He early came to the attention of juvenile authorities, quit school at 16, [and] started a series of incarcerations in and out Penna. often of assaultive nature and commonly related to over-indulgence in alcoholic beverages.' The same file discloses test results that the defense's mental health experts would have viewed as pointing to schizophrenia and other disorders, and test scores showing a third grade level of cognition after nine years of schooling.[8]

---

[8] The dissent would ignore the opportunity to find this evidence on the ground that its discovery (and the consequent analysis of prejudice) "rests on serendipity." But once counsel had an obligation to examine the file, counsel had to make reasonable efforts to learn its contents; and once having done so, they could not reasonably have ignored mitigation evidence or red flags simply because they were unexpected. The dissent, however, assumes that counsel could reasonably decline even to read what was in the file, (if counsel had reviewed the case file for mitigating evidence, "[t]here would have been no reason for counsel to read, or even to skim, this obscure document"). While that could well have been true if counsel had been faced with a large amount of possible evidence, there is no indication that examining the case file in question here would have required significant labor. Indeed, Pennsylvania has conspicuously failed to contest Rompilla's claim that because the information was located in the prior conviction file, reasonable efforts would have led counsel to this information.

"The accumulated entries would have destroyed the benign conception of Rompilla's upbringing and mental capacity defense counsel had formed from talking with Rompilla himself and some of his family members, and from the reports of the mental health experts. With this information, counsel would have become skeptical of the impression given by the five family members and would unquestionably have gone further to build a mitigation case. Further effort would presumably have unearthed much of the material postconviction counsel found, including testimony from several members of Rompilla's family, whom trial counsel did not interview. * * * This evidence adds up to a mitigation case that bears no relation to the few naked pleas for mercy actually put before the jury, and although we suppose it is possible that a jury could have heard it all and still have decided on the death penalty, that is not the test. It goes without saying that the undiscovered mitigating evidence, taken as a whole, 'might well have influenced the jury's appraisal' of [Rompilla's] culpability,' *Wiggins,* and the likelihood of a different result if the evidence had gone in is 'sufficient to undermine confidence in the outcome' actually reached at sentencing, *Strickland.*"

Justice Kennedy's dissent (joined by Chief Justice Rehnquist, and Justices Scalia and Thomas), responded, in part:

"A *per se* rule requiring counsel in every case to review the records of prior convictions used by the State as aggravation evidence is a radical departure from *Strickland* and its progeny. We have warned in the past against the creation of 'specific guidelines' or 'checklist[s] for judicial evaluation of attorney performance.' *Strickland.* * * * [So too, while] we have referred to the ABA Standards for Criminal Justice as a useful point of reference, we have been careful to say these standards 'are only guides' and do not establish the constitutional baseline for effective assistance of counsel. The majority, by parsing the guidelines as if they were binding statutory text, ignores this admonition. * * * The Court's opinion makes clear it has imposed on counsel a broad obligation to review prior conviction case files where those priors are used in aggravation—and to review every document in those files if not every single page of every document, regardless of the prosecution's proposed use for the prior conviction. * * * One member of the majority tries to limit the Court's new rule by arguing that counsel's decision here was 'not the result of an informed tactical decision,' (O'Connor, J., concurring), but the record gives no support for this notion.[g]

"The majority also disregards the sound strategic calculation supporting the decisions made by Rompilla's attorneys. Charles and Dantos were 'aware of [Rompilla's] priors' and 'aware of the circumstances' surrounding these convictions. At the postconviction hearing, Dantos also indicated that she had reviewed documents relating to the prior conviction. Based on this information, as well as their numerous conversations with Rompilla and his family, Charles and Dantos reasonably could conclude that reviewing the full prior conviction case file was not the best allocation of resources. * * *

"In imposing this new rule, the Court states that counsel in this case could review the 'entire file' with 'ease.' There is simply no support in the record for this assumption. Case files often comprise numerous boxes. The file may contain, among other things, witness statements, forensic evidence, arrest reports, grand jury transcripts, testimony and exhibits relating to any pretrial suppression hearings, trial transcripts, trial exhibits, post-trial motions and presentence reports. Full review of even a single prior conviction case file could be time consuming, and many of the

[g] Justice O'Connor joined the opinion of the Court, but also wrote separately. Defense attorney Dantos testified at the postconviction hearing that she had examined some files regarding the prior conviction (see dissent, infra), but offered no explanation of why she had not looked at the entire file. Justice O'Connor concluded that the decision not to examine the entire file "was not the result of an informed tactical decision about how the lawyers' time would best be spent" (as the dissent suggested). Their failure would "not necessarily have been deficient" if based on such a "careful exercise of judgment," as where they determined, for example, "that the file was inaccessible or so large that examining it would necessarily divert them from other trial-preparation tasks they thought more promising." Here, however, the failure was "the result of inattention" and thus could not be justified under *Strickland.*

documents in a file are duplicative or irrelevant. * * * Today's decision will not increase the resources committed to capital defense. (At the time of Rompilla's trial, the Lehigh County Public Defender's Office had two investigators for 2,000 cases.) If defense attorneys dutifully comply with the Court's new rule, they will have to divert resources from other tasks. The net effect of today's holding in many cases—instances where trial counsel reasonably can conclude that reviewing old case files is not an effective use of time—will be to diminish the quality of representation. * * *

"Even accepting the Court's misguided analysis of the adequacy of representation by Rompilla's trial counsel, Rompilla is still not entitled to habeas relief. *Strickland* assigns the defendant the burden of demonstrating prejudice. Rompilla cannot satisfy this standard, and only through a remarkable leap can the Court conclude otherwise. * * * The Court's theory of prejudice rests on serendipity. Nothing in the old case file diminishes the aggravating nature of the prior conviction. * * * The Court, recognizing this problem, instead finds prejudice through chance. If Rompilla's attorneys had reviewed the case file of his prior rape and burglary conviction, the Court says, they would have stumbled across 'a range of mitigation leads.' The range of leads to which the Court refers is in fact a handful of notations within a single 10-page document. The document, an 'Initial Transfer Petition,' appears to have been prepared by the Pennsylvania Department of Corrections after Rompilla's conviction to facilitate his initial assignment to one of the Commonwealth's maximum-security prisons. * * * [N]othing in the record indicates that Rompilla's trial attorneys would have discovered the transfer petition, or the clues contained in it, if they had reviewed the old file. The majority faults Rompilla's attorneys for failing to 'learn what the Commonwealth knew about the crime,' 'discover any mitigating evidence the Commonwealth would downplay,' and 'anticipate the details of the aggravating evidence the Commonwealth would emphasize.' Yet if Rompilla's attorneys had reviewed the case file with these purposes in mind, they almost surely would have attributed no significance to the transfer petition following only a cursory review. * * * The Court claims that the transfer petition would have been discovered because it was in the 'same file' with the transcript, but this characterization is misleading and the conclusion the Court draws from it is accordingly fallacious. The record indicates only that the transfer petition was a part of the same case file, but Rompilla provides no indication of the size of the file, which for all we know originally comprised several boxes of documents."

4. In CULLEN v. PINHOLSTER, 563 U.S. 170 (2011), the Ninth Circuit had found that the state court unreasonably applied *Strickland* in summarily denying an IAC claim alleging counsel's failure to adequately investigate and present mitigating evidence in a capital sentencing proceeding. A divided Supreme Court reversed (5–3, with Justice Breyer not reaching the merits of the claim). Justice Thomas's opinion for the Court and Justice Sotomayor's dissent (joined by Justices Ginsburg and Kagan) agreed as to the standards of § 2254(d) review, but disagreed as to a reasonable reading of the record and the validity of the Ninth Circuit's reasoning.

The majority found that the record supported the state court having reasonably concluded that counsel had followed the strategic path outlined in the Ninth Circuit dissent. That path had the following elements: (1) counsel were fully aware of the need to deal with the mitigation issue; (2) counsel had in fact spent "considerable time and effort on investigating mitigation," interviewing defendant Pinholster's mother and brother, (who provided information on possible brain injuries, school placement in an "educationally handicapped class," time spent in a state hospital for emotionally handicapped children, and treatment for epilepsy), and consulting a psychiatrist (who reviewed Pinholster's personality traits and offered a diagnosis limited to an "antisocial personality disorder"); (3) counsel recognized that "they represented a psychotic client whose performance at trial hardly endeared him to the jury," presenting a substantial impediment to a successful mitigation strategy; and (4) counsel therefore adopted the strategy of "presenting only Pinholster's mother in the penalty phase to create sympathy not for Pinholster, but for his mother" (such a family-sympathy mitigation defense "at the time of the trial [was a strategy that] the defense bar in California had been using").

The majority concluded that the Ninth Circuit had failed to give proper weight to this "reasonable tactical basis" for counsels' actions because it erroneously "attribut[ed] strict rules to this Court's recent case law." Those cases (including *Wiggins* and *Rompilla*) were described by the Ninth Circuit as establishing "a constitutional duty to investigate" the issue of mitigation, rendering "it * * * prima facie ineffective assistance * * * to abandon * * * [that investigation] after acquiring only rudimentary knowledge * * * from a narrow set of sources." Thus, the Ninth Circuit noted, it could not "lightly disregard, a failure to introduce evidence of 'excruciating life history' or 'nightmarish childhood'." This approach, the majority countered, ignored both *Strickland's* rejection of the use of "specific guidelines," and *Strickland's* recognition that "there comes a point where a defense attorney will reasonably decide that another strategy is in order, thus mak[ing] particular investigation unnecessary." The Court quoted in this connection a passage from Judge Kozinski's dissent below: "The current infatuation with 'humanizing' the defendant as the be-all and end-all of mitigation disregards the possibility that this may be the wrong tactic in some cases because experienced lawyers conclude that the jury won't buy it." Such decisions by counsel, the majority noted, "are due a heavy measure of deference."

As discussed in Note 3, p. 159, the dissent viewed the record as refuting the finding that counsel gave serious consideration to a traditional mitigation defense. But even with such consideration, it argued, the state court's acceptance of counsels' strategic decision constituted an unreasonable application of *Strickland* under § 2254(d); the investigation of a traditional mitigation defense was far too limited to abandon that strategy in favor of a family-sympathy mitigation defense. The dissent cited the skimpy information given to the psychiatrist, the mother's natural interest in painting a more favorable picture of the family situation than actually existed, and the ready availability of other sources, such as schooling and medical records, and various health care providers who had treated Pinholster. Although Pinholster was an unsympathetic client, "that fact," the dissent noted, "compounds, rather than excuses, counsel's deficiency in ignoring the glaring avenues of investigation that could explain why Pinholster was the way he was."

§ 4. THE *CRONIC* EXCEPTIONS AND OTHER POSSIBLE PER SE VIOLATIONS

1. ***Recognizing exceptions.*** *Strickland* presents the dominant standards for resolving ineffective assistance claims, but as *Strickland* itself noted, those standards are not universal. Thus *Strickland* distinguished (pp. 130–131) two settings in which the Court departs from the *Strickland* two-pronged test: (1) where the trial court had prevented counsel from utilizing certain adversarial procedures (commonly described as the "interference cases") (Note 5, p. 170); and (2) where counsel had been "burdened by an actual conflict of interest," as in *Cuyler v. Sullivan* (Note 1, p. 183). The Court's opinion in *United States v. Cronic*, Note 2, infra, recognized additional exceptions while stressing the general applicability of the *Strickland* standards. The Notes that follow discuss the scope of those additional exceptions, and the Court's rejection of still broader exceptions.

2. ***Rejection of a broad inferential exception.*** In UNITED STATES v. CRONIC, 466 U.S. 648 (1984), decided on the same day as *Strickland*, the Court rejected an attempt to create a broad exception to the *Strickland* approach.

Respondent Cronic and two associates were indicted on mail fraud charges involving a "check kiting" scheme. When, shortly before the scheduled trial date, respondent's trial counsel withdrew, the district court appointed a young lawyer with a real estate practice who had never participated in a jury trial to represent respondent. Appointed counsel was allowed only 25 days for pretrial preparation, although it had taken the government over four and a half years to investigate the case and it had reviewed thousands of documents during that investigation. Without referring to any specific error or inadequacy in appointed counsel's performance, the Tenth Circuit reversed respondent's conviction, inferring from the circumstances surrounding the representation of respondent that his right to the effective assistance of counsel had been violated. The Tenth Circuit based this conclusion on five factors: (1) the limited time afforded counsel for investigation and preparation; (2) counsel's inexperience; (3) the gravity of the charge; (4) the complexity of possible defenses; and (5) the inaccessibility of witnesses.

The Supreme Court (per Stevens, J.) rejected the "inferred incompetence" approach of the Tenth Circuit. Citing the underlying function of the right to counsel in protecting the adversary process (see Note 3, p. 123), the Court reasoned that a determination that counsel failed to fulfill that function ordinarily requires some showing of an adverse effect on that process. The Tenth Circuit had not pointed to anything in the actual conduct of the trial "indicating a breakdown in the adversarial process." The five factors it cited were "relevant to an evaluation of a lawyer's ineffectiveness in a particular case, * * * but neither separately nor in combination [did] they provide a basis for concluding that competent counsel was not able to provide the guiding hand that the Constitution guarantees." The Court had indicated as much in earlier rulings recognizing that not every refusal to give counsel more time to prepare results in ineffective assistance. The additional circumstances here did not present "surrounding circumstances that justify a presumption of ineffectiveness * * * without inquiry into counsel's actual performance at trial."

The *Cronic* opinion noted, however, that the Court previously had recognized exceptions to this general rule "requiring inquiry into counsel's actual performance." These situations presented "circumstances that are so likely to prejudice the accused that the cost of litigating their effect in a particular case is unjustified." The opinion included a brief, frequently quoted, description of those situations:

"Most obvious, of course, is the complete denial of counsel. The presumption that counsel's assistance is essential requires us to conclude that a trial is unfair if the accused is denied counsel at a critical stage of his trial.[25] Similarly, if counsel entirely fails to subject the prosecution's case to meaningful adversarial testing, then there has been a denial of Sixth Amendment rights that makes the adversary process itself presumptively unreliable. * * * Circumstances of that magnitude also may be present on some occasions when, although counsel is available to assist the accused during trial, the likelihood that any lawyer, even a fully competent one, could provide effective assistance is so small that a presumption of prejudice is appropriate without inquiry into the actual conduct of the trial. *Powell v. Alabama* [Note 1, p. 122] was such a case.

"The defendants [in *Powell*] had been indicted for a highly publicized capital offense. Six days before trial, the trial judge appointed 'all the members of the bar' for purposes of arraignment. 'Whether they would represent the defendants thereafter if no counsel appeared in their behalf, was a matter of speculation only, or, as the judge indicated, of mere anticipation on the part of the court.' On the day of trial, a lawyer from Tennessee appeared on behalf of persons 'interested' in the defendants, but stated that he had not had an opportunity to prepare the case or to familiarize himself with local procedure, and therefore was unwilling to represent the defendants on such short notice. The problem was resolved when the court decided that the Tennessee lawyer would represent the defendants, with whatever help the local bar could provide. * * * This Court held that 'such designation of counsel as was attempted was either so indefinite or so close upon the trial as to amount to a denial of effective and substantial aid in that regard.' * * * "

3. *The constructive denial of counsel.* Relying on both *Cronic*'s discussion of *Powell* and its reference to a counsel who "entirely fails to subject the prosecution's case to meaningful

[25] The Court has uniformly found constitutional error without any showing of prejudice when counsel was either totally absent or prevented from assisting the accused during a critical stage of the proceeding. [The Court here cited the "interference" cases discussed in Note 5, p. 170, and cases such as *Hamilton v. Alabama*, Note 2, p. 68, where the state failed to provide counsel at an arraignment deemed a critical stage].

adversary testing," lower courts developed a doctrine of "constructive denial of counsel" (a phrase first used in *Strickland*, see p. 130). Those cases held that where counsel was absent at a critical proceeding, or counsel's lack of effort there was so extensive as to produce a "complete failure" of representation, a presumption of prejudice was justified. BELL v. CONE, 535 U.S. 685 (2002), presented a typical lower court ruling of this type.

At respondent's trial the prosecution provided overwhelming evidence that he had killed an elderly couple in brutal fashion. Respondent's defense was that he was not guilty by reason of insanity due to substance abuse and posttraumatic stress disorder related to his Vietnam military service. The jury found respondent guilty of the murders, and a sentencing hearing followed. The prosecution introduced evidence of aggravating factors and the defense called the jury's attention to the mitigating evidence already before it. The defense also cross-examined prosecution witnesses, but called no witnesses of its own. After the junior prosecutor made a closing argument, defense counsel waived final argument, which prevented the lead prosecutor from arguing in rebuttal. The jury found four aggravating factors and no mitigating factors. Under state law, these findings required the death penalty.

The Sixth Circuit granted federal habeas relief, concluding that counsel's failures at the sentencing hearing amounted to a constructive denial of counsel and that justified a presumption of prejudice under the analysis of *Cronic*. But an 8–1 majority, per Rehnquist, C.J., held that the lower court's reliance on *Cronic* was misplaced:

"When we spoke in *Cronic* of the possibility of presuming prejudice based on an attorney's failure to test the prosecutor's case, we indicated that the attorney's failure must be complete. [Here] respondent's argument is not that his counsel failed to oppose the prosecution throughout the sentencing proceeding as a whole, but that his counsel failed to do so at specific points. For purposes of distinguishing between the rule of *Strickland* and that of *Cronic*, this difference is not of degree but of kind. The aspects of counsel's performance challenged by respondent—the failure to adduce mitigating evidence and the waiver of closing argument—are plainly of the same ilk as other specific attorney errors we have held subject to *Strickland*'s performance and prejudice components."

4. Does *Bell v. Cone* require reconsideration of a series of pre-*Bell* rulings that applied the constructive denial doctrine to situations in which counsel was absent from an arguably critical portion of the criminal justice process but otherwise participated in the proceedings leading to conviction? One such situation was that in which counsel fell asleep at different times during the trial. See e.g., *Burdine v. Johnson*, 262 F.3d 336 (5th Cir.2001) (en banc) (majority refuses to adopt a "per se rule that any dozing by defense counsel during trial merits a presumption of prejudice," but will presume prejudice based on "repeated unconsciousness of * * * counsel through not insubstantial portions of the critical guilt-innocence phase of Burdine's murder trial"; dissent concludes that the only specific factual finding is that counsel dozed during unidentified portions of the trial, with precise reconstruction impossible due to the passage of time, and these circumstances do not distinguish situations where the Circuit previously had insisted on a *Strickland* showing of specific prejudice, such as where counsel's capacity was allegedly restricted by alcohol use or a mental condition). Another is the situation in which the trial court conducted part of the trial or a pretrial proceeding in the absence of counsel, either because of counsel's tardiness or some misunderstanding relating to counsel's presence. See e.g., French v. Jones, 282 F.3d 893 (6th Cir.2002), reaffirmed after remand for reconsideration in light of *Cone*, 332 F.3d 430 (6th Cir.2003) (counsel not present when trial judge gave supplemental jury instruction to deadlocked jury).

As noted in CRIMPROC § 11.10(d): "Several post-*Cone* lower court rulings have continued to [apply the *Cronic* presumption] to such absences. They read *Cronic's* [fn. 25] reference to 'counsel totally absent or prevented from assisting * * * during a critical stage' to encompass not only the state's failure to provide counsel (or its restriction of counsel's representation [see Note 5, infra]), but also an appointed counsel's failure to represent the defendant during a critical stage. *Bell v. Cone* is distinguished as involving a separate category for presuming prejudice (the total failure to subject the prosecution's case to adversarial testing)." The contrary position is that the *Bell* ruling suggests no such limitation. The *Cronic* reference in fn. 25 to counsel's absence during a critical stage clearly does not apply, as that footnote was discussing only situations in which the judiciary is responsible for the absence, by denying the appointment of counsel or precluding counsel from participation, as indicated by the cases fn. 25 cited.

5. ***The interference cases.*** As noted in fn. 25 of *Cronic* and in *Strickland* (see p. 130), the Court has found per se violations of the Sixth Amendment in what have come to be known as the "state interference" cases. The leading interference cases, as described in *Strickland*, are: "*Geders v. United States*, 425 U.S. 80 (1976) (bar on attorney-client consultation during overnight recess); *Herring v. New York*, 422 U.S. 853 (1975) (bar on summation at bench trial); *Brooks v. Tennessee*, 406 U.S. 605 (1972) (requirement that defendant be first defense witness); *Ferguson v. Georgia*, 365 U.S. 570 (1961) (bar on direct examination of defendant)."

The reasoning of the interference rulings is summarized in CRIMPROC § 11.8(a): "The 'right to the assistance of counsel,' the Supreme Court noted in *Herring v. New York*, 'has been understood to mean that there can be no restrictions upon the function of counsel in defending a criminal prosecution in accord with the traditions of the adversary factfinding process.' Accordingly, state action, whether by statute or trial court ruling, that prohibits counsel from making full use of traditional trial procedures may be viewed as denying defendant the effective assistance of counsel. In considering the constitutionality of such 'state interference,' courts are directed to look whether the interference denied counsel 'the opportunity to participate fully and fairly in the adversary factfinding process.' If the interference had that effect, then both the overall performance of counsel apart from the interference and the lack of any showing of actual outcome prejudice become irrelevant."

Prospective Challenges to Delivery System Deficiencies

Commentators have long contended that the various state delivery systems for providing state-funded counsel (see Notes 3–5, pp. 71–73) are woefully lacking in funding and quality controls, and therefore institutionally incapable of providing adequate representation of indigent defendants on a regular basis. They recognize that *Cronic* precludes overturning a conviction based on systemic conditions impeding representation, but argue that challenges brought prospectively and tied to systemic deficiencies that produce "structural ineffectiveness" present a quite different legal issue. As discussed in CRIMPROC § 11.8(c), the initial prospective challenges to alleged systemic deficiencies were presented in the course of criminal litigation (e.g., in a pretrial motion by defense counsel claiming that a heavy caseload or inadequate compensation would preclude effective representation). Most courts rejected such challenges as inconsistent with *Cronic* and *Strickland*, which were seen as requiring a review, after trial, as to whether counsel's performance actually failed to meet the *Strickland* standards. Prospective relief was granted in some cases (e.g., lifting the cap on compensation of the appointed attorney), but those rulings were generally based on grounds other than the Sixth Amendment.

The general lack of success for challenges raised pretrial in criminal cases led to a shift to a new form of systemic challenge. Civil class actions were brought, typically on behalf of accused persons, alleging that systemic deficiencies present a substantial risk of irreparable injury through specific flaws in representation, and seeking either injunctive relief relating to the alleged deficiencies or an appropriate declaratory judgment. This litigation has been grounded in part on the Sixth Amendment and state counterparts to the Sixth Amendment, but other sources of judicial authority have also been considered. The results have been mixed. Where the suits have survived a motion to dismiss, they often have resulted in settlements. See CRIMPROC § 11.8(c). *Kuren v. Luzerne County*, set forth below, provides perhaps the most comprehensive judicial discussion of the Sixth Amendment grounding for such civil class actions, as well as constituting the most recent major class action ruling by a state Supreme Court.

KUREN V. LUZERNE COUNTY

637 Pa. 33, 146 A.3d 715 (2016).

JUSTICE WECHT.

The question that we confront today is whether a cause of action exists entitling a class of indigent criminal defendants to allege prospective, systemic violations of the right to counsel due to underfunding [of a county's Office of Public Defender (OPD)], and to seek and obtain an injunction forcing a county to provide adequate funding to a public defender's office. Pursuant to *Gideon* and its progeny, and because remedies for Sixth Amendment violations need not await conviction and sentencing, we hold that such a cause of action exists, so long as the class action plaintiffs demonstrate "the likelihood of substantial and immediate irreparable injury, and the inadequacy of remedies at law." *O'Shea v. Littleton*, 414 U.S. 488 (1974).

In the amended complaint, Appellants detailed the effects that the inadequate funding had upon the OPD's ability to meet its constitutional mandate. Appellants first delineated six essential components of competent "legal representation" that offices servicing indigent defendants require in order to comply with the Sixth Amendment: (1) the attorneys must have adequate knowledge of the relevant areas of the law; (2) the attorneys must be assigned to represent indigent clients at the earliest possible stage; (3) the attorneys must be present at every critical stage of the client's case; (4) the office and attorneys must be able to conduct reasonable factual and legal pre-trial investigations, pursue and comply with the discovery rules, and utilize investigators when necessary; (5) the attorneys must be able to consult with their clients to discuss the material aspects of the case, as well as the client's substantive and procedural rights, to ensure that the client is making informed decisions regarding the case; and (6) the attorneys must be able to perform their work with reasonable diligence and promptness. These criteria, according to Appellants, comprised the necessary elements of constitutional representation of indigent defendants. Due to the lack of funds and resources, Appellants alleged that the OPD could not satisfy any one of these six criteria, let alone all of them, and, therefore, could not provide constitutionally adequate representation. * * *

[The trial court dismissed the amended complaint and, on appeal, the Commonwealth Court affirmed] Appellants contend that the Commonwealth Court erroneously held that a violation of the right to counsel can be remedied only after trial and conviction upon a showing of *Strickland* prejudice. To the contrary, Appellants assert, there are multiple remedies available for violations of the rights guaranteed by the Bill of Rights and the Fourteenth Amendment, including injunctive relief. * * * Appellants are supported by numerous amici curiae. [The opinion here discussed the supporting briefs of the U.S. Department of Justice, the Innocence Network and Pennsylvania Innocence Project, the National Association of Criminal Defense Lawyers and the Pennsylvania Association of Criminal Defense Lawyers, and the American Bar Association. Each argued that granting prospective relief was required, under somewhat differently defined circumstances, to implement the Sixth Amendment] * * *

Appellants allege that the circumstances in Luzerne County amount to a constructive denial of counsel. Although *Cronic* recognized such a denial as a constitutional violation, the circumstances in that case were markedly different than those present in the case at bar. *Cronic* addressed a post-conviction claim, and focused upon whether a post-conviction petitioner must demonstrate prejudice after being constructively denied counsel. The *Cronic* Court did not address whether constructive denial of counsel claims could be brought prospectively in a civil suit, nor did it address whether injunctive relief was a viable remedy for such a deprivation. Thus, *Cronic*'s value to Appellants is limited. Because this Court also has never addressed the viability of such claims, we turn our focus to the leading cases from jurisdictions that have done so, cases upon which the parties and the lower courts have relied.

In *Luckey v. Harris*, 860 F.2d 1012 (11th Cir. 1988), a class claiming to represent indigent criminal defendants who had been charged with crimes * * * filed a section 1983 action against the governor of Georgia and other state officials alleging that: "systemic deficiencies including inadequate resources, delays in the appointment of counsel, pressure on attorneys to hurry their clients' case to trial or to enter a guilty plea, and inadequate supervision in the Georgia indigent criminal defense system deny indigent criminal defendants their Sixth Amendment right to counsel, their due process rights under the Fourteenth Amendment, their right to bail under the Eighth and Fourteenth Amendments and equal protection of the laws guaranteed by the Fourteenth Amendment." The United States District Court for the Northern District of Georgia dismissed the suit * * * and the Court of Appeals for the Eleventh Circuit reversed.

The District Court had ruled that, in order to obtain prospective, injunctive relief, the class plaintiffs had to prove the inevitability of constitutionally ineffective assistance by appointed counsel. The Court of Appeals overturned this ruling, explicitly rejecting as "inappropriate" the notion that *Strickland* is the governing standard in a civil suit seeking prospective relief. The Court of Appeals elaborated as follows: "The Sixth Amendment protects rights that do not affect the outcome of a trial. Thus, deficiencies that do not meet the 'ineffectiveness' standard may nonetheless violate a defendant's rights under the Sixth Amendment. In the post-trial context, such errors may be deemed harmless because they did not affect the outcome of the trial. Whether an accused has been prejudiced by the denial of a right is an issue that relates to relief—whether the defendant is entitled to have his or her conviction overturned—rather than to the question of whether such a right exists and can be protected prospectively." * * *

The Court of Appeals held that, for prospective claims of constitutional violations, the class plaintiffs' burden is to demonstrate "the likelihood of substantial and immediate irreparable injury, and the inadequacy of remedies at law." *Luckey*, 860 F.2d at 1017 (quoting *O'Shea*, supra). "[W]ithout passing on the merits of [the allegations in the suit]," the Court of Appeals concluded that those allegations, as set forth above, were sufficient to state a claim upon which relief could be granted.

In *Duncan v. Michigan*, 284 Mich.App. 246, 774 N.W.2d 89 (2009), the Court of Appeals of Michigan addressed a similar set of circumstances. * * * In a "highly detailed complaint," the class alleged that the indigent defense systems in several Michigan counties were "underfunded, poorly administered, and [did] not ensure that the participating defense attorneys have the necessary tools, time, and qualifications to adequately represent indigent defendants and to put the cases presented by prosecutors to the crucible of meaningful adversarial testing." The class averred that the system, as it existed at the time of the complaint, was deficient in, inter alia: client eligibility standards; attorney hiring; attorney training; conflict of interest guidelines; and independence from the prosecution and judiciary. These deficiencies, the class asserted, resulted in wrongful convictions, longer terms of incarceration, guilty pleas lacking in evidentiary foundations, unprepared counsel at hearings and trials, and introduction of evidence that should have been suppressed or ruled inadmissible had counsel had the time and resources to prepare and file pretrial motions. Additionally, the class set forth various specific instances in which appointed counsel failed adequately to represent members of the class during their criminal cases. For instance, the class noted that counsel met with clients for the first time minutes before preliminary hearings commenced; advised clients to waive hearings and rights without full, confidential discussions of the consequences of such decisions; failed to provide police reports and other discovery materials to the client; and neglected to discuss the nature and factual support—or lack thereof—of the charges against the client. * * *

Regarding injunctive relief, *Duncan* employed the same test utilized by the *Luckey* Court, requiring a party seeking such relief to demonstrate the danger of irreparable and immediate injury with no other available remedy at law. * * * [In describing the requisite "justiciable harm," the Michigan Court of Appeals noted]: "We hold that injury or harm is shown when court-appointed counsel's performance or representation is deficient relative to a critical stage in the proceedings and, absent a showing that it affected the reliability of the verdict, the deficient performance results in a detriment to a criminal defendant that is relevant and meaningful in some fashion, e.g. unwarranted pretrial detention. Finally, we hold that, when it is shown that court-appointed counsels' representation falls below an objective standard of reasonableness with respect to a critical stage in the proceedings, there has been an invasion of a legally protected interest and harm occurs." * * *

The Court of Appeals then rejected the argument that class plaintiffs could find a remedy at law in *Strickland*. Relying upon *Luckey* and other * * * decisions that also have rejected the application of *Strickland* to this type of case, as well as the presumption of prejudice established by the *Cronic* Court, the Court of Appeals explained that the *Strickland* rubric simply is too rigid to address the "many shapes and forms" that harm resulting from a violation of the right to counsel can take. The court noted that when *Strickland*-type prejudice results, justiciable harm certainly has occurred. However, harm also may occur when "there are instances of deficient performance by counsel at critical stages in the criminal proceedings that are detrimental to an indigent defendant in some relevant and meaningful fashion, even without neatly wrapping the justiciable harm around a verdict and trial." Examples of such harm include unnecessarily prolonged detention before trial or plea, failure to file potentially meritorious motions, and the entry of guilty pleas lacking a factual basis.

In the case *sub judice*, the Commonwealth Court found the *Duncan* dissent persuasive. That dissent vehemently disagreed with the majority's analysis, accusing the majority of simply reformulating *Strickland* to create a prospective cause of action while simultaneously disavowing *Strickland*'s relevance. The dissent would have required satisfaction of the *Strickland* formula, including the traditional proof of actual prejudice, because prejudice "is an essential element of any Sixth Amendment violation." Because the class in the case could not allege traditional prejudice prospectively, the dissent would have held that the class did not state a justiciable cause of action.

In *Hurrell-Harring v. New York*, 15 N.Y.3d 8, 904 N.Y.S.2d 296, 930 N.E.2d 217 (2010), the Court of Appeals of New York noted that, at the time the case commenced, New York delegated to the counties the duty to comply with *Gideon*. The class plaintiffs alleged that the delegation to the counties of the duty to provide indigent defendants with counsel was a "costly, largely unfunded and politically unpopular mandate" that "has functioned to deprive [indigent defendants] of constitutionally and statutorily guaranteed representational rights." The plaintiffs sought declaratory and injunctive relief; they did not seek individual relief in their respective criminal cases. The defendants sought dismissal of the action, claiming that the suit was non-justiciable. The trial court denied the motion, but the intermediate appellate court reversed the trial court's order, and ruled that a violation of the right to counsel could not be vindicated in a civil proceeding seeking increased funding from county officials. * * * The New York Court of Appeals reversed the intermediate appellate court's decision.

First, the Court of Appeals acknowledged that a *Strickland*-based argument had "a measure of merit." However, the court ultimately rejected the argument, holding that *Strickland*'s approach "is expressly premised on the supposition that the fundamental underlying right to representation under *Gideon* has been enabled by the State in a manner that would justify the presumption that the standard of objective reasonableness will ordinarily be satisfied." The Court of Appeals explained that the crux of a prospective cause of action is not rooted in whether counsel, individually or systematically, are ineffective under *Strickland*, but "rather [in] whether the State has met its foundational obligation under *Gideon* to provide legal representation." * * * The Court of Appeals examined the pleadings, and, viewing the averments in plaintiffs' favor, ruled that the plaintiffs had advanced more than mere allegations of deficient performance. The plaintiffs claimed that half of the class members named in the complaint did not have counsel assigned to them for their preliminary arraignments, and most of them were incarcerated because their bail was greater than they could afford. Those who were assigned counsel alleged that their attorneys were unavailable to them, sometimes for months; that those lawyers waived the accused's constitutional rights without consultation; and that counsel served only "as conduits for plea offers, some of which purportedly were highly unfavorable." Attorneys frequently missed court hearings, and were unprepared when they did appear. These allegations, the Court of Appeals held, went well beyond routine claims of ineffective assistance of counsel, and stated "a claim for constructive denial of the right to counsel by reason of insufficient compliance with the constitutional mandate of *Gideon*." * * *

Like the dissent in *Duncan*, the dissent in *Hurrell-Harring* would not have recognized a cause of action for prospective relief. * * * In the dissent's view, the constructive denial claim that the majority recognized "is nothing more than an ineffective assistance of counsel claim under another name." The *Hurrell-Harring* dissent agreed with the majority that *Strickland* was inapplicable, but would nonetheless have declined to recognize a constructive denial claim premised upon *Cronic*'s presumed prejudice rationale. Such a claim, according to the dissent, was merely *Strickland* stripped of the prejudice prong, and it, too, generally should be restricted to individual claims of deficient stewardship. Interestingly, the dissent did not opine that systemic constructive denial of counsel claims can never be cognizable. The dissent merely would have held that the plaintiffs' allegations did not rise to the level that would justify such a claim.

Unlike the Commonwealth Court, we find the majorities' reasoning in *Luckey*, *Duncan*, and *Hurrell-Harring* to be persuasive, and indeed, compelling. We now hold that there is a cognizable cause of action whereby a class of indigent defendants may seek relief for a widespread, systematic and constructive denial of counsel when alleged deficiencies in funding and resources provided by the county deny indigent defendants their constitutional right to counsel. The consequences of holding otherwise would be untenable, and would be fundamentally irreconcilable with the United States Supreme Court's pronouncements on the role of the right to counsel in our system of justice. * * * Because the right to a lawyer occupies a unique station in our system of justice, we must recognize that harm necessarily inheres in the deprivation of counsel, including at the earlier stages of a criminal case. The right to counsel is as important in the initial stages of a criminal case as it is at trial. To remedy only deprivations of the latter would foster subversion of the right as soon as it has attached. As the Court of Appeals of Michigan stated in *Duncan*, "there are instances of deficient performance at critical stages in the criminal proceedings that are detrimental to an indigent defendant in some relevant and meaningful fashion, even without neatly wrapping the justiciable harm around a verdict and trial." * * * In *Maine v. Moulton*, 474 U.S. 159 (1985), the Supreme Court explained that "to deprive a person of counsel during the period prior to trial may be more damaging than denial of counsel during the trial itself." * * * Certain types of harm are easily identifiable at this stage, harms that may not have an effect upon a trial itself. These include prolonged pretrial detention, potentially meritorious motions that go unfiled, and inadequate or nonexistent factual investigation, to name a few. Without an avenue to pursue relief for these harms, and countless others that arise from pretrial deprivations of the right to counsel, the Sixth Amendment right to counsel would erode into a right without a remedy. * * *

Because the justiciable harm alleged is prospective, in order to successfully plead the cause of action for equitable relief, a claimant must satisfy the test that the United States Supreme Court articulated in *O'Shea*. The claimant must demonstrate "the likelihood of substantial and immediate irreparable injury, and the inadequacy of remedies at law." The first prong of the *O'Shea* test requires a party seeking injunctive relief to prove the "likelihood of substantial and immediate irreparable injury." This is not an insignificant burden, and it is apt in light of the fact that the claimant is seeking prospective relief. Nonetheless, relief is available, because the denial of the right to counsel, whether actual, or as here, constructive, poses a significant, and tangible threat to the fairness of criminal trials, and to the reliability of the entire criminal justice system. * * *

The right to be assisted by competent counsel attaches to nearly every aspect of the criminal process. For this reason, and because of the myriad circumstances in which the right can be denied or withheld, it would be impossible to delineate an exhaustive list of factors that an indigent plaintiff, or a class comprised of same, must satisfy in order to satisfy the first element of the *O'Shea* test. Nonetheless, we find that the standard proposed by the Department of Justice offers a workable, if non-exhaustive, paradigm for weighing such claims. The test bears repeating here. In setting forth a cause of action for prospective injunctive relief based upon the constructive denial of counsel, to prove the "likelihood of substantial and immediate irreparable injury," the plaintiff should focus upon the following factors: "(1) when, on a system-wide basis, the traditional markers of representation—such as timely and confidential consultation with clients, appropriate investigation, and meaningful adversarial testing of the prosecution's case—are absent or significantly compromised; and (2) when substantial structural limitations—such as a severe lack of resources, unreasonably high workloads, or critical understaffing of public defender offices—cause that absence or limitation on representation." See Amicus Brief for the United States at 11. * * *

The second prong of the [*O'Shea*] test requires a plaintiff to demonstrate that no other adequate remedy at law exists for redress of the harm asserted. Appellees and the Commonwealth Court assert that *Strickland* provides the exclusive remedy for claims pertaining to violations of the right to counsel and that the relief it offers is sufficient. This argument ignores both the nature of Appellants' claims and the interests that the Supreme Court sought to protect in *Strickland*. * * * Applying the *Strickland* test to the category of claims at bar would be illogical. Appellants are not arguing individual claims of ineffective assistance of counsel. Appellants point to no specific instances in which an attorney failed to provide constitutionally effective stewardship. Rather, Appellants' claim centers upon the widespread and endemic inability of the OPD's attorneys to provide counsel to indigent defendants. * * * These general allegations in no way resemble the individual ineffectiveness claims that the Court considered in *Strickland*.[a] * * *

NOTES AND QUESTIONS

1. ***Compensation for appointed attorneys.*** Does the reasoning of *Kuren* extend to challenging fee caps and hourly rates for appointed attorneys? Successful challenges often have been based on judicial authority other than fulfilling the command of the Sixth Amendment. See e.g., *State v. Lynch*, 796 P.2d 1150 (1990) (relying on the court's "constitutional responsibilities relating to the managerial and superintending control of the district courts"). As to the argument that totally inadequate compensation will lead to ineffective representation, consider the response of *Ex parte Grayson*, 479 So.2d 76 (Ala. 1985) (rejecting a challenge to a $1000 cap for a capital case): "These contentions are made on the premise that lawyers will not provide effective

[a] Justice Baer, concurring in the result, argued that "the action * * * should be viewed as a mandamus action," directing the County to fund adequately the OPD, a statutory obligation that "corresponds with Appellant's legal right to effective assistance of counsel."

assistance unless paid a certain amount of money. But the legal profession requires its members to give their best efforts in 'advancing the undivided interests of [their] client[s].' * * * We reaffirm this belief that attorneys appointed to defend capital clients will serve them as directed by their consciences and the ethical rules enforced by the state bar association."

Consider also *Kerr v. Parsons*, 378 A.3d 1 (N.M. 2016). On a general challenge to use of a flat fee arrangement for contract counsel, the court distinguished its earlier ruling that held such an arrangement invalid. In that case, the court addressed a specific fee ($19,500 for first chair and $9,500 for each second chair) in "one of the most complex death penalty cases ever tried in New Mexico." Presuming ineffective assistance by all contract attorneys operating under the current flat fee statute (which prohibits hourly payments) would "constitute a huge departure from *Cronic*." The court refused to assume that flat fee attorneys "do as little as possible," as that fails to respect the attorney's contractual obligation "to provide legal services in accord with the Sixth Amendment." The court warned, however, "that some limitations on funding * * * could be so severe as to create a presumption of ineffective assistance."

2. ***Public defender withdrawal.*** In 2006, the ABA Standing Committee on Ethics and Professional Responsibility issued Formal Ethics Opinion No. 06–441, advising lawyers who represent indigents in criminal cases to refuse new cases or withdraw from current cases when excessive caseloads prevented them from providing "competent and diligent representation" to their clients. The opinion relied not only on the general ethical obligation to provide such representation, but also on professional standards imposing specific duties unlikely to be fulfilled where caseloads are excessive (e.g., keeping the client reasonably informed). Public defender offices in several states have been allowed to refuse to carry their caseload beyond a certain limit (typically one set by a state commission, see Note 5, p. 72). Consider, however, *State ex rel. Public Defender Commission v. Pratte*, 298 S.W.3d 870 (Mo. 2009) (Commission authority to maintain caseload standards did not extend to adopting a rule automatically excluding representation of indigent defendants on probation violations when public defender office is on "limited availability" status, as public defender statute requires representation in such hearings).

The Right to the Assistance of Experts

1. ***The* Ake *ruling.*** In AKE v. OKLAHOMA, 470 U.S. 68 (1985), the defendant Ake, an indigent, was charged with first-degree murder. At his arraignment, Ake's behavior was so bizarre that the trial judge ordered that he be examined by a psychiatrist. The examining psychiatrist found Ake incompetent to stand trial, but Ake later was found to be competent to stand trial as long as he continued to be sedated with an antipsychotic drug. Ake's attorney informed the court that he would raise an insanity defense, but his motion for a psychiatric evaluation at state expense was denied. The jury rejected the insanity defense and Ake was convicted of first-degree murder. At the capital sentencing proceeding, the state asked for the death penalty, relying on the examining psychiatrist's testimony to establish Ake's future dangerousness. Ake had no expert witness to rebut this testimony or to give evidence in mitigation of his punishment, and he was sentenced to death. The Supreme Court (8–1) reversed. The majority opinion, per Marshall, J., reasoned:

"This Court has long recognized that when a State brings its judicial power to bear on an indigent defendant in a criminal proceeding, it must take steps to assure that the defendant has a fair opportunity to present his defense. This elementary principle, grounded in significant part in the Fourteenth Amendment's due process guarantee of fundamental fairness, derives from the belief that justice cannot be equal where, simply as a result of his poverty, a defendant is denied the opportunity to participate meaningfully in a judicial proceeding in which his liberty is at stake. * * * [A] criminal trial is fundamentally unfair if the State proceeds against an individual defendant without making certain that he has access to the raw materials integral to the building of an effective defense. Thus, while the Court has not held that a State must purchase for the indigent defendant all the assistance that his wealthier counterpart might buy, see *Ross v. Moffitt* [p. 95], it has often reaffirmed that fundamental fairness entitles indigent defendants to 'an adequate opportunity to present their claims fairly within the adversary system,' id. To implement this principle, we have focused on identifying the 'basic tools of an adequate defense or appeal,' and we have required that such tools be provided to those defendants who cannot afford to pay for them.

"[W]ithout the assistance of a psychiatrist to conduct a professional examination on issues relevant to the defense, to help determine whether the insanity defense is viable to present testimony, and to assist in preparing the cross-examination of a State's psychiatric witnesses, the risk of an inaccurate resolution of sanity issues is extremely high. With such assistance, the defendant is fairly able to present at least enough information to the jury, in a meaningful manner, as to permit it to make a sensible determination.

"A defendant's mental condition is not necessarily at issue in every criminal proceeding, however, and it is unlikely that psychiatric assistance of the kind we have described would be of probable value in cases where it is not. The risk of error, from denial of such assistance * * * is most predictably at its height when the defendant's mental condition is seriously in question. When the defendant is able to make an ex parte threshold showing to the trial court that his sanity is likely to be a significant factor in his defense, the need for the assistance of a psychiatrist is readily apparent. It is in such cases that a defense may be devastated by the absence of a psychiatric examination and testimony; with such assistance, the defendant might have a reasonable chance of success. In such a circumstance, where the potential accuracy of the jury's determination is so dramatically enhanced, and where the interests of the individual and the State in an accurate proceeding are substantial, the State's interest in its fisc must yield.

"[This] is not to say, of course, that the indigent defendant has a constitutional right to choose a psychiatrist of his personal liking or to receive funds to hire his own. Our concern is that the indigent defendant have access to a competent psychiatrist for the purpose we have discussed, and as in the case of provision of counsel we leave to the State the decision on how to implement this right.

"Ake also was denied the means of presenting evidence to rebut the State's evidence of his future dangerousness. The foregoing discussion compels a similar conclusion in the context of a capital sentencing proceeding, when the State presents psychiatric evidence of the defendant's future dangerousness. * * * [W]here the consequence of error is so great, the relevance of responsive psychiatric testimony so evident, and the burden on the State so slim, due process requires access to a psychiatric examination on relevant issues, to the testimony of the psychiatrist, and to assistance in preparation at the sentencing phase."

2. ***The Sixth Amendment vs. Fourteenth Amendment due process.*** Although one might maintain that a right to a court-appointed psychiatrist under certain circumstances is implicit in the right to counsel, as it implements or effectuates that right, *Ake* is not written that way. It is a free-standing procedural due process decision (Note 4, p. 30)—one that applies "the Fourteenth Amendment's due process guarantee of fundamental fairness." (The *Ake* Court added in a footnote: "Because we conclude that the Due Process Clause guaranteed to Ake the assistance he requested and was denied, we have no occasion to consider the applicability of the Equal Protection Clause, or the Sixth Amendment, in this context.")

Does reliance on the due process clause provide a stronger foundation for limiting the scope of the "fair opportunity" principle? Does it provide a barrier against extension beyond experts to encompass the general resources often utilized by a defense attorney, including supporting personnel, and, in turn, to evaluating such factors as caseloads and compensation? Consider

A.B.A. Standards § 5–1.4(a) (2d ed., 1980) (commentary): "Quality legal representation, * * * cannot be rendered either by defenders or by assigned counsel unless the lawyers have available for their use adequate supporting services. These [include] expert witnesses * * *, personnel skilled in social work and related disciplines to provide assistance at pretrial release hearings and at sentencing, and trained investigators to interview witnesses and to assemble demonstrative evidence. * * * If the defense attorney must personally conduct factual investigations, the financial cost to the justice system is likely to be greater. Moreover, when an attorney personally interviews witnesses, [the attorney] may be placed in the untenable position of either taking the stand to challenge their credibility if their testimony conflicts with statements previously given or withdrawing from the case."

3. ***Other basic tools.*** In *Caldwell v. Mississippi*, 472 U.S. 320 (1985), the Court found it unnecessary to rule on the extension of *Ake*. The defendant there argued that due process had been denied when the trial judge refused to grant appointed counsel's request for "the appointment of a criminal investigator, a fingerprint expert, and a ballistics expert." The Court responded (in a footnote): "Given that petitioner offered little more than undeveloped assertions that the requested assistance would be beneficial, we find no deprivation of due process in the trial judge's decision. Cf. *Ake v. Oklahoma*, (discussing showing that would entitle defendant to psychiatric assistance as matter of federal constitutional law). We therefore have no need to determine as a matter of federal constitutional law what if any showing would have entitled a defendant to assistance of the type here sought."

Only a handful of lower courts have concluded that psychiatric expertise is so unique that the due process reasoning of *Ake* should not extend to other assistance. Most courts addressing the issue have concluded that due process may require appointment of other types of scientific experts and some have suggested that providing defense investigators with special expertise might also be required. These courts uniformly stress that the defense showing of need must set forth in detail "what assistance is being requested and why it is needed" (and not all will permit that filing to be made ex parte[b]). They vary considerably, however, in describing the level of need that must be met by this particularized showing—both as to the importance of the issue on which the expert's assistance is sought and as to the need for an expert's assistance in contesting that issue. In particular, where the scientific methodology is well established and its application is viewed as largely mechanical, the defense often carries a special burden in convincing the court that a defense expert might assist in a successful challenge to the state's evidence. Fundamental fairness, lower courts have noted, does not demand that the defense be given an offsetting expert whenever the prosecution will use an expert in establishing a critical element of its case.

4. ***Local law alternatives.*** In many jurisdictions, expert assistance can be obtained without relying on the constitutional right recognized in *Ake*. Many jurisdiction have statutes granting indigent defendants funding for a broad range of experts under standards less rigorous than the constitutional standards discussed above. The federal statute, for example, employs a "private attorney standard, which directs the district court to authorize defense services under circumstances in which a reasonable attorney would engage such services for a client having the independent means to pay." CRIMPROC § 11.2(e). Where a public defender office's budget includes an allocation for retaining experts, there will be no need to use the constitutional or

---

[b] Some jurisdictions give the judge discretion to choose between an ex parte proceeding and an adversary proceeding in which the prosecution may participate, with the judge also determining how much information the prosecutor will be given as to the defense's explanation of why its case presents the need for an expert (and how it will use the expert). See CRIMPROC § 11.2(e). Of course, even if the funding for an expert is granted ex parte, the prosecutor will be made aware of the defense's use of an expert if that expert must examine physical evidence in the possession of the state. As to the possible prosecution discovery of the report of an expert that the defense will not use at trial, see Note 4, p. 1117.

statutory right if that allocation is sufficient to cover all cases in which the defender office desires the assistance of experts.

5. ***Reversible error.*** Upon finding that the defendant had made a showing that "entitled [him] to the assistance of a psychiatrist and that the denial of that assistance deprived him of due process," the *Ake* Court reversed the defendant's conviction. The Court did not stop to examine how well the defense has done at trial and in the sentencing proceeding without that assistance. An occasional lower court ruling has viewed that performance as relevant to the conclusion that fundamental fairness was denied. See e.g., *Conklin v. Schofield*, 366 F.3d 1191 (11th Cir.2004) (trial court acted unreasonably in denying indigent's motion for funds for expert assistance after the defense made an appropriate showing, but fundamental fairness was not denied since defense expert's testimony would have undermined state's position that stab wounds occurred before death, but prosecution expert conceded on cross-examination that the wounds could have been inflicted shortly after death, and defense expert's additional support "would not have likely altered the jury's decision"). Most courts, however, reason that the due process violation occurs when the court denies assistance notwithstanding a defense showing that meets the *Ake* prerequisites. On the other hand, many of those courts also have concluded that the violation is subject to a state showing of "harmless error," although others disagree. See CRIMPROC § 27.6(c) (courts rejecting harmless error view the violation as "structural" since it "eliminates a basic tool of an adequate defense," while others view it as akin to errors of the improper admission or exclusion of evidence, which are subject to harmless error analysis).

§ 5. CONFLICTS OF INTEREST

A. POTENTIAL CONFLICTS AND THE DUTY TO INQUIRE

1. ***Range of conflicts.*** The Supreme Court first held, in *Glasser v. United States*, 315 U.S. 60 (1942), that the right to the assistance of counsel is not satisfied by a counsel whose actions are influenced by a conflict of interest. The conflict in *Glasser* arose out of an attorney's joint representation of codefendants in the same trial. While that is the paradigm conflict setting, many other settings may also produce an "actual conflict of interest"—i.e., a situation in which action or inaction by defense counsel which would be favorable to the defendant would also be contrary to an obligation that counsel owes to another person or to counsel's self-interest. Those other settings include: (1) defense counsel simultaneously representing another defendant who will be tried separately for the same offense (either because charged separately or jointly charged and granted a severance); (2) defense counsel has previously represented, or is currently representing, in another matter or the same matter, a victim of the alleged offense; (3) defense counsel has previously represented, or is currently representing, in another matter or the same matter, a likely prosecution witness; (4) a third party with some interest in the case is paying defense counsel's fee; (5) a fee arrangement that creates a possible conflict between counsel's financial interests and the defendant's interests (e.g., a publication agreement giving counsel an interest in royalties received from a movie or book relating to the trial); (6) counsel faces a potential liability that might be impacted by choices made in representing the defendant, e.g., where counsel (i) was involved in the alleged crime and fears possible criminal prosecution, (ii) is under investigation or being actively prosecuted by the same prosecutor's office as to another matter, or (iii) is facing possible criminal or disciplinary consequences as a result of questionable behavior in representing the defendant; (7) counsel has delivered to police (or possesses with a legal obligation to deliver), physical evidence that can be used against the defendant; and (8) counsel is to be called as a prosecution witness.[a]

[a] In many of the above situations, conflicts also arise where the potentially conflicting representation is by another attorney in the same law firm as the defendant's counsel. Under ethics codes, conflicts generally are

2. ***Conflicts and professional responsibility standards.*** While the various settings noted above each carry a significant potential for presenting an actual conflict in the course of representation, that result is not inevitable—even in the case of joint representation of codefendants in the same trial. Moreover, if an actual conflict should arise, the ABA's Model Rules of Professional Conduct do not always preclude continued representation. See e.g., Rule 1.7 (where a defense counsel has another client whose interests are "directly adverse" to the defendant, the lawyer may nonetheless represent the defendant if the lawyer "reasonably believes that [he or she] will be able to provide competent and diligent representation to each affected client," and each client consents after full disclosure); Rule 1.8 (lawyer is not prohibited from representing a client where the representation of that client "will be materially limited by the lawyer's responsibilities to another client, a former client, * * * or by a personal interest of the lawyer" if the lawyer believes the representation will be competent and diligent and there is adequate consultation and consent).

The profession's willingness to tolerate arrangements that create a high potential for dividing the attorney's loyalty is not based simply upon the fact that those arrangements may not, in the end, result in an actual conflict. Its decision not to absolutely prohibit such arrangements is also based in part on the potential value of many of these arrangements to the client. Initially, they may permit the client to obtain the services of the one lawyer that he wants to represent him. Some defendants put their trust in a particular lawyer and would want that lawyer even though she may have previously represented one of the prosecution's witnesses or even the victim. Some would prefer a privately retained lawyer and can afford one only if their employer, a codefendant, or some other interested person will pay that lawyer.

While Sixth Amendment standards stand apart from Professional Responsibility standards, courts often will look to Professional Responsibility standards for guidance, particularly in the context of disqualifications. See Pt. C, infra. Courts also take note of the considerations that have led Professional Responsibility standards not to automatically bar representation in certain conflict settings. Thus the Supreme Court has noted: "Joint representation is a means of ensuring against reciprocal recrimination. A common defense often gives strength against a common attack." *Holloway v. Arkansas*, Note 5, infra.

3. ***Prohibiting representation in potential-conflict situations.*** As one might anticipate, even as to the most obvious potential conflict situations, neither courts nor legislatures have been willing to adopt prophylactic prohibitions (in court rules or statutes) where the profession has been unwilling to do so in its regulations. See CRIMPROC § 11.9(b) (describing state law). However, in many jurisdictions, public defender offices are prohibited from representing multiple defendants charged with the same offense (typically by an internal policy, applied with judicial approval). No jurisdiction has applied a similar absolute prohibition to joint representation by retained counsel. A few states, however, have taken a partial step in this direction by viewing joint representation of codefendants as "inherently prejudicial," and therefore allowed only with an appropriate waiver by each defendant. Several other jurisdictions require a judicial inquiry when jointly charged defendants are represented by the same attorney, and as discussed infra (see Note 4, and *Wheat v. United States*), that inquiry may lead to a judicial

---

vicariously imputed to all members of a law firm. While the Supreme Court has not ruled directly on this approach, *Burger v. Kemp* (Note 5, p. 187) "assumed without deciding that two law partners are considered as one attorney" in analyzing the conflict potential of representing codefendants. Some states treat the lawyers in a public defender office in much the same manner. Many other jurisdictions, however, hold the "same firm" principle generally inapplicable to public defenders, in part because "the salaried government employee does not have the financial interest in the success of the departmental representation that is inherent in private practice." In these jurisdictions, where the defender office's potential conflict stems from confidential information received from a past client now a prosecution witness, the common solution is to utilize an internal ethical wall of separation which keeps that information away from the attorney representing the defendant. That device tends not to be viewed as sufficient, however, to allow separate defenders in the same office to represent codefendants. See Note 3, infra.

preclusion of joint representation even where each defendant waives—though such judicial disqualification is not mandated.

4. ***Non-constitutional requirements of judicial inquiry.*** Federal Rule 44 requires the trial court to conduct an inquiry whenever defendants have been jointly charged under Rule 8(b) or joined for trial under Rule 13 and are represented by "the same counsel or counsel who are associated in the practice of law." The trial court is directed to "promptly inquire about the propriety of the joint representation," and to "personally advise each defendant of the right to the effective assistance of counsel, including separate representation." Moreover, "unless there is good cause to believe that no conflict of interest is likely to arise," the trial court "must take appropriate measures to protect each defendant's right to counsel." Several states impose similar obligations on their trial courts. The Advisory Committee Notes on Rule 44(c) clearly indicate that the failure to comply with Rule 44(c) should not in itself constitute a per se reversible error. Accordingly, on review after a conviction, appellate courts will look to whether the reversal is required under the Sixth Amendment. See Pt. B, infra.

5. ***The initial recognition of a constitutional duty of inquiry.*** The Supreme Court first recognized a constitutional duty to inquire into a potential conflict in HOLLOWAY v. ARKANSAS, 435 U.S. 475 (1978). In that case, an appointed counsel representing three codefendants in a joint trial requested pretrial that the trial court appoint separate counsel for each defendant (counsel noting that confidential information revealed to him by the different defendants could place him in an actual conflict in addressing their testimony). The trial court denied the request without conducting an inquiry, and when the issue arose again, directed counsel to have each defendant give unguided direct testimony. The Supreme Court majority (per Burger, C.J.) reversed the convictions of all three defendants. *Glasser* (Note 1, supra), the majority noted, had established that "joint representation * * * is not per se violative of constitutional guarantees of effective counsel," and subsequent lower court rulings on joint representation had diverged as to: (1) what showing was needed postconviction to establish that an actual conflict had existed and had resulted in a denial of effective assistance; and (2) "the scope and nature of the affirmative duty of the trial judge to assure that criminal defendants are not deprived of their right to the effective assistance of counsel by joint representation of conflicting interests." However, there was no need here "to resolve these two issues," as this case presented a situation in which trial counsel's motion pretrial had given the trial court notice of the "probable risk of a conflict of interests." In that setting, the Court concluded, the judge's inadequate response was itself grounds for reversal of the convictions. It noted: "The judge * * * failed either to appoint separate counsel or to take adequate steps to ascertain whether the risk was too remote to warrant separate counsel. We hold that the failure, in the face of the representations made by counsel weeks before trial and again before the jury was impaneled, deprived petitioners of the guarantee of 'assistance of counsel.' "

The three dissenters in *Holloway* agreed that under the special circumstances presented there, the trial court "should have held an appropriate hearing on defense motion," but argued that this failure should do no more than shift to the prosecution the burden of showing the "improbability of conflict or prejudice." The majority rejected this approach, noting that *Glasser* had held that "whenever a trial court improperly requires joint representation over timely objection reversal is automatic." Admittedly, *Glasser* was decided before the Supreme Court, in *Chapman v. California* (p. 1417) had recognized that certain constitutional violations could constitute harmless error. But that standard was not suited to a denial of the right to counsel, including a denial due to a conflict of interest. In "the normal case where harmless error is applied, the reviewing court can undertake with some confidence its relatively narrow task of assessing the likelihood that error materially affected the deliberations of the jury." But as *Glasser* had pointed out: "In the case of joint representation of conflicting interests, the evil is in what the advocate finds himself compelled to *refrain* from doing, not only at trial but also as to possible pretrial plea negotiations and in the sentencing process. It may be possible in some cases to identify from the record the prejudice resulting from an attorney's failure to undertake certain trial tasks, but even with a record of the sentencing hearing available it would be difficult to judge intelligently the impact of a conflict on the attorney's representation of a client. And to assess the impact of a conflict of interests on the attorney's options, tactics, and decisions in plea negotiations would be virtually impossible. Thus an inquiry into a claim of harmless error here would require, unlike most cases, unguided speculation."

Two years after *Holloway,* in *Cuyler v. Sullivan*, the Court addressed two issues that *Holloway* declined to decide. Its response on the first issue, what postconviction review standard applies where there is no duty to inquire, is discussed in Note 1, p. 183. Its response to the second, how far does the duty to inquire extend beyond the special situation presented in *Holloway,* is discussed in Note 6 below.

6. *Defining the scope of the duty.* In CUYLER v. SULLIVAN, 446 U.S. 335 (1980), defendant Sullivan[b] had been indicted, along with two codefendants, for the first degree murders of two victims. Sullivan accepted representation from the two lawyers retained by his codefendants because he could not afford to retain a lawyer. Sullivan came to trial first and counsel challenged the prosecution's case, but did not put on any defense evidence. The jury found Sullivan guilty and set his sentence at life imprisonment. Sullivan's two codefendants were later acquitted in separate trials. Sullivan then sought collateral relief under state law, raising for the first time a claim that his counsel had represented conflicting interests. Although the Third Circuit, on federal habeas review, held that there had been an actual conflict of interest, the Supreme Court initially considered the contention that Sullivan was entitled to a reversal of his conviction, without examining whether an actual conflict had occurred, because, as in *Holloway*, the trial court had violated a constitutional duty to conduct an inquiry into the possibility of a conflict. The Court majority (per Powell, J.) rejected that contention:

"*Holloway* requires state trial courts to investigate timely [defense counsel] objections to multiple representation. But nothing in our precedents suggests that the Sixth Amendment requires state courts themselves to initiate inquiries into the propriety of multiple representation in every case. Defense counsel have an ethical obligation to avoid conflicting representations and to advise the court promptly when a conflict of interest arises during the course of trial. Absent special circumstances, therefore, trial courts may assume either that multiple representation entails no conflict or that the lawyer and his clients knowingly accept such risk of conflict as may exist. * * * Unless the trial court knows or reasonably should know that a particular conflict exists, the court need not initiate an inquiry.

"Nothing in the circumstances of this case indicates that the trial court had a duty to inquire whether there was a conflict of interest. The provision of separate trials for Sullivan and his codefendants significantly reduced the potential for a divergence in their interests. No participant in Sullivan's trial ever objected to the multiple representation. [Counsel's] opening argument for Sullivan outlined a defense compatible with the view that none of the defendants was connected with the murders. The opening arguments also suggested that counsel was not afraid to call witnesses whose testimony might be needed at the trials of Sullivan's codefendants. Finally counsel's critical decision to rest Sullivan's defense was on its face a reasonable tactical response to the weakness of the circumstantial evidence presented by the prosecutor. On these facts, we conclude that the Sixth Amendment imposed upon the trial court no affirmative duty to inquire into the propriety of multiple representation."

---

[b] Since appellant Cuyler was the prison warden, also involved in many other reported cases, the case is often referred to as *Sullivan*, although some judges prefer *Cuyler*. See e.g., the different opinions in *Mickens v. Taylor,* infra.

Justices Brennan and Marshall, in separate opinions, disagreed with the Court's analysis on this issue. Justice Brennan noted: "[As the Court observes], 'a possible conflict inheres in almost every instance of multiple representation.' Therefore, upon discovery of joint representation, the duty of the trial court is to ensure that the defendants have not unwittingly given up their constitutional right to effective counsel. * * * [T]he trial court cannot safely assume that silence indicates a knowledgeable choice to proceed jointly. The court must at least affirmatively advise the defendants that joint representation creates potential hazards which the defendants should consider before proceeding with the representation. * * * "

7. ***The "reasonably should know" standard.*** CRIMPROC. § 11.9(b) notes that lower courts generally have confined the "reasonably should know" standard to situations in which "actual conflicts were obvious," such as "where the record established that the defense counsel had previously represented a [prosecution] witness in connection with the same or a related matter [or] that the defense counsel was facing a disciplinary complaint in connection to this case." The courts have held that the standard is not met "where indicators were ambiguous, or suggested no more than a potential conflict."

8. Although the Court's ruling was far from clear, *Wood v. Georgia*, 450 U.S. 261 (1981), appeared to conclude that the trial court reasonably should have known of a conflict (and the case was so interpreted in the subsequent decision of *Mickens v. Taylor*, Note 2, p. 184). The Supreme Court granted certiorari in *Wood* to determine whether a state could constitutionally revoke the probation of defendants who were unable to pay fines imposed for a previous conviction. The case was remanded, however, for an evidentiary hearing on a conflict issue raised by the Court sua sponte. The defendants had been charged with an offense committed in the course of their employment and their counsel had been provided by their employer. They had been sentenced to pay substantial fines on the assumption that the employer would provide them with the necessary funds. When the employer refused to give them the funds, counsel did not immediately move for modification of the fines or ask for leniency. Instead, he pressed the argument that a probation revocation for the failure to pay fines that were beyond a defendant's means was unconstitutional, a contention which, if accepted, would work to the long range benefit of the employer. The Supreme Court (per Powell, J.) noted that the record of the revocation proceedings was not sufficiently complete for it to determine whether a conflict actually existed. "Nevertheless," it noted, "the record does demonstrate that the possibility of a conflict of interest was sufficiently apparent at the time of the revocation hearing to impose upon the [state] court a duty to inquire further." All of the relevant facts relating to the employer's retention of counsel, the employer's failure to pay the fines, and "counsel's insistence upon pressing a constitutional attack" were known to the state court. Moreover, "any doubt as to whether th[at] court should have been aware of the problem [was] dispelled by the fact that the [prosecutor] had raised the conflict problem."

9. ***Scope of the inquiry.*** Appellate courts note that where an inquiry is required under *Sullivan*, that inquiry should not be "perfunctory," but should include "probing and specific questions" regarding the apparent conflict. They also note, however, that the trial court is "entitled to rely on the attorney's representations" as to the "underlying facts." If the trial court determines that a potential or actual conflict exists, but disqualification is not needed (see Pt. C), it has an obligation to explain the situation to the defendant and obtain a waiver. See CRIMPROC § 11.9(b). As to waivers, see Note 4, p. 194.

B. POSTCONVICTION REVIEW

1. ***The* Cuyler *"actual conflict" standard.*** Having determined that the joint representation there did not impose a constitutional duty of inquiry (see Note 6, p. 182), Justice Powell's majority opinion in in CUYLER v. SULLIVAN, 466 U.S. 335 (1980), turned to the Third

Circuit's ruling that a conflict had materialized during the trial, thereby requiring a reversal of the defendant's conviction. The opinion reasoned:

"In order to establish a violation of the Sixth Amendment, a defendant who raised no objection at trial must demonstrate that an actual conflict of interest adversely affected his lawyer's performance. In *Glasser v. United States* [Note 1, p. 179], for example, the record showed that defense counsel failed to cross-examine a prosecution witness whose testimony linked Glasser with the crime and failed to resist the presentation of arguably inadmissible evidence. The Court found that both omissions resulted from counsel's desire to diminish the jury's perception of a codefendant's guilt. * * * Since this actual conflict of interest impaired Glasser's defense, the Court reversed his conviction. *Glasser* [thus] established that unconstitutional multiple representation is never harmless error. But until a defendant shows his counsel actively represented conflicting interests, he has not established the constitutional predicate for his claim of ineffective assistance."

"The Court of Appeals granted Sullivan relief because he had shown that multiple representation in this case involved a possible conflict of interest. We hold that the possibility of conflict is insufficient to impugn a criminal conviction. In order to demonstrate a violation of his Sixth Amendment rights, a defendant must establish that an actual conflict of interest adversely affected his lawyer's performance. Sullivan believes he should prevail even under this standard. He emphasizes [attorney] Peruto's admission that the decision to rest Sullivan's defense reflected a reluctance to expose witnesses who later might have testified for the other defendants. The petitioner, on the other hand, points to [attorney] DiBona's contrary testimony and to evidence that Sullivan himself wished to avoid taking the stand. Since the Court of Appeals did not weigh these conflicting contentions under the proper legal standard, its judgment is vacated and the case is remanded * * *."

Justice Marshall's partial dissent challenged the Court's insistence on a showing that the conflict "adversely affected" his lawyer's performance. "Such a test," he noted," is not only unduly harsh, but incurably speculative as well." It should be rejected, he argued, under the reasoning set forth in *Holloway* (see Note 5, p. 181) in explaining why harmless error doctrine did not apply there. Where no objection was made at trial, the "appropriate inquiry" should simply be whether a "conflict actually existed during the course of the representation."

2. *Violations of the "knows-or-reasonably-should-know" duty of inquiry.* MICKENS V. TAYLOR, 535 U.S. 162 (2002), presented an issue not considered in *Cuyler*—whether the *Cuyler* standard also applied where no objection had been raised at trial, but the trial court had violated that portion of the duty of inquiry that extends beyond *Holloway* (see Notes 6 and 7, pp. 182–183). The federal habeas petitioner Mickens had been convicted of the murder and sexual assault of a juvenile, Timothy Hall. Habeas counsel uncovered that one of the two trial counsel representing Mickens (Sanders) had been representing Hall on assault and concealed weapons charges at the time he was killed. Moreover, the same state judge who had appointed Sanders to represent Mickens had three weeks earlier dismissed the charges against Hall upon his death, and the docket sheet before him listed Sanders as Hall's counsel. The federal habeas court assumed that, under these circumstances, the state judge "knew or should have known" of the conflict and inquiry therefore was required under the *Cuyler* extension of that duty beyond *Holloway*. That assumption was not challenged by the state, and the Third Circuit and the Supreme Court proceeded to address the question of whether the automatic reversal standard of *Holloway* or the "actual conflict" standard of *Cuyler* applied in this setting. The Third Circuit held that the *Cuyler* standard applied, and a closely divided Supreme Court (5–4) agreed. Justice Scalia's opinion for the Court reasoned:

"The question presented in this case is what a defendant must show in order to demonstrate a Sixth Amendment violation where the trial court fails to inquire into a potential conflict of interest about which it knew or reasonably should have known. * * *"

"Petitioner argues that the remand instruction in *Wood* [Note 8, p. 183] established an 'unambiguous rule' that where the trial judge neglects a duty to inquire into a potential conflict, the defendant, to obtain reversal of the judgment, need only show that his lawyer was subject to a conflict of interest, and need not show that the conflict adversely affected counsel's performance. He relies upon the language in the remand instruction directing the trial court to grant a new revocation hearing if it determines that 'an actual conflict of interest existed,' without requiring a further determination that the conflict adversely affected counsel's performance. As used in the remand instruction, however, we think 'an actual conflict of interest' meant precisely a conflict *that affected counsel's performance*—as opposed to a mere theoretical division of loyalties. It was shorthand for the statement in *Sullivan* that 'a defendant who shows that a conflict of interest *actually affected the adequacy of his representation* need not demonstrate prejudice in order to obtain relief.' (emphasis added)

"Petitioner's proposed rule of automatic reversal when there existed a conflict that did not affect counsel's performance, but the trial judge failed to make the *Sullivan*-mandated inquiry, makes little policy sense. As discussed, the rule applied when the trial judge is not aware of the conflict (and thus not obligated to inquire) is that prejudice will be presumed only if the conflict has significantly affected counsel's performance—thereby rendering the verdict unreliable, even though *Strickland* prejudice cannot be shown. The trial court's awareness of a potential conflict neither renders it more likely that counsel's performance was significantly affected nor in any other way renders the verdict unreliable. Nor does the trial judge's failure to make the *Sullivan*-mandated inquiry often make it harder for reviewing courts to determine conflict and effect, particularly since those courts may rely on evidence and testimony whose importance only becomes established at the trial.

"Nor, finally, is automatic reversal simply an appropriate means of enforcing *Sullivan*'s mandate of inquiry. Despite Justice Souter's belief that there must be a threat of sanction (to-wit, the risk of conferring a windfall upon the defendant) in order to induce "resolutely obdurate" trial judges to follow the law, we do not presume that judges are as careless or as partial as those police officers who need the incentive of the exclusionary rule.* * * And in any event, the *Sullivan* standard, which requires proof of effect upon representation but (once such effect is shown) presumes prejudice, already creates an "incentive" to inquire into a potential conflict. * * *

"Since this was not a case in which (as in *Holloway*) counsel protested his inability simultaneously to represent multiple defendants;[c] and since the trial court's failure to make the *Sullivan*-mandated inquiry does not reduce the petitioner's burden of proof; it was at least necessary, to void the conviction, for petitioner to establish that the conflict of interest adversely affected his counsel's performance. The Court of Appeals having found no such effect, the denial of habeas relief must be affirmed."

Of the four dissenters, Justice Souter was the only one to reach the issue of whether a violation of a duty of inquiry under the know-or-reasonably-should-have-known-standard required automatic reversal. Justice Souter disagreed with the Court's reading of *Wood* and argued that the *Holloway* reasoning applied equally to the second prong of the duty to inquire: "While a

[c] The Court had previously noted that *Holloway* presented unique features: the objection was raised by the defense counsel, the person who is "in the best position to determine when a [disabling] conflict exists"; it came in a setting of joint representation, which is "inherently suspect"; and that setting placed on counsel obligations that "effectively seal his lips in crucial matters and make it difficult to measure the precise harm arising from counsel's errors." These features combined to justify a presumption of a 'disabling conflict" which "undermined the adversarial process."

defendant can fairly be saddled with the characteristically difficult burden of proving adverse effects of conflicted decisions after the fact when the judicial system was not to blame in tolerating the risk of conflict, the burden is indefensible when a judge was on notice of the risk but did nothing." Justice Kennedy, joined by Justice O'Connor, though concurring in the opinion of the Court, wrote separately to emphasize how "the facts of this case will illustrate why [such] a wooden rule requiring reversal is inappropriate." The concurring opinion stressed the federal district court's finding that "counsel [Sander's] brief representation of the victim had no effect whatsoever on the course of petitioner's trial." As the district court noted, "although Sanders probably did learn some matters that were confidential, * * * nothing the attorney learned was relevant to the murder case" and Sanders "labored under the impression he had had no continuing duty at all to his deceased client."

Justice Breyer, joined by Justice Ginsburg, dissented on the ground that the special circumstances of this case required automatic reversal. These circumstances included a "representational incompatibility [that]* * * is egregious on its face," a "trial court [that] itself created the conflict," and a case in which capital punishment was imposed. Justice Stevens' dissent also stressed the special circumstances of the case. He added that defense counsel had violated his obligation to disclose to the client that he had been representing the alleged victim, information which would have enabled the defendant to refuse the appointment.

3. ***Inadequate inquiries.*** Where the trial judge does conduct an inquiry, as required by *Holloway* or *Cuyler*, but that inquiry is inadequate, resulting in the failure to recognize and respond to the likely presence of an actual conflict, should that failure result in an automatic reversal of the conviction or should counsel's actual performance be examined under the *Cuyler* standard. The few lower courts considering this scenario have been divided, at least as to an inquiry commanded by *Holloway*. See CRIMPROC § 11.9(d).

4. ***Limiting the presumption of prejudice.*** After holding that the *Cuyler* standard applied to the case before it, the Justice Scalia's majority opinion in MICKENS v. TAYLOR, Note 2 supra, added a caveat as to the scope of the presumption of prejudice that follows from finding an adverse impact upon performance. The Court noted:

"Lest today's holding be misconstrued, we note that the only question presented was the effect of a trial court's failure to inquire into a potential conflict upon the *Sullivan* rule that deficient performance of counsel must be shown. The case was presented and argued on the assumption that (absent some exception for failure to inquire) *Sullivan* would be applicable—requiring a showing of defective performance, but *not* requiring in addition (as *Strickland* does in other ineffectiveness-of-counsel cases), a showing of probable effect upon the outcome of trial. That assumption was not unreasonable in light of the holdings of Courts of Appeals, which have applied *Sullivan* "unblinkingly" to "all kinds of alleged attorney ethical conflicts," *Beets v. Scott*, 65 F.3d 1258, 1266 (CA5 1995) (en banc).[d] They have invoked the *Sullivan* standard not only when (as here) there is a conflict rooted in counsel's obligations to *former* clients, but even when representation of the defendant somehow implicates counsel's personal or financial interests, including a book deal, * * * a job with the prosecutor's office, * * * the teaching of classes to

[d] In *Beets*, a closely divided Fifth Circuit concluded that *Cuyler v. Sullivan*'s prejudice presumption should apply only to conflicts presented by "multiple representation" situations (i.e., defense counsel represented codefendants or represented the defendant and witnesses or other interested parties), as opposed to conflicts arising from some self-interest of the attorney. In the latter situation, a claim of ineffective assistance based on a conflict should be treated no differently than any other ineffective assistance claim, with the court applying the *Strickland* standard, which requires a showing of prejudicial impact upon the outcome. The *Beets* majority reasoned that attorney ethical conflicts that do not result from obligations owed to current or former clients simply reflect another form of incompetent performance. To allow a "recharacterization of ineffectiveness claims to duty of loyalty claims," thereby importing "*Cuyler*'s lesser standard of prejudice" was to "blu[r] the *Strickland* standard" and undercut its role as the "uniform standard of constitutional ineffectiveness."

Internal Revenue Service agents, * * * a romantic 'entanglement' with the prosecutor, * * * or fear of antagonizing the trial judge.

"It must be said, however, that the language of *Sullivan* itself does not clearly establish, or indeed even support, such expansive application. '[U]ntil,' it said, 'a defendant shows that his counsel *actively represented* conflicting interests, he has not established the constitutional predicate for his claim of ineffective assistance' (emphasis added). Both *Sullivan* itself and *Holloway* stressed the high probability of prejudice arising from multiple concurrent representation, and the difficulty of proving that prejudice. Not all attorney conflicts present comparable difficulties. Thus, the Federal Rules of Criminal Procedure treat concurrent representation and prior representation differently, requiring a trial court to inquire into the likelihood of conflict whenever jointly charged defendants are represented by a single attorney (Rule 44(c)), but not when counsel previously represented another defendant in a substantially related matter, even where the trial court is aware of the prior representation.

"This is not to suggest that one ethical duty is more or less important than another. The purpose of our *Holloway* and *Sullivan* exceptions from the ordinary requirements of *Strickland*, however, is not to enforce the Canons of Legal Ethics, but to apply needed prophylaxis in situations where *Strickland* itself is evidently inadequate to assure vindication of the defendant's Sixth Amendment right to counsel. * * * In resolving this case on the grounds on which it was presented to us, we do not rule upon the need for the *Sullivan* prophylaxis in cases of successive representation. Whether *Sullivan* should be extended to such cases remains, as far as the jurisprudence of this Court is concerned, an open question."

Justice Stevens' dissent criticized the Court's "foray into an issue that is not implicated by the question presented." He noted that lower courts had "applied *Sullivan* to claims of successive representation as well as to some insidious conflicts arising from a lawyer's self-interest," and *Wood* had "applied *Sullivan* to a conflict stemming from a third-party payment arrangement." In doing so, "neither we nor the Court of Appeals have applied this standard 'unblinkly' * * * but rather have relied upon principled reason"—recognizing situations in which a lawyer's representation would be so "materially and adversely affected" that "a presumption of prejudice is appropriate."

Post *Mickens*, several circuits have recognized the possible restriction of the presumption of prejudice but have not ruled on the issue. See CRIMPROC § 11.9(d) (collecting cases). These cases have suggested that the Supreme Court may well find that *Strickland* rather than *Cuyler* applies to: (1) "cases of successive representation" (but not where that representation involved "substantial relatedness," as where counsel represented successively defendants on charges "arising from identical facts"); (2) a counsel who would be a defense witness (resulting in his disqualification) and therefore decided not to present an "advice of counsel" defense; and (3) "all ethical conflicts" of counsel other than "multiple or serial [representation] conflicts." Several state courts have held *Strickland* applicable in various conflict situations not involving multiple representation (e.g., prior representation of a witness on an unrelated matter). Ibid. Of course, state courts are free under state law to reject the "*Mickens* invitation" and refuse to "dra[w] any distinctions between 'types' of conflict of interest that may form the basis of a claim of ineffective assistance." *Acosta v. State*, 233 S.W.3d 349 (Tex.Crim.App. 2007).

5. ***Applying the "adverse impact" requirement.*** The leading Supreme Court ruling on the application of the adverse impact standard is BURGER v. KEMP, 483 U.S. 776 (1987). In that case Burger and Stevens were indicted for murder, but tried separately. Each made a confession that emphasized the culpability of the other. Leaphart, described as an experienced and well-respected criminal lawyer, was appointed to represent Burger. Leaphart's law partner was appointed to represent Stevens in his later, separate trial. Leaphart, however, did assist his

partner in the representation of Stevens. Moreover, he prepared the briefs for both defendants on their second appeal to the Georgia Supreme Court.

At their separate trials, each of the defendants sought to underscore the culpability of the other in order to avoid the death penalty. Although he had relied on Burger's lesser culpability as a trial defense, Leaphart did not make a "lesser culpability" argument in his appellate brief on behalf of Burger. In a subsequent federal habeas petition, defendant Burger argued that this omission, along with others, established Leaphart's incompetency under the *Cuyler* standard. Two lower federal courts rejected that claim, and a divided Supreme Court, per Stevens, J., affirmed:

"In an effort to identify an actual conflict of interest, petitioner points out that Leaphart prepared the briefs for both Burger and Stevens on their second appeal to the Georgia Supreme Court, and that Leaphart did not make a 'lesser culpability' argument in his appellate brief on behalf of Burger even though he had relied on Burger's lesser culpability as a trial defense. Given the fact that it was petitioner who actually killed Honeycutt [and] the further fact that the Georgia Supreme Court expressed the opinion that petitioner's actions were 'outrageously and wantonly vile and inhuman under any reasonable standard of human conduct,' [the] decision to forgo this omission had a sound strategic basis. * * *

"In addition, determining that there was an actual conflict of interest requires the attribution of Leaphart's motivation for not making the 'lesser culpability' argument to the fact that his partner was Stevens' lawyer, or to the further fact that he assisted his partner in that representation. The District Court obviously credited his testimony to the contrary, and its findings were twice sustained by the Court of Appeals. It would thus be most inappropriate, and factually unsupportable, for this Court to speculate that the drafting of a brief on appeal was tainted by a lawyer's improper motivation. Our duty to search for constitutional error with painstaking care is never more exacting than it is in a capital case. Nevertheless, when the lower courts have found that a lawyer has performed his or her solemn duties in such a case at or above the lower boundary of professional competence, both respect for the bar and deference to the shared conclusion of two reviewing courts prevent us from substituting speculation for their considered opinions. The district judge, who presumably is familiar with the legal talents and character of the lawyers who practice at the local bar and who saw and heard the witness testify, is in a far better position than we are to evaluate a charge of this kind, and the regional courts of appeals are in a far better position than we are to conduct appellate review of these heavily fact-based rulings."

In dissent, Justice Blackmun, joined by Justices Brennan and Marshall, responded: "It is difficult to imagine a more direct conflict than existed here, where counsel was preparing the appellate brief for petitioner at the same time that he was preparing the appellate brief for Stevens, and where the state statute specifies that one of the roles of that appellate process is to consider the comparative culpability and sentences of defendants involved in similar crimes. Counsel's abandonment of the lesser-culpability argument on appeal, the stage at which the two cases would be reviewed contemporaneously, is indicative of the 'struggle to serve two masters.' This record *compels* a finding that counsel's representation of the conflicting interests of petitioner and Stevens had an adverse effect on his performance as petitioner's counsel."[e]

---

[e] Consider also the reasoning in *West v. People*, 341 P.3d 520 (Colo. 2015). Because "research indicates that attorneys systematically understate both the existence of conflicts and their deleterious effects," the court's focus should be on "whether the alternative strategy or tactic [not pursued] was objectively reasonable under the facts known to the attorney at the time of the strategic decision"—a standard that "promotes conflict free counsel by eliminating a defendant's forced reliance on attorney's subjective assessment of his representation." If objective reasonableness is established, the failure to pursue that strategy can be "linked to the actual conflict" by showing either that it "was inherently in conflict with the attorneys other loyalty or interest" or "was not undertaken due to those other loyalties or interests." This approach, also utilized by some federal courts, is characterized as implementing the *Mickens* "adverse effect" requirement.

6. ***Presuming an adverse impact.*** Federal appellate rulings have held that an adverse impact on counsel's performance can be presumed in the instance of certain flagrant conflicts. See e.g., *United States v. Fulton*, 5 F.3d 605 (2d Cir.1993) (*per se* rule applies where the "attorney has engaged in the defendant's crimes," and also where a prosecution witness alleged that "he has direct knowledge of criminal conduct by defense counsel"; "the danger arising from a counsel who has been implicated in related criminal activity by a government witness is of a different order of magnitude"); Walberg v. Israel, 766 F.2d 1071 (7th Cir.1985) (adverse impact presumed where trial judge indicated to appointed counsel that approval of his fee and future appointments would depend upon counsel "pulling his punches"). Does *Mickens* require reexamination of such rulings?

C. DISQUALIFICATION OF COUNSEL

WHEAT V. UNITED STATES

486 U.S. 153, 108 S.Ct. 1692, 100 L.Ed.2d 140 (1988).

CHIEF JUSTICE REHNQUIST delivered the opinion of the Court.

[Petitioner, along with numerous codefendants, including Gomez-Barajas and Bravo, was charged with participating in a far-flung drug conspiracy. Both Gomez-Barajas and Bravo were represented by attorney Eugene Iredale. Gomez-Barajas was tried first and was acquitted on drug charges overlapping with those against petitioner. To avoid a second trial on other charges, Gomez-Barajas offered to plead guilty to certain offenses stemming from the conspiracy. At the commencement of petitioner's trial, the district court had not yet accepted the plea of Gomez-Barajas; thus he was free to withdraw his plea and proceed to trial. Bravo had pled guilty.]

[At the conclusion of Bravo's guilty plea proceedings and two court days before his trial was to commence, petitioner moved for the substitution of Iredale as his counsel. The government objected on the ground that Iredale's representation of the two other codefendants created a serious conflict of interest: (1) In the event that Gomez-Barajas's plea and the sentencing arrangement negotiated between him and the government were rejected by the court, petitioner was likely to be called as a witness for the prosecution at Gomez-Barajas's trial. This scenario would pose a conflict of interest for Iredale, who would be prevented from cross-examining petitioner and thereby from effectively representing Gomez-Barajas. (2) In the likely event that Bravo was called as a witness for the prosecution against petitioner, ethical proscriptions would prevent Iredale from cross-examining Bravo in any meaningful way. Thus, Iredale would be unable to provide petitioner with effective assistance of counsel.]

[In response, petitioner emphasized his right to have counsel of his own choosing and his willingness, and the willingness of the other codefendants, to waive the right to conflict-free counsel. Moreover, maintained petitioner, the circumstances posited by the government that would create a conflict of interest were highly speculative and bore no connection to the true relationship among the co-conspirators. If called to testify against petitioner, Bravo would simply say that he did not know petitioner and had had no dealings with him. In the unlikely event that Gomez-Barajas went to trial, petitioner's lack of involvement in his alleged crimes made his appearance as a witness highly improbable. According to petitioner, the government was "manufacturing implausible conflicts" in an attempt to disqualify Iredale, who had already proved extremely effective in representing the other codefendants.]

[The district court denied petitioner's request to substitute Iredale as his attorney, concluding, on the basis of the representation of the government, that it "really has no choice at this point other than to find that an irreconcilable conflict of interest exists." Petitioner proceeded to trial with his original counsel and was convicted of various drug offenses. The Court of Appeals for the Ninth Circuit affirmed.] * * *

[While] the right to select and be represented by one's preferred attorney is comprehended by the Sixth Amendment, the essential aim of the Amendment is to guarantee an effective advocate for each criminal defendant rather than to ensure that a defendant will inexorably be represented by the lawyer whom he prefers. * * * The Sixth Amendment right to choose one's own counsel is circumscribed in several important respects. Regardless of his persuasive powers, an advocate who is not a member of the bar may not represent clients (other than himself) in court. Similarly, a defendant may not insist on representation by an attorney he cannot afford or who for other reasons declines to represent the defendant. Nor may a defendant insist on the counsel of an attorney who has a previous or ongoing relationship with an opposing party, even when the opposing party is the Government. The question raised in this case is the extent to which a criminal defendant's right under the Sixth Amendment to his chosen attorney is qualified by the fact that the attorney has represented other defendants charged in the same criminal conspiracy. * * *

Petitioner insists that the provision of waivers by all affected defendants cures any problems created by the multiple representation. But no such flat rule can be deduced from the Sixth Amendment presumption in favor of counsel of choice. Federal courts have an independent interest in ensuring that criminal trials are conducted within the ethical standards of the profession and that legal proceedings appear fair to all who observe them. Both the American Bar Association's Model Code of Professional Responsibility and its Model Rules of Professional Conduct, as well as the rules of the California Bar Association (which governed the attorneys in this case), impose limitations on multiple representation of clients. Not only the interest of a criminal defendant but the institutional interest in the rendition of just verdicts in criminal cases may be jeopardized by unregulated multiple representation.

For this reason, the Federal Rules of Criminal Procedure direct trial judges to investigate specially cases involving joint representation. In pertinent part, Rule 44(c) [requires an inquiry in cases of joint representation]. * * * Although Rule 44(c) does not specify what particular measures may be taken by a district court, one option suggested by the Notes of the Advisory Committee is an order by the court that the defendants be separately represented in subsequent proceedings in the case. This suggestion comports with our instructions in *Holloway* and in *Glasser* that the trial courts, when alerted by objection from one of the parties, have an independent duty to ensure that criminal defendants receive a trial that is fair and does not contravene the Sixth Amendment.

To be sure, this need to investigate potential conflicts arises in part from the legitimate wish of district courts that their judgments remain intact on appeal. As the Court of Appeals accurately pointed out, trial courts confronted with multiple representations face the prospect of being "whip-sawed" by assertions of error no matter which way they rule. If a district court agrees to the multiple representation, and the advocacy of counsel is thereafter impaired as a result, the defendant may well claim that he did not receive effective assistance. On the other hand, a district court's refusal to accede to the multiple representation may result in a challenge such as petitioner's in this case. Nor does a waiver by the defendant necessarily solve the problem, for we note, without passing judgment on, the apparent willingness of Courts of Appeals to entertain ineffective assistance claims from defendants who have specifically waived the right to conflict-free counsel.

Thus, where a court justifiably finds an actual conflict of interest, there can be no doubt that it may decline a proffer of waiver, and insist that defendants be separately represented. * * * Unfortunately for all concerned, a district court must pass on the issue of whether or not to allow a waiver of a conflict of interest by a criminal defendant not with the wisdom of hindsight after the trial has taken place, but the murkier pretrial context when relationships between parties are seen through a glass, darkly. The likelihood and dimensions of nascent conflicts of interest are notoriously hard to predict, even for those thoroughly familiar with criminal trials. It is a rare attorney who will be fortunate enough to learn the entire truth from his own client, much less be fully apprised before trial of what each of the Government's witnesses will say on the stand. A few bits of unforeseen testimony or a single previously unknown or unnoticed document may significantly shift the relationship between multiple defendants. These imponderables are difficult enough for a lawyer to assess, and even more difficult to convey by way of explanation to a criminal defendant untutored in the niceties of legal ethics. Nor is it amiss to observe that the willingness of an attorney to obtain such waivers from his clients may bear an inverse relation to the care with which he conveys all the necessary information to them.

For these reasons we think the District Court must be allowed substantial latitude in refusing waivers of conflicts of interest not only in those rare cases where an actual conflict may be demonstrated before trial, but in the more common cases where a potential for conflict exists which may or may not burgeon into an actual conflict as the trial progresses. In the circumstances of this case, with the motion for substitution of counsel made so close to the time of trial, the District Court relied on instinct and judgment based on experience in making its decision. We do not think it can be said that the court exceeded the broad latitude which must be accorded it in making this decision. Petitioner of course rightly points out that the government may seek to "manufacture" a conflict in order to prevent a defendant from having a particularly able defense counsel at his side; but trial courts are undoubtedly aware of this possibility, and must take it into consideration along with all of the other factors which inform this sort of a decision.

Here the District Court was confronted not simply with an attorney who wished to represent two coequal defendants in a straightforward criminal prosecution; rather, Iredale proposed to defend three conspirators of varying stature in a complex drug distribution scheme. The Government intended to call Bravo as a witness for the prosecution at petitioner's trial. The Government might readily have tied certain deliveries of marijuana by Bravo to petitioner, necessitating vigorous cross-examination of Bravo by petitioner's counsel. Iredale, because of his prior representation of Bravo, would have been unable ethically to provide that cross-examination.

Iredale had also represented Gomez-Barajas, one of the alleged kingpins of the distribution ring, and had succeeded in obtaining a verdict of acquittal for him. Gomez-Barajas had agreed with the Government to plead guilty to other charges, but the District Court had not yet accepted the plea arrangement. If the agreement were rejected, petitioner's probable testimony at the resulting trial of Gomez-Barajas would create an ethical dilemma for Iredale from which one or the other of his clients would likely suffer.

Viewing the situation as it did before trial, we hold that the District Court's refusal to permit the substitution of counsel in this case was within its discretion and did not violate petitioner's Sixth Amendment rights. Other district courts might have reached differing or opposite conclusions with equal justification, but that does not mean that one conclusion was "right" and the other "wrong." The District Court must recognize a presumption in favor of petitioner's counsel of choice, but that presumption may be overcome not only by a demonstration of actual conflict but by a showing of a serious potential for conflict. The evaluation [of the] circumstances of each case under this standard must be left primarily to the informed judgment of the trial court. * * *

JUSTICE MARSHALL, with whom JUSTICE BRENNAN joins, dissenting.

[I] disagree [with] the Court's suggestion that the trial court's decision as to whether a potential conflict justifies rejection of a defendant's chosen counsel is entitled to some kind of special deference on appeal. The Court grants trial courts "broad latitude" over the decision to accept or reject a defendant's choice of counsel; although never explicitly endorsing a standard of appellate review, the Court appears to limit such review to determining whether an abuse of discretion has occurred. * * * [This approach] accords neither with the nature of the trial court's decision nor with the importance of the interest at stake. * * *

The interest at stake in this kind of decision is nothing less than a criminal defendant's Sixth Amendment right to counsel of his choice. The trial court simply does not have "broad latitude" to vitiate this right. In my view, a trial court that rejects a criminal defendant's chosen counsel on the ground of a potential conflict should make findings on the record to facilitate review, and an appellate court should scrutinize closely the basis for the trial court's decision. Only in this way can a criminal defendant's right to counsel of his choice be appropriately protected.

The Court's resolution of the instant case flows from its deferential approach to the District Court's denial of petitioner's motion to add or substitute counsel; absent deference, a decision upholding the District Court's ruling would be inconceivable. Indeed, I believe that even under the Court's deferential standard, reversal is in order. * * *

At the time of petitioner's trial, Iredale's representation of Gomez-Barajas was effectively completed. * * * Gomez-Barajas was not scheduled to appear as a witness at petitioner's trial; thus, Iredale's conduct of that trial would not require him to question his former client. The only possible conflict this Court can divine from Iredale's representation of both petitioner and Gomez-Barajas rests on the premise that the trial court would reject the negotiated plea agreement and that Gomez-Barajas then would decide to go to trial. In this event, the Court tells us, "petitioner's probable testimony at the resulting trial of Gomez-Barajas would create an ethical dilemma for Iredale."

This argument rests on speculation of the most dubious kind. The Court offers no reason to think that the trial court would have rejected Gomez-Barajas's plea agreement; neither did the Government posit any such reason in its argument or brief before this Court. The most likely occurrence at the time petitioner moved to retain Iredale as his defense counsel was that the trial court would accept Gomez-Barajas's plea agreement, as the court in fact later did. Moreover, even if Gomez-Barajas had gone to trial, petitioner probably would not have testified. * * * [The] only alleged connection between petitioner and Gomez-Barajas sprang from the conspiracy to distribute marijuana, and a jury already had acquitted Gomez-Barajas of that charge. It is therefore disingenuous to say that representation of both petitioner and Gomez-Barajas posed a serious potential for a conflict of interest.

Similarly, Iredale's prior representation of Bravo was not a cause for concern. * * * Contrary to the Court's inference, Bravo could not have testified about petitioner's involvement in the alleged marijuana distribution scheme. As all parties were aware at the time, Bravo did not know and could not identify petitioner; indeed, prior to the commencement of legal proceedings, the two men never had heard of each other. Bravo's eventual testimony at petitioner's trial related to a shipment of marijuana in which petitioner was not involved; the testimony contained not a single reference to petitioner. Petitioner's counsel did not cross-examine Bravo, and neither petitioner's counsel nor the prosecutor mentioned Bravo's testimony in closing argument. * * * Moreover, even assuming that Bravo's testimony might have "necessitat[ed] vigorous cross-examination," the District Court could have insured against the possibility of any conflict of interest without wholly depriving petitioner of his constitutional right to the counsel of his choice. Petitioner's motion requested that Iredale either be substituted for petitioner's current counsel or be added to petitioner's defense team. Had the District Court allowed the addition of Iredale and then ordered that he take no part in the cross-examination of Bravo, any possibility of a conflict would have been removed. * * *

JUSTICE STEVENS, with whom JUSTICE BLACKMUN joins, dissenting.

[The] Court gives inadequate weight to the informed and voluntary character of the clients' waiver of their right to conflict-free representation. Particularly, the Court virtually ignores the fact that the additional counsel representing petitioner had provided him with sound advice concerning the wisdom of a waiver and would have remained available during the trial to assist in the defense. Thus, [the] question before [the District Judge] was whether petitioner should be permitted to have *additional* counsel of his choice. I agree with Justice Marshall that the answer to that question is perfectly clear.

NOTES AND QUESTIONS

1. ***Viewing* Wheat *from different perspectives.*** Commentators have approached the issue of disqualification from quite diverse perspectives, producing equally diverse evaluations of the *Wheat* ruling. Consider:

(a) William J. Stuntz, *Waiving Rights in Criminal Procedure*, 75 Va. L. Rev. 761 (1989): "One might try to explain *Wheat* as nothing more than a paternalistic attempt to protect Iredale's clients against their own irrationality * * * [but] that approach to the case seems strained. * * *[Professor Stuntz notes that Wheat was involved in a large-scale conspiracy, where defendants often are more "sophisticated."] * * * There are two reasons why the coconspirators [in Wheat] might have wished to use Iredale as common counsel. The first, offered by the defendants, is unobjectionable: the defendants believed Iredale to be a very good attorney, better than the likely alternatives. But the second is troubling. If the three defendants in question were guilty, they may well have faced a classic prisoners' dilemma: it may have been in each individual's interest to 'sell out' to the government and implicate his colleagues, but may have been far better for all if all either lied or remained silent. Common counsel may have removed the dilemma by facilitating the enforcement of an agreement not to finger each other. * * * If an objective observer familiar with the local bar would have concluded that Iredale was not any better than the lawyers who might have taken his place, then the defendants' motive for retaining him seems suspect. The district judge was in a good position to make that judgment. The ability of district judges to make case-by-case assessments of defendants' counsel of choice may be why the Court left the matter in the district courts' discretion, rather than promulgate a blanket rule either barring or allowing waiver."

(b) Bruce A. Green, *"Through a Glass, Darkly": How the Court Sees Motions to Disqualify Criminal Defense Lawyers,* 89 Colum.L.Rev. 1201, 1215–16, 1221–22 (1989): "In light of the nature of the potential conflict in *Wheat* and the manner in which it is addressed by the prevailing ethical standards, the district judge in that case had no basis for concluding that, if Bravo were to be a government witness at Wheat's trial, Iredale's representation of Wheat would violate the prevailing ethical norms. * * * Even if Iredale were called upon to cross-examine Bravo, the client's consent to the potential conflict would have eliminated the ethical barrier to the representation, notwithstanding Iredale's possession of confidences that needed to be preserved. * * * Thus, the *Wheat* decision is bottomed on the Court's misunderstanding of the ethical rules. [The] Court upheld the denial of Wheat's choice of counsel in a case where the ethical rules plainly would have permitted that choice."

(c) Note, 102 Harv.L.Rev. 143 (1988). "By allowing the government successfully to oppose Wheat's attempted waiver on the basis of institutional concerns external to Wheat, the Court in effect vested the right to conflict-free defense counsel in the state as well as in Wheat. * * * Recognizing such a right transforms the Sixth Amendment, presumably a shield to help criminal defendants receive fair treatment in their battle against a more powerful adversary, into an additional weapon for their prosecutors to use against them. The state might now intentionally manufacture conflicts in order to disqualify a particularly formidable opposing attorney. Indeed, the relative insignificance of Bravo's testimony against Wheat, the late date at which the government expressed interest in that testimony, and the success of Iredale in representing Wheat's alleged co-conspirators together suggest that Wheat's prosecutor succeeded in doing just that."

2. ***"Manufactured conflicts."*** Assume that the defense claims, in responding to a motion to disqualify, that the prosecution has "manufactured a conflict" based on: (i) a prosecution offer of a plea bargain (in exchange for testifying for the government) to one of several jointly represented codefendants; (ii) the prosecution's current investigation of defense counsel as to events relating to the charges against the client; or (iii) the prosecution's intent to call the defense counsel as a witness. What type of inquiry, if any, is needed to satisfy *Wheat*'s directive that the trial court "must take * * * into consideration" the possibility that the conflict was "manufactured" by the prosecution to "prevent a defendant from having a particularly able defense counsel at his side" (p. 191). Consider *United States v. Diozzi*, 807 F.2d 10 (1st Cir.1986) (to ensure against a "manufactured conflict," where conflict is based on prosecution's use of defense counsel as a witness, the trial court should seek to determine whether the testimony of counsel is truly needed or whether the same facts could be established through other means, but the government should not be forced "to settle for less than its best evidence").

3. ***Disqualification in other conflict settings.*** "Recognizing [*Wheat*'s acceptance of trial court] discretion and applying a deferential standard of review, appellate courts have sustained the disqualification of counsel not only in cases involving multiple representation of codefendants (as in *Wheat*), but also in a broad range of other settings that present a realistic potential for a conflict of interest. These include cases in which: (1) defense counsel currently was representing an anticipated prosecution witness on either a related or different matter; (2) defense counsel has previously represented a prosecution witness on a related matter; (3) co-defendants (or co-targets of an investigation) had separate counsel, but shared information under a joint defense agreement, and one of the participants 'flipped,' leaving the agreement and agreeing to testify for the government; (4) defense counsel was a potential witness for the prosecution; (5) defense counsel's participation in events that would be described before the jury could lead to calling him as a defense witness, and would make him an 'unsworn' witness for the defense even if he were not called to testify; (6) defense counsel was a former member of the prosecution's staff who had participated in the bringing of these charges or otherwise had access through that position to confidential information relevant to the prosecution; (7) defense counsel was alleged to have been involved in criminal activity or professional misconduct that would bear upon his representation of the defendant; and (8) defense counsel also represented the entity with which defendant was associated (with that entity having interests separate from the defendant)." CRIMPROC § 11.9(c). Do all of these situations present the justifications for broad judicial discretion that were cited in *Wheat*?

4. ***Waivers.*** Where the conflict creates the potential of giving the defendant an adversarial advantage (e.g., where defense counsel is a former prosecutor and acquired confidential information relating to the prosecution's case), disqualification is virtually automatic. Where, however, the primary concern is that the particular conflict will adversely impact the defendant (or the related "judicial integrity" concern that such representation will appear less than fair), many trial courts will refuse to disqualify if they can obtain a satisfactory waiver of the conflict. Although *Wheat* spoke of federal appellate decisions that appeared to allow a defendant to press a postconviction conflict of interest challenge notwithstanding defendant's waiver of the right to conflict-free counsel, "post-*Wheat* circuit court rulings have established that a knowing and intelligent waiver precludes a subsequent competency challenge based on the conflict." CRIMPROC § 11.9(c).

Various appellate courts have offered fairly detailed instructions for advising defendants of potential and actual conflicts in the course of obtaining a waiver, and some courts also insist that a defendant consult with independent counsel before entering the waiver. *United States v. Newell*, 315 F.3d 510 (5th Cir.2002), indicates, however, that even such precautions may not provide a waiver that is an acceptable response to a postconviction challenge.

petitioner's dubious mental condition, the jury would surely have gotten the message that English was essentially conceding that petitioner killed the victims. But according to petitioner's current attorney, the difference is fundamental. The first formulation, he admits, is perfectly fine. The latter, on the other hand, is a violation so egregious that the defendant's conviction must be reversed even if there is no chance that the misstep caused any harm. It is no wonder that the Court declines to embrace this argument and instead turns to an issue that the case at hand does not actually present.

II

The constitutional right that the Court has now discovered—a criminal defendant's right to insist that his attorney contest his guilt with respect to all charged offenses—is like a rare plant that blooms every decade or so. Having made its first appearance today, the right is unlikely to figure in another case for many years to come. Why is this so?

First, it is hard to see how the right could come into play in any case other than a capital case in which the jury must decide both guilt and punishment. * * * Second, few rational defendants facing a possible death sentence are likely to insist on contesting guilt where there is no real chance of acquittal and where admitting guilt may improve the chances of avoiding execution. * * * Third, where a capital defendant and his retained attorney cannot agree on a basic trial strategy, the attorney and client will generally part ways unless, as in this case, the court is not apprised until the eve of trial. Fourth, if counsel is appointed, and unreasonably insists on admitting guilt over the defendant's objection, a capable trial judge will almost certainly grant a timely request to appoint substitute counsel. * * * Finally, even if all the above conditions are met, the right that the Court now discovers will not come into play unless the defendant expressly protests counsel's strategy of admitting guilt. Where the defendant is advised of the strategy and says nothing, or is equivocal, the right is deemed to have been waived. See *Nixon*. * * * In short, the right that the Court now discovers is likely to appear only rarely, and because the present case is so unique, it is hard to see how it meets our stated criteria for granting review. * * *

III

While the question that the Court decides is unlikely to make another appearance for quite some time, a related—and difficult—question may arise more frequently: When guilt is the sole issue for the jury, is it ever permissible for counsel to make the unilateral decision to concede an element of the offense charged? If today's decision were understood to address that question, it would have important implications.

Some criminal offenses contain elements that the prosecution can easily prove beyond any shadow of a doubt. A prior felony conviction is a good example. Suppose that the prosecution is willing to stipulate that the defendant has a prior felony conviction but is prepared, if necessary, to offer certified judgments of conviction for multiple prior violent felonies. If the defendant insists on contesting the convictions on frivolous grounds, must counsel go along? Does the same rule apply to all elements? If there are elements that may not be admitted over the defendant's objection, must counsel go further and actually contest those elements? Or is it permissible if counsel refrains from expressly conceding those elements but essentially admits them by walking the fine line recommended at argument by petitioner's current attorney?

What about conceding that a defendant is guilty, not of the offense charged, but of a lesser included offense? That is what English did in this case. He admitted that petitioner was guilty of the noncapital offense of second-degree murder in an effort to prevent a death sentence.[4] Is

---

[4] The Court asserts that, under Louisiana law, English's "second-degree strategy would have encountered a shoal" and necessarily failed. *Ante*, n. 1 [p. 197]. But the final arbiter of Louisiana law—the Louisiana Supreme Court—disagreed. It held that "[t]he jury was left with several choices" after English's second-degree concession, "including returning a responsive verdict of second degree murder" and "not returning the death penalty."

admitting guilt of a lesser included offense over the defendant's objection always unconstitutional? Where the evidence strongly supports conviction for first-degree murder, is it unconstitutional for defense counsel to make the decision to admit guilt of any lesser included form of homicide—even manslaughter? What about simple assault?

These are not easy questions, and the fact that they have not come up in this Court for more than two centuries suggests that they will arise infrequently in the future. I would leave those questions for another day and limit our decision to the particular (and highly unusual) situation in the actual case before us. And given the situation in which English found himself when trial commenced, I would hold that he did not violate any fundamental right by expressly acknowledging that petitioner killed the victims instead of engaging in the barren exercise that petitioner's current counsel now recommends.

IV

Having discovered a new right not at issue in the real case before us, the Court compounds its error by summarily concluding that a violation of this right "ranks as error of the kind our decisions have called 'structural.' " * * * The Court concedes that the Louisiana Supreme Court did not decide the structural-error question and that we " 'did not grant certiorari to review' that question." *Ante*, n. 4 [p. 201]. We have stated time and again that we are "a court of review, not of first view" and, for that reason, have refused to decide issues not addressed below. * * * Under comparable circumstances, we have refrained from taking the lead on the question of structural error. * * * There is no good reason to take a different approach in this case. * * *

NOTES AND QUESTIONS

1. ***What distinguishes "personal choice" decisions.*** In *Gonzalez v. United States*, 553 U.S. 242 (2008), Justice Scalia, in a concurring opinion, argued that defense counsel should be able to bind the defendant on the waiver of all rights, absent a client objection before the court, which would establish the client's revocation of lawyer-client "agency." In that connection, he criticized the Court's previous efforts to distinguish "personal choice" decisions from decisions assigned to counsel's expertise (as explained by the *Gonzalez* majority, see fn. a, supra). Justice Scalia noted: "I would not adopt the tactical-vs.-fundamental approach, which is vague and derives from nothing more substantial than this Court's say-so. One respected authority has noted that the approach has a 'potential for uncertainty,' and that our precedents purporting to apply it 'have been brief and conclusionary.' 3 W. LaFave, J. Israel, N. King & O. Kerr, *Criminal Procedure* §§ 11.6(a), (c), pp. 784, 796 (3d ed. 2007). That is surely an understatement. What makes a right tactical? Depending on the circumstances, waiving *any* right can be a tactical decision. Even pleading guilty, which waives the right to trial, is highly tactical, since it usually requires balancing the prosecutor's plea bargain against the prospect of better and worse outcomes at trial. * * * Whether a right is 'fundamental' is equally mysterious. One would think that any right guaranteed by the Constitution would be fundamental. But I doubt many think that the Sixth Amendment right to confront witnesses cannot be waived by counsel. * * * Perhaps, then, specification in the Constitution is a necessary, but not sufficient, condition for 'fundamental' status. But if something more is necessary, I cannot imagine what it might be. Apart from constitutional guarantee, I know of no objective criterion for ranking rights. * * * [Following the reasoning in today's decision], the essence of 'fundamental' rights continues to elude."

Does the *McCoy* majority provide a less "elusive" touchstone in its emphasis on the client's "objective" and "autonomy"? Does that emphasis nonetheless leave the issues posed in Pt. III of Justice Alito's dissent as not "easy questions"? Is Justice Alito assuming a "complex balancing process" in assigning decisions to the personal choice category? Consider CRIMPROC § 11.6(c) (classification appears to be the product of a pragmatic balancing process, considering the likely importance of the decision to defendants, the "inherently personal quality" of the decision, the practical necessities of litigation, and concern that lawyers maintain sufficient control over the case to remain "the manager of the lawsuit" and thereby ensure their zealous representation).

2. ***Lawyer/client disagreements and replacement of counsel.*** Lower courts uniformly agree that the indigent defendant has a right to substitution of new counsel upon a showing of "good cause," but a lawyer's refusal to accept defendant's directions on strategy, where ultimate decisionmaking authority does not rest with the client, does not constitute "good cause". Rather, "good cause" is created by a conflict of interest (see § 4, infra) or a "complete breakdown in communication," and the latter cannot have been the product of defendant's abusive or uncooperative behavior (indeed, such behavior may lead the court to allow counsel to withdraw, leaving defendant to proceed *pro se*). See CRIMPROC § 11.4(b). Where counsel is retained, but scheduling difficulties would otherwise prevail over defendant's right to retain counsel of choice, the same "good cause" standard applies. Does *McCoy* suggest that on a motion for replacement subject to the good cause standard, a conclusion that the lawyer-client disagreement related to "personal choice" defense also need not be viewed as good cause because, even if defense counsel believes that defendant's choice is foolish, the court has the option of directing defense counsel to proceed with the representation in accord with the defendant's choice?

3. ***Ineffective assistance and acceptance of defendant's directions.*** Even where the ultimate authority lies with counsel, can defense counsel invariably adopt the position that, "on balance, it is better to go against [your] best professional judgment, and [follow] [your] client's strongly felt views, than run the risk of a breakdown in lawyer-client communications that would be even more likely to preclude a successful defense"? CRIMPROC § 11.6(a). In applying *Strickland,* should a distinction be drawn between following the client's wishes (against the lawyer's best professional judgment) as to decisions within counsel's control (1) where the client described his choice as a reflection of personal values, and (2) where the client described the choice as a tactical decision? Justice Brennan's dissent in *Jones v. Barnes,* see fn. a, p. 195, has been characterized as stressing acceptance of all personal-value decisions in arguing that the attorney should function as "the instrument and defender of the client's autonomy and dignity *in all phases* of the criminal process." (emphasis added)

4. May a client's desire not to pursue a strategy that portrays him in a certain way justify the failure even to investigate the evidentiary strength of that strategy? The ABA Guidelines on Capital Representation provide that the investigation of a possible mitigation presentation in capital sentencing should be conducted "regardless of any initial assertion by the client that mitigation is not to be offered." Without such an investigation, it is noted, the defendant will not be able to make an informed decision. The Court majority in *Schriro v. Landrigan*, 550 U.S. 465 (2007), viewed the state court ruling there as having addressed such a situation (in contrast to the dissent's reading of the record). Among the several errors made by the Ninth Circuit on habeas review was that court's insistence that counsel should have explored "additional grounds for arguing mitigating evidence" notwithstanding defendant's instruction that a mitigation defense not be presented. The majority (per Thomas, J.) reasoned:

"The Court of Appeals held that, even if Landrigan did not want any mitigating evidence presented, the Arizona courts' determination that Landrigan's [ineffective assistance] claims were 'frivolous' and 'meritless' was an 'unreasonable application of United States Supreme Court precedent." This holding was founded on the belief, derived from *Wiggins v. Smith* [Note 2, p. 162], that 'Landrigan's apparently last-minute decision cannot excuse his counsel's failure to conduct an adequate investigation prior to the sentencing.' * * * Neither *Wiggins* nor *Strickland* addresses a situation in which a client interferes with counsel's efforts to present mitigating evidence to a sentencing court. * * * Indeed, we have never addressed a situation like this. * * * In short, at the time of the Arizona postconviction court's decision, it was not objectively unreasonable for that court to conclude that a defendant who refused to allow the presentation of any mitigating evidence could not establish *Strickland* prejudice based on his counsel's failure to investigate further possible mitigating evidence."

5. ***Failing to consult and per se prejudice.*** In *Nixon*, where defendant consulted and the defendant failed to take a position, the Court held that a challenge to counsel's representation was subject to the *Strickland* standards, including a showing of prejudice if counsel's performance did not meet the reasonably competent attorney standard. In *McCoy*, where the attorney consulted and the defendant disagreed, the failure to abide by the defendant's instructions constituted prejudice per se. What standard would apply where the defense counsel failed to consult as to a personal choice decision, followed his preferred strategy, and the defendant (aware of counsel's decision) did not object, but now states that he would have done so if he had known that his personal choice governed?

In ROE v. FLORES-ORTEGA, 528 U.S. 470 (2000), counsel failed to consult with the client as to filing an appeal, and failed to file an appeal. The Court majority, per O'Connor, J., concluded that per se prejudice did not apply. The case involved a first appeal of right, which carried a constitutional right to effective assistance. The Court had previously held that when the defendant has requested that an appeal be filed, the failure to file was per se prejudicial (without considering the likely outcome of the appeal). Here, however, the failure to consult did not in itself establish either inherently incompetent performance or per se prejudice.

Justice O'Connor concluded that, to establish *Strickland*'s first prong of professional unreasonableness based upon a failure to consult, it must be shown either that (1) the circumstances of the case were such that a "rational defendant would [have] want[ed] the appeal," or (2) that "this particular defendant reasonably demonstrated to counsel that he was interested in appealing." Thus, a "highly relevant factor would be whether the conviction follows a trial or a guilty plea, both because a guilty plea reduces the scope of potentially appealable issues and because such a plea may indicate that the defendant seeks an end to judicial proceedings." Where a guilty plea was entered, the court therefore should look to surrounding circumstances, including "whether the defendant received the sentence bargained for" and whether the plea "expressly reserved or waived some or all appeal rights."

As for the *Strickland* element of prejudicial impact, even if "all the information counsel knew or should have known" establishes that the rational defendant would want to appeal or that this defendant demonstrated an interest in an appeal, that did not invariably establish that the failure to consult "actually caus[ed] the forfeiture of the appeal." To meet the prejudice prerequisite, the defendant must "demonstrate that there is a reasonable probability that, but for counsel's deficient failure to consult with him about an appeal, he would have timely appealed." Justice O'Connor acknowledged that this inquiry "is not wholly dissimilar from the inquiry into whether counsel performed deficiently" by failing to consult. Thus, where the defendant shows nonfrivolous grounds for appeal, that will establish both that a "rational defendant would [have] want[ed] to appeal" and a "reasonable probability" that this defendant would have chosen to appeal after consultation. On the other hand, where the failure to consult constituted deficient performance because defendant had "sufficiently demonstrated to counsel his interest in an appeal," the defendant must also be able to establish that after consultation (which might suggest an appeal was fruitless), he would have continued that interest and instructed his counsel to file the appeal.

Justice Breyer, who provided the sixth vote for the majority, noted that the question presented to the Court concerned only the "filing of a notice of appeal following a guilty plea," and the opinion of the Court, "in my view, makes clear that counsel 'almost always' has a constitutional duty to consult with a defendant about an appeal after a trial." Justice Ginsburg, dissenting in part, also described the majority ruling as limited. She described the issue before the Court as "whether, after a defendant pleads guilty or is convicted, the Sixth Amendment permits the defense counsel to simply walk away, leaving defendant uncounseled about his appeal rights," and she characterized the majority's answer as "effectively respond[ing]: hardly ever." Justice Souter, in dissent, similarly described the issue, but characterized the majority's answer as being "sometimes," while "mine is 'almost always' in cases in which a plea of guilty has not obviously waived any claims of error."

PART 3

THE COMMENCEMENT OF FORMAL PROCEEDINGS

■ ■ ■

CHAPTER 13

PRETRIAL RELEASE

■ ■ ■

Except in the case of relatively minor offenses, the criminal process is usually invoked by arrest, meaning that most defendants will have occasion to seek release on bail either at the police station or at the first judicial appearance. The two central questions that arise regarding pretrial release, discussed herein, are: (1) Under what circumstances may such release be denied altogether? and (2) When release must be made available, what financial or other conditions may be imposed?

§ 1. THE RIGHT TO BAIL; PRETRIAL RELEASE PROCEDURES

A. STATE AND FEDERAL BAIL SYSTEMS

1. ***State bail.*** "Bail practices vary, but most jurisdictions adhere to the following methods: After charges are filed against someone, a judge or magistrate first determines whether to jail the person without the possibility of release until the case is over. In most jurisdictions, a person may be detained pretrial only if there is a high risk that the person will not appear in court or that the person will be a danger to the community before trial. * * *

"A judge can then decide to release the person if they promise to return to court (release on personal recognizance), conditionally release the person, or release the person on bail. With conditional release, a person must fulfill conditions such as checking in with pretrial services, drug testing, or electronic monitoring. With bail, a person can be released on a secured or unsecured bond. For an unsecured bond, the defendant doesn't have to pay anything up front but will owe the court money if they miss upcoming court dates.

" 'Cash bail' or 'money bail' almost always refers to secured bonds. For a secured bond, the defendant will be released from jail only upon paying the bond amount to the court. Many jurisdictions assign a defendant a predetermined bond amount based on the criminal charge, without an assessment of the defendant's ability to pay. Bail bondsmen will charge the defendant a fee, often 10% of the bail amount, to pay the bond on the defendant's behalf. When the defendant arrives at a later court date, the court will return the money to the bail bondsman, who retains the defendant's fee as profit. If someone is unable to pay for bail or unable to pay a bail bondsman's fee, the state will jail them until their case is over or the bond is paid.

"Cash bail results in excessive detention, wealth- and race-based discrimination, and high costs to taxpayers and communities. Nearly two-thirds of the people in jails in the United States have not been convicted of a crime. On any given day, that's more than 450,000 people, many of whom don't need to remain in jail: a judge has already determined that they are not a flight or dangerousness risk. If they could pay their bail or bail bondsman's fee, they could walk out the front door and go home. * * * People jailed pretrial are disproportionately black and Hispanic, and one study has found that 'Hispanic and black defendants are more likely to be detained [pretrial] than similarly situated white defendants.'

"With staggering incarceration numbers come staggering costs—for the public and for those who are detained, their families, and their communities. Taxpayers spend approximately $38 million a day—or $14 billion a year—on pretrial detention. Those who are detained face a cascading avalanche of difficulties. They can lose their jobs because they cannot go to work; without work and trapped in jail, they can lose their homes because they cannot pay rent; separated from their families and unable to support them, they can lose custody of their children or leave an elderly or sick family member without a caregiver. As the Supreme Court has observed, someone detained pretrial 'is hindered in his ability to gather evidence, contact witnesses, or otherwise prepare his defense.' Innocent people sometimes accept plea offers because pleading guilty allows them to go home, whereas maintaining their innocence would require staying in jail for months or years awaiting trial. Suicide remains the leading cause of death in American jails.

"And those are just the most visible problems. Empirical studies are beginning to confirm what many have long suspected: Pretrial detention results in worse case outcomes and has a criminogenic effect on people—that is, detaining someone pretrial makes that person more likely to commit a crime in the future. One study found that people who were detained pretrial were more likely to be sentenced to jail or prison than similarly situated people who were released before trial. People detained pretrial are also more likely to face longer sentences. Even brief stays in jail increase someone's likelihood of committing crimes in the future. And those who spend more than twenty-four hours in jail but are released pretrial are less likely to make their court dates than those who spend less time in jail. * * *

"The rise of bail reform activism and legislation has been sudden and meteoric. Nonprofits are funding efforts to eliminate money bail in at least thirty-six states. * * *

"Some reform advocates champion the adoption of pretrial risk assessment tools that use algorithms to predict a defendant's risk of dangerousness and flight. According to one developer of a risk assessment tool, adopting a system 'in which judges have access to scientific, objective risk assessment tools could further our central goals of increasing public safety, reducing crime, and making the most effective, fair, and efficient use of public resources.' Other models for reform * * * include community bail funds and switching from secured to unsecured bonds.

"Pretrial risk assessment tools typically use actuarial data to predict how likely it is that someone will miss an upcoming court date or commit a crime before trial. These tools use a checklist of risk factors that statistically correlate with nonappearance in court or commission of a crime pretrial. For example, New Jersey teamed up with the Laura and John Arnold Foundation, which has created one of the most popular risk assessment tools: the Public Safety Assessment (PSA). The PSA looks to nine risk factors: age at current arrest, current violent offense, pending charges, prior misdemeanor conviction, prior felony conviction, prior violent conviction, prior failure to appear in past two years, prior failure to appear older than two years, and prior sentence to incarceration. Based on a combination of these factors, a person receives three prediction scores: a 'failure to appear' score, a 'new criminal activity' score, and a 'new violent criminal activity' score. * * *

"There are substantial criticisms of risk assessment tools. Risk assessments depend upon criminal justice data that is neither neutral nor objective. American criminal justice has been shaped by our country's legacy of slavery and racial discrimination, by decades of mass incarceration, by preventative policing and profiling that targets minority communities, by a gulf between those who vote on criminal justice and those who are affected by it, and by the explicit and implicit biases of people working in the system. * * * Risk assessment tools may also be deficient because the data that inform the tools come from an environment where the only pretrial options are jail and personal recognizance. For example, the prediction that someone will miss a court date doesn't consider how a text message reminder or bus pass from pretrial services could improve their chances of getting to court.

"Proponents of pretrial risk assessment tools argue that even though the algorithms cannot fully shed the race or class bias inherent in the data, they are a net improvement over the current system in which judges' and prosecutors' biases are opaque and unknown. To minimize bias, the creators of tools like the PSA have chosen not to use demographic or socioeconomic data and have tried to calibrate the algorithms' use of criminal histories to reduce racial disparities. There has been little empirical research to see how these tools perform in practice, and more research is needed. It's also unsettled whether algorithms will produce more transparency than the black box of a judge's mind. The aura and complexity of big data pose the risk of concealing racial biases. The notions of objective data and computer algorithms can give false assurances of neutrality." Note, *Bail Reform and Risk Assessment*, 131 Harv.L.Rev. 1125, 1126–33 (2018).

2. ***Federal bail.*** Under the Bail Reform Act of 1984, set out in Supp. App. B, in the federal system "release of the person on his personal recognizance, or upon execution of an unsecured appearance bond in an amount specified by the court" is the preferred form of release, as it is to be utilized "unless the judicial officer determines that such release will not reasonably assure the appearance of the person as required."[a] Otherwise, the judicial officer may release the person "on a condition or combination of conditions," but he must select "the least restrictive * * * condition, or combination of conditions, that [he] determines will reasonably assure the appearance of the person as required." The Act lists many possible conditions, including that the person "execute a bail bond" or that he do various things while on release (e.g., maintain employment, comply with a curfew, return to custody during evening hours). However, the judicial officer "may not impose a financial condition that results in the pretrial detention of the person."[b] A person may be detained pending trial in certain situations (e.g., where there is "a serious risk that the person will flee") when "no condition or combination of conditions will reasonably assure the appearance of the person as required."[c]

The Act was amended by the Adam Walsh Child Protection and Safety Act of 2006 to provide in § 3142(c)(1)(B) that "[i]n any case that involves a minor victim * * * any release order shall contain, at a minimum, a condition of electronic monitoring and each of the conditions specified at subparagraphs (iv), (v), (vi), (vii), and (viii)." In *United States v. Merritt*, 612 F.Supp.2d 1074 (D.Neb.2009), the court held that enforcement of this provision "would violate the defendant's right to procedural due process" because it would infringe upon defendant's "liberty interest" "even in the absence of any showing that the defendant is a flight risk or that the conditions will protect the public or any person." The defendant in *Merritt* was charged with receiving and possessing child pornography, and the court noted defendant had "not been charged with any crime involving personal contact or direct observation of a minor" and there was "no evidence before the court that

[a] Another consideration is whether release "will endanger the safety of any other person or the community." This preventive detention aspect of the Act is considered in § 2 of this Chapter.

[b] In *United States v. Mantecon-Zayas*, 949 F.2d 548 (1st Cir.1991), defendant, after posting a $200,000 bond on Florida drug charges, was charged with additional drug offenses in Puerto Rico, where bail was set at an additional $200,000, which the lower court declined to reduce after defendant complained that raising the prior bond had "left him close to financial exhaustion." On appeal, the court held that such action was proper if that financial condition was necessary to ensure defendant's appearance, but if defendant could not meet that financial condition it then would be necessary for the court to comply with the statutory requirements for a detention order, including "written findings of fact and a written statement of the reasons for the detention."

[c] In *United States v. Orta*, 760 F.2d 887 (8th Cir.1985), the court stated: "In this case, the district court erred in interpreting the 'reasonably assure' standard set forth in the statute as a requirement that release conditions 'guarantee' community safety and the defendant's appearance. Such an interpretation contradicts both the framework and the intent of the pretrial release and detention provisions of the 1984 Act. Congress envisioned the pretrial detention of only a fraction of accused individuals awaiting trial. The district court's interpretation, however, virtually mandates the detention of almost every pretrial defendant: no other safeguards can 'guarantee' the avoidance of the statutory concerns."

this defendant poses any risk whatsoever of offending against a minor" or "any risk of flight during the pendency of this case."[d]

Bureau of Justice Statistics, *Federal Justice Statistics, 2013–2014* (March 2017), reports: "More than 3 in 4 defendants (78%) in cases terminated in 2014 had been detained by the court prior to case disposition (table 10). Two-thirds (67%) of defendants had been detained for the entire pretrial period and about a tenth (12%) were detained for part of the period and released. The defendants most likely to be detained were those charged with immigration (89%), weapons (87%), drug (85%), and violent (83%) offenses as the most serious charge. * * * Immigration defendants made up 41% of all defendants in cases terminated in 2014 and 47% of all defendants detained prior to case disposition. Eighty-seven percent of immigration defendants were detained for the entire period, while 2% of immigrant defendants were detained for part of the pretrial period and then released. Eleven percent of immigration defendants were not detained prior to case disposition in 2014.

"Of the 36% of property defendants detained, the majority were more likely to be detained for part of the period—rather than the entire period—than defendants charged with other offenses. For cases terminated in 2014, 81% of defendants charged with a sex offense were detained prior to case disposition. More than half (59%) of sex offenders were detained for the entire pretrial period, and nearly a quarter (22%) were detained for part of the period."

B. CONSTITUTIONAL LIMITS ON PRETRIAL RELEASE PROCESS

1. ***"Excessive" bail.*** In STACK v. BOYLE, 342 U.S. 1 (1951), indictments had been returned charging the 12 petitioners with conspiring to violate the Smith Act (which made it a crime to advocate the overthrow of the government by force or violence). Bail was fixed in the district court in the uniform amount of $50,000 for each petitioner. Petitioners then moved to reduce bail on the ground that the bail as fixed was excessive under the Eighth Amendment, and in support submitted statements as to their financial resources, family relationships, health, prior criminal records, and other information. The only evidence offered by the government was a certified record showing that four persons previously convicted under the Smith Act had forfeited bail. Though the petitioners' factual statements were uncontroverted at the hearing on the motion, the motion was denied. The same district court thereafter denied writs of habeas corpus applied for by the petitioners, and the court of appeals affirmed. The Supreme Court granted the petition for certiorari, and held that bail had "not been fixed by proper methods" and that "petitioners' remedy is by [a renewed] motion to reduce bail" in the district court. Vinson, C.J., stated for the Court:

"From the passage of the Judiciary Act of 1789, to the present * * *, federal law has unequivocally provided that a person arrested for a non-capital offense *shall* be admitted to bail. This traditional right to freedom before conviction permits the unhampered preparation of a defense, and serves to prevent the infliction of punishment prior to conviction. * * * Unless this right to bail before trial is preserved, the presumption of innocence, secured only after centuries of struggle, would lose its meaning.

"The right to release before trial is conditioned upon the accused's giving adequate assurance that he will stand trial and submit to sentence if found guilty. * * * Like the ancient practice of

---

[d] Compare *United States v. Peeples*, 630 F.3d 1136 (9th Cir.2010) (rejecting facial challenge to this provision because no showing the mandatory release provisions are inappropriate for *all* child pornography defendants, and rejecting defendant's "as applied" challenge on ground that it sufficient judge here exercised discretion, as statute deemed to permit, by tailoring the curfew and electronic monitoring conditions based upon the defendant's individual circumstances), criticized in *United States v. Karper*, 847 F.Supp.2d 350 (N.D.N.Y.2011) ("when the Adam Walsh Act is at play, there is no judicial discretion to be exercised in any respect").

securing the oaths of responsible persons to stand as sureties for the accused, the modern practice of requiring a bail bond or the deposit of a sum of money subject to forfeiture serves as additional assurance of the presence of an accused. Bail set at a figure higher than an amount reasonably calculated to fulfill this purpose is 'excessive' under the Eighth Amendment.

"Since the function of bail is limited, the fixing of bail for any individual defendant must be based upon standards relevant to the purpose of assuring the presence of that defendant. The traditional standards as expressed in the Federal Rules of Criminal Procedure[e] are to be applied in each case to each defendant. In this case petitioners are charged with offenses under the Smith Act and, if found guilty, their convictions are subject to review with the scrupulous care demanded by our Constitution. * * * Upon final judgment of conviction, petitioners face imprisonment of not more than five years and a fine of not more than $10,000. It is not denied that bail for each petitioner has been fixed in a sum much higher than that usually imposed for offenses with like penalties and yet there has been no factual showing to justify such action in this case. The Government asks the courts to depart from the norm by assuming, without the introduction of evidence, that each petitioner is a pawn in a conspiracy and will, in obedience to a superior, flee the jurisdiction. To infer from the fact of indictment alone a need for bail in an unusually high amount is an arbitrary act. Such conduct would inject into our own system of government the very principles of totalitarianism which Congress was seeking to guard against in passing the statute under which petitioners have been indicted.

"If bail in an amount greater than that usually fixed for serious charges of crimes is required in the case of any of the petitioners, that is a matter to which evidence should be directed in a hearing so that the constitutional rights of each petitioner may be preserved. In the absence of ...g, we are of the opinion that the fixing of bail before trial in these cases cannot be ...e statutory and constitutional standards for admission to bail."

...eme Court noted in *Schilb v. Kuebel,* p. 849, "the Eighth Amendment's ...essive bail has been assumed to have application to the States through the ...ment." See also Note 2, p. 865 infra.

...*edules.* The common use of bail schedules, which take account of only the ...se and not the individual defendant's circumstances, to authorize release prior ...nce, has sometimes been questioned, e.g., Lindsey Carlson, *Bail Schedules*, 26 (Spring 2011): "Regular use of bail schedules often unintentionally fosters the ...tion of misdemeanants, indigents, and nondangerous defendants because they ...rd the sum mandated by the schedule. * * * On the other hand, bail schedules ... or risky defendants to purchase release without judicial review or other ...l to prevent danger or flight."

Fields v. Henry County, 701 F.3d 180 (6th Cir.2012), where Fields was arrested ...domestic assault, denied any post-booking bail because of a county 12-hour hold ...state law, did not apply in the instant case, and then appeared the next morning before a judge, who set Fields' bail at $5,000 by using a bond schedule. As for the delay, the court stated: "The Eighth Amendment's protections address the amount of bail, not the timing. There is no constitutional right to speedy bail." As for any "procedural due process claim" regarding the delay, the court responded it would necessitate a "liberty interest" created by state law, not the case here because Fields had no "right to be released earlier than he was." Regarding the judicial use of a bond schedule, the court rejected Fields' contention "that he was entitled to a 'particularized examination' before having his bond set," as "nothing in the Eighth Amendment

[e] The reference is to Rule 46(c), which then stated: "Amount. If the defendant is admitted to bail, the amount thereof shall be such as in the judgment of the commissioner or court or judge or justice will insure the presence of the defendant, having regard to the nature and circumstances of the offense charged, the weight of the evidence against him, the financial ability of the defendant to give bail and the character of the defendant."

requires a particular type of 'process' or examination." Rather, use of a bond schedule violates the Eighth Amendment only if the amount specified for a particular offense is "grossly disproportional to the gravity of that offense," which Fields did not allege.

3. ***Indigent defendants.*** Justice Jackson, in a separate opinion in *Stack v. Boyle,* declared it would not be correct to say "that every defendant is entitled to such bail as he can provide." Compare the observations of Justice Douglas in *Bandy v. United States,* 81 S.Ct. 197 (1960): "To continue to demand a substantial bond which the defendant is unable to secure raises considerable problems for the equal administration of the law. We have held that an indigent defendant is denied equal protection of the law if he is denied an appeal on equal terms with other defendants, solely because of his indigence. *Griffin v. Illinois* [p. 92]. Can an indigent be denied freedom, where a wealthy man would not, because he does not happen to have enough property to pledge for his freedom?

"It would be unconstitutional to fix excessive bail to assure that a defendant will not gain his freedom. *Stack v. Boyle.* Yet in the case of an indigent defendant, the fixing of bail in even a modest amount may have the practical effect of denying him release. * * * The wrong done by denying release is not limited to the denial of freedom alone. That denial may have other consequences. In case of reversal, he will have served all or part of a sentence under an erroneous judgment. Imprisoned, a man may have no opportunity to investigate his case, to cooperate with his counsel, to earn the money that is still necessary for the fullest use of his right to appeal."

Under the Douglas approach, is it equally objectionable to *grant* a wealthy person freedom on conditions an indigent could not meet, as in *United States v. Madoff,* 586 F.Supp.2d 240 (S.D.N.Y.2009)? Consider *United States v. Patriarca*, 948 F.2d 789 (1st Cir.1991) (concurring judge raises question of fairness to indigents with respect to upholding district court's innovative set of release conditions, including all-hours video surveillance of defendant's home at defendant's expense); Note, 47 Harv.J.Legis. 555 (2010) (questioning the practice).

4. ***Equal protection challenge.*** In *ODonnell v. Harris County, Texas*, 251 F.Supp.3d 1052 (S.D.Tex.2017), the court concluded that county judges in Harris County had followed a policy of detaining "misdemeanor defendants before trial who are otherwise eligible for release, but whose indigence makes them unable to pay secured financial conditions of release," deemed "not narrowly tailored to meet the County's compelling interest in having misdemeanor defendants appear for hearings or refrain from new criminal activity before trial." The court then concluded that to pass equal protection muster, "when a secured financial condition of release works an absolute deprivation of pretrial liberty because a defendant is indigent or so impecunious that he or she cannot pay even a bondsman's premium required for release, the County must show that requiring a secured money bail is at least more effective than a less restrictive alternative at meeting the County's interests, even if it is not the least restrictive means to do so," which the county was unable to do.

The court of appeals, 892 F.3d 147 (5th Cir.2018) affirmed the district court's equal protection analysis, which it said "can be boiled down to the following: take two misdemeanor arrestees who are identical in every way—same charge, same criminal backgrounds, same circumstances, etc.—except that one is wealthy and one is indigent. Applying the County's current custom and practice, with their lack of individualized assessment and mechanical application of the secured bail schedule, both arrestees would almost certainly receive identical secured bail amounts. One arrestee is able to post bond, and the other is not. As a result, the wealthy arrestee is less likely to plead guilty, more likely to receive a shorter sentence or be acquitted, and less likely to bear the social costs of incarceration. The poor arrestee, by contrast, must bear the brunt of all of these, simply because he has less money than his wealthy counterpart. The district court held that this state of affairs violates the equal protection clause, and we agree."[f]

5. ***Bail credit.*** "Bail credit was designed, in large part, to remove from jail populations those pretrial detainees who, due to their own economic circumstances, are unable to post relatively modest bonds and are not otherwise a danger to the community. It is these same defendants, who are often unable to post bonds of just a few hundred dollars, who contribute substantially to jail overcrowding.

"In a typical misdemeanor case under the bail credit statute, a court may, for example, place a $500 full cash bond against a defendant. This is usually accomplished at arraignment. If the defendant remains unable to post the bond, $100 per day is credited for each day of confinement toward the unposted bond, with the defendant released on his or her own recognizance after five days without the necessity of posting any monetary bond.

" 'Bail credit' is not, however, limited to misdemeanor cases; it applies in felony cases as well. In some situations, a person charged with a felony offense may have access to some monetary funds to post as bail, but not enough to meet the amount of the bail imposed. Under those circumstances, the bail credit statute would permit the pretrial detainee through his or her confinement to earn enough bail credits to add to his or her own funds to make bail." Jay Lambert & J. Vincent April, *Bail Credit*, 32 Crim.Just. 32 (Winter 2018), discussing Ky. statute.

6. ***10% deposit alternative.*** SCHILB v. KUEBEL, 404 U.S. 357 (1971), upheld against a due process and equal protection challenge an Illinois statute providing for the pretrial release of an eligible accused by: (1) personal recognizance; (2) execution of a bail bond and deposit of cash equal to 10% of the bond, in which event 10% of the amount deposited (i.e., 1% of the amount of the bond) was retained by the state as "bail bond costs"; or (3) execution of bail bond and deposit of the full amount of the bail, in which event there is no charge or retention. Appellant Schilb had utilized the 10% provision, depositing $75 on a $750 bond, and his challenge was directed to the $7.50 that was retained by the state after he was subsequently acquitted on one charge and convicted on another. Justice Blackmun's opinion for the majority noted:

"Prior to 1964 the professional bail bondsman system with all its abuses was in full and odorous bloom in Illinois. Under that system the bail bondsman customarily collected the maximum fee (10% of the amount of the bond) permitted by statute, and retained that entire amount even though the accused fully satisfied the conditions of the bond. Payment of this substantial 'premium' was required of the good risk as well as of the bad. The results were that a heavy and irretrievable burden fell upon the accused, to the excellent profit of the bondsman, and that professional bondsmen, and not the courts, exercised significant control over the actual workings of the bail system. One of the stated purposes of the new bail provisions in the 1963 Code was to rectify this offensive situation. The purpose appears to have been accomplished. It is said that the bail bondsman abruptly disappeared in Illinois 'due primarily to the success of the ten percent bail deposit provision.'[g]

"Bail, of course, is basic to our system of law, and the Eighth Amendment's proscription of excessive bail has been assumed to have application to the States through the Fourteenth Amendment. But we are not at all concerned here with any fundamental right to bail or with any Eighth Amendment-Fourteenth Amendment question of bail excessiveness. Our concern, instead, is with the 1% cost-retention provision. This smacks of administrative detail and of procedure and

[f] "*ODonnell v. Harris County, Texas* might be the most important case ever decided on money bail. * * * As a direct result of the preliminary injunction that was issued in June 2017, as of this writing, over 11,000 people have been released from jail. The pretrial detention rate has gone from roughly 40 percent to roughly 5.6 percent." Thea Sebastian & Alec Karakatsanis, *Challenging Money Bail in the Courts*, 57 No. 3 Judges' J. 23, 26 (2018).

[g] Only four states have abolished commercial bail bonds. Shima Baughman, *The Bail Book* 49 (2018).

is hardly to be classified as a 'fundamental' right or as based upon any suspect criterion. The applicable measure, therefore, must be the traditional one: Is the distinction drawn by the statutes invidious and without rational basis?

"[Appellant argues] * * * that [the 1% charge] is imposed on the poor and nonaffluent and not on the rich and affluent * * *. But it is by no means certain, as the appellants suggest, that the 10% deposit provision under § 110–7 is a provision for the benefit of the poor and the less affluent and that the full-deposit provision of § 110–8 is one for the rich and the more affluent. It should be obvious that the poor man's real hope and avenue for relief is the personal recognizance provision of § 110–2. We do not presume to say, as the appellants in their brief intimate, that § 110–2 is not utilized by Illinois judges and made available for the poor and the less affluent. Neither is it assured, as the appellants also suggest, that the affluent will take advantage of the full-deposit provision of § 110–8 with no retention charge, and that the less affluent are relegated to the 10% deposit provision of § 110–7 and the 1% retention charge. The record is silent, but the flow indeed may be the other way. The affluent, more aware of and more experienced in the marketplace, may see the advantage, in these days of high interest rates, in retaining the use of 90% of the bail amount. A 5% or greater return on this 90% in a short period of time more than offsets the 1% retention charge. In other words, it is by no means clear that the route of § 110–8 is more attractive to the affluent defendant than the § 110–7 route. The situation, therefore, wholly apart from the fact that appellant Schilb himself has not pleaded indigency, is not one where we may assume that the Illinois plan works to deny relief to the poor man merely because of his poverty."[h]

But, is there a point at which the *Schilb* 10% scheme is too much of a burden on the rich? Consider *Platt v. Brown*, 872 F.3d 848 (7th Cir.2017) (under Ill. scheme at issue in *Schilb*, defendant whose bail set at $2 million paid 10% bond of $200,000 and after acquittal was refunded all but $20,000, loses on arguments that scheme as applied to him resulted in procedural due process violation, equal protection violation, and substantive due process violation, with latter rejected because fee "bears a rational relationship to Illinois's legitimate interests in encouraging the use of the full deposit system, creating a simple method of administration, and defraying the expenses of administering the bail bond system").

7. ***Proper sources of bail funds.*** In *Fleury v. State*, 2018 WL 3559916 (Fla.App.2018), defendant, charged with drug trafficking, challenged a court-imposed pretrial release condition that he show none of the funds used to post his bail in the amount of $138,000 would be derived from illegal activity. The court distinguished earlier court decisions supporting defendant's position, as in the interim the applicable state statute had been amended, now requiring a court to consider whether the "source of funds used to post bail * * * may be linked to or derived from the crime alleged to have been committed or from any other criminal or illicit activities." While the statutory language was unqualified, the court limited its holding to the conclusion that the requirement of such a showing was not "unreasonable under the circumstances of this case," as "there is probable cause to believe the Defendant engaged in drug trafficking, and police allegedly found $14,308 in cash in Defendant's bedroom."

Are certain other sources of bail money open to question? Consider Note, 44 Hofstra L.Rev. 1319, 1321 (2016), arguing money from crowdsourcing websites is one such source, as it "creates an easy way to legitimize money, which would have otherwise been rejected by the court due to its likely being the proceeds of criminal activity"; and Jocelyn Simonson, *Bail Nullification,* 115 Mich.L.Rev. 585, 587–88 (2017), noting that "community groups in jurisdictions across the United States have increasingly begun to use bail funds to post bail on behalf of strangers, using a

---

[h] Justices Stewart and Brennan dissented on other grounds relating to the state's failure to impose a similar retention fee upon persons who utilized the full-deposit provision. Justice Douglas dissented on the ground that the fee actually amounted to the imposition of court costs upon persons subsequently acquitted.

revolving pool of money," and objecting that whenever "a community bail fund pays bail for a stranger, the people in control of the fund reject a judge's determination that a certain amount of the defendant's personal money was necessary for the defendant's release."

8. ***Release to facilitate preparation of defense.*** *Kinney v. Lenon*, 425 F.2d 209 (9th Cir.1970), involved a 17-year-old detained in a juvenile detention home pending trial in juvenile court on charges arising out of a schoolyard fight. He alleged that there were many potential witnesses to the fight, that he could not identify them by name but would recognize them by sight, that his attorneys were white though he and the potential witnesses were black, that his attorneys would consequently have great practical difficulty in interviewing and lining up the witnesses, and that he was the sole person who could do so. The court concluded:

"We * * * are of the opinion that, in the peculiar circumstances of this case, failure to permit appellant's release for the purpose of aiding the preparation of his defense unconstitutionally interfered with his due-process right to a fair trial.

"The ability of an accused to prepare his defense by lining up witnesses is fundamental, in our adversary system, to his chances of obtaining a fair trial. Recognition of this fact of course underlies the bail system. But it is equally implicit in the requirements that trial occur near in time, and place (U.S.Const.Amend. VI) to the offense, and that the accused have compulsory process to obtain witnesses in his behalf. Indeed, compulsory process as a practical matter would be of little value without an opportunity to contact and screen potential witnesses before trial.

"This is not a case where release from detention is sought simply for the convenience of the appellant. There is here a strong showing that the appellant is the only person who can effectively prepare his own defense. We may take notice, as judges and lawyers, of the difficulties often encountered, even by able and conscientious counsel, in overcoming the apathy and reluctance of potential witnesses to testify. It would require blindness to social reality not to understand that these difficulties may be exacerbated by the barriers of age and race. Yet the alternative to some sort of release for appellant is to cast the entire burden of assembling witnesses onto his attorneys, with almost certain prejudice to appellant's case."

9. ***Right to counsel.*** A recent study, John P. Gross, *The Right to Counsel But Not the Presence of Counsel: A Survey of State Criminal Procedures for Pre-Trial Release*, 69 Fla.L.Rev. 831, 841 (2017), "reveals that in thirty-two states, counsel for indigent defendants is not physically present at the initial appearance," when bail is set. Is a bail hearing a "critical stage" at which there is a constitutional right to counsel? Cf. *Coleman v. Alabama*, p. 922 (preliminary hearing is a critical stage because, inter alia, "counsel can also be influential * * * in making effective arguments for the accused on such matters as * * * bail"); *Rothgery v. Gillespie County*, p. 80 (reaffirming "that the right to counsel guaranteed by the Sixth Amendment applies at the first appearance before a judicial officer at which a defendant is told of the formal accusation against him and restrictions are imposed on his liberty"); *Hurrell-Harring v. New York*, pp. 86, 175 (Court divides on whether Sixth Amendment right requires counsel's presence when bail set).

Sandra Thompson, *Do Prosecutors Matter? A Proposal to Ban One-Sided Bail Hearings*, 44 Hofstra L.Rev. 1161, 1164 (2016), noting that the ABA Standards for Criminal Justice, Prosecution Function § 3–5.1 (4th ed. 2015), "take the position that defendants are better off if a prosecutor is present at the bail hearing, even if defense counsel is not," argues, id. at 1162, "that time has proven this approach to protecting the rights of defendants at bail hearings is unrealistic and that defendants are actually better off if prosecutors are ethically barred from participating unless defense counsel is present."

10. ***Burden of production and proof.*** Who should have the burden of producing evidence and the burden of proof at the bail hearing? Consider *Van Atta v. Scott,* 613 P.2d 210 (Cal.1980), holding (1) that the burden of *producing evidence* to establish defendant's ties to the community

is on the defendant, as he "is clearly the best source for this information and for names of individuals who could verify such information" and "has a substantial incentive to cooperate in providing this information"; (2) that the burden of *producing evidence* regarding defendant's prior appearances or flight and the severity of the sentence he faces is on the prosecution, as "this information should be relatively easy and inexpensive for the prosecution to secure"; and (3) that "due process requires the burden of *proof* concerning the detainee's likelihood of appearing for future court proceedings to be borne by the prosecution," as so placing the burden "helps to preserve the respect for the individual's liberty and for the presumption of innocence that lies at the foundation of our judicial system, to maintain the respect and confidence of the community in the uniform application of the law and to systematically correct certain biases inherent in the OR decision-making process." With respect to the uniformity point, the court noted that because "the decision being made is predictive in nature" it is "peculiarly subject to abuse." On the matter of inherent biases, the court reasoned that anti-defendant distortion can easily occur because defendant's "incarceration prevents him from effectively locating witnesses or gathering other evidence to establish his local contacts and personal reliability"[i] and because the "not infrequent practice" of overcharging "gives an inaccurate picture to the trial court of the detainee's likelihood of fleeing."

11. *Defendant's testimony.* In *State v. Williams,* 343 A.2d 29 (N.H.1975), the court held: "Defendant's own testimony regarding the crime may be critical to a court's determination whether he should be set free pending trial. Since the 'law favors the release of defendants pending determination of guilt or innocence', a defendant should be encouraged to testify at a hearing on a motion to set bail without the fear that what he says may later be used to incriminate him."

Compare *United States v. Dohm,* 618 F.2d 1169 (5th Cir.1980), holding that defendant's statements at his bail hearing were inadmissible at trial because "the magistrate failed to accurately advise Dohm of his *Miranda* rights." But, the court rejected the broader claim by Dohm that in any event "he was compelled to forfeit his fifth amendment right to remain silent, in order to safeguard his eighth amendment right to reasonable bail." The defendant's analogy to *Simmons v. United States,* p. 802, was rejected by the court because in *Simmons* the Supreme Court stressed that "at one time, a defendant who wished to assert a fourth amendment objection was required to show that he was the owner or possessor of the seized property or that he had a possessory interest in the searched premises," while by contrast "a defendant at a bail bond hearing need not divulge the facts in his case in order to receive the benefits of the eighth amendment right to bail." A dissent questioned the latter conclusion, noting that the constitutional guarantee was "not just the right to bail, but the right to non-excessive bail," and that in the instant case "the defendant not unreasonably concluded that the recommended amount of bail would be determined to be appropriate for him unless he rebutted the government testimony portraying him as a big-time drug dealer." See also Note, 94 Harv.L.Rev. 426, 437 (1980), concluding that "*Dohm* represents a clearly impermissible compelled election."

12. *Victim's testimony.* Should the crime victim have a right to testify at defendant's bail hearing, as provided in 18 U.S.C.A. § 3771(a)(4), Supp. App. B, and comparable state provisions? About what? Consider Lynne Henderson, *Revisiting Victim's Rights*, 1999 Utah L. Rev. 383, 406,

---

[i] "Although there is widespread recognition of the need for reliable information when making a pretrial release decision, many jurisdictions have failed to implement pretrial services programs. A 2009 survey identified only about 300 jurisdictions that have such programs. The majority of respondents served a single jurisdiction, such as a county or city, and about fifteen percent were relatively new, having been established within the past ten years of the survey. In addition, nine percent of respondents reported that defendants charged with misdemeanors were excluded from their programs. Moreover, the Pretrial Justice Institute does not have any record for pretrial services programs in at least eleven of the jurisdictions that are among the fifty largest jail populations in the United States. There are several reasons why pretrial services programs have failed to gain widespread implementation in local communities, but it is primarily due to the fact that their very existence is at the whim of local governments." Note, 66 Rutgers L.Rev. 241, 255–56 (2013) .

regarding an earlier but similar proposal: "None of these proceedings necessarily invites the telling of the whole story, and it is absolutely unclear how many times in the criminal process it would be necessary for victims to be allowed to tell their stories for therapeutic value. Related to this is the question of the weight that authorities ought to give such statements.

"The provisions * * * are mostly silent on the reasons for victims presenting statements in court—that is, what the relevance and substantive effects of those statements should be—and what procedures ought to be followed in permitting those statements. It seems doubtful—or remains to be proved—that victims would be content to make statements knowing that they would have very little, if any, legal effect."

13. *Conditional release.* So-called conditional release, which "most often * * * includes certain nonfinancial requirements," Shima Baughman, *The Bail Book* 52 (2018), raises two questions: (i) whether the condition may be imposed for purposes other than ensuring the defendant's appearance; and (ii) whether, in any event, the condition is excessive. Compare, e.g., *United States v. Gates*, 709 F.3d 58 (1st Cir.2013) (where defendant charged with disorderly conduct and resisting arrest, bail condition that he submit to search of his person and residence at any time, even absent reasonable suspicion, upheld); with *Ex parte Allen-Pieroni*, 524 S.W.3d 252 (Tex.App.2016) (where defendant, charged with illegal possession of a weapon, "has no criminal record" and "has longtime and strong ties to the community," imposition of pretrial bail condition of home confinement and electronic monitoring constituted abuse of discretion).

14. *Bail after conviction.* In *Harris v. United States,* 404 U.S. 1232 (1971), Justice Douglas, acting as Circuit Justice on an application for bail pending appeal, noted: "While there is no automatic right to bail after convictions, 'The command of the Eighth Amendment that "Excessive bail shall not be required* * * " *at the very least* obligates judges passing on the right to bail to deny such relief only for the strongest of reasons.' "

Most state constitutions guarantee the right to bail in noncapital cases, but only "before conviction." In *State v. Patel*, 171 A.3d 1037 (Conn.2017), the court concluded that notwithstanding elimination of the qualifying words "before conviction" from the bail provision in the state constitution, such a limitation still existed and thus defendant here was not entitled to bail after the guilty verdict but before sentencing. The court added: "We observe that courts in other jurisdictions with constitutional provisions imposing no textual limitation on the right to bail (except capital offenses) have concluded that their constitutions do not afford a right to bail after the defendant is deemed to be convicted of a crime."

As elaborated in Doug Keller, *Resolving a "Substantial Question": Just Who is Entitled to Bail Pending Appeal Under the Bail Reform Act of 1984?*, 60 Fla.L.Rev. 825, 837–41 (2008), the Third Circuit was the first appellate court to work through the meaning of 18 U.S.C. § 3143(b), in Supp. App. B, concluding that a "substantial question" was one that is either "novel, which has not been decided by controlling precedent, or which is fairly doubtful," and that "likely to result in reversal or an order for a new trial" only meant that the district court should determine whether, if the substantial question were decided in the defendant's favor, it would likely result in a reversal or an order for a new trial. But the Eleventh Circuit criticized the Third Circuit's definition of substantial question and came up a different one: a substantial question is a "close question." Then the Ninth Circuit adopted the historical definition of substantial question: a question that is "fairly debatable." Keller concludes:

"[I]n short order, every other circuit sided with the Eleventh Circuit and essentially parroted its reasoning: the fairly debatable standard failed to go far enough to effectuate Congress's intent in restricting bail pending appeal. As an en banc Eighth Circuit succinctly put it: 'We believe [the close question standard] is more responsive to the announced purpose of Congress, which was, bluntly, that fewer convicted persons remain at large while pursuing their appeals.' The court's terse reasoning typifies the analysis of the other circuits, whose support in selecting the close question standard rarely stretched beyond a single sentence.

"The state of the law on the meaning of 'substantial question' has not changed since. On one side of the road sits the Ninth Circuit. On the other side sits every other circuit except for the Third Circuit, which sits in the road near the Ninth Circuit's curb."

§ 2. PREVENTIVE DETENTION

The term "preventive detention" is ordinarily used to describe pretrial detention of a defendant to protect other persons or the community at large from criminal conduct by that defendant. Even in bail systems limited, in theory, to the single legitimate function of assuring the defendant's appearance at trial, the preventive detention function is often served sub rosa. But in recent years preventive detention has been more openly discussed, and in many jurisdictions some form of preventive detention is now expressly authorized.

Such is the case with the federal Bail Reform Act of 1984, set out in Supp. App. B. For one thing, in determining the manner and conditions of release (discussed on p. 845), the Act makes ensuring "the safety of any other person or the community" a relevant consideration. Moreover, a detention hearing is to be held, upon motion of the attorney for the government, where the case involves a crime of violence, an offense for which the maximum penalty is death or life imprisonment, certain serious drug offenses, or any felony by one with two or more convictions of the aforementioned type offenses. Also, such a hearing is to be held on motion of either the attorney for the government or the judicial officer asserting the case involves a serious risk that the person will flee or will obstruct or attempt to obstruct justice or interfere with a prospective witness or juror. If at the hearing the judicial officer "finds that no condition or combination of conditions will reasonably assure the appearance of the person as required and the safety of any other person and the community," then detention is to be ordered. (A rebuttable presumption in support of such a finding exists in certain circumstances.) The Act also makes nonviolation of any federal, state or local crime a condition of any release under the Act, and upon violation of that condition revocation of the release is required upon a finding of probable cause that such a crime was committed while on release, if there is also a finding that the person is unlikely to abide by any conditions of release or that there is no combination of release conditions that will assure the person will not flee or pose a danger. A person ordered detained may obtain review of the order from the court with original jurisdiction over the offense charged, and may appeal from the detention order.

Post-9/11 antiterrorist investigations have often involved preventive detention of one kind or another. See, e.g., Note 3, p. 339 (re material witnesses). There has also occurred a "revision of guidelines prosecutors use to determine when to oppose bail for people charged with relatively minor crimes. Federal prosecutors have in many cases urged judges not to release people suspected of involvement in terrorist activities even if they are charged with minor and unrelated crimes." Neil A. Lewis & Christopher Marquis, *Longer Visa Waits for Arabs; Stir Over U.S. Eavesdropping,* www.nytimes.com/2001/11/10/us/nation-challenged-immigration-longer-visa-waits-for-arabs-stir-over-us.html.

UNITED STATES V. SALERNO

481 U.S. 739, 107 S.Ct. 2095, 95 L.Ed.2d 697 (1987).

CHIEF JUSTICE REHNQUIST delivered the opinion of the Court.

The Bail Reform Act of 1984 allows a federal court to detain an arrestee pending trial if the government demonstrates by clear and convincing evidence after an adversary hearing that no release conditions "will reasonably assure . . . the safety of any other person and the community."

The United States Court of Appeals for the Second Circuit struck down this provision of the Act as facially unconstitutional, because, in that court's words, this type of pretrial detention violates "substantive due process." We granted certiorari because of a conflict among the Courts of Appeals regarding the validity of the Act. We hold that, as against the facial attack mounted by these respondents, the Act fully comports with constitutional requirements. We therefore reverse.

Responding to "the alarming problem of crimes committed by persons on release," Congress formulated the Bail Reform Act of 1984, 18 U.S.C. § 3141 et seq., as the solution to a bail crisis in the federal courts. The Act represents the National Legislature's considered response to numerous perceived deficiencies in the federal bail process. By providing for sweeping changes in both the way federal courts consider bail applications and the circumstances under which bail is granted, Congress hoped to "give the courts adequate authority to make release decisions that give appropriate recognition to the danger a person may pose to others if released."

To this end, § 3141(a) of the Act requires a judicial officer to determine whether an arrestee shall be detained. Section 3142(e) provides that "[i]f, after a hearing pursuant to the provisions of subsection (f), the judicial officer finds that no condition or combination of conditions will reasonably assure the appearance of the person as required and the safety of any other person and the community, he shall order the detention of the person prior to trial." Section 3142(f) provides the arrestee with a number of procedural safeguards. He may request the presence of counsel at the detention hearing, he may testify and present witnesses in his behalf, as well as proffer evidence, and he may cross-examine other witnesses appearing at the hearing. If the judicial officer finds that no conditions of pretrial release can reasonably assure the safety of other persons and the community, he must state his findings of fact in writing, § 3142(i), and support his conclusion with "clear and convincing evidence," § 3142(f).

The judicial officer is not given unbridled discretion in making the detention determination. Congress has specified the considerations relevant to that decision. These factors include the nature and seriousness of the charges, the substantiality of the government's evidence against the arrestee, the arrestee's background and characteristics, and the nature and seriousness of the danger posed by the suspect's release. § 3142(g). Should a judicial officer order detention, the detainee is entitled to expedited appellate review of the detention order. §§ 3145(b), (c).

Respondents Anthony Salerno and Vincent Cafaro were arrested on March 21, 1986, after being charged in a 29-count indictment alleging various Racketeer Influenced and Corrupt Organizations Act (RICO) violations, mail and wire fraud offenses, extortion, and various criminal gambling violations. The RICO counts alleged 35 acts of racketeering activity, including fraud, extortion, gambling, and conspiracy to commit murder. At respondents' arraignment, the Government moved to have Salerno and Cafaro detained pursuant to § 3142(e), on the ground that no condition of release would assure the safety of the community or any person. The District Court held a hearing at which the Government made a detailed proffer of evidence. The Government's case showed that Salerno was the "boss" of the Genovese Crime Family of La Cosa Nostra and that Cafaro was a "captain" in the Genovese Family. According to the Government's proffer, based in large part on conversations intercepted by a court-ordered wiretap, the two respondents had participated in wide-ranging conspiracies to aid their illegitimate enterprises through violent means. The Government also offered the testimony of two of its trial witnesses, who would assert that Salerno personally participated in two murder conspiracies. Salerno opposed the motion for detention, challenging the credibility of the Government's witnesses. He offered the testimony of several character witnesses as well as a letter from his doctor stating that he was suffering from a serious medical condition. Cafaro presented no evidence at the hearing, but instead characterized the wiretap conversations as merely "tough talk."

The District Court granted the Government's detention motion, concluding that the Government had established by clear and convincing evidence that no condition or combination of conditions of release would ensure the safety of the community or any person * * * .

Respondents appealed, contending that to the extent that the Bail Reform Act permits pretrial detention on the ground that the arrestee is likely to commit future crimes, it is unconstitutional on its face. Over a dissent, the United States Court of Appeals for the Second Circuit agreed. Although the court agreed that pretrial detention could be imposed if the defendants were likely to intimidate witnesses or otherwise jeopardize the trial process, it found "§ 3142(e)'s authorization of pretrial detention [on the ground of future dangerousness] repugnant to the concept of substantive due process, which we believe prohibits the total deprivation of liberty simply as a means of preventing future crimes." * * * The Court of Appeals also found our decision in *Schall v. Martin,* 467 U.S. 253 (1984), upholding postarrest pretrial detention of juveniles, inapposite because juveniles have a lesser interest in liberty than do adults. The dissenting judge concluded that on its face, the Bail Reform Act adequately balanced the Federal Government's compelling interests in public safety against the detainee's liberty interests.

A facial challenge to a legislative Act is, of course, the most difficult challenge to mount successfully, since the challenger must establish that no set of circumstances exists under which the Act would be valid. The fact that the Bail Reform Act might operate unconstitutionally under some conceivable set of circumstances is insufficient to render it wholly invalid, since we have not recognized an "overbreadth" doctrine outside the limited context of the First Amendment. We think respondents have failed to shoulder their heavy burden to demonstrate that the Act is "facially" unconstitutional.[3]

Respondents present two grounds for invalidating the Bail Reform Act's provisions permitting pretrial detention on the basis of future dangerousness. First, they rely upon the Court of Appeals' conclusion that the Act exceeds the limitations placed upon the Federal Government by the Due Process Clause of the Fifth Amendment. Second, they contend that the Act contravenes the Eighth Amendment's proscription against excessive bail. We treat these contentions in turn.

The Due Process Clause of the Fifth Amendment provides that "No person shall . . . be deprived of life, liberty, or property, without due process of law. . . ." This Court has held that the Due Process Clause protects individuals against two types of government action. So-called "substantive due process" prevents the government from engaging in conduct that "shocks the conscience," or interferes with rights "implicit in the concept of ordered liberty." When government action depriving a person of life, liberty, or property survives substantive due process scrutiny, it must still be implemented in a fair manner. This requirement has traditionally been referred to as "procedural" due process.

Respondents first argue that the Act violates substantive due process because the pretrial detention it authorizes constitutes impermissible punishment before trial. The Government, however, has never argued that pretrial detention could be upheld if it were "punishment." The Court of Appeals assumed that pretrial detention under the Bail Reform Act is regulatory, not penal, and we agree that it is.

---

[3] We intimate no view on the validity of any aspects of the Act that are not relevant to respondents' case. Nor have respondents claimed that the Act is unconstitutional because of the way it was applied to the particular facts of their case. [Editors' Note: This issue has often been litigated in the lower courts. Typical is *United States v. El-Hage*, 213 F.3d 74 (2d Cir.2000) (confinement expected to last 30–33 months not a violation of due process, considering that "prosecution appears to bear very little responsibility for the delay of trial" and defendant "charged with playing a vital role in a worldwide terrorist organization"). Consider Floralynn Einesman, *How Long is Too Long? When Pretrial Detention Violates Due Process*, 60 Tenn.L.Rev. 1, 2 (1992), concluding that "the due process tests used to determine whether the pretrial detention has become punitive * * * are deficient because they fail to effectively protect the liberty interest of the accused."]

As an initial matter, the mere fact that a person is detained does not inexorably lead to the conclusion that the government has imposed punishment. To determine whether a restriction on liberty constitutes impermissible punishment or permissible regulation, we first look to legislative intent. Unless Congress expressly intended to impose punitive restrictions, the punitive/regulatory distinction turns on " 'whether an alternative purpose to which [the restriction] may rationally be connected is assignable for it, and whether it appears excessive in relation to the alternative purpose assigned [to it].' "

We conclude that the detention imposed by the Act falls on the regulatory side of the dichotomy. The legislative history of the Bail Reform Act clearly indicates that Congress did not formulate the pretrial detention provisions as punishment for dangerous individuals. Congress instead perceived pretrial detention as a potential solution to a pressing societal problem. There is no doubt that preventing danger to the community is a legitimate regulatory goal.

Nor are the incidents of pretrial detention excessive in relation to the regulatory goal Congress sought to achieve. The Bail Reform Act carefully limits the circumstances under which detention may be sought to the most serious of crimes. See 18 U.S.C. § 3142(f) (detention hearings available if case involves crimes of violence, offenses for which the sentence is life imprisonment or death, serious drug offenses, or certain repeat offenders). The arrestee is entitled to a prompt detention hearing, *ibid.* and the maximum length of pretrial detention is limited by the stringent time limitations of the Speedy Trial Act.[4] See 18 U.S.C. § 3161 *et seq.* Moreover, as in *Schall v. Martin,* the conditions of confinement envisioned by the Act "appear to reflect the regulatory purposes relied upon by the" government. As in *Schall,* the statute at issue here requires that detainees be housed in a "facility separate, to the extent practicable, from persons awaiting or serving sentences or being held in custody pending appeal." 18 U.S.C. § 3142(i)(2). We conclude, therefore, that the pretrial detention contemplated by the Bail Reform Act is regulatory in nature, and does not constitute punishment before trial in violation of the Due Process Clause.

The Court of Appeals nevertheless concluded that "the Due Process Clause prohibits pretrial detention on the ground of danger to the community as a regulatory measure, without regard to the duration of the detention." Respondents characterize the Due Process Clause as erecting an impenetrable "wall" in this area that "no governmental interest—rational, important, compelling or otherwise—may surmount."

We do not think the Clause lays down any such categorical imperative. We have repeatedly held that the government's regulatory interest in community safety can, in appropriate circumstances, outweigh an individual's liberty interest. For example, in times of war or insurrection, when society's interest is at its peak, the government may detain individuals whom the government believes to be dangerous. See *Ludecke v. Watkins,* 335 U.S. 160 (1948) (approving unreviewable Executive power to detain enemy aliens in time of war); *Moyer v. Peabody,* 212 U.S. 78 (1909) (rejecting due process claim of individual jailed without probable cause by Governor in time of insurrection). Even outside the exigencies of war, we have found that sufficiently compelling governmental interests can justify detention of dangerous persons. Thus, we have found no absolute constitutional barrier to detention of potentially dangerous resident aliens pending deportation proceedings. *Carlson v. Landon,* 342 U.S. 524 (1952); *Wong Wing v. United States,* 163 U.S. 228 (1896). We have also held that the government may detain mentally unstable individuals who present a danger to the public, *Addington v. Texas,* 441 U.S. 418 (1979), and dangerous defendants who become incompetent to stand trial, *Jackson v. Indiana,* 406 U.S. 715 (1972); *Greenwood v. United States,* 350 U.S. 366 (1956). We have approved of postarrest regulatory detention of juveniles when they present a continuing danger to the community. *Schall v. Martin.* Even competent adults may face substantial liberty restrictions as a result of the

[4] We intimate no view as to the point at which detention in a particular case might become excessively prolonged, and therefore punitive, in relation to Congress' regulatory goal.

operation of our criminal justice system. If the police suspect an individual of a crime, they may arrest and hold him until a neutral magistrate determines whether probable cause exists. *Gerstein v. Pugh.* Finally, respondents concede and the Court of Appeals noted that an arrestee may be incarcerated until trial if he presents a risk of flight or a danger to witnesses.

Respondents characterize all of these cases as exceptions to the "general rule" of substantive due process that the government may not detain a person prior to a judgment of guilt in a criminal trial. Such a "general rule" may freely be conceded, but we think that these cases show a sufficient number of exceptions to the rule that the congressional action challenged here can hardly be characterized as totally novel. Given the well-established authority of the government, in special circumstances, to restrain individuals' liberty prior to or even without criminal trial and conviction, we think that the present statute providing for pretrial detention on the basis of dangerousness must be evaluated in precisely the same manner that we evaluated the laws in the cases discussed above.

The government's interest in preventing crime by arrestees is both legitimate and compelling. In *Schall,* we recognized the strength of the State's interest in preventing juvenile crime. This general concern with crime prevention is no less compelling when the suspects are adults. Indeed, "[t]he harm suffered by the victim of a crime is not dependent upon the age of the perpetrator." The Bail Reform Act of 1984 responds to an even more particularized governmental interest than the interest we sustained in *Schall.* The statute we upheld in *Schall* permitted pretrial detention of any juvenile arrested on any charge after a showing that the individual might commit some undefined further crimes. The Bail Reform Act, in contrast, narrowly focuses on a particularly acute problem in which the government interests are overwhelming. The Act operates only on individuals who have been arrested for a specific category of extremely serious offenses. 18 U.S.C. § 3142(f). Congress specifically found that these individuals are far more likely to be responsible for dangerous acts in the community after arrest. Nor is the Act by any means a scattershot attempt to incapacitate those who are merely suspected of these serious crimes. The government must first of all demonstrate probable cause to believe that the charged crime has been committed by the arrestee, but that is not enough. In a full-blown adversary hearing, the government must convince a neutral decisionmaker by clear and convincing evidence that no conditions of release can reasonably assure the safety of the community or any person. 18 U.S.C. § 3142(f). While the government's general interest in preventing crime is compelling, even this interest is heightened when the government musters convincing proof that the arrestee, already indicted or held to answer for a serious crime, presents a demonstrable danger to the community. Under these narrow circumstances, society's interest in crime prevention is at its greatest.

On the other side of the scale, of course, is the individual's strong interest in liberty. We do not minimize the importance and fundamental nature of this right. But, as our cases hold, this right may, in circumstances where the government's interest is sufficiently weighty, be subordinated to the greater needs of society. We think that Congress' careful delineation of the circumstances under which detention will be permitted satisfies this standard. When the government proves by clear and convincing evidence that an arrestee presents an identified and articulable threat to an individual or the community, we believe that, consistent with the Due Process Clause, a court may disable the arrestee from executing that threat. Under these circumstances, we cannot categorically state that pretrial detention "offends some principle of justice so rooted in the traditions and conscience of our people as to be ranked as fundamental."

Finally, we may dispose briefly of respondents' facial challenge to the procedures of the Bail Reform Act. To sustain them against such a challenge, we need only find them "adequate to authorize the pretrial detention of at least some [persons] charged with crimes," whether or not they might be insufficient in some particular circumstances. We think they pass that test. As we stated in *Schall,* "there is nothing inherently unattainable about a prediction of future criminal conduct."

Under the Bail Reform Act, the procedures by which a judicial officer evaluates the likelihood of future dangerousness are specifically designed to further the accuracy of that determination. Detainees have a right to counsel at the detention hearing. 18 U.S.C. § 3142(f). They may testify in their own behalf, present information by proffer or otherwise, and cross-examine witnesses who appear at the hearing.[a] *Ibid.* The judicial officer charged with the responsibility of determining the appropriateness of detention is guided by statutorily enumerated factors, which include the nature and the circumstances of the charges, the weight of the evidence, the history and characteristics of the putative offender, and the danger to the community. § 3142(g). The government must prove its case by clear and convincing evidence. § 3142(f). Finally, the judicial officer must include written findings of fact and a written statement of reasons for a decision to detain. § 3142(i). The Act's review provisions, § 3145(c), provide for immediate appellate review of the detention decision.

We think these extensive safeguards suffice to repel a facial challenge. The protections are more exacting than those we found sufficient in the juvenile context, see *Schall,* and they far exceed what we found necessary to effect limited postarrest detention in *Gerstein v. Pugh.* Given the legitimate and compelling regulatory purpose of the Act and the procedural protections it offers, we conclude that the Act is not facially invalid under the Due Process Clause of the Fifth Amendment.

Respondents also contend that the Bail Reform Act violates the Excessive Bail Clause of the Eighth Amendment. The Court of Appeals did not address this issue because it found that the Act violates the Due Process Clause. We think that the Act survives a challenge founded upon the Eighth Amendment.

The Eighth Amendment addresses pretrial release by providing merely that "Excessive bail shall not be required." This Clause, of course, says nothing about whether bail shall be available at all. Respondents nevertheless contend that this Clause grants them a right to bail calculated solely upon considerations of flight. They rely on *Stack v. Boyle* [p. 846], in which the Court stated that "Bail set at a figure higher than an amount reasonably calculated [to ensure the defendant's presence at trial] is 'excessive' under the Eighth Amendment." In respondents' view, since the Bail Reform Act allows a court essentially to set bail at an infinite amount for reasons not related to the risk of flight, it violates the Excessive Bail Clause. Respondents concede that the right to bail they have discovered in the Eighth Amendment is not absolute. A court may, for example, refuse bail in capital cases. And, as the Court of Appeals noted and respondents admit, a court may refuse bail when the defendant presents a threat to the judicial process by intimidating witnesses. Respondents characterize these exceptions as consistent with what they claim to be the sole purpose of bail—to ensure integrity of the judicial process.

While we agree that a primary function of bail is to safeguard the courts' role in adjudicating the guilt or innocence of defendants, we reject the proposition that the Eighth Amendment categorically prohibits the government from pursuing other admittedly compelling interests through regulation of pretrial release. The above-quoted *dicta* in *Stack v. Boyle* is far too slender a reed on which to rest this argument. The Court in *Stack* had no occasion to consider whether the Excessive Bail Clause requires courts to admit all defendants to bail, because the statute before the Court in that case in fact allowed the defendants to be bailed. Thus, the Court had to determine

[a] Compare *Aime v. Commonwealth,* 611 N.E.2d 204 (Mass.1993) (state preventive detention statute unconstitutional under *Salerno,* as defendant without right to testify in own behalf or to cross-examine state's witnesses).

only whether bail, admittedly available in that case, was excessive if set at a sum greater than that necessary to ensure the arrestees' presence at trial.

The holding of *Stack* is illuminated by the Court's holding just four months later in *Carlson v. Landon*. In that case, remarkably similar to the present action, the detainees had been arrested and held without bail pending a determination of deportability. The Attorney General refused to release the individuals, "on the ground that there was reasonable cause to believe that [their] release would be prejudicial to the public interest and *would endanger the welfare and safety of the United States*." (emphasis added). The detainees brought the same challenge that respondents bring to us today: the Eighth Amendment required them to be admitted to bail. The Court squarely rejected this proposition:

> "The bail clause was lifted with slight changes from the English Bill of Rights Act. In England that clause has never been thought to accord a right to bail in all cases, but merely to provide that bail shall not be excessive in those cases where it is proper to grant bail. When this clause was carried over into our Bill of Rights, nothing was said that indicated any different concept. The Eighth Amendment has not prevented Congress from defining the classes of cases in which bail shall be allowed in this country. Thus, in criminal cases bail is not compulsory where the punishment may be death. Indeed, the very language of the Amendment fails to say all arrests must be bailable."

Carlson v. Landon was a civil case, and we need not decide today whether the Excessive Bail Clause speaks at all to Congress' power to define the classes of criminal arrestees who shall be admitted to bail. For even if we were to conclude that the Eighth Amendment imposes some substantive limitations on the National Legislature's powers in this area, we would still hold that the Bail Reform Act is valid. Nothing in the text of the Bail Clause limits permissible government considerations solely to questions of flight. The only arguable substantive limitation of the Bail Clause is that the government's proposed conditions of release or detention not be "excessive" in light of the perceived evil. Of course, to determine whether the government's response is excessive, we must compare that response against the interest the government seeks to protect by means of that response. Thus, when the government has admitted that its only interest is in preventing flight, bail must be set by a court at a sum designed to ensure that goal, and no more. We believe that when Congress has mandated detention on the basis of a compelling interest other than prevention of flight, as it has here, the Eighth Amendment does not require release on bail.

In our society liberty is the norm, and detention prior to trial or without trial is the carefully limited exception. We hold that the provisions for pretrial detention in the Bail Reform Act of 1984 fall within that carefully limited exception. The Act authorizes the detention prior to trial of arrestees charged with serious felonies who are found after an adversary hearing to pose a threat to the safety of individuals or to the community which no condition of release can dispel. The numerous procedural safeguards detailed above must attend this adversary hearing. We are unwilling to say that this congressional determination, based as it is upon that primary concern of every government—a concern for the safety and indeed the lives of its citizens—on its face violates either the Due Process Clause of the Fifth Amendment or the Excessive Bail Clause of the Eighth Amendment.

JUSTICE MARSHALL, with whom JUSTICE BRENNAN joins, dissenting.

This case brings before the Court for the first time a statute in which Congress declares that a person innocent of any crime may be jailed indefinitely, pending the trial of allegations which are legally presumed to be untrue, if the Government shows to the satisfaction of a judge that the accused is likely to commit crimes, unrelated to the pending charges, at any time in the future. Such statutes, consistent with the usages of tyranny and the excesses of what bitter experience teaches us to call the police state, have long been thought incompatible with the fundamental human rights protected by our Constitution. Today a majority of this Court holds otherwise. Its decision disregards basic principles of justice established centuries ago and enshrined beyond the reach of governmental interference in the Bill of Rights. * * *

The majority approaches respondents' challenge to the Act by dividing the discussion into two sections, one concerned with the substantive guarantees implicit in the Due Process Clause, and the other concerned with the protection afforded by the Excessive Bail Clause of the Eighth Amendment. This is a sterile formalism, which divides a unitary argument into two independent parts and then professes to demonstrate that the parts are individually inadequate.

On the due process side of this false dichotomy appears an argument concerning the distinction between regulatory and punitive legislation. The majority concludes that the Act is a regulatory rather than a punitive measure. The ease with which the conclusion is reached suggests the worthlessness of the achievement. The major premise is that "[u]nless Congress expressly intended to impose punitive restrictions, the punitive/regulatory distinction turns on 'whether an alternative purpose to which [the restriction] may rationally be connected is assignable for it, and whether it appears excessive in relation to the alternative purpose assigned [to it].' " The majority finds that "Congress did not formulate the pretrial detention provisions as punishment for dangerous individuals," but instead was pursuing the "legitimate regulatory goal" of "preventing danger to the community." Concluding that pretrial detention is not an excessive solution to the problem of preventing danger to the community, the majority thus finds that no substantive element of the guarantee of due process invalidates the statute.

This argument does not demonstrate the conclusion it purports to justify. Let us apply the majority's reasoning to a similar, hypothetical case. After investigation, Congress determines (not unrealistically) that a large proportion of violent crime is perpetrated by persons who are unemployed. It also determines, equally reasonably, that much violent crime is committed at night. From amongst the panoply of "potential solutions," Congress chooses a statute which permits, after judicial proceedings, the imposition of a dusk-to-dawn curfew on anyone who is unemployed. Since this is not a measure enacted for the purpose of punishing the unemployed, and since the majority finds that preventing danger to the community is a legitimate regulatory goal, the curfew statute would, according to the majority's analysis, be a mere "regulatory" detention statute, entirely compatible with the substantive components of the Due Process Clause.

The absurdity of this conclusion arises, of course, from the majority's cramped concept of substantive due process. The majority proceeds as though the only substantive right protected by the Due Process Clause is a right to be free from punishment before conviction. The majority's technique for infringing this right is simple: merely redefine any measure which is claimed to be punishment as "regulation," and, magically, the Constitution no longer prohibits its imposition. Because, as I discuss infra, the Due Process Clause protects other substantive rights which are infringed by this legislation, the majority's argument is merely an exercise in obfuscation.

The logic of the majority's Eighth Amendment analysis is equally unsatisfactory. The Eighth Amendment, as the majority notes, states that "[e]xcessive bail shall not be required." The majority then declares, as if it were undeniable, that: "[t]his Clause, of course, says nothing about whether bail shall be available at all." If excessive bail is imposed the defendant stays in jail. The same result is achieved if bail is denied altogether. Whether the magistrate sets bail at $1 billion or refuses to set bail at all, the consequences are indistinguishable. It would be mere sophistry to suggest that the Eighth Amendment protects against the former decision, and not the latter. Indeed, such a result would lead to the conclusion that there was no need for Congress to pass a preventive detention measure of any kind; every federal magistrate and district judge could simply refuse, despite the absence of any evidence of risk of flight or danger to the community, to set bail. This would be entirely constitutional, since, according to the majority, the Eighth Amendment "says nothing about whether bail shall be available at all."

But perhaps, the majority says, this manifest absurdity can be avoided. Perhaps the Bail Clause is addressed only to the judiciary. "[W]e need not decide today," the majority says, "whether the Excessive Bail Clause speaks at all to Congress' power to define the classes of criminal arrestees who shall be admitted to bail." The majority is correct that this question need not be decided today; it was decided long ago. Federal and state statutes which purport to accomplish what the Eighth Amendment forbids, such as imposing cruel and unusual punishments, may not stand. The text of the Amendment, which provides simply that "[e]xcessive bail shall not be required, nor excessive fines imposed, nor cruel and unusual punishments inflicted," provides absolutely no support for the majority's speculation that both courts and Congress are forbidden to inflict cruel and unusual punishments, while only the courts are forbidden to require excessive bail.[5]

The majority's attempts to deny the relevance of the Bail Clause to this case are unavailing, but the majority is nonetheless correct that the prohibition of excessive bail means that in order "to determine whether the government's response is excessive, we must compare that response against the interest the government seeks to protect by means of that response." The majority concedes, as it must, that "when the government has admitted that its only interest is in preventing flight, bail must be set by a court at a sum designed to ensure that goal, and no more." But, the majority says, "when Congress has mandated detention on the basis of a compelling interest other than prevention of flight, as it has here, the Eighth Amendment does not require release on bail." This conclusion follows only if the "compelling" interest upon which Congress acted is an interest which the Constitution permits Congress to further through the denial of bail. The majority does not ask, as a result of its disingenuous division of the analysis, if there are any substantive limits contained in both the Eighth Amendment and the Due Process Clause which render this system of preventive detention unconstitutional. The majority does not ask because the answer is apparent and, to the majority, inconvenient.

The essence of this case may be found, ironically enough, in a provision of the Act to which the majority does not refer. Title 18 U.S.C. § 3142(j) provides that "[n]othing in this section shall be construed as modifying or limiting the presumption of innocence." But the very pith and purpose of this statute is an abhorrent limitation of the presumption of innocence. The majority's untenable conclusion that the present Act is constitutional arises from a specious denial of the role of the Bail Clause and the Due Process Clause in protecting the invaluable guarantee afforded by the presumption of innocence.

"The principle that there is a presumption of innocence in favor of the accused is the undoubted law, axiomatic and elementary, and its enforcement lies at the foundation of the administration of our criminal law." *Coffin v. United States,* 156 U.S. 432 (1895). Our society's belief, reinforced over the centuries, that all are innocent until the state has proven them to be guilty, like the companion principle that guilt must be proved beyond a reasonable doubt, is "implicit in the concept of ordered liberty," and is established beyond legislative contravention in the Due Process Clause.

The statute now before us declares that persons who have been indicted may be detained if a judicial officer finds clear and convincing evidence that they pose a danger to individuals or to the community. The statute does not authorize the government to imprison anyone it has evidence is

---

[5] The majority refers to the statement in *Carlson v. Landon* that the Bail Clause was adopted by Congress from the English Bill of Rights Act of 1689, 1 Wm. & Mary, Sess. 2, ch. II, § I(10), and that "[i]n England that clause has never been thought to accord a right to bail in all cases, but merely to provide that bail shall not be excessive in those cases where it is proper to grant bail." A sufficient answer to this meagre argument was made at the time by Justice Black: "The Eighth Amendment is in the American Bill of Rights of 1789, not the English Bill of Rights of 1689." *Carlson v. Landon* (dissenting opinion). Our Bill of Rights is contained in a written Constitution one of whose purposes is to protect the rights of the people against infringement by the Legislature, and its provisions, whatever their origins, are interpreted in relation to those purposes.

dangerous; indictment is necessary. But let us suppose that a defendant is indicted and the government shows by clear and convincing evidence that he is dangerous and should be detained pending a trial, at which trial the defendant is acquitted. May the government continue to hold the defendant in detention based upon its showing that he is dangerous? The answer cannot be yes, for that would allow the government to imprison someone for uncommitted crimes based upon "proof" not beyond a reasonable doubt. The result must therefore be that once the indictment has failed, detention cannot continue. But our fundamental principles of justice declare that the defendant is as innocent on the day before his trial as he is on the morning after his acquittal. Under this statute an untried indictment somehow acts to permit a detention, based on other charges, which after an acquittal would be unconstitutional. The conclusion is inescapable that the indictment has been turned into evidence, if not that the defendant is guilty of the crime charged, then that left to his own devices he will soon be guilty of something else.

To be sure, an indictment is not without legal consequences. It establishes that there is probable cause to believe that an offense was committed, and that the defendant committed it. Upon probable cause a warrant for the defendant's arrest may issue; a period of administrative detention may occur before the evidence of probable cause is presented to a neutral magistrate. See *Gerstein v. Pugh.* Once a defendant has been committed for trial he may be detained in custody if the magistrate finds that no conditions of release will prevent him from becoming a fugitive. But in this connection the charging instrument is evidence of nothing more than the fact that there will be a trial, and

> "release before trial is conditioned upon the accused's giving adequate assurance that he will stand trial and submit to sentence if found guilty. Like the ancient practice of securing the oaths of responsible persons to stand as sureties for the accused, the modern practice of requiring a bail bond or the deposit of a sum of money subject to forfeiture serves as additional assurance of the presence of an accused." *Stack v. Boyle.*[6]

The finding of probable cause conveys power to try, and the power to try imports of necessity the power to assure that the processes of justice will not be evaded or obstructed.[7] "Pretrial detention to prevent future crimes against society at large, however, is not justified by any concern for holding a trial on the charges for which a defendant has been arrested." The detention purportedly authorized by this statute bears no relation to the government's power to try charges supported by a finding of probable cause, and thus the interests it serves are outside the scope of interests which may be considered in weighing the excessiveness of bail under the Eighth Amendment. * * *

JUSTICE STEVENS, dissenting. * * *

If the evidence of imminent danger is strong enough to warrant emergency detention, it should support that preventive measure regardless of whether the person has been charged, convicted, or acquitted of some other offense. In this case, for example, it is unrealistic to assume that the danger to the community that was present when respondents were at large did not justify

---

6 The majority states that denial of bail in capital cases has traditionally been the rule rather than the exception. And this of course is so, for it has been the considered presumption of generations of judges that a defendant in danger of execution has an extremely strong incentive to flee. If in any particular case the presumed likelihood of flight should be made irrebuttable, it would in all probability violate the Due Process Clause. Thus what the majority perceives as an exception is nothing more than an example of the traditional operation of our system of bail.

7 It is also true, as the majority observes, that the government is entitled to assurance, by incarceration if necessary, that a defendant will not obstruct justice through destruction of evidence, procuring the absence or intimidation of witnesses, or subornation of perjury. But in such cases the government benefits from no presumption that any particular defendant is likely to engage in activities inimical to the administration of justice, and the majority offers no authority for the proposition that bail has traditionally been denied *prospectively,* upon speculation that witnesses would be tampered with. Cf. *Carbo v. United States,* 82 S.Ct. 662 (1962) (Douglas, J., in chambers) (bail pending appeal denied when more than 200 intimidating phone calls made to witness, who was also severely beaten).

their detention before they were indicted, but did require that measure the moment that the grand jury found probable cause to believe they had committed crimes in the past. It is equally unrealistic to assume that the danger will vanish if a jury happens to acquit them. Justice Marshall has demonstrated that the fact of indictment cannot, consistent with the presumption of innocence and the Eighth Amendment's Excessive Bail Clause, be used to create a special class the members of which are, alone, eligible for detention because of future dangerousness.* * *

NOTES AND QUESTIONS

1. **Salerno *and amount of bail.*** Reconsider *Stack v. Boyle*, p. 846, in light of *Salerno*. Can the safety of others now be made a factor bearing on the *amount* of bail? Consider *Galen v. County of Los Angeles*, 477 F.3d 652 (9th Cir.2007), where Galen was arrested for domestic violence after his fiancée showed police photographs of injuries (large bruises on her arms and legs and a 7-inch laceration on her arm) she claimed Galen had inflicted on her. The police decided to request an increase in Galen's bail from the default amount of $50,000 for such an offense to $1,000,000 because "the victim was in fear for her safety" and Galen "could easily post $50,000 bail because he was an attorney and lived in a 'fairly nice house.'" The Bail Commissioner set the bail at $1,000,000, and Galen, fearing he would otherwise spend the weekend in jail, obtained a bail bond in that amount by paying the $50,000 premium, but he was soon released when his fiancée signed a "request not to prosecute." Galen's § 1983 Eighth Amendment action resulted in summary judgment for the defendants, which was affirmed on appeal. The court stated:

"We also reject Galen's argument that flight risk is the only factor the Commissioner was allowed to consider in setting bail, and, accordingly, that his bail was excessive because it exceeded the amount necessary to prevent flight in light of his ties to the community and partial custody of his two school-age children. California law not only authorized, but required, the Commissioner to 'take into consideration the protection of the public, the seriousness of the offense charged, the previous criminal record of the defendant, and the probability of his or her appearing at trial or hearing of the case,' Cal.Penal Code § 1275(a), and 'to set bail in an amount that he . . . deems sufficient . . . to assure the protection of a victim . . . of domestic violence.' *Salerno* holds that these non-flight-related considerations are permissible and therefore forecloses Galen's argument that his bail was unconstitutionally excessive to the extent it was designed to serve interests other than prevention of flight."

2. **Salerno *and risk of flight.*** Consider *Lopez-Valenzuela v. Arpaio*, 770 F.3d 772 (9th Cir. 2014), concerning laws implementing a recently-added provision to the Arizona Constitution commanding that bail not be set for "serious felony offenses as prescribed by the legislature if the person charged has entered or remained in the United States illegally and if the proof is evident or the presumption great as to the present charge." No discretion was left to the judge to grant bail, and the underlying concern was not with dangerousness of the defendant but rather the defendant's risk of flight. The court held that under *Salerno* this provision violated substantive due process, for these laws (a) do not address "a particularly acute problem," as "the record contains no findings, studies, statistics or other evidence * * * showing that undocumented immigrants as a group pose either an unmanageable flight risk or a significantly greater flight risk than lawful residents"; (b) are not limited to "a specific category of extremely serious offenses," but instead "encompass an exceedingly broad range of offenses, including * * * relatively minor ones"; and (c) employ "an overbroad, irrebuttable presumption rather than an individualized hearing to determine whether a particular arrestee poses an unmanageable flight risk," even though there "is no evidence that undocumented status correlates closely with unmanageable flight risk. The defendants speculate that undocumented immigrants pose a greater flight risk than lawful residents because they supposedly lack strong ties to the community and have a 'home' in another country to which they can flee. But this assumption ignores those undocumented

immigrants who do have strong ties to their community or do not have a home abroad. As our own court's immigration docket reveals, many undocumented immigrants were brought here as young children and have no contacts or roots in another country. Many have 'children born in the United States' and 'long ties to the community.' "

3. ***Proof of dangerousness.*** In *State ex rel. Torrez v. Whitaker*, 410 P.3d 201 (N.M.2018), the court addressed "the nature of evidentiary presentation required" to establish a degree of dangerousness meriting denial of release on bail: "We agree with courts in all other federal and state bail reform jurisdictions that have considered the same issues, and we hold that the showing of dangerousness required by the new constitutional authority is not bound by formal rules of evidence but instead focuses on judicial assessment of all reliable information presented to the court in any format worthy of reasoned consideration. The probative value of the information, rather than the technical form, is the proper focus of the inquiry at a pretrial detention hearing.

"In most cases, credible proffers and other summaries of evidence, law enforcement and court records, or other nontestimonial information should be sufficient support for an informed decision that the state either has or has not met its constitutional burden. But we also agree with other jurisdictions that a court necessarily retains the judicial discretion to find proffered or documentary information insufficient to meet the constitutional clear and convincing evidence requirement in the context of particular cases."

Notes on Preventive Detention in the States

1. **Salerno *in the states.*** In *McDonald v. City of Chicago*, 561 U.S. 742 (2010), the Court included the bail clause in a list of incorporated Bill of Rights protections. Scott W. Howe, *The Implications of Incorporating the Eight Amendment Prohibition on Excessive Bail,* 43 Hofstra L.Rev. 1039, 1043–44 (2015), reasons "that incorporation implies that the *Excessive Bail Clause* imposes significant limits on government. In *McDonald,* the Supreme Court emphasized that incorporation is 'selective' among the *Bill of Rights* provisions, and that the incorporated protection must be 'fundamental' to our 'scheme of ordered liberty and system of justice.' Based on this perspective, [it can be concluded] that incorporation of the bail clause implies answers to the two basic riddles about the definition of excessive bail that the Court noted in *Salerno.* First, incorporation should mean that the clause confers an implicit right to bail for criminal defendants in broad circumstances. Second, incorporation should mean that the clause defines the proper function of bail and, thus, the measure of excessiveness. Without these basic premises, the clause is unworthy of incorporation."

2. ***Variety in state constitutions.*** Preventive detention practice in the fifty states is quite diverse, largely because of the different state constitutional provisions on bail to be found:

(a) In 9 states, these provisions are essentially the same as the Eighth Amendment, and thus probably lack independent significance, as they are likely to be interpreted as not foreclosing any variety of preventive detention allowed under *Salerno.* Most of these states have adopted preventive detention statutes. Some are of a more limited type, as where a detention-justifying danger to persons or the community may be found or is presumed when the defendant has been charged with a certain crime after conviction for an earlier crime of that type, while on bail, or while on probation or parole, or when the defendant has violated some condition of pretrial release. But others are among the most expansive preventive detention provisions to be found, declaring as to a rather broad range of offenses that denial of bail is permissible upon a finding of such danger or upon the defendant's failure to rebut a declared presumption of danger.

(b) In 20 states, the constitution declares a right to bail subject to very limited exceptions; 14 of them adhere to the traditional approach ("All prisoners shall, before conviction, be bailable by sufficient sureties, except for capital offenses, where the proof is evident and the presumption great"), while 6 others instead or in addition declare an exception where the punishment was once capital, where the punishment is life imprisonment, or where some specified very serious offenses (e.g., murder, treason, rape) are charged.

(c) In the remaining 21 states there is once again a constitutional declaration of a right to bail, typically with an exception for capital cases or some other limited exception as in (b) above, but significantly the constitutional provision then, by virtue of recent amendment, goes on to describe other situations in which a form of preventive detention may be utilized. These amendments vary by the kinds of preventive detention provision included therein (some include more than one kind): (i) 14 states authorize preventive detention whenever the charge is of a certain type and in addition there is a finding that the defendant, if released, would present a danger to another person or the community. (ii) Others require a certain type of charge plus only some condition precedent, either that the defendant at the time of the alleged crime was already on bail for another offense of a certain type (5 states), that he was then on probation or parole (3 states), or that at the time of the alleged crime the defendant had previously been convicted of one or (usually) more offenses of a certain type (4 states). (iii) The provisions in 3 states combine the features of the other two categories, so that the defendant may be detained pending trial only if there was a specified condition precedent and in addition a finding of dangerousness.

3. ***Excepted offenses provisions.*** In the great majority of states where the applicable constitutional provision declares a right to bail but then states that capital offenses (or life imprisonment offenses, or specified very serious crimes) are excepted, a variety of issues have arisen as to the meaning of the exception. There is, for example, the question of whether a capital case exception applies when the state's death penalty provisions have been declared unconstitutional; compare *People v. Anderson*, 493 P.2d 880 (Cal.1972) (yes, as the "underlying gravity of those offenses endures"); with *Commonwealth v. Truesdale*, 296 A.2d 829 (Pa.1972) (no, as the "strong flight urge because of the possibility of an accused forfeiting his life" is then removed). As for the proof-evident/presumption-great requirement, this requires a "fair likelihood"[b] that defendant would be convicted of capital murder, which, under the Supreme Court's decisions on constitutionally-mandated sentencing procedures in capital cases, means the question is whether or not an aggravating factor exists that would allow the jury to impose the death penalty. *State v. Engel*, 493 A.2d 1217 (N.J.1985). But this leads to such questions as who has the burden of proof, compare *Phillips v. State*, 550 N.E.2d 1290 (Ind.1990) (burden on defendant in custody to show status quo should be changed), with *State v. Konigsberg*, 164 A.2d 740 (N.J.1960) ("burden should rest on the party relying on the exception," the prosecution); what rules of evidence apply at the hearing, compare *Engel*, supra ("a defendant does not have a right *per se* to insist upon the opportunity for cross-examination at a bail hearing, and thus no bar to consideration of co-defendant's confession not admissible at trial against defendant because of lack of opportunity for cross-examination"), with *State v. Kastanis,* 848 P.2d 673 (Utah 1993) (impermissible, over defendant's objection, to rely upon evidence received at preliminary hearing); and what the consequences are of a determination that "the proof is evident, or the presumption great," compare *Harnish v. State*, 531 A.2d 1264 (Me.1987) (such showing of defendant's guilt of capital offense, "while defeating a capital defendant's constitutional right to bail, leaves intact the discretionary power of the court to admit any defendant to bail"), with *People v. District Court*, 529 P.2d 1335 (Colo.1974) (in such circumstances court without power to release defendant).

Assume that a constitutional provision of the kind discussed in the preceding paragraph is challenged on the federal due process grounds explored in *Salerno*. Does the outcome depend upon

---

[b] Actually, as for the extent of this burden, there is considerable variation among the states, which have selected from among the following possibilities, ranging from least to most demanding: fair likelihood, preponderance of the evidence, substantial showing or substantial evidence, clear and convincing, and evidence which viewed in the light most favorable to the state would suffice to sustain a jury's guilty verdict. See *Fry v. State*, 990 N.E.2d 429 (Ind.2013), assessing the various approaches.

whether the provision adheres to the traditional capital offense exception or not, or perhaps upon how some of the issues mentioned in the previous paragraph are resolved? Consider *Hunt v. Roth*, 648 F.2d 1148 (8th Cir.1981), judgment vacated for mootness, 455 U.S. 478 (constitutional exception in cases of "sexual offenses involving penetration by force or against the will of the victim * * * where the proof is evident or the presumption great" has a "fatal flaw" because "the state has created an irrebuttable presumption that every individual charged with this particular offense is incapable of assuring his appearance by conditioning it upon reasonable bail or is too dangerous to be granted release"); *State v. Blackmer*, 631 A.2d 1134 (Vt.1993) (constitutional exception for offenses punishable by life imprisonment; no *Hunt* defect because "the trial court's discretion is extremely broad," and no *Salerno* defect though dangerousness inquiry not focused as in the federal statute, for "most or all of the procedural protections of the federal law" were followed, and information on which judge acted sufficed to support a presumption of danger to the public and "was unrebutted by defendant"). Compare *State v. Furgal*, 13 A.3d 272 (N.H.2010) (upholding statute providing a person "shall not be allowed bail" when that person is charged with an offense punishable by life imprisonment and "the proof is evident or the presumption great," notwithstanding fact statute "does not permit the trial court to consider a defendant's risk of flight or dangerousness when deciding whether to deny bail").

4. ***Broader preventive detention provisions.*** Consider next the more expansive preventive detention provisions to be found in many states, either as a result of a constitutional amendment proclaiming the right of the state to so detain in specified circumstances, or as a result of legislation in a state lacking a "right to bail" constitutional guarantee. Here again, the question is whether, in light of the analysis in *Salerno*, these provisions violate federal due process. As for that variety of state preventive detention most resembling that utilized in the federal act, which contemplates (sometimes by reliance upon a rebuttal presumption) a showing of dangerousness on a case-by-case basis, it has been suggested that even here several of the state provisions are vulnerable because many of them lack a sufficiently narrow "serious crime" limitation, fail to "limit detention to situations where proof of probable cause and clear and convincing evidence of potential danger are shown," or "contain only some" of the "procedural protections" enumerated in *Salerno*. Note, 22 Ga.L.Rev. 805, 823, 828 (1988). As for the serious crime requirement, consider *Aime v. Commonwealth*, 611 N.E.2d 204 (Mass.1993) (state statute permitting denial of bail upon a finding of dangerousness, applicable as to all arrestees without regard to charge, unconstitutional); *Mendonza v. Commonwealth*, 673 N.E.2d 22 (Mass.1996) (though state list "is more extensive" than in federal act, this only "reflects the different roles of State and Federal law enforcement," and thus offenses involving violence or threats of violence within the family, even including some misdemeanors, properly included, as such offenses "are peculiarly within the province of State concern"). As for the lack of sufficient procedural protections, some state courts have responded by engrafting onto their preventive detention provisions those protections emphasized in *Salerno*. See, e.g., *Brill v. Gurich*, 965 P.2d 404 (Okl.Cr.1998).

What then of those state preventive detention provisions that substitute some sort of condition precedent (one or more prior convictions, or release on bail or on parole or probation at time of offense charged) for a case-by-case dangerousness determination? Should all the *Salerno* requirements apply there as well? Note, supra, at 825–27, suggests the answer is no as to a defendant who has a prior conviction or is out on probation or parole from such conviction "because such individuals pose a statistically greater danger to the community upon release than do first-time offenders," but that this argument is weaker where defendant has been charged with a crime allegedly committed while he was released on bail from an earlier charge, as such a defendant differs from others only in that he "has been accused twice rather than once," so that in the latter situation "each of the *Salerno* substantive due process conditions" must be met. Is that so? What then of the statute upheld in *Rendel v. Mummert*, 474 P.2d 824 (Ariz.1970), providing that a felony defendant released on bail may have his bail revoked upon a showing of probable cause that he has thereafter committed another felony? And what of a provision allowing revocation of prior pretrial release if the defendant was thereafter charged with *any* subsequent offense, upheld in *Paquette v. Commonwealth*, 795 N.E.2d 521 (Mass.2003), on the ground that the purpose of such a provision is *not* protection of the public, but rather "to assure compliance with [the state's] laws and to preserve the integrity of the judicial process by exacting obedience with its lawful orders"?

5. ***State "right to bail" as bar to preventive detention.*** Finally, there is the question of whether the very common "right to bail" provision in a state constitution provides a barrier to many (or all) preventive detention schemes that are not themselves specifically excepted in that constitution, but which would pass muster under *Salerno*. Unquestionably such a state constitutional guarantee forbids many varieties of such detention that do not necessarily violate the federal constitution. Consider, e.g., *Simms v. Oedekoven*, 839 P.2d 381 (Wyo.1992) (on issue "of first impression" as to which no precedent found elsewhere, namely, whether state rule modeled after 18 U.S.C. § 3142, and allowing detention if "judicial officer finds that no condition or combination of conditions will reasonably assure the appearance of the defendant as required," violates state constitutional right to bail, court concludes state right-to-bail provision "does not permit denial of bail on the ground that the accused is considered to be a serious flight risk").

This is not to suggest, however, that a state right-to-bail clause will bar preventive detention under any circumstances not encompassed within a declared exception thereto. Perhaps the easiest case is where the defendant, while on release pending trial, made an effort to obstruct the fair disposition of the charges against him, as in *In re Mason*, 688 N.E.2d 552 (Ohio App.1996) (upon defendant's efforts at witness intimidation, it proper for judge to respond "by revoking bail and detaining the person attempting to thwart the proper functioning of the criminal justice system"). Does it follow that a right-to-bail clause does not stand in the way of bail revocation in *any* case where there has been a showing of some sort of criminal conduct or violation of some sort of release condition? Consider the *Rendel* case, Note 3 supra, where the statute was deemed not to violate the right-to-bail provision in the state constitution.

Compare *State v. Sauve*, 621 A.2d 1296 (Vt.1993), concluding that the "absolute right to bail" in the state constitution means that "liberty must remain the norm" and that exceptions must thus be limited to " 'special circumstances' where the state's interest is 'legitimate and compelling.' " The defendant in *Sauve* was on pretrial release after being charged with burglary, unlawful mischief, and trespass for entering the residence of the complaining witness, who continued to carry on an intimate relationship with defendant thereafter. When defendant later was determined to have committed another trespass and to have consumed alcohol, each a violation of an express condition of his release, his release was revoked on the basis of a statutory provision permitting such action for "repeatedly violated conditions of release." But that language, the appellate court concluded, "does not rise to the level of a compelling interest," as even repeated violations do "not show that the judicial process is endangered." For example, those defendants who "violate conditions of release by continuing to use drugs or alcohol" may be "uncooperative" or even "potentially dangerous," but they "will not necessarily threaten justice." Likewise, repeated crimes "may show disrespect for the judicial system, but these violations do not necessarily threaten the integrity of the judicial system, in the constitutionally limited sense that they thwart the prosecution of the defendant." Revocation in the instant case thus violated the state constitution, for to "justify a compelling state interest * * * there must be a nexus between defendant's repeated violations and a disruption of the prosecution."

CHAPTER 14

THE DECISION WHETHER TO PROSECUTE

■ ■ ■

The American prosecutor possesses vast discretion in deciding whether or not to prosecute (including the choice of either no action or pretrial diversion in lieu of prosecution and, if prosecution is undertaken, often the choice between a greater and lesser offense or between a single offense and multiple offenses). This Chapter assesses the need for and scope of such discretion and the extent to which the exercise of that discretion is subject to challenge.

§ 1. THE OFFICE OF PROSECUTOR AND THE NATURE OF THE DECISION WHETHER TO PROSECUTE

1. ***Federal prosecutors.*** There are 93 United States Attorneys, one for each of the federal judicial districts except two Pacific districts that share one. Those offices range in size from just a few assistants in the sparsely populated districts to over 350 lawyers in the most populous district, with more than 6,000 lawyers over all. The U.S. Attorney is a presidential appointee, confirmed by the Senate. In practice, the appointee is almost invariably a member of the President's political party and is appointed on the recommendation of the Senators or Representatives from the particular state who are members of that party. When a president of a different political party takes office, the U.S. Attorney usually is replaced (tradition dictates that the U.S. Attorney, though appointed to a four year term, resign upon presidential request). The assistants are hired by the U.S. Attorney, usually without reference to their political affiliation. When a new U.S. Attorney is appointed, even after a shift in political party, the assistants no longer are replaced en masse. Nevertheless, assistants do not view their jobs as career positions, and the vast majority stay no more than several years (usually leaving to return to private practice). Although U.S. Attorneys are subject to the supervisory authority of the Attorney General, they are given considerable autonomy in their exercise of prosecutorial discretion.[a]

In a typical year, the United States Attorneys' offices open matters for investigation against about 180,000 criminal suspects, about 50% of whom are ultimately prosecuted in the district courts while another 35% are disposed of by magistrates. But various divisions within the Justice Department also exercise prosecutorial authority as to particular types of offenses. Criminal antitrust prosecutions are developed and presented by the Antitrust Division, and the Civil Rights

---

[a] "In practice, [the Department of Justice] has exercised control fairly selectively through the adoption of internal rules and regulations. Some of these rules require U.S. Attorneys to cede categories of case-sensitive decisions to the Attorney General (or his designee)—for example, whether or not to seek the death penalty. Other regulations require U.S. Attorneys to obtain the approval of the Attorney General for specific types of decisions made in the course of investigating and charging defendants, including whether to immunize a witness, whether to subpoena certain witnesses (e.g., a defense lawyer, a journalist, or a family member of the target), or whether to bring certain charges (e.g., tax or racketeering charges)." Bruce A. Green & Fred. C. Zacharias, *"The U.S. Attorneys Scandal" and the Allocation of Prosecutorial Power*, 69 Ohio St.L.J. 187, 197, 200 (2008).

The exercise of discretion by federal prosecutors is also affected by memoranda issued by the Attorney General, often upon a change of administrations. See Alan Vinegrad, *Justice Department's New Charging, Plea Bargaining and Sentencing Policy*, N.Y.Law Journal (June 10, 2010). The most recent is Memorandum from Attorney General Sessions on Department Charging and Sentencing Policy (May 10, 2017) ("prosecutors should charge and pursue the most serious, readily provable offense," i.e., "those that carry the most substantial guidelines sentence, including mandatory minimum sentences," except when a variance is approved by a supervisor and the reasons "documented in the file").

Division often brings prosecutions within its area of expertise. The Criminal Division itself initiates prosecutions in several fields (e.g., organized crime, public corruption, and narcotics distribution), acting through its special Strike Forces and regional offices located in 25 major cities.

2. ***Local prosecutors: the rural and small suburban office.*** There are about 2,330 prosecutors' offices handling felony cases in state trial courts, in addition to those municipal and county attorneys who primarily operate in courts of limited jurisdiction. 74% of these offices serve districts with populations of less than 100,000. In contrast to large urban or suburban offices, many prosecutors in the smaller districts operate with only one full-time assistant. Indeed, in 15% of all local prosecutors' offices the prosecutor is a part-time official, maintaining a private practice in addition to his public office.

The criminal caseload in small districts often is fairly light, particularly as to felonies. One recent survey found that only half of all local prosecutors' offices processed 300 or more felony cases per year. Of course, in most of these districts, the prosecutor's responsibility is not limited to criminal prosecution. The prosecutor also handles juvenile cases and often has extensive civil responsibilities.

Small prosecutor's offices have no need for a bureaucratic structure. The assistants, if any, work closely with the prosecutor and should fully understand his prosecutorial policies. Dealings with defense counsel, who are likely to be known socially as well as professionally, require no formal guidelines. There are neither the resources nor the need for highly structured programs dealing with matters such as diversion or the investigation and prosecution of complex fraud or narcotics offenses. The former can be handled through relatively informal arrangements, and the latter is often best handled by turning the matter over to the state attorney general or federal authorities.

3. ***Local prosecutors: the urban and large suburban office.*** Prosecuting attorneys in metropolitan districts not uncommonly have a larger legal staff than even the largest of the private law firms in the community. Los Angeles County, with the largest prosecutorial office in the nation, has nearly 1,000 assistant prosecutors. Full-time prosecutor's offices in the 43 jurisdictions with 1,000,000 or more population have a median total staff size of 445, with a median of 133 assistant prosecutors. Notwithstanding their size, these offices commonly have extraordinarily heavy caseloads per prosecutor, often four or five times that found in smaller offices. In a recent year, the median number of felony cases closed for these 43 offices was 14,304. To assist the local prosecutor in handling that caseload, some counties have relieved the prosecutor's office of most of its civil responsibilities, or provided a separate staff for civil cases.

In a large office, the assignment of prosecutors may have a substantial bearing on the operation of the office. The two most common assignment systems are the vertical or integrated system and the horizontal or process system. The vertical system is most commonly found in districts in which a complaint once filed will be assigned to a specified caseflow resulting in its eventual presentation in a particular courtroom or before a particular judge. A single assistant prosecutor or a team of assistants will then be assigned to all cases docketed for that courtroom or judge, with the assistant handling those cases from the point of filing through their final disposition. The horizontal assignment system, in contrast, revolves around each process step rather than the individual case. Thus, separate assistants may be assigned to intake, preliminary hearings, grand jury review, arraignments, trials, and appeals. As the case moves from one step to another, a new prosecutor will take over. Under this system, the newest assistants are commonly assigned to the preliminary steps or to misdemeanor trials, with the more seasoned prosecutors handling felony trials or supervising at one of the other stages.

Large offices also vary in the degree to which they seek to control the assistants in their exercise of discretion. Some assign experienced assistants to major areas of discretionary decisionmaking (e.g., charging and plea negotiation) and allow basically autonomous exercise of that authority by each assistant. Others utilize detailed guidelines, require assistants to justify their decision in writing by reference to those guidelines, and require all variations to be approved by one of a selected group of senior assistants. Spot checks and statistical analyses are run to ensure that all prosecutors are adhering basically to the same policies. Even here, however, individual prosecutors retain considerable flexibility, particularly in evaluating the factual elements of the case.

4. ***The charging decision: in general.*** "The decision whether to file formal charges is a vitally important stage in the criminal process. It provides an opportunity to screen out cases in which the accused is apparently innocent, and it is at this stage that the prosecutor must decide in cases of apparent guilt whether criminal sanctions are appropriate." *Task Force Report, The Courts* 5 (1967). In making this decision, the prosecutor must decide: (1) whether there is sufficient evidence to support a prosecution; (2) if so, whether there are nonetheless reasons for not subjecting the defendant to the criminal process; (3) if so, whether nonprosecution should be conditioned upon the defendant's participation in a diversion program; and (4) if prosecution is to be undertaken, with what offense or offenses the defendant should be charged.

"[Most] cases come to the attention of the prosecutor only after the police have instituted the criminal process by arresting a suspect. * * * As a consequence, the police exercise a very important influence over the initial decision as to whether to invoke the criminal process. Where a decision is made to arrest, there are procedures for review by the prosecutor and, ultimately, the court.[b] Where, however, the police decide not to invoke the criminal process, effective methods of review and control are largely lacking, and this issue of the proper scope and function of police discretion is of great, current importance and difficulty." Frank W. Miller & Frank J. Remington, *Procedures Before Trial,* 339 Annals 111, 115 (1962).

"A prosecutor should have several kinds of information if he is to make sound charge decisions. He must evaluate the strength of his case. Police reports usually provide him with some facts about the offense, but often he needs more. Before a prosecutor decides whether to charge or dismiss in any case that is not elementary, he should review the case file to determine whether more evidence and witnesses are available than the police have uncovered. In addition, the prosecutor needs to know enough about the offender to determine whether he should be diverted from the criminal track. * * * Often the prosecutor needs to know whether there are facilities in the community for treating such medical or behavioral problems as the offender may have and whether those facilities will accept him.[c] * * *

"Defense counsel has an important role to play at this stage, and he should be involved wherever an intrusive disposition or significant penalty is likely. Counsel can assist in gathering information and formulating a treatment program; he can help persuade the prosecutor of the appropriateness of a noncriminal disposition." *Task Force Report,* supra, at 7.

---

[b] But consider Andrew Horwitz, *Taking the Cop Out of Copping a Plea: Eradicating Police Prosecution of Criminal Cases*, 40 Ariz.L.Rev. 1305, 1306 (1998), observing that "a surprising number of jurisdictions in the United States entrust the prosecution of criminal cases to police officers who are not licensed to practice law, who are not obligated to follow a legal code of ethics, and who have no particular obligation to be responsive to the electorate," and concluding "that police officers who are not licensed attorneys should not be allowed to prosecute criminal cases."

[c] Compare Ronald F. Wright, *Prosecutor Institutions and Incentives*, in 3 *Reforming Criminal Justice: Pretrial and Trial Processes* 49 (E.Luna ed. 2017), asserting that the "typical local prosecutor, working within the current legal framework, must 'fly blind' * * *. The prosecutor flies blind because so little information is available about overall trends in case processing, prevention programs, corrections costs, and voter concerns about public safety."

5. ***Charging: evidence sufficiency.*** "[A.B.A.] Model Rule [of Professional Conduct] 3.8(a) is brief and to the point. It succinctly mandates that:

> The prosecutor in a criminal case shall: (a) refrain from prosecuting a charge that the prosecutor knows is not supported by probable cause.

A large majority of jurisdictions (41 states) have adopted the Model Rule's 3.8(a) language verbatim. The remaining ten jurisdictions (including the District of Columbia) maintain the Model Rule's probable cause level as the ethical minimum standard for a prosecutor to institute a criminal charge. * * *

"A disciplinary proceeding against a prosecutor for violating the knowing standard of 3.8(a) is exceedingly rare, presumably for the simple reason that the rule expresses the bare essential in terms of what is required in order to charge. Presumably the majority of prosecutors heed the clear language of both the National District Attorneys Association Prosecution Standard 43.3 that a 'prosecutor should file only those charges which he reasonably believes can be substantiated by admissible evidence,'[d] and the American Bar Association Prosecution Standard 3–3.9 that a 'prosecutor should not institute, cause to be instituted, or permit the continued pendency of criminal charges in the absence of sufficient admissible evidence to support a conviction.'[e] While filing charges without probable cause clearly is unethical, and although filing charges with only probable cause meets the minimum ethical standard, the better practice clearly is not to file charges unless the prosecutor knows there is sufficient evidence to sustain a conviction." Hans Sinha, *Prosecutorial Ethics: The Charging Decision*, 41 Prosecutor 32, 36, 38 (Oct. 2007).

As noted in Daniel Medwed, *Emotionally Charged: The Prosecutorial Charging Decision and the Innocence Revolution*, 31 Cardozo L.Rev. 2187, 2005, 2008 (2010), "tunnel vision often infuses a prosecutor's decision-making in screening a case for potential criminal charges. The principal effect of tunnel vision in this phase is to heighten a prosecutor's belief in the original suspect's guilt and minimize any countervailing impression that someone else may have committed the crime. * * *

"The formation of an internal review committee to evaluate charging decisions would force the prosecutor handling the case to communicate the precise reasons for her decision, a process that could trigger the type of critical self-reflection necessary to curb tunnel vision. Even if the charging prosecutor remained gripped by tunnel vision despite this exercise in introspection, the members of the review committee would likely not suffer from this malady, provided of course that they had no previous exposure to the case. The practice of seeking internal review of charging decisions is relatively common at the federal level, with some U.S. Attorneys' Offices requiring line prosecutors to consult supervisors and/or committees before proceeding with particular types of cases."

6. ***Charging: screening out cases.*** "In some cases invocation of the criminal process against marginal offenders seems to do more harm than good. Labeling a person a criminal may set in motion a course of events which will increase the probability of his becoming or remaining one. The attachment of criminal status itself may be so prejudicial and irreversible as to ruin the future of a person who previously had successfully made his way in the community, and it may foreclose legitimate opportunities for offenders already suffering from social, vocational, and educational disadvantages. Yet a criminal code has no way of describing the difference between a petty thief who is on his way to becoming an armed robber and a petty thief who succumbs once

[d] Substantially the same in Standard 4–2.2 (3d ed. 2012).

[e] Later revised to provide: "A prosecutor should seek or file criminal charges only if the prosecutor reasonably believes that the charges are supported by probable cause, that admissible evidence will be sufficient to support conviction beyond a reasonable doubt, and that the decision to charge is in the interests of justice." A.B.A. Standards for Criminal Justice, Prosecution Function § 3–4.3(a) (4th ed. 2015).

to a momentary impulse. The same criminal conduct may be the deliberate act of a professional criminal or an isolated aberration in the behavior of a normally law abiding person. The criminal conduct describes the existence of a problem, but not its nature or source. The system depends on prosecutors to recognize these distinctions when bringing charges.

"Among the types of cases in which thoughtful prosecutors commonly appear disinclined to seek criminal penalties are domestic disturbances;[f] assaults and petty thefts in which victim and offender are in a family or social relationship; statutory rape when both boy and girl are young; first offense car thefts that involve teenager taking a car for a short joyride; checks that are drawn upon insufficient funds; shoplifting by first offenders, particularly when restitution is made; and criminal acts that involve offenders suffering from emotional disorders short of legal insanity." *Task Force Report,* supra, at 5.

7. ***Charging: diversion.*** "The term 'diversion' is defined as the channeling of criminal defendants into rehabilitative programs after a criminal complaint has been filed. The term implies a halting or suspending of formal criminal proceedings against the alleged criminal perpetrator in favor of a noncriminal proceeding which, if successful, is the final disposition of the criminal offense.

> The pretrial . . . 'diversion' program represents one of the most promising correctional treatment innovations in recent years. Adaptable both to adult and juvenile correctional populations, the concept has received increasing recognition and endorsement as a rehabilitative technique for early and youthful offenders . . . . The technique is to be distinguished from informal diversion practices . . . in that pretrial [diversion] referrals are based on (i) formalized eligibility criteria, (ii) required participation in manpower, counseling, job placement, and educational services for defendants placed in the programs, and (iii) utilization of a real alternative to official court processing, i.e., dismissal of formal charges for successful participants.

"Pretrial diversion programs are based on the belief that not every criminal violation warrants a formal courtroom prosecution. The subjects of diversion have fallen into two general groups. One such group is comprised or persons charged with offenses of arguably dubious criminality, such as drug abuse and juvenile offenses. A second group includes persons for whom ordinary criminal processing may be ineffectual, such as misdemeanants, juveniles, and domestic assaulters. The rationale for using diversion in both groups is the avoidance of costly criminal processing 'of questionable benefit to the individual and society, while maintaining social controls through services aimed at altering behavior.' Thus, through pretrial diversion, the benefits of rehabilitative social services can be received without allowing the offender to completely escape criminal culpability." Note, 3 Ohio St.J. on Disp.Resol. 415, 422–23 (1988).

8. ***Charging: selection of the charge.*** "Once the prosecutor is personally convinced of the guilt of the accused, he then must determine the charge. * * * There is seldom difficulty in the heinous murder or simple petty theft. But what of the case where the offense could be aggravated battery, aggravated assault, battery, or simple assault? Should a charge be burglary, felonious theft, or petty theft? Should a 16-year-old boy be charged with a technical burglary or should he be handled as a juvenile before the family court?[g] These are the situations that pose a real test to

---

[f] This was an accurate description of the practice when this *Report* was written in 1967, but today many prosecutors follow a "no-drop" policy or some variation thereof under which the victim's expressed wish for no prosecution is much less often followed. See Cheryl Hanna, *No Right to Choose: Mandated Victim Participation in Domestic Violence Prosecutions*, 109 Harv.L.Rev. 1849, 1860 (1996).

[g] See Wallace J. Mlyniec, *Juvenile Delinquent or Adult Convict—The Prosecutor's Choice,* 14 Am.Crim.L.Rev. 29 (1976), discussing and criticizing the discretion given to prosecutors in 16 states to decide whether a juvenile goes to criminal court or juvenile court. In *Manduley v. Superior Court,* 41 P.3d 3 (Cal.2002), the court followed "[n]umerous decisions from other jurisdictions" agreeing "that prosecutorial decisions whether to charge minors as

prosecutorial discretion. Further, evidence may be insufficient, witnesses may be unavailable, the complaining witness may not wish to prosecute, the evidence may have been illegally seized, witnesses may lack credibility, or the case may appear too weak to justify prosecution on the major, technical, or primary offense under the statute. Perhaps the offender has no previous criminal record; perhaps the injuries were too slight; perhaps the offense was the result of mutual combat; perhaps it was a domestic squabble; perhaps there was a considerable delay by the prosecuting witness in reporting the crime; perhaps identification witnesses are weak and unsure of themselves; perhaps the witnesses themselves are convicted criminals and subject to impeachment. These are some of the factors which must be weighed and given proper consideration by the prosecutor * * *." Richard Mills, *The Prosecutor: Charging and "Bargaining,"* 1966 U.Ill.L.F. 511, 514–15.

"Very often, an offender's conduct violates more than one criminal statute. This may be the situation because: (1) the offender has committed a series of offenses prior to apprehension, as, for example, a number of burglaries; (2) the offender may, by a single course of criminal conduct, violate more than one criminal statute of the jurisdiction where his conduct occurred, as, for example, in a situation where conduct may constitute both forgery and theft; (3) the offender may violate both state and federal law, as, for example, where theft of an automobile may violate a state statute and a federal statute if the vehicle is driven across a state line. In these situations, prosecutors must decide whether the offender's conduct is to be subjected to a single prosecution for more than one offense or to more than one prosecution.

"There is variation in practice, and there is, therefore, risk of oversimplification in generalizing. There is adequate evidence to show that charging more than one offense is routine practice in many jurisdictions. This gives to the sentencing judge the power to impose consecutive sentences, which occurs frequently in some jurisdictions and rarely in others where, typically, sentences for all of the offenses are made to run concurrently. It is apparent that the processes of charging, convicting, and sentencing the multiple offender are so closely interrelated as to make it impossible to understand completely the one without understanding the other. Charging a single offense may be the practice where the sentencing range available to the judge is adequate to deal with the offender taking cognizance of the totality of his criminal conduct. Charging a number of offenses may be the practice where the penalty for one offense is thought to be disproportionately low in relation to the conduct involved. Also, here, as in relation to the selection of charge, the willingness of the defendant to plead guilty may be reflected in the number of offenses for which he is prosecuted."[h] Frank W. Miller & Frank J. Remington, supra, at 118–20.

---

adults or juveniles fall within ' "the long and widely accepted concept of prosecutorial discretion * * *" ' " and thus are permissible without an evidentiary hearing or judicial review.

[h] If a lower and higher court have concurrent jurisdiction over the charge or charges filed, then the prosecutor may also have the discretion to determine the forum for the prosecution. *State v. Pruitt*, 805 A.2d 177 (Del.2002) (but holding "that, absent compelling circumstances not present here, once the State engages in a prosecution in a court of competent jurisdiction, it should be prohibited from pursuing that prosecution to its ultimate conclusion in any forum other than one it initially chose").

§ 2. SOME VIEWS ON DISCRETION IN THE CRIMINAL PROCESS AND THE PROSECUTOR'S DISCRETION IN PARTICULAR

WAYNE R. LAFAVE—THE PROSECUTOR'S DISCRETION IN THE UNITED STATES

18 Am.J.Comp.L. 532, 533–35 (1970).

The American prosecutor has traditionally exercised considerable discretion in deciding whether or not to prosecute, that is, in determining whether prosecution is called for in a given case as a matter of enforcement policy. Insufficient attention has been given to the question of precisely why this is so, but the most common explanations are these:

(1) Because of legislative "overcriminalization." As one commentator has said, "The criminal code of any jurisdiction tends to make a crime of everything that people are against, without regard to enforceability, changing social concepts, etc. The result is that the criminal code becomes society's trash bin." Examination of the typical state code of criminal law supports this judgment. Included therein are likely to be crimes which are over-defined for administrative convenience (e.g., the gambling statute which bars *all* forms of gambling so as "to confront the professional gambler with a statutory facade that is wholly devoid of loopholes"); crimes which merely constitute "state-declared ideals" (e.g., the crime of adultery, which is "unenforced because we want to continue our conduct, and unrepealed because we want to preserve our morals"); and now outdated crimes which found their way into the law because of "the mood that dominated a tribunal or legislature at strategic moments in the past, a flurry of public excitement on some single matter."

(2) Because of limitations in available enforcement resources. No prosecutor has available sufficient resources to prosecute all of the offenses which come to his attention. To deny the authority to exercise discretion under these circumstances, it is said, is "like directing a general to attack the enemy on all fronts at once." Thus, so the argument goes, the prosecutor must remain free to exercise his judgment in determining what prosecutions will best serve the public interest.

(3) Because of a need to individualize justice. A criminal code can only deal in general categories of conduct. * * * Individualized treatment of offenders, based upon the circumstances of the particular case, has long been recognized in sentencing, and it is argued that such individualized treatment is equally appropriate at the charging stage so as to relieve deserving defendants of even the stigma of prosecution. * * *

The current practice, as set forth in a recently-published empirical study of the charging decision, clearly reflects these three considerations. * * *

A full appreciation of the extent of the prosecutor's power, however, requires consideration of the fact that his discretion may be exercised in the other direction; a particular individual may be selected out for prosecution notwithstanding the fact that the case is one which ordinarily would not result in an affirmative charging decision. Sometimes the purpose is to benefit the offender in some way,[20] but usually it is not. Such selection may occur in response to press and public pressure for "law and order," to rid society of certain "bad actors" who are thought to have committed more serious crimes, and for similar reasons.

[20] See, e.g., Francis A. Allen, *The Borderland of Criminal Justice* 5–6 (1964), describing the practice of prosecution and conviction of prospective mothers for some offense relating to extramarital sexual relations when they are without the financial resources to pay for the medical expenses of childbirth or the subsequent care of their offspring.

Should this aspect of the prosecutor's discretion be a matter of concern? Some would undoubtedly say no, on the ground that only acts of leniency are involved, but there are two answers to this. For one thing, not all leniency is consistent with the public interest in effective law enforcement. Moreover, as Professor Kenneth Davis has aptly pointed out:

"A fundamental fact about the discretionary power to be lenient is extremely simple and entirely clear and yet is usually overlooked: *The discretionary power to be lenient is an impossibility without a concomitant discretionary power not to be lenient, and injustice from the discretionary power not to be lenient is especially frequent; the power to be lenient is the power to discriminate.*"

BRUCE A. GREEN & FRED C. ZACHARIAS—PROSECUTORIAL NEUTRALITY

2004 Wis.L.Rev. 837, 902–03.

[T]he fact remains that, for better or worse, prosecutors are among the least accountable public officials. As a result, in evaluating prosecutors' work, the public tends to overemphasize the measurable or obvious aspects of what prosecutors do (e.g., the number of convictions they obtain, the length of sentences, and prosecutors' behavior in public trials) and tend to overlook more momentous decisions that occur behind the scenes. Prosecutors' limited public accountability might be acceptable, or at least more acceptable, if there were well-established normative standards governing prosecutors' discretionary decision-making. In that event, the public could elect people of integrity to serve as prosecutors, or higher officials could appoint them, and then trust them faithfully to apply accepted criteria. But our analysis of the concept of "prosecutorial neutrality" demonstrates that there are no settled understandings, except perhaps at the most general and abstract level. All might agree that prosecutors should be "neutral," just as they might agree that prosecutors should be "fair" or that they should "seek justice." But none of these terms has a fixed meaning. They are proxies for a constellation of other, sometimes equally vague, normative expectations about how prosecutors should make decisions.

As we have shown, neutrality has been used in different contexts to denote a range of expectations that can be grouped under three different conceptions: nonbias, nonpartisanship, and principled decision-making. These dimensions of neutrality, though somewhat more concrete than the umbrella term, still have variable content. Nor is it clear how the conceptions fit together. In the end, therefore, these too fall short in providing meaningful guidance for the discretionary decisions that prosecutors routinely must make.

Consequently, there is a need for more robust commentary and analysis. It is neither helpful simply to ask prosecutors to be "neutral" nor fair to criticize prosecutors for alleged failures to act "neutrally." Indeed, the neutrality rhetoric is singularly unpersuasive as criticism, because even the most egregious prosecutorial decisions can ordinarily be defended as "neutral" in some sense of the term.

JOSH BOWERS—LEGAL GUILT, NORMATIVE INNOCENCE, AND THE EQUITABLE DECISION NOT TO PROSECUTE

110 Colum.L.Rev. 1655, 1657–58, 1600 (2010).

The conventional wisdom is that the prosecutor is best situated to exercise charging discretion. The argument has two parts. First, it makes sense to leave legal reasons for charging (or not) principally to the prosecutor, because she knows most about the evidentiary support for a given charge. Second, it makes sense to leave administrative reasons for charging decisions exclusively to the prosecutor, because she knows most about her strategic priorities and limitations. This assumption of prosecutorial competency holds as far as it goes. The problem is that it does not go far enough. Left unaddressed is the harder, further question of whether prosecutors are also better situated (than laypersons or some other screening body) to reach commonsense determinations of whether defendants normatively ought to be charged. Significantly, such determinations turn not on legal or factual guilt or innocence, but on evaluations of relative blameworthiness or, put differently, what Akhil Amar once dubbed "normative guilt or innocence." Specifically, a defendant may be normatively innocent where he "did it . . . [but] did not thereby offend the public's moral code." * * *

For several reasons, prosecutors may be ill-suited to adequately consider relevant equitable factors in petty cases. Significantly, none of these reasons arises out of bad faith or ill will on prosecutors' parts. Instead, prosecutors' limitations are attributable to their institutional perspectives and incentives. First, based on their experience and training, prosecutors, like many lawyers, come to think primarily in terms of legal boxes, categories, and types, and not in terms of equitable specifics. Second, to the extent prosecutors are competent to evaluate equitable considerations, they are motivated to charge petty offenses reflexively and to consider the equities as part of summary plea bargains only. Prosecutors adopt near-categorical charging strategies in petty cases, because petty charges provide cover to the police for consummated arrests and institutional advantages to prosecutors in the form of cheap and expeditious plea convictions.

THURMAN W. ARNOLD—LAW ENFORCEMENT—AN ATTEMPT AT SOCIAL DISSECTION

42 Yale L.J. 1, 7–8, 17–18 (1932).

* * * It is impossible to understand the "principles" of the Criminal Law without analyzing [certain] contradictions. A few of them may be stated as follows: * * * (2) *Assumption.* Criminal Law is a body of governing rules, protecting certain social interests which are generally known and guide the ordinary citizen in his conduct. *Contradiction.* Substantive criminal law for the most part consists, not in a set of rules to be enforced, but in an arsenal of weapons to be used against such persons as the police or prosecutor may deem to be a menace to public safety. The choice of weapons is sufficiently elastic that the prosecutor may select a large number of offenses with different penalties to cover any single course of conduct. (3) *Assumption.* It is the duty of the prosecuting attorney to enforce all criminal laws regardless of his own judgment of public convenience or safety. Compromises and "bargain days" in criminal courts lead to disrespect for law because this process conflicts with enforcement of law. *Contradiction.* It is the duty of the prosecuting attorney to solve the problem of public order and safety using the criminal code as an instrument rather than as a set of commands. This makes it proper and necessary that some laws should be enforced, others occasionally enforced, and others ignored according to the best judgment of the enforcing agency. The criminal problem must be looked at as a war on dangerous individuals and not as a law enforcement problem, unless we want to escape from reality by taking refuge in an ideal world of false assumptions concerning both criminal codes and criminals.

GLENN HARLAN REYNOLDS—HAM SANDWICH NATION: DUE PROCESS WHEN EVERYTHING IS A CRIME

113 Colum.L.Rev. Sidebar 102, 103–04 (2013).

Attorney General (and later Supreme Court Justice) Robert Jackson once commented: "If the prosecutor is obliged to choose his cases, it follows he can choose his defendants." This method results in "[t]he most dangerous power of the prosecutor: that he will pick people he thinks he should get, rather than pick cases that need to be prosecuted." Prosecutors could easily fall prey to the temptation of "picking the man, and then searching the law books . . . to pin some offense on him." In short, prosecutors' discretion to charge—or not to charge—individuals with crimes is a tremendous power, amplified by the large number of laws on the books. * * *

With so many more federal laws and regulations than were present in Jackson's day,[a] a prosecutor's task of first choosing a possible target and then pinning the crime on him or her has become much easier. If prosecutors were not motivated by politics, revenge, or other improper motives, the risk of improper prosecution would not be particularly severe. However, such motivations do, in fact, encourage prosecutors to pursue certain individuals * * * while letting others off the hook * * *.

The result of overcriminalization is that prosecutors no longer need to wait for obvious signs of a crime. Instead of finding Professor Plum dead in the conservatory and launching an investigation, authorities can instead start an investigation of Colonel Mustard as soon as someone has suggested he is a shady character. And since * * * everyone is a criminal if prosecutors look hard enough, they are guaranteed to find something eventually.

Overcriminalization has thus left us in a peculiar place: Though people suspected of a crime have extensive due process rights in dealing with the police, and people charged with a crime have even more extensive due process rights in court, the actual decision of whether or not to charge a person with a crime is almost completely unconstrained. Yet, * * * the decision to prosecute is probably the single most important event in the chain of criminal procedure.

WAYNE R. LAFAVE—THE PROSECUTOR'S DISCRETION IN THE UNITED STATES

18 Am.J.Comp.L. 532, 536–39 (1970).

The discretion of the American prosecutor to decide, as a matter of policy, when to prosecute and when not to prosecute is clearly recognized in the case law. It is said, for example, that the prosecutor must be allowed to consider whether "a prosecution will promote the ends of justice, instill a respect for law, and advance the cause of ordered liberty," and to take into account "the degree of criminality, the weight of the evidence, the credibility of witnesses, precedent, policy, the climate of public opinion, timing, and the relative gravity of the offense." Indeed, it would hardly make sense to contend that the prosecutor should have *no* discretion; full enforcement would be neither possible nor tolerable. The issue is not discretion versus no discretion, but rather how discretion should be confined, structured, and checked. As Davis notes: "Half the problem is to cut back *unnecessary* discretionary power. The other half is to find effective ways to control *necessary* discretionary power."

1. *Confining the prosecutor's discretion to decide when to prosecute.* A significant part of the discretion currently exercised by American prosecutors is "unnecessary," in the sense that adequate reform of the substantive criminal law would eliminate, as a matter of law, many cases now screened out only at the option of the prosecutor. Clearly, "one of the major consequences of the state of penal law today is that administration has so largely come to dominate the field without effective guidance from the law."

---

[a] "So entrenched is the expectation of discretion within this system that it may drive the expansion of substantive prohibitions in the first place, in a sort of vicious cycle. Because legislators expect prosecutors to exercise discretion over which offenders and offenses to prosecute, Congress has little disincentive for passing ever-broader criminal prohibitions. Quite the opposite, a tough-on-crime electorate may create incentives to expand substantive criminal law, while prosecutorial discretion mitigates the costs of such legislation because Congress may anticipate that prosecutors will not in fact prosecute individuals within the scope of the law whom the public would not consider culpable. The end result of this 'pathological' political structure is ever-increasing prosecutorial discretion: '[L]aw enforcers, not the law, determine who goes to prison and for how long.'" Zachary S. Price, *Discretion and Executive Duty*, 67 Vand.L.Rev. 671, 682 (2014).

No one would seriously contend that the prosecutor's discretion could be eliminated by penal law reform. It is clear, however, from even the most casual inspection of the typical state criminal code, that some significant portion of that discretion would be unnecessary if many obsolete or largely unenforceable statutes were repealed and if other statutes were more narrowly drawn. The principal benefit of such reform would be that it would eliminate that part of the prosecutor's discretion which carries with it the greatest potential for misuse * * *.

2. *Structuring the prosecutor's discretion to decide when to prosecute.* Nearly forty years ago, Thurman Arnold noted that "the idea that a prosecuting attorney should be permitted to use his discretion concerning the laws which he will enforce and those which he will disregard appears to the ordinary citizen to border on anarchy." This may be the reason why this particular aspect of the prosecutor's discretion has traditionally been exercised sub rosa and on an ad hoc basis, and has thus remained largely unstructured.

The President's Commission on Law Enforcement and Administration of Justice identified three basic needs which must be met before the prosecutor's charging discretion may become more structured and thus more rational. They are:

(a) The need for more information. More detailed background information about the offender is needed so that it may be determined whether he is a dangerous or only marginal offender. (In the absence of any information, or only the limited information provided by a brief police report, the temptation is great to resort to rule-of-thumb policies based only upon the nature of the crime.) In addition, most prosecutors lack sufficient information about alternative treatment facilities and programs in the community to be able to make a rational determination of whether there exists some better course than prosecution.

(b) The need for established standards. "Standards should pertain to such matters as the circumstances that properly can be considered mitigating or aggravating, or the kinds of offenses that should be most vigorously prosecuted in view of the community's law enforcement needs." In large offices, the absence of such standards often results in a lack of uniformity in decision-making by the several assistant prosecutors. But even in a one-man office, consistency would seem more likely if the prosecutor had beforehand attempted to articulate general enforcement standards.

(c) The need for established procedures. These procedures might include a "precharge conference" at which the prosecutor and defense counsel could discuss the appropriateness of a noncriminal disposition. At least in serious cases, a decision not to prosecute should be supported by a written statement of the underlying reasons, and this statement should become a public record.

3. *Checking the prosecutor's discretion to decide when to prosecute.* Although the American criminal justice system has reasonably effective controls to ensure that the prosecutor does not abuse his power by prosecuting upon less than sufficient evidence, there are—as a practical matter—no comparable checks upon his discretionary judgment of whether or not to prosecute one against whom sufficient evidence exists. * * *

While it may be apparent that this is an unfortunate state of affairs, it is not so apparent how the situation might be best remedied. A system of close administrative review, perhaps modeled after the practice in West Germany, would seem to require a hierarchical arrangement quite different from the present structure of most state governments. Whether such a significant change in structure would be an improvement is not readily apparent. As for judicial review, it is probably true that courts have exercised undue restraint in responding to challenges of prosecutorial discretion. Yet, there may be something to the contention that courts are ill-equipped to make enforcement policy. Finally, greater control by the electorate could readily be achieved by exposing the prosecutor's nonenforcement decisions to the public, but it is by no means clear that the soundest enforcement policies are those which would draw approval from the "silent majority."

A.B.A. STANDARDS FOR CRIMINAL JUSTICE: PROSECUTION FUNCTION

(4th ed., 2017).

Standard 3–4.4 Discretion in Filing, Declining, Maintaining, and Dismissing Criminal Charges

(a) In order to fully implement the prosecutor's functions and duties, including the obligation to enforce the law while exercising sound discretion, the prosecutor is not obliged to file or maintain all criminal charges which the evidence might support. Among the factors which the prosecutor may properly consider in exercising discretion to initiate, decline, or dismiss a criminal charge, even though it meets the requirements of Standard 3–4.3, are:

(i) the strength of the case;

(ii) the prosecutor's doubt that the accused is in fact guilty;

(iii) the extent or absence of harm caused by the offense;

(iv) the impact of prosecution or non-prosecution on the public welfare;

(v) the background and characteristics of the offender, including any voluntary restitution or efforts at rehabilitation;

(vi) whether the authorized or likely punishment or collateral consequences are disproportionate in relation to the particular offense or the offender;

(vii) the views and motives of the victim or complainant;

(viii) any improper conduct by law enforcement;

(ix) unwarranted disparate treatment of similarly situated persons;

(x) potential collateral impact on third parties, including witnesses or victims;

(xi) cooperation of the offender in the apprehension or conviction of others;

(xii) the possible influence of any cultural, ethnic, socioeconomic or other improper biases;

(xiii) changes in law or policy;

(xiv) the fair and efficient distribution of limited prosecutorial resources;

(xv) the likelihood of prosecution by another jurisdiction; and

(xvi) whether the public's interests in the matter might be appropriately vindicated by available civil, regulatory, administrative, or private remedies.

(b) In exercising discretion to file and maintain charges, the prosecutor should not consider:

(i) partisan or other improper political or personal considerations;

(ii) hostility or personal animus towards a potential subject, or any other improper motive of the prosecutor; or

(iii) the impermissible criteria described in Standard 1.6 above.

(c) A prosecutor may file and maintain charges even if juries in the jurisdiction have tended to acquit persons accused of the particular kind of criminal act in question.

(d) The prosecutor should not file or maintain charges greater in number or degree than can reasonably be supported with evidence at trial and are necessary to fairly reflect the gravity of the offense or deter similar conduct.

(e) A prosecutor may condition a dismissal of charges, *nolle prosequi*, or similar action on the accused's relinquishment of a right to seek civil redress only if the accused has given informed consent, and such consent is disclosed to the court. A prosecutor should not use a civil waiver to avoid a bona fide claim of improper law enforcement actions, and a decision not to file criminal charges should be made on its merits and not for the purpose of obtaining a civil waiver.

(f) The prosecutor should consider the possibility of a noncriminal disposition, formal or informal, or a deferred prosecution or other diversionary disposition, when deciding whether to initiate or prosecute criminal charges. The prosecutor should be familiar with the services and resources of other agencies, public or private, that might assist in the evaluation of cases for diversion or deferral from the criminal process.

RONALD F. WRIGHT—PROSECUTORIAL GUIDELINES AND THE NEW TERRAIN IN NEW JERSEY

109 Penn.St.L.Rev. 1087, 1102–03 (2005).

Many practicing attorneys and legal scholars conclude that meaningful guidelines for prosecutors are impossible to draft. According to these scholars, the rules will either be phrased so generally that they will change no prosecutor choices, or they will be phrased too specifically and lead to improper outcomes in some cases because the rules cannot anticipate the complex reality of criminal charging.

The New Jersey experience, however, makes this critique less believable. Over time, prosecutors can draft guidelines on their own that promote some reasonable uniformity in case processing, while allowing for the variety that criminal justice makes necessary. Indeed, there are many parallels between this task and the maturing efforts to create sentencing guidelines that strike a useful balance between uniformity and individualization. The familiar sentencing concept of a favored "presumptive" outcome, coupled with potential "departures" from the norm that are discouraged by some degree of review and possible reversal, already exists in embryonic form in the * * * guidelines for prosecutors. The successes and failures of sentencing guidelines over the last two decades have marked the path for the prosecutorial guidelines that might follow behind.

Notes on Prosecutorial (and Other) Discretion

1. ***Police discretion.*** Should the prosecutor have the sole responsibility for determining when, on policy grounds, an offender should not be subjected to the criminal process, or should the police also be expected to make such decisions, as they frequently do when they decide not to arrest an offender who is lawfully subject to arrest? "It has been traditional to give explicit recognition to the propriety of discretion on the part of the prosecutor and either to deny or, more commonly, to ignore the issue of police discretion.[b] [There is apparently an] assumption that the average

[b] This issue seldom surfaces in appellate cases. A noteworthy exception, indicating *some* police discretion is properly exercised, is *City of Cambridge v. Phillips,* 612 N.E.2d 638 (Mass.1993), where the defendant, cited by a police officer for an illegal left turn, challenged a statute expressly declaring with respect to such minor traffic violations that "the police officer may direct that a written warning be issued or may cite the violator." After noting that the defendant had *not* claimed a denial of equal protection, the court commented: "Police have some discretion in their administration and enforcement of the law. The defendant advances no authority to indicate that nondiscriminatory, nonarbitrary exercise of discretion by a police officer is unlawful if no standard guides the decision-making process. Prosecutors have wide ranges of discretion in deciding whether to bring charges and which specific charges to bring. In the administration of the law concerning civil motor vehicle infractions, the police act as prosecutors as a practical matter in presenting such infractions to clerk-magistrates and to judges. In any event, in the absence of unfair discrimination or some other improper exercise of discretion, the judgment of the 'cop on the beat' is not subject to a valid constitutionally-based criticism where the range of clearly defined, available options is

municipal police agency lacks any special competence to make policy decisions * * *. For example, the United States Supreme Court held it proper for the Federal Trade Commission to follow a policy of proceeding criminally against only major violators because there were insufficient resources to proceed against all violators.[c] This kind of judgment was said to be within the expertness of the enforcement agency, which is familiar with the economic problems being dealt with. Under similar circumstances, a Philadelphia court held an identical policy of the Philadelphia Police Commissioner to be improper.[d] The Philadelphia court gave no indication that it believed that the police commissioner was particularly qualified to decide how best to allocate the limited enforcement resources made available to him."[e]

"Although the prosecutor is legally accorded a wider area of discretion than the policeman, the setting of the policeman's role offers greater opportunity to behave inconsistently with the rule of law. Police discretion is 'hidden' insofar as the policeman often makes decisions in direct interaction with the suspect. * * * By contrast, prosecutorial discretion frequently takes place at a later stage in the system, after the initial charge has been made public. The public character of the charge may restrict the prosecutor's discretion in practice more than the policeman's, even though the scope of the prosecutor's discretion is far wider in theory."[f]

Does this mean "the police should operate in an atmosphere which exhorts and commands them to invoke impartially all criminal laws within the bounds of *full enforcement*," so that "[r]esponsibility for the enactment, amendment, and repeal of the criminal laws will not, then, be abandoned to the whim of each police officer or department, but retained where it belongs in a democracy—with elected representatives"?[g] Consider in this regard that in some locales with respect to certain offenses the police have been placed in essentially a "full enforcement" posture. "At least 15 states and the District of Columbia have enacted mandatory arrest laws for misdemeanor violence calls. * * * In these jurisdictions, officers must arrest the defendant when they have probable cause to believe that a domestic violence assault has occurred.[h] * * * Although these policies have received mixed reviews, the clear trend in police practice is to arrest the batterer at the scene, regardless of the victim's wishes."[i]

2. *Jury discretion.* The prosecutor's decision not to prosecute is often based upon the expectation that the judge or jury would refuse to convict notwithstanding proof of guilt beyond a reasonable doubt. The jury in a criminal case has uncontrolled discretion to acquit the guilty. An empirical study has shown that juries acquit the guilty because: (a) they sympathize with the defendant as a person; (b) they apply personal attitudes as to when self-defense should be recognized; (c) they take into account the contributory fault of the victim; (d) they believe the offense is *de minimis;* (e) they take into account the fact that the statute violated is an unpopular

as narrow as it is in this case. This case does not involve the delegation of a basic policy matter to the police for resolution."

[c] *Moog Industries, Inc. v. FTC,* 355 U.S. 411 (1958).

[d] *Bargain City U.S.A., Inc. v. Dilworth,* 29 U.S.L. Week 2002 (Pa.C.P., June 10, 1960), aff'd, 179 A.2d 439 (Pa.1962).

[e] Wayne R. LaFave, Arrest: The Decision to Take a Suspect Into Custody 72–73 (1965).

[f] Jerome H. Skolnick, *Justice Without Trial* 233–34 (1966).

[g] Joseph Goldstein, *Police Discretion Not to Invoke the Criminal Process,* 69 Yale L.J. 543, 586 (1960). For more on police discretion, see Symposium, 47 Law & Contemp.Prob. 1 (1984).

[h] But see *Town of Castle Rock v. Gonzalez,* 545 U.S. 748 (2005), holding that a statute declaring that police "shall use every reasonable means to enforce a restraining order" and "shall arrest, or, if arrest would be impractical under the circumstances, seek a warrant" on probable cause, did *not* make enforcement of restraining orders mandatory, as it "is hard to imagine that a Colorado peace officer would not have some discretion to determine that—despite probable cause to believe a restraining order has been violated—the circumstances of the violation or the competing duties of that officer or his agency counsel decisively against enforcement in a particular instance."

[i] Cheryl Hanna, *No Right to Choose: Mandated Victim Participation in Domestic Violence Prosecutions*, 109 Harv.L.Rev. 1849, 1860 (1996).

law; (f) they feel the defendant has already been punished enough; (g) they feel the defendant was subjected to improper police or prosecution practices; (h) they refuse to apply strict liability statutes to inadvertent conduct; (i) they apply their own standards as to when mental illness or intoxication should be a defense; and (j) they believe the offense is accepted conduct in the subculture of the defendant and victim. See Harry Kalven & Hans Zeisel, *The American Jury* chs. 15–27 (1966). Regarding such nullification by a *grand* jury, see *United States v. Navarro-Vargas*, p. 973.

3. ***Judicial discretion.*** Because there is not agreement on whether such discretionary action by a jury is a desirable safety valve in the criminal justice system or an unavoidable evil, it is a debatable point whether it is proper for the trial judge to act in a similar fashion when a case is tried before him without a jury. The *Model Penal Code* would give the trial judge discretion to acquit the guilty under certain circumstances,[j] and an empirical study has established that judges acquit guilty defendants for the same reasons that juries do. See Donald J. Newman, *Conviction: The Determination of Guilt or Innocence Without Trial* chs. 9–12, 14 (Frank J. Remington ed. 1966).[k]

Should the trial judge, even in a jury case, be recognized as possessing authority essentially the same as that of the prosecutor, so that he might dismiss or reduce charges? Consider *United States v. Giannattasio*, 979 F.2d 98 (7th Cir.1992) (district judge exceeded authority in dismissing indictment after prosecutor refused to dismiss 10 counts of 15-count indictment in order to shorten the trial); *State v. Williamson*, 853 P.2d 56 (Kan.1993) (court may not dismiss aggravated assault charge on ground civil treatment of mental illness would be better, as that choice up to prosecutor subject to possibility of acquittal via insanity defense). However, about a dozen states have statutes or court rules authorizing a trial judge to dismiss criminal charges sua sponte in furtherance of justice. See *State v. Sauve*, 666 A.2d 1164 (Vt.1995) (collecting and discussing these provisions).

About the same number of states have a "compromise statute," covering most or all misdemeanors, providing that if the injured party appears in court and acknowledges that he has received satisfaction for the injury, then the judge may terminate the prosecution. These provisions only apply to those crimes overlapping a civil remedy, so that, e.g., compromise with a person injured in an automobile accident is no defense to a charge of leaving the scene of an accident. Most compromise statutes allow termination even over the prosecutor's objection, and this is deemed not to violate the separation of powers doctrine. *Commonwealth v. Guzman*, 845 N.E.2d 270 (Mass.2006).

4. ***Victim's role.*** Consider CRIMPROC § 13.1: "While it has been said that under a 'victim participation model' of the criminal process victims 'should have a veto power over whether a charge is brought,' 'should be able to determine what charges are appropriate,' and 'should be

---

[j] When "the defendant's conduct:

"(1) was within a customary license or tolerance, neither expressly negatived by the person whose interest was infringed nor inconsistent with the purpose of the law defining the offense; or

"(2) did not actually cause or threaten the harm or evil sought to be prevented by the law defining the offense or did so only to an extent too trivial to warrant the condemnation of conviction; or

"(3) presents such other extenuations that it cannot reasonably be regarded as envisaged by the legislature in forbidding the offense." *Model Penal Code* § 2.12.

Five states have adopted this provision; see, e.g., *State v. Kargar*, 679 A.2d 81 (Me.1996) (where defendant, an Afghani, charged with gross sexual assault for kissing his young son's penis, charge properly dismissed on finding conduct "is accepted practice in his culture" and there "is nothing sexual" about it).

[k] Under the traditional view, the double jeopardy clause bars retrial after such an acquittal, *Fong Foo v. United States*, 369 U.S. 141 (1962), but if the judge acknowledged he was acting on policy grounds it might be claimed there is no acquittal unless "the ruling of the judge, whatever its label, actually represents a resolution, correct or not, of some or all of the factual elements of the offense charged." *United States v. Martin Linen Supply*, p. 1352.

[able] to challenge the prosecutor's decision not to charge,' the reformers have been unwilling (or unable) to bring about such 'a monumental shift of the victims' rights pendulum.' * * *

"As for the victims' rights statute applicable in the federal criminal justice system, a crime victim is granted a 'reasonable right to confer with the attorney for the Government in the case,' [18 U.S.C.A. § 3771(a)(5)] but it is nowhere specified that the conference must precede or concern the prosecutor's charging decision * * * Moreover, the federal statute specifically declares: 'Nothing in this chapter shall be construed to impair the prosecutorial discretion of the Attorney General or any officer under his direction.' [18 U.S.C.A. § 3771(d)(6)]

"[S]omewhat less than half of all the states have a constitutional or statutory provision recognizing a right of the crime victim to 'confer,' 'consult' or 'communicate' with the prosecutor. More significantly, the great majority of these provisions make it apparent that consultation about the initial charge is not contemplated * * *. It is hardly surprising, therefore, that state courts have viewed these various victims' rights provisions as not limiting the prosecutor's charging discretion and not as conferring upon victims any right to judicial review of the exercise of that discretion."

Regarding an equal protection challenge to the prosecutor's charging decision (see p. 891), "[w]hile it is well settled that defendants subjected to or threatened with discriminatory prosecution have standing to bring an equal protection claim, * * * this right has not been extended to crime victims." *Parkhurst v. Tabor,* 569 F.3d 861 (8th Cir.2009). As stated in *Linda R.S. v. Richard D.*, 410 U.S. 614 (1973), such "a private citizen lacks a judicially cognizable interest in the prosecution or nonprosecution of another." Why? Should the victim at least be entitled to seek "a declaratory judgment that a prosecutor has abused his discretion not to prosecute," as proposed in Note, 97 Yale L.J. 488, 489 (1988)?

5. *Prosecutorial discretion.* What decision would you, as prosecuting attorney, reach in the following cases? What additional facts, if any, would you desire in each case prior to making a decision?

(a) A man lured several 14-year-old boys to a mountain cabin, bound them up, and sexually molested them. One of the lads managed to free himself and the others, found a rifle in the cabin, and then shot and killed their abductor upon his later return to the cabin. The juvenile court law of the state gives the criminal courts exclusive jurisdiction over juveniles when they are charged with murder. The law of self-defense in the jurisdiction only permits the use of deadly force "to prevent imminent death or great bodily harm to himself or another," which was not the case here. See Joseph Sax, *Civil Disobedience,* Saturday Review, Sept. 28, 1968, p. 22.

(b) A woman returned home from work a few hours late in a disheveled condition and told her husband that she had been kidnapped and raped. The husband called the police, and on the basis of the information given by the woman two suspects were arrested the next day. Upon questioning the woman in more detail the following day, the police discovered some discrepancies in her story, and she finally admitted that she was carrying on an affair with a man and that she had fabricated the story in order to explain her absence to her husband. Filing a false felony report is a criminal offense punishable by a fine of up to $500 and imprisonment up to six months. See Wayne R. LaFave, *Arrest: The Decision to Take a Suspect Into Custody* 140 (Frank J. Remington ed. 1965).

(c) A woman called police to her residence because of a domestic dispute. When the police arrived, they saw that she had swelling on her face and arms. After she told police she had dialed 911 because her boyfriend had beaten her, the officers arrested him. Two weeks later, the woman met with the prosecutor and said that, despite the fact she had suffered abuse throughout the relationship, she did not want to proceed with the case. "I have AIDS," she said, "and I'm sure that the stress of my illness caused him to beat me." She added that she did not want her family to discover that she had AIDS, and that she and her boyfriend were now "working things out." See Cheryl Hanna, supra note j, at 1873–74.

(d) An applicant for temporary employment as a mail carrier during the Christmas season completed a government employment application form in which he falsely denied ever having been arrested. A subsequent investigation disclosed that he had a record of several arrests for such offenses as drunkenness and vagrancy. This, however, did not become known until the man had been hired and had completed his temporary service for the post office department. His false statements were in violation of 18 U.S.C. § 1001, and are punishable by a fine of not more than $10,000 and imprisonment for five years. See John Kaplan, *The Prosecutorial Discretion—A Comment,* 60 Nw.U.L.Rev. 174, 189–90 (1965).

§ 3. CHALLENGING THE PROSECUTOR'S DISCRETION

A. THE DECISION NOT TO PROSECUTE

In *Inmates of Attica Correctional Facility v. Rockefeller,* 477 F.2d 375 (2d Cir.1973), the inmates and others brought a class action seeking to require federal and state officials to investigate and prosecute persons who allegedly had violated certain federal and state criminal statutes in connection with treatment of inmates during and following the Attica prison uprising. The district court dismissed the complaint, and the court of appeals, per Mansfield, J., affirmed:

"With respect to the defendant United States Attorney, plaintiffs seek mandamus to compel him to investigate and institute prosecutions against state officers, most of whom are not identified, for alleged violations of 18 U.S.C. §§ 241 and 242. Federal mandamus is, of course, available only 'to compel an officer or employee of the United States * * * to perform a duty owned to the plaintiff.' 28 U.S.C. § 1361. And the legislative history of § 1361 makes it clear that ordinarily the courts are 'not to direct or influence the exercise of discretion of the officer or agency in the making of the decision.' More particularly, federal courts have traditionally and, to our knowledge, uniformly refrained from overturning, at the instance of a private person, discretionary decisions of federal prosecuting authorities not to prosecute persons regarding whom a complaint of criminal conduct is made.

"This judicial reluctance to direct federal prosecutions at the instance of a private party asserting the failure of United States officials to prosecute alleged criminal violations has been applied even in cases such as the present one where, according to the allegations of the complaint, which we must accept as true for purposes of this appeal, serious questions are raised as to the protection of the civil rights and physical security of a definable class of victims of crime and as to the fair administration of the criminal justice system.

"The primary ground upon which this traditional judicial aversion to compelling prosecutions has been based is the separation of powers doctrine. * * *

"In the absence of statutorily defined standards governing reviewability, or regulatory or statutory policies of prosecution, the problems inherent in the task of supervising prosecutorial decisions do not lend themselves to resolution by the judiciary. The reviewing courts would be placed in the undesirable and injudicious posture of becoming 'superprosecutors.' In the normal case of review of executive acts of discretion, the administrative record is open, public and reviewable on the basis of what it contains. The decision not to prosecute, on the other hand, may be based upon the insufficiency of the available evidence, in which event the secrecy of the grand jury and of the prosecutor's file may serve to protect the accused's reputation from public damage based upon insufficient, improper, or even malicious charges. *In camera* review would not be meaningful without access by the complaining party to the evidence before the grand jury or U.S. Attorney. Such interference with the normal operations of criminal investigations, in turn, based solely upon allegations of criminal conduct, raises serious questions of potential abuse by persons seeking to have other persons prosecuted. Any person, merely by filing a complaint containing allegations in general terms (permitted by the Federal Rules) of unlawful failure to prosecute, could gain access to the prosecutor's file and the grand jury's minutes, notwithstanding the secrecy normally attaching to the latter by law. See Rule 6(e), F.R.Cr.P.

"Nor is it clear what the judiciary's role of supervision should be were it to undertake such a review. At what point would the prosecutor be entitled to call a halt to further investigation as unlikely to be productive? What evidentiary standard would be used to decide whether prosecution should be compelled? How much judgment would the United States Attorney be allowed? Would he be permitted to limit himself to a strong 'test' case rather than pursue weaker cases? What collateral factors would be permissible bases for a decision not to prosecute, e.g., the pendency of another criminal proceeding elsewhere against the same parties? What sort of review should be available in cases like the present one where the conduct complained of allegedly violates state as well as federal laws? With limited personnel and facilities at his disposal, what priority would the prosecutor be required to give to cases in which investigation or prosecution was directed by the court?

"These difficult questions engender serious doubts as to the judiciary's capacity to review and as to the problem of arbitrariness inherent in any judicial decision to order prosecution. On balance, we believe that substitution of a court's decision to compel prosecution for the U.S. Attorney's decision not to prosecute, even upon an abuse of discretion standard of review and even if limited to directing that a prosecution be undertaken in good faith, would be unwise.

"Plaintiffs urge, however, that Congress withdrew the normal prosecutorial discretion for the kind of conduct alleged here by providing in 42 U.S.C. § 1987 that the United States Attorneys are 'authorized *and required* * * * to institute prosecutions against all persons violating any of the provisions of [18 U.S.C. §§ 241, 242]' (emphasis supplied), and, therefore, that no barrier to a judicial directive to institute prosecutions remains. This contention must be rejected. The mandatory nature of the word 'required' as it appears in § 1987 is insufficient to evince a broad Congressional purpose to bar the exercise of executive discretion in the prosecution of federal civil rights crimes. * * *

"Such language has never been thought to preclude the exercise of prosecutorial discretion. Indeed the same contention made here was specifically rejected in *Moses v. Kennedy,* 219 F.Supp. 762, 765 (D.D.C.1963), aff'd 342 F.2d 931 (1965), where seven black residents and one white resident of Mississippi sought mandamus to compel the Attorney General of the United States and the Director of the F.B.I. to investigate, arrest, and prosecute certain individuals, including state and local law enforcement officers, for willfully depriving the plaintiffs of their civil rights. There the Court noted that 'considerations of judgment and discretion apply with special strength to the area of civil rights, where the Executive Department must be largely free to exercise its considered judgment on questions of whether to proceed by means of prosecution, injunction, varying forms of persuasion, or other types of action.' * * *

"With respect to the state defendants, plaintiffs also seek prosecution of named and unknown persons for the violation of state crimes. However, they have pointed to no statutory language even arguably creating any mandatory duty upon the state officials to bring such prosecutions. To the contrary, New York law reposes in its prosecutors a discretion to decide whether or not to prosecute in a given case, which is not subject to review in the state courts."[a]

[a] Many comparable decisions are to be found concerning the discretion of state prosecutors. See, e.g., *Manning v. Municipal Court,* 361 N.E.2d 1274 (Mass.1977) (spectator at Fenway Park, allegedly struck by baseball thrown from visiting team's bullpen by Ross Grimsley, cannot compel prosecutor to undertake assault and battery prosecution).

United States v. Cox, 342 F.2d 167 (5th Cir.1965), concerned the refusal of a United States Attorney, upon instructions from the Acting Attorney General, to prepare or sign indictments for a federal grand jury in the Southern District of Mississippi charging with perjury two blacks who had testified in a civil rights action brought by the United States against a county voting registrar. A federal judge held the United States Attorney in contempt and also ordered that the Acting Attorney General show cause why he should not also be adjudged guilty of contempt. Three members of the court took the view that the United States Attorney was not obligated to either prepare or sign the indictments, three others that he was obligated to do both, and the seventh (who determined the majority) that he must prepare but need not sign the indictments.

Judge Jones, in the first group, wrote: "The role of the grand jury is restricted to a finding as to whether or not there is probable cause to believe that an offense has been committed. The discretionary power of the attorney for the United States in determining whether a prosecution shall be commenced or maintained may well depend upon matters of policy wholly apart from any question of probable cause. Although as a member of the bar, the attorney for the United States is an officer of the court, he is nevertheless an executive official of the Government, and it is as an officer of the executive department that he exercises a discretion as to whether or not there shall be a prosecution in a particular case. * * * [S]ince the United States Attorney cannot be required to give validity to an indictment by affixing his signature, he should not be required to indulge in an exercise of futility by the preparation of the form of an indictment which he is unwilling to vitalize with his signature."

Judges Rives, Gewin and Bell explained their vote to compel the United States Attorney to both prepare and sign the indictments in this way:

"The grand jury may be permitted to function in its traditional sphere, while at the same time enforcing the separation of powers doctrine as between the executive and judicial branches of the government. This can best be done, indeed, it is mandatory, by requiring the United States Attorney to assist the grand jury in preparing indictments which they wish to consider or return, and by requiring the United States Attorney to sign any indictment that is to be returned. Then, once the indictment is returned, the Attorney General or the United States Attorney can refuse to go forward. That refusal will, of course, be in open court and not in the secret confines of the grand jury room. To permit the district court to compel the United States Attorney to proceed beyond this point would invest prosecutorial power in the judiciary, power which under the Constitution is reserved to the executive branch of the government."

Judge Brown noted that his conclusion that the United States Attorney must prepare but need not sign the indictments "lacks logical consistency," but thought there were sound reasons for both positions. Since the signature of the federal prosecutor, together with that of the jury's foreman, "is a formal, effective initiation of a prosecution," so that "what was previously an unfettered discretionary right on the part of the executive not to initiate prosecution has now been set in motion and can be stopped only on the executive taking affirmative action for dismissal with all of the uncertainties which F.R.Crim.P. 48(a) generates," the signature should not be required. However, he concluded, the grand jury should be entitled to the legal assistance of the U.S. Attorney in the preparation of the indictment so that the document, as drafted, "would clearly

---

Compare *State ex rel. Ginsberg v. Naum,* 318 S.E.2d 454 (W.Va.1984) (court grants mandamus, on petition of Dep't of Human Services, for prosecution of welfare fraud cases; court relies on statute declaring it to be duty of every prosecutor "when he has information of the violation *of any penal law* committed within such county" to "institute and prosecute all necessary and proper proceedings against the offender," which makes it a prosecutor's non-discretionary duty to institute proceedings against persons when he has information giving him probable cause to believe that *any* penal law has been violated, "even if the prosecutor has insufficient manpower"). But see Note 5, p. 904.

reflect the conscientious conclusion of the Grand Jury itself" and "reveal the difference of view as between the Grand Jury and the prosecuting attorney."

NOTES AND QUESTIONS

1. ***The court as a check on the prosecutor's decision not to prosecute.*** Although all jurisdictions recognize that the prosecutor has a substantial range of discretion in deciding whether or not to prosecute, many have placed some controls on his discretion after initial steps toward prosecution have been taken. There is a split of authority, for example, on the question whether a prosecutor may nol pros (from the Latin phrase *nolle prosequi*—an entry on the record by the prosecutor declaring that he will not prosecute) after the magistrate has sent the case to the grand jury but before the grand jury has had an opportunity to make a formal accusation. When the law permits the prosecutor to forego indictment and prosecute by information (a formal charge prepared by the prosecutor), almost all jurisdictions permit the prosecutor to nol pros after the preliminary hearing and before an information has been filed, although some states require that he file a statement of his reasons with the court. After formal accusation by indictment or information, a few states still recognize the power that the prosecutor possessed in the common law to nol pros on his own. Some other states, however, have now placed this authority entirely within the discretion of the court, while others require the court's approval for entry of a nol pros. Which system is preferable?

In *State ex rel. Unnamed Petitioners v. Connors,* 401 N.W.2d 782 (Wis.1987), two professional football players allegedly assaulted a female dancer in a dressing room of a Milwaukee night club. The prosecutor, after investigation, decided not to issue a criminal complaint, "not on the basis of a lack of probable cause but upon his perceived inability to prove guilt [beyond a reasonable doubt] at trial." Upon petition of the dancer the matter was then assigned to a circuit judge, and she directed that proceedings be commenced under a statute reading: "If a district attorney refuses or is unavailable to issue a complaint, a circuit judge may permit the filing of a complaint, if the judge finds there is probable cause to believe that the person to be charged has committed an offense after conducting a hearing." The football players then sought a writ of prohibition. In holding that the statute "violates the separation-of-powers principle of the Wisconsin Constitution that prohibits a substantial encroachment by one branch on a function that is within the delegated province of another branch,"[b] the court distinguished its holding in an earlier case that judicial approval is required for dismissal of a charge already filed:

"The right of a court to refuse to accept prosecutorial discretion as the final word where a case has commenced is vastly different from a situation where no crime has been charged. It is obviously factually different. In addition, it is jurisprudentially different. A prosecutor who dismisses an already initiated claim is free to reprosecute it later. To allow on-again, off-again prosecutions that cease before a defendant has been subjected to jeopardy would be to permit the court system to be used for harassment and would expose a defendant to some of the hazards of attachment of jeopardy, i.e., damage to reputation, expense, and threat of criminal sanctions, without the protection that the constitutional prohibition against double jeopardy affords. In addition, the 'public interest' and that of third parties is implicated by a pending prosecution—a situation not present where a prosecution has not been commenced."

The Supreme Court has explained that the "principal object of the 'leave of court' requirement" for dismissal of charges under Fed.R.Crim.P. 48(a) "is apparently to protect a defendant against prosecutorial harassment, *e.g.,* charging, dismissing, and recharging, when the

---

[b] Regarding such statutes elsewhere, Darryl Brown, *The Judicial Role in Criminal Charging and Plea Bargaining,* 46 Hofstra L.Rev. 63, 74–75 (2017), notes that "in a few states" there are "statutes that authorized judges to review public prosecutors' decisions not to charge based on private criminal complaints," but there "is little published evidence of courts using this statutory power to overrule prosecutors."

Government moves to dismiss an indictment over the defendant's objection." *Rinaldi v. United States*, 434 U.S. 22 (1977). "Where a defendant consents to the government's move to dismiss, it is not clear that the district court has any discretion to deny the government's motion. The Supreme Court reserved judgment on this question in *Rinaldi* * * *. The only standard that we have recognized as possibly being appropriate to such cases is 'whether the motion was clearly contrary to manifest public interest.'" *United States v. Garcia-Valenzuela*, 232 F.3d 1003 (9th Cir.2000).

2. ***The grand jury as a check.*** Most jurisdictions permit the grand jury to initiate prosecution by indictment even though the prosecutor opposes prosecution. Some require only that the foreman, acting on behalf of the grand jury, sign the indictment. Others have provisions similar to Rule 7 requiring the prosecutor's signature; some of them take the *Cox* position, while others hold the view that the signature requirement mandates essentially a "clerical act" by the prosecutor. It takes a most unusual case, however, for a grand jury to act as a "runaway" and indict notwithstanding the prosecutor's opposition. See pp. 715, 723.

3. ***The state attorney general as a check.*** At common law, the attorney general exercised wide powers of supervision over all criminal prosecutions, and in states in which he retains these powers he may initiate and prosecute criminal cases and may, at his discretion, supersede and replace the local prosecutor. Also, many states by statute confer upon the attorney general the power to initiate prosecution in cases where the local prosecutor has failed to act. In practice, however, attorneys general have seldom exercised much control over local prosecuting attorneys, except perhaps in the three states where all prosecutors are part of the office of the attorney general.

Consider *Johnson v. Pataki*, 655 N.Y.S.2d 463, aff'd 691 N.E.2d 1002 (N.Y.1997). Upon adoption by the legislature of new death penalty legislation including a provision that a death sentence could not be given unless the prosecutor elected before trial to seek it, one prosecutor issued a public statement of his "present intention not to utilize the death penalty provision" and instead to seek life imprisonment terms in homicide cases. This prosecutor later did not seek the death penalty against a defendant who had killed five people. Still later, another person was charged in that county with murder of a police officer, at which point the governor directed the Attorney General to assume control of that prosecution. The prosecutor and county taxpayers then unsuccessfully sought to challenge the governor's order. On appeal, the court held: "In furtherance of his Constitutional mandate to see that the laws of New York are faithfully executed, the Governor's apparent objective was to assure that those laws are being applied in a uniform fashion throughout the State's 62 counties. The wide discretionary authority that any district attorney does retain in executing the heavy responsibilities of his office must be held subservient to that overriding interest. The Governor had the power to determine the scope of this prosecution, before what he perceived to be the legislative will could be locally frustrated. Within Constitutional limits, the exercise of discretionary authority by the chief executive of the State in enforcing statutes is not subject to judicial review."

4. ***Private prosecution when the prosecutor does not act.*** Noting that some foreign jurisdictions permit private criminal prosecution when the public prosecutor fails to act, Comment, 65 Yale L.J. 209, 233 (1955), recommends that state legislatures enact statutes providing: "A trial court may in its discretion, upon petition of any person, substitute an attorney hired by the petitioner to replace a public prosecutor for any criminal prosecution if (a) the public prosecutor fails or refuses to prosecute the defendant or proceeds improperly, and (b) the crime charged is open and notorious or the petitioner has a cause of action against the defendant in tort on the facts alleged."

Compare *In re Richland County Magistrate's Court*, 699 S.E.2d 161 (S.C.2010), where, in holding that representatives of business entities allegedly given worthless checks by the defendants could not prosecute bad check charges against them in magistrate's court, the court declared: "If a private party is permitted to prosecute a criminal action, we can no longer be assured that the powers of the State are employed only for the interest of the community at large. In fact, we can be absolutely certain that the interests of the private party will influence the prosecution, whether the self-interest lies in encouraging payment of a corporation's debt, influencing settlement in a civil suit, or merely seeking vengeance."

Consider *In re Robertson*, 940 A.2d 1050 (D.C.App.2008), where on 6/26/99 Robertson violated a civil protection order by assaulting his girl friend Watson; he thereafter entered a plea agreement re an earlier assault in which the prosecutor agreed not to "pursue any charges concerning an incident on 6–26–99." Later, Watson filed a motion to initiate criminal contempt proceedings against Robertson for violating the protective order on 6/26/99, and he was found guilty and sentenced. The court of appeals held there had been no violation of the plea bargain, as "the criminal contempt prosecution in this case was conducted as a private action brought in the name and interest of Ms. Watson." Four Justices, dissenting from dismissal of cert. as improvidently granted, asserted: "The terrifying force of the criminal justice system may only be brought to bear against an individual by society as a whole, through prosecution brought on behalf of the government." *Robertson v. U.S. ex rel. Watson*, 560 U.S. 272 (2010). (The lower court subsequently held in *In re Jackson*, 51 A.3d 529 (D.C.App.2012), that in such cases a trial judge must go through a two-step process to ensure that neutral counsel, representing the government, prosecutes the offense." The court must first ask one of the District's two public prosecutor's offices "to prosecute the criminal contempt in the name of and pursuant to the sovereign power of the United States," and if both decline the judge may then "appoint a private attorney to prosecute the criminal contempt in the name and on behalf of the United States," but any court-appointed counsel must be "disinterested.")

5. ***Substitution of special prosecutor.*** Consider *People v. Adams*, 987 N.E.2d 272 (N.Y.2013), where the court concluded that appointment of a special prosecutor was improperly denied. The court noted that while a "conflict of interest" is usually required, this was one of the "rare situations" in which "the appearance of impropriety" was itself sufficient, i.e., the appearance that the prosecutor refused to accept a reduced-charge plea bargain because "the complainant was a sitting judge who demanded that the matter go to trial," contrary to the usual practice as to comparable charges.

In *Morrison v. Olson*, 487 U.S. 654 (1988), the Court upheld, 7–1, a federal statute (which lapsed in 1999) requiring the Attorney General to conduct a preliminary investigation of allegations that enumerated high-ranking federal officials have committed a crime and, unless the allegations prove insubstantial, to ask a special three-judge panel to appoint an "independent counsel" to complete the investigation and conduct any prosecutions. The Court, per Rehnquist, C.J., held that the Act did not violate the separation of powers doctrine, reasoning that while "the Act reduces the amount of control or supervision that the Attorney General and, through him, the President exercises over the investigation and prosecution of a certain class of alleged criminal activity," it "does give the Attorney General several means of supervising or controlling the prosecutorial powers that may be wielded by an independent counsel," most importantly the power to remove for "good cause."

B. THE DECISION TO PROSECUTE

UNITED STATES V. ARMSTRONG

517 U.S. 456, 116 S.Ct. 1480, 134 L.Ed.2d 687 (1996).

CHIEF JUSTICE REHNQUIST delivered the opinion of the Court. * * *

In April 1992, respondents were indicted in the United States District Court for the Central District of California on charges of conspiring to possess with intent to distribute more than 50 grams of cocaine base (crack) and conspiring to distribute the same, in violation of 21 U.S.C. §§ 841 and 846, and federal firearms offenses. For three months prior to the indictment, agents of the Federal Bureau of Alcohol, Tobacco, and Firearms and the Narcotics Division of the Inglewood, California, Police Department had infiltrated a suspected crack distribution ring by using three confidential informants. On seven separate occasions during this period, the informants had bought a total of 124.3 grams of crack from respondents and witnessed respondents carrying firearms during the sales. The agents searched the hotel room in which the sales were transacted, arrested respondents Armstrong and Hampton in the room, and found more crack and a loaded gun. The agents later arrested the other respondents as part of the ring.

In response to the indictment, respondents filed a motion for discovery or for dismissal of the indictment, alleging that they were selected for federal prosecution because they are black. In support of their motion, they offered only an affidavit by a "Paralegal Specialist," employed by the Office of the Federal Public Defender representing one of the respondents. The only allegation in the affidavit was that, in every one of the 24 §§ 841 or 846 cases closed by the office during 1991, the defendant was black. Accompanying the affidavit was a "study" listing the 24 defendants, their race, whether they were prosecuted for dealing cocaine as well as crack, and the status of each case.

The Government opposed the discovery motion, arguing, among other things, that there was no evidence or allegation "that the Government has acted unfairly or has prosecuted non-black defendants or failed to prosecute them." The District Court granted the motion. It ordered the Government (1) to provide a list of all cases from the last three years in which the Government charged both cocaine and firearms offenses, (2) to identify the race of the defendants in those cases, (3) to identify what levels of law enforcement were involved in the investigations of those cases, and (4) to explain its criteria for deciding to prosecute those defendants for federal cocaine offenses.

The Government moved for reconsideration of the District Court's discovery order. With this motion it submitted affidavits and other evidence to explain why it had chosen to prosecute respondents and why respondents' study did not support the inference that the Government was singling out blacks for cocaine prosecution. The federal and local agents participating in the case alleged in affidavits that race played no role in their investigation. An Assistant United States Attorney explained in an affidavit that the decision to prosecute met the general criteria for prosecution, because "there was over 100 grams of cocaine base involved, over twice the threshold necessary for a ten year mandatory minimum sentence; there were multiple sales involving multiple defendants, thereby indicating a fairly substantial crack cocaine ring; . . . there were multiple federal firearms violations intertwined with the narcotics trafficking; the overall evidence in the case was extremely strong, including audio and videotapes of defendants; . . . and several of the defendants had criminal histories including narcotics and firearms violations." The Government also submitted sections of a published 1989 Drug Enforcement Administration report which concluded that "[l]arge-scale, interstate trafficking networks controlled by Jamaicans, Haitians and Black street gangs dominate the manufacture and distribution of crack."

In response, one of respondents' attorneys submitted an affidavit alleging that an intake coordinator at a drug treatment center had told her that there are "an equal number of caucasian users and dealers to minority users and dealers." Respondents also submitted an affidavit from a criminal defense attorney alleging that in his experience many nonblacks are prosecuted in state court for crack offenses, and a newspaper article reporting that Federal "crack criminals . . . are being punished far more severely than if they had been caught with powder cocaine, and almost every single one of them is black."

The District Court denied the motion for reconsideration. When the Government indicated it would not comply with the court's discovery order, the court dismissed the case.[2]

A divided three-judge panel of the Court of Appeals for the Ninth Circuit reversed, holding that, because of the proof requirements for a selective-prosecution claim, defendants must "provide a colorable basis for believing that 'others similarly situated have not been prosecuted' " to obtain discovery. The Court of Appeals voted to rehear the case en banc, and the en banc panel affirmed the District Court's order of dismissal, holding that "a defendant is not required to demonstrate that the government has failed to prosecute others who are similarly situated." We granted certiorari to determine the appropriate standard for discovery for a selective-prosecution claim. * * *[c]

A selective-prosecution claim is not a defense on the merits to the criminal charge itself, but an independent assertion that the prosecutor has brought the charge for reasons forbidden by the Constitution. Our cases delineating the necessary elements to prove a claim of selective prosecution have taken great pains to explain that the standard is a demanding one. These cases afford a "background presumption" that the showing necessary to obtain discovery should itself be a significant barrier to the litigation of insubstantial claims.

A selective-prosecution claim asks a court to exercise judicial power over a "special province" of the Executive. The Attorney General and United States Attorneys retain " 'broad discretion' " to enforce the Nation's criminal laws. They have this latitude because they are designated by statute as the President's delegates to help him discharge his constitutional responsibility to "take Care that the Laws be faithfully executed." U.S. Const., Art. II, § 3. As a result, "[t]he presumption of regularity supports" their prosecutorial decisions and "in the absence of clear evidence to the contrary, courts presume that they have properly discharged their official duties." In the ordinary case, "so long as the prosecutor has probable cause to believe that the accused committed an

---

[2] We have never determined whether dismissal of the indictment, or some other sanction, is the proper remedy if a court determines that a defendant has been the victim of prosecution on the basis of his race. Here, "it was the government itself that suggested dismissal of the indictments to the district court so that an appeal might lie."

[c] In an omitted portion of the opinion the Court considered the respondents' claim they were entitled to discovery under then Fed.R.Crim.P. 16(a)(1)(C), now 16(a)(1)(E). The Court concluded "that in the context of Rule 16 'the defendant's defense' means the defendant's response to the Government's case-in-chief." In support, two reasons were given: (1) "If 'defense' means an argument in response to the prosecution's case-in-chief, there is a perceptible symmetry between documents 'material to the preparation of the defendant's defense,' and, in the very next phrase, documents 'intended for use by the government as evidence in chief at the trial.' " (2) "Rule 16(a)(2), as relevant here, exempts from defense inspection 'reports, memoranda, or other internal government documents made by the attorney for the government or other government agents in connection with the investigation or prosecution of the case.' * * * Because respondents construction of 'defense' creates the anomaly of a defendant's being able to examine all Government work product except the most pertinent, we find their construction implausible."

Justice Souter, concurring, joined the Court's discussion of Rule 16 "only to the extent of its application to the issue in this case." Justice Ginsburg, concurring, emphasized that the "Court was not called upon to decide here whether Rule 16(a)(1)(C) applies in any other context, for example, to affirmative defenses unrelated to the merits." Justice Breyer, concurring in part and concurring in the judgment, though concluding that "neither the alleged 'symmetry' in the structure of Rule 16(a)(1)(C), nor the work product exception of Rule 16(a)(2), supports the majority's limitation of discovery under Rule 16(a)(1)(C) to documents related to the government's 'case-in-chief,' " concluded that the defendants' discovery request failed to satisfy the Rule's requirement that the discovery be "material to the preparation of the defendant's defense."

offense defined by statute, the decision whether or not to prosecute, and what charge to file or bring before a grand jury, generally rests entirely in his discretion."

Of course, a prosecutor's discretion is "subject to constitutional constraints." One of these constraints, imposed by the equal protection component of the Due Process Clause of the Fifth Amendment, is that the decision whether to prosecute may not be based on "an unjustifiable standard such as race, religion, or other arbitrary classification," *Oyler v. Boles*, 368 U.S. 448 (1962). A defendant may demonstrate that the administration of a criminal law is "directed so exclusively against a particular class of persons . . . with a mind so unequal and oppressive" that the system of prosecution amounts to "a practical denial" of equal protection of the law. *Yick Wo v. Hopkins*, 118 U.S. 356 (1886).

In order to dispel the presumption that a prosecutor has not violated equal protection, a criminal defendant must present "clear evidence to the contrary." We explained in *Wayte* [*v. United States*, 470 U.S. 598 (1985)], why courts are "properly hesitant to examine the decision whether to prosecute." Judicial deference to the decisions of these executive officers rests in part on an assessment of the relative competence of prosecutors and courts. "Such factors as the strength of the case, the prosecution's general deterrence value, the Government's enforcement priorities, and the case's relationship to the Government's overall enforcement plan are not readily susceptible to the kind of analysis the courts are competent to undertake." It also stems from a concern not to unnecessarily impair the performance of a core executive constitutional function. "Examining the basis of a prosecution delays the criminal proceeding, threatens to chill law enforcement by subjecting the prosecutor's motives and decisionmaking to outside inquiry, and may undermine prosecutorial effectiveness by revealing the Government's enforcement policy."

The requirements for a selective-prosecution claim draw on "ordinary equal protection standards." The claimant must demonstrate that the federal prosecutorial policy "had a discriminatory effect and that it was motivated by a discriminatory purpose." To establish a discriminatory effect in a race case, the claimant must show that similarly situated individuals of a different race were not prosecuted. This requirement has been established in our case law since *Ah Sin v. Wittman*, 198 U.S. 500 (1905). Ah Sin, a subject of China, petitioned a California state court for a writ of habeas corpus, seeking discharge from imprisonment under a San Francisco county ordinance prohibiting persons from setting up gambling tables in rooms barricaded to stop police from entering. He alleged in his habeas petition "that the ordinance is enforced 'solely and exclusively against persons of the Chinese race and not otherwise.'" We rejected his contention that this averment made out a claim under the Equal Protection Clause, because it did not allege "that the conditions and practices to which the ordinance was directed did not exist exclusively among the Chinese, or that there were other offenders against the ordinance than the Chinese as to whom it was not enforced."

The similarly situated requirement does not make a selective-prosecution claim impossible to prove. Twenty years before *Ah Sin*, we invalidated an ordinance, also adopted by San Francisco, that prohibited the operation of laundries in wooden buildings. *Yick Wo*, supra. The plaintiff in error successfully demonstrated that the ordinance was applied against Chinese nationals but not against other laundry-shop operators. The authorities had denied the applications of 200 Chinese subjects for permits to operate shops in wooden buildings, but granted the applications of 80 individuals who were not Chinese subjects to operate laundries in wooden buildings "under similar conditions." We explained in *Ah Sin* why the similarly situated requirement is necessary: "No latitude of intention should be indulged in a case like this. There should be certainty to every intent. Plaintiff in error seeks to set aside a criminal law of the State, not on the ground that it is unconstitutional on its face, not that it is discriminatory in tendency and ultimate actual operation as the ordinance was which was passed on in the *Yick Wo* case, but that it was made so by the manner of its administration. This is a matter of proof, and no fact should be omitted to make it out completely, when the power of a Federal court is invoked to interfere with the course of criminal justice of a State." Although *Ah Sin* involved federal review of a state conviction, we think a similar rule applies where the power of a federal court is invoked to challenge an exercise of one of the core powers of the Executive Branch of the Federal Government, the power to prosecute. * * *

Having reviewed the requirements to prove a selective-prosecution claim, we turn to the showing necessary to obtain discovery in support of such a claim. If discovery is ordered, the Government must assemble from its own files documents which might corroborate or refute the defendant's claim. Discovery thus imposes many of the costs present when the Government must respond to a prima facie case of selective prosecution. It will divert prosecutors' resources and may disclose the Government's prosecutorial strategy. The justifications for a rigorous standard for the elements of a selective-prosecution claim thus require a correspondingly rigorous standard for discovery in aid of such a claim.

The parties, and the Courts of Appeals which have considered the requisite showing to establish entitlement to discovery, describe this showing with a variety of phrases, like "colorable basis," "substantial threshold showing," "substantial and concrete basis," or "reasonable likelihood." However, the many labels for this showing conceal the degree of consensus about the evidence necessary to meet it. The Courts of Appeals "require some evidence tending to show the existence of the essential elements of the defense," discriminatory effect and discriminatory intent.

In this case we consider what evidence constitutes "some evidence tending to show the existence" of the discriminatory effect element. The Court of Appeals held that a defendant may establish a colorable basis for discriminatory effect without evidence that the Government has failed to prosecute others who are similarly situated to the defendant. We think it was mistaken in this view. The vast majority of the Courts of Appeals require the defendant to produce some evidence that similarly situated defendants of other races could have been prosecuted, but were not, and this requirement is consistent with our equal protection case law. * * *[3]

The Court of Appeals reached its decision in part because it started "with the presumption that people of all races commit all types of crimes—not with the premise that any type of crime is the exclusive province of any particular racial or ethnic group." It cited no authority for this proposition, which seems contradicted by the most recent statistics of the United States Sentencing Commission. Those statistics show that: More than 90% of the persons sentenced in 1994 for crack cocaine trafficking were black; 93.4% of convicted LSD dealers were white; and 91% of those convicted for pornography or prostitution were white. Presumptions at war with presumably reliable statistics have no proper place in the analysis of this issue.

The Court of Appeals also expressed concern about the "evidentiary obstacles defendants face." But all of its sister Circuits that have confronted the issue have required that defendants produce some evidence of differential treatment of similarly situated members of other races or protected classes. In the present case, if the claim of selective prosecution were well founded, it should not have been an insuperable task to prove that persons of other races were being treated differently than respondents. For instance, respondents could have investigated whether similarly situated persons of other races were prosecuted by the State of California, were known to federal law enforcement officers, but were not prosecuted in federal court. We think the required threshold—a credible showing of different treatment of similarly situated persons—adequately balances the Government's interest in vigorous prosecution and the defendant's interest in avoiding selective prosecution.

---

[3] We reserve the question whether a defendant must satisfy the similarly situated requirement in a case "involving direct admissions by [prosecutors] of discriminatory purpose."

In the case before us, respondents' "study" did not constitute "some evidence tending to show the existence of the essential elements of" a selective-prosecution claim. The study failed to identify individuals who were not black, could have been prosecuted for the offenses for which respondents were charged, but were not so prosecuted. This omission was not remedied by respondents' evidence in opposition to the Government's motion for reconsideration. The newspaper article, which discussed the discriminatory effect of federal drug sentencing laws, was not relevant to an allegation of discrimination in decisions to prosecute. Respondents' affidavits, which recounted one attorney's conversation with a drug treatment center employee and the experience of another attorney defending drug prosecutions in state court, recounted hearsay and reported personal conclusions based on anecdotal evidence. The judgment of the Court of Appeals is therefore reversed, and the case is remanded for proceedings consistent with this opinion.

It is so ordered.

JUSTICE STEVENS, dissenting. * * *

The Court correctly concludes that in this case the facts presented to the District Court in support of respondents' claim that they had been singled out for prosecution because of their race were not sufficient to prove that defense. Moreover, I agree with the Court that their showing was not strong enough to give them a right to discovery, either under Rule 16 or under the District Court's inherent power to order discovery in appropriate circumstances. Like Chief Judge Wallace of the Court of Appeals, however, I am persuaded that the District Judge did not abuse her discretion when she concluded that the factual showing was sufficiently disturbing to require some response from the United States Attorney's Office. Perhaps the discovery order was broader than necessary, but I cannot agree with the Court's apparent conclusion that no inquiry was permissible.

The District Judge's order should be evaluated in light of three circumstances that underscore the need for judicial vigilance over certain types of drug prosecutions. First, the Anti-Drug Abuse Act of 1986 and subsequent legislation established a regime of extremely high penalties for the possession and distribution of so-called "crack" cocaine. * * * These penalties result in sentences for crack offenders that average three to eight times longer than sentences for comparable powder offenders.

Second, the disparity between the treatment of crack cocaine and powder cocaine is matched by the disparity between the severity of the punishment imposed by federal law and that imposed by state law for the same conduct. For a variety of reasons, often including the absence of mandatory minimums, the existence of parole, and lower baseline penalties, terms of imprisonment for drug offenses tend to be substantially lower in state systems than in the federal system. * * *

Finally, it is undisputed that the brunt of the elevated federal penalties falls heavily on blacks. While 65% of the persons who have used crack are white, in 1993 they represented only 4% of the federal offenders convicted of trafficking in crack. Eighty-eight percent of such defendants were black. * * * The Sentencing Commission acknowledges that the heightened crack penalties are a "primary cause of the growing disparity between sentences for Black and White federal defendants."

The extraordinary severity of the imposed penalties and the troubling racial patterns of enforcement give rise to a special concern about the fairness of charging practices for crack offenses. Evidence tending to prove that black defendants charged with distribution of crack in the Central District of California are prosecuted in federal court, whereas members of other races charged with similar offenses are prosecuted in state court, warrants close scrutiny by the federal judges in that District. In my view, the District Judge, who has sat on both the federal and the state benches in Los Angeles, acted well within her discretion to call for the development of facts that would demonstrate what standards, if any, governed the choice of forum where similarly situated offenders are prosecuted.

Respondents submitted a study showing that of all cases involving crack offenses that were closed by the Federal Public Defender's Office in 1991, 24 out of 24 involved black defendants. To supplement this evidence, they submitted affidavits from two of the attorneys in the defense team. * * *

The majority discounts the probative value of the affidavits, claiming that they recounted "hearsay" and reported "personal conclusions based on anecdotal evidence." But the Reed affidavit plainly contained more than mere hearsay; Reed offered information based on his own extensive experience in both federal and state courts. * * *

The criticism that the affidavits were based on "anecdotal evidence" is also unpersuasive. I thought it was agreed that defendants do not need to prepare sophisticated statistical studies in order to receive mere discovery in cases like this one. Certainly evidence based on a drug counselor's personal observations or on an attorney's practice in two sets of courts, state and federal, can "ten[d] to show the existence" of a selective prosecution.

Even if respondents failed to carry their burden of showing that there were individuals who were not black but who could have been prosecuted in federal court for the same offenses, it does not follow that the District Court abused its discretion in ordering discovery. There can be no doubt that such individuals exist, and indeed the Government has never denied the same. In those circumstances, I fail to see why the District Court was unable to take judicial notice of this obvious fact and demand information from the Government's files to support or refute respondents' evidence. The presumption that some whites are prosecuted in state court is not "contradicted" by the statistics the majority cites, which show only that high percentages of blacks are convicted of certain federal crimes, while high percentages of whites are convicted of other federal crimes. Those figures are entirely consistent with the allegation of selective prosecution. The relevant comparison, rather, would be with the percentages of blacks and whites who commit those crimes. But, as discussed above, in the case of crack far greater numbers of whites are believed guilty of using the substance. The District Court, therefore, was entitled to find the evidence before her significant and to require some explanation from the Government.[6] * * *

NOTES AND QUESTIONS

1. ***Discovery limitations.*** As concluded in the en banc decision in UNITED STATES v. DAVIS, 793 F.3d 712 (7th Cir.2015), whether the *Armstrong* discovery limitations apply depends upon the locus of the suspected discrimination. The defendants in that case alleged that the prosecutor, the FBI, and the Bureau of Alcohol, Tobacco, Firearms and Explosives (ATF) had engaged in racial discrimination with respect to the investigation and prosecution of stash-house stings. To their request for discovery, the prosecutor responded that *Armstrong* "forbids discovery into prosecutorial selectivity unless the defense first shows that similarly situations persons have not been prosecuted," lacking here. The court of appeals concluded:

"To the extent that Davis and the other six defendants want information about how the United States Attorney has exercised prosecutorial discretion, *Armstrong* is an insuperable obstacle (at least on this record). But the defendants' principal targets are the ATF and the FBI.

[6] Also telling was the Government's response to respondents' evidentiary showing. It submitted a list of more than 3,500 defendants who had been charged with federal narcotics violations over the previous 3 years. It also offered the names of 11 nonblack defendants whom it had prosecuted for crack offenses. All 11, however, were members of other racial or ethnic minorities. The District Court was authorized to draw adverse inferences from the Government's inability to produce a single example of a white defendant, especially when the very purpose of its exercise was to allay the Court's concerns about the evidence of racially selective prosecutions. As another court has said: "Statistics are not, of course, the whole answer, but nothing is as emphatic as zero. . . ."

They maintain that these agencies offer lucrative-seeming opportunities to black and Hispanic suspects, yet not to those similarly situated in criminal background and interests but of other ethnicity. If the agencies do that, they have violated the Constitution—and the fact that the United States Attorney may have prosecuted every case the agencies presented, or chosen 25% of them in a race-blind lottery, would not matter, since the constitutional problem would have preceded the prosecutor's role and could not be eliminated by the fact that things didn't get worse at a later step. * * *

"Agents of the ATF and FBI are not protected by a powerful privilege or covered by a presumption of constitutional behavior. Unlike prosecutors, agents regularly testify in criminal cases, and their credibility may be relentlessly attacked by defense counsel. They also may have to testify in pretrial proceedings, such as hearings on motions to suppress evidence, and again their honesty is open to challenge. Statements that agents make in affidavits for search or arrest warrants may be contested, and the court may need their testimony to decide whether if shorn of untruthful statements the affidavits would have established probable cause. * * * Before holding hearings (or civil trials) district judges regularly, and properly, allow discovery into nonprivileged aspects of what agents have said or done. In sum, the sort of considerations that led to the outcome in *Armstrong* do not apply to a contention that agents of the FBI or ATF engaged in racial discrimination when selecting targets for sting operations, or when deciding which suspects to refer for prosecution."

2. ***Discriminatory purpose.*** (a) *Armstrong* says the defendant must show not only that the prosecutorial policy had "a discriminatory effect," but also "that it was motivated by a discriminatory purpose." Compare Daniel I. Givelber, *The Application of Equal Protection Principles to Selective Enforcement of the Criminal Law,* 1973 U.Ill.L.F. 88, 106: "Rather than requiring a defendant to prove the prosecutor's knowledge and motivation in order to establish a denial of equal protection, a court should hold that the burden of going forward shifts to the state once the defendant proves that only a few of the knowable violators of a law have been prosecuted or that the group prosecuted for violating a law differs from the group not prosecuted in characteristics irrelevant to law enforcement purposes. Only after the state explains what has produced the unequal treatment can the court determine whether the selective enforcement results from the application of unjustifiable or arbitrary enforcement criteria."

(b) In WAYTE v. UNITED STATES, relied upon in *Armstrong*, petitioner sent letters to government officials stating he had not registered for the draft and did not intend to do so. The letters were added to a Selective Service file of men who had written similar letters or who had been reported by others as having failed to register. Later the Service adopted a policy of passive enforcement under which only nonregistration cases in the file were brought to prosecution, and only if the individual remained unregistered after having been warned that failure to register could result in prosecution and after repeated urgings by government authorities to register. When petitioner was then indicted, he claimed a denial of equal protection because of selective enforcement against "vocal" nonregistrants who were exercising their First Amendment Rights. But the Supreme Court did not agree:

" * * *All petitioner has shown here is that those eventually prosecuted, along with many not prosecuted, reported themselves as having violated the law. He has not shown that the enforcement policy selected nonregistrants for prosecution on the basis of their speech. Indeed, he could not have done so given the way the 'beg' policy was carried out. The Government did not prosecute those who reported themselves but later registered. Nor did it prosecute those who protested registration but did not report themselves or were not reported by others. In fact, the Government did not even investigate those who wrote letters to Selective Service criticizing registration unless their letters stated affirmatively that they had refused to comply with the law. The Government, on the other hand, did prosecute people who reported themselves or were reported by others but who did not publicly protest. These facts demonstrate that the Government treated all reported nonregistrants similarly. It did not subject vocal nonregistrants to any special burden. Indeed, those prosecuted in effect selected themselves for prosecution by refusing to register after being reported and warned by the Government.

"Even if the passive policy had a discriminatory effect, petitioner has not shown that the Government intended such a result. The evidence he presented demonstrated only that the Government was aware that the passive enforcement policy would result in prosecution of vocal objectors and that they would probably make selective prosecution claims. As we have noted, however, " '[d]iscriminatory purpose" * * * implies more than * * * intent as awareness of consequences. It implies that the decisionmaker * * * selected or reaffirmed a particular course of action at least in part "because of," not merely "in spite of," its adverse effects upon an identifiable group.' In the present case, petitioner has not shown that the Government prosecuted him *because of* his protest activities. Absent such a showing, his claim of selective prosecution fails."

(c) In McCLESKEY v. KEMP, 481 U.S. 279 (1987), the black defendant, sentenced to death for murdering a white victim, claimed racial discrimination in violation of equal protection. He relied upon a statistical study of over 2,000 murder cases arising in Georgia during the 1970s showing, inter alia, that prosecutors sought the death penalty in 70% of the cases involving black defendants and white victims; 32% of the cases involving white defendants and white victims; 15% of the cases involving black defendants and black victims; and 19% of the cases involving white defendants and black victims.

The Court, per White, J., held such statistics insufficient, for "McCleskey must prove that the decision-makers in *his* case acted with discriminatory purpose." The Court asserted that while it had "accepted statistics as proof of intent to discriminate in certain limited contexts," such as jury selection, where "the statistics relate to fewer entities, and fewer variables are relevant to the challenged decisions," the same approach would not be appropriate here. For one thing, state-wide statistics would not support an inference as to the policy of the prosecutor in this county: "Since decisions whether to prosecute and what to charge necessarily are individualized and involve infinite factual variations, coordination among DA offices across a State would be relatively meaningless." Secondly, "the policy considerations behind a prosecutor's traditionally 'wide discretion' suggest the impropriety of requiring prosecutors to defend their decisions to seek death penalties, 'often years after they were made.' " Moreover, the Constitution does not bar the exercise of discretion by the prosecutor as to when to seek the death penalty, as "discretion in the criminal justice system offers substantial benefits to the criminal defendant," and "the capacity of prosecutorial discretion to provide individualized justice is 'firmly entrenched in American law.' "[d]

Blackmun, J., for the four dissenters, argued that the defendant had established a prima facie case under the *Castaneda* [p. 951] three-factor standard (factors one and two were established by the study, and factor three by testimony assistant prosecutors in the county operated without any guidelines as to when to seek the death penalty); disagreed with the majority's assertion "that there are fewer variables relevant to the decisions of jury commissioners or prosecutors in their selection of jurors," or that such decisions "are 'made by fewer entities' "; and asserted that the "Court's refusal to require that the prosecutor provide an explanation for

[d] The part of the statistical study purporting to show racial discrimination by *juries* in opting for the death penalty was similarly assessed by the Court. Thus, the Court stressed the difficulty in deducing a policy "by studying the combined effects of the decisions of hundreds of juries that are unique in their composition"; the fact this disparity could not be explained because " 'considerations of . . . public policy' dictate that jurors 'cannot be called . . . to testify to the motives and influences that led to their verdict' "; and that "it is the jury's function to make the difficult and uniquely human judgments that defy codification and that 'buil[d] discretion, equity, and flexibility into a legal system.' "

his actions * * * is completely inconsistent with this Court's longstanding precedents" and with the recent decision in *Batson v. Kentucky,* p. 1250.[e]

(d) Bass, charged with two intentional killings, received notice of the government's intent to seek the death penalty. (Since 1995, only the Attorney General can authorize seeking the death penalty; individual prosecutors retain discretion in only three areas: whether to bring federal charges or defer to state prosecutions, whether to charge defendants with a capital-eligible offense, and whether to enter into a plea agreement.) Relying upon a 2000 Department of Justice survey showing, e.g., a significant difference between the percentage of white and black prisoners in federal prisons (57% and 38%, respectively) and those charged with death-eligible crimes (20% and 48%, respectively), and upon public comments by the then-Attorney General and then-Deputy Attorney General expressing concern about this disparity, the defendant sought discovery under *Armstrong* of the government's charging practices. The court of appeals affirmed the district court's grant of discovery, but Supreme Court summarily reversed, UNITED STATES v. BASS, 536 U.S. 862 (2002): "We need go no further in the present case than consideration of the evidence supporting discriminatory effect. As to that, *Armstrong* says that the defendant must make a 'credible showing' that 'similarly situated individuals of a different race were not prosecuted.' The Sixth Circuit concluded that respondent had made such a showing based on nationwide statistics demonstrating that '[t]he United States charges blacks with a death-eligible offense more than twice as often as it charges whites' and that the United States enters into plea bargains more frequently with whites than it does with blacks. Even assuming that the *Armstrong* requirement can be satisfied by a nationwide showing (as opposed to a showing regarding the record of the decisionmakers in respondent's case), raw statistics regarding overall charges say nothing about charges brought against *similarly situated defendants.* And the statistics regarding plea bargains are even less relevant, since respondent *was* offered a plea bargain but declined it. Under *Armstrong,* therefore, because respondent failed to submit relevant evidence that similarly situated persons were treated differently, he was not entitled to discovery."

(e) Is *Armstrong* satisfied on the facts of *Commonwealth v. Bernardo B.,* 900 N.E.2d 834 (Mass.2009), where "[t]he boy sought material from the Commonwealth concerning the district attorney's policies and decisions to prosecute in cases alleging statutory rape where both a defendant and any complainants were minors, on the grounds that the information was relevant to his claim that the disparity in treatment between him and the complainant girl children was based on gender discrimination," and the supporting evidence is that "both the boy and the three complaining witnesses appeared to have engaged in 'mutually consensual acts of oral sex,' the district attorney did not dispute that the activity was consensual, all four children were under the age of consent, and the district attorney refused the request of the boy's counsel that the girls be charged with statutory rape of the boy"?

3. ***The "arbitrary classification" requirement.*** (a) What is an arbitrary classification? Is the enforcement policy proper if the distinction being drawn in practice is one that the legislature could have drawn? See *Taylor v. City of Pine Bluff,* 289 S.W.2d 679 (Ark.1956), holding that enforcement of a Sunday blue law only against groceries was not a violation of equal protection because the legislature could have so limited the statute. Is this view incorrect, in that it is not the function of enforcement officials "to make the broad policy judgments that may require

---

[e] In *Armstrong,* respondents relied upon *Batson,* but the Court responded that *Batson* was different: "During jury selection, the entire res gestae take place in front of the trial judge. Because the judge has before him the entire venire, he is well situated to detect whether a challenge to the seating of one juror is part of a 'pattern' of singling out members of a single race for peremptory challenges. He is in a position to discern whether a challenge to a black juror has evidentiary significance; the significance may differ if the venire consists mostly of blacks or of whites. Similarly, if the defendant makes out a prima facie case, the prosecutor is called upon to justify only decisions made in the very case then before the court. The trial judge need not review prosecutorial conduct in relation to other venires in other cases."

such classification"? Comment, 61 Colum.L.Rev. 1103, 1118 (1961). Or, does this position not go far enough, in that a prosecutor must be free "to choose whom to prosecute after weighing such factors as the likelihood of successful prosecution, the social value of obtaining a conviction as against the time and expense to the state, and his own sense of justice in the particular case," id. at 1119, which are factors that could not be expressed in legislation? See *Futernick v. Sumpter Township*, 78 F.3d 1051 (6th Cir.1996), so concluding.

(b) In *United States v. Ojala,* 544 F.2d 940 (8th Cir.1976), defendant, a state legislator, established that he was targeted for prosecution for his failure to file income tax returns (while many others were not) because he publicly announced his refusal to comply with the filing requirements in order to protest the Vietnam war. Said the court: "It is difficult to conceive of a more legitimate object of prosecution than one who exploits his own public office and reputation to urge a political position by announcing publicly that he had gone on strike against the tax laws of the nation." Is this so? What then of the IRS's "Project ACE," which gave "special priorities" to the prosecution of tax crimes by attorneys and accountants because of their "special obligation and responsibility to the tax laws"? See *United States v. Swanson,* 509 F.2d 1205 (8th Cir.1975). What if, as concluded in *United States v. Hastings*, 126 F.3d 310 (4th Cir.1997), the defendant was selected for failure-to-file prosecution because of "his general prominence in the community"?

(c) After more traditional efforts to curb vice in the Times Square area had failed, city officials obtained federal funding for the Midtown Enforcement Project. A task force of fire, safety and health inspectors made frequent inspections only of "sex related" businesses in that area. Defendants, operators of an adult book store, sought dismissal of the charges of health and building code violations brought against them. In *People v. Mantel,* 388 N.Y.S.2d 565 (1976), the court declared that the test is "whether a particular classification bears a rational relationship to the broad purposes of the criminal law and is reasonably related to law enforcement objectives," and then concluded: "It cannot be seriously doubted that this concentrated effort, even assuming it is aimed at sex related establishments, is rationally related to legitimate law enforcement objectives. Any area of activity that carries with it a high incidence of crime is an appropriate choice for strenuous law enforcement."

(d) Compare *People v. Kail,* 501 N.E.2d 979 (Ill.App.1986), involving an arrest for violation of an otherwise unenforced city ordinance requiring bicycles to be equipped with bells, made "under a police-department policy requiring strict enforcement of all laws against suspected prostitutes," where the court held: "The purpose of the ordinance requiring a bell on a bicycle clearly does not envision the eradication of prostitution. There is no conceivable set of facts which would establish a rational relationship between the class of suspected prostitutes and the State's legitimate interest in enforcing the ordinance requiring bells on bicycles. We can conceive of no such set of facts, and the State has failed to propound any. To suggest that the requirement of a bell on one's bicycle should be enforced only against suspected prostitutes because it helps combat prostitution is clearly so attenuated as to render the classification arbitrary or irrational."

(e) It is the prosecutor's policy to prosecute for violations of the Sunday closing law only upon receipt of a citizen complaint, but for many years he never received one. Then the business manager of the meatcutters' union filed complaints against all supermarkets in the county but not against any so-called "Mom and Pop" groceries. What result if the supermarkets defend on equal protection grounds? Are the private complainant's reasons (concern over union members working on Sunday) relevant, or are they irrelevant because the prosecutor proceeds on all complaints without regard to what motivated them? If they are relevant, is this "an unseemly state of affairs openly inviting discrimination and harassment of one group by another," or may it be said that the complaints were designed "to achieve exactly what the statute intends"? See *People v. Acme Markets, Inc.*, 334 N.E.2d 555 (N.Y.1975).

(f) In *United States v. Moore*, 543 F.3d 891 (7th Cir.2008), the court considered "a class-of-one equal protection challenge," which "asserts that an individual has been 'irrationally singled out,' without regard for any group affiliation, for discriminatory treatment." Relying on the Supreme Court's recent explanation in *Engquist v. Oregon Dept. of Agriculture*, 553 U.S. 591 (2008), that class-of-one equal protection theory is a "poor fit" where the challenged government action is the product of a broadly discretionary decision-making process, the court concluded: "This logic is equally applicable to the exercise of prosecutory discretion. To treat like individuals differently in this context, even without a strictly rational justification, 'is not to classify them in a way that raises equal protection concerns,' [as stated in *Engquist*]; the discretion conferred on prosecutors in choosing whom and how to prosecute is flatly inconsistent with a presumption of uniform treatment. Indeed, in this context, there is no readily apparent standard against which departures can be assessed for arbitrariness. Therefore, a class-of-one equal protection challenge, at least where premised solely on arbitrariness/irrationality is just as much a 'poor fit' in the prosecutorial discretion context as in the public employment context."

Compare Steven D. Clymer, *Unequal Justice: The Federalization of Criminal Law*, 70 So.Cal.L.Rev. 643, 713–14 (1997), rejecting "the view that purely random or unprincipled selection is constitutional," as it "is difficult to reconcile the guarantee of equal protection with the intentional use of a policy that randomly subjects one offender to a small fine and another who is similarly situated to the near certainty of a ten-year term of imprisonment."

(g) If, as has been recommended,[f] the prosecutor has a handbook setting out guidelines for the exercise of his discretion, is any deviation from them a denial of equal protection? If not, should a deviation from published policies be a defense anyway? Consider *Nichols v. Reno*, 931 F.Supp. 748 (D.Colo.1996), aff'd 124 F.3d 1376 (10th Cir.1997) (where U.S. Attorneys' Manual contemplates that decision to seek death penalty be made by Attorney General after review by U.S. Attorney and Attorney General's committee and upon consideration of aggravating circumstances plus mitigating circumstances submitted by defense counsel, but promptly following Oklahoma City bombing Attorney General stated at press conference that death penalty would be sought for then unknown perpetrators, Nichols entitled to no relief, as Manual does not provide him with any judicially enforceable rights). Cf. *United States v. Caceres*, p. 216.

4. ***Discriminatory effect.*** Given the discriminatory effect requirement, said in *Armstrong* to necessitate a showing that others "similarly situated * * * were not prosecuted," can intentional or purposeful discrimination existing within a scheme of general or random enforcement ever constitute a violation of equal protection? (a) In *People v. Walker*, 200 N.E.2d 779 (N.Y.1964), where the defendant claimed a violation of equal protection when she was prosecuted for violations of the Multiple Dwelling Law closely following her exposure of corrupt practices in the Department of Buildings, the court ordered a retrial at which she could have "a fair opportunity to establish" such intentional discrimination. A dissenting judge objected:

"If the constitutional defense of unequal protection of the laws were maintainable solely upon a showing of bad motive on the part of those responsible for the placing of the violations of which appellant is admittedly guilty, then I would concur for reversal. This, however, is not the law; nor does the court say it is. Since the legislation under which appellant has been convicted is itself valid, and since appellant is admittedly guilty of the violations, the defense of unequal protection is established only upon a showing of both bad motive in the subject case and nonenforcement as to others similarly situated * * *. The violations, among which are the creation of an additional room by a partition, an additional class B room out of a vestibule, and the maintenance of a defective sprinkler valve, are, in my experience, commonly enforced in New York City. * * *

---

[f] See *A.B.A. Standards for Criminal Justice: Prosecution Function* § 3–2.4 (4th ed. 2017).

"[Appellant's] offers of proof went solely to the point of bad motive in her individual case. Sympathetic as we may be toward appellant's unfortunate position as the result of what she alleges were numerous bribe solicitations by Building Department officials, we have no license to play fast and loose with the elements of so volatile a doctrine as equal protection of the laws. If the statutory requirements to which appellant was held were generally enforced, then there was no infringement of her constitutional right when she was prosecuted for their violation—no matter how contemptible may have been the motives of those who enforced the law. Were the law otherwise all enforcement proceedings could be turned into subjective expeditions into motive without the stabilizing, objectively verifiable, element of an unequal pattern of enforcement. No one has a constitutional right to random enforcement of the law. No one has a constitutional right to sincere enforcement of the law. The right is to equal enforcement of the law."[g]

(b) Consider Recent Case, 78 Harv.L.Rev. 884, 885–86 (1965): "Once it is recognized that the equal protection clause requires each state to enact and enforce its laws in an impartial manner, it follows that Miss Walker should be given the opportunity to prove that even though there was general or random enforcement of the statute in question she would not have been prosecuted but for the purposeful discrimination on the part of the borough superintendent. For example, assume that the superintendent has a list of 1,000 known violators and reasonably exercises his discretion to enforce the law selectively by prosecuting every other person on the list, namely, even numbers. If Miss Walker's name is 149th on the list and the superintendent admits deviating from his selective enforcement formula in order to vent his personal prejudice against her, she has been deprived of equal protection of the laws and should be permitted to quash the prosecution."

Compare Note, 50 Cornell L.Q. 309, 315 (1965): "While a prosecutor does have the obligation to act in good faith in performing his duty, he ought not to be obligated to forego prosecuting a violator whom he believes to be guilty, merely because of some personal feeling or antagonism he has toward that violator.[h] A contrary rule might in fact result in discrimination against other violators." Would such an extension of the equal protection guarantee "be anomalous to criminal law as it is known today, for regardless of the motives of the prosecutor, the policy reasons which led to the enactment of the penal statute are being carried out, since society is still being protected from forbidden conduct"? Recent Decision, 39 St. John's L.Rev. 145, 149 (1964). And what of the point that "even if it can be proved that the prosecution might have been improperly motivated, it will be exceedingly difficult to prove that the defendant would not have been selected for prosecution in the normal course of events"? Recent Decision, 51 Va.L.Rev. 499, 507 (1965).

(c) But if the defendant shows the prosecutor had a "bad motive," why shouldn't the defendant prevail on that basis alone, even if there is no equal protection violation? Consider *State v. Annala,* 484 N.W.2d 138 (Wis.1992): When he was 15 years old, defendant molested an 8-year-old child he was babysitting; no criminal charges were pursued because even the victim's parents

[g] Defendant Walker finally prevailed, but the decision in her favor was in part based upon more traditional notions of equal protection, in that "the manner of prosecution was not the same as that used in the case of other property owners similarly situated" because "the time allowed to defendant for correction of alleged housing violations was so unreasonably short as to make correction an impossibility and criminal conviction a certainty." *People v. Walker,* 271 N.Y.S.2d 447 (1966).

Should Ms. Walker prevail even on these facts? Consider *Futernick v. Sumpter Township,* Note 2(a) supra: "We do not believe that choosing to enforce the law against a particular individual is a 'classification' as that term is normally understood. *Webster's Third New International Dictionary* 417 (1986) (defining 'classify' as 'to group or segregate in classes that have systematic relations usually founded on common properties or characters; sort')."

[h] In *United States v. Bourque,* 541 F.2d 290 (1st Cir.1976), where defendant alleged that his prosecution for wilful failure to file corporate income tax returns was brought about because of a dispute between him and the IRS District Director of Intelligence on a personal matter, the court held that even if this were so, defendant was entitled to no relief because he failed to show that "prosecutions are normally not instituted for the offenses with which he was charged."

agreed that the best disposition would be for defendant to seek counseling, which he did. Five years later the prosecutor charged defendant with the sexual assault, apparently because of a letter from the victim's therapist indicating such action would be in the best interests of the victim. In response to the defendant's claim "that abuse of discretion should be found because the prosecutor brought the charges based on an improper motive," the court stated: "When probable cause exists for prosecution, the court should not consider the subjective motivations of the district attorney in making his charging decision, except to determine whether a discriminatory basis was involved. * * * Political review through the electoral process is sufficient to ensure the proper application of prosecutorial discretion. If this court placed the nondiscriminatory subjective motivations of the district attorney under scrutiny with respect to the charging decision, it would likely create an enormous amount of litigation challenging prosecutorial discretion that had little or nothing to do with the defendant's guilt or innocence." Is it significant that the majority in *Annala* went on to conclude that the prosecutor's decision to prosecute in order to aid the victim's rehabilitation was not an abuse of discretion, while the dissent states it was "Shylockian retribution"?

(d) *United States v. Aguilar*, 883 F.2d 662 (9th Cir.1989), illustrates that when the statute is being selectively enforced, there may arise the critical question of just who is and is not "similarly situated." The defendants in *Aguilar*, members of the sanctuary movement (which operated a modern-day underground railroad that smuggled Central American natives into the U.S. and dispersed them to safehouses throughout the country), contended they were singled out for prosecution because of their "vocal opposition to U.S. refugee and asylum policy and to U.S. foreign policy in Central America." They acknowledged that government enforcement of the immigration laws was not limited to those opposing government policies, but they claimed they should nonetheless prevail because "growers and ranchers employing illegal aliens had not been prosecuted in the previous ten years." The court responded:

"Appellants' definition of similarly situated fails because it does not insure that all distinctions extraneous to the first amendment expression are removed. The government argues that appellants are similarly situated to 'well-organized and structured alien smuggling conspiracies that were smuggling high volumes of aliens.' Agent Rayburn testified that immigration authorities had never uncovered a similar conspiracy by Arizona farmers or growers to transport illegal aliens outside the State of Arizona. The United States Attorney testified that the office's focus was upon organized smuggling rings.

"Appellants' suggested definition of similarly situated excludes the one class of immigration law violators with whom they are most analogous: organized smugglers operating for financial gain. This group is unlikely to have a political motivation for their conduct and is consequently unlikely to be a vocal opponent of United States foreign policy. They represent the perfect control group because they present a similar threat to immigration policy in terms of the numbers of aliens they smuggle, but they do not engage in the expression that appellants' claim motivated this prosecution.

"Appellants do not contend that the government generally does not prosecute organized alien smugglers. Their suggested focus exclusively upon agricultural employers seeks to distract attention away from the fact that the government generally *does* prosecute organized alien smugglers, albeit organized smugglers following the dollar instead of the cross. We reject appellants' suggested definition of the similarly situated class and thus their selective prosecution claim."

5. ***Selective enforcement vs. selective nonenforcement.*** If a certain statute is generally enforced except as to a certain identifiable group, does a defendant not in that group have a valid equal protection claim? See *United States v. Robinson,* 311 F.Supp.1063 (W.D.Mo.1969) (conviction of private detective for wiretapping in violation of federal law overturned upon a

showing that federal agents were not prosecuted for similar violations), commented on as follows in 55 Minn.L.Rev. 1234, 1243 (1971): "Implicit in the *Robinson* decision is the belief that presence of an invidious motive for prosecution is not required for a finding of discriminatory enforcement. The absence of a proper justification for not fully enforcing the statute makes any partial enforcement discriminatory. Though this seems to expand *Yick Wo,* it is probably justified."

Consider Larry Alexander, *Equal Protection and the Prosecution and Conviction of Crime*, 2002 U.Chi.Legal F. 155, hypothesizing "a county somewhere in the United States with a large and diverse population. Assume the following facts about it: (1) There is a particular crime—say, cockfighting—that is committed disproportionately more by one ethnic group than by others. Assume for the purposes of this hypothetical that the group is Guatemalan. (2) Not only do members of that ethnic group disproportionately commit the crime, but the prosecution and conviction rates mirror the commission rate. That is, if Guatemalans commit 50 percent of the cockfighting crimes in the county (although they are but 10 percent of the population), they also make up approximately 50 percent of those prosecuted for the crime and approximately 50 percent of those convicted of it. (3) Every prosecutor but one prosecutes cockfighting without regard to the ethnicity of the defendant. One prosecutor, 'P,' is prejudiced against Guatemalans, however, and in one case failed to prosecute a non-Guatemalan in circumstances where, counterfactually, had the defendant been Guatemalan, he would have prosecuted him. Assume counterfactuals like this can be true, and that this one is. On the other hand, P has never prosecuted a Guatemalan defendant for cockfighting whom he did not believe was guilty." On such facts, how should one answer Alexander's later queries, id. at 157, 159: (a) "of what significance is it that Guatemalans are disproportionately (by one person) prosecuted and convicted of cockfighting relative to their commission of it?"; and (b) "If ['P'] denied equal protection, to whom did [he] deny it, and what is the appropriate remedy for the denial?"

6. ***Selective enforcement vs. full enforcement.*** Is the prosecutor's *failure* to exercise any discretion objectionable? In *State v. Pettitt,* 609 P.2d 1364 (Wash.1980), the defendant, after his conviction for taking a motor vehicle without permission, was charged under the habitual criminal statute pursuant to the prosecutor's "mandatory policy of filing habitual criminal complaints against all defendants with three or more prior felonies," as he had prior convictions for taking a motor vehicle without permission, second degree burglary, and unauthorized use of a vehicle. The defendant argued that "a policy which prevents the prosecutor from considering mitigating factors is a failure to exercise discretion, which may, as in this case, result in an unfair and arbitrary result." The court agreed:

"In the present case, the prosecutor (now former prosecutor) admitted that he relied on the record alone in deciding to file the habitual criminal information. He testified that he did not consider any mitigating circumstances in reaching his decision, and that he could imagine no situation which would provide for an exception to the mandatory policy.

"In our view, this fixed formula which requires a particular action *in every case* upon the happening of a specific series of events constitutes an abuse of the discretionary power lodged in the prosecuting attorney."

However, a dissenting judge objected:

"The statute makes it clear that every person who falls into the ambit of the statute *shall* be sentenced to life imprisonment. This statute is mandatory and requires that the prosecutor file a supplemental information charging each such person with being a habitual criminal. It does not say that certain persons may be charged and others may not, and it provides no standards for the exercise of prosecutorial discretion. Here the prosecutor followed the mandate of the statute."

Compare that dissent with *State v. Rice,* 279 P.3d 849 (Wash.2012) (if statutory command that prosecutors "shall" prosecute any kidnapping with sexual motivation and juvenile victim deemed "mandatory" it would be unconstitutional, as prosecutors' "broad charging discretion" under state constitution includes "the authority to be merciful and to seek individualized justice").

7. ***Selective reversal of prior nonenforcement decisions.*** In *Wayte*, the Court declared that "the decision to prosecute may not be ' "deliberately based upon an unjustifiable standard such as race, religion, or other arbitrary classification," ' including the exercise of protected statutory and constitutional rights." But when the exercise of those rights prompting prosecution comes *after* the prosecutor had decided not to prosecute, does it (should it) make any difference why the particular nonenforcement decision was made? Consider *Dixon v. District of Columbia*, 394 F.2d 966 (D.C.Cir.1968), which involved a black defendant stopped by two white police officers for alleged traffic violations. He was neither charged nor ticketed at that time, and two days later the defendant—a retired detective sergeant—filed a complaint with the police department concerning the conduct of the officers. Shortly thereafter defendant and the Corporation Counsel's office entered into a tacit agreement: defendant would proceed no further with his complaint and the government would not prosecute the traffic charges. Later, defendant did file a formal complaint with the D.C. Council on Human Relations, and after he refused to withdraw the complaint he was charged and convicted for the two traffic offenses. The Court of Appeals reversed; Chief Judge Bazelon had this to say:

"Of course prosecutors have broad discretion to press or drop charges. But there are limits. If, for example, the Government had legitimately determined not to prosecute appellant and had then reversed its position solely because he filed a complaint, this would clearly violate the first amendment. The Government may not prosecute for the purpose of deterring people from exercising their right to protest official misconduct and petition for redress of grievances. Moreover, a prosecution under such circumstances would be barred by the equal protection clause since the Government employs an impermissible classification when it punishes those who complain against police misconduct and excuses those who do not.

"Appellant's case, however, is more complicated. The record indicates that the Government's initial decision not to prosecute was based on appellant's tentative agreement not to proceed with his complaint. It would therefore be naive to say that the Government made a legitimate decision not to prosecute and then reversed it solely because appellant decided to complain. On the contrary, it may be that the Government should have prosecuted Dixon and that its failure to do so stemmed from an illegitimate desire to protect the two police officers. And if the Government should have prosecuted Dixon in the first place, there is arguably no reason why it should be barred from prosecuting him now.

"But I believe reason is to be found in the need to prevent the type of agreement which was attempted in this case. * * *

"The major evil of these agreements is not that charges are sometimes dropped against people who probably should be prosecuted. Much more important, these agreements suppress complaints against police misconduct which should be thoroughly aired in a free society. And they tempt the prosecutor to trump up charges for use in bargaining for suppression of the complaint. The danger of concocted charges is particularly great because complaints against the police usually arise in connection with arrests for extremely vague offenses such as disorderly conduct or resisting arrest.

"Courts may not become the 'enforcers' of these odious agreements. We must therefore bar prosecutions which are brought because the defendant refused to promise or reneged on a promise not to file a complaint against the police. Prosecutors will then have no incentive to offer or make such agreements."

Judge Bazelon, relying on the federal entrapment cases, based his decision on the supervisory power of federal courts to grant immunity from prosecution because of government misconduct.

Could *Dixon* instead have been decided as it was on equal protections grounds? On the grounds that there had been a vindictive prosecution under the *Goodwin* case, Note 6, p. 913?

Was the earlier agreement between the prosecutor and the defendant in *Dixon* "odious"? Compare *MacDonald v. Musick*, 425 F.2d 373 (9th Cir.1970) (state prosecutor's offer not to prosecute defendant for driving while intoxicated if defendant stipulated his arrest was made on probable cause, thus foreclosing possibility of false arrest suit, deemed to constitute the crime of extortion and also ethical misconduct of misuse of the criminal process to gain advantage in a civil case); with *Town of Newton v. Rumery*, 480 U.S. 386 (1987) ("a court properly may enforce an agreement in which a criminal defendant releases his right to file a § 1983 action in return for a prosecutor's dismissal of pending criminal charges," as while "a promise is unenforceable if the interest in its enforcement is outweighed in the circumstances by a public policy harmed by enforcement of the agreement," the court of appeals was incorrect in concluding "that all release-dismissal agreements offend public policy," for these agreements also "protect public officials from the burdens of defending * * * unjust claims," and in this case the prosecutor "had an independent, legitimate reason to make this agreement directly related to his prosecutorial responsibilities," namely, sparing a sexual assault victim the "public scrutiny and embarrassment she would have endured if she had to testify in either" the criminal or § 1983 trial).

In other cases, courts have enforced prosecutors' nonprosecution agreements because of the "consideration" the defendant supplied, *Bowers v. State*, 500 N.E.2d 203 (Ind.1986) (information constituting probable cause for search warrant), the defendant's detrimental reliance, *State v. Johnson*, 360 S.W.3d 104 (2010) (spending $300 and compromising self-incrimination privilege in supplying required mental evaluation), or simply the "bond of public trust" involved, *State v. Howington*, 907 S.W.2d 403 (Tenn.1995).

8. ***Desuetude.*** (a) In *State ex rel. Canterbury v. Blake,* 584 S.E.2d 512 (W.Va.2003), defendant, the long-time owner of pawn shop, was indicted on two counts of violating W.Va.Code § 61–3–51, a statute requiring a purchaser of precious metals and gems to obtain "proof of lawful ownership" from the seller. He petitioned for a writ of prohibition to preclude prosecution, relying on the doctrine of desuetude, because no one in the county had been prosecuted under the statute since its enactment 20 years earlier. The court stated: "Desuetude is defined as '1. Lack of use; obsolescence through disuse. 2. The doctrine holding that if a statute or treaty is left unenforced long enough, the courts will no longer regard it as having any legal effect even though it has not been repealed.' Stated more clearly, '[t]he doctrine of desuetude, the concept that a statute may be void because of its lack of use, is founded on the constitutional concept of fairness embodied in federal and state constitutional due process and equal protection clauses.' * * *

"[This court has previously] held that:

> Penal statutes may become void under the doctrine of desuetude if: (1) The statute proscribes only acts that are malum prohibitum and not malum in se; (2) There has been open, notorious and pervasive violation of the statute for a long period; and (3) There has been a conspicuous policy of nonenforcement of the statute.

We believe all three elements are satisfied in this case.

"First, we must distinguish between crimes that are malum prohibitum and crimes that are malum in se. * * * The [lower] court made its ruling by stating, 'I don't think there's any question that it's a regulatory statute [.]' We need not belabor this point. We agree with the circuit court.

" 'Second, there must be an open, notorious, and pervasive violation of the statute for a long period before desuetude will take hold.' In the case before us, the defense argued that the statute had been violated 'for the entire period of time the statute has been in place[.]' The assistant prosecutor did not contest this contention, but rather argued that the statute was not old enough to fall into desuetude. Finally, there is no doubt that a conspicuous policy of nonenforcement exists in Fayette County. At the October 12, 2001 hearing, the Sheriff of Fayette County * * * testified that he believes W.Va.Code § 61–3–51 has never been enforced in the county since its inception in 1981. He testified that he 'looked through the records that are available to me in the Fayette County Sheriff's Department, and found no such records.' Richard Kemp, an investigator, 'did a survey of businesses in Fayette County which pawn or purchase gems or precious metals, to see if they have been following the provisions of 61–3–51[.]' The State stipulated Mr. Kemp would report that no business in Fayette County was making such report. * * *

"Because W.Va.Code § 61–3–51 (1981) has fallen into desuetude, the petitioner cannot be made to stand trial for violating the statute."

(b) In *John R. Thompson Co. v. District of Columbia,* 203 F.2d 579 (D.C.Cir.1953), the court, although holding a criminal statute on refusal to serve blacks unenforceable on other grounds, added: "But we think it appropriate to comment, in this connection, that the enactments having lain unenforced for 78 years, in the face of a custom of race disassociation in the District, the decision of the municipal authorities to enforce them now, by the prosecution of the instant case, was, in effect, a decision legislative in character. That is to say, it was a determination that the enactments reflect a social policy which is now correct, although it was not correct—else the enactments would have been enforced—heretofore. Such a decision were better left, we think, to the Congress." On review, in *District of Columbia v. John R. Thompson Co.,* 346 U.S. 100 (1953), the Supreme Court disagreed: "The repeal of laws is as much a legislative function as their enactment. * * * Cases of hardship are put where criminal laws so long in disuse as to be no longer known to exist are enforced against innocent parties. But that condition does not bear on the continuing validity of the law; it is only an ameliorating factor in enforcement."

(c) Compare Arthur E. Bonfield, *The Abrogation of Penal Statutes by Nonenforcement,* 49 Iowa L.Rev. 389, 415–16 (1964): "The depth of the American commitment to the abrogation of enacted law by desuetude is perhaps best revealed by analogy to the due-process fair-notice or fair-warning cases. Where both the community and its law-enforcement agencies have notoriously ignored an enactment for an unduly protracted period, it should be constitutionally impermissible to suddenly prosecute its violation because the act's proscriptions have disappeared from the legal consciousness of the body politic. The statute has neither been obeyed nor applied for such an extended period that ample justification as long existed for the public's feeling that the act has lost the force of binding law."

(d) Compare also the defense in *Model Penal Code* § 2.04 where a defendant believes "that conduct does not legally constitute an offense [and] acts in reasonable reliance upon an official statement of the law, afterward determined to be invalid or erroneous, contained in * * * an official interpretation of the public officer or body charged by law with responsibility for the interpretation, administration or enforcement of the law defining the offense." Should it make any difference whether the prosecutor says that the contemplated conduct is not covered by the law or that it is covered by the law but that it is not his policy to prosecute for such conduct?

C. THE DIVERSION DECISION

1. ***Prosecutor's discretion.*** In *Billis v. State*, 800 P.2d 401 (Wyo.1990), consolidating the cases of several defendants who challenged that part of a statute establishing a process for pretrial diversion (called probation without entry of judgment) that permitted the court to order diversion only upon the prosecutor's consent, the court concluded: "Despite the prosecutor's long-recognized possession of the power to charge, to reduce charges, to dismiss some or all of the charges, to plea bargain, and to dismiss the prosecution * * *, these criminal defendants wish that the power to consent to a criminal defendant's probation without entry of a judgment resided in the judicial department rather than in the executive department. Under the state constitution, that cannot be. Once the prosecutor has decided to file the criminal charge, a criminal defendant has no

constitutional right to a preferred disposition of that charge. He has no right to a reduced charge, to a dismissal of some charges, or to a plea bargain."[i]

2. ***Risks and remedies.*** One danger "attending the practice of pre-charge diversion * * * is the risk that individuals who would not otherwise be prosecuted or convicted will be persuaded to enter into deferred prosecution agreements, thus expanding the net of social control in the name of 'diversion.' The psychological pressure to resolve the matter as quickly as possible may also prevent accused individuals from invoking constitutional rights and other protections they would possess in a formal prosecution." *Model Penal Code: Sentencing* § 6.02A (2017). The Code's provision on deferred prosecution addresses those concerns in various ways, including by (1) limiting deferred prosecution to cases in which "a prosecutor has probable cause to believe that an individual has committed a crime and reasonably anticipates that sufficient admissible evidence can be developed to support conviction at trial"; (2) providing for right to counsel whenever a defendant is tendered a deferred prosecution agreement, even "before the initiation of formal charges"; and (3) providing that the existence of a deferred-prosecution agreement "does not relieve the prosecuting agency of any duty to disclose exculpatory evidence."

3. ***Court review.*** If, as concluded in *Billis,* diversion is an aspect of the prosecutor's discretion, then to what extent are the prosecutor's diversion decisions subject to court review? Consider the applicability in this context of the separation of powers doctrine invoked in *Inmates of Attica,* p. 885, and the equal protection challenge discussed in *Armstrong,* p. 891 (as invoked, e.g., in *Flynt v. Commonwealth,* 105 S.W.3d 415 (Ky.2003), re exclusion of all "employee-theft defendants"; and *Chavez v. United States,* 499 A.2d 813 (D.C.App.1985), re exclusion of all "illegal aliens"). Consider also:

(a) *State v. Leonardis,* 375 A.2d 607 (N.J.1977): Noting that pretrial diversion was adopted in the state by the supreme court pursuant to its rule-making power, conferred by the state constitution, the court concluded that the "authority to engage in rule-making also includes the power to interpret and enforce court rules."[j] Thus, "our rule-making power must be held to include the power to order the diversion of a defendant * * * where either the prosecutor or the program director arbitrarily fails to follow the [judicial] guidelines in refusing to consent to diversion.[k] Conversely, where the program director or the prosecutor would subvert the goals of the program by approving diversion, meaningful judicial review must also be cognizable."

(b) *United States v. Smith,* 354 A.2d 510 (D.C.App.1976): After defendant was charged with the misdemeanor of marijuana possession, he moved to dismiss on the ground that criminal penalties for such conduct constitutes cruel and unusual punishment. The trial judge granted the motion, but this motion was reversed on appeal. Defendant then sought diversion pursuant to the prosecutor's program whereunder young people without prior records accused of minor

---

[i] What then if the program *does* limit the prosecutor's discretion? In *State v. Greenlee,* 620 P.2d 1132 (Kan.1980), where the program was adopted by legislation which listed diversion criteria for prosecutors to apply, the court concluded the resulting limitation on the prosecutor's discretion did not violate the separation of powers doctrine, as the statute "does not * * * destroy or unreasonably restrict" that discretion. The court added that if such a statute had specifically provided the courts were to administer the program, or if the program had been adopted by rule of court, it would be clear that the setting of standards would not encroach on the executive power because then "a judicial function" would be involved.

[j] Compare *Cleveland v. State,* 417 So.2d 653 (Fla.1982) (because statutory pretrial diversion program "requires consent of the administrator of the program, victim, judge, and state attorney, but fails to provide for *any* form of review," "the pretrial diversion decision of the state attorney is prosecutorial in nature and, thus, is not subject to judicial review").

[k] Illustrative is *State v. Negran,* 835 A.2d 301 (N.J.2003) (prosecutor committed an abuse of discretion by basing his denial of diversion re charge of eluding police upon defendant's past driving history; not justified by statutory criterion of defendant's "record of criminal and penal violations," as motor vehicle violations not crimes; not justified by statutory criterion of defendant's "continuing pattern of anti-social behavior," as last traffic offense ten years earlier; also, prosecutor failed to consider such other relevant factors as "the applicant's efforts to seek help for a disorder and the applicant's progress in such program or therapy").

misdemeanors not involving force or violence were ordinarily diverted. The prosecutor declined because it was his policy to deny such treatment to defendants who had chosen to litigate any issues in their case. The trial court found this objectionable and therefore dismissed the charges. On appeal, the court first distinguished this diversion program from that in New Jersey because the former "owes its existence and operation solely to prosecutorial discretion," and then concluded:

"We have no quarrel with the trial court's ruling that a policy intended to deter defendants from exercising their legal rights cannot be tolerated in the name of prosecutorial discretion. We disagree, however, with the court's finding that the defendant has made an adequate showing that the policy questioned here has any such objective or effect. The record makes clear that if a defendant applies for, is accepted into the program, and successfully completes the requisite activities, charges are dropped without his having to go to court, and no conviction or criminal record results.

"The beneficiary of such a disposition of charges against him can scarcely be said to be deterred from exercising his right to defend himself, for, by dismissing such charges, the government has done away with any reason for him to do so. Should the prosecutor deny first offender treatment to a defendant, the latter is in no way barred from then invoking his legal rights and defenses in any manner he chooses. An accused is not prejudiced, therefore, by any official policy that no issues be litigated while his application for diversionary treatment is pending.

" * * * If it is permissible, in plea bargaining, to induce a defendant to plead guilty and waive his right to trial, *a fortiori* no substantial constitutional question is presented when a prosecutor offers to drop all charges provided the accused conforms to certain conditions, including, *inter alia,* foregoing the filing of any motions or pleas in defense."

(c) *Morse v. Municipal Court,* 529 P.2d 46 (Cal.1974): By statute, certain defendants charged with drug offenses could be diverted upon their consent. Defendant, charged with possession of marijuana, moved to suppress the evidence on Fourth Amendment grounds, and only after that motion was denied did he consent to diversion. In the course of rejecting the prosecutor's contention that the consent was untimely, the court commented: "As a practical matter, the People's insistence upon a deferral of suppression motions requires that a defendant choose between potential diversion and the possibility of an immediate dismissal of charges. His opportunity to test the strength of the evidence against him *at the outset* of the case is entirely lost if he elects diversion. Although no loss of constitutional rights thereby occurs in view of the defendant's ability to move to suppress at any later resumption of criminal proceedings by reason of a failure to complete successfully a drug treatment program, such a choice may tend to discourage defendants from consenting to consideration for diversion. As in the case of petitioner, defendants may be wont to try for even a remote chance of dismissal by virtue of the exclusionary rule in lieu of immediately committing themselves to the restrictions imposed by required participation in a rehabilitation program."

4. ***Termination basis.*** If the defendant and prosecutor agree to diversion, is the prosecutor free to renege for any reason? Consider:

(a) *United States v. Bethea,* 483 F.2d 1024 (4th Cir.1973): Defendant claimed his prosecution for failure to report for induction breached an agreement with the United States attorney, who said he would seek dismissal of the case if defendant submitted to induction. Defendant did submit, but the Army refused to induct him upon moral grounds. As to defendant's reliance upon *Santobello v. New York,* p. 1174, the court responded: "The concern of *Santobello* was to protect a defendant who by pleading guilty has surrendered valuable constitutional rights in exchange for the prosecution's assurances. That concern has no application to the facts of this case. Appellant's submission for induction surrendered none of the rights protected by *Santobello*. In the context of this case, Bethea's conduct was at most only a factor to be considered by the prosecutor in deciding whether or not to prosecute, a decision not reviewable here."

(b) *State v. Russo*, 942 A.2d 694 (Me.2008): Defendant and the prosecutor entered into a "filing agreement," approved by the court, whereby an assault charge would be filed for one year and then dropped if defendant complied with all conditions of the agreement (payment of $750, no further criminal activity, no contact with the victim). But shortly thereafter the prosecutor, in response to the victim's objections to such disposition, canceled the agreement and lodged an aggravated assault charge based upon the same incident. Asserting that "[f]iling agreements, like plea agreements, are an essential and desirable part of the criminal justice system," citing *Santobello*, the court concluded defendant was entitled to enforcement of the agreement, by which he "waived his right to a speedy trial and voluntarily subjected himself to the conditions set forth in the agreement."

5. ***Termination procedures.*** "The similar rights at stake in probation revocation, plea bargain agreements, and pretrial diversions persuade us that appellant is entitled to have factual disputes resolved by a neutral fact finder. This includes an independent determination that the deferred prosecution agreement was violated, by a preponderance of the evidence with the burden of proof on the State." *State v. Marino*, 674 P.2d 171 (Wash.1984). Compare *Wood v. United States*, 622 A.2d 67 (D.C.App.1993) (where diversion agreement said termination proper if prosecutor "determines" defendant breached agreement, no due process right to hearing, as termination does not involve "deprivation of a constitutionally protected liberty interest" comparable to that of probationers or parolees).

D. SELECTION OF THE CHARGE

1. ***"Overlapping" statutes.*** UNITED STATES v. BATCHELDER, 442 U.S. 114 (1979), concerned two federal criminal statutes that were "overlapping," in the sense that, while each prohibited convicted felons from receiving firearms, their coverage as to other types of receivers was not identical. After defendant, a previously convicted felon, was charged and convicted under one of these statutes and received the maximum authorized prison term of 5 years, the court of appeals expressed "serious doubts about the constitutionality of two statutes that provide different penalties for identical conduct" and consequently changed the sentence to 2 years, the maximum under the other statute. But a unanimous Supreme Court, per Marshall, J., found "no constitutional infirmities" in the three concerns expressed by the court of appeals.

(1) As for concern that the statutes might be void for vagueness, the Court responded that this was not so, for the two provisions "unambiguously specify the activity proscribed and the penalties available upon conviction" and "create uncertainty as to which crime may be charged and therefore what penalties may be imposed," but "do so to no greater extent than would a single statute authorizing various alternative punishments." (2) As for concern with "avoiding excessive prosecutorial discretion," the Court responded that the prosecutor's "selection of which of two penalties to apply" would not be "unfettered," as the court of appeals claimed, for that discretion was "subject to constitutional restraints" (e.g., equal protection) and, in any event, did not empower the prosecutor to "predetermine ultimate criminal sanctions," as the prosecutor's choice between the two statutes would authorize but not mandate a longer prison term in one instance and a higher fine in the other. (3) As for concern with the impermissible delegation of congressional authority, the Court replied that because the "provisions at issue plainly demarcate the range of penalties that prosecutors and judges may seek and impose," the power delegated to prosecutors "is no broader than the authority they routinely exercise in enforcing the criminal laws."

2. ***Penalty-only distinction.*** It has been suggested that the situation specifically at issue in *Batchelder*, concerning statutes with different total coverage but overlapping as to defendant's

conduct, should be distinguished from a case where instead the two statutes are identical in coverage yet different in the penalties they permit, for in the latter situation "the prosecutor finds not the slightest shred of guidance" in other parts of the statute as to which of the offenses to charge. Comment, 71 J.Crim.L. & C. 226, 236 (1980). Does this mean, contrary to the position generally taken, see, e.g., *State v. Rooney*, 19 A.3d 92 (Vt.2011), that *Batchelder* should be deemed inapplicable in the latter situation?

3. ***Substantial penalty disparity.*** Should *Batchelder* be deemed applicable no matter how dramatic or more certain the disparities between the sentences allowed or required under the two statutes? For example, what of the pre-*Batchelder* case of *Hutcherson v. United States,* 345 F.2d 964 (D.C.Cir.1965), where defendant was prosecuted under the federal statute (providing that a third-time narcotics offender was to be sentenced from 10 to 40 years imprisonment without suspension of sentence) rather than the D.C. statute (providing for imprisonment up to 10 years, with suspension of sentence possible)? The court rejected defendant's due process claim, but Bazelon, C.J., objected: "Here, however, prosecution under Federal rather than District narcotics law precluded any sentence less than ten years. No correction of a prosecutorial 'mistake' would be possible. When the prosecutor 'chooses' a mandatory minimum sentence, he makes a sentencing decision, without either sentencing information or expertise in sentencing."

4. ***Violation of guidelines.*** Judge Bazelon's dissent in *Hutcherson* continued: "Recent instructions from the Attorney General relating to prosecutorial decisions in narcotic cases suggest that the United States Attorney does have certain administrative guidelines for his choice. Thus Title 2, § 86.2–86.3 of the United States Attorneys' Manual provides:

" 'The principal object of enforcement is * * * to prosecute the importers, dealers and traffickers * * *. The emphasis should be on prosecutions of the sellers or purveyors, particularly those who deal with minors, *and not the mere addict possessors.* * * * [C]riminal prosecutions of [addicts] in some instances may be justified so as *to compel an addict to undergo complete [rehabilitative] treatment.* * * * *[P]rosecutions for such minor offenses which are considered to be local in character may well be and often are left to the state or local authorities.* Not falling within such minor category are cases against persons, whether addicts or not, who engage in the importation or transportation or are in possession of these drugs under circumstances reasonably indicating that the drugs were intended for use in the illegal traffic. * * *

" 'In prosecutions for *serious* offenses by *traffickers* * * * *two* counts may be charged, one under the internal revenue laws and the other under [21 U.S.C. § 174].' [Emphasis supplied.] * * *

"These instructions may provide a suitable framework for structuring prosecutorial choice. The reference in the first instructions above to 'minor offenses which are considered to be local in character' suggests use of the 'local' or District statute in the absence of special circumstances. * * *

"I think it would have been open to defendant to attempt to show abuse of prosecutorial discretion on a pretrial motion to dismiss the indictment."

Is Judge Bazelon suggesting that Hutcherson should prevail if he shows the charging decision was not in accordance with the guidelines in the United States Attorneys' Manual? Can this be squared with the reasoning in *United States v. Caceres* (p. 216)? Is it relevant that the Manual states: "This Manual provides only internal Department of Justice guidance. It is not intended to, does not, and may not be relied upon to create any rights, substantive or procedural, enforceable at law by any party in any matter civil or criminal. Nor are any limitations hereby placed on otherwise lawful litigative prerogatives of the Department of Justice."

5. ***Vindictive charge selection.*** A somewhat different situation is where the prosecutor "revises" his charge selection upward following the exercise of some right by the defendant, as in BLACKLEDGE v. PERRY, 417 U.S. 21 (1974). After Perry's conviction of misdemeanor assault in

district court (for which he received a sentence of 6 months), he exercised his right under state law to obtain a trial de novo in the superior court. The applicable statute provided that in such a situation the slate is wiped clean, the prior conviction is annulled, and the prosecution and defense begin anew in the superior court. Prior to Perry's appearance in superior court, the prosecutor obtained an indictment, based on the same conduct for which Perry had been tried, charging him with the felony of assault with a deadly weapon with intent to kill. Perry pleaded guilty[l] to that charge and was sentenced to a term of 5–7 years. Relying upon *North Carolina v. Pearce,* p. 1403 (holding that due process prohibits a judge from imposing a more severe sentence for the purpose of discouraging defendants from exercising their statutory right to appeal), Perry later claimed that the felony charge deprived him of due process. The Court, per Stewart, J., agreed:

"The lesson that emerges from *Pearce* [and its progeny] is that the Due Process Clause is not offended by all possibilities of increased punishment upon retrial after appeal, but only by those that pose a realistic likelihood of 'vindictiveness.' Unlike the circumstances presented by those cases, however, in the situation here the central figure is not the judge or the jury, but the prosecutor. The question is whether the opportunities for vindictiveness in this situation are such as to impel the conclusion that due process of law requires a rule analogous to that of the *Pearce* case. We conclude that the answer must be in the affirmative.

"A prosecutor clearly has a considerable stake in discouraging convicted misdemeanants from appealing and thus obtaining a trial *de novo* in the Superior Court, since such an appeal will clearly require increased expenditures of prosecutorial resources before the defendant's conviction becomes final, and may even result in a formerly convicted defendant going free. And, if the prosecutor has the means readily at hand to discourage such appeals—by 'upping the ante' through a felony indictment whenever a convicted misdemeanant pursues his statutory appellate remedy—the State can insure that only the most hardy defendants will brave the hazards of a *de novo* trial.

"There is, of course, no evidence that the prosecutor in this case acted in bad faith or maliciously in seeking a felony indictment against Perry. The rationale of our judgment in the *Pearce* case, however, was not grounded upon the proposition that actual retaliatory motivation must inevitably exist. Rather, we emphasized that 'since the fear of such vindictiveness may unconstitutionally deter a defendant's exercise of the right to appeal his first conviction, due process also requires that a defendant be freed of apprehension of such a retaliatory motivation on the part of the sentencing judge.' We think it clear that the same considerations apply here. A person convicted of an offense is entitled to pursue his statutory right to a trial *de novo,* without apprehension that the State will retaliate by substituting a more serious charge for the original one thus subjecting him to a significantly increased potential period of incarceration.[m]

"Due process of law requires that such a potential for vindictiveness must not enter into North Carolina's two-tiered appellate process. We old, therefore, that it was not constitutionally

---

l The Court held that the guilty plea did not bar Perry from later raising the due process claim. See *Class v. United States,* p. 1224.

m In *Thigpen v. Roberts,* 468 U.S. 27 (1984), the relevant facts were essentially identical to those in *Blackledge* except that the first trial was the responsibility of the county prosecutor while the indictment and trial on the felony was the responsibility of the district attorney. The Court noted: "It might be argued that if two different prosecutors are involved, a presumption of vindictiveness, which arises in part from assumptions about the individual's personal stake in the proceedings, is inappropriate. On the other hand, to the extent the presumption reflects 'institutional pressure that * * * might * * * subconsciously motivate a vindictive prosecutorial * * * response to a defendant's exercise of his right to obtain a retrial of a decided question,' it does not hinge on the continued involvement of a particular individual. A district attorney burdened with the retrial of an already-convicted defendant might be no less vindictive because he did not bring the initial prosecution." But the Court then found it unnecessary to "determine the correct rule when two independent prosecutors are involved," for here the county prosecutor participated fully in the later proceedings, as was his statutory duty, and thus "the addition of the district attorney to the prosecutorial team changes little."

permissible for the State to respond to Perry's invocation of his statutory right to appeal by bringing a more serious charge against him at the trial *de novo*.[7]"

Rehnquist, J., dissenting, objected: "The prosecutor here elected to proceed initially in the state district court where felony charges could not be prosecuted for reasons which may well have been unrelated to whether he believed respondent was guilty of and could be convicted of the felony with which he was later charged. Both prosecutor and defendant stand to benefit from an initial prosecution in the District Court, the prosecutor at least from its less burdensome procedures and the defendant from the opportunity for an initial acquittal and the limited penalties. With the countervailing reasons for proceeding only on the misdemeanor charge in the District Court no longer applicable once the defendant has invoked his statutory right to a trial *de novo*, a prosecutor need not be vindictive to seek to indict and convict a defendant of the more serious of the two crimes of which he believes him guilty."

6. ***Presumption of vindictiveness.*** Goodwin was charged with several misdemeanor and petty offenses, including assault, and his case was assigned to a Department of Justice attorney detailed temporarily to try such cases before a magistrate and who did not have authority to seek indictments or try felony cases. Goodwin indicated a desire for jury trial, not then available in a trial before a magistrate, so the case was transferred to the district court, where an assistant U.S. Attorney obtained a four-count indictment charging Goodwin with a felony count of forcibly assaulting a federal officer and three related counts. After his conviction of the felony count and a misdemeanor count, Goodwin sought to set aside the verdict on the ground of prosecutorial vindictiveness; the district court denied relief, but the court of appeals reversed, stating that *Blackledge* entitled Goodwin to such relief even though "the prosecutor did not act with actual vindictiveness." In UNITED STATES v. GOODWIN, 457 U.S. 368 (1982), the Court, per Stevens, J., disagreed:

"There is good reason to be cautious before adopting an inflexible presumption of prosecutorial vindictiveness in a pretrial setting. In the course of preparing a case for trial, the prosecutor may uncover additional information that suggests a basis for further prosecution or he simply may come to realize that information possessed by the State has a broader significance. At this stage of the proceedings, the prosecutor's assessment of the proper extent of prosecution may not have crystallized. In contrast, once a trial begins—and certainly by the time a conviction has been obtained—it is much more likely that the State has discovered and assessed all of the information against an accused and has made a determination, on the basis of that information, of the extent to which he should be prosecuted. Thus, a change in the charging decision made after an initial trial is completed is much more likely to be improperly motivated than is a pretrial decision.

"In addition, a defendant before trial is expected to invoke procedural rights that inevitably impose some 'burden' on the prosecutor. Defense counsel routinely file pretrial motions to suppress evidence; to challenge the sufficiency and form of an indictment; to plead an affirmative defense; to request psychiatric services; to obtain access to Government files; to be tried by jury. It is unrealistic to assume that a prosecutor's probable response to such motions is to seek to penalize and to deter. The invocation of procedural rights is an integral part of the adversary process in which our criminal justice system operates.

---

7 This would clearly be a different case if the State had shown that it was impossible to proceed on the more serious charge at the outset, as in *Diaz v. United States,* 223 U.S. 442 (1912). In that case the defendant was originally tried and convicted for assault and battery. Subsequent to the original trial, the assault victim died, and the defendant was then tried and convicted for homicide. Obviously, it would not have been possible for the authorities in *Diaz* to have originally proceeded against the defendant on the more serious charge, since the crime of homicide was not complete until after the victim's death.

"Thus, the timing of the prosecutor's action in this case suggests that a presumption of vindictiveness is not warranted. A prosecutor should remain free before trial to exercise the broad discretion entrusted to him to determine the extent of the societal interest in prosecution. An initial decision should not freeze future conduct. As we made clear in *Bordenkircher* [*v. Hayes,* p. 1160], the initial charges filed by a prosecutor may not reflect the extent to which an individual is legitimately subject to prosecution.

"The nature of the right asserted by the respondent confirms that a presumption of vindictiveness is not warranted in this case. After initially expressing an interest in plea negotiation, respondent decided not to plead guilty and requested a trial by jury in District Court. In doing so, he forced the Government to bear the burdens and uncertainty of a trial. This Court in *Bordenkircher* made clear that the mere fact that a defendant refuses to plead guilty and forces the Government to prove its case is insufficient to warrant a presumption that subsequent changes in the charging decision are unjustified. Respondent argues that such a presumption is warranted in this case, however, because he not only requested a trial—he requested a trial by jury.

"We cannot agree. The distinction between a bench trial and a jury trial does not compel a special presumption of prosecutorial vindictiveness whenever additional charges are brought after a jury is demanded. To be sure, a jury trial is more burdensome than a bench trial. The defendant may challenge the selection of the venire; the jury itself must be impaneled; witnesses and arguments must be prepared more carefully to avoid the danger of a mistrial. These matters are much less significant, however, than the facts that before either a jury or a judge the State must present its full case against the accused and the defendant is entitled to offer a full defense. As compared to the complete trial *de novo* at issue in *Blackledge* a jury trial—as opposed to a bench trial—does not require duplicative expenditures of prosecutorial resources before a final judgment may be obtained. Moreover, unlike the trial judge in *Pearce,* no party is asked 'to do over what it thought it had already done correctly.' A prosecutor has no 'personal stake' in a bench trial and thus no reason to engage in 'self-vindication' upon a defendant's request for a jury trial. Perhaps most importantly, the institutional bias against the retrial of a decided question that supported the decisions in *Pearce* and *Blackledge* simply has no counterpart in this case.

"There is an opportunity for vindictiveness, [but] a mere opportunity for vindictiveness is insufficient to justify the imposition of a prophylactic rule. As *Blackledge* makes clear, 'the Due Process Clause is not offended by all possibilities of increased punishment * * * but only by those that pose a realistic likelihood of "vindictiveness." ' The possibility that a prosecutor would respond to a defendant's pretrial demand for a jury trial by bringing charges not in the public interest that could be explained only as penalty imposed on the defendant is so *unlikely* that a presumption of vindictiveness certainly is not warranted.

"In declining to apply a presumption of vindictiveness, we of course do not foreclose the possibility that a defendant in an appropriate case might prove objectively that the prosecutor's charging decision was motivated by a desire to punish him for doing something that the law plainly allowed him to do."

Blackmun, J., concurring in the judgment, found "no support in our prior cases for any distinction between pretrial and post-trial vindictiveness," but concluded there had been a permissible adjustment of the charges "based on 'objective information concerning identifiable conduct on the part of the defendant occurring after the time of the original' charging decision."[n]

---

[n] In support he referred to footnote 2 of the majority opinion, reading: "By affidavit, the Assistant United States Attorney later set forth his reasons for this action: (1) he considered respondent's conduct on the date in question to be a serious violation of law, (2) Goodwin had a lengthy history of violent crime, (3) the prosecutor considered respondent's conduct to be related to major narcotics transactions, (4) the prosecutor believed that respondent had committed perjury at his preliminary hearing, and (5) Goodwin had failed to appear for trial as

Brennan, J., joined by Marshall, J., dissenting, objected: "The Court suggests that the distinction between a bench trial and a jury trial is unimportant in this context. Such a suggestion is demonstrably fallacious. Experienced criminal practitioners, for both prosecution and defense, know that a jury trial entails far more prosecutorial work than a bench trial. Defense challenges to the potential-juror array, *voir dire* examination of potential jurors, and suppression hearings all take up a prosecutor's time before a jury trial, adding to his scheduling difficulties and caseload. More care in the preparation of his requested instructions, of is witnesses, and of his own remarks is necessary in order to avoid mistrial or reversible error. And there is always the specter of the 'irrational' acquittal by a jury that is unreviewable on appeal. Thus it is simply inconceivable that a criminal defendant's election to be tried by jury would be a matter of indifference to his prosecutor. On the contrary, the prosecutor would almost always prefer that the defendant waive such a 'troublesome' right. And if the defendant refuses to do so, the prosecutor's subsequent elevation of the charges against the defendant manifestly poses a realistic likelihood of vindictiveness."

7. **Goodwin *applied.*** What would be the proper application of *Goodwin* on these facts, from *United States v. LaDeau*, 734 F.3d 561 (6th Cir.2013)? LaDeau was indicted on a single count of possessing child pornography, punishable by a sentence range of zero to ten years. LaDeau moved pretrial to suppress evidence that he had any such materials in his possession; the motion was granted, which "eviscerated the government's possession case" and "eliminated its ability to prosecute the charge alleged in the first indictment." This left the government with three charging options: (1) conspiracy to possess child pornography, in violation of 18 U.S.C. § 2252A(b)(2), punishable by zero to ten years; (2) conspiracy to receive child pornography, in violation of 18 U.S.C. § 2252A(b)(2), punishable by five to twenty years; or (3) conspiracy to receive or possess child pornography, in violation of the general conspiracy statute, 18 U.S.C. § 371, punishable by zero to five years. The government opted for the second alternative, "based on evidence that had been in the government's possession since before the initial indictment."

8. ***Overcoming the presumption.*** In a situation where *Blackledge* does apply, may a prosecutor escalate the charge only in the particular situation described in footnote 7 of that case? Of what significance is it that the Court has more recently stated in *Goodwin* that the *Blackledge* presumption "could be overcome by objective evidence justifying the prosecutor's action"? That in *Texas v. McCullough*, p. 1404, the Court declared that if the *Pearce* presumption were applicable there it could be overcome "by objective information * * * justifying the increased sentence"?

9. ***Vindictiveness by others.*** Consider *United States v. Spears*, 159 F.3d 1081 (7th Cir.1998), stating that a vindictive motive by an investigative agency "will not be imputed to a federal prosecutor" and that, likewise, if there was a prior state prosecution a vindictive motive by the state prosecutor in then seeking federal prosecution is not sufficient as to a subsequent federal prosecution absent evidence it was the *state* prosecutor who "actually made the decision to prosecute * * * in federal court." Cf. *Hartman v. Moore*, 547 U.S. 250 (2006) (where federal prosecution brought at urging of postal inspectors, against whom person unsuccessfully prosecuted brought § 1983 action claiming "they had engineered the prosecution in retaliation for his lobbying efforts," in such circumstances plaintiff must plead and show the absence of probable cause for pressing the underlying criminal charges, as "a retaliatory motive on the part of an official urging prosecution combined with an absence of probable cause supporting the prosecutor's decision to go forward are reasonable grounds to suspect the presumption of regularity behind the charging decision * * *, and enough for a prima facie inference that the unconstitutionally motivated inducement infected the prosecutor's decision to bring the charge").

---

originally scheduled. The Government attorney stated that his decision to seek a felony indictment was not motivated in any way by Goodwin's request for a jury trial in District Court."

10. *Breach of agreement.* Sometimes the charges are not escalated, but yet are not reduced as the prosecutor earlier indicated would be done. Illustrative is *People v. Navarroli,* 521 N.E.2d 891 (Ill.1988), where, at a hearing on defendant's motion for specific performance, it was established (i) that after defendant was charged with three drug offenses the prosecutor promised a reduction in the charges if defendant would act as an informant in various drug investigations, and (ii) that defendant had fully performed his portion of the agreement. The lower court granted the motion, but on appeal it was decided that the prosecutor's "refusal to carry out the claimed bargain did not deprive the defendant of due process, and that therefore, the defendant was not entitled to have the assumed agreement enforced." The court distinguished *Santobello v. New York,* p. 1174, as a case where "the prosecutor breached the plea agreement after the defendant entered a plea of guilty," and asserted that in the instant case "the defendant has not entered a plea of guilty in reliance on the proposed plea agreement. He cannot say he was deprived of liberty by virtue of the State's refusal to abide by the terms of the claimed plea agreement." As for defendant's assertion that "he performed his part of the bargain in reliance on the agreement, making restoration of the pre-plea-agreement status impossible," the court responded that because "the defendant still has the option of pleading not guilty and going to trial," it could not be said "that specific performance of the bargain is the only adequate remedy."

A dissent declared that from a contracts perspective the majority was in error because it ignored the fact that the defendant provided "actual consideration" when "he provided the State with new information," and that from a public policy perspective the majority's conclusion was unsound because now "a prosecutor's promise to reduce the charges for a defendant in exchange for the defendant's assistance will not be enforceable; few informed defendants will aid the prosecution in return for a promise when they know that it is not enforceable by a trial court."

Query, does the *Navarroli* majority or dissent have the better of the argument? Consider *People v. Boyt,* 488 N.E.2d 264 (Ill.1985) (defendant agreed to testify against her codefendant in exchange for the state's promise to reduce the charge against her, but before defendant could testify the codefendant pleaded guilty, so the state refused to reduce the charges; held, defendant has no right to enforce the agreement, as the state's repudiation deprived defendant of no constitutionally protected interest);[o] and *People v. Starks,* 478 N.E.2d 350 (Ill.1985) (defendant submitted to polygraph examination in exchange for prosecutor's promise to dismiss charges against him if he passed the test; held, when defendant passed the test he was entitled to enforcement of the agreement, as he had surrendered his Fifth Amendment privilege against self-incrimination as part of the agreement). The *Navarroli* majority found the instant case more like *Boyt* than *Starks,* while the dissent reached the exact opposite conclusion.

Some jurisdictions follow the approach of the *Navarroli* dissent, so that a prosecutor's promise to reduce (or even drop) charges in exchange for some consideration provided by the defendant, even if not involving surrender of a constitutional right, is enforceable if the defendant has kept his side of the bargain. Illustrative is *Bowers v. State*, 500 N.E.2d 203 (Ind.1986), where, following defendant's arrest for burglary, the prosecutor entered into an agreement with him to dismiss charges related to defendant's arrest if defendant would provide information sufficient to obtain a search warrant for the residence of another person, as he did. What if Bowers had struck that agreement with the *police*? Cf. *United States v. Flemmi*, 225 F.3d 78 (1st Cir.2000).

---

[o] In *Boyt,* what if the codefendant did not plead guilty but instead opted for trial and then claimed the testimony should be suppressed because improperly induced? Cf. *United States v. Singleton,* 165 F.3d 1297 (10th Cir.1999), where the court rejected the contention that the government had violated 18 U.S.C.A. § 201(c)(2), which makes it a criminal offense to give or offer "anything of value to any person for or because of the testimony under oath or affirmation given or to be given by such person as a witness upon a trial." The court concluded that given the "longstanding" and "ingrained" practice of granting leniency in exchange for testimony, reading the statute as restricting that power would be "a diminution of sovereignty not countenanced in our jurisprudence."

CHAPTER 15

THE PRELIMINARY HEARING

■ ■ ■

The preliminary hearing is an adversary hearing at which the magistrate court determines whether the evidence presented by the prosecution, as challenged by the defense, is sufficient to send the prosecution on to the next step in the process.[a] States typically provide for a preliminary hearing only on felony charges, so that next step will either be a grand jury determination as to whether to indict (in states requiring prosecution by indictment) or the prosecutor's filing of an information in the court of general trial jurisdiction (in states allowing prosecution by information). Section one addresses the availability of the preliminary hearing; it is not a guaranteed right under the federal constitution, and variations in state law and practice produce substantial differences among the states in the availability of the hearing. If a preliminary hearing is held, the defense can use it for various purposes other than simply challenging evidentiary sufficiency, and defense strategies vary in implementing such uses. Section two discusses these different defense uses and the extent to which they are acknowledged in different aspects of the law governing preliminary hearings. Sections three and four look at the key structural elements of preliminary hearings and state variations in shaping those elements. Section three focuses on standards that relate to the magistrate's determination as to whether to send the prosecution on to the next stage (the "bindover determination"), and section four considers the procedural rules applied in the preliminary hearing.

§ 1. THE DEFENDANT'S RIGHT TO A PRELIMINARY HEARING

1. ***Independent screening and the federal constitution.*** *Hurtado v. California,* 110 U.S. 516 (1884), was the first in a series of cases considering the contention that the federal constitution requires a pretrial screening of the prosecution's proposed charge by a neutral agency to ensure that there is adequate evidentiary support for that charge. In *Hurtado,* the defendant argued that the Fourteenth Amendment due process clause required such screening by a grand jury through its incorporation of the Fifth Amendment requirement that felony prosecutions be instituted only by grand jury indictment. For reasons discussed at p. 946, the Court rejected defendant's contention. It held that the Fifth Amendment guarantee of prosecution by indictment was *not* a fundamental right, and therefore was not applicable to the states through the due process clause of the Fourteenth Amendment.

The California procedure challenged in *Hurtado* provided for charging by prosecutor's information, rather than by indictment, but it also required a magistrate's initial determination that probable cause existed, made at what was essentially a preliminary hearing. It therefore was not clear from *Hurtado* whether due process permitted a state to dispense with all forms of independent screening or just screening by a grand jury. Although there traditionally had been no screening procedure for misdemeanor offenses, states commonly required either an indictment or

[a] While most states refer to this hearing as the "preliminary hearing," other commonly used descriptions include "preliminary examination," "probable cause hearing," "commitment hearing" and "bindover hearing" (the decision to send the case forward commonly being described as a "bindover"). This hearing should be distinguished from the ex parte magistrate determination as to whether there is probable cause to arrest, which is made at or before the first appearance and commonly is called the "*Gerstein* review." See step 7 in Ch. 1, § 2.

a magistrate's preliminary hearing bindover for a felony prosecution. In *Lem Woon v. Oregon,* 229 U.S. 586 (1913), the elimination of all screening procedures was squarely presented by an Oregon procedure permitting direct filing of an information without "any examination, or commitment by a magistrate * * * or any verification other than [the prosecutor's] official oath." A unanimous Court held that the Oregon procedure did not violate due process. Justice Pitney's opinion for the Court relied primarily upon the reasoning of *Hurtado.* It rejected as "untenable" an attempt to distinguish *Hurtado* on the ground that the California procedure upheld there required an initial finding of probable cause by the magistrate. The *Lem Woon* opinion noted: "[T]his court has * * * held [that] the 'due process of law' clause does not require the State to adopt the institution and procedure of a grand jury, [and] we are unable to see upon what theory it can be held that an examination or the opportunity for one, prior to the formal accusation by the district attorney, is obligatory upon the States."

In *Gerstein v. Pugh,* 420 U.S. 103 (1975), the Court also rejected the contention that a preliminary hearing was required by the Fourth Amendment. The Court there held that the Fourth Amendment "requires a judicial determination of probable cause as a prerequisite to extended restraint following arrest," but added that such determination may be made ex parte, in a fashion similar to a judge issuing an arrest warrant. Justice Stewart, in a concurring opinion, asked why the Constitution "extends less procedural protection" to an arrested person who might not gain his release prior to trial than to defendants in civil cases, held to be constitutionally entitled to an adversary pretrial hearing on the plaintiff's temporary seizure of their property to secure any future judgment. Justice Powell, speaking for the Court, responded that the "historical basis of the probable cause requirement is quite different from the relatively recent application of variable procedural due process in debtor-creditor disputes," and that the Fourth Amendment had always been thought "to define the 'process that is due' for seizure of person or property in criminal cases."

The *Gerstein* Court specifically reaffirmed *Lem Woon,* noting that

> In holding that the prosecutor's assessment of probable cause is not sufficient alone to justify restraint on liberty pending trial, we do not imply that the accused is entitled to judicial oversight or review of the decision to prosecute. Instead, we adhere to the Court's prior holding that a judicial hearing is not prerequisite to prosecution by information. * * * *Lem Woon v. Oregon.*

Justice Powell saw no need to further explore why procedural due process does not protect the criminal defendant from the significant burdens imposed upon him apart from the seizure of his person (i.e., the burdens of accusation and litigation) and therefore require some form of independent screening that is not tied to that Fourth Amendment concern. *Albright v. Oliver*, 510 U.S. 266 (1994), did not address that issue, but it did address a closely related issue: why substantive due process fails to protect an individual even against the burdens of a baseless prosecution. *Albright* rejected a civil rights action brought by a former criminal defendant (Albright) who claimed that a police detective (Oliver) had instituted charges against him based solely on information received from an informant known to be unreliable. Albright alleged that Oliver had relied on that information initially to have Albright arrested, and then to have the charge against Albright sustained at a preliminary hearing. Following the later dismissal of the charge (as failing to state an offense under state law), Albright filed his civil rights action, basing his claim entirely on substantive due process, with no reference to possible violations of the Fourth Amendment or procedural due process. The Supreme Court majority (7–2) rejected that claim.

Four justices in the majority concluded that the defendant could not look to due process, as substantive due process is not available where the Constitution "otherwise provides * * * an explicit textual source of constitutional protection" and here the Fourth Amendment addresses relief for deprivations accompanying the charging of a defendant without probable cause; *Gerstein* had recognized "the Fourth Amendment's relevance to the deprivations that go hand in hand with criminal prosecutions." Another justice in the majority viewed Fourth Amendment doctrine as controlling where (as here) the arrest coincided with the charging, but noted that a baseless prosecution could present a separate due process issue "where some quantum of harm occurs in the interim after groundless charges are filed but before any Fourth Amendment seizure." The final two justices in the majority concluded that being prosecuted presents personal interests that are separate from Fourth Amendment interests and could be protected by substantive due process. However, due process was not violated here because due process, read in light of the common law, simply does not impose a "standard * * * for the initiation of prosecution" (indeed, they noted, even the Fifth Amendment's grand jury clause does not prescribe such a standard—as evidenced by *Costello*, p. 957).

2. ***Independent screening: state law alternatives.*** Although not required to do so by the federal constitution, all but a handful of states (discussed below) provide a defense right to evidentiary review of the prosecution's case, by either a magistrate at a preliminary hearing or a grand jury in considering an indictment, for all felony charges (and in a few states, for more serious misdemeanors that are triable in the trial court of general jurisdiction). These states require for a felony prosecution (absent a defense waiver) either an indictment issued by grand jury or a prosecutor's information supported by a preliminary hearing finding of sufficient evidence (a magistrate's "bindover"). Notes 4 and 5, infra, describe the law and practice that largely determine whether one or the other (or both of these screenings) will be used in a particular case. They discuss separately the law and practice in: (1) states which require prosecution by indictment, and (2) states which allow prosecution by information, as that distinction tends to produce different legal and practice patterns.

Direct filing. A handful of states do not require prosecution by indictment and allow prosecution by information without the support of a preliminary hearing bindover. The procedure followed by those states is commonly described as "direct filing," as the prosecution files the information "directly" (i.e., without a preliminary hearing bindover).[b] This procedure finds its roots in the procedure upheld in *Lem Woon*, but today provides for a judicial review of the grounding for the information more extensive than that involved in *Lem Woon*. In some direct-filing states, judicial screening is mandated prior to filing the information and consists basically of an *ex parte* judicial determination of whether probable cause exists. That determination is based upon a prosecutor's affidavit summarizing the available evidence, although the judge has authority to ask for a further presentation of evidence. The review tends to be similar to the *Gerstein* review (see fn. a, supra), but the sufficiency determination relates to proceeding with the prosecution rather than justifying the arrest. In others, the screening is introduced at the option of the defendant when the defendant makes a motion to dismiss the information. That motion is presented after defendant has obtained complete discovery of the prosecution's evidence (including the use of depositions in two states), allowing the motion to operate in a fashion roughly similar to the motion for summary judgment in civil cases. Having before it a complete picture of the evidence, the court determines whether, if the case should go to trial, the prosecution's evidence would survive a motion for directed verdict of acquittal. Proponents of this procedure argue that it is preferable to the preliminary hearing because it: (1) concentrates on screening, and leaves the other functions associated with preliminary hearings (see § 2 infra) to procedures specifically designed to serve those functions; (2) is far less time consuming and less expensive, as motions are made only in the small percentage of cases where some question exists as to the sufficiency of the evidence to proceed (usually because of a total lack of evidence on a particular element of the

[b] Not all direct filing states have eliminated the preliminary hearing. Some provide for a preliminary hearing, but give the prosecution the option of "bypassing" the preliminary hearing by direct filing. In those states, prosecutors will commonly use the bypass, but may prefer the preliminary hearing in particular cases for the reasons discussed in Note 6(b).

crime); (3) comes at a time when the court can gain a better picture of the full case; and (4) avoids issues of credibility, which are appropriately for the jury to decide. Proponents of the preliminary hearing respond that such an alternative procedure fails to provide prompt relief for those improperly charged and loses the advantages of subjecting witnesses to cross-examination.

3. ***Preliminary hearings in the federal system.*** The basic federal statutory provision on the defendant's right to a preliminary hearing is contained in the Federal Magistrate's Act, 18 U.S.C. § 3060. See also Fed.R.Crim.P. 5.1 (largely duplicating that provision). Section 3060 initially provides for a preliminary hearing in all felony cases, to be held (unless waived) within "a reasonable time following initial appearance, but in any event not later than (1) the tenth day following * * * the initial appearance * * * [if the arrested person remains in custody] or (2) the twentieth day following * * * initial appearance if the arrested person is released from custody * * *." It then adds, however, a critical proviso: "No preliminary examination * * * shall be required to be accorded an arrested person * * * if at [a] time * * * prior to the date fixed for the preliminary examination * * * an indictment is returned * * * against such person." See also Fed.R.Crim.P. 5.1(a).[c]

The § 3060 proviso restated the position that federal courts had reached under earlier versions of the Federal Rules that made no reference to the impact of intervening indictments. In a long line of decisions, the federal courts had held that the issuance of an indictment rendered "moot" the defendant's statutory right to a preliminary hearing. As stated in *Sciortino v. Zampano,* 385 F.2d 132 (2d Cir.1967): "The return of an indictment, which establishes probable cause, eliminates the need for a preliminary examination. * * * A post-indictment preliminary examination would be an empty ritual, as the government's burden of showing probable cause would be met merely by offering the indictment. Even if the [magistrate] disagreed with the grand jury, he could not undermine the authority of its finding." The practical impact of the § 3060 proviso has been to eliminate virtually all preliminary hearings. Even where grand juries do not sit daily, the U.S. Attorney is able to regularly bypass the preliminary hearing by obtaining indictments within the time frames set forth in § 3060 and Rule 5.1.

4. ***Indictment states.*** Eighteen states, as in the federal system, require prosecution by indictment (unless waived) for all felonies (see fn. b, p. 946). All of these "indictment states" also have statutes or court rules granting the defendant a right to a preliminary hearing within a specified period after his arrest. The language of the provisions, or judicial interpretations, commonly allows bypassing by obtaining an indictment within a specific time frame, just as in the federal system. While the use of bypassing varies from one prosecutorial district to another, bypassing as frequently as in the federal system is rare.

In many prosecutorial districts in indictment states, preliminary hearings are commonly available in all but a small group of exceptional cases. In some of these districts, regular mooting would not be feasible since the grand jury meets too infrequently or its caseload is too heavy to regularly obtain indictments prior to the scheduled preliminary hearing. In others, prompt grand jury review is feasible, but prosecutors have decided against regularly bypassing the preliminary hearing. In some instances, that decision may be attributed to a tradition dating back to a time when prompt grand jury review was not available. In others, it may reflect a determination that the additional costs of a preliminary hearing are more than offset by various advantages for the prosecution (e.g., the better preparation of witnesses and the facilitation of plea negotiations). Other prosecutors in the same states favor holding preliminary hearings for much the same reasons, but view administrative and other factors as justifying bypassing in a more substantial group of cases, not just the exceptional case. See Note 6(b), (c), infra.

[c] While Rule 5.1(a) repeats the exemption of § 3060's proviso, Rule 5.1(a) also contains four other exemptions. Those exemptions, however, either require a waiver or apply only to misdemeanors, and therefore are also in accord with § 3060.

On the other side, many prosecutors in indictment states view the preliminary hearing as generally undesirable, either because of the benefits it affords the defense or because they believe that it generally is a waste of prosecutorial resources. This typically leads to bypassing in the vast majority of cases, while recognizing exceptions for certain classes of cases based upon the factors cited in Note 6(a), infra. The breadth of those exceptions may result in preliminary hearings in a significant portion of the felony docket (e.g., 20%) or only in a very small portion of the docket (e.g., 2%).

5. ***Information states.*** Thirty-two states permit felony prosecutions to be brought by information (although four deny that option as to capital offenses alone, or as to both capital and life-imprisonment offenses, where they require prosecution by indictment). Only a handful of those states have legal requirements that preclude bypassing via grand jury indictment (either by eliminating indicting grand juries or granting a right to a preliminary hearing notwithstanding an indictment). On the other side, a handful allow bypassing by direct filing of an information, which tends to be used regularly. See Note 2, supra. For a substantial majority of the information states, bypassing is available only through a prior indictment and whether it is used depends upon the choice of the local prosecutor. With the exception of one state, in the vast majority of the prosecutorial districts in these states, prosecutors either never use bypassing or using it sparingly. Preliminary hearings are available for all felony prosecutions (a grand jury has not been used in decades), or for almost all felony prosecutions (see Note 6(b), infra). However, in some of these information states, one or more prosecutors, almost always in a large metropolitan district, will choose the convenience of the grand jury process and bypass in almost all cases (see Note 6(a), infra). So too, in some of those states, a small group of prosecutors, also in metropolitan districts, will use bypassing for a significant but lesser portion of the felony docket (typically identified by the type of crime, see Note 6(c)).

6. ***Prosecutorial discretion.*** (a) *Bypassing in all but exceptional cases.* Where prosecutors have the capacity to bypass preliminary hearings on a regular basis, and ordinarily favor that approach, what factors identify the exceptional cases in which prosecutors allow the defendant the option to have a preliminary hearing (or even insist upon the hearing, where the prosecutor can force a hearing over a defense waiver)? CRIMPROC § 14.2(c) notes that the exceptions are likely to be based on one or more of the following "special circumstances": (1) to perpetuate the testimony of a witness who might well be unavailable at trial; (2) some special reason for putting a prosecution witness to the test of testifying in public; (3) promoting the victim's interest in pursuing the matter by presenting it in a public forum; (4) gaining the defense perspective as to the events involved where there is some uncertainty as to what actually happened and the defense has indicated a willingness to present its side of the story at a preliminary hearing; (5) gaining a further eyewitness identification of the suspect by having the witness make that identification at the hearing; (6) lending support to defense counsel's recommendation that the defendant accept a guilty plea offer by educating the defendant as to strength of the prosecution's case and the firm commitment of the victim (see Note 7, p. 925); (7) promoting public confidence in a sensitive prosecutorial decision by having the government's evidence presented in a public forum and the decision to proceed ratified by a magistrate (or if the case is likely to be dismissed, by inviting dismissal in an open proceeding rather than a grand jury proceeding, where the prosecutor might be accused of having "dumped" the case due to political pressure).[d]

---

[d] Where the prosecutor believes the evidence is insufficient to bindover, using the preliminary to ensure that the public is satisfied with the decision not to proceed presents an ethical obstacle; the preliminary hearing is available only upon filing a complaint and that ethically requires a belief that probable cause exists. See Note 5, p. 872. The same obstacle does not arise in presenting the case to the grand jury. The basic function of grand jury screening permits the prosecution to ask it to screen (and possibly override) the prosecutor's conclusion that the evidence is insufficient to indict. Cf. ABA Standards §§ 3–4.6(a) (Note 5, p. 976). So too, where the prosecutor is

(b) *Bypassing only in exceptional cases.* Critics of the bypass procedure often contend that bypassing is used where the prosecution recognizes that its evidence is weak and prefers the "easier route" of grand jury screening. Available studies do not support that contention, particularly as to districts in which the bypass procedure is used in only a small percentage of cases (reflecting "exceptional-case bypassing"). See CRIMPROC § 14.2(c). The prime candidates for exceptional bypassing are cases in which: (1) a grand jury investigation develops the evidence (with the grand jury taking the investigation to the final step, the indictment, even where the prosecutor might have the authority to remove the case at that point and proceed by information); (2) the prospective defendant is a fugitive and therefore any preliminary hearing would have to be postponed indefinitely; (3) the prospective defendant is outside the jurisdiction and the formal charge (provided by the indictment) facilitates extradition; and (4) there is a need not to reveal publicly at this point some aspect of the prosecution's case (e.g., protecting an ongoing investigation or avoiding a disclosure that might impact the ability to select a jury).

(c) *More substantial bypassing.* Where bypassing is not the norm, but is used in more than exceptional cases, the selection process does focus on indictment alternatives being the "easier" route, but typically easier for reasons other than gaining a charge in a weaker case. The primary considerations here tend to be: (1) the desire to save time where the preliminary hearing would be protracted due to the number of exhibits or witnesses or the number of separate hearings that would have to be held for separate defendants (the grand jury could save time in such situations due to the absence of cross-examination, less stringent application of evidentiary rules, and its capacity to consider a series of related cases in a single presentation); (2) the desire to avoid some aspect of the defense discovery inherent in a preliminary hearing (see Note 6, p. 925); and (3) the desire to limit the number of times that a particular type of complainant (e.g., a victim of a sex offense) will be required to give testimony in public.

§ 2. DEFENSE BENEFITS AND STRATEGIES

A. JUDICIAL RECOGNITION OF MULTIPLE DEFENSE USES

1. ***The influence of* Coleman.** In COLEMAN v. ALABAMA, 399 U.S. 1 (1970), a divided Court (6–2) held that the Sixth Amendment rights of indigent defendants were violated by the state's failure to appoint counsel to assist them at their preliminary hearings. Though the state had no constitutional obligation to provide a preliminary hearing, once it did so, the Sixth Amendment right to the assistance of counsel applied. All states subsequently moved to providing indigents with appointed counsel at preliminary hearings, but the influence of *Coleman* extended substantially beyond that single issue. The *Coleman* majority, as discussed below, recognized that the preliminary hearing could be used by the defense for more purposes than challenging the evidentiary sufficiency of the prosecution's case. State courts, in turn, took note of such additional defense uses, and began to ask whether they should play a role in shaping the procedures at a preliminary hearing (see Note 8 infra). *Coleman* also raised the issue, as discussed in Pt. B infra, as to what role those defense uses should play in determining an appellate court's response, upon

---

uncertain about proceeding because of critical credibility issues, the prosecutor may prefer grand jury screening since the grand jury is a lay body, reflecting the likely perspective of a petit jury, and has full authority to judge credibility, in contrast to the magistrate at the preliminary hearing (see Note 5, p. 933). The primary difficulty in relying upon the grand jury as a buffer against public criticism of a non-prosecution is the secrecy requirement that precludes disclosure of the evidence considered by the grand jury. The controversial Ferguson, Missouri grand jury proceeding involving a police shooting was unique in this regard because state law there did not preclude prosecutor disclosure of the grand jury transcripts. A California statute prohibiting a prosecutor from using grand jury screening rather than preliminary hearing screening where police use of force led to a fatal injury was held unconstitutional in *People v. Superior Court of El Dorado County*, 7 Cal.App. 5th 402 (2017) (statute violates state constitutional provision that authorized prosecution by grand jury as an alternative to prosecution by information).

review following a conviction, to error in the preliminary hearing. Here too, *Coleman* led to a reconsideration of state standards.

Coleman considered the multiple uses of a preliminary hearing in the course of determining whether the preliminary hearing was a "critical stage" of the criminal prosecution, which was a prerequisite for requiring the assistance of counsel in a pretrial proceeding. See Pt. B, p. 80. The critical-stage test required the *Coleman* Court to ask whether the assistance of counsel at Alabama's preliminary hearing "[was] necessary to preserve the defendant's basic right to a fair trial as affected by his right meaningfully to cross-examine the witnesses against him and to have effective assistance of counsel at the trial itself." The Court majority was not persuaded by the argument of the state (and the dissenters) that counsel was not needed because state law ensured that the defendant would not be harmed by any defects in his self-representation at the hearing: his failure to raise a particular defense or objection would not preclude raising that defense or objection at trial; any testimony presented against him (including any admissions in his own testimony) would not be admissible against him at trial; and the determination as to whether there was sufficient evidence to charge ultimately rested with the grand jury. Speaking for the majority on this issue, Justice Brennan responded:

"[F]rom the fact that in cases where the accused has no lawyer at the hearing the Alabama Courts prohibit the State's use at trial of anything that occurred at the hearing, it does not follow that the Alabama preliminary hearing is not a 'critical stage' * * *. Plainly the guiding hand of counsel at the preliminary hearing is essential to protect the indigent accused against an erroneous or improper prosecution. First, the lawyer's skilled examination and cross-examination of witnesses may expose fatal weaknesses in the State's case that may lead the magistrate to refuse to bind the accused over. Second, in any event, the skilled interrogation of witnesses by an experienced lawyer can fashion a vital impeachment tool for use in cross-examination of the State's witnesses at the trial, or preserve testimony favorable to the accused of a witness who does not appear at the trial. Third, trained counsel can more effectively discover the case the State has against his client and make possible the preparation of a proper defense to meet that case at the trial. Fourth, counsel can also be influential at the preliminary hearing in making effective arguments for the accused on such matters as the necessity for an early psychiatric examination or bail. The inability of the indigent accused on his own to realize these advantages of a lawyer's assistance compels the conclusion that the Alabama preliminary hearing is a 'critical stage' of the State's criminal process at which the accused is 'as much entitled to such aid [of counsel] * * * as at the trial itself.' "

2. ***Challenging evidentiary sufficiency.*** Although the purpose of the preliminary hearing is to determine whether there is sufficient evidence to "bind the case over," defense strategy often will not include any effort to challenge the evidentiary sufficiency beyond making a *pro forma* motion to dismiss. The focus, instead, will be on the other potential benefits of the preliminary hearing. The most significant factor in deciding whether to actively challenge the evidentiary sufficiency will be the likely strength and character of the prosecution's evidence. However, variations in the structural elements of the preliminary hearing may bear upon that assessment, including: (1) differences in the standard of proof needed for a bindover (see Notes 1–4, pp. 932–933); (2) whether the magistrate has authority to judge credibility (see Note 5, p. 933); (3) what limitations are placed upon the scope of the defense's cross-examination of prosecution witnesses (see Notes 2, 3, pp. 939–941); and (4) what limitations are placed upon the defense's capacity to present its own witnesses (see Notes 1–3, pp. 942–944).[a]

[a] The evidentiary review provided by the preliminary hearing arguably has increased significance in a criminal justice system now dominated by guilty pleas. The right to a preliminary hearing, particularly a mini-trial hearing (see Note 2, p. 932) is seen as a key safeguard against the prosecutorial practice of "factual overreaching" in the charging and plea negotiation process. See Crespo, The Hidden Law of Plea Bargaining, 118 Colum.L.Rev. 1303 (2018) (stressing particularly the right to cross-examine the prosecution's witnesses "where the prosecutor is

3. ***The rate of successful challenges.*** Studies of the preliminary hearings in different judicial districts (typically involving different states) report quite disparate statistics on the percentage of preliminary hearings that produce a dismissal of felony charges. That percentage has ranged from a low of 2% to a high of 33%. See CRIMPROC § 14.1(a). However, a higher percentage does not necessarily indicate that the hearing provides a superior screening device as compared to the hearing in a jurisdiction with a lower percentage. A series of institutional factors also can contribute to substantial differences in dismissal rates. These include: (1) whether prosecutorial screening before cases reach the preliminary hearing stage is extensive (as in jurisdictions where 30–50% of the felony cases presented by the police do not result in the filing of felony charges) or is superficial or not even utilized for all but exceptional cases; (2) whether the prosecutor most often bypasses the preliminary hearing by taking cases directly to the grand jury (so that preliminary hearing cases constitute a minor portion of the total docket); (3) whether the use of the bypass procedure is tied to the strength of the particular case; (4) whether the caseload at the trial level necessarily precludes trial of all cases which could justifiably be boundover (thereby encouraging the magistrate to either dismiss the felony charges or reduce charges to lesser-included misdemeanors in cases more appropriately disposed of at the misdemeanor level); (5) whether cases commonly are settled by plea bargains prior to the preliminary hearing stage (weeding out many open-and-shut cases) or plea bargaining begins and cases are settled largely after the case reaches the trial level court; (6) whether defense counsel regularly insist upon a preliminary hearing even in strong prosecution cases (largely to obtain discovery) or usually waive the hearing in such cases; and (7) whether the prosecution, even though not required to do so in order to satisfy the bindover standard, follows the practice of presenting all of its key witnesses, or instead seeks to limit defense discovery and reduce the burden on its witnesses by introducing just enough evidence to meet the bindover standard.

4. ***Laying the groundwork for future impeachment.*** As Justice Brennan noted in *Coleman*, the skillful extraction of statements from a witness at the preliminary hearing may provide a solid foundation for effective cross-examination of that witness at trial. In many instances, witnesses are more likely to make damaging admissions or contradictory statements at the preliminary hearing because they are less thoroughly briefed for that proceeding than they are for trial. Also, with respect to some witnesses, the more they say before trial, the more likely that there will be some inconsistency between their trial testimony and their previous statements. Arguably, such inconsistencies may have a more damaging impact upon the witness' credibility when the inconsistency is with preliminary hearing testimony, as opposed to unsworn statements given to the police during interviews. Of course, cross-examination designed to lay the foundation for future impeachment carries with it certain dangers for the defense. If the cross-examination focuses too much on potential weaknesses in the witness' testimony, it may educate the witness as to those weaknesses. The witness may then attempt to rehabilitate himself at trial by stating that he was confused at the hearing, that caused him to review the events, and he now has everything clear in his mind. If the witness is one who otherwise might "soften" his view of the facts as time passes and his emotional involvement lessens, extensive cross-examination at the preliminary hearing may only harden his position and make him less able to retreat to a more friendly position.

5. ***Preserving favorable testimony.*** As discussed in Note 4, p. 941, preliminary hearing testimony not only is available for subsequent impeachment use at trial, but if a witness should become unavailable to testify at trial (due to specified conditions, see fn. f, p. 941), that witness' preliminary hearing testimony will be admissible at trial under the "prior testimony" exception to the hearsay rule. In *Coleman*, Justice Brennan viewed this potential for perpetuating testimony as beneficial to the defense, noting that the hearing may be used by the defense to "preserve

required to produce the principal witness"; also noting how relatively few states establish such a right, looking to the law rather than the practice, on bypasses and hearing procedures, see § 1, supra and § 4, infra).

testimony favorable to the accused of a witness who does not appear at trial." In general, however, the possibility of perpetuating testimony tends to be "viewed by the defense as a negative feature of the hearing," as it is more likely to benefit the prosecution than the defense. CRIMPROC § 14.1(d).

Where either the defense or the prosecution has a substantial basis for believing that a witness will be unavailable to testify at trial, that witness' testimony may be preserved through a deposition designed to perpetuate testimony. See e.g., Fed.R.Crim.P. 15(a). Thus, the preliminary hearing's value in perpetuating testimony lies primarily in perpetuating the testimony of a witness who was not viewed at the time as likely to become "unavailable." Because conventional defense wisdom argues against the defense presenting its own witnesses at the preliminary hearing (see Note 1, p. 942), the defense is unlikely to go against that wisdom where the potential for unavailability is less than what would be needed to utilize a deposition. On the other hand, the prosecution will of necessity be presenting its witnesses, and in some instances, those witnesses will unexpectedly become unavailable at trial, with the prosecution then using their preliminary hearing testimony.

6. ***Defense discovery.*** In meeting the evidentiary standard for a bindover, the prosecutor will necessarily provide the defense with some discovery of the prosecution's case. The defendant may obtain even more discovery by cross-examining the prosecution's witnesses at the hearing and by subpoenaing other potential trial witnesses, not called by the prosecution, to testify as defense witnesses. The extent of the discovery that can be obtained in this manner will depend upon several factors, including the following: (1) whether the prosecution can rely entirely on hearsay reports and thereby sharply limit the number of witnesses it presents; (2) whether, even assuming hearsay cannot be used, the bindover standard may be satisfied by the presentation of a minimal amount of testimony on each element of the offense; (3) whether, notwithstanding the ease with which the bindover standard is met, the prosecution still follows a general practice of presenting most of its case; and (4) whether the defendant is limited, both in cross-examination and in the presentation of witnesses, to direct rebuttal of material presented by the prosecution.

The importance to the defense of the limited discovery available through the preliminary hearing will depend in large part on the availability (and timing) of alternative discovery procedures. Where state law and practice provide very little pretrial discovery, the preliminary hearing may serve as the primary discovery device under local practice. On the other hand, where state law provides discovery of the prior recorded statements of prospective prosecution witnesses, including the arresting officer's report, the discovery will be less important. Even here, however, the preliminary hearing can provide the additional discovery commonly associated with discovery depositions (which are readily available in only a small group of states). The defense has the opportunity to see how the witness testifies in a courtroom setting and to compel the witness to answer questions on matters that may not have been covered in his prior recorded statement. The former advantage, at least, applies even where the witness was willing to be interviewed by the defense and to respond fully in that interview. Finally, even where state law provides extensive discovery, if that discovery is not available until after the critical time for plea settlements has passed, preliminary hearing discovery may still be critical simply to prepare for plea negotiation. Another limitation of the state discovery law in many jurisdictions is that its use requires that the defendant provide reciprocal discovery to the prosecution. See Note 5, p. 1118. Thus, if the defense is able to gain sufficient discovery through the preliminary hearing, it can avoid making a pretrial discovery request and preclude prosecution discovery.

7. ***Other benefits.*** *Coleman* also pointed to the potential use of the preliminary hearing "to make effective arguments for the accused in such matters as the necessity for early psychiatric examinations or bail." The general reference here is to building a record relating to the defendant or the offense that might bear upon the reconsideration of decisions already made by the

magistrate (e.g., bail) and the defense's future presentation of motions to the trial court (e.g., for a psychiatric examination). The latter use can extend to several different types of motions. Thus, while most jurisdictions do not allow the defense to challenge the legality of the government's acquisition of evidence at the preliminary hearing, the defense may seek, in cross-examining government witnesses who acquired that evidence, to build a record that will be useful when a motion to suppress is made before the trial court. So too, the preliminary hearing may be used to develop mitigating evidence that will later be helpful on sentencing following a guilty plea.

The preliminary hearing also may serve as integral part of the plea bargaining process, with the objective of the defense being to convince the prosecution that the circumstances of the offense justify a substantial reduction in the level of the charge in return for a guilty plea. So too, the hearing may serve as a valuable "educating process" for a defendant who is not persuaded by his counsel's opinion that the prosecution has such a strong case that a negotiated plea is in the defendant's best interest.

8. ***"Incidental" benefits and preliminary hearing procedures.*** Prior to *Coleman*, the dominant view was that the screening involved in the bindover decision was "the sole legally cognizable purpose of the preliminary hearing." CRIMPROC § 14.1(a). While the hearing might provide the defense with other benefits, such as discovery, those were no more than "incidental byproducts" of the screening function, and did not shape preliminary hearing procedures. Those procedures should be designed exclusively to allow the defense to challenge evidentiary sufficiency under the jurisdiction's bindover standard, and they should not be expanded to facilitate other potential uses of the hearing. Following *Coleman*, many states reconsidered this position. With few exceptions, however, they did not alter relevant legal standards based upon that position. Thus, states continued to adhere to prohibitions against questioning on cross-examination that is aimed at discovery. See Note 2, p. 939. They have also retained or added restrictions on the defense's presentation of evidence, seeking to confine that presentation by reference to the sole function of applying a probable-cause bindover standard. See e.g., Notes 1–3, pp. 942–944. *Coleman* generally is viewed as a case holding only that the various incidental defense benefits were relevant to a critical stage analysis, not as indicating that the state had any obligation to provide or expand those benefits. See, e.g., *State v. O'Brien*, fn. b, p. 936 (argument that defendant was denied effective assistance of counsel because state allowed unlimited use of hearsay failed to take account of the "limited purpose of the hearing," as a counsel's role is "necessarily limited" by that purpose, and ineffective assistance must be assessed in light of that role).

9. ***Defense waivers.*** The range of potential defense benefits might suggest that defense waivers of the right to a preliminary hearing would be rare. In fact, waivers by the defense exceed 50% in a substantial number of jurisdictions, including some which provide the most extensive preliminary hearings (commonly described as "mini-trial" hearings, see Note 2, p. 932). A variety of factors may influence the waiver rate in a particular jurisdiction, including: "(1) the availability of alternative discovery devices; (2) the inadequacy of the payment schedule of appointed counsel for representation at a preliminary hearing; (3) a prosecution practice of offering significant concessions to defendants who waive their preliminary hearings; and (4) the conventional wisdom of the local defense bar that the preliminary hearing is (i) unnecessary where the prosecution has a strong case and the defendant intends to plead guilty, or (ii) an inherently risky process because * * * [certain] disadvantages [e.g., revealing that the case is "undercharged" in light of the evidence, "calling the prosecution's attention to a curable defect in its case that otherwise would not be noticed until trial," and antagonizing a complainant/witness who otherwise was likely to "mellow with time"] often cannot be foreseen until after the hearing is underway." CRIMPROC § 14.2(f).

B. "INCIDENTAL BENEFITS" AND APPELLATE REVIEW

1. ***Postconviction review of defense challenges.*** Defense challenges to magistrate rulings regarding the preliminary hearing tend to fall into three categories: (1) the magistrate's ruling denied the defendant his right to a preliminary hearing (e.g., by accepting a waiver that was not voluntary and knowledgeable, or by granting an unjustified extension in time that resulted in a bypass by prior indictment); (2) the magistrate erred in finding the evidence sufficient to meet the jurisdiction's bindover standard (see Note 7, p. 935); and (3) the magistrate erred in a procedural ruling at the preliminary hearing. These challenges will first be presented to the felony trial court, typically by a pretrial motion to dismiss after an information or indictment has been filed in that court. If that motion is denied, immediate appellate review typically is not available. See Note 1, p. 1405, and Note 4, p. 1409. The defense will, however, be able to seek review of that denial on an appeal following a conviction. At that point, the appellate court must consider what remedy, if any, is appropriate if it finds that the defendant's challenge had merit and the trial court erred in denying that challenge. As described below, state courts are divided on this issue among three basic approaches.

2. ***The* Coleman *approach.*** In *Coleman v. Alabama*, Note 1, p. 922, the prosecution argued that even if defendant's right to counsel had been denied, the constitutional violation had proven harmless in light of defendant's subsequent conviction following a fair trial. It stressed in this regard that no testimony given at the preliminary hearing had been used at trial, where defendant had been represented by counsel and guilt had been proven beyond a reasonable doubt. Speaking for a Court majority on this issue, Justice Brennan responded: "The trial transcript indicates that the prohibition against use by the State at trial of anything that occurred at the preliminary hearing was scrupulously observed. But on the record it cannot be said whether or not petitioners were otherwise prejudiced by the absence of counsel at the preliminary hearing. That inquiry in the first instance should more properly be made by the Alabama courts. The test to be applied is whether the denial of counsel at the preliminary hearing was harmless error under *Chapman v. California* [p. 1417]. We accordingly vacate the petitioners' convictions and remand the case to the Alabama courts for such proceedings not inconsistent with this opinion as they may deem appropriate to determine whether such denial of counsel was harmless error * * *."

Justices Harlan and White, each writing separate opinions, also commented on the appropriate relief. Justice Harlan noted: "I consider the scope of the Court's remand too broad and amorphous. I do not think that reversal of these convictions, for lack of counsel at the preliminary hearing, should follow unless petitioners are able to show on remand that they have been prejudiced in their defense at trial, in that favorable testimony that might otherwise have been preserved was irretrievably lost by virtue of not having counsel to help present an affirmative case at the preliminary hearing."

Justice White expressed a somewhat similar view: "I would expect the application of the harmless-error standard on remand to produce results approximating those contemplated by Mr. Justice Harlan's separately stated views. * * * [The assessment of harmless error] cannot ignore the fact that petitioner has been tried and found guilty by a jury. The possibility that counsel would have detected preclusive flaws in the State's probable cause showing is for all practical purposes mooted by the trial where the State produced evidence satisfying the jury of the petitioner's guilt beyond a reasonable doubt. Also, it would be wholly speculative in this case to assume either (1) that the State's witnesses at the trial testified inconsistently with what their testimony would have been if petitioner had counsel to cross-examine them at the preliminary hearing, or (2) that counsel, had he been present at the hearing, would have known so much more about the State's case than he actually did when he went to trial that the result of the trial might have been different. So too it seems extremely unlikely that matters related to bail * * * would ever raise reasonable doubts about the integrity of the trial. There remains the possibility, as Mr.

Justice Harlan suggests, that important testimony of witnesses unavailable at the trial could have been preserved had counsel been present to cross-examine opposing witnesses or to examine witnesses for the defense."

Lower courts, in applying *Coleman,* have adopted the analysis suggested by Justice White. Violation of the right to counsel at the preliminary hearing has been held to constitute reversible error only where the defense is able to point to specific aspects of the trial where defendant was adversely impacted by having lacked counsel at the preliminary hearing. CRIMPROC § 14.4(a).

Several state courts have adopted a modified version of the *Coleman* approach in analyzing other types of preliminary hearing errors. If the error relates only to the magistrate's bindover ruling, it is per se harmless because the trial verdict establishes guilt beyond a reasonable doubt. If the error involves the denial of a procedural right that might have had a bearing on the defense's presentation at trial, it may require reversal of the conviction upon a sufficient showing of trial prejudice. The same is true of a complete denial of a preliminary hearing if defendant there could have utilized a right that would bear on the defense's trial presentation. Unlike *Coleman*, which applied the constitutional harmless error standard of *Chapman* to potential trial prejudice, state courts dealing with such errors tend to start from the assumption that the error was harmless, and require the defense to show particular trial prejudice (i.e., to show what would have been done differently at trial if not for the preliminary hearing procedural error—or the denial of the hearing entirely—and how that difference could have impacted the outcome of trial). See CRIMPROC § 14.4(e) (noting that these rulings typically have not identified the type of prejudice that would justify reversal, although "it has been suggested that the loss of a critical witness would be sufficient").

3. ***The "per se harmless" approach.*** Most state courts appear to take the position that any type of error relating to the preliminary hearing (apart from the constitutional violation of denial of counsel, which is governed by *Coleman*) is automatically rendered harmless by the trial conviction. The sole function of the preliminary hearing, they note, is to determine evidentiary sufficiency under the bindover standard and the conviction at trial finds guilt under an even higher standard. The defense may have lost the opportunity to use the hearing for "trial preparation," but to reverse a conviction based on the loss of such an incidental benefit would convert the hearing into something it is not. CRIMPROC §§ 14.2(g), 14.3(d), 14.4(e).

4. ***The "jurisdictional defect" approach.*** In a handful of information states, courts read the state's statutory or constitutional requirement that an information be based on a preliminary hearing bindover (or its waiver) as a jurisdictional defect that cannot be cured by a subsequent trial and conviction. The absence of a valid bindover produces a setting comparable to a case in which no charge was ever filed. Although the defect is described as "jurisdictional," it does not establish a lack of subject matter jurisdiction, as it can be "waived" by the failure to make a timely objection. See *State v. Niblack*, 596 A.2d 407 (Conn.1991) (defect relates to jurisdiction, over the person and thus must be "seasonably raised"). Consider also Note 1, p. 1423 (describing errors that are non-jurisdictional, but characterized as "structural" and therefore require automatic reversal rather than application of harmless error analysis). Under this view, automatic reversal is required where the magistrate erroneously denied the defendant's right to a hearing or held a hearing, but issued a bindover on insufficient evidence. See CRIMPROC §§ 14.2(g), 14.3(d). An erroneous procedural ruling may produce the same result, but only if that error "could have altered the magistrate's decision to bind over." CRIMPROC § 14.4(e).

5. ***Post-indictment review.*** In indictment jurisdictions, where an indictment is issued promptly after the preliminary hearing (or the denial of hearing), the defendant's challenge to a magistrate's ruling commonly will be considered by the trial court in a post-indictment setting. In jurisdictions that view preliminary hearing errors as per se harmless on post-conviction review (see Note 3 supra), the indictment will similarly be viewed as rendering moot any preliminary

hearing error. Courts here reason that the sole cognizable function of the preliminary hearing is the bindover determination, and even if the magistrate should have decided against a bindover, the grand jury would have remained free to indict, as it did. See Note 6, p. 934; CRIMPROC §§ 14.2(g), 14.3(d).

Where a jurisdiction treats the *Coleman* analysis as having a bearing beyond the right-to-counsel issue, the appropriate remedy becomes more complex. In *Coleman v. Burnett*, 477 F.2d 1187 (D.C. Cir.1973), the defendant challenged, in a post-indictment, pretrial setting the preliminary hearing magistrate's denial of a defense request to subpoena an unnamed undercover agent who apparently was the sole available eyewitness to the marijuana transactions for which the defendant was charged. The D.C. Circuit, on review of a trial court's denial of a writ of mandamus, concluded that the magistrate had denied the defendant his right under the governing court rule to introduce at the preliminary hearing "evidence on his own behalf." The importance of that right, as it might bear upon trial preparation, was "reinforced by the holding in *Coleman v. Alabama*", as the restriction placed on counsel's performance could operate to "deprive [the accused] of the very benefit which the Sixth Amendment right of counsel was designed to confer." Turning to the question of how the magistrate's mistake should be corrected, the D.C. Circuit noted that the "[indictment] itself establishes probable cause," and thus precluded a new preliminary hearing. However, the magistrate's error could be remedied through other procedures directed at ensuring that the defense was not prejudiced at trial through its inability to call the witness at the preliminary hearing. Thus, the district court might make the undercover agent's grand jury testimony available to defense counsel, have the agent produced for a voluntary interview of "appropriate bounds" as set by the judge, or allow a "deposition by written interrogatories to the agent." These suggestions were not meant to "exhaust the possibilities," and the case would be remanded to the trial court to fashion "suitable relief."

§ 3. THE BINDOVER DETERMINATION

STATE V. CLARK

20 P.3d 300 (Utah 2001).

DURRANT, JUSTICE:

In two separate prosecutions, Cory H. Smith and John L. Clark were charged with forgery. In each case, the charges were based on allegations that [1] the defendant had requested a bank to cash [a check made out to himself as payee], that [2] * * * [the check came from a recently stolen book of blank checks, with the account holder later testifying that she had not written the check], and, [3] * * * [defendant produced the identification and fingerprint needed for check cashing, but] when the bank did not readily comply, left the check and exited the bank. In each case, the defendant was initially bound over by a magistrate, but the bindover was subsequently quashed by the district court, on the ground that the State had failed to meet its evidentiary burden at the preliminary hearing. The State appeals both cases. Due to the similarity of the issues presented, the appeals have been consolidated. * * *

The determination of whether to bind a criminal defendant over for trial is a question of law. Accordingly, we review that determination without deference to the court below. * * * The issue on appeal is whether the district court judges erred in quashing the magistrates' findings that there was probable cause to bind Smith and Clark over for trial.

I. The Probable Cause Standard

To bind a defendant over for trial, the State must show "probable cause" at a preliminary hearing by "present[ing] sufficient evidence to establish that 'the crime charged has been committed and that the defendant has committed it.' " *State v. Pledger* (1995) (quoting Utah R.Crim.P. 7(h)(2)). At this stage of the proceeding, "the evidence required [to show probable cause] . . . is relatively low because the assumption is that the prosecution's case will only get stronger as the investigation continues." * * * Accordingly, "[w]hen faced with conflicting evidence, the magistrate may not sift or weigh the evidence . . . but must leave those tasks 'to the fact finder at trial.' " Instead, "[t]he magistrate must view all evidence in the light most favorable to the prosecution and must draw all reasonable inferences in favor of the prosecution." Yet, "[t]he magistrate's role in this process, while limited, is not that of a rubber stamp for the prosecution. . . . Even with this limited role, the magistrate must attempt to ensure that all 'groundless and improvident prosecutions' are ferreted out no later than the preliminary hearing."

With these principles in mind, we turn to the question of what quantum of evidence is sufficient to support a finding of probable cause at the preliminary hearing stage of a prosecution. We have taken various approaches in articulating an answer to this question. In some cases, we have described the State's burden of proof at a preliminary hearing by comparing it to the burdens applicable to other stages of a criminal prosecution. We have held that the quantum of evidence necessary to establish probable cause at the preliminary hearing is "more than [is] required to establish probable cause for arrest." *State v. Anderson* (1980). To issue an arrest warrant, "the facts presented must be sufficient to establish that an offense has been committed and a *reasonable belief* the defendant committed it. * * *" *Anderson*[1] We have further held that the probable cause standard is also "less than would prove the defendant guilty beyond a reasonable doubt." *Anderson* Indeed, we recently stated, "[The probable cause] standard is lower, even, than a preponderance of the evidence standard applicable to civil cases." *Pledger*. * * * Thus, our case law to this point places the level of proof necessary to support a preliminary hearing bindover somewhere between the reasonable belief necessary to support a warrant and the preponderance of the evidence standard applicable in the civil context.

In a number of cases, we have equated the preliminary hearing probable cause standard with the motion for directed verdict standard, i.e., "to survive a motion to quash a bindover, the State must produce enough evidence sufficient to survive a *motion for directed verdict* with respect to each element of the crime." *State v. Talbot* (1998). We have justified the use of a single standard in both these contexts as follows: "Since both a directed verdict and a motion to quash [a magistrate's bindover order] serve gatekeeping functions, it is sensible for them to share a common standard." *Talbot*. The court of appeals has correctly summarized the directed verdict standard as follows:

> "[T]he trial court should dismiss the charge if the State did not establish a prima facie case against the defendant by producing 'believable evidence of all the elements of the crime charged.' " * * * If, however, " '*the jury acting fairly and reasonably could find the defendant guilty beyond a reasonable doubt,* the judge is required to submit the case to the jury for determination of the guilt or innocence of the defendant.' " * * * We will uphold the trial court's decision to submit a case to the jury " 'if, upon reviewing the evidence and all inferences that can be reasonably drawn from it, the court concludes that some evidence exists from which a reasonable jury could find that the elements of the crime had been proven beyond a reasonable doubt.' " * * *

However, any conclusion that the preliminary hearing probable cause standard is the same as the directed verdict standard is weakened by our other descriptions of the preliminary hearing

[1] The probable cause standard necessary to support an arrest warrant has been worded differently by other courts. In federal court, to demonstrate probable cause for an arrest warrant, there must be a " 'fair probability," *Illinois v. Gates* (1983). * * * Though phrased differently, there is little, if any, difference in these arrest warrant standards. * * * Indeed, the court of appeals notes that both the "fair probability" wording and the "reasonable belief" wording have been applied to search warrants in federal courts. See *State v. Brooks*, 849 P.2d 640, 643 (Ut. App.1993).

standard. In *Pledger* we held that the probable cause standard at a preliminary hearing is "lower, even, than a preponderance of the evidence standard applicable to civil cases." In retrospect, this guidance was more confusing than helpful. As noted earlier, "[w]hen faced with conflicting evidence, the magistrate may not sift or weigh the evidence . . . but must leave those tasks 'to the fact finder at trial.' " However, the preponderance of the evidence standard can only be met by weighing the evidence. * * * Thus, our comparison of the probable cause standard to the preponderance standard was, essentially, a comparison of apples to oranges that could lead magistrates at the preliminary hearing stage of a criminal proceeding to improperly weigh the evidence before them as permitted by the civil preponderance standard. As a result, despite our recent efforts to clarify the exact meaning of the probable cause standard, it remains somewhat confusing. Therefore, we take this opportunity to elucidate that standard.

We hold that to prevail at a preliminary hearing, the prosecution must still produce "believable evidence of all the elements of the crime charged," *State v. Emmett* (1992), just as it would have to do to survive a motion for a directed verdict. However, unlike a motion for a directed verdict, this evidence need not be capable of supporting a finding of guilt beyond a reasonable doubt. Instead, we hold that the quantum of evidence necessary to support a bindover is less than that necessary to survive a directed verdict motion. Specifically, we see no principled basis for attempting to maintain a distinction between the arrest warrant probable cause standard and the preliminary hearing probable cause standard. Our efforts to articulate a standard that is more rigorous than the arrest warrant standard and is still lower than a preponderance of the evidence standard have only resulted in confusion. Therefore, at both the arrest warrant and the preliminary hearing stages, the prosecution must present sufficient evidence to support a reasonable belief that an offense has been committed and that the defendant committed it.[3] This "reasonable belief" standard has the advantage of being more easily understood while still allowing magistrates to fulfill the primary purpose of the preliminary hearing, "ferreting out . . . groundless and improvident prosecutions." *Anderson*.

II. Applying The Standard To Clark and Smith

The Utah Code defines the crime of forgery as follows: "A person is guilty of forgery if, *with purpose to defraud anyone, or with knowledge that he is facilitating a fraud to be perpetrated by anyone,* he: (a) alters any writing of another without his authority or utters any such altered writing; (b) makes, completes, executes, authenticates, issues, transfers, publishes, or utters any writing so that the writing * * * purports to be the act of another, whether the person is existent or nonexistent * * *." Utah Code Ann. 76–6–501(1) (1999) (emphasis added).

The district court dismissed the forgery charges against both Clark and Smith because the State failed to demonstrate that they had acted with the requisite intent. However, in doing so, the district court applied the directed verdict standard. Because we reject the notion that the probable cause standard is equivalent to the directed verdict standard, we apply the clarified probable cause standard.

Viewed in the light most favorable to the prosecution, the facts presented at the preliminary hearing were sufficient to meet the reasonable belief standard. The State presented evidence that

---

[3] In a pragmatic sense, however, the State still has a higher bar at the preliminary hearing stage than at the arrest warrant stage: Although the hearing is not a trial per se, it is not an ex parte proceeding nor [a] one-sided determination of probable cause, and the accused is granted a statutory right to cross-examine the witnesses against him, and the right to subpoena and present witnesses in his defense. Thus, the preliminary examination is an adversarial proceeding in which certain procedural safeguards are recognized as necessary to guarantee the accused's substantive right to a fair hearing. *Anderson*. However, this distinction has been somewhat reduced by the recent amendment to the Utah Constitution allowing for the admission of "reliable hearsay evidence" at "preliminary examinations." See also Utah R.Crim.P. 7(h)(2) (noting that at a preliminary examination, "[t]he findings of probable cause may be based on hearsay in whole or in part"); Utah R. Evid. 1102 (outlining admissible hearsay evidence at a preliminary hearing).

both Clark and Smith attempted to cash forged checks at local banks mere hours after those checks were reported stolen. After a brief delay while bankers told Smith that they were seeking approval to cash the check, Smith exited the bank, abandoning the forged check. Similarly, when told that there was a problem with the account and that he would have to take it up with the account holder, Clark abandoned the forged check and left the bank.

The issue is whether this evidence is sufficient to support a reasonable belief that Smith and Clark uttered forged checks "with purpose to defraud anyone, or with knowledge that [they were] facilitating a fraud to be perpetrated by anyone." Here, the facts give rise to two alternate inferences. On the one hand, Clark and Smith may have been unaware the checks were stolen. After the delays, they may have simply assumed they had themselves been defrauded and, thus, felt there was no reason to take the checks with them. On the other hand, one could reasonably infer an intent to defraud. If Smith were a holder in due course he would have waited for approval rather than leaving when he had been given no other explanation for the delay. If Clark were a holder in due course, he would have taken the check with him to "take that up with the account holder." Further, both Clark and Smith presented the checks only hours after the reported thefts. While one could infer that Clark and Smith received the checks in otherwise legitimate transactions, this does not negate the reasonable inference that, in light of the timing, they either stole the checks or knew they were stolen. Viewing the evidence, and all reasonable inferences therefrom, in a light most favorable to the State, the State has shown probable cause. Therefore, the district courts' findings to the contrary are reversed. * * *

NOTES AND QUESTIONS

1. ***Bindover standards.*** *Clark* probably represents the dominant reading of the bindover standard in accepting an arrest warrant standard. See CRIMPROC § 14.3. Critics note that the initial formulation of an arrest-warrant bindover standard came in most states long before the Supreme Court's ruling in *Gerstein v. Pugh*, p. 918 (Note 1)—i.e., at a time when there was no assurance that the probable cause needed to sustain an arrest would otherwise be determined by a neutral magistrate. Now that *Gerstein* requires that such a determination be made either in the magistrate's issuance of an arrest warrant prior to the arrest, or on the magistrate's review of a warrantless arrest at the arrestee's first appearance, an arrest-warrant bindover standard, the critics argue, is largely "duplicative," notwithstanding the distinctions noted in fn. 3 of *Clark*.

2. Only a few jurisdictions appear to have moved to a true prima facie case bindover standard, asking whether there is evidence, viewed in the light most favorable to the prosecution, from which a jury could find guilt beyond a reasonable doubt. See CRIMPROC § 14.3. One reason for this sparse support may be the timing requirements for the preliminary hearing. New York, which had formerly used the prima facie case standard, moved to a probable cause standard when it shortened the time period within which the preliminary hearing had to be held. See Staff Comments, Proposed New York Procedure Law § 90.60 (1969) (noting further that a prima facie standard "does not really benefit a defendant" as it "may cause an arrested person to be held for a considerable time" while the case is being further investigated to meet that standard). Utilizing a prima facie case standard also has been criticized as not in tune with the procedural limitations of the preliminary hearing. A screening standard resembling that imposed by the trial court, it is argued, is most appropriately applied where the hearing has the characteristics of a mini-trial—i.e., with the rules of evidence fully applicable, procedural rights (particularly confrontation and subpoena authority) basically parallel to that at trial, and the magistrate having an authority to weigh credibility close to that of a trial judge in a bench trial (see Note 5 infra). A substantial majority of the states do not provide for such a hearing. However, even among the minority that do provide for a mini-trial type hearing, many more use a probable cause standard than a prima facie case standard.

3. Where courts have utilized a "probable cause" bindover standard, but describe that standard as "greater" or "more rigorous" than the arrest warrant standard, they typically have not suggested that such a standard requires the magistrate to weigh conflicting evidence (compare the *Clark* discussion of the implications of its previous reference to the preponderance of the evidence standard). Those courts apparently "have in mind differences in the type of evidence required at each stage." CRIMPROC § 14.3(a). For example, "under the arrest standard, considerable uncertainty must be tolerated on occasion because of the need to allow the police to take affirmative action in ambiguous circumstances, but no comparable exigencies are presented as the charging decision is made. Thus, a police officer may make an arrest where the circumstances suggest that the property possessed by the suspect may have been stolen, but the prosecutor ordinarily has no justification for proceeding to charge without first determining that a theft actually did occur." Ibid.

4. ***A forward looking perspective.*** Commentators have argued that an important component of the bindover analysis, no matter what the standard, should be its "forward looking" perspective. While the arrest warrant standard looks to probability based upon the information available at the time of arrest, the preliminary hearing bindover, in reviewing a decision to charge, should insist on the likelihood that the government will be able to develop further evidence to establish guilt at trial. See e.g., Kenneth Graham Jr. & Leon Letwin, *The Preliminary Hearing* in Los Angeles, 18 U.C.L.A. L. Rev. 635, 655–56 (1971) (citing this forward looking approach as the grounding for a California case in which bindover was denied on a narcotics possession charge where, inter alia, an informant told the arresting officer that the accused was involved in narcotics activities, the officer confronted the accused and saw in his mouth several multicolored balloons, the accused was able to flee and flush the balloons down the toilet before he could be arrested, and narcotics experts testified that persons transporting narcotics often placed narcotic-filled balloons in their mouth, but the balloons also occasionally were used in that fashion by persons selling "phony narcotics").

This view of probable cause, "as encompassing consideration of the prosecution's likely future development of the case, finds support in occasional language in appellate opinions and magistrate explanations of bindover rejections. * * * However, 'a forward looking' interpretation of probable cause has been rejected by the few courts speaking directly to the issue." CRIMPROC § 14.3(a). They note that the adoption of a probable cause standard carries with it an inherent presumption (not subject to revision by the magistrate in the individual case) that the prosecution may be able to "strengthen its case on trial." *Kennedy v. State*, 839 P.2d 667 (Okla.Crim.App.1992). Is that the approach endorsed in *Clark* when it refers to "the assumption that the prosecutor's case will only get stronger as the investigation continues" (p. 930)?

5. ***Weighing credibility.*** Appellate opinions in numerous states note that the magistrate has authority to judge the credibility of witnesses. In several states, those statements appear to refer to the full authority vested in a factfinder at trial. *Hunter v. District Court*, 543 P.2d 1265 (Colo.1995), suggests, however, that in most of these states, the magistrate's authority to judge credibility actually is far more limited. Thus, *Hunter* notes, one such state restricts the inquiry into credibility to judging "the plausibility of the story and not general trustworthiness," another holds that the magistrate can resolve conflicts in testimony "only where the evidence is overwhelming," and still another stresses that the magistrate must not usurp the role of the trial jury in determining the "weight to be accorded the testimony of witnesses." In *Hunter,* the court held that the magistrate could consider credibility "only when, as a matter of law, the testimony is implausible or incredible. When there is a mere conflict in the testimony, a question of fact exists for the jury, and the [magistrate] must draw the inference favorable to the prosecution." Consider also, in this connection, the directive in *Clark* that the magistrate not "sift or weigh" evidence (p. 930).

The majority opinion in *Hunter* also suggested that the degree of authority given to the magistrate to judge credibility follows in large part from other aspects of preliminary hearing procedure. In refusing to follow California decisions granting the magistrate extensive authority in judging credibility, the *Hunter* majority stressed the more limited role of the Colorado preliminary hearing:

"The preliminary hearing in Colorado under Crim.P. 7(h) is not a mini-trial, but rather is limited to the purpose of determining whether there is probable cause to believe that a crime was committed and that the defendant committed it. * * * It focuses upon a probable cause determination, rather than a consideration of the probability of conviction at the ensuing trial. See Note, 83 Yale L.J. 771 (1974) [contrasting the prima facie case standard]. * * * In light of its limited purpose, evidentiary and procedural rules in the preliminary hearing in Colorado are relaxed [e.g., hearsay evidence may be used]. * * * The preliminary hearing in California is a 'mini-trial,' emphasizing the probability of conviction at trial on admissible evidence.[a] In such a situation, California * * * properly allows the judge to act as a trier of fact. In Colorado, however, the preliminary hearing is not a 'mini-trial,' and the judge in such a role is not a trier of fact. Rather, his function is solely to determine the existence or absence of probable cause."

6. ***Consequences of a dismissal.*** The states are divided as to granting the prosecution an appeal of right to the next highest court (typically the trial court) to contest a dismissal at a preliminary hearing. Where such an appeal is not provided, review may still be obtained by application for an extraordinary writ (e.g., mandamus), but that remedy is available only if the magistrate's ruling constitutes a "gross abuse" of his authority. The prosecution is more likely to look, in any event, to two alternative strategies for obtaining a "reversal" of a dismissal ruling—obtaining an indictment from the grand jury or seeking a second run at a preliminary hearing.

Since the preliminary hearing dismissal is prior to the attachment of jeopardy (see Note 1, p. 1339), there is no constitutional bar against reinstituting proceedings, and state law commonly imposes few, if any, restrictions on starting over again following a dismissal. If a grand jury is readily available, the prosecutor may present the same case to the grand jury for indictment. The grand jury may indict notwithstanding the magistrate's refusal to bindover, and most often the prosecutor need not even inform the grand jury that the magistrate refused to bindover on the same evidence. See CRIMPROC § 14.3(c). A substantial majority of the states also allow the prosecutor to refile the charges and seek another preliminary hearing on the same evidence. Use of this authority, however, may be subject to powerful institutional restraints. In some smaller judicial districts, the prosecutor may not be able to avoid having the refiled charge come before the same magistrate. Even where the charge comes before a different magistrate, he or she may be hesitant to reach a result inconsistent with the first ruling and to thereby call attention to the importance of the differing perspectives of members of the same bench.

A minority group of states prohibit refiling on the same evidence. These states typically provide for prosecution appeal from a dismissal and consider that the only appropriate avenue for challenge. However, such jurisdictions do allow the prosecutor to refile and seek a new preliminary hearing when it has "new evidence." *Jones v. State,* 481 P.2d 169 (Okla.Cr.App.1971). One view of new evidence for this purpose limits such evidence to that which was "[not] known at the time of the first preliminary hearing and which could [not] easily have been acquired at that time." *Jones*

[a] The *Hunter* reference apparently was to the traditional California preliminary hearing, rather than the California hearing as modified in the early 1990s. In a complicated case, the traditional California mini-trial hearing could be substantially longer than the typical state felony trial. The record was set in the preliminary hearing in the McMartin Preschool case (involving over 200 counts of alleged child molestation), which produced "19 months of testimony [and] over 143,000 pages of transcript." Paul Eberle & Shirley Eberle, *The Abuse of Innocence* 29 (1997).

The elements that produce the mini-trial characterization are described in note 2, supra. That characterization clearly applies to a small group of states, and some commentators would apply it to the Utah preliminary hearing as described in *Clark*, prior to the adoption of the hearsay provisions cited in *Clark*'s fn. 3.

v. State, supra. Others simply require that the evidence adds substantially to what was presented at the first hearing. They note that prosecutors have a natural reluctance to disclose all available evidence at the preliminary hearing, and that the prosecutor's misjudgment as to the evidence needed should not immunize the defendant from further prosecution. But compare *Harper v. District Court,* 484 P.2d 891 (Okla.Cr.App.1971) (suggesting that the proper approach for a prosecutor who misjudges the evidence is to simply seek a continuance for the purpose of presenting additional available evidence in the initial hearing).

7. ***Consequences of a bindover.*** In an indictment state, if the defendant does not waive the right to be prosecuted by indictment, the bindover only leads to the presentation of the case before the grand jury. In making its decision on indictment, the grand jury is in no way controlled by the bindover. It may refuse to indict despite the bindover or may indict for a higher or lesser offense. Once the grand jury indicts, the indictment serves as the basis for the continued detention of the defendant and all further proceedings.

In an information state, the bindover leads directly to the filing of charges by information. In most information states, the information may charge only the offense on which the magistrate boundover. A small group of states do not impose that limitation. They require only that the charge in the information be transactionally related to the bindover offense and be supported by evidence presented in the preliminary hearing, as independently assessed by the trial court. In some jurisdictions, this can include both a charge that was presented to the magistrate and rejected (thus eliminating the need to "appeal" the dismissal) and a charge that the prosecutor first selected as more appropriate after the bindover.

Restricting the prosecutor's charge to the bindover does not dictate the standard of appellate review. Some courts view the existence of probable cause as a legal issue, and therefore review de novo. In others, both the initial review by the trial court and any subsequent appellate review gives deference to the magistrate's bindover determination. The reviewing court asks whether that decision was "clearly erroneous" or reflected an "abuse of discretion." See CRIMPROC § 14.3(d). Some of the states giving deference to the magistrate's determination also restrict sharply the magistrate's authority to judge credibility, apparently justifying a deferential review standard on factors other than the magistrate having heard the witnesses.

§ 4. PRELIMINARY HEARING PROCEDURES

A. APPLICATION OF THE RULES OF EVIDENCE

1. ***Variations in state law.*** While all jurisdictions require magistrates to recognize testimonial privileges,[a] jurisdictions vary considerably in their application of the other rules of evidence at preliminary hearings. See CRIMPROC § 14.4(b). A handful of states require full application of the rules of evidence, i.e., the magistrate may receive only evidence normally admissible at trial. These jurisdictions will not reject a bindover, however, simply because the magistrate relied erroneously on incompetent evidence. If the reviewing court concludes that there was sufficient competent evidence before the magistrate to sustain a finding of probable cause, the bindover will be upheld notwithstanding the magistrate's error.

[a] The reference here is to a witness' exercise of a testimonial privilege or the defendant's authority to preclude the testimony of a particular witness because of the defendant's relationship to that witness (e.g., preclude the testimony of a spouse or lawyer). The provisions recognizing the application of privileges, see e.g., Fed.R.Evid. 1101(d)(3), are not read as encompassing challenges to the government's introduction of evidence allegedly acquired through the invasion of a privilege (e.g., where the government seized documents protected by the lawyer-client privilege). The defendant's capacity to raise such a challenge will depend upon whether the state applies to the preliminary hearing the evidentiary remedy that would require exclusion of unlawfully acquired evidence at trial (e.g., a constitutional exclusionary rule). See CRIMPROC § 14.4(b), and the discussion in Notes 3 and 4, infra.

A somewhat larger group of jurisdictions hold the rules of evidence to be "largely applicable" to the preliminary hearings, but allow the magistrate to consider certain types of inadmissible evidence. In most of these jurisdictions, the exceptions are recognized by statute or court rule and are fairly limited. See e.g., Tenn.R.Crim.P. 5.1(a) (excepting a limited class of hearsay). In others, the directive to the magistrate is to follow generally the rules of evidence, making exceptions only upon some general principle relating to need or the special character of the preliminary hearing. See Mo.Stat. § 544.280 (evidence standards "same as governs in the trial of criminal cases * * * as far as practicable").

A third group of jurisdictions, perhaps a majority, have provisions stating that the rules of evidence (apart from privileges) "do not apply" to the preliminary hearing. See e.g., Fed.R.Evid. 1101(d)(3). Magistrates here generally have discretion to follow or not follow evidentiary rules as they choose, although that discretion may be limited by provisions requiring acceptance of a specific type of evidence that would not be admissible at trial (most frequently found with respect to hearsay, see Note 2 infra).

2. ***Hearsay.*** Where magistrates are not held to a full application of the rules of evidence, the most common class of otherwise inadmissible evidence considered at the preliminary hearing is hearsay. The primary arguments advanced for allowing use of hearsay in preliminary examinations are: (1) many witnesses will give evidence on matters not really in dispute (e.g., the scientific expert testifying on drug content, or the burglary victim who can testify only as to what was missing from his home), and it places an undue burden on those persons to make them testify at the preliminary hearing as well as the trial; (2) witnesses in general will be less likely to assist police if they believe that, as a general rule, they will be required to make court appearances both for the preliminary hearing and the trial; (3) the prosecutor should be able to take into account the special concerns of victims (especially victims of violent crime) and exercise the option, where appropriate, of excusing these victims from testifying and having their statements presented through the testimony of the investigating officer (fn. b, infra); (4) the grand jury can consider hearsay in most jurisdictions (see Notes 1–2, p. 964) and imposing a stricter standard at the preliminary hearing will simply encourage the prosecutor to bypass the preliminary hearing by obtaining a prior indictment; and (5) magistrates, even when laypersons, are sufficiently familiar with the limitations of hearsay evidence to appropriately judge its degree of reliability.

In many jurisdictions, no limit is placed on the prosecution's use of hearsay. Those jurisdictions typically have provisions which state that the "finding of probable cause may be based upon hearsay evidence in whole or in part."[b] Other jurisdictions have provisions that hold admissible certain specific types of hearsay or all types of hearsay under specific conditions. In the former category are provisions declaring automatically admissible the "written reports of experts," the written statements of persons attesting to their ownership of stolen or damaged property, and the written statements of persons attesting to the authenticity of their signature on a document. In the latter category are provisions that declare hearsay admissible if it is "demonstrably inconvenient to summon witnesses able to testify to facts from personal knowledge" or "there is a

[b] This provision was included in the original version of Federal Rule 5.1 and was adopted by many of the states with court rules modeled on the Federal Rules. Additional adoptions have occurred in recent years, as the provision has been endorsed by victims' rights advocates, along with a less well-received provision restricting defense use of its subpoena authority to call victims. See La. Stat. Ann § 46.1844(d)(3) (defendant must show "good cause" to subpoena victim). Constitutional challenges to the hearsay provision have uniformly failed. Because state and federal constitutional provisions on confrontation establish only a trial right, see Note 1, p. 939, the challenges have claimed, unsuccessfully, that prosecution reliance on only hearsay violates procedural due process. In the leading rejection of that claim, *State v. O'Brien*, 850 N.W. 2d 8 (Wis. 2014), the court emphasized that procedural fairness here was measured by reference to the limited function of the hearing and the "narrow scope" of probable cause. Reliance on hearsay did not deprive the defendant of "means * * * sufficient to address" the probable-cause issue "as [defendant] retains the ability to challenge the plausibility of hearsay * * * through cross-examination, the presentation of evidence and argument to the court," and "the court has discretion in determining what evidence is sufficiently reliable to establish probable cause."

substantial basis for believing the source of the hearsay is credible and for believing there is a factual basis for the information furnished."

3. ***Unconstitutionally obtained evidence.*** A substantial majority of the states, including most which require adherence to the rules of evidence, do not recognize exclusionary rule objections at the preliminary hearing. See e.g., *State v. Moats,* 457 N.W.2d 299 (Wis.1990) (rules of evidence do not in themselves bar unconstitutionally obtained evidence). On the other hand, several states either specifically require or permit magistrates to exclude unconstitutionally obtained evidence. In a few of these states, defendants are authorized to make a suppression motion at the preliminary hearing. In the others, the defendant may present an exclusionary rule objection only if the prosecutor seeks to use at the hearing evidence that appears to have been obtained in a manner that may have been unconstitutional. States recognizing preliminary hearing challenges to the government's acquisition of evidence typically treat the magistrate's ruling on such objections as binding only in the preliminary hearing—i.e., the exclusion or admission of the evidence at trial will depend upon the outcome of a suppression motion made to the trial court, rather than the magistrate's determination.

In deciding whether to allow or disallow challenges to evidence as obtained unlawfully, states have assumed that choosing to disallow is compatible with the federal constitution. In light of the limited purpose of the preliminary hearing, the exclusionary remedies of the Fourth Amendment, the Fifth Amendment self-incrimination clause, the Sixth Amendment counsel clause, and the due process clause are viewed as inapplicable to the preliminary hearing. While there is no Supreme Court ruling directly on point, the Court has: (1) held that the Sixth Amendment's confrontation clause does not apply to the preliminary hearing, see Note 1, p. 939; (2) stated that in the federal counterpart process for determining probable cause, grand jury review, the Fourth Amendment exclusionary rule does not apply, *United States v. Calandra*, 414 U.S. 338 (1974), Note 1, p. 235, and held that issuance of an indictment cannot be challenged based on the grand jury's consideration of unconstitutionally obtained evidence, Note 5, p. 960; (3) approved Federal Rule 5.1 which provides that the "defendant may not object to evidence on the ground that it was unlawfully acquired"; and (4) described the self-incrimination prohibition of use of compelled statements as a "trial right," because a constitutional violation occurs only with admission at trial, *United States v. Verdugo-Urquidez*, 494 U.S. 259 (1990).

Recent circuit court rulings have questioned the 4th grounding noted above. The Supreme Court in *Chavez v. Martinez*, 538 U.S. 760 (2003), concluded that compelling an incriminatory statement did not in itself constitute a violation of the self-incrimination, but in describing the subsequent government use of the compelled statement that would complete the violation, noted only that the prohibited use in a "criminal case" did not include pre-complaint activities. See Note 4, p. 613. Subsequent circuit court rulings divided as to whether the prohibition could include use in proceedings that came after the prosecution was initiated but before trial. See CRIMPROC § 2.10(b). That, in turn, led to rulings regarding the use of a compelled statement in a preliminary hearing, as discussed in Note 4, below.

4. ***Self-incriminations and compelled statements.*** Is the self-incrimination clause violated when the government uses, at a preliminary hearing, an incriminating statement of the defendant obtained by means deemed to constitute compulsion under that clause? The circuit court rulings speaking to this issue have not involved challenges to preliminary hearing bindovers, but § 1983 actions brought by former defendants who were never convicted but had a compelled statement (and/or evidence discovered through that statement) used by the government in a pretrial proceeding. Among the circuits rejecting the position that the clause prohibits use only at trial (and sentencing, see Note 1.c., p. 1449), the Tenth Circuit has advanced the most extensive reasoning centering on the preliminary hearing.

Vogt v. City of Hayes, 844 F.3d 1235 (10th Cir. 2017), held that plaintiff Vogt set forth a sustainable § 1983 cause of action in alleging that the police department of the City of Hayes (his former employer): (1) utilized compulsion (as established in *Garrity v. New Jersey*[c]) to obtain from him several incriminating statements, and (2) then caused those statements to be admitted into evidence (along with derivative evidence) in the Kansas preliminary hearing that followed the filing of a criminal charge as to an incident revealed in those statements. The Tenth Circuit viewed the critical issue as to whether the "criminal case" reference in the self-incrimination clause included pretrial proceedings such as the Kansas "probable cause hearing." It reasoned that the "text of Fifth Amendment, * * * interpret[ed] in light of the common understanding of the phrase 'criminal case,' " and the "Framer's understanding of the right against self-incrimination," clearly established that the self-incrimination clause is "more than a trial right." The Supreme Court had previously noted that the term "criminal case" is broader than the Sixth Amendment's "criminal prosecution," and it therefore appears to encompass all of the proceedings involved in a "criminal prosecution," which includes a preliminary hearing (see Note 1, p. 922). Relevant sources (founding-era dictionaries and caselaw) similarly indicate that the terms "case" and "cause" were used synonymously. Also, "there was consensus that the right against self-incrimination was not limited to the suspect's trial," as the "right against self-accusation was understood to arise primarily in pretrial or pre-prosecution settings [e.g., the grand jury] rather than in the context of a person's own criminal trial, * * * [where] criminal defendants were then unable to testify." While it was true that "courts have held in other contexts that evidence may be used in pretrial proceedings [such as preliminary hearings], even if the evidence would be inadmissible at trial, * * * [t]he defendant's attempt to impart this practice into the Fifth Amendment context * * * avoid[ed] the question by assuming that use of compelled statements in pretrial proceedings is not rendered inadmissible by the Fifth Amendment."

The Supreme Court subsequently granted certiorari in *City of Hayes v. Vogt*, on a petition which described the question presented as: "Whether the Fifth Amendment is violated when allegedly compelled statements are used at a probable cause hearing but not a criminal trial." The Court also granted the motion of the United States Solicitor General to participate in oral argument as amicus curiae (supporting the City of Hayes). In their briefs and oral arguments, neither the City of Hayes nor the Solicitor General challenged the Tenth Circuit's conclusion that the Kansas preliminary hearing was part of a "criminal case." They argued that the use of the compelled statements at the preliminary hearing did not make Vogt "a witness against himself"; that could occur only in proceedings that ultimately determine guilt and punishment because those are the only stages in the criminal case where the defendant's statement may be used to "incriminate" him. At oral argument, apart from discussion of whether this was an appropriate interpretation of the Fifth Amendment,[d] several justices raised issues relating to the record. One concern was the lack of information as to whether Vogt had filed a motion to suppress his statements or otherwise objected to their use in the preliminary hearing (Kansas allowed such an objection), with Justice Sotomayor strongly suggesting that such a failure would constitute a waiver that foreclosed § 1983 relief. Other questions related to whether the statements or their

---

[c] In *Garrity v. New Jersey*, 385 U.S. 493 (1967), police officers suspected of involvement in ticket fixing were summoned to answer questions under oath in an internal investigation. They were told that, while they had a right to remain silent, they could be fired for refusing to answer questions pertaining to their official actions. They responded with incriminating answers that subsequently were used against them in a criminal prosecution. The Supreme Court held that those statements had been compelled in violation of the Fifth Amendment (i.e., they were basically coerced confessions) and use of those statements to convict of a crime was therefore barred.

[d] One issue raised in this connection was whether the preliminary hearing could be distinguished from other pretrial proceedings—in particular, whether a ruling rejecting the governments argument and sustaining Vogt's claim would also extend to the grand jury proceeding, see Note 6, p. 961, the competency to stand trial proceeding (and require reexamination of the suggestion in *Estelle v. Smith*, Note 1, p. 544, that the statement obtained in a compelled psychiatric examination could be used in that proceeding, though not in sentencing), and the *Gerstein* determination.

fruits had actually been used in the preliminary hearing (which had ended in a dismissal). Not surprisingly, in light of the concerns expressed about the record, the Court subsequently dismissed the writ of certiorari as improvidently granted. *City of Hayes, Kansas v. Vogt*, certiorari dismissed as improvidently granted, 138 S.Ct. 1683 (2018).

B. THE DEFENDANT'S RIGHT OF CROSS-EXAMINATION

1. The Supreme Court has long held that the Sixth Amendment's confrontation clause is a trial right and does not apply to the preliminary hearing. See *Goldsby v. United States,* 160 U.S. 70 (1895). In all jurisdictions, however, local law (usually statute or court rule) grants to the accused a right to cross-examine "adverse witnesses" who testify at the preliminary hearing. See e.g., Fed.R.Crim.P. 5.1(e). In general, the right to cross-examine at the preliminary hearing is not quite as extensive as the right to cross-examine at trial. Fairly typical is the standard set forth in *People v. Horton,* 358 N.E.2d 1121 (Ill.1976): "It [cross-examination] may not extend beyond the scope of direct examination and such further interrogation as is directed to show interest, bias, prejudice or motive of the witness to the extent that these factors are relevant to the question of probable cause." In restricting cross-examination at the preliminary hearing, magistrates most commonly cite two grounds: (1) that the defendant is attempting improperly to use cross-examination as a pretrial discovery device, and (2) that further cross-examination is unnecessary since it would only raise issues of credibility more appropriately left to the trial jury. As indicated in the notes that follow, states vary considerably in their treatment of each of these grounds.

2. ***Discovery and cross-examination.*** Almost all jurisdictions have recognized the magistrate's authority to cut-off cross-examination which appears to be aimed primarily at obtaining discovery. They differ, however, in the leeway granted to the magistrate in determining whether cross-examination is being used primarily to obtain discovery rather than to refute the prosecution's showing of probable cause.[e] Consider, for example, the following cases:

(a) In *Wilson v. State,* 208 N.W.2d 134 (Wis.1973), the victim's wife identified the defendant at the preliminary hearing as the man who shot her husband. On cross-examination, she acknowledged that she had given a description of the assailant to the police. Defense counsel was not allowed to question her, however, as to the details of that description or her subsequent identification of the defendant at a lineup. In holding that the magistrate erred in treating those questions as aimed primarily at discovery, the Wisconsin court noted: "There is a point where attacks on credibility become discovery. That point is crossed when one delves into general trustworthiness of the witness, as opposed to plausibility of the story. Because all that need be established for a bindover is probable cause, all that is needed is a believable account of the defendant's commission of a felony. Applying this standard to the case now before this court, defense counsel should have been allowed to cross-examine the state's witness on her prior description of the man who shot her husband. * * * [T]he question propounded did not merely go to the witness's general trustworthiness, but also to the plausibility of her description of the defendant, upon which the finding of probable cause rested."

(b) In *People ex rel. Pierce v. Thomas,* 334 N.Y.S.2d 666 (Sup.Ct.1972), the complaining witness identified the defendants at the preliminary hearing as the persons who had robbed him while he was riding a subway train. On cross-examination, defense counsel elicited the complainant's acknowledgment that he had never seen the defendants prior to the three-minute long incident. Counsel was not allowed to ask, however, whether other persons had been present

---

[e] Differing views of the relationship between discovery and effective cross-examination also are reflected in the rules governing defendant's access to prior recorded statements of preliminary hearing witnesses possessed by the prosecution. Several jurisdictions grant the defense access to those statements for possible use in impeaching the witnesses. See e.g. Fed. R. Crim. P. 26.2(g). Others hold, however, that disclosure of those statements is part of the pretrial or trial discovery process and access will not be granted until the time provided for such discovery.

at the time or whether the complainant had ever recovered his possessions. In sustaining the magistrate's refusal to permit such questions, the trial court noted that the "hearing is not intended as a pre-trial discovery device nor is it a substitute for the trial itself." While defense counsel's questions would be permitted at trial, they were "beyond the scope of the hearing."

3. ***Cross-examination and the magistrate's judgment of credibility.*** Magistrates commonly assume that they have the authority to limit (or even bar) cross-examination on the ground that the direct testimony clearly establishes probable cause and "nothing that the cross-examination might reveal is likely to change the result." The few appellate courts that have considered and sustained that authority have emphasized either that (1) the magistrate has only a limited authority to judge credibility and can readily assess when a line of cross-examination would fail to establish the implausibility needed to reject a witness' testimony (see Note 5, p. 933) or (2) the magistrate, as a finder of fact, may conclude that prospective cross-examination, because it follows a certain path, simply will not be persuasive. Such reasoning did not prevail, however, in the case presenting the leading judicial discussion of the magistrate's authority to so limit cross-examination (or to use the same rationale to limit the evidence presented by the defense). *Myers v. Commonwealth*, 298 N.E.2d 819 (Mass. 1973), involved a preliminary hearing on a rape charge, at which only the complainant testified for the prosecution. When defense counsel questioned the complainant about her alleged belief in witchcraft, the magistrate terminated the preliminary hearing, noting that he had "heard enough testimony to find probable cause." The magistrate rejected defense counsel's objection that he wished to complete the cross-examination and to introduce evidence, including a psychiatric evaluation of the complaining witness. On review prior to trial, the appellate court (per Tauro, C.J.) ordered that a new preliminary hearing be held:

"The Commonwealth argues that once a prima facie showing of probable cause has been made by prosecution testimony, the examining magistrate can end the hearing before the defendant's attorney has had an opportunity to make a complete cross-examination of the prosecution witness or to present an affirmative defense. We fail to see how such a limited procedure could possibly effectuate the hearing's primary function of screening out cases that should not go to trial.* * * The primary function of the probable cause hearing of screening out 'an erroneous or improper prosecution,' *Coleman v. Alabama* [Note 1, p. 922], can only be effectuated by an adversary hearing where the defendant is given a meaningful opportunity to challenge the credibility of the prosecution's witnesses and to raise any affirmative defenses he may have. * * * The facts of the instant case provide an excellent illustration of this point. The only witness at the petitioner's probable cause hearing was the complaining witness who repeated her accusation that the petitioner had raped her. If the petitioner had been afforded his statutory rights, he would have introduced testimony challenging the complaining witness's credibility and supporting his defense of a consensual sexual relationship. The examining magistrate could not have possibly made an informed judgment on the question of whether there was sufficient credible evidence of the defendant's guilt to support a bindover until he had considered all of this evidence."

"In some cases, the evidence introduced in behalf of the defendant will do no more than raise a conflict which can best be resolved by a jury at the actual trial where the Commonwealth must prove the defendant's guilt beyond a reasonable doubt. But, in other cases, the evidence elicited by defense counsel on cross-examination or from the testimony of defense witnesses or from other evidence may lead the examining magistrate to disbelieve the prosecution's witnesses and discharge the defendant for lack of probable cause. * * * Regardless of whether the petitioner's evidence in the instant case would have been sufficient to overcome the prosecution's case for probable cause, he had a statutory right to have the judge consider it before making his decision."

Myers also held that the proper bindover standard was a prima facie case standard. See Note 2, p. 932. Would the reasoning of the *Myers* court be less persuasive under a traditional probable cause standard? Would it be less persuasive in a jurisdiction that sharply limits the magistrate's authority to judge credibility?

4. ***The perpetuation of testimony.*** Preliminary hearing testimony traditionally has been admitted at trial as substantive evidence, under the "prior testimony" exception to the hearsay rule, where the witness is currently unavailable to testify. Thus, the hearing perpetuates the testimony of witnesses, ensuring that it may be used even if the witness should die, disappear, or otherwise become unavailable to testify.[f] In CALIFORNIA v. GREEN, 399 U.S. 149 (1970), the Supreme Court sustained this traditional position against a Sixth Amendment confrontation clause challenge. The Court there upheld the constitutionality of admitting preliminary hearing testimony where the prosecution witness was "unavailable" solely because of a loss of memory. The primary point of concern in *Green* was the treatment of the witness' loss of memory as a type of "unavailability," but both the majority and dissent commented as well on the application of the "prior testimony" exception to preliminary hearing testimony. The majority opinion, per White, J., noted in this regard:

"[The witness] Porter's statement at the preliminary hearing had already been given under circumstances closely approximating those that surround the typical trial. Porter was under oath; respondent was represented by counsel—the same counsel in fact who later represented him at the trial; respondent had every opportunity to cross-examine Porter as to his statement; and the proceedings were conducted before a judicial tribunal, equipped to provide a judicial record of the hearings. * * * This Court long ago held that admitting the prior testimony of any unavailable witness does not violate the Confrontation Clause. *Mattox v. United States,* 156 U.S. 237 (1895). That case involved testimony given at the defendant's first trial by a witness who had died by the time of the second trial, but we do not find the instant preliminary hearing significantly different from an actual trial to warrant distinguishing the two cases for purposes of the Confrontation Clause. * * * In the present case respondent's counsel does not appear to have been significantly limited in any way in the scope or nature of his cross-examination of the witness Porter at the preliminary hearing."

Justice Brennan, dissenting, argued that the admission of a witness' preliminary hearing statement violates the accused's right of confrontation "where the witness is in court and either is unwilling or unable to testify regarding the pertinent events." The dissent argued that such "unavailability" was particularly suspect, and in that context (in contrast to the situation where the witness is "physically unavailable"), cross-examination at a preliminary hearing could not provide sufficient countervailing indicia of reliability. On the latter point, the dissent noted:

"Cross-examination at the [preliminary] hearing pales beside that which takes place at trial. This is so for a number of reasons. First, as noted, the objective of the hearing is to establish the presence or absence of probable cause, not guilt or innocence proved beyond a reasonable doubt; thus, if evidence suffices to establish probable cause, defense counsel has little reason at the preliminary hearing to show that it does not conclusively establish guilt—or, at least, he had little reason before today's decision. Second, neither defense nor prosecution is eager before trial to

---

[f] See Fed.R.Evid. 804(a) setting forth the traditional grounds of unavailability: " 'Unavailability as a witness' includes situations in which the declarant: (1) is exempted by ruling of the court on the ground of privilege from testifying concerning the subject matter of the declarant's statement; or (2) persists in refusing to testify concerning the subject matter of the declarant's statement despite an order of the court to do so; or (3) testifies to a lack of memory of the subject matter of the declarant's statement; or (4) is unable to be present or to testify at the hearing because of death or then existing physical or mental illness or infirmity; or (5) is absent from the hearing and the proponent of a statement has been unable to procure the declarant's attendance * * * by process or other reasonable means. * * * "

It should be noted, in connection with the 5th ground, that persons located outside the trial jurisdiction will not necessarily be "unavailable." If his whereabouts are known, a witness located in another state ordinarily may be subjected to compulsory process under the Uniform Act to Secure The Attendance of Witnesses From Without a State in Criminal Proceedings, 11 U.L.A. 2 (1974).

disclose its case by extensive examination at the preliminary hearing; thorough questioning of a prosecution witness by defense counsel may easily amount to a grant of gratis discovery to the state. Third, the schedules of neither court nor counsel can easily accommodate lengthy preliminary hearings. Fourth, even were the judge and lawyers not concerned that the proceedings be brief, the defense and prosecution have generally had inadequate time before the hearing to prepare for extensive examination. * * * It appears, then, that in terms of the purposes of the Confrontation Clause, an equation of face-to-face encounter at the preliminary hearing with confrontation at trial must rest largely on the fact that the witness testified at the hearing under oath, subject to the penalty for perjury and in a courtroom atmosphere. These factors are not insignificant, but by themselves they fall far short of satisfying the demands of constitutional confrontation. Moreover, the atmosphere and stakes are different in the two proceedings. In the hurried, somewhat *pro forma* context of the average preliminary hearing, a witness may be more careless in his testimony than in the more measured and searching atmosphere of a trial. Similarly, a man willing to perjure himself when the consequences are simply that the accused will stand trial may be less willing to do so when his lies may condemn the defendant to loss of liberty. In short, it ignores reality to assume that the purposes of the Confrontation Clause are met during a preliminary hearing. * * * "[g]

In *Crawford v. Washington*, 541 U.S. 36 (2004), where the Court reexamined the function of the confrontation clause (see p. 1308), the Court referred to the prior preliminary hearing testimony of an unavailable witness as being admissible "if the defendant had an *adequate opportunity* to cross-examine" (emphasis added). Lower courts subsequently have noted that, in light of *Green's* rejection of Justice Brenan's arguments concerning the basic structure of the preliminary hearing, the core elements of that structure may not be viewed as per se rendering inadequate the opportunity to cross-examine. On the other hand, the specific circumstances of the case can undercut that opportunity (e.g., where counsel, lacking discovery, could not obtain critical information that would have altered completely the preliminary hearing cross-examination). So too, a few courts have concluded that state law sharply restricting cross-examination may render the opportunity inadequate. See CRIMPROC § 14.1(d).

C. DEFENDANT'S RIGHT TO PRESENT WITNESSES

1. ***Use of defense witnesses.*** Most jurisdictions recognize, specifically or by implication, a general defense right of subpoena authority to present witnesses at the preliminary hearing. See e.g., Fed.R.Crim.P. 5.1(e). In several states, however, defense witnesses (other than the defendant himself) may be called only with the permission of the magistrate. The conventional wisdom on the use of defense witnesses appears to be much the same in both types of jurisdictions. Defense counsel generally adhere to the principle that defense witnesses should not be presented unless the case is quite exceptional.

In many hearings, defense counsel's primary objectives are to obtain discovery and to establish a basis for the impeachment of the prosecution's witnesses at trial. Presenting defense witnesses ordinarily will not help in achieving either of these objectives. In other instances, counsel also may seek to vigorously challenge the prosecution's showing of probable cause, but

---

[g] The majority responded that, notwithstanding these limitations, Justice Brennan acknowledged that Porter's preliminary hearing testimony would have been admissible if Porter had died. "As a constitutional matter," it reasoned, "it is untenable to construe the confrontation clause to permit the use of the prior testimony * * * where the declarant never appears, but to bar the testimony where the declarant is present at trial." The key to unavailability was whether "the State * * * has made every effort to introduce its evidence through the live testimony of the witness" and that condition had been met here. It further noted: "Surely in terms of protecting the defendant's interests, and the jury's ability to assess the reliability of the evidence it hears, it seems most unlikely that respondent in this case would have been better off, as the dissent seems to suggest, if Porter had died, and his prior testimony were admitted, than he was in the instant case where Porter's conduct on the stand cast substantial doubt on his prior statement."

even then, the usual approach is to rely entirely on cross-examination of prosecution witnesses. Unless the credibility of prosecution witnesses has been shaken substantially on cross-examination, the contrary testimony of defense witnesses is likely to be treated by the magistrate as simply presenting a credibility conflict that should be resolved by the fact-finder at trial. Moreover, by presenting the defense witness at the preliminary hearing, the defendant runs the risk of making that witness' testimony less effective at trial. Just as the defense may use its cross-examination of prosecution witnesses to gain discovery and to prepare for future impeachment, the prosecution may use its cross-examination of the defense witnesses to achieve the same goals. Whatever value defense witnesses may have in rebutting the prosecution's probable cause showing is generally thought to be outweighed by the tactical advantages given the prosecution if the case should go to trial.

2. ***Credibility and discovery limitations.*** A magistrate's authority to deny a defense subpoena because the testimony of a proposed witness would do no more than raise a credibility issue presents issues similar to the restriction of cross-examination on that ground. See Note 3, p. 940. The prohibition against use of subpoena authority for the purpose of obtaining discovery also is a counterpart to a limitation on cross-examination. Here, however, one special setting stands out in the application of the prohibition—the defense calling a prospective prosecution trial witness (typically, where only the investigating officer testifies, calling the victim). The division in *State v. O'Brien*, 850 N.W. 2d 8 (Wis. 2014), reflects the importance of judicial perspective in analyzing that situation.

The *O'Brien* defendants were charged with counts of child abuse and disorderly conduct relating to their adopted children. The state investigator testified as to statements that the children had made in interviews by a social worker and in her interview of one of the children, S.M.O. On cross-examination, the investigator acknowledged that the complaint she had filed did not "contain the complete statement from S.M.O. that provided the factual basis for count one, but was a summary." On cross-examination also, the investigator "provided some additional detail * * * [but] could not remember enough about the interviews to respond to many of counsel's questions." Defense counsel then sought to subpoena S.M.O., explaining that S.M.O.'s testimony was relevant because it would "fill in the gaps in the Investigator's story," that with the complete story, "it may appear that the [O'Briens'] actions were accidental as opposed to intentional," but "they were not sure what S.M.O. would actually say." This showing was deemed inadequate and the subpoena was quashed. A divided Wisconsin Supreme Court affirmed.

The Court majority (per Wilson, J) considered the denial in the context of a claim that the subpoena could only be quashed to implement the provision allowing bindover reliance on hearsay testimony (see fn. b, p. 936). It rejected that contention, finding ample ground for quashing the subpoena in the general principles governing preliminary hearing subpoena authority. The defendant "must be able to show that the evidence is relevant to the probable cause determination," and that excluded "issues relating to weight and credibility," as opposed to "plausibility." It also excluded use for discovery. "Absent any idea what S.M.O. would testify to, counsel's proffer was insufficient to show that S.M.O.'s testimony would be relevant." The dissent (per Abrahamson, C.J.) agreed that defense counsel is "limited to presenting evidence at the preliminary examination relevant to probable cause and plausibility (not credibility)," and that discovery was not a proper function. However, consideration had to be given to the limited ability of the defendant to make a proffer. "When a defendant has no way of knowing exactly what a witness knows or will testify to at a preliminary examination, the law does not place a significant burden on the defendant to demonstrate relevance." Otherwise, "with the limited tools of criminal discovery available in pretrial proceedings, how can a defendant ever challenge double or triple hearsay in a police report read by an individual who never interviewed the hearsay declarant." Here, "the offer of proof, although admittedly weak, sufficed to call the declarant."

3. ***"Affirmative defenses."*** The states are divided as to the defendant's right to present at the preliminary hearing what are commonly characterized as "affirmative defenses"—i.e., defenses which do not negate any element of the crime, but operate, in effect, as a confession and avoidance that relieves the actor of liability. Caselaw on this issue is sparse because the conventional wisdom argues against the defense disclosing such a defense at a preliminary hearing. "Not surprisingly, the leading cases deal with attempts to present a defense of entrapment"; since "presentment of the entrapment defense [to the jury at trial] is a highly risky venture, counsel might readily conclude that entrapment defense should be presented at the preliminary hearing with an eye toward not repeating it as a trial defense should it not persuade or come close to persuading the magistrate." CRIMPROC § 14.4(D). A jurisdiction that accepts presentation of entrapment will also allow presentation of other affirmative defenses. But does rejecting the presentation of an entrapment defense necessarily preclude presentation of all affirmative defenses? As noted in CRIMPROC, supra "no court has suggested that a defendant can be precluded from introducing evidence of self-defense at a preliminary hearing." Factors that might lead to disallowing presentation of a particular affirmative defense include: (1) the defendant bears the burden of proof in establishing the defense; (2) the defense relates to events and circumstances other than those which the prosecution would investigate in the course of establishing the elements of the crime; and (3) raising the defense carries with it special defense responsibilities in providing access to the prosecution (e.g., insanity). Where an affirmative defense (e.g., self-defense) is cognizable, the issue for the magistrate is whether there is probable cause that the defense might *not* apply.

4. ***Exculpatory evidence.*** *State v. Mitchell,* 512 A.2d 140 (Conn.1986), holds that the prosecutor's constitutional duty under the *Brady* doctrine [Pt. A, p. 1130], to disclose material exculpatory evidence within its control, extends to the preliminary hearing, as well as the trial. In light of the hearing's status in Connecticut as "an essential part of the defendant's criminal prosecution," disclosure at that point was consistent with the "unmistakable tone" of *Brady* "that the exculpatory evidence be disclosed at a time when it can be used." Compare *State v. Benson,* 661 P.2d 908 (Okl.Crim.App.1983) (*Brady* disclosure relates to the trial and trial preparation, and therefore is within the exclusive authority of the trial court). Consider also Notes 1–4, pp. 1141–1142 (division on requiring pretrial disclosure of *Brady* material).

CHAPTER 16

GRAND JURY REVIEW

■ ■ ■

The grand jury traditionally has been assigned two functions in the criminal justice process. One is its investigative function, described briefly in Chapter 1 (p. 8) and more fully in Chapter 11. This chapter considers the grand jury's other major function, commonly characterized as its "shielding" or "screening" function. One of the most frequently cited descriptions of this function is found in *Wood v. Georgia*, 370 U.S. 375 (1962):

> "Historically, this body [the grand jury] has been regarded as a primary security to the innocent against hasty, malicious and oppressive persecution; it serves the invaluable function in our society of standing between the accuser and the accused, whether the latter be an individual, minority group, or other, to determine whether a charge is founded upon reason or was dictated by an intimidating power or by malice and personal ill will."

Grand jury screening is mandated through a requirement that a criminal prosecution be brought by an indictment—a charging instrument issued by the grand jury. In determining whether an indictment should issue, the grand jury first hears the prosecution's presentation of its case (in an ex parte, closed proceeding) and then decides whether that case justifies bringing a prosecution before the trial court (see Ch. 1, § 2, steps 10 and 11).

Section 1 of this chapter discusses the current use of prosecution by indictment. That section also presents a brief description of the debate over the continued effectiveness of grand jury screening, which, in large part, explains why prosecution by indictment is no longer required in a substantial majority of the states. Sections 2–4 consider legal challenges to the grand jury's exercise of its screening authority. Those challenges are presented almost exclusively through defense motions to dismiss an indictment. Sections 2–4 address the primary screening objections raised in such motions. As noted in those sections, there is considerable variation among the jurisdictions using indictments as to the range of objections that will be recognized.

§ 1. ON REQUIRING GRAND JURY REVIEW

A. PROSECUTION BY INDICTMENT: FEDERAL AND STATE REQUIREMENTS

As noted in Chapter 11, the English grand jury originally was established to assist the Crown in reporting crimes, but it was its eventual development as a shield against arbitrary prosecutions by the Crown that led to its recognition in the federal constitution. That was achieved in the Fifth Amendment, which provides that, except in certain military cases, "no person shall be held to answer for a capital, or otherwise infamous crime, unless on a presentment or indictment of a Grand Jury." The Fifth Amendment thus ensures that a federal charge for a felony offense will not be brought without granting the accused the protection of the review and acceptance of the charge by the grand jury (as expressed through its issuance of an indictment).[a]

[a] The Amendment's reference to "infamous crimes" has been held to encompass all felony offenses. See CRIMPROC § 15.1(a). In misdemeanor prosecutions, where the amendment does not apply, federal law permits the prosecution to proceed by indictment if it so chooses, but it may also use an information. See Fed.R.Crim.P. 58(b).

At the time of the adoption of the Fifth Amendment, all of the states also required that felony prosecutions be brought by indictment. Today, however, only eighteen states make a grand jury indictment mandatory for the prosecution of all felonies (although four additional states require an indictment for capital offenses or capital and/or life imprisonment offenses).[b] Almost all of the remaining states permit prosecution either by indictment or information at the option of the prosecutor. Given that choice, prosecutors in these "information states" regularly have chosen the information alternative for the vast majority of their prosecutions. See Note 5, p. 921.

The movement away from compulsory prosecution by indictment began with Michigan's adoption of the information alternative in 1859, and several states (including California) soon followed Michigan's lead. As expected, such a revolutionary change in the processing of felony cases did not go unchallenged. Its constitutionality reached the Supreme Court in HURTADO v. CALIFORNIA, 110 U.S. 516 (1884). The Court there sustained a California first degree murder conviction in which prosecution had been initiated by information rather than indictment. *Hurtado* was one of the first rulings interpreting the Fourteenth Amendment's due process clause, and Justice Matthews' opinion for the majority stressed the need for a flexible interpretation of that clause. Due process, Justice Matthews noted, should impose on the states only those "fundamental principles of liberty and justice which lie at the base of all our civil political institutions" and should emphasize the "substance" of those principles rather than their "forms and modes of attainment." The opinion concluded:

"Tried by these principles, we are unable to say that the substitution for a presentment or indictment by a grand jury of the proceeding by information, after examination and commitment by a magistrate, certifying to the probable guilt of the defendant, with the right on his part to the aid of counsel, and to the cross-examination of the witnesses produced for the prosecution, is not due process of law. It is, as we have seen, an ancient proceeding at common law, which might include every case of an offence of less grade than a felony, except misprision of treason; and in every circumstance of its administration, as authorized by the statute of California, it carefully considers and guards the substantial interest of the prisoner. It is merely a preliminary proceeding and can result in no final judgment, except as the consequence of a regular judicial trial, conducted precisely as in cases of indictments."

Justice Harlan's dissenting opinion stressed the history of the grand jury in English and American law and the recognition of the grand jury in the federal constitution. The dissent also stressed the need for screening by representatives of the community rather than by a magistrate, who will "hold office at the will of the government or at the will of the voters." Although the Supreme Court in the 1960s adopted a "selective incorporation" interpretation of the Fourteenth Amendment, and overruled various earlier decisions refusing to find in due process particular guarantees specified in the Bill of Rights, see Ch. 2, § 1, it has continued to adhere to the *Hurtado* holding that states need not prosecute by indictment. Indeed, the indictment guarantee is the only Bill of Rights guarantee relating to the criminal process that clearly has not been incorporated (and therefore will not be applied to the states). See fn. 13, p. 26; CRIMPROC § 15.1(c).

Although the Fifth Amendment refers to prosecution by "presentment" as well as "indictment," federal law now provides only for use of the indictment. See Fed.R.Crim.P. 7. Historically, a presentment was a formal charge similar to an indictment except that it was prepared by the grand jury on its own initiative. See CRIMPROC §§ 15.1(a), 15.1(d). The term "presentment" today is also used in describing reports issued by investigative grand juries that are not charging instruments.

[b] The 18 states are: Alabama, Alaska, Delaware, Georgia, Kentucky, Maine, Massachusetts, Mississippi, New Hampshire, New Jersey, New York, North Carolina, Ohio, South Carolina, Tennessee, Texas, Virginia, and West Virginia. The four "limited indictment" jurisdictions are Florida, Louisiana, Minnesota, and Rhode Island.

B. THE USE OF GRAND JURY INDICTMENTS

1. ***Indictment jurisdictions: the use of waiver.*** While the Fifth Amendment and the various state constitutional provisions requiring grand jury indictments do not mention specifically the possibility of waiver, courts have almost uniformly held that these provisions do not preclude acceptance of a defense waiver. Several courts have suggested, however, that since waiver of indictment was not permitted at common law, it should be accepted only if authorized by statute. Most indictment jurisdictions now have statutes or court rules allowing knowing and voluntary waivers. A few permit waiver in all cases; several, permit waiver in all but capital cases; and several restrict the availability of waivers to certain types of non-capital cases. The effect of the waiver, where permitted, is to allow the prosecution to charge by information (typically without a preliminary hearing). See e.g., Fed.R.Crim.P. 7(b).

2. The rate of waivers varies substantially among indictment jurisdictions. At one time the waiver rate in federal courts was as low as 5%, but in recent years, it has been in the neighborhood of 20%. Available statistics from a limited number of indictment states suggest waiver rates not quite as high as the recent federal rates. CRIMPROC § 15.1(f). Studies suggest that waivers are most frequently made where the defendant intends to plead guilty, and many waivers probably are part of a plea bargain. Where the defendant intends to go to trial, the conventional wisdom advises against waiver, although not because it is anticipated that the grand jury will refuse to indict. Prosecution by indictment may offer the defense a potential advantage since local law may make pleading defects in an indictment more difficult to cure by amendment than similar defects in an information. See Note 3, p. 1010. Also, if the jurisdiction precludes the use of hearsay before the grand jury, key witnesses will have to testify before the grand jury and that testimony, in most states, will be available for impeachment use at trial. See Note 4, p. 1096. On the other hand, the conventional wisdom also recognizes that there are some situations in which a defendant who intends to go to trial may prefer to waive. The defense may be concerned that the prosecutor will gain valuable preparation for trial in presenting the state's witnesses before the grand jury. A defendant also has an incentive to waive if he is in jail or would otherwise be inconvenienced by delay and his case cannot promptly be presented to the grand jury.

3. ***Information states.*** As discussed in Notes 5–6, pp. 921–922, prosecutors in information states vary in their use of the alternative of prosecuting by indictment, which usually allows the prosecutor to avoid having a preliminary hearing. In some information states, a significant group of prosecutors will make frequent use of indictments, but for most information states, prosecutors rarely, if at all, turn to indictments. As a result, many information states have no caselaw or very limited, older caselaw relating to challenges to the grand jury's decision to indict. Thus, surveys of the state law applied to such challenges tend to look largely to standards applied in the indictment states.

C. THE EFFECTIVENESS DEBATE

1. ***The primary positions.*** The debate over the effectiveness of grand jury screening dates back at least to Bentham's challenge to the English grand jury in the mid-1800s. See CRIMPROC § 15.3 (reviewing the debate over the years, and noting that it has become "one-sided" in current academic commentary, which "has almost uniformly been critical of relying upon grand jury screening"). Today's critics tend to fall into two groups: (1) those who characterize the grand jury as a worthless "rubber stamp" of the prosecutor, and support its elimination as a screening device, or if that cannot be done due to the difficulty of amending constitutions (federal and state), at least giving the defendant the option to choose preliminary hearing screening over grand jury screening; and (2) those who view the grand jury as having the potential to be a legitimate screening alternative to the preliminary hearing, but only if it is reformed to include various safeguards. Both groups point to statements of former prosecutors and former grand jurors that speak of the

prosecutor's absolute dominance of grand jury screening, and both point to statistics viewed as clearly establishing that dominance. They cite in particular federal system statistics which show that federal grand juries refuse to indict in less than 1% of the cases presented to them.[c]

Critics in the second category often prefer preliminary hearing screening to grand jury screening, but argue that grand jury screening, with appropriate reforms, can become an acceptable alternative. They call primarily for the following reforms (already in place in at least some jurisdictions): (1) requiring the court, in its charge to the grand jury, to fully inform the grand jurors of their independent authority, including the authority to nullify, and to impress upon the jurors their obligation to screen out unworthy prosecutions;[d] (2) giving the grand jury its own counsel (currently the practice only in Hawaii) or at least informing the grand jury that it can turn to the court for legal advice whenever it is not satisfied with the advice provided by the prosecutor (a practice specifically endorsed in several states); (3) giving the target the right to testify before the grand jury[e]; (4) requiring the prosecutor to present available exculpatory evidence (see Note 4, p. 975); (5) forbidding prosecutor use of evidence which would be constitutionally inadmissible at trial (see Note 2, p. 964); (6) prohibiting the use of hearsay evidence to support the indictment, except under narrowly defined circumstances (see Note 2, p. 964); (7) requiring the prosecution to meet a "prima facie case" standard of proof, rather than the lesser "probable cause" standard (which is favored by a slight majority of the states addressing the issue); (8) requiring an affirmative vote of a "supermajority" of grand jurors (e.g., two-thirds) to issue an indictment (as required in a majority of the states, including a majority of the indictment states, with the minority and the federal system requiring a simple majority of the jury's maximum size); (9) prohibiting prosecutorial resubmissions following a grand jury decision not to indict, absent a showing made to a court that the prosecution has newly discovered additional evidence (currently a minority position, as the dominant view allows resubmission without limitation); and (10) providing for a post-indictment, pretrial defense challenge that would require the trial court to review the grand jury transcript to ensure that were no significant

[c] See Andrew Leipold, *Prosecutorial Charging Practices and Grand Jury Screening: Some Empirical Observations,* in Grand Jury 2.0, 193 (Roger Fairfax ed. 2011) (in 2007, "federal grand juries returned a 'no bill' in fewer than two dozen cases and returned indictments more than 63,000 times, a government success rate of more than 99.9%"). Reports on rejection rates in indictment states are incomplete and often dated. Those reports include states with very low rates of no-bills (though not quite as low as the federal rate) and reports from other states with "rates as high as 10–20 percent." CRIMPROC § 15.3(b) (also noting that critics of grand jury screening suggest that the higher rates reflect a prosecutor practice of bringing to the grand jury cases in which the prosecutor would prefer not to charge, and so recommends, see fn. d, p. 921).

[d] As discussed in Note 2, p. 973, the Ninth Circuit in *United States v. Navarro-Vargas* concluded that the grand jury lacks nullification authority, although other appellate opinions have characterized nullification as a major attribute of grand jury review. See e.g., Note 7, p. 955. Reviewing the standard grand jury charges in various states, the Ninth Circuit noted that only a small group of states used language that either explicitly recognizes or arguably suggests to the grand jurors that they can refuse to indict even if the evidence is sufficient.

Grand jury charges commonly do speak to various other aspects of the grand jury's independent authority, including: "the grand jury's obligation to act as an independent body * * *; juror recognition that prosecutors present evidence 'as advocates for the government'; the authority of the grand jurors to have appropriate questions put to witnesses and to request the production of additional witnesses; * * * [and] the need for jurors to make their own judgment of the credibility of witnesses." CRIMPROC § 15.2(e).

[e] A handful of states recognize this right, see CRIMPROC § 15.2(e), but the conventional wisdom is that it will have little impact because few prospective defendants would risk going before a grand jury and being subjected to examination by a prosecutor without the protections afforded at trial (where a testifying defendant will have counsel's assistance and a judge presides). But consider William Glaberson, *New Trend Before Grand Juries, Meet the Accused,* N.Y. Times, June 20, 2004, (in Brooklyn, nearly 14 percent of felony suspects testified before the grand juries investigating their cases, and "slightly more than half of those cases have ended with no charges"; this practice "once extremely rare, is now commonplace" in all five boroughs, with similar results; its increased use is attributed to several factors, including the suspect's right to be accompanied by a lawyer, "new selection methods that broadened the pool of potential jurors," an "increased willingness by grand jurors to question official accounts of crime," and a recognition by lawyers that "the mere fact that the defendant is testifying makes the grand jury sit up and take notice").

procedural violations and that the grand jury received sufficient evidence to support its indictment decision (see Notes 2–4, pp. 964–965). See CRIMPROC § 15.3(a) (collecting citations to the large body of reform literature, including articles advancing still other reforms).

Critics in the first group view such reforms as insufficient to justify retention of grand jury screening. The basic problem, as they see it, lies not in any particular aspect of the process (e.g., in the reliance upon hearsay evidence), but in the very structure of grand jury screening. That structure asks a group of laypersons to apply an unfamiliar legal standard to a one-sided presentation, utilizing a process that is non-adversary, that allows the prosecutor to establish a close rapport with the jurors, and that forces the jurors to rely largely on the prosecutor's investigative resources and legal advice. The proposed reforms, they argue, would modify that structure only slightly. They would not provide the jurors with the experience, the adversarial debate, and the access to all relevant information that is needed to meet the objective of an effective screening process.

Supporters of grand jury review as it traditionally existed (i.e., without the various reforms noted above) reject the underlying premises of both groups of critics. Initially they maintain that the grand jury is a highly effective screening agency. They cite prosecutors who have characterized the grand jury as a valuable sounding board with a mind of its own. The supporters dispute the significance of the low rate of no-bills in many jurisdictions. The critical question, they argue, is whether the statistics on the ultimate disposition of indictments indicate relatively few instances in which indictments lacked evidentiary support for the most serious offense charged (recognizing that effective screening includes preventing prosecutorial overcharging). In the federal system, which provides the most complete statistics, the no-bill rate is low, but the rate of dispositions without conviction also is low (less than 10%, with 9% based on dismissals, which often are based on grounds other than evidence insufficiency, see fn. q, p. 18), and the vast majority of convictions are on the most serious crime charged (notwithstanding that over 95% of the convictions are based on plea bargains). See Leipold, fn. c supra. States often produce much higher post-indictment non-conviction rates (see p. 18), but supporters note that, here again, the non-convictions (almost entirely dismissals) may be based on grounds unrelated to the insufficiency of the evidence (as in the case of dismissals tied to diversions). Moreover, they note, the post-information dismissal rates for states using the supposedly superior screening of a preliminary hearing are often similar to (or even higher than) the dismissal rates in indictment states. Trial rates are so low universally that acquittals say very little about screening, especially since there is no separate category for the acquittal that reflects poor screening—the acquittal directed by the trial judge because the prosecution's evidence could not possibly lead to an acceptable jury conviction.

Supporters of grand jury review also stress that it brings a layperson's sense of reality to the evaluation of the circumstances surrounding the alleged offense. Though critics contend that grand jurors tend to "just sit there, like a bump on a log," prosecutors and others report that grand jurors do ask questions when testimony does not "ring true." Supporters further argue that the strength of grand jury review lies exactly where independent screening is most needed—in those cases in which special factors, e.g., the involvement of politics or racial animosity, are likely to result in unjust accusations. Such cases require a screening agency that can carefully judge credibility and can give consideration to community notions of fairness and justice. As a group selected from the community, the grand jury can more readily provide those qualities than a magistrate at a preliminary hearing. Indeed, they note, only the grand jury has a recognized authority to fully judge credibility (compare Note 5, p. 933 as to the magistrates), and only the grand jury has a recognized power to nullify (even if not so informed, see fn. d, p. 948). The grand jury similarly is ideally suited to leaven the rigidity of the law, and take account of mitigating circumstances in setting the level of the charge. Critics respond that the grand jury's reputation as a community evaluator is largely mythical (based in good part on a small group of celebrated cases from another era, prior to prosecutorial domination), and irrelevant, in any event, to the correction of erroneous charging and over-charging where it is most needed—in the run-of-the-mill case.

2. ***Judicial responses.*** Consider CRIMPROC § 15.3(d):

"While the debate over the effectiveness of grand jury review has been aimed primarily at legislative reform, it has not gone unnoticed by the courts. Several courts have suggested that the critics probably are correct in concluding that grand jury review almost always is a rubber stamp operation. Their response has been to downplay in various respects the significance of the indictment process. Thus, * * * courts have suggested that the safeguards required to ensure against inadvertent 'waivers' of other constitutional rights need not be applied to waivers of the right to indictment since that right is rarely of importance to the defense * * * Other courts have expressed concern as to the possible loss in effectiveness of grand jury review, but have cited that concern as a basis for insisting upon procedural safeguards designed to offset prosecutorial dominance. * * * Finally, still other courts largely reject the criticism of grand jury screening. They view grand jury review as continuing to function effectively, although that judgment may rest upon a view of the process as designed to provide screening less finely tuned than that envisaged by many of those most critical of the process. * * *

"These differences in judgment as to the potential value of grand jury screening are reflected in the judicial treatment of almost all of the various grounds urged for challenging an indictment. While some opinions treating such challenges openly discuss the merits of grand jury review, most do not speak to the issue directly. Very often the court's underlying policy perspective will be obvious from the result it reaches. At times, however, the same ruling might be supported by either of two quite different judgments as to the value of grand jury review. Thus, a court rejecting a challenge to an indictment that was based in part on illegally obtained evidence may be taking the position that: (1) even if the use of such evidence were prohibited, the grand jury still would almost always indict upon the prosecutor's request, so adding a prohibition against such use would simply cause delay without significant gain for an inherently weak screening process; or (2) the grand jury is functioning well as a rough screening body guided by a community sense of justice and the addition of prohibitions against the use of illegally obtained evidence is not needed for effective performance of its assigned role."

§ 2. CHALLENGES TO GRAND JURY COMPOSITION

1. ***Grand jury selection procedures.*** The selection of the grand jury is in some respects quite similar to, and in some respects quite different from, the selection of the petit jury. Initially, in most jurisdictions, the process utilized in selecting that body of persons who will be summoned as prospective jurors (commonly described as the "array" or "venire") is the same for both grand and petit jurors. These jurisdictions require, for both petit jury and grand jury, random selection from one or more representative source lists (see p. 1241). A small group of states, however, still allow the selectors of the grand jury venire (e.g., jury commissioners) sufficient discretion to use a "key-person" system, which was dominant in grand jury selection for many years. Under that system, the selectors will look to a pool of persons nominated by a group of civic leaders, who are directed to include well respected persons from all major racial and socio-economic segments of the community. Under either the random system or the key-person system, the prospective grand jurors will initially be screened for the same basic qualifications for jury service (e.g., residency and age) and the same automatic exemptions (e.g., military personnel) as are applied to petit jurors.

Once an array of qualified and non-exempt jurors is established, the grand jury selection process begins to depart substantially from the process used for selecting petit jurors. Initially, because the grand jury sits for a longer term, a larger portion of the array is likely to be excused on hardship grounds. Secondly, there is no regularized procedure for participation of the defense counsel and the prosecutor in the selection process. Indeed, the defense counsel ordinarily does not enter the picture until after the grand jury has completed its work and charged counsel's client with a crime. The selection process for grand jurors does not involve voir dire conducted by counsel or peremptory challenges, and its version of a challenge for cause tends to be narrower and utilized in a much different fashion.

In general, once prospective grand jurors pass the stage of hardship excuses, they are seated automatically and any challenges to their capacity to fairly judge a particular case will first be raised after indictment, as discussed in Notes 5 and 6 infra. There are, however, a few avenues that may lead to jurors being excused on that ground prior to their taking action on an indictment. In some jurisdictions, before impaneling the grand jury, the presiding judge will ask the prospective jurors general questions about their background as it relates to particular types of offenses (e.g., drug offenses) and will excuse those jurors who might have difficulties in fairly judging such cases. In many jurisdictions, the prosecutor, after briefly introducing a case, will ask the already impaneled jurors whether there is any reason that they should not participate (e.g., whether they know any of the potential defendants or witnesses), and jurors will occasionally be excused through this process.

2. ***Equal protection objections.*** Supreme Court decisions in the latter part of the nineteenth century firmly established that, while the states were not required to use a grand jury in the charging process, if they did so, they could not engage in intentional racial discrimination in selecting the grand jury. In all of its judicial procedures, whether optional or due process mandated, the state remained subject to the command of the Fourteenth Amendment's equal protection clause. The Court's rulings also established that the basic elements of a defendant's equal protection challenge to selection procedures would be the same for both grand and petit juries. This position was reaffirmed in *Campbell v. Louisiana*, 523 U.S. 392 (1998), where the Court held that the standing rule of *Powers v. Ohio* (Note 3(a), p. 1256) applies to grand jury selection as well as petit jury selection, and therefore a "white criminal defendant had standing to object to discrimination against black persons in the selection of the grand jurors." The Court rejected the state's argument that the *Powers* doctrine should not be carried over to grand juries because that doctrine had been established in the context of peremptory challenges, an aspect of jury selection not applicable to grand jury selection.

3. ***Cross-section violations.*** With respect to the petit jury, the Supreme Court has held that the Sixth Amendment, as applied to the states through the Fourteenth Amendment, requires that the jury be drawn from a "fair cross-section of the community." See *Taylor v. Louisiana* (p. 1242). A fair cross-section violation differs in several respects from an equal protection violation. It does not require purposeful discrimination and arguably encompasses underrepresentation of "distinctive groups" who would not be "suspect classes" under equal protection analysis. See Notes 1–5, pp. 1245–1246. Accordingly, the fair cross-section requirement may prohibit selection procedures that would not be prohibited under an equal protection analysis. However, whether such a constitutional requirement applies to grand jury selection remains uncertain.

Various lower federal courts have assumed that the fair cross-section requirement applies to the federal grand jury process as an attribute of the Fifth Amendment's grand jury provision. See CRIMPROC § 15.4(d). That assumption has been questioned, however, on the ground that the fair cross-section requirement has been explained by the Supreme Court as a device aimed at ensuring jury impartiality, see *Holland v. Illinois,* 493 U.S. 474 (1990), and the grand jury clause of the Fifth Amendment, unlike the petit jury clause of the Sixth Amendment, does not refer to an "impartial" jury. See also *United States v. Knowles,* Note 5 infra. Of course, even if a fair cross-section requirement is implicit in the Fifth Amendment's guarantee of prosecution by indictment, that would not carry the requirement over to the states. Here, a federal constitutional mandate that the grand jury be drawn from a fair cross-section of the community would have to be found in a due process clause that does not require grand jury screening or any other type of screening of the decision to charge. See *Hurtado*, p. 946, and Note 1, p. 917. Many indictment states have no need to consider this issue because the state statute governing the selection of the venire imposes a fair cross-section requirement. See CRIMPROC § 15.4(d).

Occasional lower court opinions have assumed that due process does impose a fair cross-section requirement on state grand jury selection. See e.g., *State v. Jenison,* 405 A.2d 3 (R.I.1979) (once state elects to use the grand jury, it must adhere to Supreme Court's view that " 'the very idea of a jury, whether it be grand or petit jury, is 'a body truly representative of the community.' ") Although not involving state grand jury selection, *Hobby v. United States*, Note 4 infra, is seen as providing support for this position. In the course of assessing the impact of discrimination in the selection of a federal grand jury's foreperson, the *Hobby* majority noted that there had been no impairment of "defendant's due process interest in ensuring that the grand jury includes persons with a range of experiences and perspectives." Quoting from *Peters v. Kiff* (see Note 4, infra), the *Hobby* majority further described this "due process concern" as ensuring that "no large and identifiable segment of the community be excluded from jury service."

In *Campbell v. Louisiana*, Note 2 supra, the Court found it unnecessary to determine the exact content of any such due process requirement. Upon finding that the defendant had standing to raise a "*Peters v. Kiff* due process claim" as to selection of a grand jury foreperson, it remanded the case to the lower court to consider the merits of that claim. The Court noted that, "as to the nature and full extent of due process in the context of grand jury selection," that "issue, to the extent it is still open based on our earlier precedents," would be determined by the lower court. However, the Court apparently viewed that due process requirement as distinct from a traditional cross-section requirement for it also noted that defendant had presented a "fair cross-section claim," but that claim was not open for review because of a procedural default in the lower courts.

4. ***Selection of the foreperson.*** A jury composition problem unique to the grand jury is presented in the selection of the foreperson. Unlike the petit jury foreperson, the grand jury foreperson commonly is appointed by the court (rather than being selected by the jurors). In *Rose v. Mitchell,* Note 6 infra, the Supreme Court "assume[d] without deciding that discrimination with regard to the selection of only the foreman requires that a subsequent conviction be set aside, just as if the discrimination proved had tainted the selection of the entire grand jury venire." In HOBBY v. UNITED STATES, 468 U.S. 339 (1984), the Court returned to the issue of discrimination in the selection of the foreperson, and held that discrimination did not demand dismissal of an indictment in the context presented there.

The defendant in *Hobby* claimed that the trial judge had discriminated against blacks and women in the selection of the grand jury foreman. Since defendant was a white male and equal protection claims were at that time thought to be available only to defendants who were members of the class discriminated against (a position later rejected, see *Campbell v. Louisiana,* Note 2 supra), he framed his claim as a due process objection, relying on the analysis of *Peters v. Kiff,* 407 U.S. 493 (1972). In that case, Justice Marshall's opinion for three justices had sustained a white defendant's due process objection to racial discrimination against blacks in the selection of a state grand jury. Justice Marshall had concluded that a "state cannot, consistent with due process, subject a defendant to indictment * * * by a jury that has been selected in an arbitrary and discriminatory manner, in violation of the Constitution." He reasoned that "the exclusion from jury service of a substantial and identifiable class of citizens has a potential impact that is too subtle and too pervasive" to assume it had an impact only upon the cases of defendants who had a class identification with the excluded persons.

Chief Justice Burger's opinion for the Court majority in *Hobby* acknowledged that "purposeful discrimination against Negroes or women in the selection of federal grand jury foremen is forbidden by the Fifth Amendment." Unlike the dissent, which argued that that was enough to justify dismissal of the indictment (in light of "injury done to public confidence in the judicial process"), the majority concluded that the discrimination did not require dismissal of the indictment unless it adversely affected the due process interests raised by the defendant. Here, there was no violation of the "representational due process values" recognized in *Peters* since the discriminatory selection of the foreman did not alter the composition "of the grand jury as a whole." Unlike the situation presented in *Rose,* where the foreperson was appointed from outside of the grand jury panel, the foreperson here already was a member of the randomly selected jury. Thus, the persons voting on the indictment had been fairly selected, without discrimination.

Chief Justice Burger also rejected the contention that the discrimination in the selection of the foreman had "impugn[ed] the fundamental fairness of the [grand jury] process itself." Again in contrast to *Rose,* where the foreman had substantial powers that might be used in influencing the other jurors (e.g., the authority to issue subpoenas for witnesses), the foreman of a federal grand jury performed basically ministerial duties that would have no bearing upon the substantive decisions of the grand jury. Accordingly, it would have made no appreciable difference in the outcome whether one jury member or another had been appointed foreman.

Both of the factors noted above would limit the significance of the issue left undecided in *Rose* to a small group of states. Only a few states appoint forepersons from outside the regularly selected grand jury panel, and only a small group give the foreperson powers significantly broader than those granted the federal foreperson. However, the *Hobby* majority also distinguished *Rose* on a third ground. Speaking to the distinctive nature of the equal protection claim presented in *Rose,* the Court noted: "As members of the class [African-Americans] allegedly excluded from service as the grand jury foreman, the *Rose* defendants had suffered the injuries of stigmatization and prejudice associated with racial discrimination." Relying on this language, several lower courts have held that discrimination in the selection of the foreperson remains subject to an equal protection challenge even if the foreperson is selected from among the grand jury members and has only ministerial duties. See CRIMPROC § 15.4(d).

5. *Personal bias.* In his dissent in *Beck v. Washington,* 369 U.S. 541 (1962), a case addressing a pretrial publicity issue, Justice Douglas asked: "Could we possibly sustain a conviction obtained in either a state or federal court where the grand jury that brought the charge was composed of the accused's political enemies?" Due process, Justice Douglas suggested, would surely require that the conviction be reversed on the basis of grand jury bias. Several federal courts, however, have held an indictment may not be challenged on the ground that a grand juror lacked impartiality due to some special interest or knowledge about the case. In adopting Federal Rule 6(b), the Supreme Court rejected a preliminary draft proposal to allow an objection to a grand juror "on the ground that * * * a state of mind exists on his part which may prevent him from acting impartially." 1943 Preliminary Draft, Rule 7(b)(1). Decisions rejecting bias objections rely upon the rejection of that proposal along with the rationale of *United States v. Knowles,* 147 F.Supp. 19 (D.D.C. 1957):

"The basic theory of the functions of a grand jury, does not require that grand jurors should be impartial and unbiased. In this respect, their position is entirely different from that of petit jurors. The Sixth Amendment to the Constitution of the United States expressly provides that the trial jury in a criminal case must be 'impartial.' No such requirement in respect to grand juries is found in the Fifth Amendment, which contains the guaranty against prosecutions for infamous crimes unless on a presentment or indictment of a grand jury. It is hardly necessary to be reminded that each of these Amendments was adopted at the same time as a part of the group consisting of the first ten Amendments. A grand jury does not pass on the guilt or innocence of the defendant, but merely determines whether he should be brought to trial. It is purely an accusatory body. This review can be demonstrated by the fact that a grand jury may undertake an investigation on its own initiative, or at the behest of one of its members. In such event, the grand juror who instigated the proceeding that may result in an indictment, obviously can hardly be deemed to be impartial, but he is not disqualified for that reason."

A few federal courts have suggested that bias objections can be recognized under the Fed.R. 6(b) provision permitting a challenge to a legally "unqualified" juror. The requirement that grand jurors be unbiased, they note, follows from the language and reasoning of various Supreme Court decisions, particularly the equal protection decisions barring racial discrimination in the grand jury selection process (see Note 1 supra). As Justice Douglas noted in his *Beck* dissent, the "systematic exclusion of Negroes from grand jury service" was barred because it "infects the accusatory process * * * [with] unfairness" in much the same way that juror bias infects the process. See also *Costello v. United States,* p. 957, where the Court referred to the validity on its face of "an indictment returned by a legally constituted and *unbiased* grand jury" (p. 958) (emphasis added). But see *Hopkins v. State,* 329 A.2d 738 (Md.App.1974): "Justice Douglas' interpretation of [the racial discrimination cases] * * * overlooks the fact that it is the manner of selection—as opposed to the mental attitude of those selected—that violates the equal protection * * * [clause]. Exclusion of Negroes from panels is not indicative of the mental attitude of white persons actually selected * * *."

A substantial minority of the states recognize at least limited bias objections. In some, that objection is tied to a narrow statutory prohibition against specified persons (e.g., relatives of the victim) serving on the grand jury. In others, it is based on more broadly worded provisions (e.g., prohibiting the seating of a person "whose state of mind prevents him from acting impartially"). In still others, it is viewed by the courts as implicit in a statutory or constitutional right to an unbiased grand jury. See *State v. Murphy,* 538 A.2d 1235 (N.J.1988) (rejecting the reasoning of cases like *Knowles,* as "rooted more to history than in justice"; in "contemporary society," we no longer expect local jurors personally to know "the character of the parties and the witnesses," but seek instead to impanel jurors who have no knowledge of the case or its participants). Even in jurisdictions adopting the broadest definition of bias in this context, the practice is to limit objections largely to the juror who has some special relationship to the victim, the target, or a key witness. CRIMPROC § 15.4(g). But consider *McGill v. Superior Court,* 194 Cal. App. 4th, 1454 (2011) (statutory requirement that grand jury be "neutral" is violated "where the same grand jury which heard the testimony directly indicts [the witness] for perjury").

6. ***Post-conviction review.*** Assume that a defendant makes a timely objection to the grand jury's composition on a ground recognized under the federal constitution or state law. Assume also that the objection is improperly denied by the trial judge, interlocutory appeal is unavailable, and the case goes to trial. On appeal from a subsequent conviction, should the illegality in the grand jury's composition now be viewed as a harmless error? In *Cassell v. Texas,* 339 U.S. 282 (1950), Justice Jackson, dissenting, argued that racial discrimination in the selection of the grand jury should constitute harmless error where the defendant had been convicted by a fairly selected petit jury. The majority rejected that contention without discussion and reversed on the basis of grand jury discrimination alone. In ROSE v. MITCHELL, 443 U.S. 545 (1979), the majority found Justice Jackson's contention worthy of reconsideration, but it was again rejected. Justice Blackmun's opinion for the Court noted:

"Discrimination on account of race was the primary evil at which the Amendments adopted after the War Between the States, including the Fourteenth Amendment, were aimed. * * * Discrimination on the basis of race, odious in all aspects, is especially pernicious in the administration of justice. Selection of members of a grand jury because they are of one race and not another destroys the appearance of justice and thereby casts doubt on the integrity of the judicial process. The exclusion from grand jury service of Negroes, or any group otherwise qualified to serve, impairs the confidence of the public in the administration of justice. As this Court repeatedly has emphasized, such discrimination 'not only violates our Constitution and the laws enacted under it but is at war with our basic concepts of a democratic society and a representative government.' * * * Because discrimination on the basis of race in the selection of members of a grand jury thus strikes at the fundamental values of our judicial system and our society as a whole, the Court has recognized that a criminal defendant's right to equal protection of the laws has been denied when he is indicted by a grand jury from which members of a racial group purposefully have been excluded. For this same reason, the Court also has reversed the conviction and ordered the indictment quashed in such cases without inquiry into whether the defendant was prejudiced in fact by the discrimination at the grand jury stage. * * * We do not deny that there are costs associated with this approach. But the remedy here is in many ways less drastic than in situations where other constitutional rights have been violated. In the case of a Fourth or Fifth Amendment violation, the violation often results in the suppression of evidence that is highly probative on the issue of guilt. Here, however, reversal does not render a defendant 'immune from prosecution,' nor is a subsequent reindictment and reprosecution 'barred altogether.' * * * In any event, we believe such costs as do exist are out-weighed by the strong policy the Court consistently has recognized of combating racial discrimination in the administration of justice. And regardless of the fact that alternative remedies remain to vindicate the rights of those members of the class denied the chance to serve on grand juries, the fact is that permitting challenges to unconstitutional state action by defendants has been, and is, the main avenue by which Fourteenth Amendment rights are vindicated in this context."

7. In VASQUEZ v. HILLERY, 474 U.S. 254 (1986), the Court majority, per Marshall, J., rejected the contention of three dissenters that the "automatic reversal" standard of *Rose v. Mitchell* should not apply where "the [grand jury] discrimination claim is pressed many years after conviction." The dissenters argued that the prophylactic remedy of *Mitchell* was unwarranted in that situation because the state was more likely to be "prejudiced in its ability to retry the defendant" and the delay will have "dilute[d] the effectiveness of the reversal rule as a deterrent." Noting that that defendant here had persistently pressed his equal protection challenge in state and federal courts over the 24 years since his first-degree murder conviction, the majority concluded that that claim was still viable under federal habeas corpus. *Rose v. Mitchell* had "ably presented * * * justifications, based on the necessity for vindicating Fourteenth Amendment rights, supporting a policy of automatic reversal," and the "six years since *Mitchell*" gave the Court "no reason to doubt" the "continuing truth" of the observations made there relating to "racial and other forms of discrimination" in the "administration of justice." In addition, the Court was not convinced that a subsequent fair trial necessarily eliminated the impact of the grand jury discrimination upon defendant's conviction. As to this point, the majority reasoned:

"The grand jury does not determine only that probable cause exists to believe that a defendant committed a crime, or that it does not. In the hands of the grand jury lies the power to charge a greater offense or a lesser offense; numerous counts or a single count; and perhaps most significant of all, a capital offense or a noncapital offense—all on the basis of the same facts. Moreover, '[t]he grand jury is not bound to indict in every case where a conviction can be obtained.' *United States v. Ciambrone,* 601 F.2d 616 (2d Cir.1979) (Friendly, J., dissenting). Thus, even if a grand jury's determination of probable cause is confirmed in hindsight by a conviction on the indicted offense, that confirmation in no way suggests that the discrimination did not impermissibly infect the framing of the indictment and, consequently, the nature or very existence of the proceedings to come. * * * Just as a conviction is void under the Equal Protection Clause if the prosecutor deliberately charged the defendant on account of his race, see *United States v. Batchelder* [Note 1, 910, a conviction cannot be understood to cure the taint attributable to a charging body selected on the basis of race. Once having found discrimination in the selection of a grand jury, we simply cannot know that the need to indict would have been assessed in the same way by a grand jury properly constituted."

Responding to the above reasoning, dissenting Justice Powell (joined by Burger, C.J., and Rehnquist, J.), noted: "The Court * * * decides that discrimination in the selection of the grand jury potentially harmed respondent, because the grand jury is vested with broad discretion in deciding whether to indict and in framing the charges, and because it is impossible to know whether this discretion would have been exercised differently by a properly selected grand jury. The point appears to be that an all-white grand jury from which blacks are systematically excluded might be influenced by race in determining whether to indict and for what charge. * * * This reasoning ignores established principles of equal protection jurisprudence. * * * This Court has never suggested that the racial composition of a grand jury gives rise to the inference that indictments are racially motivated, any more than it has suggested that a suspect arrested by a policeman of a different race may challenge his subsequent conviction on that basis. * * * There may be a theoretical possibility that a different grand jury might have decided not to indict or to indict for a less serious charge. The fact remains, however, that the grand jury's decision to indict was *correct as a matter of law,* given respondent's subsequent unchallenged conviction."

8. Commentators have argued that the *Vasquez* ruling reflects in two respects a focus on more than the possible prejudicial impact of selection discrimination on the grand jury's exercise of its screening authority. Initially, the Court reversed the conviction without considering whether the nature of the case was such that there was only a very faint likelihood that a fairly selected grand jury would have produced a different indictment. See e.g., Nancy King, *Postconviction Review of Jury Discrimination: Measuring the Effects of Juror Race on Jury Decisions*, 92 Mich.L.Rev. 62 (1993) (noting that assessing the possible impact of discrimination in jury selection upon the decision to indict in the particular case, though complex and difficult, was not unlike other inquiries demanded under Supreme Court precedent; social science studies on the impact of jury composition upon jury decision-making provides assistance, as they not only demonstrate that race affects juror evaluations, but also indicate where that effect is especially probable or improbable).

Second, the Court in *Vasquez* reversed the defendant's conviction, rather than remanding for the purpose of "permitting a grand jury selected in a race-neutral fashion to reconsider probable cause," with the convictions to be reinstated if the grand jury should reindict on the same charge. See Tom Stacy & Kim Dayton, *Rethinking Harmless Constitutional Error*, 88 Colum.L.Rev. 79 (1988). Concurring in *Ramseur v. Beyer,* 983 F.2d 1215 (3d Cir.1992) (a case involving an impanelling judge's efforts to achieve "racial balance" on a grand jury), Circuit Judge Greenberg argued that a court granting habeas relief had authority to impose such conditional relief. Since that alternative was not before the Supreme Court in *Vasquez,* it should not be deemed foreclosed by the relief granted there. Judge Greenberg further noted that this procedure "[would] not introduce a harmless error analysis into cases dealing with racial discrimination in grand jury selection. Quite to the contrary, it treats the discrimination as prejudicial and addresses the remedy for it."

9. Assuming a constitutional fair cross-section or individual bias objection applies to grand jury selection, should that objection be cognizable following a conviction? Consider *Porter v. Wainwright,* 805 F.2d 930 (11th Cir.1986). The defendant in *Porter,* on a habeas challenge to his conviction, alleged that one member of the grand jury was related by marriage to the homicide victim, that the juror had explained that relationship and his discomfort in sitting on the case to the prosecuting attorney, and that he had been told to simply sit and not vote. The court concluded that, "assuming arguendo" that those allegations made out a due process violation, the standard harmless error rationale of *United States v. Mechanik* (Note 5, p. 980) controlled, rather than the automatic reversal rule of *Rose* and *Vasquez.* In holding that a fair trial cured procedural errors in the grand jury process, the *Mechanik* majority distinguished *Vasquez* as a case "compelled by precedent directly applicable to the special problem of racial discrimination." It described *Vasquez* as grounded on the view that "racial discrimination * * * is so pernicious, and other remedies so impractical, that the remedy of automatic reversal was necessary as a prophylactic means of deterring grand jury discrimination in the future, and that one could presume that a discriminatorily selected grand jury would treat defendants of excluded races unfairly," and then added: "We think that these considerations have little force outside the context of racial discrimination in the composition of the grand jury." But compare *State v. Murphy,* Note 5, p. 954 (rule of *Mechanik* should not be applied to issues of fundamental fairness, such as possible grand juror bias).

§ 3. CHALLENGES TO THE EVIDENCE BEFORE THE GRAND JURY

COSTELLO V. UNITED STATES

350 U.S. 359, 76 S.Ct. 406, 100 L.Ed. 397 (1956).

JUSTICE BLACK delivered the opinion of the Court.

We granted certiorari in this case to consider a single question: "May a defendant be required to stand trial and a conviction be sustained where only hearsay evidence was presented to the grand jury which indicted him?"

Petitioner, Frank Costello, was indicted for wilfully attempting to evade payment of income taxes due the United States for the years 1947, 1948 and 1949. The charge was that petitioner falsely and fraudulently reported less income than he and his wife actually received during the taxable years in question. Petitioner promptly filed a motion for inspection of the minutes of the grand jury and for a dismissal of the indictment. His motion was based on an affidavit stating that he was firmly convinced there could have been no legal or competent evidence before the grand jury which indicted him since he had reported all his income and paid all taxes due. The motion was denied. At the trial which followed the Government offered evidence designed to show increases in Costello's net worth in an attempt to prove that he had received more income during the years in question than he had reported. To establish its case the Government called and examined 144 witnesses and introduced 368 exhibits. All of the testimony and documents related to business transactions and expenditures by petitioner and his wife. The prosecution concluded its case by calling three government agents. Their investigations had produced the evidence used against petitioner at the trial. They were allowed to summarize the vast amount of evidence already heard and to introduce computations showing, if correct, that petitioner and his wife had received far greater income than they had reported. We have held such summarizations admissible in a "net worth" case like this.

Counsel for petitioner asked each government witness at the trial whether he had appeared before the grand jury which returned the indictment. This cross-examination developed the fact that the three investigating officers had been the only witnesses before the grand jury. After the Government concluded its case, petitioner again moved to dismiss the indictment on the ground that the only evidence before the grand jury was "hearsay," since the three officers had no first-hand knowledge of the transactions upon which their computations were based. Nevertheless the trial court again refused to dismiss the indictment, and petitioner was convicted. The Court of Appeals affirmed. * * * Petitioner here urges: (1) that an indictment based solely on hearsay evidence violates that part of the Fifth Amendment providing that "No person shall be held to answer for a capital, or otherwise infamous crime, unless on a presentment or indictment of a Grand Jury * * *." and (2) that if the Fifth Amendment does not invalidate an indictment based solely on hearsay we should now lay down such a rule for the guidance of federal courts. * * *

[N]either the Fifth Amendment nor any other constitutional provision prescribes the kind of evidence upon which grand juries must act. The grand jury is an English institution, brought to this country by the early colonists and incorporated in the Constitution by the Founders. There is every reason to believe that our constitutional grand jury was intended to operate substantially like its English progenitor. The basic purpose of the English grand jury was to provide a fair method for instituting criminal proceedings against persons believed to have committed crimes. Grand jurors were selected from the body of the people and their work was not hampered by rigid procedural or evidential rules. In fact, grand jurors could act on their own knowledge and were free to make their presentments or indictments on such information as they deemed satisfactory. Despite its broad power to institute criminal proceedings the grand jury grew in popular favor with the years. It acquired an independence in England free from control by the Crown or judges. Its adoption in our Constitution as the sole method for preferring charges in serious criminal cases shows the high place it held as an instrument of justice. And in this country as in England of old the grand jury has convened as a body of laymen, free from technical rules, acting in secret, pledged to indict no one because of prejudice and to free no one because of special favor. As late as 1927 an English historian could say that English grand juries were still free to act on their own knowledge if they pleased to do so. And in 1852 Mr. Justice Nelson on circuit could say "No case has been cited, nor have we been able to find any, furnishing an authority for looking into and revising the judgment of the grand jury upon the evidence, for the purpose of determining whether or not the finding was founded upon sufficient proof * * *." *United States v. Reed,* 27 Fed.Cas. 727 [1852].

In *Holt v. United States,* 218 U.S. 245 (1910), this Court had to decide whether an indictment should be quashed because supported in part by incompetent evidence. Aside from the incompetent evidence "there was very little evidence against the accused." The Court refused to hold that such an indictment should be quashed, pointing out that "The abuses of criminal practice would be enhanced if indictments could be upset on such a ground." The same thing is true whereas here all the evidence before the grand jury was in the nature of "hearsay." If indictments were to be held open to challenge on the ground that there was inadequate or incompetent evidence before the grand jury, the resulting delay would be great indeed. The result of such a rule would be that before trial on the merits a defendant could always insist on a kind of preliminary trial to determine the competency and adequacy of the evidence before the grand jury. This is not required by the Fifth Amendment. An indictment returned by a legally constituted and unbiased grand jury, like an information drawn by the prosecutor, if valid on its face, is enough to call for trial of the charge on the merits. The Fifth Amendment requires nothing more.

Petitioner urges that this Court should exercise its power to supervise the administration of justice in federal courts and establish a rule permitting defendants to challenge indictments on the ground that they are not supported by adequate or competent evidence. No persuasive reasons are advanced for establishing such a rule. It would run counter to the whole history of the grand jury institution, in which laymen conduct their inquiries unfettered by technical rules. Neither justice nor the concept of a fair trial requires such a change. In a trial on the merits, defendants are entitled to a strict observance of all the rules designed to bring about a fair verdict. Defendants are not entitled, however, to a rule which would result in interminable delay but add nothing to the assurance of a fair trial. Affirmed.

JUSTICE CLARK and JUSTICE HARLAN took no part in the consideration or decision of this case.

JUSTICE BURTON, concurring.

I agree with the denial of the motion to quash the indictment. In my view, however, this case does not justify the breadth of the declarations made by the Court. I assume that this Court would not preclude an examination of grand jury action to ascertain the existence of bias or prejudice in an indictment. Likewise, it seems to me that if it is shown that the grand jury had before it no substantial or rationally persuasive evidence upon which to base its indictment, that indictment should be quashed. To hold a person to answer to such an empty indictment for a capital or otherwise infamous federal crime robs the Fifth Amendment of much of its protective value to the private citizen. * * *

Notes on the Rationale and Scope of *Costello*

1. ***The relevance of history.*** To what extent should the traditional practices of the grand jury, as developed at the time of the Constitution's adoption, control the Court's interpretation of the Fifth Amendment? Commentators have argued that the grand jury today operates in such a substantially different setting than the grand jury of the late eighteenth century that fulfillment of its screening role now requires courts to impose requirements previously thought unnecessary. While the late eighteenth century grand jury surely considered evidence that would be inadmissible at trial, it did not have the assistance of a legally trained prosecutor. Cases were presented by the sheriff, a justice of the peace, or a complainant, and those persons were not necessarily present when the grand jury heard from other witnesses. With the development of the office of the modern prosecutor, it is argued, there is less room for a grand jury remaining independent and a greater capacity in the grand jury, assisted by its legal advisor, to distinguish between admissible and inadmissible evidence.

2. ***Supervisory power.*** Commentators have suggested that *Costello* is based not so much on history as on the Court's conclusion that federal courts should not restrict grand juries to the consideration of evidence that would be admissible at trial. They note that when *Costello* was decided, the supervisory authority of federal courts was viewed as quite extensive (in contrast to the position taken in *United States v. Williams*, p. 965), and several federal courts had relied upon that authority to limit grand juries to "receive 'only legal evidence, to the exclusion of mere reports.'" Field, J., *Charge to the Grand Jury*, 30 Fed.Cas. 992 (C.C.D. Cal.1872). Thus, they argue, if the Court had concluded in *Costello* that extensive reliance upon hearsay was inappropriate, but so clearly ratified by historical practice that it could not be deemed contrary to the Fifth Amendment, it could have prohibited that practice in the "exercise [of] its power to supervise the administration of justice in federal courts [p. 958]." As evidence that *Costello* rested on the Court's policy preference for the result reached there, commentators point to the Federal Rules of Evidence, later adopted by the Court (and Congress). The Rules set forth the general standards governing the admissibility of evidence, but then provide, in Rule 1101(d) that "the[se] rules (other than with respect to privileges) to do not apply in * * * proceedings before grand juries."

3. ***Administrative burdens.*** *Costello* also has been characterized as a rule grounded in the belief that, even if a complete or partial prohibition of the use of hearsay before the grand jury would work to improve grand jury screening, imposing such a prohibition would be too costly administratively. Commentators note in this connection Justice Black's reference to frequent evidentiary challenges to indictments that would cause "interminable delay" and produce "a kind of preliminary trial" in each case (p. 958). They point out that the Court may have been influenced as well by other administrative difficulties that would flow from the position urged by the petitioner. If the Court were to permit evidentiary challenges, it also would have to require that grand jury testimony be recorded (a requirement not imposed in federal courts until 1979, with the adoption of current Rule 6(e)). So too, the implementation of such challenges logically would require that the defense be given pretrial access to that transcript to determine whether it revealed grounds for an evidentiary challenge (see Note 3, p. 964), and such disclosure would have undercut various limitations found in federal pretrial discovery (including the nondisclosure of the names of prospective government witnesses). Also, recognition of evidentiary challenges might have required separation of the investigating grand jury and the screening grand jury, since an

investigating grand jury must be able to receive inadmissible evidence if it is to fulfill its task of tracking down "every available clue," including "tips" and "rumors," *United States v. Dionisio,* 410 U.S. 1 (1973). See also Peter J. Henning, *Prosecutorial Misconduct in Grand Jury Investigations,* 51 S.Car.L.Rev. 1 (1999) (cases like *Costello* and *Williams*, pp. 957, 965, have made "the grand jury, and the prosecutors that guide its proceedings, free from oversight in order to protect the [grand jury's] investigative function from outside interference"; that "function, more than the accusatory function, defines the importance of the grand jury in the criminal justice system").

4. ***Review of evidentiary sufficiency.*** To what extent do the concerns noted in *Costello* apply to allowing a pretrial challenge as to whether the evidence before the grand jury, without regard to its potential admissibility at trial, was sufficient to establish probable cause as to each of the elements of the crimes charged? *Costello* generally has been read as rejecting even Justice Burton's suggestion that a federal court could dismiss an indictment on the ground that the grand jury had before it "no substantial or rationally persuasive evidence upon which to base its indictment." See *United States v. Alexander*, 789 F.2d 1046 (4th Cir.1986) ("Justice Burton's view * * * fails to overcome the clear command of * * * *Costello* that a facially valid indictment suffices to permit the trial of the party indicted").

5. ***Unconstitutionally obtained evidence.*** In three post-Costello decisions, including *United States v. Calandra*, 414 U.S. 338 (1974), the Supreme Court indicated quite clearly, albeit in dictum, that the Costello rationale also barred a challenge to an indictment issued on the basis of unconstitutionally obtained evidence. Calandra noted that past Supreme Court rulings established that "an indictment valid on its face is not subject to challenge on the ground that the grand jury acted on the basis of * * * incompetent evidence; or even on the basis of information obtained in violation of a defendant's Fifth Amendment privilege against self-incrimination." Consistent with those rulings, Calandra refused to fashion a witness remedy that would have precluded grand jury consideration of evidence contained through an unconstitutional search and seizure. Calandra stressed that the grand jury "traditionally has been allowed to pursue its investigative and accusatorial functions unimpeded by the evidentiary and procedural restrictions applicable to a criminal trial." Weighing the costs and benefits of applying the Fourth Amendment exclusionary rule to the grand jury setting, the Calandra ruling concluded that applying the rule in a proceeding the "does not finally adjudicate guilt or innocence" would not substantially enhance its deterrence function. On the other hand, that application "would delay and disrupt grand jury proceedings. Suppression hearings would halt the orderly progress of an investigation and might necessitate litigation of issues only tangentially related to the grand jury's primary objective."

Prior to *Calandra*, Federal Rule 41 allowed a person "aggrieved by an unlawful search and seizure" to make a pre-indictment motion for return of property lawfully owned, which was combined with an order directing that the evidence not be admissible "at any trial or hearing." If this relief was obtained prior to grand jury consideration, it precluded the government from referring to the returned property or its fruits in the grand jury presentation. This relief was not available where the item seized was contraband or the government could claim an interest in the property (e.g., it was subject to forfeiture). It also was conditioned on a showing that "irreparable injury" would result from not obtaining immediate return of the property (i.e., waiting until the investigation was complete and the property was returned or retained for a criminal prosecution, where a suppression motion would be available).[a] *Calandra* led to a revision of Rule 41. The

[a] Although the Rule 41 provision spoke to the return of "property" and illegal seizures, two circuits, pre-*Calandra*, had held that similar injunctive relief was available pre-indictment where investigators obtained an incriminating statement by compulsion that violated the self-incrimination clause. They noted that the Rule 41 provision was the successor to a previously recognized civil action for the return of property grounded in the federal court's supervisory authority over the federal official responsible for the unconstitutional seizure, and that authority similarly extended to the officials who obtained and now sought to use the incriminating compelled statement. Here too, it was argued, equitable considerations supported relief as a "wrongful indictment * * * [inflicts] a blot on a man's escutcheon * * * seldom wiped out by a subsequent judgment of not guilty. *In re Fried*, 161 F.2d 453 (2d Cir.

suppression remedy and the motion for return were separated, with the suppression remedy now available only before "the court where trial will occur." The question on return was no longer tied to whether the seizure of the property was unconstitutional, but whether the owner of the property would suffer significant hardship from a lack of immediate return. Moreover, when that hardship was established, the district court could attach to its order "reasonable conditions to protect [government] access to the property and its use in later proceedings." Fed.R.Crim.P. 41(g). Thus, in the case of seized documents needed for business purposes, the order typically will give the owner copies, allowing the government to introduce the originals before the grand jury, with any subsequent post-indictment use challenged by a suppression motion. See CRIMPROC § 8.9(a–1).

6. ***A self-incrimination clause exception?*** As discussed in Note 4, p. 938, certiorari was granted in *City of Hayes, Kansas v. Vogt*, 138 S.Ct. 55 (2017), to review a Tenth Circuit ruling that a cause of action under § 1983 was established when actions of the Hays Police Department led to the introduction of a compelled incriminating statement in a preliminary hearing. The Tenth Circuit opinion had also referred to the grand jury proceeding as an illustration of the applicability of the self-incrimination clause to pretrial proceedings, and had cited a Ninth Circuit ruling that sustained a § 1983 claim based in part on use of a compelled statement before a grand jury. See *Crowe v. County of San Diego*, 608 F.3d 406 (9th Cir. 2010). Thus, not surprisingly, the oral argument in *City of Hayes* touched upon use of compelled statements before the grand jury. Justice Breyer, in particular, questioned the reach of past rulings. He initially noted: "[S]upreme Court cases refer to a grand jury proceeding as part of a criminal case, and you cannot introduce it [the incriminating compelled statement] in a criminal case. * * * [Y]ou can't attack a grand jury proceeding later, but that's different." Official Transcript, p. 8, 2018 WL136809. Subsequently, Justice Breyer added: "I don't know what the answer is in a grand jury proceeding. I do know that you can't attack that proceeding at trial,[b] but I don't know whether, as in this case, somebody might, if they were used, bring a § 1983 claim * * *. And I don't know what would happen if, because of the circumstance, the defendant went before a judge [prior to the grand jury proceeding] and said: Judge, keep that piece of paper [i.e., the compelled statement] out of the grand jury proceedings." Official Transcript p. 15, 2018 WL1368609. Justice Alito subsequently asked petitioner's counsel whether he "was familiar with any cases * * * in federal law that allow a person who thinks that he or she may be under investigation by a grand jury to go to a federal judge and file a motion in limine regarding the evidence that may be presented to the grand jury?" Counsel replied, "I am not," and Justice Alito responded: "This would be revolutionary, wouldn't it?" Official Transcript, p. 21, 2018 WL136809.

7. ***DOJ policy.*** The United States Attorneys' Manual, §§ 9–11.231–232, draws a distinction between hearsay and unconstitutionally obtained evidence. As to hearsay, it notes that such evidence may be utilized if the evidence is clearly presented to the grand jury as hearsay and "affords the grand jurors a substantial basis for voting upon an indictment." As for evidence unconstitutionally obtained, it directs federal prosecutors "not [to] present to the grand jury for use against a person whose constitutional rights clearly have been violated evidence which the prosecutor personally knows was obtained as a direct result of the constitutional violation."

1947) (Frank, J.) Accordingly, the government officials could be prohibited from further using the statement and its fruits (along with "returning" any transcription). Other circuits concluded that Rule 41 and the previously recognized civil action were tied to the protection of property, and did not apply to compelled statements. Reliance upon the decisions accepting pre-indictment relief virtually disappeared after *Calandra* (which described past rulings as having extended *Costello* to grand jury reliance upon "information obtained in violation of a defendant's Fifth Amendment privilege").

[b] The reference here was to the self-incrimination rulings described in *Calandra*. Responding to the City of Hayes reliance upon those cases, Justice Kagan remarked: "[T]here is a kind of anomaly there, but explained, I think by a kind of historic judgment, that grand juries are sacrosanct, that everything has to be secret, that we don't want people poking around the black box, and none of that is true of just probable cause hearings." Official Transcript, p. 12, 2018 WL 136809.

8. ***Extended consequences.*** As the Court explained in KALEY V. UNITED STATES, 571 U.S. 320 (2013), the *Costello* analysis leads to treating the grand jury indictment as a "conclusively determining * * * probable cause" for purposes beyond enabling the prosecution. At issue in *Kaley* was the application of a federal money laundering provision authorizing the issuance of a pre-trial asset restraint (a "freeze order") precluding transfer of assets that would be subject to forfeiture upon conviction. *United States v. Monsanto*, 491 U.S. 600 (1989), a companion case to *Caplin & Drysdale, Chartered v. United States* (Note 5, p. 121), held that such a restraint did not violate due process or the Sixth Amendment (assuming that the asset-freeze would prevent the defendant from retaining counsel of choice), provided there is "probable cause to think (1) that the defendant has committed an offense permitting forfeiture, and (2) that the property at issue has the requisite connection to that crime." *Monsanto*, as noted, in *Kaley*, "declined to consider whether Due Process requires a hearing to establish either or both of those aspects of forfeitability." Subsequently, "lower courts generally provided a hearing to any indicted defendant seeking to lift an asset restraint to pay for a lawyer * * *. They uniformly allowed the defendant to litigate the second issue stated above [probable cause as to whether the assets are sufficiently related to the crime to be subject to forfeiture], * * * [but] divided over extending the hearing to the first issue [probable cause as to the crime]." In *Kaley*, the indicted defendants sought only to challenge probable cause as to the crime, seeking to show "that the case against them was 'baseless.' " The federal lower courts held that a hearing on that issue was not available since the grand jury indictment conclusively established the needed probable cause. Describing the only issue before it as "whether an indicted defendant has a constitutional right to contest the grand jury's prior determination of that matter," a divided Supreme Court (6–3) affirmed. The Court majority, per Kagan, J., reasoned in part:

"This Court has often recognized the grand jury's singular role in finding the probable cause necessary to initiate a prosecution for a serious crime. See, e.g., *Costello v. United States*. '[A]n indictment fair upon its face, and returned by a 'properly constituted grand jury,' we have explained, 'conclusively determines the existence of probable cause to believe the defendant perpetrated the offense alleged.' *Gerstein v. Pugh*, 430 U.S. 103 (1979) [magistrate review of continued restraint, see fn. d, p. 328, not needed where grand jury has indicted]. And 'conclusively' has meant, case in and case out, just that. * * * The grand jury gets to say—without any review, oversight, or second-guessing—whether probable cause exists to think that a person committed a crime. * * *

"And that inviolable grand jury finding, we have decided, may do more than commence a criminal proceeding (with all the economic, reputational, and personal harm that entails); the determination may also serve the purpose of immediately depriving the accused of her freedom. If the person charged is not yet in custody, an indictment triggers 'issuance of an arrest warrant without further inquiry' into the case's strength. Alternatively, if the person was arrested without a warrant, an indictment eliminates her Fourth Amendment right to a prompt judicial assessment of probable cause to support any detention. See *Gerstein*, supra. In either situation, this Court—relying on the grand jury's 'historical role of protecting individuals from unjust persecution'—has 'let [that body's] judgment substitute for that of a neutral and detached magistrate.'

"The same result follows when, as here, an infringement on the defendant's property depends on a showing of probable cause that she committed a crime. If judicial review of the grand jury's probable cause determination is not warranted (as we have so often held) to put a defendant on trial or place her in custody, then neither is it needed to freeze her property. The grand jury that is good enough—reliable enough, protective enough—to inflict those other grave consequences through its probable cause findings must be adequate to impose this one too. Indeed, *Monsanto* already noted the absence of any reason to hold property seizures to different rules: As described earlier, the Court partly based its adoption of the probable cause standard on the incongruity of subjecting an asset freeze to any stricter requirements than apply to an arrest or ensuing detention."

Dissenting in *Kaley*, Chief Justice Roberts, joined by Justices Breyer and Sotomayor, argued that the majority was giving insufficient weight to the fair trial implications of a "denial of counsel of choice" by viewing "syllogistic-type reasoning [as] effectively resolv[ing] the case." Allowing the defendant to challenge the probable cause needed for the freeze need not be viewed as "relitigating the grand jury finding." While "the grand jury decides whether a defendant should be required to stand trial, the judge decides pretrial matters," and the validity of the freeze order was a pretrial matter. Thus, the dissent noted, although the grand jury indictment identifies the property that is subject to forfeiture, there was agreement that the trial court must grant a hearing allowing the defendant to challenge "the grand jury's probable cause finding as to traceability." Responding, the majority distinguished the judicial determination of that issue, noting that (1) "the tracing of assets is a technical matter far removed from the grand jury's core competence and traditional function," and (2) "a judge's finding that the assets are not traceable to the crime charged in no way casts doubt on the prosecution itself."[c] The dissent replied, in turn, that "nothing in [*Monsanto*] or the indictment * * * justifies treating one grand jury finding differently from another."

9. *Misconduct rulings.* Following *Costello,* the federal lower courts turned to a "prosecutorial misconduct" rationale (see § 4 infra) to maintain some control over the character of the evidence presented to the grand jury. *Costello,* it was argued, did not take from the lower courts their authority "to preserve the integrity of the judicial process" by dismissing indictments that were the product of "flagrantly abusive prosecutorial conduct." Prosecutor misconduct was held to include not only such traditional forms of misconduct as inflammatory prosecutorial argument to the grand jury (see Note 5, p. 976), but also the presentation of evidence in an unfair manner. Federal lower courts varied considerably in what they deemed evidentiary misconduct, but under the broadest view, all of the following constituted grounds for dismissal where they had a possible impact on the indictment decision: the knowing presentation of perjured testimony; the introduction of false testimony by government agents where the prosecutor was patently negligent in failing to recognize its inaccuracy; the failure to return to the grand jury, during the period between indictment and trial, upon learning that a key witness had lied in testimony material to the charge; allowing the grand jury to become aware of the immunized testimony of the person subsequently indicted; the presentation of hearsay in a manner suggesting the witness was testifying based on personal observations rather than simply stating what he had been told by another (a practice sometimes used in narcotics cases, where a supervisor testified to information that actually came from an undercover agent or informant); the presentation of hearsay where there was a "high probability" that, with eyewitness rather than hearsay testimony, the grand jury might not have indicted (*United States v. Estepa,* cited in fn. 8 at p. 969); presenting the prior recorded testimony of a key witness and failing to inform the grand jury that the witness had acknowledged lying in a different portion of his testimony; and failing to produce known exculpatory evidence that clearly was material. See CRIMPROC § 15.5(b). The broad view of

[c] The majority viewed the dissent's position as opening the door to "strange and destructive consequences" via "inconsistent findings" by the judge and grand jury as to probable cause supporting the charges. While the dissent argued that the findings would not be inconsistent because the evidence the prosecutor presented in the freeze-order hearing would not necessarily be the same as that presented to the grand jury, the majority viewed any such difference as further contributing to a serious administrative flaw in the dissent's position. Because the hearing would be held "well before the rules of criminal procedure—or principles of due process—would otherwise require [disclosure]," the prosecutor ("particularly in organized crime and drug trafficking prosecutions, in which forfeiture questions often arise") would face a dilemma—provide a "sneak preview which might not just aid the defendant's preparations but also facilitate witness tampering or jeopardize witness safety" or "hold back some of its evidence" and thereby risk a negative ruling that "would diminish the likelihood of ultimately recovering stolen assets to which the public is entitled." Moreover, "any defense counsel worth his salt—whatever the merits of the case—would put the prosecutor to * * * [that] choice."

supervisory power that served as the grounding for these rulings was flatly rejected in *United States v. Williams,* discussed in § 4 infra. Indeed, after *Williams,* only a very narrow slice of these "evidentiary misconduct" challenges continue to be viable. See Note 1, p. 971.

Evidentiary Challenges in State Courts

1. **Costello *states.*** A substantial majority of the states that have addressed the issue, including all but a few indictment states, follow *Costello* in refusing to allow challenges to an indictment based on the type of evidence considered by the grand jury. Several of these states have statutory provisions requiring adherence in grand jury proceedings to all or most of the rules governing the admission of evidence at trial, but nonetheless follow *Costello* because of (1) statutory provisions precluding evidentiary challenges to an indictment, or (2) judicial rulings adopting the *Costello* arguments against "judicial revision" of the "judgment of the grand jury." Most "*Costello* states" also do not allow challenges to the sufficiency of the evidence supporting the indictment. Several, however, depart somewhat from this prong of *Costello*, and allow challenges based on the total absence of evidence as to a particular element of the crime charged, or challenges based on "the absence of any testimony from witness[es] deemed competent to testify." CRIMPROC § 15.5(c).

2. ***States rejecting* Costello.** A few indictment states and a somewhat larger group of information states (perhaps a dozen in all) allow challenges to the sufficiency and competency of the evidence underlying an indictment. See CRIMPROC § 15.5(c). Some do so by statutory command, but others have adopted this position based on the court's supervisory authority over the grand jury process. The reasoning of *Costello,* it is argued, is persuasive only "if the institution of the grand jury is viewed as an anachronism." If the grand jury is to "protect * * * the innocent against oppression and unjust prosecution," a defendant "with substantial grounds for having an indictment dismissed should not be compelled to go to trial to prove the insufficiency." *State v. Parks,* 437 P.2d 642 (Alaska 1968) (Rabinowitz, J., concurring).

Jurisdictions rejecting *Costello* uniformly insist that the trial court act with caution in reviewing the sufficiency of the evidence before the grand jury. They stress that "every legitimate inference that may be drawn from the evidence must be drawn in favor of the indictment," and note that "probable cause * * * may be based on 'slight' or even marginal evidence." *State v. Freedle,* 620 P.2d 740 (Hawai'i App.1980). As a result, most of the successful sufficiency challenges arise from the prosecution's failure to offer any competent evidence on a particular element of the crime charged.

A few of the non-*Costello* states direct the grand jury to consider only evidence that would be admissible at trial. Others, including the non-*Costello* indictment states, generally apply the rules of evidence but permit consideration of either limited types of hearsay (e.g., scientific reports) or a broad range of hearsay (determined in large part by the character of the burden that would be imposed on the prosecution and the witness in presenting direct testimony). Some would exclude evidence illegally obtained by the police, and others, looking only to the admissibility standards of the rules of evidence, would not. In general, the erroneous presentation of inadmissible evidence before the grand jury will not require dismissal of the indictment if there was sufficient competent evidence before the grand jury to sustain the charge.

3. ***Inspection of grand jury transcripts.*** Almost all of the jurisdictions which permit challenges to the competency and sufficiency of the grand jury evidence also grant the defendant an automatic right to inspect the transcript of the grand jury testimony. See CRIMPROC § 15.2(i). In *Burkholder v. State,* 491 P.2d 754 (Alaska 1971), the court concluded that the right to inspect was essential "to give meaning" to the right to challenge the indictment. The court rejected as unsatisfactory a state provision, similar to Fed.R.Crim.P. 6(e)(3)(E)(ii), that allowed disclosure only "upon a showing that grounds may exist for a motion to dismiss the indictment." The difficulty

with such a rule, it noted, was "that so far as the sufficiency of the indictment is concerned, * * * it is only by being able to have access to the grand jury proceedings without any prior showing that a defendant can know whether the indictment is subject to dismissal because of insufficiency of evidence."

Compare with *Burkholder,* the position adopted in New York. In connection with a motion to dismiss an indictment as based on insufficient legal evidence, the defendant may move for inspection of the transcript. However, the inspection initially is conducted *in camera* by the court, and further inspection by the defense may be denied if the court "determines there is not reasonable cause to believe that the evidence before the grand jury may have been legally insufficient." N.Y.Crim.P.Law § 210.30(4).

4. ***Postconviction appellate review.*** In several of the non-*Costello* states, a defendant may readily obtain interlocutory appellate review of the trial judge's rejection of a motion to dismiss. In others, however, interlocutory appellate review generally is not available (see Ch. 28, § 2), and a trial judge's adverse ruling on an indictment challenge ordinarily comes before the appellate court as part of the appeal following conviction. At this point, should any insufficiency in the evidence before the grand jury be viewed as harmless error since the trial jury found sufficient evidence to convict? Cf. *United States v. Mechanik,* Note 5, p. 980. Most non-*Costello* states apparently assume that a conviction will be reversed automatically if the trial judge erred in failing to grant the dismissal motion. See e.g., *Adams v. State,* 598 P.2d 503 (Alaska 1979) ("If we were to find that a trial could validate an otherwise invalid indictment [because based on hearsay testimony], the right to indictment by a grand jury could become a nullity"). But compare N.Y.Crim.P.Law § 210.30(6) (validity of an order denying a motion to dismiss or to inspect the grand jury transcript is "not reviewable upon an appeal from an ensuing judgment of conviction based upon legally sufficient trial evidence").

§ 4. MISCONDUCT CHALLENGES

A. MISCONDUCT CHALLENGES IN THE FEDERAL COURTS

UNITED STATES V. WILLIAMS

504 U.S. 36, 112 S.Ct. 1735, 118 L.Ed.2d 352 (1992).

JUSTICE SCALIA delivered the opinion of the Court.

The question presented in this case is whether a district court may dismiss an otherwise valid indictment because the Government failed to disclose to the grand jury "substantial exculpatory evidence" in its possession. * * *

On May 4, 1988, respondent John H. Williams, Jr., a Tulsa, Oklahoma, investor, was indicted by a federal grand jury on seven counts of "knowingly mak[ing] [a] false statement or report . . . for the purpose of influencing . . . the action [of a federally insured financial institution]," in violation of 18 U.S.C. § 1014. According to the indictment, between September 1984 and November 1985, Williams supplied four Oklahoma banks with "materially false" statements that variously overstated the value of his current assets and interest income in order to influence the banks' actions on his loan requests.

Williams' misrepresentation was allegedly effected through two financial statements provided to the banks, a "Market Value Balance Sheet" and a "Statement of Projected Income and Expense." The former included as "current assets" approximately $6 million in notes receivable from three venture capital companies. Though it contained a disclaimer that these assets were carried at cost rather than at market value, the Government asserted that listing them as "current assets"—*i.e.,* assets quickly reducible to cash—was misleading, since Williams knew that none of the venture capital companies could afford to satisfy the notes in the short term. The second document—the Statement of Projected Income and Expense—allegedly misrepresented Williams' interest income, since it failed to reflect that the interest payments received on the notes of the venture capital companies were funded entirely by Williams' own loans to those companies. The Statement thus falsely implied, according to the Government, that Williams was deriving interest income from "an independent outside source."

Shortly after arraignment, the District Court granted Williams' motion for disclosure of all exculpatory portions of the grand jury transcripts, see *Brady v. Maryland* [p. 1130]. Upon reviewing this material, Williams demanded that the District Court dismiss the indictment, alleging that the Government had failed to fulfill its obligation under the Tenth Circuit's prior decision in *United States v. Page,* 808 F.2d 723 (1987), to present "substantial exculpatory evidence" to the grand jury. His contention was that evidence which the Government had chosen not to present to the grand jury—in particular, Williams' general ledgers and tax returns, and Williams' testimony in his contemporaneous Chapter 11 bankruptcy proceeding—disclosed that, for tax purposes and otherwise, he had regularly accounted for the "notes receivable" (and the interest on them) in a manner consistent with the Balance Sheet and the Income Statement. This, he contended, belied an intent to mislead the banks, and thus directly negated an essential element of the charged offense.

The District Court * * * ordered the indictment dismissed without prejudice. It found, after a hearing, that the withheld evidence was "relevant to an essential element of the crime charged," created " 'a reasonable doubt about [respondent's] guilt,' " and thus "render[ed] the grand jury's decision to indict gravely suspect." Upon the Government's appeal, the Court of Appeals affirmed the District Court's order, following its earlier decision in *Page*, supra. * * *

Respondent does not contend that the Fifth Amendment itself obliges the prosecutor to disclose substantial exculpatory evidence in his possession to the grand jury. Instead, building on our statement that the federal courts "may, within limits, formulate procedural rules not specifically required by the Constitution or the Congress," *United States v. Hasting* [p. 33], he argues that imposition of the Tenth Circuit's disclosure rule is supported by the courts' "supervisory power." We think not. *Hasting,* and the cases that rely upon the principle it expresses, deal strictly with the courts' power to control their *own* procedures. That power has been applied not only to improve the truth-finding process of the trial, but also to prevent parties from reaping benefit or incurring harm from violations of substantive or procedural rules (imposed by the Constitution or laws) governing matters apart from the trial itself, see, *e.g., Weeks v. United States* 232 U.S., 383 (1914). Thus, *Bank of Nova Scotia v. United States* [Note 2, p. 977] makes clear that the supervisory power can be used to dismiss an indictment because of misconduct before the grand jury, at least where that misconduct amounts to a violation of one of those "few, clear rules which were carefully drafted and approved by this Court and by Congress to ensure the integrity of the grand jury's functions," *United States v. Mechanik* [Note 5, p. 980] (O'Connor, J., concurring in judgment).[6]

[6] Rule 6 of the Federal Rules of Criminal Procedure contains a number of such rules, providing, for example, that "no person other than the jurors may be present while the grand jury is deliberating or voting," Rule 6(d), and placing strict controls on disclosure of "matters occurring before the grand jury," Rule 6(e). * * * Additional standards of behavior for prosecutors (and others) are set forth in the United States Code. See 18 U.S.C. §§ 6002, 6003 (setting forth procedures for granting a witness immunity from prosecution); § 1623 (criminalizing false declarations before grand jury); § 2515 (prohibiting grand jury use of unlawfully intercepted wire or oral communications); § 1622 (criminalizing subornation of perjury). That some of the misconduct alleged in *Bank of Nova Scotia v. United States,* was not specifically proscribed by Rule, statute, or the Constitution does not make the case stand for a judicially prescribable grand jury code * * *. All of the allegations of violation were dismissed by the Court—without considering their validity in law—for failure to meet *Nova Scotia*'s dismissal standard. [See Note 2, p. 977].

We did not hold in *Bank of Nova Scotia,* however, that the courts' supervisory power could be used, not merely as a means of enforcing or vindicating legally compelled standards of prosecutorial conduct before the grand jury, but as a means of *prescribing* those standards of prosecutorial conduct in the first instance—just as it may be used as a means of establishing standards of prosecutorial conduct before the courts themselves. It is this latter exercise that respondent demands. Because the grand jury is an institution separate from the courts, over whose functioning the courts do not preside, we think it clear that, as a general matter at least, no such "supervisory" judicial authority exists, and that the disclosure rule applied here exceeded the Tenth Circuit's authority. * * *

"[R]ooted in long centuries of Anglo-American history," the grand jury is mentioned in the Bill of Rights, but not in the body of the Constitution. It has not been textually assigned, therefore, to any of the branches described in the first three Articles. It " 'is a constitutional fixture in its own right.' " *United States v. Chanen,* 549 F.2d 1306 (9th Cir.1977). In fact the whole theory of its function is that it belongs to no branch of the institutional government, serving as a kind of buffer or referee between the Government and the people. See *Stirone v. United States* [Note 5, p. 1011]. * * * Although the grand jury normally operates, of course, in the courthouse and under judicial auspices, its institutional relationship with the judicial branch has traditionally been, so to speak, at arm's length. Judges' direct involvement in the functioning of the grand jury has generally been confined to the constitutive one of calling the grand jurors together and administering their oaths of office. * * *

The grand jury's functional independence from the judicial branch is evident both in the scope of its power to investigate criminal wrongdoing, and in the manner in which that power is exercised. "Unlike [a] [c]ourt, whose jurisdiction is predicated upon a specific case or controversy, the grand jury 'can investigate merely on suspicion that the law is being violated, or even because it wants assurance that it is not.' " *United States v. R. Enterprises*, 498 U.S. 292 (1991). It need not identify the offender it suspects, or even "the precise nature of the offense" it is investigating. *Blair v. United States*, 250 U.S. 273 (1919). The grand jury requires no authorization from its constituting court to initiate an investigation, nor does the prosecutor require leave of court to seek a grand jury indictment. And in its day-to-day functioning, the grand jury generally operates without the interference of a presiding judge. * * * It swears in its own witnesses, Fed.Rule Crim.Proc. 6(c), and deliberates in total secrecy.

True, the grand jury cannot compel the appearance of witnesses and the production of evidence, and must appeal to the court when such compulsion is required. See *Brown v. United States,* 359 U.S. 41 (1959). And the court will refuse to lend its assistance when the compulsion the grand jury seeks would override rights accorded by the Constitution, see, *e.g., Gravel v. United States,* 408 U.S. 606 (1972) (grand jury subpoena effectively qualified by order limiting questioning so as to preserve Speech or Debate Clause immunity), or even testimonial privileges recognized by the common law, see *In re Grand Jury Investigation of Hugle,* 754 F.2d 863 (9th Cir.1985) (same with respect to privilege for confidential marital communications) (opinion of Kennedy, J.). Even in this setting, however, we have insisted that the grand jury remain "free to pursue its investigations unhindered by external influence or supervision so long as it does not trench upon the legitimate rights of any witness called before it." *United States v. Dionisio,* 410 U.S. 1 (1973). Recognizing this tradition of independence, we have said that the Fifth Amendment's "constitutional guarantee *presupposes* an investigative body 'acting independently of either prosecuting attorney *or judge*'. . . ." *Dionisio.*

No doubt in view of the grand jury proceeding's status as other than a constituent element of a "criminal prosecutio[n]," U.S. Const., Amdt. VI, we have said that certain constitutional protections afforded defendants in criminal proceedings have no application before that body. The Double Jeopardy Clause of the Fifth Amendment does not bar a grand jury from returning an indictment when a prior grand jury has refused to do so. * * * We have twice suggested, though not held, that the Sixth Amendment right to counsel does not attach when an individual is summoned to appear before a grand jury, even if he is the subject of the investigation. See *United States v. Mandujano*, 425 U.S. 564 (1976); *In re Groban*, 352 U.S. 330 (1957), see also Fed.Rule Crim.Proc. 6(d). And although "the grand jury may not force a witness to answer questions in violation of [the Fifth Amendment's] constitutional guarantee" against self-incrimination, our cases suggest that an indictment obtained through the use of evidence previously obtained in violation of the privilege against self-incrimination "is nevertheless valid." *United States v. Calandra* [Note 5, p. 960].

Given the grand jury's operational separateness from its constituting court, it should come as no surprise that we have been reluctant to invoke the judicial supervisory power as a basis for prescribing modes of grand jury procedure. Over the years, we have received many requests to exercise supervision over the grand jury's evidence-taking process, but we have refused them all, including some more appealing that the one presented today. In *Calandra,* supra, a grand jury witness faced questions that were allegedly based upon physical evidence the Government had obtained through a violation of the Fourth Amendment; we rejected the proposal that the exclusionary rule be extended to grand jury proceedings, because of "the potential injury to the historic role and functions of the grand jury." In *Costello v. United States* [p. 957], we declined to enforce the hearsay rule in grand jury proceedings, since that "would run counter to the whole history of the grand jury institution, in which laymen conduct their inquiries unfettered by technical rules."

These authorities suggest that any power federal courts may have to fashion, on their own initiative, rules of grand jury procedure is a very limited one, not remotely comparable to the power they maintain over their own proceedings. See *United States v. Chanen,* supra. It certainly would not permit judicial reshaping of the grand jury institution, substantially altering the traditional relationships between the prosecutor, the constituting court, and the grand jury itself. * * * As we proceed to discuss, that would be the consequence of the proposed rule here. * * *

Respondent argues that the Court of Appeals' rule can be justified as a sort of Fifth Amendment "common law," a necessary means of assuring the constitutional right to the judgment "of an independent and informed grand jury," *Wood v. Georgia* [p. 945]. Respondent makes a generalized appeal to functional notions: Judicial supervision of the quantity and quality of the evidence relied upon by the grand jury plainly facilitates, he says, the grand jury's performance of its twin historical responsibilities, *i.e.,* bringing to trial those who may be justly accused and shielding the innocent from unfounded accusation and prosecution. We do not agree. The rule would neither preserve nor enhance the traditional functioning of the institution that the Fifth Amendment demands. To the contrary, requiring the prosecutor to present exculpatory as well as inculpatory evidence would alter the grand jury's historical role, transforming it from an accusatory to an adjudicatory body.

It is axiomatic that the grand jury sits not to determine guilt or innocence, but to assess whether there is adequate basis for bringing a criminal charge. See *United States v. Calandra,* supra. That has always been so; and to make the assessment it has always been thought sufficient to hear only the prosecutor's side. As Blackstone described the prevailing practice in 18th-century England, the grand jury was "only to hear evidence on behalf of the prosecution[,] for the finding of an indictment is only in the nature of an enquiry or accusation, which is afterwards to be tried and determined." 4 W. Blackstone, Commentaries 300 (1769) * * *. So also in the United States. According to the description of an early American court, three years before the Fifth Amendment was ratified, it is the grand jury's function not "to enquire . . . upon what foundation [the charge may be] denied," or otherwise to try the suspect's defenses, but only to examine "upon what foundation [the charge] is made" by the prosecutor. *Respublica v. Shaffer,* 1 U.S. (1 Dall.) 236, 1

L.Ed. 116 (Philadelphia Oyer and Terminer 1788). * * * As a consequence, neither in this country nor in England has the suspect under investigation by the grand jury ever been thought to have a right to testify, or to have exculpatory evidence presented.

Imposing upon the prosecutor a legal obligation to present exculpatory evidence in his possession would be incompatible with this system. If a "balanced" assessment of the entire matter is the objective, surely the first thing to be done—rather than requiring the prosecutor to say what he knows in defense of the target of the investigation—is to entitle the target to tender his own defense. To require the former while denying (as we do) the latter would be quite absurd. It would also be quite pointless, since it would merely invite the target to circumnavigate the system by delivering his exculpatory evidence to the prosecutor, whereupon it would *have* to be passed on to the grand jury—unless the prosecutor is willing to take the chance that a court will not deem the evidence important enough to qualify for mandatory disclosure. * * *

Respondent acknowledges (as he must) that the "common law" of the grand jury is not violated if the *grand jury itself* chooses to hear no more evidence than that which suffices to convince it an indictment is proper. Thus, had the Government offered to familiarize the grand jury in this case with the five boxes of financial statements and deposition testimony alleged to contain exculpatory information, and had the grand jury rejected the offer as pointless, respondent would presumably agree that the resulting indictment would have been valid. Respondent insists, however, that courts must require the modern prosecutor to alert the grand jury to the nature and extent of the available exculpatory evidence, because otherwise the grand jury "merely functions as an arm of the prosecution." We reject the attempt to convert a nonexistent duty of the grand jury itself into an obligation of the prosecutor. The authority of the prosecutor to seek an indictment has long been understood to be "coterminous with the authority of the grand jury to entertain [the prosecutor's] charges." *United States v. Thompson,* 251 U.S. 407 (1920). If the grand jury has no obligation to consider all "substantial exculpatory" evidence, we do not understand how the prosecutor can be said to have a binding obligation to present it.

There is yet another respect in which respondent's proposal not only fails to comport with, but positively contradicts, the "common law" of the Fifth Amendment grand jury. Motions to quash indictments based upon the sufficiency of the evidence relied upon by the grand jury were unheard of at common law in England, see, *e.g., People v. Restenblatt,* 1 Abb.Prac. 268, 269 (Ct.Gen.Sess.N.Y.1855). * * * [In] *Costello v. United States* * * * we held that "it would run counter to the whole history of the grand jury institution" to permit an indictment to be challenged "on the ground that there was incompetent or inadequate evidence before the grand jury." And we reaffirmed this principle recently in *Bank of Nova Scotia,* where we held that "the mere fact that evidence itself is unreliable is not sufficient to require a dismissal of the indictment," and that "a challenge to the reliability or competence of the evidence presented to the grand jury" will not be heard. It would make little sense, we think, to abstain from reviewing the evidentiary support for the grand jury's judgment while scrutinizing the sufficiency of the prosecutor's presentation. A complaint about the quality or adequacy of the evidence can always be recast as a complaint that the prosecutor's presentation was "incomplete" or "misleading."[8] Our words in *Costello* bear repeating: Review of facially valid indictments on such grounds "would run counter to the whole history of the grand jury institution[,] [and] [n]either justice nor the concept of a fair trial requires [it]."

---

[8] In *Costello,* for example, instead of complaining about the grand jury's *reliance* upon hearsay evidence the petitioner could have complained about the prosecutor's *introduction* of it. See, *e.g., United States v. Estepa,* 471 F.2d 1132, 1136–1137 (2d Cir.1972) (prosecutor should not introduce hearsay evidence before grand jury when direct evidence is available); see also Arenella, *Reforming the Federal Grand Jury and the State Preliminary Hearing to Prevent Conviction Without Adjudication,* 78 Mich.L.Rev. 463, 540 (1980) ("[S]ome federal courts have cautiously begun to . . . us[e] a revitalized prosecutorial misconduct doctrine to circumvent *Costello's* prohibition against directly evaluating the sufficiency of the evidence presented to the grand jury").

* * * Echoing the reasoning of the Tenth Circuit in *United States v. Page,* supra, respondent argues that a rule requiring the prosecutor to disclose exculpatory evidence to the grand jury would, by removing from the docket unjustified prosecutions, save valuable judicial time. That depends, we suppose, upon what the ratio would turn out to be between unjustified prosecutions eliminated and grand jury indictments challenged—for the latter as well as the former consume "valuable judicial time." We need not pursue the matter; if there is an advantage to the proposal, Congress is free to prescribe it. For the reasons set forth above, however, we conclude that courts have no authority to prescribe such a duty pursuant to their inherent supervisory authority over their own proceedings. The judgment of the Court of Appeals is accordingly reversed and the cause remanded for further proceedings consistent with this opinion.

JUSTICE STEVENS, with whom JUSTICE BLACKMUN and JUSTICE O'CONNOR join, and with whom JUSTICE THOMAS joins as to Parts II and III, dissenting. * * *

II

Like the Hydra slain by Hercules, prosecutorial misconduct has many heads. * * * [It has not] been limited to judicial proceedings: the reported [lower court] cases indicate that it has sometimes infected grand jury proceedings as well. The cases contain examples of prosecutors presenting perjured testimony, questioning a witness outside the presence of the grand jury and then failing to inform the grand jury that the testimony was exculpatory, failing to inform the grand jury of its authority to subpoena witnesses, operating under a conflict of interest, misstating the law, and misstating the facts on cross-examination of a witness. [citations omitted] * * *

[As] Justice Sutherland [explained in *Berger v. United States,* Note 1, p. 1330: "The United States Attorney is the representative not of an ordinary party to a controversy, but of a sovereign whose obligation to govern impartially is as compelling as its obligation to govern at all; and whose interest, therefore, in a criminal prosecution is not that it shall win a case, but that justice shall be done. * * * It is as much his duty to refrain from improper methods calculated to produce a wrongful conviction as it is to use every legitimate means to bring about a just one." It is equally clear that the prosecutor has the same duty to refrain from improper methods calculated to produce a wrongful indictment. Indeed, the prosecutor's duty to protect the fundamental fairness of judicial proceedings assumes special importance when he is presenting evidence to a grand jury. As the Court of Appeals for the Third Circuit recognized, "the costs of continued unchecked prosecutorial misconduct" before the grand jury are particularly substantial because there

> "the prosecutor operates without the check of a judge or a trained legal adversary, and virtually immune from public scrutiny. The prosecutor's abuse of his special relationship to the grand jury poses an enormous risk to defendants as well. For while in theory a trial provides the defendant with a full opportunity to contest and disprove the charges against him, in practice, the handing up of an indictment will often have a devastating personal and professional impact that a later dismissal or acquittal can never undo. Where the potential for abuse is so great and the consequences of a mistaken indictment so serious, the ethical responsibilities of the prosecutor, and the obligation of the judiciary to protect against even the appearance of unfairness, are correspondingly heightened." *United States v. Serubo,* 604 F.2d 807, 817 (C.A.3 1979).

* * * In an opinion that I find difficult to comprehend, the Court today * * * seems to suggest that the court has no authority to supervise the conduct of the prosecutor in grand jury proceedings so long as he follows the dictates of the Constitution, applicable statutes, and Rule 6 of the Federal Rules of Criminal Procedure. The Court purports to support this conclusion by invoking the doctrine of separation of powers and citing a string of cases in which we have declined to impose categorical restraints on the grand jury. Needless to say, the Court's reasoning is unpersuasive.

Although the grand jury has not been "textually assigned" to "any of the branches described in the first three Articles" of the Constitution, it is not an autonomous body completely beyond the reach of the other branches. Throughout its life, from the moment it is convened until it is discharged, the grand jury is subject to the control of the court. As Judge Learned Hand recognized over sixty years ago, "a grand jury is neither an officer nor an agent of the United States, but a part of the court." *Falter v. United States,* 23 F.2d 420, 425 (2d Cir.1928). This Court has similarly characterized the grand jury [in discussing its subpoena authority]. *Brown v. United States*, 359 U.S. 41 (1959). * * * This Court has, of course, long recognized that the grand jury has wide latitude to investigate violations of federal law as it deems appropriate and need not obtain permission from either the court or the prosecutor. Correspondingly, we have acknowledged that "its operation generally is unrestrained by the technical procedural and evidentiary rules governing the conduct of criminal trials." *United States v. Calandra* [Note 5, p. 960]. But this is because Congress and the Court have generally thought it best not to impose procedural restraints on the grand jury; it is not because they lack all power to do so. * * *

Unlike the Court, I am unwilling to hold that countless forms of prosecutorial misconduct must be tolerated—no matter how prejudicial they may be, or how seriously they may distort the legitimate function of the grand jury—simply because they are not proscribed by Rule 6 of the Federal Rules of Criminal Procedure or a statute that is applicable in grand jury proceedings. Such a sharp break with the traditional role of the federal judiciary is unprecedented, unwarranted, and unwise. Unrestrained prosecutorial misconduct in grand jury proceedings is inconsistent with the administration of justice in the federal courts and should be redressed in appropriate cases by the dismissal of indictments obtained by improper methods. * * *

III

What, then, is the proper disposition of this case? I agree with the Government that the prosecutor is not required to place all exculpatory evidence before the grand jury. A grand jury proceeding is an *ex parte* investigatory proceeding to determine whether there is probable cause to believe a violation of the criminal laws has occurred, not a trial. Requiring the prosecutor to ferret out and present all evidence that could be used at trial to create a reasonable doubt as to the defendant's guilt would be inconsistent with the purpose of the grand jury proceeding and would place significant burdens on the investigation. But that does not mean that the prosecutor may mislead the grand jury into believing that there is probable cause to indict by withholding clear evidence to the contrary. I thus agree with the Department of Justice that "when a prosecutor conducting a grand jury inquiry is personally aware of substantial evidence which directly negates the guilt of a subject of the investigation, the prosecutor must present or otherwise disclose such evidence to the grand jury before seeking an indictment against such a person." U.S. Dept. of Justice, United States Attorneys' Manual, Title 9, ch. 11, ¶ 9–11.233, 88 (1988).

Although I question whether the evidence withheld in this case directly negates respondent's guilt, I need not resolve my doubts because the Solicitor General did not ask the Court to review the nature of the evidence withheld. Instead, he asked us to decide the legal question whether an indictment may be dismissed because the prosecutor failed to present exculpatory evidence. Unlike the Court and the Solicitor General, I believe the answer to that question is yes, if the withheld evidence would plainly preclude a finding of probable cause. I therefore cannot endorse the Court's opinion. * * *

NOTES AND QUESTIONS

1. ***Post-*Williams *"misconduct."*** Prior to *Williams,* federal lower courts had characterized a broad range of prosecutorial actions and inactions as "misconduct" that could lead to dismissal of an indictment. Whether a dismissal was in order depended upon the possible prejudicial impact of the misconduct either in itself or in conjunction with other acts of misconduct.

See Note 2, p. 977. Among those prosecutorial actions viewed as misconduct for this purpose were the various actions relating to the presentation of evidence that are described in Note 9, p. 963, and the illustrations of prosecutorial improprieties cited in the first paragraph of Part II of Justice Stevens' dissent in *Williams* (see p. 970). Still other prosecutorial actions held to constitute misconduct included the prosecutor giving testimony as a witness, making inflammatory comments to the grand jury, expressing a personal opinion of guilt, presenting to the grand jury an indictment already signed by the prosecutor, having an unauthorized person present during grand jury proceedings, attempting to clothe investigatory personnel with an aura of neutrality by swearing them in before the grand jurors as "agents of the grand jury," and various violations of the Rule 6(e) secrecy provisions. Under the standard announced in *Williams,* which of those actions can still be proscribed in the exercise of a federal court's supervisory power?

Lower courts have recognized that *Williams* cuts deeply into the prior precedent on cognizable misconduct claims. See e.g., *United States v. Fenton*, 1998 WL 356891 (W.D.Pa.1998) (speaking to allegedly improper and prejudicial comments by the prosecutor, as identified in the ABA standards discussed in Note 5, p. 976: "Well-recognized as the ABA standards are, they have not been adopted wholesale into any [federal] rule or statute to which I have been cited. Nor has the defense suggested that either standard is co-extensive with, or based upon, a constitutional principle. Accordingly, *Williams* renders this sort of prosecutorial conduct beyond the reach of my review."); *United States v. Orjuela,* 809 F.Supp. 193 (E.D.N.Y.1992) (government's failure to reconvene the grand jury after learning that its sole witness, a government agent, had relayed information from an informant that was "inaccurate and misleading" could not justify dismissal after *Williams,* which "called into question the continued viability of the Circuit cases upon which the defendant's argument relies").

But consider *United States v. Boettcher*, 164 F.Supp.2d 925 (E.D.Mich.2001) (in determining whether prosecutor's comments concerning a government witness' fear of testifying constituted misconduct justifying a pretrial indictment dismissal, court would apply the standard announced in a pre-*Williams* Sixth Circuit precedent, which allows dismissal in the exercise of the court's supervisory power if (1) the "defendant demonstrates that prosecutorial misconduct is a long-standing or common problem in grand jury proceedings in the district" and (2) "the prosecutor's actions caused the defendant actual prejudice"); *United States v. Navarro*, 608 F.3d 529 (9th Cir. 2010) (finding cognizable error in a judicial grand jury charge that erroneously told the grand jury that the prosecutor was duty bound to present exonerating evidence, and then enhanced that error by adding that the grand jury could count on the "candor, honesty, and good faith" of the prosecutor; court cites *Williams*, but only as holding that the prosecutor has no obligation to disclose exculpatory evidence, and not as limiting misconduct rulings; unlike *Navarro-Vargas*, Note 2 infra, court does not characterize defendant's challenge as presenting a constitutional claim, and it holds the error harmless under harmless-error standards addressing non-constitutional claims).

2. ***Constitutional violations.*** As the Court notes, there was no claim in *Williams* that the alleged prosecutorial misconduct amounted to a constitutional violation. The Supreme Court has said very little about what prosecutorial actions before a grand jury might amount to a constitutional violation requiring dismissal of an indictment. In *Bank of Nova Scotia* (Note 2, p. 977), the defendant claimed that the prosecutor had "violated the Fifth Amendment by calling a number of witnesses [associated with the defendant] for having them assert their privilege against self-incrimination," and thereby encouraging the grand jurors to draw adverse inferences in their decision to indict the defendant. The Court did not find it necessary to determine, however, whether such action constituted a constitutional violation, as it presumably would at trial (cf. Note 3, p. 1324), since the facts did not support the claim that the prosecutor either had acted in bad faith in calling the witnesses or had sought to have the grand jury draw adverse inferences based upon the witnesses invocation of the Fifth Amendment.

4. ***Exculpatory evidence.*** Courts in roughly twenty states have directly addressed the question of whether a prosecutor has an obligation to present known exculpatory evidence to the grand jury. A substantial majority have agreed with the *Williams* dissent rather than the *Williams* majority. In these states, including several major indictment states, the prosecutor has an obligation to disclose to the grand jury known exculpatory evidence, and violation of that obligation can lead to a dismissal of the indictment. See CRIMPROC § 15.7(p). In several of these states, the prosecutor's obligation is derived from a statute directing or authorizing the grand jury to consider known evidence that "may explain away the charge" (although other states with similar statutes view them as dealing only with the responsibilities of the grand jurors). Other states have concluded that the obligation is inherent in the prosecutor's relationship to the grand jury, for "a prosecutor who withholds substantial exculpatory evidence which would have tended to negate probable cause, destroys the existence of an independent and informed jury." The failure to disclose exculpatory evidence also has been characterized as producing a form of prosecutorial deception analogous to the use of perjured testimony.

Courts recognizing disclosure obligation have split on the scope of the obligation. The seminal California Supreme Court ruling in *Johnson v. Superior Court,* 539 P.2d 792 (Cal.1975), apparently the first case to dismiss an indictment for a failure to present exculpatory evidence, offered a broad view of the prosecutor's obligation. In that case, a magistrate had refused to bindover at a preliminary hearing after the defendant Johnson testified that his role in the drug transaction had been grossly exaggerated in the prosecution witness' testimony and that his limited participation had been part of a plan to furnish information to another local prosecutor in connection with a plea bargain on another charge. Not satisfied with the magistrate's decision, the prosecutor took the case to the grand jury. Only the arresting officers presented grand jury testimony, and the grand jury was not informed of Johnson's preliminary hearing testimony. (Indeed, the prosecutor conveyed to the jurors "the false impression that Johnson would refuse to testify if called"). The California Supreme Court held that the indictment should be dismissed because the prosecutor failed to inform the grand jury of the defendant's preliminary hearing testimony which was "evidence reasonably tending to negate guilt." This application of a "reasonable tendency" standard did not appear to hinge on the fact that defendant's testimony had previously persuaded the magistrate, but on the testimony's general character as potentially believable evidence that "explained away the charge." See also *Ostman v. Eighth Judicial Dist. Court,* 816 P.2d 458 (Nev.1991) (dismissal of indictment was required where prosecution's sole witness on a sexual assault charge was the alleged victim, the accused's girlfriend, who testified to being forced into unwanted sexual activity, with the prosecutor failing to inform the jury that the accused claimed, in a statement given to the police shortly after the incident, that the complainant had voluntarily consented; the accused's statement was exculpatory evidence "as a matter of law" since it "had a tendency to explain away the charge").

Other courts have viewed the prosecutor's obligation as encompassing a much narrower range of evidence. They hold that prosecutors must disclose before the grand jury only that exculpatory evidence which "clearly negates guilt"; dismissal therefore is required only where the grand jury almost surely would not have indicted had it considered the exculpatory evidence. See *State v. Hogan,* 676 A.2d 533 (N.J.1996) (evidence "so clearly exculpatory as to induce a rational grand juror to conclude that the state has not made out a prima facie case"). Arguably that standard would not encompass the evidence that the prosecutor failed to disclose in *Johnson,* as it could be characterized as no more than a "self-serving statement" of the defendant, and hardly evidence of an irrefutable nature. Courts adopting this narrower obligation to produce exculpatory evidence note that the broader standard was borrowed from the trial setting and is inappropriate in the grand jury setting because: (1) the prosecutor at the grand jury stage ordinarily does not have the advantage of defense motions identifying those items that the defense views as potentially exculpatory (although targets will occasionally request that the prosecutor present certain evidence to the grand jury); and (2) at such an early stage in the development of the case, both the possible charges and likely defenses are often uncertain, making it especially difficult for the prosecutor to determine what weight might be given to evidence that could be viewed as exculpatory.

5. ***Improper comments.*** A.B.A. Standards for Criminal Justice, *Prosecution Function* § 3–4.5(c) (4th ed. 2015), provides that the prosecutor "should not make statements or arguments in an effort to influence grand jury action in a manner which would be impermissible at trial before a petit jury." Are the A.B.A. Standards too rigid in importing a standard of what would be "impermissible at trial before a petit jury"? Is it improper under the A.B.A. Standards for the prosecutor to inform the grand jury: (1) that defendant had been indicted previously and the prosecution was now seeking a reindictment on the transcript of the earlier testimony; (2) that the case came out of an organized crime investigation so there was a special need to report any contacts by strangers or friends that might suggest their remotest interest in the case; or (3) that the grand jury would not be expected to investigate certain parts of the transaction because they were being considered by other grand juries? Should it matter whether such information was volunteered or provided in response to juror questions? It has been argued that, since the grand jury's authority to utilize its subpoena power and to ask questions may be based on "tips, rumors, * * * and personal knowledge" [*Dionisio*, Note 3, p. 960], and since the grand jury may reject a charge supported by sufficient evidence when it views that charge as unjust [see fn. d, p. 948, and Note 2, p. 973], it should be deemed "competent to evaluate and cope with prejudice [and] opinion" and prosecutors should be able to furnish the grand jury with the "background information" that enables them to put the charge in its proper context. Gary Woodward & Gary Ahrens, *The Iowa Grand Jury*, 26 Drake L.Rev. 241 (1976).

By and large, courts have accepted the approach of the A.B.A. Standards and have applied to prosecutorial comments in the grand jury setting the same limits that would be applied at trial. Nonetheless, some courts have found avenues for giving the prosecutor more leeway in the grand jury proceeding. Many states recognize that the prosecutor, as the legal advisor to the grand jury, may express a personal opinion as to the legal sufficiency of the evidence. CRIMPROC § 15.2(e) (noting a division, however, as to whether this authority goes beyond explaining how evidence relates to elements of the crime and also encompasses personal opinions on the credibility of witnesses). Indeed, the A.B.A. Standards acknowledge that a prosecutor may be given the authority to express personal opinions on legal sufficiency (giving "due deference to the grand jury as an independent legal body"), and impose an obligation on the prosecutor to inform the grand jury when his or her opinion is that the evidence does not warrant indictment. See A.B.A. Standards, supra, §§ 3–4.5(b), 3–4.6(a).

Courts also have taken cognizance of the multiple roles of the prosecutor in the grand jury setting in holding that trial limitations should not apply to comments that were aimed at purposes other than convincing the grand jury to indict. *State v. Schamberg,* 370 A.2d 482 (N.J.Super.App.Div.1977), illustrates this approach. In that case, the defendant moved to dismiss his indictment for perjury on the ground that the prosecutor had expressed a personal opinion on his guilt, an action traditionally prohibited at trial (see Note 1, p. 1330). In the course of examining the witness before the grand jury that later indicted him, the prosecutor had noted: "I have reason to believe that you just perjured yourself." The reviewing court noted its disapproval of "the form of [the prosecutor's] comment," but refused to quash the indictment. Though it suggested a personal opinion of guilt, the comment "was not addressed to the grand jury, nor was it intended to direct the grand jury to indict"; it reflected only the "culmination of efforts * * * to give the witness the opportunity to change his testimony," which was to be expected in the investigative setting of the grand jury.

6. ***Establishing misconduct.*** Even where the defendant testified before the grand jury, it is unlikely that prosecutor misconduct will have occurred in the presence of the defendant. Thus, the defense's ability to raise a misconduct challenge will be heavily dependent upon the availability of avenues that could enable it to learn of possible misconduct. In most jurisdictions, however, those avenues are quite limited. The best source for determining what happened before the grand jury usually is the transcript of the grand jury proceeding. However, some states do not require transcripts, and some of the states that mandate transcription extend that mandate only to the testimony of witnesses, meaning that discussions between the prosecutor and the grand jurors are not transcribed.

Many jurisdictions do provide for complete transcription, but that means very little to the defense unless it can gain access to that transcript. Automatic access to that transcript will be available only in those non-*Costello* jurisdictions that allow challenges to the sufficiency of the grand jury evidence. See Note 3, p. 964. In the many jurisdictions that follow *Costello,* which includes most of the indictment jurisdictions, the principle of grand jury secrecy sharply restricts defense access to the transcript. Federal Rule 6(e)(3)(E)(ii) is typical. It allows for court-ordered discovery on a defense showing that "a ground may exist to dismiss the indictment because of a matter that occurred before the grand jury." The requirement that the defense make a specific initial showing reflects the concern that defendants otherwise would use the motion as a fishing expedition, seeking discovery for trial preparation through the transcript disclosed as a result of the motion. Accordingly, the needed showing, for most district courts, is rigorous. It usually requires that the defense produce an affidavit of a friendly witness or a portion of the transcript otherwise released to the defense (e.g., for witness impeachment purposes) that contains a strong suggestion of impropriety. The preliminary showing cannot be made through the testimony of the grand jurors, as they typically are allowed to testify only as to "outside influences."

C. THE PREJUDICE REQUIREMENT

1. ***Variations.*** A finding of misconduct ordinarily will not in itself be sufficient to justify a remedy of dismissal. As discussed below, most jurisdictions insist also upon some showing of prejudicial impact, although a minority do allow for the possible use of dismissal as a "prophylactic tool" without regard to the presence of prejudice. Jurisdictions vary considerably in their approach to this prejudice requirement. The variations relate to the degree of the likelihood of prejudice, the treatment of some types of misconduct as inherently prejudicial, and the application of a different focus for assessing prejudice where the misconduct challenge is being considered after a conviction at a fair trial.

2. ***The federal harmless error standard.*** In BANK OF NOVA SCOTIA v. UNITED STATES, 487 U.S. 250 (1988), the Supreme Court spelled out the governing standard for dismissals issued prior to conviction. *Bank of Nova Scotia* was decided prior to *Williams* and dealt with some prosecutorial actions that did not violate the statutes and court rules identified in *Williams* (see fn. 6, p. 966), but it also applied the same prejudice standard to actions that would be subject to a supervisory-authority dismissal under *Williams,* and *Williams* itself assumed the applicability of the *Bank of Nova Scotia* standard to such misconduct.

The trial court in *Bank of Nova Scotia* had dismissed the indictment pretrial on the basis of numerous prosecutorial actions characterized as misconduct, concluding that such actions had undermined the independence of the grand jury and that, in any event, dismissal was appropriate to declare "with unmistakable intention" that "such conduct * * * will not be tolerated." A divided Court of Appeals reversed the dismissal order. It concluded that the prosecutorial actions had not "significantly infringe[d] on the grand jury ability to exercise independent judgment" and that "without a showing of such infringement," federal supervisory authority could not be used to dismiss an indictment. A dissenting judge disagreed with "the view of the majority that prejudice to the defendant must be shown before a court can exercise its supervisory power to dismiss an indictment on the basis of egregious prosecutorial misconduct." The Supreme Court, with only Justice Marshall dissenting, held in an opinion by Justice Kennedy that the Court of Appeals majority had been correct in insisting upon a prejudicial impact and in finding no such impact here. Speaking first to the requisite showing of prejudice, Justice Kennedy stated:

"We hold that, as a general matter, a District Court may not dismiss an indictment for errors in grand jury proceedings unless such errors prejudiced the defendants. In the exercise of its supervisory authority, a federal court 'may, within limits, formulate procedural rules not specifically required by the Constitution or the Congress.' *United States v. Hasting* [p. 33]. Nevertheless, it is well established that '[e]ven a sensible and efficient use of the supervisory power . . . is invalid if it conflicts with constitutional or statutory provisions.' * * * *United States v. Payner* [p. 33]. Our previous cases have not addressed explicitly whether this rationale bars exercise of a supervisory authority where, as here, dismissal of the indictment would conflict with the harmless error inquiry mandated by the Federal Rules of Criminal Procedure. We now hold that a federal court may not invoke supervisory power to circumvent the harmless error inquiry prescribed by Federal Rule of Criminal Procedure 52(a). Rule 52(a) provides that '[a]ny error, defect, irregularity or variance which does not affect substantial rights shall be disregarded.' * * * Rule 52 is, in every pertinent respect, as binding as any statute duly enacted by Congress, and federal courts have no more discretion to disregard the Rule's mandate than they do to disregard constitutional or statutory provisions. * * *

"Having concluded that our customary harmless error inquiry is applicable where, as in the cases before us, a court is asked to dismiss an indictment prior to the conclusion of the trial, we turn to the standard of prejudice that courts should apply in assessing such claims. We adopt for this purpose, at least where dismissal is sought for nonconstitutional error, the standard articulated by Justice O'Connor in her concurring opinion in *United States v. Mechanik* [Note 5, p. 980]. Under this standard, dismissal of the indictment is appropriate only 'if it is established that the violation substantially influenced the grand jury's decision to indict,' or if there is 'grave doubt' that the decision to indict was free from the substantial influence of such violations. *United States v. Mechanik*. This standard is based on our decision in *Kotteakos v. United States* [Note 2, p. 1416], where, in construing a statute later incorporated into Rule 52(a), we held that a conviction should not be overturned unless, after examining the record as a whole, a court concludes that an error may have had 'substantial influence' on the outcome of the proceeding.

"To be distinguished from the cases before us are a class of cases in which indictments are dismissed, without a particular assessment of the prejudicial impact of the errors in each case, because the errors are deemed fundamental. These cases may be explained as isolated exceptions to the harmless error rule. We think, however, that an alternative and more clear explanation is that these cases are ones in which the structural protections of the grand jury have been so compromised as to render the proceedings fundamentally unfair, allowing the presumption of prejudice. [*Neder*, at p. 1420]* * * These cases are exemplified by *Vasquez v. Hillery* [Note 7, p. 955], where we held that racial discrimination in selection of grand jurors compelled dismissal of the indictment. In addition to involving an error of constitutional magnitude, other remedies were impractical and it could be presumed that a discriminatorily selected grand jury would treat defendants unfairly. * * * We reached a like conclusion in *Ballard v. United States* [p. 1243], where women had been excluded from the grand jury. The nature of the violation allowed a presumption that the defendant was prejudiced, and any inquiry into harmless error would have required unguided speculation. Such considerations are not presented here, and we review the alleged errors to assess their influence, if any, on the grand jury's decision to indict in the factual context of the cases before us."

Turning to the application of the harmless error standard to the present case, the Court initially noted that it had before it no constitutional error as defendant's major claim of such misconduct lacked a factual grounding. See Note 2, p. 972. The Court also added two further caveats: "In the cases before us we do not inquire whether the grand jury's independence was infringed. Such an infringement may result in grave doubt as to a violation's effect on the grand jury's decision to indict, but we did not grant certiorari to review this conclusion. We note that the Court of Appeals found that the prosecution's conduct was not 'a significant infringement on the grand jury's ability to exercise independent judgment,' and we accept that conclusion here. Finally, we note that we are not faced with a history of prosecutorial misconduct, spanning several cases, that is so systematic and pervasive as to raise a substantial and serious question about the fundamental fairness of the process which resulted in the indictment."

Turning to the specific instances of misconduct cited by the trial court, the Court found no basis for concluding that, "despite the grand jury's independence, there was any misconduct * * * that otherwise may have influenced the grand jury's decision to indict" or may have left a "grave doubt as to whether the decision to indict was so influenced." The Court noted that there were two alleged instances of misconduct that could have influenced the decision to indict by affecting the substance of the evidence before the grand jury, but the record failed to support the conclusion that either involved misconduct. With respect to all of the others, they had no bearing upon the persuasiveness of the case presented to the grand jury and therefore did not present a sufficient possibility of influencing the decision to indict.

As for "several instances of misconduct found by the district court—that the prosecutors manipulated the grand jury investigation to gather evidence for use in civil audits; violated the secrecy provisions of Rule 6(e) by publicly identifying the targets and the subject matter of the grand jury investigation; and imposed secrecy obligations in violation of Rule 6(e) upon grand jury witnesses—[they] might be relevant to an allegation of a purpose or intent to abuse the grand jury process * * * [but] could not have affected the charging decision." As for the ceremony of swearing in IRS agents as agents of the grand jury, an alleged violation of Rule 6(c), there was "nothing in the record to indicate that the oaths * * * caused their reliability or credibility to be elevated, and the effect, if any, on the grand jury decision to indict was negligible." As for the violation of Rule 6(d) by allowing two IRS agents to read transcripts to the grand jury in tandem, there was "no evidence" that their joint appearance "enhanced the credibility of their testimony or otherwise allowed the agents to exercise undue influence." It was also relevant that "these incidents [of misconduct] occurred as isolated episodes in the course of a 20-month [grand jury] investigation * * * involving dozens of witnesses and thousands of documents."

3. ***State prejudice standards.*** All but a few states would appear to impose a prejudice requirement for dismissal of an indictment based on misconduct, although many will meet that requirement by attaching a presumption of prejudice to certain types of misconduct (see Note 4 infra). Most states appear to follow a standard for measuring prejudice quite similar to the "grave doubt" standard of *Bank of Nova Scotia.* Some, however, may be requiring a somewhat stronger showing of possible prejudice when they speak to the need for a "reasonable likelihood" of prejudice. Also, some courts would appear to look to a "correct result" analysis, holding misconduct harmless where the evidence before the grand jury supported the indictment. See CRIMPROC § 15.6(c).

A quite different approach was adopted in *State v. Johnson,* 441 N.W.2d 460 (Minn.1989). The court there had before it a series of improprieties in the prosecutor's general directions to the March term grand jury. Those included warning the jurors that a squad car would pick up any absentees, furnishing the jurors with informational packets from former jurors, telling the jurors that they should take account of the "county's higher standard of probable cause" (which was described as requiring that the prosecution have "a reasonable likelihood of conviction based upon the most logical defense"), and asking the jury to consider possible plea bargains in charging. Reversing a lower court that found the various improprieties to be harmless, as analyzed individually and in their "cumulative effect," the Minnesota Supreme Court ordered representment of all defendants charged by the March term grand jury who were still pressing pretrial objections. The court noted its agreement with the appellants that "today's harmless error can become the standard practice of tomorrow," and there appeared to be "no other way to preserve the integrity of the judicial process and maintain the independence of the grand jury."[a] Representment, it noted, was "necessary to protect not only the defendants but all of us as well."

4. ***Per se prejudice.*** Many of the states which ordinarily require a particularized showing of possible prejudicial impact create exceptions for one or more types of misconduct which are viewed as presumptively prejudicial and therefore providing a per se basis for dismissal. The Supreme Court in *Bank of Nova Scotia* acknowledged that federal courts too would presume prejudice, but only where "structural protections * * * have been so compromised as to render the proceeding fundamentally unfair," as illustrated by racial or gender discrimination in the selection of the grand jury (see Note 2, p. 978). Many state courts apply a presumption of prejudice in other circumstances as well. Thus, while *Bank of Nova Scotia* insisted upon a showing of possible prejudice with respect to the Rule 6(d) violation presented there (two witnesses appearing before the grand jury at the same time), those states would treat the presence of an unauthorized individual during any part of the grand jury proceedings as per se prejudicial (although others do so only when the unauthorized presence was during the jurors' deliberations or voting). CRIMPROC § 15.7(h). So too, where state law gave the accused a right to testify before the grand jury, the prosecution's failure to honor that right was held to constitute prejudice per se and mandated dismissal of the indictment. CRIMPROC § 15.7(d).

5. ***Postconviction review: the rule of* Mechanik.** In UNITED STATES v. MECHANIK, 475 U.S. 66 (1986), the defense learned during its cross-examination of a government agent that the agent had appeared together with another agent before the grand jury, where they had testified in tandem. The defense then moved for dismissal of the indictment on the ground that this practice violated Rule 6(d), which specifies those persons who may be present at grand jury proceedings and refers only to "*the* witness under examination" (emphasis added). Although Rule 12(b)(2) requires that such motions to dismiss ordinarily be raised before trial, an exception is made where there is "good cause" for the late objection. The trial judge took the motion under advisement until after the trial. It was then considered, after the jury had returned its verdict of guilty, with the trial judge ruling that Rule 6(d) had been violated but the violation was harmless because it had no impact upon the grand jury's decision to indict. The Court of Appeals then reversed, holding that a Rule 6(d) violation should require automatic reversal. That ruling was then reversed by the Supreme Court, and the conviction reinstated.

Three different approaches were advanced in the three opinions in *Mechanik.* Justice Marshall, in dissent, adopted the analysis of the Court of Appeals. Three concurring judges (in an opinion by Justice O'Connor) agreed with the trial judge's conclusion that the critical question was whether the violation was harmless as it impacted upon the grand jury's decision to indict. They concluded that it was, applying the standard later adopted in *Bank of Nova Scotia* for pre-conviction review. The opinion for the Court (per Rehnquist, J.) argued that the impact of the Rule 6(d) violation should be evaluated in light of the supervening jury verdict. It reasoned:

---

[a] The Supreme Court in *Bank of Nova Scotia* noted there were other means of remedying errors that did not have a prejudicial impact. They cited, as illustrations of alternative remedies, the punishment of a prosecutor's knowing violation of Rule 6 as contempt of court, requesting the bar or Department of Justice to initiate discipline proceedings, and the court "chastis[ing] the prosecutor in a published opinion." "Such remedies," it noted, "allow the court to focus on the culpable individual rather than granting a windfall to the unprejudiced defendant." See also p. 1331 (Note 4).

"Both the District Court and the Court of Appeals observed that Rule 6(d) was designed, in part, 'to ensure that grand jurors, sitting without the direct supervision of a judge, are not subject to undue influence that may come with the presence of an unauthorized person.' The Rule protects against the danger that a defendant will be required to defend against a charge for which there is no probable cause to believe him guilty. The error involving Rule 6(d) in these cases had the theoretical potential to affect the grand jury's determination whether to indict these particular defendants for the offenses for which they were charged. But the petit jury's subsequent guilty verdict not only means that there was probable cause to believe that the defendants were guilty as charged, but that they are in fact guilty as charged beyond a reasonable doubt. Measured by the petit jury's verdict, then, any error in the grand jury proceeding connected with the charging decision was harmless beyond a reasonable doubt.

"It might be argued in some literal sense that because the Rule was designed to protect against an erroneous charging decision by the *grand jury,* the indictment should not be compared to the evidence produced by the Government at *trial,* but to the evidence produced before the *grand jury*. But even if this argument was accepted, there is no simple way after the verdict to restore the defendant to the position in which he would have been had the indictment been dismissed before trial. He will already have suffered whatever inconvenience, expense, and opprobrium that a proper indictment may have spared him. In courtroom proceedings as elsewhere, 'the moving finger writes, and having writ moves on.' Thus reversal of a conviction after a trial free from reversible error cannot restore to the defendant whatever benefit might have accrued to him from a trial on an indictment returned in conformity with Rule 6(d). * * *

"We express no opinion as to what remedy may be appropriate for a violation of Rule 6(d) that has affected the grand jury's charging decision and is brought to the attention of the trial court before the commencement of trial. We hold only that however diligent the defendants may have been in seeking to discover the basis for the claimed violation of Rule 6(d), the petit jury's verdict rendered harmless any conceivable error in the charging decision that might have flowed from the violation. In such a case, the societal costs of retrial after a jury verdict of guilty are far too substantial to justify setting aside the verdict simply because of an error in the earlier grand jury proceedings."[b]

6. ***Interlocutory review.*** Justice Marshall, in his dissent, complained that the majority was leaving the enforcement of Rule 6(d) to the "unreviewable largesse of the district courts." He noted that if a judge should rule against a defendant on a pretrial motion to dismiss, that ruling might not be subject to appeal until after the trial, where a conviction would have precluded any relief under the majority's view. He offered the possibility of viewing the denial of the motion as a collateral order, so that it would be immediately appealable, but that position subsequently was rejected by the Court in *Midland Asphalt Corp. v. United States,* p. 1407.

7. ***The scope of* Mechanik.** Federal lower courts have disagreed as to how broadly *Mechanik* should be read. The Tenth Circuit has reasoned that *Mechanik* was "carefully crafted along very narrow lines" and involved misconduct that "at worst, was [a] technical [violation]." It would hold postconviction review available where prosecutorial misconduct reflected an "attempt

[b] As to those costs, the Court noted: "The reversal of a conviction entails substantial social costs: it forces jurors, witnesses, courts, the prosecution, and the defendants to expend further time, energy, and other resources to repeat a trial that has already once taken place; victims may be asked to relive their disturbing experiences. The '[p]assage of time, erosion of memory, and dispersion of witnesses may render retrial difficult, even impossible.' * * *. Thus, while reversal 'may, in theory, entitle the defendant only to retrial, in practice it may reward the accused with complete freedom from prosecution,' and thereby 'cost society the right to punish admitted offenders.' Even if a defendant is convicted in a second trial, the intervening delay may compromise society's 'interest in the prompt administration of justice,' * * * and impede accomplishment of the objectives of deterrence and rehabilitation. These societal costs of reversal and retrial are an acceptable and often necessary consequence when an error in the first proceeding has deprived a defendant of a fair determination of the issue of guilt or innocence. But the balance of interest tips decidedly the other way when an error has had no effect on the outcome of the trial."

to unfairly sway the grand jury or to otherwise affect the accusatory process" or the misconduct "transgressed the defendant's right to fundamental fairness." *United States v. Taylor,* 798 F.2d 1337 (10th Cir.1986) (finding reviewable a pre-*Williams* "totality of the circumstances" challenge that cited the prosecutor's failure to present exculpatory evidence, use of inadmissible and inflammatory evidence, violation of the attorney-client privilege, and unauthorized use of state officers in the grand jury's investigation). Several other circuits have rejected such a narrow reading. They acknowledge that *Mechanik* does not extend to misconduct which denies fundamental fairness and thereby presents a constitutional claim, but see it as extending to a broad range of nonconstitutional improprieties aimed at the charging process. See CRIMPROC § 15.6(e).

8. ***Postconviction review in state courts.*** Like federal courts prior to *Mechanik,* state courts traditionally were willing to consider misconduct challenges to grand jury procedures on appeal following a conviction. Since *Mechanik,* however, several state courts have adopted the rationale of the *Mechanik* rule and have applied it to a broad range of misconduct challenges. Other state courts have either rejected outright the *Mechanik* rationale or refused to extend it to what are viewed as significant errors. CRIMPROC § 15.6(f). While state Courts rejecting *Mechanik* usually have relied on the need for postconviction reversal to preserve the integrity of the grand jury process, the New York Court of Appeals in *People v. Wilkins,* 501 N.E.2d 542 (N.Y.1986), also focused on a state statutory structure governing grand jury proceedings that was quite different from that applicable to federal grand juries. In New York, unlike the federal system, automatic resubmission of a case rejected by a grand jury is not allowed. Thus, if a court can conclude that the defendant might not have been indicted but for the prosecutor's misconduct, it cannot also conclude, that the prosecution could readily have obtained an indictment notwithstanding that the first grand jury (without the misconduct) would have refused to indict. In New York, the prosecutor might not have been able to go to a second grand jury, even though the prosecutor had sufficient additional evidence (as established at trial).

CHAPTER 17

THE CHARGING INSTRUMENT

■ ■ ■

The law of pleading prescribes the contents of an information or indictment. For charging the most common offenses, the needed content will be firmly established in the law of the particular jurisdiction. However, where new or rarely used offenses are charged, a prosecutor must turn to the basics of the law of pleading, described in section 1 of this chapter, and to the case law applying those basics, described in section 2 of this chapter. In these situations, and others as well, the defense is likely to give serious attention to the pleading, evaluating whether a successful objection can be made, and if that is a possibility, what is to be gained by that success (subjects also considered in section 2). On occasion, after the pleading is filed, the prosecution learns that either the facts or the legal theory of the case are different than what was assumed in preparing the pleading. Very often this leads to an attempt to amend the pleading or to the prosecution's reliance on a factual variance at trial—the topics covers in section 3.

§ 1. PLEADING BASICS

A. THE LIBERALIZATION OF PLEADING REQUIREMENTS[a]

Common law requirements. As first developed in the common law system, the accusatory pleading was a quite simple document. In the early fourteenth century, it was sufficient to allege that "A stole an ox," "B burgled a house," or "C slew a man." Over the next few centuries, however, as the criminal law grew more complex and defendants were allowed to use counsel to challenge indictments, English courts came to demand that the pleading contain a full statement of the facts and legal theory underlying the charge. Indictments were lengthy, highly detailed, and filled with technical jargon. Pleading requirements for particular crimes often paralleled in their complexity and formalism the specialized civil pleadings required for each of the different forms of action. An indictment charging an assault, for example, had to include the phrase "*vi et armis,*" and a murder charge had to describe not only the means used but also the nature and extent of the wound inflicted.

American courts inherited the complex, formalistic, and often confusing pleading requirements of the eighteenth century common law, and they did not hesitate to require strict adherence to those requirements. Indictments were not infrequently quashed for the most picayune errors in form. Moreover, defects in an indictment were not waived by defendant's failure to raise the objection before trial; most defects could be challenged for the first time after conviction, usually by a motion in arrest of judgment. As a result, courts were often overturning convictions fully supported by the evidence simply because the underlying indictment was inartfully drawn or awkwardly worded. A conviction could also be reversed because the evidence at trial varied from the facts alleged in the indictment. Here too, the courts generally were strict, except for a variance as to the date of the offense. Thus, an early Delaware decision reversed a conviction under an indictment alleging the theft of a "pair of shoes" because the evidence established that both of the shoes stolen were for the right foot and therefore did not constitute a pair.

---

[a] This discussion is largely derived from CRIMPROC § 19.1. Supporting citations can be found there.

While the formalism and detail mandated by the common law pleading rules were designed in part to provide notice to the accused, they clearly went beyond what was needed to provide notice alone. As Sir James Stephen observed, a major function of the "strictness and technicality" in indictments was to guard against "looseness in the legal definitions of crimes." At a time when "the concepts and definitions of offenses took form largely through the experience of administration and without the aid of definitive statutes," the requirement that the offense be stated according to a particular formula, specifying in detail each element of the crime, was seen as providing assurance both that the grand jury understood what was necessary to establish an offense and that the courts did not engage in unanticipated extensions of the substance of the offense. Courts in later years suggested that perhaps an equally significant function of the complex common law requirements was to supply the judiciary with grounds that were readily available for reversing convictions in "hard cases." As one court put it: "When stealing a handkerchief worth £I was punished by death, and there were nearly 200 different capital offenses; it was to the credit of humanity that [pleading] technicalities could be invoked in order to prevent the cruelty of a strict and literal enforcement of the law."

The first round of reform. By the mid-1800s, with the increasing codification of the substantive criminal law and the reduction in the number of capital offenses, many courts no longer insisted upon strict adherence to the technical rules of pleading. That insistence, it was noted, had in many cases permitted "public justice" to be evaded and "let loose upon society" the "most dangerous malefactors." Other courts, however, insisted upon pleading strictness, and still others moved slowly in departing from common law precedents. As a result, legislative reform was deemed necessary. In general, the new legislation was directed at relaxing specific common law pleading requirements for specific crimes. Thus, it was provided that a murder indictment need not allege the manner or means of causing death, that there was no need to specify the denomination or species of money taken in a theft, and that the absence of specified phrases, such as "with force and arms," did not render an indictment invalid. More general provisions stated that variances would not be fatal unless they were "material," and that indictments should not "be deemed insufficient * * * by reason of any defect or imperfection in form only, which shall not tend to the prejudice of the defendant." Since the common law pleading requirements had been carried over from indictments to informations, the new legislation was made applicable to both pleading instruments.

The judicial response to the new legislation was mixed. Although most jurisdictions had adopted some form of pleading reform by the turn of the century, courts in many states continued to insist that offenses be charged with technical accuracy and nicety of language. In 1907, the Missouri Supreme Court reversed a conviction on appeal because the indictment charged that the offense was against the "peace and dignity of State," having left out the necessary word "the" before "State." The legislative response to such decisions was the enactment of broader pleading reform legislation. This second round of reform was part of a general movement to "modernize" criminal procedure (of Progressive Era origination, but not receiving broad support until the 1930s). A major component of that movement was to shift lawmaking authority to judicial rulemaking. As a result, this round of key pleading reforms was commonly enacted in court rules, rather than statutes, but even when included in statutory codes of criminal procedure, commonly added provisions rather than replacing the legislative enactments of the first round of reform (which can still be found in the statutes of many states).

The second round. The most widely adopted measures in this second round of legislative liberalization of pleading requirements centered upon three interrelated reforms: (1) a single simplified pleading standard; (2) official forms for the most commonly prosecuted crimes; and (3) an expanded waiver rule. These reforms, which had been instituted at an earlier point in many states, were incorporated in the Federal Rules of Criminal Procedure, which became effective in 1946. Today, they are found in almost all jurisdictions, with many states having provisions that are almost a verbatim copy of the Federal Rules provisions. Added to these provisions, in many jurisdictions, was one or more measures seeking to address the problem of variances.

Federal Rule 7(c) sets forth the most common formulation of a simplified pleading standard: "The indictment or information shall be a plain, concise, and definite written statement of the essential facts constituting the offense charged." This standard offered several advantages over the provisions adopted in the first wave of pleading reforms. Many of those provisions dealt either with a specific common law pleading requirement or a particular crime. Rule 7(c), on the other hand, established a single standard, applicable to the pleading of all crimes and all elements of the pleading. Moreover, that standard had behind it the basic thrust of an already achieved reform since it was a rough counterpart of the standard that reformers had previously used in mandating simplified pleadings in civil cases. Thus, looking to that civil reform, a court could readily conclude that Rule 7(c) required that a pleading do no more than "set forth, in factual terms, the elements of the offense sought to be charged."

Supporting the basic thrust of the Rule 7(c) standard were the official forms.[b] That Rule 7(c) did not mandate all of the detail found in the common law pleading was apparent from its reference to a "concise" statement of the "essential" facts. Exactly how little detail was needed obviously would vary with the offense, but the official forms provided useful illustrations of what the reformers had in mind. The Federal Rules include forms for 11 different crimes. In most states, forms were adopted for a much larger group of offenses. In addition to providing the prosecutor with a safe path for pleading the listed offenses, the forms served to "illustrate the simplicity of statement which the Rules were designed to achieve." Thus, Federal Rule Form 1, for the offense of murder in the first degree of a federal officer, stated:

> On or about the _______ day of _______, in the _______ District of _______, John Doe with premeditation and by means of shooting murdered John Roe, who was then an officer of the Federal Bureau of Investigation of the Department of Justice engaged in the performance of his official duties.

The third element of the second round of pleading reforms was the use of an expansive waiver doctrine that forced most pleading objections to be raised before trial. Federal Rule 12(b), for example, provided: "Defenses and objections based on defects * * * in the indictment or information other than it fails to show jurisdiction in the court or to charge an offense may be raised only by motion before trial." The Rule then added that the failure to present any such objection pretrial constituted a "waiver" of the objection (although the trial court "for good cause shown" was given discretion to "grant relief from the waiver"). The only exceptions were objections as to "lack of jurisdiction or the failure of the indictment or information to charge an offense," which were to "be noticed by the court at any time during the proceeding."

Provisions like Rule 12(b) sharply restricted the defense tactic of "sandbagging" that had been available in many jurisdictions. Recognizing that a successful objection pretrial would only result in some delay and a new pleading, counsel had followed the strategy of not objecting pretrial, going to trial on the defective pleading, and then, if the defendant was convicted, raising the pleading objection to overturn the conviction (which would be followed by a new pleading and a new trial, but would give the defendant a second chance to gain an acquittal or possibly to accept a plea bargain previously rejected). Through its waiver doctrine, provisions like Rule 12(b) precluded that tactic as to all objections except the failure of the pleading to show jurisdiction or to charge

---

[b] In 1983, the federal forms were abrogated as "unnecessary." Most states, however, continue to retain their official forms. Those forms typically reflect application of the Rule 7(c)-type pleading standard to a variety of individual offenses. Several states, however, have substituted for such a standard, as to a limited group of crimes, a separate system of "short form" pleadings. Here, an extremely truncated pleading, describing the offense by little more than its name (e.g., "A murdered B"), may be used, but the defendant then becomes entitled automatically to a bill of particulars "setting up specifically the nature of the offense charged." See CRIMPROC § 19.1(c).

an offense. For most commonly charged crimes, that exception was not significant. The primary concern was the failure to charge an offense due to the charging instrument failing to cover each element of the offense. That pleading error was most likely to arise in charging a newly enacted or rarely prosecuted offense. For commonly charged offenses, charging instruments would almost certainly include all elements of the offense; where the offense was the subject of an official form, that form set forth a judicially approved allegation as to each element, and when a form was not available, a model jury charge for the offense often provided an alternative source for a judicially approved listing of the elements.

While the requirement of a pretrial objection facilitated pretrial correction of inadequate pleadings (and thereby reduced the number of convictions that were reversed due to pleading defects), it did not respond to the problem of convictions reversed due to a variance between the allegations contained in a proper pleading and the proof introduced at trial. Many states, seeking to preclude application of the rather strict common law view of variance, added legislation permitting the pleading to be amended at trial to conform to the proof (thereby "curing" the variance), provided the defendant was not prejudiced by the amendment. The Federal Rules similarly included a liberal provision on amendments in Rule 7(e), although that provision was restricted to amendments of an information (the Supreme Court had adopted a very strict rule on amendments of indictments which had constitutional underpinnings and therefore seemed to bar extending Rule 7(e) to indictments, see Note 4, p. 1010).

The simplified pleading standards under Rule 7(c) and similar state provisions were also seen as responding, in part, to the problem of variances by reducing the likelihood that variances would occur. Since the pleading need not include a detailed description of the circumstances of the offense, there was less factual specificity from which the proof could vary. Rule 7(c) and many state provisions also included a pleading authorization that would make it easier to avoid variances; the prosecution could allege that the offense was committed by "one or more specified means." Thus, if the prosecution was uncertain as to whether its proof would establish that the offense was committed in one manner or another, it need not make a choice and hope that its proof would support that particular alternative. Similarly, where an offense encompassed more than one mental element or result, the simplified pleading standards also authorized pleadings that, in effect, set forth the various possibilities as alternatives.

The effectiveness of the second-round reforms depended, in part, upon the receptiveness of the courts. The simplified pleading standard, in particular, was not so precise as to preclude a court from retaining much of the common law approach to pleadings, at least where a specific official form was not applicable. The federal courts generally were most willing to interpret the Rules in light of the spirit of the reform movement. Most state courts followed a similar approach, although some moved to that position very slowly. The general consensus was that pleadings would no longer be dismissed for "technical defects"; and a "common sense construction would apply." Still, where the pleading failed to fulfill the basic functions of a pleading, dismissal of the charging instrument was required, and a small group of states tended to view those functions as quite demanding in their requirements.

A third round? A movement that may (or may not) eventually constitute a third round of reform was instituted toward the end of the twentieth century. It has fallen short so far of the widespread acceptance that characterizes a genuine round of reform. The focus of this movement is comparatively narrow; it seeks only to eliminate the reversal of a conviction based on a pleading defect where that conviction is the product of an otherwise acceptable proceeding.

One component of the movement is the elimination of special treatment of the pleading defect of failing to charge an offense when that defect was not timely raised. Under the exception noted in the original Rule 12(b) and similar state provisions, that defect can be raised for the first time on appeal after conviction and considered on its merits. Since it is not subject to the usual limitations governing review of untimely objections, the defendant has an incentive to engage in the type of sandbagging that Rule 12(b) sought to eliminate as to other pleading defects. As discussed on Note 2, p. 1006, this special treatment was grounded in the view that a pleading's failure to charge all the elements of an offense constituted a jurisdictional defect and, therefore, should be cognizable on appeal even if not previously raised (indeed, many jurisdictions viewed it as cognizable in challenging a guilty plea on collateral attack). However, as also discussed in Note 2, a substantial number of jurisdictions have come to reject this "jurisdictional" characterization. In the federal system and several states, this development has led to treating an untimely-raised failure-to-charge defect no differently than any other untimely objection. See Note 3, p. 1007, and Note 6, p. 1009. The end result is to eliminate the possibility that such an untimely-raised defect will produce reversal of a conviction where the conviction was supported by sufficient evidence (or in the case of a guilty plea, by a sufficient factual basis). It remains to be seen whether the 2014 amendment of Federal Rule 12 to eliminate the special treatment of the failure-to-charge defect (see Note 4, p. 1008) will lead additional states, particularly those with court rules modeled on the federal rules, to adopt a similar position.

The rejection of the jurisdictional characterization also has contributed to a reexamination of the standard of review applied on appeal to a timely raised pleading objection. Traditionally, appellate courts have treated an erroneous trial court rejection of a failure-to-charge objection as requiring automatic reversal of the ensuing conviction. As discussed in Notes 2 and 3, pp. 1004–1005, various federal circuits and a few state courts have rejected this automatic-reversal position, holding that reversal is not required where the pleading defect could not have prejudiced the defendant in the proceedings producing the conviction. Here too, it remains to be seen whether more states will accept that change, which does not as readily follow from the rejection of the jurisdictional characterization.

B. BASIC PLEADING DEFECTS

Federal Rule 7(c) is a prototype provision on the contents of a charging instrument, but perhaps more significant is Federal Rule 12(b)(3)(B). That provision implements the requirement that "defects in the indictment or information" be raised before trial by listing examples of those defects. That list includes four pleading defects (each unacceptable under Rule 7(c)) and a joinder defect (violating Rule 8). While the list of pleading defects is not exclusive (e.g., it fails to include a pleading's lack of a statutory citation), the four listed defects are the defects most commonly raised by defense challenges in every jurisdiction—in part because these four challenges, if successful, will require meaningful remedial action. The four defects are briefly described below.

1. ***"Failure to state an offense."*** The defect described by Rule 12(b)(3)(B)(iv) as the "failure to state an offense" is also commonly described as a failure to "charge" or "allege" an "offense" or "crime" (Rule 12(b) originally using "failure to charge an offense"). The primary, though not exclusive, component of a failure-to-charge is the pleading instrument's lack of reference to one of the elements needed to establish liability for the crime cited in the pleading (sometimes described as an "essential-elements defect").[c] A pleading does not charge an offense simply by asserting the violation of a crime identified by name or statutory citation (leaving aside the short-form pleading described in fn. b, p. 985). The pleading must allege the presence of each of the essential elements of the particular crime—typically the mens rea, the prohibited act, any requisite circumstances, and the necessary harm. The required identification of each element dates back to a time when pleadings played a major role in defining crimes, but the inclusion of all essential elements continued to be required after codification because stating the essential

[c] The objection of failing to state an offense also has been held to encompass (1) a claim that the offense charged is unconstitutional on its face, and (2) a claim that facts alleged as a matter of law establish exemption from liability. See CRIMPROC § 19.2. See also Note 5, p. 1008.

elements served the basic functions of modern pleadings (see Note 1, p. 994). Under the Rule 7(c) standard (calling for the "essential facts constituting the offense"), an element will be set forth in factual terms where the element lends itself to such a description (e.g., by describing the actual activities satisfying the conduct element). Other elements, most notably mens rea, commonly are set forth by reference to the statutory description of the element (see e.g., former federal form #1, p. 985, using "with premeditation" to describe the mens rea).

The essential elements requirement encompasses only the elements that the prosecution must initially establish to make its case. The pleading need not negate exemptions, excuses, or justifications that relieve the actor of liability, even where the defense presentation of such factors at trial would shift the burden of persuasion to the prosecution. Jurisdictions are divided in their treatment of so-called *Apprendi* elements. In *Apprendi v. New Jersey* (p. 1388) and its progeny, the Supreme Court concluded that any fact (other than a prior conviction) that operates to increase the maximum punishment or set a mandatory minimum is an element of the offense and must be found by a jury beyond a reasonable doubt. The Court further held that such an element must be included in the indictment, and that position is followed in several states. Other states, however, view the Court's pleading ruling as grounded in the federal grand jury clause, and therefore not binding on the states. They view an *Apprendi* element as a "sentencing factor" that need not be alleged on the charging instrument (although the defendant must otherwise be given advanced notice of the prosecution's intent to establish that element).

Essential elements defects occasionally are the product of a prosecutor's mistaken assumption that what a court later holds to be an element of the offense was a factor that stands apart from establishing liability (e.g., an affirmative defense). Much more often, the defect arises from the prosecution relying exclusively on the terms of the statutory definition to identify elements. That results in a fatal omission where courts have held that liability requires an element (e.g., mens rea) nowhere mentioned in the statute. Similarly, where courts have interpreted statutory terminology as requiring proof of factors not readily suggested by that terminology, inclusion of that statutory terminology without reference to those factors is likely to constitute an essential-elements defect. See e.g., *United States v. Keith,* 605 F.2d 462 (9th Cir. 1979), (where manslaughter statute's reference to actions taken "without due caution and circumspection" had been interpreted to require a "wanton or reckless disregard for life" based on "actual knowledge of the threat imposed," indictment could not ignore those distinctive elements and rely solely on the statutory language). Another common source of error arises when the prosecution erroneously assumes that its non-statutory description of the events establishing liability will implicitly allege the presence of a particular element. See Note 1, p. 1001.

Should a trial court find that an indictment or information fails to allege an essential element, it must dismiss the pleading. Since no offense has been charged, and amendments are limited to refining an offense already charged (as indicated by the prohibition against charging an "additional or different offense," see Note 1, p. 1009), the essential-elements defect cannot be cured by an amendment. Neither can it be cured by a bill of particulars, which only provides further detail as to elements otherwise properly pleaded. Where an essential-elements objection is timely raised pretrial, rejected by the trial court, and then raised on appeal after conviction, the appellate court will determine de novo whether the pleading was deficient. See, e.g., *United States v. Resendiz-Ponce*, p. 997. If the appellate court concludes that the trial court erred in rejecting the essential-elements challenge that error, in all but a few states, will lead to automatic reversal of the conviction, without considering whether the defendant was prejudiced by that error. See Notes 1–2, pp. 1003–1004. So too, as discussed in Note 1, p. 1005, most states continue to allow the essential-elements defect to be presented for the first time on appeal, and require automatic reversal if the charging instrument clearly failed to include an essential element. A minority position even allows the defendant to overturn a guilty plea conviction on the basis of at least one type of essential-elements pleading defect. See Note 2, p. 1006, and Note 5, p. 1008. Thus, it is not surprising that, "from the prosecutor's perspective, the essential-elements requirement clearly is the most critical pleading requirement." CRIMPROC § 19.3(a). Even in jurisdictions that have adopted the third round of reform, eliminating its special status as to late objections and automatic reversal, it remains especially significant because it cannot be cured by amendment.

2. ***Lack of specificity.*** The defect described in Rule 12 (b)(3)(B)(iii) as "lack of specificity" also is commonly described as a "factual specificity" defect, as it relates primarily to the failure to provide the accused with a sufficient description of the facts establishing the elements of the offense. As numerous cases have noted, the Rule 7(c) requirement that the charging instrument allege "the essential facts constituting the offense charged" is aimed at ensuring a "description * * * [sufficient] to enable [the accused] to defend himself adequately." The initial specificity issue is whether the pleading must go beyond the statutory language in describing an element of the offense. For example, in charging the offense covered by former Federal Form 1 (p. 985), must the charging instrument go beyond the statutory term "kill" and explain how the killing occurred, and must it go beyond the statutory description of the required circumstances—that the victim was engaged in "the performance of official duties"—and identify those duties? Form 1 reflected a determination that a factual explanation was required for the former element ("by means of shooting"), but not for the latter element. Secondly, where a factual description is required, the question arises as to how much detail is required. For example, when the pleading must identify the property that was stolen, is it satisfactory to describe that property as an "automobile" or must the make, year, and even the model of the automobile also be included?

Precisely how much specificity is required varies with the offense, the element, and even the particular aspect of the element. CRIMPROC § 19.3, for example, notes that the answer on specificity in describing conduct may depend on whether the question is who, what, where, when or how. Jurisdictions historically have allowed flexibility as to "when" (e.g., permitting the allegation that the described activity took place "on or about" a certain date) and "where" (e.g., permitting the allegation that the described activity occurred within the county or the judicial district). In determining the needed specificity as to "what" and "how", courts look to several considerations that can result in varying degrees of specificity for different offenses: "Relevant factors include the nature of the offense, the likely significance of particular factual variations in determining liability, the ability of the prosecution to identify a particular circumstance without a lengthy and basically evidentiary allegation, and the availability of alternative procedures for obtaining the particular information. It generally is agreed that the issue is not whether the alleged offense could be described with more certainty, but whether there is 'sufficient particularity' to enable the accused to 'prepare a proper defense.' "

In most jurisdictions, a specificity defect is treated differently from an essential-elements defect in one or more of the following aspects: (1) the relevance of the availability of a bill of particulars (a factor considered in determining the degree of specificity required, but not in assessing whether the essential-elements requirement was met); (2) on appeal following conviction, in most states, a finding that the trial court erred in rejecting a timely essential-elements objection requires automatic reversal of the conviction, but error on a specificity defect generally does not require reversal if it is shown that the defendant otherwise received notice of the missing content, resulting in an obvious lack of prejudice in the trial proceeding; and (3) the consequences of failing to raise the objection pretrial (a specificity objection is forfeited, while an essential-elements defect, in most states, can be raised for the first time on appeal).

In the course of applying the above distinctions, jurisdictions have divided as to proper categorization of one particular type of inadequate specification. As discussed in CRIMPROC § 19.3(a), that is "the failure to describe an element with sufficient specificity to distinguish alternative legal components of the element." Three illustrations of such rulings are noted: (1) where "offenses prohibit certain action when tied to the commission or attempted commission of another crime" (e.g., burglary), the charging instrument fails if it does not specify "the particular ulterior crime that fulfills the relationship in the particular case" (e.g., go beyond the statutory language of "intent to commit felony" and identify the felony); (2) in *United States v. Cruikshank*, 92 U.S. 542 (1875), where the statute prohibited actions intended to deprive a person of his constitutional rights, the indictment failed because it did not identify the particular constitutional rights involved; and (3) "where the statute specifies several different ways in which the crime can be committed [e.g., alternative forms of "compulsion" in a sexual misconduct statute], the pleading fails if it does not refer to the particular alternative presented in the individual case." In some states, such failures are treated simply as another form of lack of specificity. More commonly, however, jurisdictions distinguish such failures from the ordinary lack of factual specificity (e.g., in identifying the stolen property) because the failure here "looks not so much to factual detail as to further refinement in legal theory." The failure therefore is characterized as an essential-elements defect, resulting from a lack of specific identification of the particular element. That will give it the consequences cited in Note 1, supra.

3. ***Duplicity.*** As noted in Rule 12(b)(3)(B)(i), duplicity is the joining of two or more offenses in the same count. This practice is unacceptable because it prevents the jury from deciding guilt or innocence on each offense separately and may make it difficult to determine whether the conviction rested on only one of the offenses (and if so, which one). Duplicity can result in prejudice to the defendant in the shaping of evidentiary rulings, in producing a conviction on less than a unanimous verdict as to each separate offense, and in limiting review on appeal. A valid duplicity objection raised before trial will force the government to elect the offense upon which it will proceed, but will not require the dismissal of the indictment. Where the duplicity objection is erroneously rejected, the potential that the jurors convicted without being unanimous as to any one separate offense ordinarily creates a sufficient potential for prejudice to merit appellate reversal, but that may be offset if the trial judge's instructions to the jury or a special verdict form indicates that the finding of guilt was based on unanimity as to at least one offense. See CRIMPROC § 19.3(c).

4. ***Multiplicity.*** As noted in Federal Rule 12(b)(3)(B)(ii), multiplicity consists of charging the same offense in more than one count. The principle danger in multiplicity is that the defendant will receive multiple sentences for a single offense, although courts have noted that multiple counts may also work against a defendant by leading the jury to believe that the defendant's conduct is especially serious because it constitutes more than one crime. Multiplicity does not require dismissal of the indictment. The court may respond to a successful objection by requiring the prosecutor to elect one count, consolidating the various counts, or simply advising the jury that only one offense is charged. Where a multiplicity objection is erroneously rejected by the trial court, the remedy on appeal is to remand for a single sentence. The possibility that the presence of multiple charges influenced the jury's determination of guilt generally is viewed as too speculative to establish the prejudice needed for a conviction reversal. See CRIMPROC § 19.3(c).

C. PLEADING FUNCTIONS

Courts frequently note that the modern law of pleading eliminates complexity and technicality, but still requires that the pleading fulfill basic functions that were recognized in judicial opinions dating back to the nineteenth century. These functions relate to: (1) providing double jeopardy protection; (2) "fairly informing the defendant of the charge against which he must defend" (the "informing function"); (3) facilitating judicial review; and (4), in the case of indictments, safeguarding the defendant's right to be proceeded against based on a grand jury determination (the "grand jury function"). The defects discussed in Pt. B, the courts note, present unacceptable pleadings because they undercut one or more of these functions. Accordingly, where the defect is not obvious, as in determining whether a possible reference to an essential-element is sufficient or whether a factual description provides adequate specificity, courts often will base their assessment on whether the pleading fulfills key pleading functions. The majority opinion in *Russell v. United States*, set forth below, undoubtedly presents the most prominent use of such a "functional analysis" and the most frequently cited explanation of key pleading functions.[d]

RUSSELL V. UNITED STATES

369 U.S. 749, 82 S.Ct. 1038, 8 L.Ed.2d 240 (1962).

JUSTICE STEWART delivered the opinion of the Court.

Each of the petitioners was convicted [of violating 2 U.S.C. § 192 by] refusing to answer certain questions when summoned before a congressional subcommittee. In each case the indictment returned by the grand jury failed to identify the subject under congressional subcommittee inquiry at the time the witness was interrogated. [Each indictment stated that the particular defendant was summoned before a subcommittee on a particular date, that the subcommittee was conducting hearings pursuant to House Resolution 5 (authorizing the House Committee on Un-American Activities to conduct investigations of "un-American propaganda activities in the United States" and "all other questions in relation thereto that would aid Congress in any necessary remedial legislation"), that the defendant refused to answer certain questions (which were set forth verbatim), and that these questions "were pertinent to the question then under inquiry"]. In each case a motion was filed to quash the indictment before trial upon the ground that the indictment failed to state the subject under investigation at the time of the subcommittee's interrogation of the defendant. In each case the motion was denied. * * *

Sinclair v. United States, 279 U.S. 263 (1929) * * * [which extensively discussed Congressional investigative authority and the scope of § 192] established several propositions which provide a relevant starting point here. First, there can be criminality under the statute only if the question which the witness refused to answer pertained to a subject then under investigation by the congressional body which summoned him. * * * Secondly, because the defendant is presumed to be innocent, it is "incumbent upon the United States to plead and show that the question [he refused to answer] pertained to some matter under investigation." Finally, *Sinclair* held that the question of pertinency is one for determination by the court as a matter of law.

* * * The crucial importance of determining the issue of pertinency is reflected in many cases which have come here since *Sinclair*. Our decisions have pointed out that the obvious first step in determining whether the questions asked were pertinent to the subject under inquiry is to ascertain what that subject was. Identification of the subject under inquiry is also an essential preliminary to the determination of a host of other issues which typically arise in prosecutions under the statute. * * * To be sure, the fact that difficulties and doubts have beset the federal courts in trying to ascertain the subject under inquiry could hardly justify, in the abstract, a requirement that indictments under the statute contain averments which would simplify the courts' task. [But] the repeated appearance in prosecutions under a particular criminal statute of

---

[d] *Russell* was a 5–2 ruling. Justice Harlan dissented in an opinion joined by Justice Clark, and Justices Frankfurter and White did not participate. When decided, *Russell* was the latest in a substantial line of cases considering challenges to the highly controversial investigations conducted by the House Committee on Un-American Activities. *Russell* was a noteworthy addition to this line of cases because the Court was able to rule against the Committee without reexamining some arguably suspect First Amendment rulings. Not surprisingly, it was suggested that the "result in *Russell*—and the rhetoric supporting it—must be attributed in part at least to the Committee whose questions the defendant refused to answer." George Dix, *Texas Charging Instrument Law*, 35 Baylor L. Rev. 689 (1983). Justice Harlan's dissent took note of the special context, but warned that it was "not apparent how the seeds which this discussion plants in other fields of criminal pleading can well be prevented from sprouting." The *Russell* ruling has been viewed as relevant in resolving pleading specificity issues under many other statutes, although its actual impact there may be viewed as limited. See Note 2, p 1002. However, *Russell's* general discussion of pleading functions has been much more influential. In the federal courts, *Russell* has been cited in over 1400 opinions. In the states, it has been cited in appellate opinions in all but three states, with a total in excess of 300 citations.

the same critical and difficult question, which could be obviated by a simple averment in the indictment, invites inquiry into the purposes and functions which a grand jury indictment is intended to serve. * * *

Any discussion of the purpose served by a grand jury indictment in the administration of federal criminal law must begin with the Fifth and Sixth Amendments to the Constitution. * * * We need not pause to consider whether an offense under 2 U.S.C § 192 is an infamous crime, * * * since Congress had from the beginning explicitly conferred upon those prosecuted under the statute the protection which the Fifth Amendment confers. * * * This [grand jury] guarantee as well as the Fifth Amendment's Due Process Clause are, therefore, both brought to bear here. Of like relevance is the guaranty of the Sixth Amendment that "In all criminal prosecutions, the accused shall enjoy the right * * * to be informed of the nature and cause of the accusation." * * *

As we have elsewhere noted, "this Court has, in recent years, upheld many convictions in the face of questions concerning the sufficiency of the charging papers. Convictions are no longer reversed because of minor and technical deficiencies which did not prejudice the accused. This has been a salutary development in the criminal law." *Smith v. United States,* 360 U.S. 1 (1959). "But," as the *Smith* opinion went on to point out, "the substantial safeguards to those charged with serious crimes cannot be eradicated under the guise of technical departures from the rules." Resolution of the issue presented in the cases before us thus ultimately depends upon the nature of "the substantial safeguards" to a criminal defendant which an indictment is designed to provide. * * *

In a number of cases the Court has emphasized two of the protections which an indictment is intended to guarantee, reflected by two of the criteria by which the sufficiency of an indictment is to be measured. These criteria are, first, whether the indictment "contains the elements of the offense intended to be charged, 'and sufficiently apprises the defendant of what he must be prepared to meet,' " and, secondly, "in case any other proceedings are taken against him for a similar offense whether the record shows with accuracy to what extent he may plead a former acquittal or conviction."

Without doubt the second of these preliminary criteria was sufficiently met by the indictments in these cases. Since the indictments set out not only the times and places of the hearings at which the petitioners refused to testify, but also specified the precise questions which they then and there refused to answer, it can hardly be doubted that the petitioners would be fully protected from again being put in jeopardy for the same offense, particularly when it is remembered that they could rely upon other parts of the present record in the event that future proceedings should be taken against them. * * * The vice of these indictments, rather, is that they failed to satisfy the first essential criterion by which the sufficiency of an indictment is to be tested, i.e., that they failed to sufficiently apprise the defendant "of what he must be prepared to meet." * * * [T]he very core of criminality under 2 U.S.C. § 192, is pertinency to the subject under inquiry of the questions which the defendant refused to answer. * * * Where guilt depends so crucially upon such a specific identification of fact, our cases have uniformly held that an indictment must do more than simply repeat the language of the criminal statute. * * *

"It is an elementary principle of criminal pleading, that where the definition of an offense, whether it be at common law or by statute, includes generic terms, it is not sufficient that the indictment shall charge the offence in the same generic terms as in the definition; but it must state the species,—it must descend to particulars." *United States v. Cruikshank,* [Note 2, p. 990]. An indictment not framed to apprise the defendant "with reasonable certainty, of the nature of the accusation against him . . . is defective although it may follow the language of the statute." *United States v. Simmons*, 96 U.S. 360, 362 (1979). * * * That these basic principles of fundamental fairness retain their full vitality under modern concepts of pleading, and specifically under Rule 7(c) of the Federal Rule of Criminal Procedure, is illustrated by many recent federal decisions.

The vice which inheres in the failure of an indictment under 2 U.S.C. § 192 to identify the subject under inquiry is thus the violation of the basic principle "that the accused must be apprised by the indictment, with reasonable certainty, of the nature of the accusation against him, * * *." *United States v. Simmons,* supra. A cryptic form of indictment in cases of this kind requires the defendant to go to trial with the chief issue undefined. It enables his conviction to rest on one point and the affirmance of the conviction to rest on another. It gives the prosecution free hand on appeal to fill in the gaps of proof by surmise or conjecture. The Court has had occasion before now to condemn just such a practice in a quite different factual setting. *Cole v. Arkansas,* 333 U.S. 196 (1948) [due process violated where the state appellate court affirmed the conviction of defendants charged and tried for one offense on the ground that the evidence established their commission of another offense, which was "separate, distinct, and substantially different"]. And the unfairness and uncertainty which have characteristically infected criminal proceedings under this statute which were based upon indictments which failed to specify the subject under inquiry are illustrated by the cases in this Court already discussed. The same uncertainty and unfairness are underscored by the records of the cases now before us. A single example will suffice to illustrate the point.

In No. 12, *Price v. United States,* the petitioner refused to answer a number of questions put to him by [the subcommittee]. * * * At the beginning of the hearing in question, the Chairman and other subcommittee members made widely meandering statements purporting to identify the subject under inquiry. It was said that * * * the investigation was of "such attempt as may be disclosed on the part of the Communist Party . . . to influence or to subvert the American Press." It was also said that "we are simply investigating communism wherever we find it." In dealing with a witness who testified shortly before Price, counsel for the subcommittee emphatically denied that it was the subcommittee's purpose "to investigate Communist infiltration of the press and other forms of communication." But when Price was called to testify before the subcommittee no one offered even to attempt to inform him of what subject the subcommittee did have under inquiry. At the trial the Government took the position that the subject under inquiry had been Communist activities generally. The district judge before whom the case was tried found that "the questions put were pertinent to the matter under inquiry" without indicating what he thought the subject under inquiry was. The Court of Appeals, in affirming the conviction, likewise omitted to state what it thought the subject under inquiry had been. In this Court the Government contends that the subject under inquiry at the time the petitioner was called to testify was "Communist activity in news media." It is difficult to imagine a case in which an indictment's insufficiency resulted so clearly in the indictment's failure to fulfill its primary office—to inform the defendant of the nature of the accusation against him. * * *

It has long been recognized that there is an important corollary purpose to be served by the requirement that an indictment set out "the specific offence, coming under the general description," with which the defendant is charged. This purpose, as defined in *United States v. Cruikshank,* supra, is "to inform the court of the facts alleged, so that it may decide whether they are sufficient in law to support a conviction, if one should be had." This criterion is of the greatest relevance here, in the light of the difficulties and uncertainties with which the federal trial and reviewing courts have had to deal in cases arising under 2 U.S.C. § 192, to which reference has already been made. * * *

It is argued that any deficiency in the indictments in these cases could have been cured by bills of particulars. But it is a settled rule that a bill of particulars cannot save an invalid indictment. * * * When Congress provided that no one could be prosecuted under 2 U.S.C. § 192, except upon an indictment, Congress made the basic decision that only a grand jury could determine whether a person should be held to answer in a criminal trial for refusing to give testimony pertinent to a question under congressional committee inquiry. A grand jury, in order to make that ultimate determination, must necessarily determine what the question under inquiry was. To allow the prosecutor, or the court, to make a subsequent guess as to what was in the minds of the grand jury at the time they returned the indictment would deprive the defendant of a basic protection which the guaranty of the intervention of a grand jury was designed to secure. For a defendant could then be convicted on the basis of facts not found by, and perhaps not even presented to, the grand jury which indicted him. * * * This underlying principle is reflected by the settled rule in the federal courts that an indictment may not be amended except by resubmission to the grand jury, unless the change is merely a matter of form. *Ex parte Bain* [Note 4, p. 1010].

For these reasons we conclude that an indictment under 2 U.S.C. § 192, 2 U.S.C.A. § 192 must state the question under congressional committee inquiry as found by the grand jury. * * * Reversed.[e]

NOTES AND QUESTIONS

1. ***Essential elements.*** The Court refers to the pleading "protections" reflected by "criteria" which ask whether the pleading "contains the elements of the offense intended to be charged, and sufficiently apprises the defendant of what he must be prepared to meet" (p. 992). Sufficiently informing the defendant clearly constitutes a basic function of the pleading. Is the same true of the reference to the essential-elements requirement? "Courts quite often refer to the essential-elements requirement as a pleading objective in itself." CRIMPROC § 19.2(a). One explanation of that characterization is that the pleading of the essential-elements serves a purpose standing apart from the other functions noted in *Russell*—namely the function of providing a jurisdictional grounding (i.e., "providing a formal basis for the judgment," which requires a pleading necessary for a complete case on paper"). See CRIMPROC § 19.2(e). Consider, however, Note 2, p. 1006, discussing the rejection of such a "jurisdictional" characterization of the essential-elements requirement. Another explanation is that the essential-elements requirement is included in the discussion of functions because it is one aspect of sufficiently informing the defendant—indeed, the initial prerequisite for fulfilling that function. Commentators have questioned, however, whether a pleading's reference to all essential-elements is more appropriately viewed as a special facet of the "informing" function, than of the double jeopardy function, the judicial review function, or the grand jury function. See CRIMPROC § 19.2 (discussing judicial opinions that have tied the essential-elements requirements to each of these functions).

2. ***The double jeopardy function.*** At common law, the pleading played a critical role in determining whether a second prosecution was for the "same offense," as the practice was to compare the two pleadings. The essential-elements requirement ensured that the two crimes charged could be analyzed under the *Blockburger* standard, p. 1036, but the pleading's required factual specificity was less than perfect in assessing whether the two charges were based on the same events. A major weakness in this regard were the relaxed requirements in identifying time and place. See *United States v. Stringer,* 730 F.3d 120 (2d Cir. 2013) ("when a crime, unlike a

---

[e] Justice Harlan's dissent responded that the lack of specificity did not deprive the accused of notice or create uncertainty. It reasoned that (1) the defendants had available the transcripts of committee proceedings, containing all discussions of the subject matter of the investigations, and (2) there should be no concern relating a shifting analysis on appeal, as the "Government cannot * * * travel outside the confines of the trial record" and is free, as to a matter of law, to shift its "connective reasoning." The dissent pointed to *United States v. Debrow,* 346 U.S. 374 (1953), where the Court upheld a perjury indictment which failed to allege either the name or authority of the person administering the oath, noting the indictment alleged all essential elements and a bill of particulars was available if the defendant wanted "more definite information" on the administration of the oath.

The dissent also rejected the Court's reliance on the "corollary purpose" of furthering judicial review, noting that "pertinency is something that must be determined on the record made at trial, not upon the allegations of the indictment." As for insuring that the pertinency determination is tied to a subject matter found by the grand jury, that proposition was "unsound," since the prosecution is not prohibited from "introduce[ing] or advocate[ing] at trial evidence or theories, however relevant to the crime charged in the indictment, which it had not presented to the grand jury."

murder of a specified individual, is capable of repetition on the same day, or within a specified time period, the indictment will rarely provide sufficient detail, so that, on its face, it guarantees protection against double jeopardy"). Today, as *Russell* notes, the defendant raising a double jeopardy objection may also point to "other parts of the record" in determining the offense at issue (typically the trial transcript, but in the case of a guilty plea, the factual basis supporting the plea, Pt. D., p. 1217). This has led commentators and some courts to question whether double jeopardy protection should still be included in the list of pleading objectives.

3. ***The "informing" function.*** *Russell* initially notes the "relevance" of the Sixth Amendment right to be informed of the charge Does a pleading's failure to fulfill the "informing" function therefore constitute a Sixth Amendment violation? Some federal courts have found a Sixth Amendment violation, on federal habeas review of a state conviction, where the pleading was viewed as totally inadequate in failing to factually identify the offense. See e.g., *Valentine v. Konteh*, 395 F.3d 626 (8th Cir. 2005) (indictment charged 20 identically worded counts of child rape and 20 identically worded counts of felonious sexual penetration, all involving the same victim, and alleged to have occurred over a period of 10 months, with no attempt to distinguish between the "carbon copy" counts by reference to location, type of sexual action, or time of day). In general, however, "in applying the Sixth Amendment notice requirement to * * * objections relating to pleadings, courts have looked to * * * the actual notice provided in light of the totality of the information available to the defendant" CRIMPROC § 19.2(c). See e.g., *Parker v. State*, 917 P.2d 980 (Okla. Crim. App. 1998) (notice must be assessed in light of the "four corners of the information" together with the material that was made available to defendant at the preliminary hearing and through discovery).

Assuming adequate notification is satisfied by looking beyond the pleading, the informing function arguably also includes a broader goal that typically cannot be satisfied by other sources—forcing the prosecution to identify in an instrument that precludes variance its choices among potential factual grounds for establishing an element of the crime, primarily where that choice can readily call for differing factual and legal responses by the defense. This objective responds in particular to the situation in which all potential groundings for establishing the element are knows to the defense (e.g., through discovery), but they present so many alternatives as to preclude adequate defense preparation. Moreover, even when the alternatives are fewer, the broader goal responds to the difficulties created by prosecutorial shifts in grounding as noted in *Russell.*

4. ***The judicial review function.*** The judicial review function, which *Russell* describes as a "corollary purpose" of pleading specificity, is mentioned by courts far less frequently than the other functions. This may be because it commonly takes more than what *Russell* described as a "simple averment" to determine whether the government's case rests on an erroneous interpretation of a statutory requirement. See CRIMPROC § 19.2(d) ("to squarely present that issue [commonly] will require an extensive recitation of the factual circumstances the government intends to prove" and "factual specificity standards * * * generally do not require [such] extensive development of the underlying factual circumstances"). See e.g., *United States v. Bergin,* 650 F.3d 257 (3d Cir. 2011) (overturning a district court dismissal of a RICO indictment based on that court's analysis of "what the government would be able to prove at trial" as to the element of relatedness to the racketeering enterprise—the indictment having sufficiently alleged that the predicate crimes were committed for "the same or similar purposes" and to "promote the enterprise").

Of course, the prosecutor, where the interpretation of the element is unsettled, may prefer to have a pretrial ruling (with a dismissal being subject to appeal, see Note 1, p. 1409). In that situation the prosecution may provide specificity beyond the minimum required in order to set the stage for a defense motion to dismiss. See also CRIMPROC § 15.5(a) (noting the willingness of some federal courts to entertain a motion to dismiss based on the insufficiency of operative facts acknowledged by the government to be undisputed, while other courts conclude that the motion to dismiss is limited to defects in the charging instrument, stressing that the Federal Rules do not provide for a summary judgment procedure).

5. ***The grand jury function.*** Jurisdictions differ on the extent to which grand jury determinations control the prosecution's presentation at trial and how that position shapes pleading requirements. All agree that the prosecution is bound by the charge found by the grand jury, and that the indictment must refer to each element of the crime, thereby ensuring that the grand jury found sufficient evidence to proceed as to all elements of the offense. [f] All jurisdictions agree as well that the prosecution, in proving that charge, is not limited to the evidence presented before the grand jury. The disagreement relates to possible shifts from the activities and circumstances viewed by the grand jury as establishing a particular element of a crime. The jurisdiction's position here is revealed, in part, in the law governing the prosecutor's authority to amend the indictment, either directly or through introducing evidence at variance with the pleading (a "constructive amendment").

As discussed in Note 1, p. 1009, where a defendant is not taken by surprise, many jurisdictions allow amendment of an indictment under the same standards as the amendment of an information. The amendment is allowed provided that a "different offense" is not charged. While these jurisdictions vary in their definition of a "different offense," that prohibition typically allows a basic shift in the factual grounding of an element from that set forth in the indictment approved by the grand jury. Thus, the critical limit on such shifting is the prohibition of creating trial prejudice due to surprise. Since the "informing function" of the charging instrument also relates to that concern, commentators suggest that in these jurisdictions the "grand jury function" does not require any more specificity than the informing function.

As discussed in Notes 3 and 4, p. 1010, and Note 8, p. 1013, in the federal system and in several states, the range of permissible prosecution amendments is very limited. In addressing "constructive amendments" through variances, these jurisdictions similarly bar any significant shift from the grand jury's finding. See Note 5, p. 1011 and Note 5, p. 1015. Commentators question, however, the extent to which this approach necessarily ties the prosecution to the grand jury's determinations and thereby rigorously enforces the grand jury function. Consideration must be given to what is included in the indictment in the first place. Where a shift from a grand jury determination set forth in the indictment would be prohibited by the law governing formal and constructive amendments, does it follow that inclusion of that determination in the indictment is required to implement the pleading's grand jury function? Courts finding improper formal or constructive amendments do not always indicate that the impermissibly altered finding of the grand jury was a finding that had to be included in the indictment under pleading law (although they sometimes do so). So too, in addressing specificity, courts in these limited-amendment jurisdictions commonly emphasize notice, rather than the grand jury function, and rarely suggest that a specificity defect in an indictment would not also be a defect in an information.

6. ***The bill of particulars.*** The function of the bill of particulars is to provide the defendant with such information about the details of the charge against him as is needed for the "preparation of his defense, and the avoidance of prejudicial surprise" at the trial. See CRIMPROC § 19.2(f). The exact relationship of the bill to the pleadings is not always clear. As noted in *Russell,* the bill does not cure an "invalid indictment." As an instrument filed by the prosecutor, it cannot satisfy a pleading's grand jury function. So too, it cannot remedy the charging instrument's failure

[f] This grounding for the essential-elements requirement was recognized long before grand jury transcripts became available. "With that record available, continued use of pleading requirements as an indirect means of safeguarding the defendant's right to grand jury screening has been questioned." CRIMPROC § 19.2(f) However, courts continue to look only to the pleading in assessing whether the grand jury considered all the elements of the crime. This position arguably follows from the perspective of cases like *Costello*, p. 957, which, in another context, refused to look behind the indictment and asked only whether the "indictment is valid on its face."

to charge an offense. But the additional detail provided by the bill of particulars can serve the "informing" and "judicial review" functions. Thus, in assessing whether a charging instrument provides sufficient specificity, courts often look to the possibility of obtaining that specificity through a bill of particulars (which, like a pleading, will bind the prosecutor, so a departure in proof will constitute a variance.)

Apart from the special requirements of short form pleading (see fn. b, p. 985), whether to grant or deny a request for a bill of particulars lies in the discretion of the trial court. Moreover, appellate courts will give considerable deference to trial courts in their exercise of that discretion. Although appellate courts frequently offer general guidelines for the use of the bill, those guidelines tend to provide only limited assistance in ruling on a particular request. For example, the directive that the bill should be used to protect the defendant against "prejudicial surprise," combined with the traditional assumption that the defendant is innocent and "has no knowledge of the facts charged," could be read literally to require disclosure of almost every basic factual claim that defendant will have to meet at trial; yet even those trial judges most liberal in allowing a bill of particulars will stop far short of requiring such complete disclosure. So too, though it is commonly said that a bill of particulars "may not call for evidentiary matters," courts commonly order disclosure of information (e.g., the names of alleged coconspirators) that will identify the source of the government's evidence, if not set forth the evidence itself. The end result, as courts and commentators have noted, is a flood of trial court rulings that tend to be highly individualized and that often produce differing decisions on similar requests for a wide range of particulars.

§ 2. APPLYING THE BASIC PLEADING STANDARDS

UNITED STATES V. RESENDIZ-PONCE

549 U.S. 549, 127 S.Ct. 782, 166 L.Ed.2d 591 (2007).

JUSTICE STEVENS delivered the opinion of the Court.

A jury convicted respondent Juan Resendiz-Ponce, a Mexican citizen, of illegally attempting to reenter the United States. Because the indictment failed to allege a specific overt act that he committed in seeking reentry, the Court of Appeals set aside his conviction and remanded for dismissal of the indictment. We granted the Government's petition for certiorari to answer the question whether the omission of an element of a criminal offense from a federal indictment can constitute harmless error. * * * Although the Government expressly declined to "seek review of the court of appeals' threshold holdings that the commission of an overt act was an element of the offense of attempted unlawful reentry and that the indictment failed to allege that element," * * * "[i]t is not the habit of the Court to decide questions of a constitutional nature unless absolutely necessary to a decision of the case." * * * For that reason, after oral argument we ordered the parties to file supplemental briefs directed to the question whether respondent's indictment was in fact defective. We conclude that it was not and therefore reverse without reaching the harmless-error issue.

Respondent was deported twice, once in 1988 and again in 2002, before his attempted reentry on June 1, 2003. On that day, respondent walked up to a port of entry and displayed a photo identification of his cousin to the border agent. Respondent told the agent that he was a legal resident and that he was traveling to Calexico, California. Because he did not resemble his cousin, respondent was questioned, taken into custody, and ultimately charged with a violation of 8 U.S.C. § 1326(a).[1] The indictment alleged:

[1] 8 U.S.C. § 1326 provides, in part: "any alien who (1) has been denied admission, excluded, deported, or removed * * * and thereafter (2) enters, attempts to enter, or is at any time found in, the United States, unless (A) prior to his reembarkation * * * the Attorney General has expressly consented to such alien's reapplying for

"On or about June 1, 2003, JUAN RESENDIZ-PONCE, an alien, knowingly and intentionally attempted to enter the United States of America at or near San Luis in the District of Arizona, after having been previously denied admission, excluded, deported, and removed from the United States at or near Nogales, Arizona, on or about October 15, 2002, and not having obtained the express consent of the Secretary of the Department of Homeland Security to reapply for admission. In violation of Title 8, United States Code, Sections 1326(a) and enhanced by (b)(2)."

Respondent moved to dismiss the indictment, contending that it "fail[ed] to allege an essential element, an overt act, or to state the essential facts of such overt act." * * * The District Court denied the motion and, after the jury found him guilty, sentenced respondent to a 63-month term of imprisonment. * * * The Ninth Circuit reversed, reasoning that an indictment's omission of "an essential element of the offense is a fatal flaw not subject to mere harmless error analysis." In the court's view, respondent's indictment was fatally flawed because it nowhere alleged "any specific overt act that is a substantial step" toward the completion of the unlawful reentry.[2] The panel majority explained:

"The defendant has a right to be apprised of what overt act the government will try to prove at trial, and he has a right to have a grand jury consider whether to charge that specific overt act. Physical crossing into a government inspection area is but one of a number of other acts that the government might have alleged as a substantial step toward entry into the United States. The indictment might have alleged the tendering a bogus identification card; it might have alleged successful clearance of the inspection area; or it might have alleged lying to an inspection officer with the purpose of being admitted. . . . A grand jury never passed on a specific overt act, and Resendiz was never given notice of what specific overt act would be proved at trial."

* * * At common law, the attempt to commit a. crime was itself a crime if the perpetrator not only intended to commit the completed offense, but also performed " 'some open deed tending to the execution of his intent.' " 2 W. LaFave, *Substantive Criminal Law* § 11.2(a), p. 205 (2d ed. 2003) (quoting E. Coke, Third Institute 5 (6th ed. 1680)) * * * . More recently, the requisite "open deed" has been described as an "overt act" that constitutes a "substantial step" toward completing the offense. LaFave, supra, § 11.4. * * * As was true at common law, the mere intent to violate a federal criminal statute is not punishable as an attempt unless it is also accompanied by significant conduct.

The Government does not disagree with respondent's submission that he cannot be guilty of attempted reentry in violation of 8 U.S.C. § 1326(a) unless he committed an overt act qualifying as a substantial step toward completion of his goal. Nor does it dispute that "[a]n indictment must set forth each element of the crime that it charges." * * * It instead contends that the indictment at bar implicitly alleged that respondent engaged in the necessary overt act "simply by alleging that he 'attempted to enter the United States.' " We agree.

Not only does the word "attempt" as used in common parlance connote action rather than mere intent, but more importantly, as used in the law for centuries, it encompasses both the overt

---

admission, or (B) with respect to an alien previously denied admission and removed, unless such alien shall establish that he was not required to obtain such advance consent, * * * shall be fined under title 18, or imprisoned not more than 2 years, or both." [Under subsection b(2), the two year maximum is enhanced to 20 years where the alien's previous removal was subsequent to commission of an aggravated felony].

[2] In the opinion of the Ninth Circuit, the five elements of the offense of attempted reentry in violation of § 1326(a) are: "(1) the defendant had the purpose, i.e., conscious desire, to reenter the United States without the express consent of the Attorney General; (2) the defendant committed an overt act that was a substantial step towards reentering without that consent; (3) the defendant was not a citizen of the United States; (4) the defendant had previously been lawfully denied admission, excluded, deported or removed from the United States; and (5) the Attorney General had not consented to the defendant's attempted reentry.' "

act and intent elements. Consequently, an indictment alleging attempted illegal reentry under § 1326(a) need not specifically allege a particular overt act or any other "component par[t]" of the offense. See *Hamling v. United States,* 418 U.S. 87 (1974). Just as it was enough for the indictment in *Hamling* to allege that the defendant mailed "obscene" material in violation of 18 U.S.C. § 1461, it was enough for the indictment in this case to point to the relevant criminal statute and allege that "[o]n or about June 1, 2003," respondent "attempted to enter the United States of America at or near San Luis in the District of Arizona."

In *Hamling,* we identified two constitutional requirements for an indictment: "first, [that it] contains the elements of the offense charged and fairly informs a defendant of the charge against which he must defend, and, second, [that it] enables him to plead an acquittal or conviction in bar of future prosecutions for the same offense." In this case, the use of the word "attempt," coupled with the specification of the time and place of respondent's attempted illegal reentry, satisfied both. Indeed, the time-and-place information provided respondent with more adequate notice than would an indictment describing particular overt acts. After all, a given defendant may have approached the border or lied to a border-patrol agent in the course of countless attempts on innumerable occasions. For the same reason, the time-and-date specification in respondent's indictment provided ample protection against the risk of multiple prosecutions for the same crime.[4]

Respondent nonetheless maintains that the indictment would have been sufficient only if it had alleged any of three overt acts performed during his attempted reentry: that he walked into an inspection area; that he presented a misleading identification card; or that he lied to the inspector. Individually and cumulatively, those acts tend to prove the charged attempt—but none was essential to the finding of guilt in this case. All three acts were rather part of a single course of conduct culminating in the charged "attempt."

Respondent is of course correct that while an indictment parroting the language of a federal criminal statute is often sufficient, there are crimes that must be charged with greater specificity. * * * A clear example is the statute making it a crime for a witness summoned before a congressional committee to refuse to answer any question "pertinent to the question under inquiry." 2 U.S.C. § 192. As we explained at length in our opinion in *Russell v. United States* [p. 991], a valid indictment for such a refusal to testify must go beyond the words of § 192 and allege the subject of the congressional hearing in order to determine whether the defendant's refusal was "pertinent." Based on a number of cases arising out of congressional investigations, we recognized that the relevant hearing's subject was frequently uncertain but invariably "central to every prosecution under the statute." Both to provide fair notice to defendants and to assure that any conviction would arise out of the theory of guilt presented to the grand jury, we held that indictments under § 192 must do more than restate the language of the statute.

Our reasoning in *Russell* suggests that there was no infirmity in the present indictment. First, unlike the statute at issue in *Russell,* guilt under 8 U.S.C. § 1326(a) does not "depen[d] so crucially upon such a specific identification of fact." Second, before explaining the special need for particularity in charges brought under 2 U.S.C. § 192, Justice Stewart noted that, in 1872, Congress had enacted a statute reflecting "the drift of the law away from the rules of technical and formalized pleading which had characterized an earlier era." * * * As we have said, the]Federal Rules "were designed to eliminate technicalities in criminal pleadings and are to be

---

4 There is little practical difference between our holding and Justice Scalia's position. Apparently, Justice Scalia would have found the indictment to be sufficient if it also stated that respondent " 'took a substantial step' " toward entering the United States. * * * Unlike the Ninth Circuit, then, Justice Scalia would not have required the indictment to allege a particular overt act such as tendering a false identification to a border inspector. * * * With all due respect to his principled position, we think that the "substantial step" requirement is implicit in the word "attempt," and we do not believe that adding those four words would have given respondent any greater notice of the charges against him or protection against future prosecution.

construed to secure simplicity in procedure." * * * While detailed allegations might well have been required under common-law pleading rules, * * * they surely are not contemplated by Rule 7(c)(1), which provides that an indictment "shall be a plain, concise, and definite written statement of the essential facts constituting the offense charged."[7]

Because we are satisfied that respondent's indictment fully complied with that Rule and did not deprive him of any significant protection that the constitutional guarantee of a grand jury was intended to confer, we reverse the judgment of the Court of Appeals and remand the case for further proceedings consistent with this opinion.

JUSTICE SCALIA, dissenting.

It is well established that an indictment must allege all the elements of the charged crime. * * * As the Court acknowledges, it is likewise well established that "attempt" contains two substantive elements: the *intent* to commit the underlying crime, and the undertaking of *some action* toward commission of that crime.* * * It should follow, then, that when the Government indicts for attempt to commit a crime, it must allege both that the defendant had the intent to commit the crime, *and* that he took some action toward its commission. Any rule to the contrary would be an exception to the standard practice.

The Court gives two reasons for its special "attempt" exception. First, it says that in "common parlance" the word attempt "connote[s]," and therefore "impli[es]," both the intent and overt-act elements. This strikes me as certainly irrelevant, and probably incorrect to boot. It is irrelevant because, as I have just discussed, we have always required the elements of a crime to be explicitly set forth in the indictment, *whether or not* they are fairly called to mind by the mere name of the crime. Burglary, for example, connotes in common parlance the entry of a building with felonious intent, yet we require those elements to be set forth. Our precedents make clear that the indictment must "fully, directly, and *expressly,* without any uncertainty or ambiguity, set forth all the elements necessary to constitute the offence intended to be punished." *United States v. Carll*, 105 U.S. 611, 612 (1882) (emphasis added). And the Court's argument is probably incorrect because I doubt that the common meaning of the word "attempt" conveys with precision what conviction of that crime requires. A reasonable grand juror, relying on nothing but that term, might well believe that it connotes intent plus any minor action toward the commission of the crime, rather than the " 'substantial step' " that the Court acknowledges is required.

Besides appealing to "common parlance," the Court relies on the fact that attempt, "as used in the law for centuries . . . encompasses both the overt act and intent elements." Once again, this argument seems to me certainly irrelevant and probably incorrect. Many common-law crimes have retained relatively static elements throughout history, burglary among them; that has never been thought to excuse the specification of those elements in the indictment. And the argument is probably incorrect, because the definition of attempt has not been nearly as consistent as the Court suggests. * * * Nearly a century ago, a leading criminal-law treatise pointed out that "attempt' is a term peculiarly indefinite" with "no prescribed legal meaning." 1 F. Wharton, *Criminal Law* § 229, p. 298 (11th ed. 1912) . Even the modern treatise the Court relies upon, explains—in a subsection entitled "The Confusion"—that jurisdictions vary widely in how they define the requisite actus reus. LaFave, supra, § 11.4(a) * * *.

In this case, the indictment alleged that respondent "knowingly and intentionally attempted to enter the United States of America," so that the Court focuses only on whether the indictment

---

[7] Federal Rule of Criminal Procedure 31(c) is also instructive. It provides that a defendant may be found guilty of "an attempt to commit the offense charged; or . . . an attempt to commit an offense necessarily included in the offense charged, if the attempt is an offense in its own right." Fed. Rule Crim. Proc. 31(c)(2)–(3). If a defendant indicted only for a completed offense can be convicted of attempt under Rule 31(c) without the indictment ever mentioning an overt act, it would be illogical to dismiss an indictment charging "attempt" because it fails to allege such an act.

needed to allege the second element of attempt, an overt act. If one accepts the Court's opinion, however, the indictment could just as well have omitted the phrase "knowingly and intentionally," since that is understood in "common parlance," and has been an element of attempt "for centuries." Would we say that, in a prosecution for first-degree murder, the element of "malice aforethought" could be omitted from the indictment simply because it is commonly understood, and the law has always required it? Surely not. * * *

The Court finds another point "instructive": "If a defendant indicted only for a completed offense can be convicted of attempt . . . without the indictment's ever mentioning an overt act, it would be illogical to dismiss an indictment charging 'attempt' because it fails to allege such an act." *Ante,* n. 7. I disagree; it seems to me entirely logical. To indict for commission of a *completed offense,* the prosecutor must persuade the grand jury that the accused's acts and state of mind fulfilled all the elements of the offense. If they did so, and if the offense has *a mens rea* element (which almost all crimes, including burglary, do), then they unquestionably fulfilled all the elements of an attempt as well—i.e., the accused meant to commit the crime and took the requisite step (no matter how demanding the requirement) in that direction. That is to say, attempt to commit a crime is simply a lesser included offense. A grand jury finding that the accused committed the crime is *necessarily* a finding that he attempted to commit the crime, and therefore the attempt need not be separately charged. When, however, the prosecutor seeks only an indictment for attempt, it is not enough to tell the grand jury that it requires a finding of "some, but not all, of the elements of the substantive crime"; he must specify what the elements of attempt consist of. He must do that for the same reason a court must *instruct* the petit jury on the attempt elements, even when the indictment has not separately *charged* attempt: without such specification, the jury, grand or petit, cannot intelligently find attempt.

* * * Despite the clear answer provided by straightforward application of the oft-recited principles of our jurisprudence, I might have been persuaded to recognize an (illogical) exception to those principles if the Government had demonstrated that mere recitation of the word "attempt" in attempt indictments has been the traditional practice. But its effort to do so falls far short; in fact, it has not even undertaken such an effort. The Government has pointed to some cases that allow an indictment simply to use the word "attempt," and many others that invalidate an indictment for failure to allege an overt act. * * * To be clear, I need not decide in this case whether, as the Ninth Circuit held, the Government was required to specify in the indictment which particular overt act it would be relying on at trial. Cf. *Russell v. United States.* It suffices to support the judgment, that the Government *was* required to state not only that Resendiz-Ponce "knowingly and intentionally attempted to enter the United States of America," but also that he "took a substantial step" toward that end.

My dissenting view that the indictment was faulty (a point on which we requested supplemental briefing) puts me in the odd position of being the sole Justice who must decide the question on which we granted certiorari: whether a constitutionally deficient indictment is structural error, as the Ninth Circuit held, or rather is amenable to harmless-error analysis. I cannot vote to affirm or to reverse the judgment without resolving that issue. Since the full Court will undoubtedly have to speak to the point on another day (it dodged the bullet today by inviting and deciding *a different* constitutional issue-albeit, to be fair, a narrower one) there is little use in my setting forth my views in detail. It should come as no surprise, given my opinions in *United States v. Gonzalez-Lopez,* [pp. 115–116], and *Neder v. United States,* [pp. 1422–1423] that I would find the error to be structural. I would therefore affirm the judgment of the Ninth Circuit.

NOTES AND QUESTIONS

1. ***Explicit vs. implicit allegations.*** Justice Scalia's dissent quotes from the 1882 *Carll* opinion that refers to each element being expressly pleaded without "any uncertainty or

ambiguity." More recent federal cases arguably have allowed greater leeway. They have noted, for example, that it is sufficient if the words or facts contained in the indictment "necessarily or fairly import" an allegation of the element. A series of First Circuit rulings provides a representative sample of pleadings held to have satisfied and to have failed a "fair import" standard. See *Hughes v. United States,* 338 F.2d 651 (1st Cir. 1964) (indictment charging defendants with "unlawfully" removing merchandise while it was in customs' custody failed to allege requisite mens rea element; use of word "unlawfully" does not necessarily suggest defendants acted "knowingly"); *Portnoy v. United States,* 316 F.2d 486 (1st Cir.1963) (indictment charging assault against a federal official, when it alleged that the assault was committed by defendant "on account of [the victim's] official duties," necessarily implied that defendant had the requisite knowledge that his victim was an official); *United States v. McLennan,* 672 F.2d 239 (1st Cir. 1982) (that principal acted "willfully" in jumping bail was implicit in other allegations of the indictment, which stated that principal failed to appear "after having been ordered to do so," that his failure constituted a violation of 18 U.S.C. § 3150, that the district court entered a "default," and that defendant as an accomplice acted "in order to hinder and prevent [the principal's] apprehension"; the indictment fell "somewhere between" *Hughes* and *Portnoy,* but was closer to "Portnoy").

Does *Resendiz-Ponce* establish as a prerequisite for finding that an element is pleaded by implication that the language used is understood to encompass that element in "common parlance" or in a well-established legal tradition? Lower courts have drawn distinctions in this regard between use of the term "steal" (sufficient to allege the intent to permanently deprive required for larceny) and "convert" (insufficient to allege such intent because conversion traditionally has been a tort concept limited to exercising control without permission). See CRIMPROC § 19.3(a).

2. ***Limiting* Russell.** In a leading post-*Resendiz-Ponce* ruling, *United States v. Stringer,* 730 F.3d 120 (2d Cir. 2013), the Second Circuit held that an indictment charging aggravated identity theft was not defective for failing to name the persons whose identification documents were used to open bank accounts funded with forged checks and to subsequently withdraw the proceeds. It was sufficient that the indictment tracked the statutory language, specified the means used, and identified the banks involved. Defendant's reliance on *Russell,* the opinion noted, was completely misplaced:

"*Russell* [is] a 50 year-old precedent, which is one of the rare cases in which an indictment that tracked the statutory language and furnished the pertinent dates was held insufficient. [The opinion here described the *Russell* ruling, noting, inter alia, that "the case arose out of the controversial McCarthy-era hearings of the Committee on Un-American Activities, see fn. d, p. 991. * * * [I]t is clear that the Supreme Court's decision in *Russell* must be seen as addressed to the special nature of a refusal to answer questions in a congressional inquiry, and not as a broad requirement, applicable to all criminal charges, that the indictment specify how each essential element is met. This view of *Russell* was confirmed by the Supreme Court's more recent decision in *United States v. Resendiz-Ponce*. [The opinion here quotes the *Resendez-Ponce* discussion of *Russell*] * * * The message of the Supreme Court's discussion in *Russell* and *Resendez-Ponce* is that for certain statutes specification of how a particular element of a criminal charge will be met (as opposed to categorical recitation of the element) is of such importance to the fairness of the proceeding that it must be spelled out in the indictment, but there is no such universal requirement. * * * Other examples that courts have found to fall in that less-common category have been specification of what statements are alleged to be false, and in what respect they are false, in charges of criminal falsity, * * *, and the type of controlled substance * * * when charging under the controlled substances statute. We do not believe the name of the victim in a charge under § 1028A falls in that narrow category. It is, of course, an essential-element of the charge, unquestionably important, and the defendant is of course entitled on demand to its disclosure in a bill of particulars or otherwise."

3. ***Federal practice.*** Federal indictments for many offenses are not nearly as spare as the *Resendez-Ponce* indictment for the 8 U.S.C. § 1326(a) offense. See e.g., U.S. Department of Justice, Criminal Division Guides for Drafting Indictments (1990) (containing draft indictments for numerous offenses). Indeed, indictments in white collar cases are often filled with details (set forth in dozens of pages) as to the "when, where, what, who, and how" of fraudulent schemes. A variety of factors—including the character of the government's proof (documents vs. witness memory) and the likely response of defense counsel—may influence the decision to include more or less detail as to particular offenses. Commentators have noted that in high profile cases, likely to receive media coverage, a detailed indictment may circumvent restrictions on extrajudicial statements by the prosecution. See Ch. 23, § 2, Pt. A. So too, where the judge will provide the jury with a copy of the indictment, a detailed pleading may serve as a useful roadmap for the jury in following a complicated set of events.

4. ***Prosecutorial and defense interests.*** The primary prosecution interest in limiting specificity is the avoidance of variance problems if the prosecution should go to trial. See Note 7, p. 1015. In some instances, the defense may hope for a significant procedural advantage—e.g., in forcing the prosecution to more precisely shape its case, in creating a potential for a variance in proof at trial, or in gaining a favorable interpretation of the statute—as a result of a successful challenge to the pleading. Very often, however, the result of success (a second filing of the charging instrument) is unlikely to produce any of those advantages; the primary benefit consists of imposing upon the prosecution the delay and other administrative burdens associated with obtaining a second charging instrument and possibly obtaining a benefit in plea negotiation for waiving the objection and relieving the prosecution of those burdens. Because of the distinct limitations of that "advantage," *Dix*, fn. d p. 991, suggests that the most beneficial strategy for the defense often is to raise the objection pretrial so as to ensure that it is preserved, but then hope that it will be erroneously rejected by the trial court so that it will then be available as a reversible error (see Note 1, p. 1003) should the defendant subsequently be convicted at trial.

Conviction Reversals and Timely Raised Pleading Objections

1. ***The traditional rule.*** The traditional rule holds that an essential-elements defect in a pleading requires automatic reversal of a trial conviction where that defect was timely challenged. This rule was well established prior to the adoption of harmless error standards in the mid 1800's (see Note 1, p. 1415), although the primary vehicle for overturning the conviction at that time was the motion in arrest of judgment rather than an appellate reversal. The harmless error statutes were viewed as leaving the traditional rule intact because the harmless error doctrine did not apply to jurisdictional defects. The law of pleading at the time was tied to the role of the grand jury and the failure of the indictment to refer to all the elements of a crime meant that the grand jury had not truly charged the defendant with a crime. Improper amendments to the indictment were also viewed as jurisdictional (see Note 4, p. 1010), and that led to a similar characterization of certain specificity failures, the key being a deficiency so great that it would allow the prosecutor a basic grounding for liability entirely different from the grounding that might have led the grand jury to indict. Thus, both essential-elements defects and many specificity defects, when erroneously rejected by the trial court, required an automatic conviction reversal without considering how the defect impacted the trial that produced the conviction.

Although the traditional rule came out of the law governing indictments, it was carried over to informations without reconsideration of its grounding. As a result, it was followed in the federal system and in both indictment and information states throughout most of the twentieth century. The initial departure, as discussed below, related to specificity defects, and that was followed by a departure in far fewer jurisdictions as to essential-elements defects. Whether more jurisdictions will move in that direction remains to be seen, with the Supreme Court's eventual ruling on the harmless error issue, reserved in *Resendiz-Ponce*, likely to be influential.

2. *State departures.* The initial state movement away from the traditional rule came in the analysis of alleged specificity defects. Focusing on the notice function of specificity requirements, courts in numerous states now look to whether the pleading's lack of specificity had resulted in trial prejudice (with the possible exception of the alternative-legal-element defect, see Note 2, p. 9901417). Consideration is given to the notice provided through other sources, including that which could have been obtained by a bill of particulars. CRIMPROC § 19.3(b). With only a few exceptions, this approach has not been extended in these states to an essential-elements defect. State appellate courts continue to automatically reverse trial convictions where the trial court erroneously denied a timely objection to the pleading's failure to state an offense. CRIMPROC § 19.3(a).

3. *Federal departures.* In *United States v. Prentiss*, 256 F.3d 971 (10th Cir.2001) (en banc), a divided Tenth Circuit concluded that, in light of recent Supreme Court rulings on the scope of the harmless error doctrine, an indictment's failure to allege an essential element of the charged offense should no longer be exempt from harmless error analysis. That position was subsequently adopted by several other circuits, but the Ninth Circuit disagreed, and continued to adhere to the traditional rule. This produced the conflict which led to the grant of certiorari in *Resendiz-Ponce*. The opinions arguing for and against application of the harmless error rule have differed in their view of the lessons to be drawn from the following Supreme Court precedents:

(a) *Russell and Stirone*. The Supreme Court applied the traditional rule in both *Russell* (p. 991) and *Stirone v. United States*, Note 5, p. 1011. Neither case discussed harmless error, but both were decided before *Chapman v. California* (p. 1417) introduced harmless error analysis to the appellate review of constitutional errors. See also Note 6, p. 1012.

(b) *Neder*. A divided Supreme Court, in *Neder v. United States* (p. 1420), applied harmless error analysis to the failure to submit an essential-element to the trial jury. *Prentiss* viewed that situation as analogous to the defect underlying an indictment's failure to allege an essential element—the possibility that the grand jury had not considered that essential element in its decision to indict. That analogy is challenged, however, as failing to recognize other functions of the essential-elements requirement, and as failing to take account of the "structural" role of the pleading as a prerequisite for further proceedings. However, *Neder*, in its extensive listing of structural errors (which are exempt from harmless error analysis), did not include an indictment's failure to allege an offense.

(c) *Cotton*. As discussed in Note 3, p. 1007, *United States v. Cotton* concluded that an indictment's failure to charge an offense is not a jurisdictional defect. *Cotton* held that an indictment's failure to allege an *Apprendi*-type element (see p. 988), where not timely raised before the trial court, would be recognized on appeal only if it met the stringent requirements of the "plain error" standard of Rule 52(b). Application of Rule 52(a)'s harmless error standard does not necessarily follow from the application of Rule 52(b)'s plain error standard to the same objection where not timely raised. Nonetheless, courts viewing the harmless error standard as applicable to essential-elements defects find support for that position in the general thrust of *Cotton*, including its conclusion that the defect there did not seriously affect the "integrity" of the judicial proceeding. On the other side, however, it is noted that *Cotton* specifically found no need to decide whether the defect before it was a "structural error" (see p. 1008). Also, *Cotton*, in distinguishing the citation to *Bain* [Note 4, p. 1010] in both *Stirone* and *Russell*, noted that these were cases in which (in contrast to the case before it) "proper objection had been made in the District Court to the sufficiency of the indictment."

(d) *Grand jury cases. Prentiss* noted that the Supreme Court in *Mechanik* (Note 5, p. 980) and *Bank of Nova Scotia* (Note 2, p. 977) had applied harmless error analysis to "errors, defects, irregularities or variances occurring before a grand jury." The only exception was discrimination in the selection of the grand jury, as reflected in *Vasquez v. Hillery* [Note 7, p. 955]. Responding to the *Prentiss* argument, the briefs filed in *Resendiz-Ponce* in favor of the traditional rule argued that *Vasquez* provided the closer analogy. They argued that the premise underlying the traditional rule is that a reviewing court should not attempt to estimate how a grand jury would exercise the "broad [charging] discretion" recognized in *Vasquez*. See Brief of National Association of Federal Public Defenders, 2006 WL 2506638.

4. ***Applying harmless error.*** What should be required to establish that a pleading error was harmless? Consider *United States v. Lee*, 833 F.3d 56 (2d Cir. 2016), where the indictment failed to allege that the value of the stolen property (described as "U.S. Postal pellets") exceeded $1,000. The court there noted that its primary concerns were "fair notice and double jeopardy protection." In assessing notice, the court looked initially to whether the indictment gave notice of the "nature of the offense and the core of the criminal conduct to be proven at trial." It then looked to notice of the missing valuation element, which was provided in the more detailed description of the offense in the criminal complaint and the government's requested jury charge, advanced two weeks before trial. Also significant was the trial judge's comment, in response to the missing-element objection first being raised after the government rested its case, that the defense had long been on notice " 'not by virtue of the indictment, but by virtue of the way the case was prosecuted, discovery, the complaint, * * * whatever [plea] discussions have been made, plus the evidence at the trial.' " As for double jeopardy protection, the court pointed to the trial evidence establishing the missing element. The court also considered whether that evidence might be considered an impermissible constructive amendment, but found that limitation inapplicable because the core conduct considered by the grand jury was not altered and there was "no semblance of any uncertainty" as to whether the grand jury would have included the missing element in its charge.

Appellate Review of Untimely Objections

1. ***The traditional position.*** As noted previously (pp. 985–986), a critical element of the second round of pleading reforms was to provide for the "waiver" or "forfeiture" of pleading objections that were not raised before trial. That reform was not carried over, however, to two pleading objections—the "failure to show jurisdiction in the court" and the "failure to charge an offense". These two objections were "to be noticed * * * at any time during the pendency of the proceedings". Fed.R.Crim.P. 12(b) (original version). The "failure to charge an offense" exception creates a distinction in the treatment of the essential-elements and inadequate-specificity defects. The former is at the core of the failure to charge an offense (see Note 1, p. 987), while the later is subject to the usual standards for untimely objections (except possibly for the alternative-legal-element inadequacy, categorized as an essential-elements defect in some jurisdictions, see Note 2, p. 989).

In applying the exception for essential-elements defects, the appellate courts repeatedly stress that an untimely challenge faces a special obstacle. Here, the court will go beyond a "fair import" standard (see Note 1, p. 1001) in determining whether the pleading did include a particular element. A charging instrument not previously challenged will be construed, they note, "liberally in favor of sufficiency," absent a specific showing of prejudice (which is deemed unlikely, as the failure to object suggests that the defense was not concerned about notice). Indeed, the pleading will be held sufficient unless "so defective that it does not by any reasonable construction" charge the necessary elements. See CRIMPROC § 19.3(e). However, the caselaw reflects "considerable variation * * * from one appellate court to another in their willingness to stretch the language of the pleading to find that an allegedly missing element was sufficiently set forth by implication. One will find satisfactory, against a late objection, a pleading that simply alleged 'the commission of a battery,' without referring to any of the elements of the crime. Another will hold invalid a murder indictment that alleged that the defendant 'unlawfully, willfully, deliberately and with premeditation' killed a particular person, reasoning that such language could not reasonably be construed as alleging the necessary element of 'malice aforethought.' " Ibid.

If the appellate court concludes that the pleading fails, even with liberal construction, then the remedy applied is the same remedy that would apply to an objection timely raised before trial and erroneously denied by the trial court—automatic reversal in all but the few jurisdictions that apply harmless-error analysis to an essential-elements defects. This stands in contrast to the treatment of pleading objections other than the failure-to-charge when not timely made. In most jurisdictions, as under Rule 12(b), an untimely objection here may not be considered by the trial court unless that court excuses the delay in objecting with a finding of "good cause." Where the untimely trial court objection is raised after conviction (e.g., in a new trial motion), good cause "requires a showing both a reason for [objecting] late and trial prejudice due to the error that is the subject of the [late] objection" CRIMPROC § 19.3(e); Where the pleading objection (other than the failure-to-charge objection) is first raised on appeal, some jurisdictions will allow appellate court consideration of the objection if it meets the rigorous standards of plain error review. Since pleading errors are apparent on the face of the charging instrument, they can readily meet the "plain" prerequisite but the other prerequisites present a far greater obstacle. See Note 3(c), (d), pp. 1413–1414. Other jurisdictions will not consider the plain-error possibility because the failure to timely raise the objection is viewed as a binding waiver (rather than merely an objection forfeiture), see Note 3(a), p. 1411.

2. ***Jurisdictional grounding.*** The two exceptions recognized in the original Rule 12(b) were grounded in the principal that jurisdictional defects can never be waived and therefore always are available for review. Placing the failure-to-charge in this category initially was based on treating a pleading that did not charge all the elements of the crime as, in effect, no pleading at all. Its jurisdictional characterization was explained as reflecting the common law position that waiver of prosecution by indictment was not allowed. See Note 1, p. 947. However, that position had long been discarded when Rule 12(b) and similar state provisions were enacted, and the failure-to-charge exception historically has been applicable to charging by information as well as indictment. This led to another explanation. The common law viewed the accusatory instrument (whether indictment, information or complaint) as providing "a formal basis for the judgment"; without an accusatory instrument before it, the trial court had no subject matter to resolve and that was equally true, courts reasoned, when the instrument was a nullity because it failed to charge an offense.

Treating the defective pleading as a nullity meant, for many courts, that there was no charge to which the defendant could enter a guilty plea. This led to allowing a defendant to utilize a failure-to-charge claim to challenge a guilty plea, including a challenge on collateral attack (although the Rule 12(b) exception stated only that the objection "shall be noticed * * * at any time during the pendency of the proceedings," which presumably ended with direct appeal). As many as a dozen states still allow such challenges to a guilty plea. See CRIMPROC § 19.3(a). The much larger group rejecting such challenges do so on various grounds. Many states have rejected their prior reasoning and concluded that a charging instrument defective in failing to allege all essential-elements does not present a jurisdictional defect. See CRIMPROC § 19.2(e) These rulings have been based on analysis of jurisdiction similar to that advanced by the Supreme Court in *Cotton v. United States,* discussed in Note 3 infra. However, unlike *Cotton,* most have not extended their rejection of the jurisdictional characterization beyond guilty pleas. They do not similarly reject the special treatment of untimely raised failure-to-charge objections in challenging trial convictions. See Note 6, p. 1009.

3. ***The* Cotton *departure from the traditional position.*** In UNITED STATES v. COTTON, 535 U.S. 625 (2002), the defendant on appeal raised for the first time the failure of the indictment to allege that the quantity of cocaine he conspired to distribute exceeded 50 grams. Since the defendant's sentence had been increased under a statutory enhancement based on drug quantity, this *Apprendi*-type element should have been included in the indictment. The government acknowledged its error, but argued that, since defendant's objection had not been timely presented, relief should be available only if the defendant could meet the stringent prerequisites for recognition of error under Rule 52(b)'s plain error provision (see Note 3, p. 1411).[a] Relying basically on language in the Supreme Court's ruling in *Ex parte Bain* [Note 4, p. 1010], the Fourth Circuit held that an indictment's failure to include an essential element of an offense was a "jurisdictional" defect, and therefore the enhanced sentence had to be vacated even though not timely challenged below. Rejecting that reasoning, a unanimous Supreme Court (per Rehnquist C.J.) held that the indictment defect was not jurisdictional and should be cognizable only if it met the rigorous standards of the plain error doctrine (which was not the case, here). The Court reasoned:

"We first address the Court of Appeals' conclusion that the omission from the indictment was a 'jurisdictional defect and thus required vacating respondents' sentences. *Ex parte Bain* is the progenitor of this view. * * * Bain challenged the amendment to [his] indictment in a petition for a writ of habeas corpus. The Court concluded that the amendment was improper and that therefore 'the jurisdiction of the offence [was] gone, and the court [had] no right to proceed any further in the progress of the case for want of an indictment.' * * * *Bain,* however, is a product of an era in which this Court's authority to review criminal convictions was greatly circumscribed. * * * In 1887, [t]his Court could examine constitutional errors in a criminal trial only on a writ of habeas corpus, and only then if it deemed the error 'jurisdictional.' The Court's desire to correct obvious constitutional violations led to a 'somewhat expansive notion of jurisdiction,' which was 'more a fiction than anything else,' *Wainwright v. Sykes* [p. 1434].

"*Bain*'s elastic concept of jurisdiction is not what the term 'jurisdiction' means today, *i.e.,* 'the courts' statutory or constitutional *power* to adjudicate the case.' *Steel Co. v. Citizens for a Better Environment,* 523 U.S. 83 (1998). This latter concept of subject-matter jurisdiction, because it involves a court's power to hear a case, can never be forfeited or waived. * * * In contrast, the grand jury right can be waived. See Fed. Rule Crim. Proc. 7(b). * * *

"Post-*Bain* cases confirm that defects in an indictment do not deprive a court of its power to adjudicate a case. In *Lamar v. United States,* 240 U.S. 60 (1916), the Court rejected the claim that 'the court had no jurisdiction because the indictment does not charge a crime against the United States.' Justice Holmes explained that a district court 'has jurisdiction of all crimes cognizable under the authority of the United States . . . [and][t]he objection that the indictment does not charge a crime against the United States goes only to the merits of the case.' Similarly, *United States v. Williams,* 341 U.S. 58 (1951), held that a ruling 'that the indictment is defective does not affect the jurisdiction of the trial court to determine the case presented by the indictment.'

"Freed from the view that indictment omissions deprive a court of jurisdiction, we proceed to apply the plain-error test of Federal Rule of Criminal Procedure 52(b) to respondents' forfeited claim. See *United States v. Olano* [Note 3, p. 1411]. Under that test, before an appellate court can correct an error not raised at trial, there must be (1) 'error,' (2) that is 'plain,' and (3) that 'affect[s] substantial rights.' *Johnson v. United States* [Note 3, p. 1411]. 'If all three conditions are met, an

[a] The government argued that the Rule 12(b) provision on noticing untimely failure-to-charge objections did not require that the objection be reviewed as if timely made, but merely established that the objection was not "waived"—i.e., Rule 12(b)'s exception provision merely made certain that the Rule 52(b) provision on plain error could be applied. "The government's argument as to the interface of Rule 52 and Rule 12(b) was inconsistent with a long line of lower court cases," CRIMPROC § 19.3(c), but the Fourth Circuit did not address the argument and neither did the Supreme Court.

appellate court may then exercise its discretion to notice a forfeited error, but only if (4) the error seriously affect[s] the fairness, integrity, or public reputation of judicial proceedings.' *Johnson.*

"The Government concedes that * * * [there was error and] that such error was plain. * * * The third inquiry is whether the plain error 'affect[ed] substantial rights.' This usually means that the error 'must have affected the outcome of the district court proceedings.' *Olano.* Respondents argue that an indictment error falls within the 'limited class' of 'structural errors,' that 'can be corrected regardless of their effect on the outcome,' *Olano.* * * * As in *Johnson*, we need not resolve whether respondents satisfy this element of the plain-error inquiry, because even assuming respondents' substantial rights were affected, the error did not seriously affect the fairness, integrity, or public reputation of judicial proceedings. * * * The evidence that the conspiracy involved at least 50 grams of cocaine base was 'overwhelming' and 'essentially uncontroverted.' * * * Surely the grand jury, having found that the conspiracy existed, would have also found that the conspiracy involved at least 50 grams of cocaine base."

4. ***The Rule 12 Amendment.*** Defendants sought to limit *Cotton* to *Apprendi* elements, but the Federal circuits uniformly held that it applied to the failure to allege any type of essential element. Following this development, in 2006, the Department of Justice urged the Judicial Conference to consider deleting the reference to "fails * * * to state an offense" in the noticed-at-any-time proviso in Rule 12(b). That objection, it noted, had been placed alongside the "fails to invoke the court's jurisdiction" objection, but *Cotton* had clearly established that the "failure to state an offense" was not a jurisdictional defect. After extensive discussion in the Criminal Rules Advisory Committee and the Judicial Conference Committee on Rules (including consideration of three different amendment proposals and public comments from various sources), the Judicial Conference adopted a proposal that was later approved by the Supreme Court. That revision took effect on December 1, 2014. Under the new Rule 12(b)(3)(B) provision, objections that must be made before trial continue to include "a defect in the indictment or information," and the list of encompassed defects includes "failure to state an offense." In accord with this change, the Rule 12(b)(2) provision on objections that may be made "at any time while the case is pending" now refers only to the "motion that the court lacks jurisdiction."

5. **A Cotton *exception?*** *United States v. Brown*, 752 F.3d 1344 (11th Cir. 2014), reviewed the Eleventh Circuit caselaw governing a challenge to a guilty plea (on an appeal or on collateral attack) based on the indictment's failure-to-charge an offense. In light of *Cotton,* such a challenge could not be based on an "indictment's omission of an element of the crime" since that failure "does not create a jurisdictional defect." However, "an indictment does fail to invoke [the court's] subject matter jurisdiction" where the "indictment affirmatively alleges conduct that does not constitute a crime at all because that conduct falls outside the scope of the charging statute," or otherwise charges "a crime that simply does not exist" (e.g., "a violation of a regulation that was not intended to be 'law' for the purposes of a criminal liability").

Other circuits have refused to distinguish the "failure to state an offense" that is based on "the indictment's factual allegations alleg[ing] a so-called 'non-offense'." *United States v. Rubin*, 744 F.3d 31 (2d Cir. 2014). In the most extensive response to the Eleventh Circuit position, *Rubin*, supra, concluded that distinguishing such a "failure to state an offense" was inconsistent with *Cotton*. The *Cotton* opinion "did not speak merely of omissions [of essential elements]; rather it invoked the broader concepts of 'indictment defects'." Moreover, *Cotton* relied on *Lamar* and *Williams* (p. 1007 supra) and the opinions there implicitly rejected such a distinction. *Lamar* rejected a jurisdictional defect argument as to a claim that the charged impersonation of a U. S. Representative did not violate the impersonation statute because the statutory reference to "officer of the United States" did not include a Congressman, and the *Williams* Court stressed that jurisdiction existed even though an appellate court might subsequently conclude "that the statute is unconstitutional or that the facts stated in the indictment do not constitute a crime." *Rubin*, like *Brown* addressed challenges to a guilty plea based on a pleading error. Neither *Rubin* nor *Brown* considered the defendant's potential alternative path of claiming a plea receiving error due to the "non-offense." See *Bousley v. United States*, 523 U.S. 614 (1993) (where Supreme Court subsequently held that firearm offense required "active employment of the firearm," in a ruling given retroactive application, earlier plea would be invalid if defendant could establish that he was misinformed when he pled guilty, as counsel and the court were not aware of this element, such notice being needed for an intelligent plea).

6. ***State departures.*** So far, only a handful of states have departed from the traditional position on considering untimely failure-to-charge objections to trial convictions. See CRIMPROC § 19.3(e) All of these states hold that the availability of a remedy for the defect, when the challenge is untimely, is subject to a more rigorous standard than applied to timely challenges. However, their varying approaches include treating the untimely objection as waived, applying plain error review, and requiring the defense to make a showing that the pleading defect resulted in trial prejudice. All of these jurisdictions apply this more rigorous standard to essential-elements defects, but at least one follows an approach similar to the Eleventh Circuit in distinguishing a non-offense factual pleading.

§ 3. AMENDMENTS AND VARIANCES

A. THE PERMISSIBLE SCOPE OF AMENDMENTS

1. ***The prejudice/different-offense standard.*** The dominant standard governing the amendment of felony pleadings is that set forth in Federal Rule 7(e):

> Unless an additional or different offense is charged or a substantial right of the defendant is prejudiced, the court may permit an information to be amended at any time before the verdict or finding.

Although Federal Rule 7(e) is limited to amendments of the information, most states apply a Rule 7(e)-type standard to both informations and indictments. That standard has two prongs, barring amendments that either result in prejudice to the accused or charge a new offense.

The prejudice prong, though referring generally to prejudice to the "substantial rights of accused," focuses almost exclusively upon the element of surprise. To oppose an amendment on this ground, the defense ordinarily must make some showing that the amendment will catch it by surprise and thereby interfere with its ability to defend against the charges. Since such prejudice may be avoided before trial by granting an appropriate continuance, an amendment made before trial is unlikely to be held to have injured the substantial rights of the defendant where a continuance was granted or none was requested. Amendments made during trial will cause more difficulty, but are often held not to be prejudicial where they do not change the factual basis of the offense as set forth in the original pleading, the bill of particulars, or pretrial discovery obtained by the defense. See *State v. Price*, 940 S.W.2d 534 (Mo.App.1997) (test for prejudice is whether defendant's evidence would be equally applicable and his defense equally available under the amended information).

The second prong of the Rule 7(e) standard—prohibiting amendments that charge additional or different offenses—stands apart from any showing of surprise, and will bar an amendment notwithstanding an obvious lack of surprise. As noted in CRIMPROC § 19.5(b), "the precise content of the 'different offense' standard has been the source of disagreement at its edges." A different offense clearly is presented where the indictment alleges an offense under a different statutory provision and that offense requires proof of different elements under the traditional jeopardy standard (i.e., the *Blockburger* standard, see p. 652). Consistent with double jeopardy analysis, a charge under the same statute also is viewed as producing a new offense if the "factual identity" of the original charge is changed by relying on an entirely different series of events as the basis for the violation. Division arises when the statute remains the same, the basic incident remains the same, but the statute lists alternative means of commission, harms, or circumstances, and the shift is from one alternative to another. Many courts "view such [an amendment] * * * as merely shifting the facts [or the interpretation of the facts] that will be relied upon to establish the same basic element of the crime [which happens to be broken down by the statute into alternatives rather than stated in general terms that would encompass those alternatives]. * * * Carrying this single-element analysis to its logical extreme, one court allowed a shift in a first degree murder charge from premeditated killing to a killing in the course of a felony since all that was altered was the means of establishing the mens rea element for a single statutory offense." Id. Other courts would not accept such an amendment, as they define the elements of the offense far more narrowly. The most confining position in this regard treats each statutory alternative as establishing a separate element (and therefore a separate offense) if it requires proof that the other alternative does not.

2. ***The "form/substance" distinction***. Not all jurisdictions follow an amendment policy as liberal as that provided in Federal Rule 7(e). A substantial group of states adhere to the formulation that amendments are permitted as to "form," but not as to "substance." Although some states apply this distinction to allow roughly the same type of amendments that would be permitted under Rule 7(e), others construe it to allow only a much narrower range of amendments. In these jurisdictions, an amendment that falls short of changing the basic character of the offense charged can nevertheless readily be characterized as one of substance. Amendments are said to fall in that category if they alter or supply "essential facts that must be proved to make the act complained of a crime." *Brown v. State,* 400 A.2d 1133 (Md.1979). Thus, apart from any question of surprise, jurisdictions following a form/substance distinction are likely to bar an amendment that substantially alters the factual description of the criminal act, statutorily required circumstances, or the consequences of that act. See e.g., *Brown v. State,* supra (prohibiting amendment that changed the original allegation that defendant defrauded an automobile dealer of a dollar amount to an allegation that he defrauded the dealer of an automobile worth that amount); *State v. Abraham*, 451 S.E.2d 131 (N.C. 1994) (indictment amendment could not change the name of the victim of an assault, although it referred to the same person, who originally gave police an alias).

3. ***Amendments to indictments.*** The federal courts and several states draw a sharp distinction between amendments of indictments and informations, allowing considerably less latitude for the indictment amendments. Indeed, some of these jurisdictions are commonly said to follow "the historic rule that an indictment may not be amended." None actually go so far as to adhere to the early common law prohibition that barred even amendments to cure misnomers, but they do follow what is sometimes described as the "rule of *Ex parte Bain.*" *Bain* and the Supreme Court cases discussing *Bain* are set forth below.

4. EX PARTE BAIN, 121 U.S. 1 (1887), involved a habeas corpus challenge to a conviction based on an amended indictment. The original indictment charged the defendant with having made a false statement in a bank report "with intent to deceive the Comptroller of the Currency and the agent appointed to examine the affairs of said [bank]." The trial court initially sustained a demurrer to the indictment. That court apparently read the cited statute as making it an offense only to deceive the agent appointed to examine the bank records. Under common law pleading standards the indictment therefore was fatally defective since it alleged as an offense an alternative action (deceiving the Comptroller) that was not a crime. To cure this defect, the trial court allowed the government to amend the indictment by striking the reference to the Comptroller. In a unanimous opinion, the Supreme Court concluded that the amendment was impermissible, depriving the trial court of the power to proceed, and therefore requiring habeas relief. Speaking for the Court, Justice Miller, noted:

"The learned judge who presided in the Circuit Court at the time the change was made in this indictment, says that the court allowed the words 'Comptroller of the Currency and' to be stricken out as surplusage,[a] * * *. He goes on to argue that the grand jury would have found the indictment without this language. But it is not for the court to say whether they would or not. The party can only be tried upon the indictment as found by such grand jury, and especially upon all its language found in the charging part of that instrument. While it may seem to the court, with its better instructed mind in regard to what the statute requires to be found as to the intent to deceive, that it was neither necessary nor reasonable that the grand jury should attach importance to the fact that it was the Comptroller who was to be deceived, yet it is not impossible nor very improbable that the grand jury looked mainly to that officer as the party whom the prisoner intended to deceive by a report which was made upon his requisition and returned directly to him. * * * How can the court say that there may not have been more than one of the jurors who found this indictment, who was satisfied that the false report was made to deceive the Comptroller, but was not convinced that it was made to deceive anybody else? And how can it be said that, with these words stricken out, it is the indictment which was found by the grand jury? If it lies within the province of a court to change the charging part of an indictment to suit its own notions of what it ought to have been, or what the grand jury would probably have made it if their attention had been called to suggested changes, the great importance which the common law attaches to an indictment by a grand jury, as a prerequisite to a prisoner's trial for a crime, and without which the Constitution says 'no person shall be held to answer,' may be frittered away until its value is almost destroyed."

5. In STIRONE v. UNITED STATES, 361 U.S. 212 (1960), the Court relied on *Bain* in concluding that the government could not accomplish through a variance between proof and charge what it could not achieve through an amendment. The indictment there, brought under the Hobbs Act, charged defendant with extortion affecting interstate commerce through wrongful use of a threatened labor dispute. The dispute was directed against Rider, a Pennsylvania supplier of ready-mixed concrete used in the construction of a Pennsylvania steel processing plant. The indictment alleged that Stirone's activities had obstructed the interstate flow of sand shipments into Rider's concrete plant. At trial, over defense objection, the judge admitted evidence concerning (and instructed the jury that their verdict could rest upon) Stirone's interference with interstate commerce by preventing shipments that the steel plant would have made had it been built on time. A unanimous court, per Black, J., found this variance "fatal":

"We agree with the Court of Appeals that Rider's dependence on shipments of sand from outside Pennsylvania to carry on his ready-mixed concrete business entitled him to the Hobbs Act's protection. * * * Whether prospective steel shipments from the new steel mills would be enough, alone, to bring this transaction under the Act is a more difficult question. We need not decide this, however, since we agree with the dissenting judges in the Court of Appeals that it was error to submit that question to the jury and that the error cannot be dismissed as merely an insignificant variance between allegation and proof and thus harmless error as in *Berger v. United States* [Note 2, p. 1014]. The crime charged here is a felony and the Fifth Amendment requires that prosecution be begun by indictment.

"Ever since *Ex parte Bain* was decided in 1887, it has been the rule that after an indictment has been returned its charges may not be broadened through amendment except by the grand jury itself. * * * The *Bain* case, which has never been disapproved, stands for the rule that a court cannot permit a defendant to be tried on charges that are not made in the indictment against him. Yet the court did permit that in this case. * * * The grand jury which found this indictment was

[a] While Federal Rule 7(d) today provides for the striking of surplusage, it uses that term with a different point of reference. Rule 7(d) is aimed at inflammatory and prejudicial language that is irrelevant to the description of the events alleged in the indictment. Accordingly, it provides only for the striking of surplusage on motion of the defendant (who is viewed as thereby waiving his right not to have the indictment amended).

satisfied to charge that Stirone's conduct interfered with interstate importation of sand. But neither this nor any other court can know that the grand jury would have been willing to charge that Stirone's conduct would interfere with interstate exportation of steel from a mill later to be built with Rider's concrete. * * * Although the trial court did not permit a formal amendment of the indictment, the effect of what it did was the same. And the addition charging interference with steel exports here is neither trivial, useless, nor innocuous."

6. In *United States v. Prentiss*, discussed in Note 3, p. 1004, the dissenters argued that application of a harmless error analysis to the failure of an indictment to allege the essential elements of the offense was inconsistent with the automatic reversal in *Stirone*. The *Prentiss* majority, however, saw *Stirone* as involving a flaw quite different from an essential-elements defect. Where an indictment simply failed to expressly include all the elements of the offense charged, the crime the indictment presented nonetheless was basically that on which the jury later convicted, based on its guilt finding as to the elements alleged in the indictment and the additional, missing element. On the other hand, the jury in *Stirone* may have convicted for an offense that had been changed in character from that found by the grand jury, through the variance that amounted to a constructive indictment amendment. Is it significant that the Supreme Court's subsequent *Cotton* opinion, Note 3, p. 1007, did not draw this distinction? Instead, it distinguished both *Stirone* (a constructive amendment case) and *Russell* (a pleading deficiency case) on the same ground—that in each case the objection had been timely presented before the trial court. See Note 3(c), p. 1004.

7. In UNITED STATES v. MILLER, 471 U.S. 130 (1985), the indictment alleged that the defendant defrauded an insurance company by both arranging for a burglary at his place of business and by lying to the insurer as to the value of the loss. The evidence at trial, however, established only the lying. Although there was no element of surprise involved, the trial court denied the government's motion to amend the indictment by striking the allegation that defendant arranged the burglary. After the case was submitted to the jury on the full indictment, and the defendant was convicted, the defense challenged the conviction on the ground that the government's proof had fatally varied from the scheme alleged in the indictment by failing to cover both aspects of that scheme. In the course of rejecting that contention, a unanimous Supreme Court (per Marshall, J) noted that the government's proposed amendment would have been permissible under a proper reading of *Bain*. The opinion noted:

"*Bain* may best be understood in terms of two distinct propositions. Most generally, *Bain* stands for the proposition that a conviction cannot stand if based on offense that is different from that alleged in the grand jury's indictment. But more specifically, *Bain* can support the proposition that the striking out of parts of an indictment invalidates the whole of the indictment, for a court cannot speculate as to whether the grand jury had meant for any remaining offense to stand independently, even if that remaining offense clearly was included in the original text. Under this latter proposition, the narrowing of an indictment is no different from the adding of a new allegation that had never been considered by the grand jury; both are treated as 'amendments' that alter the nature of the offense charged. In evaluating the relevance of *Bain* to the instant case, it is necessary to examine these two aspects of *Bain* separately, for the Court has treated these two propositions quite differently in the years since *Bain*.

"The proposition that a defendant cannot be convicted of an offense that is different from that which was included in the indictment * * * has been reaffirmed in a number of subsequent cases. * * * But this aspect of *Bain* gives no support to Miller in this case, for the offense that formed the basis of Miller's conviction was clearly and fully set out in the indictment. Miller must instead rest on the second, and more specific, proposition found in *Bain*, that a narrowing of the indictment constitutes an amendment that renders the indictment void. * * *

"As is clear from [our previous] discussion of * * * the decisions in *Ford v. United States*, 273 U.S. 593 (1927) and *Salinger v. United States*, 272 U.S. 542 (1926), this second proposition did not long survive *Bain*. Indeed, when defendants have sought to rely on *Bain* for this point, this Court has limited or distinguished the case, sustaining convictions where courts had withdrawn or ignored independent and unnecessary allegations in the indictments. Modern criminal law has generally accepted that an indictment will support each offense contained within it. To the extent *Bain* stands for the proposition that it constitutes an unconstitutional amendment to drop from an indictment those allegations that are unnecessary to an offense that is clearly contained within it, that case has simply not survived. To avoid further confusion, we now explicitly reject that proposition. * * *

"[The] proper disposition of this case is clear. The variance complained of added nothing new to the grand jury's indictment and constituted no broadening. As in *Salinger* and *Ford*, what was removed from the case was in no way essential to the offense on which the jury convicted."

8. Consider the pleading strategy suggested by CRIMPROC § 19.5(d): "For the federal prosecutor who wishes to avoid repeated trips to the grand jury, the *Bain* rule, as modified by *Miller,* offers two obvious lessons. First, all possible factual theories of liability should be included in the initial indictment. If post-indictment investigation should reveal that a theory is not worthy of carrying forward at trial, it may always be deleted; on the other hand, if a factual theory originally is omitted on the ground that it is not as strong as other theories, and post-indictment investigation reveals its strength was underestimated, the addition of that theory will require a new indictment under the *Bain* rule. Second, there is an advantage in utilizing less specificity so that allegations can cover more factual variations that might arise as a result of post-indictment investigation. * * * Of course, the prosecution often walks a fine line in adopting this tact, as the lack of factual specificity * * * may provide a basis for a successful defense challenge to the sufficiency of the pleading."

As to the consequences of not following this strategy, consider CRIMPROC § 19.5(d): "Lower federal courts applying the *Bain* rule have rejected amendments that added a different drug to the list of drugs possessed by defendant with an intent to distribute, that altered the service provided for a 'kickback' from referring 'medical patients' to referring 'medical services,' and that shifted the deadly weapon under a charge of possession during a felony from a 'chair' to a 'chair and/or table.' "

B. THE SCOPE OF PERMISSIBLE VARIANCES

1. ***The procedural setting.*** A variance arises when the proof offered at trial departs from the allegations in the indictment or information. The defense may object to the introduction of that evidence, arguing that it is irrelevant to the offense pleaded, but most often the key objection comes after the presentation of evidence is complete and the case is ready to go to the jury. At this point, the defendant objecting to a variance typically states, in effect: "The prosecution may have offered evidence sufficient to establish a crime, but it is not the crime alleged in its accusatory pleading and I therefore am entitled to an acquittal." On occasion, the state has introduced evidence covering all the allegations in its pleading and the variance relates to evidence establishing an additional theory of liability. The defense objection then is to the instruction to the jury that would permit it to consider this additional theory of liability. Very often, the prosecution, recognizing the existence of a variance, will seek to amend the pleading to conform to the evidence. If this is permitted, the issue raised on appeal will be whether the amendment was properly allowed. Where there was no amendment (either because the trial judge disallowed the amendment or no request for amendment was made), the defendant's claim on appeal speaks directly to the variance, arguing that the submission of the case to the jury on the basis of the variance constituted reversible error.

2. ***The* Berger *standard.*** The source of the prevailing standard for judging the scope of permissible variance is the frequently cited statement of Justice Sutherland in *Berger v. United States,* 295 U.S. 78 (1935):

> The true inquiry, * * * is not whether there has been a variance in proof, but whether there has been such a variance as to "affect the substantial rights" of the accused.[b] The general rule that allegations and proof must correspond is based upon the obvious requirements (1) that the accused shall be definitely informed as to the charges against him, so that he may be enabled to present his defense and not be taken by surprise by the evidence offered at the trial; and (2) that he may be protected against another prosecution for the offense.

In light of this statement, most states hold that a "variance requires reversal of a conviction only when it deprives the defendant of a right to fair notice[c] or leaves him open to a risk of double jeopardy." CRIMPROC § 19.2(h).

3. In applying the notice element of the *Berger* standard, courts look to the record to determine whether it suggests "a possibility that the defendant may have been misled or embarrassed in the preparation or presentation of his defense." *Marshall v. State,* 381 So.2d 276 (Fla.App.1980). A failure to object to the variance at trial is generally viewed as a waiver of a claim of prejudice, and an eleventh-hour objection is taken as strong evidence belying any such claim. If the defendant was previously aware of the prosecution's proof as a result of pretrial discovery or a preliminary hearing, that factor also will weigh against a finding of prejudice. The court will also look to the relationship of the variance to the defense presented by the defendant. Consider *United States v. Wozniak,* 126 F.3d 105 (2d Cir.1997) (although indictment could simply have charged member of motorcycle club with offenses involving "controlled substances," the indictment specifically identified the substances as "cocaine and methamphetamine," while others were charged with marijuana offenses; accordingly, defendant was prejudiced by introduction of evidence of his marijuana transactions and a charge to the jury on those transactions; had "defendant been aware that the government would seek a conviction mostly on marijuana evidence, he might have chosen a different trial strategy," which did not put his credibility in issue by testifying in his own defense and stating that he did not use marijuana and had never seen a large bale of marijuana).

4. What additional restrictions should the double jeopardy prong of the *Berger* standard add to scope of permissible variances? Consider CRIMPROC § 19.6(b): "The possibility of actual prejudice at trial is put aside when courts test a variance against the risk of exposing the defendant to double jeopardy. The only element considered here is the extent to which the variance alters the scope of the charge. Indeed, a challenge based on this ground may be raised by a defendant who failed to object to the variance at trial. The concern of *Berger* apparently was that if defendant were tried on the proof presented in the variance and the jury concluded that such proof did not establish the offense charged, the record would be such that a reprosecution on the theory of the variance would not necessarily be barred. The original pleading would establish the

[b] The reference was to the federal harmless error statute which directed an appellate or trial court, on challenge to a conviction, to "give judgment * * * without regard to technical errors, defects, or exceptions which do not affect the substantial rights of the parties." See Note 1, p. 1415.

[c] The first prong of this standard is sometimes more broadly stated as whether the defendant suffered "actual prejudice at trial." Although notice is the primary concern in determining whether the defendant suffered such prejudice, *Berger* itself recognized that a variance could also cause prejudice where it resulted in the introduction of evidence that would not otherwise have been admissible against defendant. The defendant in *Berger* objected to the additional evidence that had been introduced at his trial because the government charged a single larger conspiracy rather than the two smaller conspiracies its proof sustained, but the Court found that the "incompetent" evidence thereby admitted was not prejudicial under the facts of that case. In *Kotteakos v. United States,* 328 U.S. 750 (1946), it found otherwise where thirteen parties were jointly tried, and as to all but one, the variance resulted in the jury having before it evidence of additional conspiracies which had no bearing on the individual defendant's liability.

scope of the jeopardy that attached at the first trial, and it would not bar a second trial on the theory of the variance if that theory established a different offense. Today, however, the pleading alone would not control the scope of the jeopardy that attached at the original proceeding, as the trial record would be available to show that the defendant had been placed in jeopardy on the theory of the variance. Since the defendant went to trial on the original pleading, a reprosecution on that charge alone would also be barred."

5. ***The constructive amendment limitation.*** Relying on *Stirone,* Note 5, p. 1011, some jurisdictions characterize as a separate limitation on permissible variances the standard applied in determining the permissible scope of an amendment to the charging instrument. Insofar as the jurisdiction's amendment standard looks to notice (see p. 1009, Note 1), it will largely duplicate the first prong of the *Berger* standard. Insofar as the amendment standard also prohibits the allegation of a "different offense" (see p. 1009, Note 1), it arguably should only duplicate the double jeopardy prong of *Berger.* But where the jurisdiction follows *Bain* in restricting permissible amendments to an indictment, even as *Bain* is limited by *Miller,* the end result will be a limitation upon variances somewhat more stringent than that imposed by *Berger's* double jeopardy prong. Consider, for example, the variance found to be fatal in *Stirone.* Would that variance have been acceptable under the double jeopardy prong of *Berger?*

6. In those jurisdictions that follow a "form/substance" distinction as to allowable amendments and view broadly what constitutes a change of substance (see Note 2, p. 1010), the constructive amendment limitation is likely to restrict permissible variances even further than would *Bain.* Thus, one such jurisdiction holds that the prosecution's proof must adhere to any allegation of the indictment "which is not impertinent or foreign to the cause * * * though a prosecution for the same offense might [have] been supported without such allegation." *State v. Brooks,* 462 S.W.2d 491 (Tenn.1970) (where defendant was charged with robbery "by use of a deadly weapon; to wit * * * a pistol," evidence that defendant used a .22 caliber rifle constituted a "material variance"); *Wilson v. State,* 292 S.W.2d 188 (Tenn.1956) (proof of theft of bronze rollers constitutes a fatal variance from indictment charging theft of brass rollers).

7. ***Pleading to avoid variances.*** Does the combination of a state requirement of substantial specificity in pleading and a prohibition against significant variance in proof place the prosecutor on the "horns of a dilemma"? Assume, for example, that in a homicide case, the available evidence indicates that death probably was caused by blows inflicted by the defendant, but there is additional evidence suggesting that death may have been caused by the exposure of the deceased to the elements following the assault. Moreover, assume that further evidence may become available at trial that will furnish greater support for exposure as the cause of death. To avoid the possibility of a variance, the prosecutor may prefer that the charge simply state that defendant "caused" the death of the deceased. But what if the state law requires greater specificity in pleading the manner in which death was caused? May the prosecutor utilize alternative allegations as to this element of the offense? Some courts have rejected alternative allegations as failing to fully inform the defendant of the charge against him. See e.g., *Shreveport v. Bryson,* 33 So.2d 60 (La.1947) (rejecting allegation of reckless driving by driving under the influence of "intoxicating liquor or drugs"). But other courts have approved disjunctive pleading—at least where the alternatives are not extensive. See e.g., *Commonwealth v. Schuler,* 43 A.2d 646 (Pa.Super.1945) (driving under influence of "intoxicating liquor or a narcotic or habit forming drug").

CHAPTER 18

THE LOCATION OF THE PROSECUTION

■ ■ ■

Determining the proper location of the prosecution—the issue of proper venue—is not troublesome in the vast majority of prosecutions. Venue clearly lies in a single judicial district, and that district is easily identified. Even when venue is readily identified, however, other issues relating to venue may arise. Section one of this chapter discusses those other issues, as well as the basics that determine the venue district. Section two considers the application of the standards that determine whether a particular offense may have proper venue in more than one district. It is in the application of these standards that the determination of venue is most likely to be troublesome.

§ 1. BASIC CONCEPTS

1. ***Distinguishing territorial jurisdiction.*** "Venue" sets the particular judicial district in which a criminal charge is to be filed and tried. As discussed below, the traditional standard for determining venue is the crime-committed formula, which places venue in the judicial district in which the charged crime allegedly was committed. "Jurisdiction" refers to a variety of limitations upon judicial authority, including restrictions upon the permissible geographical applicability of penal legislation adopted by the particular legal entity. A primary standard setting that geographical scope is the principle of "territorial jurisdiction," which allows the political entity to apply its criminal law to crimes committed within the territorial limits of the entity. In the federal system, the territorial principle is a basic grounding for applying federal criminal law, but other principles of jurisdiction (e.g., protection of national security) allow the federal government to reach crimes committed outside of its national territory. See CRIMPROC § 16.4(b). For the states, the territorial principle tends to be the exclusive determinant of the geographical applicability of a state's penal law.

Since the territorial principle asks whether a crime was committed within the state and venue's crime-committed formula asks whether a crime was committed within a particular judicial district within the state, they raise quite similar issues. The classic jurisdiction cases will have their venue counterparts. Where a defendant in state A mails poisoned candy to a victim in state B, who eats the candy there, but dies in state C, the jurisdictional question is whether jurisdiction to prosecute for murder lies with only one of those states (and if so, which one) or whether more than one state has jurisdiction (and if so, does that include all three). Cf. *People v. Botkin,* 64 P. 286 (Cal.1901) (sustaining jurisdiction for a murder prosecution in the state of the mailing). Assuming that the same events occurred in three different counties within the same state, the venue issues similarly would be whether venue lies in only one county (and if so, which one) or whether venue lies in more than one county (and if so, does that include all three).

Though the issues presented in applying the crime-committed formula of venue and the territorial principle of jurisdiction are quite similar, important distinctions exist. First the governing statutory language of a territorial scope provision may not be the same as the language describing permissible multi-venue situations (see Note 3 infra), and that may produce different results. Second, the standards governing proof of jurisdiction may be higher than the standards governing proof of venue (see Note 5 infra). Third, whereas venue limitations are subject to voluntary waiver or to forfeiture by failure to raise a timely objection (see Note 6 infra), jurisdictional limitations are said not to be subject to waiver and can be raised at any time in the proceeding (including collateral attack) where apparent on the face of the record. See CRIMPROC § 16.4(d).

Finally, and most significantly, the interests at stake in determining which state may prosecute are quite different from those at stake in determining where the trial will be held within a state. This is evident from the consequence of a decision that more than one state has jurisdiction. Under the dual sovereignty doctrine (Ch. 26, § 4), the double jeopardy clause does not prohibit prosecution of the defendant for the same criminal activity by each of those states. On the other hand, a determination that multi-venue exists because the crime extended over more than one judicial district still leaves the defendant subject to a single prosecution, although the state now has a choice of location. The different interests at stake also are reflected in the absence of any provision for transfer from a state with jurisdiction to a state without jurisdiction, in contrast to venue provisions, which allow for transfer from a judicial district in which the crime-committed formula applies to one in which it does not apply (see Note 7 infra).

2. ***Distinguishing vicinage.*** Whereas venue refers to the locality in which charges will be brought and adjudicated, vicinage refers to the locality from which jurors will be drawn. At common law, the defendant was entitled to a jury drawn from the "vicinage," i.e., the "neighborhood" in which the crime was committed. See Drew Kershen, *Vicinage,* 29 Okla.L.Rev. 801 (1976), 30 Okla.L.Rev. 1 (1977). As with venue, to determine vicinage, one had to identify the locale of the crime. Vicinage also required determining the appropriate geographical boundary of the "neighborhood" (or "vicinity") of the crime, which the common law most often made the county. The Sixth Amendment's recognition of a defendant's right to a "jury of the State and district wherein the crime shall have been committed" is often described as a vicinage provision, but it fails to meet the common law requirement that the jury be of the "neighborhood." Indeed, all but two of the original federal districts covered entire states. When Congress decided in the First Judiciary Act to recognize a true right of vicinage, it required for capital offenses that the jurors were to be selected from "the county where the offence was committed." See Kershen, supra.

In contrast to the Sixth Amendment, a substantial minority of the states have constitutional vicinage provisions which are true to the common law in limiting jury selection to a geographical district (usually the county) that fits within the vicinage concept of "the neighborhood." These provisions are often treated as also setting venue, on the assumption that the jury will be drawn from the judicial district in which the trial also should take place. In theory, state law could provide that the jury be selected from the county of the crime, as required by the concept of vicinage, and that the trial be placed in another county, within a much larger crime-committed district designated by the law of venue. However, all of these states use the districts designated in their vicinage provision as the appropriate judicial districts for their venue statute. A small group of states do have provisions authorizing selection of jurors from a district other than the district of trial, but they do so only where an unbiased jury cannot be obtained in the district of the crime. See Note 2, p. 1283.

3. ***The crime-committed formula.*** The standard formula for setting venue calls for placing the trial in the judicial district in which the crime was committed. This crime-committed formula is imposed as a constitutional requirement in the federal system (Article III, § 2, requiring the trial of all crimes "to be held in the State where said crimes shall have been committed") and in a handful of states. A substantial number of other states and the federal system (through the Sixth Amendment) impose the same formula indirectly through constitutional vicinage provisions (assuming that the place of jury selection will be the place of trial). In both jurisdictions with and without constitutional provisions adopting the crime-committed formula, that formula is set forth as the general venue standard in either the code of criminal procedure or the court rules of criminal procedure. See e.g., Fed.R.Crim.P. 18.

When the framers of the Constitution included the crime-committed formula in both Article III, Section 2, and the Sixth Amendment, they referred in the singular to the "state" and the "district" in which the crime "shall have been committed." This reflected the assumption that a crime ordinarily would be committed in a single place. At a time when travel was difficult and slow, and communications systems were rudimentary, all of the action constituting an offense and all of the immediate harm flowing from that action commonly occurred within a limited geographic area. Even at that time, however, there were certain federal offenses that could occur in more than one place and those two or more places would occasionally be in two different states. At the state level, where the judicial districts typically were counties, offenses committed in more than one judicial district were not quite so unique.

The offenses most likely to be multi-venue offenses were those commonly described as "continuing offenses." These were offenses having basic elements that continued (or, as some would say, "repeated themselves") over a period of time as part of a single crime. A prime illustration is kidnapping, which starts when the victim is taken into custody and continues until the victim is no longer under the control of the kidnappers. If the kidnapped victim was moved from one district to another in the course of the kidnapping, the offense was committed in each of those districts. At common law, larceny was placed in the same category, as the continued possession of the stolen property by the thief was viewed as a continuation of the trespassory taking.

A crime could also occur in more than one place when it had two or more distinct parts. Such offenses created a multi-venue potential when they required two separate elements that could occur at separate places. A criminal statute, for example, might define the offense as requiring first the doing of a prohibited act and then the causing of a certain victim response, with the act and response capable of occurring in two different localities. Similarly a statute might require distinct acts by the defendant which could occur in different places. The classic example here was the crime of conspiracy when it required both an agreement and an overt act in furtherance of that agreement.

Finally, multi-venue also was possible where the offense could be committed by a single act that could start in one place and finish in another. Thus, some courts viewed the act of conversion as one that could start with the decision to convert a financial account or instrument held in trust to one's own use and end when that scheme was fulfilled by obtaining funds for personal use. See CRIMPROC § 16.1(d).

By the mid-nineteenth century, with significant advances made in transportation and communications, crimes committed in more than one judicial district became much more common. This was particularly true for the federal system, which dealt with many crimes relating to commerce. In 1867, Congress adopted a general provision governing offenses committed in more than one district. That provision, in a slightly modified form, is now contained in Section 3237 of the federal criminal code. It provides:

> Except as otherwise expressly provided by enactment of Congress, any offense against the United States begun in one district and completed in another, or committed in more than one district, may be inquired of and prosecuted in any district in which such offense was begun, continued, or completed.

Most states also have adopted provisions, similar to § 3237, authorizing multi-district venue when the commission of an offense involves more than one district. These provisions typically refer to offenses "committed partly" in more than one district. See e.g., Ala.Code § 15–2–6. Several state provisions provide for multi-venue based on "acts or effects thereof constituting or requisite to the consummation of the offense" occurring in more than one district. See e.g., Ky.Rev.Stat. § 452.550. Others provide for multi-venue based on "acts," "conduct," and "results" that are elements of the offense occurring in more than one district. See e.g., Iowa Code Ann. § 803.3. The broader language of such statutes can lead to having venue based on acts that would not be sufficient under § 3237. See e.g., *People v. Thomas,* 274 P.2d 1170 (Cal. 2012) ("requisite acts" include "preparatory acts" that are not elements of the crime).

4. ***Legislative exceptions.*** Legislatures have adopted statutory exceptions to the crime-committed formula for various situations that prove troubling in applying that formula. Thus state venue statutes include provisions authorizing venue in: (1) either county where the crime was committed within a specified distance (e.g., 500 yards) of the boundary between two counties; (2) any county through which a vehicle passed where the crime was committed in a moving vehicle (with some states conditioning the application of this provision on a prosecution showing that the exact location cannot "readily be determined"); (3) any district selected by the attorney general where "it is impossible to determine in which county the crime occurred"; (4) in the case of child abuse, either in the county where the child was abused or the county in which the child was found; and (5) where state law requires joinder of offenses committed in the same criminal episode or transaction (see Note 10, p. 1057), in any county in which the crime-committed formula establishes venue for any one of those offenses. See CRIMPROC § 16.1(e), (f).

Where a state has either a constitutional venue guarantee of a trial in the county in which the crime was committed, or a constitutional guarantee of a jury of the vicinage, special venue legislation can pose constitutional difficulties. Thus, courts have divided on the constitutionality of provisions allowing venue in either county where the crime was committed near the border between two counties. See e.g., *State v. Chalikes,* 170 N.E. 653 (Ohio 1930) (unconstitutional where locus of crime readily determined); *State v. Lehman,* 279 P. 283 (Or.1929) (constitutional on theory that legislature has simply created judicial districts with slightly expanded and overlapping boundaries for such crimes, so venue is still in the district in which the crime was committed). The majority of states, however, do not have such constitutional provisions, leaving the legislature free to create such exceptions to the crime-committed formula as it deems appropriate.

Of course, where the venue is set by legislation in a district other than the district of commission of the crime, the jury too will be selected from that special venue district, and that could create federal constitutional difficulties. The Sixth Amendment guarantees a jury from "the State and district wherein the crime shall have been committed, which district shall have previously been ascertained by law." However, courts have advanced two different rationales in finding no Sixth Amendment difficulties in the selection of the state juries from special venue districts: (1) the Sixth Amendment's "vicinage" guarantee should not apply to the states, as it is a peculiarly federal guarantee, not of the fundamental character needed to make it applicable to the states (see Ch. 2, § 1); and (2) the Sixth Amendment's "district" requirement (assuming its application to the states) demands only (i) a trial somewhere within the state, in light of the acceptance of districts covering the complete state in the federal system, and (ii) that the special venue district be previously designated by legislation. See CRIMPROC §§ 2.6(b), 16.1(e).

5. ***Proof of venue.*** Only a handful of jurisdictions treat venue in much the same manner as other procedural prerequisites for prosecution (e.g., a valid preliminary hearing bindover, or a grand jury charge). In these jurisdictions, the defendant must put the venue prerequisite in issue by a pretrial motion to dismiss, with the court then making a determination that venue does or does not exist. In the federal system and the vast majority of the states, venue is not simply a prerequisite that the defendant may choose to challenge pretrial; it is viewed as part of the case that the prosecution must prove at trial. These jurisdictions offer a variety of explanations for requiring that venue be established at trial. Venue is described as: "a jurisdictional fact put in issue by a plea of not guilty"; a "material allegation of the indictment" which must be proven along with other indictment allegations; an "element of the crime" to be treated no differently than the

substantive elements of the offense; and an "issuable fact" most appropriately addressed in the course of the proof of the offense and presented to the finder of fact.[a]

As might be expected from the above explanations, all but a few of these jurisdictions treat venue as a factual question to be decided by the jury in a jury trial. The court has the responsibility for determining whether, as a matter of law, the events alleged to have occurred in a particular place could be sufficient to establish that the crime was committed at least in part in that district (or whether venue could otherwise be justified under special legislation). The jury then decides the underlying factual issues, such as whether a particular act did occur in the district, or whether that act had the impact or other quality that the court deems necessary to characterize it as involving the commission of the crime.

Though most jurisdictions treat proof of venue as a jury issue, they ordinarily do not view venue as one of those matters that must invariably be submitted to the jury. Courts frequently state that a jury charge on venue is required only "when trial testimony puts venue in issue." Thus, a jury charge on venue is not required "where the entirety of the defendant's illegal activity is alleged to have taken place within the trial * * * [district] and no trial evidence is proffered that the illegal act was committed in some other place or that the place alleged is not within the * * * [district]." *United States v. Miller,* 111 F.3d 747 (10th Cir.1997). Courts also have concluded that the failure to charge on venue should not constitute error, even when the evidence would justify such a charge, where the defendant failed to request a charge on venue. See Note 6, infra.

Jurisdictions requiring prosecution proof of venue at trial are divided as to the level of persuasiveness of the prosecution's proof of venue. The federal courts and a substantial number of state courts hold that the facts supporting venue only need be established by a preponderance of the evidence. Other states require that venue be proved beyond a reasonable doubt. Courts explaining this higher proof requirement point to state law that treats venue as an "element of the offense," the characterization of venue as a "material allegation" of the charging instrument, and the status of venue as a jurisdictional prerequisite (therefore requiring the same proof standard as traditionally applied to proof of the territorial jurisdiction of the state). See CRIMPROC § 16.1(g).

6. *Waiver.* A defendant can waive his right to proper venue by an express statement of relinquishment (e.g., a statement consenting to be tried in a judicial district even though the crime is not alleged to have been committed there, or a request for a transfer to another district from the district of proper venue). In addition, in the federal system and in a substantial majority of the states, in contrast to such trial guarantees as trial by jury and representation by counsel, venue can be "waived"—or more accurately, "forfeited"—by a defendant's "silence," in the form of a failure to make a timely objection. Where the pleading on its face establishes as a matter of law that venue does not exist, a failure to raise that issue pretrial will constitute a forfeiture. See Fed.R.Crim.P. 12(b)(3)(A)(i). Where the lack of venue first appears in the evidence at trial, a

[a] Consider, however, the response in *People v. Posey,* 82 P.3d 755 (Cal.2004), citing three reasons for finding "unsound" the "rule * * * that declares the issue whether a criminal action has been brought in a place appropriate for trial to be a question of fact to be decided by the jury at the conclusion of trial rather than a question of law to be decided by the Court prior to trial": "First, the rule impedes the purposes underlying the venue provisions, especially their 'principal purpose . . . from a defendant's perspective' of 'protect[ing] a defendant from being required to stand trial in a distant and unduly burdensome locale' * * * by putting off any finding on venue until *after* 'the defendant [has been] required to undergo the rigors and hardship of standing trial in an assertedly improper locale,' and *after* 'the state [has] incur[red] the time and expense of conducting a trial' there. Second, the rule is 'inconsistent with contemporary treatment of other analogous . . . issues,' inasmuch as venue is a procedural question involving the appropriateness of a place for a defendant's trial on a criminal charge, and not a substantive question relating to the defendant's guilt or innocence of the crime charged. * * * Third, the rule threatens the untoward consequence of an 'unwarranted acquittal' when the jury returns a verdict of not guilty predicated solely on lack of proper venue."

failure to object at that point (including a failure to seek a jury charge on venue where the evidence on venue is disputed) will constitute a forfeiture. See CRIMPROC § 16.1(h).

7. ***Change of venue.*** The federal system and every state has a statute or court rule (or both) authorizing a trial court to order that a case be moved from its original district of prosecution, proper under the jurisdiction's venue laws, to a district that otherwise would not be proper under those laws. In some states, additional authorization is provided through the recognition of an inherent judicial authority to order a change of venue, which supplements the statutory authorization. Together, these sources establish a quite varied law governing venue changes. Initially, the jurisdictions divide as to the grounds that justify ordering a venue change. Some limit changes to ensuring that the ensuing trial will be fair, while others add to that ground, allowing changes in the interest of witness convenience or sound judicial administration. Jurisdictions also vary as to whether changes are allowed only on motion of the defendant, on the motion of the prosecution as well as the defendant, and on the court's own initiative over the objection of one or both parties.

Provisions authorizing venue changes to ensure a fair trial are found in every jurisdiction. Those changes are discussed in Ch. 24, § 2. Far less common are provisions authorizing a change to promote convenience. Federal Rule 21(b) and a substantial minority of states authorize such changes on motion of the defendant. Only a handful of states authorize such changes on motion of the prosecution. Provisions authorizing convenience transfers typically state that the court "may transfer" on convenience grounds, and courts recognize that such a transfer lies in the discretion of the trial court, subject only to the prohibition against arbitrary or capricious exercise of that discretion. However, federal district courts have been advised with respect to Federal Rule 21(b) that: "Nothing in Rule 21(b) or in the cases interpreting it place on the defendant seeking a change of venue the burden of establishing 'truly compelling circumstances' for such a change. It is enough if, all relevant things considered, the case would be better off transferred to another district." *Matter of Balsimo,* 68 F.3d 185 (7th Cir.1995).

What factors are relevant in determining whether another district would be a more convenient forum and a transfer to that district would be in the interest of justice? In the leading Supreme Court ruling on a Federal Rule 21(b), *Platt v. Minnesota Mining and Manufacturing Co.,* 376 U.S. 240 (1964), the Court cited a ten factor list that had been considered by the district court, and while the Court's ruling related to another point, it did add that both the parties and the appellate court had agreed that the consideration of those ten factors was "appropriate." Those ten factors, frequently relied upon in subsequent federal lower court decisions, are: "(1) location of the corporate defendant [which was the apparent counterpart of the location of one's residence for an individual]; (2) location of possible witnesses; (3) location of events likely to be in issue; (4) location of documents and records likely to be involved; (5) disruption of defendant's business unless the case is transferred; (6) expense to the parties; (7) location of counsel; (8) relative accessibility of place of trial; (9) docket condition of each district or division involved; and (10) any other special elements which might affect the transfer." In a jurisdiction with victims' rights legislation, that legislation ordinarily would also require weighing any logistical difficulties that a transfer would create for a victim who desired to regularly attend the trial. See e.g., Fed.R.Crim.P. 21(b) (including "convenience of * * * any victim").

§ 2. APPLYING THE CRIME-COMMITTED FORMULA

UNITED STATES V. RODRIGUEZ-MORENO

526 U.S. 275, 119 S.Ct. 1239, 143 L.Ed.2d 388 (1999).

JUSTICE THOMAS delivered the opinion of the Court.

This case presents the question whether venue in a prosecution for using or carrying a firearm "during and in relation to any crime of violence, in violation of 18 U.S.C. § 924(c)(1)", is proper in any district where the crime of violence was committed, even if the firearm was used or carried only in a single district. * * * During a drug transaction that took place in Houston, Texas, a New York drug dealer stole 30 kilograms of a Texas drug distributor's cocaine. The distributor hired respondent, Jacinto Rodriguez-Moreno, and others to find the dealer and to hold captive the middleman in the transaction, Ephrain Avendano, during the search. In pursuit of the dealer, the distributor and his henchmen drove from Texas to New Jersey with Avendano in tow. * * * They [then] moved to a house in New York and then to a house in Maryland, taking Avendano with them. Shortly after respondent and the others arrived at the Maryland house, the owner of the home passed around a .357 magnum revolver and respondent took possession of the pistol. As it became clear that efforts to find the New York drug dealer would not bear fruit, respondent told his employer that he thought they should kill the middleman and end their search for the dealer. He put the gun to the back of Avendano's neck but, at the urging of his cohorts, did not shoot. Avendano eventually escaped through the back door and ran to a neighboring house. The neighbors called the Maryland police, who arrested respondent along with the rest of the kidnappers. The police also seized the .357 magnum, on which they later found respondent's fingerprint.

Rodriguez-Moreno and his codefendants were tried jointly in the United States District Court for the District of New Jersey. Respondent was charged with, inter alia, conspiring to kidnap Avendano, kidnaping Avendano, and using and carrying a firearm in relation to the kidnaping of Avendano, in violation of 18 U.S.C. § 924(c)(1). At the conclusion of the Government's case, respondent moved to dismiss the § 924(c)(1) count for lack of venue. He argued that venue was proper only in Maryland, the only place where the Government had proved he had actually used a gun. The District Court denied the motion, and the jury found respondent guilty on the kidnaping counts and on the § 924(c)(1) charge as well. He was sentenced to 87 months' imprisonment on the kidnaping charges, and was given a mandatory consecutive term of 60 months' imprisonment for committing the § 924(c)(1) offense.

On a 2-to-1 vote, the Court of Appeals for the Third Circuit reversed respondent's § 924(c)(1) conviction. A majority of the Third Circuit panel applied what it called the "verb test" to § 924(c)(1), and determined that a violation of the statute is committed only in the district where a defendant "uses" or "carries" a firearm. Id., at 849. Accordingly, it concluded that venue for the § 924(c)(1) count was improper in New Jersey even though venue was proper there for the kidnaping of Avendano. * * *

As we confirmed just last Term, the " 'locus delicti [of the charged offense] must be determined from the nature of the crime alleged and the location of the act or acts constituting it.' " *United States v. Cabrales* [Note 1, p. 1025], quoting *United States v. Anderson*, 328 U.S. 699 (1946). * * * In performing this inquiry, a court must initially identify the conduct constituting the offense (the nature of the crime) and then discern the location of the commission of the criminal acts.[3] * * * At the time respondent committed the offense and was tried, 18 U.S.C. § 924(c)(1) provided:

> "Whoever, during and in relation to any crime of violence . . . for which he may be prosecuted in a court of the United States, uses or carries a firearm, shall, in addition to the punishment provided for such crime of violence . . . be sentenced to imprisonment for five years. . . ."

The Third Circuit, as explained above, looked to the verbs of the statute to determine the nature of the substantive offense. But we have never before held, and decline to do so here, that verbs are the sole consideration in identifying the conduct that constitutes an offense. While the "verb test" certainly has value as an interpretative tool, it cannot be applied rigidly, to the exclusion of other relevant statutory language. The test unduly limits the inquiry into the nature of the offense and thereby creates a danger that certain conduct prohibited by statute will be missed.

In our view, the Third Circuit overlooked an essential conduct element of the § 924(c)(1) offense. Section 924(c)(1) prohibits using or carrying a firearm "during and in relation to any crime of violence . . . for which [a defendant] may be prosecuted in a court of the United States." That the crime of violence element of the statute is embedded in a prepositional phrase and not expressed in verbs does not dissuade us from concluding that a defendant's violent acts are essential conduct elements. To prove the charged § 924(c)(1) violation in this case, the Government was required to show that respondent used a firearm, that he committed all the acts necessary to be subject to punishment for kidnaping (a crime of violence) in a court of the United States, and that he used the gun "during and in relation to" the kidnaping of Avendano. In sum, we interpret § 924(c)(1) to contain two distinct conduct elements—as is relevant to this case, the "using and carrying" of a gun and the commission of a kidnaping.[4]

Respondent, however, argues that for venue purposes "the New Jersey kidnaping is completely irrelevant to the firearm crime, because respondent did not use or carry a gun during the New Jersey crime." In the words of one amicus, § 924(c)(1) is a "point-in-time" offense that only is committed in the place where the kidnaping and the use of a gun coincide. Brief for National Association of Criminal Defense Lawyers as Amicus Curiae 11. We disagree. Several Circuits have determined that kidnaping, as defined by 18 U.S.C. § 1201 (1994 ed. and Supp. III), is a unitary crime, and we agree with their conclusion. A kidnaping, once begun, does not end until the victim is free. It does not make sense, then, to speak of it in discrete geographic fragments. Section 924(c)(1) criminalized a defendant's use of a firearm "during and in relation to" a crime of violence; in doing so, Congress proscribed both the use of the firearm and the commission of acts that constitute a violent crime. It does not matter that respondent used the .357 magnum revolver, as the Government concedes, only in Maryland because he did so "during and in relation to" a kidnaping that was begun in Texas and continued in New York, New Jersey, and Maryland. In

[3] The Government argues that venue also may permissibly be based upon the effects of a defendant's conduct in a district other than the one in which the defendant performs the acts constituting the offense. Brief 16–17. Because this case only concerns the *locus delicti*, we express no opinion as to whether the Government's assertion is correct.

[4] By the way of comparison, last Term in *United States v. Cabrales* [Note 1, p. 1025], we considered whether venue for money laundering, in violation of 18 U.S.C. §§ 1956(a)(1)(B)(ii) and 1957, was proper in Missouri, where the laundered proceeds were unlawfully generated, or rather, only in Florida, where the prohibited laundering transactions occurred. As we interpreted the laundering statutes at issue, they did not proscribe "the anterior criminal conduct that yielded the funds allegedly laundered." *Cabrales*. The existence of criminally generated proceeds was a circumstance element of the offense but the proscribed conduct—defendant's money laundering activity—occurred " 'after the fact' of an offense begun and completed by others." Here, by contrast, given the "during and in relation to" language, the underlying crime of violence is a critical part of the § 924(c)(1) offense.

our view, § 924(c)(1) does not define a "point-in-time" offense when a firearm is used during and in relation to a continuing crime of violence. * * *

As we said in *United States v. Lombardo* [Note 2(a), p. 1025], "where a crime consists of distinct parts which have different localities the whole may be tried where any part can be proved to have been done." * * * The kidnaping, to which the § 924(c)(1) offense is attached, was committed in all of the places that any part of it took place, and venue for the kidnaping charge against respondent was appropriate in any of them. (Congress has provided that continuing offenses can be tried "in any district in which such offense was begun, continued, or completed," 18 U.S.C. § 3237(a).) Where venue is appropriate for the underlying crime of violence, so too it is for the § 924(c)(1) offense. As the kidnaping was properly tried in New Jersey, the § 924(c)(1) offense could be tried there as well.

JUSTICE SCALIA, with whom JUSTICE STEVENS joins, dissenting.

* * * [Section 924(c)] prohibits the act of using or carrying a firearm "during" (and in relation to) a predicate offense. The provisions of the United States Code defining the particular predicate offenses already punish all of the defendant's alleged criminal conduct except his use or carriage of a gun; § 924(c)(1) itself criminalizes and punishes such use or carriage "during" the predicate crime, because that makes the crime more dangerous. This is a simple concept, and it is embodied in a straightforward text. To answer the question before us we need only ask where the defendant's alleged act of using a firearm during (and in relation to) a kidnaping occurred. Since it occurred only in Maryland, venue will lie only there. * * *

[T]he crime before us does *not* consist of "distinct" parts that can occur in different localities. Its two parts are bound inseparably together by the word "during." Where the gun is being used, the predicate act must be occurring as well, and vice versa. The Court quite simply reads this requirement out of the statute—as though there were no difference between a statute making it a crime to steal a cookie and eat it (which could be prosecuted either in New Jersey, where the cookie was stolen, or in Maryland, where it was eaten) and a statute making it a crime to eat a cookie while robbing a bakery (which could be prosecuted only where the ingestive theft occurred). * * *

The Court believes its holding is justified by the continuing nature of the kidnaping predicate offense, which invokes the statute providing that "any offense * * * begun in one district and completed in another, or committed in more than one district, may be * * * prosecuted in any district in which such offense was begun, continued, or completed." To disallow the New Jersey prosecution here, the Court suggests, is to convert § 924(c)(1) from a continuing offense to a "point-in-time" offense. That is simply not so. I in no way contend that the kidnaping, or, for that matter, the use of the gun, can occur only at one point in time. Each can extend over a protracted period, and in many places. But § 924(c)(1) is violated only so long as, and where, both continuing acts are being committed simultaneously. That is what the word "during" means. Thus, if the defendant here had used or carried the gun throughout the kidnaping, in Texas, New Jersey, New York, and Maryland, he could have been prosecuted in any of those States. As it was, however, he used a gun during a kidnaping only in Maryland.

The short of the matter is that this defendant, who has a constitutional right to be tried in the State and district where his alleged crime was "committed," U.S. Const., Art. III, § 2, cl. 3; Amdt. 6, has been prosecuted for using a gun during a kidnaping in a State and district where all agree he did not use a gun during a kidnaping. If to state this case is not to decide it, the law has departed further from the meaning of language than is appropriate for a government that is supposed to rule (and to be restrained) through the written word.

NOTES AND QUESTIONS

1. ***Supreme Court precedent.*** As the Court notes, UNITED STATES v. CABRALES, 524 U.S. 1 (1998), distinguished in footnote 4 (p. 1023), also applied the "general guide" of *United States v. Anderson*, that venue "[should] be determined from the nature of the crime alleged and the location of the acts or acts constituting it." *Cabrales* involved a prosecution under a money laundering statute making it a crime to "knowing[ly] * * * conduct * * * a financial transaction which * * * involves proceeds of specified unlawful activity * * * knowing that the transaction is designed * * * to avoid a transaction reporting requirement." The prosecution was brought in Missouri, where drug trafficking had produced the criminally derived funds, but the alleged financial transactions were deposits and withdrawals made in Florida (and it was not alleged that the defendant had transported the funds from Missouri to Florida[a]). The government argued that venue was proper in the district of the underlying criminality that produced the funds (here Missouri) because (1) that underlying crime was an essential element of the money laundering offense, (2) the laundering activity impacts the underlying criminal activity by making it profitable and impeding its detection, and (3) the district of the underlying offense is a most appropriate district for trial because of the need to prove that the funds were criminally derived and the important "interests of the community victimized by [the] drug dealers." The Supreme Court in a unanimous ruling found these arguments unpersuasive.

Justice Ginsburg's opinion for the Court reasoned that the money laundering offense was "defined in statutory proscriptions * * * that interdict only the financial transactions (acts located entirely in Florida), not the anterior criminal conduct that yielded the funds allegedly laundered." To be criminally liable, "the money launderer must know she is dealing with funds [criminally] derived," but "it is immaterial whether * * * [she] knew where the first crime was committed." Admittedly, "whenever a defendant acts 'after the fact' to conceal a crime, * * * it might be said that the first crime is an essential element of the second; * * * and that the second facilitated the first," but that does not establish the venue for the second in the district of the first. The government had available to it the potential for trial in the district of drug trafficking if it charged the defendant with a conspiracy with the drug dealers and treated the money laundering as an overt act. It could not use charges of money laundering, which "described activity of the [defendant] alone, untied to others," as a substitute for a conspiracy charge.

2. Although the Court in *Rodriguez-Moreno* rejects the lower court's sole reliance upon a "verb test,"[b] does that test have solid support as a key factor in determining venue under the Supreme Court precedent described below?

(a) In UNITED STATES v. LOMBARDO, 241 U.S. 73 (1916), the defendant, an operator of a house of prostitution in Seattle, was charged in the Western District of Washington with failing to comply with a federal statute requiring any person who harbored an alien for the purpose of prostitution to report that alien's identity to the Commissioner General of Immigration. The district court sustained a demurrer to the indictment on the ground that the offense was not committed in Seattle, but in the District of Columbia, where the offices of the Commissioner General were located. Affirming that ruling, the Supreme Court initially quoted with approval from the district court's analysis of the critical statutory verb:

---

[a] Congress later adopted a special venue provision dealing with this situation. 18 U.S.C.A. § 1956(i) provides that a money-laundering prosecution can be brought "in any district where a prosecution for the underlying specified unlawful activity could be brought, if the defendant participated in the transfer of the proceeds * * * from that district to the district where the financial or monetary transaction is conducted."

[b] Consider as to this test, John Dobie, *Venue in Criminal Cases in the United States District Court*, 12 Va.L.Rev. 287 (1926): "Crimes are defined, hidden away amid pompous verbosity, in terms of a single verb," which "usually contains the key to the solution to the question: In what district was the crime committed." For many years, Judge Dobie's article was one of the most frequently cited commentaries on federal venue.

"The word 'file' was not defined by Congress. No definition having been given, the etymology of the word must be considered and ordinary meaning applied. The word 'file' is derived from the Latin word 'filum,' and relates to the ancient practice of placing papers on a thread or wire for safekeeping and ready reference. Filing, it must be observed, is not complete until the document is delivered and received. 'Shall file' means to deliver to the office and not send through the United States mails. A paper is filed when it is delivered to the proper official and by him received and filed."

The Court then rejected the government's response that this was an unduly narrow reading of the term "shall file." The government contended that a filing could begin in the place where the document was sent and therefore the defendant's failure to send the document from Seattle marked the beginning of the crime. The Court's answer to this contention was that it "was constrained by the meanings of the words of the statute." The requirement of a filing demanded delivery at a specific place; it had never been deemed satisfied by "a deposit in a post office at some distant place." The Court also offered several administrative justifications for its ruling. Those included difficulties relating to proof of mailing (or the lack thereof) and to setting "the instant of time" for compliance if a mailing was to be taken as compliance.

(b) In TRAVIS v. UNITED STATES, 364 U.S. 631 (1961), a union official in Colorado was charged under a statute applicable to any person who, "in a matter within the jurisdiction of any department or agency of the United States," knowingly "makes" any false statement. The false statements at issue were non-Communist affidavits executed and mailed in Colorado to the offices of the National Labor Relations Board in Washington, D.C. The defendant contended, and the Court majority agreed, that the government had erred in bringing the prosecution in Colorado as the offense only could be committed in the District of Columbia. The majority stressed that the offense required that the false statement be "within the jurisdiction" of the Board. Section 9(h) of the National Labor Relations Act did not require union officers to file non-Communist affidavits, but provided for their voluntary filing as a prerequisite to invoking the Board's authority in the investigation and issuance of complaints against employers. Accordingly, "filing [of the affidavit] must be completed before there is a 'matter within the jurisdiction' of the Board." *Lombardo* had held that "when a place is explicitly designated where a paper must be filed, a prosecution for failure to file lies only at that place." The same was true where an element of the charged offense was tied to an actual filing. Accordingly, the charge could be brought only in the District of Columbia, where the affidavit was filed.

The *Travis* majority acknowledged that "Colorado, the residence of the [defendant] might offer conveniences and advantages to him which a trial in the District of Columbia might lack." It did not disagree with the dissent's contention that "the witnesses and relevant circumstances surrounding the contested issues in such cases more probably will be found in the district of the execution of the affidavit than at the place of filing."[c] Its response was that the "constitutional requirement is as to the locality of the offense and not the personal presence of the offender," and here the nature of the offense set that locality in only one place. To argue, as the government did, that the offense started in Colorado because the defendant there "irrevocably set in motion and placed beyond his control the train of events which would normally result (and here did result) in the consummation of the offense" was to ignore that Congress here "has so carefully indicated the locus of the crime." That was done in the "explicit provision of 9(h)," which combined with the

[c] The dissent did not rely on this factor alone. It noted that the prohibited act was the "making" of a false statement to the government, which would "begin at the place where the false affidavit is actually made, sworn, and subscribed." At this point, the process that constituted the crime was started and it was in bringing the statement within the jurisdiction of the N.L.R.B. that the crime was completed. This analysis, the dissent argued, was supported by the *Anderson* directive to examine the "nature of the crime." The majority described the *Anderson* directive as applicable only "where Congress is not explicit."

"agency jurisdiction" requirement of the false statement statute to render the crime incapable of commission until the affidavit was delivered to the Board.

(c) In UNITED STATES v. JOHNSON, 323 U.S. 273 (1944), the Court split 5–4 over appropriate venue for a charge of "using" the mails for the purpose of "sending" dentures into another state in violation of the Federal Denture Act. The government argued that venue was proper in the receiving state (Delaware), while the defendant claimed that he could only be tried in his home district of Chicago, from which the dentures had been mailed. The majority found that the crucial element of the offense was the act of "sending," and therefore venue could only lie in Chicago since the offense was completed there. Although the majority recognized Congress' right to specifically provide for broader venue, it considered its interpretation of the statute "more consistent" with the "underlying spirit of the constitutional concern for trial in the vicinage." Where legislative history leaves the issue open, a court should, it noted, prefer an interpretation that avoids (1) placing upon the defendant "the serious hardship of defending prosecutions in places remote from home (including the accused's difficulties, financial and otherwise * * * of marshaling his witness)" and (2) establishing multiple permissible venues, and thereby creating the "appearance of abuses * * * in the prosecution's selection of what may be deemed a tribunal favorable to the prosecution." The four dissenting judges sharply rejected this analysis: "The Court misapprehends the purpose of the Constitutional provisions. We understand them to assure a trial in the place where the crime is committed and not to be concerned with the domicile of the criminal nor with his familiarity with the environment of the place of trial."

(d) In JOHNSTON v. UNITED STATES, 351 U.S. 215, 100 L.Ed. 1097 (1956), the Court split 6–3 in holding that persons charged with the crime of failing to perform civilian work as ordered by a local draft board (as alternative service for conscientious objectors) could be prosecuted only in the district where that work was to be performed rather than their home districts in which their boards were located. The majority opinion by Justice Reed (who had dissented in *Johnson*) noted that the "requirement of venue states the public policy that fixes the situs of the trial in the vicinage of the crime rather than the residence of the accused," and the crime here was a failure to perform a duty at the location of the assigned workplace. The dissent (written by Justice Douglas, who also wrote the majority opinion in *Travis*) argued that it would be preferable to "read the statute with an eye to history and try the offenders at home where our forefathers thought that normally men would receive their fairest trial." The basic element of the crime, the dissent contended, was the failure to obey the draft board's order, which occurred when the registrant "refus[ed] to budge from his home town."

3. ***Policy.*** Commentators contend that in identifying the "nature of the offense," there commonly is sufficient flexibility to take account of Justice Frankfurter's admonition that "questions of venue in criminal cases * * * raise deep issues of public policy in the light of which legislation must be construed." *United States v. Johnson,* Note 2(c) supra. In such instances, it is noted, a court should resolve ambiguities in favor of an interpretation of the offense that will best serve the underlying policy objective of venue requirements—"insur[ing] a fair trial for persons accused of crime." Drew Kershen, *Vicinage,* 29 Okla.L.Rev. 801 (1976). However, at least three conflicting guidelines have been advanced as to what construction will best serve that policy objective:

> (1) One position maintains that liberal provisions for change of venue (see Note 7, p. 1021) provide adequate protection against forcing defendants to defend in an inconvenient forum. Accordingly, venue provisions should be broadly construed so that a conviction following a fair trial will not be reversed simply on the ground that the prosecutor selected the wrong district.
>
> (2) Another viewpoint would place greater emphasis on the defendant's home district. Supporters of this position acknowledge that the draftsmen of Article III, § 2

chose the place of the commission of the crime, rather than the place of the accused's residence, as the appropriate test for venue, but they note that that test was selected primarily because it "accorded with the concept of jurisdiction held * * * in the late eighteenth century," and everyone assumed "that the place of commission of the crime and the place of residence would almost always be identical." Drew Kershen, *Vicinage,* 30 Okla.L.Rev. 1, 22 (1977). Under this guideline, where the structure of the offense reasonably permits the court to conclude that it was committed in part in the home district, that interpretation should be adopted.

(3) A third view would stress limiting the prosecutor's discretion to choose where the prosecution will be initiated. Under this view, where possible, the court should treat an offense as non-continuing, thereby permitting venue only in a single district. Where venue is held to be proper in several districts, the prosecutor controls the choice of district (absent a rarely granted defense motion for change of venue), and that choice, it is argued, may be based on inappropriate considerations—such as where the prosecution feels it will obtain the most favorable jury or where it can impose the greatest logistical difficulties for the defense in presenting its case.

To what extent do *Rodriguez-Moreno*, *Cabrales*, and the cases cited in Note 2 reflect the application of such guidelines? The Court has frequently discussed the "home district" consideration (with the justices often differing on the weight it should be given). See e.g., *Johnson*, and *Johnston*. It occasionally had taken note of the position that would limit the prosecutor's discretion to choose. See e.g., *Travis* ("Congress should not be so freely construed to give the Government the choice of a 'tribunal favorable to it'," quoting *Johnson*).

4. ***Use of the mails.*** Following *Johnson,* Note 2(c) supra, Congress added a second paragraph to § 3237(a) providing that: "Any offense involving the use of the mails, or transportation in interstate or foreign commerce, is a continuing offense and, except as otherwise expressly provided by enactment of Congress, may be inquired of and prosecuted in any district from, through, or into which such commerce or mail matter moves." Is there any justification for allowing venue on a charge such as mail fraud to be brought in any district through which the mail moved as opposed to limiting such venue to the "sending" and "receiving" districts, as considered in *Johnson*? Consider *United States v. Peraino*, 645 F.2d 548 (6th Cir.1981) (venue in federal obscenity prosecutions lies in any district from, through, or into which the obscene material moves). While § 3237(a)'s second paragraph does not apply simply because the mails or interstate transportation were used in committing the crime, the concept of an offense "involving" interstate transportation has been held to encompass offenses in which interstate transportation is a "circumstance" inherent in the offense, though not an element of the offense. See *United States v. Solan,* 792 F.Supp. 99 (M.D.Fla.1992) (paragraph two applies to the offense of delivery of firearms to a contract carrier for the purpose of interstate shipment).

5. ***Conspiracy venue.*** Perhaps the most extensive choice of venue arises in conspiracy cases. The prosecutor there may initiate prosecution on the conspiracy charge in any district in which any overt act in furtherance of the conspiracy was committed by any of the conspirators, even though the defendant himself was not present in that district. Courts have advanced two theories in support of this position, each resting on the proposition that conspiracy offense is "committed" in the place of the overt act (as well as the place of the agreement). Where the conspiracy offense requires no more than the agreement itself, they note that each overt act constitutes a "renewal" or "continuation" of the agreement. Where the offense requires both an agreement and an overt act, each overt act is viewed as an element of the offense.

Each count in an indictment or information must have proper venue. Thus, substantive offenses committed in furtherance of a conspiracy can be joined with the conspiracy count only if each of these offenses was committed in the same judicial district. As to the possibility of expanding venue for the substantive offenses committed in furtherance of a conspiracy, consider the theory advanced by the government, but rejected by the court, in *United States v. Walden*, 464 F.2d 1015 (4th Cir.1972). There a federal prosecution was brought in South Carolina charging the ten defendants with a conspiracy to rob federally insured banks and with the substantive counts of violating 18 U.S.C. § 2113 (entering a bank with intent to rob) as to the various banks, which were located in states other than South Carolina. The government argued that the conspiratorial acts (which did occur in South Carolina) made each of the co-conspirators an accomplice to the robberies, and the substantive counts therefore could be brought in South Carolina under the doctrine that "an accomplice may be tried where his accessorial act took place." Rejecting that contention, the Court of Appeals noted: "If we accept the [government's] argument, we would have, with respect to these substantive counts, the conceptual difficulty of a bank robbery or unlawful entry being perpetrated entirely by accessories in South Carolina without the assistance of principals at place of entry. * * * [W]here all persons charged as accessories for purposes of obtaining venue at the place where the crime was planned (South Carolina) are physically present and actively engaged in unlawful entry of a bank in another jurisdiction, we think it would distort both the substantive criminal law and the law of criminal venue to allow prosecution for the substantive offense of unlawful entry at the place (South Carolina) where the crime was planned."

CHAPTER 19

JOINDER AND SEVERANCE

■ ■ ■

While the simplest form of a criminal trial is one involving a single charge against a single defendant, often a defendant will face multiple charges or a group of defendants will be together charged with the same offense, and, indeed, it is not uncommon for there to be both multiple charges and multiple defendants in a single trial. As a general matter, it is commonly assumed to be to a defendant's disadvantage to face multiple charges or to be tried with other defendants, though there are some circumstances in which a defendant might prefer disposition of all charges in a single trial. The prevailing rules on when charges and defendants may be initially joined and must be subsequently severed are discussed in this Chapter, together with various constitutional doctrines (e.g., collateral estoppel) that have an impact in this context.

§ 1. JOINDER AND SEVERANCE OF OFFENSES

PEOPLE V. MERRIMAN

60 Cal.4th 1, 177 Cal.Rptr.3d 1, 332 P.3d 1187 (2014).

CANTIL-SAKAUYE, C.J. * * *

Defendant contends that the trial court abused its discretion by refusing to sever trial on the murder count from trial on the rest of the charges against him. He furthermore asserts that a joint trial on all charges deprived him of his constitutional rights to a fair trial and due process. His claim fails, as we explain below.

1. Background

The Ventura County Grand Jury initially returned a 25-count indictment against defendant in January 1999. The first three counts of the indictment charged defendant with special circumstance murder and other crimes involving Katrina. Seven of the counts charged defendant with sexually assaulting Robyn G. and Billie B., and nine counts arose from the circumstances surrounding defendant's attempt to evade arrest in January 1998. The remaining six counts charged defendant with being under the influence of a controlled substance at various times predating his arrest. A second, five-count indictment was issued in May 1999, about four months after the first indictment, charging defendant with crimes stemming from various attempts to dissuade witnesses who had testified at the earlier grand jury proceeding.

In 2000, the court conducted a hearing on two pretrial motions by the parties, granting the prosecution's motion to consolidate the two indictments, and granting as to certain counts a defense motion to sever trial on the murder charge from trial on the other charges in the first indictment.[5] The court denied the request to sever the murder count from all other charges, however. * * *

---

[5] The court severed trial on (1) drug- and firearm-possession charges connected with defendant's arrest that required proof of defendant's status as a convicted felon and drug addict and (2) five counts charging defendant with being under the influence of a controlled substance that were based upon events unrelated to his arrest. As to these charges, the court found that joinder would prejudice defendant.

2. Statutory requirements for joinder of charges

Section 954 authorizes the joinder of "two or more different offenses connected together in their commission . . . or two or more different offenses of the same class of crimes or offenses, under separate counts." The statute further provides that "if two or more accusatory pleadings are filed in such cases in the same court, the court may order them to be consolidated."

As a threshold matter, we conclude that the charges in question met the statutory requirements for joinder. The sexual offense charges were properly joined with the murder count because they are assaultive crimes against the person and therefore belong to the same class of crimes. The counts involving defendant's attempts to evade arrest and to dissuade and intimidate the witnesses who testified at the grand jury proceeding were connected together in their commission with the murder count because defendant's apparent motive for resisting arrest and intimidating witnesses was to avoid criminal liability for Katrina's murder. We observe that the one count charging defendant with being under the influence of a controlled substance at the time of his arrest is neither in the same class of crimes nor connected together in its commission with the murder charge. Because the drug offense occurred in conjunction with the other crimes stemming from defendant's arrest, however, it was connected together in its commission with those offenses and therefore properly joined.

Defendant does not suggest there was any failure in meeting the statutory requirements for joinder. He points out, however, that a court has discretion to order severance of charges "in the interests of justice and for good cause shown," even when the requirements of section 954 are satisfied. Defendant contends that the court abused its discretion by refusing to sever trial on the murder charge from trial on all other joined counts.

3. A court has discretion to order separate trials

The law favors the joinder of counts because such a course of action promotes efficiency. Nonetheless, as defendant correctly observes, a trial court has discretion to order that properly joined charges be tried separately. Likewise, although a trial court is authorized to consolidate two or more accusatory pleadings for trial in an appropriate case, it is not required to do so.

In exercising its discretion in this regard, the court weighs "the potential prejudice of joinder against the state's strong interest in the efficiency of a joint trial." * * *

If the evidence underlying the joined charges would have been cross-admissible at hypothetical separate trials, "that factor alone is normally sufficient to dispel any suggestion of prejudice and to justify a trial court's refusal to sever properly joined charges." Relevant to our inquiry here, it is sufficient that evidence supporting the various noncapital crimes would be admissible in a separate murder trial. As this court has explained, " 'two-way' cross-admissibility is not required." * * *

a. Joinder of the sexual assault counts

* * * Defendant argues that the court's findings regarding the factual similarities between the sexual assaults against Robyn G. and Billie B. and the sexual assaults underlying the murder charge were insufficient to establish cross-admissibility under Evidence Code section 1101, subdivision (b).[6] * * *

[6] Evidence Code section 1101, subdivision (b) (Evidence Code section 1101(b)) states, "(b) Nothing in this section prohibits the admission of evidence that a person committed a crime, civil wrong, or other act when relevant to prove some fact (such as motive, opportunity, intent, preparation, plan, knowledge, identity, absence of mistake or accident, or whether a defendant in a prosecution for an unlawful sexual act or attempted unlawful sexual act did not reasonably and in good faith believe that the victim consented) other than his or her disposition to commit such an act."

We need not resolve the parties' debate concerning whether the evidence supporting the sexual assault crimes was sufficiently similar to the evidence underlying the murder charge to permit admission under Evidence Code section 1101(b) to prove intent, common plan, or identity in a separate trial on the murder count. This is because the sexual assaults evidence would have been cross-admissible pursuant to Evidence Code section 1108 to show defendant's propensity to commit the rape and forcible oral copulation upon which both the murder charge and the special circumstance allegations were based.

Evidence Code section 1108 provides that "[i]n a criminal action in which the defendant is accused of a sexual offense, evidence of the defendant's commission of another sexual offense or offenses is not made inadmissible by Section 1101 if the evidence is not inadmissible pursuant to Section 352." Defendant was "accused of a sexual offense" within the meaning of Evidence Code section 1108 because it was alleged he murdered Katrina during the commission of rape and forcible oral copulation, both of which are "sexual offenses" as defined by Evidence Code section 1108, subdivision (d)(1).

We are persuaded furthermore that the evidence supporting the sexual assault crimes that was known to the court at the time of the severance motion would not have been inadmissible under Evidence Code section 352 in a separate trial on the murder count. A court deciding whether evidence of one or more sexual offenses meeting the definitional requirements of Evidence Code section 1108 should nonetheless be excluded pursuant to Evidence Code section 352 undertakes a careful and specialized inquiry to determine whether the danger of undue prejudice from the propensity evidence substantially outweighs its probative value. * * *

The probative value of the sexual assaults evidence was substantial. First, the evidence supporting the sexual assault charges involving Robyn G. and Billie B. was relatively similar to that supporting the murder count. Each of the victims was an SHD "groupie," in each incident defendant raped his victim and forced her to orally copulate him and, in each instance, defendant forcibly prevented the victim from leaving and ignored her pleas to stop. The sexual assaults occurred no more than three years after the murder and were therefore not remote, which further increased their probative value. * * *

If the prejudicial effect of the sexual assaults evidence would substantially outweigh its probative value in a separate trial on the murder count, it would defeat cross-admissibility of the evidence. The admission of this evidence would not have been unduly prejudicial, however. Although the sexual assaults were demeaning, disturbing, and unsavory, their underlying facts paled in comparison to the horrendous nature of the murder. The sexual assaults evidence was considerably less inflammatory than the murder and, therefore, its admission would not likely have had an unduly prejudicial impact on a jury. * * *[a]

Finally, defendant emphasizes that at the time of the court's ruling he had not been convicted of the sexual assaults against Robyn G. and Billie B. We agree that the absence of a conviction would increase the prejudicial impact of the evidence at a separate trial on the murder count because the jury might be tempted to convict defendant of murder as punishment for having escaped criminal liability for subsequent crimes. This circumstance does not tip the balance against cross-admissibility, however. Just as defendant bears a heavy burden to overcome the preference for a single trial of properly joined counts, he likewise faces a presumption favoring the admissibility of sexual offense evidence under Evidence Code section 1108 to show propensity to commit the charged offense. * * *

[a] Compare *Hughes v. United States*, 150 A.3d 289 (D.C.2016) (where defendant jointly charged with sexual abuse in workplace and related charges concerning three women under his supervision, the case against one of the women should be severed from the other two, for the "graphic" evidence of the crimes against her—kidnapping and forcible oral and anal intercourse—would prejudice defendant in the trial of the misdemeanor sexual contact counts involving the two others).

b. Joinder of the resisting arrest counts

The indictment charged defendant with nine crimes in connection with the incident in late January 1998 in which he fled from officers and then barricaded himself inside a residence until tear gas forced him outside and he was apprehended. As relevant here, the charges included two counts of resisting an executive officer, two counts of brandishing a handgun to resist arrest, and one count each of assault on a peace officer, felony vandalism, and being under the influence of a controlled substance.

The prosecution made the following offer of proof in opposition to the defense motion to sever trial on these counts from trial on the murder count. By late 1997, defendant was aware he was a suspect in Katrina's murder. On the evening of January 30, 1998, officers noticed two individuals, one of whom was later identified as defendant, riding bicycles without headlights. When they approached the pair, defendant fled, ignoring the officers' order to stop. The officers gave chase. As they got closer, defendant pulled a gun from his waistband and threatened to shoot himself. Defendant then jumped a fence and ran to a nearby home, where he beat on the door and demanded to be let inside. The occupants complied, but eventually left the house. Meanwhile, defendant barricaded himself inside. A Ventura County SWAT team was called to the scene but the standoff continued for hours. After tear gas was deployed, defendant went out of the house and back inside several times. On one occasion, he crawled on his hands and knees with a knife in his hand, and slashed at one of the approaching officers, then retreated into the house. He was apprehended the next time he emerged when a group of officers managed to tackle and handcuff him. A blood sample taken from defendant shortly after the incident showed the presence of methamphetamine. Subsequent to defendant's arrest, he told an acquaintance that he felt like a "dumb fuck" for running from the police because he thought he was being arrested for murder, not for a bicycle infraction. * * *

Evidence that defendant, thinking he was being arrested for murder, fled from police and resisted arrest by engaging in a dramatic, hours-long standoff generally would be admissible at a separate trial on the murder charge to show his consciousness of guilt for killing Katrina. Likewise, evidence of the murder generally would be cross-admissible in a separate trial on the resisting arrest charges to help explain the intensity of his efforts to evade police. We reject defendant's assertion that the bulk of the evidence of events surrounding his arrest served no purpose other than to prejudice him.

Defendant repeats the argument advanced by his trial counsel at the hearing that there were any number of reasons why defendant would have fled the police other than a consciousness of guilt for Katrina's murder. His argument demonstrates only that the evidence proffered by the prosecution regarding defendant's motive for evading police was disputed by the defense. He points to no case, and we have located none, suggesting that a finding of cross-admissibility is an abuse of discretion simply because the defense has challenged the inferences that may be drawn from the proffered evidence.

Because any inference of prejudice from the joinder was dispelled by the cross-admissibility of the evidence, the court did not abuse its discretion in declining to sever trial on the murder count from trial on the charges arising from incident relating to defendant's arrest.

c. Consolidation of the witness dissuasion counts

After defendant was charged with Katrina's murder, the sexual assaults on her and two other victims, and the crimes stemming from the incident relating to his arrest, a second indictment was issued in May 1999 charging defendant with five counts that involved various attempts to dissuade witnesses who had testified at the earlier grand jury proceeding. Specifically, defendant was charged with three counts of dissuading a witness by force or threat, and the solicitation of, and conspiracy to commit, those crimes. In connection with the conspiracy count, it was alleged that the crime was committed for the benefit of and in association with a criminal street gang, for purposes of sentence enhancement under section 186.22, subdivision (b). * * *

We conclude the court did not abuse its discretion in ordering consolidation. Notably, the victims identified in the second indictment were the witnesses who testified against defendant in the grand jury proceeding that led to the original 25-count indictment. Evidence supporting the witness dissuasion charges therefore generally would have been cross-admissible in a separate trial on all of the charges in the first indictment to show defendant's consciousness of guilt as to those counts.

On appeal, defendant again acknowledges that evidence of his attempts to dissuade witnesses from testifying was relevant to show his consciousness of guilt as to the murder count. He asserts, however, that the inference of prejudice was not dispelled by the cross-admissibility of the evidence because of the voluminous amount of highly inflammatory evidence relating to his gang membership and White supremacist views, his obscene and vulgar writings, his "Mansonesque" psychosexual power over young women, and his perverse relationship with his mother that was admitted to prove the witness dissuasion counts and the associated gang enhancement.

In these respects, defendant's argument is based on evidence developed later at trial, not on the facts known to the trial court at the time it ruled on the motion to consolidate the indictments. Although the points he raises are relevant to the question whether consolidation of the charges and denial of severance resulted in gross unfairness in violation of his right to due process (see post), these argument have no bearing on the question whether the court's ruling on the motion to consolidate was an abuse of discretion.

4. Constitutionality of trial on the joined charges

Even when we conclude, as we do here, that the trial court acted well within its discretion in denying severance or consolidating charges, we must further inquire whether events after the court's ruling demonstrate that joinder actually resulted in "gross unfairness" amounting to a denial of defendant's constitutional right to fair trial or due process of law. Our review of the trial record in the case discloses there was no gross unfairness. * * *

Defendant argues more generally that the result of the court's refusal to sever the trial on the murder count from trial on all other counts was a trial in which the "jury's view of the actual evidence of the capital crime was hopelessly entangled with evidence of defendant's character." For example, defendant argues, joinder permitted the admission of evidence of his "bizarre and scary behavior" while attempting to evade arrest, as well as evidence of the vulgar, antisocial, and frightening beliefs he embraced by virtue of his membership in a White supremacist gang. According to defendant, the "sheer amount of evidence that was extraneous and fundamentally irrelevant" to the murder charge "had everything to do with the jury's willingness to convict defendant of it."

We disagree with defendant that the evidence supporting the sexual offenses, resisting arrest, and witness dissuasion counts was extraneous and irrelevant to the murder count. Rather, for the reasons previously discussed, all three groups of crimes were bound up with proving defendant's guilt of the murder and the evidence developed at trial was properly admitted for that purpose. For example, the evidence regarding the SHD gang explained the code of silence, which tended to show why the two eyewitnesses did not report the murder to law enforcement until years after the incident. Nor was the evidence of guilt of the murder count substantially weaker than the evidence supporting defendant's guilt of the other crimes so as to render his trial grossly unfair. * * *

Pointing to the prosecutor's closing argument, which urged the jury to consider the various sexual crimes against the different victims as "not just one evil act [but as] all the evil together," defendant argues finally that the jury could not reasonably have been expected to "compartmentalize the evidence" so as to decide each count individually on the evidence presented. The record does not support his assertion. The prosecutor's point was that were the jury to find defendant committed rape and forcible oral copulation against some of the victims, it could infer that defendant had a disposition to commit, and likely did commit, all of the charged sexual offenses, an argument he was entitled to make. The record shows moreover that the jury was instructed on the elements of each of the charged crimes, told that "each count charges a distinct crime," and directed to "decide each count separately." Absent some showing to the contrary, we presume the jury followed the court's instructions. No such showing was made here.

In resolving a claim that joinder resulted in gross unfairness in violation of a defendant's right to a fair trial and due process, we have observed that a judgment will be reversed on this ground only if it is "reasonably probable that the jury was influenced [by the joinder] in its verdict of guilt." For all the reasons explained above, we conclude there was no reasonable probability that the joinder of counts tainted the jury's verdicts in this case.

NOTES AND QUESTIONS

1. ***"Conflicting testimonial imperatives."*** While "a need for severance arises when a defendant 'makes a convincing showing that he has both important testimony to give concerning one count and a strong need to refrain from testifying on the other count,' " *United States v. Best*, 235 F.Supp.2d 923 (N.D.Ind.2002), defendants have rarely succeeded in obtaining a severance on this basis. *Best* is an exception. The court found there were "conflicting testimonial imperatives," as (i) "Defendant's previously asserted alibi defense to the murder-related counts (i.e., that he was at a hospital with his son and others at the time of the murder) * * * may be critically important if the jury accepts it"; and (ii) "his best hope for acquittal is to remain silent on the drug-related counts and force the Government to prove its case without the benefit of his testimony." The court emphasized that the instant case was "different" from most involving such a severance question, as (a) this was "a death penalty case" and (b) because "the drug distribution conspiracy charge * * * is an offense element for the murder-related charge," an acquittal on that charge would, under *Ashe v. Swenson*, p. 1049, "almost certainly" bar a subsequent murder prosecution.

2. ***Prejudicial effect of joinder.*** In Andrew D. Leipold & Hossein A. Abbasi, *The Impact of Joinder and Severance on Federal Criminal Cases: An Empirical Study*, 59 Vand.L.Rev. 349, 401 (2006), the authors present extensive statistics and analysis of nearly 20,000 federal criminal trials over a five-year period, which clearly establish "that the joinder of charges has a prejudicial effect on the defendant, increasing the chances of conviction of the most serious charge by more than 10%." From this, the authors conclude "that courts currently miscalculate the defense and governmental interests when deciding whether to sever. In particular, we claim that judges undervalue the defendants' interests, in part because they may assume that defendants are trying to gain some tactical or unfair advantage from separate trials. This fear seems exaggerated; we could not identify any illegitimate reason why a defendant would seek severance. At the same time, the fear of increased trials in a world of more generous severance also seems overdone. More severance would undoubtedly lead to some increase in the number of proceedings, but given the predictive effect of the first trial outcome on the rest of the cases, it is questionable whether all, or even most, subsequent trials would find their way to the courtroom. At a minimum, the existence of the joinder effect calls for a reexamination of the doctrine. A significant increase in the likelihood of conviction, one that appears to be based on factors that detract from the fairness of the proceedings and even the accuracy of the outcome, is a steep price to pay for more efficient proceedings. The critical need to reduce those costs without materially undermining the benefits of consolidation means that even dry and technical issues, like joinder and severance, warrant another look." Id. at 401. As for specific remedies, they suggest: (i) placing "a heavy thumb on the defense side of the balance," either by providing "that a 'colorable' or 'prima facie' claim of prejudice

by the defense is sufficient to shift the burden to the government to prove that joinder will not cause undue harm," or at least by eliminating "the judicial requirement of 'substantial' or 'compelling' prejudice before severance is ordered"; or (ii) "perhaps a simple judicial refocus on the interests at stake, realizing that defendants' interests may be greater and the government's interest smaller than conventional wisdom suggests, might help avoid the routine approval of consolidated cases, decisions that now often seem reflexive rather than nuanced." Id. at 398–99.

§ 2. FAILURE TO JOIN RELATED OFFENSES

UNITED STATES V. DIXON

509 U.S. 688, 113 S.Ct. 2849, 125 L.Ed.2d 556 (1993).

JUSTICE SCALIA announced the judgment of the Court and delivered the opinion of the Court with respect to Parts I, II, and IV, and an opinion with respect to Parts III and V, in which JUSTICE KENNEDY joins. * * *

I

[Dixon, arrested for murder in D.C., was released on bail on the condition he not commit "any criminal offense," violation of which could result in, inter alia, contempt of court. While awaiting trial, Dixon was arrested and indicted for possession of cocaine with intent to distribute; on proof of that conduct he was found guilty of criminal contempt and sentenced to 180 days in jail. Dixon later moved to dismiss the cocaine indictment on double jeopardy grounds; the trial court granted the motion. Foster's wife obtained a civil protection order (CPO) in a D.C. court because of his prior physical attacks upon her; the order required that he not "molest, assault, or in any manner threaten or physically abuse" her. Later, the wife with apparent knowledge of the prosecutor sought to have Foster held in contempt for numerous violations of the CPO, including threats on Nov. 12, March 26 and May 17 and assault on Nov. 6 and May 21. Foster was acquitted on the threats counts but was convicted on those two assault counts and other charges, resulting in him being sentenced to 600 days imprisonment. He was later charged by indictment with assault on Nov. 6 (Count I), threatening to injure on Nov. 12, March 26 and May 17 (Counts II-IV), and assault with intent to kill on May 21 (Count V). Foster's motion to dismiss on double jeopardy grounds was denied. The D.C. Court of Appeals consolidated the cases and, relying on *Grady v. Corbin*, 495 U.S. 508 (1990), ruled that both prosecutions were barred.]

II

* * *

The Double Jeopardy Clause * * * provides that no person shall "be subject for the same offence to be twice put in jeopardy of life or limb." This protection applies both to successive punishments and to successive prosecutions for the same criminal offense. It is well established that criminal contempt, at least the sort enforced through nonsummary proceedings, is "a crime in the ordinary sense." * * *

In both the multiple punishment and multiple prosecution contexts, this Court has concluded that where the two offenses for which the defendant is punished or tried cannot survive the "same-elements" test, the double jeopardy bar applies. See, e.g., *Brown v. Ohio,* 432 U.S. 161 (1977); *Blockburger v. United States,* 284 U.S. 299 (1932) (multiple punishment); *Gavieres v. United States,* 220 U.S. 338 (1911) (successive prosecutions). The same-elements test, sometimes referred to as the *"Blockburger"* test, inquires whether each offense contains an element not contained in the other; if not, they are the "same offence" and double jeopardy bars additional punishment and successive prosecution. * * *

We recently held in *Grady* that in addition to passing the *Blockburger* test, a subsequent prosecution must satisfy a "same-conduct" test to avoid the double jeopardy bar. The *Grady* test provides that, "if, to establish an essential element of an offense charged in that prosecution, the government will prove conduct that constitutes an offense for which the defendant has already been prosecuted," a second prosecution may not be had.

III

A

The first question before us today is whether *Blockburger* analysis permits subsequent prosecution in this new criminal contempt context, where judicial order has prohibited criminal act. If it does, we must then proceed to consider whether *Grady* also permits it.

We begin with *Dixon*. The statute applicable in Dixon's contempt prosecution provides that "[a] person who has been conditionally released . . . and who has violated a condition of release shall be subject to . . . prosecution for contempt of court." Obviously, Dixon could not commit an "offence" under this provision until an order setting out conditions was issued. The statute by itself imposes no legal obligation on anyone. Dixon's cocaine possession, although an offense under [the] D.C. Code, was not an offense under [the aforementioned contempt statute] until a judge incorporated the statutory drug offense into his release order.

In this situation, in which the contempt sanction is imposed for violating the order through commission of the incorporated drug offense, the later attempt to prosecute Dixon for the drug offense resembles the situation that produced our judgment of double jeopardy in *Harris v. Oklahoma,* 433 U.S. 682 (1977). There we held that a subsequent prosecution for robbery with a firearm was barred by the Double Jeopardy Clause, because the defendant had already been tried for felony-murder based on the same underlying felony. We have described our terse per curiam in *Harris* as standing for the proposition that, for double jeopardy purposes, "the crime generally described as felony murder" is not "a separate offense distinct from its various elements." So too here, the "crime" of violating a condition of release cannot be abstracted from the "element" of the violated condition. The Dixon court order incorporated the entire governing criminal code in the same manner as the *Harris* felony-murder statute incorporated the several enumerated felonies. Here, as in *Harris,* the underlying substantive criminal offense is "a species of lesser-included offense."

Both the Government and Justice Blackmun contend that the legal obligation in Dixon's case may serve "interests . . . fundamentally different" from the substantive criminal law, because it derives in part from the determination of a court rather than a determination of the legislature. That distinction seems questionable, since the court's power to establish conditions of release, and to punish their violation, was conferred by statute; the legislature was the ultimate source of both the criminal and the contempt prohibition. More importantly, however, the distinction is of no moment for purposes of the Double Jeopardy Clause, the text of which looks to whether the offenses are the same, not the interests that the offenses violate. And this Court stated long ago that criminal contempt, at least in its nonsummary form, "is a crime in every fundamental respect." Because Dixon's drug offense did not include any element not contained in his previous contempt offense, his subsequent prosecution violates the Double Jeopardy Clause.

The foregoing analysis obviously applies as well to Count I of the indictment against Foster, charging assault, based on the same event that was the subject of his prior contempt conviction for violating the provision of the CPO forbidding him to commit simple assault. The subsequent prosecution for assault fails the *Blockburger* test, and is barred.

B

The remaining four counts in Foster, assault with intent to kill (Count V) and threats to injure or kidnap (Counts II–IV), are not barred under *Blockburger*. As to Count V: * * * At the contempt hearing, the court stated that Ana Foster's attorney, who prosecuted the contempt, would have to prove first, knowledge of a CPO, and second, a willful violation of one of its conditions, here simple assault as defined by the criminal code.[5] On the basis of the same episode, Foster was then indicted for assault with intent to kill. Under governing law, that offense requires proof of specific intent to kill; simple assault does not. Similarly, the contempt offense required proof of knowledge of the CPO, which assault with intent to kill does not. Applying the *Blockburger* elements test, the result is clear: These crimes were different offenses and the subsequent prosecution did not violate the Double Jeopardy Clause.[7]

Counts II, III, and IV of Foster's indictment are likewise not barred. These charged Foster under § 22–2307 (forbidding anyone to "threate[n] . . . to kidnap any person or to injure the person of another or physically damage the property of any person") for his alleged threats on three separate dates. Foster's contempt prosecution included charges that, on the same dates, he violated the CPO provision ordering that he not "in any manner threaten" Ana Foster. Conviction of the contempt required willful violation of the CPO—which conviction under § 22–2307 did not; and conviction under § 22–2307 required that the threat be a threat to kidnap, to inflict bodily injury, or to damage property—which conviction of the contempt (for violating the CPO provision that Foster not "in any manner threaten") did not.[8] Each offense therefore contained a separate element, and the *Blockburger* test for double jeopardy was not met.

IV

Having found that at least some of the counts at issue here are not barred by the *Blockburger* test, we must consider whether they are barred by the new, additional double jeopardy test we announced three Terms ago in *Grady v. Corbin*. They undoubtedly are, since *Grady* prohibits "a subsequent prosecution if, to establish an essential element of an offense charged in that prosecution [here, assault as an element of assault with intent to kill, or threatening as an element of threatening bodily injury], the government will prove conduct that constitutes an offense for

---

[5] Given this requirement of willful violation of the order, Justice White's desire to "put to the side the CPO," because it only "triggered the court's authority" cannot be reconciled with his desire to "compar[e] the substantive offenses of which respondents stood accused." The "substantive offense" of criminal contempt is willful violation of a court order. Far from a mere jurisdictional device, that order (or CPO) is the centerpiece of the entire proceeding. Its terms define the prohibited conduct, its existence supports imposition of a criminal penalty, and willful violation of it is necessary for conviction. To ignore the CPO when determining whether two offenses are the "same" is no more possible than putting aside the statutory definitions of criminal offenses. * * *

[7] Justice White's suggestion that if Foster received a lesser-included-offense instruction on assault at his trial for assault with intent to kill, we would uphold a conviction on that lesser count is simply wrong. Under basic *Blockburger* analysis, Foster may neither be tried a second time for assault nor again convicted for assault, as we have concluded as to Count I (charging simple assault). Thus, Foster certainly does receive the "full constitutional protection to which he is entitled": he may neither be tried nor convicted a second time for assault. That does not affect the conclusion that trial and conviction for assault with intent to kill are not barred. It merely illustrates the unremarkable fact that one offense (simple assault) may be an included offense of two offenses (violation of the CPO for assault, and assault with intent to kill) that are separate offenses under *Blockburger*.

[8] We think it is highly artificial to interpret the CPO's prohibition of threatening "in any manner," as Justice White would interpret it, to refer only to threats that violate the District's criminal laws. The only threats meeting that definition would have been threats to do physical harm, to kidnap, or to damage property. Threats to stalk, to frighten, to cause intentional embarrassment, to make harassing phone calls, to make false reports to employers or prospective employers, to harass by phone calls or otherwise at work—to mention only a few of the additional threats that might be anticipated in this domestic situation—would not be covered. Surely "in any manner threaten" should cover at least all threats to commit acts that would be tortious under D.C. law (which would be consistent with the trial court's later reference to a "legal threat"). Thus, under our *Blockburger* analysis the aggravated threat counts and the assault-with-intent-to-kill count come out the same way.

which the defendant has already been prosecuted [here, the assault and the threatening, which conduct constituted the offense of violating the CPO]."

We have concluded, however, that *Grady* must be overruled. Unlike *Blockburger* analysis, whose definition of what prevents two crimes from being the "same offence," has deep historical roots and has been accepted in numerous precedents of this Court, *Grady* lacks constitutional roots. The "same-conduct" rule it announced is wholly inconsistent with earlier Supreme Court precedent and with the clear common-law understanding of double jeopardy. We need not discuss the many proofs of these statements, which were set forth at length in the *Grady* dissent. We will respond, however, to the contrary contentions of today's pro-*Grady* dissents.

The centerpiece of Justice Souter's analysis is an appealing theory of a "successive prosecution" strand of the Double Jeopardy Clause that has a different meaning from its supposed "successive punishment" strand. We have often noted that the Clause serves the function of preventing both successive punishment and successive prosecution, but there is no authority, except *Grady,* for the proposition that it has different meanings in the two contexts. That is perhaps because it is embarrassing to assert that the single term "same offence" (the words of the Fifth Amendment at issue here) has two different meanings—that what is the same offense is yet not the same offense. * * *[14]

But *Grady* was not only wrong in principle; it has already proved unstable in application. Less than two years after it came down, in *United States v. Felix,* 503 U.S. 378 (1992), we were forced to recognize a large exception to it. There we concluded that a subsequent prosecution for conspiracy to manufacture, possess, and distribute methamphetamine was not barred by a previous conviction for attempt to manufacture the same substance. We offered as a justification for avoiding a "literal" (i.e., faithful) reading of *Grady* "longstanding authority" to the effect that prosecution for conspiracy is not precluded by prior prosecution for the substantive offense. Of course the very existence of such a large and longstanding "exception" to the *Grady* rule gave cause for concern that the rule was not an accurate expression of the law. This "past practice" excuse is not available to support the ignoring of *Grady* in the present case, since there is no Supreme Court precedent even discussing this fairly new breed of successive prosecution (criminal contempt for violation of a court order prohibiting a crime, followed by prosecution for the crime itself).

A hypothetical based on the facts in *Harris* reinforces the conclusion that *Grady* is a continuing source of confusion and must be overruled. Suppose the State first tries the defendant for felony-murder, based on robbery, and then indicts the defendant for robbery with a firearm in the same incident. Absent *Grady,* our cases provide a clear answer to the double-jeopardy claim in this situation. Under *Blockburger,* the second prosecution is not barred—as it clearly was not barred at common law * * *.[15]

---

[14] It is unclear what definition of "same offence" Justice Souter would have us adopt for successive prosecution. At times, he appears content with our having added to *Blockburger* the *Grady* same-conduct test. At other times, however, he adopts an ultra-*Grady* "same transaction" rule, which would require the Government to try together all offenses (regardless of the differences in the statutes) based on one event. Of course, the same-transaction test, long espoused by Justice Brennan, see, e.g., *Brown v. Ohio,* (concurring opinion), has been consistently rejected by the Court.

[15] Justice Souter dislikes this result because it violates "the principles behind the protection from successive prosecution included in the Fifth Amendment." The "principles behind" the Fifth Amendment are more likely to be honored by following longstanding practice than by following intuition. But in any case, Justice Souter's concern that prosecutors will bring separate prosecutions in order to perfect their case seems unjustified. They have little to gain and much to lose from such a strategy. Under *Ashe v. Swenson,* an acquittal in the first prosecution might well bar litigation of certain facts essential to the second one—though a conviction in the first prosecution would not excuse the Government from proving the same facts the second time. Surely, moreover, the Government must be deterred from abusive, repeated prosecutions of a single offender for similar offenses by the sheer press of other demands upon prosecutorial and judicial resources. Finally, even if Justice Souter's fear were well founded, no double-jeopardy bar short of a same-transaction analysis will eliminate this problem; but that interpretation of the

Having encountered today yet another situation in which the pre-*Grady* understanding of the Double Jeopardy Clause allows a second trial, though the "same-conduct" test would not, we think it time to acknowledge what is now, three years after *Grady,* compellingly clear: the case was a mistake. We do not lightly reconsider a precedent, but, because *Grady* contradicted an "unbroken line of decisions," contained "less than accurate" historical analysis, and has produced "confusion," we do so here. Although stare decisis is the "preferred course" in constitutional adjudication, "when governing decisions are unworkable or are badly reasoned, 'this Court has never felt constrained to follow precedent.' " We would mock stare decisis and only add chaos to our double jeopardy jurisprudence by pretending that *Grady* survives when it does not. We therefore accept the Government's invitation to overrule *Grady* * * *.

V

Dixon's subsequent prosecution, as well as Count I of Foster's subsequent prosecution, violate the Double Jeopardy Clause.[18] For the reasons set forth in Part IV, the other Counts of Foster's subsequent prosecution do not violate the Double Jeopardy Clause.[19] * * *

CHIEF JUSTICE REHNQUIST, with whom JUSTICE O'CONNOR and JUSTICE THOMAS join, concurring in part and dissenting in part.

[I] join Parts I, II, and IV of the Court's opinion, and write separately to express my disagreement with Justice Scalia's application of *Blockburger* in Part III.

In my view, *Blockburger*'s same-elements test requires us to focus not on the terms of the particular court orders involved, but on the elements of contempt of court in the ordinary sense. Relying on *Harris v. Oklahoma,* a three-paragraph per curiam in an unargued case, Justice Scalia concludes otherwise today, and thus incorrectly finds in Part III-A of his opinion that the subsequent prosecutions of Dixon for drug distribution and of Foster for assault violated the Double Jeopardy Clause. In so doing, Justice Scalia rejects the traditional view—shared by every federal court of appeals and state supreme court that addressed the issue prior to *Grady*—that, as a general matter, double jeopardy does not bar a subsequent prosecution based on conduct for which a defendant has been held in criminal contempt. * * *

At the heart of this pre-*Grady* consensus lay the common belief that there was no double-jeopardy bar under *Blockburger.* There, we stated that two offenses are different for purposes of double jeopardy if "each provision requires proof of a fact which the other does not." Applying this test to the offenses at bar, it is clear that the elements of the governing contempt provision are entirely different from the elements of the substantive crimes. Contempt of court comprises two elements: (i) a court order made known to the defendant, followed by (ii) willful violation of that order. Neither of those elements is necessarily satisfied by proof that a defendant has committed the substantive offenses of assault or drug distribution. Likewise, no element of either of those substantive offenses is necessarily satisfied by proof that a defendant has been found guilty of contempt of court.

Justice Scalia grounds his departure from *Blockburger*'s customary focus on the statutory elements of the crimes charged on *Harris v. Oklahoma,* an improbable font of authority. A summary reversal, like *Harris,* "does not enjoy the full precedential value of a case argued on the merits." Today's decision shows the pitfalls inherent in reading too much into a "terse per curiam." Justice Scalia's discussion of *Harris* is nearly as long as *Harris* itself and consists largely of a quote not from *Harris,* but from a subsequent opinion analyzing *Harris.* Justice Scalia then concludes that *Harris* somehow requires us to look to the facts that must be proven under the particular

Double Jeopardy Clause has been soundly rejected, and would require overruling numerous precedents, the latest of which is barely a year old, *United States v. Felix.*

[18] Justices White, Stevens, and Souter concur in this portion of the judgment.

[19] Justice Blackmun concurs only in the judgment with respect to this portion.

court orders in question (rather than under the general law of criminal contempt) in determining whether contempt and the related substantive offenses are the same for double jeopardy purposes. This interpretation of *Harris* is both unprecedented and mistaken.

Our double jeopardy cases applying *Blockburger* have focused on the statutory elements of the offenses charged, not on the facts that must be proven under the particular indictment at issue—an indictment being the closest analogue to the court orders in this case. By focusing on the facts needed to show a violation of the specific court orders involved in this case, and not on the generic elements of the crime of contempt of court, Justice Scalia's double-jeopardy analysis bears a striking resemblance to that found in *Grady*—not what one would expect in an opinion that overrules *Grady*. * * *

But there is a more fundamental reason why the offenses in this case are not analogous to greater and lesser included offenses. A lesser included offense is defined as one that is "necessarily included" within the statutory elements of another offense. Taking the facts of *Harris* as an example, a defendant who commits armed robbery necessarily has satisfied one of the statutory elements of felony murder. The same cannot be said, of course, about this case: A defendant who is guilty of possession with intent to distribute cocaine or of assault has not necessarily satisfied any statutory element of criminal contempt. Nor, for that matter, can it be said that a defendant who is held in criminal contempt has necessarily satisfied any element of those substantive crimes. In short, the offenses for which Dixon and Foster were prosecuted in this case cannot be analogized to greater and lesser included offenses; hence, they are separate and distinct for double jeopardy purposes.[3] * * *

JUSTICE WHITE, with whom JUSTICE STEVENS joins, and with whom JUSTICE SOUTER joins as to Part I, concurring in the judgment in part and dissenting in part. * * *

[I]n this case, the offense for which Dixon was held in contempt was possession with intent to distribute drugs. Since he previously had been indicted for precisely the same offense, the double jeopardy bar should apply. * * * All of the offenses for which Foster was either convicted or acquitted in the contempt proceeding were similar to, or lesser included offenses of, those charged in the subsequent indictment. Because "the Fifth Amendment forbids successive prosecution * * * for a greater and lesser included offense," *Brown v. Ohio,* (1977), the second set of trials should be barred in their entirety.

Professing strict adherence to *Blockburger*'s so-called "same elements" test, Justice Scalia opts for a more circuitous approach. The elements of the crime of contempt, he reasons, in this instance are (1) the existence and knowledge of a court, or CPO; and (2) commission of the underlying substantive offense. Where the criminal conduct that forms the basis of the contempt order is identical to that charged in the subsequent trial, Justice Scalia concludes, *Blockburger* forbids retrial. All elements of Foster's simple assault offense being included in his previous contempt offense, prosecution on that ground is precluded. The same is true of Dixon's drug offense. I agree with this conclusion, though would reach it rather differently: Because in a successive prosecution case the risk is that a person will have to defend himself more than once against the same charge, I would have put to the side the CPO (which, as it were, triggered the

[3] Assuming, arguendo, that Justice Scalia's reading of *Harris v. Oklahoma* is accurate, and that we must look to the terms of the particular court orders involved, I believe Justice Scalia is correct in differentiating among the various counts in Foster. The court order there provided that Foster must "not molest, assault, or in any manner threaten or physically abuse" his estranged wife. For Foster to be found in contempt of court, his wife need have proved only that he had knowledge of the court order and that he assaulted or threatened her, but not that he assaulted her with intent to kill (Count V) or that he threatened to inflict bodily harm (Counts II-IV). So the crime of criminal contempt in Foster, even if analyzed under Justice Scalia's reading of *Harris,* is nonetheless a different offense under *Blockburger* than the crimes alleged in Counts II-V of the indictment, since "each provision requires proof of a fact which the other does not." Because Justice Scalia finds no double-jeopardy bar with respect to those counts, I agree with the result reached in Part III-B of his opinion.

court's authority to punish the defendant for acts already punishable under the criminal laws) and compared the substantive offenses of which respondents stood accused in both prosecutions.

The significance of our disaccord is far more manifest where an element is added to the second prosecution. Under Justice Scalia's view, the double jeopardy barrier is then removed because each offense demands proof of an element the other does not: Foster's conviction for contempt requires proof of the existence and knowledge of a CPO, which conviction for assault with intent to kill does not; his conviction for assault with intent to kill requires proof of an intent to kill, which the contempt conviction did not. Finally, though he was acquitted in the contempt proceedings with respect to the alleged threats, his conviction under the threat charge in the subsequent trial required the additional proof that the threat be to kidnap, to inflict bodily injury, or to damage property. As to these counts, and absent any collateral estoppel problem, Justice Scalia finds that the Constitution does not prohibit retrial.

The distinction drawn by Justice Scalia is predicated on a reading of the Double Jeopardy Clause that is abstracted from the purposes the constitutional provision is designed to promote. To focus on the statutory elements of a crime makes sense where cumulative punishment is at stake, for there the aim simply is to uncover legislative intent. The *Blockburger* inquiry, accordingly, serves as a means to determine this intent, as our cases have recognized. But, as Justice Souter shows, adherence to legislative will has very little to do with the important interests advanced by double jeopardy safeguards against successive prosecutions. The central purpose of the Double Jeopardy Clause being to protect against vexatious multiple prosecutions, these interests go well beyond the prevention of unauthorized punishment. The same-elements test is an inadequate safeguard, for it leaves the constitutional guarantee at the mercy of a legislature's decision to modify statutory definitions. Significantly, therefore, this Court has applied an inflexible version of the same-elements test only once, in 1911, in a successive prosecution case, see *Gavieres v. United States,* and has since noted that "[t]he *Blockburger* test is not the only standard for determining whether successive prosecutions impermissibly involve the same offense." *Brown.* Rather, "[e]ven if two offenses are sufficiently different to permit the imposition of consecutive sentences, successive prosecutions will be barred in some circumstances where the second prosecution requires the relitigation of factual issues already resolved by the first."

Take the example of Count V in Foster: For all intents and purposes, the offense for which he was convicted in the contempt proceeding was his assault against his wife. The majority, its eyes fixed on the rigid elements-test, would have his fate turn on whether his subsequent prosecution charges "simple assault" or "assault with intent to kill." Yet, because the crime of "simple assault" is included within the crime of "assault with intent to kill," the reasons that bar retrial under the first hypothesis are equally present under the second: These include principles of finality; protecting Foster from "embarrassment" and "expense"; and preventing the government from gradually fine-tuning its strategy, thereby minimizing exposure to a mistaken conviction.

Analysis of the threat charges (Counts II-IV) makes the point more clearly still. In the contempt proceeding, it will be recalled, Foster was acquitted of the-arguably lesser-included-offense of threatening "in any manner." As we have stated, "the law attaches particular significance to an acquittal. To permit a second trial after an acquittal, however mistaken the acquittal might have been, would present an unacceptably high risk that the Government, with its vastly superior resources, might wear down the defendant so that 'even though innocent he may be found guilty.'" To allow the government to proceed on the threat counts would present precisely the risk of erroneous conviction the Clause seeks to avoid. That the prosecution had to establish the existence of the CPO in the first trial, in short, does not in any way modify the prejudice potentially caused to a defendant by consecutive trials.

To respond, as the majority appears to do, that concerns relating to the defendant's interests against repeat trials are "unjustified" because prosecutors "have little to gain and much to lose" from bringing successive prosecutions and because "the Government must be deterred from abusive, repeated prosecutions of a single offender for similar offenses by the sheer press of other demands upon prosecutorial and judicial resources," is to get things exactly backwards. The majority's prophesies might be correct, and double jeopardy might be a problem that will simply take care of itself. Not so, however, according to the Constitution, whose firm prohibition against double jeopardy cannot be satisfied by wishful thinking. * * *

JUSTICE SOUTER, with whom JUSTICE STEVENS joins, concurring in the judgment in part and dissenting in part.

* * * I join Part I of Justice White's opinion, and I would hold, as he would, both the prosecution of Dixon and the prosecution of Foster under all the counts of the indictment against him to be barred by the Double Jeopardy Clause. * * *

In addressing multiple punishments, "the role of the constitutional guarantee is limited to assuring that the court does not exceed its legislative authorization by imposing multiple punishments for the same offense." *Brown v. Ohio.* Courts enforcing the federal guarantee against multiple punishment therefore must examine the various offenses for which a person is being punished to determine whether, as defined by the legislature, any two or more of them are the same offense. * * * We ask what the elements of each offense are as a matter of statutory interpretation, to determine whether the legislature intended "to impose separate sanctions for multiple offenses arising in the course of a single act or transaction." *Iannelli v. United States,* 420 U.S. 770 (1975). * * *

The interests at stake in avoiding successive prosecutions are different from those at stake in the prohibition against multiple punishments, and our cases reflect this reality. The protection against successive prosecutions is the central protection provided by the Clause. * * *

The Double Jeopardy Clause prevents the government from "mak[ing] repeated attempts to convict an individual for an alleged offense, thereby subjecting him to embarrassment, expense and ordeal and compelling him to live in a continuing state of anxiety and insecurity." The Clause addresses a further concern as well, that the government not be given the opportunity to rehearse its prosecution, "honing its trial strategies and perfecting its evidence through successive attempts at conviction," because this "enhanc[es] the possibility that even though innocent [the defendant] may be found guilty."

Consequently, while the government may punish a person separately for each conviction of at least as many different offenses as meet the *Blockburger* test, we have long held that it must sometimes bring its prosecutions for these offenses together. If a separate prosecution were permitted for every offense arising out of the same conduct, the government could manipulate the definitions of offenses, creating fine distinctions among them and permitting a zealous prosecutor to try a person again and again for essentially the same criminal conduct. While punishing different combinations of elements is consistent with the Double Jeopardy Clause in its limitation on the imposition of multiple punishments (a limitation rooted in concerns with legislative intent), permitting such repeated prosecutions would not be consistent with the principles underlying the Clause in its limitation on successive prosecution. The limitation on successive prosecution is thus a restriction on the government different in kind from that contained in the limitation on multiple punishments, and the government cannot get around the restriction on repeated prosecution of a single individual merely by precision in the way it defines its statutory offenses. Thus, "[t]he *Blockburger* test is not the only standard for determining whether successive prosecutions impermissibly involve the same offense. Even if two offenses are sufficiently different to permit the imposition of consecutive sentences, successive prosecutions will be barred in some circumstances where the second prosecution requires the relitigation of factual issues already resolved by the first." *Brown.*[*]

An example will show why this should be so. Assume three crimes: robbery with a firearm, robbery in a dwelling and simple robbery. The elements of the three crimes are the same, except that robbery with a firearm has the element that a firearm be used in the commission of the robbery while the other two crimes do not, and robbery in a dwelling has the element that the robbery occur in a dwelling while the other two crimes do not.

If a person committed a robbery in a dwelling with a firearm and was prosecuted for simple robbery, all agree he could not be prosecuted subsequently for either of the greater offenses of robbery with a firearm or robbery in a dwelling. Under the lens of *Blockburger,* however, if that same person were prosecuted first for robbery with a firearm, he could be prosecuted subsequently for robbery in a dwelling, even though he could not subsequently be prosecuted on the basis of that same robbery for simple robbery.[3] This is true simply because neither of the crimes, robbery with a firearm and robbery in a dwelling, is either identical to or a lesser-included offense of the other. But since the purpose of the Double Jeopardy Clause's protection against successive prosecutions is to prevent repeated trials in which a defendant will be forced to defend against the same charge again and again, and in which the government may perfect its presentation with dress rehearsal after dress rehearsal, it should be irrelevant that the second prosecution would require the defendant to defend himself not only from the charge that he committed the robbery, but also from the charge of some additional fact, in this case, that the scene of the crime was a dwelling.[4] If, instead, protection against successive prosecution were as limited as it would be by *Blockburger* alone, the doctrine would be as striking for its anomalies as for the limited protection it would provide. Thus, in the relatively few successive prosecution cases we have had over the years, we have not held that the *Blockburger* test is the only hurdle the government must clear. * * *

NOTES AND QUESTIONS

1. ***Multiple punishment.*** Pre-*Dixon*, the Supreme Court's treatment of the cumulative punishment branch of double jeopardy had taken on a somewhat different character. In *Albernaz v. United States*, 450 U.S. 333 (1981), the Court treated *Blockburger* as only a method for ascertaining legislative intent when nothing more concrete was available, stating that "the question of what punishments are constitutionally permissible is not different from the question of what punishment the Legislative Branch intended to be imposed." As the Court later put it in *Missouri v. Hunter*, 459 U.S. 359 (1983), where "a legislature specifically authorizes cumulative punishment under two statutes, regardless of whether those two statutes proscribe the 'same' conduct under *Blockburger*, a court's task of statutory construction is at an end and the prosecutor may seek and the trial court or jury may impose cumulative punishment under such statutes in a single trial."

---

* [Transposed footnote] In *Brown* we recognized that "[a]n exception may exist where the State is unable to proceed on the more serious charge at the outset because the additional facts necessary to sustain that charge have not occurred or have not been discovered despite the exercise of due diligence." [Editors' note: Lower courts have recognized such an exception, e.g., *Whittlesey v. State,* 606 A.2d 225 (Md.1992), stating it "would apply if a reasonable prosecutor, having full knowledge of the facts which were known and in the exercise of due diligence should have been known to the police and the prosecutor at the time, would not be satisfied that he or she would be able to establish the suspect's guilt beyond a reasonable doubt."]

3 Our cases have long made clear that the order in which one is prosecuted for two crimes alleged to be the same matters not in demonstrating a violation of double jeopardy. See *Brown v. Ohio* (1977) ("the sequence is immaterial").

4 The irrelevance of additional elements can be seen in the fact that, as every Member of the Court agrees, the Double Jeopardy Clause does provide protection not merely against prosecution a second time for literally the same offense, but also against prosecution for greater offenses in which the first crime was lesser-included, offenses that by definition require proof of one or more additional elements.

Consider now the post-*Dixon* case of *People v. Ream*, 750 N.W.2d 536 (Mich.2008), applying the *Albernaz-Hunter* approach. After Ream's trial at which he was convicted of both felony-murder and the predicate felony of criminal sexual assault, he was sentenced on both offenses. On appeal, in response to Ream's contention that such sentencing "violates the 'multiple punishments' strand of the Double Jeopardy Clause," the court affirmed. Because the two crimes had independent elements—killing a human being for felony murder, sexual penetration for criminal sexual assault—this manifested "a relatively clear legislative intent to allow multiple punishments."

Recalling that five Justices in *Dixon* agreed it would be "embarrassing to assert that the single term 'same offense' * * * has two different meanings," depending upon whether the issue is successive prosecution or multiple punishment, must it be concluded (1) that *Dixon* trumps *Albernaz* and *Hunter,* meaning *Ream* was wrongly decided; (2) that, on the other hand, by reconciling *Dixon* with *Albernaz* and *Hunter*, it is *Harris v. Oklahoma,* p. 1037, that is trumped, so that now (at least in Michigan) it would also be constitutionally permissible to have separate *prosecutions* for felony-murder and the underlying felony; or (3) that neither is the case?

As for option (2), at least one court has declined to go that route on the ground that "[m]ultiple punishments that result from a single prosecution do not subject a defendant to the evils attendant upon successful prosecutions," namely, "the 'embarrassment, expense and ordeal' of repetitive trials, 'compelling [the accused] to live in a continuing state of anxiety and insecurity,' and creating 'a risk of conviction through sheer governmental perseverance.' " *Ex parte Chaddock*, 369 S.W.3d 880 (Tex.Crim.App.2012). A concurring opinion in *Chaddock* suggested the "two different meanings" objection in *Dixon* should not be taken too seriously given Justice Scalia's view that the multiple punishment issue should be considered under the due process clause rather than the double jeopardy clause.

2. ***Lesser included offense instruction.*** When only the greater offense has been charged, as in *Harris v. Oklahoma*, joinder sometimes occurs as a consequence of the well-established rule of procedure under which a defendant is entitled to a jury instruction on the uncharged lesser included offense whenever such an alternative disposition is rationally justified by the evidence in the case. As noted in BECK v. ALABAMA, 447 U.S. 625 (1980): "In the federal courts, it has long been 'beyond dispute that the defendant is entitled to an instruction on a lesser included offense if the evidence would permit a jury rationally to find him guilty of the lesser offense and acquit him of the greater.' Similarly, the state courts that have addressed the issue have unanimously held that a defendant is entitled to a lesser included offense instruction where the evidence warrants it. * * * Although the States vary in their descriptions of the quantum of proof necessary to give rise to a right to a lesser included offense instruction, they agree that it must be given when supported by the evidence." This procedure, the Court noted in *Beck*, "originally developed as an aid to the prosecution in cases in which the proof failed to establish some element of the crime charged. But it has long been recognized that it can also be beneficial to the defendant because it affords the jury a less drastic alternative than the choice between conviction of the offense charged and acquittal."

In *Beck*, the Court concluded that "the nearly universal acceptance of the rule in both state and federal courts establishes the value to the defendant of this procedural safeguard," which is "especially important * * * when the evidence unquestionably establishes that the defendant is guilty of a serious, violent offense—but leaves some doubt with respect to an element that would justify conviction of a capital offense." Thus the Court held as a matter of due process that when "the unavailability of a lesser included offense instruction enhances the risk of an unwarranted conviction," that option may not be withdrawn from the jury in a capital case. The *Beck* rule does not require a state court to instruct the jury on offenses that, under state law, are not considered lesser included offenses of the crime charged. *Hopkins v. Reeves*, 524 U.S. 88 (1998) (second-degree murder, which requires intent, is not lesser included offense of felony-murder, which does not).

3. ***Continuing criminal enterprise.*** GARRETT v. UNITED STATES, 471 U.S. 773 (1985), involved these facts: Two months after pleading guilty to a federal charge of importing marijuana off the coast of Washington, defendant was indicted in a Florida federal court for several offenses, including that of engaging in a continuing criminal enterprise. That crime requires proof of three or more successive violations of a specified type within a specified period of time, and at trial the government's proof in that respect included the importation offense to which defendant had earlier pleaded guilty. Defendant claimed that his conviction of engaging in a continuing criminal enterprise violated *Brown v. Ohio,* p. 1036, in that the importation charge was a "lesser included offense" of the continuing criminal enterprise offense. Rehnquist, J., for the plurality, assuming but not deciding that this latter characterization was correct, concluded that the case nonetheless fell outside *Brown* because "the continuing criminal enterprise charged against Garrett in Florida had not been completed at the time that he was indicted in Washington":

"Were we to sustain Garrett's claim, the Government would have been able to proceed against him in either one of only two ways. It would have to have withheld the Washington charges, alleging crimes committed in October 1979 and August 1980, from the grand jury which indicted Garrett in March 1981, until it was prepared to present to a grand jury the continuing criminal enterprise charges which were alleged to have been, and found by a jury to be, continuing on each of those dates; or it would have to have submitted the continuing criminal enterprise charge to the Washington grand jury in March 1981, even though the indictment ultimately returned against Garrett on that charge alleged that the enterprise had continued until July 1981. We do not think that the Double Jeopardy Clause may be employed to force the Government's hand in this manner, however we were to resolve Garrett's lesser-included-offense argument. One who insists that the music stop and the piper be paid at a particular point must at least have stopped dancing himself before he may seek such an accounting."

The plurality deemed it irrelevant "whether the Government could in March 1981 have successfully indicted and prosecuted Garrett for a different continuing criminal enterprise—one ending in March 1981," explaining that a determination of that question is not "required at the behest of one who at the time the first indictment is returned is continuing to engage in other conduct found criminal by the jury which tried the second indictment."[a] Stevens, J., joined by Brennan and Marshall, JJ., dissenting, objected that the instant case did not come within the exception noted in *Brown* (see fn. * on p. 1044) because, while the government alleged that the enterprise continued to the date of the Florida indictment, all the facts necessary to prove a continuing criminal enterprise charge had occurred before the Washington indictment was returned. The other participating member of the Court,[b] O'Connor, J., concurring, found "merit to this position" of the dissenters, but reached "a different conclusion upon balancing the interests protected by the Double Jeopardy Clause," including the desirability of allowing the government

---

[a] It has been aptly noted that "the *Blockburger* test is insufficient where * * * the concern is not multiple charges under separate statutes, but rather successive prosecutions for conduct that may constitute the same act or transaction." *Rashad v. Burt,* 108 F.3d 677 (6th Cir.1997). This is because when "a defendant is convicted for violating one statute multiple times, the same evidence test will never be satisfied." *State v. Adel,* 965 P.2d 1072 (Wash.1998). The "appropriate inquiry" in such a case "asks what 'unit of prosecution' was intended by the Legislature as the punishable act. * * * The inquiry requires us to look to the language and purpose of the statutes, to see whether they speak directly to the issue of the appropriate unit of prosecution, and if they do not, to ascertain that unit, keeping in mind that any ambiguity that arises in the process must be resolved, under the rule of lenity, in the defendant's favor." *Commonwealth v. Rabb,* 725 N.E.2d 1036 (Mass.2000) (concluding that allegedly multiple drug possessions justify multiple charges if the possessions are sufficiently differentiated by time, place or intended purpose, the case here regarding defendant's possession of drugs at his residence for immediate sale and his possession of drugs at motel for future sales).

[b] Powell, J., took no part in the decision.

to decide prosecution is warranted whenever "the defendant continues unlawful conduct after the time the Government prosecutes him for a predicate offense."

4. ***Defendant's election of separate trials.*** In JEFFERS v. UNITED STATES, 432 U.S. 137 (1977), two indictments were returned against petitioner: the first charged him and nine others under 21 U.S.C. § 846 with conspiracy to distribute drugs; the second charged him with violation of 21 U.S.C. § 848, which prohibits conducting a continuing criminal enterprise to violate the drug laws. The government filed a motion to join the charges for trial, but petitioner objected, pointing out that "much of the evidence in the conspiracy trial would not inculpate petitioner and would therefore be inadmissible against him in the continuing criminal enterprise trial." The court denied the government's motion, and trial on the § 846 charge commenced. Petitioner later moved to dismiss the § 848 charge on double jeopardy grounds, but that motion was denied, and petitioner was separately convicted of both offenses.

Blackmun, J., announced the judgment of the Court in an opinion in which the Chief Justice and Powell and Rehnquist, JJ., joined.[c] He first assumed, "*arguendo,* that * * * § 846 is a lesser included offense of § 848,"[d] and then continued:

"If the defendant expressly asks for separate trials on the greater and the lesser offenses, or, in connection with his opposition to trial together, fails to raise the issue that one offense might be a lesser included offense of the other, [an] exception to the *Brown* [same-elements] rule emerges. * * * [A]lthough a defendant is normally entitled to have charges on a greater and a lesser offense resolved in one proceeding, there is no violation of the Double Jeopardy Clause when he elects to have the two offenses tried separately and persuades the trial court to honor his election.[20]

"In this case, trial together of the conspiracy and continuing criminal enterprise charges could have taken place without undue prejudice to petitioner's Sixth Amendment right to a fair trial.[21] If the two charges had been tried in one proceeding, it appears that petitioner would have been entitled to a lesser included offense instruction. If such an instruction had been denied on the ground that § 846 was not a lesser included offense of § 848, petitioner could have preserved his point by proper objection. Nevertheless, petitioner did not adopt that course. Instead, he was solely responsible for the successive prosecutions for the conspiracy offense and the continuing criminal enterprise offense. Under the circumstances, we hold that his action deprived him of any right that he might have had against consecutive trials."

---

c White, J., concurred as to the issue here considered.

d The Court later so held. *Rutledge v. United States,* 517 U.S. 292 (1996).

20 The considerations relating to the propriety of a second trial obviously would be much different if any action by the Government contributed to the separate prosecutions on the lesser and greater charges. No hint of that is present in the case before us, since the Government affirmatively sought trial on the two indictments together.

Unlike the dissenters, we are unwilling to attach any significance to the fact that the grand jury elected to return two indictments against petitioner for the two statutory offenses. As the Court of Appeals' opinion made clear, before this case it was by no means settled law that § 846 was a lesser included offense of § 848. Even now, it has not been necessary to settle that issue definitively. If the position reasonably could have been taken that the two statutes described different offenses, it is difficult to ascribe any improper motive to the act of requesting two separate indictments. Furthermore, as noted supra, it was the Government itself that requested a joint trial on the two indictments, which also indicates that no sinister purpose was behind the formal method of proceeding.

21 Petitioner argues that a finding of waiver is inconsistent with the decision in *Simmons v. United States* [p. 802, where the Court held that a defendant could not be required to surrender his Fifth Amendment privilege against compulsory self-incrimination in order to assert an arguably valid Fourth Amendment claim. In petitioner's case, however, the alleged Hobson's choice between asserting the Sixth Amendment fair trial right and asserting the Fifth Amendment double jeopardy claim is illusory. Had petitioner asked for a Rule 14 severance from the other defendants, the case might be different. In that event, he would have given the court an opportunity to ensure that prejudicial evidence relating only to other defendants would not have been introduced in his trial. Assuming that a valid Fifth Amendment point was in the background, due to the relationship between §§ 846 and 848, petitioner could have had no complaint about a trial of the two charges together. No such motion, however, was made. Under the circumstances of this case, therefore, no dilemma akin to that in *Simmons* arose.

Stevens, J., joined by Brennan, Stewart, and Marshall, JJ., dissented: "The defendant surely cannot be held responsible for the fact that two separate indictments were returned,[2] or for the fact that other defendants were named in the earlier indictment, or for the fact that the Government elected to proceed to trial first on the lesser charge.[3] The other defendants had valid objections to the Government's motion to consolidate the two cases for trial.[4] Most trial lawyers will be startled to learn that a rather routine joint opposition to that motion to consolidate has resulted in the loss of what this Court used to regard as 'a vital safeguard in our society, one that was clearly won and one that should continue to be highly valued.' "

5. ***Invalid first conviction.*** Hall, charged with felony sexual assault upon the 12-year-old daughter of his ex-wife, moved to dismiss on the ground that because the victim was his stepdaughter he could only be prosecuted for incest. The motion was granted, after which Hall was charged with and convicted of incest. The Montana Supreme Court reversed because the incest statute did not apply to stepchildren at the time of Hall's conduct, and went on to rule that under the *Brown* same-elements test Hall could not now be prosecuted for sexual assault, deemed the same offense as incest for double jeopardy purposes. In *Montana v. Hall*, 481 U.S. 400 (1987), the Supreme Court reversed per curiam, explaining that "the *Brown* analysis is not apposite in this case. In *Brown,* the defendant did not overturn the first conviction; indeed, he served the prison sentence assessed as punishment for that crime. Thus, when the State sought to try him for auto theft, it actually was seeking a second conviction for the same offense. By contrast, the respondent in this case sought, and secured, the invalidation of his first conviction. This case falls squarely within the rule that retrial is permissible after a conviction is reversed on appeal."

6. ***Civil-criminal distinction.*** While it has long been settled that the Double Jeopardy Clause has to do only with multiple *criminal* punishment, the Supreme Court has encountered difficulty over the years in determining how to go about making the civil-criminal distinction in this context. The method used in *United States v. Halper,* 490 U.S. 435 (1989), under which the outcome depended primarily on whether the sanction imposed served the traditional "goals of punishment," namely "retribution and deterrence," was abandoned in HUDSON v. UNITED STATES, 522 U.S. 93 (1997). There, bank officers indicted for misapplication of bank funds claimed the prosecution was barred because monetary penalties and occupational debarment had previously been imposed upon them by the Office of Comptroller of Currency. The Court, per Rehnquist, C.J., rejected that contention:

"Whether a particular punishment is criminal or civil is, at least initially, a matter of statutory construction. A court must first ask whether the legislature, 'in establishing the penalizing mechanism, indicated either expressly or impliedly a preference for one label or the other.' Even in those cases where the legislature 'has indicated an intention to establish a civil penalty, we have inquired further whether the statutory scheme was so punitive either in purpose or effect,' as to 'transfor[m] what was clearly intended as a civil remedy into a criminal penalty.'

"In making this latter determination, the factors listed in *Kennedy v. Mendoza-Martinez*, 372 U.S. 144 (1963), provide useful guideposts, including: (1) '[w]hether the sanction involves an affirmative disability or restraint'; (2) 'whether it has historically been regarded as a punishment';

---

[2] The plurality implies that the result in this case would be different "if any action by the Government contributed to the separate prosecutions on the lesser and greater charges." I wonder how the grand jury happened to return two separate indictments.

[3] The Government retained the alternative of trying petitioner on both charges at once, while trying the other defendants separately for conspiracy. The prosecutor never attempted this course, and defense counsel—not having had an opportunity to read today's plurality opinion—had no reason to believe he had a duty to suggest it. Until today it has never been the function of the defense to give legal advice to the prosecutor.

[4] When the Government attempted to obtain a joint trial on all the charges against all the defendants, the attorney representing all the defendants resisted the Government motion. He did so largely because of the possible prejudice to petitioner's codefendants, and gave relatively little emphasis to arguments relating to petitioner alone.

(3) 'whether it comes into play only on a finding of scienter'; (4) 'whether its operation will promote the traditional aims of punishment-retribution and deterrence'; (5) 'whether the behavior to which it applies is already a crime'; (6) 'whether an alternative purpose to which it may rationally be connected is assignable for it'; and (7) 'whether it appears excessive in relation to the alternative purpose assigned.' It is important to note, however, that 'these factors must be considered in relation to the statute on its face,' and 'only the clearest proof' will suffice to override legislative intent and transform what has been denominated a civil remedy into a criminal penalty."

As for the instant case, the Court concluded "that Congress intended the OCC money penalties and debarment sanctions * * * to be civil in nature," and found "little evidence" that the sanctions were so punitive as to make them criminal, considering that "neither money penalties nor debarment have historically been viewed as punishment," and that the sanctions imposed "do not involve an 'affirmative disability or restraint'" or come "into play 'only' on a finding of scienter." Moreover, "though the conduct for which OCC sanctions are imposed may also be criminal" and though the sanctions will serve to deter others, "a traditional goal of criminal punishment," neither of those factors "renders such sanctions 'criminal' for double jeopardy purposes."[e]

ASHE V. SWENSON

397 U.S. 436, 90 S.Ct. 1189, 25 L.Ed.2d 469 (1970).

JUSTICE STEWART delivered the opinion of the Court. * * *

Sometime in the early hours of the morning of January 10, 1960, six men were engaged in a poker game in the basement of the home of John Gladson at Lee's Summit, Missouri. Suddenly three or four masked men, armed with a shotgun and pistols, broke into the basement and robbed each of the poker players of money and various articles of personal property. The robbers—and it has never been clear whether there were three or four of them—then fled in a car belonging to one of the victims of the robbery. Shortly thereafter the stolen car was discovered in a field, and later that morning three men were arrested by a state trooper while they were walking on a highway not far from where the abandoned car had been found. The petitioner was arrested by another officer some distance away.

The four were subsequently charged with seven separate offenses—the armed robbery of each of the six poker players and the theft of the car. In May 1960 the petitioner went to trial on the charge of robbing Donald Knight, one of the participants in the poker game. At the trial the State called Knight and three of his fellow poker players as prosecution witnesses. Each of them described the circumstances of the holdup and itemized his own individual losses. The proof that an armed robbery had occurred and that personal property had been taken from Knight as well as from each of the others was unassailable. The testimony of the four victims in this regard was consistent both internally and with that of the others. But the State's evidence that the petitioner had been one of the robbers was weak. Two of the witnesses thought that there had been only three robbers altogether, and could not identify the petitioner as one of them. Another of the victims, who was the petitioner's uncle by marriage, said that at the "patrol station" he had positively identified each of the other three men accused of the holdup, but could say only that the

---

[e] *Hudson* produced four concurring opinions by six Justices. All but one of them agreed that a departure from pre-*Hudson* doctrine was necessary, but three expressed reservations about the extent of the departure in the Rehnquist opinion.

In *Seling v. Young*, 531 U.S. 250 (2001), the Court held that a provision deemed civil under *Hudson* cannot be deemed punitive "as applied" to a single individual, for an "as applied" approach would be unworkable because it could never be fully determined whether a scheme was valid under the double jeopardy clause.

petitioner's voice "sounded very much like" that of one of the robbers. The fourth participant in the poker game did identify the petitioner, but only by his "size and height, and his actions."

The cross-examination of these witnesses was brief, and it was aimed primarily at exposing the weakness of their identification testimony. Defense counsel made no attempt to question their testimony regarding the holdup itself or their claims as to their losses. Knight testified without contradiction that the robbers had stolen from him his watch, $250 in cash, and about $500 in checks. His billfold, which had been found by the police in the possession of one of the three other men accused of the robbery, was admitted in evidence. The defense offered no testimony and waived final argument.

The trial judge instructed the jury that if it found that the petitioner was one of the participants in the armed robbery, the theft of "any money" from Knight would sustain a conviction. He also instructed the jury that if the petitioner was one of the robbers, he was guilty under the law even if he had not personally robbed Knight. The jury—though not instructed to elaborate upon its verdict—found the petitioner "not guilty due to insufficient evidence."

Six weeks later the petitioner was brought to trial again, this time for the robbery of another participant in the poker game, a man named Roberts. The petitioner filed a motion to dismiss, based on his previous acquittal. The motion was overruled, and the second trial began. The witnesses were for the most part the same, though this time their testimony was substantially stronger on the issue of the petitioner's identity. For example, two witnesses who at the first trial had been wholly unable to identify the petitioner as one of the robbers, now testified that his features, size, and mannerisms matched those of one of their assailants. Another witness who before had identified the petitioner only by his size and actions now also remembered him by the unusual sound of his voice. The State further refined its case at the second trial by declining to call one of the participants in the poker game whose identification testimony at the first trial had been conspicuously negative. The case went to the jury on instructions virtually identical to those given at the first trial. This time the jury found the petitioner guilty, and he was sentenced to a 35-year term in the state penitentiary. * * *

"Collateral estoppel" is an awkward phrase, but it stands for an extremely important principle in our adversary system of justice. It means simply that when an issue of ultimate fact has once been determined by a valid and final judgment, that issue cannot again be litigated between the same parties in any future lawsuit. Although first developed in civil litigation, collateral estoppel has been an established rule of federal criminal law at least since this Court's decision more than 50 years ago in *United States v. Oppenheimer,* 242 U.S. 85 [1916]. As Justice Holmes put the matter in that case, "It cannot be that the safeguards of the person, so often and so rightly mentioned with solemn reverence, are less than those that protect from a liability in debt." As a rule of federal law, therefore, "[i]t is much too late to suggest that this principle is not fully applicable to a former judgment in a criminal case, either because of lack of 'mutuality' or because the judgment may reflect only a belief that the Government had not met the higher burden of proof exacted in such cases for the Government's evidence as a whole although not necessarily as to every link in the chain."

The federal decisions have made clear that the rule of collateral estoppel in criminal cases is not to be applied with the hypertechnical and archaic approach of a 19th century pleading book, but with realism and rationality. Where a previous judgment of acquittal was based upon a general verdict, as is usually the case, this approach requires a court to "examine the record of a prior proceeding, taking into account the pleadings, evidence, charge, and other relevant matter, and conclude whether a rational jury could have grounded its verdict upon an issue other than that which the defendant seeks to foreclose from consideration." The inquiry "must be set in a practical frame, and viewed with an eye to all the circumstances of the proceedings." Any test more technically restrictive would, of course, simply amount to a rejection of the rule of collateral estoppel in criminal proceedings, at least in every case where the first judgment was based upon a general verdict of acquittal.

Straightforward application of the federal rule to the present case can lead to but one conclusion. For the record is utterly devoid of any indication that the first jury could rationally have found that an armed robbery had not occurred, or that Knight had not been a victim of that robbery. The single rationally conceivable issue in dispute before the jury was whether the petitioner had been one of the robbers. And the jury by its verdict found that he had not. The federal rule of law, therefore, would make a second prosecution for the robbery of Roberts wholly impermissible.

The ultimate question to be determined, then, in the light of *Benton v. Maryland*,[f] is whether this established rule of federal law is embodied in the Fifth Amendment guarantee against double jeopardy. We do not hesitate to hold that it is. For whatever else that constitutional guarantee may embrace, it surely protects a man who has been acquitted from having to "run the gantlet" a second time.

The question is not whether Missouri could validly charge the petitioner with six separate offenses for the robbery of the six poker players. It is not whether he could have received a total of six punishments if he had been convicted in a single trial of robbing the six victims. It is simply whether, after a jury determined by its verdict that the petitioner was not one of the robbers, the State could constitutionally hale him before a new jury to litigate that issue again. * * *

In this case the State in its brief has frankly conceded that following the petitioner's acquittal, it treated the first trial as no more than a dry run for the second prosecution: "No doubt the prosecutor felt the state had a provable case on the first charge and, when he lost, he did what every good attorney would do—he refined his presentation in light of the turn of events at the first trial." But this is precisely what the constitutional guarantee forbids. * * *

Reversed and remanded.

JUSTICE BRENNAN, whom JUSTICE DOUGLAS and JUSTICE MARSHALL join, concurring.

I agree that the Double Jeopardy Clause incorporates collateral estoppel as a constitutional requirement and therefore join the Court's opinion. However, even if the rule of collateral estoppel had been inapplicable to the facts of this case, it is my view that the Double Jeopardy Clause nevertheless bars the prosecution of petitioner a second time for armed robbery. * * *

In my view, the Double Jeopardy Clause requires the prosecution, except in most limited circumstances,[7] to join at one trial all the charges against a defendant which grow out of a single criminal act, occurrence, episode, or transaction. This "same transaction" test of "same offence" not only enforces the ancient prohibition against vexatious multiple prosecutions embodied in the Double Jeopardy Clause, but responds as well to the increasingly widespread recognition that the consolidation in one lawsuit of all issues arising out of a single transaction or occurrence best promotes justice, economy, and convenience. * * *

CHIEF JUSTICE BURGER, dissenting.

The Fifth Amendment to the Constitution of the United States provides in part: "nor shall any person be subject for the same offense to be twice put in jeopardy of life or limb * * *." Nothing in the language and none of the gloss previously placed on this provision of the Fifth Amendment

---

[f] Page 1337, holding that the Fifth Amendment guarantee against double jeopardy is enforceable against the States through the Fourteenth Amendment.

[7] For example, where a crime is not completed or not discovered, despite diligence on the part of the police, until after the commencement of a prosecution for other crimes arising from the same transaction, an exception to the "same transaction" rule should be made to permit a separate prosecution. Another exception would be necessary if no single court had jurisdiction of all the alleged crimes. * * *

remotely justifies the treatment which the Court today accords to the collateral estoppel doctrine. * * *

The collateral estoppel concept—originally a product only of civil litigation—is a strange mutant as it is transformed to control this criminal case. In civil cases the doctrine was justified as conserving judicial resources as well as those of the parties to the actions and additionally as providing the finality needed to plan for the future. It ordinarily applies to parties on each side of the litigation who have the same interest as or who are identical with the parties in the initial litigation. Here the complainant in the second trial is not the same as in the first even though the State is a party in both cases. Very properly, in criminal cases, finality and conservation of private, public, and judicial resources are lesser values than in civil litigation. Also, courts which have applied the collateral concept to criminal actions would certainly not apply it to *both* parties, as is true in civil cases, i.e., here, if Ashe had been convicted at the first trial, presumably no court would then hold that he was thereby foreclosed from litigating the identification issue at the second trial. * * *[g]

[T]he majority's analysis of the facts completely disregards the confusion injected into the case by the robbery of Mrs. Gladson.[h] To me, if we are to psychoanalyze the jury, the evidence adduced at the first trial could more reasonably be construed as indicating that Ashe had been at the Gladson home with the other three men but was not one of those involved in the basement robbery. Certainly, the evidence at the first trial was equivocal as to whether there were three or four robbers, whether the man who robbed Mrs. Gladson was one of the three who robbed the six male victims, and whether a man other than the three had robbed Mrs. Gladson. Then, since the jury could have thought that the "acting together" instruction given by the trial court in both trials only applied to the actual taking from the six card players, and not to Mrs. Gladson, the jury could well have acquitted Ashe but yet believed that he was present in the Gladson home. On the other hand, the evidence adduced at the second trial resolved issues other than identity which may have troubled the first jury. If believed, that evidence indicated that a fourth robber, Johnson, not Ashe, was with Mrs. Gladson when Ashe, Larson, and Brown were robbing the male victims. Johnson did go to the basement where the male victims were located, but only after the other three had already taken the stolen items and when the robbers were preparing for their departure in a car to be stolen from Roberts.[i]

Accordingly, even the facts in this case, which the Court's opinion considers to "lead to but one conclusion," are susceptible to an interpretation that the first jury did not base its acquittal on the identity ground which the Court finds so compelling. The Court bases its holding on sheer "guesswork," which should have no place particularly in our review of state convictions by way of habeas corpus. * * *

---

[g] In *Simpson v. Florida,* 403 U.S. 384 (1971), the Court, noting that "mutuality" is not an ingredient of the *Ashe* rule, held that defendant's conviction at his first trial (reversed on appeal for failure to instruct the jury on a lesser included offense) did not estop him from claiming that the state failed to prove his identity at the second trial.

[h] Earlier in his opinion, the Chief Justice notes certain facts not stated in the opinion of the Court: "During the same period in which the men were being robbed in the basement, one man entered Mrs. Gladson's bedroom three floors above, ripped out the telephone there, tied her with the telephone cord, and removed the wedding ring from her finger. * * * Mrs. Gladson did not testify [at the first trial] because she was ill on the day of trial. * * * [At the second trial,] she said that she was able to identify the robber by his voice, and that he was Johnson, not Ashe."

[i] In *Harris v. Washington,* 404 U.S. 55 (1971), the state court held *Ashe* inapplicable where the issue of identity had not been "fully litigated" at the first trial because the trial judge had excluded evidence on grounds having "no bearing on the quality of the evidence." The Supreme Court reversed, holding that "the constitutional guarantee applies, irrespective of whether the jury considered all relevant evidence, and irrespective of the good faith of the State in bringing successive prosecutions."

NOTES AND QUESTIONS

1. ***What issues foreclosed?*** In *Turner v. Arkansas,* 407 U.S. 366 (1972), where, some time after petitioner, his brother, Yates and another played poker, Yates was robbed and murdered. Turner was charged with murder on a felony-murder theory and acquitted, after which he was charged with the robbery the state conceded arose out of the same facts and circumstances. Under the Arkansas statutory provisions on joinder of offenses, these two charges could not have been joined together for trial. The Court, per curiam, ruled: "The jury was instructed that it must find petitioner guilty of first degree murder if it found that he had killed the decedent Yates either with premeditation or unintentionally during the course of a robbery. The jury's verdict thus necessarily means that it found petitioner not guilty of the killing. The State's theory, however, is that the jury might have believed that petitioner and his brother robbed Yates but that this brother actually committed the murder. This theory is belied by the actual instructions given the jury. The trial judge charged that:

> 'An accessory is one who stands by, aids, abets, or assists * * * the perpetration of the crime * * *.
>
> 'All persons being present, aiding and abetting, or ready and consenting to aid and abet, in any felony, shall be deemed principal offenders, and indicted or informed against, and punished as such.'

Had the jury found petitioner present at the crime scene, it would have been obligated to return a verdict of guilty of murder even if it believed that he had not actually pulled the trigger. The only logical conclusion is that the jury found him not present at the scene of the murder and robbery, a finding which negates the possibility of a constitutionally valid conviction for the robbery of Yates."

But in *Schiro v. Farley,* 510 U.S. 222 (1994), the Court held that the "failure to return a verdict does not have collateral estoppel effect * * * unless the record establishes that the issue was actually and necessarily decided in the defendant's favor." In that case, defendant's trial for a single killing resulted in the jury being given ten possible verdicts, including three murder counts ("knowingly" killing, rape felony-murder, deviate conduct felony-murder), voluntary and involuntary manslaughter, guilty but mentally ill, not guilty by reason of insanity, and not guilty. Because the jury returned a guilty verdict as to rape felony murder and left the other verdict sheets blank, defendant claimed the state was collaterally estopped from now showing intentional killing as an aggravated factor supporting a death sentence. The Court disagreed, concluding that because the jury (i) was not instructed to return more than one verdict but (ii) was instructed that intent was required for each variety of murder, defendant had "not met his 'burden . . . to demonstrate that the issue whose relitigation he seeks to foreclose was actually decided' in his favor."

2. ***Defendant-caused severance.*** In CURRIER v. VIRGINIA, 138 S.Ct. 2144 (2018), Currier, charged with burglary, grand larceny and unlawful possession of a firearm by a convicted felon, sought a severance of the latter charge, concerned that certain evidence as to it, his prior burglary and larceny convictions, might prejudice the jury's consideration of the other charges. He and the government agreed to a severance and that the burglary and larceny charges should be tried first. Acquitted in the first trial, he then sought to stop the second trial, arguing that it would amount to double jeopardy, but the trial court disagreed, and Currier was then convicted on the felony-in-possession charge. Gorsuch, J., for five Justices, rejecting Currier's claim that the severance and conviction violated the Double Jeopardy Clause, concluded that *Jeffers v. United States*, p. 1079, "points the other way":

"What was true in *Jeffers*, we hold, can be no less true here. If a defendant's consent to two trials can overcome concerns lying at the historic core of the Double Jeopardy Clause, so too we think it must overcome a double jeopardy complaint under *Ashe.* Nor does anything in *Jeffers* suggest that the outcome should be different if the first trial yielded an acquittal rather than a conviction when a defendant consents to severance. While we acknowledge that *Ashe*'s protections apply only to trials following acquittals, as a general rule, the Double Jeopardy Clause " 'protects against a second prosecution for the same offense after conviction' " as well as " 'against a second prosecution for the same offense after acquittal.' " Because the Clause applies equally in both situations, consent to a second trial should in general have equal effect in both situations. * * *

"Mr. Currier replies that he had no real choice but to seek two trials. Without a second trial, he says, evidence of his prior convictions would have tainted the jury's consideration of the burglary and larceny charges. And, he notes, Virginia law guarantees a severance in cases like his unless the defendant and prosecution agree to a single trial. But no one disputes that the Constitution permitted Virginia to try all three charges at once with appropriate cautionary instructions. So this simply isn't a case where the defendant had to give up one constitutional right to secure another. Instead, Mr. Currier faced a lawful choice between two courses of action that each bore potential costs and rationally attractive benefits. It might have been a hard choice. But litigants every day face difficult decisions."

Concluding that those points "suffice to resolve this case in a full and proper way," Justice Kennedy did not join the balance of the Gorsuch opinion, where four Justices went on to conclude that civil issue preclusion principles cannot be imported into the criminal law via the Double Jeopardy Clause to prevent parties from retrying any issue or retrying any evidence about a previously tried issue. Thus, even assuming Currier's consent to holding a second trial didn't more broadly imply consent to the manner in which it was conducted, his argument must be rejected.

A dissent by Justice Ginsburg, for four Justices, citing *Ashe* for the proposition that the Double Jeopardy Clause also shields "the issue-preclusion effect of an acquittal," and distinguishing *Jeffers* because it "presented a claim-preclusion question," rejected the notion "that Currier surrendered his right to assert the issue-preclusive effect of his first-trial acquittals by consenting to two trials. * * *

"Currier took no action inconsistent with assertion of an issue-preclusion plea. To understand why, one must comprehend just what issue preclusion forecloses. Unlike the right against a second trial for the same offense (claim preclusion), issue preclusion prevents relitigation of a previously rejected theory of criminal liability without necessarily barring a successive trial. Take *Ashe*, for example. Issue preclusion prevented the prosecution from arguing, at a second trial, that Ashe was one of the robbers who held up the poker players at gunpoint. But if the prosecution sought to prove, instead, that Ashe waited outside during the robbery and then drove the getaway car, issue preclusion would not have barred that trial. Similarly here, the prosecution could not again attempt to prove that Currier participated in the break-in and theft of the safe at the Garrisons' residence. But a second trial could be mounted if the prosecution alleged, for instance, that Currier was present at the river's edge when others showed up to dump the safe in the river, and that Currier helped to empty out and replace the guns contained in the safe."

3. ***"Evidentiary" vs. "ultimate" facts.*** Phillips was tried for robbery of a federally insured bank. In response to a question from the jury, the court instructed that Phillips could not be convicted unless the jury believed he was one of those in the bank; the court also gave instructions on the "lesser included offense" of possessing what were known to be the proceeds of the robbery. Ten minutes later the jury returned a verdict of guilty of the lesser offense, which the court later set aside on the ground it was not included in the indictment. Phillips was then prosecuted for the possession offense, and evidence of his presence in the bank was admitted to prove his knowledge that the funds he received were stolen. In *Phillips v. United States,* 502 F.2d 227 (4th Cir.1974), his conviction was reversed on the authority of *Ashe.* Craven, J., dissenting, gave "two independent reasons why collateral estoppel should not apply in this case.

"First, Phillips' acquittal of bank robbery was only an implicit acquittal, arising by operation of law from the verdict of guilt on a lesser included offense. I would hold that such an implicit acquittal cannot be the basis for collateral estoppel because it leaves doubt whether the jury has made any factual determination in favor of the accused. * * *

"Second, * * * I would not allow its use to restrict proof on retrial of the *lesser* charge. Retrial in cases like this one harbors none of the prosecutorial abuses that supplied the rationale of *Ashe* * * * ."

Are these reasons sound? Is there yet a third reason, namely, that the defendant's presence in the bank was, in the second prosecution, an "evidentiary" fact rather than an "ultimate" fact (i.e., presence did not have to be proved in the second trial, showing presence was merely of evidentiary value on the knowledge element)? See *Dowling v. United States,* 493 U.S. 342 (1990) (earlier acquittal, even if it established a reasonable doubt as to the existence of a matter to be proved as an evidentiary fact at a later trial, is no bar to proof of the evidentiary fact by a lesser standard).[j] But in *York v. State*, 342 S.W.3d 528 (Tex.Crim.App.2011), it is noted that (i) there "is a split among the federal circuits and various other jurisdictions on whether collateral estoppel can ever apply to facts that are merely evidentiary, in the second prosecution," (ii) Restatement (Second) of Judgments § 27, comment j (1982), "eschews any distinction between 'evidentiary' and 'ultimate' facts," and (iii) the Supreme Court has never cited to that comment or otherwise indicated such is the case as to constitutionally-grounded collateral estoppel.

4. ***Hung jury; implicit acquittal.*** As for Judge Craven's first reason in *Phillips*, does it find support in *Yeager v. United States*, 557 U.S. 110 (2009)? A jury acquitted Yeager on securities and wire fraud counts, but hung on the counts of insider trading and money laundering, which the government undertook to prosecute again. The lower court concluded that the fact the jury hung on those two counts cast sufficient doubt upon whether the acquittals decided factual matters that would bar the reprosecution under *Ashe*. The Supreme Court reversed, reasoning that "the consideration of hung counts has no place in the issue-preclusion analysis," as a "host of reasons—sharp disagreement, confusion about the issues, exhaustion after a long trial, to name but a few—could work alone or in tandem to cause a jury to hang."

5. ***Directed verdict; evidence suppression.*** In *York,* Note 3 supra, a city policeman outside his jurisdiction stopped York when he was found parked outside a closed gas station at 3 a.m., obtained consent to search and found methamphetamine on his person, and then arrested him, after which York gave a false name. At York's trial for failure-to-identify (requiring that a person "gives a false or fictitious name * * * to a peace officer who has (1) lawfully arrested the person [or] (2) lawfully detained the person"), the judge outside the presence of the jury considered York's two motions, a motion to suppress evidence and a motion for a directed verdict of acquittal, both based upon the assertion that the state had not proved York's detention or arrest was lawful. The judge granted the motion to suppress and then entered a directed verdict of acquittal. York was then prosecuted for meth possession; the judge denied York's motion to suppress notwithstanding his collateral estoppel claim, and York was convicted. On York's appeal, based "solely on the motion to suppress," should he prevail (a) because of the directed verdict in the first trial? (b) because of the granting of the suppression motion in the first trial?

6. ***Contradictory theories.*** The "same parties" limitation in *Ashe* means that a defendant may not base a collateral estoppel claim upon another case involving a different defendant. But relief has sometimes been obtained in such circumstances on a different basis, "that the use of

---

[j] So too as to proof of an "ultimate fact" in the second trial if a lower burden of proof then applies. *One Lot Emerald Cut Stones and One Ring v. United States*, 409 U.S. 232 (1972) (defendant's acquittal of federal charge that he willfully and knowingly, with intent to defraud, smuggled jewels into U.S. no bar to civil forfeiture action with respect to same jewels, under which government must prove by a preponderance of the evidence that the property was brought into the U.S. without the required declaration).

inconsistent, irreconcilable theories to secure convictions against more than one defendant in prosecutions for the same crime violates the due process clause." *Stumpf v. Mitchell,* 367 F.3d 594 (6th Cir.2004). Illustrative is *Smith v. Groose,* 205 F.3d 1045 (8th Cir.2000) (where prosecutor used two directly conflicting statements by a codefendant at successive trials to convict defendant and another, such "use of inherently contradictory theories violates the principles of due process" where, as here, those theories "exist at the core of the prosecutor's case against defendants for the same crime"); distinguishing *Nichols v. Scott,* 69 F.3d 1255 (5th Cir.1995) (another case where prosecutor argued in two separate cases that different defendants had done the shooting, but there both defendants could have been convicted under a felony-murder theory without regard to which one did the shooting).

When the *Stumpf* case reached the Supreme Court, *Bradshaw v. Stumpf,* p. 1215, the Court concluded that when the state in the later trial of Stumpf's robbery accomplice Wesley put in evidence that Wesley admitted shooting one Mrs. Stout, this was in any event not inconsistent with Bradshaw's earlier guilty plea to aggravated murder, as the precise identity of the triggerman was immaterial to Stumpf's aggravated murder conviction. As for Stumpf's claim that such evidence at Wesley's trial was inconsistent with the claim at Stumpf's penalty hearing, resulting a sentence of death, that Stumpf had killed Mrs. Stout, the Court found such ambiguity in the court of appeal's view on that distinct issue that it remanded the case to that court. (Upon remand, the court in *Stumpf v. Houk,* 653 F.3d 426 (6th Cir.2011), concluded "it would amount to nothing short of complete abdication of our sworn responsibilities to ensure the reliability of capital sentencing were we to presume that the state's later-recanted argument that the petitioner was the triggerman in Mrs. Stout's murder did not affect the panel's sentencing decision" in sentencing Stumpf to death.)

7. ***Lack of incentives to contest.*** An exception to *Ashe* was later recognized under the unusual circumstances that obtained in *Bobby v. Bies,* 556 U.S. 825 (2009), brought about by the Court's earlier holding in *Atkins v. Virginia,* 536 U.S. 304 (2002), that mental retardation is a constitutional barrier to execution rather than merely a mitigating factor. Years before *Atkins,* state courts affirmed Bies' death sentence, concluding that his mental retardation was entitled to "some weight" as a mitigator but was outweighed by the aggravating circumstances. When Bies challenged his death sentence post-*Atkins*, a federal court on habeas ruled that *Ashe* barred the state from relitigating the mental retardation issue. The Supreme Court disagreed because (1) the earlier ruling did not involve an "ultimate fact,"[k] and (2) even assuming "the core requirements of issue preclusion[l] are met" here, an exception to *Ashe* applies because of the intervening "change in [the] applicable legal context." Mental retardation pre- and post-*Atkins* involved "discrete legal issues," as prosecutors had "little incentive" to contest retardation evidence pre-*Atkins* because such evidence would likely prompt the jury also to find the presence of the aggravating factor of future dangerousness. Because *Atkins* "substantially altered the State's incentive to contest Bies' mental capacity, applying preclusion would not advance the equitable administration of the law."

8. ***Beyond* Ashe*?*** In a case not covered by *Ashe*, can a double jeopardy violation occur if evidence resulting in acquittal at the first trial comes into play in a significant way at a retrial of a related charge as to which the jury in the first trial could not agree? Consider *Garrett v. State,* 992 N.E.2d 710 (Ind.2013), where defendant was charged with two counts of rape involving the

[k] The Court explained that to qualify as an "ultimate fact" the fact must be "essential to the judgment," which was not the case in *Bies,* for while the state courts, in earlier upholding Bies' death penalty, had concluded his mental retardation was entitled to "some weight" as a mitigating factor but was outweighed by the aggravating factors, such "determinations of his mental capacity were not necessary to the ultimate imposition of the death penalty" and thus did not foreclose a new inquiry as to whether Bies qualified as mentally retarded under the intervening decision in *Atkins.*

[l] The Court in *Bies* used the term "issue preclusion" to mean the same thing as "collateral estoppel" in *Ashe.* Lower courts use both terms, not always limited to claims constitutionally grounded in the double jeopardy clause. See CRIMPROC § 17.4(a).

same victim alleged to have occurred at the same place and in close temporal proximity. The defendant was found not guilty of the first-in-time alleged rape, but the jury hung as to the other rape count, which was the subject of a second trial, at which the sum total of the evidence was essentially the same as at the first trial, covering the entire episode. On appeal, the court, although apparently of the view that defendant could not prevail under *Ashe*, went on "to conclude there is a reasonable possibility that the evidentiary facts used by the jury in the first trial to establish the essential elements of Rape, for which Garrett was acquitted, may also have been used on retrial to establish all of the essential elements of Rape for which Garrett was convicted," meaning "that Garrett was twice prosecuted for the same offense in violation * * * of the Indiana Constitution."

9. ***"Offensive collateral estoppel."*** In *State v. Allen*, 31 A.3d 476 (Md.2011), defendant was convicted of robbery and felony-murder at his first trial, but the felony-murder conviction was reversed on appeal because of faulty jury instructions. Defendant was then convicted of felony-murder at his second trial, at which the jury was told that whether defendant committed the robbery "is not before you" because that was settled at the prior trial. On appeal, the court rejected such "offensive collateral estoppel," disagreeing "with the State's contention that the Sixth Amendment's jury trial guarantee was not violated in this case because the robbery and murder elements were decided by 'a jury,' (i.e. the jury who sat on Respondent's first trial) if not 'the jury' that sat on Respondent's second trial. The State's assertion finds no support in the law. When a jury is impaneled, it must discharge all of its constitutional-fact finding duties in order to fulfill the guarantee of the Sixth Amendment. The right to a jury in a criminal trial necessarily includes 'the right to have the *same* trier of the fact decide *all* of the elements of the charged offense.' "

10. ***"Same transaction" joinder.*** Several state courts have adopted a "same transaction" joinder-of-offenses requirement. Is this position sound? Consider *State v. Conrad,* 243 So.2d 174 (Fla.App.1971): "The absurdity of the 'same transaction' standard can be easily illustrated. Assume that one breaks and enters a building to commit larceny of an automobile, does thereafter in fact steal the automobile and drive away, killing the night watchman in the process, and two blocks away runs a red light which brings about his arrest by the municipal police. Could it be said with any logic that a plea of guilty to breaking and entering would bar a subsequent prosecution for murder? If so, presumably a plea of guilty to the traffic offense would likewise, since all arise out of the 'same transaction.' "

Does this mean that some intermediate position is desirable? What of Ill.Comp.Stat. ch. 720, § 5/3–3(b), mandating joinder only if the offenses "are based on the same act"? Or N.Y.Crim.P.Law § 40.20(2)(b), which permits successive prosecutions where "the offenses * * * [contain] an element which is not an element of the other, and the statutory provisions defining such offenses are designed to prevent very different kinds of harm or evil"? Are there, in any event, other limits which are necessary to meet the concerns of the court in *Conrad?* What, for example, of the additional requirement in the above Illinois statute that "the several offenses are known to the proper prosecuting officer at the time of commencing the prosecution and are within the jurisdiction of a single court"?

§ 3. JOINDER AND SEVERANCE OF DEFENDANTS

Fed.R.Crim.P. 8(b) provides that two or more defendants may be charged in the same indictment or information "if they are alleged to have participated in the same act or transaction, or in the same series of acts or transactions, constituting an offense or offenses." Some states have identical provisions, while others utilize similar language. These rules and statutes are intended to promote economy and efficiency and to avoid a multiplicity of trials.

One common joinder situation is that in which the several defendants are connected by virtue of a charged conspiracy relationship, as where the joined defendants are all charged in a conspiracy count and some or all are also charged with substantive offenses alleged to have been committed in furtherance of the conspiracy. Joinder of multiple conspiracies is permissible if they are sufficiently related, which is not shown merely by a slight membership overlap. Even absent a conspiracy count, defendants may be joined when their acts were part of a common plan (e.g., individual acts of income tax evasion related to joint gambling activities) or were so closely connected in respect to time, place and occasion that it would be difficult to separate the proof of one charge from proof of the other (e.g., negligent homicide charges against several drivers involved in same accident).

Although a few states still grant defendants an absolute right to separate trials, in most jurisdictions joined defendants may obtain a severance only by a showing of prejudice flowing from the joinder.

SCHAFFER V. UNITED STATES

362 U.S. 511, 80 S.Ct. 945, 4 L.Ed.2d 921 (1960).

JUSTICE CLARK delivered the opinion of the Court. * * *

The indictment charged transportation in interstate commerce of goods known to have been stolen and having a value in excess of $5,000. It contained three substantive counts. Count 1 charged the two Schaffers (petitioners in No. 111) and the three Stracuzzas (defendants below, who either pleaded guilty or had the charges against them *nolle prossed* at trial) with transporting stolen ladies' and children's wearing apparel from New York to Pennsylvania. Count 2 charged petitioner Marco and the Stracuzzas with a similar movement of stolen goods from New York to West Virginia. Count 3 charged petitioner Karp and the Stracuzzas with like shipments from New York to Massachusetts. The fourth and final count of the indictment charged all of these parties with a conspiracy to commit the substantive offenses charged in the first three counts. The petitioners here were tried on the indictment simultaneously in a single trial. On motion of petitioners for acquittal at the close of the Government's case, the court dismissed the conspiracy count for failure of proof. This motion was denied, however, as to the substantive counts, the court finding that no prejudice would result from the joint trial. Upon submission of the substantive counts to the jury on a detailed charge, each petitioner was found guilty and thereafter fined and sentenced to prison. * * *

It is admitted that the three Stracuzzas were the common center of the scheme to transport the stolen goods. The four petitioners here participated in some steps of the transactions in the stolen goods, although each was involved with separate interstate shipments. The separate substantive charges of the indictment employed almost identical language and alleged violations of the same criminal statute during the same period and in the same manner. This made proof of the over-all operation of the scheme competent as to all counts. The variations in the proof related to the specific shipments proven against each petitioner. This proof was related to each petitioner separately and proven as to each by different witnesses. It included entirely separate invoices and other exhibits, all of which were first clearly identified as applying only to a specific petitioner and were so received and shown to the jury under painstaking instructions to that effect. In short, the proof was carefully compartmentalized as to each petitioner. The propriety of the joinder prior to the failure of proof of conspiracy was not assailed. When the Government rested, however, the petitioners filed their motion for dismissal and it was sustained as to the conspiracy count. The petitioners then pressed for acquittal on the remaining counts, and the court decided that the evidence was sufficient on the substantive counts. The case was submitted to the jury on each of these counts, and under a charge which was characterized by petitioners' counsel as being "extremely fair." This charge meticulously set out separately the evidence as to each of the petitioners and admonished the jury that they were "not to take into consideration any proof against one defendant and apply it by inference or otherwise to any other defendant."

Petitioners contend that prejudice would nevertheless be implicit in a continuation of the joint trial after dismissal of the conspiracy count. They say that the resulting prejudice could not be cured by any cautionary instructions, and that therefore the trial judge was left with no discretion. Petitioners overlook, however, that the joinder was authorized under Rule 8(b) and that subsequent severance was controlled by Rule 14, which provides for separate trials where "it appears that a defendant * * * is prejudiced * * * by such joinder for trial * * *." It appears that not only was no prejudice shown, but both the trial court and the Court of Appeals affirmatively found that none was present. We cannot say to the contrary on this record. Nor can we fashion a hard-and-fast formula that, when a conspiracy count fails, joinder is error as a matter of law. We do emphasize, however, that, in such a situation, the trial judge has a continuing duty at all stages of the trial to grant a severance if prejudice does appear. And where, as here, the charge which originally justified joinder turns out to lack the support of sufficient evidence, a trial judge should be particularly sensitive to the possibility of such prejudice. However, the petitioners here not only failed to show any prejudice that would call Rule 14 into operation but even failed to request a new trial. Instead they relied entirely on their motions for acquittal. Moreover, the judge was acutely aware of the possibility of prejudice and was strict in his charge—not only as to the testimony the jury was not to consider, but also as to that evidence which was available in the consideration of the guilt of each petitioner separately under the respective substantive counts. The terms of Rule 8(b) having been met and no prejudice under Rule 14 having been shown, there was no misjoinder. * * *

JUSTICE DOUGLAS, with whom THE CHIEF JUSTICE, JUSTICE BLACK, and JUSTICE BRENNAN concur, dissenting. * * *

[O]nce it becomes apparent during the trial that the defendants have not participated "in the same series" of transactions, it would make a mockery of Rule 8(b) to hold that the allegation alone, now known to be false, is enough to continue the joint trial.

* * * It is not enough to say that evidence of the guilt of each of the present petitioners may have been clear. Reasons for severance are founded on the principle that evidence against one person may not be used against a codefendant whose crime is unrelated to the others. Instructions can be given the jury and admonitions can be made explicit that the line between the various defendants must be kept separate. The district judge conscientiously made that effort here. But where, as here, there is no nexus between the several crimes, the mounting proof of the guilt of one is likely to affect another. * * *

This is unlike the case where the conspiracy count and the substantive counts are submitted to the jury, the verdict being not guilty of conspiracy but guilty on the other counts. There is then no escape from the quandary in which defendants find themselves. Once the conspiracy is supported by evidence, it presents issues for the jury to decide. What may motivate a particular jury in returning a verdict of not guilty on the conspiracy count may never be known. * * *

NOTES AND QUESTIONS

1. **Schaffer *criticized.*** Is the *Schaffer* rule unsound because it "may have the effect of encouraging an unscrupulous prosecutor to frame a baseless conspiracy count in order that several defendants, accused of similar but unrelated offenses, may be tried together"? Note, 42 N.Y.U.L.Rev. 513, 518 (1967). Or, is the dissent's position unsound because it "could militate against the very result that the argument seeks to achieve," in "that a trial judge, faced with a rigid rule requiring severance as a matter of law and consequent time consuming multiple trials,

might be extremely reluctant to dismiss the charge upon which joinder is founded." Note, 45 Minn.L.Rev. 1066, 1073 (1961).

2. ***Harmless error.*** While in *Schaffer* the Court could say "that the joinder was authorized under Rule 8(b)," such was not the case in UNITED STATES v. LANE, 474 U.S. 438 (1986). The indictment charged (count #1) James Lane with mail fraud in connection with a 1979 restaurant fire; (counts #2, 3, and 4) James and Dennis Lane with mail fraud in connection with a 1980 duplex fire; (count #5) James and Dennis Lane with conspiracy to commit mail fraud in connection with a planned flower shop fire; and (count #6) Dennis Lane with perjury before a grand jury when testifying about a person involved in the duplex and flower shop schemes. The court of appeals concluded that when "a case involves multiple defendants as well as multiple counts, we look to Rule 8(b) for the relevant standards," that consequently the issue "in this case is whether all of the counts are part of the same series of acts or transactions," that the answer is no because, between count #1 and the other counts, there is neither a "substantial identity of facts" nor "a common scheme," that thus there was a misjoinder of count #1, and that such misjoinder "is inherently prejudicial." The Supreme Court, per Burger, C.J., disagreed. Noting that the harmless error doctrine is applicable even to many constitutional violations [see, Ch. 28, § 5B], the Court asserted: "In this case, the argument for applying harmless-error analysis is even stronger because the specific joinder standards of Rule 8 are not themselves of constitutional magnitude."[a] Such application, the Court added, "follows" from *Kotteakos* and from *Schaffer,* which involved "a clear error of misjoinder" at that point when the trial court concluded there was insufficient evidence supporting the conspiracy count.

Stevens and Marshall, JJ., dissenting, argued: "In my view, harmless-error analysis is inappropriate in at least three situations: (1) when it is clear that a statute or Rule was not intended to be subject to such a rule; (2) when an independent value besides reliability of the outcome suggests that such analysis is inappropriate; and (3) when the harmlessness of an error cannot be measured with precision. In my view, misjoinder clearly falls into the first category.[b] It also has elements of the second and third. Misjoinder implicates the independent value of individual responsibility and our deep abhorrence of the notion of 'guilt by association.' Our criminal justice system has expanded considerably in its tolerance of multiple joinders and massive conspiracy trials. The rule against misjoinder remains, however, as an ultimate safeguard of our cherished principle that one is tried for one's own deeds, and not for another's. The

---

[a] A footnote by the majority stated: "Respondents argue that application of the harmless-error rule to Rule 8(b) misjoinder will eviscerate Rule 14, which provides the trial court with discretion to grant a severance even if the joinder is proper under Rule 8 when it believes the defendants or the Government may be prejudiced by a joinder. We see no conflict with our holding and the applicability of Rule 14. Rule 14's concern is to provide the trial court with some flexibility when a joint trial may appear to risk prejudice to a party; review of that decision is for an abuse of discretion. Rule 8(b), however, requires the granting of a motion for severance unless its standards are met, even in the absence of prejudice; review on appeal is for an error of law. Applying the harmless-error rule to Rule 8(b) misjoinder simply goes to the additional question whether the error requires setting aside the convictions. We need not decide whether the degree of prejudice necessary to support a Rule 14 motion for severance is identical to that necessary to require reversal for a Rule 8(b) error.

"The dissent fails to recognize that the Rule 14 prejudice component involves a different inquiry from the Rule 8 technical requirements. Indeed, the express language of Rule 14, as well as the Advisory Committee Note, shows that Congress tolerates some Rule 8 joinders even when there is prejudice. The first hurdle in obtaining a severance under Rule 14 is a showing of prejudice, and if shown, it remains in the district court's discretion whether to grant the motion."

[b] As explained earlier in this dissent, "if one reads Rule 8 in conjunction with Rule 14, it is immediately apparent that the draftsmen of the Rules regarded every violation of Rule 8 as inherently prejudicial. For Rule 14 authorizes the Court to grant a severance, even in the absence of a Rule 8 violation, if either the defendant or the Government is prejudiced by a joinder of offenses or defendants. Thus, it seems clear that the draftsmen of the Rules regarded violations of Rule 8 as inherently prejudicial, and recognized that even joinders that were not prohibited by the rule should be forbidden if a party could demonstrate actual prejudice."

harmfulness of misjoinder is also the type of error that has consequences that are difficult to measure with precision."

Brennan and Blackmun, JJ., concurring on this branch of the case, responded to those three points as follows: (1) "nothing in the language or history of either the statutory harmless-error provisions or Rule 8 indicates that Congress chose to except misjoinder from harmless-error scrutiny"; (2) "joinder rules do not serve 'an independent value besides reliability of the outcome' justifying an exception to the harmless-error principle"[c], and (3) "the prejudice that may result from misjoinder is not so difficult to ascertain that it must always be presumed to be present."

GRAY V. MARYLAND

523 U.S. 185, 118 S.Ct. 1151, 140 L.Ed.2d 294 (1998).

JUSTICE BREYER delivered the opinion of the Court.

The issue in this case concerns the application of *Bruton v. United States*, 391 U.S. 123 (1968). *Bruton* involved two defendants accused of participating in the same crime and tried jointly before the same jury. One of the defendants had confessed. His confession named and incriminated the other defendant. The trial judge issued a limiting instruction, telling the jury that it should consider the confession as evidence only against the codefendant who had confessed and not against the defendant named in the confession. *Bruton* held that, despite the limiting instruction, the Constitution forbids the use of such a confession in the joint trial.[d]

The case before us differs from *Bruton* in that the prosecution here redacted the codefendant's confession by substituting for the defendant's name in the confession a blank space or the word "deleted." We must decide whether these substitutions make a significant legal difference. We hold that they do not and that *Bruton*'s protective rule applies.

[Bell confessed to Baltimore police that he, Gray, and Vanlandingham had participated in the beating that resulted in Stacey Williams' death. Bell and Gray were indicted for murder. The trial judge, after denying Gray's motion for a separate trial, permitted the State to introduce a redacted version of Bell's confession. Other witnesses said that six persons (including Bell, Gray,

---

[c] As to this point, Justice Brennan noted: "Rules respecting joinder are based on recognition that the multiplication of charges or defendants may confuse the jury and lead to inferences of habitual criminality or guilt by association. * * * Apart from this, however, joinder rules do not serve 'an independent value besides reliability of the outcome' justifying an exception to the harmless-error principle." Chief Justice Burger's opinion for the Court adopted a similar view of the joinder rules in its application of the harmless error standard. The Chief Justice stressed that: when evidence on the misjoined count was introduced, the trial judge provided a limiting instruction directing the jury to consider each count and defendant separately; the same evidence on the misjoined count 1 would likely have been admissible in any event under Evidence Rule 404(b) (governing evidence of other crimes); and the evidence of guilt was "overwhelming."

[d] *Bruton* stated the proposition more narrowly, i.e., that "effective confrontation * * * was possible only if [the witness] affirmed the statement as his." But in *Nelson v. O'Neil,* 402 U.S. 622 (1971), where a police officer testified as to Runnels' confession implicating O'Neil and Runnels took the stand, denied making the confession, and asserted that the substance of the purported confession was false, the Court held there had been no *Bruton* violation: "The short of the matter is that, given a joint trial and a common defense, Runnels' testimony respecting his out-of-court statement was more favorable to the respondent than any that cross-examination by counsel could possibly have produced had Runnels 'affirmed the statement as his.' It would be unrealistic in the extreme in the circumstances here presented to hold that the respondent was denied either the opportunity or the benefits of full and effective cross-examination of Runnels."

Nelson must be distinguished from *Lilly v. Virginia,* 527 U.S. 116 (1999), where petitioner's accomplice in a 2-day crime spree, *not* joined for trial with petitioner, was called by the prosecution as a witness and invoked his privilege against self-incrimination, after which the court admitted his confession to police, blaming petitioner for the homicide occurring during the spree, as a declaration of an unavailable witness against penal interest. While the state court affirmed defendant's confession on the ground that the accomplice's confession fell within an exception to the hearsay rule, the Supreme Court, although divided as to the breadth of the applicable rule, concluded that "admission of the untested confession" in such circumstances "violated petitioner's Confrontation Clause rights."

and Vanlandingham) participated in the beating. Gray testified and denied his participation; Bell did not testify. The jury was instructed not to use the confession as evidence against Gray. Bell and Gray were convicted.]

In deciding whether *Bruton*'s protective rule applies to the redacted confession before us, we must consider both *Bruton*, and a later case, *Richardson v. Marsh*, 481 U.S. 200 (1987), which limited *Bruton's* scope. We shall briefly summarize each of these two cases.

Bruton, as we have said, involved two defendants—Evans and Bruton—tried jointly for robbery. Evans did not testify, but the Government introduced into evidence Evans' confession, which stated that both he (Evans) and Bruton together had committed the robbery. The trial judge told the jury it could consider the confession as evidence only against Evans, not against Bruton.

This Court held that, despite the limiting instruction, the introduction of Evans' out-of-court confession at Bruton's trial had violated Bruton's right, protected by the Sixth Amendment, to cross-examine witnesses. The Court recognized that in many circumstances a limiting instruction will adequately protect one defendant from the prejudicial effects of the introduction at a joint trial of evidence intended for use only against a different defendant. But it said that

> there are some contexts in which the risk that the jury will not, or cannot, follow instructions is so great, and the consequences of failure so vital to the defendant, that the practical and human limitations of the jury system cannot be ignored. Such a context is presented here, where the powerfully incriminating extrajudicial statements of a codefendant, who stands accused side-by-side with the defendant, are deliberately spread before the jury in a joint trial. Not only are the incriminations devastating to the defendant but their credibility is inevitably suspect. . . . The unreliability of such evidence is intolerably compounded when the alleged accomplice, as here, does not testify and cannot be tested by cross-examination.

The Court found that Evans' confession constituted just such a "powerfully incriminating extrajudicial statemen[t]," and that its introduction into evidence, insulated from cross-examination, violated Bruton's Sixth Amendment rights.

In *Richardson v. Marsh*, the Court considered a redacted confession. The case involved a joint murder trial of Marsh and Williams. The State had redacted the confession of one defendant, Williams, so as to "omit all reference" to his codefendant, Marsh—"indeed, to omit all indication that *anyone* other than . . . Williams" and a third person had "participated in the crime." (emphasis in original). The trial court also instructed the jury not to consider the confession against Marsh. As redacted, the confession indicated that Williams and the third person had discussed the murder in the front seat of a car while they traveled to the victim's house. The redacted confession contained no indication that Marsh—or any other person—was in the car. Later in the trial, however, Marsh testified that she was in the back seat of the car. For that reason, in context, the confession still could have helped convince the jury that Marsh knew about the murder in advance and therefore had participated knowingly in the crime.

The Court held that this redacted confession fell outside *Bruton's* scope and was admissible (with appropriate limiting instructions) at the joint trial. The Court distinguished Evans' confession in *Bruton* as a confession that was "incriminating on its face" and which had "expressly implicat[ed]" Bruton. By contrast, Williams' confession amounted to "evidence requiring linkage" in that it "became" incriminating in respect to Marsh "only when linked with evidence introduced later at trial." The Court held

> that the Confrontation Clause is not violated by the admission of a nontestifying codefendant's confession with a proper limiting instruction when, as here, the confession is redacted to eliminate not only the defendant's name, but any reference to his or her existence.

The Court added: "We express no opinion on the admissibility of a confession in which the defendant's name has been replaced with a symbol or neutral pronoun."

Originally, the codefendant's confession in the case before us, like that in *Bruton*, referred to, and directly implicated another defendant. The State, however, redacted that confession by removing the nonconfessing defendant's name. Nonetheless, unlike *Richardson's* redacted confession, this confession refers directly to the "existence" of the nonconfessing defendant. The State has simply replaced the nonconfessing defendant's name with a kind of symbol, namely the word "deleted" or a blank space set off by commas. The redacted confession, for example, responded to the question "Who was in the group that beat Stacey," with the phrase, "Me, and a few other guys." And when the police witness read the confession in court, he said the word "deleted" or "deletion" where the blank spaces appear. We therefore must decide a question that *Richardson* left open, namely whether redaction that replaces a defendant's name with an obvious indication of deletion, such as a blank space, the word "deleted," or a similar symbol, still falls within *Bruton's* protective rule. We hold that it does.

Bruton, as interpreted by *Richardson*, holds that certain "powerfully incriminating extrajudicial statements of a codefendant"—those naming another defendant—considered as a class, are so prejudicial that limiting instructions cannot work. Unless the prosecutor wishes to hold separate trials or to use separate juries or to abandon use of the confession, he must redact the confession to reduce significantly or to eliminate the special prejudice that the *Bruton* Court found. Redactions that simply replace a name with an obvious blank space or a word such as "deleted" or a symbol or other similarly obvious indications of alteration, however, leave statements that, considered as a class, so closely resemble Bruton's unredacted statements that, in our view, the law must require the same result.

For one thing, a jury will often react similarly to an unredacted confession and a confession redacted in this way, for the jury will often realize that the confession refers specifically to the defendant. This is true even when the State does not blatantly link the defendant to the deleted name, as it did in this case by asking whether Gray was arrested on the basis of information in Bell's confession as soon as the officer had finished reading the redacted statement. Consider a simplified but typical example, a confession that reads "I, Bob Smith, along with Sam Jones, robbed the bank." To replace the words "Sam Jones" with an obvious blank will not likely fool anyone. A juror somewhat familiar with criminal law would know immediately that the blank, in the phrase "I, Bob Smith, along with _______, robbed the bank," refers to defendant Jones. A juror who does not know the law and who therefore wonders to whom the blank might refer need only lift his eyes to Jones, sitting at counsel table, to find what will seem the obvious answer, at least if the juror hears the judge's instruction not to consider the confession as evidence against Jones, for that instruction will provide an obvious reason for the blank. A more sophisticated juror, wondering if the blank refers to someone else, might also wonder how, if it did, the prosecutor could argue the confession is reliable, for the prosecutor, after all, has been arguing that Jones, not someone else, helped Smith commit the crime.

For another thing, the obvious deletion may well call the jurors' attention specially to the removed name. By encouraging the jury to speculate about the reference, the redaction may overemphasize the importance of the confession's accusation—once the jurors work out the reference. That is why Judge Learned Hand, many years ago, wrote in a similar instance that blacking out the name of a codefendant not only "would have been futile. . . . [T]here could not have been the slightest doubt as to whose names had been blacked out" but "even if there had been, that blacking out itself would have not only laid the doubt, but underscored the answer."

Finally, *Bruton's* protected statements and statements redacted to leave a blank or some other similarly obvious alteration, function the same way grammatically. They are directly accusatory. Evans' statement in *Bruton* used a proper name to point explicitly to an accused defendant. And *Bruton* held that the "powerfully incriminating" effect of what Justice Stewart called "an out-of-court accusation," creates a special, and vital, need for cross-examination—a need that would be immediately obvious had the codefendant pointed directly to the defendant in the courtroom itself. The blank space in an obviously redacted confession also points directly to the defendant, and it accuses the defendant in a manner similar to Evans' use of Bruton's name or to a testifying codefendant's accusatory finger. By way of contrast, the factual statement at issue in *Richardson*—a statement about what others said in the front seat of a car—differs from directly accusatory evidence in this respect, for it does not point directly to a defendant at all.

We concede certain differences between *Bruton* and this case. A confession that uses a blank or the word "delete" (or, for that matter, a first name or a nickname) less obviously refers to the defendant than a confession that uses the defendant's full and proper name. Moreover, in some instances the person to whom the blank refers may not be clear: Although the follow-up question asked by the State in this case eliminated all doubt, the reference might not be transparent in other cases in which a confession, like the present confession, uses two (or more) blanks, even though only one other defendant appears at trial, and in which the trial indicates that there are more participants than the confession has named. Nonetheless, as we have said, we believe that, considered as a class, redactions that replace a proper name with an obvious blank, the word "delete," a symbol, or similarly notify the jury that a name has been deleted are similar enough to *Bruton*'s unredacted confessions as to warrant the same legal results.

The State, in arguing for a contrary conclusion, relies heavily upon *Richardson*. But we do not believe *Richardson* controls the result here. We concede that *Richardson* placed outside the scope of *Bruton*'s rule those statements that incriminate inferentially. We also concede that the jury must use inference to connect the statement in this redacted confession with the defendant. But inference pure and simple cannot make the critical difference, for if it did, then *Richardson* would also place outside *Bruton*'s scope confessions that use shortened first names, nicknames, descriptions as unique as the "red-haired, bearded, one-eyed man-with-a-limp," and perhaps even full names of defendants who are always known by a nickname. This Court has assumed, however, that nicknames and specific descriptions fall inside, not outside, *Bruton*'s protection. * * *

That being so, *Richardson* must depend in significant part upon the kind of, not the simple fact of, inference. *Richardson*'s inferences involved statements that did not refer directly to the defendant himself and which became incriminating "only when linked with evidence introduced later at trial." The inferences at issue here involve statements that, despite redaction, obviously refer directly to someone, often obviously the defendant, and which involve inferences that a jury ordinarily could make immediately, even were the confession the very first item introduced at trial. Moreover, the redacted confession with the blank prominent on its face, in *Richardson*'s words, "*facially* incriminat[es]" the codefendant. (emphasis added). Like the confession in *Bruton* itself, the accusation that the redacted confession makes "is more vivid than inferential incrimination, and hence more difficult to thrust out of mind."

Nor are the policy reasons that *Richardson* provided in support of its conclusion applicable here. *Richardson* expressed concern lest application of *Bruton*'s rule apply where "redaction" of confessions, particularly "confessions incriminating by connection," would often "not [be] possible," thereby forcing prosecutors too often to abandon use either of the confession or of a joint trial. Additional redaction of a confession that uses a blank space, the word "delete," or a symbol, however, normally is possible. Consider as an example a portion of the confession before us: The witness who read the confession told the jury that the confession (among other things) said,

Question: Who was in the group that beat Stacey?

Answer: Me, deleted, deleted, and a few other guys.

Why could the witness not, instead, have said:

Question: Who was in the group that beat Stacey?

Answer: Me and a few other guys.

Richardson itself provides a similar example of this kind of redaction. The confession there at issue had been "redacted to omit all reference to respondent—indeed, to omit all indication that anyone other than Martin and Williams participated in the crime," and it did not indicate that it had been redacted. * * *

The *Richardson* Court also feared that the inclusion, within *Bruton's* protective rule, of confessions that incriminated "by connection" too often would provoke mistrials, or would unnecessarily lead prosecutors to abandon the confession or joint trial, because neither the prosecutors nor the judge could easily predict, until after the introduction of all the evidence, whether or not *Bruton* had barred use of the confession. To include the use of blanks, the word "delete," symbols, or other indications of redaction, within *Bruton's* protections, however, runs no such risk. Their use is easily identified prior to trial and does not depend, in any special way, upon the other evidence introduced in the case. We also note that several Circuits have interpreted *Bruton* similarly for many years, yet no one has told us of any significant practical difficulties arising out of their administration of that rule.

For these reasons, we hold that the confession here at issue, which substituted blanks and the word "delete" for the respondent's proper name, falls within the class of statements to which *Bruton's* protections apply. * * *

JUSTICE SCALIA, with whom THE CHIEF JUSTICE, JUSTICE KENNEDY, and JUSTICE THOMAS join, dissenting. * * *

The almost invariable assumption of the law is that jurors follow their instructions. This rule "is a pragmatic one, rooted less in the absolute certitude that the presumption is true than in the belief that it represents a reasonable practical accommodation of the interests of the state and the defendant in the criminal justice process." * * * In *Bruton*, we recognized a "narrow exception" to this rule: "We held that a defendant is deprived of his Sixth Amendment right of confrontation when the facially incriminating confession of a nontestifying codefendant is introduced at their joint trial, even if the jury is instructed to consider the confession only against the codefendant."

We declined in *Richardson*, however, to extend *Bruton* to confessions that incriminate only by inference from other evidence. When incrimination is inferential, "it is a less valid generalization that the jury will not likely obey the instruction to disregard the evidence." Today the Court struggles to decide whether a confession redacted to omit the defendant's name is incriminating on its face or by inference. On the one hand, the Court "concede[s] that the jury must use inference to connect the statement in this redacted confession with the defendant," but later asserts, on the other hand, that "the redacted confession with the blank prominent on its face . . . 'facially incriminat[es]' " him. The Court should have stopped with its concession: the statement "Me, deleted, deleted, and a few other guys" does not facially incriminate anyone but the speaker. The Court's analogizing of "deleted" to a physical description that clearly identifies the defendant (which we have assumed *Bruton* covers, see *Harrington v. California*, 395 U.S. 250 (1969)) does not survive scrutiny. By "facially incriminating," we have meant incriminating independent of other evidence introduced at trial. *Richardson*, supra. Since the defendant's appearance at counsel table is not evidence, the description "red-haired, bearded, one-eyed man-with-a-limp," would be facially incriminating—unless, of course, the defendant had dyed his hair black and shaved his beard before trial, and the prosecution introduced evidence concerning his former appearance. Similarly, the statement "Me, Kevin Gray, and a few other guys" would be facially incriminating, unless the defendant's name set forth in the indictment was not Kevin Gray, and evidence was introduced to the effect that he sometimes used "Kevin Gray" as an alias.

By contrast, the person to whom "deleted" refers in "Me, deleted, deleted, and a few other guys" is not apparent from anything the jury knows independent of the evidence at trial. Though the jury may speculate, the statement expressly implicates no one but the speaker.

Of course the Court is correct that confessions redacted to omit the defendant's name are more likely to incriminate than confessions redacted to omit any reference to his existence. But it is also true—and more relevant here—that confessions redacted to omit the defendant's name are less likely to incriminate than confessions that expressly state it. The latter are "powerfully incriminating" as a class, *Bruton*, supra; the former are not so. Here, for instance, there were two names deleted, five or more participants in the crime, and only one other defendant on trial. The jury no doubt may "speculate about the reference," as it speculates when evidence connects a defendant to a confession that does not refer to his existence. The issue, however, is not whether the confession incriminated petitioner, but whether the incrimination is so "powerful" that we must depart from the normal presumption that the jury follows its instructions. *Richardson*, supra. I think it is not—and I am certain that drawing the line for departing from the ordinary rule at the facial identification of the defendant makes more sense than drawing it anywhere else.

The Court's extension of *Bruton* to name-redacted confessions "as a class" will seriously compromise "society's compelling interest in finding, convicting, and punishing those who violate the law." We explained in *Richardson* that forgoing use of codefendant confessions or joint trials was "too high" a price to insure that juries never disregard their instructions. The Court minimizes the damage that it does by suggesting that "[a]dditional redaction of a confession that uses a blank space, the word 'delete,' or a symbol . . . normally is possible." In the present case, it asks, why could the police officer not have testified that Bell's answer was "Me and a few other guys"? The answer, it seems obvious to me, is because that is not what Bell said. Bell's answer was "Me, Tank, Kevin and a few other guys." Introducing the statement with full disclosure of deletions is one thing; introducing as the complete statement what was in fact only a part is something else. And of course even concealed deletions from the text will often not do the job that the Court demands. For inchoate offenses—conspiracy in particular—redaction to delete all reference to a confederate would often render the confession nonsensical. If the question was "Who agreed to beat Stacey?", and the answer was "Me and Kevin," we might redact the answer to "Me and [deleted]," or perhaps to "Me and somebody else," but surely not to just "Me"—for that would no longer be a confession to the conspiracy charge, but rather the foundation for an insanity defense. To my knowledge we have never before endorsed—and to my strong belief we ought not endorse—the redaction of a statement by some means other than the deletion of certain words, with the fact of the deletion shown. The risk to the integrity of our system (not to mention the increase in its complexity) posed by the approval of such free-lance editing seems to me infinitely greater than the risk posed by the entirely honest reproduction that the Court disapproves.

The United States Constitution guarantees, not a perfect system of criminal justice (as to which there can be considerable disagreement), but a minimum standard of fairness. Lest we lose sight of the forest for the trees, it should be borne in mind that federal and state rules of criminal procedure—which can afford to seek perfection because they can be more readily changed—exclude non-testifying-codefendant confessions even where the Sixth Amendment does not. Under the Federal Rules of Criminal Procedure (and Maryland's), a trial court may order separate trials if joinder will prejudice a defendant. See Fed. Rule Crim. Proc. 14; Md.Crim. Rule 4–253(c) (1998). * * * Here, petitioner moved for a severance on the ground that the admission of Bell's confession would be unfairly prejudicial. The trial court denied the motion, explaining that where a confession names two others, and the evidence is that five or six others participated, redaction of petitioner's name would not leave the jury with the "unavoidable inference" that Bell implicated Gray.

I do not understand the Court to disagree that the redaction itself left unclear to whom the blank referred.[2] That being so, the rule set forth in *Richardson* applies, and the statement could constitutionally be admitted with limiting instruction. This remains, insofar as the Sixth Amendment is concerned, the most "reasonable practical accommodation of the interests of the state and the defendant in the criminal justice process." * * *

NOTES AND QUESTIONS

1. ***The* Crawford *exception.*** In *State v. Nieves*, 897 N.W.2d 363 (Wis.2017), Nieves, convicted of homicide at a trial where a jailhouse informant testified about a codefendant's statements implicating both himself and Nieves, invoked *Bruton* on appeal. The court, reaching a result "in accord with the majority of federal circuit courts that have addressed the issue," rejected the appeal on the ground that *Crawford v. Washington*, p. 1307, had "engendered a seismic shift in how courts analyze the Confrontation Clause," and had thereby "limited the application of the *Bruton* doctrine to instances in which a codefendant's statements are testimonial." Per *Ohio v. Clark*, p. , this was *not* so in the instant case, where the codefendant's statements "were not taken in * * * a formal setting," "were made in a jail and were the product of the casual conversation of two inmates," and where there "is nothing to suggest that an objective observer would believe that these statements would later be used at trial."

2. ***"Interlocking" confessions.*** Benjamin and Eulogio were jointly tried for felony murder. The prosecution admitted against Benjamin his videotaped confession implicating Eulogio, and also called Norberto, who testified about his conversation with the two defendants, when each of them described the circumstances of the felony murder to him. Both defendants were convicted. Eulogio's conviction was affirmed on appeal; the court adopted the reasoning of the plurality in *Parker v. Randolph,* 442 U.S. 62 (1979), that *Bruton* was inapplicable to "interlocking" confessions because in such circumstances the codefendant's confession "will seldom, if ever, be of the 'devastating' character referred to in *Bruton*." The Supreme Court, in the 5–4 decision of CRUZ v. NEW YORK, 481 U.S. 186 (1987), reversed. Scalia, J., for the majority, declared:

" * * * While 'devastating' practical effect was one of the factors that *Bruton* considered in assessing whether the Confrontation Clause might sometimes require departure from the general rule that jury instructions suffice to exclude improper testimony, it did not suggest that the existence of such an effect should be assessed on a case-by-case basis. Rather, that factor was one of the justifications for excepting from the general rule the entire category of codefendant confessions that implicate the defendant in the crime. It is impossible to imagine why there should be excluded from that category, as generally not 'devastating,' codefendant confessions that 'interlock' with the defendant's own confession. '[T]he infinite variability of inculpatory statements (whether made by defendants or codefendants), and of their likely effect on juries, makes [the assumption that an interlocking confession will preclude devastation] untenable.' *Parker* (Stevens, J., dissenting). In this case, for example, the precise content and even the existence of the

[2] The Court does believe, however, that the answer to a "follow-up question"—"All right, now, officer, after he gave you that information, you subsequently were able to arrest Mr. Kevin Gray; is that correct?" ("That's correct")—"eliminated all doubt" as to the subject of the redaction. That is probably not so, and is certainly far from clear. Testimony that preceded the introduction of Bell's confession had already established that Gray had become a suspect in the case, and that a warrant had been issued for his arrest, before Bell confessed. Respondent contends that, given this trial background, and in its context, the prosecutor's question did not imply any connection between Bell's confession and Gray's arrest, and was simply a means of making the transition from Bell's statement to the next piece of evidence, Gray's statement. That is at least arguable, and an appellate court is in a poor position to resolve such a contextual question de novo. * * * But if the question did bring the redaction home to the defendant, surely that shows the impropriety of the question rather than of the redaction—and the question was not objected to. The failure to object deprives petitioner of the right to complain of some incremental identifiability added to the redacted statement by the question and answer. Of course the Court's reliance upon this testimony belies its contention that name-redacted confessions are powerfully incriminating "as a class."

petitioner's own confession were open to question, since they depended upon acceptance of Norberto's testimony, whereas the incriminating confession of codefendant Benjamin was on videotape.

"In fact, it seems to us that 'interlocking' bears a positively inverse relationship to devastation. A codefendant's confession will be relatively harmless if the incriminating story it tells is different from that which the defendant himself is alleged to have told, but enormously damaging if it confirms, in all essential respects, the defendant's alleged confession. It might be otherwise if the defendant were *standing by* his confession, in which case it could be said that the codefendant's confession does no more than support the defendant's very own case. But in the real world of criminal litigation, the defendant is seeking to *avoid* his confession—on the ground that it was not accurately reported, or that it was not really true when made. In the present case, for example, the petitioner sought to establish that Norberto had a motive for falsely reporting a confession that never in fact occurred. In such circumstances a codefendant's confession that corroborates the defendant's confession significantly harms the defendant's case, whereas one that is positively incompatible gives credence to the defendant's assertion that his own alleged confession was nonexistent or false. Quite obviously, what the 'interlocking' nature of the codefendant's confession pertains to is not its *harmfulness* but rather its *reliability:* If it confirms essentially the same facts as the defendant's own confession it is more likely to be true. Its reliability, however, may be relevant to whether the confession should (despite the lack of opportunity for cross-examination) be *admitted as evidence* against the defendant, see *Lee v. Illinois* [p. 1069], but cannot conceivably be relevant to whether, assuming it cannot be admitted, the jury is likely to obey the instruction to disregard it, or the jury's failure to obey is likely to be inconsequential. The law cannot command respect if such an inexplicable exception to a supposed constitutional imperative is adopted. Having decided *Bruton,* we must face the honest consequences of what it holds."

White, J., for the dissenters, objected: "*Bruton* held that where the defendant has not himself confessed, there is too great a chance that the jury would rely on the codefendant's confession. But here, Cruz had admitted the crime and this fact was before the jury. I disagree with the Court's proposition that in every interlocking confession case, the jury, with the defendant's confession properly before it, would be tempted to disobey its instructions and fail to understand that presumptively unreliable evidence must not be used against the defendant. Nor is it remotely possible that in every case the admission of an interlocking confession by a codefendant will have the devastating effect referred to in *Bruton.*[2]"

3. *Limiting instruction.* In *Tennessee v. Street*, 471 U.S. 409 (1985), Street testified at trial that his confession to murder and burglary had been coerced by the sheriff reading to him the prior confession of severed co-defendant Peele and then directing Street to say the same thing. Peele's confession was then admitted in rebuttal to show the several differences in the two confessions. The Court, per Chief Justice Burger, after concluding that use of Peele's confession for this "legitimate, nonhearsay purpose" itself "raises no Confrontation Clause concerns," noted that the "only similarity to *Bruton* is that Peele's statement, like the codefendant's confession in *Bruton,* could have been misused by the jury." But in the present context the Court concluded that the trial court's limiting instruction (that Peele's confession was to be considered "for the purpose

---

[2] The Court is of the view that " 'interlocking' bears a positively inverse relationship to devastation." In so reasoning, the Court gives no weight whatsoever to the devastating effect that the defendant's own confession is likely to have upon his case. The majority's excuse for ignoring this consideration apparently is that the damaging effect of the defendant's confession may vary somewhat from case to case. But the *Bruton* rule is prophylactic in nature, and, in view of the fact that it imposes significant burdens on the prosecution, the rule should be confined to those cases where the jury's ignoring of limiting instructions is most likely to change the verdict, which is to say, those cases where there is the greatest risk that jury misconduct will lead to the conviction of an innocent defendant. It is self-evident that, as a class, cases where the defendant has not confessed fit that description far better than cases where the defendant has confessed.

of rebuttal only") constituted an "appropriate way to limit the jury's use of that evidence in a manner consistent with the Confrontation Clause." This was because here, "unlike the situation in *Bruton,* there were no alternatives that would have both assured the integrity of the trial's truthseeking function and eliminated the risk of the jury's improper use of evidence." The already-granted severance did not solve the problem, and redaction of Peele's confession "would have made it more difficult for the jury to evaluate" Street's claim that his confession was a coerced imitation of Peele's.

4. ***Opportunity to cross-examine.*** *In re Hill,* 458 P.2d 449 (Cal.1969), held that "the Sixth Amendment right to confrontation is intended to give to defendants in criminal cases the right to cross-examine as to statements made by the witness *at the time the witness makes those statements,*" so that *Bruton* applies even when the confessing co-defendant "took the stand and testified consistently with his prior extra-judicial statements." However, that position was rejected in *California v. Green,* [p. 941] upholding a California statute permitting the admission of a witness' prior inconsistent statement to prove the truth of the matter asserted therein, whether or not the defense had an opportunity for cross-examination when it was made. After noting that "there is little difference as far as the Constitution is concerned" between that situation and *Bruton,* the Court held that "the Confrontation Clause does not require excluding from evidence the prior statements of a witness who concedes making the statements, and who may be asked to defend or otherwise explain the inconsistency between his prior and his present version of the events in question, thus opening himself to full cross-examination at trial as to both stories." What then, in a *Bruton*-type situation, of a case in which the confessing co-defendant does *not* take the stand at trial, but did testify in earlier proceedings?

In *Lee v. Illinois,* 476 U.S. 530 (1986),[e] the Court dropped this footnote: "Illinois makes the somewhat surprising argument—an argument, incidentally, that was not made before the state court—that this case does not present any Confrontation Clause issue since Lee was afforded an opportunity to cross-examine Thomas during the suppression hearing. We disagree.

"The function of a suppression hearing is to determine the voluntariness, and hence the admissibility for Fifth Amendment purposes, of a confession. The truth or falsity of the statement is not relevant to the voluntariness inquiry, and no such testimony was given by Thomas. Counsel for both Lee and Thomas specifically stated that their clients were testifying 'for purposes of the motion to suppress the confession only.' Before either defendant took the stand, the court announced, 'Let the record show the testimony of this defendant will be used solely for the purpose of sustaining the motion to suppress previously made.'

"Thus there was no opportunity to cross-examine Thomas with respect to the reliability of the statement, especially as it may have related to Lee, and thus no opportunity for cross-examination sufficient to satisfy the demands of the Confrontation Clause."

5. ***Other severance grounds.*** Other grounds upon which defendants sometimes obtain severances are: (a) because the number of defendants or the complexity of the evidence as to the several defendants is such that the trier of fact probably will be unable to distinguish the evidence and apply the law intelligently as to the charges against each defendant; (b) because the several defendants have antagonistic defenses; and (c) because it would otherwise be impossible to call a codefendant as a witness. As to (a), the question is "whether it is within the jury's capacity, given the complexity of the case, to follow admonitory instructions and to keep separate, collate and

---

[e] The issue before the Court in *Lee,* Justice Brennan had previously noted, was "not strictly speaking a *Bruton* [problem] * * * because we are not here concerned with the effectiveness of limiting instructions in preventing spill-over prejudice to a defendant when his codefendant's confession is admitted against the codefendant at a joint trial." Here, the codefendant's confession was used as substantive evidence against the petitioner. Accordingly, under the standards set forth in *Ohio v. Roberts* [p. 1308], the critical question was whether that statement of an unavailable witness bore "sufficient indicia of reliability" to allow its admission consistent with the Confrontation Clause.

appraise the evidence relevant only to each defendant." *United States v. Warner*, 498 F.3d 666 (7th Cir.2007). As to (b), "defendants are not entitled to severance merely because they may have a better chance of acquittal in separate trials" or "whenever codefendants have conflicting defenses"; rather, a court should grant a severance "only if there is a serious risk that a joint trial would compromise a specific trial right of one of the defendants, or prevent the jury from making a reliable judgment about guilt or innocence," as "might occur when evidence that the jury should not consider against a defendant and that would not be admissible if a defendant were tried alone is admitted against a codefendant." *Zafiro v. United States,* 506 U.S. 534 (1993). As to (c), "the defendant must establish a bona fide need for the testimony, the substance of the desired testimony, the exculpatory effect of the desired testimony, and indication that the co-defendant would indeed testify at a separate trial," shown by "an affidavit from the co-defendant himself or other similar proof." *United States v. Nguyen*, 493 F.3d 613 (5th Cir.2007).

6. ***Comment on co-defendant's failure to testify.*** In *De Luna v. United States,* 308 F.2d 140 (5th Cir.1962), de Luna and Gomez, after denial of a severance motion, were jointly tried on a narcotics charge. They were the occupants of a moving car from which police had seen Gomez throw a package of narcotics. Gomez testified that he was innocent, explaining that de Luna had thrown the package to him and told him to throw it out the window when the police approached. De Luna did not testify, but his lawyer argued that Gomez had the package at all times. Gomez's attorney commented on de Luna's failure to take the stand. Gomez was acquitted; de Luna was found guilty. On appeal, de Luna's conviction was reversed because of the violation of his privilege against self-incrimination. Two members of the court went on to say that under these circumstances the proper result below would have been to permit the comment and then grant a severance. Gomez's "attorneys should be free to draw all rational inferences from the failure of a co-defendant to testify, just as an attorney is free to comment on the effect of any interested party's failure to produce material evidence in his possession or to call witnesses who have knowledge of pertinent facts." Is the analogy an apt one? Given the analysis in *Griffin v. California,* p. 1322, what "rational inferences" may be drawn from de Luna's failure to testify? What if Gomez's attorney had merely called attention to the fact that his client had taken the stand?

7. ***Joint sentencing hearing.*** In *Kansas v. Carr,* 136 S.Ct. 633 (2016), defendant claimed the joint capital-sentencing proceeding in the murder prosecution of him and his brother violated his Eighth Amendment right to an individualized sentencing determination. Citing its prior holding that it is not the role of the Eighth Amendment to establish a special "federal code of evidence" governing "the admissibility of evidence at capital sentencing proceedings," the Court instead assessed the defendant's claim under the due process clause, where the question is whether the evidence "so infected the sentencing proceeding with unfairness as to render the jury's imposition of the death penalty a denial of due process." Thus concluding that the "mere admission of evidence that might not otherwise have been admitted in a severed proceeding does not demand the automatic vacatur of a death sentence," the Court went on to hold that the admission of mitigating evidence by defendant's brother did not constitute a due process violation with respect to him, given (i) the trial court's careful instructions to the jury to give separate consideration to each defendant and to decide each sentence on the evidence applicable to that defendant; and (ii) the preference accorded to joint proceedings: "Better that the two defendants who have together committed the same crimes be placed side-by-side to have their fates determined by a single jury."

CHAPTER 20

SPEEDY TRIAL AND OTHER SPEEDY DISPOSITION

■ ■ ■

While defendants may be prejudiced by undue delay in the trial of charges against them, certainly many defendants would prefer to delay their trials as long as possible, perhaps to the detriment of the public interest in prompt trials. These conflicting considerations largely account for the existing array of federal and state constitutional and statutory provisions dealing with the matter of speedy trial, discussed herein together with constitutional limitations upon delay at other stages of the criminal process.

§ 1. SPEEDY TRIAL

BARKER V. WINGO

407 U.S. 514, 92 S.Ct. 2182, 33 L.Ed.2d 101 (1972).

JUSTICE POWELL delivered the opinion of the Court.

Although a speedy trial is guaranteed the accused by the Sixth Amendment to the Constitution, this Court has dealt with that right on infrequent occasions. The Court's opinion in *Klopfer v. North Carolina,* 386 U.S. 213 (1967), established that the right to speedy trial is "fundamental" and is imposed by the Due Process Clause of the Fourteenth Amendment on the States. [I]n none of these cases have we attempted to set out the criteria by which the speedy trial right is to be judged. This case compels us to make such an attempt.

On July 20, 1958, in Christian County, Kentucky, an elderly couple was beaten to death by intruders wielding an iron tire tool. Two suspects, Silas Manning and Willie Barker, the petitioner, were arrested shortly thereafter. The grand jury indicted them on September 15. Counsel was appointed on September 17, and Barker's trial was set for October 21. The Commonwealth had a stronger case against Manning, and it believed that Barker could not be convicted unless Manning testified against him. Manning was naturally unwilling to incriminate himself. Accordingly, on October 23, the day Silas Manning was brought to trial, the Commonwealth sought and obtained the first of what was to be a series of 16 continuances of Barker's trial. Barker made no objection. By first convicting Manning, the Commonwealth would remove possible problems of self-incrimination and would be able to assure his testimony against Barker.

The Commonwealth encountered more than a few difficulties in its prosecution of Manning. The first trial ended in a hung jury. A second trial resulted in a conviction, but the Kentucky Court of Appeals reversed because of the admission of evidence obtained by an illegal search. At his third trial, Manning was again convicted, and the Court of Appeals again reversed because the trial court had not granted a change of venue. A fourth trial resulted in a hung jury. Finally, after five trials, Manning was convicted, in March 1962, of murdering one victim, and after a sixth trial, in December 1962, he was convicted of murdering the other.

The Christian County Circuit Court holds three terms each year—in February, June, and September. Barker's initial trial was to take place in the September term of 1958. The first continuance postponed it until the February 1959 term. The second continuance was granted for one month only. Every term thereafter for as long as the Manning prosecutions were in process, the Commonwealth routinely moved to continue Barker's case to the next term. When the case was continued from the June 1959 term until the following September, Barker, having spent 10 months in jail, obtained his release by posting a $5,000 bond. He thereafter remained free in the community until his trial. Barker made no objection, through his counsel, to the first 11 continuances.

When on February 12, 1962, the Commonwealth moved for the twelfth time to continue the case until the following term, Barker's counsel filed a motion to dismiss the indictment. The motion to dismiss was denied two weeks later, and the State's motion for a continuance was granted. The State was granted further continuances in June 1962 and September 1962, to which Barker did not object.

In February 1963, the first term of court following Manning's final conviction, the Commonwealth moved to set Barker's trial for March 19. But on the day scheduled for trial, it again moved for a continuance until the June term. It gave as its reason the illness of the ex-sheriff who was the chief investigating officer in the case. To this continuance, Barker objected unsuccessfully.

The witness was still unable to testify in June, and the trial, which had been set for June 19, was continued again until the September term over Barker's objection. This time the court announced that the case would be dismissed for lack of prosecution if it were not tried during the next term. The final trial date was set for October 9, 1963. On that date, Barker again moved to dismiss the indictment, and this time specified that his right to a speedy trial had been violated. The motion was denied; the trial commenced with Manning as the chief prosecution witness; Barker was convicted and given a life sentence.

Barker appealed his conviction to the Kentucky Court of Appeals, relying in part on his speedy trial claim. The court affirmed. In February 1970 Barker petitioned for habeas corpus in the United States District Court for the Western District of Kentucky. Although the District Court rejected the petition without holding a hearing, the Court granted petitioner leave to appeal *in forma pauperis* and a certificate of probable cause to appeal. On appeal, the Court of Appeals for the Sixth Circuit affirmed the District Court. * * * We granted Barker's petition for certiorari.

The right to a speedy trial is generically different from any of the other rights enshrined in the Constitution for the protection of the accused. In addition to the general concern that all accused persons be treated according to decent and fair procedures, there is a societal interest in providing a speedy trial which exists separate from and at times in opposition to the interests of the accused. The inability of courts to provide a prompt trial has contributed to a large backlog of cases in urban courts which, among other things, enables defendants to negotiate more effectively for pleas of guilty to lesser offenses and otherwise manipulate the system. In addition, persons released on bond for lengthy periods awaiting trial have an opportunity to commit other crimes. It must be of little comfort to the residents of Christian County, Kentucky, to know that Barker was at large on bail for over four years while accused of a vicious and brutal murder of which he was ultimately convicted. Moreover, the longer an accused is free awaiting trial, the more tempting becomes his opportunity to jump bail and escape. Finally, delay between arrest and punishment may have a detrimental effect on rehabilitation.

If an accused cannot make bail, he is generally confined, as was Barker for 10 months, in a local jail. This contributes to the overcrowding and generally deplorable state of those institutions. Lengthy exposure to these conditions "has a destructive effect on human character and makes the rehabilitation of the individual offender much more difficult." At times the result may even be violent rioting. Finally, lengthy pretrial detention is costly. The cost of maintaining a prisoner in jail varies from $3 to $9 per day, and this amounts to millions across the Nation. In addition, society loses wages which might have been earned, and it must often support families of incarcerated breadwinners.

A second difference between the right to speedy trial and the accused's other constitutional rights is that deprivation of the right may work to the accused's advantage. Delay is not an uncommon defense tactic. As the time between the commission of the crime and trial lengthens, witnesses may become unavailable or their memories may fade. If the witnesses support the prosecution, its case will be weakened, sometimes seriously so. And it is the prosecution which carries the burden of proof. Thus, unlike the right to counsel or the right to be free from compelled self-incrimination, deprivation of the right to speedy trial does not *per se* prejudice the accused's ability to defend himself.

Finally, and perhaps most importantly, the right to speedy trial is a more vague concept than other procedural rights. It is, for example, impossible to determine with precision when the right has been denied. We cannot definitely say how long is too long in a system where justice is supposed to be swift but deliberate. As a consequence, there is no fixed point in the criminal process when the State can put the defendant to the choice of either exercising or waiving the right to a speedy trial. If, for example, the State moves for a 60-day continuance, granting that continuance is not a violation of the right to speedy trial unless the circumstances of the case are such that further delay would endanger the values the right protects. It is impossible to do more than generalize about when those circumstances exist. There is nothing comparable to the point in the process when a defendant exercises or waives his right to counsel or his right to a jury trial. * * *

The amorphous quality of the right also leads to the unsatisfactorily severe remedy of dismissal of the indictment when the right has been deprived. This is indeed a serious consequence because it means that a defendant who may be guilty of a serious crime will go free, without having been tried. Such a remedy is more serious than an exclusionary rule or a reversal for a new trial, but it is the only possible remedy.

Perhaps because the speedy trial right is so slippery, two rigid approaches are urged upon us as ways of eliminating some of the uncertainty which courts experience in protecting the right. The first suggestion is that we hold that the Constitution requires a criminal defendant to be offered a trial within a specified time period. The result of such a ruling would have the virtue of clarifying when the right is infringed and of simplifying courts' application of it. Recognizing this, some legislatures have enacted laws, and some courts have adopted procedural rules which more narrowly define the right. * * *

But such a result would require this Court to engage in legislative or rulemaking activity, rather than in the adjudicative process to which we should confine our efforts. We do not establish procedural rules for the States, except when mandated by the Constitution. We find no constitutional basis for holding that the speedy trial right can be quantified into a specified number of days or months. The States, of course, are free to prescribe a reasonable period consistent with constitutional standards, but our approach must be less precise.

The second suggested alternative would restrict consideration of the right to those cases in which the accused has demanded a speedy trial. Most States have recognized what is loosely referred to as the "demand rule," although eight States reject it. It is not clear, however, precisely what is meant by that term. Although every Federal Court of Appeals that has considered the question has endorsed some kind of demand rule, some have regarded the rule within the concept of waiver, whereas others have viewed it as a factor to be weighed in assessing whether there has been a deprivation of the speedy trial right. We shall refer to the former approach as the demand-waiver doctrine. The demand-waiver doctrine provides that a defendant waives any consideration of his right to speedy trial for any period prior to which he has not demanded a trial. Under this rigid approach, a prior demand is a necessary condition to the consideration of the speedy trial right. This essentially was the approach the Sixth Circuit took below.

Such an approach, by presuming waiver of a fundamental right from inaction, is inconsistent with this Court's pronouncements on waiver of constitutional rights. The Court has defined waiver as "an intentional relinquishment or abandonment of a known right or privilege." Courts should "indulge every reasonable presumption against waiver," and they should "not presume acquiescence in the loss of fundamental rights." * * *

In excepting the right to speedy trial from the rule of waiver we have applied to other fundamental rights, courts that have applied the demand-waiver rule have relied on the assumption that delay usually works for the benefit of the accused and on the absence of any readily ascertainable time in the criminal process for a defendant to be given the choice of exercising or waiving his right. But it is not necessarily true that delay benefits the defendant. There are cases in which delay appreciably harms the defendant's ability to defend himself. Moreover, a defendant confined to jail prior to trial is obviously disadvantaged by delay as is a defendant released on bail but unable to lead a normal life because of community suspicion and his own anxiety.

The nature of the speedy-trial right does make it impossible to pinpoint a precise time in the process when the right must be asserted or waived, but that fact does not argue for placing the burden of protecting the right solely on defendants. A defendant has no duty to bring himself to trial; the State has that duty as well as the duty of insuring that the trial is consistent with due process. Moreover, for the reasons earlier expressed, society has a particular interest in bringing swift prosecutions, and society's representatives are the ones who should protect that interest.

It is also noteworthy that such a rigid view of the demand rule places defense counsel in an awkward position. Unless he demands a trial early and often, he is in danger of frustrating his client's right. If counsel is willing to tolerate some delay because he finds it reasonable and helpful in preparing his own case, he may be unable to obtain a speedy trial for his client at the end of that time. Since under the demand-waiver rule no time runs until the demand is made, the government will have whatever time is otherwise reasonable to bring the defendant to trial after a demand has been made. Thus, if the first demand is made three months after arrest in a jurisdiction which prescribes a six months rule, the prosecution will have a total of nine months—which may be wholly unreasonable under the circumstances. The result in practice is likely to be either an automatic, *pro forma* demand made immediately after appointment of counsel or delays which, but for the demand-waiver rule, would not be tolerated. Such a result is not consistent with the interests of defendants, society, or the Constitution.

We reject, therefore, the rule that a defendant who fails to demand a speedy trial forever waives his right. This does not mean, however, that the defendant has no responsibility to assert his right. We think the better rule is that the defendant's assertion of or failure to assert his right to a speedy trial is one of the factors to be considered in an inquiry into the deprivation of the right. Such a formulation avoids the rigidities of the demand-waiver rule and the resulting possible unfairness in its application. It allows the trial court to exercise a judicial discretion based on the circumstances, including due consideration of any applicable formal procedural rule. It would permit, for example, a court to attach a different weight to a situation in which the defendant knowingly fails to object from a situation in which his attorney acquiesces in long delay without adequately informing his client or from a situation in which no counsel is appointed. It would also allow a court to weigh the frequency and force of the objections as opposed to attaching significant weight to a purely *pro forma* objection.

In ruling that a defendant has some responsibility to assert a speedy-trial claim, we do not depart from our holdings in other cases concerning the waiver of fundamental rights, in which we have placed the entire responsibility on the prosecution to show that the claimed waiver was knowingly and voluntarily made. Such cases have involved rights which must be exercised or waived at a specific time or under clearly identifiable circumstances, such as the rights to plead not guilty, to demand a jury trial, to exercise the privilege against self-incrimination, and to have the assistance of counsel. We have shown above that the right to a speedy trial is unique in its uncertainty as to when and under what circumstances it must be asserted or may be deemed waived. But the rule we announce today, which comports with constitutional principles, places the primary burden on the courts and the prosecutors to assure that cases are brought to trial. We hardly need add that if delay is attributable to the defendant, then his waiver may be given effect under standard waiver doctrine, the demand rule aside.

We, therefore, reject both of the inflexible approaches—the fixed time period because it goes further than the Constitution requires; the demand-waiver rule because it is insensitive to a right which we have deemed fundamental. The approach we accept is a balancing test, in which the conduct of both the prosecution and the defendant are weighed.

A balancing test necessarily compels courts to approach speedy-trial cases on an *ad hoc* basis. We can do little more than identify some of the factors which courts should assess in determining whether a particular defendant has been deprived of his right. Though some might express them in different ways, we identify four such factors: Length of delay, the reason for the delay, the defendant's assertion of his right, and prejudice to the defendant.

The length of the delay is to some extent a triggering mechanism. Until there is some delay which is presumptively prejudicial, there is no necessity for inquiry into the other factors that go into the balance. Nevertheless, because of the imprecision of the right to speedy trial, the length of delay that will provoke such an inquiry is necessarily dependent upon the peculiar circumstances of the case. To take but one example, the delay that can be tolerated for an ordinary street crime is considerably less than for a serious, complex conspiracy charge.

Closely related to length of delay is the reason the government assigns to justify the delay. Here, too, different weights should be assigned to different reasons. A deliberate attempt to delay the trial in order to hamper the defense should be weighed heavily against the government. A more neutral reason such as negligence or overcrowded courts should be weighed less heavily but nevertheless should be considered since the ultimate responsibility for such circumstances must rest with the government rather than with the defendant. Finally, a valid reason, such as a missing witness, should serve to justify appropriate delay.

We have already discussed the third factor, the defendant's responsibility to assert his right. Whether and how a defendant asserts his right is closely related to the other factors we have mentioned. The strength of his efforts will be affected by the length of the delay, to some extent by the reason for the delay, and most particularly by the personal prejudice, which is not always readily identifiable, that he experiences. The more serious the deprivation, the more likely a defendant is to complain. The defendant's assertion of his speedy trial right, then, is entitled to strong evidentiary weight in determining whether the right is being deprived. We emphasize that failure to assert the right will make it difficult for a defendant to prove that he was denied a speedy trial.

A fourth factor is prejudice to the defendant. Prejudice, of course, should be assessed in the light of the interests of defendants which the speedy trial right was designed to protect. This Court has identified three such interests: (i) to prevent oppressive pretrial incarceration; (ii) to minimize anxiety and concern of the accused; and (iii) to limit the possibility that the defense will be impaired. Of these, the most serious is the last, because the inability of a defendant adequately to prepare his case skews the fairness of the entire system. If witnesses die or disappear during a delay, the prejudice is obvious. There is also prejudice if defense witnesses are unable to recall accurately events of the distant past. Loss of memory, however, is not always reflected in the record because what has been forgotten can rarely be shown.

We have discussed previously the societal disadvantages of lengthy pretrial incarceration, but obviously the disadvantages for the accused who cannot obtain his release are even more serious. The time spent in jail awaiting trial has a detrimental impact on the individual. It often means loss of a job; it disrupts family life; and it enforces idleness. Most jails offer little or no recreational or rehabilitative programs. The time spent in jail is simply dead time. Moreover, if a defendant is locked up, he is hindered in his ability to gather evidence, contact witnesses, or otherwise prepare his defense. Imposing those consequences on anyone who has not yet been convicted is serious. It is especially unfortunate to impose them on those persons who are ultimately found to be innocent. Finally, even if an accused is not incarcerated prior to trial, he is still disadvantaged by restraints on his liberty and by living under a cloud of anxiety, suspicion, and often hostility.

We regard none of the four factors identified above as either a necessary or sufficient condition to the finding of a deprivation of the right of speedy trial. Rather, they are related factors and must be considered together with such other circumstances as may be relevant. In sum, these factors have no talismanic qualities; courts must still engage in a difficult and sensitive balancing process. But, because we are dealing with a fundamental right of the accused, this process must be carried out with full recognition that the accused's interest in a speedy trial is specifically affirmed in the Constitution.

The difficulty of the task of balancing these factors is illustrated by this case, which we consider to be close. It is clear that the length of delay between arrest and trial—well over five years—was extraordinary. Only seven months of that period can be attributed to a strong excuse, the illness of the ex-sheriff who was in charge of the investigation. Perhaps some delay would have been permissible under ordinary circumstances, so that Manning could be utilized as a witness in Barker's trial, but more than four years was too long a period, particularly since a good part of that period was attributable to the Commonwealth's failure or inability to try Manning under circumstances that comported with due process.

Two counter-balancing factors, however, outweigh these deficiencies. The first is that prejudice was minimal. Of course, Barker was prejudiced to some extent by living for over four years under a cloud of suspicion and anxiety. Moreover, although he was released on bond for most of the period, he did spend 10 months in jail before trial. But there is no claim that any of Barker's witnesses died or otherwise became unavailable owing to the delay. The trial transcript indicates only two very minor lapses of memory—one on the part of a prosecution witness—which were in no way significant to the outcome.

More important than the absence of serious prejudice, is the fact that Barker did not want a speedy trial. Counsel was appointed for Barker immediately after his indictment and represented him throughout the period. No question is raised as to the competency of such counsel. Despite the fact that counsel had notice of the motions for continuances, the record shows no action whatever taken between October 21, 1958, and February 12, 1962, that could be construed as the assertion of the speedy-trial right. On the latter date, in response to another motion for continuance, Barker moved to dismiss the indictment. The record does not show on what ground this motion was based, although it is clear that no alternative motion was made for an immediate trial. Instead the record strongly suggests that while he hoped to take advantage of the delay in which he had acquiesced, and thereby obtain a dismissal of the charges, he definitely did not want to be tried. Counsel conceded as much at oral argument:

"Your honor, I would concede that Willie Mae Barker—probably—I don't know this for a fact—probably did not want to be tried. I don't think any man wants to be tried. And I don't consider this a liability on his behalf. I don't blame him."

The probable reason for Barker's attitude was that he was gambling on Manning's acquittal. The evidence was not terribly strong against Manning, as the reversals and hung juries suggest, and Barker undoubtedly thought that if Manning were acquitted, he would never be tried. Counsel also conceded this:

"Now, it's true that the reason for this delay was the Commonwealth of Kentucky's desire to secure the testimony of the accomplice, Silas Manning. And it's true that if Silas Manning were never convicted, Willie Mae Barker would never have been convicted. We concede this."

That Barker was gambling on Manning's acquittal is also suggested by his failure, following the *pro forma* motion to dismiss filed in February 1962, to object to the Commonwealth's next two motions for continuances. Indeed, it was not until March 1963, after Manning's convictions were final, that Barker, having lost his gamble, began to object to further continuances. At that time, the Commonwealth's excuse was the illness of the ex-sheriff, which Barker has conceded justified the further delay.

We do not hold that there may never be a situation in which an indictment may be dismissed on speedy-trial grounds where the defendant has failed to object to continuances. There may be a situation in which the defendant was represented by incompetent counsel, was severely prejudiced, or even cases in which the continuances were granted *ex parte.* But barring extraordinary circumstances, we would be reluctant indeed to rule that a defendant was denied this constitutional right on a record that strongly indicates, as does this one, that the defendant did not want a speedy trial. We hold, therefore, that Barker was not deprived of his due process right to a speedy trial. * * *[a]

NOTES AND QUESTIONS

1. ***The* Barker *balancing test.*** H. Richard Uviller, *Barker v. Wingo: Speedy Trial Gets a Fast Shuffle,* 72 Colum.L.Rev. 1376, 1399–1400 (1972), objects that "the Court in its pronouncements and in their application to the facts before it seems to arrive at a distorted formula for the interplay of the elements of the speedy trial guarantee. It runs something like this: notwithstanding the lapse of a substantial period of time to which the accused did not affirmatively consent, he is not denied a speedy trial if the court determines as a fact that he did not really want to be sooner tried, and he fails to demonstrate concretely some actual and significant deterioration of his defensive case suffered by reason of the delay. With all due deference, it is here submitted that a formulation more closely harmonious with traditional concepts and prior insights from other quarters, might be shaped thus: absent an explicit and competent waiver for the period in question, the accused is denied his right to a speedy trial by the passage of an unreasonable period of time without a demonstration by the state of good and sufficient reason or necessity therefor; and further, prejudice presumptively increases with the length of elapsed time, imposing upon the

[a] White, J., joined by Brennan, J., concurring, emphasized that the crowded dockets could not justify an unreasonable delay in providing a trial: "[F]or those who desire an early trial, * * * [the defendant's interests] should prevail if the only countervailing considerations offered by the State are those connected with crowded dockets and prosecutorial case loads. A defendant desiring a speedy trial, therefore, should have it within some reasonable time; and only special circumstances presenting a more pressing public need with respect to the case itself should suffice to justify delay. * * * Of course, cases will differ among themselves as to the allowable time between charge and trial so as to permit prosecution and defense adequately to prepare their case. But unreasonable delay in run-of-the-mill criminal cases cannot be justified by simply asserting that the public resources provided by the State's criminal justice system are limited and that each case must await its turn."

state the increasing burden of proving the delay harmless by reasons more particular and persuasive than convenience, negligence, or the hope of tactical advantage."

Doggett was indicted on drug charges in February 1980; officers seeking to arrest him learned he had left for Colombia; in September 1981 it was learned he was imprisoned in Panama; Panama authorities agreed to "expel" him to the U.S. but instead released him the following July; he then went to Colombia but reentered the U.S. unhindered in September 1982 and settled in Virginia, where he lived openly under his own name until September 1988, when the Marshal's Service ran a simple credit check on several thousand people subject to outstanding arrest warrants and, within minutes, found out where he lived and worked; upon his arrest, he moved without success to dismiss the indictment. In DOGGETT v. UNITED STATES, 505 U.S. 647 (1992), the Supreme Court reversed, applying the *Barker* balancing test in this fashion: (1) Re *length of delay*, "the extraordinary 8 ½-year lag between Doggett's indictment and arrest clearly suffices to trigger the speedy trial enquiry." (2) The *reason for the delay* was government negligence, as for "six years, the Government's investigators made no serious effort to test their progressively more questionable assumption that Doggett was living abroad, and, had they done so, they could have found him within minutes." (3) Re *defendant's assertion of his right*, "Doggett is not to be taxed for invoking his speedy trial right only after his arrest," as the government conceded he was unaware of the indictment prior to his arrest. (4) Re *prejudice to the defendant*, there was no pretrial detention or anxiety, leaving only the possibility of impairment of the defense, about which Doggett made no specific showing. Recognizing "that excessive delay presumptively compromises the reliability of a trial in ways that neither party can prove or, for that matter, identify," the Court then concluded: "When the Government's negligence thus causes delay six times as long as that generally sufficient to trigger judicial review, and when the presumption of prejudice, albeit unspecified, is neither extenuated, as by the defendant's acquiescence, nor persuasively rebutted, the defendant is entitled to relief."

In *Vermont v. Brillon*, 556 U.S. 81 (2009), the Court concluded that "delay caused by the defense weighs against the defendant," that "delay caused by the defendant's counsel is also charged against the defendant," and that this is so "whether counsel is privately retained or publicly assigned," for "[u]nlike a prosecutor or the court, assigned counsel ordinarily is not considered a state actor." This means, the Court added, that an "assigned counsel's failure 'to move the case forward' does not warrant attribution of delay to the State," a sensible conclusion, for a contrary rule "could encourage appointed counsel to delay proceedings by seeking unreasonable continuances, hoping thereby to obtain a dismissal of the indictment on speedy-trial grounds." But the Court cautioned that the above-stated general rule "is not absolute," for "[d]elay resulting from a systemic 'breakdown in the public defender system' * * * could be charged to the State."

In *Boyer v. Louisiana*, 569 U.S. 238 (2013), cert. had been granted to decide whether a delay caused by a State's failure to fund counsel for an indigent's defense should weigh against the State in determining whether there was a deprivation of defendant's Sixth Amendment right to a speedy trial. The writ was dismissed, per curiam, as improvidently granted; three concurring Justices explained this was because the record did not support the state court's assertion most of the 7-year delay was attributable to a "funding crisis." The other four Justices opted to "defer to" the state court's "factual determination," and then concluded that a "State's failure to provide adequate funding for an indigent's defense that prevents a case from going to trial is no different" than the "overcrowded courts" cited in *Barker* or the "systemic breakdown" mentioned in *Brillon*.

2. Barker *"rebalanced"?* Was the *Barker* test "revised" in *Reed v. Farley*, 512 U.S. 339 (1994)? The Court there held that a state court's failure to observe the 120-day time-for-trial rule of the Interstate Agreement on Detainers[b] was not cognizable on federal habeas corpus when, as

---

[b] The IAD, a Compact adopted by the federal government and virtually all states, provides that a prisoner "serving a term of imprisonment" (which excludes a pretrial detainee, a person serving a misdemeanor sentence in

there, the defendant registered no objection to the trial date when it was set and suffered no prejudice from the delay. In responding to Reed's argument the result should be otherwise because the IAD's speedy trial provision "effectuates" the Sixth Amendment speedy trial guarantee, the Court asserted, citing *Barker:* "A showing of prejudice is required to establish a violation of the Sixth Amendment Speedy Trial Clause, and that necessary ingredient is entirely missing here."

3. ***The imprisoned defendant.*** In the pre-*Barker* case of SMITH v. HOOEY, 393 U.S. 374 (1969), the Court, per Stewart, J., rejected the state court's conclusion that the state had no duty under the Sixth Amendment to make a good faith effort to obtain the presence for trial of petitioner, who repeatedly demanded trial while confined in a federal prison:

"At first blush it might appear that a man already in prison under a lawful sentence is hardly in a position to suffer from 'undue and oppressive incarceration prior to trial.' But the fact is that delay in bringing such a person to trial on a pending charge may ultimately result in as much oppression as is suffered by one who is jailed without bail upon an untried charge. First, the possibility that the defendant already in prison might receive a sentence at least partially concurrent with the one he is serving may be forever lost if trial of the pending charge is postponed. Secondly, under procedures now widely practiced, the duration of his present imprisonment may be increased, and the conditions under which he must serve his sentence greatly worsened, by the pendency of another criminal charge outstanding against him.

"And while it might be argued that a person already in prison would be less likely than others to be affected by 'anxiety and concern accompanying public accusation,' there is reason to believe that an outstanding untried charge (of which even a convict may, of course, be innocent) can have fully as depressive an effect upon a prisoner as upon a person who is at large. * * * In the opinion of the former Director of the Federal Bureau of Prisons, '[I]t is in their effect upon the prisoner and our attempts to rehabilitate him that detainers are most corrosive. The strain of having to serve a sentence with the uncertain prospect of being taken into the custody of another state at the conclusion interferes with the prisoner's ability to take maximum advantage of his institutional opportunities. His anxiety and depression may leave him with little inclination towards self-improvement.'

"Finally, it is self-evident that 'the possibilities that long delay will impair the ability of an accused to defend himself' are markedly increased when the accused is incarcerated in another jurisdiction. Confined in a prison, perhaps far from the place where the offense covered by the outstanding charge allegedly took place, his ability to confer with potential defense witnesses, or even to keep track of their whereabouts, is obviously impaired. And, while 'evidence and witnesses disappear, memories fade, and events lose their perspective,' a man isolated in prison is powerless to exert his own investigative efforts to mitigate these erosive effects of the passage of time.

"[As] is fully confirmed by the brief that the Solicitor General has filed in the present case:

'[T]he Bureau of Prisons would doubtless have made the prisoner available if a writ of habeas corpus *ad prosequendum* had been issued by the state court. It does not appear, however, that the State at any point sought to initiate that procedure in this case.' "

---

the county jail, and perhaps a person still in a facility for temporary custody) in another jurisdiction against whom a detainer (a request filed by a criminal justice agency asking the detaining institution to hold the prisoner for the agency or to notify the agency when release is imminent) has been filed must be promptly notified of that fact and of his right to demand trial. If the prisoner demands trial, that constitutes a waiver of extradition and mandates surrender of the prisoner by the incarcerating jurisdiction. If trial is not had within 180 days from the date the prosecutor and court in the requesting jurisdiction received notice of the demand, and good cause for the delay is not shown, the charges must be dismissed with prejudice. Also, under the IAD's antishuttling provision, if the prisoner is returned to his original place of imprisonment without trial, the charge "shall not be of any further force or effect."

4. ***Federal statute.*** The Speedy Trial Act of 1974, set out in Supp.App. B, establishes specific time limits within which the trial and certain other steps must commence in a federal prosecution.

5. ***Speedy trial in the states; constitution vs. statute.*** Although the Sixth Amendment right to a speedy trial was not applied to the states until *Klopfer,* all state constitutions also provide such a guarantee. An overwhelming majority of the states have enacted statutes setting forth the time within which a defendant must be tried following the date he was arrested, held to answer, committed, or indicted, and it is these statutes that have received principal attention. If a statutory violation is found, there is seldom any inquiry into the alleged constitutional denial; and if the statute has not been violated, it is typically assumed that the constitutional provision has been satisfied. But, while "the statutory and constitutional provisions address similar concerns, the rights established by each are not necessarily coextensive." *People v. Hall,* 743 N.E.2d 521 (Ill.2000).

6. ***Excuses for delay.*** Speedy trial statutes declare that trial must commence within a fixed period—expressed in days, months, or terms of courts—following some prior event, such as arrest, indictment, or holding to answer, but also recognize that certain periods of time are not to be counted in determining whether this time has run. A majority of jurisdictions merely provide for additional time upon a showing of "good cause," while some statutes enumerate some of the more common legitimate reasons for delay. See, e.g., the excluded periods in § 3161(h) of the Speedy Trial Act of 1974. Because of the excluded periods, a substantial number of cases will not come to trial within the period specified in the statute. (When excluded periods in the federal Act are described in terms of "delay resulting from" a specified event, this does *not* mean that the event must have actually caused, or be expected to cause, delay in starting the trial. *United States v. Tinklenberg,* 563 U.S. 647 (2011).)

A central feature of the federal statute is that subparagraph (7) in the statutory list of excluded periods expressly provides that the "period of delay resulting from a continuance" will be excluded *only* if the judge makes findings for the record as to why "the ends of justice served by the granting of such continuance outweigh the best interests of the public and the defendant in a speedy trial." Given that language, a unanimous Court decided in *Zedner v. United States,* 547 U.S. 489 (2006), a defendant may not prospectively waive application of the Act so as to make a continuance effective notwithstanding the failure of the judge to place the necessary findings on the record. "If a defendant could simply waive the application of the Act whenever he or she wanted more time, no defendant would ever need to put such considerations before the court under the rubric of an ends-of-justice exclusion." The Court then went on to hold (i) that the district court could not supply the findings on remand, as "at the very least the Act implies that those findings must be put on the record by the time a district court rules on a defendant's motion to dismiss under § 3162(a)(2)"; and (ii) that the harmless error doctrine (see p. 1413) is inapplicable in this context given the language of the statute (e.g., the statement in § 3162(a)(2) that if the trial is not commenced within the prescribed time "the information or indictment shall be dismissed on motion of the defendant").

Bloate v. United States, 559 U.S. 196 (2010), raised the question of whether the findings required under the above-mentioned subparagraph were unnecessary because the delay was instead covered under another subparagraph—specifically, whether the time granted to *prepare* pretrial motions instead fits within subparagraph (1) dealing with "delay resulting from * * * proceedings concerning the defendant." The Court answered that in the negative, noting that subparagraph (1) further particularized its coverage by referencing "delay resulting from any pretrial motion, from the filing of the motion through the conclusion of the hearing," which thus excludes the period before the filing (even if filing subsequently occurs).

7. ***Consequences of denial of speedy trial.*** In *United States v. Strunk*, 467 F.2d 969 (7th Cir.1972), where defendant's constitutional right to speedy trial was found to have been violated while he was serving a state sentence for another offense, but defendant made "no claim of having been prejudiced in presenting his defense," the court took note of the traditional remedies of "dismissal of the indictment or the vacation of the sentence" and then ruled that in the instant case "the proper remedy is to * * * credit the defendant with the period of time elapsing between the return of the indictment and the date of arraignment." But a unanimous Supreme Court disagreed, noting that delay in a case such as this "may subject the accused to an emotional stress" by which "the prospect of rehabilitation may also be affected," and concluding: "In light of the policies which underlie the right to a speedy trial, dismissal must remain, as *Barker* noted, 'the only possible remedy.' " *Strunk v. United States*, 412 U.S. 434 (1973).

As for denial of a statutory speedy trial right, "one group of states treats it as a bar to another prosecution for the same offense, while another group does not. The third position is that [denial] prevents subsequent prosecutions for the same charge if it is a misdemeanor, but not if it is a felony." Note, 57 Colum.L.Rev. 846, 859–60 (1957). Under § 3162(a) of the federal Act, the sanction is dismissal "with or without prejudice," depending upon the court's assessment of various factors. In *United States v. Taylor,* 487 U.S. 326 (1988), the Court concluded that neither remedy has priority, that the legislative history of the Act reveals that prejudice to the defendant is a factor to be taken into account in addition to those listed in the Act, and that under the Act a district judge "must carefully consider those factors as applied to the particular case and, whatever its decision, clearly articulate their effect in order to permit meaningful appellate review." The Court overturned a district court's order of dismissal with prejudice for a delay 14 days longer than permitted by the Act because the district court (i) "did not explain how it factored in the seriousness of the offenses with which respondent stood charged," (ii) "relied heavily on its unexplained characterization of the Government conduct as 'lackadaisical,' while failing to consider other relevant facts and circumstances leading to dismissal," and (iii) apparently ignored "the brevity of the delay and the consequential lack of prejudice to the respondent," as well as his "own illicit contribution to the delay" by fleeing the day before the original trial date.

What then should the district judge do upon remand in *Zedner*?

8. ***Interlocutory appeal.*** If a defendant's pretrial motion to dismiss on speedy trial grounds is denied, he need not be allowed an interlocutory appeal to fully protect his rights under *Barker v. Wingo,* as it "is the delay before trial, not the trial itself, that offends against the constitutional guarantee of a speedy trial." See *United States v. MacDonald,* discussed at p. 1087.

Assuming an interlocutory appeal by either the defense or the prosecution on some issue, *Barker* applies only "when the defendant is subject to indictment or restraint" during that interval. *United States v. Loud Hawk,* p. 1087. "Given the important public interests in appellate review, it hardly need be said that an interlocutory appeal by the Government ordinarily is a valid reason that justifies delay. In assessing the purpose and reasonableness of such an appeal, courts may consider several factors. These include the strength of the Government's position on the appealed issue, the importance of the issue in the posture of the case, and—in some cases—the seriousness of the crime." In the limited circumstances "where pretrial appeal by the defendant is appropriate, delays from such an appeal ordinarily will not weigh in favor of a defendant's speedy trial claims. A defendant with a meritorious appeal would bear the heavy burden of showing an unreasonable delay caused by the prosecution in that appeal, or a wholly unjustifiable delay by the appellate court," but in the instant case the respondents' "position was so lacking in merit that the time consumed by this appeal should not weigh in support of respondents' speedy trial claim."

9. ***When does the time begin to run?*** Under state speedy trial statutes, the time usually runs from the date the defendant first appears in court following his arrest, except that it typically runs from the date of the formal charge if it precedes arrest. As to the constitutional right to speedy

trial, only the delay following arrest or formal charge (whichever comes first) is taken into account. See *United States v. Lovasco,* below.

§ 2. OTHER SPEEDY DISPOSITION

UNITED STATES V. LOVASCO

431 U.S. 783, 97 S.Ct. 2044, 52 L.Ed.2d 752 (1977).

JUSTICE MARSHALL delivered the opinion of the Court. * * *

On March 6, 1975, respondent was indicted for possessing eight firearms stolen from the United States mail, and for dealing in firearms without a license. The offenses were alleged to have occurred between July 25 and August 31, 1973, more than 18 months before the indictment was filed. Respondent moved to dismiss the indictment due to the delay.

The District Court conducted a hearing on respondent's motion at which the respondent sought to prove that the delay was unnecessary and that it had prejudiced his defense. In an effort to establish the former proposition, respondent presented a Postal Inspector's report on his investigation that was prepared one month after the crimes were committed, and a stipulation concerning the post-report progress of the probe. The report stated, in brief, that within the first month of the investigation respondent had admitted to Government agents that he had possessed and then sold five of the stolen guns, and that the agents had developed strong evidence linking respondent to the remaining three weapons.[1] The report also stated, however, that the agents had been unable to confirm or refute respondent's claim that he had found the guns in his car when he returned to it after visiting his son, a mail handler, at work. The stipulation into which the Assistant United States Attorney entered indicated that little additional information concerning the crimes was uncovered in the 17 months following the preparation of the Inspector's report.

To establish prejudice to the defense, respondent testified that he had lost the testimony of two material witnesses due to the delay. The first witness, Tom Stewart, died more than a year after the alleged crimes occurred. At the hearing respondent claimed that Stewart had been his source for two or three of the guns. The second witness, respondent's brother, died in April 1974, nine months after the crimes were completed. Respondent testified that his brother was present when respondent called Stewart to secure the guns, and witnessed all of respondent's sales. Respondent did not state how the witnesses would have aided the defense had they been willing to testify.[4]

The Government made no systematic effort in the District Court to explain its long delay. The Assistant United States Attorney did expressly disagree, however, with defense counsel's suggestion that the investigation had ended after the Postal Inspector's Report was prepared. The prosecutor also stated that it was the Government's theory that respondent's son, who had access to the mail at the railroad terminal from which the guns were "possibly stolen," was responsible

---

[1] The report indicated that the person to whom respondent admitted selling five guns had told Government agents that respondent had actually sold him eight guns which he, in turn, had sold to one Martin Koehnken. The report also indicated that Koehnken had sold three of these guns to undercover federal agents and that a search of his house had uncovered four others. Finally the report stated that the eighth gun was sold by one David Northdruft to Government agents, and that Northdruft claimed Koehnken had sold him the gun.

At the hearing on the motion to dismiss, respondent for the first time admitted that he had possessed and sold eight guns.

[4] Respondent admitted that he had not mentioned Stewart to the Postal Inspector when he was questioned about his source of the guns. He explained that this was because Stewart "was a bad tomato" and "was liable to take a shot at me if I told [on] him." Respondent also conceded that he did not mention either his brother's or Stewart's illness or death to the Postal Inspector on the several occasions in which respondent called the Inspector to inquire about the status of the probe.

for the thefts. Finally, the prosecutor elicited somewhat cryptic testimony from the Postal Inspector indicating that the case "as to these particular weapons involves other individuals"; that information had been presented to a grand jury "in regard to this case other than . . . [on] the day of the indictment itself"; and that he had spoken to the prosecutors about the case on four or five occasions.

Following the hearing, the District Court filed a brief opinion and order. The court found that by October 2, 1973, the date of the postal inspector's report, "The Government had all the information relating to defendant's alleged commission of the offense charged against him," and that the 17-month delay before the case was presented to the grand jury "had not been explained or justified" and was "unnecessary and unreasonable." The Court also found that "[a]s a result of the delay defendant has been prejudiced by reason of the death of Tom Stewart, a material witness on his behalf." Accordingly, the court dismissed the indictment.

The Government appealed to the United States Court of Appeals for the Eighth Circuit. In its brief the Government explained the months of inaction by stating:

> "[T]here was a legitimate Government interest in keeping the investigation open in the instant case. The defendant's son worked for the Terminal Railroad and had access to mail. It was the Government's position that the son was responsible for the theft and therefore further investigation to establish this fact was important.
>
> ". . . Although the investigation did not continue on a full time basis, there was contact between the United States Attorney's office and the Postal Inspector's office throughout . . . and certain matters were brought before a Federal Grand Jury prior to the determination that the case should be presented for indictment. . . ."

The Court of Appeals accepted the Government's representation as to the motivation for the delay, but a majority of the court nevertheless affirmed the District Court's finding that the Government's actions were "unjustified, unnecessary, and unreasonable." The majority also found that respondent had established that his defense had been impaired by the loss of Stewart's testimony because it understood respondent to contend that "were Stewart's testimony available it would support [respondent's] claim that he did not know that the guns were stolen from the United States mails." * * *

We granted certiorari, and now reverse.[7]

In *United States v. Marion,* 404 U.S. 307 (1971), this Court considered the significance, for constitutional purposes, of a lengthy preindictment delay. We held that as far as the Speedy Trial Clause of the Sixth Amendment is concerned, such delay is wholly irrelevant, since our analysis of the language, history, and purposes of the Clause persuaded us that only "a formal indictment or information or else the actual restraints imposed by arrest and holding to answer a criminal charge . . . engage the particular protections" of that provision. We went on to note that statutes of limitations, which provide predictable, legislatively enacted limits on prosecutorial delay, provide "the primary guarantee, against bringing overly stale criminal charges."[a] But we did

---

7 In addition to challenging the Court of Appeals' holding on the constitutional issue, the United States argues that the District Court should have deferred action on the motion to dismiss until after trial, at which time it could have assessed any prejudice to the respondent in light of the events at trial. This argument, however, was not raised in the District Court or in the Court of Appeals. Absent exceptional circumstances, we will not review it here. * * *

a The statute of limitations, in contrast to the speedy trial time limitations, runs from the date the offense is committed (or, in a few states, from the date the offense is discovered) to the date prosecution is commenced (in some states this means the date an indictment or information is filed, in others the date a warrant of arrest is issued). The typical statute specifies situations in which time is not counted against the period of limitation, such as when the defendant is out of the state or is away from his usual residence for the purpose of avoiding prosecution. "There are several reasons for the imposition of time limitations: First, and foremost, is the desirability that prosecutions be based upon reasonably fresh evidence. With the passage of time memories fade, witnesses die or leave the area, and physical evidence becomes more difficult to obtain, identify, or preserve. In short, possibility of erroneous acknowledge that the "statute of limitations does not fully define [defendants'] rights with respect to the events occurring prior to indictment," and that the Due Process Clause has a limited role to play in protecting against oppressive delay.

Respondent seems to argue that due process bars prosecution whenever a defendant suffers prejudice as a result of preindictment delay. To support that proposition respondent relies on the concluding sentence of the Court's opinion in *Marion* where, in remanding the case, we stated that "[e]vents of the trial may demonstrate actual prejudice, but at the present time appellees' due process claims are speculative and premature." But the quoted sentence establishes only that proof of actual prejudice makes a due process claim concrete and ripe for adjudication, not that it makes the claim automatically valid. Indeed, two pages earlier in the opinion we expressly rejected the argument respondent advances here:

> "[W]e need not . . . determine when and in what circumstances actual prejudice resulting from preaccusation delay requires the dismissal of the prosecution. Actual prejudice to the defense of a criminal case may result from the shortest and most necessary delay; and no one suggests that every delay-caused detriment to a defendant's case should abort a criminal prosecution."

Thus *Marion* makes clear that proof of prejudice is generally a necessary but not sufficient element of a due process claim, and that the due process inquiry must consider the reasons for the delay as well as the prejudice to the accused.

The Court of Appeals found that the sole reason for the delay here was "a hope on the part of the Government that others might be discovered who may have participated in the theft. . . ." It concluded that this hope did not justify the delay, and therefore affirmed the dismissal of the indictment. But the Due Process Clause does not permit courts to abort criminal prosecutions simply because they disagree with a prosecutor's judgment as to when to seek an indictment. Judges are not free, in defining "due process," to impose on law enforcement officials our "personal and private notions" of fairness and to "disregard the limits that bind judges in their judicial function." Our task is more circumscribed. We are to determine only whether the actions complained of—here, compelling respondent to stand trial after the Government delayed indictment to investigate further—violates those "fundamental conceptions of justice which lie at the base of our civil and political institutions," and which define "the community's sense of fair play and decency."

It requires no extended argument to establish that prosecutors do not deviate from "fundamental conceptions of justice" when they defer seeking indictments until they have probable cause to believe an accused is guilty; indeed it is unprofessional conduct for a prosecutor to recommend an indictment on less than probable cause. It should be equally obvious that prosecutors are under no duty to file charges as soon as probable cause exists but before they are satisfied they will be able to establish the suspect's guilt beyond a reasonable doubt. To impose such a duty "would have a deleterious effect both upon the rights of the accused and upon the ability of society to protect itself." From the perspective of potential defendants, requiring prosecutions to commence when probable cause is established is undesirable because it would increase the likelihood of unwarranted charges being filed, and would add to the time during which

---

conviction is minimized when prosecution is prompt. Second, if the actor long refrains from further criminal activity, the likelihood increases that he has reformed, diminishing the necessity for imposition of the criminal sanction. If he has repeated his criminal behavior, he can be prosecuted for recent offenses committed within the period of limitation. Hence, the need for protecting society against the perpetrator of a particular offense becomes less compelling as the years pass. Third, after a protracted period the retributive impulse which may have existed in the community is likely to yield to a sense of compassion aroused by the prosecution for an offense long forgotten. Fourth, it is desirable to reduce the possibility of blackmail based on a threat to prosecute or to disclose evidence to enforcement officials. Finally, statutes of limitations 'promote repose by giving security and stability to human affairs.'" *Model Penal Code* § 1.06, Comment (1985).

defendants stand accused but untried. * * * From the perspective of law enforcement officials, a requirement of immediate prosecution upon probable cause is equally unacceptable because it could make obtaining proof of guilt beyond a reasonable doubt impossible by causing potentially fruitful sources of information to evaporate before they are fully exploited. And from the standpoint of the courts, such a requirement is unwise because it would cause scarce resources to be consumed on cases that prove to be insubstantial, or that involve only some of the responsible parties or some of the criminal acts.[12] Thus, no one's interests would be well served by compelling prosecutors to initiate prosecutions as soon as they are legally entitled to do so.

It might be argued that once the Government has assembled sufficient evidence to prove guilt beyond a reasonable doubt, it should be constitutionally required to file charges promptly, even if its investigation of the entire criminal transaction is not complete. Adopting such a rule, however, would have many of the same consequences as adopting a rule requiring immediate prosecution upon probable cause.

First, compelling a prosecutor to file public charges as soon as the requisite proof has been developed against one participant on one charge would cause numerous problems in those cases in which a criminal transaction involves more than one person or more than one illegal act. In some instances, an immediate arrest or indictment would impair the prosecutor's ability to continue his investigation, thereby preventing society from bringing lawbreakers to justice. In other cases, the prosecutor would be able to obtain additional indictments despite an early prosecution, but the necessary result would be multiple trials involving a single set of facts. Such trials place needless burdens on defendants, law enforcement officials, and courts.

Second, insisting on immediate prosecution once sufficient evidence is developed to obtain a conviction would pressure prosecutors into resolving doubtful cases in favor of early—and possibly unwarranted—prosecutions. The determination of when the evidence available to the prosecution is sufficient to obtain a conviction is seldom clear-cut, and reasonable persons often will reach conflicting conclusions. In the instant case, for example, since respondent admitted possessing at least five of the firearms, the primary factual issue in dispute was whether respondent knew the guns were stolen as required by 18 U.S.C. § 1708. Not surprisingly, the Postal Inspector's report contained no direct evidence bearing on this issue. The decision whether to prosecute, therefore, required a necessarily subjective evaluation of the strength of the circumstantial evidence available and the credibility of respondent's denial. Even if a prosecutor concluded that the case was weak and further investigation appropriate, he would have no assurance that a reviewing court would agree. To avoid the risk that a subsequent indictment would be dismissed for preindictment delay, the prosecutor might feel constrained to file premature charges with all the disadvantages that entails.

Finally, requiring the Government to make charging decisions immediately upon assembling evidence sufficient to establish guilt would preclude the Government from giving full consideration to the desirability of not prosecuting in particular cases. The decision to file criminal charges, with the awesome consequences it entails, requires consideration of a wide range of factors in addition to the strength of the Government's case, in order to determine whether prosecution would be in the public interest. Prosecutors often need more information than proof of a suspect's guilt, therefore, before deciding whether to seek an indictment. Again the instant case provides a useful illustration. Although proof of the identity of the mail thieves was not necessary to convict respondent of the possessory crimes with which he was charged, it might have been crucial in assessing respondent's culpability, as distinguished from his legal guilt. If, for example, further investigation were to show that respondent had no role in or advance knowledge of the theft and

[12] Defendants also would be adversely affected by trials involving less than all of the criminal acts for which they are responsible, since they likely would be subjected to multiple trials growing out of the same transaction or occurrence.

simply agreed, out of paternal loyalty, to help his son dispose of the guns once respondent discovered his son had stolen them, the United States Attorney might have decided not to prosecute, especially since at the time of the crime respondent was over 60 years old and had no prior criminal record. Requiring prosecution once the evidence of guilt is clear, however, could prevent a prosecutor from awaiting the information necessary for such a decision.

We would be most reluctant to adopt a rule which would have these consequences absent a clear constitutional command to do so. We can find no such command in the Due Process Clause of the Fifth Amendment. In our view, investigative delay is fundamentally unlike delay undertaken by the Government solely "to gain tactical advantage over the accused," precisely because investigative delay is not so one-sided.[17] Rather than deviating from elementary standards of "fair play and decency," a prosecutor abides by them if he refuses to seek indictments until he is completely satisfied that he should prosecute and will be able promptly to establish guilt beyond a reasonable doubt. Penalizing prosecutors who defer action for these reasons would subordinate the goal of "orderly expedition" to that of "mere speed." This the Due Process Clause does not require. We therefore hold that to prosecute a defendant following investigative delay does not deprive him of due process, even if his defense might have been somewhat prejudiced by the lapse of time.

In the present case, the Court of Appeals stated that the only reason the Government postponed action was to await the results of additional investigation. * * * In light of this explanation, it follows that compelling respondent to stand trial would not be fundamentally unfair. The Court of Appeals therefore erred in affirming the District Court's decision dismissing the indictment.

In *Marion* we conceded that we could not determine in the abstract the circumstances in which preaccusation delay would require dismissing prosecutions. More than five years later, that statement remains true. Indeed, in the intervening years so few defendants have established that they were prejudiced by delay that neither this Court nor any lower court has had a sustained opportunity to consider the constitutional significance of various reasons for delay.[19] We therefore leave to the lower courts, in the first instance, the task of applying the settled principles of due process that we have discussed to the particular circumstances of individual cases. We simply hold that in this case the lower courts erred in dismissing the indictment.[b]

---

[17] In *Marion* we noted with approval that the Government conceded that a "tactical" delay would violate the Due Process Clause. The Government renews that concession here, and expands it somewhat by stating that "A due process violation might also be made out upon a showing of prosecutorial delay incurred in reckless disregard of circumstances, known to the prosecution, suggesting that there existed an appreciable risk that delay would impair the ability to mount an effective defense." As the Government notes, however, there is no evidence of recklessness here.

[19] Professor Amsterdam has catalogued some of the noninvestigative reasons for delay:

"[P]roof of the offense may depend upon the testimony of an undercover informer who maintains his 'cover' for a period of time before surfacing to file charges against one or more persons with whom he has dealt while disguised. . . .[I]f there is more than one possible charge against a suspect, some of them may be held back pending the disposition of others in order to avoid the burden upon the prosecutor's office of handling charges that may turn out to be unnecessary to obtain the degree of punishment that the prosecutor seeks. There are many other motives for delay, of course, including sinister ones, such as a desire to postpone the beginning of defense investigation or the wish to hold a 'club' over the defendant.

"Additional reasons for delay may be partly or completely beyond the control of the prosecuting authorities. Offenses may not be immediately reported; investigation may not immediately identify the offender; an identified offender may not be immediately apprehendable. . . .[A]n indictment may be delayed for weeks or even months until the impaneling of the next grand jury. It is customary to think of these delays as natural and inevitable . . . but various prosecutorial decisions—such as the assignment of manpower and priorities among investigations of known offenses—may also affect the length of such delays." Amsterdam, *Speedy Criminal Trial: Rights and Remedies,* 27 Stan.L.Rev. 525, 527–528 (1975).

[b] Stevens, J., dissenting, agreed with the foregoing principles, but concluded the majority had erred in not deciding the case on the record made in the district court, wherein the government's delay was unexplained.

NOTES AND QUESTIONS

1. ***Charge dismissal interval.*** *Marion* was also relied upon in *United States v. MacDonald*, 456 U.S. 1 (1982), holding that the time between dismissal of military charges and the subsequent indictment on civilian charges may not be considered in determining whether the delay in bringing the defendant to trial violated his Sixth Amendment right to speedy trial. Burger, C.J., stated for the Court:

"Once charges are dismissed, the speedy trial guarantee is no longer applicable.[8] At that point, the formerly accused is, at most, in the same position as any other subject of a criminal investigation. Certainly the knowledge of an ongoing criminal investigation will cause stress, discomfort and perhaps a certain disruption in normal life. This is true whether or not charges have been filed and then dismissed. This was true in *Marion,* where the defendants had been subjected to a lengthy investigation which received considerable press attention. But with no charges outstanding, personal liberty is certainly not impaired to the same degree as it is after arrest while charges are pending. After the charges against him have been dismissed, 'a citizen suffers no restraints on his liberty and is [no longer] the subject of public accusation: his situation does not compare with that of a defendant who has been arrested and held to answer.' *United States v. Marion.* Following dismissal of charges, any restraint on liberty, disruption of employment, strain on financial resources, and exposure to public obloquy, stress and anxiety is no greater than it is upon anyone openly subject to a criminal investigation."

Four members of the Court[c] found that conclusion to be "inconsistent with the language and policies of the Speedy Trial Clause and with this Court's decisions," such as *Klopfer,* said to teach "that the anxiety suffered by an accused person, even after the initial prosecution has terminated and after he has been discharged from custody, warrants application of the speedy trial protection." They added that the majority's conclusion was "also senseless" because "[a]ny legitimate government reason for delay during the period between prosecutions can, indeed must, be weighed when a court determines whether the defendant's speedy trial right has been violated. No purpose is served by simply ignoring that period for speedy trial purposes."

2. ***Appeal interval.*** Relying on *MacDonald,* the Court in *United States v. Loud Hawk*, 474 U.S. 302 (1986), held, 5–4, that the Sixth Amendment speedy trial clock was not running during the government's appeals of the district court's successive dismissals of the indictment with prejudice, during which time the respondents were free on their own recognizance, as "respondents were neither under indictment nor subject to bail." A contrary result, the Court added, was not called for merely "because the Government's desire to prosecute them was a matter of public record" or because of "respondents' need for counsel while their case was technically dismissed," as "the Speedy Trial Clause's core concern is impairment of liberty; it does not shield a suspect or a defendant from every expense or inconvenience associated with criminal defense." The dissenters argued that the instant case was distinguishable from *MacDonald* because (a) the "respondents did not enjoy the protection of the statute of limitations while the Government prosecuted its appeal"; (b) there was no dismissal by the government "acknowledging that the first formal accusation had been a mistake and extinguishing the prior probable cause determination," and instead the government "continues to align its full resources against respondents in judicial

---

[8] *Klopfer v. North Carolina* [p. 1071], is not to the contrary. There, under an unusual state procedure, a prosecutor was able to suspend proceedings on an indictment indefinitely. The prosecutor could activate the charges at any time and have the case restored for trial, "without further order" of the court. The charges against the defendant were thus never dismissed or discharged in any real sense so the speedy trial guarantee continued to apply.

[c] Marshall, J., joined by Brennan and Blackmun, JJ., dissenting, took a different view of the scope of the Sixth Amendment speedy trial protection and then, applying the four factors from *Barker,* concluded that MacDonald's speedy trial rights were violated. Stevens, J., concurring, agreed with the dissenters' scope analysis but disagreed with their application of the *Barker* factors.

proceedings"; and (c) "respondents' liberty could have been taken from them at any time during the Government's appeal," as 18 U.S.C. § 3731 says "that a person in respondents' position shall be subject to the same restraints as an arrested defendant awaiting trial."

3. **Lovasco *construed.*** Assess these interpretations of *Lovasco*: (a) in *State v. Whiting*, 702 N.E.2d 1189 (Ohio 1998), that "the *Lovasco* court burdened the defendant with establishing actual prejudice from the delay and charged the government with the burden of producing evidence of a justifiable reason for the delay"; (b) in *United States v. Ross*, 123 F.3d 1181 (9th Cir.1997), that "[p]reindictment delay that results from negligence or worse may violate due process," but"[i]f mere negligent conduct by the prosecutors is asserted, then obviously the delay and/or prejudice suffered by the defendant will have to be greater."

4. ***Speedy disposition at other stages.*** As to what other steps in the criminal process should the defendant have a constitutional right to speedy disposition? What about a right to "speedy judgment" when a criminal case is tried before a judge? See *State v. Doughman*, 92 N.E.3d 30 (Ohio App.2017). To "speedy sentencing"? See *United States v. Ray*, 578 F.3d 184 (2d Cir.2009). To a speedy decision on a motion for a new trial? See *Veal v. State,* 800 S.E.2d 325 (Ga.2017). To a "speedy appeal"? See *Chatman v. Mancill*, 626 S.E.2d 102 (Ga.2006). To a "speedy probation revocation proceeding"? See *State v. West*, 194 P.3d 683 (Mont.2008). To a "speedy parole revocation proceeding"? See *Morrissey v. Brewer,* p. 88 fn. c, and compare *Moody v. Daggett,* 429 U.S. 78 (1976), where the Court, per Burger, C.J., held that a federal parolee imprisoned for a crime committed while on parole was not constitutionally entitled to a prompt parole revocation hearing when a parole violator warrant was issued and lodged with the institution of his confinement but not served on him. The Court stressed (i) his present confinement did not derive from the warrant, (ii) the warrant did not diminish his opportunity for parole on the intervening sentence, and (iii) it would be more appropriate to hold the revocation hearing at the expiration of the intervening sentence because at that time a more relevant and accurate prediction of the parolee's ability to live at large in a law-abiding way can be made.

Regarding the source and dimensions of any post-trial right to "speedy" disposition, consider BETTERMAN v. MONTANA, 136 S.Ct. 1609 (2016), holding that "the Sixth Amendment's speedy trial guarantee * * * does not apply once a defendant has been found guilty at trial or has pled guilty to criminal charges," for "[a]s a measure protecting the presumptively innocent, the speedy trial right—like other similarly aimed measures—loses force upon conviction." Such a reading of the Sixth Amendment, the Court emphasized, "comports with the historical understanding," as "[a]t the founding, 'accused' described a status preceding 'convicted,' " "[a]nd 'trial' meant a discrete episode after which judgment (i.e., sentencing) would follow."

"The sole remedy for a violation of the speedy trial right—dismissal of the charges—fits the preconviction focus of the Clause. It would be an unjustified windfall, in most cases, to remedy sentencing delay by vacating validly obtained convictions. Betterman concedes that a dismissal remedy ordinarily would not be in order once a defendant has been convicted. * * *

"As we have explained, at the third phase of the criminal-justice process, i.e., between conviction and sentencing, the Constitution's presumption-of-innocence-protective speedy trial right is not engaged. That does not mean, however, that defendants lack any protection against undue delay at this stage. The primary safeguard comes from statutes and rules. The federal rule on point directs the court to "impose sentence without unnecessary delay." Fed. Rule Crim. Proc. 32(b)(1). Many States have provisions to the same effect, and some States prescribe numerical time limits. Further, as at the prearrest stage, due process serves as a backstop against exorbitant delay. After conviction, a defendant's due process right to liberty, while diminished, is still present. He retains an interest in a sentencing proceeding that is fundamentally fair. But because Betterman advanced no due process claim here, we express no opinion on how he might fare under that more pliable standard."

PART 4

THE ADVERSARY SYSTEM AND THE DETERMINATION OF GUILT OR INNOCENCE

■ ■ ■

CHAPTER 21

PRETRIAL DISCOVERY AND RELATED RIGHTS

■ ■ ■

This chapter treats two subjects that are often considered together but are only partially related. The first is pretrial discovery—i.e., the legal rights of the defense and the prosecution to each obtain from the other information that relates to the evidence they might use at trial. The law of pretrial discovery is largely governed by statutes and court rules which vary from one jurisdiction to another. Sections 1–4 of this chapter discuss the basic patterns found in those provisions, along with the policy preferences and constitutional limitations that have contributed to those patterns. Section one provides an introduction to both the basic structure of discovery provisions and the critical elements of those provisions that shape both prosecution and defense discovery. Section two considers the discovery made available to the defense,[a] and section three considers the discovery made available to the prosecution. Section four considers the sanctions and remedies imposed for prosecution or defense violations of their respective statutory discovery obligations.

Pretrial discovery provides a major avenue for defense acquisition of evidence (or leads to evidence) that the defense might use at trial. Another major avenue is a series of constitutional standards combining to create "what might loosely be called the area of constitutionally guaranteed access to evidence." *Arizona v. Youngblood*, 488 U.S. 51 (1988). These standards are considered in section 5 of this chapter. Some of these constitutional standards are analagous to pretrial discovery standards, as they relate to the prosecution's duty to disclose evidence within its possession (though not necessarily disclosure pretrial). Others involve obligations imposed upon the government with respect to the defense's efforts to obtain evidence from third parties. Even here, the standards may be seen as somewhat related to pretrial discovery as it is usually pretrial discovery that leads the defense to seek such evidence.

---

[a] Section two deals only with the discovery provided under discovery provisions. Defense discovery is sometimes available as well through evidentiary rules (e.g., in provisions requiring the prosecution to provide pretrial notice when it intends to introduce evidence of uncharged misconduct) or provisions implementing suppression motions (e.g., requiring pretrial notice of the prosecution's intent to use evidence acquired through a search). Civil actions of different types also may provide defense discovery, although the proceeding that might appear on the surface to hold the greatest promise, an action under the jurisdiction's Freedom of Information Act, is actually of little value. Such Acts typically include an exemption for records "compiled for law enforcement purposes" which precludes disclosure during the pendency of a criminal investigation or prosecution. See CRIMPROC § 20.2(d).

Other procedures within the criminal justice process, although aimed at serving different defense interests, also provide discovery as an incidental byproduct. Those procedures include the preliminary hearing (see Ch. 15, § 2), challenges to the grand jury's indictment decision (see Note 3, p. 964 and Note 6, p. 977), the bail hearing, particularly where the prosecution seeks preventive detention, and the hearing on a motion to suppress. As to the potential use of procedural objections to gain a "sneak preview" of the prosecution's case, "whatever the merits" of the objection, see the discussion by the Court majority in *Kaley v. United States,* described in fn. c, p. 963.

Section two also does not exam patterns of discretionary prosecution disclosures to the defense, going beyond what is required by the discovery provision. Such disclosures tend to be quite common, particularly in connection with plea bargaining. See CRIMPROC § 20.1(b) (discussing prosecution use of "open file" informal discovery).

§ 1. PRETRIAL DISCOVERY: THE STATUTORY FRAMEWORK

A. PATTERNS IN DISCOVERY PROVISIONS

1. ***The common structure.*** In the federal system and all but one state, discovery is governed by statutes or court rules which are comprehensive in their coverage. In many states, there is a single court rule or statute governing all aspects of discovery by both sides. Other jurisdictions, following the pattern of the Federal Rules, utilize both a basic provision governing discovery in general and separate provisions setting forth the obligations of pretrial disclosure where defense seeks to advance a claim of alibi or an insanity defense. In some states, these provisions are applicable to all prosecutions in all courts. In others, the basic provisions apply only to trial courts of general jurisdictions (and thus may be limited to felonies). Other provisions, allowing for narrower discovery, apply in the magistrate court. See CRIMPROC § 20.2. The discussion that follows focuses on the provisions that apply, at a minimum, to the courts of general jurisdiction.

Although the basic discovery provisions vary in content, they tend to be similar in structure. Typically, the basic discovery statute or court rule performs the following major tasks: (1) it establishes a procedure by which the defense and the prosecution can put into effect the other side's obligation to make pretrial disclosure;[a] (2) it designates those items which must be disclosed (within a specified time frame), either automatically or when ordered by the court, by the prosecution to the defense; (3) it designates those items which must be disclosed, either automatically or when ordered by the court, by the defense to the prosecution; (4) it establishes certain exemptions from disclosure based upon content (e.g., work product) or, in some instances, based on the nature of the item (e.g., witness' recorded statements); (5) it authorizes the trial court to issue, under special circumstances, a protective order that will bar or limit disclosures that would otherwise be required; (6) it imposes a continuing duty to disclose discoverable items so that the process automatically encompasses items acquired after the initial disclosure; and (7) it provides a procedure for judicial administration and enforcement of the discovery provisions, including the imposition of sanctions.

2. ***Variations.*** Although numerous aspects of the law of discovery produce variations from one jurisdiction to another, three aspects tend to be most significant. Initially, there are major differences in the provisions in discovery statutes or rules that describe what is and what is not discoverable. Items listed as discoverable as a matter of right in one jurisdiction may be discoverable only by judicial discretion in a second or even barred from discovery by a third. Second, even when the statutory language is similar, it may be so general in its directive as to leave ample room for differences in interpretation.

---

[a] Discovery provisions typically do not take effect prior to the filing of the indictment or information with the trial court. At that point, the discovery which is granted as a matter of right, in all but a small group of jurisdictions, is provided without resort to judicial action. A motion seeking a court order directing a party to provide discovery is required only where there is a dispute as to what must be disclosed as a matter of right or the particular item is discoverable only at the discretion of the court. Under many state discovery provisions, the prosecution has an automatic obligation to disclose the items discoverable as of right within a specified number of days following the filing of the indictment or information. Under other discovery provisions, the defense must make a request of the prosecutor. That request, however, need contain no more than a listing of those categories of items specified in the discovery provision as to which disclosure is desired. Where the prosecution's right to discovery is conditioned on the defense having received similar discovery (see Note 5, p. 1118), the request serves to trigger the prosecution's authority to seek parallel discovery. In some jurisdictions, the prosecution's right is not so conditioned, and the defense, like the prosecution, has an automatic obligation to provide disclosure within a specified period following the filing of the indictment or information.

Third, jurisdictions differ on the interaction of trial court's inherent authority and the jurisdiction's discovery statute or court rule. In some states, the basic discovery provision clearly is intended to be preemptive. Judicial authority to order discovery is limited to the items identified in the discovery provisions (although some of these states include a "catchall section," authorizing such additional discovery as meets the general objectives of the discovery provision). In other jurisdictions (including the federal), the statute or court rule is not viewed as setting forth the full range of the trial court's authority to order discovery. Where the discovery provision neither authorizes nor prohibits discovery as to a particular item, the court retains its inherent authority to order disclosure as an element of its control over the trial process (an authority first recognized in the mid-1900's, when courts rejected the common law position that a court could not order the prosecution to disclose its evidence in advance of trial without legislative authorization). However, in the federal system and in most of the states recognizing such inherent authority, that authority cannot be used to fill in the "gaps" in the coverage of the provisions authorizing discovery from the defense by the prosecutor. Because of the controversial nature of prosecution discovery, the sections on prosecution discovery are read as requiring defense disclosure of the items specified, and, by implication, barring courts from granting prosecution discovery as to all other items. See CRIMPROC § 20.2(b).

3. ***Basic patterns.*** Notwithstanding the variations in state discovery provisions, those provisions have been loosely categorized by reference to the basic coverage patterns in three models—(1) the Federal Rules of Criminal Procedure; (2) the first edition of the A.B.A.'s *Standards Relating to Discovery and Procedure Before Trial* (1st ed. 1970) (hereafter cited as A.B.A.1st); and (3) the latest revision of those Standards. A.B.A. Standards for Discovery (3d ed. 1996) (hereafter cited as A.B.A.3d). See CRIMPROC § 20.2(b).

With respect to discovery by the defense, roughly three-fourths of the states provide discovery that closely matches one of the three models. Those models illustrate the narrowest discovery allowed (in states using the Federal Rule 16 model), the broadest discovery allowed (in states with provisions patterned on A.B.A.3d), and the discovery in most of the states with provisions that fall somewhere in-between (largely states with provisions patterned on A.B.A.1st).[b]

Prosecution discovery provisions contain more variations, so fewer state provisions precisely match one of the models. However, if the distinction between conditional and mandatory discovery provisions (see Note 5, p. 1118) is ignored, and the comparison is based solely on the categories of discoverable material, the Federal Rules model and the A.B.A.3d model each have a substantial number of state counterparts. The first edition of the A.B.A. standards is less significant here as

[b] States with provisions that do not fit these models typically started with a discovery provision based on the Federal Rules and then added several, but not all, of the more expansive provisions of A.B.A.1st. See CRIMPROC § 20.2(b).

A significant exception is the North Carolina provision, which is based on the concept of "open file" discovery advanced in the second edition of the A.B.A. standards. See Robert P. Mosteller, *Exculpatory Evidence, Ethics, and the Road to the Disbarment of Mike NiFong: The Critical Importance of Full Open-File Discovery*, 15 George Mason L.Rev. 257 (2008) (describing the legislative background and the reach of the statute): "The [North Carolina] discovery law * * * requires that, upon motion, the court must order the prosecution to '[m]ake available to the defendant the complete files of all law enforcement and prosecutorial agencies involved in the investigation of the crimes committed or the prosecution of the defendant.' The term 'file' is broadly defined to include statements by defendants or codefendants and 'witness statements, investigating officers' notes, results of tests and examinations, or any other matter or evidence obtained during the investigation. . . .' [The statute also] mandates that '[o]ral statements shall be in written or recorded form.' * * * [T]his is 'full open-file discovery' in the sense that the prosecution is responsible for providing the defense, not only with the material that it has in its file, but also with relevant materials in the files of law enforcement agencies, which it may never have seen or possessed."

Commentators sometimes place in the "open file" category defense discovery provisions that include an exceptionally broad range of items. Some of those provisions "probably encompass every matter that would be included in the North Carolina open file provision," but only that provision defines discovery by reference to law enforcement and prosecutorial files. CRIMPROC § 20.1(c) (also noting that the North Carolina provision, like these state provisions, includes a "narrow work product" exemption).

it provided for prosecution discovery roughly as narrow as that provided under Federal Rule 16(b). States with defense discovery provisions based on either the Federal Rules or the first edition of the A.B.A. standards both tend to have prosecution discovery provisions roughly similar in scope to the combination of Rule 16(b), Rule 12.1 (notice of alibi), and Rule 12.2 (notice of an insanity defense). Almost half of the states have broader provisions, with many modeled on the prosecution discovery provided in the third edition of the A.B.A. Standards, and others providing even broader discovery in certain areas, such as the defense's scientific testing. See Note 4, p. 1117.

4. ***Comparing defense and prosecution discovery.*** Although discovery provisions are commonly characterized as presenting a "two-way street" to the avoidance of "trial by surprise," defense discovery provisions uniformly are broader than prosecution discovery provisions. The differences tend to be created by three distinctions drawn in identifying discoverable material. The first relates to disclosure that goes beyond the evidence that the party making the disclosure intends to utilize at trial. All jurisdictions require the prosecution to make some disclosures that fit in this category. See Note 2, p. 1099 In many states, prosecution discovery provisions will match defense discovery provision as to evidence that will be introduced at trial, but will not require the defense to match any additional types of prosecution disclosure that go beyond anticipated trial evidence. Second, where states do require defense disclosure to go beyond anticipated trial evidence, they add a limitation that does not apply to the prosecution's disclosure responsibilities. Defense disclosures beyond trial evidence are always limited to information that directly relates to the anticipated trial evidence (e.g., disclosure of the recorded defense interviews of prospective defense witnesses, see Note 1, p. 1114). The prosecution on the other hand is required in some instances to make disclosures unrelated to trial evidence (e.g., the names of other persons who may have pertinent information, see Notes 7 & 8, pp. 1103–1105). Finally, even to as disclosing material relating to possible trial evidence, the defense obligation always includes an exemption for statements made by the defendant to the defense staff. See Note 1, p. 1114.

Providing somewhat narrower prosecution discovery is justified in some instances by doubts as to the constitutionality of requiring greater disclosure by the defense. See Pt. C. pp. 1114–1119. In other instances, imposing a broader disclosure obligation upon the prosecutor is justified by the investigative advantages of the prosecution, and the obligation of the prosecution to ensure that "justice" (including avoidance of the conviction of the innocent) is achieved. See Note 2, p. 1099.

B. GENERAL PROVISIONS

Discovery statutes or court rules commonly include various provisions that apply to both prosecution and defense discovery and provide a basic structure shaping the scope of the provisions dealing with specific items of discovery. The varied approaches to several of these provisions are briefly described below.

1. ***"Scope provisions."*** Discovery provision for both defense and prosecution discovery commonly limit the obligation to disclose to items within the "possession, custody, or control" of the particular party. See e.g., Fed.R.Crim.P. 16(a)(1), 16(b)(1). Litigation relating to these "scope provisions" usually centers on the reach of the prosecutor's control. That control clearly extends to items within the files of those investigative agencies that have participated in the development of the particular prosecution. Some courts have held that the prosecutor's "control" also extends to records in the possession of state law enforcement agencies that typically make the particular type of record (e.g., fingerprints) available to the prosecution, even though that agency was not involved in the investigation of the particular case. Should that position be extended to other case-specific records held by agencies with frequent ties to the prosecutor, but not involved in the particular investigation? Consider *Commonwealth v. Daye*, 587 N.E.2d 194 (Mass.1992) (prosecutor's control did not extend to investigator reports on another murder that conceivably could have a relationship to the charged murder where that investigation was by a police

department that had not been involved in investigating the murder charges against the defendant).

Responding to such issues, A.B.A.3d, St.11–4.3 provides, that "the obligations of the prosecuting attorney and of the defense attorney * * * extend to material and information in the possession or control of members of the attorney's staff and of any others who either regularly report to or, with reference to the particular case, have reported to the attorney's office." When the prosecution "is aware that information which would be discoverable if in the possession of the prosecution" is in the possession of a "governmental agency" that does not fall within the above definition, the prosecutor is directed to "disclose the fact of the existence of such information to the defense." If the defense requests, the prosecution must make a "diligent good faith effor[t] to cause such material to be made available," and if that effort is unsuccessful and the agency is subject to the court's jurisdiction, the court is directed to issue "suitable subpoenas or orders to cause such material to be available."

2. ***Protective orders.*** Where discovery provisions provide for mandatory disclosure, such discovery is always made subject to possible restriction through judicial issuance of a protective order. Where discovery is discretionary, the trial court's discretion allows it to limit or deny discovery based on the same interests that would justify issuance of a protective order. As to what those interests might be, compare the open ended language of A.B.A.1st, St.4.4 (upon "a showing of cause") and Federal Rule 16(d)(1) (upon a "sufficient showing") with Ill.Sup.Ct.R. 412(j) (based on A.B.A.3d, St.11–6.1). Rule 412(j) requires a "substantial risk to any person of physical harm, intimidation, bribery, economic reprisals, or unnecessary annoyance or embarrassment resulting from such disclosure which outweighs the usefulness of disclosure to counsel." Is there a special need for a fairly specific standard governing the issuance of protective orders in light of protective order provisions also authorizing courts to rely upon *ex parte* showings by the prosecution?

Assuming a particular factor (e.g., threats to a witness) justifies issuance of a protective order, how far may that order extend? Should the court be able to eliminate completely disclosure pretrial, so the opposing party first learns of the non-disclosed evidence when it is used at trial? Compare A.B.A.1st, St.4.4 (disclosure may be restricted or deferred, "provided that all material and information to which a party is entitled must be disclosed in time to permit * * * beneficial use"); Fed.R.Crim.P. 16(d)(1) ("court may * * * *deny*, restrict, or defer discovery") (emphasis added); A.B.A.3d, St.11–6.1 ("deny, delay, or otherwise condition").

3. ***The "work product" exemption.*** Discovery provisions all exempt from discovery some form of prosecution and defense work product. The concept of exempting work product from discovery stems from the law of civil discovery, but the nature of the exemption in criminal discovery is different in several respects. The leading civil discovery ruling, *Hickman v. Taylor,* 329 U.S. 495 (1947), recognized a general policy against discovery of the opposing party's work product in order to protect against "unwarranted inquiries [through discovery] into the files and mental impressions of an attorney." As incorporated in the Federal Rules of Civil Procedure 26(b)(3), the *Hickman* work product doctrine is broad in its coverage, extending to almost all documents and tangible things prepared in anticipation of litigation. However, it does not produce an absolute bar against discovery. The court may order discovery of such material if the party seeking discovery shows "a substantial need" for the item and an inability without "undue hardship" to obtain equivalent materials. When ordering such discovery, however, the court must "protect against disclosure of the mental impressions, conclusions, opinions, or legal theories of an attorney or other representative concerning the litigation." The portion of litigation-preparation material reflecting such tactical perspectives is commonly described as "opinion" work product, with the remainder of the litigation-preparation material constituting "non-opinion" work product.

Some commentators have contended that, as to defense discovery, there should be no work product exemption. They argue that the prosecutor's role, as representative of the people, is to do justice, not simply to be an adversary, and therefore the prosecution should have no interest in keeping its work product from the defense where that material would be helpful to the defense in preparing its case. This contention has not convinced either legislatures or courts. In *United States v. Nobles*, p. 1114 (Note 1), the Supreme Court advanced the position that the work product exemption should be a two-way street. In the course of holding that a work product exemption applied to litigation material prepared by the defense, the Court drew no distinction between prosecution and defense in commenting on the need for a work product doctrine in criminal cases. That doctrine, the Court noted, was "even more vital" in criminal cases than in civil cases because "the interests of society and the accused in obtaining a fair and accurate resolution of the question of guilt or innocence demand that adequate safeguards assure the thorough preparation and presentation of *each* side of the case" (emphasis added).

However, arguably because the work production exemption was initially adopted in the context of limiting defense discovery from the prosecution, many states adhere to a much narrower view of work product than is found in civil procedure. They utilize the work product definition proposed in all editions of the A.B.A. Standards: "legal research or * * * records, correspondence, reports, or memoranda to the extent they contain the opinions, theories, or conclusions of the prosecuting attorney or the defense attorney, or members of the attorney's legal staff." A.B.A.3d, St.11–6.1. This exemption furnishes absolute protection, but is limited to "opinion" work product and then only that of the legal staff. It avoids the possible application of the work product exemption to reports of investigators (e.g., police reports) or reports of experts (see fn. a, p. 1117), since the authors of those reports are not part of the legal staff. It often even avoids work product exemption of the written record of a witness interview (a staple of work product protection in civil discovery), notwithstanding that the witness' statement was recorded by a prosecutor or defense attorney. Where that record consists of a substantially verbatim quotation of the witness, it most often will be deemed not to reflect the opinions or theories of the attorney (although a contrary conclusion is possible where the witness responded to pointed questions presented by the attorney). Even should the questioning reflect "some legal theory or factual judgment" of the attorney, that material may be "capable of deletion without detracting from the flow of the witness' statement." CRIMPROC § 20.3(j).

In civil discovery, as the Supreme Court noted in *United States v. Nobles*, supra, the work product doctrine has taken account of "the realities of litigation in our adversary system," as it recognizes that "attorneys often must rely on their investigators," and extends coverage to litigation materials prepared by investigators. *Nobles* concluded that the federal common law work product protection would apply to defense investigators working at the direction of defense counsel. Many of the states that otherwise follow the A.B.A. Standards in limiting the work product exemption to opinion work product do extend their exemption to investigators and others who are "agents" of the prosecutor or defense attorneys. To ensure that these provisions include police officers, who may not be operating under the specific direction of the prosecutor, some refer specifically to the police. Here, police reports, where they reflect opinion, will be exempt from pretrial discovery. Separate written descriptions of police interviews with witnesses will also be exempt as to any portion that reflects the officer's opinions.

In contrast to the A.B.A. Standards, jurisdictions following the Federal Rules model commonly have an "internal documents" exemption that goes beyond the work product doctrine of civil discovery. Federal Rule 16(a)(2) exempts from discovery "reports, memoranda, or other internal documents made by an attorney for the government or other government agent in connection with the case"—except for those internal documents explicitly made discoverable under 16(a)(1)(A)–(D), (F), and (G) (basically records of the defendant's statements to government agents, the defendant's criminal record, reports of examinations and tests, and a summary of anticipated expert testimony). The internal-memoranda exemption encompasses non-opinion as well as opinion work product and applies to investigators as well as government lawyers.[c] It covers such items as investigator reports, recorded communications among investigators and prosecutors, and investigator or prosecutor summaries of statements given by witnesses (except where the particular jurisdiction adds an exception for witness statements to its version of the internal-memorandum exemption). Since the exemption is not tied to the concept of work product, it does not provide for the possibility of being overridden by a special showing of need for non-opinion materials.

4. ***"Written or recorded statements."*** All discovery provisions treat as one class of discoverable material the "written or recorded" statements of certain persons. Under Federal Rule 16 (and many similar state provisions), the written or recorded category extends only to statements of the defendant. In other jurisdictions, the category also includes statements of codefendants, witnesses that the prosecution intends to present at trial, witnesses that the defense intends to present at trial, and in several states, statements of all persons "known to the prosecution to have information concerning the offense charged." The same definition of "written or recorded statements" (shortened in A.B.A.3d. to "written statements") applies in each context. As to defendants and codefendants, the prosecution's obligation may also include disclosing "oral statements" under the same conditions, so the limitations of the "written or recorded" definition may not be so significant. But see Note 1, p. 1100 (describing special limits that some jurisdictions place on the obligation to disclose oral statements).

Neither the original A.B.A. Standards nor the Federal Rules sought to define the phrase "written or recorded statement." The drafting committees in both instances recognized the possible incorporation of the definition of "statement" used in the Jencks Act (18 U.S.C.A. § 3500). That Act, which applies only to federal courts, gives the defendant a right to inspect the prior statements of a prosecution witness, following that witness' testimony at trial, for the purpose of possible impeachment of the witness. See Note 8, p. 1104. The Jencks Act defines "statement" for this purpose as (1) "a written statement made by said witness and signed or otherwise adopted by him," (2) "a stenographic, mechanical, electrical or other recording, or a transcription thereof, which is a substantially verbatim recital of an oral statement made by said witness and recorded contemporaneously with the making of such oral statement," and (3) grand jury testimony.

The drafters of both the original A.B.A. Standards and Federal Rule 16 agreed that the "written or recorded statement" phrase in their respective discovery provisions should include all statements that fell within the Jencks Act definition of "statement." The unresolved issue was whether the discovery provision should also have a broader scope. Since the character of a person's "written" statement is fairly clear (basically meaning statements actually written or signed or otherwise approved by the individual), the primary uncertainty centered upon possibly going beyond the Jencks Act limitations as to a "recording" of an oral statement—i.e., not insisting that a "recorded statement" be both substantially verbatim and recorded contemporaneously. Proponents of broad discovery argued that discovery provisions should be broader than the Jencks Act, which had in mind "recordings" of sufficient completeness and likely reliability to be fairly used for impeachment. The issue here was simply discovery, and that should include material which could not itself be used at trial if that material could provide leads to useful information; even the most sketchy and non-contemporaneous records of oral statements could provide such leads.

---

[c] The Rule 16 internal-memoranda provision refers only to defense discovery, since federal prosecution discovery is limited to specific items that the defense intends to use at trial (and therefore would not include the defense's internal memoranda). Where the jurisdiction provides broader prosecution discovery, the internal-memoranda exemption will refer also to internal documents prepared by the defense attorney's staff (including defense investigators).

The federal judiciary eventually settled on a Jencks-type standard. Since Jencks requires a substantially verbatim recording, an officer's notes on statements made by the defendant were held not to constitute a recorded statement. Similarly when a person who had spoken to the defendant later presented an account of that conversation to the police, that description of defendant's statement, even if it sought to recount verbatim what the defendant had said, was not a recorded statement because it was not recorded contemporaneously. See CRIMPROC § 20.3(b) (collecting cases). In states with provisions similar to Federal Rule 16, and in many of the states with provisions modeled on the original A.B.A. Standards, courts similarly adopted a Jencks-type definition.

In other states, however, broader definitions were either added to the discovery provision or adopted by the courts. These definitions are similar to A.B.A.3d, St.11–1.3, which states that a "written statement" shall include: "(i) any statement in writing that is made, signed or adopted by that person; and (ii) the substance of a statement of any kind made by that person that is embodied or summarized in any writing or recording, whether or not specifically signed or adopted by that person. The term ['written statement'] is intended to include statements contained in police or investigative reports, but does not include attorney work product."

One factor that may well influence a jurisdiction's position on the definition of recorded statements is the range of discovery situations to which it applies. In particular, where the definition applies to the discovery of the statements of witnesses, particularly defense witnesses (whose statements are often taken by defense counsel), additional reasons may be found for not going beyond the Jencks definition. Thus *People v. Holtzman*, 593 N.W.2d 617 (Mich.App.1999), cited the following reasons for refusing to adopt a definition that would include an interviewer's notes: (1) "if trial counsel's witness interview notes were discoverable," it would open the door to placing opposing counsel on the stand "to explain discrepancies surrounding the notes"; and (2) counsel's interview notes often reflect counsel's analysis of the case, and while a distinction could be drawn between the factual content and the opinion content of the notes, "the distinction is [not] clear cut and [it] would probably lead to endless legal wrangles over which portions of the notes are work product and which are not."

5. *Discovery depositions.* Another important feature dividing jurisdictions is their approach to the use of the deposition as a discovery device. The deposition is a primary component of civil discovery. A party may depose any person thought to have relevant information, including the opposing party, without making any showing of need or justification. The witness is subpoenaed to appear at a particular time and place to be deposed, and at the deposition is questioned under oath by the party that subpoenaed him, with opportunity given to the other side to object to improper questions and to ask questions of its own. The deposition is stenographically transcribed and in many jurisdictions may also be videotaped.

All jurisdictions authorize use of depositions in the criminal justice process, but the vast majority sharply restrict their use to purposes other than discovery. Many make the deposition available in criminal cases only to preserve the testimony of a favorable witness who is likely to be unavailable at trial. To utilize a deposition, the side seeking to depose a prospective witness must obtain a court order upon a showing that the proposed deponent would be a material witness at trial but is unlikely to be available to testify there due to illness or other difficulty. In other jurisdictions, the language of the deposition provision is somewhat broader, but still is aimed at preserving testimony rather than discovery. Thus, Federal Rule 15(a) allows for depositions upon court order "whenever due to the exceptional circumstances of the case it is in the interest of justice that testimony of a prospective witness of a party be taken and preserved for use at trial."

Less than a dozen states provide for use of the deposition as a basic discovery device, and they vary as to the extent of its availability for that purpose. In some, discovery depositions are not available automatically, but require court approval upon a special showing of need. One feature is universal: although depositions generally are available to both the defense and prosecution, one prospective defense witness—the defendant—is off-limits to the prosecution. See CRIMPROC § 20.2(e) (describing the various provisions).

Why have so few states been willing to adopt the discovery deposition, a mainstay of civil discovery? Most of the reasons offered relate to administrative difficulties. It is noted, for example, that civil discovery depositions are used in conjunction with interrogatories which allow the parties to discover from each other the names of all persons thought to have relevant information. In the criminal discovery process, many jurisdictions do not even require reciprocal pretrial disclosure of witness lists (although each side is likely to be aware of at least some of the other side's witnesses). Another administrative argument is that depositions are very costly, and with the state footing the bill for indigent defendants, there is no financial sacrifice that would provide a restraint against appointed counsel conducting unnecessary depositions. The traditional civil deposition procedure, which allows the party to be in attendance, is seen as providing further administrative difficulties—forcing the victim/witness to be confronted (without the security provided by the courtroom setting) by a person he or she may fear, and requiring, for defendant's attendance, the temporary release of the defendant who is being held in custody (although deposition jurisdictions often respond to custody concerns by providing that only defense counsel need be present at the deposition).

Finally, depositions are opposed as imposing an unnecessary burden on prosecution witnesses. There is no need, it is argued, to subject the witness to a further loss of time, beyond that consumed first in providing information to the police for a police report, then in testifying at a screening procedure (preliminary hearing or grand jury proceeding or both), and finally in testifying at trial. If there is need for discovery prior to trial of what a witness knows about the crime, it is sufficient, so the argument goes, to provide for disclosure of the witness' prior recorded statements. (In civil pretrial discovery, the prior recorded statements taken by the opposing party generally are not discoverable as it is expected that the witness will be deposed). Of course, in jurisdictions with provisions modeled on the Federal Rules, those prior recorded statements will not be made available until trial, but that is deemed sufficient in light of offsetting considerations. See Note 8, p. 1104. In jurisdictions which make regular use of a "mini-trial" preliminary hearing (see Ch. 15, § 4), it also is argued that defendant will have the opportunity to question at least the most critical prosecution witnesses (and to call other witnesses) at the preliminary hearing.

§ 2. DISCOVERY BY THE DEFENSE

A. SCOPE: GENERAL CONSIDERATIONS

1. ***Constitutional overtones.*** Pretrial discovery by the defense has been treated by the Supreme Court as largely a matter to be determined by state legislative or judicial policy, with each state free to set discovery requirements as broadly or narrowly as it pleases. The Court has recognized, however, certain constitutional requirements that limit that freedom of choice. The *Wardius* ruling, discussed at Note 4, p. 1111, requires a state granting discovery to the prosecution to provide at least reciprocal discovery for the defense. More significantly, the *Brady* doctrine, discussed in § 5 of this chapter, imposes upon the prosecution a due process obligation to disclose to the defense such evidence within the prosecution's possession as is both exculpatory and material. Insofar as that due process doctrine may require disclosure prior to trial, rather than simply during trial (see Notes 1–4, pp. 1141–1142), it creates a constitutional right to discovery that overrides any limitations found in the particular jurisdiction's discovery statutes or rules.

Apart from the need to reciprocate for prosecution discovery and the *Brady* rule as to exculpatory evidence, the Supreme Court has found no significant constitutional objection to a state's determination to sharply limit defendant's pretrial discovery. The Court has noted, for example, that while it may be the "better practice" to grant to the defense pretrial discovery of a defendant's confession that the prosecution intends to use at trial, the failure to follow that practice does not violate due process. *Cicenia v. La Gay,* 357 U.S. 504 (1958). It also has held that a state does not violate due process when it fails to grant pretrial disclosure as to other material relevant to defense preparation but not exculpatory. See *Moore v. Illinois,* 408 U.S. 786 (1972) (prior recorded statement of witness); *Weatherford v. Bursey,* 429 U.S. 545 (1977) (failure to inform defendant that an associate was an undercover agent and would testify for the prosecution at trial). See also *Pennsylvania v. Ritchie,* Note 1, p. 1144. State courts, however, have occasionally found that the prosecution's failure to disclose before trial certain critical portions of its evidence deprived the defendant of an adequate opportunity to prepare to meet the government's case and therefore violated due process. See e.g., *Gilchrist v. Commonwealth,* 317 S.E.2d 784 (Va.1984) (failure to furnish key autopsy report until chief medical examiner testified at trial).

2. ***Discovery beyond avoiding surprise.*** A basic objective of defense discovery in all jurisdictions is to avoid having the defense being disadvantaged by surprise. The primary focus in achieving this objective is on the prosecution providing advance notice of the evidence it intends to produce at trial, either in its case-in-chief or on rebuttal. All jurisdictions, however, also provide for discovery of at least some items within the prosecution's control that the prosecution does not intend to introduce at trial. The theory here is that "the state in its might and power ought to be * * * too jealous of according [defendant] a fair and impartial trial to hinder him in intelligently preparing his defense and in availing him of all competent material and relevant evidence that tends to throw light on the subject matter on trial." *Powell v. Superior Court,* 312 P.2d 698 (Cal.1957). The need to ensure against the conviction of the innocent, it is argued, overrides the concept that the state, in an adversary system, has a proprietary interest in the relevant information it develops that might be useful to the defense.

As will be seen in Pt. B of this section, jurisdictions vary in the extent to which they will require disclosure beyond the evidence that the prosecution intends to introduce at trial. All jurisdictions require disclosure of relevant prior recorded statements of the defendant, whether or not the prosecution intends to use that statement. See Note 1, p. 1099. Mandatory disclosure of reports on physical and mental examinations and scientific tests commonly encompasses all those reports "made in connection with the particular case," see A.B.A.1st, St. 2.1(a)(iii), without regard to whether the prosecution intends to introduce at trial the results of those examinations or tests. See Note 4, p. 1101. So too, the defense commonly gains discovery of physical evidence and documents taken from or belonging to the accused, whether or not they will be used at trial. See Note 5, p. 1101. Jurisdictions following the model of Federal Rule 16 also mandate disclosure of additional physical items and documents where "material to the preparation of the defense." See Note 5, p. 1101.

On the other side, only a small group of jurisdictions require pretrial disclosure of the names and prior recorded statements of all persons known to the government to have relevant information. Where pretrial disclosure of the names and prior recorded statements of persons with knowledge is required, it generally is limited to the persons that the prosecution intends to call as its witnesses. See Notes 7–8, pp. 1103–1105. So too, while jurisdictions following either A.B.A. model usually add to their listing of discoverable items a requirement of prosecution disclosure of any "material or information within [its] possession or control which tends to negate the guilt of accused," other jurisdictions commonly leave the prosecution's obligation to disclose exculpatory evidence to the due process mandate. See Note 9, p. 1105.

B. SPECIFIC ITEMS

1. ***Defendant's statements.*** All jurisdictions provide for discovery of the defendant's written or recorded statements (see Note 4, p. 1096) within the prosecution's possession or control

(see Note 1, p. 1093). Such disclosure is required as a matter of right in all but the few states with discovery provisions that grant judicial discretion as to all discovery categories. In most states, this disclosure provision does not include a "relevancy" restriction. However, Federal Rule 16 and state provisions modeled on Federal Rule 16(a)(1) refers to disclosure of "any *relevant* written or record statement by the defendant" (emphasis added). In jurisdictions with such provisions, courts generally have taken "a broad view of relevancy," noting that, "while the government can assess relevance to its own case, it can only guess as to what would be relevant from the defense viewpoint." CRIMPROC § 20.3(c). Accordingly, relevancy is presumed as to all written or recorded statements made by defendant to investigators during the course of the investigation. The relevancy limitation, under this view, exists primarily because of the possibility that a particular defendant may have made statements in connection with other inquiries by an agency involved in the investigation (particularly in the federal system, where that agency may also have a regulatory function). This concern also arguably underlies the additional limitation imposed in the Rule 16(a)(1) provision—"that the attorney for the government knows—or through due diligence could know—that the statement exists."

Almost all states also require prosecution disclosure of the "substance of oral statements" made by the defendant. In most of the states with discovery provisions based on the A.B.A. Standards, that disclosure requirement is stated without including any limitation, or including only the limitation that the oral statement "relate to the subject matter of the offense charged." A.B.A.3d, St.11–2.1(i). In other states, however, discovery is limited to oral statements that the prosecution "intends to offer in evidence at the trial." One function of such a limitation arguably is to avoid disclosure of statements that might be used only for impeachment (which assumes that "offer in evidence" refers only to the prosecution's case-in-chief). Another function arguably is to limit the prosecutor's responsibility in seeking out discoverable items that the investigating agency may not have conveyed to the prosecutor's office (the range of unrecorded oral statements being much broader than the range of written or recorded statements).

A 1991 amendment of Federal Rule 16 discarded the intended use requirement as to a written record containing the substance of defendant's oral statements (although intended use remains a prerequisite for disclosing oral statements where there is no such writing). However, Federal Rule 16 here retains a second limitation applied to oral statements—the oral statement summarized in the writing must have been made "in response to interrogation by a person the defendant knew was a government agent." This limitation allows the prosecution to keep from the defense the fact that the persons he conversed with were undercover agents or non-agent witnesses who will be testifying against him at trial. It is seen as flowing from concerns relating to the defendant's misuse of that information, which are similar to those concerns—discussed in Notes 7 and 8, infra—that led Federal Rule 16 not to require disclosure of witness lists and to bar pretrial disclosure of a witness' prior recorded statements. Accordingly, the Federal Rules (and similar state provisions) added this "known agent" limitation to the provision on oral statements, notwithstanding its restriction to statements that the prosecution intends to use in its case-in-chief.

2. ***Codefendant's statements.*** Unlike Federal Rule 16, discovery provisions in a substantial majority of the states requires disclosure of statements of codefendants under at least some circumstances. Many states, following A.B.A.3d, St.11–2.1, require disclosure of all relevant "written or recorded" and oral statements of a codefendant. Others, following the original A.B.A. model, restrict the required disclosure of a codefendant's recorded or oral statements to cases in which the codefendants will be jointly tried. The focus here is on giving the defense that information which will be critical in its determination as to whether to seek a severance.

3. ***Criminal records.*** Federal Rule 16 and a substantial majority of the state discovery provisions grant the defendant a right to discovery of his criminal record. Disclosure of the prior

record does not disadvantage the prosecution while the contents of the record are important to the defense on various issues (e.g., whether the defendant should testify at trial, or should move to restrict the use of prior convictions for impeachment purposes). The prior record also will show whether the defendant faces sentencing under enhanced sentencing provisions. In general, pretrial discovery provides a very limited vehicle for making a sentencing assessment. Much of the material that would be considered relevant under sentencing guidelines will be unrelated to the proof of the crime charged and therefore not be discoverable pretrial under even the broadest discovery provisions. Thus, disclosure of the criminal record tends to be viewed primarily as assisting in the evaluation of potential impeachment. This function leads to including disclosure of the criminal records of prosecution witnesses in states that require disclosure of the names of those witnesses (see Note 7, infra).

4. ***Scientific reports.*** Federal Rule 16 and almost all state discovery provisions provide for the disclosure of various reports of medical and physical examinations, scientific tests, and experiments. Most jurisdictions encompass all such reports that are "made in connection with the particular case." Several, however, limit required disclosure to reports the prosecution intends to use at trial, while several follow the federal formula of requiring disclosure only if the reports are either "material to preparing the defense" or intended to be used by the government "in its case-in-chief at the trial."

Automatic disclosure of scientific reports is justified on several grounds. Once the report is prepared, the scientific expert's position is not readily influenced, and therefore disclosure presents little danger of prompting perjury or intimidation. Very often such disclosure is needed to "lessen the imbalance which results from the State's early and complete investigation in contrast to [defendant's] * * * late and limited investigation." *State v. Cook*, 206 A.2d 359 (N.J. 1965). Also, a scientific report typically cannot be challenged adequately at trial without the opportunity to examine it closely and seek the assistance of defense experts, which requires disclosure well in advance of trial.

Although a written report is needed for many types of examinations and tests, experts in some instances will be able to testify on the basis of their notes alone. Also, a full evaluation of an expert's report often requires more than the report itself. Accordingly A.B.A.3d, St.11–2.1 goes beyond the expert's written report in a provision adopted in various states. It states: "With respect to each expert whom the prosecution intends to call as a witness at trial, the prosecutor should also furnish to the defense a curriculum vitae and a written description of the substance of the proposed testimony of the expert, the expert's opinion, and the underlying basis of that opinion." See also Fed.R.Crim.P. 16(a)(1)(G).

5. ***Documents and tangible objects.*** All state discovery provisions provide for defense discovery of certain documents and tangible objects in the possession or control of the prosecution. Provisions based on the first edition of the A.B.A. Standards include both items that the prosecution intends to use at trial and items obtained from or belonging to the defendant. See A.B.A.1st, St. 2.1(a)(u). The need for pretrial disclosure of documents and tangible objects to be used as evidence is similar to the need for pretrial disclosure of scientific tests that will be used in evidence. Adding disclosure of items obtained from, or belonging to, the defendant is justified by the combination of defendant's proprietary interest in the items and their potential relevance in presenting a defense. Several states with A.B.A.-type provisions, stressing the relevance factor, have rejected limiting disclosure by reference to defendant owning or having surrendered the item. Following the lead of A.B.A.3d, St.11–2.1(u), they require disclosure of all tangible objects "which pertain to the case" (although intended use at trial remains a separate disclosure identification, which assists the defense in understanding the prosecution's case).

Federal Rule 16 (and state provisions modeled on Federal Rule 16) also utilize a discovery category that goes beyond items to be used in evidence and items that were obtained from, or belong to, the defendant. Rule 16(a)(E)(i) requires prosecution disclosure of documents and tangible items that are "material to preparing the defense."[a] Some federal lower courts have stated that materiality under this provision requires more than a showing of "relevancy," that the defense must also show some grounding for believing that the line of defense to which the document has relevance would be productive. Since the defense typically will be unaware of the exact content of the document, that standard may be met by pointing to the document's possible relationship to information known to the defense that could prove helpful in challenging the prosecution's case or presenting a defense. CRIMPROC § 20.3(g).

A materiality request must be sufficiently specific; it cannot use terms that largely leave the identification of the document to the subjective assessment of the prosecutor. In white collar cases, in particular, the prosecution will often have obtained from a third-party (e.g., the defendant's employer), a substantial quantity of electronically stored information (ESI). Although Rule 16 and state discovery provisions do not include specific provisions on e-discovery, such discovery is available under Rule 16(a)(E)(i)-type provisions, with the defense describing the demanded ESI by reference to key-word or other search protocols. See CRIMPROC § 20.1(a).

6. *Police reports.* Where a police report contains a description of a statement made to the police by a defendant, codefendant, or prosecution witness that is sufficiently complete to constitute a "recorded statement" of that person, that portion of the report commonly will be governed by the jurisdiction's discovery rule governing such statements. So too, the portion of the report containing an abridged description of an oral statement is likely to be within a discovery provision that encompasses summaries of oral statements. Where the officer is to be a prosecution witness, the police report will be governed by the jurisdiction's discovery rule on the prior recorded statements of witnesses. See Note 8 infra.

The critical issue with respect to police reports is whether there should be pretrial discovery of additional information in those reports that would not fall under the provisions governing statements of defendants, codefendants, or prosecution witnesses. This would include the officer's comments on his own observations (where the officer is not himself a prosecution witness), and references to conversations with persons who are not defendants, codefendants, or prosecution witnesses. These portions of the report might conceivably fit under several other discovery provisions, including: (1) provisions for discovery of documents "which are material to the preparation of the defense" (see Note 5, supra); (2) provisions requiring disclosure of statements of persons having knowledge of relevant facts (see Note 8, infra); and (3) provisions authorizing discretionary disclosure of "relevant material and information" not otherwise specified in the discovery rule (see A.B.A.1st, St. 2.5). However, a substantial number of jurisdictions exempt police reports from discovery under such provisions. Some do so by a specific exemption referring to police reports, some rely on an internal-memorandum exemption provision, and others extend the work product doctrine to investigators and view it as automatically encompassing all police reports.

Although police reports will sometimes reflect the "mental impressions" of police officers that a state might desire to protect as "opinion work product," see Note 3, p. 1094, the general exemption of police reports obviously rests on other justifications. Such provisions are said to reflect a combination of several concerns, including: (1) preserving the confidentiality of police sources, continuing investigations, and investigative tactics without requiring a protective order, (2) avoiding defense "misuse" of police reports to build "red herring" defenses which seek to shift the focus of the case from the weight of the evidence against the defendant to a trial of the

---

[a] In *United States v. Armstrong*, as described in fn. c, p. 892, the Supreme Court held that the reference here was to the defense's preparation of its "defense against the government's case-in-chief" and Rule 16's materiality provision therefore did not encompass documents that might be material to establishing that the prosecution was precluded as a racially discriminatory prosecution.

thoroughness of the police investigation, and (3) encouraging police to file complete reports that will be more useful for internal review purposes. CRIMPROC § 20.3(k). Are these concerns met by a provision that specifically provides for discovery of "all police and investigative reports of any kind prepared for or in connection of the case," but then states that the court may "prohibit or partially restrict the disclosure" if it "determines, *in camera*, that * * * [the] report contains irrelevant, sensitive information interrelated with other crimes or criminal activities and the disclosure * * * may seriously impair enforcement or jeopardize the investigation of these other crimes or activities"? See Fla.R.Crim.P. 3.220(b).[b]

7. ***Witness lists.*** State provisions patterned after the original A.B.A. Standards generally require the prosecution to provide the defense with "the names and addresses of persons whom the State intends to call as witnesses." See A.B.A.1st, St.2.1(a)(1). Several states have a broader provision, as recommended in A.B.A.3d, St.11–2.1(ii). They require the prosecutor to list the names and addresses of all persons "known by the government to have knowledge of relevant facts" without regard to whether they will be called as witnesses. See e.g., Alaska R.Crim.P. 16(b)(1)(i).

In those jurisdictions that do not have a provision mandating pretrial disclosure of the names of prosecution witnesses, the trial court generally is held to have discretionary authority to order pretrial discovery of the names of all or some of those witnesses. The prevailing presumption in most such jurisdictions, however, is against the affirmative exercise of that discretion; trial courts are to order disclosure only upon a strong defense showing of special need. To make such a showing, defense ordinarily must establish that there is some barrier to its ability to conduct its own investigation and that there is no reason to believe that disclosure will result in the intimidation of the listed witnesses.

CRIMPROC § 20.3(h) contends that the strong presumption against disclosure found in many "discretionary jurisdictions" is "based only partly on the need to protect against possible intimidation of witnesses." Noting that the presumption is applied in many situations in which there is no realistic fear that defendant "will intimidate or otherwise improperly influence witnesses," the authors suggest that these jurisdictions "apparently are concerned that the adoption of a policy which sought to distinguish such situations, * * * [and] thereby allowed disclosure in a substantial number of cases, would inevitably reinforce the natural reluctance of many persons to offer to testify at trial." Is this a legitimate ground for refusing to require disclosure? Various federal prosecutors relied largely on such reasoning in opposing a 1974 proposed amendment to Federal Rule 16 (approved by the Supreme Court but subsequently rejected by Congress) that would have required the government to provide defendants with witness lists unless it established grounds for a protective order. Those prosecutors noted that (1)

[b] As discussed in CRIMPROC § 20.3(K), the provisions discussed above with respect to police reports also bear upon the discovery of "video/audio recordings of police dashboard cameras and body-worn cameras," although the outcomes may differ in that context. The questions presented here include: (1) where the video does not include a voice recording but depicts the actions of the defendant or a prospective government witness (e.g., the police officer), does it fall within discovery provisions applicable to "recorded statements" (arguably not, on the ground that the "substantially verbatim" requirement limits those provisions to verbal communications, see Note 4, p. 1096); and (2) assuming that the video otherwise meets the relevancy or materiality requirement of a tangible items discovery provision (which typically will refer specifically to videos or video-counterparts, e.g., "photographs"), see Note 5, p. 1101, will disclosure be barred under an internal documents provision, which overrides the tangible items provision (see e.g., Fed.R.Crim. 16(a)(2), discussed at p. 1095) (arguably not since dash-camera and body-camera recording requirements were adopted to increase the public transparency in policing, not as work-product protected investigative tools). As CRIMPROC § 20.3(K) further notes: "[S]tanding apart from discovery provisions, defense access may be available through [statutory] provisions regulating public access to police videos, particularly provisions granting access to a person who is a subject of a recording (although that may be conditioned on filing a complaint against the police)." While state law commonly leaves the use of body-worn cameras to the discretion of the police agency, more than 20 states have adopted statutes governing such issues as recording preservation and disclosures. See CRIMPROC § 1.5(i).

gaining victim/witness cooperation was one of the most difficult tasks facing law enforcement, (2) that many potential witnesses, with or without justification in the particular case, were fearful of retaliation or harassment, and (3) that the protective order procedure could not screen out all cases of likely intimidation or provide assurance to witnesses in general. With most cases resolved by a plea bargain it was possible that a prosecutor might never have to reveal to the defendant the identity of a particular witness (either because there was no need to disclose the substance of that witness' prospective testimony in the plea bargaining process, or because the testimony could be disclosed without identifying the witness). In any event, the witness would know that his or her identity would not be revealed until the witness testified at trial, at least eliminating attempts to persuade or force the witness to alter that testimony.

8. ***Witness' recorded statement.*** Undoubtedly the most controversial item of potential defense discovery is the prior recorded statement of the prosecution witness. Here the states are divided between those that require discovery, those that make discovery discretionary, and those that prohibit court ordered discovery of such statements. See CRIMPROC § 20.3(i).

Almost all of the states requiring prosecutor disclosure of the names of its prospective witnesses also require disclosure of the written or recorded statements of those witnesses. Where the required disclosure goes beyond witnesses to all persons known to have information relating to the offense, it will also include the written or recorded statements of such persons. Both groups together account for roughly half of the states. In over a dozen of these states, the disclosure requirement is extended to the substance of oral statements.

The other half of the states either allow the court at its discretion to order disclosure of a witness' written or recorded statements or prohibit pretrial discovery of all witness statements. The group prohibiting disclosure includes the states with discovery provisions modeled on the Federal Rules and other states as well. Many of these states include in their discovery rules or statutes a specific prohibition similar to that contained in Federal Rule 16(a)(2).

Federal Rule 16(a)(2) provides that Rule 16 does not "authorize the discovery or inspection of statements made by prospective government witnesses except as provided in 18 U.S.C. § 3500." The statutory reference is to the "Jencks Act." That Act was adopted in 1958 in response to the Supreme Court's decision in *Jencks v. United States*, 353 U.S. 657 (1957). The Court there held, in the exercise of its supervisory power, that defendant was entitled to inspect the internal reports that had been filed by two FBI undercover officers who testified at trial, for possible use in cross-examining those witnesses. The dissent there (by Justice Clark, a former Attorney General) predicted that the decision would lead to defendants "rummaging through confidential material."

The Jencks Act adopted the core of the *Jencks* decision, but prohibited its possible judicial expansion. First, the Act restricted the potential scope of the witness' statements subject to disclosure through its definition of a "statement." (See Note 4 at p. 1096). Second, it provided that "no statement * * * in the possession of the United States which was made by a government witness or prospective government witness (other than the defendant) shall be the subject of subpoena, discovery, or inspection until said witness has testified on direct examination in the trial of the case." Third, once the witness testified, the Act required automatic disclosure of the witness' prior statements (i.e., the defense need not make a showing that the statement was likely to be inconsistent with the witness' trial testimony—the pre-*Jencks* position). Fourth, it also provided, on government request, for a judicial *in camera* review of the prior statement and excision of any portion that was unrelated to "the subject matter as to which the witness testified."[c]

[c] In 1975, Federal Rule 26.2 incorporated the Jencks Act standards to require disclosure at trial of the prior statements of both defense and prosecution witnesses (excepting only the defense witness who is also the defendant). States which have a Rule-16 type pretrial discovery prohibition commonly either have a Jencks-type statute, a provision similar to Rule 26.2, or a common law requirement of disclosure at trial for impeachment purposes.

While the opposition to pretrial disclosure of a prosecution witness' prior recorded statement is based in some jurisdictions on essentially the same concern for the protection of the witness that led those jurisdictions to sharply restrict court ordered disclosure of witness lists (see Note 7 supra), that concern does not fully explain the position taken in many of the jurisdictions that either prohibit disclosure of witness statements or create a strong presumption against the exercise of trial court discretion to order such disclosure. Discovery of a witness' statement is prohibited or sharply restricted even where the defense already knows that the particular person will be a prosecution witness. Indeed, some of the states that require automatic disclosure of the names of witnesses make discretionary the disclosure of a witness' statements, and many of the states making disclosure of witness names discretionary prohibit discovery of witness statements.

What justifies treating the disclosure of witness statements far more restrictively than the disclosure of other items tied to the prosecution's prospective evidence? Consider the following arguments: (1) disclosure of such statements is more likely to facilitate defense perjury than disclosure of any other aspect of the prosecution's case; (2) assuming defendant knows the identity of the prosecution's witnesses, the defendant's alternative means for preparing for the witnesses' testimony are more adequate here than as to other prosecution evidence (e.g., scientific reports), as it will be sufficient merely to interview the witness and investigate possible grounds for bias[d]; (3) the witness' statement is primarily of value in impeachment and disclosure at trial is sufficient for that purpose; (4) disclosure of witness statements tends to undermine the adversary system by giving the defense the benefit of the litigation analysis of the prosecution (the work product exemption will be insufficient because many jurisdictions do not extend it to statements recorded by police officers, and, in any event, the typical witness' statement—a narrative response to an open-ended question (e.g., what happened?)—will not be viewed as protected work product, see Note 3, p. 1095); (5) delaying disclosure of witness statements until trial is in the defendant's best interest as it encourages defense counsel to pursue his or her own investigation by interviewing witnesses rather than relying on statements obtained by the police; and (6) requiring disclosure of a witness' recorded statement will only lead police and prosecutors opposed to such discovery to avoid recording those statements, relying instead on brief notes and their memory of the substance of what the witness told them.

9. ***Exculpatory evidence.*** As discussed in Notes 1–4, pp. 1141–1142, the prosecution's *Brady* obligation as to the disclosure of exculpatory evidence generally does not require pretrial disclosure. However, over half of the states have adopted provisions requiring the prosecution to disclose pretrial exculpatory evidence within its possession or control. See CRIMPROC § 20.3(n). Indeed, those provisions are often broader than the *Brady* obligation, which arguably is limited to admissible evidence (see Note 4, p. 1140), and ties materiality to the likelihood that the disclosure would alter the outcome of the proceeding (see Note 2, p. 1139). See e.g. A.B.A.3d, St.11–2.1(viii) (material subject to pretrial discovery by the defense includes "any material or information within the prosecutor's possession or control which tends to negate the guilt of the defendant as to the offense charged or which would tend to reduce the punishment of the defendant").[e]

---

[d] Courts have uniformly held that the prosecution and police cannot advise or direct witnesses not to cooperate with defense counsel. However, they have also stated that, since "the witness is free to decide whether to grant or refuse an interview, * * * it is not improper for the government to inform the witness of that right." *United States v. White,* 454 F.2d 435 (7th Cir.1971).

[e] A substantially larger number of states have a professional responsibility rule modeled on Rule 3.8(d) of the Model Rules of Professional Conduct. Rule 3.8(d) requires prosecutors to "make timely disclosure to the defense of all evidence or information known to the prosecutor that tends to negate the guilt of the accused or mitigates the offense, and, in connection with sentencing, disclose to the defense and to the tribunal all unprivileged mitigating information known to the prosecutor." ABA Standing Committee on Ethics and Professional Responsibility, in its Formal Opinion 09–454 (7/8/2009), reads this rule as going beyond *Brady* and arguably beyond the typical exculpatory-evidence discovery rule as well. The Formal Opinion concluded that the Rule 3.8(d) obligation is not conditioned on materiality, is not limited to admissible evidence, is not subject to waiver, and requires disclosure at an early point. Professional responsibility provisions are designed for application only in disciplinary proceedings,

§ 3. PRETRIAL DISCOVERY BY THE PROSECUTION

A. CONSTITUTIONAL CONSIDERATIONS

WILLIAMS V. FLORIDA

399 U.S. 78, 90 S.Ct. 1893, 26 L.Ed.2d 446 (1970).

JUSTICE WHITE delivered the opinion of the Court.

Prior to his trial for robbery in the State of Florida, petitioner filed a "Motion for a Protective Order," seeking to be excused from the requirements of Rule 1.200 [now Rule 3.200] of the Florida Rules of Criminal Procedure. That rule requires a defendant, on written demand of the prosecuting attorney, to give notice in advance of trial if the defendant intends to claim an alibi, and to furnish the prosecuting attorney with information as to the place he claims to have been and with the names and addresses of the alibi witnesses he intends to use. In his motion petitioner openly declared his intent to claim an alibi, but objected to the further disclosure requirements on the ground that the Rule "compels the defendant in a criminal case to be a witness against himself" in violation of his Fifth and Fourteenth Amendment rights. The motion was denied. * * *

Florida's notice-of-alibi rule is in essence a requirement that a defendant submit to a limited form of pretrial discovery by the State whenever he intends to rely at trial on the defense of alibi. In exchange for the defendant's disclosure of the witnesses he proposes to use to establish that defense, the State in turn is required to notify the defendant of any witnesses it proposes to offer in rebuttal to that defense. Both sides are under a continuing duty promptly to disclose the names and addresses of additional witnesses bearing on the alibi as they become available. The threatened sanction for failure to comply is the exclusion at trial of the defendant's alibi evidence—except for his own testimony—or, in the case of the State, the exclusion of the State's evidence offered in rebuttal to the alibi.

In this case, following the denial of his Motion for a Protective Order, petitioner complied with the alibi rule and gave the State the name and address of one Mary Scotty. Mrs. Scotty was summoned to the office of the State Attorney on the morning of the trial, where she gave pretrial testimony. At the trial itself, Mrs. Scotty, petitioner and petitioner's wife all testified that the three of them had been in Mrs. Scotty's apartment during the time of the robbery. On two occasions during cross-examination of Mrs. Scotty, the prosecuting attorney confronted her with her earlier deposition in which she had given dates and times which in some respects did not correspond with the dates and times given at trial. Mrs. Scotty adhered to her trial story, insisting that she had been mistaken in her earlier testimony. The State also offered in rebuttal the testimony of one of the officers investigating the robbery who claimed that Mrs. Scotty had asked him for directions on the afternoon in question during the time when she claimed to have been in her apartment with petitioner and his wife.

We need not linger over the suggestion that the discovery permitted the State against petitioner in this case deprived him of "due process" or a "fair trial." Florida law provides for liberal discovery by the defendant against the State, and the notice-of-alibi rule is itself carefully hedged with reciprocal duties requiring state disclosure to the defendant. Given the ease with which an alibi can be fabricated, the State's interest in protecting itself against an eleventh hour defense is both obvious and legitimate. Reflecting this interest, notice-of-alibi provisions, dating at least from

---

and the relatively few reported instances of prosecutors being subjected to bar discipline for inadequate disclosures have all involved flagrant due process violations. See CRIMPROC § 1.7(j) (also citing state courts that have rejected reading Rule 3.8(d) as going beyond *Brady*, and questioning whether such a reading would apply to federal prosecutors under a statute requiring that they adhere to relevant state professional conduct standards, see 28 U.S.C. § 530 B). Consider also Note 5, p. 1144.

1927, are now in existence in a substantial number of States. The adversary system of trial is hardly an end to itself; it is not yet a poker game in which players enjoy an absolute right always to conceal their cards until played. We find ample room in that system, at least as far as "due process" is concerned, for the instant Florida rule, which is designed to enhance the search for truth in the criminal trial by insuring both the defendant and the State ample opportunity to investigate certain facts crucial to the determination of guilt or innocence.

Petitioner's major contention is that he was "compelled to be a witness against himself" contrary to the commands of the Fifth and Fourteenth Amendments because the notice-of-alibi rule required him to give the State the name and address of Mrs. Scotty in advance of trial and thus to furnish the State with information useful in convicting him. No pretrial statement of petitioner was introduced at trial; but armed with Mrs. Scotty's name and address and the knowledge that she was to be petitioner's alibi witness, the State was able to take her deposition in advance of trial and to find rebuttal testimony. Also, requiring him to reveal the elements of his defense is claimed to have interfered with his right to wait until after the State had presented its case to decide how to defend against it. We conclude, however, as has apparently every other court which has considered the issue, that the privilege against self-incrimination is not violated by a requirement that the defendant give notice of an alibi defense and disclose his alibi witnesses.[14]

The defendant in a criminal trial is frequently forced to testify himself and to call other witnesses in an effort to reduce the risk of conviction. When he presents his witnesses, he must reveal their identity and submit them to cross-examination which in itself may prove incriminating or which may furnish the State with leads to incriminating rebuttal evidence. That the defendant faces such a dilemma demanding a choice between complete silence and presenting a defense has never been thought an invasion of the privilege against compelled self-incrimination. The pressures generated by the State's evidence may be severe but they do not vitiate the defendant's choice to present an alibi defense and witnesses to prove it, even though the attempted defense ends in catastrophe for the defendant. However "testimonial" and "incriminating" the alibi defense proves to be, it cannot be considered "compelled" within the meaning of the Fifth and Fourteenth Amendments.

Very similar constraints operate on the defendant when the State requires pretrial notice of alibi and the naming of alibi witnesses. Nothing in such a rule requires the defendant to rely on an alibi or prevents him from abandoning the defense; these matters are left to his unfettered choice.[15] That choice must be made, but the pressures which bear on his pretrial decision are of the same nature as those which would induce him to call alibi witnesses at the trial: the force of historical fact beyond both his and the State's control and the strength of the State's case built on these facts. Response to that kind of pressure by offering evidence or testimony is not compelled self-incrimination transgressing the Fifth and Fourteenth Amendments.

---

[14] We emphasize that this case does not involve the question of the validity of the threatened sanction, had petitioner chosen not to comply with the notice-of-alibi rule. Whether and to what extent a State can enforce discovery rules against a defendant who fails to comply, by excluding relevant, probative evidence is a question raising Sixth Amendment issues which we have no occasion to explore. It is enough that no such penalty was exacted here.

[15] * * * The mere requirement that petitioner disclose in advance his intent to rely on an alibi in no way "fixed" his defense as of that point in time. The suggestion that the State, by referring to petitioner's proposed alibi in opening or closing statements might have "compelled" him to follow through with the defense in order to avoid an unfavorable inference is a hypothetical totally without support in this record. * * * On these facts, then, we simply are not confronted with the question of whether a defendant can be compelled in advance of trial to select a defense from which he can no longer deviate. We do not mean to suggest, though, that such a procedure must necessarily raise serious constitutional problems. See *State ex rel. Simos v. Burke,* 163 N.W.2d 177, 181 (Wis.1968) ("[i]f we are discussing the right of a defendant to defer until the moment of his testifying the election between alternative and inconsistent alibis, we have left the concept of the trial as a search for truth far behind").

In the case before us, the notice-of-alibi rule by itself in no way affected petitioner's crucial decision to call alibi witnesses or added to the legitimate pressures leading to that course of action. At most, the rule only compelled petitioner to accelerate the timing of his disclosure, forcing him to divulge at an earlier date information which the petitioner from the beginning planned to divulge at trial. Nothing in the Fifth Amendment privilege entitles a defendant as a matter of constitutional right to await the end of the State's case before announcing the nature of his defense, any more than it entitles him to await the jury's verdict on the State's case-in-chief before deciding whether or not to take the stand himself.

Petitioner concedes that absent the notice-of-alibi rule the Constitution would raise no bar to the court's granting the State a continuance at trial on the grounds of surprise as soon as the alibi witness is called. Nor would there be self-incrimination problems if, during that continuance, the State was permitted to do precisely what it did here prior to trial: to depose the witness and find rebuttal evidence. But if so utilizing a continuance is permissible under the Fifth and Fourteenth Amendments, then surely the same result may be accomplished through pretrial discovery, as it was here, avoiding the necessity of a disrupted trial.[17] We decline to hold that the privilege against compulsory self-incrimination guarantees the defendant the right to surprise the state with an alibi defense.

CHIEF JUSTICE BURGER, concurring.

I join fully in Justice White's opinion for the Court. I see an added benefit to the alibi notice rule in that it will serve important functions by way of disposing of cases without trial in appropriate circumstances—a matter of considerable importance when courts, prosecution offices and legal aid and defender agencies are vastly overworked. [The Chief Justice noted that a prosecutor receiving the names of alibi witnesses in advance of trial often would be able to determine whether an alibi defense was "reliable and unimpeachable" or "contrived and fabricated." The former determination "would very likely lead to dismissal of the charges," while the latter could lead to a defense decision to plead guilty. In either instance, the Chief Justice noted, "the ends of justice will have been served and the processes expedited."]

JUSTICE BLACK, with whom JUSTICE DOUGLAS joins, dissenting. * * *

The core of the majority's decision is an assumption that compelling a defendant to give notice of an alibi defense before a trial is no different from requiring a defendant, after the State has produced the evidence against him at trial, to plead alibi before the jury retires to consider the case. * * * [But] when a defendant is required to indicate whether he might plead alibi in advance of trial, he faces a vastly different decision than that faced by one who can wait until the State has presented the case against him before making up his mind. Before trial the defendant knows only what the State's case *might* be. Before trial there is no such thing as the "strength of the State's case," there is only a range of possible cases. At that time there is no certainty as to what kind of case the State will ultimately be able to prove at trial. Therefore any appraisal of the desirability of pleading alibi will be beset with guesswork and gambling far greater than that accompanying the decision at the trial itself. * * * Clearly the pressures on defendants to plead an alibi created by this procedure are not only quite different than the pressures operating at the trial itself, but are in fact significantly greater. Contrary to the majority's assertion, the pretrial decision cannot be analyzed as simply a matter of "timing," influenced by the same factors operating at the trial itself.

The Court apparently also assumes that a defendant who has given the required notice can abandon his alibi without hurting himself. Such an assumption is implicit in and necessary for

[17] It might also be argued that the "testimonial" disclosures protected by the Fifth Amendment include only statements relating to the historical facts of the crime, not statements relating solely to what a defendant proposes to do at trial.

the majority's argument that the pretrial decision is no different than that at the trial itself. I, however, cannot so lightly assume that pretrial notice will have no adverse effects on a defendant who later decides to forego such a defense. Necessarily the defendant will have given the prosecutor the names of persons who may have some knowledge about the defendant himself or his activities. Necessarily the prosecutor will have every incentive to question these persons fully, and in doing so he may discover new leads or evidence. Undoubtedly there will be situations in which the State will seek to use such information—information it would probably never have obtained but for the defendant's coerced cooperation.

It is unnecessary for me, however, to engage in any such intellectual gymnastics concerning the practical effects of the notice-of-alibi procedure, because the Fifth Amendment itself clearly provides that "[n]o person * * * shall be compelled in any criminal case to be a witness against himself." If words are to be given their plain and obvious meaning, that provision, in my opinion, states that a criminal defendant cannot be required to give evidence, testimony, or any other assistance to the State to aid it in convicting him of crime. The Florida notice-of-alibi rule in my opinion is a patent violation of that constitutional provision because it requires a defendant to disclose information to the State so that the State can use that information to destroy him. * * *

It is no answer to this argument to suggest that the Fifth Amendment as so interpreted would give the defendant an unfair element of surprise, turning a trial into a "poker game" or "sporting contest," for that tactical advantage to the defendant is inherent in the type of trial required by our Bill of Rights. The Framers were well aware of the awesome investigative and prosecutorial powers of government and it was in order to limit those powers that they spelled out in detail in the Constitution the procedure to be followed in criminal trials. * * *

On the surface this case involves only a notice-of-alibi provision, but in effect the decision opens the way for a profound change in one of the most important traditional safeguards of a criminal defendant. The rationale of today's decision is in no way limited to alibi defenses, or any other type or classification of evidence. The theory advanced goes at least so far as to permit the State to obtain under threat of sanction complete disclosure by the defendant in advance of trial of all evidence, testimony and tactics he plans to use at that trial. In each case the justification will be that the rule affects only the "timing" of the disclosure, and not the substantive decision itself. * * *

NOTES AND QUESTIONS

1. ***The accelerated disclosure doctrine.*** The reach of the accelerated disclosure rationale of *Williams* was sharply questioned in a large body of excellent commentary that analyzed the *Williams* ruling. See CRIMPROC § 20.4(d). The commentators agreed that accelerated disclosure provides the prosecution with several potential benefits. They disagreed as whether *Williams* was saying only that providing some—or that providing all—of these benefits did not violate the self-incrimination privilege.

Accelerated disclosure is seen as giving the prosecution at least four possible benefits it would not receive if the defendant were allowed to delay disclosing the nature of his evidence until he was ready to introduce it at trial. First, accelerated disclosure may provide the prosecution with information that will lead it to other evidence useful in presenting its case-in-chief. Admittedly, the information disclosed pretrial most often would be disclosed later at trial, but the prosecutor frequently can make more effective use of the information when it is received before trial, with more time to develop leads. More significantly, there will be instances in which the information revealed under accelerated disclosure would not later be disclosed because the defense eventually would find that it did not have to use that information at trial—e.g., where the prosecution was unable to establish a sufficient case-in-chief based on its own sources, or where the defendant decided to rely on a different defense at trial. Second, the prosecution similarly may obtain information through accelerated disclosure that will lead it to evidence establishing defendant's involvement in unrelated offenses. Here again, this could be information the prosecution might not have eventually received at trial. Third, the accelerated disclosure may provide the prosecution with information useful in developing a rebuttal to the defendant's defense. Of course, the prosecution eventually would receive this information when the defense was presented at trial, but it would often be much more difficult for the prosecution to make effective use of the information at that point (particularly in a jurisdiction in which trial judges frown on granting continuances). Fourth, accelerated disclosure, by indicating the direction the defense is likely to take, permits the prosecution to husband its resources and thereby to do a better job in presenting both its case-in-chief and its rebuttal to the defense.

Some commentators, reading *Williams* narrowly, argued that it went no farther than to reject a constitutional challenge to the third and fourth advantages. *Williams*, they note, did not present a case in which the prosecution obtained either the first or second advantages. Although Justice Black in dissent raised the possibility that an accelerated disclosure might be used directly or derivatively to enhance the prosecution's case-in-chief, the Court had noted specifically that the prosecution used the alibi disclosure there simply to lay the groundwork for impeaching the alibi witness. Moreover, the commentators note, the very nature of the alibi defense made the potential suggested by Justice Black so remote that the Court had no need to discuss it. Alibi witnesses, as persons who were elsewhere, are not likely to be helpful sources in proving the elements of the offense charged, and defendants are unlikely to offer an alibi which involves the commission of a different crime. As these commentators viewed *Williams*, it did not foreclose successfully raising a self-incrimination objection where the defendant could point to a specific likelihood of incrimination that would flow from his pretrial identification of a particular witness or possibly from pretrial identification of an entire class of witnesses (e.g., self-defense witnesses, as all would have been at the scene of the crime)—as evidenced by the ability of the witness or witnesses to tie the defendant to other criminal activity or to furnish information that would bolster the prosecution's case-in-chief.

Commentators on the other side offered a far broader reading of *Williams*. The majority opinion, they noted, placed only one possible condition on its rejection of the contention that the self-incrimination clause protected the defendant from compulsory pretrial disclosure of anticipated defense witnesses—the defense could insist that it receive sufficient information regarding the nature of the prosecution's case (provided in Florida by broad discovery) as to enable it to make a reasonable tactical judgment as to what defenses (and what witnesses) might be presented. The key to *Williams*, they argued, is that, under these circumstances, accelerating a choice (particularly one that is not final, see fn. 15, p. 1107) does not produce "compulsion," and without compulsion, the self-incrimination privilege affords no protection no matter how likely the potential for incrimination in revealing that choice.

2. Does *Brooks v. Tennessee*, described in Note 4 at p. 1325, provide any assistance in determining the scope of the *Williams* rationale? In *Brooks*, a divided Supreme Court held unconstitutional a state's rule that a defendant, if he desired to testify in his own defense, had to do so before any other defense witnesses gave testimony. The majority found that rule imposed an unjustifiable burden upon defendant's constitutional right not to testify since he was being forced to decide whether or not to testify before he could evaluate the strength of the testimony of his other witnesses. The Court acknowledged that the state had an interest in ensuring that a defendant not shape his testimony to conform to that of the defense witnesses testifying before him (an interest achieved as to other witnesses by their sequestration prior to testifying). It concluded, however, that barring defendant's later testimony if he does not testify as the first defense witness "is not a constitutionally permissible means of insuring his honesty." The majority in *Brooks* did not refer to *Williams*, but the dissent thought *Williams* to be highly relevant. It argued that the burden imposed upon the defendant here was no worse than the analogous burden held constitutionally acceptable in *Williams*. Here too, the state was simply accelerating a decision that was not "compelled," but only the voluntary product of defendant's evaluation of the strength of the prosecution's case.

Is *Brooks* inconsistent with either or both of the readings of *Williams* advanced in Note 1 supra? Consider Broussard, J., dissenting in *Izazaga v. Superior Court*, 815 P.2d 304 (Cal.1991) ("*Brooks* * * * establishes that in some circumstances a rule which requires a defendant to 'accelerate' the disclosure of witnesses or evidence that he may disclose at trial can impinge on the defendant's Fifth Amendment right," and suggests the need for a "sensitive analysis of both the purpose of the state law and the effect of acceleration," which should lead to the narrower of the two readings of *Williams* described in Note 1 supra).

Is it significant that *Brooks* involved the defendant's own testimony? See *Izazaga v. Superior Court*, supra (*Brooks* dealt with "the special component of the Fifth Amendment protecting an accused choice of whether or not to testify" and therefore is "inapposite" to the constitutionality of requiring pretrial disclosure of a "witness 'other than the defendant.' ").

Commentators have suggested that *Brooks* and *Williams* are distinguishable because the defendant in *Brooks* was being forced to do more than make the accelerated disclosure of potential trial evidence that was upheld in *Williams,* as he was required to make an accelerated "final decision" as to whether he would testify.

3. ***Lower court interpretations.*** CRIMPROC § 20.4(d) notes that, "initially, some lower courts were cautious in their reading of *Williams*." Though they accepted as facially valid broad reciprocal discovery provisions that included, for example, defense disclosure of the names of its anticipated trial witnesses, those courts also held open the possibility that the defense would be excused from its discovery obligation if it could show that, in the particular case, the required disclosure would lead the prosecution to evidence that could be used against the defendant in the prosecution's case-in-chief or in establishing another crime. The authors note, however, that "a growing group of [later] cases," such as *Izazaga v. Superior Court*, described at p. 1113 (Note 2), have "sustained reciprocal disclosure without seeking to accommodate the concerns reflected [in those earlier rulings]." They conclude: "Thus, the narrower reading of *Williams* advanced by the commentators today has virtually no support in the caselaw. Lower court rulings, looking to *Williams*, have accepted without limitation reciprocal defense notification of defenses, expert witnesses, all other witnesses, and documents and tangible items."

4. ***Reciprocal discovery.*** In WARDIUS v. OREGON, 412 U.S. 470 (1973), a unanimous Court held unconstitutional a state alibi-notice provision which made no provision for reciprocal discovery. The Court noted (per Marshall, J.): "We hold that the Due Process Clause of the Fourteenth Amendment forbids enforcement of alibi rules unless reciprocal discovery rights are given to criminal defendants. * * * [A]lthough the Due Process Clause has little to say regarding the amount of discovery which the parties must be afforded, it does speak to the balance of forces between the accused and his accuser. The *Williams* court was therefore careful to note that 'Florida law provides for liberal discovery by the defendant against the State, and the notice-of-alibi rule is itself carefully hedged with reciprocal duties requiring state disclosure to the defendant.' The same cannot be said of Oregon law. As the State conceded at oral argument, Oregon grants no discovery rights to criminal defendants, and, indeed, does not even provide defendants with bills of particulars. More significantly, Oregon, unlike Florida, has no provision which requires the State to reveal the names and addresses of witnesses it plans to use to refute an alibi defense.

"We do not suggest that the Due Process Clause of its own force requires Oregon to adopt such provisions. But we do hold that in the absence of a strong showing of state interests to the contrary, discovery must be a two-way street. The State may not insist that trials be run as a 'search for truth' so far as defense witnesses are concerned, while maintaining 'poker game' secrecy for its own witnesses. It is fundamentally unfair to require a defendant to divulge the details of his own case while at the same time subjecting him to the hazard of surprise concerning refutation of the very pieces of evidence which he disclosed to the State."

5. ***Impeachment use of defense notice.*** While an alibi-notice ordinarily may be used in impeachment where that is an appropriate remedy for a violation of the notice provision (as where defendant shifts at trial to an alternative and inconsistent alibi as to which notice was not given), many jurisdictions will not permit its impeachment use as a relevant prior inconsistent statement where defendant simply adopts a different type of defense at trial. See e.g., Federal Rule 12.1(f). Others, however, do allow such use. "The statement is considered an evidentiary admission, * * * [and] the attorney-client privilege is held to be waived because the disclosure is knowingly made to persons outside the scope of the confidential relationship." Robert Mosteller, *Discovery Against the Defense: Tilting the Adversarial Balance*, 74 Cal. L. Rev. 1567 (1986). See e.g., *State v. Howell,* 641 P.2d 37 (Or.App.1982) (defense listing of alibi defense during pretrial conference properly used to impeach defendant's trial testimony in rape case that he had consensual sex with complainant). Allowing such use has been challenged as going beyond the discovery function upheld in *Williams*. See *Moesteller*, supra.

6. ***The aftermath of* Williams.** As noted in *Moesteller*, Note 5 supra, "discovery against the criminal defendant expanded tremendously in many states" in the aftermath of *Williams*. Today, "all jurisdictions provide for some degree of prosecution discovery (although that discovery may be conditioned on the defense first requesting discovery). The jurisdictions vary substantially, however, in the scope of [that] discovery, and in how it compares to defense discovery in the particular jurisdiction." CRIMPROC § 20.5(a). Apart from the traditional alibi-notice provisions considered in *Williams*, and similar mental-illness notice provisions, prosecution discovery now extends to: defenses to be raised; prospective defense witnesses; written or recorded statements of prospective witnesses; reports of experts (to be used in evidence, or simply made in connection with the case); and documents and tangible items which the defense intends to introduce as evidence at trial. The Notes that follow explore the scope of such provisions and, where applicable, constitutional challenges advanced against the particular type of provision. Because *Williams* emphasized intended use at trial and defense discovery obligations restricted to intended use at trial are far more common, the discussion considers separately the required defense disclosure of defenses and evidence that it will use at trial and the required defense disclosure of information and material that it does not intend to introduce at trial.

B. DISCOVERY OF DEFENSES AND SUPPORTING EVIDENCE THAT WILL BE USED AT TRIAL

1. ***Notice of defenses.*** Approximately a dozen states require the defendant to give pretrial notice of the intent to rely on various defenses besides alibi. The broadest provisions extend to "any defense, other than that of not guilty, on which the defendant intends to rely on trial." See e.g., Minn.R.Crim.P. 9.02(1)(3)(a). Under these provisions, the defense must give advance notice of the intent to rely on such defenses as self-defense, entrapment, duress, intoxication, and claim of authority. As with most alibi-notice provisions, the defendant is not bound to raise the listed defense at trial, and the prosecution cannot use against the defendant his failure to do so.

2. ***Witness lists.*** Almost half of the states provide for defense disclosure of the names and addresses of the witnesses that the defense intends to introduce at trial ("other than the defendant")—a position advanced in A.B.A.3d, St.11–2.2 (also recommending, however, that the defense obligation not extend to "disclosure of the identity * * * of a person who will be called for the sole purpose of impeaching a prosecution witness"). In all of these states, the prosecution must list its intended witnesses and in some, must also list other persons with pertinent information.

See Note 7, p. 1103. Courts have noted that the defense obligation to list likely defense witnesses extends to persons the defense "reasonably anticipates it is likely to call." This includes persons who will be called only if the prosecution pursues a certain line of evidence where that prosecution tactic is "reasonably predicted." CRIMPROC § 20.5(e).

In *Prudhomme v. Superior Court,* 466 P.2d 673 (Cal.1970), the California Supreme Court struck down a trial court's discovery order in a murder case which included reciprocal disclosure of witnesses. Although the California Court had earlier accepted an accelerated disclosure analysis in upholding the pretrial disclosure of a scientific report that defendant intended to introduce at trial, it concluded that precedent could not justify a wholesale listing of witnesses. The court reasoned: "It is apparent that the principle element in determining whether a particular demand for discovery should be allowed is not simply whether * * * defendant intends to introduce or rely upon the evidence at trial, but whether disclosure thereof conceivably might lighten the prosecution's burden of proving its case-in-chief. * * * [T]he order herein is not limited to any particular defense or category of witnesses from which a court could attempt to determine its incriminatory effect. It requires no great effort or imagination to conceive of a variety of situations wherein the disclosure of the expected testimony of defense witnesses, or even their names and addresses, could easily provide an essential link in a chain of evidence underlying the prosecution's case-in-chief. For example, if a defendant in a murder case intended to call witness A to testify that defendant killed in self-defense, pretrial disclosure of that information could provide the prosecution with its sole eyewitness to defendant's homicide."

In *Izazaga v. Superior Court*, 815 P.2d 304 (Cal.1991), *Prudhomme* was distinguished as resting on an interpretation of the state constitution " 'more solicitous of the privilege against self-incrimination than federal law currently requires.' " The California Supreme Court there upheld an amendment of the state constitution providing generally for reciprocal discovery. Finding no federal self-incrimination bar to requiring the defense to make reciprocal disclosure of the "names and addresses of all of the witnesses it intends to call at trial, rather than merely its alibi witnesses," the *Izazaga* majority (per Lucas, C.J.) noted:

"Under cases of the Supreme Court, there are four requirements that together trigger this privilege: the information sought must be (i) incriminating; (ii) personal to the defendant; (iii) obtained by compulsion; and (iv) testimonial or communicative in nature. Statutorily mandated discovery of evidence that meets these four requirements is prohibited. Conversely, discovery of evidence that does not meet each of these requirements is not barred by the self-incrimination clause. This is so even in the absence of special state interests such as protection against easily fabricated eleventh-hour defenses. The absence of particular state interests in disclosure affects none of these four requirements, and thus cannot itself trigger the self-incrimination clause.

"In *Williams,* the high court held that discovery of the names and addresses of a defendant's alibi witnesses is not 'compelled' self-incrimination, and therefore does not violate the Fifth Amendment. The Court reasoned, 'At most, the rule only compelled [defendant] to accelerate the timing of this disclosure, by forcing him to divulge at an earlier date information that the [defendant] from the beginning planned to divulge at trial.' Thus, discovery of the names and addresses of the witnesses that the defense intends to call at trial, whether or not in support of an alibi defense, merely forces the defendant 'to divulge at an earlier date information that the [defendant] from the beginning planned to divulge at trial.' (Ibid.) Under the rationale of *Williams*, such discovery does not constitute compelled self-incrimination, and therefore does not implicate the privilege."

3. ***Documents, scientific reports, and tangible objects.*** State provisions patterned after the Federal Rules or either version of the A.B.A. Standards commonly provide for court-ordered defense disclosure of documents, tangible items, and scientific reports that the defense intends to use in evidence at trial. Such provisions are said to present the easiest case for pretrial

disclosure because the government most often will need to consult its own experts in advance of trial to prepare its response to evidence of this type. It also is noted that such evidence typically does not reflect information that came from the defendant although that is not always the case. See Conn.Sup.Ct.R. 40–26(1) (disclosure required of any document defendant intends to offer in evidence "except to the extent it contains any communication by the defendant").

C. DISCOVERY OF MATERIALS AND INFORMATION THAT DEFENSE DOES NOT INTEND TO USE AT TRIAL

1. ***Disclosure of defense witness statements: self-incrimination objections.*** Many of the states requiring the defense to list its potential witnesses (other than the defendant), see Note 2, p. 1112, also require the defense to disclose all "written or recorded" statements of the listed witness that are in its possession (typically statements recorded verbatim during interviews with defense counsel or defense investigators), insofar as they do not contain "opinion work product," see Note 3, p. 1094). State courts sustaining these provisions against self-incrimination challenges have relied in part upon the Supreme Court's rejection of a self-incrimination objection in UNITED STATES v. NOBLES, 422 U.S. 225 (1975), a case involving trial rather than pretrial disclosure.

In *Nobles,* defense counsel asked two key prosecution witnesses about statements they allegedly had made to a defense investigator. Those statements indicated that the witnesses' recollection of the bank robber had been considerably less clear than their current testimony suggested. One witness denied making the alleged statement and the other claimed counsel's description was inaccurate. Defense counsel later called the investigator as a defense witness for the purpose of testifying as to the statements. The trial judge then granted the prosecutor the right to inspect those portions of the investigator's report relating to the witnesses' statements for the purpose of cross-examining the investigator. When defense counsel stated that he would not produce the report, the court ruled that the investigator would not be allowed to testify about the witnesses' statements. On appeal following conviction, the Court of Appeals held that the trial court's disclosure order had violated the Fifth Amendment. The Supreme Court, per Powell, J., reversed:

"The Court of Appeals concluded that the Fifth Amendment renders criminal discovery 'basically a one-way street.' Like many generalizations in constitutional law, this one is too broad. The relationship between the accused's Fifth Amendment rights and the prosecution's ability to discover materials at trial must be identified in a more discriminating manner. The Fifth Amendment privilege against compulsory self-incrimination is an 'intimate and personal one,' which protects 'a private inner sanctum of individual feeling and thought and proscribes state intrusion to extract self-condemnation.' *Couch v. United States*, 409 U.S. 322 (1973). As we noted in *Couch,* the 'privilege is a *personal* privilege: it adheres basically to the person, not to information that may incriminate him.'

"In this instance disclosure of the relevant portions of the defense investigator's report would not impinge on the fundamental values protected by the Fifth Amendment. The court's order was limited to statements allegedly made by third parties who were available as witnesses to both the prosecution and the defense. [Defendant] did not prepare the report, and there is no suggestion that the portions subject to the disclosure order reflected any information that he conveyed to the investigator. The fact that these statements of third parties were elicited by a defense investigator on [defendant's] behalf does not convert them into [defendant's] personal communications. Requiring their production from the investigator therefore would not in any sense compel [defendant] to be a witness against himself or extort communications from him."

2. Does *Nobles'* analysis carry over to the pretrial disclosure of a witness' recorded statements? Consider *Izazaga v. Superior Court,* Note 2, p. 1113, rejecting defendant's "attempt

to distinguish *Nobles* [on the ground] * * * that the Supreme Court has never upheld disclosure of statements of defense witnesses *before* trial." The *Izazaga* court reasoned that "the timing of the disclosure, whether before or during trial, does not affect any of the four requirements that trigger the privilege against self-incrimination [see p. 1113], and therefore cannot implicate the privilege." The key to *Nobles* was its conclusion that "the compelled statements are those of 'third parties,' " and therefore the triggering requirement that the compelled statements be "personal" to the person claiming the privilege simply was not met.

The *Izazaga* court acknowledged that the third-party character of the materials to be disclosed did not always resolve the personal-communication issue. The Supreme Court has recognized that the act of producing a document can itself be testimonial and incriminating under certain circumstances. See *Fisher v. United States*, 425 U.S. 391 (1976). "[H]owever, [here] * * * the *act of handing over* the statements of defense witnesses to the prosecutor does not implicate the privilege. This act is not 'testimonial or communicative in nature' because the act does not 'reveal, directly or indirectly (defendant's) *knowledge* of facts relating him to the offense or . . . (require defendant) to share *his thoughts* and beliefs with the government.' *Doe v. United States*, 487 U.S. 201 (1988) (italics added)."

3. ***Disclosure of prosecution witness statements.*** In *Commonwealth v. Durham*, 843 N.E.2d 1035 (Mass.2006), the trial court directed the defendant, as part of reciprocal discovery, to furnish the prosecution with any recorded statements, in the possession of the defense, of persons who had been listed by the prosecution as its likely prosecution witnesses. Upon a motion for reconsideration, the trial court imposed the following limitations upon its order: "(1) the defendant was only required to turn over statements of Commonwealth witnesses that he intended to use at trial, including statements made to third parties unconnected to the defendant's case; (2) the defendant was not required to disclose statements of a witness for the Commonwealth unless the Commonwealth previously supplied discovery (in the form of grand jury minutes, police reports, recorded witness statements or some other form) containing or describing that witness's statements; (3) to the extent that any statements of the Commonwealth's witnesses included information concerning the identity of any person whom discovery produced to date indicated that the Commonwealth was unaware of, and whom the defendant did not intend to call as a witness at trial, the defendant was not required to provide that portion of the statement to the Commonwealth; and (4) the Commonwealth was permitted to disclose to its witnesses prior to trial the substance of the witnesses' respective statements that had been obtained by the defendant."

Although the defendant subsequently pled guilty, the Supreme Judicial Court agreed to review the legality of the order on a "moot appeal." A divided Court upheld the order as: (1) authorized under the Massachusetts discovery rule; (2) not requiring the disclosure of work product; (3) not invalid as administratively "unworkable"; and (4) not contrary to the defendant's constitutional right to confront witnesses against him. Speaking to the confrontation-clause issue, the Court majority, per Greany, J. noted:

"There is no question that effective cross-examination is an important safeguard of liberty and a valuable tool for testing the reliability of evidence, thereby ensuring a truthful verdict. We also have no disagreement with the view that, as a tactical matter, surprise can be an important element of effective cross-examination. But neither of these propositions is affected by the order to a degree where it can be held that the defendant's constitutional right to confront witnesses against him would be violated.

"The statements the defendant would have had to turn over under the order were presumably already known to the Commonwealth's witnesses who gave them. The defendant, if appropriate, might have received reciprocal discovery of written statements obtained by the Commonwealth from defense witnesses. As such, both sides are given a fair opportunity to investigate the veracity of statements and are not faced with confronting them for the first time at trial. See *United States v. Nobles* [Note 1, p. 1114] * * *. Indeed, such investigation might even have revealed beneficial information for the defense. Had there been a trial, the defendant's trial counsel would have been afforded an adequate opportunity to cross-examine effectively the witnesses who gave the statements. In addition to asking each witness about the substance of his or her statement, defense counsel could have questioned the witness about pretrial preparation. Such questioning could negate any mistaken impression that the witness was encountering the material for the first time and also could suggest that the witness may have conveniently crafted an explanation for any variations in former testimony or statements. * * * The trial process seeks to ascertain the truth. Our conclusion recognizes that 'the truth is most likely to emerge when each side seeks to take the other by reason rather than by surprise.' * * *

"In summary, we acknowledge, as the defendant had emphasized, that cross-examination is important for determining credibility and assisting the trier of fact in arriving at a fair verdict. We acknowledge as well that some 'imbalance' exists between the resources of the State and those of the defendant. The imbalance, however, has been considerably adjusted in modern criminal practice by requiring the State to assist the defense with full discovery, by the provision of considerable funds to hire an investigator and to retain experts to conduct evaluations and other tests (and then to testify), and by nonconstitutionally compelled prophylactic measures, such as permitting jury instruction on topics like the failure of the police to record a confession, * * * and mistaken identification, * * *. The foregoing lists just a few measures. The role of cross-examination, and the existence of an imbalance, should not override the right of the people, and the victims of crimes, to have the evidence evaluated by a fully informed trier of fact. These considerations are responsibly achieved by the interpretation of the rule we reach * * * ".

In dissent, Cordy, J., noted that discovery provisions of other states limited the defense obligation to disclose the recorded statements of witnesses to the defense's own witnesses, and argued that the Massachusetts Court Rule on discovery should be similarly interpreted. The majority's reading of the Rule was characterized as inconsistent with the general thrust of the state's discovery law and "other aspects of our criminal procedures." The dissent noted in this regard:

"Our discovery rule favors liberal discovery * * *. But the discovery authorized under the Court's interpretation of Rule 14(a) does not promote the search for truth. In fact, such discovery will significantly impair that search by disabling the 'greatest legal engine' ever invented in that search—cross-examination. * * * The reason the Commonwealth seeks to obtain statements made by its witnesses that the defense may use to impeach them is crystal clear and perfectly understandable: advance notice that Commonwealth witnesses have made inconsistent statements or admissions—the grist of impeachment—allows the Commonwealth to take any number of anticipatory actions to mute or disable the cross-examination. See *State v. Kinney*, 635 N.W.2d 449 (Neb.2001) ('State was provided with advance notice of [the defendant's] potential rebuttal and impeachment evidence. . . . [This] knowledge might allow the prosecutor to . . . craft the opening statement anticipating [the] defenses and minimizing [the defendant's] case, including deflating the impeachment evidence . . . anticipate the cross-examination . . . and prepare the witnesses [for] that cross . . . orchestrate the order of witnesses [or] forgo calling certain witnesses because of the knowledge that impeachment evidence exists . . . '). Having obtained the statements, the Commonwealth can now inform the witness of their discovery, thereby permitting the witness in advance to think of and craft a response to the cross-examination. The discovery thus provides a hitherto unavailable opportunity to reshape what the jury would otherwise see in unvarnished form. The 'greatest legal engine' in the search for truth is reduced to a mere sputter. * * *

"The rules of our criminal justice system, including our discovery rules, serve to ensure that defendants are treated fairly. In recognition of the State's power and resources, and the advantage such a position gives the prosecution over the defense in a criminal case, a variety of constitutional, statutory, rule-based and common-law rights are afforded the accused in part to even the playing field. * * * It is therefore unsurprising that '[p]rosecutorial discovery was strongly condemned in early American jurisprudence.' * * * I do not disagree with the modern trend toward liberalizing discovery for both parties. * * * Liberalizing, discovery does not come without its price. I am cognizant that 'the more liberal the discovery rules become, the greater the advantage the Commonwealth has in prosecuting its case.' * * * Our discovery rules have always sought to maintain a balance between limiting ambushes at trial and preserving time-tested techniques that offer vital protections for the defendant and aid the trier of fact in assessing credibility. There is a world of difference between eliminating surprise defenses and eliminating surprise cross-examinations designed to test the credibility of the witnesses. The court wrongly conflates the two and embarks on a wholly new direction that all of the Federal courts and the vast majority of State jurisdictions have not sanctioned."

4. ***Disclosure of scientific reports.*** Some state provisions governing prosecution discovery of scientific reports in the possession of the defendant are sufficiently broad to encompass all reports made in connection with the particular case, without regard to whether the defendant intends to rely upon the particular report or the expert who prepared the report. See CRIMPROC § 20.5(h). Does the defendant's privilege against self-incrimination protect against pretrial discovery of a report which defendant does not intend to use because it is not favorable to the defense? Is the short answer to such a claim that, under *Nobles,* the self-incrimination clause cannot apply since the defendant himself is not being asked to testify? See e.g., *Gipson v. State,* 609 P.2d 1038 (Alaska 1980) (compelled disclosure of defense expert's ballistics test did not violate defendant's self-incrimination privilege because the report was not "testimonial" as to defendant, but disclosure was barred as unauthorized under state discovery rule). But see *Binegar v. Eighth Judicial District Court*, 915 P.2d 889 (Nev.1996) (statute requiring defense disclosure of "any relevant witness statements and any reports or results of physical examinations or scientific tests, even if the defendant does not intend [to call the witnesses or] introduce those statements and materials at trial," violates defendant's privilege against self-incrimination because "the defendant would be compelled to do more than simply accelerate the timing of intended disclosures of materials; the defendant would be forced to disclose information that he never intended to disclose at trial, some of which could be incriminating.").

Does the Sixth Amendment bar pretrial discovery of an expert's report which the defense does not intend to use at trial? Consider *State v. Mingo,* 392 A.2d 590 (N.J.1978). The defendant, charged with robbery, requested that the state allow the defense's handwriting experts to examine a note written by the robber. The trial court ordered disclosure to the defense, conditioned on the prosecution having access to the resulting reports, and the prosecution, after reviewing one report, called that expert to testify on behalf of the state. The New Jersey Supreme Court initially rejected the contention that the discovery order violated the work product privilege as codified in N.J.R.Crim.P. 3:13–3(c) (barring discovery of "internal reports, memoranda, or documents" prepared by defense agents). The report of the handwriting expert did not fall "within the intent of the foregoing delineation of work product as its constitute[d] a species of evidence admissible under some circumstances whereas true work product is [nonevidential]."[a] Nevertheless, the

[a] Other jurisdictions would disagree. Where work product is not limited to material that reflects the opinions, theories, or conclusions of legal personnel, and the expert operates at the direction of counsel, they have held reports of experts to be work product, exempt from discovery unless the defense waives the work product protection by having the witness testify. See e.g., *People v. Spiezer*, 735 N.E.2d 1017 (Ill.App.2000) (work product doctrine, rather than Sixth Amendment, provides the more appropriate basis for precluding disclosure of the report of a nontestifying defense expert; to hold that required disclosure constitutes such a substantial interference with the ability of counsel

discovery order did violate the defendant's right to effective assistance of counsel (although the other evidence introduced at trial rendered that violation harmless). To safeguard that right, the court noted, it was essential to afford counsel "the maximum freedom to seek the guidance of expert advice in assessing the soundness and advisability of offering a particular defense without the fear that any unfavorable material so obtained can be used against his client. * * * Reliance upon the confidentiality of an expert's advice itself is a crucial aspect of a defense attorney's ability to consult with and advise his client. If the confidentiality of that advice cannot be anticipated, the attorney might well forego seeking such assistance, to the consequent detriment of his client's cause."

As noted in CRIMPROC § 20.4(f), other state courts have rejected Sixth Amendment challenges to prosecution discovery of the reports of non-testifying defense experts. In doing so, they often have drawn an analogy to the rationales advanced to support the constitutionality of requiring a defendant raising an insanity defense to submit to a psychiatric examination. See Note 6 infra. They note "that the defendant has put into issue the scientific claim on which the non-testifying expert reported and will introduce other expert testimony on that claim. The state, in the interest of having objective scientific evidence freely available to all sides, may insist that the defense, once it raises the issue, make all of its experts available, just as it allows the defense discovery of the reports of all experts consulted by the prosecution, including those that the prosecution may later decide not to use at trial."

5. ***Conditional discovery.*** Assuming arguendo that required defense disclosure of any of the items discussed in Notes 1–4 supra (or Notes 1–3, pp. 1112–1114) would be unconstitutional, would that constitutional barrier be overcome by conditioning the disclosure on a defendant's exercise of a statutory right to discover similar material from the prosecution? A number of the jurisdictions condition the defense's obligation to disclose on an initial defense request for disclosure of the same type of item from the prosecutor. See e.g., Fed.R.Crim.P. 16(b)(1)(A), (B). The Nebraska provision specifically notes, in authorizing such conditional disclosure, that a defendant requesting discovery from the prosecution "shall be deemed to have waived his privilege of self-incrimination" for the purposes of that provision. Neb.Stat. § 29–1916(2). Is such a "waiver" invalid on the ground that "an option [i.e., discovery from the prosecution] which exacts a 'penalty' upon the exercise of the privilege against self-incrimination violates the Fifth Amendment"? *United States v. Fratello,* 44 F.R.D. 444 (S.D.N.Y.1968) (raising, but not deciding the issue). Consider also *State v. Lucious*, 518 S.E.2d 677 (Ga.1999) [defendant had no constitutional right to discovery of state's scientific reports, scientific work product, and witness list, and conditioning that discovery and other discovery not constitutionally required on defendant making reciprocal discovery does not violate either due process, defendant's right to confrontation (rejecting defendant's theory that the confrontation clause gives him a constitutional right to pretrial disclosure of information in the prosecution's possession needed to make confrontation effective), or defendant's right to counsel (rejecting defense claim that a reciprocal discovery obligation interferes with "defense counsel's judgment of whether and when to reveal aspects of his case to the State"); dissent argues that defendant has a constitutional right to discover scientific reports and other material needed to confront witnesses, and that right cannot be burdened by requirement of reciprocity].

6. ***The "special case" of the insanity defense.*** Insanity-notice provisions commonly require that the defendant not only give advance notice of the intent to rely on that defense but also that he submit to a psychiatric exam that can then be used by the prosecution to rebut the defendant's insanity defense. See e.g., Federal Rule 12.2. While the notice requirement has been upheld without difficulty under the rationale of *Williams,* the compelled psychiatric examination

---

to make independent decisions as to violate the Sixth Amendment is to create an absolute prohibition, in contrast to the work product exemption, which is never absolute).

requirement has caused more difficulty. Varying rationales were initially offered, but the dominant explanation today is that set forth in *Kansas v. Cheever*, 571 U.S. 87 (2013): "[w]hen a defendant chooses to testify in a criminal case, the Fifth Amendment does not allow him to refuse to answer related questions on cross-examination. * * * When a defendant presents evidence through a psychological expert who has examined him, the government likewise is permitted to use the only effective means of challenging that evidence: testimony from an expert who also examined him." *Cheever* held that this rationale sustained introducing the testimony of a government expert relating to a court-ordered psychiatric examination where defendant did not raise a traditional mental illness defense, but did rely on a psychiatric expert's testimony to support the claim that brain damage rendered him incapable of meeting the statutory requirement of specific intent. The Court distinguished *Estelle v. Smith*, 451 U.S. 454 (1981), which held that the Fifth Amendment was violated in admitting the testimony of the state physician who performed a court-ordered competency exam on the issue of defendant's "future dangerousness" in a capital sentencing hearing. There the defendant had not sought the competency exam and "neither 'introduced' any 'psychiatric evidence' nor even 'indicated that he might do so.' "

§ 4. DISCOVERY VIOLATIONS: REMEDIES AND SANCTIONS

1. ***The range of relief.*** Comprehensive discovery statutes or court rules commonly include a provision authorizing the trial court to take certain actions upon learning that a party has failed to comply with its disclosure obligations. The range of authorized remedies is broad. The measures noted in Federal Rule 16(d)(2)—ordering immediate disclosure, granting a continuance, and excluding evidence—are the three most commonly mentioned, but "judicial opinions and statutory provisions also recognize several other sanctions or remedies, including (1) a charge directing the jury to assume certain facts that might have been established through the nondisclosed material, (2) granting a mistrial, (3) holding in contempt the party responsible for the nondisclosure, and (4) dismissal of the prosecution." CRIMPROC § 20.6(a). Alibi-notice and insanity-notice statutes usually have their own remedial provisions, which often are more narrowly drawn. Those provisions sometimes refer to a single remedial measure, excluding the testimony of any unlisted witness. However, the statutes commonly refer to imposing that remedy "except for good cause shown," and that phrase tends to be viewed as making available almost all of those measures short of exclusion that are specified in the general discovery provisions.

2. ***Selecting the appropriate remedy.*** The statutes or court rules tend to provide little direction to the trial courts in their choice of response to a violation of a discovery obligation. On the defense side, perhaps no claim relating to discovery has more frequently reached the appellate courts than the claim that the trial court failed to utilize the proper remedy when it discovered shortly before or during trial that the prosecution had breached a discovery responsibility. The usual defense complaint is that the trial court should have granted the remedy requested by the defense (typically the exclusion of prosecution evidence that had not been timely disclosed) rather than some lesser remedy (commonly the ordering of immediate disclosure and the granting of a continuance). While appellate courts frequently note that the trial court must be given "broad latitude" in its selection of an appropriate remedy, they also often set forth some general guidelines for the exercise of that discretion, and reversals for the failure to follow those guidelines are not infrequent.

The appellate courts have not spoken as frequently to the proper trial court response to violations of discovery obligations by the defense. Where they have done so, they commonly have spoken of trial court discretion but also have set forth some fairly specific guiding principles. Indeed, in some jurisdictions, the appellate courts regulate far more tightly the imposition of severe sanctions (exclusion or mistrial) when applied to the defense.

3. ***The preference for continuances.*** Upon learning that there has been a discovery violation, the first step to be taken by the trial court is to order immediate disclosure to the full extent required by the discovery provisions. Appellate opinions then direct the trial court to determine why disclosure was not previously made and whether the lack of previous disclosure could result in prejudice. At least where the party responsible for the violation acted in good faith, the preferred remedy is to offer to the other party a continuance that will permit it to take advantage of the delayed discovery and thereby avoid any prejudice. Thus, where the non-compliance consists of the prosecution's failure to have previously listed one of its witness, the trial court is advised to allow the witness to testify, but first grant the defendant sufficient time to interview the witness. Similarly, where the violation relates to the prosecution's failure to make timely disclosure of the existence of some item that defendant might want to offer in evidence, the trial court is advised to grant a continuance sufficient to permit the defendant to obtain that evidence. In the counterpart situation, a continuance would be offered to the prosecution where it was the defense that failed to list a witness or disclose a report or prior recorded statement.

While the continuance is the preferred response to potential prejudice arising from a delay in disclosure, the appellate cases also recognize that there are situations in which a continuance will not be a satisfactory remedy. In some instances, the length of the needed continuance will cause too great a disruption in the trial process. So too, there are circumstances in which the continuance simply will not respond to the potential prejudice. The latter situation arises primarily where the delayed disclosure comes at trial after the opposing side has committed itself to a position inconsistent with the evidence that should have been made available under pretrial discovery. One issue that has divided the lower courts in this setting is what weight should be given to the undercutting of a defense position that arguably was designed to mislead the jury as to the true facts. See e.g., the cases discussed in Notes 4 and 5 below.

4. ***Late disclosures that contradict a misleading defense.*** In *People v. Taylor*, 406 N.W.2d 859 (Mich.App.1987), the defendant, responding to the testimony of his friend Veldt that defendant had been the person who sold Veldt a stolen pickup truck, testified that he had merely told Veldt where a truck might be purchased "cheap" and had not otherwise been involved in the actual purchase of the truck. As the Court of Appeals noted (per Peterson, J.): "Unfortunately for defendant, his version of events, which might otherwise have seemed persuasive, and the depiction of his good character and truthfulness were destroyed during his cross-examination by a letter he had written to a friend, and by his ineffectual attempts to disavow the letter and then to explain it. The letter, received as an exhibit over objection, clearly demonstrated defendant's guilt and asked the friend to put pressure on Veldt to change his story so as not to implicate the defendant."

When defendant objected to the prosecutor's failure to have made pretrial disclosure of the letter, as required by an enforceable discovery agreement between the prosecution and defense, the prosecutor responded that he had only learned of the letter on the night before the trial and had received it on the day of the trial. This did not excuse the prosecutor's failure to disclose the letter to the defense immediately prior to the commencement of the trial, as the prosecutor's duty to disclose was a "continuing obligation," but the prosecutor's explanation, accepted by the trial court, indicated that that failure was the product of negligence rather than a deliberate attempt to sandbag. In light of that explanation and its conclusion that the defendant was not prejudiced (based on defense counsel's rejection of an offer to "reopen proofs" to allow the defense to call any further witnesses), the trial court held that any discovery violation was harmless. On appeal, the defense counsel argued that "had he known of the statements, he *might* have advised his client not to testify or *might* have adopted some strategy for minimizing their impact" (emphasis in original). Accordingly, the defense contended, the trial court should have excluded the letter from evidence, and its failure to do so required reversal of his conviction in light of two earlier Court of Appeals rulings. Those cases had stated that, "where a prosecutor has violated a discovery order—

even if done inadvertently in good faith—unless it is clear that the failure to divulge was harmless beyond a reasonable doubt, we will reverse."

The *Taylor* court initially overturned the standard announced in the earlier rulings. That standard, the court noted, erred in its inflexibility. It "exclud[ed] consideration of the causes of the noncompliance, good faith, degrees of negligence, the nature and degree of prejudice, and whether some other remedy would be appropriate." Moreover, it allowed "no exception * * * for evidence of which defendant had independent knowledge, such as his own statements, not even for impeachment when the defendant testified differently if not downright perjuriously." The trial court, it was noted, must have discretion to fashion a remedy for noncompliance that encompasses "a fair balancing of the interests of the courts, the public, and the parties," recognizing that "exclusion of otherwise admissible evidence is a remedy which should follow only in the most egregious cases." In this case, under that standard, "the defendant was entitled to no remedy for the prosecutor's nondisclosure of the letter in question since the defendant, having written it himself, had knowledge of it independent of discovery." Indeed, to exclude the evidence under the circumstances of this case would be "anomalous" in light of Supreme Court rulings (see Ch. 12, § 3) allowing evidence unconstitutionally obtained to be used to "impeach a perjurious defendant."

5. In *United States v. Noe*, 821 F.2d 604 (11th Cir.1987), the government's case against defendant rested largely on the testimony of two undercover agents. They testified to several discussions with defendant concerning the establishment of a clandestine methamphetamine laboratory and to their purchase from defendant of a sample of the drugs to be produced. Testifying in his defense, defendant denied that he was involved in any of the events recounted by the agents. He claimed that he was in Costa Rica during the period in question, and produced a receipt for an airline ticket in support of that claim. On rebuttal, the government offered into evidence a tape recording of a telephone conversation in which one of the undercover agents spoke to a man he identified on the phone as defendant and that person agreed to meet with the agent at a local Atlanta bar that evening. The agent then testified as to the date of the tape, which was during the period when defendant claimed to be in Costa Rica. The district court admitted the tape into evidence over defendant's objection that the prosecution had failed to make pretrial disclosure of the tape pursuant to Federal Rule 16(a)(1)(A), notwithstanding the defense's timely request for discovery. Although "conceding that the tape should have been provided * * *, the government asserted the failure to do so was inadvertent." On appeal, the government contended that its failure to provide discovery did not require reversal of defendant's conviction in light of the "strength of the government's case" against the defendant. Rejecting that position, the Court of Appeals majority reasoned:

"As [this] court * * * [previously] noted, the purpose of Rule 16(a) is 'to protect the defendant's rights to a fair trial.' And, contrary to the government's contentions, the degree to which those rights suffer as a result of a discovery violation is determined not simply by weighing all the evidence introduced, but rather by considering how the violation affected the defendant's ability to present a defense. Where the government at trial introduces undisclosed evidence that tends to undermine one aspect of the defense * * *, the existence of actual prejudice often will turn on the strength of the remaining elements of the government's case. Here, however, the government introduced evidence that attacked the very foundation of the defense strategy. As [this] court [previously] observed, the failure of the government to disclose 'statement[s] made by the defendant is so serious a detriment to the preparation for trial and the defense of serious criminal charges that where it is apparent, as here, that [the] defense strategy may have been determined by the failure to [disclose], there should be a new trial.' * * * Although Noe certainly does not have a right to 'fabricate' an alibi story, the Federal Rules of Criminal Procedure provide him a right to discover all statements that he made to law enforcement officials, and, correspondingly, to devise a defense strategy on the basis of the evidence disclosed."

6. ***Exclusion of prosecution evidence.*** Consistent with their advice to trial courts to first look to the continuance as a remedy, appellate courts frequently warn against the unnecessary use of the preclusion sanction. The trial court, it is noted, "should seek to apply sanctions that affect the evidence at trial and the merits of the case as little as possible." Sanctions generally should not have "adverse effects on the rights of the parties, rather than the offending attorneys themselves," and exclusion of prosecution evidence necessarily has such an adverse effect on the interests of the community, which is the party represented by the prosecutor. *State v. Lewis,* 632 P.2d 547 (Alaska App.1981). Accordingly, some courts treat exclusion as a remedy that should be available only where there was actual prejudice and where no other remedy will respond adequately to that prejudice. It is a "remedy of last resort," to be used only where absolutely needed. Other jurisdictions, while viewing exclusion as a remedy to be used sparingly, will not place the trial court in a position where it can exclude previously undisclosed evidence only upon finding that lesser sanctions clearly could not eliminate the prejudice to the defense. Here, the trial court is given greater leeway. It may, for example, choose exclusion over a continuance where a continuance would be disruptive or would not provide the same degree of assurance that the prejudice would be eliminated.

The jurisdictions also are divided as to the possible use of exclusion simply as a deterrent, without regard to the presence of prejudice. Some courts would allow such use where the trial court finds that the discovery violation was intentional or reflects a recurring prosecutorial disregard for discovery obligations. These courts view exclusion as offering the same prophylactic impact in the enforcement of discovery rules as the exclusion of illegally seized evidence offers in the enforcement of the Fourth Amendment. Indeed, a few courts have gone beyond that position and approved the use of a dismissal with prejudice to respond to glaring prosecutorial discovery violations that suggest either gross negligence or purposeful misconduct. Other jurisdictions reject the prophylactic use of exclusion. Similarly, dismissal is allowed only where the prosecution is ordered to provide discovery as to a certain item and prefers dismissal to complying with the court's order. Where the trial court believes that there is need for a deterrent measure, it is directed to make use of contempt orders directed against the offending prosecutor.[a] A sanction, these courts note, should "not be regarded as a bonus awarded without regard to its need in the furtherance of fair trial rights." *Miller v. State,* 405 N.E.2d 909 (1980).

7. ***Exclusion of defense evidence.*** Where a jurisdiction gives the trial court some leeway in using the sanction of exclusion, not limiting its use just to those situations in which "less drastic means" clearly will not respond to prejudice, should that flexibility apply equally to exclusion as used against both the prosecution and the defense? Prior to *Taylor v. Illinois,* discussed below, many states appeared to demand greater restraint in imposing exclusion against the defense. Some did so on general policy grounds, but others assumed that exclusion posed serious

[a] The primary contempt sanction is a fine imposed directly upon the offending prosecutor, calculated either to reimburse for the wasted time of the public defender or to be punitive. While various opinions take note of the judicial authority to impose fines as a disciplinary measure, see CRIMPROC § 1.7(j), courts do not keep track of how frequently that sanction is used.

Bar discipline is also available, as Model Rule 3.4(d) requires that attorneys "make [a] reasonably diligent effort to comply with a legally proper discovery request." See also fn. e, p. 1105(discussing Model rule 3.8(d)). Notwithstanding some prominent instances of bar authorities disciplining prosecutors who failed to provide discovery (typically also involving *Brady* violations), the general consensus is that such discipline is rarely imposed. See Note 4, p. 1331.

As to the potential for applying internal sanctions in the federal system, see CRIMPROC § 20.2(c), ("a judicial finding that the prosecution violated the disclosure requirements of federal discovery law or *Brady* ordinarily leads to internal review by the DOJ office of Professional Responsibility (OPR)"; over a three year period, the OPR complaint-category of "failure to comply with *Brady, Giglio* [fn. a, p. 1133], or Fed.R.Crim.P. 16 discovery" produced 99 investigations and 62 "inquiries" (i.e., requests for further information); "while the OPR reports do not identify findings of 'intentional misconduct' (i.e., knowing or reckless disregard violations) by reference to a misconduct category, the limited number of findings of intentional misconduct indicate that OPR could not have found such culpability in the vast majority of the *Brady, Giglio,* and Rule 16 rulings that required OPR review").

constitutional difficulties as applied to the defense—the issue considered by the Supreme Court in *Taylor*.

TAYLOR V. ILLINOIS

484 U.S. 400, 108 S.Ct. 646, 98 L.Ed.2d 798 (1988).

JUSTICE STEVENS delivered the opinion of the Court.

As a sanction for failing to identify a defense witness in response to a pretrial discovery request, an Illinois trial judge refused to allow the undisclosed witness to testify. The question presented is whether that refusal violated the petitioner's constitutional right to obtain the testimony of favorable witnesses. We hold that such a sanction is not absolutely prohibited by the Compulsory Process Clause of the Sixth Amendment and find no constitutional error on the specific facts of this case.

A jury convicted petitioner in 1984 of attempting to murder Jack Bridges in a street fight on the south side of Chicago on August 6, 1981. The conviction was supported by the testimony of Bridges, his brother, and three other witnesses. They described a twenty-minute argument between Bridges and a young man named Derrick Travis, and a violent encounter that occurred over an hour later between several friends of Travis, including the petitioner, on the one hand, and Bridges, belatedly aided by his brother, on the other. The incident was witnessed by twenty or thirty bystanders. It is undisputed that at least three members of the group which included Travis and petitioner were carrying pipes and clubs that they used to beat Bridges. Prosecution witnesses also testified that petitioner had a gun, that he shot Bridges in the back as he attempted to flee, and that, after Bridges fell, petitioner pointed the gun at Bridges' head but the weapon misfired.

Two sisters, who are friends of petitioner, testified on his behalf. In many respects their version of the incident was consistent with the prosecution's case, but they testified that it was Bridges' brother, rather than petitioner, who possessed a firearm and that he had fired into the group hitting his brother by mistake. No other witnesses testified for the defense.

Well in advance of trial, the prosecutor filed a discovery motion requesting a list of defense witnesses. In his original response, petitioner's attorney identified the two sisters who later testified and two men who did not testify. On the first day of trial, defense counsel was allowed to amend his answer by adding the names of Derrick Travis and a Chicago Police Officer; neither of them actually testified. * * * On the second day of trial, after the prosecution's two principal witnesses had completed their testimony, defense counsel made an oral motion to amend his "Answer to Discovery" to include two more witnesses, Alfred Wormley and Pam Berkhalter. In support of the motion, counsel represented that he had just been informed about them and that they had probably seen the "entire incident."

In response to the court's inquiry about the defendant's failure to tell him about the two witnesses earlier, counsel acknowledged that defendant had done so, but then represented that he had been unable to locate Wormley. After noting that the witnesses' names could have been supplied even if their addresses were unknown, the trial judge directed counsel to bring them in the next day, at which time he would decide whether they could testify. The judge indicated that he was concerned about the possibility "that witnesses are being found that really weren't there."

The next morning Wormley appeared in court with defense counsel. After further colloquy about the consequences of a violation of discovery rules, counsel was permitted to make an offer of proof in the form of Wormley's testimony outside the presence of the jury. It developed that Wormley had not been a witness to the incident itself. He testified that prior to the incident he saw Jack Bridges and his brother with two guns in a blanket, that he heard them say "they were after Ray [petitioner] and the other people," and that on his way home he "happened to run into Ray and them" and warned them "to watch out because they got weapons." On cross-examination, Wormley acknowledged that he had first met the defendant "about four months ago" (i.e., over two years after the incident). He also acknowledged that defense counsel had visited him at his home on the Wednesday of the week before the trial began. Thus, his testimony rather dramatically contradicted defense counsel's representations to the trial court.

After hearing Wormley testify, the trial judge concluded that the appropriate sanction for the discovery violation was to exclude his testimony. The judge explained:

> "THE COURT: All right, I am going to deny Wormley an opportunity to testify here. He is not going to testify. I find this is a blatant violation of the discovery rules, willful violation of the rules. I also feel that defense attorneys have been violating discovery in this courtroom in the last three or four cases blatantly and I am going to put a stop to it and this is one way to do so. * * * Further, for whatever value it is, because this is a jury trial, I have a great deal of doubt in my mind as to the veracity of this young man that testified as to whether he was an eyewitness on the scene, sees guns that are wrapped up. He doesn't know Ray but he stops Ray. * * * " App. 28.

The Illinois Appellate Court affirmed petitioner's conviction. * * * The court concluded that in this case "the trial court was within its discretion in refusing to allow the additional witnesses to testify." The Illinois Supreme Court denied leave to appeal and we granted the petition for certiorari.

In this Court petitioner makes two arguments. He first contends that the Sixth Amendment bars a court from ever ordering the preclusion of defense evidence as a sanction for violating a discovery rule. Alternatively, he contends that even if the right to present witnesses is not absolute, on the facts of this case the preclusion of Wormley's testimony was constitutional error. Before addressing these contentions, we consider the State's argument that the Compulsory Process Clause of the Sixth Amendment is merely a guarantee that the accused shall have the power to subpoena witnesses and simply does not apply to rulings on the admissibility of evidence.

In the State's view, no Compulsory Process Clause concerns are even raised by authorizing preclusion as a discovery sanction, or by the application of the Illinois rule in this case. The State's argument is supported by the plain language of the Clause, by the historical evidence that it was intended to provide defendants with subpoena power that they lacked at common law, by some scholarly comment, and by a brief excerpt from the legislative history of the Clause. We have, however, consistently given the Clause the broader reading reflected in contemporaneous state constitutional provisions.

As we noted just last Term, "[o]ur cases establish, at a minimum, that criminal defendants have the right to the government's assistance in compelling the attendance of favorable witnesses at trial and the right to put before a jury evidence that might influence the determination of guilt." *Pennsylvania v. Ritchie* [Note 1, p. 1144]. Few rights are more fundamental than that of an accused to present witnesses in his own defense. Indeed, this right is an essential attribute of the adversary system itself. * * * The right to compel a witness' presence in the courtroom could not protect the integrity of the adversary process if it did not embrace the right to have the witness' testimony heard by the trier of fact. The right to offer testimony is thus grounded in the Sixth Amendment even though it is not expressly described in so many words * * *.

Petitioner's claim that the Sixth Amendment creates an absolute bar to the preclusion of the testimony of a surprise witness is just as extreme and just as unacceptable as the State's position that the Amendment is simply irrelevant. The accused does not have an unfettered right to offer testimony that is incompetent, privileged, or otherwise inadmissible under standard rules of evidence. The Compulsory Process Clause provides him with an effective weapon, but it is a weapon that cannot be used irresponsibly.* * *

The defendant's right to compulsory process is itself designed to vindicate the principle that the "ends of criminal justice would be defeated if judgments were to be founded on a partial or speculative presentation of the facts." * * * Rules that provide for pretrial discovery of an opponent's witnesses serve the same high purpose. Discovery, like cross-examination, minimizes the risk that a judgment will be predicated on incomplete, misleading, or even deliberately fabricated testimony. The "State's interest in protecting itself against an eleventh hour defense" is merely one component of the broader public interest in a full and truthful disclosure of critical facts.

To vindicate that interest we have held that even the defendant may not testify without being subjected to cross-examination. *Brown v. United States,* 356 U.S. 148 (1958). Moreover, in *United States v. Nobles* [p. 1114 (Note 1)], we upheld an order excluding the testimony of an expert witness tendered by the defendant because he had refused to permit discovery of a "highly relevant" report. * * *

Petitioner does not question the legitimacy of a rule requiring pretrial disclosure of defense witnesses, but he argues that the sanction of preclusion of the testimony of a previously undisclosed witness is so drastic that it should never be imposed. He argues, correctly, that a less drastic sanction is always available. Prejudice to the prosecution could be minimized by granting a continuance or a mistrial to provide time for further investigation; moreover, further violations can be deterred by disciplinary sanctions against the defendant or defense counsel.

It may well be true that alternative sanctions are adequate and appropriate in most cases, but it is equally clear that they would be less effective than the preclusion sanction and that there are instances in which they would perpetuate rather than limit the prejudice to the State and the harm to the adversary process. One of the purposes of the discovery rule itself is to minimize the risk that fabricated testimony will be believed. Defendants who are willing to fabricate a defense may also be willing to fabricate excuses for failing to comply with a discovery requirement. The risk of a contempt violation may seem trivial to a defendant facing the threat of imprisonment for a term of years. A dishonest client can mislead an honest attorney, and there are occasions when an attorney assumes that the duty of loyalty to the client outweighs elementary obligations to the court.

We presume that evidence that is not discovered until after the trial is over would not have affected the outcome.[18] It is equally reasonable to presume that there is something suspect about a defense witness who is not identified until after the eleventh hour has passed. If a pattern of discovery violations is explicable only on the assumption that the violations were designed to conceal a plan to present fabricated testimony, it would be entirely appropriate to exclude the tainted evidence regardless of whether other sanctions would also be merited.

In order to reject petitioner's argument that preclusion is *never* a permissible sanction for a discovery violation it is neither necessary nor appropriate for us to attempt to draft a comprehensive set of standards to guide the exercise of discretion in every possible case. It is elementary, of course, that a trial court may not ignore the fundamental character of the defendant's right to offer the testimony of witnesses in his favor. But the mere invocation of that right cannot automatically and invariably outweigh countervailing public interests. The integrity of the adversary process, which depends both on the presentation of reliable evidence and the rejection of unreliable evidence; the interest in the fair and efficient administration of justice; and

---

[18] [The Court here cites lower court cases setting forth the Rule 33 standard as to defendant's burden in gaining a new trial based on newly discovered evidence. See fn. c, p. 1134.]

the potential prejudice to the truth-determining function of the trial process must also weigh in the balance.

A trial judge may certainly insist on an explanation for a party's failure to comply with a request to identify his or her witnesses in advance of trial. If that explanation reveals that the omission was willful and motivated by a desire to obtain a tactical advantage that would minimize the effectiveness of cross-examination and the ability to adduce rebuttal evidence, it would be entirely consistent with the purposes of the Confrontation Clause simply to exclude the witness' testimony.[20] Cf. *United States v. Nobles*.

The simplicity of compliance with the discovery rule is also relevant. As we have noted, the Compulsory Process Clause cannot be invoked without the prior planning and affirmative conduct of the defendant. Lawyers are accustomed to meeting deadlines. Routine preparation involves location and interrogation of potential witnesses and the serving of subpoenas on those whose testimony will be offered at trial. The burden of identifying them in advance of trial adds little to these routine demands of trial preparation.

It would demean the high purpose of the Compulsory Process Clause to construe it as encompassing an absolute right to an automatic continuance or mistrial to allow presumptively perjured testimony to be presented to a jury. We reject petitioner's argument that a preclusion sanction is never appropriate no matter how serious the defendant's discovery violation may be.

Petitioner argues that the preclusion sanction was unnecessarily harsh in this case because the *voir dire* examination of Wormley adequately protected the prosecution from any possible prejudice resulting from surprise. Petitioner also contends that it is unfair to visit the sins of the lawyer upon his client. Neither argument has merit.

More is at stake than possible prejudice to the prosecution. We are also concerned with the impact of this kind of conduct on the integrity of the judicial process itself. The trial judge found that the discovery violation in this case was both willful and blatant.[22] In view of the fact that petitioner's counsel had actually interviewed Wormley during the week before the trial began and the further fact that he amended his Answer to Discovery on the first day of trial without identifying Wormley while he did identify two actual eyewitnesses whom he did not place on the stand, the inference that he was deliberately seeking a tactical advantage is inescapable. Regardless of whether prejudice to the prosecution could have been avoided in this particular case, it is plain that the case fits into the category of willful misconduct in which the severest sanction is appropriate. After all, the court, as well as the prosecutor, has a vital interest in protecting the trial process from the pollution of perjured testimony. Evidentiary rules which apply to categories of inadmissible evidence—ranging from hearsay to the fruits of illegal searches—may properly be enforced even though the particular testimony being offered is not prejudicial. The pretrial conduct

---

[20] There may be cases in which a defendant has legitimate objections to disclosing the identity of a potential witness. See Note, *The Preclusion Sanction—A Violation of the Constitutional Right to Present a Defense*, 81 Yale L.J. 1342, 1350 (1972). Such objections, however, should be raised in advance of trial in response to the discovery request and, if the parties are unable to agree on a resolution, presented to the court. Under the Federal Rules of Criminal Procedure and under the rules adopted by most states, a party may request a protective order if he or she has just cause for objecting to a discovery request. See e.g., Fed.Rule Crim.Proc. 16(d)(1); Ill.Sup.Ct.Rule 412(i). In this case, there is no issue concerning the validity of the discovery requirement or petitioner's duty to comply with it. There is also no indication that petitioner ever objected to the prosecution's discovery request.

[22] The trial judge also expressed concern about discovery violations in other trials. If those violations involved the same attorney, or otherwise contributed to a concern about the trustworthiness of Wormley's eleventh hour testimony, they were relevant. Unrelated discovery violations in other litigation would not, however, normally provide a proper basis for curtailing the defendant's constitutional right to present a complete defense.

revealed by the record in this case gives rise to a sufficiently strong inference "that witnesses are being found that really weren't there," to justify the sanction of preclusion.[23]

The argument that the client should not be held responsible for his lawyer's misconduct strikes at the heart of the attorney-client relationship. Although there are basic rights that the attorney cannot waive without the fully informed and publicly acknowledged consent of the client, the lawyer has—and must have—full authority to manage the conduct of the trial. The adversary process could not function effectively if every tactical decision required client approval. Moreover, given the protections afforded by the attorney-client privilege and the fact that extreme cases may involve unscrupulous conduct by both the client and the lawyer, it would be highly impracticable to require an investigation into their relative responsibilities before applying the sanction of preclusion. In responding to discovery, the client has a duty to be candid and forthcoming with the lawyer, and when the lawyer responds, he or she speaks for the client. Putting to one side the exceptional cases in which counsel is ineffective, the client must accept the consequences of the lawyer's decision to forgo cross-examination, to decide not to put certain witnesses on the stand, or to decide not to disclose the identity of certain witnesses in advance of trial. In this case, petitioner has no greater right to disavow his lawyer's decision to conceal Wormley's identity until after the trial had commenced than he has to disavow the decision to refrain from adducing testimony from the eyewitnesses who were identified in the Answer to Discovery. Whenever a lawyer makes use of the sword provided by the Compulsory Process Clause, there is some risk that he may wound his own client. The judgment of the Illinois Appellate Court is affirmed.

JUSTICE BRENNAN, with whom JUSTICE MARSHALL and JUSTICE BLACKMUN join, dissenting.

* * * The Compulsory Process and Due Process Clauses * * * require courts to conduct a searching substantive inquiry whenever the government seeks to exclude criminal defense evidence. * * * [T]his Court defined the standard governing [that] constitutional inquiry just last Term in *Rock v. Arkansas* [Note 5, p. 1325], concluding that restrictions on the right to present criminal defense evidence can be constitutional only if they " 'accommodate other legitimate interests in the criminal trial process' " and are not "arbitrary or disproportionate to the purposes they are designed to serve." The question at the heart of this case, then, is whether precluding a criminal defense witness from testifying bears an arbitrary and disproportionate relation to the purposes of discovery, at least absent any evidence that the defendant was personally responsible for the discovery violations. * * *

The use of the preclusion sanction as a corrective measure—that is, as a measure for addressing the adverse impact a discovery violation might have on truthseeking in the case at hand—is asserted to have two justifications: (1) it bars the defendant from introducing testimony that has not been tested by discovery, and (2) it screens out witnesses who are inherently suspect because they were not disclosed until trial. The first justification has no bearing on this case because the defendant does not insist on a right to introduce a witness' testimony without giving the prosecution an opportunity for discovery. He concedes that the trial court was within its authority in requiring the witness to testify first out of the presence of the jury, and he concedes that the trial court could have granted the prosecution a continuance to give it sufficient time to conduct further discovery concerning the witness and the proffered testimony. He argues only that he should not be completely precluded from introducing the testimony. * * *

---

23 It should be noted that in Illinois, the sanction of preclusion is reserved for only the most extreme cases. In *People v. Rayford,* the Illinois Appellate Court explained: "The exclusion of evidence is a drastic measure; and the rule in civil cases limits its application to flagrant violations, where the uncooperative party demonstrates a 'deliberate contumacious or unwarranted disregard of the court's authority.' The reasons for restricting the use of the exclusion sanction to only the most extreme situations are even more compelling in the case of criminal defendants. * * *."

Nor, despite the Court's suggestions, is the preclusion at issue here justifiable on the theory that a trial court can exclude testimony that it presumes or finds suspect. * * * [P]reventing a jury from hearing the proffered testimony based on its presumptive or apparent lack of credibility would be antithetical to the principles laid down in *Washington v. Texas,* 388 U.S. 14 (1967) [holding unconstitutional a statute that rendered accomplices incompetent to testify for one another, though competent to testify for the state]. The Court in *Washington* * * * concluded that "arbitrary rules that prevent whole categories of defense witnesses from testifying on the basis of *a priori* categories that presume them unworthy of belief" are unconstitutional. Although persons who are not identified as defense witnesses until trial may not be as trustworthy as other categories of persons, surely any presumption that they are so suspect that the jury can be prevented from even listening to their testimony is at least as arbitrary as [a] presumption excluding an accomplice's testimony, *Washington v. Texas* * * *. The proper method, under Illinois law and *Washington v. Texas,* for addressing the concern about reliability is for the prosecutor to inform the jury about the circumstances casting doubt on the testimony: thus allowing the jury to determine the credit and weight it wants to attach to such testimony. * * *

Of course, discovery sanctions must include more than corrective measures. They must also include punitive measures that can deter future discovery violations from taking place. * * * In light of the availability of direct punitive measures, however, there is no good reason, at least absent evidence of the defendant's complicity, to countenance the arbitrary and disproportionate punishment imposed by the preclusion sanction. The central point to keep in mind is that witness preclusion operates as an effective deterrent only to the extent that it has a possible effect on the outcome of the trial. Indeed, it employs in part the possibility that a distorted record will cause a jury to convict a defendant of a crime he did not commit. * * * In contrast, direct punitive measures (such as contempt sanctions or, if the attorney is responsible, disciplinary proceedings) can graduate the punishment to correspond to the severity of the discovery violation.

The arbitrary and disproportionate nature of the preclusion sanction is highlighted where the penalty falls on the defendant even though he bore no responsibility for the discovery violation. In this case, although there was ample evidence that the defense attorney willfully violated Rule 413(d), there was no evidence that the defendant played any role in that violation. Nor did the trial court make any effort to determine whether the defendant bore any responsibility for the discovery violation. Indeed, reading the record leaves the distinct impression that the main reason the trial court excluded Wormley's testimony was the belief that the defense counsel had purposefully lied about when he had located Wormley. * * * Deities may be able to visit the sins of the father on the son, but I cannot agree that courts should be permitted to visit the sins of the lawyer on the innocent client. * * * Although we have sometimes held a defendant bound by tactical errors his attorney makes that fall short of ineffective assistance of counsel, we have not previously suggested that a client can be punished for an attorney's *misconduct.* * * *

JUSTICE BLACKMUN, dissenting.

I join Justice Brennan's dissenting opinion on the understanding—at least on my part—that it is confined in its reach to general reciprocal-discovery rules. I do not wish to have the opinion express for me any position as to permissible sanctions for noncompliance with rules designed for specific kinds of evidence as, for example, a notice-of-alibi rule. In a case such as that, the State's legitimate interests might well occasion a result different from what should obtain in the factual context of the present case.

NOTES AND QUESTIONS

1. ***Binding the defendant.*** As to courts typically holding the client to the consequences of procedural decisions made by counsel, consider also the discussion of the division of authority between counsel and client in Note 1, p. 195. See also Ch. 29, § 4. In general, a defendant can

escape the consequences of counsel's actions only by establishing a constitutional claim of ineffective assistance of counsel. Had defendant Taylor challenged counsel's action as ineffective assistance, he would have failed to meet the prevailing *Strickland* standard (see p. 128). In light of the weakness of the testimony of the excluded witnesses, the prejudice prong of *Strickland* could not have been met. Moreover, though counsel willfully violated the discovery rules (and thereby risked the exclusion of the witnesses), he did so as a strategic gamble which presumably would not be deemed "irrational" even though it involved a rules violation. See *Strickland* at p. 130. Thus, Taylor arguably also would not be able to meet the second *Strickland* prerequisite of a performance by counsel that fell below the standard of a "reasonably competent attorney."

2. ***Excluding reliable evidence.*** Was the potential unreliability of the evidence being excluded critical to the *Taylor* decision? Consider *Michigan v. Lucas,* 500 U.S. 145 (1991). In that case, defense counsel failed to notify the prosecution within 10 days after arraignment of the defense's intent to introduce evidence of the defendant's past sexual relationship with the rape complainant, as required by Michigan's rape-shield statute. The trial judge imposed a sanction of exclusion, which was held unconstitutional by the Michigan Court of Appeals. It reasoned that the required advance notice would not have contributed to ensuring evidentiary reliability as the prior sexual incidents were " 'personal between the parties' and therefore impossible to investigate." Justice O'Connor, writing for the Court majority, treated the case as presenting a limited question: whether the Michigan Court had erred in "adopt[ing] a *per se* rule that preclusion is unconstitutional in all cases where the victim has a prior sexual relationship with the defendant." That ruling, Justice O'Connor concluded, simply "cannot be squared" with the Court's rulings in cases such as *Nobles* and *Taylor.* The Sixth Amendment "was not so rigid": "[A] notice and hearing requirement [as to prior sexual contact evidence] * * * serves legitimate state interests in protecting against surprise, harassment, and undue delay. Failure to comply with this requirement may in some cases justify even the severe sanction of preclusion."

3. ***Negligent violations.*** Lower courts have divided as to whether the reasoning of *Taylor* is restricted to the type of "willful" discovery violation involved there. See CRIMPROC § 20.6(c), describing these rulings: "Some courts suggest that the tactically motivated willful violation may be the only situation on which preclusion is constitutionally acceptable. Others, noting the broad range of interests cited by *Taylor* as relevant to the constitutional balancing process, have looked to several additional factors that may justify imposing the preclusion sanction. They would consider the degree of fault in the violation that was not intentional (asking, for example, whether the discovery requirement was clear and whether compliance was relatively simple), the degree of prejudice suffered by the prosecution, the impact of preclusion upon the total evidentiary showing (including consideration of factors suggesting that the precluded evidence is unreliable), and the degree of effectiveness of less severe sanctions."

4. ***Defendant's testimony.*** Alibi-notice provisions typically limit the exclusion sanction to the testimony of persons other than defendant himself. See e.g., Fed.R.Crim.P. 12.1(e). Some exclusion provisions, however, are sufficiently broad to encompass defendant's own testimony, and state courts have occasionally barred defendant from giving alibi testimony beyond a denial of his presence at the scene of the crime (e.g., precluding defendant's testimony as to where he was) when no alibi-notice was provided. Does the rationale of *Taylor* extend to such exclusion, or is the exclusion of defendant's own alibi testimony distinguishable because: (1) the surprise element is less substantial as to defendant's testimony since the state ordinarily has to prove defendant's presence as an essential element of the crime, see *Alicea v. Gagnon,* 675 F.2d 913 (7th Cir.1982); or (2) defendant's right to testify requires greater constitutional protection than his right to present the testimony of others, cf. *Rock v. Arkansas,* Note 5, p. 1325?

§ 5. THE DEFENDANT'S "CONSTITUTIONALLY GUARANTEED ACCESS TO EVIDENCE"

Pretrial discovery assists the defense in preparing for adjudication both in (1) providing the defense with a preview of the prosecution's evidence, and (2) providing the defense with items within the possession or control of the prosecution that may identify possible sources of defense evidence or actually be used as defense evidence. See Note 2, p. 1099. Closely related to the latter aspect of defense discovery are a series of constitutional obligations and prohibitions, directed at the government, in "what might loosely be called the area of [defendant's] constitutionally guaranteed access to evidence." *Arizona v. Youngblood*, Note 1, p. 1151. Like pretrial discovery, these constitutional regulations enhance the capacity of the defense to discover and obtain potential defense evidence. Although they may be stated as standards applicable to the trial, they bear as well on pretrial preparation, and therefore are considered here, rather than in Chapter 25.

A. THE *BRADY* OBLIGATION

The "*Brady* obligation" refers to a constitutional obligation of the prosecutor to disclose certain exculpatory material. It draws its name from the seminal ruling in *Brady v. Maryland,* 373 U.S. 83 (1963), which first established the obligation. Matter subject to disclosure under that obligation is commonly described as "*Brady* material." The Court's opinion in *Brady* was relatively short and offered only a brief description of the obligation. *United States v. Bagley*, set forth below, subsequently provided a more complete exposition of the obligation, and is a source commonly referenced in rulings applying the *Brady* obligation.

UNITED STATES V. BAGLEY

473 U.S. 667, 105 S.Ct. 3375, 87 L.Ed.2d 481 (1985).

JUSTICE BLACKMUN announced the judgment of the Court and delivered an opinion of the Court except as to Part III.

In *Brady v. Maryland*, this Court held that "the suppression by the prosecution of evidence favorable to an accused upon request violates due process where the evidence is material either to guilt or punishment." The issue in the present case concerns the standard of materiality to be applied in determining whether a conviction should be reversed because the prosecutor failed to disclose requested evidence that could have been used to impeach Government witnesses.

I

In October 1977, respondent Hughes Anderson Bagley was indicted on 15 charges of violating federal narcotics and firearms statutes. On November 18, 24 days before trial, respondent filed a discovery motion. The sixth paragraph of that motion requested:

> "The names and addresses of witnesses that the government intends to call at trial. Also the prior criminal records of witnesses, and any deals, promises or inducements made to witnesses in exchange for their testimony."

The Government's two principal witnesses at the trial were James F. O'Connor and Donald E. Mitchell. O'Connor and Mitchell were state law-enforcement officers employed by the Milwaukee Railroad as private security guards. Between April and June 1977, they assisted the federal Bureau of Alcohol, Tobacco and Firearms (ATF) in conducting an undercover investigation of respondent.

The Government's response to the discovery motion did not disclose that any "deals, promises or inducements" had been made to O'Connor or Mitchell. In apparent reply to a request in the motion's ninth paragraph for "[c]opies of all Jencks Act material," the Government produced a series of affidavits that O'Connor and Mitchell had signed between April 12 and May 4, 1977, while the undercover investigation was in progress. These affidavits recounted in detail the undercover dealings that O'Connor and Mitchell were having at the time with respondent. Each affidavit concluded with the statement, "I made this statement freely and voluntarily without any threats or rewards, or promises of reward having been made to me in return for it."

Respondent waived his right to a jury trial and was tried before the court in December 1977. At the trial, O'Connor and Mitchell testified about both the firearms and the narcotics charges. On December 23, the court found respondent guilty on the narcotics charges, but not guilty on the firearms charges.

In mid-1980, respondent filed requests for information pursuant to the Freedom of Information Act and to the Privacy Act of 1974, 5 U.S.C. §§ 552 and 552a. He received in response copies of ATF form contracts that O'Connor and Mitchell had signed on May 3, 1977. Each form was entitled "Contract for Purchase of Information and Payment of Lump Sum Therefor." The printed portion of the form stated that the vendor "will provide" information to ATF and that "upon receipt of such information by the Regional Director, Bureau of Alcohol, Tobacco and Firearms, or his representative, and upon the accomplishment of the objective sought to be obtained by the use of such information to the satisfaction of said Regional Director, the United States will pay to said vendor a sum commensurate with services and information rendered." Each form contained the following typewritten description of services:

> "That he will provide information regarding T–I and other violations committed by Hughes A. Bagley, Jr.; that he will purchase evidence for ATF; that he will cut [*sic*] in an undercover capacity for ATF; that he will assist ATF in gathering of evidence and testify against the violator in federal court."

The figure "$300.00" was handwritten in each form on a line entitled "Sum to Be Paid to Vendor."

Because these contracts had not been disclosed to respondent in response to his pretrial discovery motion,[4] respondent moved under 28 U.S.C. § 2255 to vacate his sentence. He alleged that the Government's failure to disclose the contracts, which he could have used to impeach O'Connor and Mitchell, violated his right to due process under *Brady v. Maryland.*

The motion came before the same District Judge who had presided at respondent's bench trial. An evidentiary hearing was held before a Magistrate. The Magistrate found that the printed form contracts were blank when O'Connor and Mitchell signed them and were not signed by an ATF representative until after the trial. He also found that on January 4, 1978, following the trial and decision in respondent's case, ATF made payments of $300 to both O'Connor and Mitchell pursuant to the contracts. Although the ATF case agent who dealt with O'Connor and Mitchell testified that these payments were compensation for expenses, the Magistrate found that this characterization was not borne out by the record. * * * The District Court adopted each of the Magistrate's findings except for the last one to the effect that "[n]either O'Connor nor Mitchell expected to receive the payment of $300 or any payment from the United States for their testimony." Instead, the court found that it was "probable" that O'Connor and Mitchell expected to receive compensation, in addition to their expenses, for their assistance, "though perhaps not for their testimony." The District Court also expressly rejected the Magistrate's conclusion that "the United States did not withhold, during pretrial discovery, information as to any 'deals, promises or inducements' to these witnesses." The District Court found beyond a reasonable doubt,

---

[4] The Assistant United States Attorney who prosecuted respondent stated in stipulated testimony that he had not known that the contracts existed and that he would have furnished them to respondent had he known of them.

however, that had the existence of the agreements been disclosed to it during trial, the disclosure would have had no effect upon its finding that the Government had proved beyond a reasonable doubt that respondent was guilty of the offenses for which he had been convicted. The District Court reasoned: Almost all of the testimony of both witnesses was devoted to the firearms charges in the indictment. Respondent, however, was acquitted on those charges. The testimony of O'Connor and Mitchell concerning the narcotics charges was relatively very brief. On cross-examination, respondent's counsel did not seek to discredit their testimony as to the facts of distribution but rather sought to show that the controlled substances in question came from supplies that had been prescribed for respondent's personal use. The answers of O'Connor and Mitchell to this line of cross-examination tended to be favorable to respondent. Thus, the claimed impeachment evidence would not have been helpful to respondent and would not have affected the outcome of the trial. Accordingly, the District Court denied respondent's motion to vacate his sentence.

The United States Court of Appeals for the Ninth Circuit reversed. * * * [It] apparently based its reversal, on the theory that the Government's failure to disclose the requested *Brady* information that respondent could have used to conduct an effective cross-examination impaired respondent's right to confront adverse witnesses. The court noted: "In *Davis v. Alaska,* . . . the Supreme Court held that the denial of the 'right of *effective* cross-examination' was 'constitutional error of the first magnitude' requiring 'automatic reversal.' " 719 F.2d, at 1464, quoting *Davis v. Alaska* [Note 2, p. 1145]. In the last sentence of its opinion, the Court of Appeals concluded: "we hold that the government's failure to provide requested *Brady* information to Bagley so that he could effectively cross-examine two important government witnesses requires an automatic reversal." * * *

II

The holding in *Brady v. Maryland* requires disclosure only of evidence that is both favorable to the accused and "material either to guilt or punishment." The Court explained in *United States v. Agurs,* 427 U.S. 97 (1976): "A fair analysis of the holding in *Brady* indicates that implicit in the requirement of materiality is a concern that the suppressed evidence might have affected the outcome of the trial." The evidence suppressed in *Brady* would have been admissible only on the issue of [capital] punishment and not on the issue of guilt, and therefore could have affected only Brady's sentence and not his conviction. Accordingly, the Court affirmed the lower court's restriction of Brady's new trial to the issue of punishment.

The *Brady* rule is based on the requirement of due process. Its purpose is not to displace the adversary system as the primary means by which truth is uncovered, but to ensure that a miscarriage of justice does not occur. Thus, the prosecutor is not required to deliver his entire file to defense counsel, but only to disclose evidence favorable to the accused that, if suppressed, would deprive the defendant of a fair trial. * * * As *Agurs* noted: "For unless the omission deprived the defendant of a fair trial, there was no constitutional violation requiring that the verdict be set aside; and absent a constitutional violation, there was no breach of the prosecutor's constitutional duty to disclose. . . . "

In *Brady* and *Agurs,* the prosecutor failed to disclose exculpatory evidence. In the present case, the prosecutor failed to disclose evidence that the defense might have used to impeach the Government's witnesses by showing bias or interest. Impeachment evidence, however, as well as exculpatory evidence, falls within the *Brady* rule. Such evidence is "evidence favorable to an accused," *Brady,* so that, if disclosed and used effectively, it may make the difference between conviction and acquittal. Cf. *Napue v. Illinois* [fn. 8 infra] ("The jury's estimate of the truthfulness and reliability of a given witness may well be determinative of guilt or innocence, and it is upon such subtle factors as the possible interest of the witness in testifying falsely that a defendant's life or liberty may depend").

The Court of Appeals treated impeachment evidence as constitutionally different from exculpatory evidence. According to that court, failure to disclose impeachment evidence is "even more egregious" than failure to disclose exculpatory evidence "because it threatens the defendant's right to confront adverse witnesses." Relying on *Davis v. Alaska*, supra, the Court of Appeals held that the Government's failure to disclose requested impeachment evidence that the defense could use to conduct an effective cross-examination of important prosecution witnesses constitutes " 'constitutional error of the first magnitude' " requiring automatic reversal.

This Court has rejected any such distinction between impeachment evidence and exculpatory evidence. In *Giglio v. United States,* 405 U.S. 150 (1972), the Government failed to disclose impeachment evidence similar to the evidence at issue in the present case, that is, a promise made to the key government witness that he would not be prosecuted if he testified for the Government.[a] This Court said:

> "When the 'reliability of a given witness may well be determinative of guilt or innocence,' nondisclosure of evidence affecting credibility falls within the general rule [of *Brady*]. We do not, however, automatically require a new trial whenever 'a combing of the prosecutors' files after the trial has disclosed evidence possibly useful to the defense but not likely to have changed the verdict. . . .' A finding of materiality of the evidence is required under *Brady*. . . . A new trial is required if 'the false testimony could . . . in any reasonable likelihood have affected the judgment of the jury. . . .' "

Thus, the Court of Appeals' holding is inconsistent with our precedents.

Moreover, the court's reliance on *Davis v. Alaska* for its "automatic reversal" rule is misplaced. In *Davis,* the defense sought to cross-examine a crucial prosecution witness concerning his probationary status as a juvenile delinquent. * * * Pursuant to a state rule of procedure and a state statute making juvenile adjudications inadmissible, the trial judge prohibited the defense from conducting the cross-examination. This Court reversed the defendant's conviction, ruling that the direct restriction on the scope of cross-examination denied the defendant "the right of effective cross-examination which would be constitutional error of the first magnitude and no amount of showing of want of prejudice would cure it." The present case, in contrast, does not involve any direct restriction on the scope of cross-examination. The defense was free to cross-examine the witnesses on any relevant subject, including possible bias or interest resulting from inducements made by the Government. The constitutional error, if any, in this case was the Government's failure to assist the defense by disclosing information that might have been helpful in conducting the cross-examination.[b] As discussed above, such suppression of evidence amounts to a constitutional violation only if it deprives the defendant of a fair trial. Consistent with "our overriding concern with the justice of the finding of guilt," *United States v. Agurs,* a constitutional error occurs, and the conviction must be reversed, only if the evidence is material in the sense that its suppression undermines confidence in the outcome of the trial.

---

[a] In *Giglio*, the defense counsel "vigorously cross-examined [a key witness] seeking to discredit his testimony by revealing possible agreements or arrangements for prosecutorial leniency." The witness denied the existence of such agreements, and in his summation, the government attorney stated that the witness "received no promises that he would not be indicted." In fact, a promise had been made by another government attorney, but the trial attorney had been unaware of that discussion. The Court held that reversal was required "under the due process requirements enunciated in *Napue* [described infra at fn. 8]." Although the government's trial counsel was not aware that the witness' testimony was false, that was no excuse as the nondisclosure was still the responsibility of the government. "The prosecutor's office is an entity" said the Court, and a promise made by one of its attorneys, even if unauthorized, "must be attributed, for these purposes, to the Government."

[b] Consider also the plurality's discussion in *Pennsylvania v. Ritchie,* set forth at Note 2, p. 1145 (explaining why the Sixth Amendment's confrontation clause did not bear upon the defendant's attempt to subpoena possible impeachment material possessed by a state agency).

III

It remains to determine the standard of materiality applicable to the nondisclosed evidence at issue in this case. Our starting point is the framework for evaluating the materiality of *Brady* evidence established in *United States v. Agurs.* The Court in *Agurs* distinguished three situations involving the discovery, after trial, of information favorable to the accused that had been known to the prosecution but unknown to the defense. The first situation was the prosecutor's knowing use of perjured testimony or, equivalently, the prosecutor's knowing failure to disclose that testimony used to convict the defendant was false. The Court noted the well-established rule that "a conviction obtained by the knowing use of perjured testimony is fundamentally unfair, and must be set aside if there is any reasonable likelihood that the false testimony could have affected the judgment of the jury."[8] Although this rule is stated in terms that treat the knowing use of perjured testimony as error subject to harmless-error review,[9] it may as easily be stated as a materiality standard under which the fact that testimony is perjured is considered material unless failure to disclose it would be harmless beyond a reasonable doubt. The Court in *Agurs* justified this standard of materiality on the ground that the knowing use of perjured testimony involves prosecutorial misconduct and, more importantly, involves "a corruption of the truth-seeking function of the trial process."

At the other extreme is the situation in *Agurs* itself, where the defendant does not make a *Brady* request and the prosecutor fails to disclose certain evidence favorable to the accused. The Court rejected a harmless-error rule in that situation, because under that rule every nondisclosure is treated as error, thus imposing on the prosecutor a constitutional duty to deliver his entire file to defense counsel. At the same time, the Court rejected a standard that would require the defendant to demonstrate that the evidence if disclosed probably would have resulted in acquittal.[c] The Court reasoned: "If the standard applied to the usual motion for a new trial based on newly

---

[8] In fact, the *Brady* rule has its roots in a series of cases dealing with convictions based on the prosecution's knowing use of perjured testimony. In *Mooney v. Holohan,* 294 U.S. 103 (1935), the Court established the rule that the knowing use by a state prosecutor of perjured testimony to obtain a conviction and the deliberate suppression of evidence that would have impeached and refuted the testimony constitutes a denial of due process. The Court reasoned that "a deliberate deception of court and jury by the presentation of testimony known to be perjured" is inconsistent with "the rudimentary demands of justice." The Court reaffirmed this principle in broader terms in *Pyle v. Kansas,* 317 U.S. 213 (1942), where it held that allegations that the prosecutor had deliberately suppressed evidence favorable to the accused and had knowingly used perjured testimony were sufficient to charge a due process violation. The Court again reaffirmed this principle in *Napue v. Illinois,* 360 U.S. 264 (1959). In *Napue,* the principal witness for the prosecution falsely testified that he had been promised no consideration for his testimony. The Court held that the knowing use of false testimony to obtain a conviction violates due process regardless of whether the prosecutor solicited the false testimony or merely allowed it to go uncorrected when it appeared. The Court explained that the principle that a State may not knowingly use false testimony to obtain a conviction—even false testimony that goes only to the credibility of the witness—is "implicit in any concept of ordered liberty." Finally, the Court held that it was not bound by the state court's determination that the false testimony "could not in any reasonable likelihood have affected the judgment of the jury." The Court conducted its own independent examination of the record and concluded that the false testimony "may have had an effect on the outcome of the trial." Accordingly, the Court reversed the judgment of conviction.

[9] The rule that a conviction obtained by the knowing use of perjured testimony must be set aside if there is any reasonable likelihood that the false testimony could have affected the jury's verdict derives from *Napue v. Illinois.* See n. 8. *Napue* antedated *Chapman v. California* [p. 1417], where the "harmless beyond a reasonable doubt" standard was established. The Court in *Chapman* noted that there was little, if any, difference between a rule formulated, as in *Napue,* in terms of " 'whether there is a reasonable possibility that the evidence complained of might have contributed to the conviction,' " and a rule " 'requiring the beneficiary of a constitutional error to prove beyond a reasonable doubt that the error complained of did not contribute to the verdict obtained.' " It is therefore clear, as indeed petitioner concedes, that this Court's precedents indicate that the standard of review applicable to the knowing use of perjured testimony is equivalent to the *Chapman* harmless-error standard.

[c] The reference here was to what *Agurs* described as the "Rule 33 Standard"—the test applied in federal courts to a motion for a new trial based on newly discovered evidence. That standard typically requires that the defendant establish (1) that the failure to learn of the evidence previously was not due to a lack of diligence, (2) that the evidence is material, not merely "cumulative or impeaching," and (3) that it is more probable than not that the new evidence would have "produced an acquittal." See CRIMPROC § 24.11(d).

discovered evidence were the same when the evidence was in the State's possession as when it was found in a neutral source, there would be no special significance to the prosecutor's obligation to serve the cause of justice." The standard of materiality applicable in the absence of a specific *Brady* request is therefore stricter than the harmless-error standard but more lenient to the defense than the newly discovered evidence standard.

The third situation identified by the Court in *Agurs* is where the defense makes a specific request and the prosecutor fails to disclose responsive evidence. The Court did not define the standard of materiality applicable in this situation, but suggested that the standard might be more lenient to the defense than in the situation in which the defense makes no request or only a general request. The Court also noted: "When the prosecutor receives a specific and relevant request, the failure to make any response is seldom, if ever, excusable."

The Court has relied on and reformulated the *Agurs* standard for the materiality of undisclosed evidence in two subsequent cases arising outside the *Brady* context. In neither case did the Court's discussion of the *Agurs* standard distinguish among the three situations described in *Agurs*. In *United States v. Valenzuela-Bernal* [Note 1, p. 1148], the Court held that due process is violated when testimony is made unavailable to the defense by Government deportation of witnesses "only if there is a reasonable likelihood that the testimony could have affected the judgment of the trier of fact." And in *Strickland v. Washington* [p. 131], the Court held that a new trial must be granted when evidence is not introduced because of the incompetence of counsel only if "there is a reasonable probability that, but for counsel's unprofessional errors, the result of the proceeding would have been different." The *Strickland* Court defined a "reasonable probability" as "a probability sufficient to undermine confidence in the outcome."

We find the *Strickland* formulation of the *Agurs* test for materiality sufficiently flexible to cover the "no request," "general request," and "specific request" cases of prosecutorial failure to disclose evidence favorable to the accused: The evidence is material only if there is a reasonable probability that, had the evidence been disclosed to the defense, the result of the proceeding would have been different. A "reasonable probability" is a probability sufficient to undermine confidence in the outcome.

The Government suggests that a materiality standard more favorable to the defendant reasonably might be adopted in specific request cases. The Government notes that an incomplete response to a specific request not only deprives the defense of certain evidence, but has the effect of representing to the defense that the evidence does not exist. In reliance on this misleading representation, the defense might abandon lines of independent investigation, defenses, or trial strategies that it otherwise would have pursued.

We agree that the prosecutor's failure to respond fully to a *Brady* request may impair the adversary process in this manner. And the more specifically the defense requests certain evidence, thus putting the prosecutor on notice of its value, the more reasonable it is for the defense to assume from the nondisclosure that the evidence does not exist, and to make pretrial and trial decisions on the basis of this assumption. This possibility of impairment does not necessitate a different standard of materiality, however, for under the *Strickland* formulation the reviewing court may consider directly any adverse effect that the prosecutor's failure to respond might have had on the preparation or presentation of the defendant's case. The reviewing court should assess the possibility that such effect might have occurred in light of the totality of the circumstances and with an awareness of the difficulty of reconstructing in a post-trial proceeding the course that the defense and the trial would have taken had the defense not been misled by the prosecutor's incomplete response.

In the present case, we think that there is a significant likelihood that the prosecutor's response to respondent's discovery motion misleadingly induced defense counsel to believe that

O'Connor and Mitchell could not be impeached on the basis of bias or interest arising from inducements offered by the Government. Defense counsel asked the prosecutor to disclose any inducements that had been made to witnesses, and the prosecutor failed to disclose that the possibility of a reward had been held out to O'Connor and Mitchell if the information they supplied led to "the accomplishment of the objective sought to be obtained . . . to the satisfaction of [the Government]." This possibility of a reward gave O'Connor and Mitchell a direct, personal stake in respondent's conviction. The fact that the stake was not guaranteed through a promise or binding contract, but was expressly contingent on the Government's satisfaction with the end result, served only to strengthen any incentive to testify falsely in order to secure a conviction. Moreover, the prosecutor disclosed affidavits that stated that O'Connor and Mitchell received no promises of reward in return for providing information in the affidavits implicating respondent in criminal activity. In fact, O'Connor and Mitchell signed the last of these affidavits the very day after they signed the ATF contracts. While petitioner is technically correct that the blank contracts did not constitute a "promise of reward," the natural effect of these affidavits would be misleadingly to induce defense counsel to believe that O'Connor and Mitchell provided the information in the affidavits, and ultimately their testimony at trial recounting the same information, without any "inducements."

The District Court, nonetheless, found beyond a reasonable doubt that, had the information that the Government held out the possibility of reward to its witnesses been disclosed, the result of the criminal prosecution would not have been different. If this finding were sustained by the Court of Appeals, the information would be immaterial even under the standard of materiality applicable to the prosecutor's knowing use of perjured testimony. Although the express holding of the Court of Appeals was that the nondisclosure in this case required automatic reversal, the Court of Appeals also stated that it "disagreed" with the District Court's finding of harmless error. In particular, the Court of Appeals appears to have disagreed with the factual premise on which this finding expressly was based. The District Court reasoned that O'Connor's and Mitchell's testimony was exculpatory on the narcotics charges. The Court of Appeals, however, concluded, after reviewing the record, that O'Connor's and Mitchell's testimony was in fact inculpatory on those charges. Accordingly, we reverse the judgment of the Court of Appeals and remand the case to that court for a determination whether there is a reasonable probability that, had the inducement offered by the Government to O'Connor and Mitchell been disclosed to the defense, the result of the trial would have been different.

JUSTICE POWELL took no part in the decision of this case.

JUSTICE WHITE, with whom THE CHIEF JUSTICE and JUSTICE REHNQUIST join, concurring in part and concurring in the judgment.

I agree with the Court that respondent is not entitled to have his conviction overturned unless he can show that the evidence withheld by the Government was "material," and I therefore join Parts I and II of the Court's opinion. I also agree with Justice Blackmun that for purposes of this inquiry, "evidence is material only if there is a reasonable probability that, had the evidence been disclosed to the defense, the result of the proceeding would have been different." As the Justice correctly observes, this standard is "sufficiently flexible" to cover all instances of prosecutorial failure to disclose evidence favorable to the accused. Given the flexibility of the standard and the inherently factbound nature of the cases to which it will be applied, however, I see no reason to attempt to elaborate on the relevance to the inquiry of the specificity of the defense's request for disclosure, either generally or with respect to this case. I would hold simply that the proper standard is one of reasonable probability and that the Court of Appeals' failure to apply this standard necessitates reversal. I therefore concur in the judgment.

JUSTICE MARSHALL, with whom JUSTICE BRENNAN joins, dissenting.

* * * We have long recognized that, within the limit of the State's ability to identify so-called exculpatory information, the State's concern for a fair verdict precludes it from withholding from the defense evidence favorable to the defendant's case in the prosecutor's files. [This] recognition no doubt stems in part from the frequently considerable imbalance in resources between most criminal defendants and most prosecutors' offices. Many, perhaps most, criminal defendants in the United States are represented by appointed counsel, who often are paid minimal wages and operate on shoestring budgets. In addition, unlike police, defense counsel generally is not present at the scene of the crime, or at the time of arrest, but instead comes into the case late. Moreover, unlike the Government, defense counsel is not in the position to make deals with witnesses to gain evidence. Thus, an inexperienced, unskilled, or unaggressive attorney often is unable to amass the factual support necessary to a reasonable defense. When favorable evidence is in the hands of the prosecutor but not disclosed, the result may well be that the defendant is deprived of a fair chance before the trier of fact, and the trier of fact is deprived of the ingredients necessary to a fair decision. * * *

Since *Brady* was decided, this Court has struggled, in a series of decisions, to define how best to effectuate the right recognized. To my mind, the *Brady* decision, the reasoning that underlay it, and the fundamental interest in a fair trial, combine to give the criminal defendant the right to receive from the prosecutor, and the prosecutor the affirmative duty to turn over to the defendant, *all* information known to the government that might reasonably be considered favorable to the defendant's case. * * * My view is based in significant part on the reality of criminal practice and on the consequently inadequate protection to the defendant that a different rule would offer. * * *

At the trial level, the duty of the state to effectuate *Brady* devolves into the duty of the prosecutor; the dual role that the prosecutor must play poses a serious obstacle to implementing *Brady*. The prosecutor is by trade, if not necessity, a zealous advocate. He is a trained attorney who must aggressively seek convictions in court on behalf of a victimized public. At the same time, as a representative of the State, he must place foremost in his hierarchy of interests the determination of truth. Thus, for purposes of *Brady,* the prosecutor must abandon his role as an advocate and pore through his files, as objectively as possible, to identify the material that could undermine his case. Given this obviously unharmonious role, it is not surprising that these advocates oftentimes overlook or downplay potentially favorable evidence, often in cases in which there is no doubt that the failure to disclose was a result of absolute good faith. * * *

Once the prosecutor suspects that certain information might have favorable implications for the defense, either because it is potentially exculpatory or relevant to credibility, I see no reason why he should not be required to disclose it. After all, favorable evidence indisputably enhances the truth-seeking process at trial. And it is the job of the defense, not the prosecution, to decide whether and in what way to use arguably favorable evidence. In addition, to require disclosure of all evidence that might reasonably be considered favorable to the defendant would have the precautionary effect of assuring that no information of potential consequence is mistakenly overlooked. * * * A clear rule of this kind, coupled with a presumption in favor of disclosure, also would facilitate the prosecutor's admittedly difficult task by removing a substantial amount of unguided discretion. * * *

The Court, however, offers a complex alternative. It defines the right not by reference to the possible usefulness of the particular evidence in preparing and presenting the case, but retrospectively, by reference to the likely effect the evidence will have on the outcome of the trial. * * * By adhering to the view articulated in *United States v. Agurs*—that there is no constitutional duty to disclose evidence unless nondisclosure would have a certain impact on the trial—the Court permits prosecutors to withhold with impunity large amounts of undeniably favorable evidence, and it imposes on prosecutors the burden to identify and disclose evidence pursuant to a pretrial standard that virtually defies definition. * * * At best, this standard places on the prosecutor a responsibility to speculate, at times without foundation, since the prosecutor will not normally know what strategy the defense will pursue or what evidence the defense will find useful. At worst, the standard invites a prosecutor, whose interests are conflicting, to gamble, to play the odds, and to take a chance that evidence will later turn out not to have been potentially dispositive. * * *

* * * The State's interest in nondisclosure at trial is minimal, and should therefore yield to the readily apparent benefit that full disclosure would convey to the search for truth. After trial, however, the benefits of disclosure may at times be tempered by the State's legitimate desire to avoid retrial when error has been harmless. However, in making the determination of harmlessness, I would apply our normal constitutional error test and reverse unless it is clear beyond a reasonable doubt that the withheld evidence would not have affected the outcome of the trial. See *Chapman v. California.*[6] * * *

JUSTICE STEVENS, dissenting.

* * * [T]wo situations in which the [same rule should apply] * * * are those demonstrating the prosecution's knowing use of perjured testimony, exemplified by *Mooney v. Holohan,* and the prosecution's suppression of favorable evidence specifically requested by the defendant, exemplified by *Brady* itself. In both situations, the prosecution's deliberate nondisclosure constitutes constitutional error—the conviction must be set aside if the suppressed or perjured evidence was "material" and there was "any reasonable likelihood" that it "could have affected" the outcome of the trial. * * * The combination of willful prosecutorial suppression of evidence and, "more importantly," the potential "corruption of the truth seeking function of the trial process" requires that result. *Agurs.* * * *

[S]uppression [in response to a request] is far more serious than mere nondisclosure of evidence in which the defense has expressed no particular interest. A reviewing court should attach great significance to silence in the face of a specific request, when responsive evidence is later shown to have been in the Government's possession. Such silence actively misleads in the same way as would an affirmative representation that exculpatory evidence does not exist when, in fact, it does (*i.e.,* perjury)—indeed, the two situations are aptly described as "sides of a single coin." Babcock, *Fair Play: Evidence Favorable to An Accused and Effective Assistance of Counsel,* 34 Stan.L.Rev. 1133 (1982).

Accordingly, although I agree that the judgment of the Court of Appeals should be vacated and that the case should be remanded for further proceedings, I disagree with the Court's statement of the correct standard to be applied.

NOTES AND QUESTIONS

1. **Brady *and the false testimony cases.*** Is there a distinction in the rationales underlying the perjured testimony cases and the nondisclosure cases that justifies imposing a less strict standard of materiality in nondisclosure cases, whether or not involving a specific request? The *Brady* opinion described the due process ruling in that case as a logical extension of the perjured testimony cases. In describing the relationship between the two lines of cases, *Brady* noted: "We now hold that the suppression by the prosecution of evidence favorable to an accused upon request violates due process where the evidence is material either to guilt or to punishment, irrespective of the good faith or bad faith of the prosecution. The principle of *Mooney v. Holohan*

---

[6] In a case of deliberate prosecutorial misconduct, automatic reversal might well be proper. Certain kinds of constitutional error so infect the system of justice as to require reversal in all cases, such as discrimination in jury selection. A deliberate effort of the prosecutor to undermine the search for truth clearly is in the category of offenses anathema to our most basic vision of the role of the State in the criminal process.

[fn. 8, p. 1134] is not punishment of society for misdeeds of a prosecutor but avoidance of an unfair trial to the accused."

Not all found *Brady*'s analysis satisfactory, at least in its characterization of *Mooney*. Commentators suggested that in the perjured testimony cases, there was an element of "deliberate misconduct" in the misleading of the trier of fact by presenting testimony known to be false (under the "collective knowledge" of the prosecution, including the investigating police agency), which distinguished those cases from the *Brady* violation. Has *Bagley*, in treating the knowing use of perjured testimony as subject to a different and less demanding standard of materiality, recognized such a distinction in the groundings of the *Brady* rule and the *Mooney* principle? Consider Steven Reiss, *Prosecutorial Intent in Constitutional Criminal Procedure*, 135 U.Pa.L.Rev. 1365, 1408 (1987) (distinction in the materiality standards implicitly reflects the "high degree of culpability" inherent in the perjured testimony situation, as a rationale which rested solely on the "corruption of the truth seeking process" would not provide a "persuasive basis for treating perjured testimony differently from other types of prosecutorial suppression"). Does the *Brady* rejection of Justice Steven's position indicate that the distinction rests on some other factor? Might the distinction be based on differences in the level of deception? See CRIMPROC § 24.3(b) (*Agurs* noted "that there was no reason to question the veracity of any of the prosecution witnesses," and that rendered inapplicable "the test of materiality followed in the *Mooney* line of cases"; in "*Agurs* and other exculpatory evidence cases, the nondisclosure might detract from the strength of the government's evidence, and indeed contradict the incriminating inference * * *, but it never directly established the falsity of the evidence").

2. ***The character of the* Bagley *"materiality" standard.*** A long line of post-*Bagley* Supreme Court rulings have explored the application of *Brady*, with most focusing on the materiality standard. Those rulings have involved a fact-sensitive analysis, often dividing the Court (largely in the context of capital cases). Many rulings have presented the additional complexities of federal habeas review of state decisions that considered and rejected the *Brady* claims. See Pt. A, p. 1451. *Kyles v. Whitley*, 514 U.S. 419 (1995), was such a case, but the majority opinion there (per Souter, J.) also set forth four guiding principles, adding to *Bagley*, on applying the materiality standard. First, "a showing of materiality does not require demonstration by a preponderance that disclosure of the suppressed evidence would have resulted ultimately in the defendant's acquittal * * *. *Bagley*'s touchstone of materiality is a 'reasonable probability' of a different result, and the adjective is important. The question is not whether the defendant would more likely than not have received a different verdict with the evidence, but whether in its absence he received a fair trial, understood as a trial resulting in a verdict worthy of confidence." Second, "the *Bagley* materiality [test] * * * is not a sufficiency of evidence test. A defendant need not demonstrate that after discounting the inculpatory evidence in light of the undisclosed evidence, there would not have been enough to convict." Third, "once a reviewing court applying *Bagley* has found constitutional error there is no need for further harmless-error review." [See Note 2, p. 1419] Fourth, "*Bagley* materiality" is to be judged by reference to the "suppressed evidence considered collectively, not item-by-item," with the focus on the "cumulative effect of suppression."

3. In *Strickler v. Greene*, 527 U.S. 263 (1999), Justice Souter again analyzed the general character of the materiality—here speaking only for himself and Justice Kennedy, in a partial dissent from the majority's holding:

"The circuitous path by which the Court came to adopt 'reasonable probability' of a different result as the rule of *Brady* materiality suggests several things. First, while [the standard we have applied to the knowing use of perjured testimony], 'reasonable possibility' or 'reasonable likelihood,' the *Kotteakos* standard [error "may have had substantial influence" on the outcome, see Note 2, p. 1416], and 'reasonable probability' express distinct levels of confidence concerning the hypothetical effects of errors on decisionmakers' reasoning, the differences among the standards are slight. Second, the gap between all three of those formulations and 'more likely than not' is greater than any differences among them. Third, because of that larger gap, it is misleading in *Brady* cases to use the term 'probability,' which is naturally read as the cognate of 'probably' and thus confused with 'more likely than not.' * * * We would be better off speaking of a 'significant possibility' of a different result to characterize the *Brady* materiality standard. Even then, given the soft edges of all these phrases, the touchstone of the enquiry must remain whether the evidentiary suppression 'undermines our confidence' that the factfinder would have reached the same result."

4. ***The nature of* Brady *material.*** Does *Brady* encompass information that clearly is favorable to the defense, but could not be used as evidence at trial (e.g., the hearsay report of an informant that some other person was commonly rumored to have committed the crime)? The lower courts are divided on this issue. See CRIMPROC § 24.3(b). Some maintain that *Brady* applies only to material that would be admissible at trial. Others view admissibility as a crucial factor but would extend *Brady* to inadmissible material that could readily lead the defense to the discovery of admissible evidence. Do the several opinions in *Bagley* or the four principles announced in *Kyles* suggest a Court majority clearly favoring one or the other of these positions? Consider also *Wood v. Bartholomew*, 516 U.S. 1 (1995) (since polygraph tests would not have been admissible in evidence, prosecutor had no *Brady* obligation to disclose them).

5. ***Specific requests.*** Although the exact bearing of a specific request is debated, lower courts generally share the view expressed in *Lindsey v. King,* 769 F.2d 1034 (5th Cir.1985): "Viewing the [*Bagley*] opinions as a whole, it is fair to say that all the participating Justices agreed on one thing at least: that reversal for suppression of evidence by the government is most likely where the request for it was specific." The Supreme Court has provided only limited direction, however, on distinguishing between "general" and "specific" requests. *Agurs* characterized a general request as "really giv[ing] the prosecutor no better notice than no request," and offered only one illustration of such a request (where defendant asks for "all *Brady* material").

Accepting Justice Blackmun's view that a specific request makes a difference only in increasing the potential for prejudice by leading counsel to forego a particular line of inquiry, does the reasonableness of counsel's detrimental reliance provide a touchstone for determining whether the request was sufficiently specific? Consider CRIMPROC § 24.3(b): "Where the request is narrow and precise, giving the prosecutor considerable direction as to what is wanted, such as a request for statements of a particular person, or a request for reports by particular experts, defense counsel is more likely to treat the prosecutor's failure to disclose as an indication that the evidence does not exist. Where the request does not have those qualities, such as a request for any material bearing on the credibility of witnesses or for any material that corroborates the defense, the defense counsel must also account for the possibility that the disclosure made was not complete because the prosecution adopted a somewhat different interpretation of what was included in the request or could not readily put together all that was encompassed by the request."

Does a sufficiently specific request from this perspective require not only a description that narrows the request to specific items of evidence, but also a description of favorable content that leaves no room for the prosecutor to conclude that the evidence is not sufficiently favorable to the defense to constitute *Brady* material? That standard was met in *Bagley*, where the character of the item requested—"deals, promises, or inducements made to witnesses in exchange for their testimony"—automatically established its status as critical impeachment evidence.

6. ***Defense diligence.*** Consider CRIMPROC § 24.3(b) "Even undisclosed favorable and material information in the possession of the government is not 'suppressed' in violation of *Brady* if the defendant knew of it or could have obtained it with reasonable effort. In *Agurs*, the Court described the '*Brady* rule' as applicable to situations involv[ing] the discovery, after trial, of information which had been known to the prosecution but unknown to the defense. Looking to this

language, courts have held that the prosecutor's constitutional obligation was not violated, notwithstanding the nondisclosure of apparently exculpatory evidence, where the defense knew of the evidence and could have obtained it from a source other than the prosecutor. Before holding the defense responsible for its lack of diligence, courts have insisted on proof that the defense was aware of the potentially exculpatory nature of the evidence as well as its existence [looking to the knowledge of both the defendant and the defense counsel]. * * * Some decisions, however, have rejected the due diligence concept entirely in applying *Brady* [reasoning "the *Brady* rule is aimed at defining an important prosecutorial duty; it is not a tool to ensure competent defense counsel"]."

7. ***Prosecution possession or control.*** Lower courts have regularly held that the prosecutor's *Brady* obligation extends not only to materials within its own files, but also to material within the files of the various investigative agencies participating in the case. Addressing the special problems presented in prosecutions that are the product of joint task forces (frequently involving federal, state, and local law enforcement agencies), a DOJ internal guidance memo offers detailed guidelines on determining what agencies are part of the "prosecutor team" (pursuant to requiring the prosecutor to determine whether each such agency possesses discoverable material under *Brady* or Federal Rule 16). Factors considered include whether (1) the local agency works under control of the federal prosecutor, (2) the extent to which resources are shared, and (3) whether the federal prosecutor has "ready access" to evidence possessed by the local agency.

In *Kyles v. Whitley*, Note 2, p. 1139, the state contended that a "more lenient" standard of materiality should apply where the "favorable evidence in issue * * * was known only to police investigators and not the prosecutor." Rejecting that contention, the Court noted: "[N]o one doubts that police investigators sometimes fail to inform a prosecutor of all they know, * * * [but] neither is there any serious doubt that 'procedures and regulations can be established to carry [the prosecutor's] burden and to insure communication of all relevant information on each case to every lawyer who deals with it.' "

The Timing of *Brady* Disclosures

1. **Brady *and pretrial discovery.*** All of the Supreme Court's *Brady* rulings have involved situations in which it was learned after trial that the prosecution had failed to disclose certain evidence, and the Court therefore had no reason to comment on the needed timing of a *Brady* disclosure. Lower courts generally have agreed that the prosecutor's *Brady* obligation is satisfied if the exculpatory material is disclosed "in time for its effective use at trial," and for many types of exculpatory evidence, disclosure at trial itself will be satisfactory. CRIMPROC § 20.3(m). To sustain a claim that the disclosure of exculpatory material at trial came too late, the defendant must show that delay in disclosure violated *Brady's* materiality requirement—that is, there is a reasonable probability that had the evidence been disclosed in a pretrial proceeding, rather than at trial the "result of the proceeding would have been different." Ibid. Where would such a showing most readily be made? Commentators suggest that one possibility is a setting in which scientific expertise is needed to evaluate the exculpatory evidence and the time needed for such an evaluation simply cannot be obtained (through a continuance) when the evidence is first disclosed at trial. However, the evidence most likely to fit in this category—an exculpatory test result or expert's analysis—typically must be disclosed pretrial under discovery provisions that encompass all results of scientific tests and not just those the prosecution intends to use in evidence. See Note 4, p. 1117. Another candidate is a setting in which the exculpatory evidence would lead the defense to other helpful evidence not disclosed as part of discovery and the disclosure at trial fails to give the defense sufficient time to explore the leads to that other evidence.

2. The timing issue is commonly mooted in practice by the willingness of prosecutors to make pretrial disclosure of *Brady* material in response to specific requests for such material. In some jurisdictions, the prosecutor has no choice because state discovery provisions require pretrial

disclosure. See Note 9, p. 1105. In others, the prosecutor simply finds no advantage in delaying the disclosure. Indeed, where the prosecution possesses the requested item, but questions whether it is likely to be viewed as exculpatory material, the practice in some jurisdictions is to seek a pretrial ruling by the trial court and to disclose pretrial if the trial court concludes that *Brady* disclosure will be required. Some courts discourage such efforts, noting that the prosecutor is in a better position to evaluate the total fact situation and anticipate defense uses of the information, and a court ruling that disclosure is not needed would be subject to a distinct caveat because of the court's limited knowledge of the case. See CRIMPROC § 24.3(b) (also noting judicial concern as to the administrative burden, as pretrial "Brady review" can become "a ponderous, time-consuming task if utilized in every case merely on demand").

3. **Brady *and* Jencks.** Though following a general practice of providing pretrial disclosure of *Brady* material, a prosecutor may resist such disclosure where it is specifically prohibited by statute, as in the case of the *Jenck*'s Act prohibition of the pretrial disclosure of prior recorded statements of prospective government witnesses (p. 1104). Defense efforts to force pretrial disclosure of *Jencks* material have met with mixed success. Some courts have concluded that even if the *Jencks* material is clearly exculpatory and material, the *Brady* obligation will not conflict with the *Jencks* prohibition, as such material is primarily useful for impeachment and disclosure at trial therefore will provide the defense with adequate time to utilize the material. Other courts, however, have concluded that disclosure at trial could be insufficient, and the trial court therefore has the authority to "trump" the *Jencks* prohibition and require pretrial production of Jencks material that falls under *Brady*. Some courts would do this "automatically and others would do so based on the character of the exculpatory evidence and the likely need for pretrial disclosure to permit the defense to use it effectively (distinguishing in this regard between impeachment material and other exculpatory materials)". CRIMPROC § 20.3(m).

In *United States v. Presser*, 844 F.2d 1275 (6th Cir.1988), the Sixth Circuit suggested that, even assuming arguendo that *Brady* would be violated by failing to reveal until trial exculpatory material within a witness' prior recorded statement (notwithstanding the court's capacity to grant a recess at that point if the defense needs more time to explore that material), the *Brady* doctrine does not thereby give the trial court the authority to override Jencks and order pretrial disclosure. *Brady* imposes an obligation upon the prosecutor and leaves to the prosecution the initial determination of when to disclose. If it fails to comply adequately, "it acts at its own peril." Under this view, Jencks is not necessarily compatible with *Brady* under all circumstances, and clearly does not "trump" *Brady*, but does leave to the government the opportunity to control the timing of its disclosure, with the court determining after the case is completed whether a delay in disclosure so prejudiced the defendant as to deny due process.

4. In *United States v. Ruiz* (p. 1208), the Supreme Court sustained against a due process challenge a government policy of requiring a defendant's waiver of any failure to be informed of impeachment material prior to entering a fast-track guilty plea. Consider *Ruiz's* discussion (p. 1209) of the lack of relevance of *Brady* in that situation. What bearing, if any, does that discussion have upon the issues discussed in Notes 1 and 3 supra? Does the *Ruiz* discussion indicate that, at least as to impeachment material, *Brady* never requires disclosure prior to trial, given the government interests in avoiding "premature disclosure," as described by the *Ruiz* Court? Is *Ruiz* better read as simply declaring that *Brady* rights are "trial related" and have no bearing unless a trial occurs (as it did in the cases discussed in Notes 1–3 supra)? Commentators have noted that, if *Ruiz* adopts this view of *Brady*, then the *Ruiz* precedent cannot readily be limited to the non-disclosure of impeachment evidence in the guilty plea context, an issue considered in Notes 1–4, pp. 1211–1212.

Ensuring Compliance with *Brady*

1. ***The extent of* Brady *violations.*** Commentators disagree as to (1) how frequently *Brady* violations occur (in particular, whether the known violations are "just the tip of the iceberg"), (2) the comparative significance of inadvertence, reckless disregard, and bad faith in producing violations, and (3) as to inadvertent violations, the comparative significance of prosecutors misreading the materiality requirement, prosecutors failing to thoroughly review their files, and police failing to provide a complete file. See CRIMPROC §§ 1.9(b), and 21.3 (citing a "sampling of the voluminous commentary"). See also Ellen Yaroshefsky, *Forward: New Perspectives on Brady and Other Disclosure Obligations: What Really Works,* 31 Cardozo L.Rev. 1943 (2010) ("*Brady* is a hidden problem for which it is impossible to gather accurate data"; "prosecutors believe that defense attorneys accuse them all too often of intentional violations * * * when, in fact, most disclosure failures are the result of negligence that may not be the fault of the individual prosecutor," and [prosecutors] believe, "to the extent it is a problem, * * * disclosure errors are an episodic problem"; "defense lawyers have a very different view and find that problems of nondisclosure are endemic to the system").

2. ***Supplementing* Brady.** As noted in CRIMPROC § 24.3(a); "Scores of judges and commentators have complained that [the 'case specific remedy' of *Brady*] may do little to prevent future violations." They point to the difficulty in uncovering potential *Brady* violations, in part because of the limited availability of the assistance of counsel in collateral proceedings and in part because of the difficulty in gaining access to relevant files (the allowed use of a Freedom of Information request in *Bagley* constituting a limited exception, see fn. a, p. 1090, and Note 6, p. 1167). Added to that difficulty is a materiality requirement that may excuse even an intentional failure to disclose clearly exculpatory evidence. What is needed, they argue, are reforms that will deter intentional nondisclosures and make inadvertent nondisclosures less likely. Several of the proposed reforms are discussed below.

3. ***Broader discovery provisions.*** As discussed in Note 9, p. 1105, many states have exculpatory-evidence discovery provisions which do not include a materiality element. A proposal to add such a provision to Federal Rule 16 led to strong opposition by the DOJ. See CRIMPROC §§ 20.4(c), 24.3(b). Critics note that, under such provisions, prosecutors and police still must make an assessment as to whether particular information is exculpatory, a judgment that may be clouded by "tunnel vision". A better alternative, they suggest, is to adopt open-file discovery (see fn. b, p. 1092). But note CRIMPROC § 20.2(c) ("open-file disclosure will not invariably meet all [*Brady*] requirements" as those requirements "go beyond information contained in documents," including statements never reduced to writing; the open-file in certain types of cases will be "so massive" that critical information will be buried; and in the end, there remains the problem of "ensuring that the prosecutor has obtained from the police, all of their documents"). Would the better approach be to give the defense the capacity to unearth exculpatory evidence from potential sources—e.g., requiring that the prosecution identify all persons known to have knowledge of relevant facts (see Note 7, p. 1103), and granting the defense the right to depose all such persons (see Note 5, p. 1097)?

4. ***Direct sanctions.*** Commentators often view direct sanctions as having potential for deterring *Brady* violations, but also view those sanctions as currently ineffective due to institutional and legal restrictions. See CRIMPROC § 24.3(a). For example, ethics prohibitions encompass *Brady* violations, but enforcement of those provisions is rare. See Note 4, p. 1331. A major defect here is the lack of a system of automatic inquiry (cf. fn. a, p. 1122, describing the DOJ's internal review process). So too, civil actions might be effective, but that would require altering the current law granting prosecutors absolute immunity. See Note 4, p. 1331 (discussing *Connick v. Thompson*); Justice John Paul Stevens (Ret.), Equal Justice Initiative Speech

(5/2/2011), available at http://www.eji.org/ (urging adoption of legislation that would subject governments to tort liability under *respondeat superior* for prosecutor misconduct).

5. ***"Brady compliance" orders.*** Some judges have utilized "Brady compliance" directives as a regular practice. The order allows the judge to gain control over sanctions (through the use of the contempt sanction) and to provide more detailed directions as to the prosecutor's responsibilities. A New York Court Rule requires trial courts to issue such orders and the Chief Administrator of the Courts has issued a model order based on this directive. See CRIMPROC § 20.3(m). The model order requires disclosure of "all information favorable to the defense," but also identifies specific qualifying information. Thus, Paragraph (a) refers to: "information that impeaches the credibility of a testifying prosecution witness, including (i) benefits, promises, or inducements, express or tacit, made to a witness by a law enforcement official or law enforcement victim services agency in connection with giving testimony or cooperating in the case; (ii) a witness's prior inconsistent statements, written or oral; (iii) a witness's prior convictions and uncharged criminal conduct; (iv) information that tends to show that a witness has a motive to lie to inculpate the defendant, or a bias against the defendant or in favor of the complainant or the prosecution; and (v) information that tends to show impairment of a witness's ability to perceive, recall, or recount relevant events, including impairment resulting from mental or physical illness or substance abuse." Similarly, Paragraph (d) refers to: "Information that tends to undermine evidence of the defendant's identity as a perpetrator of a charged crime, such as a non-identification of the defendant by a witness to a charged crime or an identification or other evidence implicating another person in a manner that tends to cast doubt on a defendant's guilt."

The New York model compliance order also cites the prosecutor's "duty to learn of such favorable information that is known to others acting on the government's behalf in the case," and requires that the prosecutor personally review all police files "directly related to the case." It also requires timely disclosure, with disclosure " 'presumptively timely' if completed no later than 30 days before commencement of a trial in a felony case, and 15 days before commencement of a trial in a misdemeanor case." The order is described as implementing not just *Brady*, but also state constitutional and professional responsibility obligations (see fn. e, p. 1105).

6. ***Institutional changes.*** Other commentators have argued that training and controls within prosecutors' offices offer the most promising avenue for preventing *Brady* violations. In recent years, various prosecutors' offices (typically larger offices) have adopted internal procedures designed to ensure compliance with both *Brady* and discovery rules. The Department of Justice, for example, has adopted a four-pronged approach which includes: (1) training programs; (2) structural changes (in particular, the establishment of the position of "discovery coordinator" in "each USAO office and litigating component handling criminal cases"); (3) directives as to specific steps to be taken in discovery compliance (e.g., a "review process" that directs prosecutors to examine various sources, including case agent investigative files, confidential informant and cooperating witness files, documents or evidence gathered by civil attorneys or regulatory agencies in parallel investigations, and "substantive case related communications * * * memorialized in e-mails, memoranda, or notes"); and (4) directing individual offices to "adopt written local policies directives further shaping the discovery process." See Understanding DOJ Discovery Policies, 2011 WL 190330, 190331, 190333, 190334. An occasional local prosecutor's office has gone so far as to utilize compliance audits. CRIMPROC § 20.2(c)

B. THE *RITCHIE* RULINGS

1. **Ritchie.** In PENNSYLVANIA v. RITCHIE, 480 U.S. 39 (1987), defendant Ritchie, charged with the rape and sexual abuse of a daughter, sought through a pretrial subpoena to inspect various records of the Children and Youth Services (CYS), a state protective service agency charged with investigating the suspected mistreatment or neglect of children. The subpoena was

not a typical trial subpoena aimed at the production of specific evidence for admission at trial, but a discovery device (as permitted under state law). It sought to gain for the defense access to all CYS records relating to its investigation of the events that were the grounding for the current criminal charges as well as the records of an earlier investigation of possible child abuse (both investigations included counselor interviews of the daughter). CYS opposed the subpoena on the ground that state law rendered its records "privileged," and the trial judge, without examining the entire CYS file, quashed the subpoena. Following defendant's trial conviction, the Pennsylvania appellate courts held that: (1) the CYS records were confidential, but not privileged; (2) the failure to order disclosure of the CYS files therefore violated defendant's Sixth Amendment rights to confrontation and compulsory process insofar as they deprived the defense of materials useful in cross-examining his daughter and in presenting a defense; and (3) the trial court, in determining whether the defense had been denied such materials, could not rely on an *in camera* review of the CYS files, but was required constitutionally to give the defense full access to the files for the purpose of arguing that they contained material that should have been disclosed under the Sixth Amendment.

The Supreme Court, in an opinion by Powell, J., rejected the reasoning and holding of the Pennsylvania appellate courts. Speaking for a plurality, Justice Powell concluded that the Sixth Amendment right of confrontation did not include a right to discover and obtain possible impeachment materials (see Note 2 infra). Speaking for a majority, Justice Powell held that (1) the denial of the subpoena might have resulted in a due process violation by denying the defendant access to *Brady* material (see Notes 3–5 infra); (2) there was no need to determine whether the Sixth Amendment right to compulsory process included a right to discovery, because any such right would not extend beyond the due process right to *Brady* material (see Note 3 infra); and (3) in light of the confidential nature of the CYS records, it was constitutionally acceptable for the trial court to conduct an *in camera* review to determine whether those records included *Brady* material (see Note 6 infra).

2. ***Confrontation and access.*** Justice Powell's plurality opinion on the bearing of the confrontation clause rejected the lower court reading of *Davis v. Alaska*, 415 U.S. 308 (1974). It noted:

"In *Davis,* the trial judge prohibited defense counsel from questioning a witness about the latter's juvenile criminal record, because a state statute made this information presumptively confidential. We found this restriction on cross-examination violated the Confrontation Clause, despite Alaska's legitimate interest in protecting the identity of juvenile offenders. The Pennsylvania Supreme Court apparently interpreted our decision in *Davis* to mean that a statutory privilege cannot be maintained when a defendant asserts a need, prior to trial, for the protected information that might be used at trial to impeach or otherwise undermine a witness' testimony. * * * If we were to accept this broad interpretation of *Davis,* the effect would be to transform the Confrontation Clause into a constitutionally-compelled rule of pretrial discovery. Nothing in the case law supports such a view. The opinions of this Court show that the right of confrontation is a *trial* right, designed to prevent improper restrictions on the types of questions that defense counsel may ask during cross-examination. * * * The ability to question adverse witnesses, however, does not include the power to require the pretrial disclosure of any and all information that might be useful in contradicting unfavorable testimony."

Justice Powell's analysis of the confrontation clause was similar to that advanced in *Bagley* (in an opinion by Justice Blackmun), where the Court also rejected a the lower court's reliance upon *Davis*. See p. 1133. However, Justice Blackmun, who otherwise joined the Powell opinion in *Ritchie*, expressed disagreement with this portion of the opinion. He noted: "I do not accept the plurality's conclusion * * * that the Confrontation Clause protects only a defendant's trial rights and has no relevance to pretrial discovery. In this, I am in substantial agreement with much of what Justice Brennan says, in dissent. In my view, there might well be a confrontation violation if, as here, a defendant is denied pretrial access to information that would make possible effective cross-examination of a crucial prosecution witness."

Justice Brennan, joined by Marshall, J., dissented on the merits (two other justices dissented on the ground that the state court ruling did not present a final order). Expressing disagreement with the proposition that the confrontation clause applies "only to events at trial," he noted:

"That interpretation ignores the fact that the right of cross-examination also may be significantly infringed by events occurring outside the trial itself, such as the wholesale denial of access to material that would serve as the basis for a significant line of inquiry at trial. In this case, the trial court properly viewed Ritchie's vague speculations that the agency file might contain something useful as an insufficient basis for permitting general access to the file. However, in denying access to the prior statements of the victim [made to the CYS counselor] the court deprived Ritchie of material crucial to any effort to impeach the victim at trial. I view this deprivation as a violation of the Confrontation Clause. * * * *Jencks v. United States* [p. 1104] held that the defendant was entitled to obtain the prior statements of persons to government agents when those persons testified against him at trial. * * * As I later noted in *Palermo v. United States,* 360 U.S. 343 (1959), *Jencks* was based on our supervisory authority rather than the Constitution, 'but it would be idle to say that the commands of the Constitution were not close to the surface of the decision.' * * * Essential to testing a witness' account of events is the ability to compare that version with other versions the witness has earlier recounted. Denial of access to a witness' prior statements thus imposes a handicap that strikes at the heart of cross-examination.

"The ability to obtain material information through reliance on a Due Process claim will not in all cases nullify the damage of the Court's overly restrictive reading of the Confrontation Clause. As the Court notes, evidence is regarded as material only if there is a reasonable probability that it might affect the outcome of the proceeding. Prior statements on their face may not appear to have such force, since their utility may lie in their more subtle potential for diminishing the credibility of a witness. The prospect that these statements will not be regarded as material is enhanced by the fact that due process analysis requires that information be evaluated by the trial judge, not defense counsel. By contrast, *Jencks,* informed by confrontation and cross-examination concerns, insisted that defense counsel, not the court, perform such an evaluation, '[b]ecause only the defense is adequately equipped to determine the effective use for the purpose of discrediting the Government's witness and thereby furthering the accused's defense.' Therefore, while Confrontation Clause and due process analysis may in some cases be congruent, the Confrontation Clause has independent significance in protecting against infringements on the right to cross-examination."

3. ***Due process and compulsory process.*** Speaking to the Pennsylvania Supreme Court's conclusion that the suppression of the subpoena violated the Sixth Amendment right of compulsory process by "preventing [defendant] from learning the names of 'witnesses in his favor' as well as other evidence that might be contained in the file," Justice Powell reasoned:

"This Court has never squarely held that the Compulsory Process Clause guarantees the right to discover the *identity* of witnesses, or to require the Government to produce exculpatory evidence. * * * Instead, the Court traditionally has evaluated claims such as those raised by Ritchie under the broader protections of the Due Process Clause of the Fourteenth Amendment. See *United States v. Bagley* [p. 1130] Because the applicability of the Sixth Amendment to this type of case is unsettled, and because our Fourteenth Amendment precedents addressing the fundamental fairness of trials establish a clear framework for review, we adopt a due process analysis for purposes of this case. Although we conclude that compulsory process provides no *greater* protections in this area than those afforded by due process, we need not decide today whether and how the guarantees of the Compulsory Process Clause differ from those of the

Fourteenth Amendment. It is enough to conclude that on these facts, Ritchie's claims more properly are considered by reference to due process.

"It is well-settled that the Government has the obligation to turn over evidence in its possession that is both favorable to the accused and material to guilt or punishment. * * * At this stage, of course, it is impossible to say whether any information in the CYS records may be relevant to Ritchie's claim of innocence, because neither the prosecution nor defense counsel has seen the information, and the trial judge acknowledged that he had not reviewed the full file. The Commonwealth, however, argues that no materiality inquiry is required, because a statute renders the contents of the file privileged. Requiring disclosure here, it is argued, would override the Commonwealth's compelling interest in confidentiality on the mere speculation that the file 'might' have been useful to the defense. * * * Although we recognize that the public interest in protecting this type of sensitive information is strong, we do not agree that this interest necessarily prevents disclosure in all circumstances. This is not a case where a state statute grants CYS the absolute authority to shield its files from all eyes. Cf. 42 Pa.Cons.Stat. § 5945.1(b) (unqualified statutory privilege for communications between sexual assault counselors and victims).[14] Rather, the Pennsylvania law provides that the information shall be disclosed in certain circumstances, including when CYS is directed to do so by court order."

4. Commentators have questioned the scope of *Ritchie's* ruling that due process gave the defendant a right to *Brady* material in the possession of the CYS. Did the Court simply view the CYS as part of the "prosecution team" and therefore subject to the prosecutor's duty to disclose *Brady* material? See Note 7, p. 1141. Did the Court extend due process to recognize a defense right of access to *Brady* material in the possession of government agencies that are not within the scope of the prosecutor's *Brady* obligation? Did it go beyond that and recognize a due process right to obtain *Brady* material from third parties in general? Consider *State v. Percy*, 548 A.2d 408 (Vt.1988) ("The pretrial discovery right set out in *Ritchie* applies solely to information in the hands of the State"); *State v. Behnke*, 553 N.W.2d 265 (Wis.App.1996) (*Ritchie* extends to private records that the government does not possess or control); CRIMPROC § 24.3(f) (collecting cases applying *Ritchie* to non-governmental entities).

5. Lower courts have divided in addressing the issue left open in footnote 14 of *Ritchie*. See CRIMPROC § 24.3(f). Some have held that the defendant's access to *Brady* material does not extend to material that is privileged under state law. Others have held that an absolute privilege poses no greater barrier to *in camera* review than the "qualified privilege" presented in *Ritchie*. It is noted in this regard that *Washington v. Texas*, 388 U.S. 14 (1967), applied the compulsory process clause to hold admissible and subject to subpoena evidence that was inadmissible under state law. *Washington* held unconstitutional a local rule that made accomplices incompetent to testify for one another, although allowing them to testify for the state. As to the special protection of "personal or confidential information about a victim," consider Fed.R.Crim.P. 17(c)(3) (subpoena may be issued only on court order, with advance notice to the victim, so victim can move to quash or modify).

6. ***In camera review.*** The *Ritchie* majority flatly rejected the Pennsylvania Supreme Court's ruling that enforcement of the defendant's constitutional right of access could not be satisfied by the trial court's *in camera* review of the confidential CYS files, as the defense must be given full access to the files, so it can fully participate in the assessment of materiality. The Court reasoned:

"A defendant's right to discover exculpatory evidence does not include the unsupervised authority to search through the Commonwealth's files. See *United States v. Bagley*. Although the

[14] We express no opinion on whether the result in this case would have been different if the statute had protected the CYS files from disclosure to *anyone*, including law-enforcement and judicial personnel.

eye of an advocate may be helpful to a defendant in ferreting out information, this Court has never held—even in the absence of a [state] statute restricting disclosure—that a defendant alone may make the determination as to the materiality of the information. Settled practice is to the contrary. In the typical case where a defendant makes only a general request for exculpatory material under *Brady v. Maryland,* it is the State that decides which information must be disclosed. Unless defense counsel becomes aware that other exculpatory evidence was withheld and brings it to the court's attention, the prosecutor's decision on disclosure is final. Defense counsel has no constitutional right to conduct his own search of the State's files to argue relevance. * * * We find that Ritchie's interest (as well as that of the Commonwealth) in ensuring a fair trial can be protected fully by requiring that the CYS files be submitted only to the trial court for *in camera* review. Although this rule denies Ritchie the benefits of an 'advocate's eye,' we note that the trial court's discretion is not unbounded. If a defendant is aware of specific information contained in the file (e.g., the medical report), he is free to request it directly from the court, and argue in favor of its materiality. * * * An *in camera* review by the trial court will serve Ritchie's interest without destroying the Commonwealth's need to protect the confidentiality of those involved in child-abuse investigations."

C. ACCESS TO WITNESSES

1. ***Interference with access.*** In UNITED STATES v. VALENZUELA-BERNAL, 458 U.S. 858 (1982), the Supreme Court reversed a Ninth Circuit ruling that had relied on both due process and the Sixth Amendment compulsory process clause to hold unconstitutional a government practice of promptly deporting aliens who had been smuggled into the country. The defendant, charged with the smuggling of the aliens, had challenged the practice because it resulted in the aliens being shipped back to Mexico before defense counsel had an opportunity to interview them. The majority, per Rehnquist, J., reasoned that the Court of Appeals had failed to give sufficient weight to the government's "manifold responsibilities" in immigration cases. Those responsibilities included not only the enforcement of the criminal law, but also the faithful execution of congressional policy favoring prompt deportations of illegal aliens and the avoidance of unnecessary financial and physical burdens involved in prolonged detentions, as well as the "human cost" to the detained witness-alien. In light of these additional responsibilities, the majority noted, the Government's decision to deport was "not to be judged by standards which might be appropriate if the Government's only responsibility were to prosecute criminal offenses." Accordingly, appropriate analogies were to be found in decisions such as *Brady v. Maryland* and *Roviaro v. United States* [Note 3 infra], all of which required a showing as to the materiality and favorable nature of lost evidence in establishing a constitutional violation. The majority concluded:

"To summarize, the responsibility of the Executive Branch faithfully to execute the immigration policy adopted by Congress justifies the prompt deportation of illegal-alien witnesses upon the Executive's good-faith determination that they possess no evidence favorable to the defendant in a criminal prosecution. The mere fact that the Government deports such witnesses is not sufficient to establish a violation of the Compulsory Process Clause of the Sixth Amendment or the Due Process Clause of the Fifth Amendment. A violation of these provisions requires some showing that the evidence lost would be both material and favorable to the defense. * * * As in other cases concerning the loss of material evidence, sanctions will be warranted for deportation of alien witnesses only if there is a reasonable likelihood that the testimony could have affected the trier of fact. In making such a determination, courts should afford some leeway for the fact that the defendant necessarily proffers a description of the material evidence rather than the evidence itself. Because determinations of materiality are often best made in light of all of the evidence adduced at trial, judges may wish to defer ruling on motions until after the presentation of evidence."

2. The state may also deprive the defendant of the testimony of a subpoenaed witness by imposing pressure on that witness not to testify. Consider *Webb v. Texas,* 409 U.S. 95 (1972). The defendant's sole witness had an extensive criminal record and currently was serving a prison sentence. Before the witness took the stand, the trial judge, on his own initiative, warned him against committing perjury. The judge told the witness that if he told the truth, he would be "all right," but if he lied, he could "get into real trouble." The judge warned that he would "personally see" that any lies were brought to the attention of the grand jury. A conviction for perjury, the judge added "is probably going to mean several years" and "will be held against you * * * when you're up for parole." The judge also noted that the witness "didn't owe anybody anything to testify." After hearing these remarks and the judge's comment to defense counsel that the witness could "decline to testify," the witness refused to give testimony. The Supreme Court reversed the defendant's conviction on due process grounds. "In the circumstances of this case," the Court concluded, the judge's remarks violated defendant's right to a fair trial. The judge's admonition had been cast in "unnecessarily strong terms" and "effectively drove the witness off the stand."

Although *Webb* involved judicial action, the caselaw has even more often applied *Webb* to prosecutorial efforts to discourage prospective defense witnesses from testifying. The critical questions, the courts note, are whether (1) the witness was important to the defense,[d] and (2) as a result of the prosecution's action, the defendant was denied the witness' testimony or the witness changed his testimony to be less favorable to the defense. Prosecutorial action held to constitute a due process violation typically involves threats to prosecute the witness for perjury, with the courts noting that a prosecutor's good faith belief that the witness was about to commit perjury does not preclude a finding of a constitutional violation. See *In re Martin*, 744 P.2d 374 (Cal.1987) (arrest of one witness for perjury caused remaining witnesses not to testify); Bruce Green, *Limits on a Prosecutor's Communications With Prospective Defense Witnesses,* 25 Crim.L.Bull. 139 (1989) ("By far the safest course for a prosecutor seeking to warn a defense witness about the risks of self-incrimination or perjury is to convey those warnings through the witness's attorney"; if the witness is unrepresented, the prosecutor might seek the appointment of counsel for this purpose).

3. ***Identifying critical informants.*** The defendant in ROVIARO v. UNITED STATES, 353 U.S. 53 (1957), was charged with (1) an illegal sale of heroin to "John Doe," and (2) illegal transportation of heroin. Before trial, defendant moved for a bill of particulars listing, inter alia, Doe's name and address. The motion was denied on the ground that Doe was an informer and his identity was privileged. At trial, the court again rejected defense attempts, through cross-examination, to learn Doe's identity. The government itself did not call Doe, but relied entirely on the testimony of two investigative officers. The first officer (Durham) had Doe under surveillance on the night of the alleged transaction. He testified that Doe picked up the defendant on a street corner and drove to another location where the defendant left the car, picked up a package near a tree, gave the package to Doe, and walked away. The second officer (Bryson), who was hidden in the trunk of Doe's car, testified that he heard defendant discuss with Doe the proposed transfer of the package (which contained narcotics). The Supreme Court reversed the defendant's conviction in the exercise of its supervisory power. Justice Burton's opinion for the (6–1) majority noted:

"Petitioner * * * argues that Doe was an active participant in the illegal activity charged and that, therefore, the Government could not withhold his identity, his whereabouts, and whether he was alive or dead at the time of trial. The Government does not defend the nondisclosure of Doe's identity with respect to Count 1, which charged a sale of heroin to John Doe, but it attempts to sustain the judgment on the basis of the conviction on Count 2, charging illegal transportation of narcotics. It argues that the conviction on Count 2 may properly be upheld since the identity of

---

[d] The *Webb* opinion did not address the issue of likely prejudice (i.e., whether the missing testimony might have influenced the outcome). Some lower courts initially viewed *Webb* as establishing a per se due process violation, but in light of the Court's subsequent ruling in *Valenzuela-Bernal*, *Webb* is viewed as a case that apparently assumed prejudicial impact in light of the witness' status as the sole defense witness. See CRIMPROC § 24.3(h).

the informer, in the circumstances of this case, has no real bearing on that charge and is therefore privileged.

"What is usually referred to as the informer's privilege is in reality the Government's privilege to withhold from disclosure the identity of persons who furnish information of violations of law to officers charged with enforcement of that law. The purpose of the privilege is the furtherance and protection of the public interest in effective law enforcement. The privilege recognizes the obligation of citizens to communicate their knowledge of the commission of crimes to law-enforcement officials and, by preserving their anonymity, encourages them to perform that obligation. * * * [But] [w]here the disclosure of an informer's identity, or of the contents of his communication, is relevant and helpful to the defense of an accused, or is essential to a fair determination of a cause, the privilege must give way. In these situations, the trial court may require disclosure and, if the Government withholds the information, dismiss the action. * * * The problem is one that calls for balancing the public interest in protecting the flow of information against the individual's right to prepare his defense. Whether a proper balance renders nondisclosure erroneous must depend on the particular circumstances of each case, taking into consideration the crime charged, the possible defenses, the possible significance of the informer's testimony, and other relevant factors. * * *

"This is a case where the Government's informer was the sole participant, other than the accused, in the transaction charged. The informer was the only witness in a position to amplify or contradict the testimony of government witnesses. Moreover, a government witness testified that Doe denied knowing petitioner or ever having seen him before. We conclude that, under these circumstances, the trial court committed prejudicial error in permitting the Government to withhold the identity of its undercover employee in the face of repeated demands by the accused for his disclosure."

Although *Roviaro* was based on the Court's supervisory authority over federal courts, both lower courts and commentators have viewed the Court's "reasoning and language" as "suggest[ing] that the decision was constitutionally compelled." Peter Westen, *The Compulsory Process Clause*, 73 Mich.L.Rev. 71, 165 (1974).

4. ***Immunity for defense witnesses.*** Lower courts have consistently rejected claims of a general constitutional right of a criminal defendant to have immunity granted to witnesses so that they can testify on the defendant's behalf. See CRIMPROC § 24.3(i). No such right has been found in the Sixth Amendment's compulsory process clause, for the subpoena is made fully available by the trial court and the compulsory process clause has been held not to override the exercise by witnesses of privileges as significant as the self-incrimination privilege. So too, "while the prosecutor may not prevent or discourage a defense witness from testifying, * * * it is difficult to see how the [compulsory process clause] of its own force places upon either the prosecutor or the court an affirmative obligation * * * of replacing the protection of the self-incrimination privilege with a grant of use immunity." *United States v. Turkish*, 623 F.2d 769 (2d Cir.1980). Finally, the due process obligation of *Brady* is held not to apply, for that deals only with the disclosure of evidence in the government's possession, not with the extraction of evidence from others.

Lower courts have held, however, that fundamental fairness may require a trial court to dismiss a case if the prosecution refuses to grant immunity to a potential defense witness under particularly egregious circumstances. In applying this fundamental fairness test, the primary focus has been on whether the prosecutor is operating with a deliberate intention to distort the factfinding process. Such a prosecutorial intention is said to establish a "clear abuse of discretion violating due process," requiring that the prosecution be dismissed unless the government shifts its position and obtains immunity for the witness. *United States v. D'Antonio,* 801 F.2d 979 (7th Cir.1986). The classic case would be that in which the government had used an undercover agent to instigate the criminal transaction and then allowed that agent to plead the privilege when the defense attempts to call him as a witness. See *United States v. Bahadar*, 954 F.2d 821 (2d Cir.1992) (court must find (1) that the government "has engaged in discriminatory use to gain a tactical advantage"; (2) the witness' testimony is "material, exculpatory, and not cumulative"; and (3) the testimony is "unobtainable from any other source").

D. THE DUTY TO PRESERVE EVIDENCE

1. The leading Supreme Court evidence on the government's failure to preserve potentially exculpatory evidence is ARIZONA v. YOUNGBLOOD, 488 U.S. 51 (1988). The state appellate court there had reversed defendant's conviction on charges of child molestation, sexual assault, and kidnapping based on the government's failure to properly preserve semen samples from the 10-year-old victim's body and clothing. After making his way home following his abduction, the victim had been taken to a hospital for medical treatment. While there, a physician used a swab from a "sexual assault kit" to collect semen samples from the boy's rectum. The police also collected the boy's clothing, which they failed to refrigerate. Ten days later, after the victim identified the defendant from a photographic lineup and before the defendant was in custody, a police criminologist examined the sexual assault kit to determine whether sexual contact occurred, but did not perform tests to identify blood group substances and did not test the clothing. Following defendant's indictment more than a month later, tests for blood group substances were performed on both the samples taken by the physician and the clothing, but proved unsuccessful. Defendant's principal defense at trial was that the boy had erred in identifying him as the perpetrator. Expert witnesses testified that if tests had been performed on the samples shortly after they were gathered, or the clothing had been properly refrigerated and later tested, the blood group testing could have been performed successfully and the results might have exonerated the defendant. The state appellate court noted that it did "not imply any bad faith on the part of the state," but the conviction nonetheless would be reversed: "[W]hen identity is an issue at trial and the police permit the destruction of evidence that could eliminate the defendant as the perpetrator, such loss is material to the defense and is a denial of due process." The Supreme Court majority, per Rehnquist, C.J., disagreed:

"Decision of this case requires us to again consider 'what might loosely be called the area of constitutionally-guaranteed access to evidence.' *United States v. Valenzuela-Bernal* [Note 1, p. 1148]. * * * Our most recent decision in this area of the law, *California v. Trombetta,* 467 U.S. 479 (1984), arose out of a drunk driving prosecution in which the State had introduced test results indicating the concentration of alcohol in the blood of two motorists. The defendants sought to suppress the test results on the ground that the State had failed to preserve the breath samples used in the test. We rejected this argument for several reasons: first, 'the officers here were acting in "good faith and in accord with their normal practice" '; second, in the light of the procedures actually used the chances that preserved samples would have exculpated the defendants were slim; and, third, even if the samples might have shown inaccuracy in the tests, the defendants had 'alternative means of demonstrating their innocence.' In the present case, the likelihood that the preserved materials would have enabled the defendant to exonerate himself appears to be greater than it was in *Trombetta,* but here, unlike in *Trombetta,* the State did not attempt to make any use of the materials in its own case in chief.

"Our decisions in related areas have stressed the importance for constitutional purposes of good or bad faith on the part of the Government when the claim is based on loss of evidence attributable to the Government. In *United States v. Marion* [p. 1083], we said that '[n]o actual prejudice to the conduct of the defense is alleged or proved, and there is no showing that the Government intentionally delayed to gain some tactical advantage over appellees or to harass them.' See also *United States v. Lovasco* [p. 1082]. Similarly, in *United States v. Valenzuela-Bernal,* supra, we * * * held that the prompt deportation of the witnesses was justified 'upon the

Executive's good-faith determination that they possess no evidence favorable to the defendant in a criminal prosecution.'

"The Due Process Clause of the Fourteenth Amendment, as interpreted in *Brady v. Maryland*, makes the good or bad faith of the State irrelevant when the State fails to disclose to the defendant material exculpatory evidence. But we think the Due Process Clause requires a different result when we deal with the failure of the State to preserve evidentiary material of which no more can be said than that it could have been subjected to tests, the results of which might have exonerated the defendant. Part of the reason for the difference in treatment is found in the observation made by the Court in *Trombetta,* supra, that '[w]henever potentially exculpatory evidence is permanently lost, courts face the treacherous task of divining the import of materials whose contents are unknown and, very often, disputed.' Part of it stems from our unwillingness to read the 'fundamental fairness' requirement of the Due Process Clause as imposing on the police an undifferentiated and absolute duty to retain and to preserve all material that might be of conceivable evidentiary significance in a particular prosecution. We think that requiring a defendant to show bad faith on the part of the police both limits the extent of the police's obligation to preserve evidence to reasonable bounds and confines it to that class of cases where the interests of justice most clearly require it, i.e., those cases in which the police themselves by their conduct indicate that the evidence could form a basis for exonerating the defendant. We therefore hold that unless a criminal defendant can show bad faith on the part of the police, failure to preserve potentially useful evidence does not constitute a denial of due process of law.

"In this case, the police collected the rectal swab and clothing on the night of the crime; respondent was not taken into custody until six weeks later. The failure of the police to refrigerate the clothing and to perform tests on the semen samples can at worst be described as negligent. * * * The Arizona Court of Appeals noted in its opinion—and we agree—that there was no suggestion of bad faith on the part of the police. It follows, therefore, from what we have said, that there was no violation of the Due Process Clause.

"The Arizona Court of Appeals also referred somewhat obliquely to the State's 'inability to quantitatively test' certain semen samples with the newer P-30 test. If the court meant by this statement that the Due Process Clause is violated when the police fail to use a particular investigatory tool, we strongly disagree. The situation here is no different than a prosecution for drunk driving that rests on police observation alone; the defendant is free to argue to the finder of fact that a breathalyzer test might have been exculpatory, but the police do not have a constitutional duty to perform any particular tests."

Concurring in the judgment, Justice Stevens noted "three factors * * * of critical importance to my evaluation of the case." First, the police at the time that they failed to refrigerate "had at least as great an interest in preserving the evidence as did the person later accused. * * * In cases such as this, even without a prophylactic sanction such as dismissal of the indictment, the State has a strong incentive to preserve the evidence." "Second," Justice Stevens noted, "although it is not possible to know whether the lost evidence would have revealed any relevant information, it is unlikely that the defendant was prejudiced by the State's omission. * * * [D]efense counsel impressed upon the jury the fact that the State failed to preserve the evidence and that the State could have conducted tests that might well have exonerated the defendant. More significantly, the trial judge instructed the jury: 'If you find that the State has . . . allowed to be destroyed or lost any evidence whose content or quality are in issue, you may infer that the true fact is against the State's interest.' As a result, the uncertainty as to what the evidence might have proved was turned to the defendant's advantage." The third relevant factor was that the jurors, in convicting the defendant notwithstanding the trial court's invitation to draw this "permissive inference" favorable to the defendant, "in effect indicated that, in their view, the other evidence at trial was so overwhelming that it was highly improbable that the lost evidence was exculpatory."

Justice Blackmun's dissent (joined by Brennan and Marshall, JJ.) initially disagreed with the majority's focus on the "good faith" of the prosecution. "The Constitution," the dissent noted, "requires that criminal defendants be provided with a fair trial, not merely a 'good faith' try at a fair trial." Past cases such as *Brady* "made plain that the prosecutor's state of mind is *not* determinative. Rather, the proper standard must focus on the materiality of the evidence, and that standard 'must reflect our overriding concern with the justice of the finding of guilt.' "

In determining whether particular evidence is "material," Justice Blackmun noted, a "court should focus on the * * * [relevancy] of the evidence, the possibility it might prove exculpatory, and the existence of other evidence going to the same point of contention." Accordingly, "where no comparable evidence is likely to be available to the defendant, police must preserve physical evidence of a type that they reasonably should know has the potential, if tested, to reveal immutable characteristics of the criminal and hence to exculpate a defendant charged with a crime." Where, as here, the evidence of guilt "was far from conclusive," and "the possibility that the evidence denied to respondent would have exonerated him was not remote," the failure to preserve the evidence must be deemed a denial of due process resulting in a lack of a fair trial.

Consider also CRIMPROC § 24.3(e): "The defendant in the *Youngblood* case, Larry Youngblood, was later exonerated after DNA testing on the remaining physical evidence using improved testing methods showed he was innocent and implicated a different perpetrator, suggesting that the misgivings expressed by the dissenting justices in his case about the strength of the evidence against him were well founded. Nevertheless, the Court has continued to adhere to the bad faith requirement established in *Youngblood.* * * * In jurisdictions that require bad faith, even gross negligence is not sufficient. But if the government loses or destroys evidence known to be helpful to the defense, despite an explicit court order to preserve that particular evidence, and can give no legitimate reason for the loss or destruction, a court should not hesitate to find a due process violation. * * * [Also], a greater obligation may flow from state law. Many states, for example, have rejected the requirement of showing bad faith destruction in interpreting their own constitutional provisions. These states employ a balancing test in which the degree of culpability on the part of the state is only one of several factors. * * * A jurisdiction may also require the preservation of evidence by statute. In particular, improvements in DNA testing have prompted some jurisdictions to mandate the preservation of biological evidence [see Note 5(b), p. 1402]."

2. As discussed in CRIMPROC § 1.5(i), the "policing transparency" movement has produced a variety of state and local enactments requiring police departments to make and preserve records relating to different types of police conduct. While those records most often are of interest to the defense in challenging the lawfulness of the police conduct, certain types of required recordings (e.g., dashboard-camera and body-worn-camera videos) can readily include exculpatory evidence, producing *Youngblood*-type concerns. See CRIMPROC § 20.6(B): "In part because retention policies [often] call for erasure (with limited exceptions) after a fairly short period, a large body of precedents address defense claims based on the destruction of video/audio recordings from dashboard-cameras and body-cameras. Those rulings overwhelmingly focus on due process claims relating to the possible exculpatory content of the recording, with the courts applying either the "bad faith" standard, or some less stringent state standard.[e] * * * Courts have viewed as analytically distinct the failure of police to utilize a dashboard-camera or a body-camera

---

[e] As noted in CRIMPROC § 24.3(e), various states "have rejected the requirement of showing bad faith destruction in interpreting their own state constitutions." The footnotes of § 20.6(B) referred to state cases discussing the remedies available under such rulings where video was lost or destroyed (in the absence of bad faith) and the subject matter of the video indicated that the unknown content could have "created a reasonable doubt" as to defendant's liability. In the cited cases involving lost or destroyed videos of field sobriety tests, the state courts concluded that remedies short of dismissal were appropriate—such as directing the factfinder to presume that the videotape would have been favorable to the driver.

to record the defendant's actions where such cameras were available to the officers involved. The initial issue here is whether the police officer was under a legal obligation to create such a video [established by state law or local ordinance]. * * * If a duty to record existed, then [whether a remedy exists will depend upon whether] the source of that duty * * * creates a judicial remedy."

CHAPTER 22

GUILTY PLEAS

■ ■ ■

Most criminal cases are disposed of by a plea of guilty,[a] typically entered after the prosecutor's promise to obtain or seek charging or sentencing concessions favorable to the defendant. This Chapter explores such a "negotiated plea" system of criminal justice, and then examines how such a system does/should affect the legal rules applicable to the conduct of prosecutors, defense counsel and judges in reaching and complying with plea agreements.

§ 1. SOME VIEWS OF NEGOTIATED PLEAS

A. INTRODUCTION

1. ***Charge and sentence negotiations.*** "There is a broad range of plea arrangements currently used by prosecutors. The three most common are the sentence recommendation, the plea to a lesser included offense, and the dismissal of charges * * *.

"Under the sentence recommendation practice, the prosecuting attorney promises that he will recommend to the court a sentence favorable to the defendant, will not seek the maximum penalty, or will refrain from making any recommendations. Most often the sentence recommendation involves a promise by the prosecutor to suggest to the trial judge a mutually satisfactory term of years as the appropriate punishment in return for a defendant's guilty plea. * * * Where there is a judicial practice of following recommendations, the promise of a recommended sentence can be tantamount to a promise of a definite term. But each defendant who pleads guilty in reliance on a prosecutor's promise to recommend a specific sentence takes the risk that in his particular case the judge will not follow the suggestion in imposing sentence. In addition, many defendants may enter into agreements with prosecutors to avoid imposition of the maximum sentence, but, unless they are informed of actual sentencing patterns, may needlessly bargain away their right to trial since sentences often fall considerably below the maximums provided by the legislatures.

"In some jurisdictions the prosecutor may recommend that the court accept a guilty plea to a lesser offense included in the offense actually charged. The court's permission to plead to a lesser included offense is usually required, and in some jurisdictions the prosecutor must file reasons for recommending the lesser plea. * * *

"The charge dismissal practice developed as a possible plea bargaining tool because of the multiplicity of crimes which often arise out of a single incident. However, an apparently advantageous bargain may actually be specious because of the tendency of many courts to sentence concurrently, or to suspend sentence on all but one or two of the multiple and similar charges arising out of the same incident." Note, 112 U.Pa.L.Rev. 865–68 (1964).

2. ***Need for.*** Although the practice of plea bargaining is a longstanding one, courts for many years were reluctant to even acknowledge its existence. But this is no longer the case; the

---

[a] "The vast majority of felony convictions are now the result of plea bargains—some 94 percent at the state level, and some 97 percent at the federal level. Estimates for misdemeanor convictions run even higher." Emily Yoffe, *Innocence is Irrelevant,* The Atlantic (Sept.2017).

Supreme Court has upheld the practice as necessary and proper,[b] as have the lower courts. Illustrative is *People v. Selikoff,* 318 N.E.2d 784 (N.Y.1974): "In budget-starved urban criminal courts, the negotiated plea literally staves off collapse of the law enforcement system, not just as to the courts but also to local detention facilities.

"Plea negotiations, of course, serve many other needs. They relieve the prosecution and the defense too, for that matter, from 'the inevitable risks and uncertainties of trial'. The negotiation process which results in a guilty plea telescopes the judicial process and the necessarily protracted intervals involved in charge, trial, and sentence, and even appeals, hopefully starting the offender on the road to possible rehabilitation. The process also serves significant goals of law enforcement by permitting an exchange of leniency for information and assistance.

"Perhaps most important, plea negotiation serves the ends of justice. It enables the court to impose 'individualized' sentences, an accepted ideal in criminology, by avoiding mandatory, harsh sentences adapted to a class of crime or a group of offenders but inappropriate, and even Draconian, if applied to the individual before the court."

B. THE PROBLEM OF DISPARITY

3. ***Sentencing disparity.*** If defendants who plead guilty receive leniency, does it follow that defendants who go to trial are being dealt with too harshly? Consider *United States v. Rodriguez,* 162 F.3d 135 (1st Cir.1998), where the government indicted six defendants for engaging in the same conspiracy to distribute cocaine. Three of them pled guilty pursuant to a plea agreement that they would be held accountable only for the drugs each had personally handled, while the defendants who went to trial were convicted and held accountable for the entire 5,000 grams of cocaine distributed by the conspiracy. Thus, under the Sentencing Guidelines the guilty plea defendants received sentences of time served, 17 months and 60 months, respectively, while the other three defendants received sentences of 235 months, 260 months, and life imprisonment (the latter attributable to an additional charge of engaging in a continuing criminal enterprise). The defendants who received the 235 and 260 month sentences argued they were entitled to be resentenced because "this vast disparity on sentencing—a difference of more than 21 years * * *—* * * discriminates against those who exercise their right to a jury trial," but to no avail. The court acknowledged that this was an "enormous sentencing disparity," one that "would strike many as unfair," but then concluded that what had been done was "within the government's discretion" and "not in and of itself * * * an unconstitutional burden on one's right to go to trial."

4. ***Bases for leniency.*** *A.B.A. Standards* § 14–1.8 (3rd ed. 1997) explains the disparity in terms of factors likely to call for leniency when a plea of guilty is entered:

"(a) The fact that a defendant has entered a plea of guilty or nolo contendere should not, by itself alone, be considered by the court as a mitigating factor in imposing sentence. It is proper for the court to approve or grant charge and sentence concessions to a defendant who enters a plea of guilty or nolo contendere when consistent with governing law and when there is substantial evidence to establish, for example, that:

"(i) the defendant is genuinely contrite and has shown a willingness to assume responsibility for his or her conduct;

"(ii) the concessions will make possible alternative correctional measures which are better adapted to achieving protective, deterrent, or other purposes of correctional treatment, or will prevent undue harm to the defendant from the form of conviction;

---

[b] E.g., *Bordenkircher v. Hayes,* p. 1160; *Santobello v. New York,* p. 1174. The Supreme Court's first extended discussion of plea bargaining came in *Brady v. United States,* decided in 1970. See fn. 1 at p. 1162.

"(iii) the defendant, by making public trial unnecessary, has demonstrated genuine remorse or consideration for the victims of his or her criminal activity; or

"(iv) the defendant has given or agreed to give cooperation when such cooperation has resulted or may result in the successful prosecution of other offenders engaged in equally serious or more serious criminal conduct.

"(b) The court should not impose upon a defendant any sentence in excess of that which would be justified by any of the protective, deterrent, or other purposes of the criminal law because the defendant has chosen to require the prosecution to prove guilt at trial rather than to enter a plea of guilty or nolo contendere."

5. ***"Uncertainty of conviction."*** In *Scott v. United States,* 419 F.2d 264 (D.C.Cir.1969), Chief Judge Bazelon commented: "Superficially it may seem that * * * the defendant who insists upon a trial and is found guilty pays a price for the exercise of his right when he receives a longer sentence than his less venturesome counterpart who pleads guilty. In a sense he has. But the critical distinction is that the price he has paid is not one imposed by the state to discourage others from a similar exercise of their rights, but rather one encountered by those who gamble and lose. After the fact, the defendant who pleads innocent and is convicted receives a heavier sentence. But, by the same token, the defendant who pleads innocent and is acquitted receives no sentence. To the extent that the bargain struck reflects only the uncertainty of conviction before trial, the 'expected sentence before trial'—length of sentence discounted by probability of conviction—is the same for those who decide to plead guilty and those who hope for acquittal but risk conviction by going to trial.

" * * * The argument [to the contrary] errs on two counts: (1) the comparison is made at the wrong time—after trial, when the uncertainty of litigation has passed, rather than before trial—and (2) the comparison is made between the wrong categories of defendants—the class of defendants convicted after trial versus the class of defendants who plead guilty or are acquitted rather than the class of defendants who exercise their right to trial versus the class of defendants who do not."

6. ***Standard discount?*** Should there instead be a "standard discount" in all cases to avoid the evils of unequal bargaining and excessive leniency previously noted, as concluded in Note, 82 Yale L.J. 286 (1972)? Or, is case-by-case discounting best because only in that way can plea bargaining serve as an element "of a well-functioning market system" which sets "the 'price' of crime * * * in the traditional market fashion," thus permitting us "to get the maximum deterrent punch out of whatever resources are committed to crime control"? Frank H. Easterbrook, *Criminal Procedure as a Market System,* 12 J.Legal Stud. 289, 289–90 (1983).

C. ACCURATE AND FAIR RESULTS

7. ***Risk to "innocent defendants."*** Consider Albert Alschuler, *A Nearly Perfect System for Convicting the Innocent*, 79 Alb.L.Rev. 919, 919–21 (2016): "Convicting defendants who would be acquitted at trial is one of the principal goals of plea bargaining. 'Half a loaf is better than none,' prosecutors say. 'When we have a weak case for any reason, we'll reduce to almost anything rather than lose.' If the correlation between 'weak cases' and actual innocence is better than random, plea bargaining surely 'convict[s] defendants who are in fact innocent (and would be acquitted [at trial]).'

"Prosecutors engage in both 'odds bargaining' and 'costs bargaining.' That is, they bargain both to ensure conviction in doubtful cases and to save the costs of trial. Were a prosecutor to engage in odds bargaining alone, he might estimate a defendant's chance of conviction at trial at 50% and this defendant's probable sentence if convicted at trial at ten years. Splitting the difference, the prosecutor then might offer to recommend a sentence of five years in exchange for a plea of guilty. Five years is what economists would call the defendant's 'expected' sentence—his predicted post-trial sentence discounted by the possibility of acquittal.

"An offer of five years, however, would leave a risk-neutral defendant indifferent between pleading guilty and standing trial, and the prosecutor hopes to avoid a trial. He does not want the defendant to be indifferent. The prosecutor therefore engages in costs bargaining as well as odds bargaining. He tailors his final offer, not to balance, but to overbalance the defendant's chances of acquittal. This prosecutor may offer four years in exchange for a plea—or two or three. One can easily discover real-world cases in which prosecutors fearful of defeat at trial have struck bargains allowing defendants facing potential life sentences to plead guilty to misdemeanors.

"When a prosecutor has no chance of obtaining a conviction at trial, he may be unable to make an offer that will overbalance the defendant's chances of acquittal. In every other case, however, the prosecutor can reduce the offered punishment to the point that it will become advantageous for the defendant to plead guilty whether he is guilty or innocent."

D. ADMINISTRATIVE CONVENIENCE

8. ***Necessity for plea bargaining?*** "Most prosecutors insist they could not do their jobs without plea bargaining. Understaffed Public Defender organizations agree. Chief Justice Burger claims that even a ten percent decline in convictions produced by plea bargaining would double the number of trials held in this country. * * *

"[A] national study group concluded that '[t]he basic problem is not financial; the cost of a model system of criminal justice is easily within the means of the American people.' Of course, we may choose not to spend the necessary resources to implement the due process model's vision. The decision to allocate more of our scarce resources to the criminal justice system rests ultimately on a normative value judgment about whether the benefits of protecting due process values in all cases outweigh the costs to society." Peter Arenella, *Rethinking the Functions of Criminal Procedure: The Warren and Burger Courts' Competing Ideologies,* 72 Geo.L.J. 185, 221–22 (1983).

E. STATE AND FEDERAL LIMITATIONS ON PLEA BARGAINING

9. ***State limitations.*** Assuming total abolition of plea bargaining is not feasible, then what limitations on the practice, imposed by statute or court rule, are feasible? Consider Cal.Penal Code § 667(g) (prior serious and/or violent felony convictions are to be pleaded and proved and not plea bargained away unless there is insufficient evidence to prove the conviction); Cal.Penal Code § 1192.7 (plea bargaining forbidden "in any case in which the indictment or information charges any serious felony" or other specified offenses, "unless there is insufficient evidence to prove the people's case, or testimony of a material witness cannot be obtained, or a reduction or dismissal would not result in a substantial change in sentence").

10. ***Federal limitations.*** In the federal system there has existed since 1987 an elaborate scheme of Sentencing Guidelines, which serve to limit plea bargaining. Under the Guidelines, 43 offense levels and 6 criminal history categories are used to identify the sentencing range applicable in a particular case, from which the sentencing judge ordinarily can deviate only when one of the bases for upward or downward departure listed in the Guidelines is found to be present. The Guidelines provide regarding a plea agreement to dismiss or not bring certain charges that "the court may accept the agreement if the court determines, for reasons stated on the record, that the remaining charges adequately reflect the seriousness of the actual offense behavior and that accepting the agreement will not undermine the statutory purposes of sentencing or the sentencing guidelines." U.S.S.G § 6B1.2. This provision gives courts wide latitude in deciding whether to accept charge bargains, *United States v. Greener*, 979 F.2d 517 (7th Cir.1992). The

Guidelines further limit the opportunity for giving concessions by dropping or not bringing some charge, as such action "shall not preclude the conduct underlying such charge from being considered" in determining the offense level and other matters bearing on sentencing under the Guidelines. U.S.S.G. § 6B1.2. But even proponents of the federal guidelines acknowledge that the "system has not worked perfectly" because "judges have often simply accepted an agreed-upon account of the conduct at issue." Breyer, J., for the Court, in *Booker*, infra.

In the case of a plea agreement for a certain sentence or sentence recommendation, "the court may" accept the agreement or follow the recommendation if satisfied that the sentence is either "within the applicable guideline range" or "is outside the applicable guideline range for justifiable reasons * * * set forth with specificity." U.S.S.G. § 6B1.2. This means existence of the plea agreement is not itself a mitigating circumstance and that in determining the proper sentence the court must, for the most part, proceed just as if the defendant had pled not guilty and been convicted at trial. If the guilty plea defendant gets a lighter sentence, this is most likely to occur by application of at least one of two sentencing factors which do take on special significance in the guilty plea context as a result of: (i) a provision for decrease of the offense by two levels where defendant "clearly demonstrates acceptance of responsibility for his offense," U.S.S.G. § 3E1.1(a), which in the case of a prompt guilty plea can actually result in a decrease by a total of three levels because of defendant's conduct in "timely notifying authorities of his intention to enter a plea of guilty," U.S.S.G. § 3E1.1(b); and (ii) a provision allowing a downward departure from the Guidelines upon a "motion of the government stating that the defendant has provided substantial assistance in the investigation or prosecution of another person," U.S.S.G. § 5K1.1. While the first factor attempts to limit the amount of the standard plea discount, it nonetheless "bulked up" over time because of prosecutor-controlled sentencing concessions. Ronald F. Wright, *Trial Distortion and the End of Innocence in Federal Criminal Justice*, 154 U.Pa.L.Rev. 79, 131 (2005).

In *United States v. Booker*, p.1394, one 5-Justice majority held the Sentencing Guidelines violated the Sixth Amendment jury trial principle that "[a]ny fact (other than a prior conviction) which is necessary to support a sentence exceeding the maximum authorized by the facts established by a plea of guilty or a jury verdict must be admitted by the defendant or proved to a jury beyond a reasonable doubt." But another 5-Justice majority, in determining whether the remedy should be (1) to "change the Guidelines by preventing the sentencing court from increasing a sentence on the basis of a fact that the jury did not find (or that the offender did not admit)," or (2) to "make the Guidelines system advisory while maintaining a strong connection between the sentence imposed and the offender's real conduct," opted for the latter. (Those Justices felt that under option (1) "plea bargaining would make matters worse," while dissenting Justices contended that option (2) "suffers from the same problem to a much greater degree.") With the Guidelines merely advisory after *Booker*, sentencing judges are now free to give as much or as little weight as they choose to the defendant's willingness to plead guilty, to the presence of serious criminal conduct that would be unpunished under the plea agreement, or to other factors, so long as the sentence is "reasonable." But *Booker* does not appear to make it either more or less likely that judges will reject plea agreements due to sentencing concerns.

§ 2. REJECTED, KEPT AND BROKEN BARGAINS; UNREALIZED EXPECTATIONS

BORDENKIRCHER V. HAYES

434 U.S. 357, 98 S.Ct. 663, 54 L.Ed.2d 604 (1978).

JUSTICE STEWART delivered the opinion of the Court. * * *

[Paul Hayes was indicted in Kentucky on a charge of uttering a forged instrument in the amount of $88.30, punishable by 2–10 years in prison. Hayes and his retained counsel met with the prosecutor, who offered to recommend a sentence of 5 years if Hayes would plead guilty and added that if Hayes did not plead guilty he would seek an indictment under the state Habitual Criminal Act, which would subject Hayes to a mandatory sentence of life imprisonment given his two prior felony convictions. Hayes chose not to plead guilty, and the prosecutor did obtain such an indictment. A jury found Hayes guilty on the principal charge of uttering a forged instrument and, in a separate proceeding, further found that he had twice before been convicted of felonies. As required by the habitual offender statute, he was sentenced to a life term in the penitentiary. The Kentucky Court of Appeals rejected Hayes' constitutional objections to the enhanced sentence, and on Hayes' petition for a federal writ of habeas corpus the district court agreed that there had been no constitutional violation. The federal Court of Appeals reversed on the ground that the prosecutor's conduct had violated the principles of *Blackledge v. Perry,* p. 911, which "protect defendants from the vindictive exercise of a prosecutor's discretion."]

It may be helpful to clarify at the outset the nature of the issue in this case. While the prosecutor did not actually obtain the recidivist indictment until after the plea conferences had ended, his intention to do so was clearly put forth at the outset of the plea negotiations. Hayes was thus fully informed of the true terms of the offer when he made his decision to plead not guilty. This is not a situation, therefore, where the prosecutor without notice brought an additional and more serious charge after plea negotiations relating only to the original indictment had ended with the defendant's insistence on pleading not guilty. As a practical matter, in short, this case would be no different if the grand jury had indicted Hayes as a recidivist from the outset, and the prosecutor had offered to drop that charge as part of the plea bargain.

The Court of Appeals nonetheless drew a distinction between "concessions relating to prosecution under an existing indictment," and threats to bring more severe charges not contained in the original indictment—a line it thought necessary in order to establish a prophylactic rule to guard against the evil of prosecutorial vindictiveness. Quite apart from this chronological distinction, however, the Court of Appeals found that the prosecutor had acted vindictively in the present case since he had conceded that the indictment was influenced by his desire to induce a guilty plea. The ultimate conclusion of the Court of Appeals thus seems to have been that a prosecutor acts vindictively and in violation of due process of law whenever his charging decision is influenced by what he hopes to gain in the course of plea bargaining negotiations.

We have recently had occasion to observe that "[w]hatever might be the situation in an ideal world, the fact is that the guilty plea and the often concomitant plea bargain are important components of this country's criminal justice system. Properly administered, they can benefit all concerned." *Blackledge v. Allison* [p. 1224]. * * * The decision of the Court of Appeals in the present case, however, * * * held that the substance of the plea offer itself violated the limitations imposed by the Due Process Clause of the Fourteenth Amendment. For the reasons that follow, we have concluded that the Court of Appeals was mistaken in so ruling.

This Court held in *North Carolina v. Pearce* [p. 1403], that the Due Process Clause of the Fourteenth Amendment "requires that vindictiveness against a defendant for having successfully attacked his first conviction must play no part in the sentence he receives after a new trial." The same principle was later applied to prohibit a prosecutor from reindicting a convicted misdemeanant on a felony charge after the defendant had invoked an appellate remedy, since in this situation there was also a "realistic likelihood of 'vindictiveness.'" *Blackledge v. Perry*.

In those cases the Court was dealing with the State's unilateral imposition of a penalty upon a defendant who had chosen to exercise a legal right to attack his original conviction—a situation "very different from the give-and-take negotiation common in plea bargaining between the prosecution and the defense, which arguably possess relatively equal bargaining power." The Court has emphasized that the due process violation in cases such as *Pearce* and *Perry* lay not in the possibility that a defendant might be deterred from the exercise of a legal right, see *Colten v. Kentucky*, 407 U.S. 104 (1972); *Chaffin v. Stynchcombe*, 412 U.S. 17 (1973), but rather in the danger that the State might be retaliating against the accused for lawfully attacking his conviction. See *Blackledge v. Perry*.

To punish a person because he has done what the law plainly allows him to do is a due process violation of the most basic sort, see *North Carolina v. Pearce* (opinion of Black, J.), and for an agent of the State to pursue a course of action whose objective is to penalize a person's reliance on his legal rights is "patently unconstitutional." *Chaffin v. Stynchcombe*. But in the "give-and-take" of plea bargaining, there is no such element of punishment or retaliation so long as the accused is free to accept or reject the prosecution's offer.

Plea bargaining flows from "the mutuality of advantage" to defendants and prosecutors, each with his own reasons for wanting to avoid trial. *Brady v. United States*[a] [p. 1164]. Defendants advised by competent counsel and protected by other procedural safeguards are presumptively capable of intelligent choice in response to prosecutorial persuasion, and unlikely to be driven to false self-condemnation. Indeed, acceptance of the basic legitimacy of plea bargaining necessarily implies rejection of any notion that a guilty plea is involuntary in a constitutional sense simply because it is the end result of the bargaining process. By hypothesis, the plea may have been induced by promises of a recommendation of a lenient sentence or a reduction of charges, and thus by fear of the possibility of a greater penalty upon conviction after a trial.

While confronting a defendant with the risk of more severe punishment clearly may have a "discouraging effect on the defendant's assertion of his trial rights, the imposition of these difficult choices [is] an inevitable"—and permissible—"attribute of any legitimate system which tolerates and encourages the negotiation of pleas." It follows that, by tolerating and encouraging the negotiation of pleas, this Court has necessarily accepted as constitutionally legitimate the simple reality that the prosecutor's interest at the bargaining table is to persuade the defendant to forego his right to plead not guilty.

---

[a] Although *Brady* did not involve a plea bargaining situation, see Note 1 at p. 1162, the Court analogized the plea involved there to a plea obtained through plea bargaining, and then commented generally on the validity of a plea produced by the "mutuality of advantage" that flows from a negotiated plea: "We decline to hold * * * that a guilty plea is compelled and invalid under the Fifth Amendment whenever motivated by the defendant's desire to accept the certainty or probability of a lesser penalty rather than face a wider range of possibilities extending from acquittal to conviction and a higher penalty authorized by law for the crime charged. * * * [B]oth the state and the defendant often find it advantageous to preclude the possibility of the maximum penalty authorized by law. For a defendant who sees slight possibility of acquittal, the advantages of pleading guilty and limiting the probable penalty are obvious—his exposure is reduced, the correctional processes can begin immediately, and the practical burdens of a trial are eliminated. For the State there are also advantages—the more promptly imposed punishment after an admission of guilt may more effectively attain the objectives of punishment; and with the avoidance of trial, scarce judicial and prosecutorial resources are conserved for those cases in which there is a substantial issue of the defendant's guilt or in which there is substantial doubt that the State can sustain its burden of proof. It is this mutuality of advantage which perhaps explains the fact that at present well over three-fourths of the criminal convictions in this country rest on pleas of guilty, a great many of them no doubt motivated at least in part by the hope or assurance of a lesser penalty than might be imposed if there were a guilty verdict after a trial to judge or jury."

It is not disputed here that Hayes was properly chargeable under the recidivist statute, since he had in fact been convicted of two previous felonies. In our system, so long as the prosecutor has probable cause to believe that the accused committed an offense defined by statute, the decision whether or not to prosecute, and what charge to file or bring before a grand jury, generally rests entirely in his discretion.[8] Within the limits set by the legislature's constitutionally valid definition of chargeable offenses, "the conscious exercise of some selectivity in enforcement is not in itself a federal constitutional violation" so long as "the selection was [not] deliberately based upon an unjustifiable standard such as race, religion, or other arbitrary classification." To hold that the prosecutor's desire to induce a guilty plea is an "unjustifiable standard," which, like race or religion, may play no part in his charging decision, would contradict the very premises that underlie the concept of plea bargaining itself. Moreover, a rigid constitutional rule that would prohibit a prosecutor from acting forthrightly in his dealings with the defense could only invite unhealthy subterfuge that would drive the practice of plea bargaining back into the shadows from which it has so recently emerged.

There is no doubt that the breadth of discretion that our country's legal system vests in prosecuting attorneys carries with it the potential for both individual and institutional abuse. And broad though that discretion may be, there are undoubtedly constitutional limits upon its exercise. We hold only that the course of conduct engaged in by the prosecutor in this case, which no more than openly presented the defendant with the unpleasant alternatives of foregoing trial or facing charges on which he was plainly subject to prosecution, did not violate the Due Process Clause of the Fourteenth Amendment. * * *

Reversed.

JUSTICE BLACKMUN, with whom JUSTICE BRENNAN and JUSTICE MARSHALL, join dissenting.

[I]n this case vindictiveness is present to the same extent as it was thought to be in *Pearce* and in *Perry;* the prosecutor here admitted that the sole reason for the new indictment was to discourage the respondent from exercising his right to a trial.[1] Even had such an admission not been made, when plea negotiations, conducted in the face of the less serious charge under the first indictment, fail, charging by a second indictment a more serious crime for the same conduct creates "a strong inference" of vindictiveness. * * * I therefore do not understand why, as in *Pearce,* due process does not require that the prosecution justify its action on some basis other than discouraging respondent from the exercise of his right to a trial. * * *

It might be argued that it really makes little difference how this case, now that it is here, is decided. The Court's holding gives plea bargaining full sway despite vindictiveness. A contrary result, however, merely would prompt the aggressive prosecutor to bring the greater charge initially in every case, and only thereafter to bargain. The consequences to the accused would still be adverse, for then he would bargain against a greater charge, face the likelihood of increased bail, and run the risk that the court would be less inclined to accept a bargain plea. Nonetheless, it is far preferable to hold the prosecution to the charge it was originally content to bring and to justify in the eyes of its public.[2]

---

[8] This case does not involve the constitutional implications of a prosecutor's offer during plea bargaining of adverse or lenient treatment for some person *other* than the accused, which might pose a greater danger of inducing a false guilty plea by skewing the assessment of the risks a defendant must consider.

[1] In *Brady v. United States,* where the Court as a premise accepted plea bargaining as a legitimate practice, it nevertheless observed:

> "We here make no reference to the situation where the prosecutor or judge, or both, deliberately employ their charging and sentencing powers to induce a particular defendant to tender a plea of guilty."

[2] [Blackman opinion] That prosecutors, without saying so, may sometimes bring charges more serious than they think appropriate for the ultimate disposition of a case, in order to gain bargaining leverage with a defendant, does not add support to today's decision, for this Court, in its approval of the advantages to be gained from plea

JUSTICE POWELL, dissenting. * * *

It seems to me that the question to be asked under the circumstances is whether the prosecutor reasonably might have charged respondent under the Habitual Criminal Act in the first place. The deference that courts properly accord the exercise of a prosecutor's discretion perhaps would foreclose judicial criticism if the prosecutor originally had sought an indictment under that act, as unreasonable as it would have seemed.[2] But here the prosecutor evidently made a reasonable, responsible judgment not to subject an individual to a mandatory life sentence when his only new offense had societal implications as limited as those accompanying the uttering of a single $88 forged check and when the circumstances of his prior convictions confirmed the inappropriateness of applying the habitual criminal statute. I think it may be inferred that the prosecutor himself deemed it unreasonable and not in the public interest to put this defendant in jeopardy of a sentence of life imprisonment.

There may be situations in which a prosecutor would be fully justified in seeking a fresh indictment for a more serious offense. The most plausible justification might be that it would have been reasonable and in the public interest initially to have charged the defendant with the greater offense. In most cases a court could not know why the harsher indictment was sought, and an inquiry into the prosecutor's motive would neither be indicated nor likely to be fruitful. In those cases, I would agree with the majority that the situation would not differ materially from one in which the higher charge was brought at the outset.

But this is not such a case. Here, any inquiry into the prosecutor's purpose is made unnecessary by his candid acknowledgement that he threatened to procure and in fact procured the habitual criminal indictment because of respondent's insistence on exercising his constitutional rights. * * *

* * * In this case, the prosecutor's actions denied respondent due process because their admitted purpose was to discourage and then to penalize with unique severity his exercise of

---

negotiations, has never openly sanctioned such deliberate overcharging or taken such a cynical view of the bargaining process. Normally, of course, it is impossible to show that this is what the prosecutor is doing, and the courts necessarily have deferred to the prosecutor's exercise of discretion in initial charging decisions.

Even if overcharging is to be sanctioned, there are strong reasons of fairness why the charges should be presented at the beginning of the bargaining process, rather than as a filliped threat at the end. First, it means that a prosecutor is required to reach a charging decision without any knowledge of the particular defendant's willingness to plead guilty; hence the defendant who truly believes himself to be innocent, and wishes for that reason to go to trial, is not likely to be subject to quite such a devastating gamble since the prosecutor has fixed the incentives for the average case.

Second, it is healthful to keep charging practices visible to the general public, so that political bodies can judge whether the policy being followed is a fair one. Visibility is enhanced if the prosecutor is required to lay his cards on the table with an indictment of public record at the beginning of the bargaining process, rather than making use of unrecorded verbal warnings of more serious indictments yet to come.

Finally, I would question whether it is fair to pressure defendants to plead guilty by threat of reindictment on an enhanced charge for the same conduct when the defendant has no way of knowing whether the prosecutor would indeed be entitled to bring him to trial on the enhanced charge. Here, though there is no dispute that respondent met the then current definition of a habitual offender under Kentucky law, it is conceivable that a properly instructed Kentucky grand jury, in response to the same considerations that ultimately moved the Kentucky Legislature to amend the habitual offender statute, would have refused to subject respondent to such an onerous penalty for his forgery charge. There is no indication in the record that, once the new indictment was obtained, respondent was given another chance to plead guilty to the forged check charge in exchange for a five year sentence.

2 [Powell opinion] The majority suggests that this case cannot be distinguished from the case where the prosecutor initially obtains an indictment under an enhancement statute and later agrees to drop the enhancement charge in exchange for a guilty plea. I would agree that these two situations would be alike *only if* it were assumed that the hypothetical prosecutor's decision to charge under the enhancement statute was occasioned not by consideration of the public interest but by a strategy to discourage the defendant from exercising his constitutional rights. In theory, I would condemn both practices. In practice, the hypothetical situation is largely unreviewable. The majority's view confuses the propriety of a particular exercise of prosecutorial discretion with its unreviewability. In the instant case, however, we have no problem of proof.

constitutional rights. Implementation of a strategy calculated solely to deter the exercise of constitutional rights is not a constitutionally permissible exercise of discretion. I would affirm the opinion of the Court of Appeals on the facts of this case.

NOTES AND QUESTIONS

1. ***Voluntariness standard.*** In BRADY v. UNITED STATES, 397 U.S. 742 (1970), Brady was charged with kidnapping in violation of 18 U.S.C. § 1201(a), which could result in a maximum penalty of death if recommended by the jury. Brady elected to plead not guilty, but upon learning that a codefendant would plead guilty and be available to testify against him, he changed his plea to guilty. He was sentenced to 50 years imprisonment, later reduced to 30. Eight years later Brady unsuccessfully challenged his plea in the district court and the court of appeals. The Supreme Court granted certiorari to consider whether Brady's plea was invalid in light of the Court's intervening decision in *United States v. Jackson,* 390 U.S. 570 (1968), holding the death penalty provision of § 1201(a) unconstitutional.[b] The Court, per White, J., held:

"Plainly, it seems to us, *Jackson* ruled neither that all pleas of guilty encouraged by the fear of a possible death sentence are involuntary pleas nor that such encouraged pleas are invalid whether involuntary or not. *Jackson* prohibits the imposition of the death penalty under § 1201(a), but that decision neither fashioned a new standard for judging the validity of guilty pleas nor mandated a new application of the test theretofore fashioned by courts and since reiterated that guilty pleas are valid if both 'voluntary' and 'intelligent.' * * *

"The standard as to the voluntariness of guilty pleas must be essentially that defined by Judge Tuttle of the Fifth Circuit Court of Appeals:

> '[A] plea of guilty entered by one fully aware of the direct consequences, including the actual value of any commitments made to him by the court, prosecutor, or his own counsel, must stand unless induced by threats (or promises to discontinue improper harassment), misrepresentation (including unfulfilled or unfulfillable promises), or perhaps by promises that are by their nature improper as having no proper relationship to the prosecutor's business (e.g. bribes).'

"Under this standard, a plea of guilty is not invalid merely because entered to avoid the possibility of a death penalty.

"The record before us also supports the conclusion that Brady's plea was intelligently made. He was advised by competent counsel, he was made aware of the nature of the charge against him, and there was nothing to indicate that he was incompetent or otherwise not in control of his mental faculties; once his confederate had pleaded guilty and became available to testify, he chose to plead guilty, perhaps to ensure that he would face no more than life imprisonment or a term of years. Brady was aware of precisely what he was doing when he admitted that he had kidnaped the victim and had not released her unharmed."

---

[b] As explained in *Brady:* "In *Jackson,* the defendants were indicted under § 1201(a). The District Court dismissed the § 1201(a) count of the indictment, holding the statute unconstitutional because it permitted imposition of the death sentence only upon a jury's recommendation and thereby made the risk of death the price of a jury trial. This Court held the statute valid, except for the death penalty provision; with respect to the latter, the Court agreed with the trial court 'that the death penalty provision * * * imposes an impermissible burden upon the exercise of a constitutional right * * *.' The problem was to determine 'whether the Constitution permits the establishment of such a death penalty, applicable only to those defendants who assert the right to contest their guilt before a jury.' The inevitable effect of the provision was said to be to discourage assertion of the Fifth Amendment right not to plead guilty and to deter exercise of the Sixth Amendment right to demand a jury trial. Because the legitimate goal of limiting the death penalty to cases in which a jury recommends it could be achieved without penalizing those defendants who plead not guilty and elect a jury trial, the death penalty provision 'needlessly penalize[d] the assertion of a constitutional right,' and was therefore unconstitutional."

As for Brady's objection that his attorney had advised him the jury could impose the death penalty, which, as later held in *Jackson,* was not the case, the Court declared:

" * * * A plea of guilty triggered by the expectations of a competently counseled defendant that the State will have a strong case against him is not subject to later attack because the defendant's lawyer correctly advised him with respect to the then existing law as to possible penalties but later pronouncements of the courts, as in this case, hold that the maximum penalty for the crime in question was less than was reasonably assumed at the time the plea was entered."[c]

2. ***"Standard discount."*** Under *Hayes* and *Brady*, would a statute providing a "standard discount" for a guilty plea, see Note 6, p. 1157, also pass muster? Cf. *Corbitt v. New Jersey*, 439 U.S. 212 (1978), concluding that where defendant, tried and convicted of first degree murder and sentenced to mandatory punishment of life imprisonment, could by statute receive either life or a term of not more than 30 years had he instead entered a nolo contendere plea,[d] there is "no difference of constitutional significance between *Bordenkircher* and this case," while there are "substantial differences between this case and *Jackson*" in that the instant case (i) did not involve the death penalty and (ii) did not involve a scheme in which the maximum penalty was reserved exclusively for those who insisted on a jury trial. Stewart, J., concurring, asked: "Could a state legislature provide that the penalty for every criminal offense to which a defendant pleads guilty is to be one-half the penalty to be imposed upon a defendant convicted of the same offense after a not guilty plea? I would suppose that such legislation would be clearly unconstitutional under *United States v. Jackson*." Three dissenting Justices also distinguished case-by-case plea bargaining from a statutory scheme, asserting that a defendant in the latter situation receives a higher penalty "simply because he has insisted on a trial," while in the former situation "individual factors relevant to the particular case may be considered by the prosecutor in charging and by the trial judge in sentencing, regardless of the defendant's plea."

3. ***"Package deal" agreements.*** Under *Hayes* and *Brady,* what is the status of a plea entered because of a prosecutor's assertion that if the defendant pleads guilty his wife or fiancée will not be prosecuted? Is the point, as stated in *Miles v. Dorsey*, 61 F.3d 1459 (10th Cir.1995), that if defendant "elects to sacrifice himself for such motives, that is his choice"? What then of a plea conditioned upon the defendant not interviewing the victim? See *State v. Draper,* 784 P.2d 259 (Ariz.1989) (not per se improper, but requires close judicial scrutiny because it "may interfere with a defendant's due process rights to prepare a defense"). Or a plea conditioned on defendant testifying in another case consistently with his prior statements? See *State v. Fisher*, 859 P.2d 179 (Ariz.1993) (unenforceable, as such pleas "taint the truth-seeking function of the courts"). What about a "package deal" plea agreement, offered to multiple defendants contingent upon acceptance of the agreement by all of them? Consider *Howell v. State*, 185 S.W.3d 319 (Tenn.2006) ("must be disclosed to the trial court prior to questioning the defendant at the plea hearing," and "trial court must conduct the colloquy with special care").

4. ***Waiver of post-conviction challenge of plea.*** What then is the status of a plea bargain that includes a waiver of any right of appeal and/or collateral attack by the defendant?

---

[c] Brennan, J., joined by Douglas and Marshall, JJ., concurred in the result in *Brady* but dissented in the companion case of *Parker v. North Carolina,* 397 U.S. 790 (1970), involving a guilty plea to first-degree burglary entered at a time when North Carolina law permitted imposition of the death penalty for this offense only following a not guilty plea and trial. They objected that "those who resisted the pressures identified in *Jackson* and after a jury trial were sentenced to death receive relief, but those who succumbed to the same pressures and were induced to surrender their constitutional rights are left without any remedy at all. Where the penalty scheme failed to produce its unconstitutional effect, the intended victims obtain relief; where it succeeded, the real victims have none." They then concluded that reversal was required in *Parker* because the "North Carolina courts have consistently taken the position that *United States v. Jackson* has no applicability to the former North Carolina capital punishment scheme," but not in *Brady,* for while "Brady was aware he faced a possible death sentence, there is no evidence that this factor alone played a significant role in his decision to enter a guilty plea."

[d] On the nature of such pleas, see Note 2, p. 1214.

Compare *State v. Wilson*, 859 P.2d 744 (Ariz.1993) (given that state constitution guarantee's "some form of appellate relief," guilty plea defendants may not bargain away the only available avenue of judicial review); *Hood v. State*, 890 P.2d 797 (Nev.1995) (waiver of appeal provision proper, but may not be extended to post-conviction remedies, as it "would be unconscionable for the state to insulate a conviction from collateral constitutional review by conditioning its willingness to enter into plea negotiations on a defendant's waiver of the right to pursue post-conviction remedies"); *United States v. Erwin*, 765 F.3d 219 (3d Cir.2014) (where a defendant's "appeal is within the scope of his appellate waiver" in his plea agreement, and he "has failed to raise any meritorious grounds for circumventing the waiver," the "ordinary procedure" of appellate courts is merely "to enforce the waiver by dismissing the defendant's appeal," but upon the prosecution's contention "that merely dismissing * * * the appeal and affirming his sentence 'would neither make the Government whole for the costs it has incurred because of [the] breach nor adequately deter other cooperating defendants from similar breaches,' " then "the appropriate remedy * * * is specific performance of the agreement's terms," in this case that "the Government will be excused from its obligation to move for a downward departure," and thus appellate court here "vacate[s] Erwin's judgment of sentence and remand[s] for de novo resentencing").

While such plea bargains are now permitted in most jurisdictions, concern about these waivers has been reflected in the law in various ways. For one thing, at least in the federal system per Fed.R.Crim.P. 11(b)(1)(N), the judge receiving defendant's plea must inform the defendant of, and determine that he understands, "the terms of any plea-agreement provision waiving the right to appeal or to collaterally attack the sentence." For another, courts are inclined to limit the scope of such waivers. Sometimes this is done merely by interpreting the language in the waiver itself, as in *United States v. Cunningham*, 292 F.3d 115 (2d Cir.2002) (because "we 'scrutinize' claimed waivers of appellate rights 'closely and apply them narrowly,' " waiver of right to appeal if sentence was "a term of imprisonment of time served" did not bar appeal when court added 2 years of supervised release). But more often courts simply "refuse to enforce an otherwise valid waiver if to do so would result in a miscarriage of justice," *United States v. Rosa-Ortiz*, 348 F.3d 33 (1st Cir.2003), as in *Crider v. State*, 984 N.E.2d 618 (Ind.2013) (express waiver of right to appeal illegal sentence invalid here, where "the plea agreement did not provide for an illegal sentence," as "when entering a contract with the prosecutor, a defendant is entitled to presume that [the] trial court will order performance of the contract in compliance with the law," but "where a plea agreement provides for the illegality later challenged, a waiver contained therein will be upheld" because "the defendant benefitted from the plea"). By doing so, they ensure that defendants, notwithstanding such waiver, may still raise such questions as whether the waiver itself is defective, e.g., *United States v. Paul*, 634 F.3d 668 (2d Cir.2011) (defendant's waiver does not foreclose appeal raising "question of whether he entered his plea agreement knowingly and voluntarily"), and whether the sentence imposed "is not in accordance with the negotiated agreement," *United States v. Navarro-Botello*, 912 F.2d 318 (9th Cir.1990), or is otherwise defective, e.g., *United States v. Gibson*, 356 F.3d 761 (7th Cir.2004) (appeal waiver not binding here, as permitting "an illegal sentence to stand would impugn the fairness, integrity, and public reputation of the judicial proceedings that have taken place"). See Nancy J. King, *Priceless Process; Nonnegotiable Features of Criminal Litigation,* 47 UCLA L.Rev. 113 (1999). What then should the result be where, as in *United States v. Archie*, 771 F.3d 217 (4th Cir.2014), *after* defendant's appeal waiver, guilty plea and sentencing: (i) the Supreme Court held in *Alleyne v. United States*, 570 U.S. 99 (2013), a decision otherwise retroactive to cases on direct appeal, that any fact increasing a mandatory minimum sentence must be submitted to the jury and found beyond a reasonable doubt; (ii) defendant filed an appeal claiming an *Alleyne* violation; and (iii) the government conceded "that Archie's sentence would now be different under *Alleyne*"?

5. *Waiver of ineffective assistance claim.* "Given the recent attention by the Supreme Court to the issue of what constitutes ineffective assistance of counsel in the plea bargaining context, a question of increasing importance is whether an unqualified plea-bargain waiver of the right to take an appeal and/or pursue a collateral attack may lawfully be deemed to encompass even a post-conviction challenge grounded in a claim of such ineffective assistance. While the issue has not been squarely addressed in many jurisdictions, and though some authority is to be found indicating that ineffective-assistance waivers are not to be enforced, the current prevailing position appears to be that 'an ineffectiveness waiver bars all claims of ineffective representation, whether counsel's alleged failings occur before or after the plea, except allegations that bad advice rendered involuntary or unknowing the defendant's decision to agree to the waiver itself.' For those who find this state of affairs 'most troublesome,' this assessment 'seems to be based on three somewhat interrelated concerns': (i) 'the belief that a defendant cannot knowingly waive the right to raise a claim if the basis of the claim is unknown to him at the time he agrees to the waiver'; (ii) 'the concern that in order to be knowing and voluntary, a plea or waiver requires advice from competent counsel'; and (iii) the 'concern that any attorney who counsels a client to waive his right to claim ineffective assistance is, necessarily, constitutionally ineffective.' As to the first of these, it has been aptly noted that the Supreme Court's 'decisions leave little doubt that a defendant can indeed waive the right to attack his plea or sentence on the basis of attorney errors of which he is not aware,' and, as to the second, that 'in multiple other cases, the Court has held that a defendant's waiver of the right to any assistance of counsel . . . can be knowing and voluntary even without the separate advice of competent counsel.' Regarding the third concern, it is noteworthy that in recent years bar authorities in several states have issued ethics opinions to the effect 'that defense counsel may not ethically counsel clients to sign a plea agreement containing an express waiver of ineffective assistance of counsel claims, either because defense counsel is inherently conflicted on that subject, or because such a waiver is the functional equivalent of prospectively limiting the lawyer's liability to the client for malpractice . . . , or on both grounds.'[e] However, it is well to note 'that whether particular plea agreements are lawful, enforceable and meet constitutional requirements are legal questions outside the scope of an ethics opinion,' so that 'a violation of a professional rule of discipline does not equate to a constitutional violation' of a guilty plea defendant's rights. Yet there is much to be said for the notion that jurisdictions, albeit 'without invoking the Constitution to invalidate waivers,' should not routinely enforce them and thereby 'effectively eliminate judicial review of representation in all criminal cases resolved by plea agreement.' And, in any event, to 'ensure that a defendant's ineffectiveness waiver is knowing and voluntary, something more than the usual guilty plea colloquy should be required.'" CRIMPROC § 21.2(b), quoting mainly Nancy King, *Plea Bargains that Waive Claims of Ineffective Assistance-Waiving Padilla and Frye*, 51 Duq.L.Rev. 647 (2013).

6. ***FOIA waivers.*** In *Price v. U.S. Department of Justice Attorney Office*, 865 F.3d 676 (D.C.Cir.2017), the court (after quoting Justice O'Connor's concurrence in *Town of Newton v. Rumery*, 480 U.S. 386 (19876), stating that a "prosecutor is permitted to consider only legitimate criminal justice concerns in striking [a plea] bargain—concerns such as rehabilitation, allocation of criminal justice resources, the strength of the evidence against the defendant, and the extent of [a defendant's] cooperation with the authorities") declared that "[t]his set of legitimate interests places boundaries on the rights that can be bargained away in plea negotiations." Hence, the court deemed invalid a prosecutor's inclusion in a plea agreement of a requirement that the defendant waive his federal statutory right to seek records related to his case under the Freedom of

---

[e] See, e.g., *United States v. Kentucky Bar Association*, 439 S.W.3d 136 (Ky.2014) (such an ethics advisory opinion by KBA deemed applicable to United States Attorneys serving in districts in Ky., given provision in 28 U.S.C.A. § 530B that all government attorneys are bound to follow "State laws and rules * * * governing attorneys in each State where such attorney engages in that attorney's duties," and thus the opinion does not violate the Supremacy Clause of the U.S. Constitution). But consider CRIMPROC § 1.7(k), concluding that "neither the language nor the history of [that statute] suggest that Congress intended to delegate to the states the power to override statutory and court rule grants of authority to federal prosecutors by subjecting to disciplinary sanction federal prosecutors who exercise that authority."

Information Act, given the government's failure to assert "any legitimate criminal-justice interest served by allowing the FOIA waivers in plea agreements."

The court stated that "Price has shown, through real-world examples, that enforcing a FOIA waiver would make it harder for litigants in his position to discover potentially exculpatory information or material supporting an ineffective-assistance-of-counsel claim. This is especially true given that, 'with rare exceptions, only the waivor' in such cases 'has the requisite knowledge and interest to lodge a FOIA request in the first place.' On the other side of the scale, the government has offered us nothing more than the unsupported blanket assertion that FOIA waivers assist in effective and efficient prosecution, without any support or explanation how. Under these particular circumstances, and based on the briefing in this case, we have little trouble in concluding that the public interest in enforcing Price's waiver is outweighed by the harm to public policy that enforcement would cause.

The dissent asserted than "[w]hen overcharging defendants, withholding material information, and permitting defendants to misperceive the evidence against them are all acceptable means to achieve the 'legitimate criminal-justice' objectives of a knowing, voluntary, and intelligent guilty plea, it makes no sense to insist limited FOIA waivers require satisfying an additional 'legitimate criminal-justice' interest,' especially since as a general matter there are 'multiple 'legitimate criminal-justice' objectives served by FOIA waivers—including the safeguarding of both scarce investigative resources and information within FOIA material that an inmate could use to harm victims or third-parties."

7. ***"Ad hoc" plea bargains.*** Consider the so-called "ad hoc" plea bargain, one that contemplates concessions to the defendant in exchange for his agreement to accept a punishment the judge would not be authorized to impose upon a conviction following a not guilty plea. Joseph A. Colquitt, *Ad Hoc Plea Bargaining*, 75 Tulane L.Rev. 695 (2001), lists varieties found in current practice: (1) "coerced contributions," as where the defendant agrees to contribute a specified amount to a specified governmental agency or to a designated charitable group; (2) "deprivation of certain rights," as where the defendant agrees to surrender an interest in some property, the right to engage in a certain occupation, or to raise one's children; (3) "scarlet letter punishments," as where the defendant agrees to a shaming type of punishment (e.g., publicizing guilt via a yard sign) not otherwise permitted by law; (4) "surrender of profits," as where the defendant agrees to surrender profits (e.g., book royalties) the law could not otherwise require him to give up; (5) "banishments," as where the defendant agrees to leave the jurisdiction; and (6) "military service," as where defendant agrees to enlist in a branch of the military upon a disposition that eliminates any disqualifying aspects of the conviction. Are such dispositions a virtue or vice of the plea bargaining system?

If the defendant accepts such a plea bargain, should he later be able to have his guilty plea nullified because the accepted punishment is not authorized by law, given the offense to which he pled guilty? Compare *State v. Setters*, 25 P.3d 893 (Mont.2001) (plea bargain that defendant would plead guilty to lesser offense of tampering with public records in exchange for dismissal of theft charge, but defendant to be responsible for restitution for latter offense, as determined at sentencing, invalid, as law does not permit restitution for the tampering offense); with *In re Flatt-Moore*, 959 N.E.2d 241 (Ind.2012) (defendant may "consent to a sentence that would be otherwise unauthorized to gain benefits in a plea agreement," and thus, regarding the unaccepted first plea offer in this case, that a Class C felony check fraud charge be reduced to a Class A misdemeanor if the defendant were to "pay his victim in excess of what the Restitution Statute may have allowed," it "would not necessarily render the agreement illegal or otherwise improper"). (But the prosecutor in *Flatt-Moore* went too far; see p. 1208.)

8. ***Coercion by generosity?*** Are some pleas "coerced" merely because of the magnitude of the prosecutor's generosity? If so, how can it be determined when this is the case? "Consider, for

example, cases involving two defendants, P and Q. P has a 98 percent chance of conviction at trial; Q has a 10 percent chance. If the sentence upon conviction at trial is 240 months, then P's expected trial sentence is 235 months; Q's is 24 months. * * * If the prosecutor's opportunity costs [punishment foregone in other cases if this case goes to trial] warrant offering each defendant a further discount of up to two-thirds off, he can propose a plea sentence as low as seventy-eight months for P and eight months for Q. Though P will be strongly tempted to plead guilty, many would find it odd to view P as having been coerced; P presumably *is* guilty, and the prosecutor's resource problem enabled P to extract a windfall price for waiving his right to trial. Analytically, Q is in the same boat as P is, and one can consistently say that Q, like P, simply enjoys a windfall profit on the sale of his right to trial. But notice that so long as P and Q have similar preferences with respect to risk and related matters, both P and Q (that is, both the guilty and the innocent) face precisely the same strong inducements to plead guilty. From the perspective of the innocent defendant, those inducements start to look very much like what the ordinary person calls 'coercion.' " Stephen J. Schulhofer, *Criminal Justice Discretion as a Regulatory System,* 17 J. Legal Stud. 43, 73 (1988).

Compare Robert E. Scott & William J. Stuntz, *Plea Bargaining as Contract,* 101 Yale L.J. 1909, 1920–21 (1992): "The argument about the size of the sentencing differential reduces to the claim that the choice to plead guilty is too generous to the defendant, an odd claim to make alongside the general claim that the system treats the defendant unfairly. To be sure, the plea favors the defendant only because the post-trial sentence is so high. But this is a complaint about background sentences, not plea bargaining. * * *

"Moreover, the argument misunderstands the doctrine of economic duress. As the preceding discussion suggests, coercion in the sense of few and unpalatable choices does not necessarily negate voluntary choice. So long as the post-trial sentences have not been manipulated by the prosecutor, the coercive elements of the plea bargaining environment do not corrupt the voluntariness of the plea agreement. A large sentencing differential does not imply coercion a priori. Rather, it is entirely consistent with the assumption that the right to take the case to trial is a valuable entitlement. The prosecutor gains something very valuable when she avoids trial. It is hardly surprising that she will pay handsomely for it."

9. ***"Illusory" bargains.*** As to the requirement (as stated in *Brady*) that the defendant know "the actual value of any commitments made to him," consider *Dillon v. United States,* 307 F.2d 445 (9th Cir.1962), where the prosecutor promised to recommend a lenient sentence if the judge asked for a recommendation. Because the prosecutor knew that the judge never asked for a recommendation, the court found the prosecutor's bargain "wholly illusory." Compare *Smith v. State,* 770 N.E.2d 290 (Ind.2002) (as to defendant's claim that "the State's promise to drop the burglary charge in return for the plea bargain was 'illusory' " because the burglary evidence "does not include any evidence of breaking and entering," court responds that it has "never required the State to be able to demonstrate evidence of every element of an offense in order to file a charge or utilize a potential charge in plea negotiations").

10. ***Defendant's statements during bargaining.*** Should the defendant be free to initiate and participate in plea discussions without having his statements used against him at trial if he does not plead guilty? Does it make any difference to whom the statements were made? Consider Fed.R.Evid. 410, declaring inadmissible against the maker "any statement made in the course of plea discussions with an attorney for the prosecuting authority which do not result in a plea of guilty or which result in a plea of guilty later withdrawn,"[f] and compare *United States v. Herman,*

[f] Rule 410 goes on to provide: "However, such a statement is admissible (i) in any proceeding wherein another statement made in the course of the same plea or plea discussions has been introduced and the statement ought in fairness be considered contemporaneously with it, or (ii) in a criminal proceeding for perjury or false statement if the statement was made by the defendant under oath, on the record and in the presence of counsel."

544 F.2d 791 (5th Cir.1977) (defendant in custody of two postal inspectors during continuance of removal hearing instigated conversation with them and at some point said he would plead guilty to armed robbery if the murder charge was dropped, but inspector then explained they were not "in position to make any deals in this regard"; held, defendant's statements inadmissible under earlier, broader version of the rule because he made them "during the course of a conversation in which he sought concessions from the government in return for a guilty plea"). Is the change objectionable because it "fails to provide protection for defendants who plea bargain under the reasonable belief that the agent has bargaining authority," as asserted in Note, 70 Geo.L.J. 315, 344 (1981)?

In *United States v. Mezzanatto*, 513 U.S. 196 (1995), when defendant and his attorney met with the prosecutor for plea discussions, the prosecutor conditioned the discussions on defendant agreeing that any statements he made could be used to impeach any contradictory testimony defendant might give if the case went to trial. Defendant, after consulting his lawyer, agreed. The case later did go to trial and such impeachment occurred, but defendant's conviction was overturned on appeal on the ground that the agreement was unenforceable. The Supreme Court disagreed, reasoning the defendant had not shown that rule 410 departs "from the presumption of waivability" which exists as to "legal rights generally, and evidentiary provisions specifically."[g]

Compare *Hutto v. Ross,* 429 U.S. 28 (1976), where the Court, per curiam, reversed the holding of the court of appeals that defendant's confession, given subsequent to a negotiated plea agreement from which the defendant later withdrew, was involuntary because it would not have been made "but for the plea bargaining." Noting that "causation in that sense has never been the test of voluntariness," the Court concluded: "The existence of the bargain may well have entered into respondent's decision to give a statement, but counsel made it clear to respondent that he could enforce the terms of the plea bargain whether or not he confessed. The confession thus does not appear to have been the result of 'any direct or implied promises' or any coercion on the part of the prosecution, and was not involuntary." The Court added that the case did not "involve the admissibility in criminal trials of statements made during the plea negotiation process."

Notes on Judicial Involvement in Plea Bargaining

1. ***Not guilty plea penalty.*** Albert W. Alschuler, *The Trial Judge's Role in Plea Bargaining, Part I,* 76 Colum.L.Rev. 1059, 1133–34 (1976), describes *People v. Dennis,* 328 N.E.2d 135 (Ill.App.1975): "A defense attorney testified in a post-conviction proceeding that a Chicago trial judge had offered to sentence his client to a term of two-to-four years if the client would plead guilty. The prosecutor recalled the pretrial conference somewhat differently and testified that the judge had proposed a sentence of two-to-six years in exchange for the defendant's plea. Whatever the trial judge's offer, however, the defendant declined it; and following his conviction by a jury, the judge sentenced him to a term of 40-to-80 years. The appellate court noted that, because the trial judge had been advised of the state's evidence and of the defendant's prior criminal record during the pretrial conference, the sentence that he imposed almost certainly did not reflect circumstances of which he had been unaware at the time of his offer. The court concluded that a ' "reasonable inference" of constitutional deprivation may be drawn where a great disparity exists between the sentence offered at a pretrial conference to which the trial judge was a participant and one imposed at the conclusion of a jury trial.' Accordingly, it exercised its authority under Illinois Supreme Court Rules to reduce the defendant's sentence. The court did not, however, reduce the sentence to the two-to-four or the two-to-six year term that the defendant would have

[g] Three concurring Justices speculated "that a waiver to use such statements in the case-in-chief would more severely undermine a defendant's incentive to negotiate, and thereby inhibit plea bargaining." Two dissenters concluded the record showed Congress found that "conditions of unrestrained candor are the most effective means of encouraging plea discussions" and thus meant to bar waiver.

served if he had pleaded guilty. Rather, it reduced the sentence to six-to-eighteen years 'in the interests of justice.' The court's rule thus seemed to be that a defendant may be penalized for exercising his right to trial by a sentence three times more severe than that he could have secured by pleading guilty, but not by a sentence twenty times more severe."

2. ***"Presumption of vindictiveness."*** In light of *Bordenkircher v. Hayes,* p. 1160, how would the Supreme Court have dealt with *Dennis?* Consider *Wilson v. State,* 845 So.2d 142 (Fla.2003) (a "presumption of vindictiveness" does not arise whenever "the trial judge participates in the plea negotiations and the defendant subsequently receives a harsher sentence after a trial or hearing," but a presumption may arise from such judicial participation plus other factors: "(1) whether the trial judge initiated the plea discussions * * *; (2) whether the trial judge * * * appears to have departed from his or her role as an impartial arbiter by either urging the defendant to accept a plea, or by implying or stating that the sentence imposed would hinge on future procedural choices * * *; (3) the disparity between the plea offer and the ultimate sentence imposed; and (4) the lack of any facts on the record that explain the reason for the increased sentence other than that the defendant exercised his or her right to a trial or hearing").

3. ***Judicial coercion.*** If the defendant in *Dennis* had *accepted* the trial judge's offer and received the promised sentence, what would be the status of that guilty plea? Can it be said, as asserted in *United States ex rel. Elksnis v. Gilligan,* 256 F.Supp. 244 (S.D.N.Y.1966), that because of the "unequal positions of the judge and the accused, one with the power to commit to prison and the other deeply concerned to avoid prison," any "guilty plea predicated upon a judge's promise of a definite sentence by its very nature does not qualify as a free and voluntary act"? Compare Recent Developments, 19 Stan.L.Rev. 1082, 1086 (1967), arguing that because "the prosecutor has many means not available to the judge of putting pressure upon the defendant * * * the 'disparity of position,' in terms of power over the accused, may be even greater between prosecutor and defendant than between judge and defendant."

In *United States ex rel. Rosa v. Follette,* 395 F.2d 721 (2d Cir.1968), holding that "the participation of the trial judge in plea discussions does not *in itself* render the plea involuntary," the court reasoned: "We cannot blind ourselves to the fact that 'it is not at all unusual for the prosecutor to predict the sentence with a high degree of accuracy and to communicate this prediction to the defendant.' * * * And, every defense attorney plays the prophet as best he can. In the instant case, Rosa was fortunate in being given the security of the Judge's beneficence by learning immediately what most defendants are tortured over, can only hope for and anticipate—that the trial judge will follow the prosecutor's recommendation."

Where there is no per se rule against judicial participation, the outcome of a later challenge to the plea will turn on the extent and character of the judge's involvement. Compare, e.g., *State v. Ditter,* 441 N.W.2d 622 (Neb.1989) (did not coerce plea, as defense initiated the discussion, judge talked only with defense counsel and defendant was not present, judge only indicated possible penalties depending on defendant's course of action, and judge made no comments on the weight of the evidence or that he thought defendant was guilty); with *Standley v. Warden,* 990 P.2d 783 (Nev.1999) (coerced the plea, as "judge effectively convinced appellant to accept the plea offer through lengthy exposition" and "evinced an unmistakable desire that appellant accept the offer").

4. ***Varieties and benefits of judicial participation.*** A 2016 study collected interviews of nearly one hundred judges, prosecutors, and defense attorneys from ten of the many states whose law does not prohibit judicial involvement before a plea is tendered, revealing a surprising variety of ways that judges participate in plea bargaining. Nancy J. King and Ronald F. Wright, *The Invisible Revolution in Plea Bargaining: Managerial Judging and Judicial Participation in Negotiations*, 95 Tex.L.Rev. 325 (2016).

Most commonly reported was a short meeting about sentencing early in the process, between the judge, prosecutor, and defense counsel. Usually the attorneys begin this conversation by summarizing key evidence, the defendant's criminal history, and scoring under sentencing guidelines, if applicable. If the parties have already reached a tentative sentence deal, the judge states whether that recommended or stipulated sentence would be acceptable. If the parties have not agreed on a recommended sentence, the judge responds with language along the lines of, "Based on the information I have now, this is what I would give him if he decides to plead guilty." The conference may be off the record in chambers, or on the record in open court or at the bench. A handful of interviewees reported that when these conversations take place in open court on the record, the defendant is sometimes present. In several states, judges hold group conferences with the attorneys for all of the cases on the day's docket present at once, allowing them to chime in on each other's cases. Case law, statutes, and court rules often control these conferences, regulating such features as whether or not the meeting may be initiated by the judge, what judges can and cannot say, provision of discovery to the defense, preparation of information for the judge, plea withdrawal if a judge who accepts a sentence at the conference later changes her mind at sentencing, and whether a different judge must preside should the defendant end up going to trial.

In many counties with multiple judges, the study revealed, these early conferences are part of a formal process called "differentiated case management," which tracks those cases that are more likely to settle to specialized dockets or to judges other than those who handle cases headed for trial. These settlement tracks have various names, including "home court," "early case resolution," "early disposition docket," and "administrative term." One jurisdiction reportedly has a settlement court set up at the jail. Maryland courts staff their "preliminary disposition dockets," or "resolution conferences" with retired judges. Cases that do not settle go to a different judge for trial.

In two of the states, Oregon and Kansas, interviewees reported full-fledged judicial mediation in felony cases. Led by a judge approved by both sides, these mediations may include detailed "Best Practice" guides for the judges, attorneys, and probation officers who participate; "shuttle diplomacy" where the judge meets with one side then the next; risk assessments for each defendant; and sometimes the participation of victims, defendants, or even the defendant's family. Another innovation is formal authorization for felony court judges to function as lower court judges so that they may talk to the parties about sentencing before the preliminary hearing.

Interviewees from jurisdictions that embraced judicial participation in the negotiation phase reported that by reducing uncertainty for both sides and prompting lawyers to evaluate their cases sooner, judicial involvement helps parties reach agreements earlier than they would without the judge's input. Earlier pleas help avoid the costs of eve-of-trial settlements that waste juror time, and unnecessary pretrial detention, for example. And when the parties seek an unusually low sentence, the opportunity to answer the judge's questions in advance helps prevent delays.

Judges reported that early involvement also allows them to suggest options for sentencing that the parties overlook, and to remedy attorney error. Prosecutors found the judge's input helped them manage relationships with police, victims, and the public. Interviewees were unconcerned that these conversations about sentence occurred without presentence reports, as the judge generally had access to information at the conference that was the same or better than information available at sentencing. Nor was there much concern that the judge's participation would force defendants to settle before they received the information they needed. Rather, most interviewees reported that the defense received discovery before the conference, and that the conference allowed the defense to hear the prosecutor answer questions from the judge, questions that the prosecutor might never address in negotiations with defense counsel alone. Judges, it was widely reported, sometimes indicated a preference for a sentence lower than the prosecutor's offer, or persuaded a prosecutor to accept more lenient sentence terms by pointing out evidentiary weaknesses, resisting draconian applications of rigid prosecutorial policy, or educating an inexperienced or overzealous assistant. Concluded the authors, "interviewees suggested that by increasing the information available to a defendant and creating a sentencing option that is often more moderate than the prosecutor's offer, judicial participation can make an already coercive situation a little less so."

But consider Darryl Brown, *The Judicial Role in Criminal Charging and Plea Bargaining,* 46 Hofstra L.Rev. 63, 81 (2017), taking note of the "general asymmetrical structure of judicial power over charges in this setting," as "judges have more discretion to reject charges in proposed plea bargains on public-interest grounds because they are too lenient than because they are too harsh. This is because prosecutors' initial charging decisions set an implicit baseline for judicial authority regarding guilty pleas (they set no such baseline for prosecutors themselves, who are generally free to file additional charges). Judges can and do reject plea bargains because the parties have proposed to dismiss too many charges (or the wrong charges) as part of a negotiated plea deal. That is, they can rule that the bargain is too lenient for the court to approve, judged against the initial charging document and the evidence in support of it. But judges are on much thinner ground if they want to reject bargains as against the public interest because a defendant has agreed to plead guilty to all filed charges, even if the judge views those as too severe in light of the defendant's conduct. To describe the law of judicial authority in this context differently, judges' power over plea bargains is generally structured more as a check against prosecutors departing from their initial charging decision in the direction of leniency than as a check against unduly severe charging and plea bargain decisions by prosecutors."

5. ***Limiting judicial involvement.*** Precisely how should judicial involvement in the plea bargaining process be limited? Is it best to provide that the judge shall not "participate" in plea discussions, as in Fed.R.Crim.P. 11(c)(1), or that the judge shall not "initiate" plea discussions, as in Ill.Sup.Ct.R. 402(d)(1)? Consider *A.B.A. Standards, Pleas of Guilty* § 14–3.3(d) (3d ed. 1997): "A judge should not ordinarily participate in plea negotiation discussions among the parties. Upon the request of the parties, a judge may be presented with a proposed plea agreement negotiated by the parties and may indicate whether the court would accept the terms as proposed and if relevant, indicate what sentence would be imposed. Discussions relating to plea negotiations at which the judge is present need not be recorded verbatim, so long as an appropriate record is made at the earliest opportunity. For good cause, the judge may order the record or transcript of any such discussions to be sealed."

Regarding the Fed.R.Crim.P. 11(c) prohibition upon judicial participation in plea discussions, in *United States v. Davila*, 569 U.S. 597 (2013), the Court concluded that since this prohibition "was adopted as a prophylactic measure, not one impelled by the Due Process Clause or any other constitutional requirement," it follows that "pre-plea exhortations to admit guilt," just as with "[p]lea colloquy requirements [that] come into play *after* a defendant has agreed to plead guilty," are subject to Fed.R.Crim.P. 11(h), declaring that a "variance from the requirements of this rule is harmless error if it does not affect substantial rights."

Does Fed.R.Crim.P. 11(c), by permitting the reaching of an agreement as to a specific sentence and its communication to the judge, who can either concur and accept the plea agreement or else reject the plea agreement, involve the judge too much? As stated in *Carwile v. Smith,* 874 F.2d 382 (6th Cir.1989), the fact "that under federal law, as well as under the law of 40 out of 49 states, a criminal defendant who has pleaded guilty must be given an opportunity to withdraw his plea when an agreed sentencing recommendation is rejected by the sentencing court" does not mean it is a violation of due process for a state not to permit withdrawal absent a showing "that petitioner was 'misled' into thinking that the judge would be bound by the prosecutor's recommendation."

In those jurisdictions that permit a judge, either incident to or apart from plea bargaining, to provide what are variously characterized as nonbinding "indicated sentences" or "sentencing inclinations," it is generally agreed, as stated in *State v. Sanney,* 404 P.3d 280 (Haw.2017): "If a defendant pleads guilty or no contest in response to a court's sentencing inclination, but the court later decides not to follow the inclination, then the court must so advise the defendant and provide the defendant with the opportunity to affirm or withdraw the plea of guilty or no contest."

In a state where a defendant must be allowed to withdraw his plea if the judge decides upon a sentence higher than contemplated in the plea agreement, should the prosecution have a corresponding right to withdraw if the judge opts for a sentence lower than the parties earlier agreed to? Compare *State v. Warren,* 558 A.2d 1312 (N.J.1989) (plea agreement to that effect invalid, as though "notions of fairness apply to each side, * * * the defendant's constitutional rights and interests weigh more heavily in the scale"); with *People v. Siebert,* 537 N.W.2d 891 (Mich.1995) ("the people must be given an opportunity to withdraw from the agreement" when the court imposes a "lower sentence than that agreed" and "such action trespasses on the prosecutor's charging authority," deemed to be the case here "where the prosecutor has lowered the charges against the defendant * * * with the understanding of a certain minimum sentence").

6. ***Negotiating directly with judge.*** Should the defendant be able to bargain with the judge over the prosecutor's objection? Consider *Commonwealth v. Corey*, 826 S.W.2d 319 (Ky.1992) (defendant charged with capital murder; judge sua sponte allowed defendant to plead guilty with right to withdraw if sentence of death or life without parole; this improper, as "whether to engage in plea bargaining is a matter reserved to the sound discretion of the prosecuting authority"); *State v. Streiff*, 673 N.W.2d 831 (Minn.2004) (Minn.R.Crim.P. 15.07 allows a trial judge to accept a plea of guilty to a lesser offense over the prosecutor's objection when "it would be [a] manifest injustice not to accept the plea," which requires "a showing of abuse of prosecutorial discretion").[h]

SANTOBELLO V. NEW YORK

404 U.S. 257, 92 S.Ct. 495, 30 L.Ed.2d 427 (1971).

CHIEF JUSTICE BURGER delivered the opinion of the Court.

[After negotiations with the prosecutor, petitioner withdrew his previous not-guilty plea to two felony counts and pleaded guilty to a lesser-included offense, the prosecutor having agreed to make no recommendation as to sentence. At petitioner's appearance for sentencing many months later a new prosecutor recommended the maximum sentence, which the judge (who stated that he was uninfluenced by that recommendation) imposed. Petitioner attempted unsuccessfully to withdraw his guilty plea, and his conviction was affirmed on appeal.]

* * * The disposition of criminal charges by agreement between the prosecutor and the accused, sometimes loosely called "plea bargaining," is an essential component of the administration of justice. Properly administered, it is to be encouraged. If every criminal charge were subjected to a full-scale trial, the States and the Federal Government would need to multiply by many times the number of judges and court facilities.

Disposition of charges after plea discussions is not only an essential part of the process but a highly desirable part for many reasons. It leads to prompt and largely final disposition of most criminal cases; it avoids much of the corrosive impact of enforced idleness during pre-trial

[h] Compare H. Richard Uviller, *Pleading Guilty: A Critique of Four Models,* 41 Law & Contemp.Prob. 102, 116–17 (1977): "When a trial judge has informed himself of the defendant's background and the circumstances of his crime, when he has formed at least a tentative decision on the appropriate sentence, and even (according to some) when the sentence concession is not contingent on the plea but would be followed even if the defendant elected to be tried, what interests of the defendant are protected by prohibiting the judge from communicating this information to him?"

confinement for those who are denied release pending trial; it protects the public from those accused persons who are prone to continue criminal conduct even while on pretrial release; and, by shortening the time between charge and disposition, it enhances whatever may be the rehabilitative prospects of the guilty when they are ultimately imprisoned. * * *

This phase of the process of criminal justice, and the adjudicative element inherent in accepting a plea of guilty, must be attended by safeguards to insure the defendant what is reasonably due in the circumstances. Those circumstances will vary, but a constant factor is that when a plea rests in any significant degree on a promise or agreement of the prosecutor, so that it can be said to be part of the inducement or consideration, such promise must be fulfilled. * * *

We need not reach the question whether the sentencing judge would or would not have been influenced had he known all the details of the negotiations for the plea. He stated that the prosecutor's recommendation did not influence him and we have no reason to doubt that. Nevertheless, we conclude that the interests of justice and appropriate recognition of the duties of the prosecution in relation to promises made in the negotiation of pleas of guilty will be best served by remanding the case to the state courts for further consideration. The ultimate relief to which petitioner is entitled we leave to the discretion of the state court, which is in a better position to decide whether the circumstances of this case require only that there be specific performance of the agreement on the plea, in which case petitioner should be resentenced by a different judge, or whether, in the view of the state court, the circumstances require granting the relief sought by petitioner, i.e., the opportunity to withdraw his plea of guilty.[2] * * *

JUSTICE DOUGLAS, concurring. * * *

I join the opinion of the Court and favor a constitutional rule for this as well as for other pending or oncoming cases. Where the "plea bargain" is not kept by the prosecutor, the sentence must be vacated and the state court will decide in light of the circumstances of each case whether due process requires (a) that there be specific performance of the plea bargain or (b) that the defendant be given the option to go to trial on the original charges. One alternative may do justice in one case, and the other in a different case. In choosing a remedy, however, a court ought to accord a defendant's preference considerable, if not controlling, weight inasmuch as the fundamental rights flouted by a prosecutor's breach of a plea bargain are those of the defendant, not of the State.

JUSTICE MARSHALL, with whom JUSTICE BRENNAN and JUSTICE STEWART join, concurring in part and dissenting in part.

* * * When a prosecutor breaks the bargain, he undercuts the basis for the waiver of constitutional rights implicit in the plea. This, it seems to me, provides the defendant ample justification for rescinding the plea. Where a promise is "unfulfilled," *Brady v. United States* [p. 1164] specifically denies that the plea "must stand." Of course, where the prosecutor has broken the plea agreement, it may be appropriate to permit the defendant to enforce the plea bargain. But that is not the remedy sought here.[*] Rather, it seems to me that a breach of the plea bargain provides ample reason to permit the plea to be vacated.

It is worth noting that in the ordinary case where a motion to vacate is made prior to sentencing, the government has taken no action in reliance on the previously entered guilty plea

---

2 If the state court decides to allow withdrawal of the plea, the petitioner will, of course, plead anew to the original charge on two felony counts.

* Justice Douglas, although joining the Court's opinion (apparently because he thinks the remedy should be chosen by the state court), concludes that the state court "ought to accord a defendant's preference considerable, if not controlling, weight." Thus, a majority of the Court appears to believe that in cases like these, when the defendant seeks to vacate the plea, that relief should generally be granted. [Ed. note: there were two vacancies on the Court at the time.]

and would suffer no harm from the plea's withdrawal. More pointedly, here the State claims no such harm beyond disappointed expectations about the plea itself. At least where the government itself has broken the plea bargain, this disappointment cannot bar petitioner from withdrawing his guilty plea and reclaiming his right to a trial. * * *

NOTES AND QUESTIONS

1. ***Ambiguous agreements.*** Sometimes it is difficult to determine what the dimensions of the bargain are, as in *United States v. Harvey,* 791 F.2d 294 (4th Cir.1986), where the problem of interpretation arose out of the fact that the defendant was involved in multiple conspiracies and there were outstanding charges in various districts. Defendant's view of the agreement was that the government would not anywhere or by any prosecutorial force prosecute him further for violations "arising from" the general investigation that led to the indictment under which he entered his guilty plea, while the government's position was that the agreement merely was that defendant would not be further prosecuted in that particular district.

On the fundamental question of how a court should deal with ambiguity in a plea agreement, *Harvey* concludes that the law of contracts is generally applicable, though "those rules have to be applied to plea agreements with two things in mind which may require their tempering in particular cases. First, the defendant's underlying 'contract' right is constitutionally based and therefore reflects concerns that differ fundamentally from and run wider than those of commercial contract law. * * * Second, with respect to federal prosecutions, the courts' concerns run even wider than protection of the defendant's individual constitutional rights—to concerns for the 'honor of the government, public confidence in the fair administration of justice, and the effective administration of justice in a federal scheme of government.' "

This means, the court continued, that "both constitutional and supervisory concerns require holding the Government to a greater degree of responsibility than the defendant (or possibly than would be either of the parties to commercial contracts) for impressions or ambiguities in plea agreements. * * * This is particularly appropriate where, as would usually be the case, the Government has proffered the terms or prepared a written agreement—for the same reasons that dictate that approach in interpreting private contracts." The court added that "derelictions on the part of defense counsel that contribute to ambiguities and imprecisions in plea agreements may not be allowed to relieve the Government of its primary responsibility for ensuring precision in the agreement," for "the validity of a plea in the final analysis depends upon the voluntariness and intelligence with which defendant (not his counsel) enters into it."

Applying those principles, the court in *Harvey* found that the agreement did not specify the geographic area in which the obligation not to prosecute existed, and thus concluded this ambiguity "must be read against the Government. This does not mean that in a proper case it might not be possible to establish by extrinsic evidence that the parties to an ambiguously worded plea agreement actually had agreed—or mutually manifested their assent to—an interpretation as urged by the Government. But here, that evidence simply does not exist."

2. ***Nonperformance adverse to defendant.*** What constitutes a broken bargain—or, at least, deserves to be treated in the same way as the broken bargain in *Santobello*? Consider:

a. ***Pre-plea withdrawal of offer.*** Is the prosecutor free to withdraw his offer at any time prior to defendant's entry of a guilty plea in reliance thereon? Not if there has been other detrimental reliance by the defendant, several courts have held. As concluded in *State v. Francis,* 424 P.3d 156 (Utah 2017), a plea agreement might require a defendant to perform by "[p]roviding information to government authorities, testifying for the government, confessing guilt, returning stolen property, making monetary restitution, failing to file a motion to have charges presented to a grand jury, submitting to a lie detector test and waiving certain procedural guarantees," which "have all been held to constitute acts made in detrimental reliance upon a prosecutor's breached promises."

The Supreme Court has not addressed that issue, but in *Mabry v. Johnson*, 467 U.S. 504 (1984), followed in *Kernan v. Cuero*, 138 S.Ct. 4 (2017), denied relief to a defendant who, after he accepted and pleaded guilty to a modified offer, raised an objection to the withdrawal of an earlier and better offer. The Court held that due process was not violated by the prosecutor's pre-plea withdrawal of an accepted offer when the defendant then accepted the prosecutor's substitute offer and pleaded guilty, finding that the defendant's ultimate guilty plea was voluntary and knowing and not "induced by" the withdrawn offer.

b. ***Unsuccessful recommendation.*** If the prosecutor agrees to recommend or not oppose the defendant's request for a particular sentence, and he then performs as promised but the court does not give such a sentence, is the defendant then entitled to relief? There is a split of authority at the state level. Which is the better view? What result under Fed.R.Crim.P. 11(c)?

c. ***Insufficient performance of promise to recommend.*** If the plea bargain is that the prosecutor will seek a certain disposition, how hard must he try? In *United States v. Benchimol*, 471 U.S. 453 (1985), defendant entered a plea of guilty in exchange for the prosecutor's promise to recommend probation with restitution. At the sentencing hearing, defense counsel informed the court of that fact, the prosecutor merely commented that defense counsel's statement was "an accurate representation," and the court then sentenced defendant to six years. The court of appeals held the government had breached the bargain because it "made no effort to explain its reasons for agreeing to recommend a lenient sentence but rather left an impression with the court of less-than-enthusiastic support for leniency." But the Supreme Court disagreed, concluding "it was error for the Court of Appeals to imply as a matter of law a term which the parties themselves did not agree upon." The Court emphasized that the instant case was unlike *United States v. Brown*, 500 F.2d 375 (4th Cir.1974), where "the Government attorney appearing personally in court at the time of the plea bargain expressed personal reservations about the agreement to which the Government had committed itself," and also that the government had not made an express commitment either to make the recommendation enthusiastically or to state reasons for it.

d. ***Acquittal of related offender.*** In *People v. Fisher*, 71 N.E.3d 932 (N.Y.2017), defendant, charged with hindering prosecution by hiding a gun used by Roche in a fatal shooting, pled guilty but thereafter sought to withdraw his plea after Roche was acquitted of murder, claiming that "his guilt is inextricably tied to Roche's criminal liability, rendering him innocent if Roche is acquitted." The court responded that "the elements of * * * hindering prosecution were established at defendant's plea allocution when he admitted rendering criminal assistance to Roche, who defendant further admitted had committed second-degree murder."

e. ***Excessive performance given promise not to recommend.*** If, on the other hand, the plea bargain was that the prosecutor would not recommend a sentence or would not oppose defendant's recommendations, it may be claimed that the prosecutor did too much. Compare *Jackson v. State*, 902 P.2d 1292 (Wyo.1995) (prosecutor's promise to remain silent at sentencing "did not require the prosecutor to withhold from the district court pertinent information on appellant's background and character"); with *United States v. Moscahlaidis*, 868 F.2d 1357 (3d Cir.1989) (prosecutor's promise he would "not take a position" on sentence violated when prosecutor's sentencing memo "drew conclusions about appellant's character").

Sometimes the prosecutor's promise is not to recommend a sentence of a particular type, as in *Smith v. Stegall*, 385 F.3d 993 (6th Cir.2004). After Smith's state conviction for first-degree murder was reversed on procedural grounds, Smith (age 21 at the time of the homicide) and the prosecutor entered into a plea agreement whereby he would plead guilty to second-degree murder in exchange for the prosecutor's promise not to recommend a sentence of life imprisonment. (Smith could have received a sentence of nonparolable life on the original charge, while second-degree murder is punishable "for life, or any term of years"; parole is possible on the life sentence after 15 years and on a term-of-years sentence when the lesser time set by the judge has expired.) After Smith's guilty plea the prosecutor (a) recommended a sentence of 70 to 100 years; (b) argued that "justice demands that the Defendant be sentenced for as long as possible under the law," and (c) in response to a question by the judge, stated that the victim's family members wanted Smith to receive a life sentence. Which, if any, of these actions constituted a breach of the plea bargain by the prosecutor?

f. ***Conduct inconsistent with fact "stipulation" and sentence "estimate."*** The federal sentencing guidelines have given rise to other types of plea bargain terms regarding the sentence to be imposed. For example, one possibility is that the prosecutor will stipulate to some fact (e.g., that defendant was a minor participant in the crime) which, if true, would permit reduction of defendant's offense level for sentencing purposes. While the court is not bound by such a stipulation, *United States v. Cole*, 569 F.3d 774 (7th Cir.2009), the prosecutor is in breach of the agreement if he provides contrary evidence at sentencing. *United States v. E.V.*, 500 F.3d 747 (8th Cir.2007).

Another common practice under the federal sentencing guidelines is for the plea agreement to express the parties "estimate" of what the sentence will be, typically with the cautionary proviso that the estimate is not binding upon the probation department or the court and that if the sentence turns out to be higher the defendant will not be allowed to withdraw his plea. While such a provision might appear to provide the defendant with no avenue of relief if he ends up with a higher sentence, this is not inevitably so. In *United States v. Palladino*, 347 F.3d 29 (2d Cir.2003), defendant entered a guilty plea to communicating a threat in interstate commerce, pursuant to a plea agreement estimating a sentence of 6–12 months, based "on information known * * * at this time." After the presentence report suggested the possibility of enhancement if sufficient proof were obtained of conduct by the defendant evincing an intent to carry out the previous threat, the prosecutor supplied a tape recording of defendant manifesting such intent, evidence known to the prosecutor prior to the plea agreement. Defendant was deemed deserving of relief given his "reasonable expectation * * * that the estimate, and the Government's stance at the sentencing hearing, would not be altered in the absence of new information."

g. ***Judge's receipt of evidence related to dismissed charge.*** If a defendant charged with armed robbery pleads guilty to the lesser offense of robbery as a result of plea negotiations, is the bargain broken if the judge later receives and considers evidence that the defendant was armed? Or, if the bargain is that the defendant will plead guilty to one count if other counts are dismissed, is the bargain broken if the judge receives and considers evidence on the other counts at the time of sentencing? Consider U.S.S.G. § 6B1.2(a), providing "that a plea agreement that includes the dismissal of a charge or a plea agreement not to pursue a potential charge shall not preclude the conduct underlying such charge from being considered under [the Guidelines section on relevant conduct] in connection with the count(s) of which the defendant is convicted."

3. ***Consequences of such nonperformance.*** If there has been nonperformance adverse to the defendant, how should this affect the ultimate outcome of the case? Consider:

a. ***Nullification of plea and agreement.*** In *Puckett v. United States*, p. 1414, the Court rejected the argument that when the government breaks a plea agreement this retroactively invalidates the agreement and the defendant's guilty plea.

b. ***Plea withdrawal vs. specific performance.*** If, as in *Santobello,* the defendant seeks to withdraw his plea because of nonperformance, should the prosecution be able to bar withdrawal by now performing as promised because, as held on remand, *People v. Santobello*, 331 N.Y.S.2d 776 (1972), "due process and the interest of justice will be fully served by * * * specific performance"? Or, if the defendant in *Santobello* had asked for specific performance of the bargain, should he be entitled to this remedy, or can the prosecution insist that he be limited to plea withdrawal? Is the defendant entitled to specific performance only when the "state has already received the benefit of its bargain," as in *State v. Rivers*, 931 A.2d 185 (Conn.2007), or the defendant "has already served a substantial portion of his sentence," as in *Gibson v. State*, 803 S.W.2d 316 (Tex.Cr.App.1991), or, more broadly, except when the state shows that such a choice of remedy would result in a miscarriage of justice, e.g., imposition of an illegal sentence, as concluded in *United States v. Greatwalker*, 285 F.3d 727 (8th Cir.2002)?

Broken-bargain issues seldom arise as to Fed.R.Crim.P. 11 type-(C) bargains for "a specific sentence," for there is a built-in remedy if the court rejects the agreement: the defendant must be given "an opportunity to withdraw the plea." But as in *United States v. Heredia*, 768 F.3d 1220 (9th Cir.2014), prosecutor breach can occur in that context and may entitle the defendant to a different remedy. At sentencing, the prosecutor and defendant Morales both asked for the agreed-upon sentence of six months imprisonment and three years of supervised release, but the prosecutor then made "repeated and inflammatory references to Morales' criminal history." Thereafter the court informed the parties it would not accept the agreement, but the defendant then objected to the prosecutor's breach and sought specific performance; when the court denied such relief, the defendant declined to withdraw his plea and was thereafter sentenced to 21 months. On appeal, the court noted that it had "not previously applied the principles governing the breach of plea agreements to Rule 11(c)(1)(C) agreements," but then proceeded to do so in the instant case. Concluding that "the government breached its agreement with Morales by denying him the united front for which he bargained," the court stated: "To conclude that Morales' choice not to withdraw his plea somehow negates the breach would force Morales to bear the burden of the government's error. * * * When the district court finds that the government breached a Rule 11(c)(2)(C) agreement and the defendant timely moves for specific performance, the district court must grant the motion, order the government to fulfill its obligations under the agreement, and immediately transfer the case to a different district judge to ensure that the decision to accept or reject the agreement will be untainted by the breach."

Peter Westen & David Westin, *A Constitutional Law of Remedies for Broken Plea Bargains*, 66 Calif.L.Rev. 471, 500, 512, 513 (1978), conclude: (1) that a constitutional right of specific performance cannot be based on the requirement that pleas be "voluntary," as "the subsequent failure of the inducement cannot have any effect on the desirability of the inducement at the time the defendant accepts it"; (2) that such a constitutional right cannot be based on the requirement that pleas be "intelligent," as that interest is protected "by vacating the plea"; and (3) that therefore "*Santobello* can be understood as extending constitutional protection to the personal expectations created in defendants by plea agreements with the state."

c. ***Harmless error?*** See *Puckett v. United States*, p. 1414, Note 2.

d. ***Timely cure.*** In *United States v. Purser,* 747 F.3d 284 (5th Cir.2014), defendant pled guilty to a conspiracy charge pursuant to a plea agreement in which the government promised to recommend only a 4-level increase with respect to a specific provision in the Sentencing Guidelines. The government instead recommended a 6-level increase, but before sentencing withdrew that recommendation in order to comply with the plea agreement; while the probation officer's final presentence report nonetheless included a proposed 6-level increase, the judge at sentencing declined to make such an increase, and instead provided for a 4-level increase to "eliminate any possible objection that the Government has breached the plea agreement." The defendant, seeking to appeal other aspects of his sentence despite the fact the plea bargain also included an appeal waiver, claimed the waiver was void because of the government's breach. The court of appeals acknowledged it had "previously read *Santobello* to foreclose a harmlessness inquiry," but then noted the Supreme Court opined in *Puckett* that "*some* breaches may be curable upon timely objection—for example, where the prosecution simply forgot its commitment and is willing to adhere to the [plea] agreement." The court then concluded:

"* * * Cure and harmless error stand on different footing from each other. Cure, unlike harmless error, is the removal of legal defect or correction of legal error; that is, performance of the contract. Simply put, with a cure of breach, the government abides by the plea agreement, while harmless error excuses a lapse of government performance. * * * Here, the Government cured its breach by withdrawing its objection and arguing the application of the lesser enhancement, both prior to and at sentencing, and the district court subsequently acted consistently with the plea agreement."

4. ***Significance of post-plea events.*** Sometimes either the prosecution or the defendant will invoke certain post-plea events in an effort to produce a different result. Consider:

a. ***Misconduct by the defendant.*** Consider *United States v. Gomez*, 326 F.3d 971 (8th Cir.2003) (where plea agreement included acceptance-of-responsibility sentence reduction, but at sentencing prosecutor instead obtained obstruction-of-justice sentence increase upon learning defendant had threatened co-conspirator, defendant's "bad faith" bars claim of "good faith reliance" on the agreement); *Commonwealth v. Wallace*, 870 A.2d 838 (Pa.2005) (upon revocation of probation, "the court is similarly free to impose any sentence permitted under the Sentencing Code and is not restricted by the bounds of a negotiated plea agreement between a defendant and prosecutor," which includes "the implicit promise that he will abide by the terms of the agreement and behave in accordance with the legal punishment imposed by the court").

b. ***Breach by the defendant.*** A common variety of plea bargain includes a promise by defendant to assist in the investigation or prosecution of others, which if broken will likewise serve as a basis for the prosecution to withhold the promised concessions.[i] It once was the view that "whether defendant did in fact fail to perform the condition precedent is an issue not to be finally determined unilaterally by the government, but only on the basis of adequate evidence by the Court." *United States v. Simmons,* 537 F.2d 1260 (4th Cir.1976). However, cases of this genre later arising under the federal sentencing guidelines, which per § 5K1.1 recognize that the prosecution may make a downward departure motion because of the defendant's substantial assistance to the government, typically received different treatment because of *Wade v. United States,* 504 U.S. 181 (1992), where it was held (i) that a sentencing court may not grant defendant a downward departure under § 5K1.1 in the absence of a government motion for same, and (ii) that whether to make such a motion is discretionary with the government, so that even a defendant who provides substantial assistance is not entitled to a remedy unless an unconstitutional motive underlies the government's refusal to so move. After *Wade* it became common procedure for federal prosecutors drafting such plea agreements to reserve the "sole discretion" as to whether or not to file a downward departure motion, in which case the courts conclude there is simply "no enforceable obligation" absent the unconstitutional motive mentioned in *Wade.* See, e.g., *United States v. Underwood,* 61 F.3d 306 (5th Cir.1995). But consider *United States v. Doe*, 865 F.3d 1295 (10th Cir.2017) ("In order to trigger good-faith review of a prosecutor's discretionary refusal to file a substantial-assistance motion, a defendant must first allege that the government acted in bad faith. The government may then rebut that allegation by providing its reasons for refusing to file the motion. Assuming those reasons are at least facially plausible, we hold that a defendant is only entitled to good-faith review if he or she "produce[s] evidence giving reason to question the justification [the government] advanced." (After *United States v. Booker*, p. 1159, made the

---

[i] May the prosecutor at the same time hold defendant to his plea? See, e.g., *United States v. Fernandez,* 960 F.2d 771 (9th Cir.1992) (where defendant failed to cooperate as promised in a type (C) plea agreement for 6-year sentence, prosecutor could not both hold defendant to his plea and obtain sentence over 6 years, as defendant "could only have reasonably understood" the agreement "to mean that if he failed to live up to his end of the bargain, the entire plea agreement would be null and void").

sentencing guidelines advisory, *Wade* is still followed as to 5K1.1 departures, *United States v. Crawford*, 407 F.3d 1174 (11th Cir.2005), and thus absent a motion by the government the judge may not sentence below the statutory minimum to reflect defendant's substantial assistance, *United States v. Castaing-Sosa*, 530 F.3d 1358 (11th Cir.2008), although without such a motion the judge apparently could take defendant's cooperation into account in deciding to vary beneath the advisory guidelines sentence. *United States v. Fernandez*, 443 F.3d 19 (2d Cir.2006).)

In *United States v. Jones*, 58 F.3d 688 (D.C.Cir.1995), the prosecution did not dispute defendant's claim of complete cooperation but nonetheless claimed the plea agreement was not violated, given that the prosecutor's Departure Committee did not find defendant's assistance substantial, as the plea agreement stated the prosecutor's office "retains its discretion" whether to file a downward departure motion. The court found two aspects of the case troubling: (1) "that prosecutors might dangle the suggestion of a [substantial assistance] motion in front of defendants to lure them into plea agreements, all the while knowing that the defendant's cooperation could not possibly constitute assistance valuable enough for the Departure Committee to find it 'substantial,' "; and (2) "the Government's contention at oral argument that, under the terms of its agreement with Jones, its decision not to file a departure motion can only be reviewed for constitutional infirmities proves too much," as even without any contractual arrangements those constitutional limitations exist, but here the plea agreement "provides additional protection" for defendant. "Like all contracts, it includes an implied obligation of good faith and fair dealing," meaning the defendant "was entitled to an honest and fully informed evaluation by the Committee." Thus, the court concluded, in cases such as this the prosecution should summarize for the trial court what information it gave the Departure Committee and provide any explanation given by that group for finding defendant's assistance insubstantial.

c. ***Death of victim.*** In *State v. Carpenter*, 623 N.E.2d 66 (Ohio 1993), defendant was indicted on one count of felonious assault for stabbing the victim. As a result of plea negotiations, defendant entered a guilty plea to attempted felonious assault and thus received a lesser sentence. Two years later the victim died. Upon his challenge to the subsequent murder indictment, the court concluded: "In the present case, the state had actual knowledge of the alleged victim's condition at the time of the plea agreement and knew death was possible. Nevertheless, the state accepted a plea in which it agreed to reduce the charge of felonious assault to attempted felonious assault and recommend the imposition of a minimum sentence of two to ten years. By accepting a plea to a lesser included charge, the state obtained a definite prison term for the defendant and avoided the uncertainties of trial. In exchange, the appellant anticipated that by pleading guilty to attempted felonious assault, and giving up rights which may have resulted in his acquittal, he was terminating the incident and could not be called on to account further on any charges regarding this incident. We think this expectation was entirely reasonable and justified and that the prosecutor was aware of this expectation. Therefore, if the state wanted to reserve its right to bring further charges later, should the victim die, the state should have made such a reservation a part of the record."

The dissent objected: "The majority decision clouds the plea bargaining process by adding extraneous factors for consideration. Where do we draw the line? At what point in the victim's struggle for survival is the prosecutor deemed to know that the victim will probably die, and at what point is that knowledge assumed to be wordlessly understood in the plea agreement?

"In cases like this defendants are in a position where they can be convicted of some crime prior to the victim's death. We have no reason to believe that the plea bargain applies to any charge but that one. I believe that it is contrary to sound public policy to allow prosecutors and defense counsel to make plea bargains on crimes that have not yet been committed, especially when the bargaining is tied to the victim's chances of survival."

*d. **Change in law regarding sentence.*** In HUGHES v. UNITED STATES, 138 S.Ct. 1765 (2018), Hughes, indicted on drug and gun charges, entered into a Type-C plea agreement, per Fed.R.Crim.P. 11(c)(1)(C), which stipulated he would receive a sentence of 180 months but did not refer to a particular Sentencing Guidelines range. After his guilty plea, the district court accepted the agreement and sentenced him to 180 months, calculating his Guidelines range as 188–235 months and determining that the sentence was in accordance with the Guidelines and other factors the court was required to consider. Shortly thereafter, the Sentencing commission adopted, and made retroactive, an amendment reducing Hughes sentencing range to 151–188 months, but the lower courts denied his motion for a reduced sentence because his plea agreement did not expressly rely on a Guidelines range. Kennedy, J., for six Justices, concluded:

"A sentence imposed pursuant to a Type-C agreement is no exception to the general rule that a defendant's Guidelines range is both the starting point and a basis for his ultimate sentence. Although in a Type-C agreement the Government and the defendant may agree to a specific sentence, that bargain is contingent on the district court accepting the agreement and its stipulated sentence. The Sentencing Guidelines prohibit district courts from accepting Type-C agreements without first evaluating the recommended sentence in light of the defendant's Guidelines range. So in the usual case the court's acceptance of a Type-C agreement and the sentence to be imposed pursuant to that agreement are 'based on' the defendant's Guidelines range.

"To be sure, the Guidelines are advisory only, and so not every sentence will be consistent with the relevant Guidelines range. See *Koons v. United States*, [138 S.Ct. 1783 (2018)]. For example, in *Koons* the Court today holds that five defendants' sentences were not 'based on' subsequently lowered Guidelines ranges because in that case the Guidelines and the record make clear that the sentencing judge 'discarded' their sentencing ranges 'in favor of mandatory minimums and substantial-assistance factors.' * * *

"If the Guidelines range was not 'a relevant part of the analytic framework the judge used to determine the sentence or to approve the agreement,' then the defendant's sentence was not based on that sentencing range, and relief under § 3582(c)(2) is unavailable. * * * Still, cases like *Koons* are a narrow exception to the general rule that, in most cases, a defendant's sentence will be 'based on' his Guidelines range. In federal sentencing the Guidelines are a district court's starting point, so when the Commission lowers a defendant's Guidelines range the defendant will be eligible for relief under § 3582(c)(2) absent clear demonstration, based on the record as a whole, that the court would have imposed the same sentence regardless of the Guidelines.

"[T]he Government contends that allowing defendants who enter Type-C agreements to seek reduced sentences under § 3582(c)(2) would deprive the Government of one of the benefits of its bargain—namely, the defendant's agreement to a particular sentence. But that has nothing to do with whether a defendant's sentence was based on the Sentencing Guidelines under § 3582(c)(2). And in any event, '[w]hat is at stake in this case is a defendant's eligibility for relief, not the extent of that relief.' Even if a defendant is eligible for relief, before a district court grants a reduction it must consider "the factors set forth in section 3553(a) to the extent that they are applicable' and the Commission's 'applicable policy statements.' The district court can consider the benefits the defendant gained by entering a Type-C agreement when it decides whether a reduction is appropriate (or when it determines the extent of any reduction), 'for the statute permits but does not require the court to reduce a sentence.' "

Roberts, J., for the three dissenters, objected: "With a Type-C agreement, the sentence is set by the parties, not by a judge applying the Guidelines. Far from being 'artificial,' that distinction is central to what makes a Type-C plea a Type-C plea. * * *

"The Government may well be able to limit the frustrating effects of today's decision in the long run. Going forward, it presumably can add a provision to every Type-C agreement in which the defendant agrees to waive any right to seek a sentence reduction following future Guidelines amendments."

As illustrated by *United States v. Ritchison*, 887 F.3d 365 (8th Cir.2018), the nature of the plea agreement may affect the extent to which a subsequent advantageous change in the law is deemed to require "adjustment" of the defendant's sentence. Ritchison was charged with one count of being a felon in possession of a firearm, and the indictment also alleged he had two prior felony convictions for burglary and one for robbery, but the parties entered into a Rule 11(c)(1)(C) plea agreement–that is, one in which the prosecutor "agree[s] that a specific sentence or sentencing range is the appropriate disposition of the case"–that if the Armed Career Criminal Act, 18 U.S.C.A. § 924(e)(1), applied he would receive a sentence of 15 years, but otherwise a sentence of 10 years. Because each of Ritchison's priors constituted a "violent felony" under the ACCA, his mandatory minimum sentence was 15 years and his Guidelines range was 180 to 210 months. But when, as a result of the Supreme Court's later decision in *Johnson v. United States,* 135 S.Ct. 2551 (2015), his two prior burglary convictions no longer qualified as ACCA predicate offenses, Ritchison moved to vacate his sentence pursuant to 28 U.S.C.A. § 2255. Upon being resentenced to 10 years, he objected, arguing that "the plea agreement was now null and void because it was based on a mutual mistake of the parties," and thus "requested a sentence within the revised Guidelines range" of 63 to 78 months, to no avail. On appeal, the court noted Ritchison's argument "that in prior cases, we have held that revisiting the entire sentence was an acceptable option under § 2255," but responded that in those cases "the district court was faced with resentencing a defendant who had been sentenced based on multiple convictions that were interdependent," while in the instant case the parties "entered a binding plea agreement on one count of conviction." "Under these circumstances, an appropriate correction to the sentence was to enforce the parties binding agreement, which specifically contemplated the possibility that Ritchison's criminal history might not trigger the enhanced penalties of the ACCA." As for Ritchison's alternative argument that the plea agreement was voidable because "negotiated based on a mutual mistake regarding the validity of the ACCA's residual clause," the court responded: "One contract principle we have declined to extend to the plea agreement context is the doctrine of mutual mistake."

e. Change in law regarding collateral consequence. In *Jideonwo v. INS*, 224 F.3d 692 (7th Cir.2000), the "whole point of the plea negotiations" leading to defendant's guilty plea to conspiracy to possess heroin with intent to distribute was to ensure that the sentence of defendant, a resident alien, was under five years so that he would remain eligible for the discretionary waiver of deportation permitted by statute. Thereafter Congress changed the law so as to preclude eligibility for such a waiver by anyone convicted of an aggravated felony, which that conspiracy was. Is Jideonwo entitled to some relief, and, if so, what?

5. *Return to status quo ante.*

a. Lesser-included-offense bargain, conviction overturned on appeal. In *Santobello*, the Court said that if the plea was withdrawn the two felony counts could be reinstated. Compare *People v. McMiller*, 208 N.W.2d 451 (Mich.1973), where defendant, charged with murder, pled guilty to manslaughter and then successfully appealed that conviction because of judicial errors in the plea-acceptance process, only to be charged and convicted of murder thereafter, and the court held "that upon the acceptance of a plea of guilty, as a matter of policy, the state may not thereafter charge a higher offense arising out of the same transaction," as "[b]y agreeing to a plea to a lesser offense the prosecutor thereby vouches that the ends of justice will be served by accepting a plea of guilty to that offense."

Is the *McMiller* rule constitutionally required in light of *Green v. United States*, p. 1363 and *Price v. Georgia*, p. 1363, or in light of *Blackledge v. Perry*, see p. 911? Is the answer to be found in *Bordenkircher v. Hayes*, p. 1160? Cf. *Alabama v. Smith*, p. 1405. Compare *McMiller* with the prevailing view, as expressed in *United States ex rel. Williams v. McMann*, 436 F.2d 103 (2d Cir.1970): "If the defendant's argument were to prevail, then a trial on the lesser charge only could result. The defendant would thus run no risks by this maneuver for his trial could end in acquittal, but if he should be convicted, he urges he could not receive a sentence greater than that imposed on the guilty plea to the lesser offense. This is nothing more than a 'heads-I-win-tails-you-lose' gamble. To frustrate this strategy, prosecutors would be restrained from entering plea bargains, thereby adding further to the staggering burdens of our criminal courts, and judges would become more rigid in exercising their discretion in favor of permitting withdrawal of a guilty plea. This would hardly enhance the administration of criminal justice."[j]

b. Lesser-included-offense bargain, disputed breach by defendant. In RICKETTS v. ADAMSON, 483 U.S. 1 (1987), the prosecutor sought to return to the status quo ante even though, unlike *McMiller* and *Williams*, the defendant had not in the interim overturned his guilty plea conviction of a lesser offense. Adamson, charged with first-degree murder, agreed to plead guilty to second-degree murder and testify against his accomplices in exchange for a specified prison term. The agreement expressly provided that if he refused to testify "this entire agreement is null and void and the original charge will be automatically reinstated" and the parties "returned to the positions they were in before this agreement." The court accepted the plea agreement and sentenced Adamson accordingly, and he thereafter testified against the others, who were convicted of first-degree murder. Upon reversal of those convictions and remand defendant refused to testify again on the ground that his obligation under the agreement had terminated. Adamson was then charged with first-degree murder, and after the trial court rejected his double jeopardy claim the Arizona Supreme Court vacated the second-degree murder conviction and reinstated the original charge on the ground the plea agreement contemplated use of his testimony upon retrial. The state declined Adamson's subsequent offer to testify, and he was then convicted of first-degree murder and sentenced to death. The Supreme Court, per White, J., concluded "that respondent's breach of the plea arrangement to which the parties had agreed removed the double jeopardy bar to prosecution of respondent on the first-degree murder charge. * * *

"* * * The terms of the agreement could not be clearer: in the event of respondent's breach occasioned by a refusal to testify, the parties would be returned to the *status quo ante*, in which case respondent would have *no* double jeopardy defense to waive. And, an agreement specifying that charges may be *reinstated* given certain circumstances is, at least under the provisions of this plea agreement, *precisely* equivalent to an agreement waiving a double jeopardy defense. * * *

"We are also unimpressed by the Court of Appeals' holding that there was a good faith dispute about whether respondent was bound to testify a second time and that until the extent of his obligation was decided, there could be no knowing and intelligent waiver of his double jeopardy defense. But respondent knew that if he breached the agreement he could be retried, and it is incredible to believe that he did not anticipate that the extent of his obligation would be decided

---

[j] To avoid any statute of limitations problems in this context, in the federal system it is provided by statute, 18 U.S.C.A. § 3296, that dismissed counts may be reinstated when "(1) the counts sought to be reinstated were originally filed within the applicable limitations period; (2) the counts were dismissed pursuant to a plea agreement approved by the district court under which the defendant pled guilty to other charges; (3) the guilty plea was subsequently vacated on the motion of the defendant; and (4) the United States moves to reinstate the dismissed counts within 60 days of the date on which the order vacating the plea becomes final."

Compare *People v. Shinaul*, 88 N.E.3d 760 (Ill.2017), where defendant pled guilty to aggravated use of a weapon in exchange for the state dropping all remaining charges, but four years later defendant was able to overturn his guilty plea on the ground that the applicable statute was facially unconstitutional. The state then attempted to reinstate some of the nol-prossed charges, but was unsuccessful because the statute of limitations had run. While the state objected such a result "could have a chilling effect on the plea bargaining process," the court was unsympathetic, noting "that prosecutors in other jurisdictions have contracted with defendants to avoid the statute of limitations defense."

by a court. Here he sought a construction of the agreement in the Arizona Supreme Court, and that court found that he had failed to live up to his promise. The result was that respondent was returned to the position he occupied prior to execution of the plea bargain: he stood charged with first-degree murder. Trial on that charge did not violate the Double Jeopardy Clause. *United States v. Scott* [p. 1350], supports this conclusion. * * *

"Finally, it is of no moment that following the Arizona Supreme Court's decision respondent offered to comply with the terms of the agreement. At this point, respondent's second-degree murder conviction had already been ordered vacated and the original charge reinstated. The parties did not agree that respondent would be relieved from the consequences of his refusal to testify if he were able to advance a colorable argument that a testimonial obligation was not owing. The parties could have struck a different bargain, but permitting the State to enforce the agreement the parties actually made does not violate the Double Jeopardy Clause."

Brennan, J., for the four dissenters, reasoned that because the plea agreement "does not contain an explicit waiver of all double jeopardy protection," "any finding that Adamson lost his protection against double jeopardy must be predicated on a finding that Adamson breached his agreement." Adamson's letter to the prosecutor declining to testify again upon retrial was not itself a breach, nor was it even an anticipatory repudiation of the plea agreement, as he "advanced an objectively reasonable interpretation of his contract," obligating the prosecution, as a matter "fundamental fairness imposed by the Due Process Clause," to inform him that the state interpreted the agreement differently, so that at that point either party could "seek to have the agreement construed by the court in which the plea was entered." Moreover, even assuming "that Adamson breached his plea agreement by offering an erroneous interpretation of that agreement," once the Arizona supreme court adopted the state's construction of the agreement Adamson advised the state "that he was ready and willing to testify," but the prosecution nonetheless decided to abandon the prosecution of the accomplices and instead "chose to make Adamson pay, not with a longer sentence, but with his life."

c. ***Multiple-offense bargain, conviction partially overturned on appeal.*** In *United States v. Barron*, 127 F.3d 890 (9th Cir.1997), defendant pleaded guilty to being a felon in possession of a firearm (count #1), possession of cocaine with intent to distribute (count #2), and use of a firearm during drug trafficking (count #3), and was sentenced to concurrent terms of 120 months on counts 1 and 2 and a consecutive term of 60 months on count 3, to be followed by an 8-year period of supervised release, pursuant to a plea agreement in which the government promised to refrain from bringing any other charges arising from the facts underlying the indictment, to refrain from seeking an enhanced penalty, and to recommend a 2-point reduction for acceptance of responsibility. After the subsequent decision in *Bailey v. United States*, 516 U.S. 137 (1995), holding that a conviction for use of a firearm during drug trafficking requires evidence that defendant "actively employed the firearm," Barron filed a section 2255 petition seeking only to vacate his count #3 conviction and 60-month consecutive sentence.

On the "difficult question" of the remedy in such circumstances, the court noted there were three possibilities: (1) treat the count #3 conviction and sentence in isolation, vacate them, and leave the remainder of the convictions, sentence and plea bargain intact (Barron's preference); (2) vacate the count #3 conviction, leave the other convictions intact, and resentence Barron de novo on all remaining convictions, "the most common response in the case law and * * * perhaps most appropriate where no counts were dismissed or uncharged pursuant to the plea agreement"; or (3) vacate the entire plea agreement, including the guilty pleas on all counts, and restore the parties to the *status quo ante* the agreement, which "might be appropriate where charges in the indictment were dismissed pursuant to the plea agreement or where the plea negotiations included potential charges and enhancements not included in the indictment." The court opted for the latter, reasoning that the " 'sentencing package' concept," namely, "that when a petitioner attacks one of several interdependent sentences, he in effect challenges the aggregate sentencing scheme," "applies with equal force here."[k]

Upon rehearing en banc, 172 F.3d 1153 (9th Cir.1999), that decision was reversed. As for the panel's "package" concept, the court concluded that "the argument that plea bargains must be treated as a package logically applies only in cases in which a petitioner challenges the entire plea as unknowing or involuntary." The court added that the "drafter of the plea agreement could have anticipated the contingency that has arisen and included a provision protecting the government's interest in the event that Barron's conviction was vacated." Because the government had not done so, the appellate court concluded, the district court may only "vacate the judgment and resentence Barron on the two counts of conviction that still stand."

NOTES AND QUESTIONS ON UNREALIZED EXPECTATIONS

1. ***Counsel's erroneous sentence prediction.*** What if there has been no breach of any plea agreement but the defendant seeks post-plea relief because of an "unrealized expectation," i.e., a belief that the sentence would be less severe than was actually imposed? One situation is that in which the defendant had no belief that there was a plea bargain, but yet expected a lesser sentence because of what his attorney said, as in *Fields v. Gibson,* 277 F.3d 1203 (10th Cir.2002). The defense attorneys "pulled out all the stops" and "strongly urged" Fields to enter a blind guilty plea to capital murder; "they never told him they had a promise or guarantee that by pleading guilty he would not receive a death sentence," but rather, based upon their assessment of the judge's prior "statements and actions," advised that the judge "was far more likely to sentence Fields to less than death if he pled guilty." Though Fields was thereafter sentenced to death, he was denied relief because of the well-established doctrine that neither an "erroneous sentence estimate by defense counsel" nor "a defendant's erroneous expectation, based on his attorney's erroneous estimate," renders a guilty plea involuntary.

2. ***Counsel's erroneous assertion of plea bargain.*** What then if the defendant is specifically but erroneously advised by his counsel that there exists a plea bargain including a particular commitment, as in *Ex parte Griffin,* 679 S.W.2d 15 (Tex.Crim.App.1984)? Holding that "a plea of guilty is invalid if it is induced by defense counsel's direct misrepresentation that the State has made a concession which in fact was not part of the plea agreement," the court explained: "While this is not a broken bargain under *Santobello v. New York,* it is nevertheless clear that applicant's plea was not knowing and intelligent under the standard of *Brady v. United States,*" p. 1164.

3. ***Defendant's erroneous assumption of plea bargain.*** What if defense counsel did not specifically state there was a plea agreement but defendant claims he interpreted the attorney's remarks as meaning there was one? In *United States ex rel. LaFay v. Fritz,* 455 F.2d 297 (2d Cir.1972), the district judge, applying a subjective test (adopted in an earlier case on the ground that if a defendant "believes that a promise has been made, the effect on his state of mind is exactly the same as if such a promise had in fact been made," meaning "any test of whether a person acts voluntarily is necessarily 'subjective' "), concluded in the instant case that, while no promises had actually been made by the prosecutor or court, the petitioner was entitled to relief because he believed the judge had promised a maximum of five years as a consequence of his counsel's

---

[k] In *United States v. Bunner,* 134 F.3d 1000 (10th Cir.1998), involving similar facts, the court reached essentially the same result on a principle of contract law, specifically, the frustration of purpose doctrine, which requires that "the frustration must be such that the intervening event cannot fairly be regarded as within the risks the frustrated party assumed under the contract." Once the defendant took action that relieved him of his burdens under the contract, the court concluded, this "resulted in the underlying purpose of the agreement being frustrated and the basis of the government's bargain being destroyed," and thus the government could reinstate the dismissed charges. But see Note, 72 N.Y.U.L.Rev. 841, 846 (1997), contending that the frustration of purpose doctrine "fails to provide relief and that there is, in fact, no valid basis in contract law for allowing the government to reindict."

observation that counsel had "an indication or an intimation" that "the Judge thought that five years was an adequate minimum sentence." But the court of appeals reversed. Why should that be? Is the point, as stated in *United States ex rel. Curtis v. Zelker,* 466 F.2d 1092 (2d Cir.1972), that "[t]o hold otherwise would be to provide every prisoner with an opportunity to start out with a guilty plea, with the assurance that if he should later be disappointed at the treatment accorded him he could withdraw his plea and demand a trial on the ground that at the time of his guilty plea he had labored under an erroneous impression as to what would happen to him after acceptance of the plea"?

§ 3. THE ROLE AND RESPONSIBILITY OF DEFENSE COUNSEL

MISSOURI V. FRYE

566 U.S. 134, 132 S.Ct. 1399, 182 L.Ed.2d 379 (2012).

JUSTICE KENNEDY delivered the opinion of the Court.

[Frye was charged with driving with a revoked license after three prior convictions of that offense, punishable by up to four years. In a letter to Frye's counsel, the prosecutor extended a choice of two plea bargains, the most lenient being reduction of the charge to a misdemeanor and recommendation of a 90-day sentence. Frye's attorney never advised him of the offers, and after their expiration (and after Frye had once again been arrested for the same offense) Frye pled guilty without any underlying plea agreement and was sentenced to three years in prison. At a later post-conviction hearing, Frye testified he would have entered a guilty plea to the misdemeanor had he known of the offer. On appeal, the state court held that counsel's performance was deficient and that Frye had been prejudiced.]

It is well settled that the right to the effective assistance of counsel applies to certain steps before trial. The "Sixth Amendment guarantees a defendant the right to have counsel present at all 'critical' stages of the criminal proceedings." Critical stages include arraignments, postindictment interrogations, postindictment lineups, and the entry of a guilty plea.

With respect to the right to effective counsel in plea negotiations, a proper beginning point is to discuss two cases from this Court considering the role of counsel in advising a client about a plea offer and an ensuing guilty plea: *Hill v. Lockhart,* [p. 135]; and *Padilla v. Kentucky,* [p. 1201].

Hill established that claims of ineffective assistance of counsel in the plea bargain context are governed by the two-part test set forth in *Strickland* [p. 126]. * * *

In *Hill,* the decision turned on the second part of the *Strickland* test. There, a defendant who had entered a guilty plea claimed his counsel had misinformed him of the amount of time he would have to serve before he became eligible for parole. But the defendant had not alleged that, even if adequate advice and assistance had been given, he would have elected to plead not guilty and proceed to trial. Thus, the Court found that no prejudice from the inadequate advice had been shown or alleged.

In *Padilla,* the Court again discussed the duties of counsel in advising a client with respect to a plea offer that leads to a guilty plea. * * * The Court made clear that "the negotiation of a plea bargain is a critical phase of litigation for purposes of the Sixth Amendment right to effective assistance of counsel."[a]

---

[a] Is this so without regard to *when* the negotiation occurs? Reconsider Ch. 4, § 1 B, and compare *United States v. Moody,* 206 F.3d 609 (6th Cir.2000) (Sixth Amendment right to counsel does not attach during pre-arrest, pre-indictment negotiation, as " 'critical stages' of criminal proceedings begin only with the initiation of formal criminal

In the case now before the Court the State, as petitioner, points out that the legal question presented is different from that in *Hill* and *Padilla*. In those cases the claim was that the prisoner's plea of guilty was invalid because counsel had provided incorrect advice pertinent to the plea. In the instant case, by contrast, the guilty plea that was accepted, and the plea proceedings concerning it in court, were all based on accurate advice and information from counsel. The challenge is not to the advice pertaining to the plea that was accepted but rather to the course of legal representation that preceded it with respect to other potential pleas and plea offers.

To give further support to its contention that the instant case is in a category different from what the Court considered in *Hill* and *Padilla*, the State urges that there is no right to a plea offer or a plea bargain in any event. See *Weatherford v. Bursey*, [p. 1209]. It claims Frye therefore was not deprived of any legal benefit to which he was entitled. Under this view, any wrongful or mistaken action of counsel with respect to earlier plea offers is beside the point.

The State is correct to point out that *Hill* and *Padilla* concerned whether there was ineffective assistance leading to acceptance of a plea offer, a process involving a formal court appearance with the defendant and all counsel present. Before a guilty plea is entered the defendant's understanding of the plea and its consequences can be established on the record. This affords the State substantial protection against later claims that the plea was the result of inadequate advice. At the plea entry proceedings the trial court and all counsel have the opportunity to establish on the record that the defendant understands the process that led to any offer, the advantages and disadvantages of accepting it, and the sentencing consequences or possibilities that will ensue once a conviction is entered based upon the plea. *Hill* and *Padilla* both illustrate that, nevertheless, there may be instances when claims of ineffective assistance can arise after the conviction is entered. Still, the State, and the trial court itself, have had a substantial opportunity to guard against this contingency by establishing at the plea entry proceeding that the defendant has been given proper advice or, if the advice received appears to have been inadequate, to remedy that deficiency before the plea is accepted and the conviction entered.

When a plea offer has lapsed or been rejected, however, no formal court proceedings are involved. This underscores that the plea-bargaining process is often in flux, with no clear standards or timelines and with no judicial supervision of the discussions between prosecution and defense. Indeed, discussions between client and defense counsel are privileged. So the prosecution has little or no notice if something may be amiss and perhaps no capacity to intervene in any event. And, as noted, the State insists there is no right to receive a plea offer. For all these reasons, the State contends, it is unfair to subject it to the consequences of defense counsel's inadequacies, especially when the opportunities for a full and fair trial, or, as here, for a later guilty plea albeit on less favorable terms, are preserved.

The State's contentions are neither illogical nor without some persuasive force, yet they do not suffice to overcome a simple reality. Ninety-seven percent of federal convictions and ninety-four percent of state convictions are the result of guilty pleas. The reality is that plea bargains have become so central to the administration of the criminal justice system that defense counsel

---

proceedings"); with *United States v. Wilson*, 719 F.Supp.2d 1260 (D.Or.2010) ("To conclude that petitioner had no right to counsel in evaluating the government's plea offer simply because the government had not yet obtained a formal indictment would elevate form over substance, and undermine the reliability of the pre-indictment plea negotiation process").

Moody, deemed "binding precedent," was reluctantly followed in *Turner v. United States*, 848 F.3d 767 (6th Cir.2017), noting that at least nine other circuits follow either such a bright-line rule or a rebuttal presumption that the right to counsel attaches only after formal charges are filed. In *State v. Farfan-Galvan*, 161 Idaho 610, 389 P.3d 155 (2016), noting "the practice by certain prosecuting entities of initiating contact with defendants while they are in custody in advance of their initial appearance or arraignment in order to extend plea offers which, if not accepted, expire at the time of the initial appearance or arraignment," thus "dissuading indigent defendants from seeking the assistance of court-appointed counsel to evaluate the offer," the court concluded such conduct violated the state's Rules of Professional Conduct.

have responsibilities in the plea bargain process, responsibilities that must be met to render the adequate assistance of counsel that the Sixth Amendment requires in the criminal process at critical stages. Because ours "is for the most part a system of pleas, not a system of trials," it is insufficient simply to point to the guarantee of a fair trial as a backstop that inoculates any errors in the pretrial process. * * * See also Barkow, *Separation of Powers and the Criminal Law*, 58 Stan.L.Rev. 989, 1034 (2006) ("[Defendants] who do take their case to trial and lose receive longer sentences than even Congress or the prosecutor might think appropriate, because the longer sentences exist on the books largely for bargaining purposes. This often results in individuals who accept a plea bargain receiving shorter sentences than other individuals who are less morally culpable but take a chance and go to trial"). In today's criminal justice system, therefore, the negotiation of a plea bargain, rather than the unfolding of a trial, is almost always the critical point for a defendant. * * *

The inquiry then becomes how to define the duty and responsibilities of defense counsel in the plea bargain process. This is a difficult question. "The art of negotiation is at least as nuanced as the art of trial advocacy and it presents questions farther removed from immediate judicial supervision." Bargaining is, by its nature, defined to a substantial degree by personal style. The alternative courses and tactics in negotiation are so individual that it may be neither prudent nor practicable to try to elaborate or define detailed standards for the proper discharge of defense counsel's participation in the process.

This case presents neither the necessity nor the occasion to define the duties of defense counsel in those respects, however. Here the question is whether defense counsel has the duty to communicate the terms of a formal offer to accept a plea on terms and conditions that may result in a lesser sentence, a conviction on lesser charges, or both.

This Court now holds that, as a general rule, defense counsel has the duty to communicate formal offers from the prosecution to accept a plea on terms and conditions that may be favorable to the accused. Any exceptions to that rule need not be explored here, for the offer was a formal one with a fixed expiration date. When defense counsel allowed the offer to expire without advising the defendant or allowing him to consider it, defense counsel did not render the effective assistance the Constitution requires.

Though the standard for counsel's performance is not determined solely by reference to codified standards of professional practice, these standards can be important guides. The American Bar Association recommends defense counsel "promptly communicate and explain to the defendant all plea offers made by the prosecuting attorney," A.B.A. Standards for Criminal Justice, Pleas of Guilty 14–3.2(a) (3d ed. 1999), and this standard has been adopted by numerous state and federal courts over the last 30 years. The standard for prompt communication and consultation is also set out in state bar professional standards for attorneys.

The prosecution and the trial courts may adopt some measures to help ensure against late, frivolous, or fabricated claims after a later, less advantageous plea offer has been accepted or after a trial leading to conviction with resulting harsh consequences. First, the fact of a formal offer means that its terms and its processing can be documented so that what took place in the negotiation process becomes more clear if some later inquiry turns on the conduct of earlier pretrial negotiations. Second, States may elect to follow rules that all offers must be in writing, again to ensure against later misunderstandings or fabricated charges. Third, formal offers can be made part of the record at any subsequent plea proceeding or before a trial on the merits, all to ensure that a defendant has been fully advised before those further proceedings commence. * * *

Here defense counsel did not communicate the formal offers to the defendant. As a result of that deficient performance, the offers lapsed. Under *Strickland*, the question then becomes what, if any, prejudice resulted from the breach of duty.

To show prejudice from ineffective assistance of counsel where a plea offer has lapsed or been rejected because of counsel's deficient performance, defendants must demonstrate a reasonable probability they would have accepted the earlier plea offer had they been afforded effective assistance of counsel. Defendants must also demonstrate a reasonable probability the plea would have been entered without the prosecution canceling it or the trial court refusing to accept it, if they had the authority to exercise that discretion under state law. To establish prejudice in this instance, it is necessary to show a reasonable probability that the end result of the criminal process would have been more favorable by reason of a plea to a lesser charge or a sentence of less prison time. * * *

In order to complete a showing of *Strickland* prejudice, defendants who have shown a reasonable probability they would have accepted the earlier plea offer must also show that, if the prosecution had the discretion to cancel it or if the trial court had the discretion to refuse to accept it, there is a reasonable probability neither the prosecution nor the trial court would have prevented the offer from being accepted or implemented. This further showing is of particular importance because a defendant has no right to be offered a plea, nor a federal right that the judge accept it. In at least some States, including Missouri, it appears the prosecution has some discretion to cancel a plea agreement to which the defendant has agreed. The Federal Rules, some state rules including in Missouri, and this Court's precedents give trial courts some leeway to accept or reject plea agreements. It can be assumed that in most jurisdictions prosecutors and judges are familiar with the boundaries of acceptable plea bargains and sentences. So in most instances it should not be difficult to make an objective assessment as to whether or not a particular fact or intervening circumstance would suffice, in the normal course, to cause prosecutorial withdrawal or judicial nonapproval of a plea bargain. The determination that there is or is not a reasonable probability that the outcome of the proceeding would have been different absent counsel's errors can be conducted within that framework. * * *

There appears to be a reasonable probability Frye would have accepted the prosecutor's original offer of a plea bargain if the offer had been communicated to him, because he pleaded guilty to a more serious charge, with no promise of a sentencing recommendation from the prosecutor. It may be that in some cases defendants must show more than just a guilty plea to a charge or sentence harsher than the original offer. For example, revelations between plea offers about the strength of the prosecution's case may make a late decision to plead guilty insufficient to demonstrate, without further evidence, that the defendant would have pleaded guilty to an earlier, more generous plea offer if his counsel had reported it to him. Here, however, that is not the case. * * *

The Court of Appeals failed, however, to require Frye to show that the first plea offer, if accepted by Frye, would have been adhered to by the prosecution and accepted by the trial court. Whether the prosecution and trial court are required to do so is a matter of state law, and it is not the place of this Court to settle those matters. * * *

We remand for the Missouri Court of Appeals to consider these state-law questions, because they bear on the federal question of *Strickland* prejudice. If, as the Missouri court stated here, the prosecutor could have canceled the plea agreement, and if Frye fails to show a reasonable probability the prosecutor would have adhered to the agreement, there is no *Strickland* prejudice. Likewise, if the trial court could have refused to accept the plea agreement, and if Frye fails to show a reasonable probability the trial court would have accepted the plea, there is no *Strickland* prejudice. In this case, given Frye's new offense for driving without a license on December 30, 2007, there is reason to doubt that the prosecution would have adhered to the agreement or that the trial court would have accepted it at the January 4, 2008, hearing, unless they were required by state law to do so. * * *

JUSTICE SCALIA, with whom THE CHIEF JUSTICE, JUSTICE THOMAS, and JUSTICE ALITO join, dissenting. * * *

The Court announces its holding that "as a general rule, defense counsel has the duty to communicate formal offers from the prosecution" as though that resolves a disputed point; in reality, however, neither the State nor the Solicitor General argued that counsel's performance here was adequate. The only issue was whether the inadequacy deprived Frye of his constitutional right to a fair trial. In other cases, however, it will not be so clear that counsel's plea-bargaining skills, which must now meet a constitutional minimum, are adequate. "[H]ow to define the duty and responsibilities of defense counsel in the plea bargain process," the Court acknowledges, "is a difficult question," since "[b]argaining is, by its nature, defined to a substantial degree by personal style." Indeed. What if an attorney's "personal style" is to establish a reputation as a hard bargainer by, for example, advising clients to proceed to trial rather than accept anything but the most favorable plea offers? It seems inconceivable that a lawyer could compromise his client's constitutional rights so that he can secure better deals for other clients in the future; does a hard-bargaining "personal style" now violate the Sixth Amendment? The Court ignores such difficulties, however, since "[t]his case presents neither the necessity nor the occasion to define the duties of defense counsel in those respects." Perhaps not. But it does present the necessity of confronting the serious difficulties that will be created by constitutionalization of the plea-bargaining process. It will not do simply to announce that they will be solved in the sweet by-and-by.

While the inadequacy of counsel's performance in this case is clear enough, whether it was prejudicial (in the sense that the Court's new version of *Strickland* requires) is not. The Court's description of how that question is to be answered on remand is alone enough to show how unwise it is to constitutionalize the plea-bargaining process. Prejudice is to be determined, the Court tells us, by a process of retrospective crystal-ball gazing posing as legal analysis. First of all, of course, we must estimate whether the defendant would have accepted the earlier plea bargain. Here that seems an easy question, but as the Court acknowledges, it will not always be. Next, since Missouri, like other States, permits accepted plea offers to be withdrawn by the prosecution (a reality which alone should suffice, one would think, to demonstrate that Frye had no entitlement to the plea bargain), we must estimate whether the prosecution would have withdrawn the plea offer. And finally, we must estimate whether the trial court would have approved the plea agreement. These last two estimations may seem easy in the present case, since Frye committed a new infraction before the hearing at which the agreement would have been presented; but they assuredly will not be easy in the mine run of cases.

The Court says "[i]t can be assumed that in most jurisdictions prosecutors and judges are familiar with the boundaries of acceptable plea bargains and sentences." Assuredly it can, just as it can be assumed that the sun rises in the west; but I know of no basis for the assumption. Virtually no cases deal with the standards for a prosecutor's withdrawal from a plea agreement beyond stating the general rule that a prosecutor may withdraw any time prior to, but not after, the entry of a guilty plea or other action constituting detrimental reliance on the defendant's part. And cases addressing trial courts' authority to accept or reject plea agreements almost universally observe that a trial court enjoys broad discretion in this regard. Of course after today's opinions there will be cases galore, so the Court's assumption would better be cast as an optimistic prediction of the certainty that will emerge, many years hence, from our newly created constitutional field of plea-bargaining law. Whatever the "boundaries" ultimately devised (if that were possible), a vast amount of discretion will still remain, and it is extraordinary to make a defendant's constitutional rights depend upon a series of retrospective mind-readings as to how that discretion, in prosecutors and trial judges, would have been exercised.

The plea-bargaining process is a subject worthy of regulation, since it is the means by which most criminal convictions are obtained. It happens not to be, however, a subject covered by the

Sixth Amendment, which is concerned not with the fairness of bargaining but with the fairness of conviction. * * * A legislature could solve the problems presented by these cases in a much more precise and efficient manner. It might begin, for example, by penalizing the attorneys who made such grievous errors. That type of sub-constitutional remedy is not available to the Court, which is limited to penalizing (almost) everyone else by reversing valid convictions or sentences. Because that result is inconsistent with the Sixth Amendment and decades of our precedent, I respectfully dissent.

The companion case of LAFLER v. COOPER, 566 U.S. 156 (2012), also 5–4 on similar analysis, involved a situation in which the favorable plea offer *was* "reported to the client but, on advice of counsel, was rejected," after which there "was a full and fair trial before a jury," resulting in a guilty verdict and "a sentence harsher than that offered in the rejected plea bargain." The conceded ineffective assistance was telling defendant Cooper that he could not be convicted at trial of assault with intent to murder because the victim had been shot below the waist. The Court, per Justice Kennedy, on the matter of prejudice, rejected the contention that a "fair trial wipes clean any deficient performance by defense counsel during plea bargaining," as such a claim "ignores the reality that criminal justice today is for the most part a system of pleas, not a system of trials."[b] Prejudice was shown here, the majority in *Cooper* concluded, because (i) "but for counsel's deficient performance there is a reasonable probability [respondent] and the trial court would have accepted the guilty plea" and (ii) "as a result of not accepting the plea and being convicted at trial, respondent received a minimum sentence 3 ½ times greater than he would have received under the plea."

The *Cooper* majority then turned to "the question of what constitutes an appropriate remedy" when, as in *Cooper* and *Frye*, "a defendant shows ineffective assistance of counsel has caused the rejection of a plea," thereby "leading to a trial [or different plea] and a more severe sentence" (a matter on which lower courts were divided[c]):

"Sixth Amendment remedies should be 'tailored to the injury suffered from the constitutional violation and should not unnecessarily infringe on competing interests.' Thus, a remedy must 'neutralize the taint' of a constitutional violation, while at the same time not grant a windfall to the defendant or needlessly squander the considerable resources the State properly invested in the criminal prosecution.

"The specific injury suffered by defendants who decline a plea offer as a result of ineffective assistance of counsel and then receive a greater sentence as a result of trial can come in at least one of two forms. In some cases, the sole advantage a defendant would have received under the plea is a lesser sentence. This is typically the case when the charges that would have been admitted as part of the plea bargain are the same as the charges the defendant was convicted of after trial. In this situation the court may conduct an evidentiary hearing to determine whether the defendant has shown a reasonable probability that but for counsel's errors he would have accepted the plea. If the showing is made, the court may exercise discretion in determining whether the defendant should receive the term of imprisonment the government offered in the plea, the sentence he received at trial, or something in between.

---

[b] See Note 8, p. 139, for excerpts from the majority and dissenting opinions in *Cooper* regarding this issue.

[c] In *Frye*, the state court deemed it sufficient to "undo" the subsequent conviction, after which the defendant would be allowed "either to insist on a trial or to plead guilty to any offense the prosecutor deemed it appropriate to charge," while in *Cooper* the federal district court on habeas ordered "specific performance of [respondent's] original plea agreement." A third view, as in *State v. Greuber*, 165 P.3d 1185 (Utah 2007), was that *neither* is "an appropriate remedy for the claimed harm": the *Frye* approach is wrong because "a new trial does not remedy the lost opportunity to plead," while the *Cooper* approach is wrong because under "the doctrine of separation of powers" a court lacks the power to order renewal of the plea offer "in the absence of prosecutorial misconduct."

"In some situations it may be that resentencing alone will not be full redress for the constitutional injury. If, for example, an offer was for a guilty plea to a count or counts less serious than the ones for which a defendant was convicted after trial, or if a mandatory sentence confines a judge's sentencing discretion after trial, a resentencing based on the conviction at trial may not suffice. In these circumstances, the proper exercise of discretion to remedy the constitutional injury may be to require the prosecution to reoffer the plea proposal. Once this has occurred, the judge can then exercise discretion in deciding whether to vacate the conviction from trial and accept the plea or leave the conviction undisturbed.

"In implementing a remedy in both of these situations, the trial court must weigh various factors; and the boundaries of proper discretion need not be defined here. Principles elaborated over time in decisions of state and federal courts, and in statutes and rules, will serve to give more complete guidance as to the factors that should bear upon the exercise of the judge's discretion. At this point, however, it suffices to note two considerations that are of relevance.

"First, a court may take account of a defendant's earlier expressed willingness, or unwillingness, to accept responsibility for his or her actions. Second, it is not necessary here to decide as a constitutional rule that a judge is required to prescind (that is to say disregard) any information concerning the crime that was discovered after the plea offer was made. The time continuum makes it difficult to restore the defendant and the prosecution to the precise positions they occupied prior to the rejection of the plea offer, but that baseline can be consulted in finding a remedy that does not require the prosecution to incur the expense of conducting a new trial.

"Petitioner argues that implementing a remedy here will open the floodgates to litigation by defendants seeking to unsettle their convictions. Petitioner's concern is misplaced. Courts have recognized claims of this sort for over 30 years, and yet there is no indication that the system is overwhelmed by these types of suits or that defendants are receiving windfalls as a result of strategically timed *Strickland* claims. In addition, the 'prosecution and the trial courts may adopt some measures to help ensure against late, frivolous, or fabricated claims after a later, less advantageous plea offer has been accepted or after a trial leading to conviction.' *Frye*. This, too, will help ensure against meritless claims. * * *

"As a remedy, the District Court ordered specific performance of the original plea agreement. The correct remedy in these circumstances, however, is to order the State to reoffer the plea agreement. Presuming respondent accepts the offer, the state trial court can then exercise its discretion in determining whether to vacate the convictions and resentence respondent pursuant to the plea agreement, to vacate only some of the convictions and resentence respondent accordingly, or to leave the convictions and sentence from trial undisturbed."

The four *Cooper* dissenters (also dissenting in *Frye*) were critical of the majority's remedy analysis. Scalia, J., speaking for three of them, stated:

"Why, one might ask, require a 'reoffer' of the plea agreement, and its acceptance by the defendant? If the district court finds (as a necessary element, supposedly, of *Strickland* prejudice) that Cooper would have accepted the original offer, and would thereby have avoided trial and conviction, why not skip the reoffer-and-reacceptance minuet and simply leave it to the discretion of the state trial court what the remedy shall be? The answer, of course, is camouflage. Trial courts, after all, regularly accept or reject plea agreements, so there seems to be nothing extraordinary about their accepting or rejecting the new one mandated by today's decision. But the acceptance or rejection of a plea agreement that has no status whatever under the United States Constitution is worlds apart from what this is: 'discretionary' specification of a remedy for an unconstitutional criminal conviction.

"To be sure, the Court asserts that there are 'factors' which bear upon (and presumably limit) exercise of this discretion—factors that it is not prepared to specify in full, much less assign some determinative weight. 'Principles elaborated over time in decisions of state and federal courts, and in statutes and rules' will (in the Court's rosy view) sort all that out. I find it extraordinary that 'statutes and rules' can specify the remedy for a criminal defendant's unconstitutional conviction. Or that the remedy for an unconstitutional conviction should ever be subject at all to a trial judge's discretion. Or, finally, that the remedy could ever include no remedy at all.

"I suspect that the Court's squeamishness in fashioning a remedy, and the incoherence of what it comes up with, is attributable to its realization, deep down, that there is no real constitutional violation here anyway. The defendant has been fairly tried, lawfully convicted, and properly sentenced, and any 'remedy' provided for this will do nothing but undo the just results of a fair adversarial process."

Alito, J., dissenting, who agreed with the criticisms in the Scalia dissent quoted above, added: "The Court, for its part, finds it unnecessary to define 'the boundaries of proper discretion' in today's opinion. In my view, requiring the prosecution to renew an old plea offer would represent an abuse of discretion in at least two circumstances: first, when important new information about a defendant's culpability comes to light after the offer is rejected, and, second, when the rejection of the plea offer results in a substantial expenditure of scarce prosecutorial or judicial resources."

NOTES AND QUESTIONS

1. ***Timely communication.*** *Helmedach v. Commissioner of Corrections,* 189 A.3d 1173 (Conn.2018), notes: "Although *Frye* specifically addressed only *whether* defense counsel must relay offers received, not *when* they must be relayed, the court's rationale in *Frye* strongly suggests that counsel must relay offers to plea bargain *promptly,"* since such a requirement is included in the A.B.A. Standards and state bar professional standards relied upon in *Frye*. The court then held counsel in the instant case had failed to carry out the latter duty, on the basis of these facts: Jennifer was charged with felony-murder (with a 25-year-mandatory minimum sentence), robbery and conspiracy on the allegation she had "helped her romantic partner" by luring the victim to an apartment where her partner committed the robbery and murder. At a pretrial conference the prosecutor "offered to agree" to a sentence of 15–20 years for a guilty plea to either robbery or conspiracy, but later "withdrew the offer because the victim's family opposed it." During jury selection the prosecutor made an offer of 22 years with execution suspended after 17 years, and near the start of trial made an offer of 14 years, but defendant rejected both "because the state's case had been weakened when a critical witness recanted an earlier oral statement." The prosecutor's fourth and final offer of 10 years was made after resting the state's case, just as defense counsel was about to spend much of the weekend preparing defendant for nearly three days testifying on her own behalf. Fearing this last offer would "negatively impact her testimony," defense counsel asked the prosecutor if "he could convey the offer to [her] after she testified, and the prosecutor replied 'that's okay.' " Soon after defendant's testimony was completed, defense counsel told the prosecutor that defendant "was interested in accepting the offer," but the prosecutor responded that the offer was withdrawn. Defense counsel did not attempt to enforce the agreement, and soon thereafter the jury returned a verdict of guilty on all counts, resulting in defendant receiving a sentence of 35 years. Is the villain in *Helmedach* defense counsel, the prosecutor, or both? In that connection, since the court "return[ed] the matter to the criminal court * * * to fashion * * * an appropriate remedy," what would that be?

2. ***Plea bargain renewal?*** In *Burt v. Titlow,* Note 5 infra, the federal court of appeals, upon finding ineffective assistance by counsel Toca, remanded with instructions that the prosecution must reoffer the original plea agreement to Titlow, and that the state court should "consul[t]" the plea agreement and "fashion" a remedy for the violation of Titlow's Sixth Amendment rights. While the Supreme Court found no such violation, Ginsburg, J., doubted that Toca had acted reasonably, but then explained her concurrence: "Nevertheless, one thing is crystal

clear. The prosecutor's agreement to the plea bargain hinged entirely on Titlow's willingness to testify at [Rogers's] trial. Once Titlow reneged on that half of the deal, the bargain failed. Absent an extant bargain, there was nothing to renew. In short, the prosecutor could not be ordered to 'renew' a plea proposal never offered in the first place. With the plea offer no longer alive, Titlow was convicted after a trial free from reversible error."

3. ***Waiver of counsel.*** Should waiver of counsel in a plea bargaining context be forbidden because the "right to an attorney interested in protecting the interests of the defendant is such a substantial factor in the guilty plea procedure that it is difficult to imagine a situation that would warrant a finding of an informed waiver of that right," as asserted in Note, 112 U.Pa.L.Rev. 865, 889 (1964)? What then of *Faretta v. California*, p. 99? If waiver is permitted, is it enough that it otherwise meets the standards for an "intelligent and competent" waiver, or must the defendant be told what counsel might accomplish through plea negotiations? See *Iowa v. Tovar,* p. 107.

4. ***Negotiation.*** "In the early phases of the negotiation, the defense attorney should begin with a competitive strategy, but in a cooperative style. Even though several practice manuals suggest that defense attorneys should be extremely cooperative and seek to achieve a guilty plea agreement early in plea bargaining, negotiation theory establishes at least four reasons that the defense attorney's early tactics should be competitive. First, the government's opening demand, usually characterized by overcharging and excessively long legislatively-determined prison sentences, is very competitive. [A] * * * negotiator who uses a cooperative strategy against a competitive negotiator is severely disadvantaged. Thus, a defense attorney risks exploitation if he begins negotiations with a cooperative strategy. Second, the defendant usually has low bargaining power; some social scientists recommend that the less powerful negotiator begin competitively and become more cooperative later in the negotiation. Third, it may be necessary to adopt a competitive strategy initially to communicate to the prosecutor that the attorney intends to zealously represent the client and that he will not 'cave in' because of his caseload or other personal or institutional pressures. Finally, early competitive moves often convince the client that his attorney intends to represent him vigorously; this improves client relations. * * * The defense attorney should attempt to obtain unilateral concessions from the prosecutor by asking the prosecutor about her sense of 'what the case is worth' and what charge reductions she can make, without indicating the defendant's willingness to plead to any charge at all." Donald Gifford, *A Content-Based Theory of Strategy Selection in Legal Negotiation*, 46 Ohio St.L.J. 41, 79–80 (1985).

"While the potential sentence at trial is obviously an important piece of information that defense counsel should gather before negotiating a plea bargain, it may not provide a strategic advantage if used in the negotiation as a criteria. Using the sentence at trial as criteria in the negotiation can be disadvantageous because a concrete sentence can anchor the negotiation at a point that is unfavorable for the defendant. An anchor is a number or outcome that focuses the other negotiator's attention and expectation. The power of anchors is substantial and affects even those with negotiation experience and expertise. Presuming that the plea negotiation is a discount from a the expected sentence at trial, starting from this point may anchor the negotiation at a high point and force the defense counsel to argue for downward leniency, rather than starting from a lower point and encouraging the prosecutor to bargain upwards." Wesley Oliver & Rishi Batra, *Standards of Legitimacy in Criminal Negotiations*, 20 Harv.Negotiations L.Rev. 61, 76–77 (2015).

5. ***Advice to reject plea bargain offer.*** In BURT v. TITLOW, 571 U.S. 12 (2013), Titlow and Rogers were charged with the murder of Rogers' husband. After explaining that the state's evidence could support a conviction for first-degree murder, Titlow's attorney negotiated a manslaughter plea and 7–15 year sentence in exchange for an agreement that Titlow would testify against Rogers, but three days before Rogers's trial Titlow's new counsel, Toca, demanded a lower minimum sentence and, when the prosecutor refused, advised Titlow to withdraw the guilty plea,

which Titlow did. Rogers was acquitted, but Titlow was then convicted of second-degree murder and sentenced to 20–40 years. Upon Titlow's appeal, claiming ineffective assistance of counsel, the state appellate court rejected the claim, concluding Toca's actions were reasonable in light of his client's protestations of innocence. On federal habeas review, the court of appeals ruled that the factual predicate of the state court's decision—that the plea withdrawal was based on Titlow's assertion of innocence—was an unreasonable interpretation of the factual record. The Supreme Court reversed; taking into account the "doubly deferential" standard of review applicable on federal habeas per *Cullen v. Pinholster*, p. 166, the Court concluded that the record supported the state court's finding that Toca advised withdrawal of the plea only after Titlow's proclamation of innocence. In the course of reaching that conclusion, the Court, per Alito, J., noted that the state court "correctly recognized that there is nothing inconsistent about a defendant's asserting innocence on the one hand and refusing to plead guilty to manslaughter accompanied by higher-than-normal punishment on the other. Indeed, a defendant convinced of his or her own innocence may have a particularly optimistic view of the likelihood of acquittal, and therefore be more likely to drive a hard bargain with the prosecution before pleading guilty. * * * Although a defendant's proclamation of innocence does not relieve counsel of his normal responsibilities under *Strickland*, it may affect the advice counsel gives."

Sotomayor, J., concurring, elaborated on that last statement as follows: "The first part of that statement bears emphasis: Regardless of whether a defendant asserts her innocence (or admits her guilt), her counsel must 'make an independent examination of the facts, circumstances, pleadings and laws involved and then . . . offer his informed opinion as to what plea should be entered.' *Von Moltke v. Gillies*, 332 U.S. 708, 721 (1948) (plurality opinion). A defendant possesses " 'the ultimate authority' " to determine her plea. *Florida v. Nixon*, 543 U.S. 175 (2004). But a lawyer must abide by his client's decision in this respect only after having provided the client with competent and fully informed advice, including an analysis of the risks that the client would face in proceeding to trial. Given our recognition that 'a defendant's proclamation of innocence does not relieve counsel of his normal responsibilities,' our further observation that such a proclamation 'may affect the advice counsel gives,' states only the obvious: that a lawyer's advice will always reflect the objectives of the representation, as determined by the adequately informed client."

6. ***Advice to accept plea bargain offer.*** In PREMO v. MOORE, 562 U.S. 115 (2011), Moore and two accomplices attacked Rogers, tied him up, threw him into the trunk of a car, and drove into the countryside, where Moore fatally shot him. Moore and an accomplice told two acquaintances they had intended to scare Rogers, but that the shooting was accidental, and later repeated this account to the police. On advice of counsel, Moore agreed to plead no contest to felony murder in exchange for the minimum sentence for that offense, 300 months. Moore unsuccessfully sought postconviction relief in state court, claiming he had been denied effective assistance of counsel because his attorney had not sought suppression of his confession to the police before advising Moore about the plea offer. Though he then prevailed on federal habeas corpus, the Supreme Court, applying the doubly-deferential standard of *Harrington v. Richter*, p. 151, reversed per Kennedy, J.:

"Whether before, during, or after trial, when the Sixth Amendment applies, the formulation of the standard is the same: reasonable competence in representing the accused. *Strickland,* [p. 126]. In applying and defining this standard substantial deference must be accorded to counsel's judgment. But at different stages of the case that deference may be measured in different ways.

"In the case of an early plea, neither the prosecution nor the defense may know with much certainty what course the case may take. It follows that each side, of necessity, risks consequences that may arise from contingencies or circumstances yet unperceived. The absence of a developed or an extensive record and the circumstance that neither the prosecution nor the defense case has been well defined create a particular risk that an after-the-fact assessment will run counter to the deference that must be accorded counsel's judgment and perspective when the plea was negotiated, offered, and entered.

"Prosecutors in the present case faced the cost of litigation and the risk of trying their case without Moore's confession to the police. Moore's counsel could reasonably believe that a swift plea bargain would allow Moore to take advantage of the State's aversion to these hazards. And whenever cases involve multiple defendants, there is a chance that prosecutors might convince one defendant to testify against another in exchange for a better deal. Moore's plea eliminated that possibility and ended an ongoing investigation. Delaying the plea for further proceedings would have given the State time to uncover additional incriminating evidence that could have formed the basis of a capital prosecution. It must be remembered, after all, that Moore's claim that it was an accident when he shot the victim through the temple might be disbelieved.

"It is not clear how the successful exclusion of the confession would have affected counsel's strategic calculus. The prosecution had at its disposal two witnesses able to relate another confession. True, Moore's brother and the girlfriend of his accomplice might have changed their accounts in a manner favorable to Moore. But the record before the state court reveals no reason to believe that either witness would violate the legal obligation to convey the content of Moore's confession. And to the extent that his accomplice's girlfriend had an ongoing interest in the matter, she might have been tempted to put more blame, not less, on Moore. Then, too, the accomplices themselves might have decided to implicate Moore to a greater extent than his own confession did, say by indicating that Moore shot the victim deliberately, not accidentally. All these possibilities are speculative. What counsel knew at the time was that the existence of the two witnesses to an additional confession posed a serious strategic concern.

"Moore's prospects at trial were thus anything but certain. Even now, he does not deny any involvement in the kidnaping and killing. In these circumstances, and with a potential capital charge lurking, Moore's counsel made a reasonable choice to opt for a quick plea bargain."[d]

7. ***Failure to advise on plea choice.*** Is a defendant always entitled to advice from counsel as to how he should plead? Consider *Purdy v. United States*, 208 F.3d 41 (2d Cir.2000), concluding that especially in the case of a defendant who had made "steadfast protestations of innocence," the necessity that the attorney "steer[ ] a course between the Scylla of inadequate advise and the Charybdis of coercing a plea" will sometimes make it advisable for the defense attorney to convey all the relevant facts to the defendant without adding "an explicit opinion as to whether a client should take a plea offer."

8. ***Pressure from counsel: too much or too little?*** If defense counsel thinks the prosecutor's offer is very good, how much pressure may he exert on defendant to accept it? Consider *Uresti v. Lynaugh,* 821 F.2d 1099 (5th Cir.1987), where defense counsel told defendant of a possible plea bargain of 35 years on a charge of aggravated rape and then, when defendant said he wanted to think it over a few days, defense counsel (purportedly fearing the offer might be withdrawn or that defendant would be advised to his detriment by jail-house lawyers to reject the bargain) warned defendant that if he did not accept the bargain that day the attorney would request permission of the court to withdraw and have someone appointed in his place. Defendant accepted the offer and later claimed ineffective assistance of counsel. The court concluded:

"We have here an attorney who on the record is acting in good faith and affording sound representation when he decides that a client should plead guilty under a plea bargain. The client indicates doubt. Without question, the attorney has the right to ask the court to allow him to withdraw as counsel and have another counsel appointed if the client refuses to plead. He has

---

[d] The Supreme Court took note of "the uncertainty inherent in plea negotiations described above" in also concluding the prejudice prong of *Strickland* was not met, as the "state court here reasonably could have determined that Moore would have accepted the plea agreement even if his second confession had been ruled inadmissible."

given his best advice. He thinks the insistence of his client that the case go to trial is foolhardy. He has done what he can, and he wants to ask to be relieved so another attorney more sympathetic to trial be appointed in his stead. Having that right, whether or not the court in its discretion would grant the request, it would be improper and unethical not to warn his client that this was the course of conduct he would follow if the client refused to accept the plea bargain. Withholding this information would withhold a material and significant fact from the accused when the accused was undertaking to decide whether or not to accept the plea bargain."

In contrast to *Uresti,* a defendant who declines a plea offer may later complain that his attorney did not put enough pressure on him to accept it. See, e.g., *State v. Bristol,* 618 A.2d 1290 (Vt.1992) (while defense "counsel has a duty to communicate to a client not only the terms of a plea bargain offer, but also its relative merits compared to the client's chances of success at trial," no ineffective assistance of counsel here, where "the error claimed by petitioner and found by the court was not a failure to inform, but a failure to aggressively pursue a plea bargain with petitioner after the latter rejected it").

9. *Failure to seek a plea bargain.* Does it follow from *Frye* that defense counsel always (or, sometimes) has an obligation to sound out the prosecutor as to what concessions would be granted in exchange for a plea of guilty by his client? In *United States ex rel. Tillman v. Alldredge,* 350 F.Supp. 189 (E.D.Pa.1972), petitioner, convicted after a plea of not guilty and sentenced to a mandatory minimum of five years for a narcotics sale, contended that "he was denied the effective assistance of counsel by his attorney's failure to explore the possibility of * * * a plea bargain." The court responded:

"An attorney is in a sensitive area, and he must carefully weigh a number of considerations, when he broaches the subject of a guilty plea to a client who asserts that he is innocent. The subject has been very recently considered in American Bar Association's Project on Standards for Criminal Justice. In Part VI of the Approved Draft of Standards Relating to the Prosecution Function and the Defense Function, the Committee proposed the following guidelines:

" '6.1 Duty to explore disposition without trial

* * *

" '(b) When the lawyer concludes, on the basis of full investigation and study, that under controlling law and the evidence, a conviction is probable, he should so advise the accused and seek his consent to engage in plea discussions with the prosecutor, if such appears desirable.

" '(c) Ordinarily the lawyer should secure his client's consent before engaging in plea discussions with the prosecutor.'

"Trial counsel's testimony at the hearing before me made it quite clear that Tillman, apparently insisting that he was innocent of all charges, 'didn't wish to plead guilty to anything.' Since it is Tillman's burden to establish ineffective assistance of counsel, it was incumbent on him to present evidence that trial counsel was aware, before trial, of facts and circumstances indicating that a conviction was probable. An effort by the court to elicit such evidence was thwarted by Tillman's present counsel. * * *

"In the absence of evidence as to what Tillman might have told his trial attorney about his involvement in the charges, all that appears is Tillman's apparent insistence to trial counsel that he was innocent and that he 'didn't wish to plead guilty to anything.' Under such circumstances I cannot say that counsel's failure to suggest to Tillman that he should consider entering a guilty plea constituted ineffective assistance of counsel."

Would the result have been different if Tillman had made a showing that his trial counsel knew that conviction was probable? If there had been no such showing, but Tillman had not asserted that he did not wish to plead guilty? Consider that in the 1993 third edition of the *A.B.A. Standards* § 4–6.1(b) the language quoted above was replaced by an unqualified assertion, "Defense counsel may engage in plea discussions with the prosecutor," but in the 2015 fourth edition § 4.6–1(a) was again changed, now reading: "Defense counsel should be open at every stage of a criminal matter and after consultation with the client, to discussions with the prosecutor concerning disposition of charges by guilty plea."

10. *Hard cases: innocent but convictable; guilty but acquittable.* Stolen property was found in an illegal search of Heirens' residence, and as a result of a "truth serum" illegally given to him he confessed to several burglaries and three murders, with which he was then charged. His attorneys concluded an insanity defense would not likely succeed and that there was some chance Heirens could get the death penalty. The attorneys and his parents, to whom Heirens had admitted the murders, agreed the best course was plea discussions. The prosecutor said that if Heirens would plead guilty and make a complete confession to the murders, he would recommend concurrent life sentences. Heirens agreed, and he thereafter pleaded guilty to the three murders and to 26 additional charges of various burglaries, robberies and assaults. Then, as reported in *People v. Heirens,* 122 N.E.2d 231 (Ill.1954):

"Prior to the pronouncement of sentence the prosecutor and the principal defense attorney addressed the court. The State's Attorney in his remarks acknowledged the 'co-operative assistance' of defense counsel and observed: 'The small likelihood of a successful murder prosecution of William Heirens early prompted the State's Attorney's office to seek out and obtain the co-operative help of defense counsel and, through them, that of their client. * * * Without the aid of the defense we would to this day have no answer for the death of Josephine Ross. Without their aid, to this day a great and sincere public doubt might remain as to the guilt of William Heirens in the killing of Suzanne Degnan and Frances Brown'. Petitioner's attorney then proceeded to state to the court the reasons which impelled him and his cocounsel to adopt the course they followed. He remarked in part: 'I have no memory of any case, certainly not in my time at the bar, when counsel on both sides were so perplexed as to the mental status of an individual and the causes which motivated him to do certain acts. In those cases we both sought psychiatrists in the hope that they might aid us. I must confess that at this time there exists in my mind many doubts as to this defendant's mental capacity for crime; and I believe doubt must exist in our minds as to just what the relation of cause and effect was, and how he could, in a manner so devoid of feeling, do the acts here charged and upon which the plea has been guilty. On acquiring knowledge, your Honor, of the facts we were further notified at a later date of his mental condition. We were collectively agreed that any thought on the part of the State to cause this man to forfeit his life would be unjust. It would be unfair. By the same token we were collectively agreed that any course on our part which would assist in having him returned to society would be equally unfair.' "

In later post-conviction proceedings, Heirens claimed his attorneys had not given him effective assistance because "their recommendation to plead guilty was made from motives of public duty as well as those of duty to their client." The court rejected this contention and asserted that although Heirens "was young, emotionally unstable and unusually susceptible to suggestions, he was of normal intelligence and able to make his own decisions."

In *United States v. Rogers,* 289 F.Supp. 726 (D.Conn.1968), the defendant was charged under three federal statutes for a single alleged sale of narcotics. Defendant told his retained counsel that he was innocent of the crimes charged and that he had two witnesses who could testify he did not make the sale, but admitted that he was a convicted felon and that the two witnesses were narcotic addicts. Counsel received a bill of particulars indicating that the alleged sale was made to a named government agent at a specified time and place. Thereafter, counsel learned the government would be willing to dismiss the two counts that carried a mandatory minimum sentence of five years if defendant would plead guilty to the count that carried a two year minimum. Counsel so advised the defendant, and despite the defendant's consistent protestations of innocence recommended that it was in defendant's best interest to plead guilty because the government agent's testimony would be given great credibility while the testimony of defendant and his two friends would not be believed. The attorney added that the decision was up to the defendant. Defendant entered a plea of guilty as recommended, but prior to sentencing (and just after learning that the government agent had been arrested for counterfeiting) he moved to withdraw the plea. Judge Timbers, in ruling for the defendant, observed:

"Trial counsel doubtless believed that he was acting in the best interest of his client in recommending a guilty plea. A plea bargain had been struck. It was reasonable to assume that a jury would more likely believe a government agent than a convicted felon and narcotics addicts. But to this Court it appears utterly unreasonable for counsel to recommend a guilty plea to a defendant without first cautioning him that, no matter what, he should not plead guilty unless he believed himself guilty. Most certainly such a recommendation should not be made when the defendant in the past has maintained his innocence and has stated that he has two witnesses whom counsel has not attempted to interview. It may well have been trial counsel's opinion that even if defendant were innocent he would still be convicted. Such a view is not only cynical but unwarranted. Innocent men in the past have been convicted; but such instances have been so rare and our judicial system has so many safeguards that no lawyer worthy of his profession justifiably may assume that an innocent person will be convicted."

Assuming *Rogers* to be a case in which the defendant was innocent but there was a strong probability of conviction, and *Heirens* to be a case in which the defendant was guilty but (as acknowledged by the state's attorney) there was a "small likelihood" of conviction, who acted more "unethically," Rogers' attorney or Heirens' attorneys?

11. *Conflict of interest.* In *Thomas v. State*, 551 S.E.2d 254 (S.C.2001), police obtained consent from petitioner and her husband to search their bag, found to contain over 200 grams of cocaine, for which they both were indicted. They retained the same attorney to represent them. "At the plea proceeding, the solicitor informed the plea judge that he offered petitioner and Husband a plea bargain, which consisted of the following: petitioner and Husband could each plead to trafficking in cocaine in an amount of more than one hundred grams and each receive an eight-year sentence or either petitioner or Husband could plead to the entire amount and receive the mandatory minimum sentence of twenty-five years, while the other person would be allowed to go free. The solicitor advised the plea judge that petitioner had agreed to claim responsibility for the entire amount of cocaine. The plea judge accepted her plea."

At petitioner's post-conviction hearing, where she alleged her counsel had a conflict of interest, "counsel testified petitioner and Husband requested that he represent them both. He stated he informed them they needed separate attorneys because if they began to implicate each other, there would be a conflict of interest. Counsel testified both confessed to the crime and waived the potential conflict of interest because they did not want separate attorneys. * * * He further testified he told them the better course of action would be if they both pled guilty and received less time. However, since he felt the decision was between the two of them, he allowed them to discuss the plea bargain out of his presence. After petitioner and Husband discussed it, petitioner decided she would plead to the entire amount. * * * Counsel testified he was 'shocked' petitioner agreed to be the one to plead guilty because he thought she was less culpable than Husband. He stated he did not recall discussing whether petitioner should retain her own counsel after the solicitor made the offer."

The court concluded: "To establish a violation of the Sixth Amendment right to effective counsel due to a conflict of interest arising from multiple representation, a defendant who did not object at trial must show an actual conflict of interest adversely affected his attorney's performance. An actual conflict of interest occurs where an attorney owes a duty to a party whose interests are adverse to the defendant's.

"In this case, an actual conflict of interest arose when the solicitor offered a plea bargain that would allow the charge against one spouse to be dismissed if the other spouse would plead guilty to the entire amount of the cocaine. The conflict arose because it was in each spouse's best interest for the other spouse to take the entire responsibility for the cocaine. At the moment the solicitor made the plea offer, petitioner's and Husband's interests became adverse to one another and counsel should have advised them accordingly. * * *

"Although petitioner initially waived a conflict of interest, once it became clear an actual conflict existed due to the plea bargain, counsel should have either withdrawn from representing one or both of them or acquired another waiver covering this specific conflict. To be valid, a waiver of a conflict of interest must not only be voluntary, it must be done knowingly and intelligently."

12. ***Advice re consequences of plea.*** In PADILLA v. KENTUCKY, 559 U.S. 356 (2010), the defendant, a Honduras native and long-time permanent U.S. resident, after conviction on drug charges, sought post-conviction relief on the ground his attorney provided ineffective assistance in failing to advise him that his plea of guilty made him subject to automatic deportation. The Kentucky Supreme Court denied relief, relying upon the commonly-held view that "collateral consequences are outside the scope of representation required by the Sixth Amendment." The Supreme Court, per Stevens, J., responded that it had "never applied a distinction between direct and collateral consequences to define the scope of constitutionally 'reasonable professional assistance' required under *Strickland*," p. 126, and did not have to consider whether "that distinction is appropriate" in the instant case given "the unique nature of deportation": it is "intimately related to the criminal process," and "recent changes in our immigration laws have made removal nearly an automatic result for a broad class of noncitizen offenders," making it "uniquely difficult to classify as either a direct or a collateral consequence." Taking note of the "weight of prevailing professional norms supporting the view that counsel must advise her client regarding the risk of deportation," the Court concluded (applying the first prong of *Strickland*[e]) that counsel's representation in the instant case "fell below an objective standard of reasonableness." The Court elaborated:

"In the instant case, the terms of the relevant immigration statute are succinct, clear, and explicit in defining the removal consequence for Padilla's conviction. See 8 U.S.C. § 1227(a)(2)(B)(i) ('Any alien who at any time after admission has been convicted of a violation of (or a conspiracy or attempt to violate) any law or regulation of a State, the United States or a foreign country relating to a controlled substance . . . , other than a single offense involving possession for one's own use of 30 grams or less of marijuana, is deportable'). Padilla's counsel could have easily determined that his plea would make him eligible for deportation simply from reading the text of the statute, which addresses not some broad classification of crimes but specifically commands removal for all controlled substances convictions except for the most trivial of marijuana possession offenses. Instead, Padilla's counsel provided him false assurance that his conviction would not result in his removal from this country. This is not a hard case in which to find deficiency: The consequences of Padilla's plea could easily be determined from reading the removal statute, his deportation was presumptively mandatory, and his counsel's advice was incorrect.

"Immigration law can be complex, and it is a legal specialty of its own. Some members of the bar who represent clients facing criminal charges, in either state or federal court or both, may not be well versed in it. There will, therefore, undoubtedly be numerous situations in which the deportation consequences of a particular plea are unclear or uncertain. The duty of the private

---

[e] As for *Strickland*'s second prong, prejudice, the Court left that "to the Kentucky courts to consider in the first instance."

practitioner in such cases is more limited. When the law is not succinct and straightforward (as it is in many of the scenarios posited by Justice Alito[f]), a criminal defense attorney need do no more than advise a noncitizen client that pending criminal charges may carry a risk of adverse immigration consequences. But where the deportation consequence is truly clear, as it was in this case, the duty to give correct advice is equally clear."

As for the Solicitor General's contention that *Strickland*'s application in this setting should be limited to "alleged affirmative misadvice," the Court responded "that there is no relevant difference 'between an act of commission and an act of omission' in this context."

Scalia, J., joined by Thomas, J., dissenting, stated: "I do not believe that affirmative misadvice about those consequences renders an attorney's assistance in defending against the prosecution constitutionally inadequate; or that the Sixth Amendment requires counsel to warn immigrant defendants that a conviction may render them removable. Statutory provisions can remedy these concerns in a more targeted fashion, and without producing permanent, and legislatively irreparable, overkill."

The Court later addressed the second *Strickland* prong, prejudice, in this context in LEE v. UNITED STATES, 137 S.Ct. 1958 (2017). Lee, a noncitizen lawful permanent resident charged with possessing drugs with intent to distribute, opted to accept a plea offer carrying a lower sentence than he would have faced at trial after his counsel erroneously assured him he would not be deported. Lee later was not allowed to withdraw his guilty plea because of that ineffective assistance, on the ground he could not show prejudice. The Government asked the Supreme Court to "accept a *per se* rule that a defendant with no viable defense cannot show prejudice from the denial of his right to trial," a proposition the Court, per Roberts, C.J., deemed erroneous because (1) it utilizes a categorical rule when a "case-by-case examination" is called for; and (2) "more fundamentally, * * * the inquiry as presented in *Hill v. Lockhart* [see p. 135] "focuses on a defendant's decisionmaking, which may not turn solely on the likelihood of conviction after trial." But, the Court cautioned: "Courts should not upset a plea solely because of *post hoc* assertions from a defendant about how he would have pleaded but for his attorney's deficiencies. Judges should instead look to contemporaneous evidence to substantiate a defendant's expressed preferences."

Given the "unusual circumstances of this case," the Court held Lee had "adequately demonstrated a reasonable probability that he would have rejected the plea[g] had he known that it would lead to mandatory deportation," considering that (a) Lee repeatedly asked his attorney about whether there was any risk of deportation; (b) both Lee and his counsel testified he would have gone to trial had he known the true deportation consequences; (c) Lee's responses at his plea colloquy indicated the importance he placed on deportation; (d) Lee had strong connections with the U.S., where he had lived nearly 30 years, most of his life, and had no ties to South Korea; and

[f] The reference is to the concurring opinion of Alito, J., joined by Roberts, C.J., concluding an "attorney must (1) refrain from unreasonably providing incorrect advice and (2) advise the defendant that a criminal conviction may have adverse immigration consequences and that, if the alien wants advice on this issue, the alien should consult an immigration attorney," and finding the majority's approach "problematic" because, inter alia, (i) "it will not always be easy to tell whether a particular statutory provision is 'succinct, clear, and explicit,' " and (ii) "if defense counsel must provide advice regarding only one of the many collateral consequences of a criminal conviction, many defendant are likely to be misled." (As for the majority's reliance upon "the seriousness of deportation as a consequence of a criminal plea," the concurrence countered that "criminal convictions can carry a wide variety of consequences other than conviction and sentencing" that are also serious, "but this Court has never held that a criminal defense attorney's Sixth Amendment duties extend to providing advice about such matters.")

[g] It is commonly said that the defendant has not shown prejudice where he put forth no evidence "that he would have proceeded to trial if he had known of the likely immigration consequences of his plea." *United States v. Kayode*, 777 F.3d 719 (5th Cir.2014). Compare *Rodriguez-Penton v. United States*, 905 F.3d 481 (6th Cir.2018) (defendant "may show prejudice if he can show that, had he known about the risk of adverse immigration consequences, he would have bargained for a more favorable plea," such as by "showing similar plea agreements that were reached by others charged with the same crime").

(e) it would not be irrational for someone in Lee's situation to risk an additional few years of prison time in exchange for even a rather remote chance of acquittal.

Noting that in *Padilla* the Supreme Court looked to "norms of practice as reflected in American Bar Association standards and the like," and taking account of "a proliferation of reference guides since the *Padilla* decision," the court in *Morales Diaz v. State*, 896 N.W.2d 723 (Iowa 2017), adopted A.B.A. Standards for the Defense Function § 4–5.5 (4th ed. 2015), reading in part: "After determining the client's immigration status and potential adverse consequences from the criminal proceedings, including removal, exclusion, bars to relief from removal, immigration detention, denial of citizenship, and adverse consequences to the client's immediate family, counsel should advise the client of all such potential consequences and determine with the client the best course of action for the client's interests and how to pursue it."

13. ***Advice re appeal.*** If defense counsel's efforts resulted in a negotiated plea of guilty, should he nonetheless consult with defendant about taking an appeal? In *Roe v. Flores-Ortega*, 528 U.S. 470 (2000), the Court, per O'Connor, J., agreed that "the better practice is for counsel routinely to consult with the defendant regarding the possibility of an appeal," but nonetheless rejected the lower court's "bright-line rule that counsel must always consult with the defendant regarding an appeal," instead holding "that counsel has a constitutionally-imposed duty to consult with the defendant about an appeal when there is reason to think either (1) that a rational defendant would want to appeal (for example, because there are nonfrivolous grounds for appeal), or (2) that this particular defendant reasonably demonstrated to counsel that he was interested in appealing. * * * [A] highly relevant factor in this inquiry will be whether the conviction follows a trial or a guilty plea, both because a guilty plea reduces the scope of potentially appealable issues and because such a plea may indicate that the defendant seeks an end to judicial proceedings. Even in cases where the defendant pleads guilty, the court must consider such factors as whether the defendant received the sentence bargained for as part of the plea and whether the plea expressly reserved or waived some or all appeal rights."

Relying on *Roe*, several courts (e.g., *United States v. Poindexter*, 492 F.3d 263 (4th Cir.2007)) have held that a waiver of appeal as part of a plea bargain does not relieve defense counsel of the duty to file a notice of appeal upon his client's request. That conclusion was questioned in *Nunez v. United States,* 546 F.3d 450 (7th Cir.2008), noting that while *Roe* refers to the filing as a "purely ministerial task," it is much more than that in the waiver of appeal context, unless the defendant has expressed a "willingness to give up the plea's benefits." That is, with "the waiver in force, counsel's duty to protect his client's interest militates against filing an appeal" in light of those decisions (e.g., *United States v. Erwin*, Note 4, p. 1166) holding "that, when a defendant violated a plea agreement by appealing despite a promise not to do so, the prosecutor may withdraw concessions made as part of the bargain." The *Poindexter* court added an "important caveat," namely, that such "analysis supposes that the defendant really has waived his entitlement to direct appeal," and thus when "a waiver is ambiguous, counsel would do well to file an appeal and let the court sort things out." Should the *Erwin* rule apply then?

§ 4. THE ROLE AND RESPONSIBILITY OF THE PROSECUTOR

NEWMAN V. UNITED STATES

127 U.S.App.D.C. 263, 382 F.2d 479 (D.C.Cir.1967).

BURGER, CIRCUIT JUDGE: * * *

Appellant and one Anderson were indicted for housebreaking and petty larceny. Negotiations between Anderson's counsel and an Assistant United States Attorney led to Anderson's being allowed to plead guilty to misdemeanors of petty larceny and attempted housebreaking. The United States Attorney declined to consent to the same plea for Appellant. The essence of Appellant's claim on appeal is that the United States Attorney's conduct denied him due process, "equal standing" and equal protection. * * *

The issue in this Court, of course, must be resolved on the basis of the constitutional powers of the Executive. Few subjects are less adapted to judicial review than the exercise by the Executive of his discretion in deciding when and whether to institute criminal proceedings, or what precise charge shall be made, or whether to dismiss a proceeding once brought.

The United States Attorney, under the direction and control of the Attorney General, is the attorney for the Executive, charged with faithful execution of the laws, protection of the interests of the United States, and prosecution of offenses against the United States. As such, he must have broad discretion. * * *

To say that the United States Attorney must literally treat every offense and every offender alike is to delegate him an impossible task; of course this concept would negate discretion. Myriad factors can enter into the prosecutor's decision. Two persons may have committed what is precisely the same legal offense but the prosecutor is not compelled by law, duty or tradition to treat them the same as to charges. On the contrary, he is expected to exercise discretion and common sense to the end that if, for example, one is a young first offender and the other older, with a criminal record, or one played a lesser and the other a dominant role, one the instigator and the other a follower, the prosecutor can and should take such factors into account; no court has any jurisdiction to inquire into or review his decision.

It is assumed that the United States Attorney will perform his duties and exercise his powers consistent with his oaths; and while this discretion is subject to abuse or misuse just as is judicial discretion, deviations from his duty as an agent of the Executive are to be dealt with by his superiors.

The remedy lies ultimately within the establishment where power and discretion reside. The President has abundant supervisory and disciplinary powers—including summary dismissal—to deal with misconduct of his subordinates; it is not the function of the judiciary to review the exercise of executive discretion whether it be that of the President himself or those to whom he has delegated certain of his powers.[9] * * *

---

[9] The concurring opinion would reserve judicial power to review "irrational" decisions of the prosecutor. We do our assigned task of appellate review best if we stay within our own limits, recognizing that we are neither omnipotent so as to have our mandates run without limit, nor omniscient so as to be able to direct all branches of government. The Constitution places on the Executive the duty to see that the "laws are faithfully executed" and the responsibility must reside with that power.

NOTES AND QUESTIONS

1. ***"Reason for mistrust."*** Compare Albert W. Alschuler, *The Prosecutor's Role in Plea Bargaining,* 36 U.Chi.L.Rev. 50, 105 (1968): "This argument * * * leaps from the prosecutor's traditional power to exercise a unilateral discretion to the conclusion that he may also engage in bilateral exchanges: he may trade his unilateral discretion for a defendant's waiver of his constitutional rights. Under traditional law, prosecutors are usually trusted to evaluate the extent of the public interest in particular prosecutions, but they usually have nothing to gain by agreeing to a lenient disposition for a particular defendant. In plea negotiations, however, prosecutors gain something of value for deciding that a certain punishment is adequate, and there may therefore be greater reason for mistrust."

2. ***Other refusal to bargain.*** Does *Newman* mean a court will *never* review a prosecutor's plea bargaining policies? What if Newman had established that he and Anderson played the same role in the crime and had identical backgrounds? That the prosecutor refused to bargain because he viewed Newman's attorney as an "asshole," as in *Bourexis v. Carroll County Narcotics Task Force*, 625 A.2d 391 (Md.App.1993)? That the prosecutor's refusal was based upon the victim's wishes? Compare *Commonwealth v. Latimore*, 667 N.E.2d 818 (Mass.1996), with *State v. McDonnell*, 794 P.2d 780 (Or.1990), and consider Note 6, p. 1207.

3. ***Equal bargains for unequal defendants.*** A more common problem may be that the prosecutor will offer equally lenient bargains to defendants whose situations are only superficially similar because "of inadequate knowledge of the facts, either as to the crime itself or the defendant's background, on the part of the prosecutor who negotiates the guilty plea. Under the pressure of a heavy, time-consuming caseload, the prosecutor may easily be seduced at an early stage of the proceedings, before such facts are more fully developed, by the offer of a quick guilty plea in exchange for a light sentence, only to discover too late that the offense, or the offender, was far more serious than originally thought." Arnold Enker, in *Task Force Report, The Courts* at 110–11. What is the solution?

4. ***Limits on downcharging?*** The old (and certainly pre-*Lawrence v. Texas*) wheeze about the man charged with sodomy who was allowed to cop a plea to violating section 837 of the Traffic Code ("Following Too Close") raises the question of just how far afield the ethical prosecutor may roam when engaged in charge bargaining. Consider *Iowa Supreme Court Attorney Disciplinary Board v. Howe*, 706 N.W.2d 360 (Iowa 2005), where prosecutor Howe was charged by the Board with having violated, on 174 like occasions, the state Code of Professional Responsibility, DR 7–103(A), stating that a prosecutor "shall not institute or cause to be instituted criminal charges when the lawyer knows or it is obvious that the charges are not supported by probable cause." On each occasion, following the established practice of his predecessor, Howe reduced a charge of a misdemeanor moving traffic violation to a charge of violating the "cowl-lamp statute, a remnant from a long-ago era" requiring side lights on the fenders, though "vehicles have not been equipped with cowl or fender lamps 'for a considerable number of years.'" These charge reductions "were made as part of plea bargains with the defendants," and such an "agreement was generally sought by the defendant to avoid an adverse impact on the defendant's license or auto insurance." In concluding that violation of the above-quoted provision had been proved and that it warranted Howe's suspension from the practice of law, the court commented (i) that the "fact that the *original* traffic citations may have been supported by probable cause is beside the point"; (ii) that "the fact that plea bargains to lesser or related charges are authorized by our rules of criminal procedure is also irrelevant"; and (iii) that Howe was incorrect in asserting that "the purpose underlying this disciplinary rule is not implicated by the facts shown" in that "there was no overreaching * * * because the defendants agreed to the filing of these charges."

Is the *Howe* decision correct? Considering that the court reached the decision it did notwithstanding Howe's observation that "there is no Iowa case or rule requiring that there be a factual basis for guilty pleas to simple misdemeanors," then may it be said that *Howe* is unquestionably correct in those instances where a factual basis for the plea *is* required? See Note 4, p. 1219. If *Howe* is correct, would the same result be proper as to charge reductions under statutes having these titles (and matching definitions): robbery armed to robbery unarmed; burglary in the nighttime to burglary in the daytime; possession of 100 grams or more of marijuana to possession of less than 100 grams of marijuana; battery to assault (attempted battery)? Is a guilty plea obtained as a result of charging in violation of *Howe* open to subsequent challenge by the defendant? Consider *Woods v. State,* 958 P.2d 91 (Nev.1998) (defendant, having "voluntarily entered into the plea agreement and accepted its attendant benefits * * * is now estopped from challenging the lawfulness of the plea agreement" under a statute prohibiting prosecutors from entering such agreement).

If *Howe* is not correct, is there some other basis upon which the above-described charge bargaining practice might be questioned? Is it that the cowl light statute has itself become irrelevant and is not otherwise enforced? See Note 7, p. 906. Is it that such bargaining is contrary to the public interest, which is best served if drivers with accumulated moving violations have their licenses suspended? Cf. *Iowa Department of Transportation v. Iowa District Court*, 670 N.W.2d 114 (Iowa 2003) ("Any plea agreement entered into between the county attorney and Naber, altering a mandatory license revocation, cannot bind the DOT").

5. ***Coercive charge bargaining.*** Andrew M. Crespo, *The Hidden Law of Plea Bargaining*, 118 Colum.L.Rev. 1303, 1311–14 (2018), asserts that while a charge bargain "may sound like an actual bargain, with each party gaining, to quote the Supreme Court, a 'mutuality of advantage' from the deal, most knowledgeable observers describe it as something else: a fundamentally coercive practice (occasionally analogized to torture) that produces involuntary pleas, sometimes to crimes the defendant did not commit. The core problem is twofold. First, while defendants always want to minimize their potential sentences, prosecutors rarely want to maximize them, hoping instead to obtain only their *preferred* sentence, in the most efficient way possible. This asymmetry allows prosecutors to trade away 'extra' years of incarceration that the defendant desperately wants to avoid but that the prosecutor doesn't particularly value. As for the second problem: This free leverage is typically overwhelming, because most criminal codes authorize sentences much higher than what a typical prosecutor–or a typical person, for that matter–would actually want to see imposed in a given case. Thus, by threatening a seriously inflated set of charges and then offering to replace it with the charges that she truly desires, the prosecutor is able to control the defendant's incentive to plead guilty, and with it the outcome of any subsequent 'negotiation.' In the aggregate, prosecutors so empowered can obtain more convictions, with longer sentences, at lower costs—all preconditions for mass incarceration.

"In practice, charge manipulation involves three interrelated moves. First, the prosecutor can inflate the quantity of charges the defendant faces, by *piling on* overlapping, largely duplicative offenses—increasing with each new charge the defendant's potential sentence, his risk of conviction, and the 'sticker shock' of intimidation that accompanies a hefty charging instrument. Second, the prosecutor can achieve similar effects by inflating the substance of the charges themselves, *overreaching* beyond what the law, the evidence, or the equities of the case support. Finally, after deploying these tactics to 'jack up the threat value of trial,' the prosecutor can capitalize on the ensuing leverage by *sliding down* from her initial threat to the lower set of charges that she actually prefers. Indeed, it is the difference between the threat and the subsequent offer that constitutes the prosecutor's power: The larger the differential, the more likely the defendant is to plead guilty—whether he is in fact guilty or not."

To the extent that charge bargaining is actually or potentially regulated by law, Crespo goes on to elaborate, it is mainly by "the subconstitutional law of criminal procedure" of the particular jurisdiction, e.g., limiting charge piling by the law of joinder and severance, limiting overreaching by the law of summary dismissal, and limiting sliding down by the law of amendment and dismissal.

6. ***Judicial intervention in the public interest.*** If, as in *Newman*, the courts will not intervene on behalf of a defendant, what then of intervention in the public interest? In *In re United States*, 345 F.3d 450 (7th Cir.2003), Bitsky, a Wisconsin police officer, had assaulted an arrested person and had then tried to induce another officer to write a false arrest report justifying his use of force and had threatened still another officer in an effort to prevent her from informing on him. He was indicted on one count of violating 18 U.S.C. § 242 (deprivation of civil rights under color of law) and two counts of violating 18 U.S.C. § 1512(b)(3) (obstruction of justice). The prosecutor and Bitsky made a plea agreement under which he would plead guilty to one of the obstruction counts and the government would dismiss the other two counts. At the sentencing hearing, the district judge asked why the civil rights count, for which the sentencing range was 24–30 months, was being dropped, when the sentencing range for the count to which Bitsky had agreed to plead guilty was only 6–12 months. The prosecutor explained that his main aim was to get a felony conviction, which would bar Bitsky from remaining in law enforcement. The judge then rejected the plea agreement on the ground that it did not reflect the gravity of Bitsky's conduct, but Bitsky pled guilty to the one count nonetheless. The judge accepted the plea and sentenced Bitsky to 16 months, the top of the guidelines range. The prosecutor then moved to dismiss the other two counts, but the district judge declined to dismiss the civil rights count, prompting the government's petition for mandamus, granted by the appellate court:

"It is true that Rule 48(a) of the Federal Rules of Criminal Procedure requires leave of court for the government to dismiss an indictment, information, or complaint—or, we add, a single count of such a charging document. But the purpose, at least the principal purpose, is to protect a defendant from the government's harassing him by repeatedly filing charges and then dismissing them before they are adjudicated. *Rinaldi v. United States,* 434 U.S. 22, 29 n. 15 (1977) (per curiam). In such a case the judge might rightly condition dismissal on its being with prejudice. There is no issue of that sort here. The government wants to dismiss the civil rights count with prejudice, and that is what Bitsky wants as well. The district judge simply disagrees with the Justice Department's exercise of prosecutorial discretion. As he explained in his response to the petition for mandamus, he thinks the government has exaggerated the risk of losing at trial: 'the evidence was strong and conviction extremely likely.' The judge thus is playing U.S. Attorney. It is no doubt a position that he could fill with distinction, but it is occupied by another person. We add that this is not a case (not that it would make a difference to our analysis) in which a federal prosecutor is operating without supervision. The filing of a petition for mandamus on behalf of the federal government requires authorization by the Solicitor General of the United States.

"We are mindful of speculations in some judicial opinions that a district judge could properly deny a motion to dismiss a criminal charge even though the defendant had agreed to it. These opinions say that such a motion should be denied if it is in bad faith or contrary to the public interest, as where 'the prosecutor appears motivated by bribery, animus towards the victim, or a desire to attend a social event rather than trial.' We are unaware, however, of any appellate decision that actually upholds a denial of a motion to dismiss a charge on such a basis. That is not surprising. The Constitution's 'take Care' clause (art. II, § 3) places the power to prosecute in the executive branch, just as Article I places the power to legislate in Congress. A judge could not properly refuse to enforce a statute because he thought the legislators were acting in bad faith or that the statute disserved the public interest; it is hard to see, therefore, how he could properly refuse to dismiss a prosecution merely because he was convinced that the prosecutor was acting in bad faith or contrary to the public interest."

7. ***Victims' rights.*** "About two-thirds of the states have adopted constitutional provisions on the subject of victims' rights, and 'all 50 States have passed some form of a statutory crime

victims' bill of rights.' One type of constitutional or statutory provision is that by which an effort is made to expand the role of the victim at various critical stages of the criminal justice process. Not surprisingly, one of those stages concerns the negotiated plea of guilty, and hence two common requirements are: (1) that the prosecutor consult with the victim about any contemplated plea bargain; and (2) that the judge receiving the plea first allow the victim to communicate to the court his views about the bargain now before the court." CRIMPROC § 21.3. Regarding the federal requirements, see 18 U.S.C.A. § 3771(a), Supp. App. B.

There are limits, however, as to how far the prosecutor may go in accommodating the victim, as illustrated by *In re Flatt-Moore*, 959 N.E.2d 241 (Ind.2012), involving a professional misconduct charge against a prosecutor. One "JH" was charged with Class C felony check fraud because of insufficient funds checks totaling $68,956.91, given to "Big Rivers" as payment for agricultural products. After consultation with Big Rivers' attorney, the prosecutor offered JH a plea agreement whereby JH would be convicted of a Class A misdemeanor "on the condition that [he] agree to whatever terms and amounts Big River was demanding." That demand was for $108,501.60 by a specified date, to cover the three checks, plus a purported billing error, attorneys' fees and interest. JH accepted, but the plea agreement was thereafter withdrawn when JH failed to pay the full amount by the specified date. In finding that the prosecutor "engaged in attorney misconduct by surrendering her prosecutorial discretion in plea negotiations entirely to the pecuniary demands of the victim of the crime," the court commented:

"This is not to suggest that prosecutors may not allow crime victims to have substantial and meaningful input into plea agreements offered to the offenders at whose hands they suffered. But by giving Big Rivers unfettered veto power in the plea negotiations leading up to the First Plea Offer, Respondent entirely gave up her prosecutorial discretion to enter into what would otherwise be a fair and just resolution of the charges. If a prosecutor puts the conditions for resolving similar crimes entirely in the hands of the victims, defendants whose victims are unreasonable or vindictive cannot receive the same consideration as defendants whose victims are reasonable in their demands. At the very least, such a practice gives the appearance that resolution of criminal charges could turn on the whims of victims rather than the equities of each case."

Consider Albert W. Alschuler, *Plea Bargaining and the Death Penalty*, 58 DePaul L.Rev. 671, 677 (2009), noting that "many prosecutors have delegated de facto control of the state's most awesome penalty to private parties, the victims' families. The attitudes of these families range from adamant opposition to the death penalty to insistence that death is the only appropriate punishment and that prosecutors should not bargain about it. People who would be immediately disqualified from serving on a defendant's jury direct the government's power to decide whether he will live or die. Deferring to survivors makes application of the death penalty more arbitrary."

UNITED STATES V. RUIZ

536 U.S. 622, 122 S.Ct. 2450, 153 L.Ed.2d 586 (2002).

JUSTICE BREYER delivered the opinion of the Court. * * *

After immigration agents found 30 kilograms of marijuana in Angela Ruiz's luggage, federal prosecutors offered her what is known in the Southern District of California as a "fast track" plea bargain. That bargain—standard in that district—asks a defendant to waive indictment, trial, and an appeal. In return, the Government agrees to recommend to the sentencing judge a two-level departure downward from the otherwise applicable United States Sentencing Guidelines sentence. In Ruiz's case, a two-level departure downward would have shortened the ordinary Guidelines-specified 18-to-24-month sentencing range by 6 months, to 12-to-18 months.

The prosecutors' proposed plea agreement contains a set of detailed terms. Among other things, it specifies that "any [known] information establishing the factual innocence of the defendant" "has been turned over to the defendant," and it acknowledges the Government's "continuing duty to provide such information." At the same time it requires that the defendant "waiv[e] the right" to receive "impeachment information relating to any informants or other witnesses" as well as the right to receive information supporting any affirmative defense the defendant raises if the case goes to trial. Because Ruiz would not agree to this last-mentioned waiver, the prosecutors withdrew their bargaining offer. The Government then indicted Ruiz for unlawful drug possession. And despite the absence of any agreement, Ruiz ultimately pleaded guilty.

At sentencing, Ruiz asked the judge to grant her the same two-level downward departure that the Government would have recommended had she accepted the "fast track" agreement. The Government opposed her request, and the District Court denied it, imposing a standard Guideline sentence instead.

* * * Ruiz appealed her sentence to the United States Court of Appeals for the Ninth Circuit. The Ninth Circuit vacated the District Court's sentencing determination. The Ninth Circuit pointed out that the Constitution requires prosecutors to make certain impeachment information available to a defendant before trial. It decided that this obligation entitles defendants to receive that same information before they enter into a plea agreement. The Ninth Circuit also decided that the Constitution prohibits defendants from waiving their right to that information. And it held that the prosecutors' standard "fast track" plea agreement was unlawful because it insisted upon that waiver. * * *

The constitutional question concerns a federal criminal defendant's waiver of the right to receive from prosecutors exculpatory impeachment material—a right that the Constitution provides as part of its basic "fair trial" guarantee. See U. S. Const., Amdts. 5, 6. See also *Brady v. Maryland,* [p. 1130] (Due process requires prosecutors to "avoi[d] . . . an unfair trial" by making available "upon request" evidence "favorable to an accused . . . where the evidence is material either to guilt or to punishment"); *United States v. Agurs,* [p. 1132] (defense request unnecessary); *Kyles v. Whitley,* [p. 1139] (exculpatory evidence is evidence the suppression of which would "undermin[e] confidence in the verdict"); *Giglio v. United States,* [p. 1133] (exculpatory evidence includes "evidence affecting" witness "credibility," where the witness' "reliability" is likely "determinative of guilt or innocence").

When a defendant pleads guilty he or she, of course, forgoes not only a fair trial, but also other accompanying constitutional guarantees. *Boykin v. Alabama,* [p. 1216] (pleading guilty implicates the Fifth Amendment privilege against self-incrimination, the Sixth Amendment right to confront one's accusers, and the Sixth Amendment right to trial by jury). Given the seriousness of the matter, the Constitution insists, among other things, that the defendant enter a guilty plea that is "voluntary" and that the defendant must make related waivers "knowing[ly], intelligent[ly], [and] with sufficient awareness of the relevant circumstances and likely consequences." *Brady v. United States,* [p. 1164]; see also *Boykin.*

In this case, the Ninth Circuit in effect held that a guilty plea is not "voluntary" (and that the defendant could not, by pleading guilty, waive his right to a fair trial) unless the prosecutors first made the same disclosure of material impeachment information that the prosecutors would have had to make had the defendant insisted upon a trial. We must decide whether the Constitution requires that preguilty plea disclosure of impeachment information. We conclude that it does not.

First, impeachment information is special in relation to the *fairness of a trial,* not in respect to whether a plea is *voluntary* ("knowing," "intelligent," and "sufficient[ly] aware"). Of course, the more information the defendant has, the more aware he is of the likely consequences of a plea, waiver, or decision, and the wiser that decision will likely be. But the Constitution does not require the prosecutor to share all useful information with the defendant. *Weatherford v. Bursey,* 429 U.S.

545 (1977) ("There is no general constitutional right to discovery in a criminal case"). And the law ordinarily considers a waiver knowing, intelligent, and sufficiently aware if the defendant fully understands the nature of the right and how it would likely apply *in general* in the circumstances—even though the defendant may not know the *specific detailed* consequences of invoking it. A defendant, for example, may waive his right to remain silent, his right to a jury trial, or his right to counsel even if the defendant does not know the specific questions the authorities intend to ask, who will likely serve on the jury, or the particular lawyer the State might otherwise provide. Cf. *Colorado v. Spring,* [p. 590] (Fifth Amendment privilege against self-incrimination waived when defendant received standard *Miranda* warnings regarding the nature of the right but not told the specific interrogation questions to be asked).

It is particularly difficult to characterize impeachment information as critical information of which the defendant must always be aware prior to pleading guilty given the random way in which such information may, or may not, help a particular defendant. The degree of help that impeachment information can provide will depend upon the defendant's own independent knowledge of the prosecution's potential case—a matter that the Constitution does not require prosecutors to disclose.

Second, we have found no legal authority embodied either in this Court's past cases or in cases from other circuits that provide significant support for the Ninth Circuit's decision. To the contrary, this Court has found that the Constitution, in respect to a defendant's awareness of relevant circumstances, does not require complete knowledge of the relevant circumstances, but permits a court to accept a guilty plea, with its accompanying waiver of various constitutional rights, despite various forms of misapprehension under which a defendant might labor. See *Brady v. United States* (defendant "misapprehended the quality of the State's case"); *ibid.* (defendant misapprehended "the likely penalties"); *ibid.* (defendant failed to "anticipate a change in the law regarding" relevant "punishments"); *McMann v. Richardson,* [p. 128] (counsel "misjudged the admissibility" of a "confession"); *United States v. Broce,* [p. 1225] (counsel failed to point out a potential defense); *Tollett v. Henderson,* [p. 1225] (counsel failed to find a potential constitutional infirmity in grand jury proceedings). It is difficult to distinguish, in terms of importance, (1) a defendant's ignorance of grounds for impeachment of potential witnesses at a possible future trial from (2) the varying forms of ignorance at issue in these cases.

Third, due process considerations, the very considerations that led this Court to find trial-related rights to exculpatory and impeachment information in *Brady* and *Giglio*, argue against the existence of the "right" that the Ninth Circuit found here. This Court has said that due process considerations include not only (1) the nature of the private interest at stake, but also (2) the value of the additional safeguard, and (3) the adverse impact of the requirement upon the Government's interests. *Ake v. Oklahoma,* [p. 176]. Here, as we have just pointed out, the added value of the Ninth Circuit's "right" to a defendant is often limited, for it depends upon the defendant's independent awareness of the details of the Government's case. And in any case, as the proposed plea agreement at issue here specifies, the Government will provide "any information establishing the factual innocence of the defendant" regardless. That fact, along with other guilty-plea safeguards, see Fed. Rule Crim. Proc. 11, diminishes the force of Ruiz's concern that, in the absence of impeachment information, innocent individuals, accused of crimes, will plead guilty. Cf. *McCarthy v. United States,* [p. 1221] (discussing Rule 11's role in protecting a defendant's constitutional rights).

At the same time, a constitutional obligation to provide impeachment information during plea bargaining, prior to entry of a guilty plea, could seriously interfere with the Government's interest in securing those guilty pleas that are factually justified, desired by defendants, and help to secure the efficient administration of justice. The Ninth Circuit's rule risks premature disclosure of Government witness information, which, the Government tells us, could "disrupt ongoing investigations" and expose prospective witnesses to serious harm. And the careful tailoring that characterizes most legal Government witness disclosure requirements suggests recognition by both Congress and the Federal Rules Committees that such concerns are valid. See, *e.g.*, 18 U. S. C. § 3432 (witness list disclosure required in capital cases three days before trial with exceptions); § 3500 (Government witness statements ordinarily subject to discovery only after testimony given); Fed. Rule Crim. Proc. 16(a)(2) (embodies limitations of 18 U. S. C. § 3500).

Consequently, the Ninth Circuit's requirement could force the Government to abandon its "general practice" of not "disclos[ing] to a defendant pleading guilty information that would reveal the identities of cooperating informants, undercover investigators, or other prospective witnesses." It could require the Government to devote substantially more resources to trial preparation prior to plea bargaining, thereby depriving the plea-bargaining process of its main resource-saving advantages. Or it could lead the Government instead to abandon its heavy reliance upon plea bargaining in a vast number—90% or more—of federal criminal cases. We cannot say that the Constitution's due process requirement demands so radical a change in the criminal justice process in order to achieve so comparatively small a constitutional benefit.

These considerations, taken together, lead us to conclude that the Constitution does not require the Government to disclose material impeachment evidence prior to entering a plea agreement with a criminal defendant.

In addition, we note that the "fast track" plea agreement requires a defendant to waive her right to receive information the Government has regarding any "affirmative defense" she raises at trial. We do not believe the Constitution here requires provision of this information to the defendant prior to plea bargaining—for most (though not all) of the reasons previously stated. That is to say, in the context of this agreement, the need for this information is more closely related to the *fairness* of a trial than to the *voluntariness* of the plea; the value in terms of the defendant's added awareness of relevant circumstances is ordinarily limited; yet the added burden imposed upon the Government by requiring its provision well in advance of trial (often before trial preparation begins) can be serious, thereby significantly interfering with the administration of the plea bargaining process. * * *

NOTES AND QUESTIONS

1. ***"Continuing duty"?*** Was inclusion in the plea bargain of the prosecutor's acknowledgment of a "continuing duty" to provide "any [known] information establishing the factual innocence of the defendant" critical to the outcome in *Ruiz*? Would the prosecutor have had such a duty even absent that acknowledgment?

2. ***Extent of impeachment category.*** Assuming the answer is yes, are "information establishing factual innocence" and "exculpatory impeachment material" mutually exclusive categories in all cases? What if the prosecutor learns but does not disclose prior to successful plea negotiations with the defendant that the purported victim and sole witness to the alleged crime (as to which defendant claims to have no independent recall because of his voluntary intoxication at the time), is a pathological liar who has on numerous past occasions made false accusations of such criminal conduct by others?

3. ***Other exculpatory information.*** After *Ruiz*, what would be the proper result in a case like *Fambo v. Smith,* 433 F.Supp. 590 (W.D.N.Y.1977), aff'd, 565 F.2d 233 (2d Cir.1977), where Fambo, charged with two counts of possession of an explosive based upon alleged possession of a tube of dynamite on Nov. 29 and Dec. 1, pleaded guilty after plea negotiations to the lesser offense of possessing an incendiary device, but it later came to light that the prosecutor had known that prior to the second possession police had removed the dynamite from the tube and replaced it with sawdust?

State v. Huebler, 275 P.3d 91 (Nev.2012), noting that "courts have split as to whether the Court's decision [in *Ruiz*] also encompasses exculpatory information," concludes: "In our opinion, the considerations that led to the decision in *Ruiz* do not lead to the same conclusion when it comes to material exculpatory information. While the value of impeachment information may depend on innumerable variables that primarily come into play at trial and therefore arguably make it less than critical information in entering a guilty plea, the same cannot be said of exculpatory information, which is special not just in relation to the fairness of a trial but also in relation to whether a guilty plea is valid and accurate. For this reason, the due-process calculus also weighs in favor of the added safeguard of requiring the State to disclose material exculpatory information before the defendant enters a guilty plea.

" * * * We therefore hold that a defendant may challenge the validity of a guilty plea based on the prosecution's failure to disclose material exculpatory information before entry of the plea. * * *

"The guilty-plea context, however, requires a different approach to the prejudice component of a *Brady* violation. Prejudice for purposes of a *Brady* violation requires a showing that the withheld evidence is 'material.' Normally, evidence is material if it 'creates a reasonable doubt.' That standard of materiality is not helpful in the guilty-plea context because the defendant has admitted guilt. In fashioning a materiality test in that context, we also must be mindful that guilty pleas are presumptively valid and that the defendant therefore bears a heavy burden when challenging the validity of a guilty plea.

"Other courts considering this issue have applied a standard of materiality that is based on the relevance of the withheld evidence to the defendant's decision to plead guilty: 'whether there is a reasonable probability that but for the failure to disclose the *Brady* material, the defendant would have refused to plead and would have gone to trial.' "

4. **Brady *vs.* Ruiz.** After *Ruiz*, what if the prosecutor learns the amount of drugs purportedly possessed by defendant was much lower than asserted in the original police report, but does not reveal this fact and instead offers the defendant a plea bargain with sentencing "concessions" that are illusory because, if defendant were *tried* and convicted of possessing such a quantity of drugs, the judge would impose such a sentence on the defendant. If the defendant accepts the bargain and pleads guilty, but later learns of the prosecutor's nondisclosure, is he entitled to relief under the *Brady* requirement that the defendant know "the actual value of any commitments made to him" (see also Note 8, p. 1169), or is that requirement trumped by *Ruiz*?

5. ***State law beyond* Ruiz.** An instance of nondisclosure that *does* fall within the *Ruiz* holding might nonetheless be deemed a basis for overturning a guilty plea on other than constitutional grounds, as in *State v. Harris*, 680 N.W.2d 737 (Wis.2004) (where under state's reciprocal discovery statute prosecutor should have disclosed to defendant before he entered his negotiated plea two weeks before scheduled trial date, in prosecution for sexual assault of child, the material exculpatory impeachment evidence that alleged victim had reported being sexually assaulted by her grandfather on a different occasion, defendant entitled to withdraw negotiated guilty plea, as the evidence could have raised serious questions about credibility of victim).

6. ***Ethical responsibility beyond* Ruiz.** Under Rule 3.8(d) of the *A.B.A. Model Rules of Professional Conduct*, a prosecutor is required to "make timely disclosure to the defense of all evidence or information known to the prosecutor that tends to negate the guilt of the accused or mitigates the offense." In assessing how this responsibility exceeds that recognized in *Ruiz*, consider the following points from *A.B.A. Standing Committee on Ethics and Professional Responsibility, Formal Opinion 09–454* (July 8, 2009): (1) "This ethical duty is separate from disclosure obligations imposed under the Constitution, statutes, procedural rules, court rules, or court orders"; (2) "Rule 3.8(d) is more demanding than the constitutional case law, in that it

requires the disclosure of evidence or information favorable to the defense without regard to the anticipated impact of the evidence or information on a trial's outcome"; (3) "this ethical duty of disclosure is not limited to admissible 'evidence,'" but "also requires disclosure of favorable 'information' * * * possible inadmissible itself"; (4) "Because the defendant's decision [whether or not to plead guilty] may be strongly influenced by defense counsel's evaluation of the strength of the prosecution's case, timely disclosure requires the prosecutor to disclose evidence and information covered by Rule 3.8(f) prior to a guilty plea proceeding"; and (5) as for whether "the prosecutor and defendant [may] agree that, as a condition of receiving leniency, the defendant will forgo evidence and information that would otherwise be provided," the "answer is 'no'"—a "defendant's consent does not absolve a prosecutor of the duty imposed by Rule 3.8(d)," and thus "a prosecutor may not solicit, accept or rely on the defendant's consent."

7. ***Prosecutor's understatement of evidence.*** What if defendant's complaint is not that he accepted a tendered plea bargain because the prosecutor withheld exculpatory evidence, but rather that he *rejected* a tendered bargain because the prosecutor significantly understated the *strength* of his case? In *Weatherford v. Bursey*, 429 U.S. 545 (1977), where defendant claimed he would have taken the prosecutor's plea offer had he known the full extent of the state's inculpatory evidence, which purportedly he did not because the prosecution had "lulled [him] into a false sense of security" and thus "denied him the opportunity * * * to consider whether plea bargaining might be the best course," the Court rather summarily dismissed that claim with the observation that "there is no constitutional right to plea bargain." In *Wooten v. Thaler*, 598 F.3d 215 (5th Cir.2010), defendant, convicted of capital murder at trial and sentenced to death, sought relief via habeas because he had rejected a plea bargain for a life sentence after his experts told him "that the prosecution's DNA evidence was faulty," which appeared to be the case from the DNA report furnished defense counsel before trial but was not the case in light of the entirety of the DNA evidence offered at trial. The court followed *Weatherford*, but emphasized that the additional evidence was "unintentionally" withheld and then noted a post-*Weatherford* "line of authority that leaves open the possibility that a defendant who is *deliberately* misled as to the full weight and import of the state's evidence might have a cognizable due process claim." Should that make a difference, or is the point, as stated in *United States v. Forrester*, 616 F.3d 929 (9th Cir.2010), that "the voluntary and intelligent requirement has never been extended to *rejections* of plea offers"?

§ 5. RECEIVING THE DEFENDANT'S PLEA; PLEA WITHDRAWAL

A. PLEADING ALTERNATIVES

1. ***Pleas available.*** When the defendant is called upon to enter his plea at arraignment, he may enter a plea of (1) not guilty; (2) guilty; (3) guilty but mentally ill (in a few jurisdictions where such a plea permits a defendant, sentenced the same way as a defendant who pleads guilty, to receive mental health treatment); (4) not guilty by reason of insanity (in a few jurisdictions where such a plea is a prerequisite to the presentation of an insanity defense at trial); or (5) nolo contendere (in the federal system and about half of the states). A plea of nolo contendere—sometimes referred to as a plea of non vult contendere or of non vult—is simply a device by which the defendant may assert that he does not want to contest the issue of guilt or innocence. Such a plea may not be entered as a matter of right, but only with the consent of the court, and it is generally the practice of courts not to consent unless the prosecutor concurs.

2. ***Effect of nolo plea.*** In most states permitting a nolo plea it has the following significance: (1) Unlike a guilty plea or a conviction after trial, such a plea may not be put into evidence in a subsequent civil action as proof that the defendant committed the offense to which he entered the plea. (2) When a nolo contendere plea has been accepted, the defendant may be

given the same sentence as if he had pleaded guilty. (3) Judgment following entry of a nolo contendere plea is a conviction, and may be admitted as such in other proceedings (e.g., to apply multiple offender penalty provisions, to deny or revoke a license because of conviction, or to claim double jeopardy in a subsequent prosecution).

3. ***Procedures.*** As for the procedures required when a federal defendant tenders a guilty plea, examine Fed.R.Crim.P. 11. State provisions are not always this elaborate. In examining the following material, consider: (i) what procedures are (or should be) constitutionally required; and (ii) what other procedures are desirable.

B. DETERMINING VOLUNTARINESS OF GUILTY PLEA AND COMPETENCY OF DEFENDANT

1. ***Voluntariness.*** When the legitimacy of plea bargaining was in doubt, the general practice was not to reveal the bargain in court. Thus, when the trial judge asked the defendant if his plea was the result of any promises, he would respond in the negative even when everyone in the courtroom knew otherwise. Most jurisdictions have now moved away from this charade, so that the voluntariness inquiry includes a determination of whether a plea agreement has been reached and, if so, what it is. See, e.g., Fed.R.Crim.P. 11(b)(2), (c).

2. ***Competency.*** Inquiry into the mental competency of a guilty-plea defendant is not routinely undertaken, but a trial court is constitutionally compelled to hold a hearing if it appears from substantial evidence that a criminal defendant is incompetent to enter a guilty plea. In *Godinez v. Moran*, 509 U.S. 389 (1993), the Court rejected the notion that competency to plead guilty must be measured by a higher standard than the competency standard for standing trial (whether the defendant has "sufficient present ability to consult with his lawyer with a reasonable degree of rational understanding" and has "a rational as well as functional understanding of the proceedings against him"), as "the decision to plead guilty is * * * not more complicated than the sum total of decisions that a defendant may be called upon to make during the course of a trial."

C. DETERMINING GUILTY PLEA IS UNDERSTANDINGLY MADE

1. ***The charge.*** Defendant, 19 years old and substantially below average intelligence, was indicted for first degree murder. His attorneys sought to have the charge reduced to manslaughter, but were only able to induce the prosecutor to reduce to second degree murder in exchange for a guilty plea. The attorneys did not tell defendant that the new charge required an intent to kill, nor was any reference made to this element at the time of defendant's plea. At sentencing, the defendant's lawyers explained his version of the offense, particularly noting that he "meant no harm to the lady" when he entered her room with a knife, but this was disputed by the prosecutor. The defendant later obtained relief via federal habeas corpus, and in HENDERSON v. MORGAN, 426 U.S. 637 (1976), the Court, per Stevens, J., affirmed, stating that "such a plea cannot support a judgment of guilt unless it was voluntary in a constitutional sense. And clearly the plea could not be voluntary in the sense that it constituted an intelligent admission that he committed the offense unless the defendant received 'real notice of the true nature of the charge against him, the first and most universally recognized requirement of due process.'

"The charge of second-degree murder was never formally made. Had it been made, it necessarily would have included a charge that respondent's assault was 'committed with a design to effect the death of the person killed.' That element of the offense might have been proved by the objective evidence even if respondent's actual state of mind was consistent with innocence or manslaughter. But even if such a design to effect death would almost inevitably have been inferred from evidence that respondent repeatedly stabbed Mrs. Francisco, it is nevertheless also true that a jury would not have been required to draw that inference. The jury would have been entitled to accept defense counsel's appraisal of the incident as involving only manslaughter in the first degree. Therefore, an admission by respondent that he killed Mrs. Francisco does not necessarily also admit that he was guilty of second-degree murder.

"There is nothing in this record that can serve as a substitute for either a finding after trial, or a voluntary admission, that respondent had the requisite intent. Defense counsel did not purport to stipulate to that fact; they did not explain to him that his plea would be an admission of that fact; and he made no factual statement or admission necessarily implying that he had such intent. In these circumstances it is impossible to conclude that his plea to the unexplained charge of second-degree murder was voluntary.

"Petitioner argues that affirmance of the Court of Appeals will invite countless collateral attacks on judgments entered on pleas of guilty, since frequently the record will not contain a complete enumeration of the elements of the offense to which an accused person pleads guilty.[18] We think petitioner's fears are exaggerated.

"Normally the record contains either an explanation of the charge by the trial judge, or at least a representation by defense counsel that the nature of the offense has been explained to the accused. Moreover, even without such an express representation, it may be appropriate to presume that in most cases defense counsel routinely explain the nature of the offense in sufficient detail to give the accused notice of what he is being asked to admit. This case is unique because the trial judge found as a fact that the element of intent was not explained to respondent. Moreover, respondent's unusually low mental capacity provides a reasonable explanation for counsel's oversight; it also forecloses the conclusion that the error was harmless beyond a reasonable doubt, for it lends at least a modicum of credibility to defense counsel's appraisal of the homicide as a manslaughter rather than a murder."

In *Bradshaw v. Stumpf*, 545 U.S. 175 (2005), where the court of appeals had held the habeas petitioner's guilty plea was invalid because he had not been informed of the aggravated murder charge's specific intent element, a unanimous Court, per O'Connor, J., disagreed: "In Stumpf's plea hearing, his attorneys represented on the record that they had explained to their client the elements of the aggravated murder charge; Stumpf himself then confirmed that this representation was true. While the court taking a defendant's plea is responsible for ensuring 'a record adequate for any review that may be later sought,' we have never held that the judge must himself explain the elements of each charge to the defendant on the record. Rather, the constitutional prerequisites of a valid plea may be satisfied where the record accurately reflects that the nature of the charge and the elements of the crime were explained to the defendant by his own, competent counsel. Where a defendant is represented by competent counsel, the court usually may rely on that counsel's assurance that the defendant has been properly informed of the nature and elements of the charge to which he is pleading guilty."

2. ***The sentence.*** Hart pled no contest to six counts of rape in exchange for deletion of the element of force from them and dismissal of 13 other counts. Hart was advised by the court "that if I chose to do so * * * I can impose maximum sentences and run those sentences consecutively, which in essence would give you penalties of 60 to 150 years," but state law "says that the maximum sentence that could be served on consecutive multiple sentences is a period of 15 years." The actual legal maximum was 75 years, and Hart was ultimately sentenced to a term of 30–75 years. On Hart's federal habeas corpus challenge, the court held in *Hart v. Marion Correctional Institution*, 927 F.2d 256 (6th Cir.1991), that his plea was not constitutionally valid, as it "was not entered with a 'sufficient awareness of the relevant circumstances and likely consequences.' "

[18] "There is no need in this case to decide whether notice of the true nature, or substance, of a charge always requires a description of every element of the offense; we assume it does not. Nevertheless, intent is such a critical element of the offense of second-degree murder that notice of that element is required."

Thus, unless he was promptly resentenced in accordance with his expectations, "he must be allowed to withdraw his plea," after which the "State may then try him under the original indictment or release him."

What if, instead, the trial judge had erred in the other direction by substantially *overstating* the possible sentence? Consider *United States v. Graves*, 98 F.3d 258 (7th Cir.1996) (plea of guilty valid notwithstanding judge's erroneous assertion good time credit not available as to one count; court says it finds no case in which defendant obtained relief because the sentence imposed was less than he was led to expect, and explains that such circumstances "will rarely induce a plea, for normally the heavier the sentence invited by the plea the less likely the defendant will be to plead rather than roll the dice for trial").

When a person convicted of the crime charged is by law ineligible for probation or parole, should the defendant be so advised before his guilty plea is accepted? "While some cases have expressed the view that eligibility and ineligibility for parole involve merely matters of 'legislative grace' rather than matters of right, and are therefore not 'consequences' of a guilty plea, other cases have rejected this view and have expressed the view that (1) the average defendant assumes that he will be eligible for parole, and (2) if a defendant, upon conviction for a particular crime, will be ineligible for parole, such a complete denial of the opportunity for him to be paroled is an inseparable part of the punishment for his crime, directly affects the duration of his incarceration, and is thus a 'consequence' of his guilty plea." Annot., 8 A.L.R.Fed. 760, 763 (1971).

3. ***Collateral consequences.*** "[M]ost jurisdictions [have] explicitly said it is not the duty of the judge to inform the defendant of collateral consequences that could prove critical to a defendant's decision to plead guilty in a particular case. * * * These consequences include, but are not limited to: future sentencing enhancements for current conviction, evidentiary of defendant's plea in later proceedings, civil actions, immigration issues, loss of right to possess firearms, right to vote, loss of public employment, loss of passport, loss of driver's or business license, inability to receive federal student loans, loss of public housing assistance, involuntary commitment, health care benefits, food stamps, and a litany of other social consequences which follow a convicted person for the rest of their life." Note, 33 Whittier L.Rev. 487, 489, 504–05 (2012).

But in *Padilla v. Kentucky*, p.1201, it is noted that "many States require trial courts to advise defendants of possible immigration consequences." Is it correct to conclude, as in *Smith v. State*, 697 S.E.2d 177 (Ga.2010), that notwithstanding *Padilla* there is no due process requirement of such judicial warnings?

4. ***Rights waived by plea.*** After Wilkins' trial for first degree murder had commenced, he pled guilty to second degree murder and was sentenced to a term of 50 years. Though the trial judge had determined that the plea was voluntary and had warned defendant that he could be sentenced to life imprisonment, Wilkins sought relief via federal habeas corpus. In *Wilkins v. Erickson*, 505 F.2d 761 (9th Cir.1974), the court stated:

"Wilkins relies upon *Boykin v. Alabama,* [395 U.S. 238 (1969)]. He contends that since he was not personally advised by the trial judge on entry of his plea that by pleading guilty he was waiving (1) his privilege against self-incrimination, (2) his right to trial by jury, and (3) his right to confront his accusers; that he was unaware of the consequences, and that his plea, therefore, was not voluntarily and intelligently made. Wilkins further argues that the failure of the trial judge to articulate these three rights on the record resulted in a 'silent' record which cannot be supplemented by a post-conviction evidentiary hearing. Accordingly, he wants the opportunity to replead.

"Wilkins relies on the following language from *Boykin:*

'We cannot presume a waiver of these three important federal rights from a silent record.

'What is at stake for an accused facing death or imprisonment demands the utmost solicitude of which courts are capable in canvassing the matter with the accused to make sure he has a full understanding of what a plea connotes and of its consequence. When the judge discharges that function, he leaves a record adequate for any review that may be later sought.'

"The district court's decision, however, is supported by Supreme Court decisions subsequent to *Boykin* and several circuits. The rigid interpretation of *Boykin* urged by Wilkins has not been adopted by the Supreme Court in subsequent decisions on voluntariness of guilty pleas. In *Brady v. United States,* [p. 1164], the Court, citing *Boykin,* upheld a guilty plea as voluntary and intelligent even though defendant had not been specifically advised of the three rights discussed in *Boykin*. The *Brady* Court clarified *Boykin* by stating, '[t]he new element added in *Boykin* was the requirement that the record must affirmatively disclose that a defendant who pleaded guilty entered his plea understandingly and voluntarily.' In *North Carolina v. Alford,* [p. 1218], the Court stated that in determining the validity of guilty pleas the 'standard was and remains whether the plea represents a voluntary and intelligent choice among the alternative courses of action open to the defendant.' Specific articulation of the *Boykin* rights is not the sine qua non of a valid guilty plea.

"* * * Accordingly, we hold that *Boykin* does not require specific articulation of the above mentioned three rights in a state proceeding."

5. ***Rights forfeited by plea.*** Quite different from the *Boykin* rights is another set of rights—those relating to the legitimate bases for taking an appeal—that are waived (or, more precisely, forfeited) by a guilty plea. See § 6 infra. But judges receiving guilty pleas are under no obligation to warn defendants of that fact. As noted in *United States v. Avila,* 733 F.3d 1258 (10th Cir.2013), the Federal "Rules do not explicitly require that the court inform a defendant that an unconditional guilty plea may limit the defendant's ability to appeal," a situation the court found "troubling." But *Avila* had to do with a judge's *mis*advice regarding the extent of a guilty plea defendant's right to appeal. The judge told defendant that if he was convicted at trial he would have the right to an "appeal," and that if he were to plead guilty and the plea was accepted, then he would "still have the right to an appeal," thus telling the defendant in effect that he "would have the same unlimited right to appeal following the entry of his plea as he would after a trial." The court held that if during a plea colloquy the court "chooses to advise the defendant concerning his right to appeal following the entry of the plea, the court must ensure that the defendant understands that his right to appeal may be limited by an unconditional guilty plea." That was not done in the instant case, so defendant was entitled to withdraw his guilty plea.

D. DETERMINING FACTUAL BASIS OF GUILTY PLEA

1. ***Manner and purpose.*** The Advisory Committee Note to Fed.R.Crim.P. 11(b)(3) states: "The court should satisfy itself, by inquiry of the defendant or the attorney for the government, or by examining the presentence report, or otherwise, that the conduct which the defendant admits constitutes the offense charged or an offense included therein to which the defendant has pleaded guilty. Such inquiry should, e.g., protect a defendant who is in the position of pleading voluntarily with an understanding of the nature of the charge but without realizing that his conduct does not actually fall within the charge." Several states have adopted a similar requirement.

2. ***Self-incrimination.*** In *Mitchell v. United States*, 526 U.S. 314 (1999), the Court focused upon the self-incrimination aspects of a factual basis inquiry and concluded: (a) because entry of a guilty plea is itself not a waiver of the privilege other than as an at-trial right lost by not standing trial, a defendant to whom a factual basis inquiry is made *could* decline to answer on Fifth Amendment grounds, but by doing so he "runs the risk the district court will find the factual basis inadequate"; (b) the guilty plea and statements made by the defendant in the plea

colloquy, including the factual basis inquiry, "are later admissible against the defendant," for example, at sentencing; and (c) the fact the defendant has made incriminating statements at the factual basis inquiry does not itself constitute a waiver of the privilege at later proceedings such as sentencing. This is so, the Court explained, because that situation is unlike the case of a witness at a single proceeding (including a defendant at trial), who "may not testify voluntarily about a subject and then invoke the privilege against self-incrimination when questioned about the details," thereby "diminishing the integrity of the factual inquiry."

3. ***Guilty plea with protestation of innocence.*** In NORTH CAROLINA v. ALFORD, 400 U.S. 25 (1970), Alford was indicted for first-degree murder, a capital offense. His appointed counsel questioned witnesses the defendant said would substantiate his claim of innocence, but these witnesses instead gave statements that strongly indicated his guilt. The attorney recommended a plea of guilty, but left the final decision to Alford. Alford thereafter pleaded guilty to second-degree murder, following which the trial court received a summary of the state's case, indicating that Alford had taken a gun from his house with the stated intention of killing the victim and had later returned with the declaration that he had carried out the killing. Alford then took the stand and testified that he had not committed the murder but that he was pleading guilty because he faced the threat of the death penalty if he did not do so. When the defendant persisted in his plea, it was accepted by the trial court. The Supreme Court, per Justice White, relied upon *Brady v. United States,* p. 1164, in concluding that Alford's desire to avoid the death penalty did not necessarily make his guilty plea involuntary, and then proceeded to consider the significance of Alford's denial of guilt:

"State and lower federal courts are divided upon whether a guilty plea can be accepted when it is accompanied by protestations of innocence and hence contains only a waiver of trial but no admission of guilt. Some courts, giving expression to the principle that '[o]ur law only authorizes a conviction where guilt is shown,' require that trial judges reject such pleas. But others have concluded that they should not 'force any defense on a defendant in a criminal case,' particularly when advancement of the defense might 'end in disaster * * *.' They have argued that, since 'guilt, or the degree of guilt, is at times uncertain and elusive * * * [a]n accused, though believing in or entertaining doubts respecting his innocence, might reasonably conclude a jury would be convinced of his guilt and that he would fare better in the sentence by pleading guilty * * *.'

"The issue in *Hudson v. United States,* 272 U.S. 451 (1926), was whether a federal court has power to impose a prison sentence after accepting a plea of *nolo contendere,* a plea by which a defendant does not expressly admit his guilt, but nonetheless waives his right to a trial and authorizes the court for purposes of the case to treat him as if he were guilty. The Court held that a trial court does have such power * * *. Implicit in the *nolo contendere* cases is a recognition that the Constitution does not bar imposition of a prison sentence upon an accused who is unwilling expressly to admit his guilt but who, faced with grim alternatives, is willing to waive his trial and accept the sentence.

" * * * The fact that [Alford's] plea was denominated a plea of guilty rather than a plea of *nolo contendere* is of no constitutional significance with respect to the issue now before us, for the Constitution is concerned with the practical consequences, not the formal categorizations of state law. Thus, while most pleas of guilty consist of both a waiver of trial and an express admission of guilt, the latter element is not a constitutional requisite to the imposition of criminal penalty. An individual accused of crime may voluntarily, knowingly, and understandingly consent to the imposition of a prison sentence even if he is unwilling or unable to admit his participation in the acts constituting the crime.

"Nor can we perceive any material difference between a plea which refuses to admit commission of the criminal act and a plea containing a protestation of innocence when, as in the instant case, a defendant intelligently concludes that his interests require entry of a guilty plea and the record before the judge contains strong evidence of actual guilt. Here the State had a strong case of first-degree murder against Alford. Whether he realized or disbelieved his guilt, he insisted on his plea because in his view he had absolutely nothing to gain by a trial and much to gain by pleading. Because of the overwhelming evidence against him, a trial was precisely what neither Alford nor his attorney desired. Confronted with the choice between a trial for first-degree murder, on the one hand, and a plea of guilty to second-degree murder, on the other, Alford quite reasonably chose the latter and thereby limited the maximum penalty to a 30-year term. When his plea is viewed in light of the evidence against him, which substantially negated his claim of innocence and which further provided a means by which the judge could test whether the plea was being intelligently entered, its validity cannot be seriously questioned. In view of the strong factual basis for the plea demonstrated by the State and Alford's clearly expressed desire to enter it despite his professed belief in his innocence, we hold that the trial judge did not commit constitutional error in accepting it.[11]"

4. ***Factual basis for a different crime.*** What if the facts show that the defendant committed a different crime and that the offense to which the plea is offered is not even a logical included offense? Consider *State v. Zhao*, 137 P.3d 835 (Wash.2006) ("a defendant can plead guilty to amended charges for which there is no factual basis, but *only* if the record establishes * * * that there at least exists a factual basis for the original charge, thereby establishing a factual basis for the plea as a whole," as "[d]oing so supports a flexible plea bargaining system through which a defendant can choose to plead guilty to a related charge that was not committed, in order to avoid near certain conviction for a greater offense"). What then of *People v. Foster,* 225 N.E.2d 200 (N.Y.1967), where defendant, charged with manslaughter in the first degree, was allowed to plead guilty to attempted manslaughter in the second degree, logically and legally impossible?

E. PLEA WITHDRAWAL GENERALLY

1. ***Timely motion.*** One means employed in an effort to "undo" a guilty plea is a motion to the trial court to withdraw the plea. Fed.R.Crim.P. 11(d), (e) permits such a motion only before sentencing, but many states (following the *former* federal approach) allow the motion thereafter as well. If the time for presenting a withdrawal motion has passed, the plea might be challenged by a timely appeal (limited to issues reflected by the record at arraignment and sentencing) or by collateral attack (typically limited to constitutional violations or other serious violations of law).

2. ***Applicable standard.*** The federal standard for presentence withdrawal, "any fair and just reason," is often used at the state level as well. As for later motions, the states typically utilize a higher standard, such as "miscarriage of justice" or "manifest injustice." As explained in *State v. Olish,* 266 S.E.2d 134 (W.Va.1980): "The basis for the distinction between these two rules is three-fold. First, once sentence is imposed, the defendant is more likely to view the plea bargain as a tactical mistake and therefore wish to have it set aside. Second, at the time the sentence is imposed, other portions of the plea bargain agreement will often be performed by the prosecutor, such as the dismissal of additional charges or the return or destruction of physical evidence, all of which may be difficult to undo if the defendant later attacks his guilty plea. Finally, a higher post-sentence standard for withdrawal is required by the settled policy of giving finality to criminal sentences which result from a voluntary and properly counseled guilty plea."

---

[11] Our holding does not mean that a trial judge must accept every constitutionally valid guilty plea merely because a defendant wishes so to plead. A criminal defendant does not have an absolute right under the Constitution to have his guilty plea accepted by the court, although the States may by statute or otherwise confer such a right. Likewise, the States may bar their courts from accepting guilty pleas from any defendants who assert their innocence. Cf. Fed.Rule Crim.Proc. 11, which gives a trial judge discretion to "refuse to accept a plea of guilty * * *." We need not now delineate the scope of that discretion.

3. ***Meaning of standards.*** Though the higher test has different meanings in different states, it is commonly treated as equivalent to the grounds for relief upon collateral attack in a post-conviction proceeding. As for the lower "fair and just reason" test, it has received different interpretations. Compare *United States v. Savage,* 561 F.2d 554 (4th Cir.1977) (any desire to withdraw the plea before sentence suffices unless the prosecution establishes it would be prejudiced by withdrawal); with *United States v. Saft,* 558 F.2d 1073 (2d Cir.1977) (there is no occasion to inquire into the matter of prejudice unless the defendant first shows good reason for being allowed to withdraw his plea). Though there remains variation at the state level, *Saft* now prevails in the federal courts.

4. ***Withdrawal before court accepts agreement.*** In *United States v. Hyde*, 520 U.S. 670 (1997), defendant and the government entered into a plea agreement whereby if defendant pleaded guilty to four of the counts in the indictment the government would dismiss the other four. The agreement was submitted to the district court, which accepted defendant's guilty plea but deferred decision on acceptance of the plea agreement pending completion of the presentence report. A month later, before sentencing and the court's decision on the plea agreement, defendant sought to withdraw his plea, but his motion was denied because he had not provided a "fair and just reason." The court of appeals reversed, reasoning that defendant had an absolute right to withdraw his guilty plea before the court accepted the plea agreement because the plea and the agreement are "inextricably bound up together." A unanimous Supreme Court, per Chief Justice Rehnquist, disagreed, noting that the court of appeals' conclusion was contradicted by what is now Fed.R.Crim.P. 11(d)(2)(A), which states the defendant may withdraw his plea as a matter of right only if "the court rejects the plea agreement" (which did not happen in the instant case). Moreover, the Court emphasized, the court of appeals' holding "debases the judicial proceeding at which a defendant pleads and the court accepts his plea" and "would degrade the otherwise serious act of pleading guilty into something akin to a move in a game of chess."

5. ***Withdrawal after court rejects agreement.*** In *United States v. Adame-Hernandez,* 763 F.3d 818 (7th Cir.2014), the parties adopted a plea agreement that (i) defendant would plead guilty to a criminal drug conspiracy, (ii) the government would drop two other charges, and (iii) the appropriate disposition would be 204 months of imprisonment plus a term of supervised release and a fine. Soon thereafter defendant entered a guilty plea to conspiracy, accepted by the judge upon the showing of a factual basis. At the sentencing hearing six months later the judge rejected the plea agreement because the proposed sentence was disparate from the sentences of codefendants, vacated defendant's earlier plea, and set the case for trial. On appeal, the court, noting that acceptance of a guilty plea is "a judicial act distinct from the acceptance of the plea agreement itself," and that once a guilty plea is accepted "the conditions under which the plea may be withdrawn are governed exclusively by Rule 11," concluded:

"Nothing in Rule 11 authorizes a district court to withdraw a defendant's guilty plea for him. Instead, '[w]here a district court accepts a plea of guilty pursuant to a plea agreement, defers acceptance of the agreement itself, and later rejects the terms of the plea agreement, it must, according to the plain language of Rule 11, "give the defendant an opportunity to withdraw the plea." ' * * * The district court had no authority under Rule 11 to withdraw Adame's plea for him. * * *

"Similarly, the court lacked the authority to withdraw Adame's plea even if he had breached some material term of the plea agreement. '[A] defendant's substantial breach of an unambiguous term of a plea agreement frees the government to rescind the deal.' It does not, however, permit the district court to rescind the plea itself and prohibit the defendant from pleading guilty"

F. SIGNIFICANCE OF NONCOMPLIANCE WITH REQUIREMENTS FOR RECEIVING GUILTY PLEA

1. ***Appeal by federal defendant.*** In McCARTHY v. UNITED STATES, 394 U.S. 459 (1969), defendant on appeal objected the trial judge failed to address him personally and determine that his plea was made voluntarily and with an understanding of the nature of the charge, as required by Rule 11. The Court rejected the government's contention that under such circumstances the government should still be allowed to prove that the defendant in fact pleaded voluntarily and with an understanding of the charge:

"From the defendant's perspective, the efficacy of shifting the burden of proof to the Government at a later voluntariness hearing is questionable. In meeting its burden, the Government will undoubtedly rely upon the defendant's statement that he desired to plead guilty and frequently a statement that the plea was not induced by any threats or promises. This prima facie case for voluntariness is likely to be treated as irrebuttable in cases such as this one, where the defendant's reply is limited to his own plaintive allegations that he did not understand the nature of the charge and therefore failed to assert a valid defense or to limit his guilty plea only to a lesser included offense. No matter how true these allegations may be, rarely, if ever, can a defendant corroborate them in a post-plea voluntariness hearing. * * *

"We thus conclude that prejudice inheres in a failure to comply with Rule 11, for noncompliance deprives the defendant of the Rule's procedural safeguards, which are designed to facilitate a more accurate determination of the voluntariness of his plea. Our holding that a defendant whose plea has been accepted in violation of Rule 11 should be afforded the opportunity to plead anew not only will insure that every accused is afforded those procedural safeguards, but also will help reduce the great waste of judicial resources required to process the frivolous attacks on guilty plea convictions that are encouraged, and are more difficult to dispose of, when the original record is inadequate."

In *United States v. Vonn*, 535 U.S. 55 (2002), where defendant challenged his guilty plea on appeal on the ground that the judge had skipped the advice (required by what is now Fed.R.Crim.P. 11(b)(10)(D)) that he would have the right to assistance of counsel, the court of appeals confined itself to considering the record of "the plea proceeding." The Supreme Court, per Souter, J., acknowledged that certain language in *McCarthy* "ostensibly supports" the court of appeals, but then observed that in *McCarthy* the "only serious alternative" to the plea record would have been "an evidentiary hearing for further factfinding by the trial court," while in the instant case "there is a third source of information," namely, the "part of the record" showing defendant was advised of his right to trial counsel "during his initial appearance" and "at his first arraignment." "Because there are circumstances in which defendants may be presumed to recall information provided to them prior to the plea proceeding," the Court concluded that source should have been considered by the court of appeals.

2. ***Collateral attack by federal defendant.*** In UNITED STATES v. TIMMRECK, 441 U.S. 780 (1979), the trial judge explained to the defendant who tendered a guilty plea that he could receive a sentence of 15 years imprisonment and a $25,000 fine, but failed to describe the mandatory special parole term of at least 3 years. The judge then accepted the plea and sentenced defendant to 10 years imprisonment, plus a special parole term of 5 years and a fine of $5,000. The defendant raised no objection to the sentence at the time, and did not take an appeal. About two years later, defendant collaterally attacked his plea in a 28 U.S.C. § 2255 proceeding on the ground that the judge had violated Rule 11 by not informing him of the mandatory special parole term. The district court concluded the Rule 11 violation did not entitle defendant to § 2255 relief because he had not suffered any prejudice, inasmuch as his sentence was within the maximum described to him when the plea was accepted. But the Court of Appeals held that "a Rule 11

violation is per se prejudicial" and thus a basis for relief via § 2255. Relying upon the limits on § 2255 relief set out in *Hill v. United States,* 368 U.S. 424 (1962), a unanimous Court stated:

"The reasoning in *Hill* is equally applicable to a formal violation of Rule 11. Such a violation is neither constitutional nor jurisdictional: the 1966 amendment to Rule 11 obviously could not amend the Constitution or limit the jurisdiction of the federal courts. Nor can any claim reasonably be made that the error here resulted in a 'complete miscarriage of justice' or in a proceeding 'inconsistent with the rudimentary demands of fair procedure.' Respondent does not argue that he was actually unaware of the special parole term or that, if he had been properly advised by the trial judge, he would not have pleaded guilty. His only claim is of a technical violation of the rule. That claim could have been raised on direct appeal, see *McCarthy v. United States,* but was not. * * *

"Indeed, if anything, this case may be a stronger one for foreclosing collateral relief than the *Hill* case. For the concern with finality served by the limitation on collateral attack has special force with respect to convictions based on guilty pleas. * * *

"As in *Hill,* we find it unnecessary to consider whether § 2255 relief would be available if a violation of Rule 11 occurred in the context of other aggravating circumstances. 'We decide only that such collateral relief is not available when all that is shown is a failure to comply with the formal requirements of the Rule.' "

3. ***Plain error.*** Because Rule 11(h), unlike the more general harmless error provision in Rule 52, does not also contain a plain-error provision, the defendant in *Vonn*, Note 1 supra, who raised his claim of a Rule 11 violation for the first time on appeal, asserted he should be entitled to prevail without showing plain error. The Supreme Court disagreed, concluding that there was no evidence supporting the conclusion that adoption of Rule 11(h) implicitly repealed Rule 52 so far as it might cover a Rule 11 case. The Court added that "the incentive to think and act early when Rule 11 is at stake," the objective of what is now Rule 11(d) & (e), "would prove less substantial if Vonn's position were law." This means, the Court later concluded in *United States v. Dominguez Benitez,* 542 U.S. 74 (2004), "that a defendant who seeks reversal of his conviction after a guilty plea, on the ground that the district court committed plain error under Rule 11, must show a reasonable probability that, but for the error, he would not have entered the plea."

4. ***Noncompliance with state provisions.*** State courts are not in complete agreement as to the significance of noncompliance with state provisions similar to Federal Rule 11, but most of the recent cases, e.g., *Brakeall v. Weber*, 668 N.W.2d 79 (S.D.2003), follow *Timmreck*.

5. ***Plea challenge by state defendant.*** *Boykin v. Alabama,* p. 1216, a direct review of defendant's guilty plea, concerned a defendant who pled guilty in state court to five armed robbery indictments and thereafter received the death penalty. At arraignment, "so far as the record shows, the judge asked no questions of petitioner concerning his plea, and petitioner did not address the court." The Supreme Court reversed, concluding that it "was error, plain on the face of the record, for the trial judge to accept petitioner's guilty plea without an affirmative showing that it was intelligent and voluntary." *Boykin*, it was said, "applied to state criminal proceedings the same standard for on-the-record establishment of the defendant's knowledge of the nature of the charge and the consequences of a guilty plea as was applied to the federal courts in *McCarthy*," *United States ex rel. Wiggins v. Pennsylvania*, 430 F.2d 650 (3d Cir.1970). But in *North Carolina v. Alford*, p. 1218, where Alford unsuccessfully challenged his guilty plea in a state postconviction hearing and then on federal habeas corpus, the Court noted in footnote 3: "At the state court hearing on post-conviction relief, the testimony confirmed that Alford had been fully informed by his attorney as to his rights on a plea of not guilty and as to the consequences of a plea of guilty. Since the record in this case affirmatively indicates that Alford was aware of the consequences of

his plea of guilty and of the rights waived by the plea, no issues of substance under *Boykin v. Alabama* would be presented even if that case was held applicable to the events here in question."

6. ***"Presumption of regularity."*** In 1986 Raley was charged with robbery and with having two prior felony convictions (based on 1979 and 1981 guilty pleas) necessitating a mandatory minimum sentence. Under state procedure, the state had to prove the *fact* of the prior convictions, after which the defendant could attack their validity.[a] Though the ultimate burden of persuasion rested with the prosecution, the defendant was first obligated to produce evidence of the invalidity of those pleas. Because the record contained no transcripts of those guilty plea proceedings, Raley claimed this was inconsistent with *Boykin's* statement that the waiver of rights essential to a valid plea cannot be presumed "from a silent record." In *Parke v. Raley,* 506 U.S. 20 (1992), the Court disagreed:

"We see no tension between the Kentucky scheme and *Boykin. Boykin* involved direct review of a conviction allegedly based upon an uninformed guilty plea. Respondent, however, never appealed his earlier convictions. They became final years ago, and he now seeks to revisit the question of their validity in a separate recidivism proceeding. To import *Boykin's* presumption of invalidity into this very different context would, in our view, improperly ignore another presumption deeply rooted in our jurisprudence: the 'presumption of regularity' that attaches to final judgments, even when the question is waiver of constitutional rights."

The Court added that there was "no good reason to suspend the presumption of regularity here," as (i) the absence of a guilty plea transcript was not itself suspicious, as under the state's procedure transcripts are made only if a direct appeal is taken and stenographic notes and tapes are not preserved more than five years; and (ii) "*Boykin* colloquies have been required for nearly a quarter-century."

G. SIGNIFICANCE OF COMPLIANCE WITH REQUIREMENTS FOR RECEIVING GUILTY PLEA

1. ***Compliance no bar to challenge.*** Is the "logical converse" of *McCarthy* and *Boykin* that if the trial judge *does* have the defendant indicate for the record that his plea is voluntary and with knowledge of the charge and the consequences, then the defendant may not thereafter challenge his plea as being involuntary and unknowing? In *Fontaine v. United States,* 411 U.S. 213 (1973), it was held that upon a federal defendant's motion under 28 U.S.C. § 2255 to vacate his sentence on the grounds that his plea of guilty had been induced by a combination of fear, coercive police tactics, and illness (including mental illness), a hearing was required "on this record" notwithstanding full compliance with Federal Rule 11, as § 2255 calls for a hearing unless "the motion and the files and records of the case conclusively show that the prisoner is entitled to no relief"; the objective of Rule 11 "is to flush out and resolve all such issues, but like any procedural mechanism, its exercise is neither always perfect nor uniformly invulnerable to subsequent challenge calling for an opportunity to prove the allegations."

2. ***Significance of plea procedure reforms.*** Allison, indicted in North Carolina for breaking and entering, attempted safe robbery and possession of burglary tools, pled guilty to the

[a] As for permitting *no* challenge of prior guilty pleas during sentencing following a later conviction, consider *Custis v. United States,* 511 U.S. 485 (1994), holding it is constitutionally permissible to bar, as in the Armed Career Criminal Act, 18 U.S.C. § 924(e), all collateral attacks upon prior state convictions being used for sentence enhancement in a federal trial, except that a defendant may raise the "unique constitutional defect" of "failure to appoint counsel for an indigent defendant." *Custis*, regarding challenging the state guilty plea conviction at a federal sentencing proceeding, was later deemed equally applicable upon a motion to vacate, set aside or correct a federal sentence pursuant to 28 U.S.C. § 2255. *Daniels v. United States*, 532 U.S. 374 (2001), in turn extended to cover § 2254 petitions directed at enhanced state sentences. *Lackawanna County District Attorney v. Coss*, 532 U.S. 394 (2001).

second charge. The judge in taking the plea read from a printed form 13 questions, each of which Allison answered as required for acceptance of the plea. He responded in the affirmative to the question, "Do you understand that upon your plea of guilty you could be imprisoned for as much as minimum [sic] of 10 years to life?"; and no to the question, "Has the Solicitor, or your lawyer, or any policeman, law officer or anyone else made any promises or threats to you to influence you to plead guilty in this case?" The only record of the proceedings was the executed form. The judge accepted the plea and at a later unrecorded sentencing hearing sentenced Allison to 17–21 years in prison. After exhausting his state remedies, Allison sought relief via federal habeas corpus, alleging that his attorney had told him an agreement had been reached with the prosecutor and judge whereby if he pleaded guilty he would get only 10 years, and that his attorney had cautioned him he should nonetheless answer the questions of the judge as he did. The district court denied the petition on the ground that the form "conclusively shows" no constitutional violation and thus met the standard of *Fontaine,* but the court of appeals reversed. In BLACKLEDGE v. ALLISON, 431 U.S. 63 (1977), the Court affirmed:

"Allison was arraigned a mere 37 days after the *Santobello* decision was announced, under a North Carolina procedure that had not been modified in light of *Santobello* or earlier decisions of this Court recognizing the process of plea bargaining. That procedure itself reflected the atmosphere of secrecy which then characterized plea bargaining generally. No transcript of the proceeding was made. The only record was a standard printed form. There is no way of knowing whether the trial judge in any way deviated from or supplemented the text of the form. The record is silent as to what statements Allison, his lawyer, or the prosecutor might have made regarding promised sentencing concessions. And there is no record at all of the sentencing hearing three days later, at which one of the participants might well have made a statement shedding light upon the veracity of the allegations Allison later advanced. * * *

"North Carolina has recently undertaken major revisions of its plea bargaining procedures in part to prevent the very kind of problem now before us. Plea bargaining is expressly legitimate. The judge is directed to advise the defendant that courts have approved plea bargaining and he may thus admit to any promises without fear of jeopardizing an advantageous agreement or prejudicing himself in the judge's eyes. Specific inquiry about whether a plea bargain has been struck is then made not only of the defendant, but also of his counsel and the prosecutor. Finally, the entire proceeding is to be transcribed verbatim.

"Had these commendable procedures been followed in the present case, Allison's petition would have been cast in a very different light. The careful explication of the legitimacy of plea bargaining, the questioning of both lawyers, and the verbatim record of their answers at the guilty plea proceedings would almost surely have shown whether any bargain did exist and, if so, insured that it was not ignored."

§ 6. THE EFFECT OF A GUILTY PLEA

CLASS V. UNITED STATES

583 U.S. ___, 138 S.Ct. 798, 200 L.Ed.2d 37 (2018).

JUSTICE BREYER delivered the opinion of the Court. * * *

[Class, indicted for possessing firearms in his vehicle while it was parked on the grounds of the U.S. Capitol, unsuccessfully sought dismissal of the indictment, claiming that the statute violated the Second Amendment. He later pled guilty pursuant to a plea agreement listing five rights he agreed to waive and three he could raise on appeal, but which said nothing about the right to raise on appeal a claim that the statute of conviction was unconstitutional.]

The question is whether a guilty plea by itself bars a federal criminal defendant from challenging the constitutionality of the statute of conviction on direct appeal. We hold that it does not. * * *

Fifty years ago this Court directly addressed a similar claim (a claim that the statute of conviction was unconstitutional). And the Court stated that a defendant's "plea of guilty did not . . . waive his previous [constitutional] claim." *Haynes v. United States*, 390 U.S. 85 (1968). Though Justice Harlan's opinion for the Court in *Haynes* offered little explanation for this statement, subsequent decisions offered a rationale that applies here.

In *Blackledge v. Perry*, 417 U.S. 21 (1974), North Carolina indicted and convicted Jimmy Seth Perry on a misdemeanor assault charge. When Perry exercised his right under a North Carolina statute to a de novo trial in a higher court, the State reindicted him, but this time the State charged a felony, which carried a heavier penalty, for the same conduct. Perry pleaded guilty. He then sought habeas relief on the grounds that the reindictment amounted to an unconstitutional vindictive prosecution. The State argued that Perry's guilty plea barred him from raising his constitutional challenge. But this Court held that it did not.

The Court noted that a guilty plea bars appeal of many claims, including some " 'antecedent constitutional violations' " related to events (say, grand jury proceedings) that had " 'occurred prior to the entry of the guilty plea' " (quoting *Tollett v. Henderson*, 411 U.S. 258 (1973)). While *Tollett* claims were "of constitutional dimension," the Court explained that "the nature of the underlying constitutional infirmity is markedly different" from a claim of vindictive prosecution, which implicates "the very power of the State" to prosecute the defendant. Accordingly, the Court wrote that "the right" Perry "asserts and that we today accept is the right not to be haled into court at all upon the felony charge" since "[t]he very initiation of the proceedings" against Perry "operated to deprive him due process of law."

A year and a half later, in *Menna v. New York*, 423 U.S. 61 (1975), this Court repeated what it had said and held in *Blackledge*. After Menna served a 30-day jail term for refusing to testify before the grand jury on November 7, 1968, the State of New York charged him once again for (what Menna argued was) the same crime. Menna pleaded guilty, but subsequently appealed arguing that the new charge violated the Double Jeopardy Clause. U.S. Const., Amdt. 5. The lower courts held that Menna's constitutional claim had been "waived" by his guilty plea.

This Court reversed. Citing *Blackledge*, the Court held that "a plea of guilty to a charge does not waive a claim that—judged on its face—the charge is one which the State may not constitutionally prosecute." Menna's claim amounted to a claim that "the State may not convict" him "no matter how validly his factual guilt is established." Menna's "guilty plea, therefore, [did] not bar the claim." * * *

In more recent years, we have reaffirmed the *Menna-Blackledge* doctrine and refined its scope. In *United States v. Broce*, 488 U.S. 563 (1989), the defendants pleaded guilty to two separate indictments in a single proceeding which "on their face" described two separate bid-rigging conspiracies. They later sought to challenge their convictions on double jeopardy grounds, arguing that they had only admitted to one conspiracy. Citing *Blackledge* and *Menna*, this Court repeated that a guilty plea does not bar a claim on appeal "where on the face of the record the court had no power to enter the conviction or impose the sentence." However, because the defendants could not "prove their claim by relying on those indictments and the existing record" and "without contradicting those indictments," this Court held that their claims were "foreclosed by the admissions inherent in their guilty pleas."

Unlike the claims in *Broce*, Class' constitutional claims here, as we understand them, do not contradict the terms of the indictment or the written plea agreement. They are consistent with

Class' knowing, voluntary, and intelligent admission that he did what the indictment alleged. Those claims can be "resolved without any need to venture beyond that record."

Nor do Class' claims focus upon case-related constitutional defects that " 'occurred prior to the entry of the guilty plea.' " *Blackledge*. They could not, for example, "have been 'cured' through a new indictment by a properly selected grand jury." Because the defendant has admitted the charges against him, a guilty plea makes the latter kind of constitutional claim "irrelevant to the constitutional validity of the conviction." *Haring v. Prosise*, 462 U.S. 306 (1983). But the cases to which we have referred make clear that a defendant's guilty plea does not make irrelevant the kind of constitutional claim Class seeks to make.

In sum, the claims at issue here do not fall within any of the categories of claims that Class' plea agreement forbids him to raise on direct appeal. They challenge the Government's power to criminalize Class' (admitted) conduct. They thereby call into question the Government's power to " 'constitutionally prosecute' " him. *Broce,* supra (quoting *Menna*, supra). A guilty plea does not bar a direct appeal in these circumstances. * * *

The Government and the dissent argue that [Fed.R.Crim.P.] 11(a)(2) means that "a defendant who pleads guilty cannot challenge his conviction on appeal on a forfeitable or waivable ground that he either failed to present to the district court or failed to reserve in writing."

The problem with this argument is that, by its own terms, the Rule itself does not say whether it sets forth the exclusive procedure for a defendant to preserve a constitutional claim following a guilty plea. At the same time, the drafters' notes acknowledge that the "Supreme Court has held that certain kinds of constitutional objections may be raised after a plea of guilty." The notes then specifically refer to the "*Menna-Blackledge* doctrine."

JUSTICE ALITO, with whom JUSTICE KENNEDY and JUSTICE THOMAS join, dissenting.

* * * I think the Court of Appeals was clearly correct. First, the Federal Constitution does not prohibit the waiver of the rights Class asserts. We have held that most personal constitutional rights may be waived, and Class concedes that this is so with respect to the rights he is asserting.

Second, no federal statute or rule bars waiver. On the contrary, Rule 11 * * * makes it clear that, with one exception that I will discuss below, a defendant who enters an unconditional plea waives all nonjurisdictional claims. Although the Rule does not say this expressly, that is the unmistakable implication of subdivision (a)(2), which allows a defendant, "[w]ith the consent of the court and the government," to "enter a conditional plea of guilty or nolo contendere, reserving in writing the right to have an appellate court review an adverse determination of a specified pretrial motion." * * *[a]

In *Blackledge*, the Court held that a defendant who pleaded guilty could nevertheless challenge his conviction on the ground that his right to due process was violated by a vindictive prosecution. The Court asserted that this right was "markedly different" from the equal protection and Fifth Amendment rights at stake in *Tollett* and the *Brady* trilogy because it "went to the very power of the State to bring the defendant into court to answer the charge brought against him." The meaning of this distinction, however, is hard to grasp.

[a] In *Commonwealth v. Gomez*, 104 N.E.3d 636 (Mass.2018), holding a defendant may enter a conditional guilty plea, the court noted that a "majority of other States * * * allow conditional pleas," "most * * * by statute or rule," often modeled on Fed.R.Crim.P. 11(a)(2). As for the claim "there is no need for conditional guilty pleas because of the availability of stipulated evidence trials," the court responded the latter "procedure is disfavored" because it requires "a comprehensive colloquy itemizing the rights surrendered confirming that the defendant understands the significance of the rights he or she gives up in a stipulated trial, and ensuring that the defendant intelligently and voluntarily relinquishes those rights," resulting in frequent "mistakes during the colloquy at a stipulated evidence trial," and even "when conducted correctly, * * * a stipulated evidence trial constitutes a flawed procedure" because it "is confusing to the defendant and to members of the public, as it is a legal fiction rather than an actual trial."

The most natural way to understand *Blackledge*'s reference to "the very power of the State" would be to say that an argument survives a guilty plea if it attacks the court's jurisdiction. * * * But that cannot be what *Blackledge* meant.

First, the defendant in *Blackledge* had been tried in state court in North Carolina for a state-law offense, and the jurisdiction of state courts to entertain such prosecutions is purely a matter of state law * * *. Second, a rule that jurisdictional defects alone survive a guilty plea would not explain the result in *Blackledge* itself. Arguments attacking a court's subject-matter jurisdiction can neither be waived nor forfeited. But the due process right at issue in *Blackledge* was perfectly capable of being waived or forfeited—as is just about every other right that is personal to a criminal defendant.

So if the "very power to prosecute" theory does not refer to jurisdiction, what else might it mean? The only other possibility that comes to mind is that it might mean that a defendant can litigate a claim if it asserts a right not to be tried, as opposed to a right not to be convicted. But we have said that "virtually all rights of criminal defendants" are "merely . . . right[s] not to be convicted," as distinguished from "right[s] not to be tried." Even when a constitutional violation requires the dismissal of an indictment, that "does not mean that [the] defendant enjoy[ed] a 'right not to be tried' " on the charges.

The rule could hardly be otherwise. Most constitutional defenses (and plenty of statutory defenses), if successfully asserted in a pretrial motion, deprive the prosecution of the "power" to proceed to trial or secure a conviction. If that remedial consequence converted them all into rights not to be prosecuted, *Blackledge* would have no discernible limit. * * *

The upshot is that the supposed "right not to be prosecuted" has no intelligible meaning in this context. * * *

If the thinking behind *Blackledge* is hard to follow, *Menna* may be worse. In that case, the Court held that a defendant who pleaded guilty could challenge his conviction on double jeopardy grounds. The case was decided by a three-page per curiam opinion, its entire analysis confined to a single footnote[, where] the Court wrote:

"[A] counseled plea of guilty is an admission of factual guilt so reliable that, where voluntary and intelligent, it quite validly removes the issue of factual guilt from the case. In most cases, factual guilt is a sufficient basis for the State's imposition of punishment. A guilty plea, therefore, simply renders irrelevant those constitutional violations not logically inconsistent with the valid establishment of factual guilt."

The wording of the final sentence is not easy to parse, but I interpret the Court's reasoning as follows: A defendant who pleads guilty does no more than admit that he committed the essential conduct charged in the indictment; therefore a guilty plea allows the litigation on appeal of any claim that is not inconsistent with the facts that the defendant necessarily admitted. * * * A holding of that scope is not what one expects to see in a footnote in a per curiam opinion, but if the Court meant less, its meaning is unclear.

When the Court returned to *Blackledge* and *Menna* in *United States v. Broce*, 488 U.S. 563 (1989), the Court essentially repudiated the theories offered in those earlier cases. * * * Like *Menna*, *Broce* involved a defendant (actually two defendants) who pleaded guilty but then sought to attack their convictions on double jeopardy grounds. This time, however, the Court held that their guilty pleas prevented them from litigating their claims.

The Court began by specifically disavowing *Menna*'s suggestion that a guilty plea admits only " 'factual guilt,' " meaning "the acts described in the indictments." Instead, the Court explained, an unconditional guilty plea admits "all of the factual and legal elements necessary to sustain a binding, final judgment of guilt and a lawful sentence." "By entering a plea of guilty, the accused is not simply stating that he did the discrete acts described in the indictment; he is admitting guilt of a substantive crime." * * * Thus, the Court concluded, a defendant's decision to plead guilty necessarily extinguishes whatever "potential defense[s]" he might have asserted in an effort to show that it would be unlawful to hold him liable for his conduct. So much for *Menna*.

As for *Blackledge*, by holding that the defendants' double jeopardy rights were extinguished by their pleas, *Broce* necessarily rejected the idea that a right not to be tried survives an unconditional guilty plea. * * *

In sum, the governing law in the present case is Rule 11 * * *. Under that Rule, an unconditional guilty plea waives all nonjurisdictional claims with the possible exception of the "*Menna-Blackledge* doctrine" created years ago by this Court. That doctrine is vacuous, has no sound foundation, and produces nothing but confusion. * * *

NOTES AND QUESTIONS

1. ***Freestanding claim of "actual innocence."*** Should states recognize a broader range of post-conviction challenges than allowed under *Class*? In *Schmidt v. State*, 909 N.W.2d 778 (Iowa 2018), the court noted that "a number of jurisdictions acknowledge freestanding claims of actual innocence," that is, where such claims are unaccompanied by an assertion of any *legal* error in the process by which the defendant's conviction was obtained.[b] In these jurisdictions, the question has sometimes been raised as to whether such an "actual innocence" claim may be made only by those defendants who asserted their innocence by standing trial. The court in *Schmidt,* stating "we do not think *Class* * * * affects our decision today," rejected its earlier holding that "[n]otions of newly discovered evidence simply have no bearing on a knowing and voluntary admission of guilt." By "now examin[ing] the phenomenon of actually innocent people pleading guilty," as manifested by the fact that the "National Registry of Exonerations reported that seventy-four exonerations in 2016 arose from pleas," the court reached the conclusion "that actually innocent people plead guilty for many different reasons." The dissent in *Schmidt,* invoking *Class* in support, objected: "Reexamining a guilty plea years after the fact is far different from reviewing a trial. Unlike with a case that actually went to trial, no trial transcript can be relied on if the witnesses no longer are around, have forgotten the events, or no longer are motivated to remember them."

2. ***Manner of proof.*** Should it make any difference in what manner the defendant's "actual innocence" is established? Acknowledging that the legislature had already provided a remedy for defendants who pled guilty where "DNA evidence exonerates them," the *Schmidt* court responded: "We see no reason why we should treat people exonerated by DNA evidence differently from people exonerated by other reliable means," as "when the court determines the police planted evidence, such as drugs." But that was not the instant case, where the defendant, who pled guilty to assault with intent to commit sexual abuse and incest, now relied upon "recantation by the victim." The dissent objected that courts would now see "applications by defendants who pled guilty to domestic assault and [then managed to] bully the survivors into recanting."

3. **Alford *plea.*** Is *Schmidt* inapplicable to an *Alford* plea, discussed at p. 1250, because, as the dissent asserts, "[s]uch a defendant always maintained he or she was innocent"?

4. ***Guilty-plea defendants with different guilt or otherwise unconvictable.*** In a state agreeing with *Schmidt* re a guilty-plea defendant's (i) "actual innocence" claim, what then of such defendants only claiming (ii) to have "different guilt" or (iii) to be "otherwise unconvictable"? Consider: (i) *Ex parte Mable*, 443 S.W.3d 129 (Tex.Crim.App.2014) ("actual innocence" can be

[b] As noted in *Schmidt*, such a "freestanding claim" must be distinguished from a "gateway claim," by which a habeas petitioner may overcome a procedural bar to habeas review by bringing a gateway claim of actual innocence such that the petitioner may obtain review of the underlying constitutional merits of his or her procedurally defaulted claim." See p. 1432, Note 2.

raised where after guilty plea to possession of controlled substance state lab tested the material and found it not a controlled substance); (ii) *Ex parte Broussard*, 517 S.W.3d 814 (Tex.Crim.App.2017) (where defendant, arrested for possession of substance field test determined was cocaine, pled guilty to delivery of cocaine, but later lab test of that substance revealed it was meth, in the same penalty group, defendant not entitled to plea withdrawal despite existing rule that "possession of *each* individual substance within the same penalty group [is] a separate and distinct offense," as "a guilty plea is not necessarily involuntary when a defendant misapprehends a known unknown"); (iii) *Ex parte Palmberg*, 491 S.W.3d 804 (Tex.Crim.App.2016) (a "guilty plea does not violate due process * * * even when the defendant enters it while operating under various misapprehensions about the nature or strength of the State's case," here unawareness that the arresting officer used up all of the substance found on defendant in preliminary testing, so that "there was no remaining unprocessed sample available for laboratory analysis," even though a test "performed by an officer in the field is inadmissible at trial."

CHAPTER 23

TRIAL BY JURY

■ ■ ■

The right to a jury trial[a] is one of the defining features of criminal procedure in the United States, setting it apart from adjudication systems in many other nations where lay persons do not determine culpability. This chapter considers first the extension of that right to state defendants, then turns to which proceedings carry the right, and what limitations the Constitution places upon jury size and decision making. Section two examines limitations on the selection of jurors in criminal cases. The final section addresses the right to an impartial judge.

§ 1. RIGHT TO JURY TRIAL

Royal interference with trial by jury in the colonies was deeply resented, and from the outset Article III of the United States Constitution commanded: "The Trial of all Crimes, except in Cases of Impeachment, shall be by Jury; and such Trial shall be held in the State where the said Crimes shall have been committed." The Bill of Rights added in the Sixth Amendment that in "all criminal prosecutions" the defendant was entitled to trial "by an impartial jury of the State and district wherein the crime shall have been committed." But neither of these provisions applied to state prosecutions; they limited only federal power.

It was in DUNCAN v. LOUISIANA, 391 U.S. 145 (1968), that the Court first held the Sixth Amendment right to trial by an impartial jury was part of the due process guaranteed to state defendants by the Fourteenth Amendment. Gary Duncan was an African-American nineteen-year-old convicted after a bench trial of committing simple battery, a crime carrying up to two years in prison but no right to a jury under Louisiana law. He was sentenced to two months in jail and additional 20 days if he failed to pay court costs and a fine of $150. Duncan's alleged slap of a white boy's arm took place outside a recently desegregated public high school. Duncan, driving by, had stopped when he noticed white students confronting two black students, his younger cousins. Trying to prevent the incident from escalating, Duncan had his cousins get into his car and suggested the white boys go home. At trial, the judge believed the white witnesses who testified that they saw Duncan slap one of the white boys, and disbelieved the black witnesses who testified that Duncan had merely touched the boy's elbow.[b] The only issue before the United States Supreme Court was whether the United States Constitution guaranteed Duncan a jury trial. Applying the selective incorporation doctrine (p. 24), the Court majority held that the right to due process under the Fourteenth Amendment included "a right of jury trial in all criminal cases which—were they to be tried in a federal court—would come within the Sixth Amendment's guarantee." Writing for the Court, White, J., reasoned:

"The guarantees of jury trial in the Federal and State Constitutions reflect a profound judgment about the way in which law should be enforced and justice administered. A right to jury trial is granted to criminal defendants in order to prevent oppression by the Government. Those

---

[a] For additional information on the criminal jury trial, see Wayne LaFave, Jerold H. Israel, Nancy J. King & Orin S. Kerr, Criminal Procedure Treatise (4th ed. 2016) (available at Westlaw at database name CRIMPROC, hereinafter cited as CRIMPROC).

[b] For the story of how Duncan, his lawyers, and the federal courts battled segregationist powers in Plaquemines Parish, see Nancy J. King, *Duncan v. Louisiana: How Bigotry in the Bayou Led to the Federal Regulation of State Juries*, in *Criminal Procedure Stories* (Carol Steiker, ed., 2006).

who wrote our constitutions knew from history and experience that it was necessary to protect against unfounded criminal charges brought to eliminate enemies and against judges too responsive to the voice of higher authority. The framers of the constitutions strove to create an independent judiciary but insisted upon further protection against arbitrary action. Providing an accused with the right to be tried by a jury of his peers gave him an inestimable safeguard against the corrupt or overzealous prosecutor and against the compliant, biased, or eccentric judge. If the defendant preferred the common sense judgment of a jury to the more tutored but perhaps less sympathetic reaction of the single judge, he was to have it. Beyond this, the jury trial provisions in the Federal and State Constitutions reflect a fundamental decision about the exercise of official power—a reluctance to entrust plenary powers over the life and liberty of the citizen to one judge or to a group of judges. Fear of unchecked power, so typical of our State and Federal Governments in other respects, found expression in the criminal law in this insistence upon community participation in the determination of guilt or innocence. The deep commitment of the Nation to the right of jury trial in serious criminal cases as a defense against arbitrary law enforcement qualifies for protection under the Due Process Clause of the Fourteenth Amendment, and must therefore be respected by the States.

"Of course jury trial has 'its weaknesses and the potential for misuse,' * * *. We are aware of the long debate, especially in this century, among those who write about the administration of justice, as to the wisdom of permitting untrained laymen to determine the facts in civil and criminal proceedings. Although the debate has been intense, with powerful voices on either side, most of the controversy has centered on the jury in civil cases. Indeed, some of the severest critics of civil juries acknowledge that the arguments for criminal juries are much stronger. In addition, at the heart of the dispute have been express or implicit assertions that juries are incapable of adequately understanding evidence or determining issues of fact, and that they are unpredictable, quixotic, and little better than a roll of dice. Yet, the most recent and exhaustive study of the jury in criminal cases concluded that juries do understand the evidence and come to sound conclusions in most of the cases presented to them and that when juries differ with the result at which the judge would have arrived, it is usually because they are serving some of the very purposes for which they were created and for which they are now employed."

" * * * We would not assert, however, that every criminal trial—or any particular trial—held before a judge alone is unfair or that a defendant may never be as fairly treated by a judge as he would be by a jury. Thus we hold no constitutional doubts about the practices, common in both federal and state courts, of accepting waivers of jury trial and prosecuting petty crimes without extending a right to jury trial. However, the fact is that in most places more trials for serious crimes are to juries than to a court alone; a great many defendants prefer the judgment of a jury to that of a court. Even where defendants are satisfied with bench trials, the right to a jury trial very likely serves its intended purpose of making judicial or prosecutorial unfairness less likely. * * * "

Harlan, J., joined by Stewart, J., dissented. Rejecting selective incorporation's complete absorption of fundamental guarantees, he argued that the issue before the Court should be "whether the State of Louisiana, which provides trial by jury to all felonies, is prohibited by the Constitution from trying charges of simple battery to the court alone." Justice Harlan noted that "through the long course of British and American history" jury trial had not been used "in a varying category of lesser crimes as a flexible response to the burden jury trial would otherwise impose," and there was no reason "why the States should not be allowed to make continuing adjustments [in identifying those offenses] based on the state of their criminal dockets and the difficulty of summoning jurors."

Justice Harlan went on to argue, "Even if I could agree that the question was whether [the] Sixth Amendment jury trial is totally 'in' or totally 'out' [of due process], I can find in the Court's opinion no real reasons for concluding that it should be 'in'. * * * The jury is of course not without virtues. It affords ordinary citizens a valuable opportunity to participate in a process of government, an experience fostering, one hopes, a respect for law. It eases the burden on judges by enabling them to share a part of their sometimes awesome responsibility. A jury may, at times, afford a higher justice by refusing to enforce harsh laws (although it necessarily does so haphazardly, raising the questions whether arbitrary enforcement of harsh laws is better than total enforcement, and whether the jury system is to be defended on the ground that jurors sometimes disobey their oaths). And the jury may, or may not, contribute desirably to the willingness of the general public to accept criminal judgments as just.

"It can hardly be gainsaid, however, that the principal original virtue of the jury trial—the limitations a jury imposes on a tyrannous judiciary—has largely disappeared. We no longer live in a medieval or colonial society. Judges enforce laws enacted by democratic decision, not by regal fiat. They are elected by the people or appointed by the people's elected officials, and are responsible not to a distant monarch alone but to reviewing courts, including this one.

"The jury system can also be said to have some inherent defects, which are multiplied by the emergence of the criminal law from the relative simplicity that existed when the jury system was devised. It is a cumbersome process, not only imposing great cost in time and money on both the State and the jurors themselves, but also contributing to delay in the machinery of justice. Untrained jurors are presumably less adept at reaching accurate conclusions of fact than judges, particularly if the issues are many or complex. And it is argued by some that trial by jury, far from increasing public respect for law, impairs it: the average man, it is said, reacts favorably neither to the notion that matters he knows to be complex are being decided by other average men, nor to the way the jury system distorts the process of adjudication."

NOTES AND QUESTIONS ON THE SCOPE OF THE RIGHT TO JURY TRIAL

1. ***Petty offenses.*** Although the Court agreed that the two-year offense Duncan faced triggered the jury right, it noted that "there is a category of petty crimes or offenses which is not subject to the Sixth Amendment jury trial provisions." In *Baldwin v. New York*, 399 U.S. 66 (1970), where Baldwin had been convicted of a misdemeanor punishable by imprisonment up to one year, a 5–3 majority held that "no offense can be deemed 'petty' for purposes of the right to trial by jury where imprisonment for more than six months is authorized." In *Blanton v. City of North Las Vegas*, 489 U.S. 538 (1989), a unanimous Court found it "appropriate to presume for purposes of the Sixth Amendment that society views" an offense carrying a maximum prison term of six months or less "as 'petty.' A defendant is entitled to jury trial in such circumstances only if he can demonstrate that any additional statutory penalties, viewed in conjunction with the maximum authorized period of incarceration, are so severe that they clearly reflect a legislative determination that the offense in question is a 'serious' one." The Court then concluded that petitioners, charged with driving under the influence, were not entitled to a jury trial where the maximum authorized prison sentence did not exceed six months, the possible additional penalty of a $1,000 fine was "well below the $5,000 level set by Congress in its most recent definition of a 'petty' offense, 18 U.S.C. § 1," and was not "out of step with state practice for offenses carrying prison sentences of six months or less." The Court also reasoned, "As for the 90-day license suspension," that "automatically" follows from conviction, "it, too, will be irrelevant if it runs concurrently with the prison sentence." It also "ascribe[d] little significance to the fact that a DUI offender faces increased penalties for repeat offenses," noting that "[r]ecidivist penalties of the magnitude imposed for DUI are commonplace and, in any event, petitioners do not face such penalties here."

Lower courts regularly find that fines well in excess of $5000 do not necessarily trigger the jury right where the maximum term of incarceration is six months or less. Typical is *United States v. Dugan*, 667 F.3d 84 (2d Cir. 2011), where the court upheld a misdemeanor conviction, without a jury, for physical obstruction of a reproductive health facility. "Because offenses carrying prison sentences of six months or less are presumed to be petty, in order to overcome this presumption, Dugan would have to demonstrate that the $10,000 monetary penalty is 'so severe' as to 'reflect a legislative determination that the offense in question is a 'serious' one.' *Blanton*. While Dugan is correct that the $10,000 maximum fine is $5,000 more than the maximum monetary penalty enumerated in the statutory definition of 'petty offense,' the Supreme Court has never adopted this statutory definition as defining the contours of the constitutional right to a jury trial, and we cannot agree that the additional $5,000 is 'so severe' as to transform this otherwise petty offense into a serious one."

What about "collateral consequences" that are not part of the sentence but that the law makes "virtually inevitable" after conviction? A majority in *People v. Suazo*, 118 N.E.3d 168, 32 N.Y.3d 491 (2018), concluded that the prospect of deportation by federal officials transformed an otherwise petty state offense into a serious one under the Sixth Amendment. The court in *Suazo* relied on the Supreme Court's special treatment of deportation in another Sixth Amendment context in *Padilla v. Kentucky*, p. 1201, and reasoned that in *Blanton,* the Court presumed that a collateral consequence could potentially render an offense serious, when it included a statement about the driver's license suspension in its analysis of whether the DUI offense in that case triggered the jury right. Nor did it matter, reasoned the *Suazo* majority, that deportation was imposed by Congress, not the state legislature. A dissenting opinion disagreed, arguing that "Federal immigration law should not override the New York State Legislature's view of the seriousness of the charged offense, as expressed by the maximum penalty authorized," and warned the decision opened the door to arguments about other federal collateral consequences such as the loss of public housing and other federal benefits. Which view do you share? If federal collateral consequences should play no role when evaluating a state offense under the Sixth Amendment, how about a collateral consequence imposed by state law, such as sex offender registration or disenfranchisement?

In criminal contempt cases where the legislature has made no judgment about the maximum penalty, the actual penalty imposed will determine whether there is a right to a jury. Contempt punished by a sentence of six months or less is considered a petty offense not requiring a jury. See *Codispoti v. Pennsylvania*, 418 U.S. 506 (1974) (holding that a defendant is entitled to a jury if the aggregate sentences for multiple counts of contempt arising from a single trial total more than six months). Evaluating when contempt *fines* trigger the jury right is often difficult. See *International Union, UMW v. Bagwell*, 512 U.S. 821 (1994). *Muniz v. Hoffman*, 422 U.S. 454 (1975), involved a contempt penalty of $10,000 against a labor union. The Court reasoned this did not trigger the jury right: "It is not difficult to grasp the proposition that six months in jail is a serious matter for any individual, but it is not tenable to argue that the possibility of a * * * fine [of $10,000] would be considered a serious risk to a large corporation or labor union."

Must a jury be provided if several petty offenses are joined in a single prosecution, so that the aggregate potential penalty exceeds six months? In *Lewis v. United States*, 518 U.S. 322 (1996), the Court answered no, noting that per *Blanton* "we determine whether an offense is serious by looking to the judgment of the legislature." The "fact that the petitioner was charged with two counts of a petty offense does not revise the legislative judgment as to the gravity of that particular offense." Stevens and Ginsburg, JJ., dissenting, could "see no basis for assuming that the dishonor associated with multiple convictions for petty offenses is less than the dishonor associated with conviction of a single serious crime."

2. ***Jury size.*** A majority of states today use juries of six jurors for trial of misdemeanors in lower trial courts, and six states have adopted juries with fewer than twelve members in noncapital felony cases. In WILLIAMS v. FLORIDA, 399 U.S. 78 (1970), the Court concluded that

use of a 6-person jury did not violate petitioner's Sixth Amendment rights. The Court found that the "intent of the Framers" did not prescribe jury size. It also emphasized that "the essential feature of a jury obviously lies in the interposition between the accused and his accuser of the common-sense judgment of a group of laymen, and in the community participation and shared responsibility which results from that group's determination of guilt or innocence. The performance of this role is not a function of the particular number of the body which makes up the jury. To be sure, the number should probably be large enough to promote group deliberation, free from outside attempts at intimidation, and to provide a fair possibility for obtaining a representative cross section of the community. But we find little reason to think that these goals are in any meaningful sense less likely to be achieved when the jury numbers six, than when it numbers 12—particularly if the requirement of unanimity is retained. And, certainly the reliability of the jury as a fact-finder hardly seems likely to be a function of its size.

". . . What few experiments have occurred—usually in the civil area—indicate that there is no discernible difference between the results reached by the two different-sized juries. In short, neither currently available evidence nor theory[49] suggests that the 12-man jury is necessarily more advantageous to the defendant than a jury composed of fewer members.

"Similarly, while in theory the number of viewpoints represented on a randomly selected jury ought to increase as the size of the jury increases, in practice the difference between the 12-man and the six-man jury in terms of the cross section of the community represented seems likely to be negligible. Even the 12-man jury cannot insure representation of every distinct voice in the community, particularly given the use of the peremptory challenge. As long as arbitrary exclusions of a particular class from the jury rolls are forbidden, the concern that the cross section will be significantly diminished if the jury is decreased in size from 12 to six seems an unrealistic one."

Eight years later in *Ballew v. Georgia,* 435 U.S. 223 (1978), a unanimous Court held that petitioner's trial before a 5-member jury deprived him of his constitutional right to jury trial. Justice Blackmun noted that there is "no significant state advantage in reducing the number of jurors from six to five." He noted that only two states had done this, and relied on new empirical studies which "suggest that progressively smaller juries are less likely to foster effective group deliberation," "raise doubts about the accuracy of the results achieved by smaller and smaller panels," "suggest that the verdicts of jury deliberation in criminal cases will vary as juries become smaller, and that the variance amounts to an imbalance to the detriment of one side, the defense," and show that "the opportunity for meaningful and appropriate [minority group] representation does decrease with the size of the panels."

Ballew relied on social science studies to draw the constitutional line at six jurors. In the field of criminal procedure, the Court generally has been reluctant to rely on empirical research as a basis for its decisions. Why? Consider Justice Powell's concurring opinion in *Ballew,* joined by Chief Justice Douglas and Justice Rehnquist, where he criticized the majority's "heavy reliance on numerology derived from statistical studies," noting that "neither the validity nor the methodology employed by the studies cited was subjected to the traditional testing mechanisms of the adversary process."

3. ***Jury unanimity.*** In APODACA v. OREGON, 406 U.S. 404 (1972), petitioners, convicted of felonies by 11–1 and 10–2 votes, unsuccessfully challenged a state constitutional provision which permitted 10 members of a jury to render guilty verdicts in noncapital cases. White, J., joined by Burger, C.J., and Blackmun and Rehnquist, JJ., announced the judgment:

---

[49] Studies of the operative factors contributing to small group deliberation and decision-making suggest that jurors in the minority on the first ballot are likely to be influenced by the proportional size of the majority aligned against them. * * *

"[T]he essential feature of a jury obviously lies in the interposition between the accused and his accuser of the commonsense judgment of a group of laymen * * *. A requirement of unanimity, however, does not materially contribute to the exercise of this commonsense judgment. As we said in *Williams,* a jury will come to such a judgment as long as it consists of a group of laymen representative of a cross section of the community who have the duty and the opportunity to deliberate, free from outside attempts at intimidation, on the question of a defendant's guilt. In terms of this function we perceive no difference between juries required to act unanimously and those permitted to convict or acquit by votes of 10 to two or 11 to one. Requiring unanimity would obviously produce hung juries in some situations where nonunanimous juries will convict or acquit. But in either case, the interest of the defendant in having the judgment of his peers interposed between himself and the officers of the State who prosecute and judge him is equally well served." The plurality also rejected the assumption that "minority groups, even when they are represented on a jury, will not adequately represent the viewpoint of those groups simply because they may be outvoted in the final result. They will be present during all deliberations, and their views will be heard."

Powell, J., concurring, disagreed with the premise that "all of the elements of jury trial within the meaning of the Sixth Amendment are necessarily embodied in or incorporated into the Due Process Clause of the Fourteenth," and thus deemed the procedure in *Apodaca* not inconsistent with the Court's long-standing presumption "that unanimous verdicts are essential in federal jury trials."

Douglas, J., joined by Brennan and Marshall, JJ., dissented: "The diminution of verdict reliability flows from the fact that nonunanimous juries need not debate and deliberate as fully as must unanimous juries. As soon as the requisite majority is attained, further consideration is not required either by Oregon or by Louisiana even though the dissident jurors might, if given the chance, be able to convince the majority. Such persuasion does in fact occasionally occur in States where the unanimous requirement applies: 'In roughly one case in ten, the minority eventually succeeds in reversing an initial majority, and these may be cases of special importance.' [citing Kalven & Zeisel, *The American Jury* 490 (1966)] * * *

"The new rule also has an impact on cases in which a unanimous jury would have neither voted to acquit nor to convict, but would have deadlocked. In unanimous jury States, this occurs about 5.6% of the time. Of these deadlocked juries, Kalven and Zeisel say that 56% contain either one, two, or three dissenters. In these latter cases, the majorities favor the prosecution 44% (of the 56%) but the defendant only 12% (of the 56%). Thus, by eliminating these deadlocks, Louisiana wins 44 cases for every 12 that it loses, obtaining in this band of outcomes a substantially more favorable conviction ratio (3.67) than the unanimous jury ratio of slightly less than two guilty verdicts for every acquittal. By eliminating the one and two dissenting juror cases, Oregon does even better, gaining 4.25 convictions for every acquittal."

In a companion case to *Apodaca, Johnson v. Louisiana,* 406 U.S. 356 (1972), a 5–4 majority upheld a 9–3 robbery conviction, rejecting appellant's argument that unanimity is necessary to give substance to the "proof beyond a reasonable doubt" standard. "[D]isagreement of three jurors does not alone establish reasonable doubt, particularly when such a heavy majority of the jury, after having considered the dissenters' views, remains convinced of guilt."

The next term in *Burch v. Louisiana,* 441 U.S. 130 (1979), a unanimous Court struck down a state constitutional provision requiring that misdemeanors punishable by more than six months "shall be tried before a jury of six persons, five of whom must concur to render a verdict." The Court stressed that the "near-uniform judgment of the Nation," reflected by the fact only two states allow nonunanimous verdicts by 6-member juries, "provides a useful guide in delimiting the line between those jury practices that are constitutionally permissible and those that are not"; and that claims that nonunanimous 6-person juries save considerable time "are speculative, at best."

In 2018, Louisiana voters restored the unanimity rule. Bipartisan support for the change developed after the publication in 2015 of a book tracing the rule's racist roots: Thomas Aiello's, "Jim Crow's Last Stand: Nonunanimous Criminal Jury Verdicts in Louisiana " Aiello explained that the Louisiana legislature removed the unanimity requirement in 1880 in order to provide more labor for the state's convict-leasing system. Prisoners, mostly black and brutally treated, were leased to private businesses for a profit. By 1898 non-unanimous verdicts became part of the Louisiana Constitution, ensuring more convictions for the state's prison workforce at Angola, where historical accounts show black prisoners remained essentially "state slaves." Opposing the return to unanimity 120 years later in 2018, "a prominent white opponent of the measure, . . . conceded that nonunanimity was a 'vestige[ ] of slavery . . . . [I]t is what it is.'" Thomas Ward Frampton, *The Jim Crow Jury*, 71 Vand. L. Rev. 1593, 1653 (2018) (also presenting data showing nonunanimity "appears to accrue to the disadvantage of black defendants more frequently than white defendants").

Oregon's rule, too, is under attack. See Aliza B. Kaplan & Amy Saack, *Overturning* Apodaca v. Oregon *Should Be Easy: Nonunanimous Jury Verdicts in Criminal Cases Undermine the Credibility of Our Justice System*, 95 Or. L. Rev. 1, 3 (2016) (Oregon's law was adopted in 1934 as the state was "simmering with anti-immigrant xenophobia (predominantly anti-Semitism and anti-Catholicism)," after "a Jewish man accused of killing a Protestant was spared a murder conviction and death sentence because a single juror held out for manslaughter").

4. ***About what must a jury agree?*** In *Schad v. Arizona*, 501 U.S. 624 (1991), the defendant was convicted of first degree murder, defined by state law as murder that is "willful, deliberate or premeditated * * * or which is committed * * * in the perpetration of, or attempt to perpetrate * * * robbery." The instructions to the jury did not require it to agree about whether the murder was premeditated or whether it was felony murder. In an opinion joined by three other members of the Court, Souter, J., declared that the Due Process Clause places "limits on a State's capacity to define different courses of conduct, or states of mind, as merely alternative means of committing a single offense, thereby permitting a defendant's conviction without jury agreement as to which course or state actually occurred." In concluding those limits were not exceeded, the plurality opinion deemed "history and widely shared practice as concrete indications of what fundamental fairness and rationality require." The plurality also found it "significant that Arizona's equation of the mental states of premeditated murder and felony murder as species of the blameworthy state of mind required to prove a single offense of first-degree murder finds substantial historical and contemporary echoes." Cautioning that it cannot be said "that either history or current practice is dispositive," the plurality emphasized the lack of "moral disparity" in the two alternative mental states. "Whether or not everyone would agree that the mental state that precipitates death in the course of robbery is the moral equivalent of premeditation, it is clear that such equivalence could reasonably be found, which is enough to rule out the argument that this moral disparity bars treating them as alternative means to satisfy the mental element of a single offense." Justice Scalia, providing the fifth vote for affirmance, was critical of the plurality's moral equivalence test and emphasized instead that the challenged practice was as old as the common law and still in existence in the vast majority of States.

The Court reached a different conclusion in *Richardson v. United States*, 526 U.S. 813 (1999), where the defendant was charged with violating a federal statute forbidding any person from "engag[ing] in a continuing criminal enterprise," defined as involving a violation of the drug statutes where "such violation is a part of a continuing series of violations." The government introduced evidence of more underlying drug offenses than the three assumed to be necessary to constitute a "series," and defendant was convicted following a jury instruction stating the jury had to agree that defendant had committed at least three such offenses but did not have to agree about which three. The Court found that "the statute's phrase 'series of violations' * * * create[s] several elements, namely the several 'violations.'" The Constitution required that the jury must agree unanimously and separately as to each of those elements." Distinguishing the statute in *Schad*, the Court noted the "statute's word 'violations' covers many different kinds of behavior of varying degrees of seriousness," which "increases the likelihood that treating violations simply as alternative means, by permitting a jury to avoid discussion of the specific factual details of each violation, will cover-up wide disagreement among the jurors about just what the defendant did, or did not, do."

For crimes lacking a common law pedigree, courts have struggled to determine when alternatives that a legislature lists in an offense definition may be considered alternative means to commit a single crime (about which jurors need not agree) or instead must be treated as elements that differentiate separate offenses (on which unanimity is required). To the extent the Court is concerned about the ability of a legislature to evade Sixth Amendment guarantees by redefining its criminal prohibitions, this problem resembles the Court's efforts to distinguish between elements and sentencing factors, examined in Ch. 27, Section 3, Part D.

5. ***Jury nullification.*** As the Court emphasized in *United States v. Gaudin*, 515 U.S. 506 (1995), the Constitution requires "criminal convictions to rest upon a jury determination that the defendant is guilty of every element of the crime with which he is charged * * * . [T]he jury's constitutional responsibility is not merely to determine the facts, but to apply the law to those facts and *draw the ultimate conclusion of guilt or innocence*." (Emphasis added). If the jury's conclusion is that the defendant is not guilty, its decision may not be appealed or reviewed. See Chapter 26. An acquittal despite proof of guilt beyond a reasonable doubt is known as "jury nullification."

Judges have long rejected claims that a defendant has a right to instructions that remind the jurors of their power to acquit despite proof of guilt. Consider *United States v. Dougherty*, 473 F.2d 1113 (D.C. Cir. 1972), where Leventhal, J., joined by Adams, J., maintained:

"The jury knows well enough that its prerogative is not limited to the choices articulated in the formal instructions of the court. The jury gets its understanding as to the arrangements in the legal system from more than one voice. There is the formal communication from the judge. There is the informal communication from the total culture—literature (novel, drama, film, and television); current comment (newspapers, magazines and television); conversation; and, of course, history and tradition. The totality of input generally convey adequately enough the idea of prerogative, of freedom in an occasional case to depart from what the judge says. Even indicators that would on their face seem too weak to notice—like the fact that the judge tells the jury it must acquit (in case of reasonable doubt) but never tells the jury in so many words that it must convict—are a meaningful part of the jury's total input. Law is a system, and it is also a language, with secondary meanings that may be unrecorded yet are part of its life.

". . . The practicalities of men, machinery and rules point up the danger of articulating discretion to depart from a rule, that the breach will be more often and casually invoked. We cannot gainsay that occasionally jurors uninstructed as to the prerogative may feel themselves compelled to the point of rigidity. The danger of the excess rigidity that may now occasionally exist is not as great as the danger of removing the boundaries of constraint provided by the announced rules.

" * * * To assign the role of mini-legislature to the various petit juries, who must hang if not unanimous, exposes criminal law and administration to paralysis, and to a deadlock that betrays rather than furthers the assumptions of viable democracy.

"Moreover, to compel a juror involuntarily assigned to jury duty to assume the burdens of mini-legislator or judge, as is implicit in the doctrine of nullification, is to put untoward strains on the jury system. It is one thing for a juror to know that the law condemns, but he has a factual power of lenity. To tell him expressly of a nullification prerogative, however, is to inform him, in effect, that it is he who fashions the rule that condemns. That is an overwhelming responsibility, an extreme burden for the jurors' psyche. And it is not inappropriate to add that a juror called upon for an involuntary public service is entitled to the protection, when he takes action that he knows is right, but also knows is unpopular, either in the community at large or in his own particular grouping, that he can fairly put it to friends and neighbors that he was merely following the instructions of the court. * * *

"What makes for health as an occasional medicine would be disastrous as a daily diet. The fact that there is widespread existence of the jury's prerogative, and approval of its existence as a 'necessary counter to case-hardened judges and arbitrary prosecutors,' does not establish as an imperative that the jury must be informed by the judge of that power. On the contrary, it is pragmatically useful to structure instructions in such ways that the jury must feel strongly about the values involved in the case, so strongly that it must itself identify the case as establishing a call of high conscience, and must independently initiate and undertake an act in contravention of the established instructions. This requirement of independent jury conception confines the happening of the lawless jury to the occasional instance that does not violate, and viewed as an exception may even enhance, the over-all normative effect of the rule of law. An explicit instruction to a jury conveys an implied approval that runs the risk of degrading the legal structure requisite for true freedom, for an ordered liberty that protects against anarchy as well as tyranny."

Dissenting on the jury nullification issue, Chief Judge Bazelon observed:

"My own view rests on the premise that nullification can and should serve an important function in the criminal process. * * * The doctrine permits the jury to bring to bear on the criminal process a sense of fairness and particularized justice. The drafters of legal rules cannot anticipate and take account of every case where a defendant's conduct is 'unlawful' but not blameworthy, any more than they can draw a bold line to mark the boundary between an accident and negligence. It is the jury—as spokesman for the community's sense of values—that must explore that subtle and elusive boundary. * * *

"I do not see any reason to assume that jurors will make rampantly abusive use of their power. * * * If a jury refuses to apply strictly the controlling principles of law, it may—in conflict with values shared by the larger community—convict a defendant because of prejudice against him, or acquit a defendant because of sympathy for him and prejudice against his victim. Our fear of unjust conviction is plainly understandable. But it is hard for me to see how a nullification instruction could enhance the likelihood of that result. The instruction would speak in terms of acquittal, not conviction, and it would provide no comfort to a juror determined to convict a defendant in defiance of the law or the facts of the case. * * *

"As for the problem of unjust acquittal, it is important to recognize the strong internal check that constrains the jury's willingness to acquit. Where defendants seem dangerous, juries are unlikely to exercise their nullification power, whether or not an explicit instruction is offered."

Dougherty reflects the judicial view rejecting a constitutional right to jury nullification and disapproving instructions that inform the jury of its power to nullify. Courts have also rejected attempts to inform jurors of the sentence that a guilty verdict would carry. *Shannon v. United States*, 512 U.S. 573 (1994) (explaining that "providing jurors sentencing information invites them to ponder matters that are not within their province, distracts them from their fact-finding responsibilities, and creates a strong possibility of confusion"). Indeed, courts have approved of the dismissal of jurors who intend to reject the applicable law, *United States v. Thomas*, 116 F.3d 606 (2d Cir. 1997), and have upheld instructions informing the jury that if it finds all of the elements of the crime beyond a reasonable doubt, it "must" convict. *United States v. Stegmeier*, 701 F.3d 574 (8th Cir. 2012); *State v. Ragland*, 519 A.2d 1361 (N.J. 1986) (the jury "was never designed * * * to protect the defendant from the law, or from the Legislature").

The Framers probably did assume that the Sixth Amendment included a right to a jury that could reject the law and could be reminded of its power to do so. The Civil War and the Fourteenth Amendment may have modified that original meaning, however. When Southern juries refused to convict those who murdered and brutalized freed blacks and their supporters, Congress enacted (and federal courts enforced) legislation that stripped from federal criminal juries all those who as Klan members swore to acquit defendants in such cases. Similar statutes barred polygamists from serving as jurors in federal prosecutions of bigamy and polygamy in the territory of Utah. This contemporaneous history lends support to an interpretation of the Fourteenth Amendment that "rejected any earlier constitutional protection *for* jury nullification in favor of constitutional protection *from* jury nullification." Nancy J. King, *Jury Nullification in the United States*, Oxford Handbooks Online (Feb. 2015) (discussing the argument by Jonathan Bressler, *Reconstruction and Transformation of Jury Nullification*, 78 U. Chi. L. Rev. 1133 (2011)).

One state has authorized a criminal defendant to argue to jurors that they have the "right to judge . . . the application of the law." N.H. Rev. Stat. § 519:23–a (2012). On what grounds would a jury's rejection of the law be appropriate? How could courts limit jurors to those grounds? Consider Jeffrey Bellin, *Is Punishment Relevant After All? A Prescription for Informing Juries of the Consequences of Conviction*, 90 B. U. L. Rev. 2223 (2010) (advocating introduction of sentencing information and collecting authority discussing sentence-based nullification); Paul Butler, *Racially Based Jury Nullification: Black Power in the Criminal Justice System*, 105 Yale L. J. 677 (1995) (arguing that a black juror can protest racial injustices of the criminal justice system by voting against convicting a black defendant who, the evidence suggests, is guilty); Andrew Leipold, *Rethinking Jury Nullification*, 82 Va. L. Rev. 253 (1996) (proposing a nullification affirmative defense limited to "certain statutory criteria"). Consider also the acquittals of six armed occupiers of a federal wildlife refuge, a standoff that "drew right-wing anti-government protesters from across the U.S. to protest the federal government's control of public land across the West." Reportedly, "During the trial, flag-waving supporters, some in boots and cowboy hats, marched around the courthouse, in part hoping jurors might see one of their signs stating 'Google: jury nullification'—effectively urging jurors to acquit the defendants out of a belief that the law under which they are charged is wrong." Pearce & Anderson, Leaders of Oregon National Wildlife Refuge are Acquitted of Federal Charges, Los Angeles Times, Oct 27, 2016. See Ch. 14, p. 882, Note 2, for additional reasons jurors may choose to acquit despite proof of guilt.

6. *Inconsistent verdicts.* Sometimes when considering multiple counts or multiple defendants, a jury will return verdicts that are not logically consistent with each other. For example, in *United States v. Powell*, 469 U.S. 57 (1984), the defendant was convicted of using the telephone to facilitate the commission of certain felonies, but acquitted of the felony counts themselves. Powell argued that her conviction could not stand because the jury must have made a mistake. Disagreeing, the Court has noted that whenever a conviction is inconsistent with an acquittal, "it is unclear whose ox [is] gored." The Court reasoned that a defendant may challenge on appeal the sufficiency of evidence supporting any guilty verdict.

This tolerant approach to inconsistent verdicts is not tied solely to the jury's nullification power. The Court has upheld inconsistent findings by judges as well, noting, "Even the unlikely possibility that the acquittal is the product of a lenity that judges are free to exercise at the time of sentencing but generally are forbidden to exercise when ruling on guilt or innocence, would not create a constitutional violation." *Harris v. Rivera*, 454 U.S. 339 (1981) (Constitution does not bar state from approving bench trial verdict that defendant was guilty and his accomplice not guilty, even if those verdicts were "logically inconsistent"). The Constitution, the Court explained, does not "prevent a State from empowering its judges to render verdicts of acquittal whenever they are convinced that no sentence should be imposed for reasons that are unrelated to guilt or innocence."

If the jury acquits on one count but cannot reach a verdict on another count, held the Court in *Yeager v. United States*, 557 U.S. 110 (2009), then there is only one verdict, not two inconsistent verdicts. Under the rule of *Ashe v. Swenson*, p. 1049, the verdict of acquittal bars a second attempt at conviction on the mistried count, if the mistried count includes an element necessarily rejected by the acquittal.

Finally, the *Powell* Court declined to consider cases in which "a defendant is convicted of two crimes, where a guilty verdict on one logically excludes the other." In this scenario—sometimes termed "mutually exclusive verdicts"—lower courts have stated that failing to grant relief "would be patently unjust because a defendant would be convicted of two crimes, at least one of which he could not have committed." *United States v. Gross*, 961 F.2d 1097, 1107 (3d Cir. 1992).

7. ***Waiving a jury in favor of a bench trial.*** In 1930, as the number of federal criminal cases skyrocketed under anti-liquor laws, the Court evaluated the jury mandate in Article III and the Sixth Amendment's Jury Clause and concluded the jury was a "privilege," not an "imperative requirement." It found that because the jury was principally for the benefit of the accused, it was a protection that a defendant could waive. *Patton v. United States*, 281 U.S. 276 (1930). Commentators have suggested that the Court's reinterpretation of Article III was based on increasing concerns about docket congestion and the quality of decisions by juries drawn from increasingly diverse populations.

Thirty-five years later, in *Singer v. United States*, 380 U.S. 24 (1965), petitioner challenged Fed.R.Crim.P. 23(a), which allows a defendant to waive a jury only with the approval of the court and the consent of the government. The Court concluded: "The ability to waive a constitutional right does not ordinarily carry with it the right to insist upon the opposite of that right. * * * We find no constitutional impediment to conditioning a waiver of [the jury] right on the consent of the prosecuting attorney and the trial judge when, if either refuses to consent, the result is simply that the defendant is subject to an impartial trial by jury—the very thing that the Constitution guarantees him. The Constitution recognizes an adversary system as the proper method of determining guilt, and the Government, as a litigant, has a legitimate interest in seeing that cases in which it believes a conviction is warranted are tried before the tribunal which the Constitution regards as most likely to produce a fair result."

The decision to waive a jury must be made by the defendant, not counsel, must be renewed if a defendant is retried, and must in most jurisdictions be made in writing or on the record. Today, more defendants are convicted after bench trials than jury trials, and those who waive a jury often receive lower sentences than those who do not. Nancy J. King, David A. Soulé, Sara Steen & Robert R. Weidner, *When Process Affects Punishment: Differences in Sentences After Guilty Plea, Bench Trial, and Jury Trial in Five Guidelines States*, 105 Colum. L. Rev. 959 (2005) (finding that no state guidelines system explicitly recommends that defendants who waive a jury trial in favor of a bench trial should be punished more leniently than defendants convicted of the very same offense who insist upon jury trial, but in many courtrooms these sentencing differences are routine). Why might a court or legislature comfortable with recognizing sentencing discounts for waiving trial altogether be reluctant to embrace sentencing discounts for waiving a jury?

8. ***Juries, accuracy, and retroactivity.*** Generally, whenever the Supreme Court announces a new rule of constitutional criminal procedure—as it did in *Duncan*—only those defendants who have not completed the direct appeal process may take advantage of that rule. If, however, the decision announces a " 'watershed rule' implicating the fundamental fairness and accuracy of the criminal proceeding," retroactive application is possible. See Ch. 29, Section 5. In *DeStefano v. Woods*, 392 U.S. 631 (1968), the Court refused to give retroactive effect to *Duncan*, noting that although "the right to jury trial generally tends to prevent arbitrariness and repression[,] * * * '[w]e would not assert * * * that every criminal trial—or any particular trial—held before a judge alone is unfair or that a defendant may never be as fairly treated by a judge

as he would be by a jury.'" Later, in *Schriro v. Summerlin*, Note 2, p. 1450, the Court again found that the "evidence is simply too equivocal to support [the] conclusion" that "judicial factfinding so 'seriously diminishe[s]' accuracy that there is an ' "impermissibly large risk" ' of punishing conduct the law does not reach." Echoing Justice Harlan's dissent in *Duncan*, the Court in *Summerlin* reasoned that "for every argument why juries are more accurate factfinders, there is another why they are less accurate," including "juries' tendency to become confused over legal standards and to be influenced by emotion or philosophical predisposition," and "judges' greater experience." The Court also noted that other countries have given the right to jury trial a "mixed reception." "When so many presumably reasonable minds continue to disagree over whether juries are better factfinders at all, we cannot confidently say that judicial factfinding seriously diminishes accuracy." Does the concern for accurate and reliable factfinding play any role in the Court's decisions interpreting the jury right? If the right to a jury trial does not advance accuracy, what principles does it safeguard?

§ 2. JURY SELECTION

Statutory as well as constitutional text regulates the process of selecting criminal juries. See, e.g., the Federal Jury Selection and Service Act of 1968, 28 U.S.C. § 1861 et seq., one of the first to require random selection. The material that follows addresses primarily the constitutional rules governing jury selection, specifically the guarantee of equal protection and the requirement that the jury be impartial. Before turning to how the Court has applied these constitutional concepts to the various steps in the jury selection process, an outline of those steps is useful.

Jury selection begins with the specification of the geographic community from which each court will draw its jurors—the *vicinage*. The vicinage typically corresponds to the judicial district for the court, in state court this is usually the county. See Ch. 18, Section 1, Note 2, p. 1017. A *master list* of persons residing in the vicinage who meet the statutory criteria for jury service is then created. For example, the jury list may include all residents who have registered to vote or who have obtained drivers' licenses. From this list, a *qualified list* or *pool* is prepared, containing the names of those on the master list who meet the statutory qualifications for jury service, such as having the ability to speak and read English. From this qualified list, a smaller group of potential jurors, known as the *venire,* is randomly selected and summoned to appear for a given trial or set of trials. Some potential jurors will be excused from jury service for hardship or health reasons. More and more jurisdictions use a "one-step" process that combines the summons and qualification questionnaire into a single mailing. *Voir dire* is the process of selecting from the venire assembled at the courthouse those persons who will be sworn in as jurors to hear an individual case. Subsection A, below, discusses constitutional limitations on the process of selecting the master list, the qualified list, and venire; Subsection B examines limits on the *voir dire* process of selecting individual jury panels from the venire.

A. SELECTING THE VENIRE

Choosing whom to summon for jury service used to be a much more subjective process than it is today. Traditionally, local officials known as jury commissioners would create the jury list and determine who would be asked to serve. By the 1990s, computers made automated list generation and random selection easier and cheaper for courts to manage. But long before computer technology, constitutional litigation also provided an incentive for change.

Defendants first challenged state jury selection procedures under the Fourteenth Amendment's Equal Protection Clause, decades before the Court decided in *Duncan* that the Sixth Amendment right to jury trial applied to the states through the Due Process Clause. In *Strauder v. West Virginia,* 100 U.S. 303 (1880), the Court held that for a state to try a black defendant before a jury from which all members of his race had been excluded by statute is a denial of the defendant's right to equal protection, and in *Neal v. Delaware,* 103 U.S. 370 (1881), the principle was extended to the discriminatory administration of ostensibly race-neutral jury selection laws to achieve the same result.

Strauder and *Neal* had very limited impact for several decades because they required the defendant to show jury officials deliberately excluded blacks from jury service, and lower court findings of fact were presumed to be true unless the defendant proved the contrary. But in *Norris v. Alabama,* 294 U.S. 587 (1935), the Court held that a defendant in a criminal case could make out a prima facie case of discrimination by showing the existence of a substantial number of blacks in the community, and their *total or virtual exclusion* from jury service. The burden then shifted to the state to show that the exclusion did not flow from discrimination. *Avery v. Georgia,* 345 U.S. 559 (1953). Later cases established that a state could not meet this burden merely by offering testimony by the jury commissioner that he did not intend to discriminate, *Eubanks v. Louisiana,* 356 U.S. 584 (1958), or that he did not know any qualified blacks. *Hill v. Texas,* 316 U.S. 400 (1942). Then, in *Castaneda v. Partida,* 430 U.S. 482 (1977), a 5–4 decision, the Court, per Blackmun, J., discarded the requirement of complete exclusion and held that the petitioner had established a prima facie case of discrimination by showing that the population of the county was 79% Mexican-American, but that over an 11-year period Mexican-Americans made up only 39% of the persons summoned for grand jury service under a "key-person" selection system (see Note 1, p. 950). Because this showing was not rebutted by any evidence that racially neutral qualifications for grand jurors had resulted in the lower proportion of Mexican-Americans, the Court agreed that an equal protection violation had been proven.

Although *Cansteneda* made it somewhat less difficult for defendants and those excluded from jury service to challenge selection practices under the Equal Protection Clause, proof of discriminatory intent remained a significant evidentiary burden. The cross-section requirement in the Sixth Amendment's guarantee of an impartial jury, developed by the Supreme Court in the cases below, does not require proof of discriminatory purpose, and regulates the exclusion of more groups than those that trigger heightened scrutiny under the Equal Protection Clause. For these reasons, the cross-section requirement has proven to be a more powerful tool than the Equal Protection Clause to persuade states to adopt more random and inclusive jury selection procedures.

TAYLOR V. LOUISIANA

419 U.S. 522, 95 S.Ct. 692, 42 L.Ed.2d 690 (1975).

[The State alleged Taylor used a butcher knife to force a woman, with her daughter and grandson, to drive him to an abandoned road, where he raped and robbed her. He was convicted of aggravated kidnapping and sentenced to death.]

JUSTICE WHITE delivered the opinion of the Court.

When this case was tried, Art. VII, § 41, of the Louisiana Constitution, and Art. 402 of the Louisiana Code of Criminal Procedure provided that a woman should not be selected for jury service unless she had previously filed a written declaration of her desire to be subject to jury service. The constitutionality of these provisions is the issue in this case. * * *

The Louisiana jury selection system does not disqualify women from jury service, but in operation its conceded systematic impact is that only a very few women, grossly disproportionate to the number of eligible women in the community, are called for jury service. [It was stipulated that no more than 10% of the persons on the jury wheel were women, that only 12 females were among the 1,800 persons drawn to fill petit jury venires, and that this discrepancy was the result of the operation of the challenged provisions.] In this case, no women were on the venire from which the petit jury was drawn. The issue we have, therefore, is whether a jury selection system which operates to exclude from jury service an identifiable class of citizens constituting 53% of eligible jurors in the community comports with the Sixth and Fourteenth Amendments.

The State first insists that Taylor, a male, has no standing to object to the exclusion of women from his jury. But Taylor's claim is that he was constitutionally entitled to a jury drawn from a venire constituting a fair cross section of the community and that the jury that tried him was not such a jury by reason of the exclusion of women. Taylor was not a member of the excluded class; but there is no rule that claims such as Taylor presents may be made only by those defendants who are members of the group excluded from jury service. In *Peters v. Kiff,* 407 U.S. 493 (1972), the defendant, a white man, challenged his conviction on the ground that Negroes had been systematically excluded from jury service. Six Members of the Court agreed that petitioner was entitled to present the issue and concluded that he had been deprived of his federal rights. Taylor, in the case before us, was similarly entitled to tender and have adjudicated the claim that the exclusion of women from jury service deprived him of the kind of fact finder to which he was constitutionally entitled.

The background against which this case must be decided includes our holding in *Duncan v. Louisiana* [p. 1230], that the Sixth Amendment's provision for jury trial is made binding on the States by virtue of the Fourteenth Amendment. Our inquiry is whether the presence of a fair cross section of the community on venires, panels or lists from which petit juries are drawn is essential to the fulfillment of the Sixth Amendment's guarantee of an impartial jury trial in criminal prosecutions. * * *

The unmistakable import of this Court's opinions, at least since 1941, and not repudiated by intervening decisions, is that the selection of a petit jury from a representative cross section of the community is an essential component of the Sixth Amendment right to a jury trial. * * *

We accept the fair cross-section requirement as fundamental to the jury trial guaranteed by the Sixth Amendment and are convinced that the requirement has solid foundation. The purpose of a jury is to guard against the exercise of arbitrary power—to make available the commonsense judgment of the community as a hedge against the overzealous or mistaken prosecutor and in preference to the professional or perhaps overconditioned or biased response of a judge. This prophylactic vehicle is not provided if the jury pool is made up of only special segments of the populace or if large, distinctive groups are excluded from the pool. Community participation in the administration of the criminal law, moreover, is not only consistent with our democratic heritage but is also critical to public confidence in the fairness of the criminal justice system. Restricting jury service to only special groups or excluding identifiable segments playing major roles in the community cannot be squared with the constitutional concept of jury trial. * * *

We are also persuaded that the fair cross-section requirement is violated by the systematic exclusion of women, who in the judicial district involved here amounted to 53% of the citizens eligible for jury service. This conclusion necessarily entails the judgment that women are sufficiently numerous and distinct from men that if they are systematically eliminated from jury panels, the Sixth Amendment's fair cross-section requirement cannot be satisfied. This very matter was debated in *Ballard v. United States,* 329 U.S. 187 (1946). Positing the fair cross-section rule—there said to be a statutory one—the Court concluded that the systematic exclusion of women was unacceptable. The dissenting view that an all-male panel drawn from various groups in the community would be as truly representative as if women were included, was firmly rejected:

> "The thought is that the factors which tend to influence the action of women are the same as those which influence the action of men—personality, background, economic status—and not sex. Yet it is not enough to say that women when sitting as jurors neither act nor tend to act as a class. Men likewise do not act as a class. But, if the shoe were on the other foot, who would claim that a jury was truly representative of the

community if all men were intentionally and systematically excluded from the panel? The truth is that the two sexes are not fungible; a community made up exclusively of one is different from a community composed of both; the subtle interplay of influence one on the other is among the imponderables. To insulate the courtroom from either may not in a given case make an iota of difference. Yet a flavor, a distinct quality is lost if either sex is excluded. The exclusion of one may indeed make the jury less representative of the community than would be true if an economic or racial group were excluded."

In this respect, we agree with the Court in *Ballard:* If the fair cross-section rule is to govern the selection of juries, as we have concluded it must, women cannot be systematically excluded from jury panels from which petit juries are drawn. This conclusion is consistent with the current judgment of the country, now evidenced by legislative or constitutional provisions in every State and at the federal level qualifying women for jury service.

There remains the argument that women as a class serve a distinctive role in society and that jury service would so substantially interfere with that function that the State has ample justification for excluding women from service unless they volunteer, even though the result is that almost all jurors are men. It is true that *Hoyt v. Florida,* 368 U.S. 57 (1961), held that such a system did not deny due process of law or equal protection of the laws because there was a sufficiently rational basis for such an exemption. But *Hoyt* did not involve a defendant's Sixth Amendment right to a jury drawn from a fair cross section of the community and the prospect of depriving him of that right if women as a class are systematically excluded. The right to a proper jury cannot be overcome on merely rational grounds. There must be weightier reasons if a distinctive class representing 53% of the eligible jurors is for all practical purposes to be excluded from jury service. No such basis has been tendered here.

The States are free to grant exemptions from jury service to individuals in case of special hardship or incapacity and to those engaged in particular occupations the uninterrupted performance of which is critical to the community's welfare. It would not appear that such exemptions would pose substantial threats that the remaining pool of jurors would not be representative of the community. A system excluding all women, however, is a wholly different matter. It is untenable to suggest these days that it would be a special hardship for each and every woman to perform jury service or that society cannot spare *any* women from their present duties. This may be the case with many, and it may be burdensome to sort out those who should serve. But that task is performed in the case of men, and the administrative convenience in dealing with women as a class is insufficient justification for diluting the quality of community judgment represented by the jury in criminal trials. * * *

It should also be emphasized that in holding that petit juries must be drawn from a source fairly representative of the community we impose no requirement that petit juries actually chosen must mirror the community and reflect the various distinctive groups in the population. Defendants are not entitled to a jury of any particular composition; but the jury wheels, pools of names, panels or venires from which juries are drawn must not systematically exclude distinctive groups in the community and thereby fail to be reasonably representative thereof. * * *

Reversed and remanded.

JUSTICE REHNQUIST, dissenting. [The majority] fails * * * to provide any satisfactory explanation of the mechanism by which the Louisiana system undermines the prophylactic role of the jury, either in general or in this case. The best it can do is to posit "a flavor, a distinct quality," which allegedly is lost if either sex is excluded. However, this "flavor" is not of such importance that the Constitution is offended if any given petit jury is not so enriched. This smacks more of mysticism than of law. * * *

NOTES AND QUESTIONS ON CROSS-SECTION CLAIMS

1. ***The test for a cross-section violation.*** In *Duren v. Missouri*, 439 U.S. 357 (1979), the defendant established (1) that 54% of the adult inhabitants of the county were women, (2) that only 15% of the persons placed on venires were women, and (3) that any woman could decline jury service (a) by claiming an exemption in response to a prominent notice on a jury-selection questionnaire, (b) by returning the summons for jury duty as indicated on the summons, or (c) by simply not reporting for jury duty. The Court, per White, J., held that the defendant had made out "a prima facie fair-cross-section violation" by showing "(1) that the group alleged to be excluded is a 'distinctive' group in the community; (2) that the representation of this group in venires from which juries are selected is not fair and reasonable in relation to the number of such persons in the community; and (3) that this underrepresentation is due to systematic exclusion of the group in the jury selection process." The Court went on to find that the state had not carried its "burden of justifying this infringement by showing attainment of a fair cross section to be incompatible with a significant state interest." Recognizing "that a State may have an important interest in assuring that those members of the family responsible for the care of children are available to do so," Justice White suggested that an exemption "appropriately tailored to this interest would * * * survive a fair-cross-section challenge."

2. ***When is a group "distinctive" for cross-section purposes?*** The Court has not clarified just what makes a group "distinctive." It did hold in *Buchanan v. Kentucky*, 483 U.S. 402 (1987), that "*Witherspoon*-excludables," see Note 3, p. 1249, do not constitute a distinctive group for fair cross-section purposes. Lower courts have looked to whether members of the group share distinct beliefs, values, or experiences that bind the group together and could not be represented adequately if the group was excluded. Consider, for example, *State v. Fulton*, 566 N.E.2d 1195 (Ohio 1991) (Amish comprise distinctive group when they make up about 35% of the population and have a "separate and distinct mode of living"); *Wells v. State*, 848 N.E.2d 1133 (Ind.App. 2006) (finding college students are not a distinctive group, declining to engage in unsupported speculation that college students think differently, on average, from other members of society).

3. ***What is "exclusion"? Determining "fair and reasonable" representation of the community.*** Cross-section claims have prompted litigation over the meaning of the "community" to be represented fairly, for just as the choice of boundaries for voting districts can affect the racial and ethnic composition of voters, the boundaries of jury districts can affect the composition of jury pools. Assuming the appropriate geographic area is settled, a court evaluating a cross-section claim will compare the proportion of the venire belonging to the group alleged to be underrepresented with the group's proportion of "citizens eligible for jury service" in that geographic area, a population sometimes difficult to quantify. Most states limit eligibility to U.S. citizens, at least 18 years old, who speak and understand English, are mentally competent, and have no felony convictions. Once the relevant comparison population is determined, what is a fair representation? An absolute disparity of 10% between the group's representation on the panel and the group's representation among those eligible for jury service is typically sufficient to show underrepresentation, but mandating such a showing would mean that the exclusion of groups constituting less than 10% of the jury eligible population would elude the cross-section guarantee. Alternative statistical measures have been proposed in such cases, including "comparative disparity," determined by dividing the absolute disparity by the group's representation in the jury-eligible population. Without "tak[ing] sides * * * on the method or methods by which underrepresentation is appropriately measured," the Court in *Berghuis v. Smith*, 559 U.S. 314 (2010), did note that "[e]ach test is imperfect. Absolute disparity and comparative disparity measurements . . . can be misleading when, as here, 'members of the distinctive group comp[ose] [only] a small percentage of those eligible for jury service.' " The Court did not reach the state's argument that proof of absolute disparity exceeding 10% should be required in order to establish a cross-section violation.

4. ***When is exclusion "systematic"?*** *Smith*, Note 3 above, is most notable for its discussion of what counts as "systematic" exclusion for a cross-section claim. The exclusion of women in *Duren* was due to the system by which juries were selected, explained the Court in *Smith*. Duren "proved that women's underrepresentation was persistent—occurring in every weekly venire for almost a year," and he identified the two stages of the selection process when the exclusion took place, namely exemptions for women at the questionnaire stage and presumptions that excluded women at the summoning stage.

In *Smith,* the petitioner argued that the practice of first assigning jurors to district courts and only then allocating those who remained to the felony Circuit Court where he had been tried had systematically excluded African Americans from his venire. But Smith's proof of systematic exclusion by "siphoning," concluded the Court, fell far short of the "particularized showing" made in *Duren*. The Court used a number of different terms to express a relationship between the selection practice and underrepresentation that would constitute "systematic exclusion." Smith had not established that the siphoning practice "caused" underrepresentation, "created" racial disparities, "made a critical difference," or even "had a significantly adverse impact on the representation of African Americans on Circuit Court venires." In light of this, the Court concluded, the state court's decision rejecting Smith's cross-section claim was reasonable and habeas relief should be denied.

Sometimes a cognizable group is underrepresented because members of that group are less likely than members of other groups to stay at one address, register to vote, or respond to juror questionnaires. Is it "systematic exclusion" if a state chooses not to modify its procedures to update addresses more frequently, draw potential jurors from drivers' lists as well as voter rolls, or follow-up on unreturned questionnaires? In *Smith*, the petitioner also argued that African Americans had been systematically excluded by 1) overly generous extension of hardship exemptions for reasons such as lack of transportation or child care, 2) reliance on mail notices to addresses at least 15 months old, and 3) failure to take action when those summoned did not respond or appear. Because Smith raised these arguments in a federal habeas proceeding, relief could be granted only if the state court ruling upholding his conviction was contrary to or an unreasonable application of Supreme Court precedent. In no decision had the Court either decided that features of that kind or "the impact of social and economic factors" could support a fair-cross-section claim. States had broad discretion to prescribe relevant qualifications for their jurors and to provide reasonable exemptions, the Court said, and in *Duren* stated that "hardship exemptions resembling those Smith assails might well 'survive a fair-cross-section challenge.' "

5. ***When is systematic exclusion tailored to a significant state interest?*** *Duren* and *Taylor* both suggested that even systematic exclusion of a distinctive group would survive constitutional attack if justified by a significant governmental interest. *Compare United States v. Greene*, 995 F.2d 793 (8th Cir. 1993) (the inclusion of jurors who have been charged with crimes is incompatible with the significant governmental interest of having jurors who can conscientiously and properly carry out their sworn duty to apply the law) with Shari Seidman Diamond & Mary R. Rose, *The Contemporary American Jury,* 14 Ann. Rev. L. Soc. Sci. 239 (2018) (noting exclusion of convicted felons "may have the largest effect on representativeness," citing research finding that the more than 16 million felons and ex-felons—7.5% of the adult population—represent 33.4% of the black adult male population, and noting study that found felons and law students did not differ on a measure of pretrial bias). *Compare also United States v. Aponte-Suarez*, 905 F.2d 483 (1st Cir. 1990) (even if it was "systematic exclusion" to require that jurors in the District of Puerto Rico be proficient in English, the requirement is justified by "the overwhelming national interest served by the use of English in a United States court") with Diamond & Rose, reporting that that including non-English speaking jurors in New Mexico state courts, where the state constitution bars the exclusion of citizens unable to speak, read or write English, has not caused difficulties).

B. SELECTING THE JURY FROM THE VENIRE: VOIR DIRE

Voir dire (to speak the truth) is the process of selecting from the venire the set of jurors that will hear a case. The number of jurors selected will be the number required for decision, plus any additional, alternate jurors who may be needed to take the place of jurors who become unable to complete their service. During voir dire, veniremembers answer questions from the judge or the attorneys. On the basis of these answers, a potential juror may be dismissed, either "for cause" or when one of the parties exercises a "peremptory challenge." This subsection first considers the defendant's access to information about potential jurors. It then turns to the standard that courts apply when ruling on challenges for cause. It concludes with the regulation of the peremptory challenge.

NOTES AND QUESTIONS ON ACCESS TO JUROR INFORMATION

1. ***Juror questionnaires.*** Many courts now utilize detailed questionnaires to obtain information about the backgrounds and attitudes of prospective jurors for particular cases. See, for example the discussion of jury questionnaires in *Skilling v. United States*, p. 1264. The completed questionnaires, as well as the veniremembers' names, however, may not be disclosed until voir dire, limiting the amount of independent research parties may conduct into veniremembers' lives. The practice of empaneling an "anonymous jury," withholding the jurors' names and addresses from the parties and the press throughout the trial, is strictly limited in most jurisdictions. A leading case is *United States v. Thomas,* 757 F.2d 1359 (2d Cir. 1985) ("there must be, first, strong reason to believe that the jury needs protection and, second, reasonable precaution must be taken to minimize the effect that such a decision might have on the jurors' opinions of the defendants"). Some courts and commentators have argued that if a legislature determines there is a need for juror anonymity, it is constitutional to require that jurors in all criminal cases be identified by number rather than by name. E.g., Nancy J. King, *Nameless Justice: The Case for the Routine Use of Anonymous Juries in Criminal Trials*, 49 Vand. L. Rev. 123 (1996).

2. ***Who questions potential jurors during voir dire?*** All but a half dozen states permit attorneys to ask questions; in the others, and in federal courts, a judge may do all the questioning. Assuming that voir dire's only function is to elicit information for cause and peremptory challenges, which do you prefer?

3. ***A right to ask certain questions?*** In *Ristaino v. Ross,* 424 U.S. 589 (1976), the Court reasoned, "The mere fact that the victim of the crimes alleged [armed robbery, assault with a dangerous weapon, and assault with intent to murder] was a white man and the defendants were Negroes" did not "suggest a significant likelihood that racial prejudice might infect Ross' trial." The judge had "acted within the Constitution in determining that the demands of due process could be satisfied by his more generalized but thorough inquiry into the impartiality of the veniremen." The Court distinguished an earlier case, *Ham v. South Carolina*, 409 U.S. 524 (1973), where it had held that the Fourteenth Amendment "required the judge . . . to interrogate the jurors upon the subject of racial prejudice," and that general questions about partiality or bias were not sufficient. The *Ristaino* Court reasoned that the special factors in *Ham,* where a black civil rights worker had claimed he had been framed of drug possession by police opposed to his civil rights activities, were more likely to distort the trial than the facts in *Ristaino*.

The Court in *Ristaino* went on to explain that although *voir dire* questioning directed to racial prejudice was not constitutionally required in the case, "the wiser course generally is to propound appropriate questions designed to identify racial prejudice if requested by the defendant. Under our supervisory power we would have required as much of a federal court faced with the circumstances here," referencing *Rosales-Lopez v. United States*, 451 U.S. 182 (1981). In *Rosales-*

Lopez, the Court held that federal trial courts must inquire about race bias "when requested by a defendant accused of a violent crime and where the defendant and the victim are members of different racial or ethnic groups." The Court explained, "It remains an unfortunate fact in our society that violent crimes perpetrated against members of other racial or ethnic groups often raise such a possibility. There may be other circumstances that suggest the need for such an inquiry, but the decision as to whether the total circumstances suggest a reasonable possibility that racial or ethnic prejudice will affect the jury remains primarily with the trial court."

In a later capital case decision, *Turner v. Murray*, 476 U.S. 28 (1986), a majority of justices agreed that the failure to question jurors about race bias invalidated the petitioner's death sentence, but did not require retrial of the guilt phase. A plurality (the Chief Justice provided a fifth, concurring vote for the result only) explained that "a capital defendant accused of an interracial crime is entitled to have prospective jurors informed of the race of the victim and questioned on the issue of racial bias," and that an "unacceptable risk of racial prejudice" infected the capital sentencing proceeding because (1) "the crime charged involved interracial violence"; (2) "the jury at the death-penalty hearing" had "broad discretion"; and (3) "the risk of improper sentencing in a capital case" carried "special seriousness." A similar right to question the jurors on race bias for the guilt phase was rejected, the plurality reasoned, because "the jury had no greater discretion than it would have had if the crime charged had been noncapital murder," as in *Ristaino*.

The Court also has declined to recognize a constitutional right to individual questioning concerning the content of media coverage that potential jurors encounter prior to trial. See *Mu'Min v. Virginia,* Note 1, p. 1285.

NOTES AND QUESTIONS ON CAUSE CHALLENGES

1. ***The "for cause" standard.*** Statutes often list the permissible grounds for challenging a potential juror for cause such as previous service as a juror on some related matter, or being related to the defendant or others involved in the case. A more general ground for challenge is often stated in these terms:

> "That the juror has a state of mind in reference to the cause or to the defendant or to the person alleged to have been injured by the offense charged, or to the person on whose complaint the prosecution was instituted, which will prevent him from acting with impartiality; but the formation of an opinion or impression regarding the guilt or innocence of the defendant shall not of itself be sufficient ground of challenge to a juror, if he declares, and the court is satisfied, that he can render an impartial verdict according to the evidence."

A trial judge's assessment of impartiality will be provided great deference on appeal, as the "judge's appraisal is ordinarily influenced by a host of factors impossible to capture fully in in the record—among them, the prospective juror's inflection, sincerity, demeanor, candor, body language, and apprehension of duty." *Skilling v. United States,* p. 1264.

2. ***Implied or presumed bias.*** Even if a prospective juror asserts impartiality, a court may discredit the juror's promise of fairness and decide the juror is biased nonetheless. Circumstances supporting such a finding of "presumed" or "implied" bias include exposure to certain types of prejudicial pretrial publicity, see the discussion in *Skilling v. United States,* p. 1264, or a close family or client relationship with the prosecutor. Generally, however, courts will not disbelieve a juror's assertion of impartiality unless circumstances make it highly unlikely that the juror can remain an impartial adjudicator, and some appear to limit this to "extreme situations."

For example, a juror employed by the government cannot for that reason be challenged for cause. *Dennis v. United States,* 339 U.S. 162 (1950), held that when the federal government is a party, its employees are not challengeable for cause solely by reason of their employment. The Court also rejected the argument that the failure to sustain the challenge denied petitioner an "impartial jury" under the "special circumstances of this case"—a prosecution of a Communist for contempt of the House Un-American Activities Committee, where the government's interest was said to be "the vindication of a direct affront, as distinguished from its role in an ordinary prosecution"; and where, because of an alleged "aura of surveillance and intimidation" said to exist because of a "Loyalty Order," government employees "would be hesitant to vote for acquittal because such action might be interpreted as 'sympathetic association' with Communism."

The bias required to warrant a cause challenge also cannot be assumed solely from membership in a group or association. In *United States v. Salamone,* 800 F.2d 1216 (3d Cir. 1986), where all prospective jurors affiliated with the National Rifle Association were excused upon the prosecution's challenge for cause because the charges were brought under the gun control statutes, the court stated: "We find the government's position untenable and potentially dangerous. To allow trial judges and prosecutors to determine juror eligibility based solely on their perceptions of the external association of a juror threatens the heretofore guarded right of an accused to a fair trial by an impartial jury as well as the integrity of the judicial process as a whole. Taken to its illogical conclusion, the government's position would sanction, inter alia, the summary exclusion for cause of NAACP members from cases seeking the enforcement of civil rights statutes, Moral Majority activists from pornography cases, Catholics from cases involving abortion clinic protests, members of NOW from sex discrimination cases, and subscribers to Consumer Reports from cases involving products liability claims."

3. ***Inability to apply sentencing options in capital cases as cause.*** In *Witherspoon v. Illinois,* 391 U.S. 510 (1968), the Court held "that a sentence of death cannot be carried out if the jury that imposed or recommended it was chosen by excluding veniremen for cause simply because they voiced general objections to the death penalty or expressed conscientious or religious scruples against its infliction." In so doing, "the State crossed the line of neutrality" and "produced a jury uncommonly willing to condemn a man to die." *Witherspoon* appeared to permit exclusion for cause only if the prospective juror made it "unmistakably clear" that he would "automatically vote against the imposition of capital punishment." But the Court later concluded it would suffice if "the trial judge is left with the definite impression that a prospective juror would be unable to faithfully and impartially apply the law." *Wainwright v. Witt*, 469 U.S. 412 (1985). Explained the Court in *Uttecht v. Brown*, 551 U.S. 1 (2007), only "a juror who is substantially impaired in his or her ability to impose the death penalty" may be removed for cause. In *Uttecht*, a case in which the law allowed either death or life without parole, the Court upheld the exclusion of a juror when some of the juror's answers suggested that he would not consider the death penalty if the alternative was a life sentence with no possibility of release on parole. A "reverse-*Witherspoon*" challenge for cause by a capital defendant must be granted where it appears the prospective juror would "automatically vote for the death penalty in every capital case." *Morgan v. Illinois*, 504 U.S. 719 (1992).

4. ***Limits on impeaching the verdict with juror testimony regarding juror bias.*** Once a trial is underway, jurors may be the best source of information about the bias of other jurors. Yet once a verdict is returned, all jurisdictions limit the use of juror testimony about what went on during deliberations to attack the verdict. E.g., Fed.R.Evid. 606(b). As a result, voir dire screening to weed out jurors who are biased or unable to comply with the rules takes on added importance. Consider *Tanner v. United States*, 483 U.S. 107 (1987), where Court agreed with the trial judge's decision to bar, on defendant's motion for a new trial, testimony from two jurors that other jurors were drinking wine and beer, smoking marijuana, and snorting cocaine during the trial. The testimony did not fall within the exception allowing statements concerning whether

"*extraneous* prejudicial information was improperly brought to the jury's attention" or "an *outside* influence was improperly brought to bear on any juror." "Allegations of juror misconduct, incompetency, or inattentiveness, raised for the first time . . . after the verdict seriously disrupt the finality of the process. Moreover, full and frank discussion in the jury room, jurors' willingness to return an unpopular verdict, and the community's trust in a system that relies on the decisions of laypeople would all be undermined by a barrage of post verdict scrutiny of juror conduct." There were sufficient "other sources of protection" for the right to an impartial and competent jury, the majority reasoned, including *voir dire*.

The Court in PEÑA-RODRIGUEZ v. COLORADO, 137 S.Ct. 855 (2017), recognized an exception to the rule barring juror testimony to impeach the verdict. After a conviction for unlawful sexual contact, affidavits supporting the defendant's motion for new trial stated that a juror had stated during deliberations that "Mexican men are physically controlling of women because of their sense of entitlement," that the defendant was guilty because, in the juror's experience as an ex-law enforcement officer, "Mexican men had a bravado that caused them to believe they could do whatever they wanted with women" and "take whatever they want," and that "nine times out of ten Mexican men were guilty of being aggressive toward women and young girls."

The Court's opinion, written by Justice Kennedy, initially noted that it would characterize "the nature of the bias" in the case as "racial," citing *Rosales-Lopez,* Note 3, p. 1247. The Court held that "where a juror makes a clear statement that indicates he or she relied on racial stereotypes or animus to convict a criminal defendant, the Sixth Amendment requires that the no-impeachment rule give way in order to permit the trial court to consider the evidence of the juror's statement and any resulting denial of the jury trial guarantee."

"Racial bias of the kind alleged in this case differs in critical ways from * * * the drug and alcohol abuse in *Tanner*, or the pro-defendant bias in [the civil case] *Warger* [*v. Shauers*, 135 S.Ct. 521 (2014)]," the Court reasoned. "The behavior in those cases is troubling and unacceptable, but each involved anomalous behavior from a single jury—or juror—gone off course. Jurors are presumed to follow their oath, and neither history nor common experience show that the jury system is rife with mischief of these or similar kinds. To attempt to rid the jury of every irregularity of this sort would be to expose it to unrelenting scrutiny. 'It is not at all clear . . . that the jury system could survive such efforts to perfect it.' *Tanner*. The same cannot be said about racial bias, a familiar and recurring evil that, if left unaddressed, would risk systemic injury to the administration of justice. This Court's decisions demonstrate that racial bias implicates unique historical, constitutional, and institutional concerns. An effort to address the most grave and serious statements of racial bias is not an effort to perfect the jury but to ensure that our legal system remains capable of coming ever closer to the promise of equal treatment under the law that is so central to a functioning democracy."

"Racial bias is distinct in a pragmatic sense as well. In past cases this Court has relied on other safeguards to protect the right to an impartial jury. Some of those safeguards, to be sure, can disclose racial bias. Voir dire at the outset of trial, observation of juror demeanor and conduct during trial, juror reports before the verdict, and nonjuror evidence after trial are important mechanisms for discovering bias. Yet their operation may be compromised, or they may prove insufficient. * * * Generic questions about juror impartiality may not expose specific attitudes or biases that can poison jury deliberations. Yet more pointed questions "could well exacerbate whatever prejudice might exist without substantially aiding in exposing it. * * * The stigma that attends racial bias may make it difficult for a juror to report inappropriate statements during the course of juror deliberations. It is one thing to accuse a fellow juror of having a personal experience that improperly influences her consideration of the case, as would have been required in *Warger*. It is quite another to call her a bigot."

The Court argued, "A constitutional rule that racial bias in the justice system must be addressed—including, in some instances, after the verdict has been entered—is necessary to prevent a systemic loss of confidence in jury verdicts, a confidence that is a central premise of the Sixth Amendment trial right." It explained, "Not every offhand comment indicating racial bias or hostility will justify setting aside the no-impeachment bar to allow further judicial inquiry. For the inquiry to proceed, there must be a showing that one or more jurors made statements exhibiting overt racial bias that cast serious doubt on the fairness and impartiality of the jury's deliberations and resulting verdict. To qualify, the statement must tend to show that racial animus was a significant motivating factor in the juror's vote to convict. Whether that threshold showing has been satisfied is a matter committed to the substantial discretion of the trial court in light of all the circumstances, including the content and timing of the alleged statements and the reliability of the proffered evidence."

Chief Justice Roberts and Justice Thomas joined Justice Alito in dissent, arguing that there are no principled grounds to prevent the expansion of the Court's holding, which will "tend to defeat full and vigorous discussion, expose jurors to harassment, and deprive verdicts of stability." "Nothing in the text or history of the [Sixth] Amendment or in the inherent nature of the jury trial right suggests that the extent of the protection provided by the Amendment depends on the nature of a jury's partiality or bias." * * * Recasting this as an equal protection case would not provide a ground for limiting the holding to cases involving racial bias," the dissenters also argued, as the rule would then reach any suspect classification such as national origin or religion as well as gender, and the exercise of First Amendment rights. The dissent also noted the difficulty of identifying which statements are " 'clear[ly]' based on racial or ethnic bias." "Suppose that the allegedly biased juror in this case never made reference to Peña-Rodriguez's race or national origin but said that he had a lot of experience with 'this macho type' and knew that men of this kind felt that they could get their way with women. Suppose that other jurors testified that they were certain that 'this macho type' was meant to refer to Mexican or Hispanic men."

BATSON V. KENTUCKY

476 U.S. 79, 106 S.Ct. 1712, 90 L.Ed.2d 69 (1986).

JUSTICE POWELL delivered the opinion of the Court.

This case requires us to reexamine that portion of *Swain v. Alabama*, 380 U.S. 202 (1965), concerning the evidentiary burden placed on a criminal defendant who claims that he has been denied equal protection through the State's use of peremptory challenges to exclude members of his race from the petit jury.

Petitioner, a black man, was indicted in Kentucky on charges of second-degree burglary and receipt of stolen goods. . . .[T]he judge conducted *voir dire* examination of the venire, excused certain jurors for cause, and permitted the parties to exercise peremptory challenges. The prosecutor used his peremptory challenges to strike all four black persons on the venire, and a jury composed only of white persons was selected. Defense counsel moved to discharge the jury before it was sworn on the ground that the prosecutor's removal of the black veniremen violated petitioner's rights under the Sixth and Fourteenth Amendments to a jury drawn from a cross section of the community, and under the Fourteenth Amendment to equal protection of the laws. Counsel requested a hearing on his motion. Without expressly ruling on the request for a hearing, the trial judge observed that the parties were entitled to use their peremptory challenges to "strike anybody they want to." The judge then denied petitioner's motion, reasoning that the cross-section requirement applies only to selection of the venire and not to selection of the petit jury itself. [The jury convicted and the Supreme Court of Kentucky affirmed.] * * *

In *Swain v. Alabama,* this Court recognized that a "State's purposeful or deliberate denial to Negroes on account of race of participation as jurors in the administration of justice violates the Equal Protection Clause." This principle has been "consistently and repeatedly" reaffirmed, in numerous decisions of this Court both preceding and following *Swain*. We reaffirm the principle today.[4] * * *

Accordingly, the component of the jury selection process at issue here, the State's privilege to strike individual jurors through peremptory challenges, is subject to the commands of the Equal Protection Clause. Although a prosecutor ordinarily is entitled to exercise permitted peremptory challenges "for any reason at all, as long as that reason is related to his view concerning the outcome" of the case to be tried, the Equal Protection Clause forbids the prosecutor to challenge potential jurors solely on account of their race or on the assumption that black jurors as a group will be unable impartially to consider the State's case against a black defendant. * * *

* * * The record in *Swain* showed that the prosecutor had used the State's peremptory challenges to strike the six black persons included on the petit jury venire. While rejecting the defendant's claim for failure to prove purposeful discrimination, the Court nonetheless indicated that the Equal Protection Clause placed some limits on the State's exercise of peremptory challenges.

The Court sought to accommodate the prosecutor's historical privilege of peremptory challenge free of judicial control, and the constitutional prohibition on exclusion of persons from jury service on account of race. While the Constitution does not confer a right to peremptory challenges, those challenges traditionally have been viewed as one means of assuring the selection of a qualified and unbiased jury. To preserve the peremptory nature of the prosecutor's challenge, the Court in *Swain* declined to scrutinize his actions in a particular case by relying on a presumption that he properly exercised the State's challenges.

The Court went on to observe, however, that a state may not exercise its challenges in contravention of the Equal Protection Clause. It was impermissible for a prosecutor to use his challenges to exclude blacks from the jury "for reasons wholly unrelated to the outcome of the particular case on trial" or to deny to blacks "the same right and opportunity to participate in the administration of justice enjoyed by the white population." Accordingly, a black defendant could make out a prima facie case of purposeful discrimination on proof that the peremptory challenge system was "being perverted" in that manner. For example, an inference of purposeful discrimination would be raised on evidence that a prosecutor, "in case after case, whatever the circumstances, whatever the crime and whoever the defendant or the victim may be, is responsible for the removal of Negroes who have been selected as qualified jurors by the jury commissioners and who have survived challenges for cause, with the result that no Negroes ever serve on petit juries." Evidence offered by the defendant in *Swain* did not meet that standard. While the defendant showed that prosecutors in the jurisdiction had exercised their strikes to exclude blacks from the jury, he offered no proof of the circumstances under which prosecutors were responsible

---

[4] In this Court, petitioner has argued that the prosecutor's conduct violated his rights under the Sixth and Fourteenth Amendments to an impartial jury and to a jury drawn from a cross section of the community. Petitioner has framed his argument in these terms in an apparent effort to avoid inviting the Court directly to reconsider one of its own precedents. On the other hand, the State has insisted that petitioner is claiming a denial of equal protection and that we must reconsider *Swain* to find a constitutional violation on this record. We agree with the State that resolution of petitioner's claim properly turns on application of equal protection principles and express no view on the merits of any of petitioner's Sixth Amendment arguments.

[Editors' Note: A challenge to the prosecutor's use of peremptories, grounded instead in the Sixth Amendment's cross-section requirement, was rejected 5–4 in *Holland v. Illinois*, 493 U.S. 474 (1990). "The tradition of peremptory challenges for both the prosecution and the accused was already venerable at the time of Blackstone, was reflected in a federal statute enacted by the same Congress that proposed the Bill of Rights, was recognized in an opinion by Justice Story to be part of the common law of the United States, and has endured through two centuries in all the States. The constitutional phrase 'impartial jury' must surely take its content from this unbroken tradition."].

for striking black jurors beyond the facts of his own case. * * * For reasons that follow, we reject this evidentiary formulation as inconsistent with standards that have been developed since *Swain* for assessing a prima facie case under the Equal Protection Clause.

* * *

The standards for assessing a prima facie case in the context of discriminatory selection of the venire have been fully articulated since *Swain*. These principles support our conclusion that a defendant may establish a prima facie case of purposeful discrimination in selection of the petit jury solely on evidence concerning the prosecutor's exercise of peremptory challenges at the defendant's trial. To establish such a case, the defendant first must show that he is a member of a cognizable racial group, and that the prosecutor has exercised peremptory challenges to remove from the venire members of the defendant's race. Second, the defendant is entitled to rely on the fact, as to which there can be no dispute, that peremptory challenges constitute a jury selection practice that permits "those to discriminate who are of a mind to discriminate." Finally, the defendant must show that these facts and any other relevant circumstances raise an inference that the prosecutor used that practice to exclude the veniremen from the petit jury on account of their race. This combination of factors in the empanelling of the petit jury, as in the selection of the venire, raises the necessary inference of purposeful discrimination.

In deciding whether the defendant has made the requisite showing, the trial court should consider all relevant circumstances. For example, a "pattern" of strikes against black jurors included in the particular venire might give rise to an inference of discrimination. Similarly, the prosecutor's questions and statements during *voir dire* examination and in exercising his challenges may support or refute an inference of discriminatory purpose. * * *

Once the defendant makes a prima facie showing, the burden shifts to the State to come forward with a neutral explanation for challenging black jurors. Though this requirement imposes a limitation in some cases on the full peremptory character of the historic challenge, we emphasize that the prosecutor's explanation need not rise to the level justifying exercise of a challenge for cause. But the prosecutor may not rebut the defendant's prima facie case of discrimination by stating merely that he challenged jurors of the defendant's race on the assumption—or his intuitive judgment—that they would be partial to the defendant because of their shared race. Just as the Equal Protection Clause forbids the States to exclude black persons from the venire on the assumption that blacks as a group are unqualified to serve as jurors, so it forbids the States to strike black veniremen on the assumption that they will be biased in a particular case simply because the defendant is black. * * * The prosecutor therefore must articulate a neutral explanation related to the particular case to be tried. The trial court then will have the duty to determine if the defendant has established purposeful discrimination.* * *

While we recognize, of course, that the peremptory challenge occupies an important position in our trial procedures, we do not agree that our decision today will undermine the contribution the challenge generally makes to the administration of justice. The reality of practice, amply reflected in many state and federal court opinions, shows that the challenge may be, and unfortunately at times has been, used to discriminate against black jurors. By requiring trial courts to be sensitive to the racially discriminatory use of peremptory challenges, our decision enforces the mandate of equal protection and furthers the ends of justice. In view of the heterogeneous population of our nation, public respect for our criminal justice system and the rule of law will be strengthened if we ensure that no citizen is disqualified from jury service because of his race. * * *[24]

---

[24] In light of the variety of jury selection practices followed in our state and federal trial courts, we make no attempt to instruct these courts how best to implement our holding today. For the same reason, we express no view on whether it is more appropriate in a particular case, upon a finding of discrimination against black jurors, for the

In this case, petitioner made a timely objection to the prosecutor's removal of all black persons on the venire. Because the trial court flatly rejected the objection without requiring the prosecutor to give an explanation for his action, we remand this case for further proceedings. If the trial court decides that the facts establish, prima facie, purposeful discrimination and the prosecutor does not come forward with a neutral explanation for his action, our precedents require that petitioner's conviction be reversed.

JUSTICE MARSHALL, concurring. * * *

The decision today will not end the racial discrimination that peremptories inject into the jury-selection process. That goal can be accomplished only by eliminating peremptory challenges entirely. * * * Any prosecutor can easily assert facially neutral reasons for striking a juror, and trial courts are ill equipped to second-guess those reasons. * * * The inherent potential of peremptory challenges to distort the jury process by permitting the exclusion of jurors on racial grounds should ideally lead the Court to * * * banning the use of peremptory challenges by prosecutors and by allowing the States to eliminate the defendant's peremptory as well. * * *

CHIEF JUSTICE BURGER, joined by JUSTICE REHNQUIST, dissenting. * * *

Permitting unexplained peremptories has long been regarded as a means to strengthen our jury system in other ways as well. One commentator has recognized:

> "The peremptory, made without giving any reason, avoids trafficking in the core of truth in most common stereotypes.... Common human experience, common sense, psychosociological studies, and public opinion polls tell us that it is likely that certain classes of people statistically have predispositions that would make them inappropriate jurors for particular kinds of cases. But to allow this knowledge to be expressed in the evaluative terms necessary for challenges for cause would undercut our desire for a society in which all people are judged as individuals and in which each is held reasonable and open to compromise.... [For example,] [a]lthough experience reveals that black males as a class can be biased against young alienated blacks who have not tried to join the middle class, to enunciate this in the concrete expression required of a challenge for cause is societally divisive. Instead we have evolved in the peremptory challenge a system that allows the covert expression of what we dare not say but know is true more often than not." Babcock, *Voir Dire: Preserving "Its Wonderful Power"*, 27 Stan. L. Rev. 545, 553–554 (1975).

For reasons such as these, this Court concluded in *Swain* that "the [peremptory] challenge is 'one of the most important of the rights' " in our justice system. For close to a century, then, it has been settled that "[t]he denial or impairment of the right is reversible error without a showing of prejudice."

* * * [I]n making peremptory challenges, both the prosecutor and defense attorney necessarily act on only limited information or hunch. The process cannot be indicted on the sole basis that such decisions are made on the basis of "assumption" or "intuitive judgment." As a result, unadulterated equal protection analysis is simply inapplicable to peremptory challenges exercised in any particular case. A clause that requires a minimum "rationality" in government actions has no application to " 'an arbitrary and capricious right' "; a constitutional principle that may invalidate state action on the basis of "stereotypic notions" does not explain the breadth of a procedure exercised on the " 'sudden impressions and unaccountable prejudices we are apt to conceive upon the bare looks and gestures of another.' " * * *

---

trial court to discharge the venire and select a new jury from a panel not previously associated with the case, or to disallow the discriminatory challenges and resume selection with the improperly challenged jurors reinstated on the venire.

JUSTICE REHNQUIST, with whom THE CHIEF JUSTICE joins, dissenting. * * *

In my view, there is simply nothing "unequal" about the State using its peremptory challenges to strike blacks from the jury in cases involving black defendants, so long as such challenges are also used to exclude whites in cases involving white defendants, Hispanics in cases involving Hispanic defendants, Asians in cases involving Asian defendants, and so on. This case-specific use of peremptory challenges by the State does not single out blacks, or members of any other race for that matter, for discriminatory treatment. Such use of peremptories is at best based upon seat-of-the-pants instincts, which are undoubtedly crudely stereotypical and may in many cases be hopelessly mistaken. But as long as they are applied across the board to jurors of all races and nationalities, I do not see—and the Court most certainly has not explained—how their use violates the Equal Protection Clause.

Nor does such use of peremptory challenges by the State infringe upon any other constitutional interests. [B]ecause the case-specific use of peremptory challenges by the State does not deny blacks the right to serve as jurors in cases involving non-black defendants, it harms neither the excluded jurors nor the remainder of the community. * * *

NOTES AND QUESTIONS ON PEREMPTORY CHALLENGES

1. ***Number of challenges.*** Most states give the prosecution a number of peremptory challenges equal to those granted the defendant (usually between 5 and 10 challenges in a felony case), but some give a lesser number (seldom below half those granted the defendant). How many is ideal?

2. ***When curing an erroneous cause ruling means losing a peremptory challenge.*** What if a trial judge fails to grant a defendant's meritorious reverse-*Witherspoon* motion, see Note 3, p. 1249, so the defendant uses one of his peremptory challenges (all of which he ultimately exhausts) to remove that juror who would not consider a sentence other than death? In *Ross v. Oklahoma*, 487 U.S. 81 (1988), the Court held 5–4 that a defendant in this position had not been denied an impartial jury, because the juror "was thereby removed from the jury as effectively as if the trial court had excused him for cause." As for the loss of the peremptory challenge to cure the trial court's error, the Court held this loss did not violate the constitutional right to an impartial jury, for "peremptory challenges are not of constitutional dimension." Rather, a state may "define their purpose and manner of exercise." Consider also *United States v. Martinez-Salazar*, 528 U.S. 304 (2000), where the Court held that Federal Rule 24(b) was not violated when defendant was forced to use a peremptory challenge to cure an erroneous cause ruling, so long as no juror who should have been dismissed for cause was seated. Likewise, if the judge's decision to disallow a defendant's peremptory challenge later proves erroneous, the defendant is not denied his right to an impartial jury when all seated jurors are unbiased. *Rivera v. Illinois*, 556 U.S. 148 (2009).

Contrast the rulings above to the Court's 5–4 holding in *Gray v. Mississippi*, 481 U.S. 648 (1987). There, the Court rejected the argument that when a trial judge erroneously grants a prosecutor's motion to exclude for cause a juror who opposes the death penalty, the *Witherspoon* violation will constitute harmless error if the prosecutor has an unexercised peremptory challenge that he states he would have used to excuse the juror anyway. The "practical result of adoption of this unexercised peremptory argument," stated the Court, "would be to insulate jury-selection error from meaningful appellate review." By "simply stating during *voir dire* that the State is prepared to exercise a peremptory challenge if the court denies its motion for cause, a prosecutor would ensure that a reviewing court would consider any erroneous exclusion harmless." Can *Gray* be reconciled with *Ross, Martinez,* and *Rivera*?

3. ***The scope of the* Batson *rule.***

a. Third-party standing to assert venireperson's rights. In *Batson*, the Court held that the defendant's individual right to equal protection of the law was violated if he could show that the state intentionally excluded members of his racial group from the jury. In 1991, the Court shifted its rationale. In *Powers v. Ohio*, 499 U.S. 400 (1991), the Court held, 7–2, that "a white defendant may object to the prosecution's peremptory challenges of black venirepersons." The majority, per Kennedy, J., reasoned that such challenges, if based upon race, violate the *venireperson*'s right to equal protection under the Fourteenth Amendment, as to which "a criminal defendant has standing" to object. Three criteria for recognizing third-party standing are present, the Court reasoned: (1) The defendant has "suffered an 'injury-in-fact' " by such peremptory challenges, adequate to give "him or her a 'sufficiently concrete interest' in the outcome of the issue in dispute," for the "overt wrong, often apparent to the entire jury panel, casts doubt over the obligation of the parties, the jury, and indeed the court to adhere to the law throughout the trial of the cause"; (2) The defendant has "a close relation to the third party" excluded venirepersons, as he or she "will be a motivated, effective advocate for the excluded venirepersons' rights" given "that discrimination in the jury selection process may lead to the reversal of a conviction"; and (3) There exists "some hindrance to the third party's ability to protect his or her own interests," for potential jurors "have no opportunity to be heard at the time of their exclusion," cannot "easily obtain declaratory or injunctive relief" later given the need to show a likely reoccurrence of their own exclusion based on race, and are unlikely to undertake an action for damages "because of the small financial stake involved and the economic burdens of litigation."

The Court emphasized, "The opportunity for ordinary citizens to participate in the administration of justice has long been recognized as one of the principle justifications for retaining the jury system. * * * Jury service preserves the democratic element of the law, as it guards the right of parties and ensures continued acceptance of the laws by all the people. It affords ordinary citizens a valuable opportunity to participate in a process of government, an experiencing fostering, one hopes, a respect for law. Indeed, with the exception of voting, for most citizens, the honor and privilege of jury duty is their most significant opportunity to participate in the democratic process."

b. Challenging peremptory strikes by the defense. In *Georgia v. McCollum*, 505 U.S. 42 (1992), where white defendants were charged with assaulting black victims, the prosecutor claimed the *defendants* should be barred from striking prospective black jurors merely because they were black. The Court agreed that "the right to discriminate against a group of citizens based upon their race" is not included in either a defendant's right to a fair trial or his Sixth Amendment rights to counsel and to an impartial jury. Prospective jurors are denied the opportunity to participate in jury service on account of their race, and public confidence in the fairness of jury verdicts is consequently undermined, the Court concluded.

Moreover, "the exercise of peremptory challenges by a criminal defendant constitutes state action." The defendant relied on government assistance to bring about the deprivation, as "the peremptory challenge system * * * 'simply could not exist' without the 'overt and significant participation of the government.' " The defendant in exercising peremptories "is performing a traditional * * * and constitutionally compelled governmental function." Also, "regardless of who precipitated the jurors' removal, the perception and the reality in a criminal trial will be that the court has excused jurors based on race, an outcome that will be attributed to the State."

Finally, the state had standing to challenge a defendant's discriminatory use of peremptory challenges because the state also suffers injury "when the fairness and integrity of its own judicial process is undermined"; the state has a close relationship with the excluded jurors as "the representative of all its citizens"; and there are significant barriers to the excluded jurors acting to vindicate their own rights.

One of the two dissenters, O'Connor, J., cautioned: "It is by now clear that conscious and unconscious racism can affect the way white jurors perceive minority defendants and the facts presented at their trials, perhaps determining the verdict of guilt or innocence. Using peremptory challenges to secure minority representation on the jury may help to overcome such racial bias, for there is substantial reason to believe that the distorting influence of race is minimized on a racially mixed jury. * * * In a world where the outcome of a minority defendant's trial may turn on the misconceptions or biases of white jurors, there is cause to question the implications of this Court's good intentions."

One commentator has observed that the *McCollum* decision reflects one aim of the Reconstruction Amendments and accompanying legislation: preventing the exclusion of black jurors from trials of white defendants charged with brutality against blacks. James Forman, Jr., *Juries and Race in the Nineteenth Century*, 113 Yale L. J. 895 (2004) . But as Justice O'Connor predicted, *McCollum* has not been limited to strikes by the defense that exclude members of *minority* racial groups.

c. ***Protection for which classifications?*** J.E.B. v. ALABAMA EX REL. T.B., 511 U.S. 127 (1994), involved a paternity action brought by the state against J.E.B. The case began before DNA testing in such cases became routine. Neil Vidmar & Valerie Hans, American Juries 95 (2007). After challenges for cause, the jury panel consisted of 10 males and 23 females. The state used 9 of its 10 peremptories to strike males, and J.E.B. used all but one of his strikes to remove females, resulting in an all-female jury. The defendant was found to be the father, and appealed. *Batson* barred gender-based peremptory challenges, found the Supreme Court, 6–3. Blackmun, J., for the majority, stated:

"Under our equal protection jurisprudence, gender-based classifications require 'an exceedingly persuasive justification' in order to survive constitutional scrutiny. Thus, the only question is whether discrimination on the basis of gender in jury selection substantially furthers the State's legitimate interest in achieving a fair and impartial trial. In making this assessment, we do not weigh the value of peremptory challenges as an institution against our . . . we consider whether peremptory challenges based on gender stereotypes provide substantial aid to a litigant's effort to secure a fair and impartial jury.

"Far from proffering an exceptionally persuasive justification for its gender-based peremptory challenges, respondent maintains that its decision to strike virtually all the males from the jury in this case 'may reasonably have been based upon the perception, supported by history, that men otherwise totally qualified to serve upon a jury might be more sympathetic and receptive to the arguments of a man alleged in a paternity action to be the father of an out-of-wedlock child, while women equally qualified to serve upon a jury might be more sympathetic and receptive to the arguments of the complaining witness who bore the child.'

"We shall not accept as a defense to gender-based peremptory challenges 'the very stereotype the law condemns.' Respondent's rationale, not unlike those regularly expressed for gender-based strikes, is reminiscent of the arguments advanced to justify the total exclusion of women from juries. Respondent offers virtually no support for the conclusion that gender alone is an accurate predictor of juror's attitudes; yet it urges this Court to condone the same stereotypes that justified the wholesale exclusion of women from juries and the ballot box.[11] Respondent seems to assume that gross generalizations that would be deemed impermissible if made on the basis of race are somehow permissible when made on the basis of gender.

---

11 Even if a measure of truth can be found in some of the gender stereotypes used to justify gender-based peremptory challenges, that fact alone cannot support discrimination on the basis of gender in jury selection. We have made abundantly clear in past cases that gender classifications that rest on impermissible stereotypes violate the Equal Protection Clause, even when some statistical support can be conjured up for the generalization. * * *

"Discrimination in jury selection, whether based on race or on gender, causes harm to the litigants, the community, and the individual jurors who are wrongfully excluded from participation in the judicial process. The litigants are harmed by the risk that the prejudice which motivated the discriminatory selection of the jury will infect the entire proceedings. The community is harmed by the State's participation in the perpetuation of invidious group stereotypes and the inevitable loss of confidence in our judicial system that state-sanctioned discrimination in the courtroom engenders. * * * The potential for cynicism is particularly acute in cases where gender-related issues are prominent, such as cases involving rape, sexual harassment, or paternity. * * *

"In recent cases we have emphasized that individual jurors themselves have a right to nondiscriminatory jury selection procedures. Contrary to respondent's suggestion, this right extends to both men and women. All persons, when granted the opportunity to serve on a jury, have the right not to be excluded summarily because of discriminatory and stereotypical presumptions that reflect and reinforce patterns of historical discrimination."[13]

Justice O'Connor, concurring, adhered to her "position that the Equal Protection Clause does not limit the exercise of peremptory challenges by private civil litigants and criminal defendants."

Justice Scalia, for the dissenters, argued "[F]or every man struck by the government petitioner's own lawyer struck a woman. To say that men were singled out for discriminatory treatment in this process is preposterous."

The Supreme Court has yet to consider whether classifications beyond race, ethnicity, and gender would trigger protection under *Batson*. Lower courts have divided over challenges based on religion. In *State v. Davis,* 504 N.W.2d 767 (Minn. 1993), the defendant objected to the prosecutor's use of a peremptory challenge against a black venireman, but the prosecutor explained she had struck the venireman because he was a Jehovah's Witness and explained that "[i]n my experience Jehovah Witness [sic] are reluctant to exercise authority over their fellow human beings in this Court House." Reading *Batson* as limited to race-based peremptory challenges, the state court affirmed. Dissenting from the denial of certiorari, Justice Thomas, joined by Justice Scalia, objected that "no principled reason immediately appears for declining to apply *Batson* to any strike based on a classification that is accorded heightened scrutiny under the Equal Protection Clause." Justice Ginsburg, concurring in the denial of certiorari, responded that the Minnesota Supreme Court also made two key observations: that '[R]eligious affiliation (or lack thereof) is not as self-evident as race or gender'; and that ordinarily "inquiry on voir dire into a juror's religious affiliation and beliefs is irrelevant and prejudicial, and to ask such questions is improper.'" *Davis v. Minnesota,* 511 U.S. 1115 (1994). Compare *United States v. Brown*, 352 F.3d 654 (2d Cir.2003) (*Batson* bars peremptory challenge based solely on a venire member's religious "affiliation," but does not bar challenge based on religious "activities," as prosecutor could believe people active in church also engaged in charitable pursuits and thus have higher "sympathy for people in distress, including criminal defendants") with *United States v. Heron*, 721 F.3d 896 (7th Cir. 2013) (rejecting *Batson* claim based on religiosity, stating "it is unclear why someone's religious affiliation ought to be entitled to greater constitutional protection than that person's religious exercise"). Should *Batson* bar challenges based on sexual orientation? Political party affiliation?

---

[13] It is irrelevant that women, unlike African-Americans, are not a numerical minority and therefore are likely to remain on the jury if each side uses it peremptory challenges in an equally discriminatory fashion. Because the right to nondiscriminatory jury selection procedures belongs to the potential jurors, as well as to the litigants, the possibility that members of both genders will get on the jury despite the intentional discrimination is beside the point. The exclusion of even one juror for impermissible reasons harms that juror and undermines public confidence in the fairness of the system.

How does the issue of which group classifications trigger the equal protection based rule of *Batson* differ from either of the following issues: 1) which groups are "distinct" under Sixth Amendment cross-section analysis, see Note 2, p. 1245, or 2) whether a juror's clear statement of bias on grounds other than race—for example, a statement indicating that a significant motivating factor in juror's vote to convict was anti-Semitism, or misogyny—should be admissible to impeach a guilty verdict under the Sixth Amendment rule in *Pena-Rodriguez,* p. 1250?

4. ***The three-step analysis.*** In *Purkett v. Elem,* 514 U.S. 765 (1995), the Court explained that *Batson* established a three-step analysis: "[O]nce the opponent of a peremptory challenge has made out a prima facie case of racial discrimination (step 1), the burden of production shifts to the proponent of the strike to come forward with a race-neutral explanation (step 2). If a race-neutral explanation is tendered, the trial court must then decide (step 3) whether the opponent of the strike has proved purposeful racial discrimination."

a. ***Step one: prima facie case.*** A "defendant satisfies the requirements of *Batson's* first step by producing evidence sufficient to permit the trial judge to draw an inference that discrimination has occurred," explained the Court in *Johnson v. California,* 545 U.S. 162 (2005). *Johnson* held that the courts below should have concluded that such a showing had been made when, at the trial of a black defendant charged with murdering a white child, the prosecutor used three of his peremptory challenges to remove the only black venirepersons remaining after challenges for cause, resulting in an all-white jury. Can the peremptory challenge of a single black venireperson be sufficient for step one? When?

b. ***Step two: race-neutral explanation.*** The justification tendered at the second step need only be race- (or gender-) neutral. There is no requirement at this step that the reason be even "minimally persuasive." Stated the Court in *Purkett,* "It is not until the *third* step that the persuasiveness of the justification becomes relevant * * *. At that stage, implausible or fantastic justifications may (and probably will) be found to be pretexts for purposeful discrimination."

In *Hernandez v. New York,* 500 U.S. 352 (1991), addressing a *Batson* claim that the prosecutor excluded Latino jurors, Kennedy, J., for a four-member plurality, concluded: "The prosecutor here offered a race-neutral basis for these peremptory strikes. As explained by the prosecutor, the challenges rested neither on the intention to exclude Latino or bilingual jurors, nor on stereotypical assumptions about Latinos or bilinguals. The prosecutor's articulated basis for these challenges divided potential jurors into two classes: those whose conduct during voir dire would persuade him they might have difficulty in accepting the translator's rendition of Spanish-language testimony and those potential jurors who gave no such reason for doubt. Each category would include both Latinos and non-Latinos. While the prosecutor's criterion might well result in the disproportionate removal of prospective Latino jurors, that disproportionate impact does not turn the prosecutor's actions into a per se violation of the Equal Protection Clause. [However, if] a prosecutor articulates a basis for a peremptory challenge that results in the disproportionate exclusion of members of a certain race, the trial judge may consider that fact as evidence that the prosecutor's stated reason constitutes a pretext for racial discrimination." The Court then concluded the state court's finding of no discriminatory intent should stand because it was not clearly erroneous. The Court cautioned: "In holding that a race-neutral reason for a peremptory challenge means a reason other than race, we do not resolve the more difficult question of the breadth with which the concept of race should be defined for equal protection purposes. We would face a quite different case if the prosecutor had justified his peremptory challenges with the explanation that he did not want Spanish-speaking jurors. It may well be, for certain ethnic groups and in some communities, that proficiency in a particular language, like skin color, should be treated as a surrogate for race under an equal protection analysis."

Stevens, J., for the three dissenters, argued that the prosecutor's justification would inevitably result in a disproportionate disqualification of Spanish-speaking venirepersons, and that an "explanation that is 'race-neutral' on its face is nonetheless unacceptable if it is merely a proxy for a discriminatory practice." Second, he argued that "the prosecutor's concern could easily have been accommodated by less drastic means. As is the practice in many jurisdictions, the jury could have been instructed that the official translation alone is evidence; bilingual jurors could have been instructed to bring to the attention of the judge any disagreements they might have with the translation so that any disputes could be resolved by the court." Third, "if the prosecutor's concern was valid and substantiated by the record, it would have supported a challenge for cause"; his failure to raise such a challenge "should disqualify him from advancing the concern as a justification for a peremptory challenge."

c. ***Step three: assessing the credibility of the neutral reason.*** The Court has emphasized repeatedly that a " 'trial court is best situated to evaluate both the words and the demeanor of jurors who are peremptorily challenged, as well as the credibility of the prosecutor who exercised those strikes.' " *Davis v. Ayala*, 135 S.Ct. 2187 (2015). An example of one circumstance that will trigger less deference to the trial judge is a prosecutor's reliance on a "race-neutral" reason for challenging a black juror that, if sincere, would have equally supported the challenge of seated white juror. In *Miller-El v. Dretke*, 545 U.S. 231 (2005), the Court rejected the state court's conclusion that the prosecutor did not violate *Batson* when only one of the 20 black members of the 108-person venire served as a juror, and ten were excused by the state's peremptory challenges. Justice Souter wrote for the Court: "If a prosecutor's proffered reason for striking a black panelist applies just as well to an otherwise-similar nonblack who is permitted to serve, that is evidence tending to prove purposeful discrimination to be considered at *Batson*'s third step. * * *. [N]onblack jurors whose remarks on rehabilitation could well have signaled a limit on their willingness to impose a death sentence were not questioned further and drew no objection, but the prosecution expressed apprehension about a black juror's belief in the possibility of reformation even though he repeatedly stated his approval of the death penalty and testified that he could impose it according to state legal standards even when the alternative sentence of life imprisonment would give a defendant (like everyone else in the world) the opportunity to reform. * * * [The] differences[6] [between the challenged juror and seated jurors] seem far from significant * * *."

The Court also noted that evidence of intentional discrimination included other patterns during jury selection, including (1) the use of a procedure to reshuffle the cards bearing panel members' names, which rearranged the panel members seated at the back and thus likely to escape *voir dire*, a shuffle that moved black panelists to the back; (2) contrasting *voir dire* questioning of black and nonblack panel members, describing the method of execution in rhetorical and clinical detail to a higher proportion of blacks than whites, and asking a "trick question" of all blacks, but not all whites, who expressed concern about the death penalty; and (3) the apparent use of a prosecution manual that outlined the reasoning for excluding minorities from jury service, as shown by the prosecutors' notes of the race of each potential juror.

Using similar comparative reasoning, the Court has invalidated other capital convictions. In *Snyder v. Louisiana*, 552 U.S. 472 (2008), the Court concluded that the Louisiana trial court had committed clear error when it failed to find that the prosecutor had excluded a young student teacher because he was black. The majority found implausible the prosecution's explanation that the young man would have allowed his worries about missing his student teaching to influence his decision when the prosecutor did not challenge two white veniremembers who expressed

[6] The dissent contends that * * * " ' "[s]imilarly situated" does not mean matching any one of several reasons the prosecution gave for striking a potential juror—it means matching *all* of them.' " None of our cases announces a rule that no comparison is probative unless the situation of the individuals compared is identical in all respects, and there is no reason to accept one. * * * A *per se* rule that a defendant cannot win a *Batson* claim unless there is an exactly identical white juror would leave *Batson* inoperable; potential jurors are not products of a set of cookie cutters.

concerns about conflicting responsibilities that were at least as pressing as the young man's course requirements. In *Foster v. Chatman*, 136 S.Ct. 1737 (2016), the Court found the state's strikes were "motivated in substantial part by discriminatory intent," when the neutral reasons provided by the prosecution had "no grounding in fact," were "difficult to credit in light of the State's acceptance" of similarly situated white jurors, and "shifted over time."

5. ***Requiring representation?*** Albert W. Alschuler, in his article *Racial Quotas and the Jury*, 44 Duke L. J. 704 (1995), argued that proposals to ensure proportionate minority representation on all jury panels would be constitutional because such "quotas would not deprive individuals of significant tangible benefits; they would not brand any group as inferior or evaluate any individual on the basis of racial stereotypes; and * * * would be likely to enhance the * * * jury's achievement of its objectives."). After years of upholding the state's "forced balancing" of its jury lists so that they included men and women and certain identifiable racial groups in proportion to the county's population as determined by the most recent census, Georgia replaced the race-conscious system with a race-neutral one in 2012. See *Ricks v. State*, 301 Ga. 171 (2017). See also Nancy J. King & G. Thomas Munsterman, *Stratified Juror Selection: Cross-section by Design*, 79 Judicature 273 (1996) (reviewing legal challenges to efforts to achieve racial or ethnic diversity in jury panels); Avern Cohn & David Sherwood, *The Rise and Fall of Affirmative Action in Jury Selection*, 32 U. Mich. J. L. Ref 323 (1999) (describing race-conscious jury selection system in Detroit, struck down as unconstitutional in 1998).

6. ***Is* Batson *futile? Should peremptories be eliminated?*** Concurring in *Miller-El v. Dretke*, Note 4.c., p. 1260, Justice Breyer endorsed Justice Marshall's conclusion in *Batson* that the only way to "end the racial discrimination that peremptories inject into the jury-selection process," was to eliminate peremptory challenges. "I am not surprised to find studies and anecdotal reports suggesting that, despite *Batson*, the discriminatory use of peremptory challenges remains a problem," he wrote, citing sources reporting that in Philadelphia race-based uses of prosecutorial peremptories declined by only 2% after *Batson*; that in a North Carolina County 71% of excused black jurors were removed by the prosecution and 81% of excused white jurors were removed by the defense. "[T]he use of race- and gender-based stereotypes in the jury-selection process seems better organized and more systematized than ever before. * * * [A] trial consulting firm advertises a new jury-selection technology: 'Whether you are trying a civil case or a criminal case, SmartJURY™ has likely determined the exact demographics (age, race, gender, education, occupation, marital status, number of children, religion, and income) of the type of jurors you should select and the type you should strike.' " Justice Breyer observed that calls for eliminating peremptories have increased, citing, e.g., Morris B. Hoffman, *Peremptory Challenges Should be Abolished: A Trial Judge's Perspective*, 64 U. Chi. L. Rev. 809 (1997) (authored by a Colorado judge), and that England "continues to administer fair trials based largely on random jury selection" without peremptories. Joined by Justice Souter in *Rice v. Collins*, 546 U.S. 333 (2006), Justice Breyer echoed this view when he concurred in the majority's decision refusing to second-guess a trial judge's conclusion that the prosecutor had not violated *Batson*. "[T]he case before us makes clear that ordinary mechanisms of judicial review cannot assure *Batson's* effectiveness." Because "[a]ppellate judges cannot on the basis of a cold record easily second-guess a trial judge's decision about likely motivation," appellate courts "must grant the trial courts considerable leeway in applying *Batson*," he explained. "The upshot is an unresolvable tension between, on the one hand, what Blackstone called an inherently ' "arbitrary and capricious" ' peremptory challenge system, and, on the other hand, the Constitution's nondiscrimination command. Given this constitutional tension, we may have to choose."

Although no state has eliminated peremptory challenges, in *State v. Saintcalle*, 178 Wash.2d 34 (2013), a majority expressed the belief that the *Batson* test is not sufficient to control discrimination in the exercise of peremptory challenges, and suggested a number of reforms, including scrapping the peremptory challenge altogether. The several opinions in the case offer an extensive collection of authority examining and critiquing *Batson* challenges and their effects.

7. ***Challenging a judge.*** A defendant has a due process right to an impartial judge. In *Williams v. Pennsylvania*, 136 S.Ct. 1899 (2016), Justice Kennedy explained for the Court that due process guarantees an absence of actual bias on the part of a judge, but this is determined using an objective standard that usually avoids having to determine whether actual bias is present. The Court asks "whether, as an objective matter, 'the average judge in his position is "likely" to be neutral, or whether there is an unconstitutional "potential for bias." ' " This standard requires recusal when the likelihood of bias on the part of the judge " 'is too high to be constitutionally tolerable.' "[a] *Williams* involved a decision of the Pennsylvania Supreme Court rejecting relief for a death row prisoner who had filed a late state post-conviction petition raising several *Brady* claims. One of the justices on the State Supreme Court had nearly three decades earlier served as the District Attorney who approved seeking the death penalty in Williams's case. When Williams moved for his recusal, he denied the motion, participated in the decision denying the stay of execution, and authored a concurring opinion denouncing the anti-death penalty agenda of the defenders' office representing Williams.

The U.S. Supreme Court concluded that due process required the former prosecutor's recusal. It explained that when "a judge had a direct, personal role in the defendant's prosecution," there is "a risk that the judge 'would be so psychologically wedded' to his or her previous position as a prosecutor that the judge 'would consciously or unconsciously avoid the appearance of having erred or changed position," and that the judge's "own personal knowledge and impression" of the case, acquired through his or her role in the prosecution, may carry far more weight with the judge than the parties' arguments to the court.' " The Court reasoned that the state justice's "significant, personal involvement in a critical decision in Williams's case gave rise to an unacceptable risk of actual bias. This risk so endangered the appearance of neutrality that his participation in the case 'must be forbidden if the guarantee of due process is to be adequately implemented.' " It also noted that "many jurisdictions" have ethical rules that "already require disqualification under the circumstances of this case."

In contrast to the situation in *Williams,* typically it is not objectionable that a judge was involved as a judge in some prior proceedings in the case. For example, as noted in *Withrow v. Larkin,* 421 U.S. 35 (1975): "Judges repeatedly issue arrest warrants on the basis that there is probable cause to believe that a crime has been committed and that the person named in the warrant has committed it. Judges also preside at preliminary hearings where they must decide whether the evidence is sufficient to hold a defendant for trial. Neither of these pretrial involvements has been thought to raise any constitutional barrier against the judge presiding over the criminal trial and, if the trial is without a jury, against making the necessary determination of guilt or innocence." Moreover, in *Liteky v. United States,* 510 U.S. 540 (1994), the Court held that both the federal challenge-for-cause statute, 28 U.S.C. § 144, and the federal recusal statute, 28 U.S.C. § 455, are subject to an "extrajudicial source" limitation, meaning: (1) "judicial rulings alone almost never constitute valid basis for a bias or partiality motion"; and (2) "opinions formed by the judge on the basis of facts introduced or events occurring in the course of the current proceedings, or of prior proceedings, do not constitute a basis for a bias or partiality motion unless they display a deep-seated favoritism or antagonism that would make fair judgment impossible."

Recusal motions are sometimes filed in response to mid-trial revelations or events. If the alleged bias is a response to the conduct of the defendant or his counsel during the proceedings, courts may be reluctant to grant recusal. See, e.g., *Bigby v. Dretke*, 402 F.3d 551 (5th Cir. 2005),

[a] The Court has emphasized that this due process standard may demand recusal even when a judge has no actual subjective bias, but, objectively speaking, considering all the circumstances alleged, the probability of actual bias is too high to be constitutionally tolerable. Rippo v. Baker, 137 S.Ct. 905 (2017).

where the court of appeals declined to find bias after Bigby, on trial for murder, attacked the judge during a trial recess and held a gun to the judge's head. The reviewing court reasoned, "Such an automatic rule would invite recusal motions from defendants whose sole purpose in attacking a judge or engaging in unruly behavior is either to manufacture constitutional due process violations or delay trial proceedings." Compare *In re Nettles*, 394 F.3d 1001 (7th Cir. 2005) (where defendant had been charged with plotting to blow up the federal courthouse in Chicago and moved pretrial for recusal of judge in that building, the court of appeals held proper the recusal of all district and appellate judges in the courthouse because of the appearance of bias when judges are "menaced by an Oklahoma City style attack").

Eighteen states also grant the defendant the right to automatic disqualification of the trial judge upon request, some requiring the defendant to file a conclusory affidavit of prejudice. What advantages does this approach have? Raymond J. McKoski, *Disqualifying Judges When Their Impartiality Might Reasonably Be Questioned: Moving Beyond A Failed Standard*, 56 Ariz. L. Rev. 411 (2014). What disadvantages? See Nancy J. King, *Batson for the Bench? The Peremptory Challenge of Judges*, 73 Chi. Kent L. Rev. 509 (1998).

CHAPTER 24

FIRST AMENDMENT INTERESTS VS. FAIR TRIALS

■ ■ ■

This Chapter addresses a series of issues relating to providing fair trials in "high-profile" cases. First Amendment interests bear on all of these issues. Section one considers Sixth Amendment and state law responses to public notoriety that is largely the product of the exercise of First Amendment rights by the media (both social and traditional). Section two presents instances in which fair trial concerns are advanced to place limits upon First Amendment rights (both the exercise of free speech and public access to judicial proceedings). Section three addresses the fair trial concerns presented by an effort to expand that public access through televised proceedings. Although the concerns here are not limited to high profile cases, they certainly are accentuated in that setting, and almost all of the leading precedent involves such cases.

§ 1. PRETRIAL PUBLICITY: VENUE CHANGES AND JURY SELECTION

SKILLING V. UNITED STATES

561 U.S. 358, 130 S.Ct. 2896, 177 L.Ed.2d 619 (2010).

JUSTICE GINSBURG delivered the opinion of the Court.[a]

In 2001, Enron Corporation, then the seventh highest-revenue-grossing company in America, crashed into bankruptcy. We consider in this opinion two questions arising from the prosecution of Jeffrey Skilling, a longtime Enron executive [and former president, COO and CEO], for crimes committed before the corporation's collapse. First, did pretrial publicity and community prejudice prevent Skilling from obtaining a fair trial? Second, did the jury improperly convict Skilling of conspiracy to commit "honest-services" wire fraud, 18 U. S. C. §§ 371, 1343, 1346?

Answering no to both questions, the Fifth Circuit affirmed Skilling's convictions. We conclude, in common with the Court of Appeals, that Skilling's fair-trial argument fails; Skilling, we hold, did not establish that a presumption of juror prejudice arose or that actual bias infected the jury that tried him. But we disagree with the Fifth Circuit's honest-services ruling. * * * Because Skilling's alleged misconduct entailed no bribe or kickback, it does not fall within § 1346's proscription. We therefore affirm in part and vacate in part [remanding for a determination as to how vacating the "honest services" conviction impacts Skilling's other convictions].

I.

The Government's investigation [of the Enron collapse] uncovered an elaborate conspiracy to prop up Enron's short-run stock prices by overstating the company's financial well-being. In the years following Enron's bankruptcy, the Government prosecuted dozens of Enron employees who participated in the scheme. In time, the Government worked its way up the corporation's chain of

[a] Part I of this opinion was joined by Chief Justice Roberts and Justices Stevens, Scalia, Kennedy, Thomas, and Alito. Part II was joined by Chief Justice Roberts and Justices Scalia, Kennedy, and Thomas. Part III, dealing with the "honest services" charge, is omitted, as is Justice Scalia's opinion addressing that charge.

command: On July 7, 2004, a grand jury indicted Skilling, Donald Lay [Enron's founder and former chairman], and Richard Causey, Enron's former chief accounting officer. Count 1 of the indictment charged Skilling with conspiracy to commit securities and wire fraud; in particular, it alleged that Skilling had sought to "depriv[e] Enron and its shareholders of the intangible right of [his] honest services." The indictment further charged Skilling with more than 25 substantive counts of securities fraud, wire fraud, making false representations to Enron's auditors, and insider trading. [The prosecution was brought in Houston, where Enron has been headquartered since its founding in 1985].

In November 2004, Skilling moved to transfer the trial to another venue; he contended that hostility toward him in Houston, coupled with extensive pretrial publicity, had poisoned potential jurors. To support this assertion, Skilling, aided by media experts, submitted hundreds of news reports detailing Enron's downfall; he also presented affidavits from the experts he engaged portraying community attitudes in Houston in comparison to other potential venues. * * * The U. S. District Court, in accord with rulings in two earlier instituted Enron-related prosecutions, denied the venue-transfer motion. Despite "isolated incidents of intemperate commentary," the court observed, media coverage "ha[d] [mostly] been objective and unemotional," and the facts of the case were "neither heinous nor sensational."[3] Moreover, "courts ha[d] commonly" favored "effective *voir dire* . . . to ferret out any [juror] bias." * * *

In the months leading up to the trial, the District Court solicited from the parties questions the court might use to screen prospective jurors. Unable to agree on a questionnaire's format and content, Skilling and the Government submitted dueling documents. On venire members' sources of Enron-related news, for example, the Government proposed that they tick boxes from a checklist of generic labels such as "[t]elevision," "[n]ewspaper," and "[r]adio." Skilling proposed more probing questions asking venire members to list the specific names of their media sources and to report on "what st[ood] out in [their] mind[s]" of "all the things [they] ha[d] seen, heard or read about Enron." The District Court rejected the Government's sparer inquiries in favor of Skilling's submission. Skilling's questions "[we]re more helpful," the court said, "because [they] [we]re generally . . . open-ended and w[ould] allow the potential jurors to give us more meaningful information." The court converted Skilling's submission, with slight modifications, into a 77-question, 14-page document that asked prospective jurors about, *inter alia*, their sources of news and exposure to Enron-related publicity, beliefs concerning Enron and what caused its collapse, opinions regarding the defendants and their possible guilt or innocence, and relationships to the company and to anyone affected by its demise.

In November 2005, the District Court mailed the questionnaire to 400 prospective jurors and received responses from nearly all the addressees. The court granted hardship exemptions to approximately 90 individuals, and the parties, with the court's approval, further winnowed the pool by excusing another 119 for cause, hardship, or physical disability. The parties agreed to exclude, in particular, "each and every" prospective juror who said that a preexisting opinion about Enron or the defendants would prevent her from impartially considering the evidence at trial.

On December 28, 2005, three weeks before the date scheduled for the commencement of trial, Causey pleaded guilty. Skilling's attorneys immediately requested a continuance, and the District Court agreed to delay the proceedings until the end of January 2006. In the interim, Skilling renewed his change-of-venue motion, arguing that the juror questionnaires revealed pervasive

---

[3] Painting a different picture of the media coverage surrounding Enron's collapse, Justice Sotomayor's opinion relies heavily on affidavits of media experts and jury consultants submitted by Skilling in support of his venue-transfer motion. * * * These Skilling-employed experts selected and emphasized negative statements in various news stories. But the District Court Judge did not find the experts' samples representative of the coverage at large; having "[m]eticulous[ly] review[ed] all of the evidence" Skilling presented, the court concluded that "incidents [of news reports using] less-than-objective language" were dwarfed by "the largely fact-based tone of most of the articles." * * *

bias and that news accounts of Causey's guilty plea further tainted the jury pool. If Houston remained the trial venue, Skilling urged that "jurors need to be questioned individually by both the Court *and* counsel" concerning their opinions of Enron and "publicity issues."

The District Court again declined to move the trial. Skilling, the court concluded, still had not "establish[ed] that pretrial publicity and/or community prejudice raise[d] a presumption of inherent jury prejudice." The questionnaires and *voir dire*, the court observed, provided safeguards adequate to ensure an impartial jury. * * * Denying Skilling's request for attorney-led *voir dire*, the court said that in 17 years on the bench: "I've found . . . I get more forthcoming responses from potential jurors than the lawyers on either side." * * * But the court promised to give counsel an opportunity to ask follow-up questions, and it agreed that venire members should be examined individually about pretrial publicity. The court also allotted the defendants jointly 14 peremptory challenges, 2 more than the standard number prescribed by Federal Rule of Criminal Procedure 24(b)(2) and (c)(4)(B).

Voir dire began on January 30, 2006. The District Court first emphasized to the venire the importance of impartiality and explained the presumption of innocence and the Government's burden of proof. The trial, the court next instructed, was not a forum "to seek vengeance against Enron's former officers," or to "provide remedies for" its victims. "The bottom line," the court stressed, "is that we want . . . jurors who . . . will faithfully, conscientiously and impartially serve if selected." In response to the court's query whether any prospective juror questioned her ability to adhere to these instructions, two individuals indicated that they could not be fair; they were therefore excused for cause.

After questioning the venire as a group, the District Court brought prospective jurors one by one to the bench for individual examination. Although the questions varied, the process generally tracked the following format: The court asked about exposure to Enron-related news and the content of any stories that stood out in the prospective juror's mind. Next, the court homed in on questionnaire answers that raised a red flag signaling possible bias. The court then permitted each side to pose follow-up questions. Finally, after the venire member stepped away, the court entertained and ruled on challenges for cause. In all, the court granted one of the Government's for-cause challenges and denied four; it granted three of the defendants' challenges and denied six. The parties agreed to excuse three additional jurors for cause and one for hardship.

By the end of the day, the court had qualified 38 prospective jurors, a number sufficient, allowing for peremptory challenges, to empanel 12 jurors and 4 alternates.[6] Before the jury was sworn in, Skilling objected to the seating of six jurors. He did not contend that they were in fact biased; instead, he urged that he would have used peremptories to exclude them had he not exhausted his supply by striking several venire members after the court refused to excuse them for cause. The court overruled this objection.

* * * Following a 4-month trial and nearly five days of deliberation, the jury found Skilling guilty of 19 counts, including the honest-services-fraud conspiracy charge, and not guilty of 9 insider-trading counts. The District Court sentenced Skilling to 292 months' imprisonment, 3 years' supervised release, and $45 million in restitution.

On appeal, Skilling raised a host of challenges to his convictions, including the fair-trial and honest-services arguments he presses here. Regarding the former, the Fifth Circuit initially determined that the volume and negative tone of media coverage generated by Enron's collapse created a presumption of juror prejudice. The court also noted potential prejudice stemming from

---

[6] Selection procedures of similar style and duration took place in three Enron-related criminal cases earlier prosecuted in Houston—*United States* v. *Arthur Andersen* (charges against Enron's outside accountants); *United States* v. *Bayly*, (charges against Merrill Lynch and Enron executives for alleged sham sales of Nigerian barges); *United States* v. *Hirko*, (fraud and insider-trading charges against five Enron Broadband Services executives). * * *

Causey's guilty plea and from the large number of victims in Houston—from the "[t]housands of Enron employees . . . [who] lost their jobs, and . . . saw their 401(k) accounts wiped out," to Houstonians who suffered spillover economic effects. * * * The Court of Appeals stated, however, that "the presumption [of prejudice] is rebuttable," and it therefore examined the *voir dire* to determine whether "the District Court empaneled an impartial jury." * * * [It found] the *voir dire* was * * * "proper and thorough," * * * that the Government had overcome the presumption of prejudice, and that Skilling had not "show[n] that any juror who actually sat was prejudiced against him." * * *

II.

Skilling's fair-trial claim raises two distinct questions. First, did the District Court err by failing to move the trial to a different venue based on a presumption of prejudice?[11] Second, did actual prejudice contaminate Skilling's jury?

We begin our discussion by addressing the presumption of prejudice from which the Fifth Circuit's analysis in Skilling's case proceeded. The foundation precedent is *Rideau* v. *Louisiana*, 373 U.S. 723 (1963). Wilbert Rideau robbed a bank in a small Louisiana town, kidnaped three bank employees, and killed one of them. Police interrogated Rideau in jail without counsel present and obtained his confession. Without informing Rideau, no less seeking his consent, the police filmed the interrogation. On three separate occasions shortly before the trial, a local television station broadcast the film to audiences ranging from 24,000 to 53,000 individuals. Rideau moved for a change of venue, arguing that he could not receive a fair trial in the parish where the crime occurred, which had a population of approximately 150,000 people. The trial court denied the motion, and a jury eventually convicted Rideau. The Supreme Court of Louisiana upheld the conviction.

We reversed. "What the people [in the community] saw on their television sets," we observed, "was Rideau, in jail, flanked by the sheriff and two state troopers, admitting in detail the commission of the robbery, kidnapping, and murder." "[T]o the tens of thousands of people who saw and heard it," we explained, the interrogation "in a very real sense *was* Rideau's trial—at which he pleaded guilty." We therefore "d[id] not hesitate to hold, without pausing to examine a particularized transcript of the *voir dire*," that "[t]he kangaroo court proceedings" trailing the televised confession violated due process.

We followed *Rideau*'s lead in two later cases in which media coverage manifestly tainted a criminal prosecution. In *Estes* v. *Texas* [Note 2, p. 1297], extensive publicity before trial swelled into excessive exposure during preliminary court proceedings as reporters and television crews overran the courtroom and "bombard[ed] . . . the community with the sights and sounds of" the pretrial hearing. The media's overzealous reporting efforts, we observed, "led to considerable disruption" and denied the "judicial serenity and calm to which [Billie Sol Estes] was entitled." Similarly, in *Sheppard* v. *Maxwell*, 384 U.S. 333 (1966), news reporters extensively covered the story of Sam Sheppard, who was accused of bludgeoning his pregnant wife to death. "[B]edlam reigned at the courthouse during the trial and newsmen took over practically the entire

---

11 [transposed footnote] Venue transfer in federal court is governed by Federal Rule of Criminal Procedure 21, which instructs that a "court must transfer the proceeding . . to another district if the court is satisfied that so great a prejudice against the defendant exists in the transferring district that the defendant cannot obtain a fair and impartial trial there." As the language of the Rule suggests, district-court calls on the necessity of transfer are granted a healthy measure of appellate-court respect. * * * Federal courts have invoked the Rule to move certain highly charged cases, for example, the prosecution arising from the bombing of the Alfred P. Murrah Federal Office Building in Oklahoma City. * * * They have also exercised discretion to deny venue-transfer requests in cases involving substantial pretrial publicity and community impact, for example, the prosecutions resulting from the 1993 World Trade Center bombing* * *. Skilling does not argue, distinct from his due process challenge, that the District Court abused its discretion under Rule 21 by declining to move his trial. We therefore review the District Court's venue-transfer decision only for compliance with the Constitution.

courtroom," thrusting jurors "into the role of celebrities." Pretrial media coverage, which we characterized as "months [of] virulent publicity about Sheppard and the murder," did not alone deny due process, we noted. But Sheppard's case involved more than heated reporting pretrial: We upset the murder conviction because a "carnival atmosphere" pervaded the trial.

In each of these cases, we overturned a "conviction obtained in a trial atmosphere that [was] utterly corrupted by press coverage"; our decisions, however, "cannot be made to stand for the proposition that juror exposure to . . . news accounts of the crime . . . alone presumptively deprives the defendant of due process." *Murphy* v. *Florida*, 421 U.S. 794 (1975).[12] See also, *e.g., Patton* v. *Yount*, 467 U.S. 1025 (1984).[13] Prominence does not necessarily produce prejudice, and juror *impartiality*, we have reiterated, does not require *ignorance*. *Irvin* v. *Dowd*, 366 U.S. 717, 722 (1961) (Jurors are not required to be "totally ignorant of the facts and issues involved"; "scarcely any of those best qualified to serve as jurors will not have formed some impression or opinion as to the merits of the case.").* * * A presumption of prejudice, our decisions indicate, attends only the extreme case. * * * Relying on *Rideau*, *Estes*, and *Sheppard*, Skilling asserts that we need not pause to examine the screening questionnaires or the *voir dire* before declaring his jury's verdict void. We are not persuaded. Important differences separate Skilling's prosecution from those in which we have presumed juror prejudice.[14]

First, we have emphasized in prior decisions the size and characteristics of the community in which the crime occurred. In *Rideau*, for example, we noted that the murder was committed in a parish of only 150,000 residents. Houston, in contrast, is the fourth most populous city in the Nation: At the time of Skilling's trial, more than 4.5 million individuals eligible for jury duty resided in the Houston area. Given this large, diverse pool of potential jurors, the suggestion that 12 impartial individuals could not be empaneled is hard to sustain. * * *

Second, although news stories about Skilling were not kind, they contained no confession or other blatantly prejudicial information of the type readers or viewers could not reasonably be expected to shut from sight. Rideau's dramatically staged admission of guilt, for instance, was likely imprinted indelibly in the mind of anyone who watched it. * * * Pretrial publicity about Skilling was less memorable and prejudicial. No evidence of the smoking-gun variety invited prejudgment of his culpability.* * *

Third, unlike cases in which trial swiftly followed a widely reported crime, *e.g., Rideau*, over four years elapsed between Enron's bankruptcy and Skilling's trial. Although reporters covered Enron-related news throughout this period, the decibel level of media attention diminished somewhat in the years following Enron's collapse. *Yount* [fn.13 supra].

Finally, and of prime significance, Skilling's jury acquitted him of nine insider-trading counts. Similarly, earlier instituted Enron-related prosecutions [see fn. 6 supra] yielded no overwhelming victory for the Government. In *Rideau*, *Estes*, and *Sheppard*, in marked contrast,

---

[12] *Murphy* involved the robbery prosecution of the notorious Jack Murphy, a convicted murderer who helped mastermind the 1954 heist of the Star of India sapphire from New York's American Museum of Natural History. Pointing to extensive press coverage about him, Murphy moved to transfer venue * * * We affirmed [the denial of that motion]. * * * Voir dire revealed no great hostility toward Murphy; "[s]ome of the jurors had a vague recollection of the robbery with which [he] was charged and each had some knowledge of [his] past crimes, but none betrayed a belief in the relevance of [his] past to the present case."

[13] In *Yount*, the media reported on Jon Yount's confession to a brutal murder and his prior conviction for the crime, which had been reversed due to a violation of *Miranda* v. *Arizona*. During *voir dire*, 77% of prospective jurors acknowledged they would carry an opinion into the jury box, and 8 of the 14 seated jurors and alternates admitted they had formed an opinion as to Yount's guilt. Nevertheless, we rejected Yount's presumption-of-prejudice claim. The adverse publicity and community outrage, we noted, were at their height prior to Yount's first trial, four years before the second prosecution; time had helped "sooth[e] and eras[e]" community prejudice.

[14] Skilling's reliance on *Estes* and *Sheppard* is particularly misplaced; those cases involved media interference with courtroom proceedings *during* trial. Skilling does not assert that news coverage reached and influenced his jury after it was empaneled.

the jury's verdict did not undermine in any way the supposition of juror bias. It would be odd for an appellate court to presume prejudice in a case in which jurors' actions run counter to that presumption. * * *

Skilling's trial, in short, shares little in common with those in which we approved a presumption of juror prejudice. The Fifth Circuit reached the opposite conclusion based primarily on the magnitude and negative tone of media attention directed at Enron. But "pretrial publicity—even pervasive, adverse publicity—does not inevitably lead to an unfair trial." * * * In this case, as just noted, news stories about Enron did not present the kind of vivid, unforgettable information we have recognized as particularly likely to produce prejudice, and Houston's size and diversity diluted the media's impact. * * * Nor did Enron's "sheer number of victims," 554 F. 3d, at 560, trigger a presumption of prejudice. Although the widespread community impact necessitated careful identification and inspection of prospective jurors' connections to Enron, the extensive screening questionnaire and follow-up *voir dire* were well suited to that task. And hindsight shows the efficacy of these devices; as we discuss infra, jurors' links to Enron were either nonexistent or attenuated. * * * Finally, although Causey's "well-publicized decision to plead guilty" shortly before trial created a danger of juror prejudice, the District Court took appropriate steps to reduce that risk. The court delayed the proceedings by two weeks, lessening the immediacy of that development. And during *voir dire*, the court asked about prospective jurors' exposure to recent publicity, including news regarding Causey. Only two venire members recalled the plea; neither mentioned Causey by name, and neither ultimately served on Skilling's jury. Although publicity about a codefendant's guilty plea calls for inquiry to guard against actual prejudice, it does not ordinarily—and, we are satisfied, it did not here—warrant an automatic presumption of prejudice.

Persuaded that no presumption arose,[18] we conclude that the District Court, in declining to order a venue change, did not exceed constitutional limitations. We next consider whether actual prejudice infected Skilling's jury. *Voir dire*, Skilling asserts, did not adequately detect and defuse juror bias. "[T]he record . . . affirmatively confirm[s]" prejudice, he maintains, because several seated jurors "prejudged his guilt." We disagree with Skilling's characterization of the *voir dire* and the jurors selected through it.

No hard-and-fast formula dictates the necessary depth or breadth of *voir dire*. Jury selection, we have repeatedly emphasized, is "particularly within the province of the trial judge." * * * When pretrial publicity is at issue, "primary reliance on the judgment of the trial court makes [especially] good sense" because the judge "sits in the locale where the publicity is said to have had its effect" and may base her evaluation on her "own perception of the depth and extent of news stories that might influence a juror." *Mu'Min v. Virginia* [Note 1, p. 1285]. Appellate courts making after-the-fact assessments of the media's impact on jurors should be mindful that their judgments lack the on-the-spot comprehension of the situation possessed by trial judges. * * * Reviewing courts are properly resistant to second-guessing the trial judge's estimation of a juror's impartiality, for that judge's appraisal is ordinarily influenced by a host of factors impossible to capture fully in the record—among them, the prospective juror's inflection, sincerity, demeanor, candor, body language, and apprehension of duty. In contrast to the cold transcript received by the appellate court, the in-the-moment *voir dire* affords the trial court a more intimate and immediate basis for assessing a venire member's fitness for jury service. We consider the adequacy of jury selection in Skilling's case, therefore, attentive to the respect due to district-court determinations of juror impartiality and of the measures necessary to ensure that impartiality.[20]

---

[18] The parties disagree about whether a presumption of prejudice can be rebutted, and, if it can, what standard of proof governs that issue. Compare Brief for Petitioner 25–35 with Brief for United States 24–32, 35–36. Because we hold that no presumption arose, we need not, and do not, reach these questions.

[20] The dissent recognizes "the 'wide discretion' owed to trial courts when it comes to jury-related issues" [quoting the dissent at p. 1277], but its analysis of the District Court's *voir dire* sometimes fails to demonstrate that awareness. For example, the dissent faults the District Court for not questioning prospective jurors regarding their

Skilling deems the *voir dire* insufficient because, he argues, jury selection lasted "just five hours," "[m]ost of the court's questions were conclusory[,] high-level, and failed adequately to probe jurors' true feelings," and the court "consistently took prospective jurors at their word once they claimed they could be fair, no matter what other indications of bias were present." Our review of the record, however, yields a different appraisal.[21] The District Court initially screened venire members by eliciting their responses to a comprehensive questionnaire drafted in large part by Skilling. That survey helped to identify prospective jurors excusable for cause and served as a springboard for further questions put to remaining members of the array. *Voir dire* thus was, in the court's words, the "culmination of a lengthy process." * * * In other Enron-related prosecutions, we note, District Courts, after inspecting venire members' responses to questionnaires, completed the jury-selection process within one day.

The District Court conducted *voir dire*, moreover, aware of the greater-than-normal need, due to pretrial publicity, to ensure against jury bias. At Skilling's urging, the court examined each prospective juror individually, thus preventing the spread of any prejudicial information to other venire members. See *Mu'Min*. To encourage candor, the court repeatedly admonished that there were "no right and wrong answers to th[e] questions." The court denied Skilling's request for attorney-led *voir dire* because, in its experience, potential jurors were "more forthcoming" when the court, rather than counsel, asked the question. The parties, however, were accorded an opportunity to ask follow-up questions of every prospective juror brought to the bench for colloquy. Skilling's counsel declined to ask anything of more than half of the venire members questioned individually, including eight eventually selected for the jury, because, he explained, "the Court and other counsel have covered" everything he wanted to know.

Inspection of the questionnaires and *voir dire* of the individuals who actually served as jurors satisfies us that, notwithstanding the flaws Skilling lists, the selection process successfully secured jurors who were largely untouched by Enron's collapse.[24] Eleven of the seated jurors and alternates reported no connection at all to Enron, while all other jurors reported at most an insubstantial link. As for pretrial publicity, 14 jurors and alternates specifically stated that they had paid scant attention to Enron-related news.[26] * * * The remaining two jurors indicated that nothing in the news influenced their opinions about Skilling.

"knowledge of or feelings about" Causey's guilty plea. But the court could reasonably decline to ask direct questions involving Causey's plea to avoid tipping off until-that-moment uninformed venire members that the plea had occurred. * * * Nothing inhibited defense counsel from inquiring about venire members' knowledge of the plea; indeed, counsel posed such a question. * * * From this Court's lofty and "panoramic" vantage point, lines of *voir dire* inquiry that "might be helpful in assessing whether a juror is impartial" are not hard to conceive. "To be constitutionally compelled, however, it is not enough that such questions might be helpful. Rather, the trial court's failure to ask these questions must render the defendant's trial fundamentally unfair." *MuMin*. According appropriate deference to the District Court, we cannot characterize jury-selection in this case as fundamentally unfair. Cf. fn. 6 supra (same selection process was used in other Enron-related prosecutions).

[21] In addition to focusing on the adequacy of *voir dire*, our decisions have also "take[n] into account . . . other measures [that] were used to mitigate the adverse effects of publicity." *Nebraska Press Assn.* v. *Stuart* [p. 1286]. We have noted, for example, the prophylactic effect of "emphatic and clear instructions on the sworn duty of each juror to decide the issues only on evidence presented in open court." Here, the District Court's instructions were unequivocal; the jurors, the court emphasized, were duty bound "to reach a fair and impartial verdict in this case based solely on the evidence [they] hear[d] and read in th[e] courtroom." Peremptory challenges, too, "provid[e] protection against [prejudice]"; the District Court, as earlier noted, exercised its discretion to grant the defendants two extra peremptories.

[24] In considering whether Skilling was tried before an impartial jury, the dissent relies extensively on venire members *not* selected for that jury [citing, inter alia, the dissent's comments on venire members 17, 29, 74, and 101, see pp. 1278–1280]. Statements by nonjurors do not themselves call into question the adequacy of the jury-selection process; elimination of these venire members is indeed one indicator that the process fulfilled its function. Critically, as discussed infra, the seated jurors showed little knowledge of or interest in, and were personally unaffected by, Enron's downfall.

[26] [The majority opinion in this footnote cited excerpts from the statements of each of these 14 jurors/alternates that supported this description. Those excerpts included the following as to those jurors deemed questionable in the

The questionnaires confirmed that, whatever community prejudice existed in Houston generally, Skilling's jurors were not under its sway. Although many expressed sympathy for victims of Enron's bankruptcy and speculated that greed contributed to the corporation's collapse, these sentiments did not translate into animus toward Skilling. When asked whether they "ha[d] an opinion about . . . Jeffrey Skilling," none of the seated jurors and alternates checked the "yes" box. And in response to the question whether "any opinion [they] may have formed regarding Enron or [Skilling] [would] prevent" their impartial consideration of the evidence at trial, every juror—despite options to mark "yes" or "unsure"—instead checked "no."

The District Court, Skilling asserts, should not have "accept[ed] *at face value* jurors' promises of fairness." In *Irvin* v. *Dowd*, 366 U.S. 717 (1961), Skilling points out, we found actual prejudice despite jurors' assurances that they could be impartial. Justice Sotomayor, in turn, repeatedly relies on *Irvin*, which she regards as closely analogous to this case. We disagree with that characterization of *Irvin*. The facts of *Irvin* are worlds apart from those presented here. Leslie Irvin stood accused of a brutal murder and robbery spree in a small rural community. In the months before Irvin's trial, "a barrage" of publicity was "unleashed against him," including reports of his confessions to the slayings and robberies. This Court's description of the media coverage in *Irvin* reveals why the dissent's "best case" is not an apt comparison:

> "[S]tories revealed the details of [Irvin's] background, including a reference to crimes committed when a juvenile, his convictions for arson almost 20 years previously, for burglary and by a court-martial on AWOL charges during the war. He was accused of being a parole violator. The headlines announced his police line-up identification, that he faced a lie detector test, had been placed at the scene of the crime and that the six murders were solved but [he] refused to confess. Finally, they announced [Irvin's] confession to the six murders and the fact of his indictment for four of them in Indiana. They reported [Irvin's] offer to plead guilty if promised a 99-year sentence, but also the determination, on the other hand, of the prosecutor to secure the death penalty, and that [Irvin] had confessed to 24 burglaries (the *modus operandi* of these robberies was compared to that of the murders and the similarity noted). One story dramatically relayed the promise of a sheriff to devote his life to securing [Irvin's] execution . . . . Another characterized [Irvin] as remorseless and without conscience but also as having been found sane by a court-appointed panel of doctors. In many of the stories [Irvin] was described as the 'confessed slayer of six,' a parole violator and fraudulent-check artist. [Irvin's] court-appointed counsel was quoted as having received 'much criticism over being Irvin's counsel' and it was pointed out, by way of excusing the attorney, that he would be subject to disbarment should he refuse to represent Irvin. On the day before the trial the newspapers carried the story that Irvin had orally admitted [to] the murder of [one victim] as well as 'the robbery-murder of [a second individual]; the murder of [a third individual], and the slaughter of three members of [a different family].'" * * * "[N]ewspapers in which the[se] stories appeared were delivered regularly to 95% of the dwellings in" the county where the trial occurred, which had a population of only 30,000; "radio and TV stations, which likewise blanketed that county, also carried extensive newscasts covering the same incidents."

dissent at pp. 1280–1281]: Juror 10 ('I haven't followed [Enron-related news] in detail of to any extreme at all.'); Juror 11 (did not 'get into the details of [the Enron case]' and 'just kind of tune[d] [it] out'); Juror 20 ('I was out of [the] state when [Enron collapsed], and then personal circumstances kept me from paying much attention.'); Juror 38 (recalled 'nothing in particular' about media coverage); Juror 63 ('I don't really pay attention.'); Juror 90 ('seldom" read the Houston Chronicle and did not watch any news programs); Juror 113 ("never really paid that much attention [to] it"); Juror 116 (had "rea[d] a number of different articles," but "since it hasn't affected me personally," could not "specifically recall" any of them).

Reviewing Irvin's fair-trial claim, this Court noted that "the pattern of deep and bitter prejudice" in the community "was clearly reflected in the sum total of the *voir dire*": "370 prospective jurors or almost 90% of those examined on the point . . . entertained some opinion as to guilt," and "[8] out of the 12 [jurors] thought [Irvin] was guilty." Although these jurors declared they could be impartial, we held that, "[w]ith his life at stake, it is not requiring too much that [Irvin] be tried in an atmosphere undisturbed by so huge a wave of public passion and by a jury other than one in which two-thirds of the members admit, before hearing any testimony, to possessing a belief in his guilt."

In this case, news stories about Enron contained nothing resembling the horrifying information rife in reports about Irvin's rampage of robberies and murders. Of key importance, Houston shares little in common with the rural community in which Irvin's trial proceeded, and circulation figures for Houston media sources were far lower than the 95% saturation level recorded in *Irvin*, see App. 15a ("The *Houston Chronicle* . . . reaches less than one-third of occupied households in Houston"). Skilling's seated jurors, moreover, exhibited nothing like the display of bias shown in *Irvin*. * * * In light of these large differences, the District Court had far less reason than did the trial court in *Irvin* to discredit jurors' promises of fairness.

The District Court, moreover, did not simply take venire members who proclaimed their impartiality at their word. As noted, all of Skilling's jurors had already affirmed on their questionnaires that they would have no trouble basing a verdict only on the evidence at trial. Nevertheless, the court followed up with each individually to uncover concealed bias. This face-to-face opportunity to gauge demeanor and credibility, coupled with information from the questionnaires regarding jurors' backgrounds, opinions, and sources of news, gave the court a sturdy foundation to assess fitness for jury service. * * * The jury's not-guilty verdict on nine insider-trading counts after nearly five days of deliberation, meanwhile, suggests the court's assessments were accurate.[31] Skilling, we conclude, failed to show that his *voir dire* fell short of constitutional requirements.

Skilling also singles out several jurors in particular and contends they were openly biased. See *United States* v. *Martinez-Salazar* [Note 2, p. 1255] ("[T]he seating of any juror who should have been dismissed for cause . . . require[s] reversal."). In reviewing claims of this type, the deference due to district courts is at its pinnacle: "A trial court's findings of juror impartiality may be overturned only for manifest error." *Mu'Min*. Skilling, moreover, unsuccessfully challenged only one of the seated jurors for cause, "strong evidence that he was convinced the [other] jurors were not biased and had not formed any opinions as to his guilt." * * * With these considerations in mind, we turn to Skilling's specific allegations of juror partiality.

Skilling contends that Juror 11—the only seated juror he challenged for cause—"expressed the most obvious bias." Juror 11 stated that "greed on Enron's part" triggered the company's bankruptcy and that corporate executives, driven by avarice, "walk a line that stretches sometimes the legality of something." But, as the Fifth Circuit accurately summarized, Juror 11 "had 'no idea' whether Skilling had 'crossed that line,' and he 'didn't say that' every CEO is probably a crook. He also asserted that he could be fair and require the government to prove its case, that he did not believe everything he read in the paper, that he did not 'get into the details' of the Enron coverage, that he did not watch television, and that Enron was 'old news.' " * * * Despite his criticism of greed, Juror 11 remarked that Skilling "earned [his] salar[y]," and said he would have "no problem" telling his co-worker, who had lost 401(k) funds due to Enron's collapse, that the jury

[31] The dissent asserts that "the Government placed relatively little emphasis on [these] insider trading counts during its closing argument." As the record shows, however, counsel described in detail the evidence supporting Count 50, one of the insider-trading counts on which the jury returned a not-guilty verdict. See Record 37008–37010. * * * Regarding the remaining insider-trading counts, counsel reminded jurors they had heard similar evidence of Skilling's other sales, and urged them to "conclude, based on the evidence," that "Skilling had information that he used to sell his stock" at the "key periods in time."

voted to acquit, if that scenario came to pass. The District Court, noting that it had "looked [Juror 11] in the eye and . . . heard all his [answers]," found his assertions of impartiality credible. We agree with the Court of Appeals that "[t]he express finding that Juror 11 was fair is not reversible error."

Skilling also objected at trial to the seating of six specific jurors whom, he said, he would have excluded had he not already exhausted his peremptory challenges. Juror 20, he observes, "said she was 'angry' about Enron's collapse and that she, too, had been 'forced to forfeit [her] own 401(k) funds to survive layoffs.' " But Juror 20 made clear during *voir dire* that she did not "personally blame" Skilling for the loss of her retirement account. Having not "pa[id] much attention" to Enron-related news, she "quite honestly" did not "have enough information to know" whether Skilling was probably guilty, and she "th[ought] [she] could be" fair and impartial. In light of these answers, the District Court did not commit manifest error in finding Juror 20 fit for jury service.

The same is true of Juror 63, who, Skilling points out, wrote on her questionnaire "that [Skilling] 'probably knew [he] w[as] breaking the law.' " During *voir dire*, however, Juror 63 insisted that she did not "really have an opinion [about Skilling's guilt] either way," she did not "know what [she] was thinking" when she completed the questionnaire, but she "absolutely" presumed Skilling innocent and confirmed her understanding that the Government would "have to prove" his guilt. In response to follow-up questions from Skilling's counsel, she again stated she would not presume that Skilling violated any laws and could "[a]bsolutely" give her word that she could be fair. "Jurors," we have recognized, "cannot be expected invariably to express themselves carefully or even consistently." *Yount*, [fn. 13 supra]. From where we sit, we cannot conclude that Juror 63 was biased. * * *

The four remaining jurors Skilling said he would have excluded with extra peremptory strikes [Jurors 38, 67, 78, and 84] exhibited no sign of prejudice we can discern. See [record as to]: (Juror 38) (remembered no media coverage about Enron and said nothing in her experience would prevent her from being fair and impartial); (Juror 67) (had no connection to Enron and no anger about its collapse); Juror 78) (did not "know much about" Enron); (Juror 84) (had not heard or read anything about Enron and said she did not "know enough to answer" the question whether she was angry about the company's demise). Skilling's counsel declined to ask follow-up questions of any of these jurors and, indeed, told Juror 84 he had nothing to ask because she "gave all the right answers." Whatever Skilling's reasons for wanting to strike these four individuals from his jury, he cannot credibly assert they displayed a disqualifying bias.

In sum, Skilling failed to establish that a presumption of prejudice arose or that actual bias infected the jury that tried him. Jurors, the trial court correctly comprehended, need not enter the box with empty heads in order to determine the facts impartially. "It is sufficient if the juror[s] can lay aside [their] impression[s] or opinion[s] and render a verdict based on the evidence presented in court." *Irvin*. Taking account of the full record, rather than incomplete exchanges selectively culled from it, we find no cause to upset the lower courts' judgment that Skilling's jury met that measure. We therefore affirm the Fifth Circuit's ruling that Skilling received a fair trial.

JUSTICE ALITO, concurring in part and concurring in the judgment.

I write separately to address petitioner's jury-trial argument. * * * The Sixth Amendment guarantees criminal defendants a trial before "an impartial jury." In my view, this requirement is satisfied so long as no biased juror is actually seated at trial. Of course, evidence of pretrial media attention and widespread community hostility may play a role in the bias inquiry. Such evidence may be important in assessing the adequacy of *voir dire*, or in reviewing the denial of requests to dismiss particular jurors for cause. There are occasions in which such evidence weighs heavily in favor of a change of venue. In the end, however, if no biased jury is actually seated, there is no violation of the defendant's right to an impartial jury.

Petitioner advances a very different understanding of the jury-trial right. Where there is extraordinary pretrial publicity and community hostility, he contends, a court must presume juror prejudice and thus grant a change of venue. I disagree. Careful *voir dire* can often ensure the selection of impartial jurors even where pretrial media coverage has generated much hostile community sentiment. Moreover, once a jury has been selected, there are measures that a trial judge may take to insulate jurors from media coverage during the course of the trial. * * * The rule that petitioner advances departs from the text of the Sixth Amendment and is difficult to apply. It requires a trial judge to determine whether the adverse pretrial media coverage and community hostility in a particular case has reached a certain level of severity, but there is no clear way of demarcating that level or of determining whether it has been met. * * * Petitioner relies chiefly on three cases from the 1960's—*Sheppard* v. *Maxwell*, *Estes* v. *Texas*, and *Rideau* v. *Louisiana*. I do not read those cases as demanding petitioner's suggested approach. As the Court notes, *Sheppard* and *Estes* primarily "involved media interference with courtroom proceedings *during* trial." *Rideau* involved unique events in a small community.

I share some of Justice Sotomayor's concerns about the adequacy of the *voir dire* in this case and the trial judge's findings that certain jurors could be impartial. But those highly fact-specific issues are not within the question presented. Pet. for Cert. i. I also do not understand the opinion of the Court as reaching any question regarding a change of venue under Federal Rule of Criminal Procedure 21.

JUSTICE SOTOMAYOR, with whom JUSTICE STEVENS and JUSTICE BREYER join, concurring in part and dissenting in part.

I respectfully dissent,* * * from the Court's conclusion that Jeffrey Skilling received a fair trial before an impartial jury. Under our relevant precedents, the more intense the public's antipathy toward a defendant, the more careful a court must be to prevent that sentiment from tainting the jury. In this case, passions ran extremely high. The sudden collapse of Enron directly affected thousands of people in the Houston area and shocked the entire community. The accompanying barrage of local media coverage was massive in volume and often caustic in tone. As Enron's one-time CEO, Skilling was at the center of the storm. Even if these extraordinary circumstances did not constitutionally compel a change of venue, they required the District Court to conduct a thorough *voir dire* in which prospective jurors' attitudes about the case were closely scrutinized. The District Court's inquiry lacked the necessary thoroughness and left serious doubts about whether the jury empaneled to decide Skilling's case was capable of rendering an impartial decision based solely on the evidence presented in the courtroom. Accordingly, I would grant Skilling relief on his fair-trial claim.

The majority understates the breadth and depth of community hostility toward Skilling and overlooks significant deficiencies in the District Court's jury selection process. The failure of Enron wounded Houston deeply. * * * Thousands of the company's employees lost their jobs and saw their retirement savings vanish. As the effects rippled through the local economy, thousands of additional jobs disappeared, businesses shuttered, and community groups that once benefited from Enron's largesse felt the loss of millions of dollars in contributions. * * * Enron's community ties were so extensive that the entire local U. S. Attorney's Office was forced to recuse itself from the Government's investigation into the company's fall.

With Enron's demise affecting the lives of so many Houstonians, local media coverage of the story saturated the community. According to a defense media expert, the Houston Chronicle—the area's leading newspaper—assigned as many as 12 reporters to work on the Enron story full time. The paper mentioned Enron in more than 4,000 articles during the 3-year period following the company's December 2001 bankruptcy filing. Hundreds of these articles discussed Skilling by name. Skilling's expert, a professional journalist and academic with 30 years' experience, could not "recall another instance where a local paper dedicated as many resources to a single topic over such an extended period of time as the Houston Chronicle . . . dedicated to Enron." Local television news coverage was similarly pervasive and, in terms of "editorial theme," "largely followed the Chronicle's lead." Between May 2002 and October 2004, local stations aired an estimated 19,000 news segments involving Enron, more than 1600 of which mentioned Skilling.

While many of the stories were straightforward news items, many others conveyed and amplified the community's outrage at the top executives perceived to be responsible for the company's bankruptcy. A Chronicle report on Skilling's 2002 testimony before Congress is typical of the coverage. It began, "Across Houston, Enron employees watched former chief executive Jeffrey Skilling's congressional testimony on television, turning incredulous, angry and then sarcastic by turns, as a man they knew as savvy and detail-oriented pleaded memory failure and ignorance about critical financial transactions at the now-collapsed energy giant." " 'He is lying; he knew everything,' said [an employee], who said she had seen Skilling frequently over her 18 years with the firm, where Skilling was known for his intimate grasp of the inner doings at the company. 'I am getting sicker by the minute.' " * * * Articles deriding Enron's senior executives were juxtaposed with pieces expressing sympathy toward and solidarity with the company's many victims. Skilling's media expert counted nearly a hundred victim-related stories in the Chronicle, including a "multi-page layout entitled 'The Faces of Enron,' " which poignantly described the gut-wrenching experiences of former employees who lost vast sums of money, faced eviction from their homes, could not afford Christmas gifts for their children, and felt "scared," "hurt," "humiliat[ed]," "helpless," and "betrayed." The conventional wisdom that blame for Enron's devastating implosion and the ensuing human tragedy ultimately rested with Skilling and former Enron Chairman Kenneth Lay became so deeply ingrained in the popular imagination that references to their involvement even turned up on the sports pages: "If you believe the story about [Coach Bill Parcells] not having anything to do with the end of Emmitt Smith's Cowboys career, then you probably believe in other far-fetched concepts. Like Jeff Skilling having nothing to do with Enron's collapse." * * *

The Sixth Amendment right to an impartial jury and the due process right to a fundamentally fair trial guarantee to criminal defendants a trial in which jurors set aside preconceptions, disregard extrajudicial influences, and decide guilt or innocence "based on the evidence presented in court." *Irvin* v. *Dowd*. Community passions, often inflamed by adverse pretrial publicity, can call the integrity of a trial into doubt. In some instances, this Court has observed, the hostility of the community becomes so severe as to give rise to a "presumption of [juror] prejudice." *Patton* v. *Yount*. * * * The Court of Appeals incorporated the concept of presumptive prejudice into a burden-shifting framework: Once the defendant musters sufficient evidence of community hostility, the onus shifts to the Government to prove the impartiality of the jury. The majority similarly envisions a fixed point at which public passions become so intense that prejudice to a defendant's fair-trial rights must be presumed. The majority declines, however, to decide whether the presumption is rebuttable, as the Court of Appeals held.

This Court has never treated the notion of presumptive prejudice so formalistically. Our decisions instead merely convey the commonsense understanding that as the tide of public enmity rises, so too does the danger that the prejudices of the community will infiltrate the jury. The underlying question has always been this: Do we have confidence that the jury's verdict was "induced only by evidence and argument in open court, and not by any outside influence, whether of private talk or public print"? *Patterson* v. *Colorado ex rel. Attorney General of Colo.*, 205 U.S. 454, 462 (1907).

This inquiry is necessarily case specific. In selecting a jury, a trial court must take measures adapted to the intensity, pervasiveness, and character of the pretrial publicity and community animus. Reviewing courts, meanwhile, must assess whether the trial court's procedures sufficed under the circumstances to keep the jury free from disqualifying bias. This Court's precedents illustrate the sort of steps required in different situations to safeguard a defendant's constitutional right to a fair trial before an impartial jury.

At one end of the spectrum, this Court has, on rare occasion, confronted such inherently prejudicial circumstances that it has reversed a defendant's conviction "without pausing to examine . . . the *voir dire* examination of the members of the jury." *Rideau* v. *Louisiana*. In *Rideau*, repeated television broadcasts of the defendant's confession to murder, robbery, and kidnaping so thoroughly poisoned local sentiment as to raise doubts that even the most careful *voir dire* could have secured an impartial jury. A change of venue, the Court determined, was thus the only way to assure a fair trial. See also 6 W. LaFave, J. Israel, N. King & O. Kerr, Criminal Procedure § 23.2(a), p. 264 (3d ed. 2007) (hereinafter LaFave) ("The best reading of *Rideau* is that the Court there recognized that prejudicial publicity may be so inflammatory and so pervasive that the voir dire simply cannot be trusted to fully reveal the likely prejudice among prospective jurors").

As the majority describes, this Court reached similar conclusions in *Estes* v. *Texas*, and *Sheppard* v. *Maxwell*. * * * [Both] involved not only massive publicity, but also media disruption * * *. It would have been difficult for the jurors not to have been swayed, at least subconsciously, by the "bedlam" that surrounded them. *Sheppard*. * * * *Estes* and *Sheppard* thus applied *Rideau*'s insight that in particularly extreme circumstances even the most rigorous *voir dire* cannot suffice to dispel the reasonable likelihood of jury bias. * * * Apart from these exceptional cases, this Court has declined to discount *voir dire* entirely and has instead examined the particulars of the jury selection process to determine whether it sufficed to produce a jury untainted by pretrial publicity and community animus. The Court has recognized that when antipathy toward a defendant pervades the community there is a high risk that biased jurors will find their way onto the panel. The danger is not merely that some prospective jurors will deliberately hide their prejudices, but also that, as "part of a community deeply hostile to the accused," "they may unwittingly [be] influenced" by the fervor that surrounds them. *Murphy* v. *Florida*. * * *

It is necessary to determine how this case compares to our existing fair-trial precedents. Were the circumstances so inherently prejudicial that, as in *Rideau*, even the most scrupulous *voir dire* would have been "but a hollow formality" incapable of reliably producing an impartial jury? * * * Though the question is close, I agree with the Court that the prospect of seating an unbiased jury in Houston was not so remote as to compel the conclusion that the District Court acted unconstitutionally in denying Skilling's motion to change venue. Three considerations lead me to this conclusion. First, as the Court observes, the size and diversity of the Houston community make it probable that the jury pool contained a nontrivial number of persons who were unaffected by Enron's collapse, neutral in their outlook, and unlikely to be swept up in the public furor. Second, media coverage of the case, while ubiquitous and often inflammatory, did not, as the Court points out, contain a confession by Skilling or similar "smoking-gun" evidence of specific criminal acts. * * * Third, there is no suggestion that the courtroom in this case became, as in *Estes* and *Sheppard*, a "carnival" in which the "calmness and solemnity" of the proceedings was compromised.

It is thus appropriate to examine the *voir dire* and determine whether it instills confidence in the impartiality of the jury actually selected.[9] * * * In concluding that the *voir dire* "adequately

[9] Whether the District Court abused its discretion in declining to change venue pursuant to the Federal Rules of Criminal Procedure is a different question. * * * As this Court has indicated, its supervisory powers confer "more latitude" to set standards for the conduct of trials in federal courts than in state courts. *Mu'Min* v. *Virginia*. While the circumstances may not constitutionally compel a change of venue "without pausing to examine . . . the *voir dire*," *Rideau* v. *Louisiana*, the widely felt sense of victimhood among Houstonians and the community's deep-seated animus toward Skilling certainly meant that the task of reliably identifying untainted jurors posed a major challenge, with no guarantee of success. It likely would have been far easier to empanel an impartial jury in a venue where the Enron story had less salience. I thus agree with the Court of Appeals that "[i]t would not have been imprudent for the [District] [C]ourt to have granted Skilling's transfer motion." Skilling, however, likely forfeited

detect[ed] and defuse[d] juror bias," the Court downplays the extent of the community's antipathy toward Skilling and exaggerates the rigor of the jury selection process. The devastating impact of Enron's collapse and the relentless media coverage demanded exceptional care on the part of the District Court to ensure the seating of an impartial jury. While the procedures employed by the District Court might have been adequate in the typical high-profile case, they did not suffice in the extraordinary circumstances of this case to safeguard Skilling's constitutional right to a fair trial before an impartial jury. * * *

I am mindful of the "wide discretion" owed to trial courts when it comes to jury-related issues. Trial courts are uniquely positioned to assess public sentiment and the credibility of prospective jurors. Proximity to events, however, is not always a virtue. Persons in the midst of a tumult often lack a panoramic view. "[A]ppellate tribunals [thus] have the duty to make an independent evaluation of the circumstances." *Sheppard*. In particular, reviewing courts are well qualified to inquire into whether a trial court implemented procedures adequate to keep community prejudices from infecting the jury. If the jury selection process does not befit the circumstances of the case, the trial court's rulings on impartiality are necessarily called into doubt. * * *

As the Court of Appeals apprehended, the District Court gave short shrift to the mountainous evidence of public hostility. For Houstonians, Enron's collapse was an event of once-in-a-generation proportions. Not only was the volume of media coverage "immense" and frequently intemperate, but "the sheer number of victims" created a climate in which animosity toward Skilling ran deep and the desire for conviction was widely shared. * * * The level of public animus toward Skilling dwarfed that present in cases such as *Murphy* and *Mu'Min*. The much closer analogy is thus to *Irvin*, which similarly featured a "barrage" of media coverage and a "huge . . . wave of public passion," although even that case did not, as here, involve direct harm to entire segments of the community. * * * Attempting to distinguish *Irvin*, the majority suggests that Skilling's economic offenses were less incendiary than Irvin's violent crime spree and that "news stories about Enron contained nothing resembling the horrifying information rife in reports about Irvin's rampage of robberies and murders." * * * The majority also points to the four years that passed between Enron's declaration of bankruptcy and the start of Skilling's trial, that "the decibel level of media attention diminished somewhat" over this time. Neither of these arguments is persuasive.

First, while violent crimes may well provoke widespread community outrage more readily than crimes involving monetary loss, economic crimes are certainly capable of rousing public passions, particularly when thousands of unsuspecting people are robbed of their livelihoods and retirement savings. Indeed, the record in this case is replete with examples of visceral outrage toward Skilling and other Enron executives. Houstonians compared Skilling to, among other things, a rapist, an axe murderer, and an Al Qaeda terrorist. * * * The bad blood was so strong that Skilling and other top executives hired private security to protect themselves from persons inclined to take the law into their own hands.

Second, the passage of time did little to soften community sentiment. Contrary to the Court's suggestion, this case in no way resembles *Yount*, where, by the time of the defendant's retrial, "prejudicial publicity [had] greatly diminished" and community animus had significantly waned. * * * The Enron story was a continuing saga, and "publicity remained intense throughout." 554 F. 3d, at 560. Not only did Enron's downfall generate wall-to-wall news coverage, but so too did a succession of subsequent Enron-related events. Of particular note is the highly publicized guilty plea of codefendant Causey just weeks before Skilling's trial. If anything, the time that elapsed between the bankruptcy and the trial made the task of seating an unbiased jury more difficult, not less. For many members of the jury pool, each highly publicized Enron-related guilty plea or

any Rule 21 or supervisory powers claim by failing to present it either in his opening brief before the Fifth Circuit, or in his petition for certiorari.

conviction likely served to increase their certainty that Skilling too had engaged in—if not masterminded—criminal acts, particularly given that the media coverage reinforced this view.

Any doubt that the prevailing mindset in the Houston community remained overwhelmingly negative was dispelled by prospective jurors' responses to the written questionnaires.* * * More than one-third of the prospective jurors either knew victims of Enron's collapse or were victims themselves, and two-thirds gave responses suggesting an antidefendant bias. In many instances their contempt for Skilling was palpable. Only a small fraction of the prospective jurors raised no red flags in their responses. And this was *before* Causey's guilty plea and the flurry of news reports that accompanied the approach of trial. One of Skilling's experts, a political scientist who had studied pretrial publicity "for over 35 years" and consulted in more than 200 high-profile cases (in which he had recommended against venue changes more often than not), "c[a]me to the conclusion that the extent and depth of bias shown in these questionnaires is the highest or at least one of the very highest I have ever encountered."

Given the extent of the antipathy evident both in the community at large and in the responses to the written questionnaire, it was critical for the District Court to take "strong measures" to ensure the selection of "an impartial jury free from outside influences." As this Court has recognized, "[i]n a community where most veniremen will admit to a disqualifying prejudice, the reliability of the others' protestations may be drawn into question." *Murphy*. * * * Perhaps because it had underestimated the public's antipathy toward Skilling, the District Court's 5-hour *voir dire* was manifestly insufficient to identify and remove biased jurors.[13]

As an initial matter, important lines of inquiry were not pursued at all. The majority accepts, for instance, that "publicity about a codefendant's guilty plea calls for inquiry to guard against actual prejudice." Implying that the District Court undertook this inquiry, the majority states that "[o]nly two venire members recalled [Causey's] plea." In fact, the court asked very few prospective jurors any questions directed to their knowledge of or feelings about that event. Considering how much news the plea generated, many more than two venire members were likely aware of it. The lack of questioning, however, makes the prejudicial impact of the plea on those jurors impossible to assess.

The court also rarely asked prospective jurors to describe personal interactions they may have had about the case, or to consider whether they might have difficulty avoiding discussion of the case with family, friends, or colleagues during the course of the lengthy trial. The tidbits of information that trickled out on these subjects provided cause for concern. In response to general media-related questions, several prospective jurors volunteered that they had spoken with others about the case. Juror 74, for example, indicated that her husband was the "news person," that they had "talked about it," that she had also heard things "from work," and that what she heard was "all negative, of course." The court, however, did not seek elaboration about the substance of these interactions. Surely many prospective jurors had similar conversations, particularly once they learned upon receiving the written questionnaire that they might end up on Skilling's jury. * * * Prospective jurors' personal interactions, moreover, may well have left them with the sense that the community was counting on a conviction. Yet this too was a subject the District Court did not adequately explore. * * *

---

[13] The majority points out that the jury selection processes in the three previous Enron trials that had been held in Houston were similarly brief. The circumstances of those cases, however, were very different. In particular, the defendants had not been personally subjected to anything approaching the withering public criticism that had been directed at Skilling and Lay. * * * [I]t was the trial of Skilling and Lay that was widely seen as the climactic event of the Enron saga. Accordingly, my conclusion that the jury selection process in this unusual case did not suffice to select an impartial jury does not cast doubt on the adequacy of the processes used in the earlier Enron prosecutions. * * *

With respect to potential nonmedia sources of bias, the District Court's exchange with Juror 101 is particularly troubling. Although Juror 101 responded in the negative when asked whether she had "read anything in the newspaper that [stood] out in [her] mind," she volunteered that she "just heard that, between the two of them, [Skilling and Lay] had $43 million to contribute for their case and that there was an insurance policy that they could collect on, also." This information, she explained, "was just something I overheard today—other jurors talking." It seemed suspicious, she intimated, "to have an insurance policy ahead of time." The court advised her that "most corporations provide insurance for their officers and directors." The court, however, did not investigate the matter further, even though it had earlier instructed prospective jurors not to talk to each other about the case. It is thus not apparent whether other prospective jurors also overheard the information and whether they too believed that it reflected unfavorably on the defendants; nor is it apparent what other outside information may have been shared among the venire members. At the very least, Juror 101's statements indicate that the court's questions were failing to bring to light the extent of jurors' exposure to potentially prejudicial facts and that some prospective jurors were having difficulty following the court's directives.

The topics that the District Court did cover were addressed in cursory fashion. Most prospective jurors were asked just a few yes/no questions about their general exposure to media coverage and a handful of additional questions concerning any responses to the written questionnaire that suggested bias. In many instances, their answers were unenlightening. Yet the court rarely sought to draw them out with open-ended questions about their impressions of Enron or Skilling and showed limited patience for counsel's followup efforts.[17] When prospective jurors were more forthcoming, their responses tended to highlight the ubiquity and negative tone of the local news coverage, thus underscoring the need to press the more guarded members of the venire for further information. Juror 17, for example, mentioned hearing a radio program that very morning in which a former Enron employee compared persons who did not think Skilling was guilty to Holocaust deniers.* * * Other jurors may well have encountered, and been influenced by, similarly incendiary rhetoric.

These deficiencies in the form and content of the *voir dire* questions contributed to a deeper problem: The District Court failed to make a sufficiently critical assessment of prospective jurors' assurances of impartiality. Although the Court insists otherwise, the *voir dire* transcript indicates that the District Court essentially took jurors at their word when they promised to be fair. Indeed, the court declined to dismiss for cause any prospective juror who ultimately gave a clear assurance of impartiality, no matter how much equivocation preceded it. Juror 29, for instance, wrote on her questionnaire that Skilling was "not an honest man." During questioning, she acknowledged having previously thought the defendants were guilty, and she disclosed that she lost $50,000–$60,000 in her 401(k) as a result of Enron's collapse. But she ultimately agreed that she would be able to presume innocence. Noting that she "blame[d] Enron for the loss of her money" and appeared to have "unshakeable bias," Skilling's counsel challenged her for cause. The court, however, declined to remove her, stating that "she answered candidly she's going to have an open mind now" and "agree[ing]" with the Government's assertion that "we have to take her at her word."[20]

---

[17] The majority's criticism of Skilling's counsel for failing to ask questions of many of the prospective jurors, is thus misplaced. Given the District Court's express warning early in the *voir dire* that it would not allow counsel "to ask individual questions if [they] abuse[d]" that right, counsel can hardly be blamed for declining to test the court's boundaries at every turn. Moreover, the court's perfunctory exchanges with prospective jurors often gave counsel no clear avenue for further permissible inquiry.

[20] The majority attempts to downplay the significance of Juror 29 by noting that she did not end up on the jury because Skilling used a peremptory challenge to remove her. * * * The majority makes a similar point with respect to other venire members who were not ultimately seated. See fn. 24. The comments of these venire members, however, are relevant in assessing the impartiality of the seated jurors, who were similarly "part of a community deeply hostile to the accused" and who may have been "unwittingly influenced by it." *Murphy* v. *Florida*. Moreover,

Worse still, the District Court on a number of occasions accepted declarations of impartiality that were equivocal on their face. Prospective jurors who "hope[d]" they could presume innocence and did "not necessarily" think Skilling was guilty were permitted to remain in the pool. * * *

The majority takes solace in the fact that most of the persons actually seated as jurors and alternates "specifically stated that they had paid scant attention to Enron-related news." In context, however, these general declarations reveal little about the seated jurors' actual knowledge or views or the possible pressure they might have felt to convict, and thus cannot instill confidence that the jurors "were not under [the] sway" of the prevailing community sentiment. Juror 63, for instance, [as quoted by the majority] told the court that she "may have heard a little bit" about Enron-related litigation but had not "really pa[id] attention." Yet she was clearly aware of some specifics. On her questionnaire, despite stating that she had not followed Enron-related news, she wrote about "whistleblowers and Arthur Andersen lying about Enron's accounting," and she expressed the view that Skilling and Lay "probably knew they were breaking the law." During questioning, which lasted barely four minutes, the District Court obtained no meaningful information about the actual extent of Juror 63's familiarity with the case or the basis for her belief in Skilling's guilt. Yet it nevertheless accepted her assurance that she could "absolutely" presume innocence.

Indeed, the District Court's anemic questioning did little to dispel similar doubts about the impartiality of numerous other seated jurors and alternates. In my estimation, more than half of those seated made written and oral comments suggesting active antipathy toward the defendants. The majority thus misses the mark when it asserts that "Skilling's seated jurors . . . exhibited nothing like the display of bias shown in *Irvin*." Juror 10, for instance, reported on his written questionnaire that he knew several co-workers who owned Enron stock; that he personally may have owned Enron stock through a mutual fund; that he heard and read about the Enron cases from the "Houston Chronicle, all three Houston news channels, Fox news, talking with friends [and] co-workers, [and] Texas Lawyer Magazine"; that he believed Enron's collapse "was due to greed and mismanagement"; that "[i]f [Lay] did not know what was going on in his company, he was really a poor manager/leader"; and that the defendants were "suspect." During questioning, he said he "th[ought]" he could presume innocence and "believe[d]" he could put the Government to its proof, but he also acknowledged that he might have "some hesitancy" "in telling people the government didn't prove its case." Juror 11 wrote * * * [about various sources of "Enron-related news" and his belief "that 'greed on Enron's part' caused the company's collapse]. During questioning, he stated that he would have 'no problem' requiring the Government to prove its case, but he also told the court * * * that corporate executives are often 'stretching the legal limits . . . I'm not going to say that they're all crooks, but you know.' Asked whether he would 'start the case with sort of an inkling that because [Lay's] greedy he must have done something illegal,' he offered an indeterminate 'not necessarily.' "[23]

the fact that the District Court failed to remove persons as dubiously qualified as Juror 29 goes directly to the adequacy of its *voir dire*. If Juror 29 made it through to the end of the selection process, it is difficult to have confidence in the impartiality of the jurors who sat, especially given how little is known about many of them. Cf. 6 LaFave § 23.2(f), at 288 ("The responses of those not seated casts light on the credibility of the seated jurors who were familiar with the same publicity").

[23] Many other seated jurors and alternates expressed similarly troubling sentiments. (Juror 20) (obtained Enron-related news from the Chronicle and "local news stations"; blamed Enron's collapse on "[n]ot enough corporate controls or effective audit procedures to prevent mismanagement of corporate assets"; and was "angry that so many people lost their jobs and their retirement savings"); (Juror 38) (followed Enron-related news from various sources, including the Chronicle; was "angry about what happened"; and "fe[lt] bad for those that worked hard and invested in the corp[oration] only to have it all taken away"); (Juror 90) (heard Enron-related news from his wife, co-workers, and television; wrote that "[i]t's not right for someone . . . to take" away the money that the "small average worker saves . . . for retirement all his life"; and described the Government's Enron investigation as "a good thing"); (Juror 113) (obtained information about Enron from a "co-worker [who] was in the jury pool for Mrs. Fastow's trial"; worked for an employer who lost money as a result of Enron's collapse; found it "sad" that the collapse had affected "such a

While several seated jurors and alternates did not make specific comments suggesting prejudice, their written and oral responses were so abbreviated as to make it virtually impossible for the District Court reliably to assess whether they harbored any latent biases. * * *

In assessing the likelihood that bias lurked in the minds of at least some of these seated jurors, I find telling the way in which *voir dire* played out. When the District Court asked the prospective jurors as a group whether they had any reservations about their ability to presume innocence and put the Government to its proof, only two answered in the affirmative, and both were excused for cause. The District Court's individual questioning, though truncated, exposed disqualifying prejudices among numerous additional prospective jurors who had earlier expressed no concerns about their impartiality. It thus strikes me as highly likely that at least some of the seated jurors, despite stating that they could be fair, harbored similar biases that a more probing inquiry would likely have exposed. Cf. *Yount*, (holding that the trial court's "particularly extensive" 10-day *voir dire* assured the jury's impartiality).[25]

The majority suggests, that the jury's decision to acquit Skilling on nine relatively minor insider trading charges confirms its impartiality. This argument, however, mistakes partiality with bad faith or blind vindictiveness. Jurors who act in good faith and sincerely believe in their own fairness may nevertheless harbor disqualifying prejudices. Such jurors may well acquit where evidence is wholly lacking, while subconsciously resolving closer calls against the defendant rather than giving him the benefit of the doubt. * * * In this regard, it is significant that the Government placed relatively little emphasis on the nine insider trading counts during its closing argument, declining to explain its theory on all but one of the counts in any detail whatsoever. The acquittals on those counts thus provide scant basis for inferring a lack of prejudice.

In sum, I cannot accept the majority's conclusion that *voir dire* gave the District Court "a sturdy foundation to assess fitness for jury service." Taken together, the District Court's failure to cover certain vital subjects, its superficial coverage of other topics, and its uncritical acceptance of assurances of impartiality leave me doubtful that Skilling's jury was indeed free from the deep-seated animosity that pervaded the community at large. "[R]egardless of the heinousness of the crime charged, the apparent guilt of the offender[,] or the station in life which he occupies," our system of justice demands trials that are fair in both appearance and fact. *Irvin*. Because I do not believe Skilling's trial met this standard, I would grant him relief.

NOTES AND QUESTIONS ON VENUE TRANSFERS

1. ***Restricting* Rideau.** While the Supreme Court found no need to rule on whether presumed prejudice established under *Rideau* can be rebutted (see fn. 18), the Fifth Circuit in *Skilling* departed from a substantial body of lower court precedent in that reading of the presumed prejudice doctrine (also described by some courts as the "inherent prejudice" doctrine). Those lower courts noted that the *Rideau* Court specifically refused to examine the *voir dire* transcript (see p. 1267) and there was no suggestion in *Estes* and *Sheppard* of any means of rebutting a presumption arising from "media interference". Under this view, the refusal to grant a venue change constitutes

huge number of people"; and thought "someone had to be doing something illegal"); (Juror 116) (knew a colleague who lost money in Enron's collapse; obtained Enron-related news from the "Houston Chronicle, Time Magazine, local TV news [and] radio, friends, family, [and] co-workers, [and] internet news sources"; and noted that what stood out was "[t]he employees and retirees that lost their savings").

[25] The majority suggests that the fact that Skilling "challenged only one of the seated jurors for cause" indicates that he did not believe the other jurors were biased. Our decisions, however, distinguish claims involving "the partiality of an individual juror" from antecedent claims directed at "the partiality of the trial jury as a whole." *Patton* v. *Yount*. If the jury selection process does not, as here, give a defendant a fair opportunity to identify biased jurors, the defendant can hardly be faulted for failing to make for-cause challenges.

a per se constitutional error where prejudicial publicly is so inflammatory and pervasive as to justify presuming prejudice.

At the same time, those same lower court rulings found *Rideau* controlling in "only a sprinkling of cases"; *Rideau* was held "not to reach even the most highly publicized cases that were covered step-by-step and scoop-by-scoop in evening newscasts and front page stories." CRIMPROC § 23.3(a). This narrow reading of *Rideau*, reinforced in *Skilling*, has been explained as a product of the need to apply a constitutional standard to all states, including the smallest. "If publicity is held to be of such a nature as to require a presumption of prejudice, a court in a small state simply may have nowhere to move the case, as the same level of publicity often is found throughout the state." Ibid. It has been suggested that if the circumstances in *Rideau* were largely replicated in Rhode Island, for example, the Court would either conclude that the presumed prejudice did no more than shift the burden of proof (see fn. 18) or possibly discard the doctrine entirely on the grounds suggested in Justice Alito's concurring opinion in *Skilling*.

2. ***Venue transfers under Federal Rule 21 and similar state rules.*** As Justice Sotomayor notes (see fn. 9): "It likely would have been far easier to empanel an impartial jury in a venue where the Enron story had less salience." Commentators have noted that another advantage of a transfer, since it requires the exclusion of fewer prospective jurors, is to produce a pool of potential jurors more likely to reflect a cross-section of the community. Federal Rule 21 provides for transfer if the trial court "is satisfied" that defendant "cannot obtain a fair and impartial trial" in the district of indictment. Many states have similar provisions. "Although interpreted literally, such provisions would require that the court find under the appropriate proof standard (presumably, the preponderance of the evidence standard) that a fair and impartial trial is not a realistic possibility, * * * federal courts and various state courts, * * * have stated that the defendant must show only a 'reasonable' or 'substantial' likelihood." CRIMPROC § 16.3(b) Moreover, that showing can be made without attempting *voir dire*, typically by presenting to the court the combination of a collection of widely distributed, prejudicial media reports and opinion polls showing widespread community prejudice. As the *Skilling* Court notes in fn. 11, "district-court calls on the necessity of transfer are granted a healthy measure of respect," so the district court in *Skilling* could readily have granted a change of venue under Rule 21 without fear of reversal (as suggested in the Fifth Circuit's opinion, see fn. 9 of the *Skilling* dissent).

In deciding not to grant a change of venue on the initial defense showing, the *Skilling* district court noted that it was following the common practice of looking to *voir dire* to "ferret out any [juror] bias" (p. 1265). As noted in CRIMPROC § 23.2(a), "the standard practice of trial judges in both federal and state courts is to postpone ruling on a change of venue * * * until after an attempt to seat an impartial jury is made, * * * [and] once jury selection has started, there is a tendency to pursue it through as many potential jurors as is deemed necessary to seat a jury believed to be immune from a successful constitutional challenge."

Commentators have cited three factors as arguably contributing to this common practice of preferring extensive *voir dire* to granting a change of venue that would be acceptable under the governing court rule. Those are: (1) the inconvenience and expense (for court and prosecutor) in transferring the trial to another location (which ordinarily will exclude nearby districts if the objective is to find a district in which the prosecution has received so little attention that a jury can easily be impaneled)[b]; (2) the belief that a transfer stamps the local community as incapable

[b] In light of the relevance of this administrative consideration, borne in large part by the state, some courts have suggested that the trial court can more readily transfer where the government is responsible for the adverse pretrial publicity (e.g., by inappropriately releasing prejudicial information). Others suggest a government source is relevant only in that it lends more credibility and weight to the information in the minds of potential jurors. Consider also *State v. Marmmone*, 13 N.E. 3d 1051 (Ohio 2014) (distinguishing *Rideau* in part because the prejudicial publicity here was largely the product of defendant's damaging admissions in a letter to the editor; the defendant would not be allowed "to benefit from the publicity he created by submitting his own confession [to the local newspaper]").

of giving the defendant a fair trial and that courts should not render that judgement unless absolutely necessary; (3) the belief that the community most directly impacted by the offense (as reflected in venue standards) should be the place of the trial; and (4) in many states, the limited gains of a venue transfer in avoiding pretrial publicity as many high-profile cases will have received statewide media coverage. Is the answer to the first and third consideration keeping the trial in the district of indictment but importing a "foreign jury"? A small group of states provide for a "change of venire" as an alternative to a change of venue; the jury is selected from another district and transferred to the trial district. CRIMPROC § 23.2(d).

3. ***Community harm.*** *Skilling* differed from the Court's earlier rulings discussing venue changes because the defendant's claim for a change of venue rested on more than the possible impact of prejudicial publicity. The defense also point to the public's association of the crime with the widespread community harm caused by the collapse of Enron, including both the economic impact on individuals and businesses and the loss of Enron's significant participation in community affairs (see dissent at p. 1274, noting both the economic impact and "Enron's community ties * * * so extensive that the * * * local U.S. Attorney's Office * * * recuse[d] itself from the Government's investigation.") Should such widespread community harm be viewed as a factor that more readily requires trial courts to grant a change of venue, as compared to prejudicial publicity, because: (1) with the dissemination of information and viewpoints through social media, blogs and similar sources added to the coverage of the traditional media, a court cannot so readily rely on the limited distribution and negativity of the traditional media coverage in assessing the level of concern relating to that harm; (2) since the harm is specific to the community, a transfer district not impacted by that harm is more readily found than a transfer district in which the community is not aware of the prejudicial publicity; and (3) "while exposure to information about a brutal murder may elicit revulsion toward the person accused of committing it, it is not the same as personal exposure to harm from a crime that threatened the entire community's well-being," Jordon Gross, *If Skilling Can't Get a Change of Venue, Who Can,* 85 Temple L. Rev. 575 (2013)? Consider *United States v. McVeigh*, 918 F.Supp. 1467 (W.D.Okla. 1996) (change of venue ordered under Rule 21(a), without first attempting voir dire, in prosecution arising out of the bombing of the federal building in Oklahoma City, which caused "the deaths of 168, injuries to hundreds of other people," structural damage assessed at 651 million, and the "immeasurable effects on the hearts and minds of the people of Oklahoma").

4. ***Transfer on prosecution motion.*** Federal Rule 21 and most state provisions on "fair trial" venue changes provide for a change of venue on motion of the defendant, with no mention of a similarly granted change on motion of the prosecution. Such provisions generally are held to preclude judicial authority to grant a change of venue on motion of the prosecution. However, a substantial minority group of states recognize a prosecution authority to obtain a change of venue where it cannot obtain a fair trial in the district of prosecution. Almost all of these states rely on statutes explicitly authorizing prosecution as well as defense motions. However, a limited body of caselaw suggests that where the venue statute does not refer to either party in authorizing venue changes, a motion by the prosecution may be recognized as consistent with a general directive to ensure a "fair trial." See CRIMPROC § 16.3(d).

Courts in states with constitutional vicinage provisions (see Note 2, p. 1017) have divided over whether such provisions render unconstitutional transfers without defense approval. Courts upholding such transfers have pointed to: (1) a common law authority of courts to order a change of venue upon prosecutorial application where needed to ensure a "fair and impartial" trial; (2) the location of the vicinage provision within a jury trial guarantee which also speaks to providing an "impartial jury" (thereby suggesting that a transfer is permissible when such a jury cannot be obtained in the vicinage district); and (3) the principle that the state constitution not be construed so as to nullify the prosecution's authority to enforce the law, which is said to be the consequence of forcing it to trial in a district where a jury is motivated by prejudice to reject any case the prosecution might present. Courts rejecting this analysis rely on: (1) what they describe as the "clear language" of the vicinage provision (recognizing, without limitation, the defendant's right to a jury from the district of the crime's commission); (2) a different reading of the common law practice and its significance; (3) a reading of the reference to jury impartiality as aimed solely at precluding a jury prejudiced against the defendant; and (4) the view that the vicinage provision implicitly places ahead of any state interest in jury impartiality the defendant's interest in a trial in the vicinage, where he is most likely to be able to benefit from his good standing with his neighbors. Several federal lower court opinions have suggested that the Sixth Amendment would prohibit Congress from authorizing a venue change without the defendant's consent.

5. ***Selecting the district of transfer.*** Notwithstanding the narrow scope of *Rideau* and the general judicial preference for *voir dire* in considering motions under state transfer provisions, changes in venue are not so rare. In several states, appellate rulings advise trial courts to favor granting a defense motion when the there is simply a "reasonable likelihood" that a fair trial cannot be obtained. Also some judges reject the usual preference for *voir dire*, particularly when jury selection otherwise will run many days and involve extensive questionnaires. Thus, not surprisingly, various states have addressed the issue of the selection of the appropriate transfer district, above and beyond the requirement that it be a district which meets the fair trial standard. The states generally have adopted one or the other of the following three approaches:

(1) Most states simply leave the choice of the district of transfer to the discretion of the court ordering the venue change. That district may or may not be a district requested by the moving party. The court is to exercise its own independent judgment in selecting the district. Of course, the first consideration is that the district be one not also subject to the influences that are likely to prevent a fair and impartial trial. Beyond that, the court will consider the convenience of the parties and witnesses, and the availability of a docket that will permit a speedy trial. The trial court's discretion in this regard is broad and will not be overturned by an appellate court absent a clear showing of reliance on improper factors.

(2) A substantial minority of the states seek to narrow the trial judge's discretion by prescribing a geographic standard for selection of the district of transfer. Some direct the trial court to select the "nearest" judicial district that is "free from exception." Others direct that the transfer be to an "adjoining" district unless a fair trial cannot be obtained there.

(3) During the 1990's, two highly publicized changes of venue in prosecutions of police officers charged with using excessive force against minority arrestees spurred a movement to have courts choose transfer districts similar in racial composition to the initial district of prosecution.[c] Critics argued that a race conscious selection would run the risk of violating the equal protection clause, at least insofar as it forced the court to choose between districts that would "favor" either the race of the victim or the race of the defendant as compared to the original district. This led to the proposal that the transfer district be similar in total demography to the original district, with race being only one component. At least two states have adopted such an approach, as have various individual trial courts in exercising their discretion. See CRIMPROC § 16.3(g).

---

[c] The cases involved were (1) *Powell v. Superior Court*, 232 Cal.App. 3d 785 (1991), where white officers were charged with beating a black arrestee (Rodney King), and the case was transferred under a geographic standard from Los Angeles to predominantly white, suburban Simi Valley (where the jury acquitted on most charges, but hung on another), and (2) *State v. Lozano*, 616 So.2d 73 (Fla.App.1993), where an Hispanic police officer was charged with manslaughter in causing the death of two black motorcyclists, his original conviction in Miami overturned based on the trial court's refusal to grant a change of venue, and the case eventually tried in Orlando (where the jury acquitted). Florida subsequently adopted a requirement of demographic similarity. See Fla.State.Ann. § 910.03(2).

NOTES AND QUESTIONS ON JURY SELECTION

1. ***Individual voir dire and content questioning.*** In *Skilling*, the trial judge included questions in the questionnaire that asked jurors about their media sources and what they recalled from those sources (p. 1265), and the judge subsequently conducted individual *voir dire* examinations that again referred to content (p. 1266). In MU'MIN v. VIRGINIA, 500 U.S. 415 (1991), a divided Court (5–4) rejected a constitutional challenge based on the trial court's rejection of a defense request for individual *voir dire* and content questions. Of 26 prospective jurors, 16 (including 8 of the actual panel) had answered affirmatively when asked if they had acquired information about the case from the news media or any other source. The defense argued that this justified asking extensive questions concerning the content of the information acquired and that should be done individually. The trial court decided, instead, to question the prospective jurors in groups of four, asking each group whether any information acquired from outside sources would affect their impartiality and whether they had formed an opinion in the case. None of the persons eventually seated responded affirmatively to those questions. Finding this procedure constitutionally adequate, Chief Justice Rehnquist's majority opinion noted:

"Acceptance of petitioner's claim [as to requiring content questions] would require that each potential juror be interrogated individually; even were the interrogation conducted in panels of four jurors, as the trial court did here, descriptions of one juror about pretrial publicity would obviously be communicated to the three other members of the panel being interrogated, with the prospect that more harm than good would be done by the interrogation. Petitioner says that the questioning can be accomplished by juror questionnaires submitted in advance at trial, but such written answers would not give counsel or the court any exposure to the demeanor of the juror in the course of answering the content questions. The trial court in this case expressed reservations about interrogating jurors individually because it might make the jurors feel that they themselves were on trial. While concern for the feelings and sensibilities of potential jurors cannot be allowed to defeat inquiry necessary to protect a constitutional right, we do not believe that content questions are constitutionally required.

"Whether a trial court decides to put questions about the content of publicity to a potential juror or not, it must make the same decision at the end of the questioning: is this juror to be believed when he says he has not formed an opinion about the case? Questions about the content of the publicity to which jurors have been exposed might be helpful in assessing whether a juror is impartial. To be constitutionally compelled, however, it is not enough that such questions might be helpful. Rather, the trial court's failure to ask these questions must render the defendant's trial fundamentally unfair.

"[T]here is no * * * consensus or even weighty authority favoring petitioner's position. Among the state-court decisions cited to us by the parties * * * [various states] have refused to adopt such a rule. * * * The Courts of Appeal [for several circuits] have held that in some circumstances such an inquiry is required, * * * [but] the Court of Appeals for the Eleventh Circuit has held that it is not. * * * Even these Federal Courts of Appeals that have required such an inquiry * * * have not expressly placed their decisions on constitutional grounds."

Justice O'Connor, who supplied the critical fifth vote for affirmance, joined the majority opinion, but also wrote a separate concurring opinion seen as more narrowly based. She stressed the character of the publicity in the case, which was known to the trial judge (the defense, in a motion for change of venue had submitted "47 newspaper articles relating to the murder"). Thus, while it was true that the trial judge "did not know precisely what each juror had read," he was aware "of the full range of the information that had been reported." With this information in mind, and with each juror having indicated that no opinion had been formed, the trial judge could not be said to have "violate[d] the Sixth Amendment" in accepting the jurors' assurances of impartiality. Three dissenters (Marshall, J, joined by Blackmun and Stevens, JJ.) characterized the publicity as so prejudicial as to have produced a "charged atmosphere", and in that setting, they noted, "a trial court cannot realistically assess the juror's impartiality without first establishing what the juror has already learned about the case." Justice Kennedy also dissented, concluding that "findings of impartiality must be based on something more than the mere silence of the individual in response to questions asked *en masse*."

2. ***The relevancy of the overall voir dire response.*** Prior to *Skilling*, lower courts, relying on *Irvin v. Dowd* (p. 1271) and *Patton v. Yount* (fn. 13, p. 1268), had looked to the totality of the *voir dire* responses, considering the responses of both the prospective jurors who were seated and the prospective jurors who were excluded. The percentage of prospective jurors who had to be excluded was often compared to the percentages in *Irvin v. Dowd*, and the percentages in the cases that rejected actual prejudice claims (primarily *Murphy v. Florida*, fn. 12, p. 1268, and *Patton v. Yount*). This led commentators to ask whether the actual prejudice standard would find acceptable a jury composed of 12 persons who claimed to have never previously heard anything about the alleged crime (and offered believable explanations on why that was so, notwithstanding the pretrial publicity), where the court had to dismiss for cause hundreds of prospective jurors who had been influenced by the pretrial publicity. Cf. N.Y. Times, May 26, 1971 (after the murder-kidnapping prosecution of Black Panther leaders Bobby Seale and Ericka Huggins ended in a hung jury, the Connecticut trial judge dismissed all charges; the judge noted that he had screened some 1,000 prospective jurors to get the jury for the first trial, and chances of drawing an unbiased jury after the added publicity of the trial would require "superhuman efforts"). Is that possibility clearly foreclosed by the analysis of the *Skilling* majority opinion, as well as Justice Alito's concurring opinion?

3. ***Supervisory power and cause exclusions.*** In *Marshall v. United States*, 360 U.S. 310 (1959), the federal district court was held to have erred in allowing a trial to continue even though some of the sitting jurors had read newspaper articles that cited defendant's two prior felony convictions and other prejudicial background information. The district court judge had questioned the jurors and then decided to proceed because he was convinced of their credibility when each stated that he would not be influenced by the news articles. The Supreme Court, relying on its supervisory power, concluded that the jurors should have been excluded because "persons who have learned of a defendant's prior record are presumed to be prejudiced." In *Murphy v. Florida* (fn. 12, p. 1268), the Court noted that the exercise of caution reflected in *Marshall* did not bear on the state case before it, as similar caution was not demanded under the federal constitution.

§ 2. PREVENTING PREJUDICIAL PUBLICITY

A. RESTRAINING MEDIA REPORTING

NEBRASKA PRESS ASS'N v. STUART, 427 U.S. 539 (1976), is widely viewed as almost absolutely barring any governmental directive that seeks to prohibit the media from publishing information because public knowledge of that information will make more difficult the selection of an unbiased jury. At issue in that case were court orders, entered prior to the trial of a mass murderer, which barred the publication of "any testimony given or evidence adduced" in court and which also barred the reporting of any confessions or incriminating statements made by the defendant to the police or to any third parties (except members of the press) or of "other facts 'strongly implicative' of the accused." The Supreme Court (per Burger, C.J.) first unequivocally concluded that the bar on reporting what happened "at the open preliminary hearing * * * plainly violated settled principles," namely, that "once a public hearing had been held, what transpired there could not be subject to prior restraint."

As for the prohibition upon publication of information from other sources, the Chief Justice concluded that the findings below clearly did not satisfy the stringent prerequisites for securing a prior restraint. In weighing the "gravity of the evil" that might justify a prior restraint on the press ("the most serious and least tolerable infringement on First Amendment rights"), the trial judge had to give adequate consideration to: "(a) the nature and extent of pretrial news coverage; (b) whether other measures would be likely to mitigate the effects of unrestrained pretrial publicity; [and] (c) how effectively a restraining order would operate to prevent the threatened danger." The judge here had failed on all three factors. With respect to the first, the trial judge's finding spoke "only [to] 'a clear and present danger that pretrial publicity *could* impinge upon the defendant's right to a fair trial,' " and his "conclusion as to that possible impact" was of necessity speculative, dealing as he was with "factors unknown and unknowable." As to the second, the record did not reflect careful consideration of "the alternatives to prior restraint," such as change of venue, continuance, *voir dire*, and admonitions to the jurors. The alternatives must prevail unless so ineffective that "12 [jurors] could not be found who would, under proper instructions, fulfill their sworn duty to render a just verdict exclusively on the evidence presented in open court." And as to the third, the trial took place in a very small community where "it is reasonable to assume" that prejudicial rumors "could well be more damaging than reasonably accurate news accounts."

Although the Chief Justice declined to "rule out the possibility of showing the kind of threat to fair trial rights that would possess the requisite degree of certainty" to justify a prior restraint of the press, the other opinions in the case suggested that this possibility was a highly unlikely one. Justice White expressed "grave doubt" that a prior restraint "would ever be justifiable," while Justice Powell emphasized the "unique burden" resting on one who would justify a prior restraint. Three other justices, in an opinion by Justice Brennan, concluded that a prior restraint simply "is a constitutionally impermissible method for enforcing" the right to a fair trial. Justice Stevens agreed with that conclusion as to "information in the public domain," and indicated he might reach the same conclusion in other circumstances as well.

In light of *Nebraska Press*, trial courts seeking to prevent prejudicial publicity are largely limited to two sources of judicial authority—(1) imposing restraints upon the dissemination of information to the press by participants in the judicial process, and (2) keeping from the press information revealed in judicial proceedings and judicial records that could readily be the subject of prejudicial pretrial publicity by closing the judicial proceedings and sealing the records.

B. RESTRICTING PARTICIPANTS' PUBLIC STATEMENTS

Sheppard v. Maxwell, 384 U.S. 333 (1966), as noted at p. 1267, presented grounds for reversal created by far more than prejudicial press coverage. Nonetheless, the Court, in describing various steps that could have been taken to avoid the *Sheppard* debacle, strongly urged exercise of the trial court's "power to control the publicity about the trial". The Court noted: "[T]he trial court might well have proscribed extra-judicial statements by any lawyer, party, witness, or court official which divulged prejudicial matters, such as the refusal of Sheppard to submit to interrogation or take any lie detector tests; any statement made by Sheppard to officials; the identity of prospective witnesses or their probable testimony; any belief in guilt or innocence; or like statements concerning the merits of the case. * * * Being advised of the great public interest in the case, the mass coverage of the press, and the potential prejudicial impact of publicity, the court could also have requested the appropriate city and county officials to promulgate a regulation with respect to dissemination of information about the case by their employees."

In GENTILE v. STATE BAR OF NEVADA, 501 U.S. 1030 (1991), the Court took a much closer look at the state's authority to proscribe extra-judicial comments by lawyers. A 5–4 majority there upheld the constitutionality of Nevada Supreme Court Rule 177, a rule governing pretrial publicity almost identical to the 1983 version of ABA Model Rule of Professional Conduct 3.6. Rule 177 prohibited a lawyer (in this case, a defense lawyer) from making extrajudicial statements to the press that he "knows or reasonably should know * * * will have a substantial likelihood of materially prejudicing an adjudicative proceeding." However, a different 5–4 majority held that Rule 177, as interpreted by the Nevada Supreme Court—taking into account that rule's "safe harbor" provision—was "void for vagueness" because it failed to furnish "fair notice to those to whom [it] is directed." The "safe harbor" provision, identical to Model Rule 3.6(c), allowed a lawyer, "notwithstanding" various prohibitions against making extrajudicial statements, to "state without elaboration [the] general nature of the claim or defense."

The case arose as follows: When undercover officers with the Las Vegas Metropolitan Police Department reported large amounts of cocaine and travelers' checks missing from a safety deposit box at Western Vault Corporation (a company owned by petitioner Gentile's client, Sanders), suspicion initially focused on Detective Scholl and another police officer. Both officers had had free access to the deposit box. But then the news reports indicated that the attention of the investigators had shifted to Sanders. The story took a sensational turn with news stories that Scholl and the other officer had been "cleared" after passing lie detector tests, but that Sanders had refused to take such a test.

The day after his client was indicted, Gentile held a press conference. At the time, Gentile knew that a jury would not be empaneled for six months. Gentile maintained that his primary motivation in holding the press conference was to counter prejudicial publicity already released by the police and prosecutors. The state disciplinary board found that he had attempted: "to counter public opinion which he perceived as adverse to Mr. Sanders"; "to fight back against the perceived efforts of the prosecution to poison the prospective juror pool"; and "to publicly present Sanders' side of the case."

At the press conference, Gentile stated, inter alia: (1) the case was similar to those in other cities, although the authorities there had been "honest enough to indict the people who did it"—"the police department, crooked cops"; (2) when the case is tried the evidence will prove "not only [that] Sanders is an innocent person," but that Detective Scholl "was in the most direct position to have stolen the drugs and money"; (3) there is "far more evidence [that] Detective Scholl took the drugs [and] travelers' checks than any other living human being"; (4) "I feel [that] Sanders is being used as a scapegoat to cover up for what has to be obvious to [law enforcement authorities]"; and (5) with respect to other theft charges alleged in the indictment against Sanders, "the so-called victims" "are known drug dealers and convicted money launderers and drug dealers." In addition, in response to a question from a reporter, Gentile strongly implied that Detective Scholl could be observed in a videotape suffering from symptoms of cocaine use.

The two newspaper stories and the two TV news broadcasts that mentioned Gentile's press conferences also mentioned a prosecution response and a police press conference in response. The chief deputy district attorney was quoted as saying that this was a legitimate indictment and that prosecutors cannot bring an indictment unless they can prove the charges in it beyond a reasonable doubt. A deputy police chief stated that Detective Scholl and another officer who had access to the safety deposit box "had nothing to do with this theft or any other" and that the police department was satisfied that both officers were "above reproach."

Some six months later, Sanders' criminal case was tried by a jury and he was acquitted on all counts. A state disciplinary board then brought proceedings against Gentile and concluded that he had violated Rule 177. The board recommended a private reprimand. The state supreme court affirmed the decision.

In concluding that the "substantial likelihood of material prejudice" standard utilized by Nevada and most other states satisfies the First Amendment, the Court majority, per Rehnquist, C.J., observed:

"* * * Currently, 31 states in addition to Nevada have adopted—either verbatim or with insignificant variations—[Model Rule 3.6]. Eleven states have adopted Disciplinary Rule 7–107 of the ABA's Code of Professional Responsibility, which is less protective of lawyer speech than Model Rule 3.6, in that it applies a 'reasonable likelihood of prejudice' standard. Only one state, Virginia, has explicitly adopted a clear and present danger standard, while four states and the District of Columbia have adopted standards that arguably approximate 'clear and present danger.'

"Petitioner maintains, however, that the First Amendment * * * requires a state [to] demonstrate a 'clear and present danger' of 'actual prejudice or an imminent threat' before any discipline may be imposed on a lawyer who initiates a press conference such as occurred here. He relies on decisions such as *Nebraska Press Ass'n v. Stuart* [p. 1286] to support his position.

"We expressly contemplated [in *Sheppard v. Maxwell*] that the speech of *those participating before the court* could be limited.[5] * * * We think that [passages in such cases as] *Sheppard v. Maxwell* rather plainly indicate that the speech of lawyers representing clients in pending cases may be regulated under a less demanding standard than that established for regulation of the press in *Nebraska Press* and the cases which preceded it. Lawyers representing clients in pending cases are key participants in the criminal justice system, and the State may demand some adherence to the precepts of that system in regulating their speech as well as their conduct. As noted by Justice Brennan in his concurring opinion in *Nebraska Press*, 'as officers of the court, court personnel and attorneys have a fiduciary responsibility not to engage in public debate that will redound to the detriment of the accused or that will obstruct the fair administration of justice'. Because lawyers have special access to information through discovery and client communications, their extrajudicial statements pose a threat to the fairness of a pending proceeding since lawyers' statements are likely to be received as especially authoritative.

"[When] a state regulation implicates First Amendment rights, the Court must balance those interests against the State's legitimate interest in regulating the activity in question. The 'substantial likelihood' test embodied in Rule 177 is constitutional under this analysis, for it is designed to protect the integrity and fairness of a state's judicial system, and it imposes only narrow and necessary limitations on lawyers' speech. The limitations are aimed at two principal evils: (1) comments that are likely to influence the actual outcome of the trial, and (2) comments that are likely to prejudice the jury venire, even if an untainted panel can ultimately be found. Few, if any, interests under the Constitution are more fundamental than the right to a fair trial by 'impartial' jurors, and an outcome affected by extrajudicial statements would violate that fundamental right. Even if a fair trial can ultimately be ensured through *voir dire,* change of venue, or some other device, these measures entail serious costs to the system. Extensive *voir dire* may not be able to filter out all of the effects of pretrial publicity, and with increasingly widespread media coverage of criminal trials, a change of venue may not suffice to undo the effects of statements such as those made by petitioner. The State has a substantial interest in preventing officers of the court, such as lawyers, from imposing such costs on the judicial system and on the litigants."

"The [Model Rule 3.6] restraint on speech is narrowly tailored to achieve those objectives. The regulation of attorneys' speech is limited—it applies only to speech that is substantially likely to have a materially prejudicial effect; it is neutral as to points of view, applying equally to all attorneys participating in a pending case; and it merely postpones the attorney's comments until after the trial. While supported by the substantial state interest in preventing prejudice to an adjudicative proceeding by those who have a duty to protect its integrity, the rule is limited on its

---

[5] The Nevada Supreme Court has consistently read all parts of Rule 177 as applying only to lawyers in pending cases and not to other lawyers or nonlawyers. We express no opinion on the constitutionality of a rule regulating the statement of a lawyer who is not participating in the pending case about which statements are made. * * *

face to preventing only speech having a substantial likelihood of materially prejudicing that proceeding."

Dissenting on the First Amendment issue, Justice Kennedy, joined by Marshall, Blackmun, and Stevens JJ., noted:

"[The] drafters of Model Rule 3.6 apparently thought the substantial likelihood of material prejudice formulation approximated the clear and present danger test. [The] difference between the requirement of serious and imminent threat found in the disciplinary rules of some States and the more common formulation of substantial likelihood of material prejudice could prove mere semantics. Each standard requires an assessment of proximity and degree of harm. Each may be capable of valid application. Under those principles, nothing inherent in Nevada's formulation fails First Amendment review; but as this case demonstrates, Rule 177 has not been interpreted in conformance with those principles by the Nevada Supreme Court. * * *

"Even if one were to accept respondent's argument that lawyers participating in judicial proceedings may be subjected, consistent with the First Amendment, to speech restrictions that could not be imposed on the press or general public, the judgment should not be upheld. The record does not support the conclusion that petitioner knew or reasonably should have known his remarks created a substantial likelihood of material prejudice, if the Rule's terms are given any meaningful content. * * *

"Neither the disciplinary board nor the reviewing court explain any sense in which petitioner's statements had a substantial likelihood of causing material prejudice. [The] Bar's whole case rests on the fact of the statement, the time it was made, and petitioner's own justifications. Full deference to these factual findings does not justify abdication of our responsibility to determine whether petitioner's statements can be punished consistent with First Amendment standards. * * *

"[An] attorney's duties do not begin inside the courtroom door. He or she cannot ignore the practical implications of a legal proceeding for the client. Just as an attorney may recommend a plea bargain or civil settlement to avoid adverse consequences of a possible loss after trial, so too an attorney may take reasonable steps to defend a client's reputation and reduce the adverse consequences of indictment, especially in the face of a prosecution deemed unjust or commenced with improper motives. A defense attorney may pursue lawful strategies to obtain dismissal of an indictment or reduction of charges, including an attempt to demonstrate in the court of public opinion that the client does not deserve to be tried.

"[On] the evening before the press conference, petitioner and two colleagues spent several hours researching the extent of an attorney's obligations under Rule 177. He decided, as we have held, see *Patton v. Yount* [fn. 13, p. 1268], that the timing of a statement was crucial in the assessment of possible prejudice and the Rule's application.

"Upon return of the indictment, the court set a trial date [for] some six months in the future. Petitioner knew, at the time of his statement, that a jury would not be empaneled for six months at the earliest, if ever. He recalled reported cases finding no prejudice resulting from juror exposure to 'far worse' information two and four months before trial, and concluded that his proposed statement was not substantially likely to result in material prejudice. * * *

"In 1988, Clark County, Nevada, had population in excess of 600,000 persons. Given the size of the community from which any potential jury venire would be drawn and the length of time before trial, only the most damaging of information could give rise to any likelihood of prejudice. The innocuous content of petitioner's statements reinforces my conclusion.

"Petitioner's statement lacks any of the more obvious bases for a finding of prejudice. Unlike the police, he refused to comment on polygraph tests except to confirm earlier reports that Sanders had not submitted to the police polygraph; he mentioned no confessions, and no evidence from searches or test results; he refused to elaborate upon his charge that the other so-called victims were not credible, except to explain his general theory that they were pressured to testify in an attempt to avoid drug-related legal trouble, and that some of them may have asserted claims in an attempt to collect insurance money.

"[Petitioner's] judgment that no likelihood of material prejudice would result from his comments was vindicated by events at trial. [The] trial took place on schedule [with] no request by either party for a venue change or continuance. The jury was empaneled with no apparent difficulty. * * *

"Only the occasional case presents a danger of prejudice from pretrial publicity. Empirical research suggests that in the few instances when jurors have been exposed to extensive and prejudicial publicity, they are able to disregard it and base their verdict upon the evidence presented in court. *Voir dire* can play an important role in reminding jurors to set aside out-of-court information, and to decide the case upon the evidence presented at trial. All of these factors weigh in favor of affording an attorney's speech about ongoing proceedings our traditional First Amendment protections. * * *

"Because attorneys participate in the criminal justice system and are trained in its complexities, they hold unique qualifications as a source of information about pending cases. [To] the extent the press and public rely upon attorneys for information because attorneys are well-informed, this may prove the value to the public of speech by members of the bar. If the dangers of their speech arise from its persuasiveness, from their ability to explain judicial proceedings, or from the likelihood the speech will be believed, these are not the sort of dangers that can validate restrictions. The First Amendment does not permit suppression of speech because of its power to command assent."

Chief Justice Rehnquist responded to Justice Kennedy's conclusion that there had been no "substantial likelihood" in part III of his opinion. Part III was joined by Justices White, Scalia, and Souter (but not by Justice O'Connor, who had joined Part II of that opinion, discussing the constitutionality of the "substantial likelihood" standard). The Chief Justice agreed that "we must review the record for ourselves," but also noted that "respectful attention" should be given to the findings below because the Nevada's disciplinary board and Supreme Court were "in a far better position than we are to appreciate the likely effect of petitioner's statements * * * in a highly publicized case like this." Petitioner's strongest points were "that the statement was made well in advance of trial, and that the statements did not in fact taint the jury panel," but the Nevada Supreme Court had responded adequately to both. It had noted that the timing of the statement, "when public interest * * * was as its height," and the highly inflammatory portrayal of prospective government witnesses presented a substantial likelihood of prejudicing the prospective jury, even though that did not in fact happen. The Chief Justice noted that there was evidence pro and con on this point, and found it persuasive that the petitioner, by his own admission, called the press conference "for the express purpose of influencing the venire." The Chief Justice rejected in this regard the suggestion of the Kennedy opinion that this purpose was irrelevant because it was aimed only at combatting adverse publicity on the other side. Such an approach would place upon a court the difficult task of trying to distinguish between publicity that would influence by neutralizing and that which would create an affirmative bias. But "more fundamentally, it misconceives the constitutional test for an impartial juror," for a "juror who may have been initially swayed from open mindedness by publicity favorable to the prosecution is not rendered fit for service by being bombarded by publicity favorable to the defense." The proper defense remedies for adverse publicity are *voir dire*, change of venue, jury instructions, and "disciplining of the prosecutor, but not self-help in the form of similarly prejudicial comments by defense counsel."

Justice O'Connor joined that portion of Justice Kennedy's opinion addressing the vagueness claim, producing a majority that overturned the sanction imposed upon Gentile. That ruling was based on a combination of the broad language of the safe harbor provision and Nevada's interpretation of that provision as inapplicable under the facts of the Gentile case. The Kennedy opinion noted:

"As interpreted by the Nevada Supreme Court, [Rule 177] is void for vagueness [for] its safe harbor provision, Rule 177(3), misled petitioner into thinking that he could give his press conferences without fear of discipline. Rule 177(3)(a) provides that a lawyer 'may state without elaboration [the] general nature of [the] defense.' Statements under this provision are protected [n]otwithstanding [the general prohibition against extrajudicial statements in subsection 1 and the specific examples of statements likely to prejudice a criminal trial in subsection 2]. * * * A lawyer seeking to avail himself of Rule 177(3)'s protection must guess at its contours. The right to explain the 'general' nature of the defense without 'elaboration' provides insufficient guidance because 'general' and 'elaboration' are both classic terms of degree. In the context before us, these terms have no settled usage or tradition of interpretation in law. The lawyer has no principle for determining when his remarks pass from the safe harbor of the general to the forbidden sea of the elaborated."

NOTES AND QUESTIONS

1. ***Responding to prior publicity.*** Chief Justice Rehnquist's opinion has been criticized for its failure to recognize the "realities" of a defendant's limited capacity to offset adverse prejudicial publicly. *Voir dire*, it is argued, will be ineffective in screening out prospective jurors who have been influenced by that publicity, and the disciplining of the prosecutor for having released that publicity will hardly help the defendant who faces a potentially biased jury. Justice Kennedy's recognition of a defense counsel's right of response has been criticized in turn as inviting an escalating "war of words" prior to trial, as each side will take advantage of any discussion of the case by the other to "respond" in a way designed to create a jury pool that would favor its position. Other commentators question treating the issue of response as an aspect of regulating the two adversaries, noting that publicity (for and against each side) most often will come from other sources, Still others suggest that courts should recognize that there is more at stake from the defendant's perspective than obtaining an unbiased jury—in particular, the defendant's interest in his public reputation (which will not necessarily be restored by an acquittal).

2. ***Changes in Rule 3.6.*** A 1994 revision of Rule 3.6 sought to respond to the *Gentile* ruling on vagueness as well as the Court's division on the protection afforded by the First Amendment as applied. In this connection, the revision made three basic changes in Rule 3.6 and added a related provision in Rule 3.8. At the same time, it retained the basic prohibition of statements that the attorney "knows or reasonably should know * * * will have a substantial likelihood of materially prejudicing an adjudicative proceeding."

To respond to *Gentile*'s overbreadth *ruling*, the revision of Rule 3.6 removed the words "without elaboration" and "general" from the safe harbor provision. As a result, the revised safe-harbor permission protects a lawyer who states "the claim, offense, or defense involved," rather than just the lawyer who states "without elaboration," the "general nature of the claim or defense."[a]

---

[a] There are eight safe-harbor provisions, with most directed at content more likely to be included in public statements of prosecutors. The eight are: (1) "the claim, offense, or defense involved"; (2) information on the public record; (3) the existence of an ongoing investigation; (4) litigation scheduling or results; (5) a request for assistance in obtaining evidence; (6) a warning of possible danger from the person where "there is reason to believe that there exists the likelihood of substantial harm" (possibly applicable where an accused is not yet apprehended); (7)

A second major change, responding to Justice Kennedy's discussion of the First Amendment issue in *Gentile*, included a new safe-harbor "right-of-reply." Paragraph (c) of the 1994 version of Rule 3.6 provides: "Notwithstanding paragraph (a), a lawyer may make a statement that a reasonable lawyer would believe is required to protect a client from the substantial undue prejudicial effect of recent publicity not initiated by the lawyer or the lawyer's client. A statement made pursuant to this paragraph shall be limited to such information as is necessary to mitigate the recent adverse publicity."

A third major change in the revised Rule 3.6 moved from the text of the Rule to the commentary the list of presumptively prejudicial statements.[b] This change apparently reflected concern that a presumptive list in the text might be viewed as detracting from and raising doubts about the safe-harbors insofar as they might overlap (e.g., where a right-of-reply statement refers to a person's criminal record).

Finally, the 1994 amendment of Rule 3.6 was accompanied by an amendment of Rule 3.8. That amendment provides: "The prosecutor in a criminal case shall . . . (g) except for statements that are necessary to inform the public of the nature and extent of the prosecutor's action and that serve a legitimate law enforcement purpose, refrain from making extrajudicial comments that have a substantial likelihood of heightening public condemnation of the accused." This change was designed to work in conjunction with Rule 3.6 by reducing the need for defense counsel to turn to the new Rule 3.6 right-of-reply. While the Rule 3.8 limitation is not tied to the "substantial likelihood of material prejudice" standard, the heightening of public condemnation was seen as almost invariably creating a substantial potential for causing such prejudice.

Many states adapted the Rule 3.6 amendments without adding the Rule 3.8 amendment. Another group of states have rejected the Rule 3.6 amendments, retaining the 1983 version of Rule 3.6. CRIMPROC § 23.4(b).

3. ***Gag orders.*** Should a lawyer "gag order"—an order of the trial court specifically prohibiting extrajudicial comments by the defense counsel and the prosecuting attorney—be subject to a First Amendment standard more restrictive than the *Gentile* standard because the gag order imposes a "prior restraint"? Consider CRIMPROC § 23.1(b): ""Where the [gag] order takes the form of simply directing counsel to abide by the limitations of the jurisdiction's professional responsibility provision on extrajudicial statements, the constitutionality of imposing contempt or other sanctions for violation of that order is tested simply by reference to the *Gentile* rulings. Where, however, the order takes the form of directing counsel not to give any statements to the media concerning the case (or not to give statements concerning specified aspects of the case), * * * courts view the order as imposing a prior restraint and therefore subject to special requirements derived from *Nebraska Press.* * * * Three prerequisites [must be met to sustain such gag orders]: (1) "potential statements to the media must present the requisite potential for prejudicing the trial [some courts requiring the "substantial likelihood," sustained in *Gentile*, some requiring the "reasonable likelihood" standard of Disciplinary Rule 7–107 (see p. 1289), and some requiring "clear and present danger" as the traditional prior restraint standard]; (2) the order must be 'narrowly tailored' to proscribe only those statements that present that potential; and (3)

---

information necessary to aid in the apprehension of the accused; and (8) basic factual information relating to the arrest of the accused (fact, time, and place), and the investigating officers (identity, investigative agency, and length of investigation).

[b] The six subjects viewed as presumptively prejudicial are: (1) the character, credibility, reputation, or criminal record of a party or witness, or the identity of a witness or the expected testimony of a party or witness; (2) the possibility of a plea of guilty, or the existence or contents of any confession, admission, or statement given by the defendant or his refusal or failure to make a statement; (3) the performance or results of any examination or test or the refusal or failure of a person to submit to examination or test, or the identity or nature of physical evidence; (4) any opinion as to the guilt or innocence of the defendant; (5) information likely to be inadmissible but prejudicial; and (6) the fact defendant has been charged, unless accompanied by a statement that the charge is only an accusation and that defendant is presumed innocent.

other, less restrictive alternatives (such as voir dire, jury instructions, jury sequestration, postponement of the trial, or change of venue) must be inadequate to prevent the threatened harm. * * * [This third requirement] * * * suggests a significant departure from the approach of *Gentile.* * * * Some courts, however, have taken [the "significant administrative cost" of the alternatives] into consideration in evaluating the effectiveness of the alternatives. Thus, in responding to defense counsel's claim that the alternative of sequestration precluded extending a gag order past the point of jury selection, one court noted that the sequestration was not an acceptable alternative in what promised to be a long trial because of the 'negative effects of sequestration'."

4. ***Extending gag orders to "agents."*** Can a court extend its gag order, relying on *Sheppard*, to "agents" on both sides? Various courts have extended gag orders to witnesses and defendants, although pre-*Gentile* precedent suggested that a stronger showing of potential prejudicial impact upon the "fair administration of justice" was needed to restrict the public comments of defendants. Gag orders directed at "trial participants" frequently include police departments, but that coverage has not produced any significant judicial challenges. See CRIMPROC § 23.1(b).

C. CLOSING THE PROCEEDINGS

1. ***Recognizing a First Amendment right.*** The Sixth Amendment right to a public trial is a right of the defendant, but *Richmond Newspapers v. Virginia*, 448 U.S. 555 (1980), concluded that the public and press had a First Amendment right to attend criminal trials. There was no opinion for the Court in *Richmond Newspapers* and the Justices differed in their explanation of this First Amendment "right of access." The Court settled on a rationale shortly thereafter in GLOBE NEWSPAPER CO. v. SUPERIOR COURT, 457 U.S. 596 (1982):

"The Court's recent decision in *Richmond Newspapers* firmly established for the first time that the press and general public have a constitutional right of access to criminal trials. * * * Of course, this right of access to criminal trials is not explicitly mentioned in terms in the First Amendment. But we have long eschewed any narrow, literal conception of the Amendment's terms, * * * for the Framers were concerned with broad principles, and wrote against a background of shared values and practices. The First Amendment is thus broad enough to encompass those rights that, while not unambiguously enumerated in the very terms of the Amendment, are nonetheless necessary to the enjoyment of other First Amendment rights. * * * Underlying the First Amendment right of access to criminal trials is the common understanding that a major purpose of that Amendment was to protect the free discussion of governmental affairs. By offering such protection, the First Amendment serves to ensure that the individual citizen can effectively participate in and contribute to our republican system of self-government. * * * Thus to the extent that the First Amendment embraces a right of access to criminal trials, it is to ensure that this constitutionally protected discussion of governmental affairs is an informed one.

"Two features of the criminal justice system, emphasized in the various opinions in *Richmond Newspapers*, together serve to explain why a right of access to *criminal trials* in particular is properly afforded protection by the First Amendment. First, the criminal trial historically has been open to the press and general public. * * * This uniform rule of openness has been viewed as significant in constitutional terms not only because the Constitution carries the gloss of history, but also because a tradition of accessibility implies the favorable judgment of experience. *Richmond Newspapers, Inc.* (Brennan, J., concurring).

"Second, the right of access to criminal trials plays a particularly significant role in the functioning of the judicial process and the government as a whole. Public Scrutiny of a criminal trial enhances the quality and safeguards the integrity of the factfinding process, with benefits to both the defendant and to society as a whole. Moreover, public access to the criminal trial fosters an appearance of fairness, thereby heightening public respect for the judicial process. And in the broadest terms, public access to criminal trials permits the public to participate in and serve as a check upon the judicial process—an essential component in our structure of self-government. In sum, the institutional value of the open criminal trial is recognized in both logic and experience."

2. ***Pretrial proceedings.*** While *Richmond Newspapers* and *Globe Newspaper* established a First Amendment right of access to the criminal trial itself, these cases left open the question whether such a right extended to pretrial proceedings. The Court, per Burger, C.J., suggested this possibility in *Press-Enterprise I (Press-Enterprise Co. v. Superior Court,* 464 U.S. 501 (1984)), when it held, without a dissent, that the First Amendment right applied to the *voir dire* examination of potential jurors. The Court emphasized two factors cited in *Globe Newspaper*—the historical tradition of openness and the functional value of openness for the particular proceeding—rather than a characterization of the jury selection process as a part of the trial itself. Two years later, in *Press-Enterprise II,* discussed below, the Court again relied on these two factors, but this time it applied the public right of access to a proceeding that clearly was not part of the trial—the preliminary hearing.

Although *Waller v. Georgia*, 467 U.S. 39 (1984), proceeded under the Sixth Amendment rather than the First Amendment, *Waller*, foreshadowed the *Press-Enterprise II* ruling. The *Waller* Court held unanimously, per Powell, J., that the defendant's Sixth Amendment right to a public trial extends to a pretrial suppression hearing; that "under the Sixth Amendment any closure of a suppression hearing over the objections of the accused must meet the [First Amendment] tests set out in *Press-Enterprise* and its predecessors"; and that, applying these tests, "the closure of the entire suppression hearing plainly was unjustified." *Waller* reformulated the standards for courtroom closure into a four-factor test: "[1] the party seeking to close the hearing must advance an overriding interest that is likely to be prejudiced, [2] the closure must be no broader than necessary to protect that interest, [3] the trial court must consider reasonable alternatives to closing the proceeding, and [4] it must make findings adequate to support the closure." The Court noted that although the analysis in recent open trial cases had proceeded largely under the First Amendment, there "can be little doubt that the explicit Sixth Amendment right of the accused is no less protective of a public trial than the implicit First Amendment right of the press and the public."

3. In PRESS-ENTERPRISE CO. v. SUPERIOR COURT [PRESS-ENTERPRISE II], 478 U.S. 1 (1986), the trial court closed a preliminary hearing at the request of the defendant. The media subsequently sought access to a transcript of the hearing, arguing that the closure bad violated the "the public's right of access under the First Amendment." The Supreme Court, per Burger, C.J., agreed.

As to the existence of a First Amendment right, the Court noted that "the considerations that led [us] to apply the First Amendment right of access to criminal trials in *Richmond Newspapers* * * * and the selection of jurors in *Press-Enterprise I* lead us to conclude that the right of access applies to preliminary hearing conducted in California." The Court recognized that "unlike a criminal trial, the California preliminary hearing cannot result in the conviction of the accused and the adjudication is before a magistrate or other judicial officer without a jury. But these features, standing alone, do not make public access any less essential to the proper functioning of the proceedings in the overall criminal justice process. Because of its extensive scope, the preliminary hearing is often the final and most important step in the criminal proceeding. * * * Similarly, the absence of a jury, long recognized as 'an inestimable safeguard against the corrupt or overzealous prosecutor and against the complaint, biased, or eccentric judge,' makes the importance of public access to a preliminary hearing even more significant." These factors combined to satisfy the "functional value of openness" for this proceeding. There was also a "historical tradition of openness" measured by the practice in California (notwithstanding the lack of any recognized legal right to an open hearing). This distinguished grand jury proceedings, which traditionally had been closed.

As to the application of the First Amendment right, the Court noted: "Since a qualified First Amendment right of access attaches * * *, the proceedings cannot be closed unless specific, on the record findings are made demonstrating that 'closure is essential to preserve higher values and is narrowly tailored to serve that interest.' *Press-Enterprise I.* * * * If the interest asserted is the right of the accused to a fair trial, the preliminary hearing shall be closed only if specific findings are made demonstrating that, first, there is a substantial probability that the defendant's right to a fair trial will be prejudiced by publicity that closure would prevent and, second, reasonable alternatives to closure cannot adequately protect the defendant's fair trial rights. *See Press-Enterprise I.* * * * The California Supreme Court, interpreting its access statute, concluded that 'the magistrate shall close the preliminary hearing upon finding a reasonable likelihood of substantial prejudice.' As the court itself acknowledged, the 'reasonable likelihood' test places a lesser burden on the defendant than the 'substantial probability' test which we hold is called for by the First Amendment. Moreover, the court failed to consider whether alternatives short of complete closure would have protected the interests of the accused. * * *

"In *Gannett Co. v. DePasquale*, 443 U.S. 368 (1979) [sustaining the closure of a suppression hearing on a defense motion], we observed * * * [that] '[p]ublicity concerning the proceedings at a pretrial hearing * * * could influence public opinion against a defendant and inform potential jurors of inculpatory information wholly inadmissible at the actual trial'. But this risk of prejudice does not automatically justify refusing public access to hearings on every motion to suppress. Through *voir dire*, cumbersome as it is in some circumstances, a court can identify those jurors whose prior knowledge of the case would disable them from rendering an impartial verdict. And even if closure were justified for the hearings on a motion to suppress, closure of an entire 41-day [preliminary hearing] proceeding would rarely be warranted. The First Amendment right of access cannot be overcome by the conclusory assertion that publicity might deprive the defendant of that right. And any limitation must be 'narrowly tailored to serve that interest.' *Press-Enterprise I, supra.*"

4. Dissenting in *Press-Enterprise II*, Justice Stevens warned that the Court's "reasoning applies to the traditionally secret grand jury * * * [for] a grand jury is just as likely to be the 'final step in a criminal proceeding' and the 'sole occasion' for public scrutiny as is a preliminary hearing." The Court made clear, however, that the right of access did not apply to grand jury proceedings in light of its long history of secrecy, and the importance of secrecy to the grand jury's screening and investigatory functions. This distinguished the preliminary hearing, which had been closed on occasion not to serve its functional objectives, but to protect the accused's right to a fair trial. Lower courts have concluded that the same secrecy elements make the right of access inapplicable to ancillary judicial hearings that involve disclosure of grand jury proceedings (e.g., grand jury witness immunity hearings).

§ 3. TELEVISING COURTROOM PROCEEDINGS

1. ***State authorization.*** In 1937, largely in response to the notorious media coverage of the 1935 trial of Bruno Hauptmann for the Lindbergh baby kidnaping, the American Bar Association adopted Judicial Canon 35 (carried forward as canon 3A(1)), banning all photographic and broadcast coverage of courtroom proceedings. In 1952 that provision was amended to proscribe television coverage as well. But the 1970s saw widespread state court experimentation with television coverage of criminal proceedings. And in *Chandler v. Florida* (1981), infra, the Court held there was no *per se* constitutional bar to such television coverage. In 1982, the A.B.A. reversed its long-standing policy in a new canon 3A(1), authorizing the broadcasting, televising and photographing of courtroom proceedings under certain conditions and subject to certain

limitations and guidelines. Today, roughly 40 states authorize the televising of trial proceedings, but only about 25 do so over the objection of the defendant. CRIMPROC § 23.3(b).

2. ***Threat to a fair trial?*** Although the media today seeks establishment of a First Amendment right to televise judicial proceedings that are subject to the First Amendment right of access, *Estes v. Texas,* 381 U.S. 532 (1965), presented the possibility of a per se due process ban on televising. As noted in *Skilling, Estes* presented a situation in which various aspects of the mechanics of televising had been disruptive and potential impacted the jury. However, in reversing defendant's conviction, the majority opinion spoke broadly of the potential pernicious consequences of televising judicial proceedings.

Writing for a 5–4 majority (which included Harlan, J., who concurred "subject to the reservations" discussed infra), Justice Clark recognized that due process deprivations usually require "a showing of identifiable prejudice to the accused," but concluded that this was one of those times when "a procedure employed by the State involves such a probability that prejudice will result that it is deemed inherently lacking in due process." He observed: "[E]xperience teaches that there are numerous situations in which [the use of television] might cause actual unfairness—some so subtle as to defy detection by the accused or control by the judge." Justice Clark then discussed how the awareness that they are being televised distracts jurors; how the medium "will often" impair the quality of the testimony in criminal cases—some witnesses may be "demoralized and frightened," others "cocky and given to overstatement"; how the presence of television is a "form of mental—if not physical—harassment" of the defendant; and how television coverage puts additional responsibilities on the trial judge.

In his special concurrence, Justice Harlan rejected the broad sweep of Clark's opinion, but concluded that "at least as to a notorious criminal trial such as this one, the considerations against allowing television in the courtroom so far outweigh the countervailing factors advanced in its support as to require a holding that what was done in this case infringed the fundamental right to a fair trial assured by [due process]."

Justice Stewart, joined by Black, Brennan and White, JJ., thought that, "at least in the present state of the art," TV coverage of courtroom proceedings was "an extremely unwise policy." But he was "unable to escalate this personal view into a *per se* constitutional rule." Nor was he able to find, "on the specific record of this case, that the circumstances attending the limited televising of the petitioner's trial resulted in the denial of any [of his constitutional rights.]"

"The suggestion that there are limits upon the public right to know what goes on in the courts," wrote Stewart, "causes me deep concern. The idea of imposing upon any medium of communication the burden of justifying its presence is contrary to where I had always thought the presumption must lie in the area of First Amendment freedoms."

3. ***Reevaluation in* Chandler.** In CHANDLER v. FLORIDA, 449 U.S. 560 (1981), the Court held that, subject to certain safeguards, a state may permit electronic media and still photography coverage of public criminal proceedings over the objection of the accused. Justices Stewart and White, in separate concurring opinions, contended that this result could be reached only by overruling *Estes*, a position they favored. However, Chief Justice Burger's opinion for the Court concluded that "*Estes'* did not announce a constitutional rule that all photographic or broadcast coverage of criminal trials is inherently a denial of due process," and the televising program presented here argued against such a "per se rule."

The case before the Court in *Chandler* involved Miami Beach police officers charged, inter alia, with conspiracy to commit burglary and grand larceny. Their trial attracted considerable media attention, and the trial judge authorized televising the trial, consistent with Cannon 3A(7) of the Florida Code of Judicial Conduct. A TV camera was in place for one entire afternoon, during which the prosecution's chief witness testified. As the Supreme Court later noted: "Only two minutes and fifty-five seconds of the trial below were broadcast—and those depicted only the prosecution's side of the case." After the jury returned a guilty verdict on all counts, appellants moved for a new trial on the ground that the television coverage had denied them a fair and impartial trial. They offered no specific evidence of prejudice, challenging the Cannon as authorizing a practice inherently prejudicial.

In upholding appellants' conviction and the constitutionality of the challenged canon, the Court deemed it "important to note that in promulgating the revised Canon 3A(7), the Florida Supreme Court pointedly rejected any state or federal constitutional right of access on the part of photographers or the broadcast media to televise or electronically record and thereafter disseminate court proceedings, [and] predicated [the canon] upon its supervisory authority over the Florida courts. [Hence,] we have before us only the limited question of the Florida Supreme Court's authority to promulgate the canon for the trial of cases in Florida courts."

Chief Justice Burger's opinion reviewed both the history of Cannon 3A(7) and the limitations it imposed. Earlier state pilot programs had been utilized to test televising various proceedings and the experience of other states allowing electronic coverage had been studied. Implementing guidelines were adopted along with the cannon. The end result was the following system: "[N]o more than one television camera and only one camera technician are allowed. Existing recording systems used by court reporters are used by broadcasters for audio pickup. Where more than one broadcast news organization seeks to cover a trial, the media must pool coverage. No artificial lighting is allowed. The equipment is positioned in a fixed location, and it may not be moved during trial. Videotaping equipment must be remote from the courtroom. Film, videotape, and lenses may not be changed while the court is in session. No audio recording of conferences between lawyers, between parties and counsel, or at the bench is permitted. The judge has sole and plenary discretion to exclude coverage of certain witnesses, and the jury may not be filmed. The judge has discretionary power to forbid coverage whenever satisfied that coverage may have a deleterious effect on the paramount right of the defendant to a fair trial."

The Court did not suggest that all of these restrictions and safeguards were needed to sustain constitutionality. Rather, they reflected a carefully crafted program, designed to safeguard against the excesses found in *Estes,* and which should not be held unconstitutional based on the *Estes* opinion's general discussion of the potentially pernicious impact of televising. The Court noted:

"Whatever may be the 'mischievous potentialities [of broadcast coverage] for intruding upon the detached atmosphere which should always surround the judicial process,' *Estes,* at present no one has been able to present empirical data sufficient to establish that the mere presence of the broadcast media inherently has an adverse impact on that process. The appellants have offered nothing to demonstrate that their trial was subtly tainted by broadcast coverage—let alone that all broadcast trials would be so tainted. * * *

"Where, as here, we cannot say that a denial of due process automatically results from activity authorized by a state, the admonition of Justice Brandeis, dissenting in *New State Ice Co. v. Liebmann,* 285 U.S. 262 (1932), is relevant: '[It] is one of the happy incidents of the federal system that a single courageous state may, if its citizens choose, serve as a laboratory; and try novel social and economic experiments without risk to the rest of the country. * * * 'This concept of federalism, echoed by the states favoring Florida's experiment, must guide our decision. * * * "

4. *Post-*Chandler *developments.* As noted in CRIMPROC § 23.3(b), in states that do not require defense consent, "defendants occasionally have been successful in precluding camera coverage where it would create difficulties for the defendant in offering testimony [e.g., witness fears] or otherwise participating in the defense. However, on postconviction review [of the denial of such motions], defendants rarely have been able to show specific prejudice on that ground, or any other [e.g., inadvertently filming the jury]."

5. ***First Amendment right?*** Courts uniformly have held that the First Amendment right of access does not include a right of the media to photograph or broadcast. Courts reason that such procedures involve administrative costs that the judicial system can find too burdensome to permit, and are hardly essential to serving the objectives of having an open proceeding. However, some courts have raised the question of whether technological advances have eliminated the concerns underlying that line of precedent. CRIMPROC § 23.3(b).

CHAPTER 25

THE CRIMINAL TRIAL

■ ■ ■

The Constitution provides a number of safeguards at trial in addition to the rights discussed in the previous chapters. It protects a defendant's right to be present and limits the use of security measures such as shackles that may suggest to the jury that the defendant is dangerous. It also grants to defendants the right to confront witnesses, the right to testify, the right to decline to testify, protection against improper statements to the jury by the prosecutor or judge, and the right to a public trial. This chapter examines each of these constitutional guarantees in turn.[a]

§ 1. PRESENCE AND PREJUDICIAL RESTRAINTS

ILLINOIS V. ALLEN

397 U.S. 337, 90 S.Ct. 1057, 25 L.Ed.2d 353 (1970).

JUSTICE BLACK delivered the opinion of the Court.

[A jury convicted Allen of armed robbery. Before trial, the judge acceded to Allen's wish to conduct his own defense, although court-appointed counsel would "sit in and protect the record." During the *voir dire* examination, when the judge directed Allen to confine his questioning to matters relating to the prospective juror's qualifications, Allen "started to argue with the judge in a most abusive and disrespectful manner." The judge then asked appointed counsel to proceed with the examination, upon which Allen continued to talk and concluded his remarks by saying to the judge, "When I go out for lunchtime, you're going to be a corpse here." The judge then warned Allen that he would be removed from the courtroom if there was another outbreak of that sort. Allen continued to talk back, saying, "There's not going to be no trial, either. I'm going to sit here and you're going to talk and you can bring your shackles out and straight jacket and put them on me and tape my mouth, but it will do no good because there's not going to be no trial." After more abusive remarks, the judge ordered the trial to proceed in Allen's absence. After a noon recess, the judge permitted Allen to return to the courtroom with the warning that he could remain only so long as he behaved himself. Shortly thereafter, Allen spoke out again, saying, "There is going to be no proceeding. I'm going to start talking all through the trial. There's not going to be no trial like this." The judge again ordered Allen removed, and he remained out of the courtroom during the presentation of the State's case-in-chief except when brought in for purposes of identification. Thereafter, Allen was permitted to return to the courtroom upon his promise to conduct himself properly, and he remained for the rest of the trial, principally his defense, which was conducted by his appointed counsel. A federal court of appeals granted a writ of habeas corpus after finding Allen's exclusion unlawful.]

* * * Although mindful that courts must indulge every reasonable presumption against the loss of constitutional rights, we explicitly hold today that a defendant can lose his right to be present at trial if, after he has been warned by the judge that he will be removed if he continues

---

[a] For a more complete discussion of the subjects discussed in this chapter, as well as other aspects of the criminal trial, see Wayne R. LaFave, Jerold H. Israel, Nancy J. King & Orin S. Kerr, Criminal Procedure Treatise § 24.1–24.11 (4th ed. 2016) (available on Westlaw under the database CRIMPROC and hereafter cited as CRIMPROC).

his disruptive behavior, he nevertheless insists on conducting himself in a manner so disorderly, disruptive, and disrespectful of the court that his trial cannot be carried on with him in the courtroom. Once lost, the right to be present can, of course, be reclaimed as soon as the defendant is willing to conduct himself consistently with the decorum and respect inherent in the concept of courts and judicial proceedings.

It is essential to the proper administration of criminal justice that dignity, order, and decorum be the hallmarks of all court proceedings in our country. The flagrant disregard in the courtroom of elementary standards of proper conduct should not and cannot be tolerated. We believe trial judges confronted with disruptive, contumacious, stubbornly defiant defendants must be given sufficient discretion to meet the circumstances of each case. No one formula for maintaining the appropriate courtroom atmosphere will be best in all situations. We think there are at least three constitutionally permissible ways for a trial judge to handle an obstreperous defendant like Allen: (1) bind and gag him, thereby keeping him present; (2) cite him for contempt; (3) take him out of the courtroom until he promises to conduct himself properly.

Trying a defendant for a crime while he sits bound and gagged before the judge and jury would to an extent comply with that part of the Sixth Amendment's purposes that accords the defendant an opportunity to confront the witnesses at the trial. But even to contemplate such a technique, much less see it, arouses a feeling that no person should be tried while shackled and gagged except as a last resort. Not only is it possible that the sight of shackles and gags might have a significant effect on the jury's feelings about the defendant, but the use of this technique is itself something of an affront to the very dignity and decorum of judicial proceedings that the judge is seeking to uphold. Moreover, one of the defendant's primary advantages of being present at the trial, his ability to communicate with his counsel, is greatly reduced when the defendant is in a condition of total physical restraint. It is in part because of these inherent disadvantages and limitations in this method of dealing with disorderly defendants that we decline to hold with the Court of Appeals that a defendant cannot under any possible circumstances be deprived of his right to be present at trial. However, in some situations which we need not attempt to foresee, binding and gagging might possibly be the fairest and most reasonable way to handle a defendant who acts as Allen did here.

In a footnote the Court of Appeals suggested the possible availability of contempt of court as a remedy to make Allen behave in his robbery trial * * * Of course, if the defendant is determined to prevent *any* trial, then a court in attempting to try the defendant for contempt is still confronted with the identical dilemma that the Illinois court faced in this case. And criminal contempt has obvious limitations as a sanction when the defendant is charged with a crime so serious that a very severe sentence such as death or life imprisonment is likely to be imposed. In such a case the defendant might not be affected by a mere contempt sentence when he ultimately faces a far more serious sanction. Nevertheless, the contempt remedy should be borne in mind by a judge in the circumstances of this case.

Another aspect of the contempt remedy is the judge's power, when exercised consistently with state and federal law, to imprison an unruly defendant such as Allen for civil contempt and discontinue the trial until such time as the defendant promises to behave himself. This procedure is consistent with the defendant's right to be present at trial, and yet it avoids the serious shortcomings of the use of shackles and gags. It must be recognized, however, that a defendant might conceivably, as a matter of calculated strategy, elect to spend a prolonged period in confinement for contempt in the hope that adverse witnesses might be unavailable after a lapse of time. A court must guard against allowing a defendant to profit from his own wrong in this way.

The trial court in this case decided under the circumstances to remove the defendant from the courtroom and to continue his trial in his absence until and unless he promised to conduct himself in a manner befitting an American courtroom. As we said earlier, we find nothing unconstitutional about this procedure. Allen's behavior was clearly of such an extreme and aggravated nature as to justify either his removal from the courtroom or his total physical restraint. Prior to his removal he was repeatedly warned by the trial judge that he would be removed from the courtroom if he persisted in his unruly conduct, and, as Judge Hastings observed in his dissenting opinion, the record demonstrates that Allen would not have been at all dissuaded by the trial judge's use of his criminal contempt powers. Allen was constantly informed that he could return to the trial when he would agree to conduct himself in an orderly manner. Under these circumstances we hold that Allen lost his right guaranteed by the Sixth and Fourteenth Amendments to be present throughout his trial. * * * The judgment of the Court of Appeals is reversed.

NOTES AND QUESTIONS

1. ***Deliberate absence as a waiver of the right to presence.*** In *Taylor v. United States,* 414 U.S. 17 (1973), the Court found that the defendant "who was at liberty on bail, had attended the opening session of his trial, and had a duty to be present at the trial," waived his right to presence by voluntarily not showing up. The Court found it "incredible" that a defendant in such circumstances " 'would not know that as a consequence the trial could continue in his absence.' " Lower courts have found it constitutional also to *begin* a trial without the defendant, so long as the defendant knew of the trial date and intentionally stayed away. See, e.g., *Jefferson v. State,* 807 So.2d 1222 (Miss. 2002). But in many jurisdictions, statute or court rule prohibits commencing a trial without the defendant's presence. For example, the Supreme Court held in *Crosby v. United States,* 506 U.S. 255 (1993), that the "language, history, and logic" of Fed.R.Crim.P. 43 "support a straightforward interpretation that prohibits the trial *in absentia* of a defendant who is not present at the beginning of trial." The Court commented: "If a clear line is to be drawn marking the point at which the costs of delay are likely to outweigh the interests of the defendant and society in having the defendant present, the commencement of trial is at least a plausible place at which to draw that line."

2. ***Presence at which proceedings?*** In KENTUCKY v. STINCER, 482 U.S. 730 (1987), in defendant's trial for the alleged commission of sodomy upon two children, aged eight and seven, the trial court conducted an in-chambers hearing to determine whether the children were competent to testify. Defense counsel participated in the in-chambers hearing, but defendant was excluded notwithstanding his request to be present. The in-chambers examination of the children was limited to questions designed to determine whether they were capable of remembering basic facts (e.g., they were asked the names of their teachers) and whether they had a moral sense of the obligation to tell the truth (e.g., they were asked "what it means to tell the truth"). Following the examination, the trial court, without objection by defense counsel, ruled that the children were competent to testify. Before each child began her substantive testimony at trial, the prosecutor repeated some of the basic questions that had been asked at the competency hearing. On cross-examination, defense counsel asked further questions designed to determine if the child could recall past events and knew the difference between the truth and a lie. The Supreme Court, per Blackmun, J., held that the exclusion of defendant from the in-chambers competency hearing had not violated defendant's constitutional rights:

Justice Blackmun began by dismissing as "not particularly helpful" the Commonwealth's attempt to characterize a competency hearing as a trial or pretrial proceeding, noting that this hearing was held after the jury was sworn and "retains a direct relationship with the trial because it determines whether a key witness will testify," and that the responsibility to determine competency is an ongoing one for the judge based on the witness' actual testimony at trial.

"[I]t is more useful to consider whether excluding the defendant from the hearing interferes with his opportunity for effective cross-examination. No such interference occurred when respondent was excluded from the competency hearing of the two young girls in this case. After the trial court determined that the two children were competent to testify, they appeared and testified in open court. At that point, the two witnesses were subject to full and complete cross-examination, and were so examined. Respondent was present throughout this cross-examination and was available to assist his counsel as necessary. * * * Any questions asked during the competency hearing, which respondent's counsel attended and in which he participated, could have been repeated during direct examination and cross-examination of the witnesses in respondent's presence. * * *

"At the close of the children's testimony, respondent's counsel, had he thought it appropriate, was in a position to move that the court reconsider its competency rulings on the ground that the direct and cross-examination had elicited evidence that the young girls lacked the basic requisites for serving as competent witnesses. Thus, the critical tool of cross-examination was available to counsel as a means of establishing that the witnesses were not competent to testify, as well as a means of undermining the credibility of their testimony. Because respondent had the opportunity for full and effective cross-examination of the two witnesses during trial, and because of the nature of the competency hearing at issue in this case, we conclude that respondent's rights under the Confrontation Clause were not violated by his exclusion from the competency hearing of the two girls. * * *

"[But] respondent [also] argues that his rights under the Due Process Clause of the Fourteenth Amendment were violated by his exclusion from the competency hearing. The Court has assumed that, even in situations where the defendant is not actually confronting witnesses or evidence against him, he has a due process right 'to be present in his own person whenever his presence has a relation, reasonably substantial, to the fullness of his opportunity to defend against the charge.' * * * [A] defendant is guaranteed the right to be present at any stage of the criminal proceeding that is critical to its outcome if his presence would contribute to the fairness of the procedure.

"We conclude that respondent's due process rights were not violated by his exclusion from the competency hearing in this case. * * * No question regarding the substantive testimony that the two girls would have given during the trial was asked at that hearing. All the questions, instead, were directed solely to each child's ability to recollect and narrate facts, to her ability to distinguish between truth and falsehood, and to her sense of moral obligation to tell the truth. Thus, although a competency hearing in which a witness is asked to discuss upcoming substantive testimony might bear a substantial relationship to a defendant's opportunity better to defend himself at trial, that kind of inquiry is not before us in this case. Respondent has given no indication that his presence at the competency hearing in this case would have been useful in ensuring a more reliable determination as to whether the witnesses were competent to testify. He has presented no evidence that his relationship with the children, or his knowledge of facts regarding their background, could have assisted either his counsel or the judge in asking questions that would have resulted in a more assured determination of competency. On the record of this case, therefore, we cannot say that respondent's rights under the Due Process Clause of the Fourteenth Amendment were violated by his exclusion from the competency hearing."

In dissent, Marshall, J. (joined by Brennan and Stevens, JJ.) argued that the presence of the defendant at a competency hearing can "enhance the reliability of the fact finding process" and helps to ensure that any inaccuracies are identified "*before* the witness takes the stand with the trial court's imprimatur of competency and testifies in front of the jury as to the defendant's commission of the alleged offense." He added, "[T]he specter of the judge, prosecutor and court-appointed attorney conferring privately with the key prosecution witnesses was understandably upsetting."

In light of *Stincer*, should the defendant have a constitutional right to be present at:

(1) an in camera inquiry into whether a juror had developed a prejudice against the defendant as a result of observing the defendant during trial sketching portraits of the jurors (the juror had expressed concern, but the judge explained that the sketching was innocuous, as the defendant was an artist, and concluded that the juror accepted this explanation and remained impartial)? No, said the Court in *United States v. Gagnon*, 470 U.S. 522 (1985). Although the right to be present is not restricted to situations where the defendant is "actually confronting witnesses or evidence against him," and encompasses all trial-related proceedings at which defendant's presence " 'has a relation, reasonably substantial, to the fullness of his opportunity to defend against the charge,' " there was no Constitutional violation when defense counsel was present and had not requested client's presence, and defendant "could have done nothing had [he] been at the conference, nor would [he] have gained anything by attending."

(2) an in-camera discussion with a juror who came to the judge's chambers to inform him of her acquaintance with a person mentioned in the trial? Yes, but denial of presence can be harmless. *Rushen v. Spain*, 464 U.S. 114 (1983) (defendant's absence was harmless as juror's acquaintance had no relationship to the case, being the victim of another crime mentioned in passing in the course of impeaching a defense witness).

3. ***Communication while removed from the courtroom.*** Concurring in *Allen,* Justice Brennan noted that "when a defendant is excluded from his trial, the court should make reasonable efforts to enable him to communicate with his attorney and, if possible, to keep apprised of the progress of his trial." Today there are more options for maintaining contact with an excluded defendant than there were in 1970. As the New Jersey Supreme Court explained "if there is no possible way to restore order and contain a defendant's insistent, defiant behavior, a judge can direct that the defendant be taken to a holding cell outfitted with a video or audio feed that will relay the proceedings to the defendant remotely." *State v. Tedesco*, 214 N.J. 177 (2013).

4. ***Constitutional limits on the use of restraints.*** DECK v. MISSOURI, 544 U.S. 622 (2005), addressed whether the conditions placed upon a defendant's presence at trial denied him his right to a fair trial. Deck had worn leg braces not visible to the jury at trial, but after his death sentence was set aside on appeal, at his resentencing, his leg irons, handcuffs, and belly chain were visible. He was again sentenced to death. Justice Breyer wrote for the Court:]

" * * * The law has long forbidden routine use of visible shackles during the guilt phase; it permits a State to shackle a criminal defendant only in the presence of a special need. This rule has deep roots in the common law. In the 18th century, Blackstone wrote that "it is laid down in our ancient books, that, though under an indictment of the highest nature," a defendant "must be brought to the bar without irons, or any manner of shackles or bonds; unless there be evident danger of an escape." Blackstone and other English authorities recognized that the rule did not apply at "the time of arraignment," or like proceedings before the judge. It was meant to protect defendants appearing at trial before a jury. * * *

"[T]his Court has suggested that a version of this rule forms part of the Fifth and Fourteenth Amendments' due process guarantee. * * * *Allen* [p. 1300] * * * Sixteen years later, the Court considered a special courtroom security arrangement that involved having uniformed security personnel sit in the first row of the courtroom's spectator section. The Court held that the Constitution allowed the arrangement, stating that the deployment of security personnel during trial is not "the sort of inherently prejudicial practice that, like shackling, should be permitted only where justified by an essential state interest specific to each trial." *Holbrook v. Flynn*, 475 U.S. 560, 568–569 (1986). * * * We now conclude that those statements identify a basic element of the "due process of law" protected by the Federal Constitution. Thus, the Fifth and Fourteenth Amendments prohibit the use of physical restraints visible to the jury absent a trial court determination, in the exercise of its discretion, that they are justified by a state interest specific to a particular trial. Such a determination may of course take into account the factors that courts have traditionally relied on in gauging potential security problems and the risk of escape at trial.

"* * * Judicial hostility to shackling may once primarily have reflected concern for the suffering—the "tortures" and "torments"—that "very painful" chains could cause. More recently, this Court's opinions have not stressed the need to prevent physical suffering (for not all modern physical restraints are painful). Instead they have emphasized the importance of giving effect to three fundamental legal principles.

"First, the criminal process presumes that the defendant is innocent until proved guilty. Visible shackling undermines the presumption of innocence and the related fairness of the factfinding process. It suggests to the jury that the justice system itself sees a "need to separate a defendant from the community at large."

"Second, the Constitution, in order to help the accused secure a meaningful defense, provides him with a right to counsel. The use of physical restraints diminishes that right. Shackles can interfere with the accused's "ability to communicate" with his lawyer. *Allen*. Indeed, they can interfere with a defendant's ability to participate in his own defense, say by freely choosing whether to take the witness stand on his own behalf.

"Third, judges must seek to maintain a judicial process that is a dignified process. The courtroom's formal dignity, which includes the respectful treatment of defendants, reflects the importance of the matter at issue, guilt or innocence, and the gravity with which Americans consider any deprivation of an individual's liberty through criminal punishment. And it reflects a seriousness of purpose that helps to explain the judicial system's power to inspire the confidence and to affect the behavior of a general public whose demands for justice our courts seek to serve. The routine use of shackles in the presence of juries would undermine these symbolic yet concrete objectives. As this Court has said, the use of shackles at trial "affront[s]" the "dignity and decorum of judicial proceedings that the judge is seeking to uphold." *Allen*.

"There will be cases, of course, where these perils of shackling are unavoidable. We do not underestimate the need to restrain dangerous defendants to prevent courtroom attacks, or the need to give trial courts latitude in making individualized security determinations. We are mindful of the tragedy that can result if judges are not able to protect themselves and their courtrooms. But given their prejudicial effect, due process does not permit the use of visible restraints if the trial court has not taken account of the circumstances of the particular case.

"The considerations that militate against the routine use of visible shackles during the guilt phase of a criminal trial apply with like force to penalty proceedings in capital cases. * * * The Court has stressed the "acute need" for reliable decisionmaking when the death penalty is at issue. The appearance of the offender during the penalty phase in shackles, however, almost inevitably implies to a jury, as a matter of common sense, that court authorities consider the offender a danger to the community—often a statutory aggravator and nearly always a relevant factor in jury decisionmaking, even where the State does not specifically argue the point. It also almost inevitably affects adversely the jury's perception of the character of the defendant. And it thereby inevitably undermines the jury's ability to weigh accurately all relevant considerations—considerations that are often unquantifiable and elusive—when it determines whether a defendant deserves death. In these ways, the use of shackles can be a "thumb [on] death's side of the scale."

* * * [W]e must conclude that courts cannot routinely place defendants in shackles or other physical restraints visible to the jury during the penalty phase of a capital proceeding. The constitutional requirement, however, is not absolute. It permits a judge, in the exercise of his or her discretion, to take account of special circumstances, including security concerns that may call

for shackling. In so doing, it accommodates the important need to protect the courtroom and its occupants. But any such determination must be case specific; that is to say, it should reflect particular concerns, say special security needs or escape risks, related to the defendant on trial.

* * * [Here] the record contains no formal or informal findings.* * * If there is an exceptional case where the record itself makes clear that there are indisputably good reasons for shackling, it is not this one. * * * [W]here a court, without adequate justification, orders the defendant to wear shackles that will be seen by the jury, the defendant need not demonstrate actual prejudice to make out a due process violation. The State must prove "beyond a reasonable doubt that the [shackling] error complained of did not contribute to the verdict obtained." *Chapman v. California*, [p. 1417]. [Reversed and remanded].

Justice Thomas, joined by Justice Scalia, dissented. He reasoned that a convicted defendant's "best opportunity to [escape] is in the courtroom," and in addition, "having been convicted, a defendant may be angry. He could turn that ire on his own counsel, who has failed in defending his innocence. Or, for that matter, he could turn on a witness testifying at his hearing or the court reporter.* * * That a defendant now convicted of his crimes appears before the jury in shackles thus would be unremarkable to the jury." He argued that the majority failed to explain "the affront to the dignity of the courts that the sight of physical restraints poses. I cannot understand the indignity in having a convicted double murderer and robber appear before the court in visible physical restraints."

Is the procedure in *Deck* limited to restraints that are visible? What if the restraint is a "stun belt" covered by defendant's clothing? Some courts require for this device the same on-the-record justification that is required for visible restraints. One court explained the reasons: 1) the belt "poses a far more substantial risk of interfering with a defendant's Sixth Amendment right to confer with counsel than do leg shackles," because of "the fear of receiving a painful and humiliating shock for any gesture that could be perceived as threatening"; 2) a defendant wearing a belt is "likely to concentrate on doing everything he can to prevent the belt from being activated and is thus less likely to participate fully in his defense at trial"; and 3) "shackles are a minor threat to the dignity of the courtroom when compared with the discharge of a stun belt, which could cause the defendant to lose control of his limbs, collapse to the floor, and defecate on himself." *United States v. Durham*, 287 F.3d 1297 (11th Cir. 2002). Compare *Mungo v. United States*, 987 A.2d 1145 (D.C. App. 2010) (noting the Court has never held that a stun belt qualifies as a type of physical restraint whose use is subject to the strictures of *Deck*, or that the reasoning of *Deck* applies equally to the limited use of restraints during jury selection); Weaver v. State, 894 So.2d 178 (Fla. 2004) (stun belt use upheld even though murder defendant had no history of violent behavior in a courtroom, because he would be moving about the courtroom, representing himself pro se).

What if the restraint is visible but the defendant has opted for a bench trial without a jury? Consider the competing views reflected in *United States v. Sanchez-Gomez*, 859 F.3d 649 (9th Cir.2017) (en banc). The majority held: "This right to be free from unwarranted shackles no matter the proceeding respects our foundational principle that defendants are innocent until proven guilty. The principle isn't limited to juries or trial proceedings. It includes the perception of any person who may walk into a public courtroom, as well as those of the jury, the judge and court personnel. A presumptively innocent defendant has the right to be treated with respect and dignity in a public courtroom, not like a bear on a chain. . . . The right also maintains courtroom decorum and dignity: The courtroom's formal dignity, which includes the respectful treatment of defendants, reflects the importance of the matter at issue, guilt or innocence, and the gravity with which Americans consider any deprivation of an individual's liberty through criminal punishment. And it reflects a seriousness of purpose that helps to explain the judicial system's power to inspire the confidence and to affect the behavior of a general public whose demands for justice our courts seek to serve. The most visible and public manifestation of our criminal justice system is the courtroom. Courtrooms are palaces of justice, imbued with a majesty that reflects the gravity of proceedings designed to deprive a person of liberty or even life. A member of the public who wanders into a criminal courtroom must immediately perceive that it is a place where justice is administered with due regard to individuals whom the law presumes to be innocent. That perception cannot prevail if defendants are marched in like convicts on a chain gang. Both the defendant and the public have the right to a dignified, inspiring and open court process. Thus, innocent defendants may not be shackled *at any point* in the courtroom unless there is an individualized showing of need." (Emphasis added.)

The dissenting judges, siding with the Second and Eleventh Circuits, argued that the majority's rule unnecessarily put those in state and federal courtrooms at risk of violence, that the Court limited *Deck* to jury proceedings, that the majority's rule was not supported by the common law, and that the question is simply whether requiring restraints is reasonably related to a legitimate governmental objective.

The Supreme Court later vacated the Ninth Circuit's decision as moot, without reaching this issue. 138 S.Ct. 1532 (2018).

§ 2. CONFRONTATION AND TESTIMONIAL HEARSAY

MICHIGAN V. BRYANT

562 U.S. 344, 131 S.Ct. 1143, 179 L.Ed.2d 93 (2011).

JUSTICE SOTOMAYOR delivered the opinion of the Court.

At respondent Richard Bryant's trial, the court admitted statements that the victim, Anthony Covington, made to police officers who discovered him mortally wounded in a gas station parking lot. A jury convicted Bryant of [second-degree murder and other crimes]. On appeal, the Supreme Court of Michigan held that the Sixth Amendment's Confrontation Clause, as explained in our decisions in *Crawford v. Washington,* 541 U.S. 36 (2004), and *Davis v. Washington,* 547 U.S. 813 (2006), rendered Covington's statements inadmissible testimonial hearsay, and the court reversed Bryant's conviction. We granted the State's petition for a writ of certiorari to consider whether the Confrontation Clause barred the admission at trial of Covington's statements to the police. We hold that the circumstances of the interaction between Covington and the police objectively indicate that the "primary purpose of the interrogation" was "to enable police assistance to meet an ongoing emergency." Therefore, Covington's identification and description of the shooter and the location of the shooting were not testimonial statements, and their admission at Bryant's trial did not violate the Confrontation Clause. We vacate the judgment of the Supreme Court of Michigan and remand.

I

Around 3:25 a.m. on April 29, 2001, Detroit, Michigan police officers responded to a radio dispatch indicating that a man had been shot. At the scene, they found the victim, Anthony Covington, lying on the ground next to his car in a gas station parking lot. Covington had a gunshot wound to his abdomen, appeared to be in great pain, and spoke with difficulty.

The police asked him "what had happened, who had shot him, and where the shooting had occurred." Covington stated that "Rick" shot him at around 3 a.m. He also indicated that he had a conversation with Bryant, whom he recognized based on his voice, through the back door of Bryant's house. Covington explained that when he turned to leave, he was shot through the door and then drove to the gas station, where police found him.

Covington's conversation with the police ended within 5 to 10 minutes when emergency medical services arrived. Covington was transported to a hospital and died within hours. The police left the gas station after speaking with Covington, called for backup, and traveled to Bryant's house. They did not find Bryant there but did find blood and a bullet on the back porch and an apparent bullet hole in the back door. Police also found Covington's wallet and identification outside the house. [At trial, which occurred prior to the Court's decisions in *Crawford* and *Davis*, the police officers who spoke with Covington at the gas station testified about what Covington had told them.][1]

* * *

II

The Confrontation Clause of the Sixth Amendment states: "In all criminal prosecutions, the accused shall enjoy the right . . . to be confronted with the witnesses against him." The Fourteenth Amendment renders the Clause binding on the States. In *Ohio v. Roberts,* 448 U.S. 56, 66 (1980), we explained that the confrontation right does not bar admission of statements of an unavailable witness if the statements "bea[r] adequate 'indicia of reliability.' " We held that reliability can be established if "the evidence falls within a firmly rooted hearsay exception," or if it does not fall within such an exception, then if it bears "particularized guarantees of trustworthiness."

Nearly a quarter century later, we decided *Crawford v. Washington.* Petitioner Michael Crawford was prosecuted for stabbing a man who had allegedly attempted to rape his wife, Sylvia. Sylvia witnessed the stabbing, and later that night, after she and her husband were both arrested, police interrogated her about the incident. At trial, Sylvia Crawford claimed spousal privilege and did not testify, but the State introduced a tape recording of Sylvia's statement to the police in an effort to prove that the stabbing was not in self-defense, as Michael Crawford claimed. The Washington Supreme Court affirmed Crawford's conviction because it found Sylvia's statement to be reliable, as required under *Ohio v. Roberts.* We reversed, overruling *Ohio v. Roberts.*[a]

Crawford examined the common-law history of the confrontation right and explained that "the principal evil at which the Confrontation Clause was directed was the civil-law mode of criminal procedure, and particularly its use of *ex parte* examinations as evidence against the accused." We noted that in England, pretrial examinations of suspects and witnesses by

---

[1] * * * The trial court ruled that the statements were admissible as excited utterances and did not address their admissibility as dying declarations. This occurred prior to our 2004 decision in *Crawford,* where we first suggested that dying declarations, even if testimonial, might be admissible as a historical exception to the Confrontation Clause. * * * Because of the State's failure to preserve its argument with regard to dying declarations, we similarly need not decide that question here.

[a] Justice Scalia wrote for the majority in *Crawford*: "Where testimonial statements are involved, we do not think the Framers meant to leave the Sixth Amendment's protection to the vagaries of the rules of evidence, much less to amorphous notions of 'reliability.' Admitting statements deemed reliable by a judge is fundamentally at odds with the right of confrontation. * * * The Clause * * * reflects a judgment, not only about the desirability of reliable evidence * * * but about how reliability can best be determined."

Chief Justice Rehnquist, joined by Justice O'Connor, concurred in the judgment in *Crawford*, but disagreed with the overruling of *Roberts.* Chief Justice Rehnquist reasoned: "The Court's distinction between testimonial and non-testimonial statements * * * is no better rooted in history than our current doctrine." While "testimonial statements such as accusatory statements to police officers likely would have been disapproved of in the 18th century, * * * [that] would not necessarily [be] because they resembled ex parte affidavits or depositions, as the Court reasons, but more likely than not, because they were not made under oath. * * * Thus, while I agree that * * * the Framers were mainly concerned about sworn affidavits and depositions, it does not follow that they were similarly concerned about the Court's broader category of testimonial statements." Moreover, "between 1700 and 1800 the rules regarding the admissibility of out-of-court statements were still being developed, * * * [with] exceptions [recognized] to the general rule of exclusion," so it was hardly "clear * * * that the Framers categorically wanted to eliminate further ones." As recognized in *Roberts*, "[e]xceptions to confrontation have been derived from the experience that some out-of-court statements are just as reliable as cross-examined in-court testimony due to the circumstances under which they were made.* * * By creating an immutable category of excluded evidence, the Court adds little to a trial's truth-finding function and ignores this longstanding guidance."

government officials "were sometimes read in court in lieu of live testimony." In light of this history, we emphasized the word "witnesses" in the Sixth Amendment, defining it as "those who 'bear testimony.' " We defined "testimony" as " '[a] solemn declaration or affirmation made for the purpose of establishing or proving some fact.' " We noted that "[a]n accuser who makes a formal statement to government officers bears testimony in a sense that a person who makes a casual remark to an acquaintance does not." We therefore limited the Confrontation Clause's reach to testimonial statements and held that in order for testimonial evidence to be admissible, the Sixth Amendment "demands what the common law required: unavailability and a prior opportunity for cross-examination." Although "leav[ing] for another day any effort to spell out a comprehensive definition of 'testimonial,' " *Crawford* noted that "at a minimum" it includes "prior testimony at a preliminary hearing, before a grand jury, or at a former trial; and . . . police interrogations." Under this reasoning, we held that Sylvia Crawford's statements in the course of police questioning were testimonial and that their admission when Michael Crawford "had no opportunity to cross-examine her" due to spousal privilege was "sufficient to make out a violation of the Sixth Amendment."

In 2006, the Court in *Davis v. Washington* and *Hammon v. Indiana,* 547 U.S. 813, took a further step to "determine more precisely which police interrogations produce testimony" and therefore implicate a Confrontation Clause bar. We explained that when *Crawford* said that " 'interrogations by law enforcement officers fall squarely within [the] class' of testimonial hearsay, we had immediately in mind (for that was the case before us) interrogations solely directed at establishing the facts of a past crime, in order to identify (or provide evidence to convict) the perpetrator. The product of such interrogation, whether reduced to a writing signed by the declarant or embedded in the memory (and perhaps notes) of the interrogating officer, is testimonial." *Davis.*

We thus made clear in *Davis* that not all those questioned by the police are witnesses and not all "interrogations by law enforcement officers," are subject to the Confrontation Clause.[2]

Davis and *Hammon* were both domestic violence cases. In *Davis,* Michelle McCottry made the statements at issue to a 911 operator during a domestic disturbance with Adrian Davis, her former boyfriend. McCottry told the operator, " 'He's here jumpin' on me again,' " and, " 'He's usin' his fists.' " The operator then asked McCottry for Davis' first and last names and middle initial, and at that point in the conversation McCottry reported that Davis had fled in a car. McCottry did not appear at Davis' trial, and the State introduced the recording of her conversation with the 911 operator.

In *Hammon,* decided along with *Davis,* police responded to a domestic disturbance call at the home of Amy and Hershel Hammon, where they found Amy alone on the front porch. She appeared " 'somewhat frightened,' " but told them " 'nothing was the matter.' " She gave the police permission to enter the house, where they saw a gas heating unit with the glass front shattered on the floor. One officer remained in the kitchen with Hershel, while another officer talked to Amy in the living room about what had happened. Hershel tried several times to participate in Amy's conversation with the police and became angry when the police required him to stay separated from Amy. The police asked Amy to fill out and sign a battery affidavit. She wrote: " 'Broke our Furnace & shoved me down on the floor into the broken glass. Hit me in the chest and threw me down. Broke our lamps & phone. Tore up my van where I couldn't leave the house. Attacked my daughter.' " Amy did not appear at Hershel's trial, so the police officers who spoke with her testified as to her statements and authenticated the affidavit. The trial court admitted the affidavit as a present sense impression and admitted the oral statements as excited utterances

---

2 We noted in *Crawford* that "[w]e use the term 'interrogation' in its colloquial, rather than any technical legal, sense," and that "[j]ust as various definitions of 'testimonial' exist, one can imagine various definitions of 'interrogation,' and we need not select among them in this case." * * *

under state hearsay rules. The Indiana Supreme Court affirmed Hammon's conviction, holding that Amy's oral statements were not testimonial and that the admission of the affidavit, although erroneous because the affidavit was testimonial, was harmless.

To address the facts of both cases, we expanded upon the meaning of "testimonial" that we first employed in *Crawford* and discussed the concept of an ongoing emergency. We explained:

"Statements are nontestimonial when made in the course of police interrogation under circumstances objectively indicating that the primary purpose of the interrogation is to enable police assistance to meet an ongoing emergency. They are testimonial when the circumstances objectively indicate that there is no such ongoing emergency, and that the primary purpose of the interrogation is to establish or prove past events potentially relevant to later criminal prosecution." *Davis.*

Examining the *Davis* and *Hammon* statements in light of those definitions, we held that the statements at issue in *Davis* were nontestimonial and the statements in *Hammon* were testimonial. We distinguished the statements in *Davis* from the testimonial statements in *Crawford* on several grounds, including that the victim in *Davis* was "speaking about events *as they were actually happening,* rather than 'describ[ing] past events,' " that there was an ongoing emergency, that the "elicited statements were necessary to be able to *resolve* the present emergency," and that the statements were not formal. In *Hammon,* on the other hand, we held that, "[i]t is entirely clear from the circumstances that the interrogation was part of an investigation into possibly criminal past conduct." There was "no emergency in progress." The officer questioning Amy "was not seeking to determine . . . 'what is happening,' but rather 'what happened.' " It was "formal enough" that the police interrogated Amy in a room separate from her husband where, "some time after the events described were over," she "deliberately recounted, in response to police questioning, how potentially criminal past events began and progressed." Because her statements "were neither a cry for help nor the provision of information enabling officers immediately to end a threatening situation," we held that they were testimonial.

Davis did not "attemp[t] to produce an exhaustive classification of all conceivable statements—or even all conceivable statements in response to police interrogation—as either testimonial or nontestimonial."[3] The basic purpose of the Confrontation Clause was to "targe[t]" the sort of "abuses" exemplified at the notorious treason trial of Sir Walter Raleigh. *Crawford.* Thus, the most important instances in which the Clause restricts the introduction of out-of-court statements are those in which state actors are involved in a formal, out-of-court interrogation of a witness to obtain evidence for trial.[4] Even where such an interrogation is conducted with all good faith, introduction of the resulting statements at trial can be unfair to the accused if they are untested by cross-examination. Whether formal or informal, out-of-court statements can evade the basic objective of the Confrontation Clause, which is to prevent the accused from being deprived of the opportunity to cross-examine the declarant about statements taken for use at trial. When,

---

[3] *Davis* explained that 911 operators "may at least be agents of law enforcement when they conduct interrogations of 911 callers," and therefore "consider[ed] their acts to be acts of the police" for purposes of the opinion. *Davis* explicitly reserved the question of "whether and when statements made to someone other than law enforcement personnel are 'testimonial.' " We have no need to decide that question in this case either because Covington's statements were made to police officers. * * *

[4] * * * For all of the reasons discussed in Justice Thomas' opinion concurring in the judgment, the situation presented in this case is nothing like the circumstances presented by Sir Walter Raleigh's trial. [Ed: In *Crawford,* Justice Scalia, writing for the Court, described that trial: "Lord Cobham, Raleigh's alleged accomplice, had implicated him in an examination before the Privy Council and in a letter. At Raleigh's trial, these were read to the jury. Raleigh argued that Cobham had lied to save himself * * * Suspecting that Cobham would recant, Raleigh demanded that the judges call him to appear, arguing that '[t]he Proof of the Common Law is by witness and jury: let Cobham be here, let him speak it. Call my accuser before my face. . . .' The judges refused, and, despite Raleigh's protestations that he was being tried 'by the Spanish Inquisition,' the jury convicted, and Raleigh was sentenced to death."]

as in *Davis,* the primary purpose of an interrogation is to respond to an "ongoing emergency," its purpose is not to create a record for trial and thus is not within the scope of the Clause. But there may be *other* circumstances, aside from ongoing emergencies, when a statement is not procured with a primary purpose of creating an out-of-court substitute for trial testimony. In making the primary purpose determination, standard rules of hearsay, designed to identify some statements as reliable, will be relevant. Where no such primary purpose exists, the admissibility of a statement is the concern of state and federal rules of evidence, not the Confrontation Clause.

Deciding this case also requires further explanation of the "ongoing emergency" circumstance addressed in *Davis*. Because *Davis* and *Hammon* arose in the domestic violence context, that was the situation "we had immediately in mind (for that was the case before us)." We now face a new context: a nondomestic dispute, involving a victim found in a public location, suffering from a fatal gunshot wound, and a perpetrator whose location was unknown at the time the police located the victim. Thus, we confront for the first time circumstances in which the "ongoing emergency" discussed in *Davis* extends beyond an initial victim to a potential threat to the responding police and the public at large. This new context requires us to provide additional clarification with regard to what *Davis* meant by "the primary purpose of the interrogation is to enable police assistance to meet an ongoing emergency."

III

To determine whether the "primary purpose" of an interrogation is "to enable police assistance to meet an ongoing emergency," *Davis,* which would render the resulting statements nontestimonial, we objectively evaluate the circumstances in which the encounter occurs and the statements and actions of the parties.

* * * The circumstances in which an encounter occurs—*e.g.,* at or near the scene of the crime versus at a police station, during an ongoing emergency or afterwards—are clearly matters of objective fact. The statements and actions of the parties must also be objectively evaluated. That is, the relevant inquiry is not the subjective or actual purpose of the individuals involved in a particular encounter, but rather the purpose that reasonable participants would have had, as ascertained from the individuals' statements and actions and the circumstances in which the encounter occurred. * * *

As our recent Confrontation Clause cases have explained, the existence of an "ongoing emergency" at the time of an encounter between an individual and the police is among the most important circumstances informing the "primary purpose" of an interrogation. The existence of an ongoing emergency is relevant to determining the primary purpose of the interrogation because an emergency focuses the participants on something other than "prov[ing] past events potentially relevant to later criminal prosecution."[8] Rather, it focuses them on "end[ing] a threatening situation." Implicit in *Davis* is the idea that because the prospect of fabrication in statements given for the primary purpose of resolving that emergency is presumably significantly diminished, the Confrontation Clause does not require such statements to be subject to the crucible of cross-examination.

This logic is not unlike that justifying the excited utterance exception in hearsay law. Statements "relating to a startling event or condition made while the declarant was under the stress of excitement caused by the event or condition," Fed. Rule Evid. 803(2) are considered reliable because the declarant, in the excitement, presumably cannot form a falsehood. An ongoing emergency has a similar effect of focusing an individual's attention on responding to the emergency. * * *

[8] The existence of an ongoing emergency must be objectively assessed from the perspective of the parties to the interrogation at the time, not with the benefit of hindsight. * * *

[W]hether an emergency exists and is ongoing is a highly context-dependent inquiry. * * * Because *Davis* and *Hammon* were domestic violence cases, we focused only on the threat to the victims and assessed the ongoing emergency from the perspective of whether there was a continuing threat *to them*. * * * An assessment of whether an emergency that threatens the police and public is ongoing cannot narrowly focus on whether the threat solely to the first victim has been neutralized because the threat to the first responders and public may continue.

The * * * duration and scope of an emergency may depend in part on the type of weapon employed. * * * Hershel Hammon was armed only with his fists when he attacked his wife, so removing Amy to a separate room was sufficient to end the emergency. If Hershel had been reported to be armed with a gun, however, separation by a single household wall might not have been sufficient to end the emergency.

* * * The medical condition of the victim is important to the primary purpose inquiry to the extent that it sheds light on the ability of the victim to have any purpose at all in responding to police questions and on the likelihood that any purpose formed would necessarily be a testimonial one. The victim's medical state also provides important context for first responders to judge the existence and magnitude of a continuing threat to the victim, themselves, and the public.

* * * [N]one of this suggests that an emergency is ongoing in every place or even just surrounding the victim for the entire time that the perpetrator of a violent crime is on the loose. As we recognized in *Davis,* "a conversation which begins as an interrogation to determine the need for emergency assistance" can "evolve into testimonial statements." This evolution may occur if, for example, a declarant provides police with information that makes clear that what appeared to be an emergency is not or is no longer an emergency or that what appeared to be a public threat is actually a private dispute. It could also occur if a perpetrator is disarmed, surrenders, is apprehended, or, as in *Davis,* flees with little prospect of posing a threat to the public. Trial courts can determine in the first instance when any transition from nontestimonial to testimonial occurs, and exclude "the portions of any statement that have become testimonial, as they do, for example, with unduly prejudicial portions of otherwise admissible evidence."

* * * [W]hether an ongoing emergency exists is simply one factor—albeit an important factor—that informs the ultimate inquiry regarding the "primary purpose" of an interrogation.

Another factor the Michigan Supreme Court did not sufficiently account for is the importance of *informality* in an encounter between a victim and police. Formality is not the sole touchstone of our primary purpose inquiry because, although formality suggests the absence of an emergency and therefore an increased likelihood that the purpose of the interrogation is to "establish or prove past events potentially relevant to later criminal prosecution," informality does not necessarily indicate the presence of an emergency or the lack of testimonial intent. The court below, however, too readily dismissed the informality of the circumstances in this case in a single brief footnote and in fact seems to have suggested that the encounter in this case was formal. As we explain further below, the questioning in this case occurred in an exposed, public area, prior to the arrival of emergency medical services, and in a disorganized fashion. All of those facts make this case distinguishable from the formal station-house interrogation in *Crawford*. * * *

In addition to the circumstances in which an encounter occurs, the statements and actions of both the declarant and interrogators provide objective evidence of the primary purpose of the interrogation. See, e.g., *Davis,* ("[T]he nature of what was *asked and answered* in *Davis,* again viewed objectively, was such that the elicited statements were necessary to be able to *resolve* the present emergency, rather than simply to learn (as in *Crawford*) what had happened in the past" (first emphasis added)). * * *

As the Michigan Supreme Court correctly recognized, *Davis* requires a combined inquiry that accounts for both the declarant and the interrogator. In many instances, the primary purpose of the interrogation will be most accurately ascertained by looking to the contents of both the questions and the answers. To give an extreme example, if the police say to a victim, "Tell us who did this to you so that we can arrest and prosecute them," the victim's response that "Rick did it," appears purely accusatory because by virtue of the phrasing of the question, the victim necessarily has prosecution in mind when she answers.

The combined approach also ameliorates problems that could arise from looking solely to one participant. Predominant among these is the problem of mixed motives on the part of both interrogators and declarants. Police officers in our society function as both first responders and criminal investigators. Their dual responsibilities may mean that they act with different motives simultaneously or in quick succession.

Victims are also likely to have mixed motives when they make statements to the police. During an ongoing emergency, a victim is most likely to want the threat to her and to other potential victims to end, but that does not necessarily mean that the victim wants or envisions prosecution of the assailant. A victim may want the attacker to be incapacitated temporarily or rehabilitated. Alternatively, a severely injured victim may have no purpose at all in answering questions posed; the answers may be simply reflexive. The victim's injuries could be so debilitating as to prevent her from thinking sufficiently clearly to understand whether her statements are for the purpose of addressing an ongoing emergency or for the purpose of future prosecution. Taking into account a victim's injuries does not transform this objective inquiry into a subjective one. The inquiry is still objective because it focuses on the understanding and purpose of a reasonable victim in the circumstances of the actual victim—circumstances that prominently include the victim's physical state.

The dissent suggests that we intend to give controlling weight to the "intentions of the police." That is a misreading of our opinion. At trial, the declarant's statements, not the interrogator's questions, will be introduced to "establis[h] the truth of the matter asserted," and must therefore pass the Sixth Amendment test. In determining whether a declarant's statements are testimonial, courts should look to all of the relevant circumstances. * * * [C]ourts making a "primary purpose" assessment should not be unjustifiably restrained from consulting all relevant information, including the statements and actions of interrogators. * * *

IV

As we suggested in *Davis,* when a court must determine whether the Confrontation Clause bars the admission of a statement at trial, it should determine the "primary purpose of the interrogation" by objectively evaluating the statements and actions of the parties to the encounter, in light of the circumstances in which the interrogation occurs. The existence of an emergency or the parties' perception that an emergency is ongoing is among the most important circumstances that courts must take into account in determining whether an interrogation is testimonial because statements made to assist police in addressing an ongoing emergency presumably lack the testimonial purpose that would subject them to the requirement of confrontation. As the context of this case brings into sharp relief, the existence and duration of an emergency depend on the type and scope of danger posed to the victim, the police, and the public.

* * *

We first examine the circumstances in which the interrogation occurred. The parties disagree over whether there was an emergency when the police arrived at the gas station. Bryant argues, and the Michigan Supreme Court accepted, that there was no ongoing emergency because "there . . . was no criminal conduct occurring. No shots were being fired, no one was seen in possession of a firearm, nor were any witnesses seen cowering in fear or running from the scene." Bryant, while conceding that "a serious or life-threatening injury creates a medical emergency for a victim," further argues that a declarant's medical emergency is not relevant to the ongoing emergency determination.

In contrast, Michigan and the Solicitor General explain that when the police responded to the call that a man had been shot and found Covington bleeding on the gas station parking lot, "they did not know who Covington was, whether the shooting had occurred at the gas station or at a different location, who the assailant was, or whether the assailant posed a continuing threat to Covington or others."

The Michigan Supreme Court stated that the police asked Covington, "what had happened, who had shot him, and where the shooting had occurred." * * * The officers basically agree on what information they learned from Covington, but not on the order in which they learned it or on whether Covington's statements were in response to general or detailed questions. They all agree that the first question was "what happened?" The answer was either "I was shot" or "Rick shot me."

As explained above, the scope of an emergency in terms of its threat to individuals other than the initial assailant and victim will often depend on the type of dispute involved. Nothing Covington said to the police indicated that the cause of the shooting was a purely private dispute or that the threat from the shooter had ended. The record reveals little about the motive for the shooting. The police officers who spoke with Covington at the gas station testified that Covington did not tell them what words Covington and Rick had exchanged prior to the shooting. What Covington did tell the officers was that he fled Bryant's back porch, indicating that he perceived an ongoing threat. The police did not know, and Covington did not tell them, whether the threat was limited to him. The potential scope of the dispute and therefore the emergency in this case thus stretches more broadly than those at issue in *Davis* and *Hammon* and encompasses a threat potentially to the police and the public.

This is also the first of our post-*Crawford* Confrontation Clause cases to involve a gun. The physical separation that was sufficient to end the emergency in *Hammon* was not necessarily sufficient to end the threat in this case; Covington was shot through the back door of Bryant's house. Bryant's argument that there was no ongoing emergency because "[n]o shots were being fired," surely construes ongoing emergency too narrowly. An emergency does not last only for the time between when the assailant pulls the trigger and the bullet hits the victim. If an out-of-sight sniper pauses between shots, no one would say that the emergency ceases during the pause. That is an extreme example and not the situation here, but it serves to highlight the implausibility, at least as to certain weapons, of construing the emergency to last only precisely as long as the violent act itself, as some have construed our opinion in *Davis*.

At no point during the questioning did either Covington or the police know the location of the shooter. In fact, Bryant was not at home by the time the police searched his house at approximately 5:30 a.m. At some point between 3 a.m. and 5:30 a.m., Bryant left his house. At bottom, there was an ongoing emergency here where an armed shooter, whose motive for and location after the shooting were unknown, had mortally wounded Covington within a few blocks and a few minutes of the location where the police found Covington.

This is not to suggest that the emergency continued until Bryant was arrested in California a year after the shooting. We need not decide precisely when the emergency ended because Covington's encounter with the police and all of the statements he made during that interaction occurred within the first few minutes of the police officers' arrival and well before they secured the scene of the shooting—the shooter's last known location.

We reiterate, moreover, that the existence *vel non* of an ongoing emergency is not the touchstone of the testimonial inquiry; rather, the ultimate inquiry is whether the "primary purpose of the interrogation [was] to enable police assistance to meet [the] ongoing emergency."

Davis. We turn now to that inquiry, as informed by the circumstances of the ongoing emergency just described. The circumstances of the encounter provide important context for understanding Covington's statements to the police. When the police arrived at Covington's side, their first question to him was "What happened?"[18] Covington's response was either "Rick shot me" or "I was shot," followed very quickly by an identification of "Rick" as the shooter. In response to further questions, Covington explained that the shooting occurred through the back door of Bryant's house and provided a physical description of the shooter. When he made the statements, Covington was lying in a gas station parking lot bleeding from a mortal gunshot wound to his abdomen. His answers to the police officers' questions were punctuated with questions about when emergency medical services would arrive. He was obviously in considerable pain and had difficulty breathing and talking. From this description of his condition and report of his statements, we cannot say that a person in Covington's situation would have had a "primary purpose" "to establish or prove past events potentially relevant to later criminal prosecution." *Davis.*

For their part, the police responded to a call that a man had been shot. As discussed above, they did not know why, where, or when the shooting had occurred. Nor did they know the location of the shooter or anything else about the circumstances in which the crime occurred.[19] The questions they asked—"what had happened, who had shot him, and where the shooting occurred,"—were the exact type of questions necessary to allow the police to " 'assess the situation, the threat to their own safety, and possible danger to the potential victim' " and to the public, including to allow them to ascertain "whether they would be encountering a violent felon," In other words, they solicited the information necessary to enable them "to meet an ongoing emergency."

Nothing in Covington's responses indicated to the police that, contrary to their expectation upon responding to a call reporting a shooting, there was no emergency or that a prior emergency had ended. Covington did indicate that he had been shot at another location about 25 minutes earlier, but he did not know the location of the shooter at the time the police arrived and, as far as we can tell from the record, he gave no indication that the shooter, having shot at him twice, would be satisfied that Covington was only wounded. In fact, Covington did not indicate any possible motive for the shooting, and thereby gave no reason to think that the shooter would not shoot again if he arrived on the scene. As we noted in *Davis,* "initial inquiries" may "*often* . . . produce nontestimonial statements." The initial inquiries in this case resulted in the type of nontestimonial statements we contemplated in *Davis.*

Finally, we consider the informality of the situation and the interrogation. This situation is more similar, though not identical, to the informal, harried 911 call in *Davis* than to the structured, station-house interview in *Crawford.* As the officers' trial testimony reflects, the situation was fluid and somewhat confused: the officers arrived at different times; apparently each, upon arrival, asked Covington "what happened?"; and, contrary to the dissent's portrayal, they did not conduct a structured interrogation. * * * The informality suggests that the interrogators' primary purpose was simply to address what they perceived to be an ongoing emergency, and the circumstances lacked any formality that would have alerted Covington to or focused him on the possible future prosecutorial use of his statements.

Because the circumstances of the encounter as well as the statements and actions of Covington and the police objectively indicate that the "primary purpose of the interrogation" was "to enable police assistance to meet an ongoing emergency," *Davis,* Covington's identification and

---

[18] Although the dissent claims otherwise, at least one officer asked Covington something akin to "how was he doing." * * *

[19] Contrary to the dissent's suggestion, and despite the fact that the record was developed prior to *Davis'* focus on the existence of an "ongoing emergency," the record contains some testimony to support the idea that the police officers were concerned about the location of the shooter when they arrived on the scene and thus to suggest that the purpose of the questioning of Covington was to determine the shooter's location. * * *

description of the shooter and the location of the shooting were not testimonial hearsay. The Confrontation Clause did not bar their admission at Bryant's trial. * * * We leave for the Michigan courts to decide on remand whether the statements' admission was otherwise permitted by state hearsay rules. The judgment of the Supreme Court of Michigan is vacated, and the case is remanded for further proceedings not inconsistent with this opinion.

JUSTICE THOMAS, concurring in the judgment.

I agree with the Court that the admission of Covington's out-of-court statements did not violate the Confrontation Clause, but I reach this conclusion because Covington's questioning by police lacked sufficient formality and solemnity for his statements to be considered "testimonial." See *Crawford*. * * * I have criticized the primary-purpose test as an "exercise in fiction" that is "disconnected from history" and "yields no predictable results" *Davis*. * * * As the majority notes, Covington interacted with the police under highly informal circumstances, while he bled from a fatal gunshot wound. The police questioning was not "a formalized dialogue," did not result in "formalized testimonial materials" such as a deposition or affidavit, and bore no "indicia of solemnity." Nor is there any indication that the statements were offered at trial "in order to evade confrontation." This interrogation bears little if any resemblance to the historical practices that the Confrontation Clause aimed to eliminate. Covington thus did not "bea[r] testimony" against Bryant, and the introduction of his statements at trial did not implicate the Confrontation Clause. I concur in the judgment.

JUSTICE SCALIA, dissenting.

* * * In its vain attempt to make the incredible plausible * * * today's opinion distorts our Confrontation Clause jurisprudence and leaves it in a shambles. * * * In *Crawford,* we held that [the Confrontation Clause] guarantees a defendant his common-law right to confront those "who 'bear testimony'" against him. A witness must deliver his testimony against the defendant in person, or the prosecution must prove that the witness is unavailable to appear at trial and that the defendant has had a prior opportunity for cross-examination.

Not all hearsay falls within the Confrontation Clause's grasp. At trial a witness "bears testimony" by providing " '[a] solemn declaration or affirmation . . . for the purpose of establishing or proving some fact.' " * * * The Confrontation Clause protects defendants only from hearsay statements that do the same. In *Davis,* we explained how to identify testimonial hearsay prompted by police questioning in the field. A statement is testimonial "when the circumstances objectively indicate . . . that the primary purpose of the interrogation is to establish or prove past events potentially relevant to later criminal prosecution." When, however, the circumstances objectively indicate that the declarant's statements were "a cry for help [o]r the provision of information enabling officers immediately to end a threatening situation," they bear little resemblance to in-court testimony. "No 'witness' goes into court to proclaim an emergency and seek help."

Crawford and *Davis* did not address whose perspective matters—the declarant's, the interrogator's, or both—when assessing "the primary purpose of [an] interrogation." In those cases the statements were testimonial from any perspective. I think the same is true here, but because the Court picks a perspective so will I: The declarant's intent is what counts. In-court testimony is more than a narrative of past events; it is a solemn declaration made in the course of a criminal trial. For an out-of-court statement to qualify as testimonial, the declarant must intend the statement to be a solemn declaration rather than an unconsidered or offhand remark; and he must make the statement with the understanding that it may be used to invoke the coercive machinery of the State against the accused.* * * A declarant-focused inquiry is also the only inquiry that would work in every fact pattern implicating the Confrontation Clause. The Clause applies to volunteered testimony as well as statements solicited through police interrogation. An inquiry into an officer's purposes would make no sense when a declarant blurts out "Rick shot me" as soon as the officer arrives on the scene.* * *

* * * From Covington's perspective, his statements had little value except to ensure the arrest and eventual prosecution of Richard Bryant. He knew the "threatening situation," had ended six blocks away and 25 minutes earlier when he fled from Bryant's back porch. Bryant had not confronted him face-to-face before he was mortally wounded, instead shooting him through a door. Even if Bryant had pursued him (unlikely), and after seeing that Covington had ended up at the gas station was unable to confront him there before the police arrived (doubly unlikely), it was entirely beyond imagination that Bryant would again open fire while Covington was surrounded by five armed police officers. And Covington knew the shooting was the work of a drug dealer, not a spree killer who might randomly threaten others.

Covington's knowledge that he had nothing to fear differs significantly from Michelle McCottry's state of mind during her "frantic" statements to a 911 operator at issue in *Davis,* Her "call was plainly a call for help against a bona fide physical threat" describing "events *as they were actually happening.*" She did not have the luxuries of police protection and of time and space separating her from immediate danger that Covington enjoyed when he made his statements.

Covington's pressing medical needs do not suggest that he was responding to an emergency, but to the contrary reinforce the testimonial character of his statements. He understood the police were focused on investigating a past crime, not his medical needs. None of the officers asked Covington how he was doing, attempted more than superficially to assess the severity of his wounds, or attempted to administer first aid. They instead primarily asked questions with little, if any, relevance to Covington's dire situation. Police, paramedics, and doctors do not need to know the address where a shooting took place, the name of the shooter, or the shooter's height and weight to provide proper medical care. Underscoring that Covington understood the officers' investigative role, he interrupted their interrogation to ask "when is EMS coming?" When, in other words, would the focus shift to his medical needs rather than Bryant's crime? * * *

[T]his is an absurdly easy case even if one (erroneously) takes the interrogating officers' purpose into account. The five officers interrogated Covington primarily to investigate past criminal events. None—absolutely none—of their actions indicated that they perceived an imminent threat. They did not draw their weapons, and indeed did not immediately search the gas station for potential shooters. To the contrary, all five testified that they questioned Covington *before conducting any investigation at the scene.* * * * Most tellingly, none of the officers started his interrogation by asking what would have been the obvious first question if any hint of such a fear existed: Where is the shooter? * * * [One Sergeant] candidly admitted that he interrogated Covington because he "ha[d] a man here that [he] believe[d] [was] dying [so he was] gonna find out who did this, period." In short, he needed to interrogate Covington to solve a crime. * * * At the very least, the officers' intentions *turned* investigative during their 10-minute encounter with Covington, and the conversation "evolve[d] into testimonial statements." * * *

* * * The Court's distorted view creates an expansive exception to the Confrontation Clause for violent crimes. Because Bryant posed a continuing threat to public safety in the Court's imagination, the emergency persisted for confrontation purposes at least until the police learned his "motive for and location after the shooting." It may have persisted in this case until the police "secured the scene of the shooting" two-and-a-half hours later. (The relevance of securing the scene is unclear so long as the killer is still at large—especially if, as the Court speculates, he may be a spree-killer.) This is a dangerous definition of emergency. Many individuals who testify against a defendant at trial first offer their accounts to police in the hours after a violent act. If the police can plausibly claim that a "potential threat to . . . the public" persisted through those first few hours, (and if the claim is plausible here it is always plausible) a defendant will have no constitutionally protected right to exclude the uncross-examined testimony of such witnesses. His

conviction could rest (as perhaps it did here) solely on the officers' recollection at trial of the witnesses' accusations.

The Framers could not have envisioned such a hollow constitutional guarantee. No framing-era confrontation case that I know of, neither here nor in England, took such an enfeebled view of the right to confrontation. * * * [I] doubt that under the Court's test English officials acted improperly by denying Raleigh and Fenwick the opportunity to confront their accusers "face to face." Under my approach, in contrast, those English trials remain unquestionably infamous. Lord Cobham did not speak with royal officials to end an ongoing emergency. He was a traitor! He spoke, as Raleigh correctly observed, to establish Raleigh's guilt and to save his own life. Cobham's statements, when assessed from his perspective, had only a testimonial purpose. The same is true of Covington's statements here.

* * * A statement during an ongoing emergency is sufficiently reliable, the Court says, "because the prospect of fabrication . . . is presumably significantly diminished," so it "does not [need] to be subject to the crucible of cross-examination." * * * The Court announces that in future cases it will look to "standard rules of hearsay, designed to identify some statements as reliable," when deciding whether a statement is testimonial. * * * We tried that approach to the Confrontation Clause for nearly 25 years before *Crawford rejected* it as an unworkable standard unmoored from the text and the historical roots of the Confrontation Clause. The arguments in Raleigh's infamous 17th-century treason trial contained full debate about the reliability of Lord Cobham's *ex parte* accusations; that case remains the canonical example of a Confrontation Clause violation, not because Raleigh should have won the debate but because he should have been allowed cross-examination.

* * * Reliability, the Court tells us, is a good indicator of whether "a statement is . . . an out-of-court substitute for trial testimony." That is patently false. Reliability tells us *nothing* about whether a statement is testimonial. Testimonial and nontestimonial statements alike come in varying degrees of reliability. An eyewitness's statements to the police after a fender-bender, for example, are both reliable and testimonial. Statements to the police from one driver attempting to blame the other would be similarly testimonial but rarely reliable.

* * * [W]e did not disavow multifactor balancing for reliability in *Crawford* out of a preference for rules over standards. We did so because it "d[id] violence to" the Framers' design. It was judges' open-ended determination of what was reliable that violated the trial rights of Englishmen in the political trials of the 16th and 17th centuries. The Framers placed the Confrontation Clause in the Bill of Rights to ensure that those abuses (and the abuses by the Admiralty courts in colonial America) would not be repeated in this country. Not even the least dangerous branch can be trusted to assess the reliability of uncross-examined testimony in politically charged trials or trials implicating threats to national security. * * *[b]

NOTES AND QUESTIONS

1. ***Forensic reports as testimony.*** The three dissenters in *Bryant*—Justices Scalia, Thomas, and Ginsburg—combined with Justices Kagan and Sotomayor to hold in *Bullcoming v. New Mexico*, 564 U.S. 647 (2011), that a forensic analyst's assertions about a defendant's blood-alcohol level, "formalized" in a signed "report" that referred to court rules providing for the admission of such analyses as evidence, were testimonial. Accordingly, admission of the report as a business record during the testimony of a government scientist who had neither observed nor

[b] Justice Ginsberg wrote a separate dissent in *Bryant*, agreeing with Justice Scalia that Covington's statements were testimonial, that "[t]he declarant's intent is what counts," and critiquing the Court for departing from earlier rulings that made it plain that "[r]eliability tells us nothing about whether a statement is testimonial." Justice Kagan did not participate in the case.

reviewed the analyses violated the defendant's confrontation rights. The decision relied on an earlier ruling, *Melendez-Diaz v. Massachusetts*, 557 U.S. 305 (2009), in which the Court had held that statements contained in forensic laboratory reports created specifically to serve as evidence in a criminal proceeding were also testimonial.

Then in *Williams v. Illinois*, 567 U.S. 50 (2012), the Court splintered over whether a defendant's Confrontation Clause rights were violated when a government expert testified about a DNA analysis that she did not conduct. No rationale commanded a majority. In a plurality opinion, the four justices who dissented in *Bullcoming* decided the statements in the DNA analyst's report discussed by the expert witness in *Williams* were not testimonial. The plurality reasoned that the report (1) was not offered for its truth but instead as a basis for the opinion of the expert witness; (2) was "not inherently inculpatory"; and (3) was "produced before any suspect was identified." All five other justices expressly rejected this reasoning. Four of the five—Justices Kagan, Sotomayor, Scalia, and Ginsburg—found the case indistinguishable from *Bullcoming* and concluded that introduction of the report through the expert witness denied Williams his right to cross examine the DNA analyst under the Confrontation Clause. Justice Thomas, however, delivered a separate opinion, which provided the fifth vote for *rejecting* the defendant's confrontation clause claim. Justice Thomas reasoned in *Williams* that the DNA report referenced by the expert witness was not "testimonial" because it lacked sufficient indicia of solemnity. "[T]he scope of the confrontation right is properly limited to extrajudicial statements similar in solemnity to the Marian examination practices that the Confrontation Clause was designed to prevent," he explained. "By certifying the truth of the analyst's representations, the unsworn *Bullcoming* report bore 'a "striking resemblance," ' to the Marian practice in which magistrates examined witnesses, typically on oath, and 'certif[ied] the results to the court.' " * * * Cellmark's report is marked by no such indicia of solemnity."

Most courts attempting to apply this confusing line of cases have ignored the solemnity standard articulated by Justice Thomas, and continue to apply only the "primary purpose" test declared prior to *Williams* in *Bryant*. Dissenting from a denial of certiorari in a subsequent case, Justice Gorsuch, joined by Justice Sotomayor, wrote that the "various opinions [in *Williams*] have sown confusion in courts across the country. * * * [W]e owe lower courts struggling to abide our holdings more clarity than we have afforded them in this area." *Stuart v. Alabama*, 139 S.Ct. 36 (2018).

2. ***Statements by young children; statements to those who must report to law enforcement.*** The Court applied its "primary purpose test" to statements made to "persons other than law enforcement officers" for the first time in OHIO v. CLARK, 135 S.Ct. 2173 (2015). There it considered whether the Confrontation Clause barred introduction into evidence of a 3-year-old's statements about physical abuse to a preschool teacher, after the trial court determined the child was incompetent to testify at trial under state law. The Court reasoned: " * * * Because at least some statements to individuals who are not law enforcement officers could conceivably raise confrontation concerns, we decline to adopt a categorical rule excluding them from the Sixth Amendment's reach. Nevertheless, such statements are much less likely to be testimonial than statements to law enforcement officers. And considering all the relevant circumstances here, L. P.'s statements clearly were not made with the primary purpose of creating evidence for Clark's prosecution. Thus, their introduction at trial did not violate the Confrontation Clause.

"L. P.'s statements occurred in the context of an ongoing emergency involving suspected child abuse. When L. P.'s teachers noticed his injuries, they rightly became worried that the 3-year-old was the victim of serious violence. Because the teachers needed to know whether it was safe to release L. P. to his guardian at the end of the day, they needed to determine who might be abusing the child. Thus, the immediate concern was to protect a vulnerable child who needed help. * * * As in *Bryant*, the emergency in this case was ongoing, and the circumstances were not entirely clear. L. P.'s teachers were not sure who had abused him or how best to secure his safety. Nor were they sure whether any other children might be at risk. As a result, their questions and L. P.'s answers were primarily aimed at identifying and ending the threat. Though not as harried, the conversation here was also similar to the 911 call in *Davis*. The teachers' questions were meant to identify the abuser in order to protect the victim from future attacks. Whether the teachers thought that this would be done by apprehending the abuser or by some other means is irrelevant. * * *

"There is no indication that the primary purpose of the conversation was to gather evidence for Clark's prosecution. * * * At no point did the teachers inform L. P. that his answers would be used to arrest or punish his abuser. L. P. never hinted that he intended his statements to be used by the police or prosecutors. And the conversation between L. P. and his teachers was informal and spontaneous. The teachers asked L. P. about his injuries immediately upon discovering them, in the informal setting of a preschool lunchroom and classroom, and they did so precisely as any concerned citizen would talk to a child who might be the victim of abuse. This was nothing like the formalized station-house questioning in *Crawford* or the police interrogation and battery affidavit in *Hammon*.

"L. P.'s age fortifies our conclusion that the statements in question were not testimonial. Statements by very young children will rarely, if ever, implicate the Confrontation Clause. * * * '[r]esearch on children's understanding of the legal system finds that' young children 'have little understanding of prosecution.' * * * Thus, it is extremely unlikely that a 3-year-old child in L. P.'s position would intend his statements to be a substitute for trial testimony. On the contrary, a young child in these circumstances would simply want the abuse to end, would want to protect other victims, or would have no discernible purpose at all.

"As a historical matter, moreover, there is strong evidence that statements made in circumstances similar to those facing L. P. and his teachers were admissible at common law. * * * It is thus highly doubtful that statements like L. P.'s ever would have been understood to raise Confrontation Clause concerns. Neither *Crawford* nor any of the cases that it has produced has mounted evidence that the adoption of the Confrontation Clause was understood to require the exclusion of evidence that was regularly admitted in criminal cases at the time of the founding. Certainly, the statements in this case are nothing like the notorious use of ex parte examination in Sir Walter Raleigh's trial for treason, which we have frequently identified as 'the principal evil at which the Confrontation Clause was directed.' *Crawford*.

"Finally, although we decline to adopt a rule that statements to individuals who are not law enforcement officers are categorically outside the Sixth Amendment, the fact that L. P. was speaking to his teachers remains highly relevant. Courts must evaluate challenged statements in context, and part of that context is the questioner's identity. Statements made to someone who is not principally charged with uncovering and prosecuting criminal behavior are significantly less likely to be testimonial than statements given to law enforcement officers. It is common sense that the relationship between a student and his teacher is very different from that between a citizen and the police. We do not ignore that reality. In light of these circumstances, the Sixth Amendment did not prohibit the State from introducing L.P.'s statements at trial.

" * * * Like all good teachers, they undoubtedly would have acted with the same purpose whether or not they had a state-law duty to report abuse. And mandatory reporting statutes alone cannot convert a conversation between a concerned teacher and her student into a law enforcement mission aimed primarily at gathering evidence for a prosecution. * * * "

Justice Thomas concurred in the judgment, finding L.Ps statements "bear no resemblance to the historical practices that the that the Confrontation Clause aimed to eliminate," as they were not "contained in formalized testimonial materials, such as affidavits, depositions, prior testimony, or confessions", nor "obtained in 'a formalized dialogue'; after the issuance of the warnings required by *Miranda*; while in police custody; or in an attempt to evade confrontation."

3. ***Virtual confrontation.*** In *Maryland v. Craig*, 497 U.S. 836 (1990), the Court upheld a state procedure that allowed the use of one-way, closed-circuit television to present at trial the testimony of a child victim in a sex abuse case. Unlike an earlier case in which the Court invalidated the use of a screen erected between the defendant and the witness in the courtroom, in this case the statute conditioned the use of the alternate procedure upon a case-specific finding that if the child had to testify from the witness stand in court, the child would suffer from such extreme emotional trauma, due to the presence of the defendant, that he or she could not "reasonably communicate." Another distinguishing factor was that the method of separation used in *Craig*—having the victim testify from another room, with the defendant, jury, and judge remaining in the courtroom—would probably be viewed by the jury as suggesting that the witness was fearful of testifying in the courtroom setting rather than fearful of testifying while looking at the defendant. Justice Scalia joined by three other justices dissented in *Craig*, arguing that the Confrontation Clause "guarantees specific trial procedures that were thought to assure reliable evidence, undeniably among which was 'face-to-face' confrontation."

Justice Scalia subsequently authored the majority opinion in *Crawford,* where he quoted Sir Walter Raleigh's cry, "Call my accuser before my face." See *Bryant,* footnote 4, p. 1310. Yet every jurisdiction authorizes testimony by child victims via closed-circuit television during which the witness does not actually see the defendant, under some conditions. Lower courts have continued to uphold witness testimony via audio visual technology under *Craig*, noting that the *Crawford* did not mention *Craig*, and addressed only *when* confrontation is required, not *what procedures* constitute confrontation. See, e.g., *United States v. Rosenau*, 870 F.Supp.2d 1109 (W.D. Wa. 2012): "It is difficult to imagine what Sir Walter Raleigh's peers would have thought of modern telecommunication technology. It seems at least plausible that a two-way videoconference allowing Raleigh and his jury to look on as Raleigh's representative cross-examined Cobham in person may have alleviated some of the injustice Raleigh faced. Given the technological progress the world has seen in the four centuries since Raleigh's trial, it seems reasonable that the requirements of confrontation could, in special circumstances, be satisfied in other ways." Do you agree?

4. ***Admissibility of testimonial statements of now unavailable witnesses, made during a proceeding in which the defendant had the opportunity to cross.*** Even if a statement is "testimonial," the Confrontation Clause permits its introduction against a defendant at trial if the person who made the statement both (1) is unavailable to testify at trial, and (2) was subject to cross-examination by the defendant when the statement was made. Death of a witness will establish "unavailability," as will the inability to secure the witness' presence despite reasonable good faith efforts. *Hardy v. Cross*, 565 U.S. 65 (2011) (citing *Barber v. Page*, 390 U.S. 719 (1968) and *Ohio v. Roberts*, 448 U.S. 56 (1980)).

The additional requirement of a "prior opportunity" to cross-examine is met when the statements to be admitted against the defendant at trial were made by a witness at a proceeding where the defendant had the *opportunity* to cross examine that witness. Testimony at a prior trial of the defendant, at the defendant's preliminary hearing, or deposition testimony taken with the defendant present would meet this requirement. *Crawford.* See also Note 4, p. 941 (discussing use of preliminary hearing testimony).

5. ***Interpreting the safeguards in the Sixth Amendment—the role of history and reliability.*** The Court in *Whorton v. Bockting*, 549 U.S. 406 (2007), unanimously held that the rule in *Crawford* would not apply retroactively, explaining: "*Crawford* overruled *Roberts* because *Roberts* was inconsistent with the original understanding of the meaning of the Confrontation Clause, not because the Court reached the conclusion that the overall effect of the *Crawford* rule

would be to improve the accuracy of fact finding in criminal trials. * * * Whatever improvement in reliability *Crawford* produced," the Court stated, "must be considered together with *Crawford's* elimination of Confrontation Clause protection against the admission of unreliable out-of-court nontestimonial statements."

How has the goal of promoting verdict accuracy affected the Court's interpretations of the several provisions of the Sixth Amendment—public trial, speedy trial, impartial jury, confrontation, compulsory process, and counsel? When and why has the Court rejected historical practice in favor of an interpretation more closely tied to the goal of promoting factually reliable verdicts? For debates on these issues in the confrontation context, see George Fisher, *The Crawford Debacle*, and Jeffrey L. Fisher, *Crawford v. Washington: The Next Ten Years* in Crawford v. Washington, A Ten-Year Retrospective, online at Mich.L.Rev. First Impressions; Ben Trachtenberg, *Testimonial Is As Testimonial Does*, 66 Fla. L. Rev. 467 (2014).

§ 3. RIGHTS TO REMAIN SILENT AND TO TESTIFY

GRIFFIN V. CALIFORNIA

380 U.S. 609, 85 S.Ct. 1229, 14 L.Ed.2d 106 (1965).

JUSTICE DOUGLAS delivered the opinion of the Court.

Petitioner was convicted of murder in the first degree after a jury trial in the California court [and sentenced to death]. He did not testify at the trial on the issue of guilt, though he did testify at the separate trial on the issue of penalty. The trial court instructed the jury on the issue of guilt, stating that a defendant has a constitutional right not to testify. But it told the jury:[2]

> "As to any evidence or facts against him which the defendant can reasonably be expected to deny or explain because of facts within his knowledge, if he does not testify or if, though he does testify, he fails to deny or explain such evidence, the jury may take that failure into consideration as tending to indicate the truth of such evidence and as indicating that among the inferences that may be reasonably drawn therefrom those unfavorable to the defendant are the more probable."

It added, however, that no such inference could be drawn as to evidence respecting which he had no knowledge. It stated that failure of a defendant to deny or explain the evidence of which he had knowledge does not create a presumption of guilt nor by itself warrant an inference of guilt nor relieve the prosecution of any of its burden of proof.

Petitioner had been seen with the deceased the evening of her death, the evidence placing him with her in the alley where her body was found. The prosecutor made much of the failure of petitioner to testify. * * *

[The Court agreed to] consider the single question whether comment on the failure to testify violated the Self-Incrimination Clause of the Fifth Amendment * * * .[3]

If this were a federal trial, reversible error would have been committed. *Wilson v. United States,* 149 U.S. 60 (1893) so holds. It is said, however, that the *Wilson* decision rested not on the

---

[2] Article I, § 13, of the California Constitution provides in part: " * * * in any criminal case, whether the defendant testifies or not, his failure to explain or to deny by his testimony any evidence or facts in the case against him may be commented upon by the court and by counsel, and may be considered by the court or the jury."

[3] The California Supreme Court later held that its "comment" rule squared with *Malloy v. Hogan,* 378 U.S. 1 (1964), [in which the court made the Clause applicable to the States]. The overwhelming consensus of the States, however, is opposed to allowing comment on the defendant's failure to testify. * * *

Fifth Amendment, but on an Act of Congress. 18 U.S.C. § 3481. * * * The question remains whether, statute or not, the comment rule, approved by California, violates the Fifth Amendment.

We think it does. It is in substance a rule of evidence that allows the State the privilege of tendering to the jury for its consideration the failure of the accused to testify. No formal offer of proof is made as in other situations; but the prosecutor's comment and the court's acquiescence are the equivalent of an offer of evidence and its acceptance. The Court in the *Wilson* case stated:

> " the act was framed with a due regard also to those who might prefer to rely upon the presumption of innocence which the law gives to every one, and not wish to be witnesses. It is not every one who can safely venture on the witness stand, though entirely innocent of the charge against him. Excessive timidity, nervousness when facing others and attempting to explain transactions of a suspicious character, and offenses charged against him, will often confuse and embarrass him to such a degree as to increase rather than remove prejudices against him. It is not every one, however honest, who would therefore willingly be placed on the witness stand. The statute, in tenderness to the weakness of those who from the causes mentioned might refuse to ask to be witnesses, particularly when they may have been in some degree compromised by their association with others, declares that the failure of a defendant in a criminal action to request to be a witness shall not create any presumption against him."

If the words "Fifth Amendment" are substituted for "Act" and for "statute" the spirit of the Self-Incrimination Clause is reflected. For comment on the refusal to testify is a remnant of the "inquisitorial system of criminal justice" which the Fifth Amendment outlaws. It is a penalty imposed by courts for exercising a constitutional privilege. It cuts down on the privilege by making its assertion costly. It is said, however, that the inference of guilt for failure to testify as to facts peculiarly within the accused's knowledge is in any event natural and irresistible, and that comment on the failure does not magnify that inference into a penalty for asserting a constitutional privilege. What the jury may infer given no help from the court is one thing. What they may infer when the court solemnizes the silence of the accused into evidence against him is quite another. * * *

We * * * hold that the Fifth Amendment, in its direct application to the federal government and its bearing on the States by reason of the Fourteenth Amendment, forbids either comment by the prosecution on the accused's silence or instructions by the court that such silence is evidence of guilt.[6]

JUSTICE STEWART, with whom JUSTICE WHITE joins, dissenting.

* * * I think that the Court in this case stretches the concept of compulsion beyond all reasonable bounds, and that whatever compulsion may exist derives from the defendant's choice not to testify, not from any comment by court or counsel. * * * How can it be said that the inferences drawn by a jury will be more detrimental to a defendant under the limiting and carefully controlling language of the instruction here involved than would result if the jury were left to roam at large with only their untutored instincts to guide them, to draw from the defendant's silence broad inferences of guilt? * * * No doubt the prosecution's argument will seek to encourage the drawing of inferences unfavorable to the defendant. However, the defendant's

---

6 We reserve decision on whether an accused can require that the jury be instructed that his silence must be disregarded. [Ed: The Court later resolved this question and held in *Carter v. Kentucky,* 450 U.S. 288 (1981), that "a trial judge has a powerful tool at his disposal to protect the constitutional privilege—the jury instruction—and he has an affirmative constitutional obligation to use that tool when a defendant seeks its employment. No judge can prevent jurors from speculating about why a defendant stands mute in the face of a criminal accusation, but a judge can, and must, if requested to do so, use the unique power of the jury instruction to reduce that speculation to a minimum." Indeed, a judge may give the instruction over the defendant's objection. *Lakeside v. Oregon,* 435 U.S. 333 (1978).]

counsel equally has an opportunity to explain the various other reasons why a defendant may not wish to take the stand, and thus rebut the natural if uneducated assumption that it is because the defendant cannot truthfully deny the accusations made. * * *

NOTES AND QUESTIONS

1. ***The constitutional right not to testify.*** Unlike most settings where a defendant must invoke his privilege against self-incrimination, a criminal defendant need not take the stand and assert the privilege at his own trial. That exception "reflects the fact that a criminal defendant has an 'absolute right not to testify.'" *Salinas v. Texas*, p. 586.

2. ***Criticisms of the* Griffin *rule barring comment on the right not to testify.*** In *Mitchell v. United States*, p. 1383, the Court, 5–4, declined to allow a sentencing judge to draw an adverse inference about the defendant's criminal conduct from the defendant's silence at sentencing. In dissent, Justice Scalia, joined by the Chief Justice and Justices O'Connor and Thomas, termed the *Griffin* rule "illogic[al]" and "counter to normal evidentiary inferences: If I ask my son whether he saw a movie I had forbidden him to watch, and he remains silent, the import of his silence is clear. Indeed, we have on other occasions recognized the significance of silence, saying that ' "[f]ailure to contest an assertion . . . is considered evidence of acquiescence . . . if it would have been natural under the circumstances to object to the assertion in question." ' *Baxter v. Palmigiano* [inference allowed in state prison disciplinary proceeding]."

"And as for history, *Griffin*'s pedigree is equally dubious. The question whether a factfinder may draw a logical inference from a criminal defendant's failure to offer formal testimony would not have arisen in 1791, because common-law evidentiary rules prevented a criminal defendant from testifying in his own behalf even if wanted to do so. * * * The longstanding common-law principle, *nemo tenetur seipsum prodere*, was thought to ban only testimony forced by compulsory oath or physical torture, not voluntary, unsworn testimony. [Under the Marian Committal Statute, the justice of the peace was required to take the examination of the arrested person not under oath and to record his response]. * * * The justice of the peace testified at trial as to the content of the defendant's statement; if the defendant refused to speak, this would also have been reported to the jury. * * * At trial, defendants were expected to speak directly to the jury. Sir James Stephen described 17th- and 18th-century English trials as follows: '[T]he prisoner in cases of felony could not be defended by counsel, and had therefore to speak for himself. He was thus unable to say . . . that his mouth was closed. On the contrary his mouth was not only open, but the evidence given against him operated as so much indirect questioning, and if he omitted to answer the questions it suggested he was very likely to be convicted.' * * * Our hardy forebearers, who thought of compulsion in terms of the rack and oaths forced by the power of law, would not have viewed the drawing of a commonsensical inference as equivalent pressure. And it is implausible that the Americans of 1791, who were subject to adverse inferences for failing to give unsworn testimony, would have viewed an adverse inference for failing to give sworn testimony as a violation of the Fifth Amendment." *"Griffin* is impossible to square with the text of the Fifth Amendment," Justices Thomas and Scalia reiterated in a later case. "A defendant is not 'compelled . . . to be a witness against himself' simply because a jury has been told that it may draw an adverse inference from his silence." *Salinas v. Texas*, (Thomas, J., concurring, joined by Scalia, J.), p. 586.

3. ***Assessing prosecution comment.*** *Griffin* has spawned an immense body of case law addressing when a particular prosecutorial statement does or does not constitute an adverse comment on the defendant's failure to take the stand. The general standard for resolving that issue is whether "(1) the prosecutor manifestly intended to refer to the defendant's silence or (2) a jury would naturally and necessarily take the remark for a comment on the defendant's silence. *United States v. Tucker*, 714 F.3d 1006 (7th Cir. 2013).

This inquiry, like that used to determine when other arguments violate due process, see Section 4, infra, is contextual. In *United States v. Robinson,* 485 U.S. 25 (1988), defense counsel in closing argument urged several times that the government had not allowed the defendant (who did not testify) to explain his side of the story and had unfairly denied him the opportunity to explain his actions. In rebuttal, the prosecutor remarked that defendant "could have taken the stand and explained it to you." Applying the "principle that prosecutorial comment must be examined in context," *Lockett v. Ohio,* 438 U.S. 586 (1978), the Court concluded: "[T]he prosecutorial comment did not treat the defendant's silence as substantive evidence of guilt, but instead referred to the possibility of testifying as one of several opportunities which the defendant was afforded, contrary to the statement of his counsel, to explain his side of the case. Where * * * the prosecutor's reference to the defendant's opportunity to testify is a fair response to a claim made by defendant or his counsel, we think there is no violation of the privilege." Once a violation of *Griffin* is established on appeal, harmless error review applies. See *Chapman*, p. 1417.

4. ***Other burdens on the right to remain silent—order of the testimony.*** In *Brooks v. Tennessee*, 406 U.S. 605 (1972), the Court invalidated a statute which required that a criminal defendant "desiring to testify shall do so before any other testimony for the defense is heard," a rule related to the ancient practice of sequestering prospective witnesses in order to prevent their being influenced by other testimony in the case. See, e.g., Fed.R.Evid. 615. The Court, per Brennan J., held first, that the statute "violates an accused's constitutional right to remain silent," as a defendant "cannot be absolutely certain that his witnesses will testify as expected or that they will be effective on the stand" and thus "may not know at the close of the State's case whether his own testimony will be necessary or even helpful to his cause." "Pressuring the defendant to take the stand, by foreclosing later testimony if he refuses, is not a constitutionally permissible means of ensuring his honesty. It fails to take into account the very real and legitimate concerns that might motivate a defendant to exercise his right of silence. And it may compel even a wholly truthful defendant, who might otherwise decline to testify for legitimate reasons, to subject himself to impeachment and cross-examination at a time when the strength of his other evidence is not yet clear." The Court also held that the statute constitutes "an infringement on the defendant's right of due process," as "by requiring the accused and his lawyer to make [the choice of whether to testify] without an opportunity to evaluate the actual worth of their evidence," the accused is "thereby deprived of the 'guiding hand of counsel' in the timing of this critical element of his defense." Chief Justice Burger, joined by Blackmun and Rehnquist, JJ., in dissent, argued that there was no violation of the right to remain silent in that the defendant was not confronted with a choice any more difficult than that approved by the Court in *Williams v. Florida,* p. 1106; and that there was no due process violation because counsel may "be restricted by ordinary rules of evidence and procedure in presenting an accused's defense" even "if it might be more advantageous to present it in some other way," as illustrated by the rule forbidding counsel from asking leading questions of the defendant. See also Note 2, p. 1110 (discussing *Brooks*).

5. ***Constitutional right to testify.*** In *Rock v. Arkansas,* 483 U.S. 44 (1987), the Court held that a state's per se exclusion of hypnotically refreshed testimony by the defendant violated the defendant's constitutional right to testify on her own behalf. That constitutional right, the Court noted, stems from three sources: (1) the Fourteenth Amendment's guarantee of due process (which includes "a right to be heard and to offer testimony"); (2) the Sixth Amendment's Compulsory Process Clause (the accused's right to call witnesses in his favor "logically include[s] * * * a right to testify himself, should he decide it is in his favor to do so"); and (3) the Fifth Amendment's self-incrimination guarantee (the "opportunity to testify is a necessary corollary to the * * * guarantee against compelled testimony"). While the defendant's constitutional right to testify is not without limitation, restrictions placed on that right by state evidentiary rules "may not be arbitrary or disproportionate to the purposes they are designed to serve." Though the state has a legitimate interest in barring unreliable evidence, that interest did not justify a per se

exclusion of defendant's hypnotically refreshed testimony without regard to procedural safeguards employed to reduce inaccuracies and the availability of corroborating evidence and other traditional means of assessing accuracy.

6. ***The impact of prior conviction impeachment on the right to testify.*** Studies of convicted defendants later exonerated by DNA evidence have demonstrated that the inference at issue in *Griffin*—that a defendant who does not testify must be guilty—is unreliable. One study found 39% of those convicted but later exonerated did not testify at their trials. The primary reason these innocent defendants stayed off the stand, the author concluded, was "the fear of impeachment with their prior convictions. Virtually all the defendants who did not testify had a prior record that likely would have been disclosed to the jury had they taken the stand." John H. Blume, *The Dilemma of the Criminal Defendant with a Prior Record—Lessons from the Wrongfully Convicted*, 5 J. Emp. Leg. Stud. 477 (2008).

Almost all jurisdictions permit impeachment with prior convictions. Jurors are instructed that they may consider a testifying defendant's prior conviction only when deciding whether to believe the defendant's testimony, not as evidence that the defendant must have committed the charged crime. But studies suggest that jurors continue to infer propensity from prior convictions anyway. For example, one study found that mock jurors convicted a burglary defendant 82% of the time when they learned that the defendant had a prior robbery conviction, 73% of the time when impeached with a fraud conviction, and only 62% of the time when no prior crimes were used for impeachment. Jeffrey Bellin, *The Silence Penalty*, 103 Iowa L. Rev. 395 (2018).

Defendants with prior convictions who go to trial must choose: stay off the stand knowing jurors may draw an improper adverse inference from silence; or testify knowing jurors may improperly infer criminal propensity from convictions introduced only for impeachment. The increased likelihood of conviction when jurors infer guilt from *silence* is about as strong as the increased likelihood of conviction when jurors infer guilt from *prior conviction*, concluded Professor Bellin. The choice also affects many more defendants today than it did back in the mid-20th Century, because of the enormous increase in the proportion of defendants, particularly African American defendants, with prior records. Writes Bellin, the "dilemma inevitably contributes to a steady increase in guilty pleas and a corresponding decrease in trials. . . . The cycle is self-perpetuating. Every new conviction leads to a decreased likelihood of success in a subsequent trial and a stronger incentive to plead guilty."

Do these studies or changed circumstances warrant modification of the rules concerning the right to testify, the right not to testify, or the use of convictions to impeach? Commentary and state law is collected in the sources cited above, as well as Anna Roberts, *Reclaiming the Importance of the Defendant's Testimony: Prior Conviction Impeachment and the Fight Against Implicit Stereotyping*, 83 U. Chi. L. Rev. 835 (2016), and Montré D. Carodine, *'The Mis-Characterization of the Negro': A Race Critique of the Prior Conviction Impeachment Rule* (2009), 84 Indiana L. J. 521 (2009).

7. ***Other burdens on the right to testify.*** In *Portuondo v. Agard*, 529 U.S. 61 (2000), the prosecutor in closing argument questioned defendant's credibility as a witness, pointing out that defendant, unlike the other witnesses, had been present throughout the trial and was thus able to hear what the others said before he testified. The defendant contended those comments "burdened his Sixth Amendment right to be present at trial and to be confronted with the witnesses against him, and his Fifth and Sixth Amendment rights to testify on his own behalf," and asked the Court to extend to the comments in his case "the rationale of *Griffin*." But the Court, per Scalia, J., after finding no "historical support" for defendant's claim, found *Griffin* to be "a poor analogue." "What we prohibited the prosecutor from urging the jury to do in *Griffin* was something *the jury is not permitted to do.* * * * By contrast, it *is* natural and irresistible for a jury, in evaluating the relative credibility of a defendant who testifies last, to have in mind and weigh in

the balance the fact that he heard the testimonial of all those who preceded him." The Court reasoned, "*Griffin* prohibited comments that suggest a defendant's silence is evidence of *guilt*. * * * The prosecutor's comments in this case, by contrast, concerned respondent's *credibility as a witness*, and were therefore in accord with the longstanding rule that when a defendant takes the stand, 'his credibility may be impeached and his testimony assailed like that of any other witness.' "

§ 4. LIMITS ON PREJUDICIAL ARGUMENT

DARDEN V. WAINWRIGHT

477 U.S. 168, 106 S.Ct. 2464, 91 L.Ed.2d 144 (1986).

JUSTICE POWELL delivered the opinion of the Court.

[The horrific facts related in detail by the Court are summarized here. A black man entered a furniture store, and left briefly after Mrs. Turman had shown him several items. Upon returning, the man forced her at gunpoint to open the register at the back of the store. Taking the cash, he was confronted at the back door by Mr. Turman, and shot him between the eyes. Leaving Mr. Turman "face-up in the rain," he told Ms. Turman to remove her false teeth, unzipped his pants, unbuckled his belt, and demanded Mrs. Turman perform oral sex on him, just "five feet from where her husband lay dying." When a 16 year-old boy arrived, the man shot him three times, after an initial misfire. The boy survived; Mr. Turman died.

Minutes after the murder and less than four miles from the store, Darden, on furlough driving a car borrowed from his girlfriend, crashed trying to avoid a head on collision. The driver of the oncoming car stopped to see if he could help, and testified that as he approached, the other driver was zipping up his pants and buckling his belt. When the police arrived at the scene, Darden was gone, having obtained a ride from a bystander. He later returned with a wrecker, only to find that police had towed the car away. A .38 revolver was found near the crash with shells showing one shot, one misfire, followed by three shots. Darden was arrested, Mrs. Turman identified him at a preliminary hearing as her husband's murderer, and the boy selected his picture from a photo array as the man who shot him.[1] An expert later testified that a bullet from a .38 killed Turman. Darden was convicted and sentenced to death. The federal district court denied habeas relief, the Eleventh Circuit affirmed.]* * *

---

[1] There are some minor discrepancies in the eyewitness identification. Mrs. Turman first described her assailant immediately after the murder while her husband was being taken to the emergency room. She told the investigating officer that the attacker was a heavyset man. When asked if he was "neat in his appearance, clean-looking, clean-shaven," she responded "[a]s far as I can remember, yes, sir." She also stated to the officer that she thought that the attacker was about her height, 5′6″ tall, and that he was wearing a pullover shirt with a stripe around the neck. The first time she saw petitioner after the attack was when she identified him at the preliminary hearing. She had not read any newspaper accounts of the crime, nor had she seen any picture of petitioner. When she was asked if petitioner was the man who had committed the crimes, she said yes. She also repeatedly identified him at trial.

Phillip Arnold first identified petitioner in a photo line-up while in the hospital. He could not speak at the time, and in response to the written question whether petitioner had a mustache, Phillip wrote back "I don't think so." Phillip also testified at trial that the attacker was a heavyset man wearing a dull, light color knit shirt with a ring around the neck. He testified that the man was almost his height, about 6′2″ tall.

A motorist who stopped at the scene of the accident testified that petitioner was wearing a white or off-grey button-down shirt and that he had a slight mustache. In fact, the witness stated that he "didn't know it was that [the mustache] or the raindrops on him or not. I couldn't really tell that much to it, it was real thin, that's all." Petitioner is about 5′10″ tall, and at the time of trial testified that he weighed about 175 pounds.

Petitioner * * * contends that the prosecution's closing argument at the guilt-innocence stage of the trial rendered his conviction fundamentally unfair and deprived the sentencing determination of the reliability that the Eighth Amendment requires.

* * * The prosecutors' comments must be evaluated in light of the defense argument that preceded it, which blamed the Polk County Sheriff's Office for a lack of evidence,[5] alluded to the death penalty,[6] characterized the perpetrator of the crimes as an "animal,"[7] and contained counsel's personal opinion of the strength of the state's evidence.[8]

The prosecutors then made their closing argument. That argument deserves the condemnation it has received from every court to review it, although no court has held that the argument rendered the trial unfair. Several comments attempted to place some of the blame for the crime on the Division of Corrections, because Darden was on weekend furlough from a prison sentence when the crime occurred.[9] Some comments implied that the death penalty would be the only guarantee against a future similar act.[10] Others incorporated the defense's use of the word "animal."[11] Prosecutor McDaniel made several offensive comments reflecting an emotional reaction to the case.[12] These comments undoubtedly were improper. But * * *, it "is not enough that the prosecutors' remarks were undesirable or even universally condemned." The relevant question is whether the prosecutors' comments "so infected the trial with unfairness as to make the resulting conviction a denial of due process." *Donnelly v. DeChristoforo,* 416 U.S. 637 (1974).

* * * [W]e agree * * * these comments * * * did not deprive petitioner of a fair trial. The prosecutors' argument did not manipulate or misstate the evidence, nor did it implicate other specific rights of the accused such as the right to counsel or the right to remain silent. Much of the objectionable content was invited by or was responsive to the opening summation of the defense. As we explained in *United States v. Young*, 470 U.S. 1 (1985), the idea of "invited response" is used not to excuse improper comments, but to determine their effect on the trial as a whole. The trial

---

5 "The Judge is going to tell you to consider the evidence or the lack of evidence. We have a lack of evidence, almost criminally negligent on the part of the Polk County Sheriff's Office in this case. You could go on and on about it."

6 "They took a coincidence and magnified that into a capital case. And they are asking you to kill a man on coincidence."

7 "The first witness you saw was Mrs. Turman, who was a pathetic figure; who worked and struggled all of her life to build what little she had, the little furniture store; and a woman who was robbed, sexually assaulted, and then had her husband slaughtered before her eyes, by what would have to be a vicious animal." Record 717. "And this murderer ran after him, aimed again, and this poor kid with half his brains blown away. . . . It's the work of an animal, there's no doubt about it."

8 * * * "The question is, do they have enough evidence to kill that man, enough evidence? And I honestly do not think they do."

9 "As far as I am concerned, there should be another Defendant in this courtroom, one more, and that is the division of corrections, the prisons. . . . Can we expect him to stay in a prison when they go there? Can we expect them to stay locked up once they go there? Do we know that they're going to be out on the public with guns, drinking?" * * *

10 "I will ask you to advise the Court to give him death. That's the only way I know that he is not going to get out on the public. It's the only way I know. It's the only way I can be sure of it. It's the only way anybody can be sure of it now, because the people that turned him loose—."

11 "As far as I am concerned, and as Mr. Maloney said as he identified this man as an animal, this animal was on the public for one reason."

12 "He shouldn't be out of his cell unless he has a leash on him and a prison guard at the other end of that leash." Record 750. "I wish [Mr. Turman] had had a shotgun in his hand when he walked in the back door and blown his [Darden's] face off. I wish I could see him sitting here with no face, blown away by a shotgun." Record 758. "I wish someone had walked in the back door and blown his head off at that point." Record 759. "He fired in the boy's back, number five saving one. Didn't get a chance to use it. I wish he had used it on himself." Record 774. "I wish he had been killed in the accident, but he wasn't. Again, we are unlucky that time." Record 775. "Don't forget what he has done according to those witnesses, to make every attempt to change his appearance from September the 8th, 1973. The hair, the goatee, even the moustache and the weight. The only thing he hasn't done that I know of is cut his throat." Record 779. After this, the last in a series of such comments, defense counsel objected for the first time.

court instructed the jurors several times that their decision was to be made on the basis of the evidence alone, and that the arguments of counsel were not evidence. The weight of the evidence against petitioner was heavy; the "overwhelming eyewitness and circumstantial evidence to support a finding of guilt on all charges," reduced the likelihood that the jury's decision was influenced by argument. Finally, defense counsel made the tactical decision not to present any witness other than petitioner. This decision not only permitted them to give their summation prior to the prosecution's closing argument, but also gave them the opportunity to make a final rebuttal argument. Defense counsel were able to use the opportunity for rebuttal very effectively, turning much of the prosecutors' closing argument against them by placing many of the prosecutors' comments and actions in a light that was more likely to engender strong disapproval than result in inflamed passions against petitioner.[14] For these reasons, we agree with the District Court below that "Darden's trial was not perfect—few are—but neither was it fundamentally unfair."[15]

JUSTICE BLACKMUN, with whom JUSTICE BRENNAN, JUSTICE MARSHALL, and JUSTICE STEVENS join, dissenting.

* * * Today's opinion * * * reveals a Court willing to tolerate not only imperfection but a level of fairness and reliability so low it should make conscientious prosecutors cringe. * * * The following brief comparison of established standards of prosecutorial conduct with the prosecutors' behavior in this case merely illustrates, but hardly exhausts, the scope of the misconduct involved:

1. "A lawyer shall not . . . state a personal opinion as to . . . the credibility [of] a witness . . . or the guilt or innocence of an accused." Model Rules of Professional Conduct, Rule 3.4(e). * * * Yet one prosecutor, White, stated: "I am convinced, as convinced as I know I am standing before you today, that Willie Jasper Darden is a murderer, that he murdered Mr. Turman, that he robbed Mrs. Turman and that he shot to kill Phillip Arnold. I will be convinced of that the rest of my life." And the other prosecutor, McDaniel, stated, with respect to Darden's testimony: " * * * If I am ever over in that chair over there, facing life or death, life imprisonment or death, I guarantee you I will lie until my teeth fall out."

2. "The prosecutor should refrain from argument which would divert the jury from its duty to decide the case on the evidence, by injecting issues broader than the guilt or innocence of the accused under the controlling law, or by making predictions of the consequences of the jury's verdict." ABA Standards, The Prosecution Function, § 3–5.8(d). * * * Yet McDaniel's argument was filled with references to Darden's status as a prisoner on furlough who "shouldn't be out of his cell unless he has a leash on him." * * *

3. "The prosecutor should not use arguments calculated to inflame the passions or prejudices of the jury." ABA Standards, § 3–5.8(c); see *Berger v. United States* [Note 1, p. 1330]. Yet McDaniel repeatedly expressed a wish "that I could see [Darden] sitting here with no face, blown away by a shotgun." Indeed, I do not think McDaniel's summation, taken as a whole, can accurately be described as anything but a relentless and single-minded attempt to inflame the jury. * * *

---

14 "Mr. McDaniel made an impassioned plea, . . . how many times did he repeat [it]? I wish you had been shot, I wish they had blown his face away. My God, I get the impression he would like to be the man that stands there and pulls the switch on him." One of Darden's counsel testified at the habeas corpus hearing that he made the tactical decision not to object to the improper comments. Based on his long experience with prosecutor McDaniel, he knew McDaniel would "get much more vehement in his remarks if you allowed him to go on." By not immediately objecting, he hoped to encourage the prosecution to commit reversible error.

15 Justice Blackmun's dissenting opinion mistakenly argues that the Court today finds, in essence, that any error was harmless, and then criticizes the Court for not applying the harmless error standard. We do not decide the claim of prosecutorial misconduct on the ground that it was harmless error. In our view of the case, that issue is not presented. Rather, we agree with the holding of every court that has addressed the issue—that the prosecutorial argument, in the context of the facts and circumstances of this case, did not render respondent's trial unfair—i.e., that it was not constitutional error. * * *

The Court presents what is, for me, an entirely unpersuasive one-page laundry list of reasons for ignoring this blatant misconduct. * * * I simply do not believe the evidence in this case was so overwhelming that this Court can conclude, on the basis of the written record before it, that the jury's verdict was not the product of the prosecutors' misconduct. The three most damaging pieces of evidence—the identifications of Darden by Phillip Arnold and Helen Turman and the ballistics evidence—are all sufficiently problematic that they leave me unconvinced that a jury not exposed to McDaniel's egregious summation would necessarily have convicted Darden. * * *. Darden testified at trial on his own behalf and denied any involvement in the robbery and murder. His account of his actions on the day of the crime was contradicted only by Mrs. Turman's and Arnold's identifications [and] a number of the State's witnesses corroborated parts of Darden's account. The trial judge who had seen and heard Darden testify found that he "emotionally and with what appeared on its face to be sincerity, proclaimed his innocence." In setting sentence, he viewed the fact that Darden "repeatedly professed his complete innocence of the charges" as a mitigating factor.

Thus, at bottom, this case rests on the jury's determination of the credibility of three witnesses—Helen Turman and Phillip Arnold, on the one side, and Willie Darden, on the other. I cannot conclude that McDaniel's sustained assault on Darden's very humanity did not affect the jury's ability to judge the credibility question on the real evidence before it. Because I believe that he did not have a trial that was fair, I would reverse Darden's conviction; I would not allow him to go to his death until he has been convicted at a fair trial.[a]

NOTES AND QUESTIONS

1. ***Prohibited argument.*** Justice Blackmun's dissent notes three categories of prosecutorial argument that are universally deemed improper. Also barred are arguments that impugn the integrity of defense counsel, that misstate the law, that refer to the possibility of a lenient sentence, that constitute impermissible comments on the defendant's silence, see Note 3, p. 1324, or that refer to evidence or witness statements not admitted into the record.

A famous statement of Justice Sutherland in *Berger v. United States*, 295 U.S. 78 (1935), explains why: "The United States Attorney is the representative not of an ordinary party to a controversy, but of a sovereignty whose obligation to govern impartially is as compelling as its obligation to govern at all; and whose interest, therefore, in a criminal prosecution is not that it shall win a case, but that justice shall be done. As such, he is in a peculiar and very definite sense the servant of the law, the twofold aim of which is that guilt shall not escape or innocence suffer. He may prosecute with earnestness and vigor—indeed, he should do so. But, while he may strike hard blows, he is not at liberty to strike foul ones. It is as much his duty to refrain from improper methods calculated to produce a wrongful conviction as it is to use every legitimate means to bring about a just one. * * * It is fair to say that the average jury, in a greater or less degree, has confidence that these obligations, which so plainly rest upon the prosecuting attorney, will be faithfully observed. Consequently, improper suggestions, insinuations, and, especially, assertions of personal knowledge are apt to carry much weight against the accused when they should properly carry none."

In barring the injecting of issues "broader than the guilt or innocence of the accused," courts have disapproved of arguments that a conviction is needed to "send a message" to other potential criminals, to relieve community fears, or to provide an example for the young people in the

---

[a] Darden was executed in 1988, still protesting his innocence. See *Florida Executes Celebrated Killer*, N.Y. Times, March 16, 1998. The case attracted worldwide attention from many who believed Darden was railroaded because he was black and the victim was white, including Nobel Peace Prize winner Andrei D. Sakharov, Democratic presidential candidate Jesse Jackson, and Amnesty International.

community. Courts have also condemned appeals to jurors as the taxpayers who pay for the costs of trial or defense counsel.

Audio visual aids, such as PowerPoint slides, provide ample opportunity for prosecutors to go "too far," leading to reversals when slides were shown containing content such as the word "GUILTY" superimposed in blood red letters in two directions forming an "X" shape across a photo of the defendant's face, or the statement "Defendant's Story is a Lie." "No legitimate purpose is served" by such displays, and they undermine the defendant's right to a fair trial.

2. ***Standard of review.*** To assess whether improper argument requires a new trial, most jurisdictions apply the due process standard set forth in *Darden*, and place the burden on the defendant to establish prejudice. In making that determination, appellate courts commonly will look to whether the improper remarks were (1) particularly egregious; (2) combined with other trial errors; (3) only isolated episodes in an otherwise proper argument; (4) invited or provoked by the improper comments of the defense; (5) objected to by the defense, thereby indicating fear of prejudice; (6) followed by corrective action by the judge, such as jury instructions to disregard; and (7) whether there was overwhelming evidence of guilt.

3. ***Defense argument.*** Rules of professional responsibility impose restrictions on defense counsel as on prosecutors: defense counsel typically will not be allowed to express a personal belief or opinion as to guilt or innocence, use arguments calculated to inflame the passions or prejudices of the jurors, or seek to inject broader issues that divert the jury from its duty to decide the case on the evidence. See Model Rules of Professional Conduct, R. 3.4 (single provision applicable to counsel for both sides). Should defense counsel be given more leeway than the prosecution in closing argument?

4. ***Sanctions and deterrence.*** For decades, appellate courts have "bemoaned the 'disturbing frequency' and the 'unheeded condemnations' " of clearly improper prosecutorial argument. Bennett Gershman, *Trial Error and Misconduct* § 10.1 (3d ed.). Although some courts have suggested that "they might well be required to reverse convictions without a showing of prejudice to deter such prosecutorial misconduct, * * * this has been done only rarely." CRIMPROC § 24.7(i). The prevailing view remains that expressed in *United States v. Modica*, 663 F.2d 1173 (2d Cir. 1981): "Reversal is an ill-suited remedy for prosecutorial misconduct; it does not affect the prosecutor directly, but rather imposes upon society the cost of retrying an individual who was fairly convicted."

In a related context, the Court has barred federal courts from granting relief for even repeated or intentional misconduct without first assessing its potential effect on the proceeding. In *United States v. Hasting*, 461 U.S. 499 (1983), the prosecutor's continuing improper references to the defendant's decision not to testify should have been reviewed under the harmless error standard established in *Chapman*, the Court held. Later, *in Bank of Nova Scotia v. United States*, Note 2, p. 977, a case of misconduct during a grand jury proceeding, the Court explained that granting a "windfall to the unprejudiced defendant" in an attempt to deter "objectionable prosecutorial misconduct" is not necessary when means "more narrowly tailored to deter . . . are available.' "

Those means include sanctions that "focus on the culpable individual," such as, for federal prosecutors, review of alleged misconduct by the Office of Professional Responsibility. Available studies, however, find that bar discipline is rarely visited on federal or state prosecutors who have been found to have engaged in misconduct. CRIMPROC § 1.7(j) (discussing studies). See also Note 3 p. 1424 and footnote a, p. 980. A day in jail or a hefty fine for contempt carries a more personal sting than losing a case, but contempt penalties are rarely imposed. Even more uncommon is the criminal prosecution of an errant prosecutor, which may require the extraordinary step of appointing a special prosecutor. A civil suit for damages, sometimes used to control constitutional violations by other actors in the criminal justice system, was taken off the table as a means of regulating prosecutors decades ago when, in a case involving a prosecutor alleged to have permitted a witness to lie at a capital murder trial, the Court held that absolute immunity bars a defendant from seeking civil damages from a prosecutor for actions taken in his role as prosecutor. *Imbler v. Pachtman*, 424 U.S. 409 (1976). See also *Connick v. Thompson*, 563 U.S. 51 (2011) (a district attorney's office may not be held liable under § 1983 for failure to train its prosecutors based on a single *Brady* violation).

§ 5. THE RIGHT TO A PUBLIC TRIAL

PRESLEY V. GEORGIA

558 U.S. 209, 130 S.Ct. 721, 175 L.Ed.2d 675 (2010).

[Before selecting a jury in Presley's trial, the trial judge excluded the lone courtroom observer, Presley's uncle, over defense counsel's objection. The judge explained, stating " '[t]here just isn't space * * * . "Each of those rows will be occupied by jurors. And his uncle cannot sit and intermingle with members of the jury panel.' " After Presley was convicted, the trial judge denied his motion for a new trial based on the exclusion of the public, and the ruling was affirmed by Georgia's appellate courts. On direct appeal, the Supreme Court reversed.]

PER CURIAM. * * * This Court's rulings with respect to the public trial right rest upon two different provisions of the Bill of Rights, both applicable to the States via the Due Process Clause of the Fourteenth Amendment. * * * The Sixth Amendment directs, in relevant part, that "[i]n all criminal prosecutions, the accused shall enjoy the right to a speedy and public trial . . . ." * * * [T]he public trial right extends beyond the accused and can be invoked under the First Amendment. *Press-Enterprise I,* [Note 2, p. 1295]. [This case] is brought under the Sixth Amendment, for it is the accused who invoked his right to a public trial. An initial question is whether the right to a public trial in criminal cases extends to the jury selection phase of trial, and in particular the *voir dire* of prospective jurors. In the First Amendment context that question was answered in *Press-Enterprise I.* The Court there held that the *voir dire* of prospective jurors must be open to the public under the First Amendment. Later in the same Term as *Press-Enterprise I,* the Court considered a Sixth Amendment case concerning whether the public trial right extends to a pretrial hearing on a motion to suppress certain evidence. *Waller v. Georgia,* [Note 2, p. 1295]. The *Waller* Court relied heavily upon *Press-Enterprise I* in finding that the Sixth Amendment right to a public trial extends beyond the actual proof at trial. It ruled that the pretrial suppression hearing must be open to the public because "there can be little doubt that the explicit Sixth Amendment right of the accused is no less protective of a public trial than the implicit First Amendment right of the press and public."

* * * The extent to which the First and Sixth Amendment public trial rights are coextensive is an open question, and it is not necessary here to speculate whether or in what circumstances the reach or protections of one might be greater than the other. Still, there is no legitimate reason, at least in the context of juror selection proceedings, to give one who asserts a First Amendment privilege greater rights to insist on public proceedings than the accused has. * * * There could be no explanation for barring the accused from raising a constitutional right that is unmistakably for his or her benefit. That rationale suffices to resolve the instant matter.

* * * While the accused does have a right to insist that the *voir dire* of the jurors be public, there are exceptions to this general rule. "[T]he right to an open trial may give way in certain cases to other rights or interests, such as the defendant's right to a fair trial or the government's interest in inhibiting disclosure of sensitive information." *Waller*. "Such circumstances will be rare, however, and the balance of interests must be struck with special care." *Waller* provided standards

for courts to apply before excluding the public from any stage of a criminal trial: "[T]he party seeking to close the hearing must advance an overriding interest that is likely to be prejudiced, the closure must be no broader than necessary to protect that interest, the trial court must consider reasonable alternatives to closing the proceeding, and it must make findings adequate to support the closure."

* * * Trial courts are obligated to take every reasonable measure to accommodate public attendance at criminal trials. Nothing in the record shows that the trial court could not have accommodated the public at Presley's trial. Without knowing the precise circumstances, some possibilities include reserving one or more rows for the public; dividing the jury venire panel to reduce courtroom congestion; or instructing prospective jurors not to engage or interact with audience members.

Petitioner also argues that, apart from failing to consider alternatives to closure, the trial court erred because it did not even identify any overriding interest likely to be prejudiced absent the closure of *voir dire*. There is some merit to this complaint. The generic risk of jurors overhearing prejudicial remarks, unsubstantiated by any specific threat or incident, is inherent whenever members of the public are present during the selection of jurors. If broad concerns of this sort were sufficient to override a defendant's constitutional right to a public trial, a court could exclude the public from jury selection almost as a matter of course. As noted in the dissent below, "the majority's reasoning permits the closure of voir dire in *every criminal case* conducted in this courtroom whenever the trial judge decides, for whatever reason, that he or she would prefer to fill the courtroom with potential jurors rather than spectators."

There are no doubt circumstances where a judge could conclude that threats of improper communications with jurors or safety concerns are concrete enough to warrant closing *voir dire*. But in those cases, the particular interest, and threat to that interest, must "be articulated along with findings specific enough that a reviewing court can determine whether the closure order was properly entered." * * * [E]ven assuming, *arguendo,* that the trial court had an overriding interest in closing *voir dire,* it was still incumbent upon it to consider all reasonable alternatives to closure. It did not, and that is all this Court needs to decide.

NOTES AND QUESTIONS

1. ***The interests protected by the public trial right.*** "The requirement of a public trial is for the benefit of the accused; that the public may see he is fairly dealt with and not unjustly condemned, and that the presence of interested spectators may keep his triers keenly alive to a sense of their responsibility and to the importance of their functions." *Waller* (quoting *In re Oliver*, 333 U.S. 257, 270, n. 25 (1948)). "In addition to ensuring that judge and prosecutor carry out their duties responsibly, a public trial encourages witnesses to come forward and discourages perjury."

In an earlier case applying the First Amendment public trial right, the Court explained, "Public scrutiny of a criminal trial enhances the quality and safeguards the integrity of the factfinding process, with benefits to both the defendant and to society as a whole. Moreover, public access to the criminal trial fosters an appearance of fairness, thereby heightening public respect for the judicial process. And in the broadest terms, public access to criminal trials permits the public to participate in and serve as a check upon the judicial process . . . ." *Globe Newspaper Co. v. Superior Court*, Note 1, p. 1294.

Also instructive is the discussion in *Weaver v. Massachusetts*, p. 143, where the Court considered potential harms from the closure of the courtroom during jury selection, resulting in the exclusion of the defendant's mother and her minister. The Court in *Weaver* confirmed that a public trial violation is a structural error that required relief on direct appeal without regard to harmlessness, but held that when a defendant raises his counsel's failure to object to closure as the basis for a post-conviction claim of ineffective assistance of counsel, a showing of prejudice under *Strickland* is still required. Finding Weaver did not show prejudice, the Court suggested various ways such a showing might have been made under different circumstances. "If, for instance, defense counsel errs in failing to object when the government's main witness testifies in secret, then the defendant might be able to show prejudice with little more detail. * * * [P]etitioner's trial was not conducted in secret or in a remote place. * * * [T]he courtroom remained open during the evidentiary phase of the trial; the closure decision apparently was made by court officers rather than the judge; there were many members of the venire who did not become jurors but who did observe the proceedings; and there was a record made of the proceedings that does not indicate any basis for concern, other than the closure itself. There has been no showing, furthermore, that the potential harms flowing from a courtroom closure came to pass in this case. For example, there is no suggestion that any juror lied during voir dire; no suggestion of misbehavior by the prosecutor, judge, or any other party; and no suggestion that any of the participants failed to approach their duties with the neutrality and serious purpose that our system demands."

2. ***When closure is justified.*** To avoid violating the defendant's Sixth Amendment right, explained the Court in *Waller*, "(1) the party seeking to close the hearing must advance an overriding interest that is likely to be prejudiced, (2) the closure must be no broader than necessary to protect that interest, (3) the trial court must consider reasonable alternatives to closing the proceeding, and (4) it must make findings adequate to support the closure." Lower courts have found that overriding interests supporting exclusion—if the other requirements of the *Waller* test are met—include protecting the welfare of a minor victim of crime, preventing harassment or physical harm to witnesses, protecting classified or confidential information, and preserving courtroom security.

3. ***A less demanding test for "trivial" closures?*** Some lower courts have applied a less stringent test for "partial" or "trivial" closures, where (unlike in *Presley* and *Weaver)* not all members of the public are excluded, or the exclusion is quite brief. These courts require only a "substantial" or "important" rather than an "overriding" reason for restricting access in order to justify such a closure, and have reasoned that these limited exclusions do not implicate the same secrecy and fairness concerns that a total closure does. *E.g., United States v. Perry*, 479 F.3d 885 (D.C.Cir.2007) (no violation by exclusion of eight-year-old son of defendant on trial for unlawfully accessing a computer resulting in damage; closure was trivial when son was only person excluded, his presence would not have ensured fair proceedings, discouraged perjury, or encouraged witnesses to come forward). Other courts have rejected this watering down of the *Waller* standard. How should courts resolve this dispute over the meaning of the Sixth Amendment?

CHAPTER 26

REPROSECUTION AND DOUBLE JEOPARDY

■ ■ ■

This chapter deals with the bearing of the Double Jeopardy Clause upon multiple prosecutions for the same offense.[a] Other aspects of the double jeopardy bar are examined in earlier chapters. Ch. 19, Section 2 examines what constitutes the "same offense" under the Clause, the effect of requesting separate trials for different statutory offenses that constitute the same offense, and when a civil penalty triggers double jeopardy protections. Ch. 22 addresses reprosecution for the same offense following breach of a plea agreement in Section 2, Note 5, p. 1183, and the loss of a potential double jeopardy claim by pleading guilty in Section 6. Double jeopardy limits on reprosecution vary depending upon whether the first prosecution results in a mistrial, an acquittal, a dismissal, or a conviction. Each context is considered below.

§ 1. REPROSECUTION AFTER MISTRIAL

A. MISTRIAL OVER THE OBJECTION OF DEFENDANT

ILLINOIS V. SOMERVILLE

410 U.S. 458, 93 S.Ct. 1066, 35 L.Ed.2d 425 (1973).

JUSTICE REHNQUIST delivered the opinion of the Court.

We must here decide whether declaration of a mistrial over the defendant's objection, because the trial court concluded that the indictment was insufficient to charge a crime, necessarily prevents a State from subsequently trying the defendant under a valid indictment. We hold that the mistrial met the "manifest necessity" requirement of our cases, since the trial court could reasonably have concluded that the "ends of public justice" would be defeated by having allowed the trial to continue. Therefore the Double Jeopardy Clause of the Fifth Amendment * * * did not bar trial under a valid indictment.

On March 19, 1964, respondent was indicted by an Illinois grand jury for the crime of theft. The case was called for trial and a jury impaneled and sworn on November 1, 1965. The following day, before any evidence had been presented, the prosecuting attorney realized that the indictment was fatally deficient under Illinois law because it did not allege that respondent intended to permanently deprive the owner of his property. Under the applicable Illinois criminal statute, such intent is a necessary element of the crime of theft, and failure to allege intent renders the indictment insufficient to charge a crime. But * * * Illinois further provides that only formal defects, of which this was not one, may be cured by amendment. The combined operation of these rules of Illinois procedure and substantive law meant that the defect in the indictment was "jurisdictional"; it could not be waived by the defendant's failure to object, and could be asserted on appeal or in a post-conviction proceeding to overturn a final judgment of conviction.

---

[a] For additional discussion of the material covered in this chapter, see Wayne R. LaFave, Jerold H. Israel, Nancy J. King & Orin S. Kerr, Criminal Procedure Treatise (4th ed. 2016) (available in Westlaw under the database CRIMPROC, and hereafter cited as CRIMPROC).

Faced with this situation, the Illinois trial court concluded that further proceedings under this defective indictment would be useless and granted the State's motion for a mistrial. On November 3, the grand jury handed down a second indictment alleging the requisite intent. Respondent was arraigned two weeks after the first trial was aborted, raised a claim of double jeopardy which was overruled, and the second trial commenced shortly thereafter. The jury returned a verdict of guilty, sentence was imposed, and the Illinois courts upheld the conviction. Respondent then sought federal habeas corpus * * *. The Seventh Circuit affirmed the denial of habeas corpus prior to our decision in *United States v. Jorn,* 400 U.S. 470 (1971). The respondent's petition for certiorari was granted, and the case remanded for reconsideration in light of *Jorn* and *Downum v. United States,* 372 U.S. 734 (1963). On remand, the Seventh Circuit held that respondent's petition for habeas corpus should have been granted because * * * jeopardy had attached when the jury was impaneled and sworn and a declaration of mistrial over respondent's objection precluded a retrial under a valid indictment. For the reasons stated below, we reverse that judgment.

The fountainhead decision construing the Double Jeopardy Clause in the context of a declaration of a mistrial over a defendant's objection is *United States v. Perez,* 9 Wheat. (22 U.S.) 579 (1824). Mr. Justice Story, writing for a unanimous Court, set forth the standards for determining whether a retrial, following a declaration of a mistrial over a defendant's objection, constitutes double jeopardy * * *. In holding that the failure of the jury to agree on a verdict of either acquittal or conviction did not bar retrial of the defendant, Mr. Justice Story wrote:

> We think, that in all cases of this nature, the law has invested Courts of justice with the authority to discharge a jury from giving any verdict, whenever, in their opinion, taking all the circumstances into consideration, there is a manifest necessity for the act, or the ends of public justice would otherwise be defeated. They are to exercise a sound discretion on the subject; and it is impossible to define all the circumstances, which would render it proper to interfere.

* * * In reviewing the propriety of the trial judge's exercise of his discretion, this Court following the counsel of Mr. Justice Story, has scrutinized the action to determine whether, in the context of that particular trial, the declaration of a mistrial was dictated by "manifest necessity" or the "ends of public justice."

In *Perez,* * * * this Court held that "manifest necessity" justified the discharge of juries unable to reach verdicts, and therefore the Double Jeopardy Clause did not bar retrial. In *Simmons v. United States,* 142 U.S. 148 (1891), a trial judge dismissed the jury, over defendant's objection, because one of the jurors had been acquainted with the defendant, and therefore was probably prejudiced against the Government; this Court held that the trial judge properly exercised his power "to prevent defeat of the ends of justice." In *Thompson v. United States,* 155 U.S. 271 (1894), a mistrial was declared after the trial judge learned that one of the jurors was disqualified, he having been a member of the grand jury that indicted the defendant. Similarly, in *Lovato v. New Mexico,* 242 U.S. 199 (1916), the defendant demurred to indictment, his demurrer was overruled and a jury sworn. The district attorney, realizing that the defendant had not pleaded to the indictment after the demurrer had been overruled, moved for the discharge of the jury and arraignment of the defendant for pleading; the jury was discharged, the defendant pleaded not guilty, the same jury was again impaneled, and a verdict of guilty rendered. In both of those cases this Court held that the Double Jeopardy Clause did not bar reprosecution.

While virtually all of the cases turn on the particular facts and thus escape meaningful categorization, it is possible to distill from them a general approach, premised on the "public justice" policy enunciated in *Perez,* to situations such as that presented by this case. A trial judge properly exercises his discretion to declare a mistrial if an impartial verdict cannot be reached, or if a verdict of conviction could be reached but would have to be reversed on appeal due to an obvious procedural error in the trial. If an error would make reversal on appeal a certainty, it would not serve "the ends of public justice" to require that the Government proceed with its proof, when, if it succeeded before the jury, it would automatically be stripped of that success by an appellate court. This was substantially the situation in both *Thompson* and *Lovato*. While the declaration of a mistrial on the basis of a rule or a defective procedure that lent itself to prosecutorial manipulation would involve an entirely different question, such was not the situation in the above cases or in the instant case.

In *Downum*, the defendant was charged with six counts of mail theft and forging and uttering stolen checks. A jury was selected and sworn in the morning, and instructed to return that afternoon. When the jury returned, the Government moved for the discharge of the jury on the ground that a key prosecution witness, for two of the six counts against defendant, was not present. The prosecution knew, prior to the selection and swearing of the jury, that this witness could not be found and had not been served with a subpoena. The trial judge discharged the jury over the defendant's motions to dismiss two counts for failure to prosecute and to continue the other four. This Court, in reversing the convictions on the ground of double jeopardy, emphasized that "[e]ach case must turn on its own facts," and held that the second prosecution constituted double jeopardy, because the absence of the witness and the reason therefor did not there justify, in terms of "manifest necessity," the declaration of a mistrial.

In *Jorn*, the Government called a taxpayer witness in a prosecution for willfully assisting in the preparation of fraudulent income tax returns. Prior to his testimony, defense counsel suggested he be warned of his constitutional right against compulsory self-incrimination. The trial judge warned him of his rights, and the witness stated that he was willing to testify and that the IRS agent who first contacted him warned him of his rights. The trial judge, however, did not believe the witness' declaration that the IRS had so warned him, and refused to allow him to testify until after he had consulted with an attorney. After learning from the Government that the remaining four witnesses were "similarly situated," and after surmising that they too had not been properly informed of their rights, the trial judge declared a mistrial to give the witnesses the opportunity to consult with attorneys. In sustaining a plea in bar of double jeopardy * * *, the plurality opinion of the Court, emphasizing the importance to the defendant of proceeding before the first jury sworn, concluded:

> It is apparent from the record that no consideration was given to the possibility of a trial continuance; indeed, the trial judge acted so abruptly in discharging the jury that, had the prosecutor been disposed to suggest a continuance, or the defendant to object to the discharge of the jury, there would have been no opportunity to do so. * * * it seems abundantly apparent that the trial judge made no effort to exercise a sound discretion to assure that, taking all the circumstances into account, there was a manifest necessity for the *sua sponte* declaration of this mistrial.

* * * [R]espondent argues that our decision in *Jorn*, which respondent interprets as narrowly limiting the circumstances in which a mistrial is manifestly necessary, requires affirmance. Emphasizing the "valued right to have his trial completed by a particular tribunal," respondent contends that the circumstances did not justify depriving him of that right. * * * We believe that in light of the State's established rules of criminal procedure the trial judge's declaration of a mistrial was not an abuse of discretion. Since this Court's decision in *Benton v. Maryland*, 395 U.S. 784 (1969) [holding the double jeopardy prohibition applicable to the states under the Fourteenth Amendment, see Ch. 2, Section 1], federal courts will be confronted with such claims that arise in large measure from the often diverse procedural rules existing in the 50 States. Federal courts should not be quick to conclude that simply because a state procedure does not conform to the corresponding federal statute or rule, it does not serve a legitimate state policy. * * *

In the instant case, the trial judge terminated the proceeding because a defect was found to exist in the indictment that was, as a matter of Illinois law, not curable by amendment. The Illinois courts have held that even after a judgment of conviction has become final, the defendant may be released on habeas corpus, because the defect in the indictment deprives the trial court of "jurisdiction." The rule prohibiting the amendment of all but formal defects in indictments is designed to implement the State's policy of preserving the right of each defendant to insist that a criminal prosecution against him be commenced by the action of a grand jury. The trial judge was faced with a situation similar to those in *Simmons, Lovato,* and *Thompson,* in which a procedural defect might or would preclude the public from either obtaining an impartial verdict or keeping a verdict of conviction if its evidence persuaded the jury. If a mistrial were constitutionally unavailable in situations such as this, the State's policy could only be implemented by conducting a second trial after verdict and reversal on appeal, thus wasting time, energy, and money for all concerned. Here the trial judge's action was a rational determination designed to implement a legitimate state policy, with no suggestion that the implementation of that policy in this manner could be manipulated so as to prejudice the defendant. This situation is thus unlike *Downum,* where the mistrial entailed not only a delay for the defendant, but also operated as a post-jeopardy continuance to allow the prosecution an opportunity to strengthen its case. Here the delay was minimal, and the mistrial was, under Illinois law, the only way in which a defect in the indictment could be corrected. Given the established standard of discretion set forth in *Perez* * * *, we cannot say that the declaration of a mistrial was not required by "manifest necessity" and the "ends of public justice." * * *

The determination by the trial court to abort a criminal proceeding where jeopardy has attached is not one to be lightly undertaken, since the interest of the defendant in having his fate determined by the jury first impaneled is itself a weighty one. *Jorn*. Nor will the lack of demonstrable additional prejudice preclude the defendant's invocation of the double jeopardy bar in the absence of some important countervailing interest of proper judicial administration. But where the declaration of a mistrial implements a reasonable state policy and aborts a proceeding that at best would have produced a verdict that could have been upset at will by one of the parties, the defendant's interest in proceeding to verdict is outweighed by the competing and equally legitimate demand for public justice. Reversed.

JUSTICE WHITE, with whom JUSTICES DOUGLAS and BRENNAN join, dissenting.

* * * The majority notes that 'the declaration of a mistrial on the basis of a rule or a defective procedure that would lend itself to prosecutorial manipulation would involve an entirely different question.' Surely there is no evidence of bad faith or overreaching on this record. However, the words of the Court in *Ball* [p. 1351, Note 1, p. 1362] seem particularly appropriate: 'This case, in short, presents the novel and unheard-of-spectacle, of a public officer, whose business it was to frame a correct bill, openly alleging his own inaccuracy or neglect, as a reason for a second trial, when it is not pretended that the merits were not fairly in issue on the first. . . . If this practice be tolerated, when are trials of the accused to end? * * *"

JUSTICE MARSHALL, dissenting.

* * * [T]he facts in *Downum*, * * * clearly show that the prosecutor's failure to have a crucial witness present was a negligent oversight. * * * I cannot understand how negligence lends itself to manipulation. And even if I could understand that, I cannot understand how negligence in failing to draw an adequate indictment is different from negligence in failing to assure the presence of a crucial witness. * * * *Downum* and *Jorn* are controlling. As in those cases, the trial judge here did not pursue an available alternative, and the reason which led him to declare a mistrial was prosecutorial negligence, a reason that this Court found insufficient in *Downum*. * * * I see no reason to * * * adopt a new balancing test whose elements are stated on such a high level of abstraction as to give judges virtually no guidance at all in deciding subsequent cases. * * *

NOTES AND QUESTIONS

1. ***When jeopardy attaches; the defendant's interest in a verdict from the original jury.*** Under the rule traditionally applied in federal courts, jeopardy attaches in a jury trial when the jury is "empaneled and sworn" and it attaches in a bench trial when the "first witness is sworn." *Somerville* apparently assumed that this federal rule was constitutionally mandated and therefore applied to state as well as federal cases. That assumption was confirmed in *Crist v. Bretz*, 437 U.S. 28 (1978), a case that also explained why, as the Court notes in *Somerville,* "the interest of the defendant in having his fate determined by the jury first impaneled is itself a weighty one."

In *Crist,* a mistrial had been granted, on grounds conceded not to constitute manifest necessity, after the jury had been sworn but before the first witness had been sworn. The state courts upheld a reprosecution on the basis of a state rule that jeopardy did not attach until the first witness was sworn in either jury or bench trials. The majority opinion (per Stewart, J.) explained that the double jeopardy guarantee initially had been viewed as applicable only after the trial had been completed and a judgment of conviction or acquittal had been entered. This reflected the Blackstonian description of the double jeopardy prohibition as the embodiment of the common law pleas of *autrefois convict* and *autrefois acquit*—a criminal law doctrine "akin to the [civil law's] *res judicata,*" and similarly designed "to preserve the finality of judgment." However, another strand of the English common law had advanced "a strong tradition that, once bonded together, a jury should not be discharged until it had completed its solemn task of announcing a verdict." This tradition was treated as an aspect of double jeopardy protection in *Perez,* and it soon became an integral part of "double jeopardy jurisprudence." Thus, Justice Stewart concluded, "regardless of its historic origin," the defendant's "valued right to have his trial completed before a particular tribunal" had become an essential element of the Fifth Amendment guarantee. It followed that the "federal rule that jeopardy attaches when the jury is empaneled and sworn" similarly had become part of that guarantee. This was so because: "[T]he federal rule * * * reflects and protects the defendant's interest in retaining a chosen jury. * * * [Basic] double jeopardy concerns—the finality of judgments, the minimization of harassing exposure to the harrowing experiences of a criminal trial, the valued right to continue with the chosen jury—have combined to produce the federal law that in a jury trial jeopardy attaches when the jury is empaneled and sworn. * * * [This standard as to] the time when jeopardy attaches in a jury trial [thereby] 'serves as the linchpin for all double jeopardy jurisprudence.' "

Justice Blackmun, in a separate concurrence, stressed that the point where the jury is sworn is where "the defendant's interest in the jury reaches its highest plateau, because the opportunity for prosecutorial overreaching thereafter increases substantially and because stress and possible embarrassment for the defendant from then on is sustained." Justice Powell, joined by the Chief Justice and Justice Rehnquist, dissented. The "one event" that should bring the defendant's interest in a particular tribunal within the constitutional guarantee, the dissent concluded, was the "beginning of the fact finder's work" through the "hearing of evidence."

2. ***When jeopardy terminates: continuing jeopardy.*** A mistrial that is supported by "manifest necessity," as in *Perez* or *Somerville*, does not terminate jeopardy on the charge mistried. Instead, in the absence of a verdict, jeopardy is said to be "continuing." Under this continuing jeopardy principle, retrial after a jury has failed to reach a verdict is not a new trial but part of the same proceeding. For example, in *Richardson v. United States*, 468 U.S. 317 (1984), a jury acquitted the defendant on one narcotics charge but hung on two others. Richardson moved to bar retrial on the hung counts, insisting that reprosecution would place him twice in jeopardy for the same offense. The Court disagreed, noting that "the failure of the jury to reach a verdict is not an event which terminates jeopardy." However, if the defendant shows that by acquitting on one count the jury necessarily rejected a fact essential to conviction on a mistried count, retrial of the

mistried count is barred by the rule of *Ashe v. Swenson*, p. 1049. See *Yeager v. United States*, 557 U.S. 110 (2009).

3. ***Mistrial for unavailable government evidence.*** What distinguishes *Downum* from *Somerville*? Can the cases be distinguished on the ground that the prosecutor's error in *Downum,* more easily "lent itself to prosecutorial manipulation"? In *Washington,* below Note 4, the Court commented: "The strictest scrutiny is appropriate when the basis for the mistrial is the unavailability of critical prosecution evidence or when there is reason to believe that the prosecutor is using the superior resources of the State to harass or to achieve a tactical advantage over the accused." In light of this statement and the *Downum* ruling, how much room is available to the trial judge to grant a mistrial for the purpose of allowing the prosecution to gain the testimony of a missing witness? Lower courts have found manifest necessity supported when the reason for the missing evidence or witness was truly unforeseeable to the government, and alternatives to mistrial were considered.

4. ***Mistrial for defense misconduct.*** In ARIZONA v. WASHINGTON, 434 U.S. 497 (1978), Washington's counsel told the jury in his opening statement that they would learn that the prosecutor had suppressed exculpatory evidence at a previous trial and that this "misconduct" had caused the Arizona Supreme Court to grant a new trial in the case. The prosecutor then moved for a mistrial, arguing that defense counsel's statement was clearly improper, that it had prejudiced the jury, and that "the prejudice could not be repaired by any cautionary instruction." Defense counsel disagreed on all points, but was unable to present any legal support for his contention that his opening statement had been proper, and the trial court granted a mistrial. In issuing its ruling, the trial court did not expressly note either that there was "manifest necessity" or that it had considered alternatives to the mistrial order. On appeal, the Supreme Court rejected Washington's double jeopardy objection to his subsequent reprosecution.

Justice Stevens, writing for the majority, noted that "along the spectrum of trial problems which may warrant a mistrial and which vary in their amenability to appellate scrutiny, the difficulty which led to the mistrial in this case also [, like the deadlocked jury,] falls in an area where the trial judge's determination is entitled to special respect." He continued, "We * * * start from the premise that defense counsel's comment was improper and may have affected the impartiality of the jury. We recognize that the extent of the possible bias cannot be measured, and that the District Court was quite correct in believing that some trial judges might have proceeded with the trial after giving the jury appropriate cautionary instructions. In a strict, literal sense, the mistrial was not 'necessary.' Nevertheless, the overriding interest in the evenhanded administration of justice requires that we accord the highest degree of respect to the trial judge's evaluation of the likelihood that the impartiality of one or more jurors may have been affected by the improper comment. * * *

"An improper opening statement unquestionably tends to frustrate the public interest in having a just judgment reached by an impartial tribunal. Indeed, such statements create a risk, often not present in the individual juror bias situation, that the entire panel may be tainted. The trial judge, of course, may instruct the jury to disregard the improper comment. In extreme cases, he may discipline counsel, or even remove him from the trial as he did in *United States v. Dinitz* [cited in *Kennedy,* at p. 1346]. Those actions, however, will not necessarily remove the risk of bias that may be created by improper argument. Unless unscrupulous defense counsel are to be allowed an unfair advantage, the trial judge must have the power to declare a mistrial in appropriate cases. * * *.

"There are compelling institutional considerations militating in favor of appellate deference to the trial judge's evaluation of the significance of possible juror bias. He has seen and heard the jurors during their *voir dire* examination. He is the judge most familiar with the evidence and the background of the case on trial. He has listened to the tone of the argument as it was delivered and has observed the apparent reaction of the jurors. In short, he is far more 'conversant with the factors relevant to the determination' than any reviewing court can possibly be.

" * * * The trial judge * * * 'must always temper the decision whether or not to abort the trial by considering the importance to the defendant of being able, once and for all, to conclude his confrontation with society through the verdict of a tribunal he might believe to be favorably disposed to his fate.' *Jorn*. In order to ensure that this interest is adequately protected, reviewing courts have an obligation to satisfy themselves that, in the words of Mr. Justice Story, the trial judge exercised 'sound discretion' in declaring a mistrial. Thus, if a trial judge acts irrationally or irresponsibly, his action cannot be condoned. But our review of this record indicates that this was not such a case."

5. ***Manifest necessity and deadlock.*** In the following case, the Court addressed a trial judge's declaration of mistrial after reported deadlock. Additional portions of the decision that discuss the standard of review under the federal habeas statute appear in Chapter 29.

RENICO V. LETT

559 U.S. 766, 130 S.Ct. 1855, 176 L.Ed.2d 678 (2010).

CHIEF JUSTICE ROBERTS. [Lett's murder trial lasted less than nine hours total, spread over more than a week. On the second day of deliberations the jury sent out a note stating that the jurors had " 'a concern about our voice levels disturbing any other proceedings that might be going on.' " Later, the jury sent out another note, asking " 'What if we can't agree? [M]istrial? [R]etrial? [W]hat?' " The judge called the jury back into the courtroom, along with the prosecutor and defense counsel. Once the jury was seated, the following exchange took place:]

"THE COURT: I received your note asking me what if you can't agree? And I have to conclude from that that that is your situation at this time. So, I'd like to ask the foreperson to identify themselves, please?

"THE FOREPERSON: [Identified herself.]

"THE COURT: Okay, thank you. All right. I need to ask you if the jury is deadlocked; in other words, is there a disagreement as to the verdict?

"THE FOREPERSON: Yes, there is.

"THE COURT: All right. Do you believe that it is hopelessly deadlocked?

"THE FOREPERSON: The majority of us don't believe that—

"THE COURT: (Interposing) Don't say what you're going to say, okay?

"THE FOREPERSON: Oh, I'm sorry.

"THE COURT: I don't want to know what your verdict might be, or how the split is, or any of that. Thank you. Okay? Are you going to reach a unanimous verdict, or not?

"THE FOREPERSON: (No response)

"THE COURT: Yes or no?

"THE FOREPERSON: No, Judge."

The judge then declared a mistrial, dismissed the jury, and scheduled a new trial for later that year. Neither the prosecutor nor Lett's attorney made any objection.

Lett's second trial was held before a different judge and jury. This time, the jury was able to reach a unanimous verdict—that Lett was guilty of second-degree murder—after deliberating for only 3 hours and 15 minutes. [After his double jeopardy challenge was rejected by the Michigan

Supreme Court, Lett obtained a writ of habeas corpus in federal court. The Supreme Court agreed to review the decision granting the writ.] * * *

* * * In *Perez*, we held that when a judge discharges a jury on the grounds that the jury cannot reach a verdict, the Double Jeopardy Clause does not bar a new trial for the defendant before a new jury. We explained that trial judges may declare a mistrial "whenever, in their opinion, taking all the circumstances into consideration, there is a manifest necessity" for doing so. The decision to declare a mistrial is left to the "sound discretion" of the judge, but "the power ought to be used with the greatest caution, under urgent circumstances, and for very plain and obvious causes."

Since *Perez*, we have clarified that the "manifest necessity" standard "cannot be interpreted literally," and that a mistrial is appropriate when there is a " 'high degree' " of necessity. *Washington*. The decision whether to grant a mistrial is reserved to the "broad discretion" of the trial judge, a point that "has been consistently reiterated in decisions of this Court." *Somerville*. In particular, "[t]he trial judge's decision to declare a mistrial when he considers the jury deadlocked is . . . accorded great deference by a reviewing court." *Washington*. A "mistrial premised upon the trial judge's belief that the jury is unable to reach a verdict [has been] long considered the classic basis for a proper mistrial." The reasons for "allowing the trial judge to exercise broad discretion" are "especially compelling" in cases involving a potentially deadlocked jury. There, the justification for deference is that "the trial court is in the best position to assess all the factors which must be considered in making a necessarily discretionary determination whether the jury will be able to reach a just verdict if it continues to deliberate." In the absence of such deference, trial judges might otherwise "employ coercive means to break the apparent deadlock," thereby creating a "significant risk that a verdict may result from pressures inherent in the situation rather than the considered judgment of all the jurors."

This is not to say that we grant *absolute* deference to trial judges in this context. *Perez* itself noted that the judge's exercise of discretion must be "sound," and we have made clear that "[i]f the record reveals that the trial judge has failed to exercise the 'sound discretion' entrusted to him, the reason for such deference by an appellate court disappears." *Washington*. Thus "if the trial judge acts for reasons completely unrelated to the trial problem which purports to be the basis for the mistrial ruling, close appellate scrutiny is appropriate." Similarly, "if a trial judge acts irrationally or irresponsibly, . . . his action cannot be condoned."

We have expressly declined to require the "mechanical application" of any "rigid formula" when trial judges decide whether jury deadlock warrants a mistrial. We have also explicitly held that a trial judge declaring a mistrial is not required to make explicit findings of " 'manifest necessity' " nor to "articulate on the record all the factors which informed the deliberate exercise of his discretion." And we have never required a trial judge, before declaring a mistrial based on jury deadlock, to force the jury to deliberate for a minimum period of time, to question the jurors individually, to consult with (or obtain the consent of) either the prosecutor or defense counsel, to issue a supplemental jury instruction, or to consider any other means of breaking the impasse. In 1981, then-Justice Rehnquist noted that this Court had never "overturned a trial court's declaration of a mistrial after a jury was unable to reach a verdict on the ground that the 'manifest necessity' standard had not been met." The same remains true today, nearly 30 years later. * * *

* * * The Michigan Supreme Court's adjudication involved a straightforward application of our longstanding precedents to the facts of Lett's case. * * * It then applied those precedents to the particular facts before it and found no abuse of discretion, especially in light of the length of deliberations after a short and uncomplicated trial, the jury notes suggesting heated discussions and asking what would happen "if we can't agree," and—"[m]ost important"—"the fact that the jury foreperson expressly stated that the jury was not going to reach a verdict." In these circumstances, it was reasonable for the Michigan Supreme Court to determine that the trial judge had exercised sound discretion in declaring a mistrial.

The Court of Appeals for the Sixth Circuit concluded otherwise. * * * it speculated that the trial judge may have misinterpreted the jury's notes as signs of discord and deadlock when, read literally, they expressly stated no such thing. It further determined that the judge's brief colloquy with the foreperson may have wrongly implied a false equivalence between "mere disagreement" and "genuine deadlock," and may have given rise to "inappropriate pressure" on her to say that the jury would be unable to reach a verdict. * * * The Court of Appeals' interpretation of the trial record is not implausible. Nor, for that matter, is the more inventive * * * speculation of the dissent. After all, the jury only deliberated for four hours, its notes were arguably ambiguous, the trial judge's initial question to the foreperson was imprecise, and the judge neither asked for elaboration of the foreperson's answers nor took any other measures to confirm the foreperson's prediction that a unanimous verdict would not be reached.

But other reasonable interpretations of the record are also possible. Lett's trial was not complex, and there is no reason that the jury would necessarily have needed more than a few hours to deliberate over his guilt. The notes the jury sent to the judge certainly could be read as reflecting substantial disagreement, even if they did not say so outright. Most important, the foreperson expressly told the judge—in response to her unambiguous question "Are you going to reach a unanimous verdict, or not?"—that the jury would be unable to agree.

Given the foregoing facts, the Michigan Supreme Court's decision upholding the trial judge's exercise of discretion—while not necessarily correct—was not objectively unreasonable. * * *. In concluding that Lett is not entitled to a writ of habeas corpus, we do not deny that the trial judge could have been more thorough before declaring a mistrial. * * * [S]he could have asked the foreperson additional followup questions, granted additional time for further deliberations, or consulted with the prosecutor and defense counsel before acting. Any of these steps would have been appropriate under the circumstances. None, however, was required * * * .

JUSTICE STEVENS, with whom JUSTICE SOTOMAYOR joins, and with whom JUSTICE BREYER joins as to Parts I and II, dissenting.

At common law, courts went to great lengths to ensure the jury reached a verdict. Fourteenth-century English judges reportedly loaded hung juries into oxcarts and carried them from town to town until a judgment " 'bounced out.' " Less enterprising colleagues kept jurors as *de facto* "prisoners" until they achieved unanimity. The notion of a mistrial based on jury deadlock did not appear in Blackstone's Commentaries; it is no surprise, then, that colonial juries virtually always returned a verdict. Well into the 19th and even the 20th century, some American judges continued to coax unresolved juries toward consensus by threatening to deprive them of heat, sleep, or sustenance or to lock them in a room for a prolonged period of time.

Mercifully, our legal system has evolved, and such harsh measures are no longer tolerated. Yet what this history demonstrates—and what has not changed—is the respect owed "a defendant's valued right to have his trial completed by a particular tribunal." * * *

II

* * * Most of the time when we worry about judicial coercion of juries, we worry about judges pressuring them, in the common-law manner, to keep deliberating until they return a verdict they may not otherwise have chosen. This judge exerted pressure so as to prevent the jury from reaching any verdict at all. In so doing, she cut off deliberations well before the point when it was clear they would no longer be fruitful. * * * [A]lmost immediately after sending the judge a note asking what would happen if they disagreed, the jury sent a note asking about lunch. Plainly, this was a group that was prepared to go on with its work. * * *

In addition to the remarkable "hast[e]," and "inexplicabl[e] abrupt[ness]," with which she acted, it is remarkable what the trial judge did not do. "Never did the trial judge consider alternatives or otherwise provide evidence that she exercised sound discretion. For example, the judge did not poll the jurors, give an instruction ordering further deliberations, query defense counsel about his thoughts on continued deliberations, or indicate on the record why a mistrial declaration was necessary." *Lett*, 466 Mich., at 227–228 (Cavanagh, J., dissenting). Nor did the judge invite any argument or input from the prosecutor, make any findings of fact or provide any statements illuminating her thought process, follow up on the foreperson's final response, or give any evident consideration to the ends of public justice or the balance between the defendant's rights and the State's interests. The manner in which this discharge decision was made contravened standard trial-court guidelines.[15] The judge may not have had a constitutional obligation to take any one of the aforementioned measures, but she did have an obligation to exercise sound discretion and thus to "assure h[er]self that the situation warrant[ed] action on h[er] part foreclosing the defendant from a potentially favorable judgment by the tribunal." *Jorn*.

NOTES AND QUESTIONS

1. ***Manifest necessity and alternatives to mistrial in cases of jury deadlock.*** Manifest necessity for declaring mistrial based on the jury's inability to reach a verdict is judged on the totality of the circumstances, including whether the defendant objected, the length of the deliberations, the length and complexity of the trial, and the instructions and actions of the trial judge. See, e.g., CRIMPROC § 25.2(e). Two years after *Lett*, in *Blueford v. Arkansas*, 566 U.S. 599 (2012), the Court again noted that it had never held that a trial judge must make particular findings or take any particular alternative steps prior to declaring a mistrial based on jury deadlock. *Blueford* upheld, on direct appeal, a state decision finding manifest necessity for mistrial after a jury reported that it had voted unanimously against murder but was deadlocked on lesser charges. The defendant argued that there was no manifest necessity for the judge's declaration of mistrial on all charges and that the trial judge "should have taken 'some action,' whether through partial verdict forms or other means," to allow the jury to give effect to its vote rejecting murder charges, and then consider mistrial only as to the remaining charges. In rejecting this argument, the Court once again stated, "We have never required a trial court, before declaring a mistrial because of a hung jury, to consider any particular means of breaking the impasse—let alone to consider giving the jury new options for a verdict."

The *Lett* Court noted that one reason to provide trial judges with broad discretion to declare mistrial upon reported jury impasse is to avoid providing an incentive to "employ coercive means to break the apparent deadlock." Even with the forgiving standard of review, however, judges routinely refuse to accept impasse when first reported, instead encouraging jurors to continue attempts to agree upon a verdict, instructions often termed "Allen charges," after an early case upholding the practice. *Allen v. United States*, 164 U.S. 492 (1896). Under some conditions, this type of "dynamite charge" will not be considered coercive, e.g., *Early v. Packer*, 537 U.S. 3 (2002); *Lowenfield v. Phelps*, 484 U.S. 231 (1988) (not coercive in capital case to poll jury twice and instruct jurors to "discuss the evidence with the objective of reaching a just verdict if you can do so without violence to [your] individual judgment," and not to "hesitate to reexamine your own views and to change your opinion if you are convinced you are wrong," while warning against "surrendering your honest belief . . . solely because of the opinion of your fellow jurors or for the mere purpose of returning a verdict"). But in exhorting a struggling jury to continue to deliberate, a judge may go too far, threatening the jury, putting undue pressure on holdouts to capitulate, or demanding unreasonably lengthy deliberations. See, e.g., *Lafayette v. State*, 90 So.3d 1215 (Miss. 2012) (coercive to tell jury: "We will call back another jury that hopefully will be reasonable and fair, and one that can be successful in reaching a decision. I hope not to put the County and the State

[15] See, e.g., A.B.A. Standards for Criminal Justice, Discovery and Trial by Jury 15–5.4, pp. 256–257 (3d ed. 1996) * * * ; Federal Judicial Center, Manual on Recurring Problems in Criminal Trials 162 (5th ed. 2001) ("Before declaring a mistrial, a trial judge must consider all the procedural alternatives to a mistrial, and, after finding none of them to be adequate, make a finding of manifest necessity for the declaration of a mistrial") * * * .

to the expense if I can get around it."); *Fortune v. United States*, 65 A.3d 75 (D.C. App. 2013) (judge coerced jurors by sending them back to continue deliberations for a third time and stating "I don't agree with the jury, and it's my job to make that kind of a decision"). Recognizing that dynamite charges often form the basis for appeal and carry the risk of coercion, many states have limited the conditions under which they may be used, or have adopted a "pattern instruction" that judges may follow. See CRIMPROC § 24.9(d).

2. ***Manifest necessity and alternatives to mistrial in non-deadlock cases.*** In situations where mistrial is based on something *other* than deadlock, the Court's statement in *Washington* that the record must demonstrate that "the trial judge acted responsibly and deliberately, and accorded careful consideration to respondent's interest in having the trial concluded in a single proceeding," suggests that trial judges must consider alternatives to mistrial as part of the manifest necessity analysis. Lower courts continue to find no manifest necessity for mistrial when obvious alternatives are by-passed or ignored. See, e.g., *United States v. Fisher*, 624 F.3d 713 (5th Cir. 2010) (no manifest necessity for mistrial after scheduling conflict prevented critical government witnesses from testifying when judge did not consider reasonable alternatives); *Morris v. Livote*, 105 A.D.3d 43, 962 N.Y.S.2d 59 (2013) (no manifest necessity for mistrial after misconduct of defense counsel in eliciting prejudicial information on cross examination, when "more specific curative instructions or a poll of the jurors to ascertain whether they could render an impartial verdict would have been appropriate"); *Meadows v. State*, 303 Ga. 507 (2018) (no manifest necessity when judge concerned about contentious deliberations did not consider alternatives such as instructing the jurors to take a break, a day off, or attempting to determine if a specific juror was responsible); *Day v. Haskell*, 799 N.W.2d 355 (N.D. 2011) (no manifest necessity after defendant left alone in the courtroom with the jurors and the bailiff, when judge failed to consider alternatives to mistrial such as curing instructions).

B. DEFENSE CONSENT TO MISTRIAL

In the cases discussed above, the mistrial was declared over the objection of the defendant or without giving the defendant an opportunity to take a position on the mistrial. The materials that follow deal with cases in which the defendant either requested the mistrial or expressly acquiesced in the court's suggestion that a mistrial be declared.

OREGON V. KENNEDY

456 U.S. 667, 102 S.Ct. 2083, 72 L.Ed.2d 416 (1982).

JUSTICE REHNQUIST delivered the opinion of the Court.

* * * Respondent was charged with the theft of an oriental rug. During his first trial, the State called an expert witness on the subject of Middle Eastern rugs to testify as to the value and the identity of the rug in question. On cross-examination, respondent's attorney apparently attempted to establish bias on the part of the expert witness by asking him whether he had filed a criminal complaint against respondent. The witness eventually acknowledged this fact, but explained that no action had been taken on his complaint. On redirect examination, the prosecutor sought to elicit the reasons why the witness had filed a complaint against respondent, but the trial court sustained a series of objections to this line of inquiry.[1] The following colloquy then ensued:

"Prosecutor: Have you ever done business with the Kennedys?

"Witness: No, I have not.

---

[1] The Court of Appeals later explained that respondent's "objections were not well taken, and the judge's rulings were probably wrong." 49 Or.App. 415, 417, 619 P.2d 948, 949 (1980).

"Prosecutor: Is that because he is a crook?"

The trial court then granted respondent's motion for a mistrial.

When the State later sought to retry respondent, he moved to dismiss the charges because of double jeopardy. After a hearing at which the prosecutor testified, the trial court found as a fact that "it was not the intention of the prosecutor in this case to cause a mistrial." On the basis of this finding, the trial court held that double jeopardy principles did not bar retrial, and respondent was then tried and convicted.

Respondent then successfully appealed to the Oregon Court of Appeals, which sustained his double jeopardy claim. * * * The Court of Appeals accepted the trial court's finding that it was not the intent of the prosecutor to cause a mistrial. Nevertheless, the court held that retrial was barred because the prosecutor's conduct in this case constituted what it viewed as "overreaching." Although the prosecutor intended to rehabilitate the witness, the Court of Appeals expressed the view that the question was in fact "a direct personal attack on the general character of the defendant." This personal attack left respondent with a "Hobson's choice—either to accept a necessarily prejudiced jury, or to move for a mistrial and face the process of being retried at a later time." * * *

Where the trial is terminated over the objection of the defendant, the classical test for lifting the double jeopardy bar to a second trial is the "manifest necessity" standard * * *. The "manifest necessity" standard provides sufficient protection to the defendant's interests in having his case finally decided by the jury first selected while at the same time maintaining "the public's interest in fair trials designed to end in just judgments." But in the case of a mistrial declared at the behest of the defendant, quite different principles come into play. Here the defendant himself has elected to terminate the proceedings against him, and the "manifest necessity" standard has no place in the application of the Double Jeopardy Clause. *United States v. Dinitz,* 424 U.S. 600 (1976). Indeed, the Court stated [in an earlier case]: "If [defendant] had *requested* a mistrial * * *, there would be no doubt that if he had been successful, the Government would not have been barred from retrying him."

Our cases, however, have indicated that even where the defendant moves for a mistrial, there is a narrow exception to the rule that the Double Jeopardy Clause is no bar to retrial. The circumstances under which respondent's first trial was terminated require us to delineate the bounds of that exception more fully than we have in previous cases.

Since one of the principal threads making up the protection embodied in the Double Jeopardy Clause is the right of the defendant to have his trial completed before the first jury empaneled to try him, it may be wondered as a matter of original inquiry why the defendant's election to terminate the first trial by his own motion should not be deemed a renunciation of that right for all purposes. We have recognized, however, that there would be great difficulty in applying such a rule where the prosecutor's actions giving rise to the motion for mistrial were done "in order to goad the [defendant] into requesting a mistrial." *Dinitz.* In such a case, the defendant's valued right to complete his trial before the first jury would be a hollow shell if the inevitable motion for mistrial were held to prevent a later invocation of the bar of double jeopardy in all circumstances.

* * * The language [of *Dinitz*] would seem to broaden the test from one of *intent* to provoke a motion for a mistrial to a more generalized standard of "bad faith conduct" or "harassment" on the part of the judge or prosecutor.[b] It was upon this language that the Oregon Court of Appeals

[b] The Court in *Dinitz* had explained: "Even when judicial or prosecutorial error prejudices a defendant's prospects of securing an acquittal, he may nonetheless desire 'to go to the first jury and, perhaps, end the dispute then and there with an acquittal.' Our prior decisions recognize the defendant's right to pursue this course in the absence of circumstances of manifest necessity requiring a *sua sponte* judicial declaration of mistrial. But it is evident that when judicial or prosecutorial error seriously prejudices a defendant, he may have little interest in completing

apparently relied in concluding that the prosecutor's colloquy with the expert witness in this case amount to "overreaching." The difficulty with the more general standards which would permit a broader exception than one merely based on intent is that they offer virtually no standards for their application. Every act on the part of a rational prosecutor during a trial is designed to "prejudice" the defendant by placing before the judge or jury evidence leading to a finding of his guilt. * * * More serious infractions on the part of the prosecutor may provoke a motion for mistrial on the part of the defendant, and may in the view of the trial court warrant the granting of such a motion. The "overreaching" standard applied by the court below and urged today by Justice Stevens, however, would add another classification of prosecutorial error, one requiring dismissal of the indictment, but without supplying any standard by which to assess that error.[5]

By contrast, a standard that examines the intent of the prosecutor, though certainly not entirely free from practical difficulties, is a manageable standard to apply. It merely calls for the court to make a finding of fact. Inferring the existence or nonexistence of intent from objective facts and circumstances is a familiar process in our criminal justice system. * * *

Prosecutorial conduct that might be viewed as harassment or overreaching, even if sufficient to justify a mistrial on defendant's motion, therefore, does not bar retrial absent intent on the part of the prosecutor to subvert the protections afforded by the Double Jeopardy Clause. A defendant's motion for a mistrial constitutes "a deliberate election on his part to forgo his valued right to have his guilt or innocence determined before the first trier of fact." *United States v. Scott* [p. 1350]. Where prosecutorial error even of a degree sufficient to warrant a mistrial has occurred, "[t]he important consideration, for purposes of the Double Jeopardy Clause, is that the defendant retain primary control over the course to be followed in the event of such error." *Dinitz.* Only where the governmental conduct in question is intended to "goad" the defendant into moving for a mistrial may a defendant raise the bar of double jeopardy to a second trial after having succeeded in aborting the first on his own motion.

Were we to embrace the broad and somewhat amorphous standard adopted by the Oregon Court of Appeals, we are not sure that criminal defendants as a class would be aided. Knowing that the granting of the defendant's motion for mistrial would all but inevitably bring with it an attempt to bar a second trial on grounds of double jeopardy, the judge presiding over the first trial might well be more loath to grant a defendant's motion for mistrial. If a mistrial were in fact warranted under the applicable law, of course, the defendant could in many instances successfully appeal a judgment of conviction on the same grounds that he urged a mistrial, and the Double Jeopardy Clause would present no bar to retrial. But some of the advantages secured to him by the Double Jeopardy Clause—the freedom from extended anxiety, and the necessity to confront the government's case only once—would be to a large extent lost in the process of trial to verdict, reversal on appeal, and subsequent retrial.

* * * We do not by this opinion lay down a flat rule that where a defendant in a criminal trial successfully moves for a mistrial, he may not thereafter invoke the bar of double jeopardy against a second trial. But we do hold that the circumstances under which such a defendant may invoke

---

the trial and obtaining a verdict from the first jury. The defendant may reasonably conclude that a continuation of the tainted proceeding would result in a conviction followed by a lengthy appeal and, if a reversal is secured, by a second prosecution. In such circumstances, a defendant's mistrial request has objectives not unlike the interests served by the Double Jeopardy Clause—the avoidance of the anxiety, expense, and delay occasioned by multiple prosecutions."

[5] If the Court were to hold, as would Justice Stevens, that such a determination requires an assessment of the facts and circumstances but without explaining how such an assessment ought to proceed, the Court would offer little guidance to the federal and state courts that must apply our decisions. Justice Stevens disagrees with this decision below because his reaction to a cold record is different from that of the Oregon Court of Appeals. The Court of Appeals found "overreaching"; Justice Stevens finds none. Neither articulates a basis for reaching their respective conclusions which can be applied to other factual situations. We are loath to adopt such an essentially standardless rule.

the bar of double jeopardy in a second effort to try him are limited to those cases in which the conduct giving rise to the successful motion for a mistrial was intended to provoke the defendant into moving for a mistrial. Since the Oregon trial court found, and the Oregon Court of Appeals accepted, that the prosecutorial conduct culminating in the termination of the first trial in this case was not so intended by the prosecutor, that is the end of the matter for purposes of the Double Jeopardy Clause of the Fifth Amendment to the United States Constitution. * * *

JUSTICE POWELL, concurring.

* * * [T]here was no sequence of overreaching prior to the single prejudicial question. Moreover, it is evident from a colloquy between counsel and the court, out of the presence of the jury, that the prosecutor not only resisted, but also was surprised by, the defendant's motion for a mistrial. Finally, at the hearing on respondent's double jeopardy motion, the prosecutor testified—and the trial found as a fact and the appellate court agreed—that there was no " 'intention . . . to cause a mistrial.' " In view of these circumstances, the Double Jeopardy Clause provides no bar to retrial.

JUSTICE STEVENS, with whom JUSTICE BRENNAN, JUSTICE MARSHALL, and JUSTICE BLACKMUN, join, concurring in the judgment.

* * * The rationale for the exception to the general rule permitting retrial after a mistrial declared with the defendant's consent is illustrated by the situation in which the prosecutor commits prejudicial error with the intent to provoke a mistrial. In this situation the defendant's choice to continue the tainted proceeding or to abort the proceeding and begin anew is inadequate to protect his double jeopardy interests. For, absent a bar to reprosecution, the defendant would simply play into the prosecutor's hands by moving for a mistrial. The defendant's other option—to continue the tainted proceeding—would be no option at all if, as we might expect given the prosecutor's intent, the prosecutorial error has virtually guaranteed conviction. There is no room in the balance of competing interests for this type of manipulation of the mistrial device. Or to put it another way, whereas we tolerate some incidental infringement upon a defendant's double jeopardy interests for the sake of society's interest in obtaining a verdict of guilt or innocence, when the prosecutor seeks to obtain an advantage by intentionally subverting double jeopardy interests, the balance invariably tips in favor of a bar to reprosecution.

Today the Court once again recognizes that the exception properly encompasses the situation in which the prosecutor commits prejudicial error with the intent to provoke a mistrial. But the Court reaches out to limit the exception to that one situation, rejecting the previous recognition that prosecutorial overreaching or harassment is also within the exception.[22]

* * * [T]he rationale for the exception extends beyond the situation in which the prosecutor intends to provoke a mistrial. There are other situations in which the defendant's double jeopardy interests outweigh society's interest in obtaining a judgment on the merits even though the defendant has moved for a mistrial. For example, a prosecutor may be interested in putting the

---

[22] The Court offers two reasons for cutting back on the exception. First, the Court states that "[t]he difficulty with the more general standards which would permit a broader exception than one merely based on intent is that they offer virtually no standards for their application." As I indicate in the text, however, some generality in the formula is a virtue and, in any event, meaningful and principled standards can be developed on a case-by-case basis that will not inhibit legitimate prosecution practices. Moreover, the general standards could hardly be more difficult to apply than the Court's subjective intent standard. * * * Second, the Court is "not sure that criminal defendants as a class would be aided" by a broader exception. If a mistrial will more frequently constitute a bar to reprosecution, the Court supposes that trial judges will tend to refuse the defendant's mistrial motion and permit the error to be corrected on appeal of the conviction, in which event there would be no bar to reprosecution. This reasoning is premised on the assumption that an appellate court that concluded not only that the defendant's mistrial motion should have been granted but also that the prosecutor intended to provoke a mistrial would not be obligated to bar reprosecution as well as reverse the conviction. The assumption is "irrational." *Commonwealth v. Potter,* 386 A.2d 918 (Pa. 1978) (Roberts, J.) (Pomeroy, J.).

defendant through the embarrassment, expense, and ordeal of criminal proceedings even if he cannot obtain a conviction. In such a case, with the purpose of harassing the defendant the prosecutor may commit repeated prejudicial errors and be indifferent between a mistrial or mistrials and an unsustainable conviction or convictions. Another example is when the prosecutor seeks to inject enough unfair prejudice into the trial to ensure a conviction but not so much as to cause a reversal of that conviction. This kind of overreaching would not be covered by the Court's standard because, by hypothesis, the prosecutor's intent is to obtain a conviction, not to provoke a mistrial. Yet the defendant's choice—to continue the tainted proceeding or to abort it and begin anew—can be just as "hollow" in this situation as when the prosecutor intends to provoke a mistrial.

To invoke the exception for overreaching, a court need not divine the exact motivation for the prosecutorial error. It is sufficient that the court is persuaded that egregious prosecutorial misconduct has rendered unmeaningful the defendant's choice to continue or to abort the proceeding. It is unnecessary and unwise to attempt to identify all the factors that might inform the court's judgment, but several considerations follow from the rationale for recognizing the exception. First, because the exception is justified by the intolerance of intentional manipulation of the defendant's double jeopardy interests, a finding of deliberate misconduct normally would be a prerequisite to a reprosecution bar. Second, because the defendant's option to abort the proceeding after prosecutorial misconduct would retain real meaning for the defendant in any case in which the trial was going badly for him, normally a required finding would be that the prosecutorial error virtually eliminated, or at least substantially reduced, the probability of acquittal in a proceeding that was going badly for the government. It should be apparent from these observations that only in a rare and compelling case will a mistrial declared at the request of the defendant or with his consent bar a retrial.

* * * The isolated prosecutorial error [here] occurred early in the trial, too early to determine whether the case was going badly for the prosecution. If anyone was being harassed at that time, it was the prosecutor who was frustrated by improper defense objections in her attempt to rehabilitate her witness. The gist of the comment that the respondent was a "crook" could fairly have been elicited from the witness, since defense counsel injected the respondent's past alleged improprieties into the trial by questioning the witness about his bias towards the defendant. The comment therefore could not have injected the kind of prejudice that would render unmeaningful the defendant's option to proceed with the trial. Because the present case quite clearly does not come within the recognized exception, I join the Court's judgment.

NOTES AND QUESTIONS

1. ***State rules offering more protection than* Kennedy.** On remand, the Oregon Supreme Court, though affirming defendant's conviction, did adopt a broader exception to the "defense-request" rule than that announced in *Kennedy,* under the Oregon Constitution. See *State v. Garner*, 234 Or.App. 486, 228 P.3d 710 (2010) (under the Oregon Constitution, retrial following a mistrial due to prosecutorial misconduct is barred when (1) the misconduct is so prejudicial that it cannot be cured by means short of mistrial; (2) the prosecutor knew that the conduct was improper and prejudicial; and (3) the prosecutor either intended or was indifferent to the resulting mistrial or reversal). Other state courts have adopted similar standards. See, e.g., *Thomas v. Eighth Judicial Dist. Court*, 402 P.3d 619 (Nev. 2017) (barring retrial after mistrial declared for *Brady* violation, holding state constitution bars retrial after mistrial whenever a prosecutor intentionally proceeds in a course of egregious and improper conduct that causes prejudice to the defendant which cannot be cured by means short of a mistrial). Most states, however, follow the *Kennedy* approach. Compare Peter J. Henning, *Prosecutorial Misconduct and Constitutional Remedies*, 77 Wash. U. L. Q. 713 (1999) ("The rationale for the *Kennedy* rule is that defendants

should not be allowed to sandbag the trial court by awaiting the outcome of the first proceeding, hoping for a not guilty verdict, and then seek to bar a second proceeding under double jeopardy on the ground that the prosecutorial misconduct tainted the conviction."), with Steven Reiss, *Prosecutorial Intent in Constitutional Criminal Procedure*, 135 U.Pa.L.Rev. 1365 (1987) (retrial should be barred where prosecutorial impropriety was sufficiently egregious to meet the "plain error standard" *and* defendant persuades the reviewing court that remedies short of a mistrial would have been "unavailing").

2. ***Burden of proving intent.*** What evidence would suggest that a prosecutor intended to provoke a defense motion for a mistrial? Misconduct so obvious that the prosecutor must have known his conduct was not permissible, and so clearly prejudicial that the prosecutor must have recognized that the defense would give serious consideration to a mistrial request? An event suggesting that the prosecutor would have had doubts as to gaining a favorable jury verdict? A basis for believing that the prosecution could do better on a new trial? See, e.g., *United States v. Hagege*, 437 F.3d 943 (9th Cir. 2006) (no error to find prosecutor did not intend to goad defendant into moving for mistrial when "the trial was going favorably for the government" and nothing in the record called into question the veracity of the prosecutor's representations that a prejudicial remark by a government witness was a complete surprise); *United States v. McCallum*, 721 F.3d 706 (D.C. Cir. 2013) (noting that "When a prosecutor deliberately causes the defendant to move for a mistrial, presumably because he believes the odds of getting a conviction will be better if he can get a fresh start, his intent is to "subvert the protections afforded by the Double Jeopardy Clause,"[and whether he] intends to obtain the mistrial by malfeasance or nonfeasance, action or inaction, is irrelevant").

3. ***Tacit or "implied" consent?*** Should the defense be viewed as having "consented" to the mistrial where the trial court informed defense counsel that it was considering ordering a mistrial and defendant counsel failed to object? The answer lower courts have given is that a court may infer consent based on a defendant's silence only if the totality of the circumstances justifies such a finding. E.g., *United States v. Buljubasic*, 808 F.2d 1260 (7th Cir. 1987) (court must consider surrounding circumstances, including whether there was sufficient time to object, and whether the trial court indicated that it would "brook no opposition" to its decision to declare a mistrial); *State v. Leon-Simaj*, 300 Neb. 317 (2018) (collecting authority, and finding implied consent when court gave defense counsel an opportunity to object to its sua sponte declaration of mistrial, and counsel failed to timely and explicitly object).

§ 2. REPROSECUTION FOLLOWING DISMISSAL, ACQUITTAL

UNITED STATES V. SCOTT

437 U.S. 82, 98 S.Ct. 2187, 57 L.Ed.2d 65 (1978).

JUSTICE REHNQUIST delivered the opinion of the Court.

On March 5, 1975, respondent, a member of the police force in Muskegon, Mich., was charged * * * with distribution of various narcotics. Both before his trial in the United States District Court and twice during the trial, respondent moved to dismiss the two counts of the indictment which concerned transactions that took place during the preceding September, on the ground that his defense had been prejudiced by preindictment delay. At the close of all the evidence, the court granted respondent's motion. Although the court did not explain its reasons for dismissing the second count, it explicitly concluded that respondent had "presented sufficient proof of prejudice with respect to the first count." * * *

The Government sought to appeal the dismissals of the first two counts to the United States Court of Appeals for the Sixth Circuit. That court * * * concluded that any further prosecution of respondent was barred by the Double Jeopardy Clause of the Fifth Amendment, and therefore dismissed the appeal. The Government has sought review in this Court only with regard to the dismissal of the first count. We granted certiorari to give further consideration to the applicability of the Double Jeopardy Clause to Government appeals from orders granting defense motions to terminate a trial before verdict. We now reverse.

* * * In 1971, Congress adopted the current language of the [Criminal Appeals] Act, permitting Government appeals from any decision dismissing an indictment, "except that no appeal shall lie where the Double Jeopardy Clause of the United States Constitution prohibits further prosecution." 18 U.S.C. § 3731. * * * In our first encounter with the new statute, we concluded "that Congress intended to remove all statutory barriers to Government appeals and to allow appeals whenever the Constitution would permit." *United States v. Wilson,* 420 U.S. 332 (1975) [discussed in Note 6, p. 1358].

* * * At the time the Fifth Amendment was adopted, its principles were easily applied, since most criminal prosecutions proceeded to final judgment, and neither the United States nor the defendant had any right to appeal an adverse verdict. The verdict in such a case was unquestionably final, and could be raised in bar against any further prosecution for the same offense. * * * It was not until 1889 that Congress permitted criminal defendants to seek a writ of error in this Court, and then only in capital cases. Only then did it become necessary for this Court to deal with the issues presented by the challenge of verdicts on appeal. And, in the very first case presenting the issues, *Ball v. United States,* 163 U.S. 662 (1896), the Court established principles that have been adhered to ever since. Three persons had been tried together for murder; two were convicted, the other acquitted. This Court reversed the convictions, finding the indictment fatally defective, whereupon all three defendants were tried again. This time all three were convicted and they again sought review here. This Court held that the Double Jeopardy Clause precluded further prosecution of the defendant who had been *acquitted* at the original trial but that it posed no such bar to the prosecution of those defendants who had been *convicted* in the earlier proceeding.

* * * These then, at least, are two venerable principles of double jeopardy jurisprudence. The successful appeal of a judgment of conviction, on any ground other than the insufficiency of the evidence to support the verdict, *Burks v. United States* [p. 1361], poses no bar to further prosecution on the same charge. A judgment of acquittal, whether based on a jury verdict of not guilty or on a ruling by the court that the evidence is insufficient to convict, may not be appealed and terminates the prosecution when a second trial would be necessitated by a reversal. What may seem superficially to be a disparity in the rules governing a defendant's liability to be tried again is explainable by reference to the underlying purposes of the Double Jeopardy Clause. * * * [T]he law attaches particular significance to an acquittal. To permit a second trial after an acquittal, however mistaken the acquittal may have been, would present an unacceptably high risk that the Government, with its vastly superior resources, might wear down the defendant so that "even though innocent, he may be found guilty." *Green v. United States* [p. 1363]. On the other hand, to require a criminal defendant to stand trial again after he has successfully invoked a statutory right of appeal to upset his first conviction is not an act of governmental oppression of the sort against which the Double Jeopardy Clause was intended to protect. * * *

Although the primary purpose of the Double Jeopardy Clause was to protect the integrity of a final judgment, this Court has also developed a body of law guarding the separate but related interest of a defendant in avoiding multiple prosecutions even where no final determination of guilt or innocence has been made. Such interests may be involved in two different situations: the first, in which the trial judge declares a mistrial; the second, in which the trial judge terminates the proceedings favorably to the defendant on a basis not related to factual guilt or innocence.

* * * We turn now to the relationship between the Double Jeopardy Clause and reprosecution of a defendant who has successfully obtained not a mistrial, but a termination of the trial in his favor before any determination of factual guilt or innocence. Unlike the typical mistrial, the granting of a motion such as this obviously contemplates that the proceedings will terminate then and there in favor of the defendant. The prosecution, if it wishes to reinstate the proceedings in the face of such a ruling, ordinarily must seek reversal of the decision of the trial court. * * * [O]nly last term, in *Lee* [*v. United States*, 432 U.S. 23 (1977)], the Government was permitted to institute a second prosecution after a midtrial dismissal of an indictment. The Court found the circumstances presented by that case "functionally indistinguishable from a declaration of a mistrial." [Ed: In *Lee*, the defendant had been charged with theft and elected a bench trial. After the prosecutor's opening statement, defense counsel moved to dismiss the information on the ground that it did not allege specific intent. The trial court took the motion under advisement and at the close of the two hour trial, explained that although the defendant's guilt had been established beyond a reasonable doubt, the information was indeed insufficient, and granted the motion. The Supreme Court held that the dismissal order had been the functional equivalent of a declaration of a mistrial, because it had been "based on the insufficiency of the information, rather than any insufficiency of the evidence."] *Lee* demonstrated that, at least in some cases, the dismissal of an indictment may be treated on the same basis as the declaration of a mistrial. * * *

[W]e are now of the view that [the] language from *Green,* ["that the State with all its resources and power should not be allowed to make repeated attempts to convict an individual for an alleged offense, thereby subjecting him to embarrassment, expense and ordeal and compelling him to live in a continuing state of anxiety and insecurity * * * "] is not a principle which can be expanded to include situations in which the defendant is responsible for the second prosecution. It is quite true that the Government with all its resources and power should not be allowed to make repeated attempts to convict an individual for an alleged offense. This truth is expressed in the three common-law pleas of *autrefois acquit, autrefois convict,* and pardon, which lie at the core of the area protected by the Double Jeopardy Clause. As we have recognized in cases from *Ball* to *Sanabria v. United States* [Note 2, p. 1355], a defendant once acquitted may not be again subjected to trial without violating the Double Jeopardy Clause.

But that situation is obviously a far cry from the present case, where the Government was quite willing to continue with its production of evidence to show the defendant guilty before the jury first empaneled to try him, but the defendant elected to seek termination of the trial on grounds unrelated to guilt or innocence. This is scarcely a picture of an all-powerful state relentlessly pursuing a defendant who had either been found not guilty or who had at least insisted on having the issue of guilt submitted to the first trier of fact. It is instead a picture of a defendant who chooses to avoid conviction and imprisonment, not because of his assertion that the Government has failed to make out a case against him, but because of a legal claim that the Government's case against him must fail even though it might satisfy the trier of fact that he was guilty beyond a reasonable doubt.

We have previously noted that "the trial judge's characterization of his own action cannot control the classification of the action." *United States v. Jorn* [p. 1336, 1337]. * * * [A] defendant is acquitted only when "the ruling of the judge, whatever its label, actually represents a resolution [in the defendant's favor], correct or not, of some or all of the factual elements of the offense charged," [*United States v. Martin Linen Supply*, 430 U.S. 564 (1977)]. Where the court, before the jury returns a verdict, enters a judgment of acquittal pursuant to Fed.R.Crim.P. 29, appeal will be barred only when "it is plain that the District Court * * * evaluated the Government's evidence and determined that it was legally insufficient to support a conviction." Id.

Our opinion in *Burks* [p. 1361] necessarily holds that there has been a "failure of proof" requiring an acquittal when the Government does not submit sufficient evidence to rebut a defendant's essentially factual defense of insanity, though it may otherwise be entitled to have its case submitted to the jury. The defense of insanity, like the defense of entrapment, arises from "the notion that Congress could not have intended criminal punishment for a defendant who has committed all the elements of a proscribed offense," *United States v. Russell*, 411 U.S. 423 (1973), where other facts established to the satisfaction of the trier of fact provide a legally adequate justification for otherwise criminal acts. Such a factual finding *does* "necessarily establish the criminal defendant's lack of criminal culpability," post, (Brennan, J., dissenting), under the existing law; the fact that "the acquittal may result from erroneous evidentiary rulings or erroneous interpretations of governing legal principles," affects the accuracy of that determination, but it does not alter its essential character. By contrast, the dismissal of an indictment for preindictment delay represents a legal judgment that a defendant, although criminally culpable, may not be punished because of a supposed constitutional violation. * * *

[I]n the present case, [defendant] successfully avoided a submission of the first count of the indictment [to the jury] by persuading the trial court to dismiss it on a basis which did not depend on guilt or innocence. He was thus neither acquitted nor convicted, because he himself successfully undertook to persuade the trial court not to submit the issue of guilt or innocence to the jury which had been empaneled to try him. * * * [Defendant] has not been "deprived" of his valued right to go to the first jury; only the public has been deprived of its valued right to "one complete opportunity to convict those who have violated its laws." *Arizona v. Washington* [p. 1340]. No interest protected by the Double Jeopardy Clause is invaded when the Government is allowed to appeal and seek reversal of such a mistrial termination of the proceedings in a manner favorable to the defendant.[13]

* * * We now conclude that where the defendant himself seeks to have the trial terminated without any submission to either judge or jury as to his guilt or innocence, an appeal by the Government from his successful effort to do so is not barred by 18 U.S.C. § 3731.

JUSTICE BRENNAN, with whom JUSTICE WHITE, JUSTICE MARSHALL, and JUSTICE STEVENS join, dissenting.

* * * The purpose of the [Double Jeopardy] Clause, which the Court today fails sufficiently to appreciate, is to protect the accused against the agony and risks attendant upon undergoing more than one criminal trial for any single offense. * * * Accordingly, the policies of the Double Jeopardy Clause mandate that the Government be afforded but one complete opportunity to convict an accused and that when the first proceeding terminates in a final judgment favorable to the defendant any retrial be barred. The rule as to acquittals can only be understood as simply an application of this larger principle.

* * * [T]he reasons that bar a retrial following an acquittal are equally applicable to a final judgment entered on a ground "unrelated to factual innocence." The heavy personal strain of the second trial is the same in either case. So too is the risk that, though innocent, the defendant may be found guilty at a second trial. If the appeal is allowed in either situation, the Government will, following any reversal, not only obtain the benefit of the favorable appellate ruling but also be permitted to shore up any other weak points of its case and obtain all the other advantages at the

---

[13] We should point out that it is entirely possible for a trial court to reconcile the public interest in the Government's right to appeal from an erroneous conclusion of law, with the defendant's interest in avoiding a second prosecution. In *Wilson*, supra, the court permitted the case to go to the jury, which returned a verdict of guilty, but it subsequently dismissed the indictment for preindictment delay on the basis of evidence adduced at trial. Most recently in *United States v. Ceccolini*, 435 U.S. 268 (1978), we described similar action with approval: "The District Court had sensibly first made its finding on the factual question of guilt or innocence, and then ruled on the motion to suppress; a reversal of these rulings would require no further proceedings in the District Court, but merely a reinstatement of the finding of guilt." We of course do not suggest that a midtrial dismissal of a prosecution, in response to a defense motion on grounds unrelated to guilt or innocence, is necessarily improper. Such rulings may be necessary to terminate proceedings marred by fundamental error. But where a defendant prevails on such a motion, he takes the risk that an appellate court will reverse the trial court.

second trial that the Double Jeopardy Clause was designed to forbid. * * * Equally significant, the distinction between the two is at best purely formal. Many acquittals are the consequence of rulings of law made on the accused's motion that are not related to the question of his factual guilt or innocence: e.g., a ruling on the law respecting the scope of the offense or excluding reliable evidence. *Sanabria v. United States* [Note 2, p. 1355] illustrates the point. * * *

* * * A critical feature of today's holding appears to be the Court's definition of acquittal as "a resolution [in the defendant's favor], correct or not, of some or all of the factual elements of the offense charged," * * *. [But] why, for purposes of its new definition of "acquittal," is not the fact *vel non* of preindictment delay one of the "factual elements of the offense charged"? The Court plainly cannot answer that preindictment delay is not referred to in the statutory definition of the offense charged in count one, for it states that dismissals based on the defenses of insanity and entrapment—neither of which is bound up with the statutory definition of federal crimes—will constitute "acquittals." How can decisions based on the trial evidence that a defendant is "not guilty by reason of insanity" or "not guilty by reason of entrapment" erect a double jeopardy bar, and a decision—equally based on evaluation of the trial evidence—that the defendant is "not guilty by reason of pre-accusation delay" not also prohibit further prosecution? * * * Ironically, it seems likely that, when all is said and done, there will be few instances indeed in which defenses can be deemed unrelated to factual innocence. If so, today's decision may be limited to disfavored doctrines like preaccusation delay. See generally *United States v. Lovasco* [p. 1082]. * * *

NOTES AND QUESTIONS

1. ***The function of the "acquittal rule."*** Professors Westen and Drubel challenged the explanations offered by both the majority and dissenting opinions in *Scott* as to the interests underlying the rule barring a retrial after an acquittal. See Peter Westen and Richard Drubel, *Towards a General Theory of Double Jeopardy,* 1978 Sup. Ct. Rev. 81; Peter Westen, *The Three Faces of Double Jeopardy: Reflections on Governmental Appeals of Criminal Sentences,* 78 Mich.L.Rev. 1001 (1980). As for the defendant's interest in avoiding the burdens and tactical disadvantages of a second trial (stressed in Justice Brennan's dissent), Professor Westen notes that those interests have been rejected as a basis for establishing an absolute bar to retrial "in every other area of double jeopardy." Thus, he notes, "the state may retry a defendant following mistrials declared over his objection, mistrials declared because of hung juries, and convictions reversed on appeal." Since the defendant in such cases is equally subject to the expense and anxiety of the second trial, to the tactical disadvantages of having disclosed his case to the prosecution, and to the possibility that the government will be able to shore up any weak points in its case, the rule prohibiting retrials following acquittals must rest, says Professor Westen, on other concerns. He rejects, however, the suggestion of the *Scott* majority that retrials following acquittals are barred because they pose "an unacceptably high risk" of resulting in the conviction of an innocent defendant. This rationale, he argues, would have to rest on the assumption that the defendant who has been acquitted, even in a trial flawed by a legal error favorable to the defendant, is more likely to be innocent than the defendant forced to face a retrial after a mistrial, after a conviction reversed on appeal due to error prejudicial to defendant, or after a dismissal based on non-acquittal grounds (such as that involved in *Scott*). Such an assumption is said to be inconsistent with an acquittal rule so absolute as to bar retrial "even where the acquittals are known to be egregiously erroneous" [quoting *Fong Foo v. United States,* 369 U.S. 141 (1962), p. 1356].

Professor Westen argues that the only sound grounding for the absolute prohibition of retrials following acquittals is the need to protect the "jury's prerogative to acquit against the evidence"—an interest that distinguishes the acquittal situation because only there does the possibility exist that the jury has exercised that prerogative. In *United States v. DiFrancesco*, 449 U.S. 117 (1980), in the course of explaining various double jeopardy principles, the Court cited both the *Scott* majority's analysis and Professor Westen's jury nullification thesis in explaining the acquittal rule. If you agree with Professor Westen's view that the ban on retrial after acquittal is linked to the jury's power to disregard the law, does it make sense to ban retrial after an acquittal by a judge not a jury?

Professor Thomas has argued that in searching for a unique grounding for the acquittal rule, Professor Westen's view ignores the common law understanding of the double jeopardy guarantee. The pleas of *autrefois acquit* and *autrefois convict* both prohibited a second prosecution for the same offense, reflecting the double jeopardy guarantee's core function of ensuring "verdict finality." The acquittal rule therefore had no special role that separated it from the conviction rule. What came to distinguish the verdict of acquittal from verdicts of conviction was the defendant's capacity "to disturb verdict finality" by electing to challenge a verdict on appeal—a capacity that applied only to verdicts of conviction, where, "naturally enough, defendants often seek to set aside the finality to which they have a right." Professor Thomas stated, "[U]ndisturbed verdicts always bar governmental action based on the same [offense], but convictions are less absolute bars than acquittals because they do not always remain undisturbed." See George C. Thomas, III, *Double Jeopardy* 233–34 (1998) (also arguing that if the principle of verdict finality is to be carried over to today's procedure, a midtrial dismissal like that in *Scott*, not based on the insufficiency of the evidence, cannot be viewed as the equivalent of an *autrefois acquit*).

2. ***Acquittals resulting from erroneous exclusions of evidence, jury instructions, or assessments of what evidence is required for conviction.*** In SANABRIA v. UNITED STATES, 437 U.S. 54 (1978), the defendant was one of several defendants charged with participation in an "illegal gambling business" in violation of 18 U.S.C. § 1955. Under that provision a gambling business violates federal law only if it also violates the law of the state in which the business is located. The single-count indictment in *Sanabria* charged that the defendants' gambling business involved wagers on a numbers pool and on horse racing in violation of Section 17 of a Massachusetts statute. The government's evidence tied *Sanabria* to the numbers operation, but not to the horsebetting. After the presentation of defendant's case, the trial judge granted defendant's earlier motion for a judgment of acquittal. It first found that Section 17 of the Massachusetts statute did not prohibit numbers betting. Another provision of the Massachusetts statute, Section 7, did make numbers betting illegal, but the government could not rely on that provision since it was not cited in the indictment. Accordingly, the court ruled, all of the evidence relating to the numbers operation had to be excluded. The court then granted the requested judgment of acquittal on the ground that there was no evidence tying the defendant to the horsebetting activities.

The government subsequently sought to appeal and asked for a new trial arguing first, that the failure to allege a violation of Section 7 of the Massachusetts statute in the indictment was harmless error and should not have barred consideration of the numbers betting as violating Massachusetts law. Second, even if it were assumed that the numbers operation could not be used to establish the illegality of the gambling business, Sanabria's participation in the numbers operation was still relevant since the federal statute would hold liable a person who participated in a lawful portion of a combined gambling venture if that venture was illegal due to its other portion, here the horse racing. On review before the Supreme Court, the Court assumed that the trial court had erred on both grounds. It held the trial court's order nevertheless was not appealable.

The opinion for the Court, per Marshall, J., initially noted that "when a defendant has been acquitted at trial, he may not be retried on the same offense, even if the legal rulings underlying the acquittal were erroneous." The government had conceded the unreviewability of "the acquittal for insufficient evidence on what it refers to as the horsebetting theory of liability." The government contended, however, that its "numbers theory of liability" was dismissed "before the judgment of acquittal was entered and therefore that petitioner was not acquitted of the numbers theory." The Court rejected this contention on two grounds: (1) the indictment had contained a single count, charging a single violation, and the acquittal therefore covered both theories of liability; and (2) even if the numbers theory was viewed as dismissed separately, a retrial on that theory would nevertheless be barred since there was only a single offense—participation in any aspect of the gambling enterprise—and the acquittal on the horsebetting necessarily constituted a final judgment as to the entire offense.

If the Supreme Court in *Sanabria* had treated the trial judge's order as similar to a *Scott*-type dismissal, would this simply have suggested to defense counsel that the better procedure would be to secure favorable jury instructions rather than a judicial "acquittal"? If the judge in *Sanabria* had let the case go to the jury and had charged the jury that defendant could be held liable only if he participated in the horsebetting, the jury presumably would have acquitted (since there was no evidence tying the defendant to horsebetting) and that acquittal clearly would have barred reprosecution.

The ruling in *Sanabria* has been enforced by the Court repeatedly. For example, in *Smith v. Massachusetts,* 543 U.S. 462 (2005), noting the "well established rule that the [double jeopardy] bar will attach to a pre-verdict acquittal that is patently wrong in law," the Court cited *Smalis v. Pennsylvania,* 476 U.S. 140 (1986) (judge alleged to have erred in deciding what degree of recklessness was required to be shown under state statute before granting acquittal) and *Fong Foo v. United States,* 369 U.S. 141 (1962) (judge directed acquittal *before* government had concluded its case, supposedly because of prosecutorial misconduct and lack of credibility of testimony by the witnesses for the prosecution who had testified up to that point).

One recurring situation is a trial court's decision to enter judgment of acquittal because the government failed to introduce sufficient evidence of a fact that, contrary to the trial judge's view, turns out not to be an element of the offense. As the Court explained in *Evans v. Michigan*, 568 U.S. 313 (2013), "There is no question the trial court's ruling was wrong; it was predicated upon a clear misunderstanding of what facts the State needed to prove under State law. But that is of no moment. *Martin Linen*, *Sanabria*, [*Arizona* v. *Rumsey*, 467 U.S. 203 (1984)], *Smalis*, and *Smith* all instruct that an acquittal due to insufficient evidence precludes retrial, whether the court's evaluation of the evidence was 'correct or not,' and regardless of whether the court's decision flowed from an incorrect antecedent ruling of law." "This case, like our previous ones, involves an antecedent legal error that led to an acquittal because the State failed to prove some fact it was not actually required to prove."

Responding to the argument that this rule allows a defendant to reap a "windfall" from the trial court's unreviewable error, the Court in *Evans* stated: "sovereigns are hardly powerless to prevent this sort of situation * * *. Nothing obligates a jurisdiction to afford its trial courts the power to grant a midtrial acquittal, and at least two States [Nevada and Louisiana] disallow the practice. Many jurisdictions, including the federal system, allow or encourage their courts to defer consideration of a motion to acquit until after the jury returns a verdict, which mitigates double jeopardy concerns. See Fed. Rule Crim. Proc. 29(b). And for cases such as this, in which a trial court's interpretation of the relevant criminal statute is likely to prove dispositive, we see no reason why jurisdictions could not provide for mandatory or expedited interlocutory appeals if they wished to prevent misguided acquittals from being entered. But having chosen to vest its courts with the power to grant midtrial acquittals, the State must bear the corresponding risk that some acquittals will be granted in error." "It should make no difference whether the court employs the formality of directing the jury to return an acquittal or whether the court enters an acquittal itself."

3. ***Distinguishing dismissals that do not bar retrial from acquittals that do.*** What distinguishes a judge's favorable mid-trial ruling regarding a defense such as insanity or entrapment, a ruling that will constitute an acquittal, from a midtrial dismissal for preindictment delay, or failure of the statute of limitations, that will not? The Court in *Evans* reviewed the difference: "an 'acquittal' includes 'a ruling by the court that the evidence is insufficient to convict,' a 'factual finding [that] necessarily establish[es] the criminal defendant's lack of criminal culpability,' and any other 'rulin[g] which relate[s] to the ultimate question of guilt or innocence.' *Scott.* These sorts of substantive rulings stand apart from procedural rulings that may also terminate a case midtrial, which we generally refer to as dismissals or mistrials. Procedural dismissals include rulings on questions that 'are unrelated to factual guilt or innocence,' but 'which serve other purposes,' including 'a legal judgment that a defendant, although criminally culpable, may not be punished' because of some problem like an error with the indictment." Continued the Court, "The distinction drawn in *Scott* has stood the test of time, and we expect courts will continue to have little 'difficulty in distinguishing between those rulings which relate to the ultimate question of guilt or innocence and those which serve other purposes.' "

In *Martinez v. Illinois*, 572 U.S. 833 (2014), after the jury was selected and sworn, the prosecution was unable to produce two of its witnesses. The state declared it was "not participating" in the trial and would produce no evidence, and the defendant moved for directed verdict of acquittal, which the trial judge granted. Because the court "acted on its view that the prosecution had failed to prove its case," the Court explained, this was a "textbook acquittal," not a dismissal. The trial judge, the Court observed, told the prosecution on the day of trial that it could "move to dismiss [its] case" before the jury was sworn, but the state declined to accept that invitation, missing its chance to avoid the double jeopardy bar. The Court added that jeopardy had attached, "even if the trial court had chosen to dismiss the case or declare a mistrial rather than granting Martinez's motion for a directed verdict, the Double Jeopardy Clause probably would still bar his retrial," noting that "precisely this scenario" took place in *Downum*.

In some cases, the trial court may be able to may control the double jeopardy consequences of an order ending trial by varying the order's rationale. If the order is based on the prosecution's failure to *prove* all of the elements, under *Sanabria* and *Evans* the government may not appeal, even when the court was mistaken in its interpretation of the necessary elements. If the order is based on the prosecution's failure to *charge* all the elements, *Lee* and *Scott* permit appeal.

4. ***The timing of the defense objection: legal defenses capable of being raised and resolved before trial.*** In *Sanabria,* the government argued that even if the trial court's ruling must be viewed as an acquittal, it should not bar retrial because of Sanabria's failure to make a pretrial objection to the government's theory that the offense could be established by reference to the gambling organization's numbers activities. Because a pretrial objection would have allowed the government to seek an amendment of the indictment, this deliberate delay, argued the government, amounted to a "waiver" of the defendant's subsequent double jeopardy objection. The Court rejected the government's theory: "Unlike questions of whether an indictment states an offense, a statute is unconstitutional, or conduct set forth in an indictment violates the statute, what proof may be presented in support of a valid indictment and the sufficiency of that proof are not 'legal defenses' required to be or even capable of being resolved before trial. In all of the former instances, a ruling in the defendant's favor completely precludes conviction, at least on that indictment. Here, even if the numbers language had been struck before trial, there was no 'legal' reason why petitioner could not have been convicted on this indictment [through the horsebetting], as were his 10 codefendants." In *Evans*, a similar argument was raised and rejected. The Court explained, "even if the Government is correct that Evans could have challenged [before trial] the charging document on the same legal theory he used to challenge the sufficiency of the evidence, it matters that he made only the latter motion, a motion that necessarily may not be made until trial is underway. Evans cannot be penalized for requesting from the court a ruling on the merits

of the State's case, as the Michigan Rules entitled him to do; whether he could have also brought a distinct procedural objection earlier on is beside the point."

Although a defendant cannot be expected to challenge the sufficiency of proof before trial, most jurisdictions do require defendants to raise pretrial those objections that can be resolved before trial, such as grand jury error, challenges to the indictment, delay in charging and trial, discovery violations, motions to suppress illegally obtained evidence, and joinder. If a defendant waits until after trial begins to raise such a claim, it is considered waived, unless the defendant can show "good cause" for not raising the claim earlier. See, e.g., Fed.R.Crim.P. 12; *Davis v. United States*, 411 U.S. 233 (1973) (discussing grand jury error), and Notes 1–6, pp. 1005–1009 (discussing pleading defects).

5. ***"Acquittals" and dismissals before jeopardy attaches.*** When a court rules *before* jeopardy has attached that the government's evidence is insufficient, reprosecution is not barred. In *Serfass v. United States*, 420 U.S. 377 (1975), petitioner, charged with willful failure to submit to military induction, filed a pretrial motion to dismiss based on the selective service board's treatment of his claim of conscientious objection. The district court then reviewed the selective service file and concluded, based on the evidence contained there, that the petitioner had submitted a "prima facie case of conscientious objector status," which invalidated the induction order due to the board's failure to provide appropriate review of that claim. The Court held that the Double Jeopardy Clause would not bar a retrial following a successful government appeal and therefore the district court's ruling was appealable (see Note 1, p. 1409). The Court stressed that the district court's ruling had come prior to the attachment of jeopardy. Defendant argued that "constructive jeopardy had attached" since the judge's ruling was the "functional equivalent of an acquittal," but the Court responded that this argument failed in light of the "history and terms" of the double jeopardy clause. Both demonstrate that the clause's protection "does not come into play until a proceeding begins before a trier having jurisdiction to try the question of guilt or innocence of the accused." That clearly was not the situation here, where the case was to be tried to a jury. See also *United States v. Sanford*, 429 U.S. 14 (1976) (government could appeal pretrial ruling dismissing unlawful hunting charge on the basis that government agents had "consented" to the defendant's conduct, a pretrial order similar to that issued in *Serfass*).

6. ***Judgments of acquittal after the verdict.*** Assume that the defendant is tried before a jury and found guilty. The trial judge then reconsiders a motion for a judgment of acquittal and concludes that, notwithstanding the jury verdict, the testimony of the chief prosecution witness was so inherently incredible that no reasonable person could find defendant guilty beyond a reasonable doubt. The trial judge then enters a judgment of acquittal notwithstanding the jury's verdict, as allowed by law. Would a prosecution appeal from that order place the defendant in double jeopardy? In *United States v. Wilson*, 420 U.S. 332 (1975), after the jury returned a verdict of guilty, the trial court reconsidered an earlier motion and dismissed the indictment on the ground that the government's preindictment delay had resulted in a denial of due process. In sustaining the government's appeal from that order, the Court found no need to determine "whether the ruling in Wilson's favor was actually an 'acquittal,' " (an issue later reached in *Scott*). It concluded that the appeal was not barred by the Double Jeopardy Clause since the defendant would not be exposed to multiple trials. Justice Marshall's opinion for the Court majority noted that "[W]here there is no threat of either multiple punishment or successive prosecutions, the Double Jeopardy Clause is not offended. * * * Since the 1907 Criminal Appeals Act, for example, the Government has been permitted without serious constitutional challenge to appeal from orders arresting judgment after a verdict has been entered against the defendant. Since reversal on appeal would merely reinstate the jury's verdict, review of such an order does not offend the policy against multiple prosecution. * * * Although review of any ruling of law discharging a defendant obviously enhances the likelihood of conviction and subjects him to continuing expense

and anxiety, a defendant has no legitimate claim to benefit from an error of law when that error could be corrected without subjecting him to a second trial before a second trier of fact."

7. ***Acquittals obtained by fraud or lacking jurisdiction.*** Should an acquittal bar reprosecution when the prosecution has established that the defendant bribed the judge or tampered with the jury? Consider David Rudstein, *Double Jeopardy and the Fraudulently Obtained-Acquittal*, 60 Mo. L. Rev. 607 (1995), and Anne Bowen Poulin, *Double Jeopardy and Judicial Accountability: When is an Acquittal Not an Acquittal*, 27 Ariz. St. L. J. 953 (1995), both taking note of an Illinois trial court ruling allowing a reprosecution where the judge had been bribed, the court concluding that the defendant had never truly been in jeopardy of conviction, *People v. Aleman*, 1994 WL 684499 (Ill.Cir.1994). See also *United States ex rel. Aleman v. Circuit Court of Cook County*, 967 F. Supp. 1022 (N.D. Ill. 1997) (recognizing exception for bench trial only). The Supreme Court has declined to address whether jeopardy fails to attach when an acquittal is obtained by fraud, or is delivered by court lacking jurisdiction. See *Martinez v. Illinois*, 572 U.S. 833 (2014).

§ 3. REPROSECUTION FOLLOWING CONVICTION

LOCKHART V. NELSON

488 U.S. 33, 109 S.Ct. 285, 102 L.Ed.2d 265 (1988).

CHIEF JUSTICE REHNQUIST delivered the opinion of the Court.

In this case a reviewing court set aside a defendant's conviction because certain evidence was erroneously admitted against him, and further held that the Double Jeopardy Clause forbade the State to retry him because the remaining evidence adduced at trial was legally insufficient to support a conviction. Nothing in the record suggests any misconduct in the prosecutor's submission of the evidence. We conclude that in cases such as this, where the evidence offered by the State and admitted by the trial court—whether erroneously or not—would have been sufficient to sustain a guilty verdict, the Double Jeopardy Clause does not preclude retrial.

Respondent Johnny Lee Nelson pleaded guilty in Arkansas state court to burglary, a class B felony, and misdemeanor theft. He was sentenced under the State's habitual criminal statute, which provides that a defendant who is convicted of a class B felony and "who has previously been convicted of . . . [or] found guilty of four [4] or more felonies," may be sentenced to an enhanced term of imprisonment of between 20 and 40 years. To have a convicted defendant's sentence enhanced under the statute, the State must prove beyond a reasonable doubt, at a separate sentencing hearing, that the defendant has the requisite number of prior felony convictions. Section 41–1003 of the statute sets out the means by which the prosecution may prove the prior felony convictions, providing that "[a] previous conviction or finding of guilt of a felony may be proved by any evidence that satisfies the trier of fact beyond a reasonable doubt that the defendant was convicted or found guilty," and that three types of documents, including "a duly certified copy of the record of a previous conviction or finding of guilt by a court of record," are "sufficient to support a finding of a prior conviction or finding of guilt." The defendant is entitled to challenge the State's evidence of his prior convictions and to rebut it with evidence of his own.

At respondent's sentencing hearing, the State introduced, without objection from the defense, certified copies of four prior felony convictions. Unbeknownst to the prosecutor, one of those convictions had been pardoned by the Governor several years after its entry. Defense counsel made no objection to the admission of the pardoned conviction, because he too was unaware of the Governor's action. On cross-examination, respondent indicated his belief that the conviction in question had been pardoned. The prosecutor suggested that respondent was confusing a pardon with a commutation to time served. Under questioning from the court, respondent agreed that the conviction had been commuted rather than pardoned, and the matter was not pursued any further.[2] The case was submitted to the jury, which found that the State had met its burden of proving four prior convictions and imposed an enhanced sentence. The State courts upheld the enhanced sentence on both direct and collateral review, despite respondent's protestations that one of the convictions relied upon by the State had been pardoned.

Several years later, respondent sought a writ of habeas corpus in the United States District Court, contending once again that the enhanced sentence was invalid because one of the prior convictions used to support it had been pardoned. When an investigation undertaken by the State at the District Court's request revealed that the conviction in question had in fact been pardoned, the District Court declared the enhanced sentence to be invalid. The State announced its intention to resentence respondent as a habitual offender, using another prior conviction not offered or admitted at the initial sentencing hearing, and respondent interposed a claim of double jeopardy. After hearing arguments from counsel, the District Court decided that the Double Jeopardy Clause prevented the State from attempting to resentence respondent as a habitual offender on the burglary charge. The Court of Appeals for the Eighth Circuit affirmed. The Court of Appeals reasoned that the pardoned conviction was not admissible under state law, and that "[w]ithout [it], the state has failed to provide sufficient evidence" to sustain the enhanced sentence. We granted certiorari to review this interpretation of the Double Jeopardy Clause.[6] * * *

It has long been settled [that] the Double Jeopardy Clause's general prohibition against successive prosecutions does not prevent the government from retrying a defendant who succeeds in getting his first conviction set aside, through direct appeal or collateral attack, because of some error in the proceedings leading to conviction. *Ball v. United States,* [p. 1351, Note 1 p. 1362] (retrial permissible following reversal of conviction on direct appeal); *United States v. Tateo,* 377 U.S. 463 (1964) (retrial permissible when conviction declared invalid on collateral attack). This rule, which is a "well-established part of our constitutional jurisprudence," is necessary in order to ensure the "sound administration of justice":

> "Corresponding to the right of an accused to be given a fair trial is the societal interest in punishing one whose guilt is clear after he has obtained such a trial. It would be a high price indeed for society to pay were every accused granted immunity from punishment because of any defect sufficient to constitute reversible error in the proceedings leading to conviction." *Tateo.*

Permitting retrial after a conviction has been set aside also serves the interests of defendants, for "it is at least doubtful that appellate courts would be as zealous as they now are in protecting

---

[2] There is no indication that the prosecutor knew of the pardon and was attempting to deceive the court. We therefore have no occasion to consider what the result would be if the case were otherwise. Cf. *Oregon v. Kennedy* [p. 1345].

[6] The State has attacked the ruling below on a single ground: that the defect in respondent's first sentence enhancement proceeding does not bar retrial. To reach this question, we would ordinarily have to decide two issues which are its logical antecedents: (1) whether the rule that the Double Jeopardy Clause limits the State's power to subject a defendant to successive capital sentencing proceedings, see *Bullington v. Missouri,* 451 U.S. 430 (1981), carries over to noncapital sentencing proceedings * * *; and (2) whether the rule that retrial is prohibited after a conviction is set aside by an *appellate* court for evidentiary insufficiency, see *Burks v. United States,* infra, is applicable when the determination of evidentiary insufficiency is made instead by a federal habeas court in a collateral attack on a state conviction. The courts below answered both questions in the affirmative, and the State has conceded both in its briefs and at oral argument the validity of those rulings. We therefore assume, without deciding, that these two issues present no barrier to reaching the double jeopardy claim raised here.

[Ed: The Court later held the answer to the first question was no. See *Monge v. California,* 524 U.S. 721 (1998), holding that *Bullington* did not extend beyond the capital sentencing context, and therefore double jeopardy did not bar a retrial on the issue of whether a prior conviction met the prerequisites for recidivist sentencing in a noncapital sentencing proceeding.]

against the effects of improprieties at the trial or pretrial stage if they knew that reversal of a conviction would put the accused irrevocably beyond the reach of further prosecution." Ibid.

In *Burks v. United States,* 437 U.S. 1 (1978), we recognized an exception to the general rule that the Double Jeopardy Clause does not bar the retrial of a defendant who has succeeded in getting his conviction set aside for error in the proceedings below. *Burks* held that when a defendant's conviction is reversed by an appellate court on the sole ground that the evidence was insufficient to sustain the jury's verdict, the Double Jeopardy Clause bars a retrial on the same charge.

Burks was based on the view that an appellate court's reversal for insufficiency of the evidence is in effect a determination that the government's case against the defendant was so lacking that the trial court should have entered a judgment of acquittal, rather than submitting the case to the jury. Because the Double Jeopardy Clause affords the defendant who obtains a judgment of acquittal at the trial level absolute immunity from further prosecution for the same offense, it ought to do the same for the defendant who obtains an appellate determination that the trial court *should* have entered a judgment of acquittal. The fact that the determination of entitlement to a judgment of acquittal is made by the appellate court rather than the trial court should not, we thought, affect its double jeopardy consequences; to hold otherwise "would create a purely arbitrary distinction" between defendants based on the hierarchical level at which the determination was made.

The question presented by this case—[is] whether the Double Jeopardy Clause allows retrial when a reviewing court determines that a defendant's conviction must be reversed because evidence was erroneously admitted against him, and also concludes that without the inadmissible evidence there was insufficient evidence to support a conviction * * * . We think the logic of *Burks* requires that the question be answered in the affirmative.

Burks was careful to point out that a reversal based solely on evidentiary insufficiency has fundamentally different implications, for double jeopardy purposes, than a reversal based on such ordinary "trial errors" as the "incorrect receipt or rejection of evidence." While the former is in effect a finding "that the government has failed to prove its case" against the defendant, the latter "implies nothing with respect to the guilt or innocence of the defendant," but is simply "a determination that [he] has been convicted through a judicial *process* which is defective in some fundamental respect."

It appears to us to be beyond dispute that this is a situation described in *Burks* as reversal for "trial error"—the trial court erred in admitting a particular piece of evidence, and without it there was insufficient evidence to support a judgment of conviction. But clearly *with* that evidence, there was enough to support the sentence: the court and jury had before them certified copies of four prior felony convictions, and that is sufficient to support a verdict of enhancement under the statute. The fact that one of the convictions had been later pardoned by the Governor vitiated its legal effect, but it did not deprive the certified copy of that conviction of its probative value under the statute. It is quite clear from our opinion in *Burks* that a reviewing court must consider all of the evidence admitted by the trial court in deciding whether retrial is permissible under the Double Jeopardy Clause—indeed, that was the *ratio decidendi* of *Burks,* and the overwhelming majority of appellate courts considering the question have agreed. The basis for the *Burks* exception to the general rule is that a reversal for insufficiency of the evidence should be treated no differently than a trial court's granting a judgment of acquittal at the close of all the evidence. A trial court in passing on such a motion considers all of the evidence it has admitted, and to make the analogy complete it must be this same quantum of evidence which is considered by the reviewing court.[a]

Permitting retrial in this instance is not the sort of governmental oppression at which the Double Jeopardy Clause is aimed; rather, it serves the interest of the defendant by affording him an opportunity to "obtai[n] a fair readjudication of his guilt free from error." *Burks*. Had the defendant offered evidence at the sentencing hearing to prove that the conviction had become a nullity by reason of the pardon, the trial judge would presumably have allowed the prosecutor an opportunity to offer evidence of another prior conviction to support the habitual offender charge. Our holding today thus merely recreates the situation that would have been obtained if the trial court had excluded the evidence of the conviction because of the showing of a pardon. The judgment of the Court of Appeals is accordingly reversed.

JUSTICE MARSHALL, with whom JUSTICE BRENNAN and JUSTICE BLACKMUN join, dissenting.

* * * It seems to me that the Court's analysis of this issue should begin with the recognition that, in deciding when the double jeopardy bar should apply, we are balancing two weighty interests: the defendant's interest in repose and society's interest in the orderly administration of justice. * * *. [O]ne might inquire into whether prosecutors tend in close cases to hold back probative evidence of a defendant's guilt; if they do not, there would be scant societal interest in permitting retrial given that the State's remaining evidence is, by definition, insufficient. Alternatively, one might inquire as to why the evidence at issue was deemed inadmissible. Where evidence was stricken for reasons having to do with its unreliability, it would seem curious to include it in the sufficiency calculus. * * *

NOTES AND QUESTIONS

1. ***The "*Ball *rule."*** While it has "long been settled" that double jeopardy "does not prevent the government from retrying a defendant who succeeds in getting his first conviction set aside * * * because of some error in the proceedings leading to conviction", that principle (first announced in *Ball* and commonly described as the "*Ball* rule") has not gone without challenge. Consider the position taken by Judge Fleming in *The Price of Perfect Justice,* 58 Judicature 340, 344 (1975). Discussing changes in procedure that would help to reduce delay in the administration of the criminal justice process, Judge Fleming notes: "My third suggestion is that a defendant be tried only once to judgment. If on appeal after judgment of conviction the trial is found substantially defective or unfair, the judgment should be reversed and the defendant should go free. If defects are found in the trial but the defects have not substantially influenced the result, the judgment should stand and become immune from further judicial examination. The occasional mistakes and mishaps discovered after judgment can be cured through executive action and the pardoning power without infringing upon the integrity of the court's judgment. This proposal may sound revolutionary, but it is actually a return to first principles. The English * * * [had] always had a system of only one trial to final judgment. [It] was not until 1896 in the case of *United States v. Ball* that multiple trials were sanctioned in the federal courts. One trial would certainly sharpen the responsibility of everyone connected with a criminal cause, trial judge, counsel, witnesses, appellate court, to whom the seriousness of what they were doing would be brought home by realization of its finality." Compare Thomas, *Double Jeopardy*, p. 1355 (*Ball* itself relied upon a "more Blackstone-like explanation" recognizing that verdict finality lies at heart of the plea of

[a] The Court emphasized this point again in *McDaniel v. Brown*, 558 U.S. 120 (2010) ("To 'make the analogy complete' between a reversal for insufficiency of the evidence and the trial court's granting a judgment of acquittal, *Lockhart*, 'a reviewing court must consider all of the evidence admitted by the trial court,' regardless whether that evidence was admitted erroneously.").

former jeopardy and that the successful defense appeal removes the verdict and therefore the plea in bar).

2. ***Convictions as implied acquittals.*** In *Green v. United States*, 355 U.S. 184 (1957), the defendant was charged with first degree murder, and the jury was informed that they could find him guilty either of first degree murder or of the lesser included offense of second degree murder. The jury returned a verdict of guilty on the second degree murder charge, saying nothing as to the first degree murder charge. Green appealed his second degree murder conviction, and the appellate court reversed on the basis of a trial error. He was then retried on the original first degree murder charge. The second jury convicted him of first degree murder, but a divided (5–4) Supreme Court reversed, holding that double jeopardy barred conviction on that charge. The majority opinion, by Black, J., noted: "Green was in direct peril of being convicted and punished for first degree murder at his first trial. He was forced to run the gauntlet once on that charge and the jury refused to convict him. When given the choice between finding him guilty of either first or second degree murder it chose the latter. In this situation the great majority of cases in this country have regarded the jury's verdict as an implicit acquittal on the charge of first degree murder. * * * [T]he jury was dismissed without returning any express verdict on that charge and without Green's consent. Yet it was given a full opportunity to return a verdict and no extraordinary circumstances appeared which prevented it from doing so. Therefore it seems clear, under established principles of former jeopardy, that Green's jeopardy for first degree murder came to an end when the jury was discharged so that he could not be retried for that offense. In brief, we believe this case can be treated no differently, for purposes of former jeopardy, than if the jury had returned a verdict which expressly read: 'We find the defendant not guilty of murder in the first degree but guilty of murder in the second degree.' "

The implied acquittal rationale does not apply where the jury convicts on the lesser charge, but notes that it cannot reach agreement on the higher charge (resulting in a mistrial—not acquittal—as to that charge). See *Sattazahn v. Pennsylvania*, 537 U.S. 101 (2003). Also, the acceptance of a guilty plea to a lesser charge does not constitute "an inferential finding of not guilty" as to a higher charge. The defendant has not really been in jeopardy as to the higher charge, and, unlike the jury in *Green,* the judge receiving the plea could not have convicted the defendant of the higher charge. Of course, if the prosecutor agrees to dismiss the higher charge in return for the plea to the lesser charge, the defendant may enforce that agreement. See Ch. 22, Section 2. But if the prosecutor does not agree to the dismissal, the prosecutor may be able to continue the prosecution on the higher charge notwithstanding the guilty plea to the lesser charge. See *Ohio v. Johnson*, 467 U.S. 493 (1984). Also, with no implied acquittal, if the defendant should overturn his guilty plea to the lesser charge, double jeopardy does not bar prosecution on the higher charge. See Note 5, p. 1183.

Assume that a manslaughter conviction impliedly acquitted the defendant of murder, but following the reversal of the manslaughter conviction for trial error, the prosecution sought retrial for murder and trial court erroneously denied defendant's double jeopardy objection. If at this second trial the defendant is convicted of manslaughter, what remedy is available to the defendant? In *Price v. Georgia,* 398 U.S. 323 (1970), the Court ordered a new trial on the manslaughter charge *alone*, noting that "we cannot determine whether or not the murder charge against the petitioner induced the jury to find him guilty of the less serious offense of voluntary manslaughter rather than to continue to debate his innocence." However, in *Morris v. Mathews,* 475 U.S. 237 (1986), the Court refused to order a new trial where the second trial on both charges resulted in a conviction for the higher, jeopardy-barred offense. Instead, the Court reduced the conviction to the lesser included offense that was not jeopardy barred. In *Price,* the *Morris* Court noted, it had been concerned that the retrial on the offense for which defendant had been implicitly acquitted had resulted in a compromise verdict. Since the jury in Morris's second trial had convicted him of the higher, jeopardy-barred count of aggravated murder, it had necessarily found, without a suggestion of a possible compromise, that the state had established all of the elements of the lesser included offense of non-aggravated murder that was not jeopardy-barred. Reasoned the Court, it would be "incongruous" to remedy the double jeopardy violation that occurred in trying the defendant on the jeopardy-barred count by ordering "yet another trial."

§ 4. REPROSECUTION BY A DIFFERENT SOVEREIGN

PUERTO RICO V. SANCHEZ VALLE ET AL.

___ U.S. ___, 136 S.Ct. 1863, 195 L.Ed.2d 179 (2016).

[Luis Sánchez Valle and Jaime Gómez Vázquez (on separate occasions) each sold a gun to an undercover police officer. Commonwealth prosecutors indicted them for, among other things, selling a firearm without a permit in violation of the Puerto Rico Arms Act of 2000. While those charges were pending, federal grand juries indicted Sánchez Valle and Gómez Vázquez, based on the same transactions, for violations of analogous U.S. gun trafficking statutes. Both defendants pleaded guilty to those federal charges. The Court granted certiorari to determine whether the Double Jeopardy Clause bars the Federal Government and Puerto Rico from successively prosecuting a defendant on like charges for the same conduct.]

JUSTICE KAGAN delivered the opinion of the Court.[a]

The Double Jeopardy Clause of the Fifth Amendment prohibits more than one prosecution for the "same offence." But under what is known as the dual-sovereignty doctrine, a single act gives rise to distinct offenses—and thus may subject a person to successive prosecutions—if it violates the laws of separate sovereigns. To determine whether two prosecuting authorities are different sovereigns for double jeopardy purposes, this Court asks a narrow, historically focused question. The inquiry does not turn, as the term "sovereignty" sometimes suggests, on the degree to which the second entity is autonomous from the first or sets its own political course. Rather, the issue is only whether the prosecutorial powers of the two jurisdictions have independent origins—or, said conversely, whether those powers derive from the same "ultimate source." *United States v. Wheeler*, 435 U.S. 313, 320 (1978). In this case, we must decide if, under that test, Puerto Rico and the United States may successively prosecute a single defendant for the same criminal conduct. We hold they may not, because the oldest roots of Puerto Rico's power to prosecute lie in federal soil.

I A

Puerto Rico became a territory of the United States in 1898, as a result of the Spanish-American War. The treaty concluding that conflict ceded the island, then a Spanish colony, to the United States, and tasked Congress with determining "[t]he civil rights and political status" of its inhabitants. * * * Acting pursuant to the U.S. Constitution's Territory Clause, Congress initially established a "civil government" for Puerto Rico possessing significant authority over internal affairs. The U.S. President, with the advice and consent of the Senate, appointed the governor, supreme court, and upper house of the legislature; the Puerto Rican people elected the lower house themselves. Federal statutes generally applied (as they still do) in Puerto Rico, but the newly constituted legislature could enact local laws in much the same way as the then-45 States. Over time, Congress granted Puerto Rico additional autonomy. * * * Public Law 600, "recognizing the principle of government by consent," authorized the island's people to "organize a government pursuant to a constitution of their own adoption." * * * The Puerto Rico Constitution created a

[a] The dissenting opinion of Justice Breyer, joined by Justice Sotomayor, is omitted, as well as the separate concurring opinion by Justice Thomas.

new political entity, the Commonwealth of Puerto Rico—or, in Spanish, Estado Libre Asociado de Puerto Rico. * * *

II A

* * * The ordinary rule under that Clause is that a person cannot be prosecuted twice for the same offense.[1] But two prosecutions, this Court has long held, are not for the same offense if brought by different sovereigns—even when those actions target the identical criminal conduct through equivalent criminal laws As we have put the point: "[W]hen the same act transgresses the laws of two sovereigns, it cannot be truly averred that the offender has been twice punished for the same offence; but only that by one act he has committed two offences." *Heath v. Alabama*, 474 U.S. 82, 88 (1985). The Double Jeopardy Clause thus drops out of the picture when the "entities that seek successively to prosecute a defendant for the same course of conduct [are] separate sovereigns."

Truth be told, however, "sovereignty" in this context does not bear its ordinary meaning. For whatever reason, the test we have devised to decide whether two governments are distinct for double jeopardy purposes overtly disregards common indicia of sovereignty. * * * [T]he inquiry (despite its label) does not probe whether a government possesses the usual attributes, or acts in the common manner, of a sovereign entity. Rather, * * * our test hinges on a single criterion: the "ultimate source" of the power undergirding the respective prosecutions. Whether two prosecuting entities are dual sovereigns in the double jeopardy context, we have stated, depends on "whether [they] draw their authority to punish the offender from distinct sources of power." *Heath*. The inquiry is thus historical, not functional—looking at the deepest wellsprings, not the current exercise, of prosecutorial authority. If two entities derive their power to punish from wholly independent sources (imagine here a pair of parallel lines), then they may bring successive prosecutions. Conversely, if those entities draw their power from the same ultimate source (imagine now two lines emerging from a common point, even if later diverging), then they may not.[3]

Under that approach, the States are separate sovereigns from the Federal Government (and from one another). See *Abbate v. United States*, 359 U.S. 187, 195 (1959); *Bartkus v. Illinois*, 359 U.S. 121, 132–137 (1959). The States' "powers to undertake criminal prosecutions," we have explained, do not "derive[ ] . . . from the Federal Government." Instead, the States rely on "authority originally belonging to them before admission to the Union and preserved to them by the Tenth Amendment." Said otherwise: Prior to forming the Union, the States possessed "separate and independent sources of power and authority," which they continue to draw upon in enacting and enforcing criminal laws. *Heath*. State prosecutions therefore have their most ancient roots in an "inherent sovereignty" unconnected to, and indeed pre-existing, the U.S. Congress.[4]

---

1 Because the parties in this case agree that the Double Jeopardy Clause applies to Puerto Rico, we have no occasion to consider that question here.

3 The Court has never explained its reasons for adopting this historical approach to the dual-sovereignty doctrine. It may appear counter-intuitive, even legalistic, as compared to an inquiry focused on a governmental entity's functional autonomy. But that alternative would raise serious problems of application. It would require deciding exactly how much autonomy is sufficient for separate sovereignty and whether a given entity's exercise of self-rule exceeds that level. The results, we suspect, would often be uncertain, introducing error and inconsistency into our double jeopardy law. By contrast, as we go on to show, the Court has easily applied the "ultimate source" test to classify broad classes of governments as either sovereign or not for purposes of barring retrials.

4 Literalists might object that only the original 13 States can claim such an independent source of authority; for the other 37, Congress played some role in establishing them as territories, authorizing or approving their constitutions, or (at the least) admitting them to the Union. And indeed, that is the tack the dissent takes. But this Court long ago made clear that a new State, upon entry, necessarily becomes vested with all the legal characteristics and capabilities of the first 13. That principle of "equal footing," we have held, is essential to ensure that the nation remains "a union of States [alike] in power, dignity and authority, each

For similar reasons, Indian tribes also count as separate sovereigns under the Double Jeopardy Clause. Originally, this Court has noted, "the tribes were self-governing sovereign political communities," possessing (among other capacities) the "inherent power to prescribe laws for their members and to punish infractions of those laws." *Wheeler*, 435 U.S., at 322–323. After the formation of the United States, the tribes became "domestic dependent nations," subject to plenary control by Congress—so hardly "sovereign" in one common sense. But unless and until Congress withdraws a tribal power—including the power to prosecute—the Indian community retains that authority in its earliest form. The "ultimate source" of a tribe's "power to punish tribal offenders" thus lies in its "primeval" or, at any rate, "pre-existing" sovereignty: A tribal prosecution, like a State's, is "attributable in no way to any delegation . . . of federal authority." * * *

Conversely, this Court has held that a municipality cannot qualify as a sovereign distinct from a State—no matter how much autonomy over criminal punishment the city maintains. See *Waller* [*v. Florida*], 397 U.S. 387, 395 (1970). Florida law, we recognized in our pivotal case on the subject, treated a municipality as a "separate sovereign entit[y]" for all relevant real-world purposes: The city possessed broad home-rule authority, including the power to enact criminal ordinances and prosecute offenses. But that functional control was not enough to escape the double jeopardy bar; indeed, it was wholly beside the point. * * * Because the municipality, in the first instance, had received its power from the State, those two entities could not bring successive prosecutions for a like offense.

And most pertinent here, this Court concluded in the early decades of the last century that U.S. territories—including an earlier incarnation of Puerto Rico itself—are not sovereigns distinct from the United States. * * *

B

* * * [I]f we go back as far as our doctrine demands—to the "ultimate source" of Puerto Rico's prosecutorial power,—we once again discover the U.S. Congress. * * * [I]f our double jeopardy decisions hinged on measuring an entity's self-governance, the emergence of the Commonwealth would have resulted as well in the capacity to bring the kind of successive prosecutions attempted here. But as already explained, the dual-sovereignty test we have adopted focuses on a different question: not on the fact of self-rule, but on where it came from. We do not care, for example, that the States presently exercise autonomous control over criminal law and other local affairs; instead, we treat them as separate sovereigns because they possessed such control as an original matter, rather than deriving it from the Federal Government. * * *

* * * [N]o one argues that when the United States gained possession of Puerto Rico, its people possessed independent prosecutorial power, in the way that the States or tribes did upon becoming part of this country. Puerto Rico was until then a colony "under Spanish sovereignty." And local prosecutors in the ensuing decades, as petitioner itself acknowledges, exercised only such power as was "delegated by Congress" through federal statutes. Their authority derived from, rather than pre-existed association with, the Federal Government.

And contrary to petitioner's claim, Puerto Rico's transformative constitutional moment does not lead to a different conclusion. * * * Back of the Puerto Rican people and their Constitution, the "ultimate" source of prosecutorial power remains the U.S. Congress, just as back of a city's charter lies a state government. * * * Put simply, Congress conferred the authority to create the Puerto

---

competent to exert that residuum of sovereignty not delegated to the United States." Thus, each later-admitted State exercises its authority to enact and enforce criminal laws by virtue not of congressional grace, but of the independent powers that its earliest counter- parts both brought to the Union and chose to maintain. The dissent's contrary view—that, say, Texas's or California's powers (including the power to make and enforce criminal law) derive from the Federal Government—contradicts the most fundamental conceptual premises of our constitutional order, indeed the very bedrock of our Union.

Rico Constitution, which in turn confers the authority to bring criminal charges. That makes Congress the original source of power for Puerto Rico's prosecutors—as it is for the Federal Government's. The island's Constitution, significant though it is, does not break the chain.

* * * So the Double Jeopardy Clause bars both Puerto Rico and the United States from prosecuting a single person for the same conduct under equivalent criminal laws.

JUSTICE GINSBURG, with whom JUSTICE THOMAS joins, concurring.

I join in full the Court's opinion, which cogently applies long prevailing doctrine. I write only to flag a larger question that bears fresh examination in an appropriate case. The double jeopardy proscription is intended to shield individuals from the harassment of multiple prosecutions for the same misconduct. Current "separate sovereigns" doctrine hardly serves that objective. States and Nation are "kindred systems," yet "parts of ONE WHOLE." The Federalist No. 82, p. 245 (J. Hopkins ed., 2d ed. 1802) (reprint 2008). Within that whole is it not "an affront to human dignity," "inconsistent with the spirit of [our] Bill of Rights," to try or punish a person twice for the same offense? * * *

NOTES AND QUESTIONS

1. ***D.O.J. guidelines.*** Shortly after *Abbate,* Attorney General Rogers issued a memorandum to U.S. Attorneys setting forth guidelines for the exercise of federal prosecutorial authority successive to a state prosecution. Now set forth in the USAM § 9–2.142, these guidelines "preclude the initiation or continuation of a federal prosecution, following a prior state prosecution * * * based on substantially the same act(s) or transaction(s) unless the following three substantive prerequisites are satisfied: (a) the matter must involve a substantial federal interest; (b) the prior prosecution must have left that interest demonstrably unvindicated; and (c) applying the same test applicable to all federal prosecutions, the government must believe that the defendant(s)' conduct constitutes a federal offense, and that the admissible evidence probably will be sufficient to obtain and sustain a conviction by an unbiased trier of fact." The determination that these conditions have been met must be approved by "the appropriate Assistant Attorney General." This policy is known as the *Petite* policy, based on its recognition by the Supreme Court in *Petite v. United States*, 361 U.S. 529 (1960). Undoubtedly the most highly publicized and controversial federal prosecutions approved under this policy have been federal civil rights prosecutions which followed state acquittals (or state convictions that produced "lenient" sentences) on the underlying assaults and homicides.

2. ***State law restrictions.*** A majority of the states would prohibit under state law a state prosecution that follows a federal prosecution in the situation presented in *Bartkus*. See CRIMPROC § 25.5(b). In a few of these states, constitutional provisions bar such a state prosecution. Most, however, rely on statutory limitations. See Adam H. Kurland, *Successive Criminal Prosecutions: The Dual Sovereignty Exception to Double Jeopardy in State and Federal Courts* (2001).

CHAPTER 27

SENTENCING

■ ■ ■

§ 1. INTRODUCTION TO SENTENCING

Sentencing is the culmination of the criminal process. Prior to sentencing, potential and expected sentences drive the choices of prosecutors, defendants, defense counsel, judges, and even police. A defendant's ability to obtain release prior to trial, his right to the assistance of counsel, and his right to a jury all depend at least in part on the sentence he may receive. And sentencing has a profound impact on charging and plea bargaining. "For most defendants," observed one judge, "sentencing is what the case is really about."[a] Because of its pervasive influence, it is, many practitioners believe, the most important aspect of the criminal process to understand. Following a short introduction to the various rationales for criminal punishment, types of criminal sentences, and possible sentencing decisionmakers, this Chapter examines the most important features of the sentencing process.[b]

A. PURPOSES OF PUNISHMENT

Punishment's major objectives—rehabilitation, deterrence, incapacitation, and retribution—should be familiar concepts from your basic course on criminal law. The prevailing rationales for inflicting punishment have varied over time. As you read the material in this chapter, consider how sentencing philosophy affects not only the choices of individual judges and juries in selecting the appropriate sentence for a particular offender, but also the choices of lawmakers in creating and administering a sentencing system.

1. ***The shift away from the rehabilitation norm.*** Professor Michael Tonry suggests that sentencing policy can be divided into "four distinct periods." Sentencing in America, 1975–2025, in *Crime and Justice in America, 1975–2025*, 143 (M. Tonry ed., 2014). From 1930 to 1975, indeterminate sentencing was pervasive. "Statutes defined crimes and set out broad ranges of authorized sentences. Few laws mandated minimum sentences, and when they did, it was typically for 1 or 2 years. Judges adjudicated cases; decided whether to impose prison, jail, probation, or monetary sentences; and set maximum and occasionally minimum prison terms. Sentence appeals were for all practical purposes unavailable. Since sentencing was supposed to be individualized and judges had broad discretion to do so, there were no standards for appellate judges to use in evaluating a challenged sentence. Parole boards decided who would be released and when and subject to what conditions. Prison systems operated extensive systems of time off for good behavior. Punishments were mostly moderate." *Id.* at 142.

"From 1975 to the mid-1980s, the second period," indeterminate sentencing came under attack. "All its premises and assumptions about rehabilitation, individualization, and broad discretion were challenged. Judge Marvin Frankel's *Criminal Sentences—Law without Order* (1973) referred to indeterminate sentencing as 'lawless' because of the absence of standards for

---

[a] *United States v. Wise*, 976 F.2d 393, 409 (8th Cir.1992) (Arnold, C.J., concurring in part and dissenting in part).

[b] For more on sentencing procedure, see Wayne R. LaFave, Jerold H. Israel, Nancy J. King & Orin S. Kerr, Criminal Procedure Treatise, Ch. 26 (4th ed. 2016) (updated annually, available on Westlaw under database name CRIMPROC, hereinafter cited as CRIMPROC).

sentencing decisions and of opportunities for appeals. Criticisms piled up. Unwarranted sentencing disparities were said to be common, and risks of racial bias and arbitrariness were said to be high. Legal academics criticized the system's lack of procedural fairness, transparency, and predictability. Researchers argued that the system did not and could not keep its rehabilitative promises. Others argued that parole release procedures were unfair and decisions inconsistent." *Id.* at 142–43. "[A] primarily liberal reform movement sought to make sentencing procedures fairer and outcomes more predictable and consistent. The totemic target was 'racial and other unwarranted disparities,' and the mechanisms for addressing them were guidelines for judges and parole boards."

"During the third period, from the mid-1980s through 1996, sentencing policy changes aimed primarily to make prison sentences longer and their imposition more certain. The principal mechanisms were mandatory minimum sentences, three-strikes, truth-in-sentencing, and life-without-possibility-of-parole laws. . . . Three-strikes laws typically required minimum 25-year sentences for people convicted of a third felony. State truth-in-sentencing laws were enacted to obtain federal funds for prison construction . . . ; to qualify, states had to demonstrate that people sentenced to imprisonment for violent crimes would serve at least 85 percent of their nominal sentences." "Sentencing ceased being something best handled by experts behind closed doors but instead became a central issue in partisan politics." *Id.* at 143. "By 1994, every state had adopted mandatory penalties; most had several." *Id.* at 165.

The fourth and present period appears to be one of experimentation. Tonry argues that unlike the goals of the first three periods, "The purposes of the initiatives of the fourth period cannot be encapsulated in any single term. Some aim at greater severity, some at greater fairness, some at reducing recidivism, some at reducing costs. New mandatory minimum sentence laws target firearms and immigration offenses, human trafficking, carjacking, and child pornography. . . . Drug and other problem-solving courts, reentry programs, and diverse treatment programs sought in many states to tailor programs and dispositions to the circumstances of individual offenders. After 2000, many state legislatures, generally in search of cost savings, enacted laws limiting the scope of some harsh sentencing provisions, reducing the numbers of revocations of parole and probation, and authorizing earlier releases from prison for selected offenders. . . ." *Id.* at 144–45.

2. ***A modern approach?*** In 2017, after fifteen years of research, drafting, and debate, the American Law Institute approved the final draft of Model Penal Code: Sentencing, a comprehensive work providing guidance to states for sentencing and sentencing procedure. The Comments and Reporters' Notes provide a rich compendium of research on sentencing law, policy, and practice across the nation. Section 1.02(2)(a) defines four purposes for sentencing decisions:

> (i) to render sentences in all cases within a range of severity proportionate to the gravity of offenses, the harms done to crime victims, and the blameworthiness of offenders;
>
> (ii) when reasonably feasible, to achieve offender rehabilitation, general deterrence, incapacitation of dangerous offenders, restitution to crime victims, preservation of families, and reintegration of offenders into the law-abiding community, provided these goals are pursued within the boundaries of proportionality in subsection (a)(i);
>
> (iii) to render sentences no more severe than necessary to achieve the applicable purposes in subsections (a)(i) and (a)(ii); and
>
> (iv) to avoid the use of sanctions that increase the likelihood offenders will engage in future criminal conduct.

B. TYPES OF SENTENCES

1. ***Capital punishment.*** The most severe punishment facing a person convicted of crime in the United States is execution. In 1972 the Supreme Court concluded then-existing capital sentencing statutes were unconstitutionally arbitrary. *Furman v. Georgia,* 408 U.S. 238 (1972). The Court soon upheld revised state sentencing statutes that it found adequately ensured that death sentences would be imposed in a more consistent, yet still individualized, manner. See *Gregg v. Georgia*, 428 U.S. 153 (1976); *Proffitt v. Florida*, 428 U.S. 242 (1976); *Jurek v. Texas*, 428 U.S. 262 (1976). The federal government and thirty states continue to authorize the death penalty as a sentence for murder. There were roughly 2740 prisoners on death row in the United States in 2018. Nearly half of those prisoners are from three states—California, Texas, and Florida. In 2018, 25 inmates were executed.

Today the sentencing phase of a capital case is a trial-like hearing before the jury that considered the defendant's guilt, at which the government presents proof of reasons it claims support a sentence of death, and the defendant has the opportunity to confront that evidence and present evidence of his own in mitigation. The jurors must determine the presence or absence of certain aggravating or mitigating factors upon which their sentencing decision must rest. Appellate and post-conviction review of death sentences tends to be more extensive than the review non-capital sentences. In large part, this is because a special set of rules under the Eighth Amendment governs the imposition of capital punishment. These special rules, recently extended by the Court to some life without parole sentences for juvenile offenders, are beyond the scope of this chapter.

2. ***Incarceration.*** Incarceration is an authorized punishment for nearly all serious offenses. Sentences of incarceration can be divided into two types: indeterminate and determinate. An *indeterminate sentence* typically includes a maximum and minimum term set by the judge within legislated limits, and leaves to the parole board the task of determining precisely when the defendant will be released from incarceration within that maximum term. This type of sentencing permits the actual sentence to track the rehabilitative progress of an offender. In use in every American jurisdiction in the first half of the Twentieth Century, Note 1, p. 1368, discretionary release on parole (indeterminate sentencing) is less pervasive today. Though more than half the states continue to use discretionary release, many now have abolished it for some or all offenses. Most states have retained a parole board or other entity to exercise release discretion. More than 44% of prisoners entering parole in 2016 were released by a paroling authority exercising its discretion. Danielle Kaeble, *Probation and Parole in the United States, 2016*, NCJ 251148 (Apr. 2018). Paroling authorities deciding whether to grant release typically use guidelines, and a growing number include "risk and needs" assessment tools to estimate a prisoner's statistical likelihood of recidivism based upon the recidivism history of prisoners with similar risk-factor profiles. See resources collected at https://nationalparoleresourcecenter.org/.

A *determinate sentence* involves mandatory release after the expiration of a fixed term set by the judge; early release by a paroling authority is not available. Federal courts and less than half of the states use this type of sentencing exclusively. A predetermined period of "supervised release" often follows the completion of a determinate sentence.

"Good time" or "earned time" credits, awarded at a rate that varies with the prisoner's classification and subject to revocation for misconduct, typically apply to reduce both determinate and indeterminate terms.

3. ***Mass incarceration and recent trends.*** The incarceration rate for federal and state inmates jumped from 150–60 per 100,000 in 1970 to more than 750 per 100,000 in 2007. Incarceration's impact on minority communities has been profound; about 60% of those incarcerated in state and federal prisons and jails are members of minority racial and ethnic

groups. "An astonishing 35 percent of black men aged twenty to thirty four without high school diplomas were estimated to be imprisoned in 2008 compared with approximately 10 percent of similarly educated and aged white men." Issa Kohler-Hausmann, Misdemeanorland: Criminal Courts and Social Control in an Age of Broken Windows Policing 9 (2018). At the end of 2010, 1 of every 33 adults in the United States was incarcerated or on probation or parole, the highest rate in the world, and about 13 percent of adult males—and over 33 percent of African American adult males—had been convicted of a felony. At year end 2013, almost 3% of black male U.S. residents of all ages were imprisoned compared to 1% of Hispanic males and 0.5% of white males. For males ages 18 to 19, blacks were more than nine times more likely to be imprisoned than whites. See generally Jeremy Travis, Bruce Western, and Steve Redburn, eds., *The Growth of Incarceration in the United States: Exploring Causes and Consequences* (National Research Council 2014), avail: www.nap.edu; E. Ann Carson, *Prisoners in 2016*, NCJ 25119 (Jan, 2018).

At the end of 2013, of state prisoners nationwide, 7% were held in private prisons (with some states delegating to private companies the responsibility for more than 44% of their prisoners); 19% of federal prisoners were in privately run facilities.

The 2008 recession prompted most states to take steps to reduce incarceration, such as increasing early release credits or expanding alternatives to incarceration for those violating conditions of supervision or those convicted of non-violent offenses. The imprisonment rate peaked in 2007 and has declined slightly since then. Prison closures and reforms to reduce incarceration often have generated resistance by correction officers' unions and the communities that have come to depend on prisons for their livelihood. More than half the states have achieved reforms using a federally supported, bipartisan process called "justice reinvestment," relying on data-driven analysis and the involvement all stakeholders to reduce spending on corrections and reinvest the savings in strategies that increase public safety. Some reforms, such as racial impact laws that mandate review of proposed legislation for evidence of inequitable racial effects, have targeted the disproportionate impact of sentencing policies on minority defendants. For the latest state sentencing reforms, see the Corrections and Sentencing web pages maintained by the National Conference of State Legislatures: www.ncsl.org, the collection of the Sentencing Project at www.sentencingproject.org, and the programs rated at www.crimesolutions.gov.

4. ***Probation or community release.*** Probation is conditional release from custody, also known as a "suspended" sentence or "community" release. At a minimum, a probationer will be required to obey the law and report periodically to his probation officer. Additional conditions must be reasonably related to the offense, the rehabilitation of the defendant, or the protection of the public, and often include the payment of restitution, costs, and fees (see Note 6, below), participation in treatment or educational programs, and community service. A few courts have experimented with conditions of probation that have come to be known as *shaming penalties*, such as requirements that a defendant wear a sign advertising his offense. E.g., *United States v. Gementera*, 379 F.3d 596 (9th Cir. 2004) (collecting authority discussing shaming sanctions and upholding condition of supervised release that required convicted mail thief to spend a day standing outside a post office wearing a signboard stating, "I stole mail. This is my punishment."). But many courts have held that conditions imposed solely for the purpose of humiliation are not authorized, as they are not reasonably related to rehabilitation. *Commonwealth v. Melvin*, 103 A.3d 1, 55–56 (Pa. Super. 2014) (collecting authority from five states).

If a probationer violates one of the conditions of his release, he may then be sentenced to incarceration. A probation violation is adjudicated in a revocation hearing where the defendant is entitled to notice of the claimed violation and given the opportunity to present evidence in his favor before an impartial adjudicator. The full constitutional protections of trial, such as a jury, proof beyond a reasonable doubt, and confrontation protections, are not applicable. For more on probation conditions and revocation, see CRIMPROC §§ 26.9 and 26.10.

5. ***Intermediate penalties; "problem solving courts."*** Intermediate penalties—somewhere in between probation and incarceration—have become more popular in recent years due in part to prison cost and overcrowding. These include *house arrest*, or *home confinement* with monitoring devices, and *day reporting programs*. "Problem solving courts" such as drug courts, mental health courts, and veterans' courts, provide structured treatment and other non-incarceration options for defendants.

6. ***Financial sanctions.*** *Fines* are the primary means of punishing misdemeanants and corporations, and are often assessed for individual felony offenders as well. *Restitution* is a common element of many sentences, more frequently imposed since the adoption of victims' rights laws. *Forfeiture* of specified assets of an offender to the government—including proceeds from criminal activity and assets used to commit crime—is also an authorized penalty for a growing number of offenses.

Conviction usually carries a number of costs and fees as well. Critics argue the growing use of such measures is counterproductive, as this "penal debt" creates a barrier to reentry, disproportionately impacts racial minorities and the poor, and distorts decisionmaking and public safety politics. See, e.g., Wayne A. Logan & Ronald F. Wright, *Mercenary Criminal Justice*, 2014 U. Ill. L. Rev. 1175 (2014) (collecting authority, also observing that that courts "often violate" the rule in *Bearden v. Georgia*, 461 U.S. 660 (1983), barring revocation of release because of non payment of fees or fines when a probationer is unable to pay after "sufficient bona fide efforts"); Note, *State Bans on Debtors' Prisons and Criminal Justice Debt*, 129 Harv.L.Rev. 1024 (2016); Beth A. Colgan, *The Excessive Fines Clause: Challenging the Modern Debtors' Prison*, 65 UCLA L. Rev. 2, 2–12 (2018) (describing various penalties imposed for the failure to pay including costs of collection and interest, loss of drivers' and occupational licenses, and loss of public benefits).

In misdemeanor cases, costs and fees often dwarf the fine authorized as punishment for the offense. For example, an Illinois report noted a defendant in McLean County convicted of DUI and fined $150, would in addition to the fine, be assessed a $75 "base fee," a $20 Court Automation fee, a $15 Court Document Storage Fund fee, $30 Circuit Court Fund fee, $25 Court Security fee, $5 E-Citation fee, $2 State's Attorney Records fee, $10 State's Attorney fee, and 15 state and local add-on fees totaling $1,560 (including fees for Children's Advocacy Centers, County Jail Medical Costs, Drug Court, Traffic School, Drivers' Education, Fire Prevention, Spinal Cord Injury, and Roadside Memorial Funds). The total $1,742 was more than ten times the $150 fine. In addition, a misdemeanor defendant may also have to pay for treatment and/or probation costs, which can cost several thousand dollars. Illinois Statutory Court Task Force, Findings and Recommendations for Addressing Barriers to Access to Justice and Additional Issues Associated with Fees and Other Court Costs in Civil, Criminal, and Traffic Proceedings 27–29 (2016).

"The vast majority of states impose 'user fees' for services commonly understood to be part of criminal justice expenditures, such as for use of a public defender, for 'room and board' for jail and prison, and for the arrested individual's probation and parole supervision. Criminal courts seek revenue from arrested individuals through booking fees at the time of arrest, bail administrative fees, dismissal fees, public defender application fees, court fees, disability and translation fees, jail and administrative fees, and postconviction fees. . . . Two-thirds of states . . . permit judges to charge defendants for at least a portion of the cost of their own public defender. . . . The fees create incentives for localities to run the criminal justice system like a business, one that creates value through imposing costs, tracking payments, and imposing additional sanctions for failure to pay. The risk is that arrest decisions are based on the institution's own organizational interest in generating revenue, rather than public considerations about safety." Elsa Jain, *Capitalizing on Criminal Justice*, 67 Duke L. J. 1381 (2018). Professor Beth Colgan summarized recent research: "Separate and distinct from the potential that inadequately designed systems for fines, fees, and forfeitures will distort criminal justice incentives, such systems can also undermine other governmental aims due to their inherently regressive nature. By entrenching or exacerbating the financial vulnerability of people and their families, fines, fees, and forfeitures can create long-term instability and familial disruption, increase criminal justice involvement, aggravate jail overcrowding, and—perhaps ironically—decrease net revenue." Beth Colgan, "Fine, Fees and Forfeitures," in Academy for Justice (2017) (collecting research), http://academyforjustice.org. See also the resources collected in Judith Resnick, et al., *Who Pays? Fines, Fees, Bail, and the Cost of Courts* (April 19, 2018), avail: https://ssrn.com/abstract=3165674.

Litigation is beginning to expose and challenge these practices. The Department of Justice report on the municipal courts in Ferguson, Missouri is the most well-known example. Another example is *Cain v. City of New Orleans*, 281 F.Supp.3d 624 (E.D. La. 2017), granting summary judgment to civil rights plaintiffs for their claims that 1) assessments of fees by the judges of the Orleans Parish Criminal District Court violated due process when "governing law . . . force[d] the Judges to generate revenue from the criminal defendants they sentence, creating a substantial conflict of interest, and 2) judges routinely imprisoned indigent defendants for the failure to pay court debts without any ability-to-pay inquiry, violating their due process rights.

The ALI's MPC Sentencing, see Note 2, p. 1369, recommends: "No economic sanction may be imposed unless the offender would retain sufficient means for reasonable living expenses and family obligations after compliance with the sanction," and "agencies or entities charged with collection of economic sanctions may not be the recipients of monies collected and may not impose fees on offenders for delinquent payments or services rendered." MPC Sentencing § 6.04 (ALI, Final Draft 2017).

7. ***Collateral consequences.*** A wide spectrum of "collateral sanctions" may impact the defendant more significantly than the sentence itself. See http://ccresourcecenter.org/ for a comprehensive, searchable catalogue for every jurisdiction and every crime. See also *United States v. Nesbeth*, 188 F.Supp.3d 179 (E.D.N.Y. 2016) (noting collateral consequences following a federal conviction "can be particularly disruptive to an ex-convict's efforts at rehabilitation and reintegration into society," and describing legal prohibitions on certain employment, the "reluctance of private employers to hire ex-convicts," as well as ineligibility for educational, tax, housing, Social Security, and nutritional benefits).

C. WHO SETS THE SENTENCE?

Who sets the sentence? Judges, for the most part, but within the limits determined by others. The legislature will set a penalty range for each offense, sometimes closely restraining judicial discretion, as Section 2 describes. The prosecutor's selection of the charge (initially, or in a subsequent charge bargain with the defendant), is everywhere one of the most important determinants of the sentence for the defendant's conduct. In most jurisdictions judges routinely approve sentences (within statutory limits set for the offense of conviction) that are negotiated by the parties, a practice that gives the parties considerable authority in defining the sentence. In a handful of states, the jury in noncapital felony cases may select the sentence. Nancy J. King & Rosevelt L. Noble, *Felony Jury Sentencing in Practice: A Three-State Study*, 57 Vand. L. Rev. 885 (2004); Jenia Iontcheva, *Jury Sentencing as Democratic Practice*, 89 Va. L. Rev. 311 (2003). Parole boards will determine the actual sentences that felony defendants will serve in states that use indeterminate sentencing. Even where discretionary parole release is not available, prison officials may change actual terms of incarceration by granting or revoking "good time." Finally, sentences may be modified by the clemency authority of the executive, a power shared in most states between the governor and an administrative board or advisory group.

What are the advantages and disadvantages of diffusing the power to set sentences among so many different decisionmakers? Consider William Stuntz, *Unequal Justice,* 121 Harv.L.Rev. 1969, 2039 (2008) ("[W]hen prosecutors have enormous discretionary power, giving other decisionmakers discretion promotes consistency, not arbitrariness. Discretion limits discretion; institutional competition curbs excess and abuse.").

The debate over who should determine punishment is an old one. In 1786, when Pennsylvania built its first penitentiary, legislators replaced capital punishment for felonies with terms of imprisonment and debated at length how the new terms of incarceration should be determined. Proponents of fixed, mandatory terms set by the legislature were outvoted by those who favored discretionary ranges. Disagreement remained about who should select an offender's sentence from within those ranges. Eventually, legislators opted to give the trial judge sentencing power, rejecting arguments that sentencing authority should rest with either the trial jury or a pardoning council. Ten years later, Virginia's legislators made a different choice, providing that the trial jury, and not the judge, would fix the offender's stay in the new penitentiary. See Nancy J. King, *The Origins of Felony Jury Sentencing in the United States*, 78 Chicago-Kent L. Rev. 937 (2003). Faced for the first time with the possibility of variable terms of imprisonment in state penitentiaries, it was not obvious to these Eighteenth Century statesmen who should select the precise penalties for crime—legislature, judge, jury, or executive. Is that choice any more obvious today? Why or why not? Consider the ALI's position: "Long experience has shown that the use of jurors as sentencers is antithetical to policies of rationality, proportionality, and restraint in the imposition of criminal sanctions, and is fundamentally inconsistent with the Code's philosophy that the public policies of sentencing should be applied consistently and even-handedly in all cases." MPC Sentencing § 6.02, Comment (ALI, Final Draft 2017).

§ 2. ALLOCATING AND CONTROLLING SENTENCING DISCRETION

Historically, with a few exceptions, trial judges have had very little guidance from the legislature or from appellate courts concerning either the selection of sentences from within the statutory ranges provided for each offense, or the decision whether to order that multiple sentences will be served consecutively rather than concurrently. This freedom has been linked to the goal of individualizing punishment so that the sentence best achieves the rehabilitation of each offender. As noted in the readings that began this chapter, many jurisdictions in the 1980s and '90s abandoned this goal and unguided sentencing discretion. Gross disparities in the sentences for similar offenders, particularly differences linked to the race of the offender or the identity of the judge, prompted efforts nationwide to limit judicial sentencing discretion at the front end and parole release discretion at the back end. Three types of restrictions on judicial discretion to set the initial sentence are considered below: mandatory minimum sentences; judicial sentencing guidelines; and appellate review of sentencing decisions.

A. MANDATORY MINIMUM SENTENCES

1. ***The rise of mandatory minimums.*** A mandatory minimum sentencing statute forbids a judge from imposing a sentence term less than the term specified in the statute. Some statutes require the minimum sentence for all offenders convicted of a certain charge; other statutes mandate a minimum term whenever designated facts about the offender or the offense are established at sentencing. By 1983 mandatory minimum penalties were enacted in 49 of 50 states. Most have some version of a "three-strikes-and-you're-out" law, imposing lengthy mandatory minimum sentences for specified repeat offenders. The "strike zone" varies, some states limiting those offenses that count as strikes to violent felonies, others including drug offenses or other non-violent crimes.

2. ***Shifting sentencing authority to the prosecutor.*** Consider Justice Breyer's concurring opinion in *Harris v. United States*, Note 4, p. 1395: "Mandatory minimum statutes are

fundamentally inconsistent with Congress' simultaneous effort to create a fair, honest, and rational sentencing system through the use of Sentencing Guidelines. Unlike Guidelines sentences, statutory mandatory minimums generally deny the judge the legal power to depart downward, no matter how unusual the special circumstances that call for leniency. * * * They transfer sentencing power to prosecutors, who can determine sentences through the charges they decide to bring, and who thereby have reintroduced much of the sentencing disparity that Congress created Guidelines to eliminate." Justice Kennedy, too, has called this transfer of sentencing power from judges to prosecutors "misguided," stating that "the trial judge is the one actor in the system most experienced with exercising discretion in a transparent, open and reasoned way." Report of the ABA Justice Kennedy Commission (2004) (quoting Justice Kennedy's address to the ABA, August 9, 2003).

3. ***Politics and sentencing policy.*** Mandatory minimum sentences have been criticized for decades as costly in terms of corrections resources, ineffective at curbing crime, and leading to questionable sentencing disparities. See, e.g., News Release, United States Sentencing Commission, *Sentencing Commission Issues Comprehensive Report on Statutory Mandatory Minimum Penalties*, October 11, 2011 ("the Commission unanimously believes that certain mandatory minimum penalties apply too broadly, are excessively severe, and are applied inconsistently across the country"); Joshua B. Fischman & Max M. Schanzenbach, *Racial Disparities Under the Federal Sentencing Guidelines: The Role of Judicial Discretion and Mandatory Minimums*, 9 J. Emp. Legal St. 729 (2012) (findings suggest that judicial discretion does not contribute to, and may in fact mitigate, racial disparities in Guidelines sentencing).

The Comment to MPC Sentencing § 6.06 (ALI, Final Draft 2017) summarized the research: "Empirical research and policy analyses have shown time and again that mandatory-minimum penalties fail to promote uniformity in punishment and instead exacerbate sentencing disparities, lead to disproportionate and even bizarre sanctions in individual cases, are ineffective measures for advancing deterrent and incapacitative objectives, distort the plea-bargaining process, shift sentencing authority from courts to prosecutors, result in pronounced geographic disparities due to uneven enforcement patterns in different prosecutors' offices, coerce some innocent defendants to plead guilty to lesser charges to avoid the threat of a mandatory term, undermine the rational ordering of graduated sentencing guidelines, penalize low-level and unsophisticated offenders more so than those in leadership roles, provoke nullification of the law by lawyers, judges, and jurors, and engender public perceptions in some communities that the criminal law lacks moral legitimacy."

If mandatory minimum sentence statutes have these effects, why are legislators so fond of them? Consider Ronald F. Wright, *Three Strikes Legislation and Sentencing Commission Objectives,* 20 Law & Pol. 429, 437 (1998) ("The fiscal costs of increased corrections, judicial, prosecutorial, and defense resources are rarely traced to particular statutes," and even when they are, "[b]y that time, most of the legislators who voted for the original punishment statute are long gone."); William J. Stuntz, *The Uneasy Relationship Between Criminal Procedure and Criminal Justice*, 107 Yale L.J. 1, 56 (1997) (higher mandatory sentences raise the risk to defendants of taking their cases to trial and thus tend to convert otherwise contested cases into guilty pleas, thereby avoiding most of the costs criminal procedure creates); Donald A. Dripps, *Criminal Procedure, Footnote Four, and the Theory of Public Choice; Or, Why Don't Legislatures Give a Damn about the Rights of the Accused?*, 44 Syracuse L. Rev. 1079, 1089 (1993) ("the group of people who might expect to be * * * defendants at a criminal trial, whether they are guilty or innocent, is largely confined to a small segment of the electorate"); Michael Tonry & Kathleen Hatlestad, *Sentencing Reform in Overcrowded Times—A Comparative Perspective* 4 (1997) (arguing that in the United States, unlike other countries, because of successful attacks on political candidates perceived as soft on crime since the 1980s, "[f]ew elected public officials dare oppose any 'toughness' proposal, whatever its unfairness, expense, or likely ineffectiveness"); Sara Sun Beale,

What's Law Got to Do with It? The Political, Social, Psychological and Other Non-Legal Factors Influencing the Development of (Federal) Criminal Law, 1 Buff. Crim. L. Rev. 23 (1997).

State legislators have been more responsive than Congress to the burdens created by mandatory minimum sentence laws, and several states have cut back on mandatory terms to cope with rising corrections costs. See, e.g., Ram Subramanian & Ruth Delaney, *Playbook for Change? States Reconsider Mandatory Sentences*, 26 Fed. Sent. Rep. 198 (2014). See also Rachel Barkow, *Federalism and the Politics of Sentencing*, 105 Colum. L. Rev. 1276, 1301–08 (2005) (Congress lacks fiscal incentives to moderate punitive sentencing policy because criminal justice makes up tiny proportion of federal spending; even if it paid attention to costs, Congress could simply leave more criminal enforcement to the states rather than amend federal statutes). Eventually, at the end of 2018, following more than a decade of sentencing reform by the states, Congress passed the First Step Act of 2018, lowering some mandatory minimum sentences.

B. SENTENCING GUIDELINES

1. ***Guidelines basics.*** Minnesota adopted the first judicial sentencing guidelines scheme in 1980; the federal government and just over a dozen states have guidelines today. Sentencing guidelines are created by sentencing commissions authorized by the legislature, or by the legislature itself. The sentence in a guidelines system is determined through the use of a sentencing table or grid that sets the presumed sentence range for each particular case. On one axis of the grid is a ranking of the criminal history of the offender, based on past convictions. The other axis ranks the severity of the particular offense. Offense severity usually is rated on a point system, starting with a certain number based on the general character of the offense. Then points are added for such aggravating factors as a leadership role, use of a weapon, commission of the offense while under supervision for another offense, or severe injury to the victim. In some systems, points may be subtracted for cooperation or other mitigating factors.

The sentencing guidelines ranges are narrower than the statutory ranges established for the offense. For example, a conviction of a serious offense carrying a statutory range of zero to ten years may result in a recommended range of 20 to 24 months for a person with no prior convictions, and 90 to 104 months for a person in the highest criminal history category who caused serious injury. Typically, they govern only felony sentences.

No two guidelines systems are identical. See Kelly Lyn Mitchell, *State Sentencing Guidelines: A Garden Full of Variety,* 81 Fed. Prob. J. 28 (Sept. 2017) (summarizing variations). Where guidelines are not binding, such as Maryland or Virginia, judges may decline to follow them without consequence. In a mandatory or binding guideline system, such as Minnesota or Washington, a judge may not impose a sentence higher or lower than the terms in the designated range, absent proof of some specified aggravating fact that would authorize a more severe sentence, or a mitigating factor that would authorize a lower sentence. As discussed in Section 3 below, the Court held in *Blakely v. Washington,* Note 2, p. 1391, that in such a binding guidelines system, these tiered ranges operate as lesser and greater offenses, and the Constitution guarantees a defendant the right to have an aggravating factor that distinguishes a higher range from a lesser range proven to a jury beyond a reasonable doubt.

2. ***Evaluating guidelines.*** Guidelines have received mixed reviews. Supporters argue that they provide greater consistency in the application of law to individual sentencing decisions, allow effective control of corrections spending, improve a state's capacity for making coherent sentencing policy, and, when a sentencing commission rather than the legislature formulates guidelines, remove "at least some policymaking about criminal punishment from the glare of the political process." See Kevin R. Reitz, *Model Penal Code: Sentencing Report* 49–50 (2004); Rachel Barkow, *Administering Crime*, 52 UCLA L. Rev. 715 (2005). Guidelines are also the centerpiece of the proposed new Model Penal Code provisions on punishment. See MPC Sentencing § 6A.01–

6B.11 (ALI, Final Draft, 2017). The Federal Sentencing Guidelines, however, have been a lightning rod for criticism. Far more complex than state guidelines, with more detailed factual findings and more severe penalties for many offenses, the federal guidelines were designed to provide fewer opportunities for judicial discretion.

C. APPELLATE REVIEW

1. ***The need for findings to review.*** One obvious way to limit the sentencing discretion of judges is to review their decisions on appeal. Until quite recently, sentencing decisions were entirely discretionary, subjected to such cursory review that few defendants bothered to appeal their sentences except to challenge procedural error. Today, in jurisdictions that use judicial sentencing guidelines or presumptive sentencing (still fewer than half of the states), the factual and legal conclusions of the trial court that form the basis for each sentence are part of the record. Many of these findings, in turn, can be tested on appeal by either prosecution (see Note 4, p. 1409) or defense for compliance with statutory command or guidelines requirements. In the federal courts, for example, the adoption of binding sentencing guidelines in the late 1980s led to a dramatic increase in sentencing appeals, and even after the guidelines became advisory, federal defendants have continued to contest on appeal the factual and legal findings made at sentencing. The bulk of criminal cases nationwide are misdemeanors, however, where access to appellate review is often limited.

2. ***Sentencing appeal waivers.*** The increased burden of sentencing appeals has created an incentive for prosecutors to seek the defendant's advance agreement or stipulation as to sentence, which in many jurisdictions bars a challenge to that sentence. Prosecutors also seek to avoid appeals by including in the plea agreement the defendant's express waiver of the right to raise on appeal all challenges to any sentence the judge later imposes and to the process by which the sentence is imposed. Should the legislature or the judiciary regulate these waivers? See Notes 4–5, p. 1165, Note 3, p. 1402, Note 3a, p. 1411 (discussing appeal waivers).

3. ***Review for compliance with the Eighth Amendment.*** Outside of the context of capital punishment, the Supreme Court has been hesitant to strike down punishment authorized by statute as unconstitutionally severe—either as a violation of "substantive" due process or as a violation of the Eighth Amendment, which prohibits the imposition of "excessive fines" and the infliction of "cruel and unusual punishments." These limitations on punishment continue to generate significant litigation, but are beyond the scope of this text. For an overview, see *Miller v. Alabama*, 567 U.S. 460 (2013) (barring mandatory life without parole sentences for juveniles) and *United States v. Bajakajian*, 524 U.S. 321 (1998) (holding, 5–4, that forfeiture of $357,144 would violate the Excessive Fines Clause, as grossly disproportionate to the gravity of the defendant's reporting offense).

§ 3. CONSTITUTIONAL LIMITS ON SENTENCING PROCEDURE

Although it was decided a half-century ago, *Williams v. New York,* below, remains the leading ruling on the content of due process as applied to sentencing. Its resilience is striking, especially when compared to the fundamental refashioning of constitutional requirements for other phases of the criminal process during the second half of the Twentieth Century.

A. INFORMATION CONSIDERED IN SETTING THE SENTENCE

WILLIAMS V. NEW YORK

337 U.S. 241, 69 S.Ct. 1079, 93 L.Ed. 1337 (1949).

MR. JUSTICE BLACK delivered the opinion of the Court.

[After a verdict finding Williams guilty of first degree murder, at sentencing Williams protested his innocence and his lawyers asked the court to accept the jury's recommendation of a life sentence, but the trial judge imposed a death sentence. (The Court decades later limited this "judicial override" procedure in capital cases, and required jury findings beyond a reasonable doubt of facts required for a death sentence, see CRIMPROC at § 26.4(i).) The judge expressed his own belief in Williams' guilt and stated that the pre-sentence investigation revealed many material facts concerning appellant's background which though relevant to the question of punishment could not properly have been brought to the attention of the jury in its consideration of the question of guilt. He referred to the experience appellant "had had on thirty other burglaries in and about the same vicinity" where the murder had been committed. The appellant had not been convicted of these burglaries although the judge had information that he had confessed to some and had been identified as the perpetrator of some of the others. The judge also referred to certain activities of appellant as shown by the probation report that indicated appellant possessed "a morbid sexuality" and classified him as a "menace to society." The accuracy of the statements made by the judge as to appellant's background and past practices was not challenged by appellant or his counsel, nor was the judge asked to disregard any of them or to afford appellant a chance to refute or discredit any of them by cross-examination or otherwise.

[Williams contended that his sentence violated due process, as it was "based upon information supplied by witnesses with whom the accused had not been confronted and as to whom he had no opportunity for cross-examination or rebuttal * * * ."]

The case presents a serious and difficult question. The question relates to the rules of evidence applicable to the manner in which a judge may obtain information to guide him in the imposition of sentence upon an already convicted defendant. Within limits fixed by statutes, New York judges are given a broad discretion to decide the type and extent of punishment for convicted defendants. Here, for example, the judge's discretion was to sentence to life imprisonment or death. To aid a judge in exercising this discretion intelligently the New York procedural policy encourages him to consider information about the convicted person's past life, health, habits, conduct, and mental and moral propensities. [A state statute provided that the court "shall cause the defendant's previous criminal record to be submitted to it, * * * and may seek any information that will aid the court in determining the proper treatment of such defendant."] The sentencing judge may consider such information even though obtained outside the courtroom from persons whom a defendant has not been permitted to confront or cross-examine. It is the consideration of information obtained by a sentencing judge in this manner that is the basis for appellant's broad constitutional challenge to the New York statutory policy.

Appellant urges that the New York statutory policy is in irreconcilable conflict with the underlying philosophy of a second procedural policy grounded in the due process of law clause of the Fourteenth Amendment. That policy as stated in *In re Oliver*, 333 U.S. 257, 273, is in part that no person shall be tried and convicted of an offense unless he is given reasonable notice of the charges against him and is afforded an opportunity to examine adverse witnesses. That the due process clause does provide these salutary and time-tested protections where the question for consideration is the guilt of a defendant seems entirely clear from the genesis and historical evolution of the clause.

Tribunals passing on the guilt of a defendant always have been hedged in by strict evidentiary procedural limitations. But both before and since the American colonies became a nation, courts in this country and in England practiced a policy under which a sentencing judge could exercise a wide discretion in the sources and types of evidence used to assist him in determining the kind and extent of punishment to be imposed within limits fixed by law. Out-of-court affidavits have been used frequently, and of course in the smaller communities sentencing judges naturally have in mind their knowledge of the personalities and backgrounds of convicted offenders. * * *

In addition to the historical basis for different evidentiary rules governing trial and sentencing procedures there are sound practical reasons for the distinction. In a trial before verdict the issue is whether a defendant is guilty of having engaged in certain criminal conduct of which he has been specifically accused. Rules of evidence have been fashioned for criminal trials which narrowly confine the trial contest to evidence that is strictly relevant to the particular offense charged. These rules rest in part on a necessity to prevent a time-consuming and confusing trial of collateral issues. They were also designed to prevent tribunals concerned solely with the issue of guilt of a particular offense from being influenced to convict for that offense by evidence that the defendant had habitually engaged in other misconduct. A sentencing judge, however, is not confined to the narrow issue of guilt. His task within fixed statutory or constitutional limits is to determine the type and extent of punishment after the issue of guilt has been determined. Highly relevant—if not essential—to his selection of an appropriate sentence is the possession of the fullest information possible concerning the defendant's life and characteristics. And modern concepts individualizing punishment have made it all the more necessary that a sentencing judge not be denied an opportunity to obtain pertinent information by a requirement of rigid adherence to restrictive rules of evidence properly applicable to the trial.

Undoubtedly the New York statutes emphasize a prevalent modern philosophy of penology that the punishment should fit the offender and not merely the crime. The belief no longer prevails that every offense in a like legal category calls for an identical punishment without regard to the past life and habits of a particular offender. This whole country has traveled far from the period in which the death sentence was an automatic and commonplace result of convictions—even for offenses today deemed trivial. Today's philosophy of individualizing sentences makes sharp distinctions for example between first and repeated offenders. Indeterminate sentences the ultimate termination of which are sometimes decided by non-judicial agencies have to a large extent taken the place of the old rigidly fixed punishments. The practice of probation which relies heavily on non-judicial implementation has been accepted as a wise policy. Execution of the United States parole system rests on the discretion of an administrative parole board. Retribution is no longer the dominant objective of the criminal law. Reformation and rehabilitation of offenders have become important goals of criminal jurisprudence.

Modern changes in the treatment of offenders make it more necessary now than a century ago for observance of the distinctions in the evidential procedure in the trial and sentencing processes. For indeterminate sentences and probation have resulted in an increase in the discretionary powers exercised in fixing punishments. In general, these modern changes have not resulted in making the lot of offenders harder. On the contrary a strong motivating force for the changes has been the belief that by careful study of the lives and personalities of convicted offenders many could be less severely punished and restored sooner to complete freedom and useful citizenship. This belief to a large extent has been justified.

Under the practice of individualizing punishments, investigational techniques have been given an important role. Probation workers making reports of their investigations have not been trained to prosecute but to aid offenders. Their reports have been given a high value by conscientious judges who want to sentence persons on the best available information rather than on guesswork and inadequate information. To deprive sentencing judges of this kind of information would undermine modern penological procedural policies that have been cautiously adopted throughout the nation after careful consideration and experimentation. We must recognize that most of the information now relied upon by judges to guide them in the intelligent imposition of sentences would be unavailable if information were restricted to that given in open court by witnesses subject to cross-examination. And the modern probation report draws on information concerning every aspect of a defendant's life. The type and extent of this information make totally impractical if not impossible open court testimony with cross-examination. Such a procedure could endlessly delay criminal administration in a retrial of collateral issues.

The considerations we have set out admonish us against treating the due process clause as a uniform command that courts throughout the Nation abandon their age-old practice of seeking information from out-of-court sources to guide their judgment toward a more enlightened and just sentence. * * * The due process clause should not be treated as a device for freezing the evidential procedure of sentencing in the mold of trial procedure. So to treat the due process clause would hinder if not preclude all courts—state and federal—from making progressive efforts to improve the administration of criminal justice. * * *

We hold that appellant was not denied due process of law. Affirmed.

JUSTICE MURPHY, dissenting.

* * * The record before us indicates that the judge exercised his discretion to deprive a man of his life, in reliance on material made available to him in a probation report, consisting almost entirely of evidence that would have been inadmissible at the trial. Some, such as allegations of prior crimes, was irrelevant. Much was incompetent as hearsay. All was damaging, and none was subject to scrutiny by the defendant.

Due process of law includes at least the idea that a person accused of crime shall be accorded a fair hearing through all the stages of the proceedings against him. I agree with the Court as to the value and humaneness of liberal use of probation reports as developed by modern penologists, but, in a capital case, against the unanimous recommendation of a jury, where the report would concededly not have been admissible at the trial, and was not subject to examination by the defendant, I am forced to conclude that the high commands of due process were not obeyed.

NOTES AND QUESTIONS

1. ***Prohibited considerations.*** In light of the sweeping description in *Williams* of information relevant to sentencing, it could be argued that every aspect of a defendant's life may be weighed in assessing the appropriate penalty. Indeed, in federal courts, 18 U.S.C. § 3661 provides: "No limitation shall be placed on the information concerning the background, character, and conduct of a person convicted of an offense which a court of the United States may receive and consider for the purpose of imposing an appropriate sentence." A small group of factors remains off limits, however.

a. ***Activity protected by the First Amendment.*** David Dawson was convicted of first degree murder and sentenced to death. At his sentencing hearing the prosecution introduced evidence that Dawson had the words "Aryan Brotherhood" tattooed on the back of his hand as well as evidence that an "Aryan Brotherhood prison gang originated in California in the 1960s, that it entertains white racist beliefs, and that a separate gang in the Delaware prison system calls itself the Aryan Brotherhood." Dawson claimed that the introduction of this evidence violated his First Amendment rights. The Court in *Dawson v. Delaware*, 503 U.S. 159 (1992), agreed. "Even if the Delaware group to which Dawson allegedly belongs is racist, those beliefs, so far as we can determine, had no relevance to the sentencing proceeding in this case. * * * [T]he murder victim was white, as is Dawson; elements of racial hatred were therefore not involved in the killing.

Because the prosecution did not prove that the Aryan Brotherhood had committed any unlawful or violent acts, or had even endorsed such acts, the Aryan Brotherhood evidence was also not relevant to help prove any aggravating circumstance. In many cases * * * associational evidence might serve a legitimate purpose in showing that a defendant represents a future danger to society. * * * But the inference which the jury was invited to draw in this case tended to prove nothing more than the abstract beliefs of the Delaware chapter. * * * [T]he evidence proved nothing more than Dawson's abstract beliefs."

b. Race and other protected classifications. The Equal Protection Clause bars a judge or jury from considering the race or national origin of the offender or victim as the basis for a more or less severe sentence. Short of an obvious statement in the record, as in *United States v. Truillo-Castillon*, 692 F.3d 575 (7th Cir. 2012) (vacating sentence when judge said the defendant's record was reminiscent of "when the Mariel people came over here and created crime waves all over the place" and that a deprived background does not "give anybody who comes from Cuba the right to . . . not value" the constitutional rights of others), it is extremely difficult for a defendant to prove either that racial animus motivated his sentencer or that a prosecutor's decision to seek a sentence was based on race or other protected classification. See *McCleskey v. Kemp*, p. 898 (rejecting equal protection claim by capital defendant who presented statistical statewide evidence demonstrating that the race of the victim was strongly correlated to the likelihood that a defendant would receive the death penalty).

The Court overturned a sentence on this ground in *Buck v. Davis*, 137 S.Ct. 759 (2017), finding ineffective assistance by defense counsel at the defendant's capital sentencing hearing. There, the jury had to determine whether the defendant was likely to be a future danger, and defense counsel allowed an expert to testify that the defendant's race increased the probability of future violence. The Court stated "when a jury hears expert testimony that expressly makes a defendant's race directly pertinent on the question of life or death, the impact of that evidence cannot be measured simply by how much air time it received at trial or how many pages it occupies in the record. Some toxins can be deadly in small doses."

In *Wisconsin v. Mitchell*, 508 U.S. 476 (1993), however, the Court upheld a sentence imposed under a statute that provided higher penalties for an offense if the defendant "intentionally selects" the victim because of the "race, religion, color, disability, sexual orientation, national origin or ancestry of that person." Rejecting the defendant's equal protection and first amendment challenges, the Court explained that bias-inspired conduct "is thought to inflict greater individual and societal harm. * * * The state's desire to redress * * * perceived harms provides an adequate explanation for its penalty enhancement provision over and above mere disagreement with the offender's beliefs or biases." (For another example of a hate crime enhancement, see *Apprendi v. New Jersey*, p. 1388). How does the claim raised by the defendant in *Mitchell* differ from the claims raised by the defendants in *McCleskey, Dawson,* or *Buck*?

Consider the facts in *Kapadia v. Tally*, 229 F.3d 641 (7th Cir. 2000). Kapadia was convicted in Cook County of burglary and arson of a Jewish community center. On his way out of the courtroom after conviction, Kapadia said to Deputy Joseph Bennett, "You can tell the Judge for me . . . that he's a b___ and f___ the Jews." Later that day, while in lockup, Kapadia asked Bennett whether "that Judge is a Jew, too?" and then answered his own question by stating, "I'll bet he is that f__g schm__." Bennett related these remarks, as well as two other epithets he'd overheard defendant utter about Jews, to the trial judge before the sentencing hearing. The trial judge told Bennett to inform both the prosecution and the defense about the remarks. At sentencing, the judge heard argument on the relevance of Bennett's information, including defense counsel's objection that "there has been absolutely no suggestion during the trial * * * that the fact that this was a Jewish synagogue had anything to do with anything, especially the conduct of my client." Bennett, under oath, testified to Kapadia's anti-Semitic remarks. The judge remarked that he had been called more names than any other professional except a tax collector, "What troubles me, of course, is the vitriol directed towards the * * * East European Jews who are the victims in this case. I did take the comments into consideration because one of the things I have to consider is the possibility of reformation of the defendant. How likely is this defendant to be restored to useful citizenship." The court went on to comment on the lessons of history, including Krystalnacht, when 1,700 synagogues and businesses were destroyed by mobs led by Nazi party members, leading to the deaths of a large number of Jewish individuals. "I take these matters into very, very serious consideration in the case of Mr. Kapadia," explained the judge, "because his virulent anti-Semitism is indicative of the fact [that] he is not likely to change his ways. He is not likely to become a productive member of society. So, it's certainly an aggravating factor." The court then sentenced Kapadia to a fourteen-year term of imprisonment, the longest term allowed under Illinois law for burglary and arson. Were Kapadia's first amendment rights violated by the court's consideration of his speech in setting his sentence?

c. Defendant's exercise of procedural rights.

(i) Right to appeal. In *North Carolina v. Pearce,* p. 1403, the Court agreed unanimously that after a defendant succeeds in winning retrial or resentencing on appeal, a judge cannot impose a higher sentence to retaliate against the defendant for the successful appeal of the first judgment. The Court acknowledged that *Williams* allowed the sentencing court on re-conviction to take into consideration the conduct of the defendant subsequent to his first conviction "that may have thrown new light upon defendant's 'moral propensities,'" but that did not authorize "punish[ing] a person because he has done what the law plainly allows him to do" in pursuing an appeal. To allow such "vindictiveness" to play a part in his sentence would be to allow the sentencing court "to put a price on an appeal" and thereby inhibit the "free and unfettered" exercise of that right. When the same judge imposes an increased sentence following reconviction for the same offense after appeal, the Court concluded, a presumption of vindictiveness attaches.

(ii) Right to testify—truthfully. *United States v. Dunnigan*, 507 U.S. 87 (1993), considered a sentencing enhancement for perjury. After five witnesses testified at trial to the defendant's trafficking in cocaine, the defendant took the stand, denied the allegations, and said she had not possessed or distributed cocaine at any time. Rebuttal witnesses for the government testified to purchasing crack cocaine from the defendant numerous times, once in a transaction monitored by law enforcement authorities. After conviction by the jury, the judge sentenced the defendant under the Guidelines. He increased her sentence applying a provision entitled "willfully obstructing or impeding proceedings," because he found that the defendant perjured herself at trial. Rejecting the defendant's contention that increasing her sentence because of her perjury interferes with her right to testify, the Court declared "[W]e have held on a number of occasions that a defendant's right to testify does not include a right to commit perjury." "The commission of perjury is of obvious relevance" to the appropriate punishment "because it reflects on a defendant's criminal history, on her willingness to accept the commands of the law and the authority of the court, and on her character in general." "The perjuring defendant's willingness to frustrate judicial proceedings to avoid criminal liability suggests that the need for incapacitation and retribution is heightened as compared with the defendant charged with the same crime who allows judicial proceedings to progress without resorting to perjury." The Court noted that "an accused may give inaccurate testimony due to confusion, mistake, or faulty memory. In other instances, an accused may testify to matters such as lack of capacity, insanity, duress, or self-defense. Her testimony may be truthful, but the jury may nonetheless find the testimony insufficient to excuse criminal liability or prove lack of intent. For these reasons, if a defendant objects to a sentence enhancement resulting from her trial testimony, a district court must review the evidence and make independent findings necessary to establish" that the defendant gave "false testimony concerning a material matter with the willful intent to provide false testimony, rather than as a result of confusion, mistake, or faulty memory."

(iii) Right to remain silent. Assume a defendant pleads guilty and admits her commission of an offense, but refuses at sentencing to answer the judge's questions about the offense and the criminal activity of her friends, choosing instead to remain silent. May the judge use this refusal as a basis for imposing a higher sentence than he would have imposed had the defendant provided the information? After *Mitchell v. United States*, 526 U.S. 314 (1999), it depends. Mitchell pleaded guilty to several drug offenses, reserving her right to contest drug quantity at sentencing. At sentencing witnesses testified that over several months the defendant had sold a total of more than 5 kilograms of cocaine, an amount carrying a mandatory minimum sentence of 10 years. In explaining why he credited the testimony, the judge explained to the defendant: "I held it against you that you didn't come forward today and tell me that you really only did this a couple of times. * * * I'm taking the position that you should come forward and explain your side of this issue." Mitchell asserted in the Supreme Court that it was a violation of her Fifth Amendment privilege against compelled self-incrimination for the trial judge to draw an adverse inference about drug amount from her silence at sentencing. Justice Kennedy's opinion for the Court agreed. "The concerns which mandate the rule [of *Griffin v. California*, p. 1322] against negative inferences at a criminal trial apply with equal force at sentencing." The rule prohibiting an inference of guilt from a defendant's silence "has become an essential feature of our legal tradition," and a "vital instrument for teaching that the question in a criminal case is not whether the defendant committed the acts of which he is accused," but "whether the Government has carried its burden to prove its allegations while respecting the defendant's individual rights." "By holding petitioner's silence against her in determining the facts of the offense at the sentencing hearing, the District Court imposed an impermissible burden on the exercise of the constitutional right against compelled self-incrimination." The Court noted "Whether silence bears upon the determination of a lack of remorse, or upon acceptance of responsibility for purposes of the downward adjustment [under the Guidelines], is a separate question. It is not before us, and we express no view on it."

Justice Scalia, writing for four Justices in dissent, noted the Court's opinion appeared to be limited to determining "facts of the offense" and may not apply to "determinations of acceptance of responsibility, repentance, character, and future dangerousness." Under this reading "we will have a system in which a state court can increase the sentence of a convicted drug possessor who refuses to say how many ounces he possessed—not because that suggests he possessed the large amount * * * but because his refusal to cooperate suggests he is unrepentant." "Ordinarily," he predicted, it will be "impossible to tell whether the sentencer has used the silence for either purpose or for neither."

In a later case, the Court observed that "*Mitchell* itself suggests that some inferences from silence regarding remorse might be permissible." *White v. Woodall*, 572 U.S. 415 (2014). While emphasizing that the question remained open, the Court suggested that it was not unreasonable for a state court to have assumed that a capital sentencing jury would be permitted to infer lack of remorse from the defendant's silence, when he had already admitted through his guilty plea every fact on which the state bore the burden of proof.

Test your understanding of *Mitchell* by applying it in the following case: After pleading guilty to distributing child pornography, the defendant refused on Fifth Amendment grounds to complete a psychosexual examination ordered by the court in preparation for sentencing—consisting of an interview, plethysmograph, and polygraph. At sentencing, the judge explained, "One of the factors that I have to consider is the need to impose a sentence that will protect the public from further crimes of the defendant. * * * By not having the results of those [tests], I can't properly assess what the risk is that you will further offend [or] what kind of danger you pose to the community. * * * I am assuming based upon what appears to the court to be your unwillingness to * * * participate in appropriate testing, that you are in fact a danger, which, therefore, requires that I impose a lifetime term of supervised release." *United States v. Kennedy*, 499 F.3d 547 (6th Cir. 2007). See also *State v. Washington*, 832 N.W.2d 650 (Iowa 2013) (violation of Fifth Amendment when "[n]either the State nor the sentencing court contends Washington's 250 hours of community service serves a legitimate penological purpose connected to his refusal to answer whether he currently is using marijuana," declining to decide if a sentencing court could order drug treatment based on defendant's refusal to answer).

2. ***Prior criminal history, uncharged criminal conduct, acquitted criminal conduct.*** As Professor Kevin Reitz has pointed out, there is more to Williams' story than the Supreme Court opinion reveals. See Kevin R. Reitz, *Sentencing Facts: Travesties of Real-Offense Sentencing*, 45 Stan. L. Rev. 523 (1993) (collecting background on the *Williams* case). At the time of the murder, Williams was 18 and had no prior convictions. He was, however, on probation for failing to appear in court after being charged at age seventeen with being a "wayward minor." The judge at sentencing noted that Williams' "difficulties" with the law dated back to age eleven, when he was accused of assisting another in a burglary, a charge that was suspended. The trial judge accepted as true allegations in the presentence report that Williams had committed an additional thirty burglaries during the months prior to the murder, based on representations in the report that these burglaries were committed in a similar manner, that victims of some of these other crimes had identified Williams, and that some property taken during these burglaries was found in his apartment. Indications that Williams "possessed 'a morbid sexuality,'" the report alleged, consisted of allegations by a seven-year-old girl that Williams had molested her during one of these uncharged burglaries, the probation department's discovery that Williams lived with two women and that "on various occasions he brought different men to the apartment for the purpose of having sexual relations with these two women," and an alleged visit to a public school "to take photographs of private parts of young children." Even assuming the allegations about Williams' other crimes are accurate, how are these other crimes relevant to the appropriate sentence for the murder?

Since *Williams*, the Court has upheld against double jeopardy challenges the practice of using uncharged and even acquitted conduct to justify a higher sentence within the range authorized for the offense of conviction. *See, e.g., United States v. Booker*, p. 1394, where the Court stated: "In *Witte v. United States,* 515 U.S. 389 (1995), we held that the Double Jeopardy Clause did not bar a prosecution for conduct that had provided the basis for an enhancement of the defendant's sentence in a prior case. We concluded that 'consideration of information about the defendant's character and conduct at sentencing does not result in "punishment" for any offense other than the one of which the defendant was convicted.' Rather, the defendant is 'punished only for the fact that the present offense was carried out in a manner that warrants increased punishment. . . .' *United States v. Watts,* 519 U.S. 148 (1997) *(per curiam)* (quoting *Witte*). In *Watts,* relying on *Witte,* we held that the Double Jeopardy Clause permitted a court to consider acquitted conduct in sentencing a defendant under the Guidelines." Since *Booker,* every circuit to have considered the question has held that acquitted conduct may be used in setting a sentence within the range authorized for the offense of conviction, so long as the conduct is established by a preponderance.

When very broad statutory sentencing ranges with high ceilings permit judges to choose severe sentences based on uncharged or acquitted conduct, critics continue to argue that this allows prosecutors "to achieve an indirect conviction" for the other criminal conduct "at the sentencing hearing, where [defendants] lack the procedural protections of trial." *Recent Case,* 125 Harv.L.Rev. 1860, 1867 (2013) (discussing *United States v. Fitch,* 659 F.3d 788 (9th Cir. 2011), which upheld sentence of nearly 22 years for fraud based on judicial finding at sentencing that defendant had murdered his wife as part of the fraudulent scheme). If you agree with critics that this is a problem, what are the possible ways to address it?

As for the use of prior *convictions* in sentencing, see the discussion of *Almendarez-Torres v. United States,* Note a., p. 1389, Note 5, p. 1398. Julian V. Roberts, *Punishing Persistent Offenders: Exploring Community and Offender Perspectives* (2008) (noting criminal record is more important than any other factor in sentencing in America). Why might judges and legislators give criminal history such a prominent role in sentencing? For one review of justifications for and criticisms of reliance on criminal history in selecting punishment, see Nancy J. King, *Sentencing and Prior Convictions: The Past, the Future, and the End of the Prior-Conviction Exception to Apprendi*, 97 Marq. L. Rev. 523 (2014) (referencing recidivism research as well as commentary criticizing the use of criminal history to predict recidivism risk as unjustified under various theories of punishment, varying in reliability, and causing disparate and corrosive racial effects).

3. ***Victim impact evidence.*** Statutes and state constitutional provisions authorize or require consideration of victim impact statements during the sentencing stage. These provisions typically allow victims the right to make an oral statement at sentencing or provide that the victim's written statement appear in the presentence report, or both. The function of the victim statement is to provide information to the sentencer about the effects of the crime on the victim and the victim's family.

What is the appropriate role for victims in the sentencing process? Should judges consider a victim's sentence recommendation as well as his description of harm from the offense? Those in favor applaud the greater satisfaction with the process that victims express when they are included, and argue that involving the victim in the process can further traditional punishment goals. Those opposed argue that victims' preferences undermine other sentencing goals, particularly consistency, because some victims may be merciful while others are vindictive, some may be interested in restitution, others in retribution. Valuing victims' views also creates incentives for others to try to influence the preferences that victims express. For a collection of commentary, see Douglas E. Beloof, et al., *Victims in Criminal Procedure* (4th ed. 2018).

What information about a victim, if any, is relevant to sentencing? Consider Steve Bogira, *Courtroom 302* at 261–262 (2005) ("[Judge] Locallo always factors in the victim's background into his sentencing calculation. * * * 'When a victim is productive and going to school and has potential, that's a greater loss to society than if he's some goof who's involved in gangs,' the judge says later."); Minnesota Sentencing Guideline 2, subd. D (listing the victim's role as aggressor as mitigating factor that would justify a downward departure, and listing as an aggravating factor justifying upward departure the victim's vulnerability due to age or infirmity).

B. NOTICE, CONFRONTATION, DEFENSE SUBMISSIONS

1. ***Discovery and disclosure of sentencing information.*** The Court in *Williams* rebuffed the defendant's claims that he should have had the opportunity to test or rebut the allegations made in the presentence report. The Court observed, "no federal constitutional objection would have been possible * * * if the judge had sentenced [defendant] to death giving no reason at all." This aspect of the *Williams* holding, at least as applied to capital cases, was modified by *Gardner v. Florida*, 430 U.S. 349 (1977), where a majority of justices agreed that the Constitution forbids a judge from sentencing a defendant to death without disclosing those portions of the presentence report that form the basis for the sentence. Rejecting the state's arguments that nondisclosure was necessary to "enable investigators to obtain relevant but sensitive disclosures from persons unwilling to comment publicly about a defendant's background or character," and to prevent delay, three justices argued the procedure violated due process, two argued that it violated the Eighth Amendment, and others concurred for separate reasons. The Court later characterized *Gardner* as a case barring "secret" but not "surprise" use of sentencing information, and upheld a death sentence despite the government's failure to inform the defendant until the night before the penalty phase that it would be presenting witnesses to testify concerning alleged prior offenses. *Gray v. Netherland,* 518 U.S. 152 (1996). In *non*-capital cases the constitutionality of failing entirely to disclose certain sentencing information to the defense in remains unsettled. Statutes in most jurisdictions entitle felony defendants to review at least some

sentencing information at some point prior to the imposition of sentence. Are there some types of sentencing information that a judge should not reveal to a defendant? Why?

Until 2005, the federal sentencing guidelines were binding, and the Court interpreted Fed.R.Crim.P. 32 to require advance notice of any ground for departure from the guideline sentence that had not already been provided to the parties in the presentence report or other documents. *Burns* v. *United States*, 501 U.S. 129 (1991). The Court justified this interpretation in part by noting that it avoided the constitutional issue of how much advance notice of sentencing information, if any, the Due Process Clause requires. After the Court's decision in *Booker* rendered the guidelines advisory and no longer binding on judges, see p. 1394, the Court in *Irizarry v. United States*, 553 U.S. 708 (2008), addressed whether Rule 32 also required advance notice of facts supporting a sentence outside the guidelines. Under advisory guidelines, reasoned the Court, "neither the Government nor the defendant may place the same degree of reliance on the type of 'expectancy' that gave rise to a special need for notice in *Burns*." The Court concluded, "The due process concerns that motivated the Court to require notice in a world of mandatory Guidelines no longer provide a basis for this Court to extend the rule" to require notice of facts relied upon by the judge in imposing a non-guidelines sentence.

2. ***Testing the reliability of sentencing information.*** The Court in *Williams* also rejected the defendant's argument that he was entitled to cross-examine those who provided sentencing information. Requiring "open court testimony with cross-examination" the Court explained, would be "totally impractical if not impossible" in the sentencing context. While statutes in most jurisdictions do provide for sentencing hearings, such hearings do not commonly include evidentiary submissions other than the presentence report itself and the allocution of the defendant (described below). Lower courts continue to cite *Williams* when rejecting a defendant's constitutional entitlement to cross-examine those who provide sentencing information, and routinely rely upon hearsay in selecting a sentence within the range authorized for the offense of conviction. See, e.g., *United States v. Powell,* 650 F.3d 388 (4th Cir. 2011) ("Once the accused has been properly convicted . . . the purposes of the proceeding—and the evidentiary rules governing it—change. . . . [T]o realize "the principle that 'the punishment should fit the offender and not merely the crime,' " the sentencing judge must have recourse to a much broader array of information than we allow the trier of fact to consider in determining a defendant's guilt").

3. ***Defense submissions and allocution.*** In capital cases, the defendant is entitled to present mitigating evidence on his own behalf at sentencing, but in non-capital cases, the governing statute may or may not provide a defendant with this opportunity. Federal Rule 32, for example, states that the court *must* afford *counsel* an opportunity to comment on matters appropriate to sentence, and *may, in its discretion,* permit parties to introduce testimony or other evidence. Many states also leave the submission of sentencing evidence to the discretion of the trial judge.

The right of the defendant to speak on his own behalf at sentencing, however, a privilege known as the right of allocution, is protected in most jurisdictions by statute or court rule. Some states require (or allow the judge to order) the defendant to testify under oath and be subject to cross examination if making a statement. Courts disagree about whether the right of allocution is guaranteed by the Due Process Clause.

C. THE ASSISTANCE OF COUNSEL

The Sixth Amendment right to counsel extends to sentencing, a "stage of a criminal proceeding where substantial rights of a criminal accused may be affected." *Mempa v. Rhay,* 389 U.S. 128 (1967). Due process provides the basis for any right to counsel at post-sentencing proceedings that are not protected by the Sixth Amendment right to counsel, specifically parole and probation revocation hearings. The revocation of probation, the Court reasoned in *Gagnon v.*

Scarpelli, p. 86, "is not a part of the criminal prosecution," but the "loss of liberty entailed is a serious deprivation requiring that the parolee be accorded due process." Rather than adopting an "inflexible" rule requiring counsel for every revocation hearing, the Court held that "counsel should be provided in cases where, after being informed of his right to request counsel, the probationer or parolee makes such a request, based on a timely and colorable claim (i) that he has not committed the alleged violation of the conditions upon which he is at liberty; or (ii) that, even if the violation is a matter of public record or is uncontested there are substantial reasons which justified or mitigated the violation and make revocation inappropriate, and that the reasons are complex or otherwise difficult to develop or present." Also relevant is "whether the probationer appears to be capable of speaking effectively for himself."

The Court in *Gagnon* noted that unlike trial, revocation hearings need not comply with the rules of evidence, proof is merely by a preponderance, the state may be represented by a non-lawyer, and the factfinder may be a layperson. In assessing the need for counsel, however, wouldn't the more appropriate comparison be sentencing, not trial? Given the lack of trial-like procedural protections at sentencing, are revocations sufficiently distinct to justify a different rule? Congress and several states think not. See, e.g., 18 U.S.C. § 3006A(a)(1)(C), (E) (providing that any indigent defendant is entitled to appointed counsel when charged with a violation of probation or facing modification or revocation of supervised release).

D. JURY TRIAL AND BURDEN OF PROOF

In 1986, in McMILLAN v. PENNSYLVANIA, 477 U.S. 79 (1986), the Court began to confront the distinction between an offense element and a sentencing factor. It rejected a challenge to a Pennsylvania statute that mandated a five-year minimum sentence for any defendant convicted of one of several specified serious felonies, if a judge found at sentencing that the defendant visibly possessed a firearm. Chief Justice Rehnquist wrote the opinion for the Court: "*Winship* held that 'the Due Process Clause protects the accused against conviction except upon proof beyond a reasonable doubt of every fact necessary to constitute the crime with which he is charged.' * * * [I]n *Patterson* [*v. New York,* 432 U.S. 197 (1977)] we rejected the claim that whenever a State links the 'severity of punishment' to 'the presence or absence of an identified fact' the State must prove that fact beyond a reasonable doubt. In particular, we upheld against a due process challenge New York's law placing on defendants charged with murder the burden of proving the affirmative defense of extreme emotional disturbance.

"*Patterson* stressed that in determining what facts must be proved beyond a reasonable doubt the state legislature's definition of the elements of the offense is usually dispositive * * *. While 'there are obviously constitutional limits beyond which the States may not go in this regard,' '[t]he applicability of the reasonable-doubt standard . . . has always been dependent on how a State defines the offense that is charged in any given case[.]'

" * * * [T]he Pennsylvania Legislature has expressly provided that visible possession of a firearm is not an element of the crimes enumerated in the mandatory sentencing statute, § 9712(b), but instead is a sentencing factor that comes into play only after the defendant has been found guilty of one of those crimes beyond a reasonable doubt. Indeed, the elements of the enumerated offenses, like the maximum permissible penalties for those offenses, were established long before the Mandatory Minimum Sentencing Act was passed. While visible possession might well have been included as an element of the enumerated offenses, Pennsylvania chose not to redefine those offenses in order to so include it, and *Patterson* teaches that we should hesitate to conclude that due process bars the State from pursuing its chosen course in the area of defining crimes and prescribing penalties.

" * * * While we have never attempted to define precisely the constitutional limits noted in *Patterson,* i.e., the extent to which due process forbids the reallocation or reduction of burdens of proof in criminal cases, and do not do so today, we are persuaded by several factors that Pennsylvania's Mandatory Minimum Sentencing Act does not exceed those limits. * * * Section 9712 neither alters the maximum penalty for the crime committed nor creates a separate offense calling for a separate penalty; it operates solely to limit the sentencing court's discretion in selecting a penalty within the range already available to it without the special finding of visible possession of a firearm. Section 9712 'ups the ante' for the defendant only by raising to five years the minimum sentence which may be imposed within the statutory plan. The statute gives no impression of having been tailored to permit the visible possession finding to be a tail which wags the dog of the substantive offense. Petitioners' claim that visible possession under the Pennsylvania statute is 'really' an element of the offenses for which they are being punished—that Pennsylvania has in effect defined a new set of upgraded felonies—would have at least more superficial appeal if a finding of visible possession exposed them to greater or additional punishment, * * * but it does not."

Fourteen years later, the Court squarely addressed a maximum-enhancing statute unlike the statute in *McMillan*.

APPRENDI V. NEW JERSEY

530 U.S. 466, 120 S.Ct. 2348, 147 L.Ed.2d 435 (2000).

[The defendant had been sentenced under New Jersey's "hate crime" statute, which provided for an "extended term" of imprisonment if the trial judge determined at sentencing, by a preponderance of the evidence, that "the defendant in committing the crime acted with a purpose to intimidate an individual or group of individuals because of race, color, gender, handicap, religion, sexual orientation or ethnicity." Apprendi had fired shots into the home of an African-American family, and agreed to plead guilty to possession of a firearm for an unlawful purpose, an offense punishable by 5–10 years' imprisonment. After accepting the plea the trial judge held an evidentiary hearing on the issue of Apprendi's "purpose" for the shooting, which included defense testimony from a psychologist, character witnesses, and Apprendi himself. The judge, however, credited the testimony of a police officer, who reported that Apprendi had stated when arrested that he did not want the occupants of the home in the neighborhood because of their race. Having found by a preponderance of the evidence that Apprendi's actions were taken "with a purpose to intimidate," the judge sentenced him to an "extended term" of 12 years, two years more than the maximum sentence that was authorized had that finding not been made. Apprendi challenged his sentence as a violation of his right to a jury trial and his right to proof beyond a reasonable doubt of every element of the offense.]

STEVENS, J., delivered the opinion of the Court, in which SCALIA, SOUTER, THOMAS, and GINSBURG, JJ., joined.

" * * * Any possible distinction between an "element" of a felony offense and a "sentencing factor" was unknown to the practice of criminal indictment, trial by jury, and judgment by court as it existed during the years surrounding our Nation's founding. As a general rule, criminal proceedings were submitted to a jury after being initiated by an indictment containing 'all the facts and circumstances which constitute the offence, . . . stated with such certainty and precision, that the defendant . . . may be enabled to determine the species of offence they constitute, in order that he may prepare his defence accordingly . . . and that there may be no doubt as to the judgment which should be given, if the defendant be convicted.' J. Archbold, Pleading and Evidence in Criminal Cases 44 (15th ed. 1862). The defendant's ability to predict with certainty the judgment from the face of the felony indictment flowed from the invariable linkage of punishment with crime. * * *

"* * * Just as the circumstances of the crime and the intent of the defendant at the time of commission were often essential elements to be alleged in the indictment, so too were the circumstances mandating a particular punishment. 'Where a statute annexes a higher degree of punishment to a common-law felony, if committed under particular circumstances, an indictment for the offence, in order to bring the defendant within that higher degree of punishment, must expressly charge it to have been committed under those circumstances, and must state the circumstances with certainty and precision. [2 M. Hale, Pleas of the Crown 170].' Archbold, Pleading and Evidence in Criminal Cases, at 51. If, then, 'upon an indictment under the statute, the prosecutor prove the felony to have been committed, but fail in proving it to have been committed under the circumstances specified in the statute, the defendant shall be convicted of the common-law felony only.' Id. at 188. * * *

"We should be clear that nothing in this history suggests that it is impermissible for judges to exercise discretion—taking into consideration various factors relating both to offense and offender—in imposing a judgment within the range prescribed by statute. We have often noted that judges in this country have long exercised discretion of this nature in imposing sentence within statutory limits in the individual case.* * * As in *Williams* [*v. New York*, p. 1378], our periodic recognition of judges' broad discretion in sentencing—since the 19th-century shift in this country from statutes providing fixed-term sentences to those providing judges discretion within a permissible range, * * * has been regularly accompanied by the qualification that that discretion was bound by the range of sentencing options prescribed by the legislature. * * *

"It was in *McMillan v. Pennsylvania,* [p. 1387], that this Court, for the first time, coined the term 'sentencing factor' to refer to a fact that was not found by a jury but that could affect the sentence imposed by the judge. * * * We did not, however, there budge from the position that (1) constitutional limits exist to States' authority to define away facts necessary to constitute a criminal offense, and (2) that a state scheme that keeps from the jury facts that 'expose [defendants] to greater or additional punishment,' may raise serious constitutional concern. * * *

"*Almendarez-Torres* [*v. United States*, 523 U.S. 224 (1998)][a] represents at best an exceptional departure from the historic practice that we have described. * * * Because Almendarez-Torres had admitted the three earlier convictions for aggravated felonies—all of which had been entered pursuant to proceedings with substantial procedural safeguards of their own—no question concerning the right to a jury trial or the standard of proof that would apply to a contested issue of fact was before the Court. * * * [T]he specific question decided concerned the sufficiency of the indictment. More important,* * * our conclusion in *Almendarez-Torres* turned heavily upon the fact that the additional sentence to which the defendant was subject was 'the prior commission of

[a] In that case, the defendant turned up in a Texas jail after he had been deported following a burglary conviction. He was charged with the federal crime of reentering the United States illegally. His indictment did not specify whether he was being charged under 18 U.S.C. § 1326(a), noting a maximum sentence of *two* years, or subsection (b) that provided for up to *twenty* years if reentry occurred after being convicted of an aggravated felony. The defendant pleaded guilty to illegal reentry, admitted his prior burglary conviction, but argued at sentencing that because his indictment had not alleged his prior conviction, he was guilty only of violating subsection (a), and faced at most two years in prison. The judge disagreed, sentenced him to seven years, and the Supreme Court in a five to four decision upheld that sentence.

The Court reasoned that Congress intended that any prior conviction that triggered the eighteen-year increase would be a sentencing factor that the judge could find after conviction, not an element of a greater offense. Admitting that the case is different than *McMillan* "for it does 'alter the maximum penalty for the crime,'" the Court nonetheless concluded that "the sentencing factor at issue here—recidivism—is a traditional, if not the most traditional, basis for a sentencing court's increasing an offender's sentence. * * * [T]o hold that the Constitution requires that recidivism be deemed an 'element' of petitioner's offense would mark an abrupt departure from a longstanding tradition of treating recidivism as 'going to the punishment only.'" Justice Scalia joined by Justices Stevens, Souter, and Ginsburg, dissented in *Almendarez-Torres*, rejecting the conclusion that the Constitution permits "a defendant's sentencing exposure to be increased tenfold on the basis of a fact that is not charged, tried to a jury, and found beyond a reasonable doubt."

a serious crime.' * * * Both the certainty that procedural safeguards attached to any 'fact' of prior conviction, and the reality that Almendarez-Torres did not challenge the accuracy of that 'fact' in his case, mitigated the due process and Sixth Amendment concerns otherwise implicated in allowing a judge to determine a 'fact' increasing punishment beyond the maximum of the statutory range.

"Even though it is arguable that *Almendarez-Torres* was incorrectly decided, and that a logical application of our reasoning today should apply if the recidivist issue were contested, Apprendi does not contest the decision's validity and we need not revisit it for purposes of our decision today to treat the case as a narrow exception to the general rule we recalled at the outset. Given its unique facts, it surely does not warrant rejection of the otherwise uniform course of decision during the entire history of our jurisprudence.

"In sum, our reexamination of our cases in this area, and of the history upon which they rely, confirms[:] Other than the fact of a prior conviction, any fact that increases the penalty for a crime beyond the prescribed statutory maximum must be submitted to a jury, and proved beyond a reasonable doubt. With that exception, we endorse the statement of the rule set forth in the concurring opinions in that case: 'It is unconstitutional for a legislature to remove from the jury the assessment of facts that increase the prescribed range of penalties to which a criminal defendant is exposed. It is equally clear that such facts must be established by proof beyond a reasonable doubt.[16]"

JUSTICE O'CONNOR, with whom THE CHIEF JUSTICE, JUSTICE KENNEDY, and JUSTICE BREYER join, dissenting. [Separate opinions by JUSTICES SCALIA, THOMAS, and BREYER are omitted.]

"[The majority's] 'increase in the maximum penalty' rule * * * rests on a meaningless formalism that accords, at best, marginal protection for the constitutional rights that it seeks to effectuate. * * * [A state could] achieve virtually the same results, by * * * prescrib[ing], in the weapons possession statute itself, a range of 5 to 20 years' imprisonment for one who commits that criminal offense," and providing "that a defendant convicted under the statute whom a judge finds, by a preponderance of the evidence, *not* to have acted with a purpose to intimidate an individual on the basis of race may receive a sentence no greater than 10 years' imprisonment. "* * * If New Jersey can, consistent with the Constitution, make precisely the same differences in punishment turn on precisely the same facts, and can remove the assessment of those facts from the jury and subject them to a standard of proof below 'beyond a reasonable doubt,' it is impossible to say that the Fifth, Sixth, and Fourteenth Amendments require the Court's rule. For the same reason, the 'structural democratic constraints' that might discourage a legislature from enacting either of the above hypothetical statutes would be no more significant than those that would discourage the enactment of New Jersey's present sentence-enhancement statute. See n. 16 (majority opinion).

[16] The principal dissent would reject the Court's rule as a 'meaningless formalism,' because it can conceive of hypothetical statutes that would comply with the rule and achieve the same result as the New Jersey statute. While a State could, hypothetically, undertake to revise its entire criminal code in the manner the dissent suggests,— extending all statutory maximum sentences to, for example, 50 years and giving judges guided discretion as to a few specially selected factors within that range—this possibility seems remote. Among other reasons, structural democratic constraints exist to discourage legislatures from enacting penal statutes that expose every defendant convicted of, for example, weapons possession, to a maximum sentence exceeding that which is, in the legislature's judgment, generally proportional to the crime. This is as it should be. Our rule ensures that a State is obliged 'to make its choices concerning the substantive content of its criminal laws with full awareness of the consequence, unable to mask substantive policy choices' of exposing all who are convicted to the maximum sentence it provides. *Patterson v. New York,* 432 U.S. at 228–229, n. 13 (Powell, J., dissenting). So exposed, 'the political check on potentially harsh legislative action is then more likely to operate.' Ibid.

In all events, if such an extensive revision of the State's entire criminal code were enacted for the purpose the dissent suggests, or if New Jersey simply reversed the burden of the hate crime finding (effectively assuming a crime was performed with a purpose to intimidate and then requiring a defendant to prove that it was not), we would be required to question whether the revision was constitutional under this Court's prior decisions. See *Patterson*, 432 U.S. at 210; *Mullaney*, 421 U.S. at 698–702. * * *"

In all three cases, the legislature is able to calibrate punishment perfectly, and subject to a maximum penalty only those defendants whose cases satisfy the sentence-enhancement criterion." The dissenters also argued that "the concerns animating the Sixth Amendment's jury trial guarantee, if they were to extend to the sentencing context at all," would appear to "apply with greater strength to a discretionary-sentencing scheme than to determinate sentencing. In the former scheme, the potential for mischief by an arbitrary judge is much greater, given that the judge's decision of where to set the defendant's sentence within the prescribed statutory range is left almost entirely to discretion."

NOTES AND QUESTIONS ON THE APPRENDI RULE

1. **Apprendi *and death sentencing.*** In *Ring v. Arizona,* 536 U.S. 584 (2002), the Court applied *Apprendi* to an Arizona law providing that no death sentence could follow a jury's decision to convict a first degree murderer without the further finding of an aggravated circumstance at sentencing. The logic of *Apprendi* required that the jury determine this aggravating circumstance. Explained the Court, "The right to trial by jury * * * would be senselessly diminished if it encompassed the factfinding necessary to increase a defendant's sentence by two years, but not the factfinding necessary to put him to death." See also *Hurst v. Florida,* 136 S.Ct. 616 (2016) (holding the Sixth Amendment does not allow a sentencing scheme that requires a judge to determine those facts, even if the jury makes an advisory recommendation).

2. **Apprendi *and sentencing guidelines.*** In BLAKELY v. WASHINGTON, 542 U.S. 296 (2004), the Court held that *Apprendi*'s rule applies to facts that raise the authorized maximum sentence under mandatory state sentencing guidelines. Blakely pleaded guilty to second-degree kidnapping involving domestic violence and use of a firearm, a class B felony carrying a sentence of no more than ten years. Washington's Sentencing Reform Act specified for petitioner's offense a "standard range" of 49 to 53 months. The Act authorized the trial judge to impose a sentence above the standard range only if he found "substantial and compelling reasons justifying an exceptional sentence," but the sentence could be vacated on appeal if there was insufficient evidence in the record to support the reasons for imposing an exceptional sentence. The judge sentenced Blakely to 90 months, 37 months beyond the standard maximum, on the ground that he had acted with "deliberate cruelty," a statutorily enumerated ground for departure in domestic-violence cases.

Justice Scalia, joined by the same justices that constituted the majority in *Apprendi,* held that Blakely had been denied his right to a jury. "[T]he 'statutory maximum' for *Apprendi* purposes is the maximum sentence a judge may impose solely on the basis of the facts reflected in the jury verdict or admitted by the defendant. * * * When a judge inflicts punishment that the jury's verdict alone does not allow, the jury has not found all the facts 'which the law makes essential to the punishment,' and the judge exceeds his proper authority. * * * Just as suffrage ensures the people's ultimate control in the legislative and executive branches, jury trial is meant to ensure their control in the judiciary. * * * *Apprendi* carries out this design by ensuring that the judge's authority to sentence derives wholly from the jury's verdict. Without that restriction, the jury would not exercise the control that the Framers intended.

"Those who would reject *Apprendi* are resigned to one of two alternatives. The first is that the jury need only find whatever facts the legislature chooses to label elements of the crime, and that those it labels sentencing factors—no matter how much they may increase the punishment—may be found by the judge. This would mean, for example, that a judge could sentence a man for committing murder even if the jury convicted him only of illegally possessing the firearm used to commit it—or of making an illegal lane change while fleeing the death scene. Not even *Apprendi*'s critics would advocate this absurd result. The jury could not function as circuitbreaker in the State's machinery of justice if it were relegated to making a determination that the defendant at some point did something wrong, a mere preliminary to a judicial inquisition into the facts of the crime the State actually seeks to punish.[19]

"The second alternative is that legislatures may establish legally essential sentencing factors within limits—limits crossed when, perhaps, the sentencing factor is a 'tail which wags the dog of the substantive offense.' *McMillan*. What this means in operation is that the law must not go too far—it must not exceed the judicial estimation of the proper role of the judge. The subjectivity of this standard is obvious. Petitioner argued below that second-degree kidnaping with deliberate cruelty was essentially the same as first-degree kidnaping, the very charge he had avoided by pleading to a lesser offense. The court conceded this might be so but held it irrelevant. Petitioner's 90-month sentence exceeded the 53-month standard maximum by almost 70%; the Washington Supreme Court in other cases has upheld exceptional sentences 15 times the standard maximum. Did the court go too far in any of these cases? There is no answer that legal analysis can provide. * * *

" * * * Of course indeterminate schemes involve judicial factfinding, in that a judge (like a parole board) may implicitly rule on those facts he deems important to the exercise of his sentencing discretion. But the facts do not pertain to whether the defendant has a legal right to a lesser sentence—and that makes all the difference insofar as judicial impingement upon the traditional role of the jury is concerned. In a system that says the judge may punish burglary with 10 to 40 years, every burglar knows he is risking 40 years in jail. In a system that punishes burglary with a 10-year sentence, with another 30 added for use of a gun, the burglar who enters a home unarmed is entitled to no more than a 10-year sentence—and by reason of the Sixth Amendment the facts bearing upon that entitlement must be found by a jury.

" * * * Justice Breyer argues that *Apprendi* works to the detriment of criminal defendants who plead guilty by depriving them of the opportunity to argue sentencing factors to a judge. But nothing prevents a defendant from waiving his *Apprendi* rights. When a defendant pleads guilty, the State is free to seek judicial sentence enhancements so long as the defendant either stipulates to the relevant facts or consents to judicial factfinding. If appropriate waivers are procured, States may continue to offer judicial factfinding as a matter of course to all defendants who plead guilty. Even a defendant who stands trial may consent to judicial factfinding as to sentence enhancements, which may well be in his interest if relevant evidence would prejudice him at trial. We do not understand how *Apprendi* can possibly work to the detriment of those who are free, if they think its costs outweigh its benefits, to render it inapplicable.[21]

"Nor do we see any merit to Justice Breyer's contention that *Apprendi* is unfair to criminal defendants because, if States respond by enacting '17-element robbery crimes,' prosecutors will have more elements with which to bargain. Bargaining already exists with regard to sentencing factors because defendants can either stipulate or contest the facts that make them applicable. If there is any difference between bargaining over sentencing factors and bargaining over elements, the latter probably favors the defendant. Every new element that a prosecutor can threaten to

---

[19] Justice O'Connor believes that a "built-in political check" will prevent lawmakers from manipulating offense elements in this fashion. But the many immediate practical advantages of judicial factfinding, suggest that political forces would, if anything, pull in the opposite direction. In any case, the Framers' decision to entrench the jury-trial right in the Constitution shows that they did not trust government to make political decisions in this area.

[21] Justice Breyer responds that States are not required to give defendants the option of waiving jury trial on some elements but not others. True enough. But why would the States that he asserts we are coercing into hard-heartedness—that is, States that want judge-pronounced determinate sentencing to be the norm but we won't let them—want to prevent a defendant from choosing that regime? Justice Breyer claims this alternative may prove "too expensive and unwieldy for States to provide," but there is no obvious reason why forcing defendants to choose between contesting all elements of his hypothetical 17-element robbery crime and contesting none of them is less expensive than also giving them the third option of pleading guilty to some elements and submitting the rest to judicial factfinding. Justice Breyer's argument rests entirely on a speculative prediction about the number of defendants likely to choose the first (rather than the second) option if denied the third.

charge is also an element that a defendant can threaten to contest at trial and make the prosecutor prove beyond a reasonable doubt. Moreover, given the sprawling scope of most criminal codes, and the power to affect sentences by making (even nonbinding) sentencing recommendations, there is already no shortage of in terrorem tools at prosecutors' disposal. See King & Klein, *Apprendi and Plea Bargaining*, 54 Stan. L. Rev. 295, 296 (2001) ("Every prosecutorial bargaining chip * * * existed pre-*Apprendi* exactly as it does post-*Apprendi*").

"Any evaluation of *Apprendi*'s 'fairness' to criminal defendants must compare it with the regime it replaced, in which a defendant, with no warning in either his indictment or plea, would routinely see his maximum potential sentence balloon from as little as five years to as much as life imprisonment, see 21 U.S.C. §§ 841(b)(1)(A), (D),[22] based not on facts proved to his peers beyond a reasonable doubt, but on facts extracted after trial from a report compiled by a probation officer who the judge thinks more likely got it right than got it wrong."

Justice O'Connor, joined by Justice Breyer, the Chief Justice and Justice Kennedy, warned in dissent, "The 'effect' of today's decision will be greater judicial discretion and less uniformity in sentencing. * * * A rule of deferring to legislative labels has no less formal pedigree and it would vest primary authority for defining crimes in the political branches, where it belongs. It also would be easier to administer than the majority's rule, inasmuch as courts would not be forced to look behind statutes and regulations to determine whether a particular fact does or does not increase the penalty to which a defendant was exposed. * * * What I have feared most has now come to pass: Over 20 years of sentencing reform are all but lost, and tens of thousands of criminal judgments are in jeopardy."

Justice Breyer's separate dissent, joined by Justice O'Connor, stated: "As a result of the majority's rule, sentencing must now take one of three forms, each of which risks either impracticality, unfairness, or harm to the jury trial right the majority purports to strengthen."

"[1] legislators [could] create a simple, pure or nearly pure 'charge offense' or 'determinate' sentencing system. In such a system, an indictment would charge a few facts which, taken together, constitute a crime, such as robbery. Robbery would carry a single sentence, say, five years' imprisonment. * * * Such a system assures uniformity, but * * * impose[s] identical punishments on people who committed their crimes in very different ways * * * [and] gives tremendous power to prosecutors to manipulate sentences through their choice of charges."

"[2] legislators [could] return to a system of indeterminate sentencing. * * * When such systems were in vogue, they were criticized, and rightly so, for producing unfair disparities, including race-based disparities, in the punishment of similarly situated defendants. The length of time a person spent in prison appeared to depend on 'what the judge ate for breakfast' on the day of sentencing, on which judge you got, or on other factors that should not have made a difference to the length of the sentence. * * * While 'the judge's authority to sentence' would formally derive from the jury's verdict, the jury would exercise little or no control over the sentence itself. It is difficult to see how such an outcome protects the structural safeguards the majority claims to be defending.

"[3] legislators [could retain] structured schemes that attempt to punish similar conduct similarly and different conduct differently, but modifying them to conform to *Apprendi*'s dictates. Judges would be able to depart downward from presumptive sentences upon finding that mitigating factors were present, but would not be able to depart upward unless the prosecutor

[22] To be sure, Justice Breyer and the other dissenters would forbid those increases of sentence that violate the constitutional principle that tail shall not wag dog. The source of this principle is entirely unclear. Its precise effect, if precise effect it has, is presumably to require that the ratio of sentencing-factor add-on to basic criminal sentence be no greater than the ratio of caudal vertebrae to body in the breed of canine with the longest tail. Or perhaps no greater than the average such ratio for all breeds. Or perhaps the median. Regrettably, *Apprendi* has prevented full development of this line of jurisprudence.

charged the aggravating fact to a jury and proved it beyond a reasonable doubt. * * * A legislature, for example, might enact a robbery statute, modeled on robbery sentencing guidelines, that increases punishment depending upon (1) the nature of the institution robbed, (2) the (a) presence of, (b) brandishing of, (c) other use of, a firearm, (3) making of a death threat, (4) presence of (a) ordinary, (b) serious, (c) permanent or life threatening, bodily injury, (5) abduction, (6) physical restraint, (7) taking of a firearm, (8) taking of drugs, (9) value of property loss, etc. * * * [This system] prejudices defendants who seek trial, for it can put them in the untenable position of contesting material aggravating facts in the guilt phases of their trials. * * * How can a Constitution that guarantees due process put these defendants, as a matter of course, in the position of arguing, 'I did not sell drugs, and if I did, I did not sell more than 500 grams'?

"* * * Is there a fourth option? Perhaps. Congress and state legislatures might, for example, rewrite their criminal codes, attaching astronomically high sentences to each crime, followed by long lists of mitigating facts, which, for the most part, would consist of the absence of aggravating facts. But political impediments to legislative action make such rewrites difficult to achieve; and it is difficult to see why the Sixth Amendment would require legislatures to undertake them."

3. *Sentencing guidelines after* Blakely. After *Blakely,* a small number of states chose to maintain appellate review of judicial compliance with their mandatory sentencing guidelines and provide a right to a jury decision finding, beyond a reasonable doubt, any aggravating fact required for a penalty exceeding the guideline range (Justice Breyer's option number 3, above). In those states the number of enhancements per crime are few and only a small number of cases per year involve contested enhancements. In other states where enhancing facts either are more plentiful or are invoked more frequently, lawmakers or courts made their formerly mandatory guidelines advisory. *E.g.* Tenn. Code Ann. § 40–35–210(c) (2006).

In UNITED STATES v. BOOKER, 543 U.S. 220 (2005), the Supreme Court adopted the second course. The many opinions in *Booker* generated two important holdings. First, in an opinion written by Justice Stevens, joined by Justices Scalia, Souter, Thomas, and Ginsburg, a majority of justices agreed that after *Blakely,* under the federal statutes as written, a federal defendant had a right to a jury determination, beyond a reasonable doubt, of any sentencing factor that raised his sentence above the base offense level specified by the guidelines. Justice Stevens reasoned: "If the Guidelines as currently written could be read as merely advisory provisions that recommended, rather than required, the selection of particular sentences in response to differing sets of facts, their use would not implicate the Sixth Amendment. We have never doubted the authority of a judge to exercise broad discretion in imposing a sentence within a statutory range. * * * The Guidelines as written, however, are not advisory; they are mandatory and binding on all judges. * * * Booker's case illustrates the mandatory nature of the Guidelines. The jury convicted him of possessing at least 50 grams of crack * * * based on evidence that he had 92.5 grams of crack in his duffel bag. Under these facts, the Guidelines specified an offense level of 32, which, given the defendant's criminal history category, authorized a sentence of 210-to-262 months. * * * The sentencing judge would therefore have been reversed had he not imposed a sentence within the level 32 Guidelines range. Booker's actual sentence, however, was 360 months, almost 10 years longer than the Guidelines range supported by the jury verdict alone. To reach this sentence, the judge found facts beyond those found by the jury: namely, that Booker possessed 566 grams of crack in addition to the 92.5 grams in his duffel bag. The jury never heard any evidence of the additional drug quantity, and the judge found it true by a preponderance of the evidence. Thus, just as in *Blakely*, 'the jury's verdict alone does not authorize the sentence. The judge acquires that authority only upon finding some additional fact.' "

Second, a different majority of the Court, in an opinion written by Justice Breyer, joined by the Chief Justice, and Justices O'Connor, Kennedy, and Ginsburg (the dissenters from the first holding, plus Justice Ginsberg), concluded that given "that it is no longer possible to maintain the judicial factfinding that Congress thought would underpin the mandatory Guidelines system that it sought to create," the appropriate response was not to require jury assessments of guideline factors, but instead to invalidate those portions of the statute that had the effect of making the Guidelines mandatory. These provisions were § 3553(b)(1), which required district courts to impose a sentence within the guidelines range (in the absence of facts justifying a departure) and § 3742(e), regarding appellate enforcement of that requirement. "So modified," Justice Breyer explained, "the Federal Sentencing Act, * * * requires a sentencing court to consider Guidelines ranges, but it permits the court to tailor the sentence in light of other statutory concerns as well." "Section 3553(a) remains in effect, and sets forth numerous factors that guide sentencing." Justice Breyer argued that "[t]o engraft the Court's constitutional requirement onto the sentencing statutes, however, would destroy the system." A system requiring jury decisions for aggravating factors would be "far more complex than Congress could have intended" as well as difficult to apply. By "prohibit[ing] the judge from basing a sentence upon any conduct other than the conduct the prosecutor chose to charge," it would "weaken the tie between a sentence and an offender's real conduct," and "undermine the sentencing statute's basic aim of ensuring similar sentences for those who have committed similar crimes in similar ways."

Under the advisory guidelines system, the Court later explained in *Peugh v. United States*, 569 U.S. 530 (2013): " 'a district court should begin all sentencing proceedings by correctly calculating the applicable Guidelines range,' " which serves as " 'the starting point and the initial benchmark.' " The court must then consider the arguments of the parties and the factors set forth in § 3553(a), may not presume that the Guidelines range is reasonable, may in appropriate cases impose a non-Guidelines sentence based on disagreement with the Sentencing Commission's views, and must explain the basis for its chosen sentence on the record. " '[A] major departure [from the Guidelines] should be supported by a more significant justification than a minor one.' " In 2017, federal courts imposed sentences that were within the applicable guideline range in 49.1 percent of all cases, a figure that varied widely by district and crime type.

4. **Apprendi *and mandatory minimum sentencing statutes.*** At first, in *Harris v. United States*, 536 U.S. 545 (2002), by a narrow 4:1:4 vote, the Court reaffirmed *McMillan* and refused to extend *Apprendi* to require proof beyond a reasonable doubt to a jury of facts triggering mandatory minimum sentences. Justice Kennedy, joined by Chief Justice Rehnquist and Justices O'Connor and Scalia explained: "*Apprendi* said that any fact extending the defendant's sentence beyond the maximum authorized by the jury's verdict would have been considered an element of an aggravated crime—and thus the domain of the jury—by those who framed the Bill of Rights. The same cannot be said of a fact increasing the mandatory minimum (but not extending the sentence beyond the statutory maximum), for the jury's verdict has authorized the judge to impose the minimum with or without the finding. * * * If facts judges consider when exercising their discretion within the statutory range are not elements, they do not become as much merely because legislatures require the judge to impose a minimum sentence when those facts are found—a sentence the judge could have imposed absent the finding. * * * There is no reason to believe that those who framed the Fifth and Sixth Amendments would have thought of them as the elements of the crime. * * * Statutes like the Pennsylvania Act [at issue in *McMillan*] which alter the minimum sentence without changing the maximum, were for the most part the product of the 20th century, when legislatures first asserted control over the sentencing judge's discretion. Courts at the founding (whose views might be relevant, given the contemporaneous adoption of the Bill of Rights) and in the mid-19th century (whose views might be relevant, given that sentencing ranges first arose then) were not as a general matter required to decide whether a fact giving rise to a mandatory minimum sentence within the available range was to be alleged in the indictment and proved to the jury. Indeed, though there is no clear record of how history treated these facts, it is clear that they did not fall within the principle by which history determined what facts were elements. That principle defined elements as 'fact[s] . . . legally essential to the

punishment to be inflicted.' This formulation includes facts that, as *McMillan* put it, 'alte[r] the maximum penalty,' but it does not include facts triggering a mandatory minimum. The minimum may be imposed with or without the factual finding; the finding is by definition not 'essential' to the defendant's punishment." Justice Breyer, concurring as the fifth vote, joined Justice Kennedy's opinion only "to the extent that it holds that *Apprendi* does not apply to mandatory minimums."

Justice Stevens, writing for the dissenters (those in the *Apprendi* majority except Justice Scalia) concluded, "Whether one raises the floor or raises the ceiling it is impossible to dispute that the defendant is exposed to greater punishment than is otherwise prescribed. * * * [H]istorical practice is not directly dispositive of the question whether facts triggering mandatory minimums must be treated like elements. The Court has not previously suggested that constitutional protection ends where legislative innovation or ingenuity begins."

Eleven years later, in ALLEYNE v. UNITED STATES, 570 U.S. 99 (2013), Justice Breyer switched sides and the position of the dissenting justices in *Harris* prevailed. The Court overruled *Harris* and *McMillan* and held that permitting judges to determine facts that trigger mandatory minimum sentences "cannot be reconciled with our reasoning in *Apprendi*." Alleyne had been convicted of violating 18 U.S.C. § 924(c)(1)(A), which provided a sentence of "not less than 5 years" for anyone who "uses or carries a firearm" in relation to a "crime of violence," and "not less than 7 years" "if the firearm is brandished." The jury that convicted Alleyne indicated on the verdict form that he had "[u]sed or carried a firearm during and in relation to a crime of violence," but did not indicate a finding that the firearm was "[b]randished." The presentence report recommended a 7-year sentence and Alleyne objected, arguing that the jury did not find brandishing beyond a reasonable doubt and that he was subject only to the five-year mandatory minimum. Relying on *Harris,* the judge overruled the objection, found Alleyne had brandished the firearm, and imposed a sentence of seven years, which was upheld on appeal.

Writing for the Court, Justice Thomas traced the "linkage of facts with particular sentence ranges (defined by both the minimum and the maximum)" at common law, and "a well-established practice of including in the indictment, and submitting to the jury, every fact that was a basis for imposing or increasing punishment * * *." This rule, he explained, allowed the defendant to predict the judgment, if convicted. "Consistent with common-law and early American practice, *Apprendi* concluded that any 'facts that increase the prescribed range of penalties to which a criminal defendant is exposed' are elements of the crime. * * * While *Harris* limited *Apprendi* to facts increasing the statutory maximum, the principle applied in *Apprendi* applies with equal force to facts increasing the mandatory minimum."

"It is indisputable that a fact triggering a mandatory minimum alters the prescribed range of sentences to which a criminal defendant is exposed. * * * And because the legally prescribed range *is* the penalty affixed to the crime, * * * it follows that a fact increasing either end of the range produces a new penalty and constitutes an ingredient of the offense. * * * It is impossible to dissociate the floor of a sentencing range from the penalty affixed to the crime. * * * Moreover, it is impossible to dispute that facts increasing the legally prescribed floor *aggravate* the punishment. * * * Elevating the low-end of a sentencing range heightens the loss of liberty associated with the crime: the defendant's 'expected punishment has increased as a result of the narrowed range' and 'the prosecution is empowered, by invoking the mandatory minimum, to require the judge to impose a higher punishment than he might wish.'). * * * This reality demonstrates that the core crime and the fact triggering the mandatory minimum sentence together constitute a new, aggravated crime, each element of which must be submitted to the jury.[2]"

---

[2] Juries must find any facts that increase either the statutory maximum or minimum because the Sixth Amendment applies where a finding of fact both alters the legally prescribed range *and* does so in a way that aggravates the penalty. Importantly, this is distinct from factfinding used to guide judicial discretion in selecting a

"Defining facts that increase a mandatory statutory minimum to be part of the substantive offense enables the defendant to predict the legally applicable penalty from the face of the indictment. * * * It also preserves the historic role of the jury as an intermediary between the State and criminal defendants. * * * As noted, the essential Sixth Amendment inquiry is whether a fact is an element of the crime. When a finding of fact alters the legally prescribed punishment so as to aggravate it, the fact necessarily forms a constituent part of a new offense and must be submitted to the jury. It is no answer to say that the defendant could have received the same sentence with or without that fact. * * * [B]ecause the fact of brandishing aggravates the legally prescribed range of allowable sentences, it constitutes an element of a separate, aggravated offense that must be found by the jury, regardless of what sentence the defendant *might* have received if a different range had been applicable. Indeed, if a judge were to find a fact that increased the statutory maximum sentence, such a finding would violate the Sixth Amendment, even if the defendant ultimately received a sentence falling within the original sentencing range (*i.e.,* the range applicable without that aggravating fact). * * * The essential point is that the aggravating fact produced a higher range, which, in turn, conclusively indicates that the fact is an element of a distinct and aggravated crime. It must, therefore, be submitted to the jury and found beyond a reasonable doubt." * * * "Our ruling today does not mean that any fact that influences judicial discretion must be found by a jury. We have long recognized that broad sentencing discretion, informed by judicial factfinding, does not violate the Sixth Amendment. * * * Our decision today is wholly consistent with the broad discretion of judges to select a sentence within the range authorized bylaw."

"The judge, rather than the jury, found brandishing, thus violating petitioner's Sixth Amendment rights," the Court concluded. "Accordingly, we vacate the Sixth Circuit's judgment with respect to Alleyne's sentence on the § 924(c)(1)(A) conviction and remand the case for resentencing consistent with the jury's verdict."

Justice Breyer concurred, explaining that although "I continue to disagree with *Apprendi,*" he agreed "the time has come to end" what he termed the "anomaly" of "read[ing] *Apprendi* as insisting that juries find sentencing facts that *permit* a judge to impose a higher sentence while not insisting that juries find sentencing facts that *require* a judge to impose a higher sentence."

Chief Justice Roberts wrote in dissent, joined by Justices Scalia and Kennedy. In this case, he noted "The jury's verdict authorized the judge to impose the precise sentence he imposed for the precise factual reason he imposed it," and the Sixth Amendment "demands nothing more." Criticizing the lack of historical evidence for the Court's position, Chief Justice Roberts also argued that the "question here is about the power of judges, not juries. Under the rule in place until today, a legislature could tell judges that certain facts carried certain weight, and require the judge to devise a sentence based on that weight—so long as the sentence remained within the range authorized by the jury. Now, in the name of the jury right that formed a barrier between the defendant and the State, the majority has erected a barrier between judges and legislatures, establishing that discretionary sentencing is the domain of judges. Legislatures must keep their respectful distance. * * * Just as the Sixth Amendment 'limits judicial power only to the extent that the claimed judicial power infringes on the province of the jury,' so too it limits *legislative* power only to the extent *that* power infringes on the province of the jury. Because the claimed infringement here is on the province of the judge, not the jury, the jury right has no work to do."

Justice Alito dissented separately, arguing that "If the Court is of a mind to reconsider existing precedent, a prime candidate should be *Apprendi.*" He questioned both the historical analysis in that "dubious" case and the illogic of accepting discretionary sentencing under its

---

punishment "within limits fixed by law." *Williams v. New York,* 337 U.S. 241, 246 (1949). While such findings of fact may lead judges to select sentences that are more severe than the ones they would have selected without those facts, the Sixth Amendment does not govern that element of sentencing.

rationale. Finally, he observed, that "if *Harris* is not entitled to *stare decisis* weight, then neither is the Court's opinion in this case. After all, only four Members of the Court think that the Court's holding is the correct reading of the Constitution."

5. ***The exception for prior convictions.*** The Court in *Alleyne* stated that it would not "revisit" *Almendarez-Torres* "[b]ecause the parties do not contest that decision's vitality." But at least three justices have contested the exception's vitality; so have many commentators. E.g., King, Note 2, p. 1384 (arguing that history, precedent, and policy does not support the exception, collecting history of law on charging prior conviction in each state, noting Justices Scalia, Thomas, and Ginsburg have already made their opposition to the exception clear, and that the concurring opinions of Justices Breyer, Sotomayor, and Kagan in *Alleyne* may provide a basis for them to join). The Supreme Court of Hawaii has rejected the exception for prior convictions, interpreting the state's constitution to require that the government allege in the charging instrument any prior conviction triggering a mandatory minimum sentence, and that the jury find that conviction beyond a reasonable doubt. *State v. Auld*, 136 Hawai'i 244, 361 P.3d 471 (2015).

6. ***Treating range-raising facts as elements—the reasons for and scope of the* Apprendi *rule.*** Notice that the problem addressed in these cases is not that judges rather than juries are selecting sentences, nor that judges, when setting sentences, are considering facts that were never proven beyond a reasonable doubt to a jury. The Court has always held there is no Sixth Amendment right to a jury's determination of punishment *within* the range authorized by law for the offense. And the Court continues to support judicial fact-finding at sentencing under the relaxed procedures authorized more than fifty years ago in *Williams,* p. 1378.

Instead, the Court adopted its rule in *Apprendi* to cope with a type of law unknown to the Founders—legislation that specified a certain fact as triggering more severe punishment but that delegated the finding of that fact to the judge at sentencing. The Court concluded that once a legislature designates that a finding of fact carries a higher range of punishment, a court must treat that fact as an element of a greater offense and the government must prove it to a jury beyond a reasonable doubt. As Justice Thomas expressed the rule in *Alleyne:* "When a finding of fact alters the legally prescribed punishment so as to aggravate it, the fact necessarily forms a constituent part of a new offense and must be submitted to the jury."

As a matter of constitutional interpretation, is this range-raising standard for differentiating between elements and sentencing facts *preferable* to the tests advanced by those who have objected to the *Apprendi* rule? These alternatives include requiring proof beyond a reasonable doubt to a jury whenever a statute is "tailored to permit the [factual] finding to be a tail which wags the dog of the substantive offense" (*McMillan*, p. 1387; *Blakely,* footnote 22, p. 1393); allowing a legislature to define what is sentencing factor and what is element "within constraints of fairness" (*Booker*, Breyer, J. dissenting); limiting trial protections to facts that are related to the offense, while allowing judges to find facts related to the offender (Douglas Berman, *Conceptualizing Booker*, 38 Ariz. St. L.J. 38 (2008)); and adopting a sliding scale of procedural protections for sentencing rather than an approach that provides some facts with "full-blown trial protections" and others "almost none" (Douglas Berman & Stephanos Bibas, *Making Sentencing Sensible*, 4 Ohio St.J.Crim.L. 37 (2006)).

Consider Justice Breyer's dissent in *Blakely*. If the second and fourth options he lists for complying with the *Apprendi* rule are permissible, is the rule merely "formalism" that legislators can easily avoid? See Justice O'Connor's dissent in *Apprendi*, at p. 1390. Is the rule essentially a "plain statement" limitation that forces the legislature to be clear about what it is doing? Compare footnote 16 of Justice Stevens' majority opinion in *Apprendi,* with footnote 19 of Justice Scalia's opinion in *Blakely*.

Is the rule doing more than ensuring the right to a jury decision rather than a judge's, and proof beyond a reasonable doubt rather than by a preponderance? Is it also mandating additional *notice* to the accused? Justice Thomas stated in *Alleyne* that the rule "enables the defendant to predict the legally applicable penalty from the face of the indictment." If so, then facts considered elements under *Apprendi/Alleyne* may have to be included in the initial charge to comply with due process, an issue the Court has yet to address. See also Note 1, p. 988.

Elemental status for range-raising sentencing facts may require more than rights to a jury decisionmaker, a higher burden of proof, and notice in the charge. Must confrontation rights be afforded? Consideration as an element for purposes of double jeopardy? Compare *United States v. Pena*, 742 F.3d 508 (1st Cir. 2014) (double jeopardy issues would be raised by the government's plan to decide on remand only the aggravating element and take the admissions of guilt from the plea for the other elements) with *Smith v. Hedgpeth*, 706 F.3d 1099 (9th Cir. 2013) (*Apprendi* did not clearly establish that sentencing enhancements that raise the penalty maximum are elements for purposes of the Double Jeopardy Clause). See also *People v. Alarcon*, 210 Cal.App.4th 432, 148 Cal.Rptr.3d 345 (2012) (*Apprendi* sentence enhancement does not function as an element for purposes of test for lesser included offenses).

7. ***Consistency and real-offense sentencing.*** Consistency in sentencing was one of the primary goals of Congress when adopting the Sentencing Reform Act, not only consistency between defendants sentenced for the same offense, but also between defendants who engaged in comparable criminal activity, but who may have been convicted of different offenses. This is the theory behind the Guidelines' policy of increasing sentences for "relevant conduct." The Guidelines "real-offense" system was meant to counteract the disparity-producing effects of charge bargaining, by enlisting probation officers to report the defendant's actual conduct to the judge before sentencing, so that the "real" offense would form the basis for the sentence rather than whatever set of facts the parties had agreed to in a plea bargain. The Guidelines also "group" similar offenses, tempering somewhat the prosecutor's ability to control the sentence by charging multiple offenses rather than a single count.

Justice Breyer in his opinion for the Court in *Booker* argued that requiring prosecutors to charge and juries to decide aggravating guideline facts would "destroy" this real offense system. Did Justice Breyer's solution in *Booker*—advisory guidelines with reasonableness review—preserve real offense sentencing? Is it worth preserving?

Inconsistency in sentencing for crime has many sources, including prosecutorial discretion in charging and settlement negotiations, judicial discretion to impose different punishments for defendants convicted of the same offense, judicial discretion to impose concurrent or consecutive sentences for multiple convictions, and variation in release decisions by paroling authorities. Does the Constitution suggest that inconsistency from any of these sources is problematic, assuming it does not amount to a violation of the Equal Protection Clause?

8. ***Consecutive sentencing.*** Consider a statute that requires a judge to impose concurrent sentences after multiple guilty verdicts issued by a single jury, and permits consecutive sentences only if the judge finds either that 1) the additional offense was not merely incidental to the commission of a more serious offense but was an indication of the defendant's willingness to commit more than one offense, or that 2) the offense caused or created a risk of causing greater or qualitatively different harm to the victim, or a risk of harm to a different victim. After *Blakely*, must these findings be made by a jury before consecutive sentences may be imposed? No, held the Court in *Oregon v. Ice*, 555 U.S. 160 (2009). Justice Ginsberg's majority opinion concluded that that the decision to impose sentences consecutively is not within the traditional jury function and "specification of the regime for administering multiple sentences has long been considered the prerogative of state legislatures." Both "historical practice" and "respect for state sovereignty," she explained, "counsel against extending *Apprendi*'s rule to the imposition of sentences for discrete

crimes." Justice Scalia, joined by the Chief Justice and Justices Souter and Thomas dissented, arguing that the Oregon "scheme allows judges rather than juries to find the facts necessary to commit defendants to longer prison sentences, and thus directly contradicts what we held eight years ago and have reaffirmed several times since. The Court's justification of Oregon's scheme is a virtual copy of the dissents in those cases."

9. ***Appellate review of sentencing under advisory guidelines.*** The Supreme Court has explained that in reviewing a federal sentence under the advisory guidelines, a court of appeals "must first ensure that the district court committed no significant procedural error, such as failing to calculate (or improperly calculating) the Guidelines range, treating the Guidelines as mandatory, failing to consider the § 3553(a) factors, selecting a sentence based on clearly erroneous facts, or failing to adequately explain the chosen sentence-including an explanation for any deviation from the Guidelines range. Assuming that the district court's sentencing decision is procedurally sound, the appellate court should then consider the substantive reasonableness of the sentence imposed under an abuse-of-discretion standard." The reviewing court "may take the degree of variance from the guidelines range into account, but may not require extraordinary circumstances to justify a sentence outside the range." *Gall v. United States*, 552 U.S. 38 (2007). "The court of appeals may, but is not required to, presume that a within-Guidelines sentence is reasonable. The reviewing court may not apply a heightened standard of review or a presumption of unreasonableness to sentences outside the Guidelines range, although it 'will, of course, take into account the totality of the circumstances, including the extent of any variance from the Guidelines range." *Peugh v. United States*, p. 1395. The Commentary to the MPC Sentencing provision on appellate review warns: "Beyond what has been specifically allowed by the Supreme Court, it is unclear how far the practice of appellate sentence review may be taken in an advisory-guidelines system without running afoul of *Blakely*." MPC: Sentencing § 7.09, Comment (ALI, Final Draft 2017).

10. ***Fines, restitution, forfeiture.*** In *Southern Union v. United States*, 567 U.S. 343 (2012), after reviewing "ample historical evidence" from the 19th Century "showing that juries routinely found facts that set the maximum amounts of fines, the Court held that rule of *Apprendi* applies to the imposition of criminal fines. The Court has yet to address *Apprendi's* application to loss findings that are required for fixing restitution as part of a sentence, or facts establishing the relationship between crime and an asset that is required before the asset may be forfeited as part of a sentence.

CHAPTER 28

APPEALS

■ ■ ■

§ 1. THE DEFENDANT'S RIGHT TO APPEAL

1. ***A constitutional right to appeal?*** "The Federal Constitution imposes on the States no obligation to provide appellate review of criminal convictions," stated the Court in *Halbert v. Michigan*, p. 98. As authority, the Court cited *McKane v. Durston,* 153 U.S. 684 (1894), where, more than a century earlier, the Court had stated in dictum that "a review by an appellate court of the final judgment in a criminal case, however grave the offense of which the accused is convicted, was not at common law and is not now a necessary element of due process." *McKane* was written at a time when appellate review had only recently been introduced into the federal judicial structure and grounds for review were limited. As the Court noted in *United States v. Scott,* p. 1350, when the Bill of Rights was adopted, "neither the United States nor the defendant had any right to appeal an adverse verdict * * * . It was not until 1889 that Congress permitted criminal defendants to seek a writ of error in this Court, and then only in capital cases." Today appellate review is a much more important element of the criminal justice process.[a] Nevertheless, the Court has never questioned the *McKane* dictum.

At least one justice has expressed doubts. Justice Brennan wrote, "there are few, if any situations in our system of justice in which a single judge is given unreviewable discretion over matters concerning a person's liberty or property, and the reversal rate of criminal convictions on mandatory appeals in the state courts, while not overwhelming, is certainly high enough to suggest that depriving defendants of their right to appeal would expose them to an unacceptable risk of erroneous conviction." *Jones v. Barnes*, 463 U.S. 745 (1983) (Brennan, J. dissenting). The reversal rate for felony appeals of right by state defendants varies considerably from one state to another. Using data from a nationwide study of state criminal appeals (see Nicole A. Waters, *et al.*, Bureau of Justice Statistics Bulletin: Criminal Appeals in State Courts (Sept. 2015)), one study found that on average, defendants received a favorable outcome in 14.9% of their felony appeals of-right, but less than 3% of their felony appeals to courts of last resort that exercised discretion whether to review the case. Michael Heise, Nancy J. King & Nicole A. Heise, *State Criminal Appeals Revealed*, 70 Vand. L. Rev. 1939 (2017). Just over half of the appeals of right produced a reasoned judicial opinion; the remainder received a summary or memorandum decision. Less than 20% received oral argument. Sentencing challenges and insufficient evidence claims were the most frequently raised claims (included in nearly 30% of first appeals of-right).

2. ***Access to appellate review provided by state law.*** Some opportunity for a defendant to obtain appellate review of a felony conviction is provided by every jurisdiction. In most states convicted felony defendants have a statutory right to appellate review of their convictions by an intermediate appellate court, but in the handful of states with no such court, appellate review is available in the state's highest court. As noted in Chapter 22, Section 6, and in Note 4, below, a guilty plea extinguishes many claims that might otherwise be raised on appeal by a defendant convicted after a trial. Several states have limited a defendant's access to appeal for those claims that remain after a guilty plea, providing only discretionary appellate review of plea-based

[a] A more extensive analysis of appellate review of criminal cases can be found in 7 Wayne R. LaFave, Jerold H. Israel, Nancy J. King & Orin S. Kerr, Criminal Procedure Treatise §§ 27.1–27.6 (4th ed. 2016) (also available on Westlaw under the database name CRIMPROC and hereafter cited as CRIMPROC).

convictions, or requiring either certification of the trial judge or permission of the appellate court. E.g. Mich. Const., Art. 1, § 20 (addressed in *Halbert*, p. 98, which also discusses the reasons for this limitation on appellate review). Law in several states bars the appeal of a sentence term the defendant agrees to accept in a plea agreement.

3. ***Express waiver of the right to appeal.*** In a plea agreement, in return for charging or sentencing concessions from the government, a defendant may expressly promise not to appeal certain claims or not to file any appeal at all. Terms that expressly waive the right to seek judicial review of a claim of ineffective assistance of counsel are considered unethical in many states, and in 2014, U.S. Attorney General Holder banned them in federal cases. A different Attorney General could rescind this directive, however. And although ethics rules or internal policy may bar attorneys from including waivers of ineffectiveness claims in plea agreements, many courts have upheld them so long as the claimed error of counsel did not affect whether the plea was knowing and voluntary. For more on appeal waivers in plea agreements, see Notes 4 and 5, p. 1165–1166, and Note 2, p. 1377.

4. ***Inherent waiver by guilty plea.*** A guilty plea "inherently waives" many potential appellate claims of error, as the Court explained in *Class v. United States,* p. 1224. Claims inherently waived by a guilty plea include claims involving the "right to fair trial" and "accompanying constitutional guarantees," claims of "case related government conduct that takes place before plea," and claims "that would contradict the 'admissions necessarily made upon entry of a voluntary plea of guilty.' "

5. ***Review by the trial judge: post-trial motion for new trial.*** After conviction but before appeal, there is in most jurisdictions a procedure that allows a defendant to ask the trial judge to grant a new trial. Motions for new trial take two forms.

a. ***Procedural error.*** A new trial motion may raise alleged procedural errors, such as the admission of improper evidence, variance between the indictment and proof, or an erroneous instruction. When a motion for new trial raises an error in the process leading to conviction, that error is reviewed under the same harmless and plain error standards that would apply had the error been raised on appeal. See Section 5.

b. ***Newly discovered evidence.*** A defendant seeking a new trial based on newly discovered evidence in most jurisdictions will be required to establish that he could not have learned of the evidence earlier by exercising due diligence, and that if considered at trial the evidence probably would produce an acquittal. The time period for making a motion based on newly discovered evidence is substantially longer than the time period allowed for a new trial motion based on procedural error. Once that time period expires, a defendant with new evidence of innocence must pursue more restrictive collateral remedies in state and federal court. See Chapter 29. The potential for DNA testing to exonerate offenders has led every state to adopt statutes regulating the post-trial provision of DNA testing upon specified showings. DNA testing and preservation statutes are collected on the website of the National Conference of State Legislatures, at www.ncsl.org, and in D. Wilkes, Jr., State Postconviction Remedies and Relief Handbook with Forms § 1.8.

Constitutional Protection for the Statutory Right to Appeal

Once a state provides for appellate review, it must ensure that review is provided to defendants consistent with the requirements of both equal protection and due process. For example, the Equal Protection and Due Process Clauses require states to appoint counsel and provide transcripts for those indigent defendants who seek to appeal and were entitled to counsel before conviction. *Halbert v. Michigan*, p. 98; *Griffin v. Illinois,* p. 92; *Douglas v. California*, p. 94.

The Due Process Clause also provides some protection for the defendant against vindictive punishment for exercising his right to appeal, as the following cases explain.

NORTH CAROLINA V. PEARCE

395 U.S. 711, 89 S.Ct. 2072, 23 L.Ed.2d 656 (1969).

[The Court had before it two cases in which defendants were initially convicted, had their convictions set aside, were then reprosecuted and reconvicted, and subsequently were sentenced to longer terms of imprisonment than they originally received. One had initially been sentenced to a term of 12 to 15 years, and after reconviction was sentenced to 15 years; the other had been sentenced initially to prison terms totaling 10 years, and after retrial was sentenced to 25 years. The defendants presented two questions relating to the sentence that constitutionally could be imposed upon a defendant's reconviction after his original conviction had been set aside—whether credit had to be given for time served under the initial, subsequently overturned conviction, and whether the sentence imposed upon reconviction could be more severe than the sentence originally imposed. The Court initially held that a double jeopardy prohibition against "multiple punishments" for the same charge required that the judge imposing a new sentence following a reconviction give credit for time served under the original sentence. Turning to the second issue, the Court majority rejected the defense contention that the double jeopardy bar prohibited the imposition of a more severe sentence on reconviction than had been imposed upon the initial conviction. Reprinted here are excerpts from the Court's opinion discussing defendants' claim that due process restricted the imposition of a more severe sentence on a reconviction.]

JUSTICE STEWART delivered the opinion of the Court.

* * * A trial judge is not constitutionally precluded * * * from imposing a new sentence, whether greater or less than the original sentence, in the light of events subsequent to the first trial that may have thrown new light upon the defendant's "life, health, habits, conduct and mental and moral propensities." *Williams v. New York,* [p. 1378]. Such information may come to the judge's attention from evidence adduced at the second trial itself, from a new presentence investigation, from the defendant's prison record, or possibly from other sources. The freedom of a sentencing judge to consider the defendant's conduct subsequent to the first conviction in imposing new sentence is no more than consonant with the principle, fully approved in *Williams,* that a State may adopt the "prevalent modern philosophy of penology that the punishment should fit the offender and not merely the crime." * * * There remains for consideration the impact of the Due Process Clause of the Fourteenth Amendment.

It can hardly be doubted that it would be a flagrant violation of the Fourteenth Amendment for a state trial court to follow an announced practice of imposing a heavier sentence upon every reconvicted defendant for the explicit purpose of punishing the defendant for his having succeeded in getting his original conviction set aside. Where, as in each of the cases before us, the original conviction has been set aside because of a constitutional error, the imposition of such a punishment, "penalizing those who choose to exercise" constitutional rights, "would be patently unconstitutional." *United States v. Jackson* [p. 1164, fn. b]. And the very threat inherent in the existence of such a punitive policy would, with respect to those still in prison, serve to "chill the exercise of basic constitutional rights." * * * But even if the first conviction has been set aside for nonconstitutional error, the imposition of a penalty upon the defendant for having successfully pursued a statutory right of appeal or collateral remedy would be no less a violation of due process of law. * * * A court is "without right to * * * put a price on an appeal. A defendant's exercise of a right of appeal must be free and unfettered. * * * "This Court has never held that the States are required to establish avenues of appellate review, but it is now fundamental that, once established, these avenues must be kept free of unreasoned distinctions that can only impede open and equal access to the courts." *Griffin v. Illinois* [p. 92].

Due process of law, then, requires that vindictiveness against a defendant for having successfully attacked his first conviction must play no part in the sentence he receives after a new trial. And since the fear of such vindictiveness may unconstitutionally deter a defendant's exercise of the right to appeal or collaterally attack his first conviction, due process also requires that a defendant be freed of apprehension of such a retaliatory motivation on the part of the sentencing judge.[20]

In order to assure the absence of such a motivation, we have concluded that whenever a judge imposes a more severe sentence upon a defendant after a new trial, the reasons for his doing so must affirmatively appear. Those reasons must be based upon objective information concerning identifiable conduct on the part of the defendant occurring after the time of the original sentencing proceeding. And the factual data upon which the increased sentence is based must be made part of the record, so that the constitutional legitimacy of the increased sentence may be fully reviewed on appeal. [The Court then found that in neither of the cases before it had the state offered "any reason or justification for that sentence beyond the naked power to impose it," and affirmed the grant of relief to both prisoners.]

NOTES AND QUESTIONS

1. ***The* Pearce *protection.*** Two questions arise when a higher sentence is imposed after a defendant's successful appeal. First, do the circumstances support a presumption of vindictiveness under *Pearce*? Second, if so, what is required to rebut that presumption? A series of cases decided after *Pearce* addressed both questions.

2. ***Resentencings that do not trigger the* Pearce *presumption.***

a. ***Different sentencers.*** In *Texas v. McCullough*, 475 U.S. 134 (1986), the Court held that the Due Process Clause is not violated when, after reconviction, a defendant received from a judge a longer sentence than he had received from a jury initially before appeal. McCullough had elected to be sentenced by the jury, as was his right under Texas law, and received 20 years. (Texas remains today one of the states authorizing sentencing by jury after trial in non-capital cases, see p. 1373). The trial judge granted his motion for a new trial on the basis of prosecutorial misconduct and he was retried before a different jury, with the same judge presiding. On retrial, the state presented testimony from two witnesses who had not testified at the first trial that McCullough rather than his accomplices had slashed the throat of the victim. After reconviction, he elected to have his sentence fixed by the trial judge, who sentenced him to 50 years. The judge indicated that in fixing the sentence she relied on the new testimony as well as new information that McCullough had been released from prison only four months before the murder, and stated that, had she fixed the first sentence instead of the jury, she would have imposed more than twenty years. The Court explained that just as in prior cases where it had not applied the *Pearce* presumption—when the second court in a two-tier trial system imposed a longer sentence, or where a *jury* imposed the increased sentence on retrial—there was "no basis for a presumption of vindictiveness." The judge had "no motivation to engage in self-vindication" or discourage what might be regarded as

---

[20] The existence of a retaliatory motivation would, of course, be extremely difficult to prove in any individual case. But data have been collected to show that increased sentences on reconviction are far from rare. See Note, 1965 Duke L.J. 395 [citing an "informal survey of North Carolina superior courts"]. A touching bit of evidence showing the fear of such a vindictive policy was noted by the [federal habeas] judge in *Patton v. North Carolina,* 256 F.Supp. 225 (W.D.N.C.1966), who quoted a letter he had recently received from a prisoner. [The Court here quoted that letter, which came from a prisoner whose original conviction had been held unconstitutional by the federal judge on habeas review and who was now being retried. The prisoner initially noted that "it is usually the [state] court's procedure to give a larger sentence when a new trial is granted I guess * * * to discourage Petitioners." He pleaded: "Please sir don't let the state re-try me * * *. I don't want a new trial. I am afraid of more time."]

"meritless appeals." Defendants may still obtain relief without the presumption if they can show actual vindictiveness upon resentencing, said the Court, citing *Wasman v. United States*, 468 U.S. 559 (1984).

b. ***Trial after vacated plea.*** In *Alabama v. Smith*, 490 U.S. 794 (1989), the Court held that the vindictiveness presumption also does not apply to a higher sentence imposed following a vacated guilty plea and a subsequent conviction after trial. In this context, "the increase in sentence is not more likely than not attributable to the vindictiveness on the part of the sentencing judge. Even when the same judge imposes both sentences, the relevant sentencing information available to the judge after the plea will usually be considerably less than that available after a trial." During trial, "the judge may gather a fuller appreciation of the nature and extent of the crimes charged" and observe the "defendant's conduct," which "may give the judge insights into his moral character and suitability for rehabilitation." "[F]actors that may have indicated leniency as consideration for the guilty plea are no longer present," and "[the] court is not simply 'do[ing] over what it thought it had already done correctly.' "

3. ***Rebutting the* Pearce *presumption.*** In *McCullough,* the Court explained that even if it had concluded that a presumption of vindictiveness applied, the findings of the trial judge had "overcome that presumption." The judge had "stated candidly her belief that the 20-year sentence respondent received initially was unduly lenient in light of significant evidence not before the sentencing jury in the first trial." The Court reasoned: "*Pearce* permits 'a sentencing authority [to] justify an increased sentence by affirmatively identifying relevant conduct or events that occurred subsequent to the original sentencing proceedings.' *Wasman* [upholding higher sentence when judge noted that after the first sentence, the defendant had been convicted on another charge pending at the time.] * * * This language, however, was never intended to describe exhaustively all of the possible circumstances in which a sentence increase could be justified. Restricting justifications for a sentence increase to *only* 'events that occurred subsequent to the original sentencing proceedings' could in some circumstances lead to absurd results." The Court here noted the example of a defendant who, it is learned after conviction on retrial following appeal, was using an alias and actually has a long, violent criminal record. Instead, the presumption of vindictiveness "may be overcome only by objective information . . . justifying the increased sentence." The Court recognized that "a defendant may be more reluctant to appeal if there is a risk that new, probative evidence supporting a longer sentence may be revealed on retrial," but noted that "this 'chilling effect' " is not "sufficient reason to create a constitutional prohibition against considering relevant information in assessing sentences."

§ 2. DEFENSE APPEALS AND THE "FINAL JUDGMENT" REQUIREMENT

1. ***Requiring a "final judgment."*** The statutory provisions governing defense appeals in the federal system and in most states restrict the defendant to an appeal from what courts commonly characterize as a "final judgment" (sometimes termed "final decision," or "final order"). Traditionally, the final judgment requirement has required defendants to postpone appeal until after a conviction and the imposition of a sentence on that conviction.

In *Cobbledick v. United States*, 309 U.S. 323 (1940), Justice Frankfurter, in an often-quoted passage, explained the policy justification for postponing defense appeals until final judgment: "Since the right to a judgment from more than one court is a matter of grace and not a necessary ingredient of justice, Congress from the very beginning has, by forbidding piecemeal disposition on appeal of what for practical purposes is a single controversy, set itself against enfeebling judicial administration. Thereby is avoided the obstruction to just claims that would come from permitting the harassment and cost of a succession of separate appeals from the various rulings to which a litigation may give rise, from its initiation to entry of judgment. To be effective, judicial administration must not be leaden-footed. Its momentum would be arrested by permitting separate reviews of the component elements in a unified cause. These considerations of policy are especially compelling in the administration of criminal justice. * * * An accused is entitled to scrupulous observance of constitutional safeguards. But encouragement of delay is fatal to the vindication of the criminal law. Bearing the discomfiture and cost of a prosecution for crime even by an innocent person is one of the painful obligations of citizenship. The correctness of a trial court's rejection even of a constitutional claim made by the accused in the process of prosecution must await his conviction before its reconsideration by an appellate tribunal."

The advantage of interlocutory review from defendant's perspective goes beyond avoiding the costs of going through a trial that must be repeated (including the disclosure of defense evidence and strategy during the trial), or the costs of going through a trial that never should occur in the first instance. Interlocutory review is advantageous for a defendant because it requires the appellate court to focus on the legal issue in isolation, while review after a conviction allows the court to conclude that an erroneous ruling was harmless given the other evidence and events at trial. Also, an overturned pretrial ruling may strengthen defendant's plea-bargaining position.

Not all jurisdictions are convinced that a defendant invariably should be forced to bear the cost of trial before seeking review, even when it seems likely that the trial will be a wasted effort given a judicial error in ruling on a pretrial motion. A substantial number of states by statute permit the defense to seek interlocutory review of a pretrial order, with the permission of the appellate court, or, in some cases, on certification by the trial judge that there is need for immediate review. Such provisions often identify a series of factors to be considered by the appellate court in determining whether to grant review, such as whether immediate review will clarify an issue of "general importance." Generally, these factors are applied so that interlocutory review remains the exception rather than the general rule. In a jurisdiction such as the federal system that does not follow such a procedure, a defendant may seek to circumvent the final judgment rule by using extraordinary writs, or the "exceptions" to the final judgment rule described in the notes below.

2. ***The collateral order exception.*** The collateral order doctrine allows the immediate appeal of "that small class [of orders] which finally determine claims of right separable from, and collateral to, rights asserted in the action, too important to be denied review and too independent of the cause itself to require that appellate consideration be deferred until the whole case is adjudicated." *Cohen v. Beneficial Industrial Loan Corp.*, 337 U.S. 541 (1949).

Coopers & Lybrand v. Livesay, 437 U.S. 463 (1978), set forth what has become the classic exposition of the prerequisites for establishing that a pretrial ruling is an immediately appealable collateral order. The Court initially summarized the key elements: "To come within the 'small class' of decisions excepted from the final-judgment rule by Cohen, the order must conclusively determine the disputed question, resolve an important issue completely separate from the merits of the action, and be effectively unreviewable on appeal from a final judgment." The first of these three prerequisites, it noted, demands that the trial court ruling not be "tentative, informal, or incomplete," but constitute a firm and final decision on the issue. If there is a reasonable prospect that the trial court might alter its ruling in light of facts that might be developed later in the proceedings, immediate appellate intrusion clearly is not appropriate. The second prerequisite demands that the issue ruled upon not "affect, or * * * be affected by" any subsequent decision on the merits of the case. If the trial court ruling is not "independent of the cause" itself, determining rights "separable from and collateral to [those] rights asserted in the action," then review prior to the ultimate disposition constitutes a wasteful use of appellate resources. Depending upon the disposition of the case, permitting appeal will produce either an unnecessary review or a review that will only be repeated. The second prerequisite also requires that the issue resolved by the trial court be not only independent but "important." Finally, interlocutory review must be withheld if review on appeal following the final disposition would provide a satisfactory remedy.

Speaking to the application of the *Coopers & Lybrand* criteria in criminal cases, the Court noted in *Flanagan v. United States*, 465 U.S. 259 (1984): "Because of the compelling interest in prompt trials, the Court has interpreted the requirements of the collateral-order exception to the final judgment rule with the utmost strictness in criminal cases. The Court has found only three types of pretrial orders in criminal prosecutions to meet the requirements. * * * An order denying a motion to reduce bail may be reviewed before trial. The issue is finally resolved and is independent of the issues to be tried, and the order becomes moot if review awaits conviction and sentence. *Stack v. Boyle* [p. 846]. Orders denying motions to dismiss an indictment on double jeopardy or Speech or Debate grounds are likewise immediately appealable. Such orders finally resolve issues that are separate from guilt or innocence, and appellate review must occur before trial to be fully effective. The right guaranteed by the Double Jeopardy Clause is more than the right not to be convicted in a second prosecution for an offense: it is the right not to be 'placed in jeopardy'—that is, not to be tried for the offense. *Abney v. United States*, 431 U.S. 651 (1977). Similarly, the right guaranteed by the Speech or Debate Clause is more than the right not to be convicted for certain legislative activities: it is the right not to 'be questioned' about them—that is, not to be tried for them. *Helstoski v. Meanor*, 442 U.S. 500 (1979). Refusals to dismiss an indictment for violation of the Double Jeopardy Clause or of the Speech or Debate Clause, like denials of bail reduction, are truly final and collateral, and the asserted rights in all three cases would be irretrievably lost if review were postponed until trial is complete."

The *Flanagan* opinion distinguished both *United States v. MacDonald*, 435 U.S. 850 (1978), and *United States v. Hollywood Motor Car Co.*, 458 U.S. 263 (1982). The Court in *MacDonald* concluded, "Unlike the protection afforded by the Double Jeopardy Clause, the Speedy Trial Clause does not, either on its face or according to the decisions of this Court, encompass a 'right not to be tried' which must be upheld prior to trial if it is to be enjoyed at all. It is the delay before trial, not the trial itself, that offends the constitutional guarantee of a speedy trial. If the factors outlined in *Barker v. Wingo* [p. 1071] combine to deprive an accused of his right to a speedy trial, that loss, by definition, occurs before trial. Proceeding with the trial does not cause or compound the deprivation already suffered. * * * [Indeed,] allowing an exception to the rule against pretrial appeals in criminal cases for speedy trial claims would threaten precisely the values manifested in the Speedy Trial Clause * * * [as] some assertions of delay-caused prejudice would become self-fulfilling prophecies during the period necessary for appeal." The determination as to whether there had been a denial of a speedy trial also was often dependent upon an assessment of the prejudice caused by the delay, which could best be considered "only after the relevant facts had been developed at trial." Hence, the pretrial denial of the defendant's motion could not be considered a "complete, formal, and final rejection" of that claim, and the prejudice element of the claim could not be viewed as separable from the trial on the merits. In *Hollywood Motor Car*, considering a claim of vindictive prosecution, the Court explained that "proceeding with the trial does not cause or compound the deprivation already suffered," as the vindictiveness claim rests on a "right whose remedy requires the dismissal of charges" rather than a "right not be tried."

The collateral order test thus rules out most interlocutory appeals. For example, in *Flanagan*, the defendant argued that he should be allowed to appeal an order disqualifying his counsel, but the Court concluded "that the second *Coopers & Lybrand* condition—that the order be truly collateral is not satisfied if petitioner's asserted right is one requiring prejudice to the defense for its violation." The validity of a disqualification order "is not independent of the issue to be tried. Its validity cannot be adequately reviewed until trial is complete. The effect of the disqualification on the defense, and hence whether the asserted right has been violated cannot be fairly assessed until the substance of the prosecution's and defendant's cases is known." And in *Midland Asphalt Corp. v. United States,* 489 U.S. 794 (1989), the Court unanimously rejected the suggestion that because the Court in another case (*United States v. Mechanik*, Note 5, p. 980), had held that a conviction renders violations of Rule 6(d) harmless, any Rule 6 ruling must be immediately appealable under the collateral order doctrine. The Court reasoned: "orders denying motions to dismiss for Rule 6(e) violations cannot be said to 'resolve an important issue completely separate from the merits of the action,'" but rather "involve considerations 'enmeshed in the merits of the dispute' and would 'affect . . . or be affected by' the decision on the merits of the case."

Sell v. United States, 539 U.S. 166 (2003), is a rare exception. There the Court considered the defendant's interlocutory appeal of a district court's pretrial order authorizing the forced administration of medication to render the defendant competent to stand trial. The majority reasoned: "The [district court] order (1) 'conclusively determine[s] the disputed question,' namely, whether Sell has a legal right to avoid forced medication. The order also (2) 'resolve[s] an important issue,' for, as this Court's cases make clear, involuntary medical treatment raises questions of clear constitutional importance. * * * At the same time, the basic issue—whether Sell must undergo medication against his will—is 'completely separate from the merits of the action,' i.e., whether Sell is guilty or innocent of the crimes charged. The issue is wholly separate as well from questions concerning trial procedures. Finally, the issue is (3) 'effectively unreviewable on appeal from a final judgment.' By the time of trial Sell will have undergone forced medication—the very harm that he seeks to avoid. He cannot undo that harm even if he is acquitted. Indeed, if he is acquitted, there will no appeal through which he might obtain review." The Court added, "the question presented here, whether Sell has a legal right to avoid forced medication, perhaps in part because medication may make a trial unfair, differs from the question whether forced medication did make a trial unfair. The first question focuses upon the right to avoid administration of the drugs. What may happen at trial is relevant, but only as a prediction. * * * The second question focuses upon the right to fair trial. It asks what did happen as a result of having administered the medication. An ordinary appeal comes too late for a defendant to enforce the first right; an ordinary appeal permits vindication of the second." In dissent, Justice Scalia (joined by Justices O'Connor and Thomas) disagreed that " '[a]n ordinary appeal comes too late for a defendant to enforce' " the right at issue, noting any violation would require reversal of the conviction. The Court's analysis, he objected, would mean that interlocutory appeal is available to any "criminal defendant who asserts that a trial court order will, if implemented, cause an immediate violation of his constitutional (or perhaps even statutory?) rights," including "an order compelling testimony" that "could be attacked as an immediate denial Fifth Amendment rights."

3. ***Independent proceedings.*** The collateral order doctrine permits an immediate appeal from an order which is viewed as part of the ongoing criminal case. Certain proceedings, though related to a criminal prosecution, are sufficiently separate from the prosecution that an order terminating such a proceeding is viewed as a final judgment in a *separate* litigation and therefore immediately appealable.

a. Third-parties; victims. For example, when a third party seeks relief, such as a media organization challenging a closure order, or an unindicted co-conspirator challenging the denial of his request to strike his name from the indictment, the proceeding is characterized as "independent" rather than "a step in the trial of the criminal case."

Some jurisdictions have provided victims of crime the right to seek review of trial court rulings denying them procedural rights granted by statute, but by writ rather than appeal. See, for example, 18 U.S.C. § 3771(d) [Supp. App. B], which provides that if the district court denies the relief sought by the victim, the victim may seek a writ of mandamus, which must be decided expeditiously. The act provides, however, "In no case shall a failure to afford a right under this chapter provide grounds for a new trial. A victim may make a motion to re-open a plea or sentence only if—(A) the victim has asserted the right to be heard before or during the proceeding at issue and such right was denied; (B) the victim petitions the court of appeals for a writ of mandamus within 10 days; and (C) in the case of a plea, the accused has not pled to the highest offense charged."

b. ***Contempt orders.*** Where a grand jury witness, civil trial witness, or criminal trial witness objects to a subpoena or to an order compelling the witness to answer a specific question, the witness may convert that ruling into an appealable order by refusing to obey and being held in contempt. In the federal system, a *nonparty* can appeal either a civil or criminal contempt sanction, but *a party* can appeal only a criminal contempt sanction. *Mohawk Indus., Inc. v. Carpenter*, 558 U.S. 100 (2009); Charles Alan Wright, Arthur R. Miller, and Edward H. Cooper, 15B *Federal Practice and Procedure: Jurisdiction 2d* §§ 3914.23, 3917 (1992 & 2018 Supp.). Since the form of contempt used against a party who refuses to comply with a discovery order almost always is civil contempt (the purpose being to coerce compliance), the disobedience and contempt route ordinarily would not be available to obtain immediate appellate review of a pretrial order directed against a criminal defendant.

4. ***Review by writ.*** Under some circumstances, appellate review of interlocutory orders in federal cases may be obtained by the procedure authorized by 18 U.S.C.A. § 1651(a), the All Writs Act. That Act empowers appellate courts to issue writs (e.g., mandamus or prohibition) where "necessary or appropriate in aid of their respective jurisdictions and agreeable to the usages and principles of law." States have similar provisions or recognize review by writ as a traditional common law process. The writs provide an avenue for review at the request of either the defense or the prosecution.

The Supreme Court has emphasized that these remedies in the federal system are exceptional. See, e.g., *Kerr v. United States District Court,* 426 U.S. 394 (1976): "[T]he writ [of mandamus] 'has traditionally been used in the federal courts only to confine an inferior court to a lawful exercise of its prescribed jurisdiction or to compel it to exercise its authority when it is its duty to do so.' *Will v. United States*, [389 U.S. 90 (1967)]. * * * '[O]nly exceptional circumstances amounting to a judicial "usurpation of power" will justify the invocation of this extraordinary remedy.' * * * [T]he party seeking issuance of the writ [must] have no other adequate means to attain the relief he desires, and [must] satisfy 'the burden of showing that [his] right to issuance of the writ is clear and indisputable.' Moreover, it is important to remember that issuance of the writ is in large part a matter of discretion with the court to which the petition is addressed." Lower federal courts frequently speak of the writs as "extraordinary remedies," to be "sparingly used" only as needed to avoid an "irreparable harm."

§ 3. PROSECUTION APPEALS

1. ***Statutory and double jeopardy limitations on prosecutor appeals of final orders.*** The federal system and all of the states have statutes that allow prosecution appeals from at least a limited class of trial court orders. Prosecution appeals were unknown at common law, so they are recognized only where specifically authorized by statute. See *Carroll v. United States*, 354 U.S. 394 (1957). Some of these statutes, like the Federal Criminal Appeals Act of 1970 (18 U.S.C. § 3731, Supp.App. B), reflect a policy to allow prosecution appeals from all final orders except where "the double jeopardy clause * * * prohibits further prosecution." This would bar appeals from verdicts of acquittal to the courts of appeals. But some states are willing to allow advisory or "moot" appeals, unlike the federal courts, and authorize the prosecution to appeal even from an acquittal so long as the appellate court in such a case is announcing rules that govern only future cases. See James Strazella, *The Relationship of Double Jeopardy to Prosecution Appeals*, 73 Notre Dame L. Rev. 1 (1997); Nancy J. King & Michael Heise, *Appeals by the Prosecution,* 15 J. Emp. Leg. Stud. 482, 494 (2018) (collecting authority in a dozen states). This allows for judicial review of potentially widespread or recurring error preceding acquittals, such as faulty jury instructions or evidentiary rulings, that would otherwise escape appellate scrutiny.

In many states, however, statutory authorization of prosecution appeals is narrower than double jeopardy would permit. Nationwide, the most commonly authorized orders are: (1) orders granting a defendant's motion to dismiss a charge, (2) sentences the government alleges are too lenient, illegal, or the result of procedural error, (3) orders granting a new trial after a guilty verdict, and (4) judgments of acquittal entered after a guilty verdict.

Prosecutors also tend to be selective about which cases they choose to appeal. In many states, criminal appeals, particularly those to the state's high court, are coordinated by a central office such as a division of the state's Attorney General's Office, rather than the local prosecutor. State intermediate appellate courts consider a drastically skewed set of direct criminal appeals—only 2% of those heard on the merits by intermediate courts were filed by prosecutors. By contrast, 41% of the decisions state high courts hear on the merits were filed by prosecutors. Not surprisingly, the success rate for the relatively small, selective set of state prosecutor direct appeals filed each year is about four times greater than that for defense appeals—roughly 40 percent of prosecutor appeals filed in both intermediate and high courts succeed, compared to 10 percent of appeals by defendants—according to the most recent nationwide data available from 2010. *Id.*

2. ***Prosecution appeals from interlocutory orders.*** Limits on the *defendant*'s right to an interlocutory appeal of an adverse pretrial order are based in part on the assumption that the defendant, if convicted, can gain review of the adverse final judgment. The prosecution, however, is in a quite different position as to an adverse pretrial order other than a pretrial dismissal. If not allowed an immediate appeal from such an order, the prosecution may have no opportunity to pursue a post-trial appeal. The erroneous pretrial order may result in the prosecution losing its case at trial, and the acquittal of the defendant will not be subject to appeal because the double jeopardy prohibition then bars further prosecution. Most jurisdictions have concluded that this circumstance justifies providing the prosecution with an immediate appeal of one or more classes of adverse pretrial interlocutory orders. Allowing for prosecutorial interlocutory appeal is also seen as reducing the potential skewing impact of the asymmetry in criminal appeals. See generally Kate Stith, *The Risk of Legal Error in Criminal Cases: Some Consequences of the Asymmetry in the Right to Appeal*, 57 U. Chi. L. Rev. 1 (1990). But commentators do not agree whether this asymmetry prompts trial judges to decide in favor of the defense on difficult questions (and thereby avoid appellate review and the possibility of reversal), or rather to rule in favor of the prosecution on the issue (and thereby preserve reviewability, assuming the defendant is convicted and appeals).

Orders granting a defendant's motion to suppress evidence are often made appealable by statute, for two reasons. First, the practical effect of the granting of a motion to suppress often is to terminate the case because the prosecution, lacking sufficient additional evidence, will be required to request dismissal of the indictment. Second, often the rules relating to searches and other police practices that lead to suppression motions are uncertain, and law enforcement officials should be entitled to base their policies on the rulings of the highest court; if appellate review of an adverse decision on a police practice is not available, the police can obtain a higher court ruling only by persisting in the challenged practice until they obtain a favorable decision from a different lower court, which would then be appealed to the higher court by the defendant. Accordingly, some jurisdictions limit prosecution appeals of suppression orders to cases in which the prosecution certifies that the suppression order will eliminate any "reasonable possibility" of a successful prosecution. Also, provisions are sometimes limited to suppression orders based on an illegality in the government's acquisition of the evidence, restricting appeals more than the federal statute, 18 U.S.C. § 3731, which speaks generally of orders "suppressing or excluding evidence." Where the prosecution can foresee difficulties in gaining admission of crucial evidence, it is to its advantage to obtain a pretrial ruling so that an adverse decision can be appealed.

§ 4. REVIEW FOR CLAIMS NOT RAISED ON TIME

If and how a court will review a claim of error depends in part upon whether the appellant complied with procedural rules for objecting to that error. This section discusses the standards that courts apply when a defendant fails to object to an error as required. The next section, Section 5, discusses the standards applied when the defendant objects to the error on time.

1. ***The "raise or waive" (forfeiture) doctrine.*** The most frequent reason for an appellate court to refuse to consider a particular defense claim on appeal is the so-called "raise-or-waive" doctrine. Simply put, appellate courts generally will not consider an error that was not properly raised and preserved at trial. Although the "raise or waive" rule speaks of a "waiver," it does not refer to a "waiver" in the traditional sense of a "knowing and intelligent relinquishment" of a right. Rather, what is involved, as the Court noted in *United States v. Olano,* quoted infra at Note 3, p. 1411, is a "forfeiture" or "procedural default" of the right to review.

What is required for proper presentation of a claim at the trial level will vary with the nature of the objection and the procedural idiosyncrasies of the particular jurisdiction. Timing requirements, for example, may require that the objection be made before trial (e.g., suppression of illegally seized evidence), or contemporaneous with the error (e.g., improper cross-examination). Among the reasons for denying review to a party who fails to adhere to rules relating to the timing and form of objections are: (1) fairness to an opponent who would lose the opportunity to respond with evidence or other factual showings, (2) preventing "sandbagging," that is, disallowing an avenue for relief for party who makes a tactical decision not to raise the objection, expecting to raise it later if the outcome turns out to be unfavorable, (3) the unseemliness of telling a lower court it was wrong when it never was presented with the opportunity to be right; and, primarily, (4) judicial economy—sparing the parties and the public the costs of appeals and retrials that could have been avoided had objections been made and resolved in the initial trial court proceedings.

2. ***General exceptions.*** It follows from this reasoning that certain circumstances may justify appellate consideration of trial court errors even though not properly presented below. For example, if a defendant never had a reasonable opportunity to comply with the state's procedural requirement, a claim will be reviewed. See, e.g., *Reece v. Georgia,* 350 U.S. 85 (1955) (state requirement that defendant challenge the grand jury composition prior to indictment held invalid as applied to indigent defendant not provided with counsel until the day after indictment). Appellate courts will consider also first-time challenges that raise "jurisdictional" or particularly fundamental questions.

3. ***The "plain error" exception.*** All but a few jurisdictions recognize, in addition to the general exceptions above, the authority of an appellate court to reverse a criminal judgment on the basis of an error that is "plain" even though the error was not properly raised and preserved at the trial level. Several states limit the doctrine's application to a specified class of errors (e.g., constitutional violations). Most have adopted standards that resemble those applied in the federal courts under Rule 52(b).

The Supreme Court in *United States v. Olano*, 507 U.S. 725 (1993), and *Johnson v. United States*, 520 U.S. 461 (1997), developed a four-step analysis for determining whether an inadequately raised error will warrant relief as "plain error" under Federal Rule 52(b). As the Court summarized in *Johnson,* "An appellate court can correct an error not raised at trial" only if there is "(1) 'error,' (2) that is 'plain,' * * * (3) that 'affects substantial rights,' " and that "(4) * * * seriously affects the fairness, integrity, or public reputation of judicial proceedings."

a. ***Error.*** The initial prerequisite of an "error" requires the appellate court to determine if the claim was actually "waived" rather than merely "forfeited," because a true waiver precludes a finding of "error." The *Olano* Court noted in this regard: "Deviation from a legal rule is 'error' unless the rule has been waived. * * * Waiver is different from forfeiture. Whereas forfeiture is the failure to make the timely assertion of a right, waiver is the 'intentional relinquishment or abandonment on a known right.' *Johnson v. Zerbst,* 304 U.S. 458 (1938). * * * If a legal rule was violated during the district court proceedings, and if the defendant did not waive the rule, then there has been an 'error' within the meaning of Rule 52(b) despite the absence of a timely objection." A claim waived as part of a plea agreement will not meet this first step of the plain error test.

Whether there is an error will also depend on the standard of review appropriate for the particular ruling being challenged. That standard will vary with the type of trial court ruling that is being reviewed. The Court has summed up the federal law on this topic succinctly: "For purposes of standard of review, decisions by judges are traditionally divided into three categories, denominated questions of law (reviewable de novo), questions of fact (reviewable for clear error), and matters of discretion (reviewable for 'abuse of discretion')." *Pierce v. Underwood,* 487 U.S. 552, 557 (1988). A trial court decision in the latter category would not pass the first prong of the *Olano* test unless it was an abuse of discretion, for example.

A claim of insufficiency of evidence to support guilt is evaluated using yet a different standard, one that asks, "whether, after viewing the evidence in the light most favorable to the prosecution, any rational trier of fact could have found the essential elements beyond a reasonable doubt." *Jackson v. Virginia,* 443 U.S. 307 (1979). A reviewing court "must presume—even if it does not affirmatively appear in the record—that the trier of fact resolved any [factual] conflicts in favor of the prosecution, and must defer to that resolution." *Cavazos v. Smith,* 565 U.S. 1 (2011).

b. That is plain at the time the error is reviewed on appeal. Speaking to the second factor, the *Olano* Court noted that the error must be "plain," which is "synonymous with 'clear' or equivalently 'obvious.'" But the error need not be obvious or clear to the trial judge, explained Justice Breyer writing for the Court in *Henderson v. United States*, 568 U.S. 266 (2013). "[P]lain-error review is not a grading system for trial judges. It has broader purposes, including in part allowing courts of appeals better to identify those instances in which the application of a new rule of law to cases on appeal will meet the demands of fairness and judicial integrity." The "plain" requirement is met not only where an unobjected-to decision of a trial judge "was *plainly incorrect* at the time it was made" but also "where the trial judge's decision was plainly *correct* at the time when it was made but subsequently becomes incorrect based on a change in law," and "where the law is unsettled at the time of error but plain at the time of review." Rejecting the "practical importance" of any increased incentive for parties to avoid objecting in hopes of better law by the time of appeal, the Court reasoned "counsel normally has other good reasons for calling a trial court's attention to potential error—for example, it is normally to the advantage of counsel and his client to get the error speedily corrected. And, even where that is not so, counsel cannot rely upon the 'plain error' rule to make up for a failure to object at trial. After all, that rule will help only if (1) the law changes in the defendant's favor, (2) the change comes after trial but before the appeal is decided, (3) the error affected the defendant's 'substantial rights,' and (4) the error 'seriously affect[ed] the fairness, integrity or public reputation of judicial proceedings.' If there is a lawyer who would deliberately forgo objection *now* because he perceives some slightly expanded chance to argue for 'plain error' *later,* we suspect that, like the unicorn, he finds his home in the imagination, not the courtroom."

In dissent, Justice Scalia, joined by Justices Thomas and Alito, argued the Court's decision contradicted the text of Rule 52, and also added the Court has repeatedly worried about counsel's "'sandbagging the court' by 'remaining silent about his objection and belatedly raising the error only if the case does not conclude in his favor.' *Puckett* [infra p. 1414]." He warned the decision would "lessen[ ] counsel's diligent efforts to identify uncertain points of law and bring them (or rather the defendant's version of them) to the court's attention, so that error will never occur."

c. ***Prejudice.*** The third requirement specified in *Olano* was that the error must "affec[t] substantial rights." The Court noted that the same language also is found in Rule 52(a)'s harmless error provision, see Note 1, p. 1415, and for "most cases," in order to affect substantial rights, the error "must have been prejudicial" in the sense of "affect[ing] the outcome" of the lower court proceedings. In contrast to a typical harmless error inquiry, to establish plain error, the defendant rather than the government bears the burden of persuasion with respect to prejudice. For example, in *United States v. Dominguez Benitez*, discussed in Note 3, p. 1222, the Court held: "A defendant who seeks reversal of his conviction after a guilty plea, on the ground that the district court committed plain error under Rule 11, must show a reasonable probability that, but for the error, he would not have entered the plea. A defendant must thus satisfy the judgment of the reviewing court, informed by the entire record, that the probability of a different result is ' "sufficient to undermine confidence in the outcome" ' of the proceeding." For a sentencing error, the defendant must "show a reasonable probability that the district court would have imposed a different sentence" had the error not occurred. *Molina-Martinez v. United States*, 136 S.Ct. 1338 (2016).

In applying the standard for reviewing claims that *were* raised on time—harmless error under Rule 52(b)—the Court has held that certain errors are "structural" and therefore require automatic reversal without inquiry as to the impact of the error on the outcome of the proceeding. See Section 5, infra. But the Court has yet to decide if any of the errors that qualify as "structural" under harmless error analysis also necessarily "affects substantial rights" under plain error review. Lower courts continue to divide over this question—some requiring a showing of prejudice for "structural" errors, others finding the "prejudice" prong met once the first two prongs of the *Olano* test have been established.

The Court in *Weaver v. Massachusetts,* p. 143, addressed a somewhat related question, and its decision suggested that if confronted with the issue, the Court would be unlikely to find that every unraised "structural" error necessarily satisfies the "prejudice" requirement of the plain error analysis. In *Weaver*, the Court held that a defendant claiming ineffective assistance based on counsel's failure to object to a courtroom closure during voir dire must demonstrate "prejudice" under *Strickland,* even though a violation of the right to a public trial is considered a "structural error" when properly preserved and raised on direct review. The Court emphasized that its decision was restricted to the context of an *ineffective assistance claim* alleging counsel's failure to object to closure of jury selection. The court's rationale, however, suggests that an unpreserved public trial right claim *raised on direct appeal* would also require a defendant to demonstrate "prejudice" for plain error relief, and that possibly other structural errors would require a showing of prejudice if not timely raised as well. The *Weaver* Court rejected the view that attempting to show prejudice from a violation of this structural error would be an impossible task, stating that "not every public-trial violation will in fact lead to a fundamentally unfair trial" or deprive "the defendant of a reasonable probability of a different outcome." Weaver failed to demonstrate prejudice, it concluded, noting that the proceedings were not conducted in secret or in a remote place; the remainder of the trial was open; the decision to close voir dire and exclude defendant's mother and her minister to make room for veniremembers was made by court officers, not the judge; during closure, the proceedings were on the record and observed by many unchosen veniremembers; and there was no suggestion that any juror or other participant misbehaved or that any of "the potential harms flowing from a courtroom closure came to pass." The ineffective assistance context in which the claim was raised also supported a requirement that the defendant demonstrate prejudice, as not raising the error until after trial deprives trial courts of the chance to cure such violations either by opening the courtroom or by explaining the reasons for closure, the Court reasoned. Moreover, preserving the claim and raising it on direct review would have allowed reviewing courts to "give instruction to the trial courts in a familiar context that allows for elaboration of the relevant principles based on review of an adequate record."[a]

The Court has also insisted on a showing of prejudice in the plain error context for a claim that would have required relief without regard to prejudice if properly preserved for appeal, but not because the claim was "structural." In *Puckett v. United States*, 556 U.S. 129 (2009), the government at sentencing refused to request a sentence reduction as promised in the agreement, Puckett's counsel made no objection, and the judge imposed the minimum sentence under the applicable guideline range. On appeal Puckett argued that relief was required once breach was shown, without regard to the likely impact of the breach on the sentence. The Court disagreed. It acknowledged that breach of a plea deal requires relief without regard to harmlessness when that breach is raised on time in the trial court, see *Santobello*, p. 1174. But the breach of a plea agreement "is not a 'structural' error as we have used that term," Justice Scalia wrote for the Court. The holding in *Santobello* "rested not upon the premise that plea-breach errors are (like 'structural' errors) somehow not *susceptible*, or not *amenable*, to review for harmlessness, but rather upon a policy interest in establishing the trust between defendants and prosecutors that is necessary to sustain plea bargaining-an 'essential' and 'highly desirable' part of the criminal process. But the rule of contemporaneous objection is equally essential and desirable, and when the two collide we see no need to relieve the defendant of his usual burden of showing prejudice."

d. Miscarriage of justice. Speaking to the fourth prong of its plain error test, the *Olano* Court stressed that Rule 52(b) is "permissive rather than mandatory," allowing rather than requiring correction when an error is found to be "plain" and "affecting substantial rights." In previous cases the Court had indicated that this discretion should be employed "in those circumstances in which a miscarriage of justice would otherwise result." However, in contrast to the meaning given the same phrase in some aspects of its habeas corpus jurisprudence (see Note 3, p. 1441), the requirement of a "miscarriage of justice" in plain-error cases was not meant to restrict plain-error review to only those errors that resulted in "the conviction or sentencing of an actually innocent defendant." An appellate court should, in addition, "correct a plain forfeited error affecting substantial rights if the error 'seriously affects' the fairness, integrity, or public reputation of judicial proceedings." This determination, the Court later explained in *Johnson*, was to be made on an analysis of the facts of the individual case.

A few examples illustrate the application of this fourth step. In *Johnson*, the record showed that the error in question—failure to submit the element of materiality to the jury—did not seriously affect either the outcome or the "fairness, integrity, or public reputation of judicial proceedings" because the evidence supporting materiality was "overwhelming." "Indeed," the Court ventured, "it would be the reversal of a conviction such as this which would have that effect." Similarly, in *Puckett* the Court reasoned, "It is true enough that when the Government reneges on a plea deal, the integrity of the system may be called into question, but there may well be countervailing factors in particular cases. Puckett is again a good example: Given that he obviously did not cease his life of crime, [having committed additional crimes before sentencing,] receipt of a sentencing reduction for *acceptance of responsibility* would have been so ludicrous as itself to compromise the public reputation of judicial proceedings."

By contrast, applying this standard (and rejecting a more stringent "shock-the-conscience" standard), the Court in *Rosales-Mireles v. United States*, 138 S.Ct. 1897 (2018), concluded that a miscalculation of the Sentencing Guidelines range will ordinarily require a court of appeals to

[a] The *Weaver* Court also mentioned that when a claim is raised in postconviction review, the costs and uncertainties of a new trial are greater than they are when a claim is raised on direct review because of the passage of time and loss of witness's memories and other evidence. This argument would support requiring prejudice for at least some structural errors under the "cause and prejudice" test for avoiding procedural default in federal habeas review, another context where the application of a "prejudice" requirement to structural errors has divided courts. See Ch. 29, Section 4, and Note 2, p. 1441.

exercise its discretion to vacate the defendant's sentence. Noting that a defendant bears the burden of persuading the reviewing court that the error seriously affected the fairness, integrity, or public reputation of judicial proceedings, Justice Sotomayor explained for the Court that an "error resulting in a higher range than the Guidelines provide usually establishes a reasonable probability that a defendant will serve a prison sentence that is more than 'necessary' to fulfill the purposes of incarceration." In asserting that any amount of actual jail time is significant to both the defendant and society, the Court relied upon social science studies of perceptions of fairness of the justice system. The Court also reasoned that the error in miscalculating the Guidelines range was a mistake by the judiciary (through its Probation Office), not a strategic error of counsel. It quoted an earlier opinion by then court of appeals Judge Gorsuch: "[W]hat reasonable citizen wouldn't bear a rightly diminished view of the judicial process and its integrity if courts refused to correct obvious errors of their own devise that threaten to require individuals to linger longer in federal prison than the law demands?" Finally, it noted that " 'remand for resentencing, while not costless, does not invoke the same difficulties as a remand for retrial does.' "

Responding to Justice Thomas's argument in dissent that the majority's decision invited sandbagging by defendants, the Court stated, "It is hard to imagine that defense counsel would 'deliberately forgo objection now' to a plain Guidelines error that would subject her client to a higher Guidelines range, 'because [counsel] perceives some slightly expanded chance to argue for "plain error" later.' " (quoting *Henderson*, Note 3.b., p. 1412). "Even setting aside the conflict such a strategy would create with defense counsel's ethical obligations to represent her client vigorously and her duty of candor toward the court," the Court wrote, "any benefit from such a strategy is highly speculative. There is no guarantee that a court of appeals would agree to a remand, and no basis to believe that a district court would impose a lower sentence upon resentencing than the court would have imposed at the original sentencing proceedings had it been aware of the plain Guidelines error."

§ 5. THE HARMLESS ERROR RULE

To understand the enforcement of rules of criminal procedure, there is probably no principle more important to grasp than harmless error. The Chief Judge of the Second Circuit Court of Appeals once observed that harmless-error principles may determine the outcome of more criminal appeals than any other doctrine. Jason M. Solomon, *Causing Constitutional Harm: How Tort Law Can Help Determine Harmless Error in Criminal Trials*, 99 Nw. U. L. Rev. 1053, 1054 (2005) (quoting Hon. John M. Walker, Jr., *Harmless Error Review in the Second Circuit*, 63 Brook. L. Rev. 395, 395 (1997)). First applied to non-constitutional errors, harmless error review was extended to constitutional errors in the 1960s as part of the Court's criminal procedure "revolution." A discussion of harmless error review of claims of non-constitutional error follows in Section A, below; review of constitutional error is discussed in Section B.

A. NON-CONSTITUTIONAL ERRORS

1. ***Development of harmless error review of non-constitutional errors.*** In the mid-1800s, American courts adopted England's Exchequer Rule, under which a trial error such as an erroneous instruction or exclusion of evidence was presumed to have caused prejudice and therefore almost automatically required a new trial. The presumption of prejudice was designed to ensure that the appellate court did not encroach upon the jury's fact-finding function by discounting the improperly admitted or excluded evidence and sustaining the verdict reached below based on its belief that that verdict was correct in light of the overall evidence. Retrials for seemingly insignificant errors mounted, and appellate courts were criticized as "impregnable citadels of technicality." Reformers finally succeeded in securing harmless error legislation in the early 1900s. The federal harmless error statute, adopted in 1919, provided the model for many of

the statutes eventually adopted by every state. It required a federal appellate court to "give judgment after an examination of the entire record before the court, without regard to technical errors, defects, or exceptions which do not affect the substantial rights of the parties." In 1944, Federal Rule of Criminal Procedure 52 took the place of the federal statute, carrying forward the statutory phrase "affect the substantial rights," which continues to require an assessment of the impact of the error on the outcome of the case.

In the federal courts today, all non-jurisdictional violations of statutes and rules are reviewed for harmless error under Rule 52(a), absent Congressional direction otherwise. See *United States v. Lane*, Note 2, p. 1060 ("Rule 52(a) admits of no broad exceptions to its applicability"); *Zedner v. United States*, Note 6, p. 1080, (Congress impliedly repealed the application of Rule 52 to a judge's failure to make certain mandated findings on the record before granting an ends-of-justice continuance under the Speedy Trial Act). Many state courts have adopted similar standards for review of violations of state law.

2. ***Harmless error standard under Rule 52(a) for non-constitutional errors.*** A court applying the federal harmless error standard is *not* supposed to ask whether in its view the finding of guilt was clearly correct despite the error. In rejecting this analysis, the Court in *Kotteakos v. United States*, 328 U.S. 750 (1946), explained that determining guilt or innocence is a judgment that is "exclusively for the jury." Instead, a court applying Rule 52(a) to non-constitutional error must consider "what effect the error had or reasonably may be taken to have had upon the jury's decision." Rephrasing the rule in later cases, the Court has stated that when a non-constitutional error has been properly raised, "a conviction should not be overturned unless, after examining the record as a whole, a court concludes that [the] error may have had "substantial influence" on the outcome of the proceeding." *Bank of Nova Scotia v. United States*, Note 2, p. 977. It requires relief if the reviewing court concludes the error "had a substantial and injurious effect or influence in determining the jury's verdict" or the court has "grave doubt" about whether an error influenced the outcome of the proceeding.

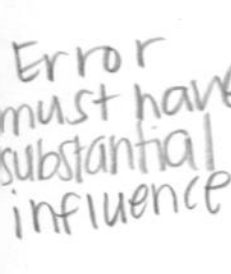

In contrast to the plain error test under Rule 52(b), when an error has been properly raised, the burden of proving prejudice is on the government, not the defendant. The Court has stated that if the reviewing court is " 'in virtual equipoise as to the harmlessness of the error' * * *, the court should 'treat the error . . . as if it affected the verdict.' " In other words, unlike the plain error standard in Rule 52(b) which *bars* relief for an error not raised in the trial court unless the *defendant* can show prejudice, an error properly preserved in the trial court *requires* relief unless the *government* can show the *absence* of prejudice.

B. CONSTITUTIONAL ERROR

Prior to the 1960s, far fewer constitutional rules governed the criminal process and although harmless error standards had been developed for reviewing non-constitutional error, as explained above, it generally was assumed that constitutional violations could never be regarded as harmless error. Prejudice was conclusively presumed, and a rule of "automatic reversal" prevailed. This changed with the due process revolution of the 1960s and its dramatic expansion of federal constitutional regulation of state procedures. *Chapman v. California,* below, first recognized a doctrine of harmless constitutional error.

CHAPMAN V. CALIFORNIA

386 U.S. 18, 87 S.Ct. 824, 17 L.Ed.2d 705 (1967).

JUSTICE BLACK delivered the opinion of the Court.

[The two petitioners were convicted of the robbery, kidnapping, and murder of a bartender. In closing, the state's attorney argued to the jury, and the trial judge instructed the jury, that it could draw adverse inferences from petitioners' failure to testify. Shortly after the trial, the Supreme Court decided *Griffin v. California,* p. 1322, holding unconstitutional such comment and instruction on a defendant's failure to testify. The California Supreme Court recognized that the comments and instructions upon petitioners' silence had violated the rule announced in *Griffin,* but affirmed the convictions and sentences under a state harmless-error provision that prohibited appellate reversal unless "the error complained of has resulted in a miscarriage of justice."]

* * * Before deciding the two questions here—whether there can ever be harmless constitutional error and whether the error here was harmless—we must first decide whether state or federal law governs. The application of a state harmless-error rule is, of course, a state question where it involves only errors of state procedure or state law. But the error from which these petitioners suffered was a denial of rights guaranteed against invasion by the Fifth and Fourteenth Amendments * * *. Whether a conviction for crime should stand when a State has failed to accord federal constitutionally guaranteed rights is every bit as much of a federal question as what particular federal constitutional provisions themselves mean, what they guarantee, and whether they have been denied. With faithfulness to the constitutional union of the States, we cannot leave to the States the formulation of the authoritative laws, rules, and remedies designed to protect people from infractions by the States of federally guaranteed rights. We have no hesitation in saying that the right of these petitioners not to be punished for exercising their Fifth and Fourteenth Amendment right to be silent—expressly created by the Federal Constitution itself—is a federal right which, in the absence of appropriate congressional action, it is our responsibility to protect by fashioning the necessary rule.

We are urged by petitioners to hold that all federal constitutional errors, regardless of the facts and circumstances, must always be deemed harmful. Such a holding, as petitioners correctly point out, would require an automatic reversal of their convictions and make further discussion unnecessary. We decline to adopt any such rule. All 50 States have harmless-error statutes or rules, and the United States long ago through its Congress established for its courts the rule that judgments shall not be reversed for "errors or defects which do not affect the substantial rights of the parties." 28 U.S.C. § 2111. None of these rules on its face distinguishes between federal constitutional errors and errors of state law or federal statutes and rules. All of these rules, state or federal, serve a very useful purpose insofar as they block setting aside convictions for small errors or defects that have little, if any, likelihood of having changed the result of the trial. We conclude that there may be some constitutional errors which in the setting of a particular case are so unimportant and insignificant that they may, consistent with the Federal Constitution, be deemed harmless, not requiring the automatic reversal of the conviction. * * *

* * * We prefer the approach of this Court in deciding what was harmless error in our recent case of *Fahy v. Connecticut*[, 375 U.S. 85 (1963) (declining to decide if admission of illegally seized evidence can be harmless)]. There we said: "The question is whether there is a reasonable possibility that the evidence complained of might have contributed to the conviction." Although our prior cases have indicated that there are some constitutional rights so basic to a fair trial that their infraction can never be treated as harmless error,[8] this statement in *Fahy* itself belies any

[8] See, e.g., *Payne v. Arkansas,* 356 U.S. 560 (1958) (coerced confession); *Gideon v. Wainwright*, 372 U.S. 335 (1963) (right to counsel); *Tumey v. Ohio*, 273 U.S. 510 (1927) (impartial judge). [Ed: The Court later overturned *Payne* in *Arizona v. Fulminante*, 499 U.S. 279 (1991), holding that admission of a coerced confession did *not* require

belief that all trial errors which violate the Constitution automatically call for reversal. At the same time, however, like the federal harmless-error statute, it emphasizes an intention not to treat as harmless those constitutional errors that "affect substantial rights" of a party. * * * Certainly error, constitutional error, in illegally admitting highly prejudicial evidence or comments, casts on someone other than the person prejudiced by it a burden to show that it was harmless. It is for that reason that the original common-law harmless-error rule put the burden on the beneficiary of the error either to prove that there was no injury or to suffer a reversal of his erroneously obtained judgment. There is little, if any, difference between our statement in *Fahy* about "whether there is a reasonable possibility that the evidence complained of might have contributed to the conviction" and requiring the beneficiary of a constitutional error to prove beyond a reasonable doubt that the error complained of did not contribute to the verdict obtained. We, therefore [hold] that before a federal constitutional error can be held harmless, the court must be able to declare a belief that it was harmless beyond a reasonable doubt. * * * .

Applying the foregoing standard, we have no doubt that the error in these cases was not harmless to petitioners. * * * [T]he state prosecutor's argument and the trial judge's instruction to the jury continuously and repeatedly impressed the jury that from the failure of petitioners to testify, to all intents and purposes, the inferences from the facts in evidence had to be drawn in favor of the State—in short, that by their silence petitioners had served as irrefutable witnesses against themselves. And though the case in which this occurred presented a reasonably strong "circumstantial web of evidence" against petitioners, it was also a case in which, absent the constitutionally forbidden comments, honest, fair-minded jurors might very well have brought in not-guilty verdicts. Under these circumstances, it is completely impossible for us to say that the State has demonstrated, beyond a reasonable doubt, that the prosecutor's comments and the trial judge's instruction did not contribute to petitioners' convictions. * * * .

NOTES AND QUESTIONS

1. ***The grounding of* Chapman.** Commentators have found puzzling the Court's reference to the "absence of appropriate congressional action" in its description of its obligation to fashion a federal harmless error rule for constitutional violations, raising the question whether Court viewed its reasonable doubt standard as constitutionally mandated. Justice Harlan suggested in a concurring opinion that the application of a state harmless error rule was an independent ground barring Supreme Court review, and "regard[ed] the Court's assumption of what amounts to a general supervisory power over the trial of federal constitutional issues in state courts as a startling constitutional development that is wholly out of keeping with our federal system and completely unsupported by the Fourteenth Amendment." Others have described such authority as an aspect of "constitutional common law," reflecting the authority of the court to fashion remedies where Congress has not chosen to do so. See Daniel J. Meltzer, *Harmless Error and Constitutional Remedies*, 61 U. Chi. L. Rev. 1 (1994). Cf. *Bivens v. Six Unknown Named Agents,* 403 U.S. 388 (1971) (Court-created tort remedy for violations of the Fourth Amendment by federal officers). Possible support for this characterization of the *Chapman* standard is found in *Brecht v. Abrahamson,* discussed at p. 1461, where the Court held that, when reviewing constitutional claims raised by state prisoners seeking habeas relief, the *Kotteakos* standard, rather than the *Chapman* standard, would apply. *United States v. Cappas*, 29 F.3d 1187, 1193 (7th Cir. 1994) (After *Brecht*, it is no longer plausible to argue that the harmless error doctrine provides a gloss on the underlying constitutional rights, or is even itself a rule derived from the Constitution. Instead, the emerging view appears to be that the *Chapman* standard is a pronouncement of "constitutional common law."); Sam Kamin, *Harmless Error and the*

---

automatic reversal, but was, like other errors in the admission and exclusion of evidence, subject to *Chapman*'s harmless error standard.]

Rights/remedies Split, 88 Va. L. Rev. 1, 17 (2002) ("Clearly, if the states were given unfettered discretion to apply whatever harmless error standards they chose, both the consistency and predictability of constitutional guarantees would suffer.").

Can a constitutional grounding for the *Chapman* standard be squared with the Court's rejection of a constitutional right to appeal (see Note 1, p. 1401)? Consider the hypothetical posed by Meltzer, supra: "[S]uppose a state conferred on its appellate courts jurisdiction to reverse a criminal conviction only if the error probably affected the outcome—a standard far less protective of defendants than that of *Chapman*. Why would affirmance of a conviction under that standard raise a federal question if the state might have provided no appeal whatsoever?"

If the Constitution may require that all violations of a particular constitutional right require reversal of a conviction (see fn. 8 of *Chapman*), then why might it not also require as to other rights that violation requires reversal unless the right was clearly harmless? If so, might a constitutional grounding for *Chapman's* standard be found in an obligation of the states, once they provide for an appeal under state law, to apply in their appellate review the commands of the federal constitution? Even if a state is obligated to provide no *less* relief than the federal harmless error standard, it could always, as a matter of state law, provide *more*. See *Washington v. Recuenco*, 548 U.S. 212, 218 n. 1 (2006) (suggesting state could apply more generous standard of review); *Danforth v. Minnesota*, Note 3, p. 1451 (state courts could give broader retroactive effect to new constitutional rules of criminal procedure in their state post-conviction proceedings than would be allowed under federal law).

2. ***Automatic reversal errors.*** The Court has recognized four types of error that once established are sufficient to require relief without applying *Chapman*'s outcome-impact standard.

First, harmless error analysis does not apply to constitutional errors that bar reprosecution entirely—e.g., Double Jeopardy Clause and Speedy Trial Clause violations.

Second, harmless error does not apply when, in order to establish the constitutional violation itself, the defense must show some probability that the error had an impact upon the outcome of the proceeding. That is often the case, for example, with due process violations, as illustrated by the *Brady/Bagley* standard for disclosing exculpatory evidence, or the due process limit on improper prosecutorial argument (see *Darden*, p. 1327). As the Court explained in *Kyles v. Whitley*, Note 5, p. 1139, "once a reviewing court applying *Bagley* has found constitutional error there is no need for further harmless error review." The Sixth Amendment *Strickland* standard for ineffective assistance of counsel also includes a finding of prejudice. Once a court has found the "reasonable probability" of impact on the outcome necessary to establish the constitutional violation under *Strickland*, that finding establishes that the error was not harmless under *Chapman*.

Third, breaches of plea agreements will not be evaluated for harmlessness. The reason, explained the Court in *Puckett v. United States*, p. 1414, is that confidence in the certainty of relief once breach is shown is necessary to maintain plea bargaining generally. The automatic reversal rule in *Santobello*, the Court stated in *Puckett*, rests "upon a policy interest in establishing the trust between defendants and prosecutors that is necessary to sustain plea bargaining—an "essential" and "highly desirable" part of the criminal process."

Finally, the Court has identified a number of errors that it has termed "structural," for which relief is available without regard to harmlessness or prejudice. The current Court's understanding of what makes an error "structural" appears in Part II of the Court's opinion in *Weaver v. Massachusetts*, reproduced at pp. 144–145. That approach is also summarized in Note 2 following the case below, which presents a particularly controversial application of this "structural error" concept.

NEDER V. UNITED STATES

527 U.S. 1, 119 S.Ct. 1827, 144 L.Ed.2d 35 (1999).

[Neder was tried for fraud and tax offenses including a statute that prohibits a person from filing a tax return "which he does not believe to be true and correct as to every material matter." Over his objection, the District Court instructed the jury that, to convict on the tax offenses, it "need not consider" the materiality of any false statements and that the question of materiality "is not a question for the jury to decide." This was error under the Court's intervening decision in *United States v. Gaudin,* Note 5, p. 1237.]

CHIEF JUSTICE REHNQUIST delivered the opinion of the Court.

* * * We have recognized that "most constitutional errors can be harmless." "[I]f the defendant had counsel and was tried by an impartial adjudicator, there is a strong presumption that any other [constitutional] errors that may have occurred are subject to harmless-error analysis." *Rose v. Clark,* 478 U.S. 570 (1986). Indeed, we have found an error to be "structural," and thus subject to automatic reversal, only in a "very limited class of cases." *Johnson v. United States,* 520 U.S. 461 (1997) (citing *Gideon v. Wainwright,* 372 U.S. 335 (1963) (complete denial of counsel); *Tumey v. Ohio,* 273 U.S. 510 (1927) (biased trial judge); *Vasquez v. Hillery,* 474 U.S. 254 (1986) (racial discrimination in selection of grand jury); *McKaskle v. Wiggins,* 465 U.S. 168 (1984) (denial of self-representation at trial); *Waller v. Georgia,* 467 U.S. 39 (1984) (denial of public trial); *Sullivan v. Louisiana,* 508 U.S. 275 (1993) (defective reasonable-doubt instruction)).

The error at issue here—a jury instruction that omits an element of the offense—differs markedly from the constitutional violations we have found to defy harmless-error review. Those cases, we have explained, contain a "defect affecting the framework within which the trial proceeds, rather than simply an error in the trial process itself." Such errors "infect the entire trial process," and "necessarily render a trial fundamentally unfair." Put another way, these errors deprive defendants of "basic protections" without which "a criminal trial cannot reliably serve its function as a vehicle for determination of guilt or innocence . . . and no criminal punishment may be regarded as fundamentally fair." *Id.*

Unlike such defects as the complete deprivation of counsel or trial before a biased judge, an instruction that omits an element of the offense does not *necessarily* render a criminal trial fundamentally unfair or an unreliable vehicle for determining guilt or innocence. * * * We have often applied harmless-error analysis to cases involving improper instructions on a single element of the offense. See, e.g., *Carella v. California,* 491 U.S. 263 (1989) *(per curiam)* (mandatory conclusive presumption); *Pope v. Illinois,* 481 U.S. 497 (1987) (misstatement of element). * * * In other cases, we have recognized that improperly omitting an element from the jury can "easily be analogized to improperly instructing the jury on an element of the offense, an error which is subject to harmless-error analysis." *California v. Roy,* 519 U.S. 2 (1996). * * * In both cases—misdescriptions and omissions—the erroneous instruction precludes the jury from making a finding on the *actual* element of the offense. The same, we think, can be said of conclusive presumptions, which direct the jury to presume an *ultimate* element of the offense based on proof of certain *predicate* facts (*e.g.,* "You must presume malice if you find an intentional killing"). Like an omission, a conclusive presumption deters the jury from considering any evidence other than that related to the predicate facts (*e.g.,* an intentional killing) and "directly foreclose[s] independent jury consideration of whether the facts proved established certain elements of the offens[e]" (*e.g.,* malice).

The conclusion that the omission of an element is subject to harmless-error analysis is consistent with the holding (if not the entire reasoning) of *Sullivan v. Louisiana,* the case upon which Neder principally relies. In *Sullivan,* the trial court gave the jury a defective "reasonable doubt" instruction in violation of the defendant's Fifth and Sixth Amendment rights to have the charged offense proved beyond a reasonable doubt. Applying our traditional mode of analysis, the Court concluded that the error was not subject to harmless-error analysis because it "vitiates *all* the jury's findings," and produces "consequences that are necessarily unquantifiable and indeterminate." By contrast, the jury-instruction error here did not "vitiat[e] *all* the jury's findings." It did, of course, prevent the jury from making a finding on the element of materiality.

* * * Neder attempts to reconcile our cases by [arguing that under our precedent] an instructional omission, misdescription, or conclusive presumption can be subject to harmless-error analysis only in three "rare situations": (1) where the defendant is acquitted of the offense on which the jury was improperly instructed (and, despite the defendant's argument that the instruction affected another count, the improper instruction had no bearing on it); (2) where the defendant admitted the element on which the jury was improperly instructed; and (3) where other facts necessarily found by the jury are the "functional equivalent" of the omitted, misdescribed, or presumed element. Neder understandably contends that *Pope*, *Carella,* and *Roy* fall within this last exception, which explains why the Court in those cases held that the instructional error could be harmless.

We believe this approach is mistaken * * *. [P]etitioner's submission * * * imports into the initial structural-error determination (*i.e.,* whether an error is structural) a case-by-case approach that is more consistent with our traditional harmless-error inquiry (*i.e.,* whether an error is harmless). Under our cases, a constitutional error is either structural or it is not. Thus, even if we were inclined to follow a broader "functional equivalence" test *e.g.,* where other facts found by the jury are "so closely related" to the omitted element "that no rational jury could find those facts without also finding" the omitted element, *Sullivan*, such a test would be inconsistent with our traditional categorical approach to structural errors. * * *

[N]o jury could reasonably find that Neder's failure to report substantial amounts of income on his tax returns was not "a material matter." * * * The evidence supporting materiality was so overwhelming, in fact, that Neder did not argue to the jury—and does not argue here—that his false statements of income could be found immaterial. Instead, he defended against the tax charges by arguing that the loan proceeds were not income because he intended to repay the loans, and that he reasonably believed, based on the advice of his accountant and lawyer, that he need not report the proceeds as income. In this situation, where a reviewing court concludes beyond a reasonable doubt that the omitted element was uncontested and supported by overwhelming evidence, such that the jury verdict would have been the same absent the error, the erroneous instruction is properly found to be harmless. We think it beyond cavil here that the error "did not contribute to the verdict obtained." *Chapman.* * * * .[2]

* * * We believe that where an omitted element is supported by uncontroverted evidence, this approach reaches an appropriate balance between "society's interest in punishing the guilty [and] the method by which decisions of guilt are to be made." * * * In a case such as this one, where a defendant did not, and apparently could not, bring forth facts contesting the omitted element, answering the question whether the jury verdict would have been the same absent the error does not fundamentally undermine the purposes of the jury trial guarantee. * * * [If a reviewing] court cannot conclude beyond a reasonable doubt that the jury verdict would have been the same absent the error—for example, where the defendant contested the omitted element and raised evidence sufficient to support a contrary finding—it should not find the error harmless.

---

[2] Justice Scalia, in his opinion * * *, also suggests that if a failure to charge on an uncontested element of the offense may be harmless error, the next step will be to allow a directed verdict against a defendant in a criminal case contrary to *Rose v. Clark*. Happily, our course of constitutional adjudication has not been characterized by this "in for a penny, in for a pound" approach. We have no hesitation reaffirming *Rose* at the same time that we subject the narrow class of cases like the present one to harmless-error review.

A reviewing court making this harmless-error inquiry does not, as Justice Traynor put it, "become in effect a second jury to determine whether the defendant is guilty." R. Traynor, *The Riddle of Harmless Error* 21 (1970). Rather a court, in typical appellate-court fashion, asks whether the record contains evidence that could rationally lead to a contrary finding with respect to the omitted element. If the answer to that question is "no," holding the error harmless does not "reflec[t] a denigration of the constitutional rights involved." *Rose*. On the contrary, it "serve[s] a very useful purpose insofar as [it] block[s] setting aside convictions for small errors or defects that have little, if any, likelihood of having changed the result of the trial." *Chapman*. We thus hold that the District Court's failure to submit the element of materiality to the jury with respect to the tax charges was harmless error. * * *

JUSTICE SCALIA, with whom JUSTICE SOUTER and JUSTICE GINSBURG join, concurring in part and dissenting in part.

* * * [T]he Court lets the defendant's sentence stand, *because we judges can tell that he is unquestionably guilty*. Even if we allowed (as we do not) other structural errors in criminal trials to be pronounced "harmless" by judges * * * it is obvious that we could not allow judges to validate *this* one. The constitutionally required step that was omitted here is distinctive, in that the basis for it is precisely that, absent voluntary waiver of the jury right, *the Constitution does not trust judges to make determinations of criminal guilt*. * * * [T]he people reserved the function of determining criminal guilt *to themselves*, sitting as jurors. It is not within the power of us Justices to cancel that reservation—neither by permitting trial judges to determine the guilt of a defendant who has not waived the jury right, nor (when a trial judge has done so anyway) by reviewing the facts ourselves and pronouncing the defendant without-a-doubt guilty. The Court's decision today is the only instance I know of (or could conceive of) in which the remedy for a constitutional violation by a trial judge (making the determination of criminal guilt reserved to the jury) is a repetition of the same constitutional violation by the appellate court (making the determination of criminal guilt reserved to the jury).

* * * The question that this raises is why, if denying the right to conviction by jury is structural error, taking *one* of the elements of the crime away from the jury should be treated differently from taking *all* of them away—since failure to prove one, no less than failure to prove all, utterly prevents conviction. * * * Indeed, we do not know, when the Court's opinion is done, *how many* elements can be taken away from the jury with impunity, so long as appellate judges are persuaded that the defendant is surely guilty. * * * The underlying theme of the Court's opinion is that taking the element of materiality from the jury did not render Neder's trial unfair, because the judge certainly reached the "right" result. But the same could be said of a directed verdict against the defendant—which would be *per se* reversible *no matter how overwhelming the unfavorable evidence*. The very premise of structural-error review is that even convictions reflecting the "right" result are reversed for the sake of protecting a basic right. For example, in *Tumey v. Ohio*, where we reversed the defendant's conviction because he had been tried before a biased judge, the State argued that "the evidence shows clearly that the defendant was guilty and that he was only fined $100, which was the minimum amount, and therefore that he cannot complain of a lack of due process, either in his conviction or in the amount of the judgment." We rejected this argument out of hand, responding that *"[n]o matter what the evidence was against him*, he had the right to have an impartial judge." The amount of evidence against a defendant who has properly preserved his objection, while relevant to determining whether a given error was harmless, has nothing to do with determining whether the error is subject to harmless-error review in the first place. * * *

* * * Where the facts *necessarily found* by the jury (and not those merely discerned by the appellate court) support the existence of the element omitted or misdescribed in the instruction,

the omission or misdescription is harmless. For there is then no "gap" *in the verdict* to be filled by the factfinding of judges.

* * * The difference between speculation directed toward *confirming* the jury's verdict *(Sullivan)* and speculation directed toward *making a judgment that the jury has never made* (today's decision) is more than semantic. * * * The right to render the verdict in criminal prosecutions belongs exclusively to the jury; reviewing it belongs to the appellate court. "Confirming" speculation does not disturb that allocation, but "substituting" speculation does. * * * [The concurring opinion of Justice Stevens is omitted.]

NOTES AND QUESTIONS

1. ***Other structural errors.*** In addition to the "structural" errors listed near the beginning of the Court's opinion in *Neder,* other procedural errors that fall within the category include: (1) discrimination in the selection of the petit jury, *Batson v. Kentucky*, p. 1250; (2) the improper exclusion of a juror based on his views of capital punishment, *Gray v. Mississippi*, p. 1255; (3) the violation of the standards governing the withdrawal of appointed counsel, *Penson v. Ohio*, 488 U.S. 75 (1988); (4) the denial of an opportunity to consult with counsel during an overnight trial recess, *Geders v. United States*, Note 5, p. 170; (5) denial of the right to select counsel of one's choice, *United States v. Gonzalez-Lopez*, p. 113; and (6) the failure to make an appropriate inquiry into a possible conflict of interest under those special circumstances that constitutionally mandate such an inquiry, *Holloway v. Arkansas*, p. 181. See CRIMPROC § 27.6(d).

2. ***The character of structural errors.*** In *Weaver,* p. 143, Court identified "at least three broad rationales" for classifying an error as structural and exempt from harmless error review.

First, it noted harmless error analysis is inappropriate if the right protects some interest other than the defendant's interest in an accurate outcome, such that harm to the defendant "is irrelevant to the basis underlying the right." As Justice Stevens observed when concurring in *Rose v. Clark*, 478 U.S. 570 (1986), "violations of certain constitutional rights are not, and should not be, subject to harmless error analysis because those rights protect important values that are unrelated to the truth-seeking function of the trial. Thus, racial discrimination in the selection of grand juries is intolerable even if the defendant's guilt is subsequently established in a fair trial. *Vasquez v. Hillery* [Note 7, p. 955]. * * * [O]ur Constitution, and our criminal justice system, protect other values besides the reliability of the guilt or innocence determination. A coherent harmless error jurisprudence should similarly respect those values."

Second, harmless error analysis may be inappropriate if the effects of the error are too hard to measure. In *Williams v. Pennsylvania,* 136 S.Ct. 1899 (2016), for example, the Court held an appellate judge's unconstitutional failure to recuse constitutes structural error even if the judge in question did not cast a deciding vote, noting this was "a defect 'not amenable' to harmless-error review, regardless of whether the judge's vote was dispositive." The Court reasoned: "The deliberations of an appellate panel, as a general rule, are confidential. As a result, it is neither possible nor productive to inquire whether the jurist in question might have influenced the views of his or her colleagues during the decisionmaking process."

The third rationale noted in *Weaver* for deeming an error structural is "if the error always results in fundamental unfairness. For example, if an indigent defendant is denied an attorney or if the judge fails to give a reasonable-doubt instruction, the resulting trial is always a fundamentally unfair one. * * * It therefore would be futile for the government to try to show harmlessness."

The *Weaver* Court noted that more than one rationale may apply, but that "an error can count as structural even if the error does not lead to fundamental unfairness in every case."

3. ***Intentional violations and the application of harmless error review.*** Justice Stewart noted in his *Chapman* concurrence that there was "no reason why the sanction of reversal should not be the result in future cases" should prosecutors "indulge in clear violations of *Griffin.*" But in *United States v. Hasting*, p. 33, the Court held that a court could not decline to apply the harmless error rule of *Chapman* and require automatic reversal as a means of disciplining prosecutors for continuing violations of *Griffin*. The federal courts' supervisory power could not be used to circumvent the balance struck by *Chapman* in fashioning a remedy for a constitutional violation. The Court has in later cases reiterated its opposition to reversal without regard to prejudice as punishment for misconduct. See Note 2, p. 977; Note 4, p. 1331.

Whether a violation was intentional may nevertheless have some influence on the willingness of appellate judges to grant relief to a defendant. See William M. Landes & Richard A. Posner, *Harmless Error*, 30 J. Legal Stud. 161 (2001) (reporting study findings that intentional errors by judges and prosecutors are more likely to be found harmful and lead the appellate court to reverse the defendant's conviction than are inadvertent errors; prosecutor errors are more likely to be forgiven than judge errors, in part because judge errors are likely to have greater influence on jurors; and appellate courts are more likely to publish an opinion when they are reversing rather than affirming the lower court).

CHAPTER 29

POST-CONVICTION REVIEW: FEDERAL HABEAS CORPUS

■ ■ ■

A state prisoner who has completed his direct appeal typically has two additional routes to attack his conviction or sentence. First, he may return to the state's courts, seeking whatever "postconviction" remedies are provided under state law. See Donald Wilkes, *State Post-Conviction Remedies and Relief Handbook with Forms* (2018–19) (annually updated comprehensive catalogue of state post-conviction remedies). If unsuccessful in state court a state prisoner may then seek relief in federal court, through the writ of habeas corpus. This federal statutory remedy is the focus of this chapter.[a] Decisions interpreting the federal habeas remedy continue to influence the scope and application of other postconviction remedies in state and federal courts. State prisoners file approximately 17,000 cases seeking habeas corpus relief annually.

§ 1. THE BASIC STRUCTURE OF FEDERAL HABEAS CORPUS RELIEF

1. ***Common law origins.*** The federal statutory remedy of habeas corpus is descended from its common law ancestor. The common law writ of habeas corpus was a judicial order directing a jailor to bring a prisoner into court. Some aspects of the common law writ are retained in the federal statutory version available today. For example, the remedy continues to be available only to a person who is in custody when the petition is filed. Those in "custody" include probationers and parolees, as well as prisoners who challenge a conviction carrying a sentence to be served after completing their present sentence. In addition, judgments other than criminal convictions may create "custody" within the meaning of the federal habeas statute, including an order of "civil commitment" or "civil contempt."

2. ***Constitutional recognition.*** In a provision known as the "Suspension Clause," Article I of the Constitution states: "[T]he privilege of the Writ of Habeas Corpus shall not be suspended, unless when in Cases of Rebellion or Invasion the Public Safety may require it." Exactly what is protected by the Clause remains unsettled. It is not clear that the Clause applies to state prisoners at all. Most of the litigation concerning the Clause has addressed detention by the executive branch of the federal government, not the detention of those convicted of crime in state court. See, e.g., *Boumediene v. Bush*, 553 U.S. 723 (2008). Some decisions have suggested that the Clause does not safeguard federal judicial review of the constitutionality of a state's incarceration of convicted prisoners, review that was first provided by statute in 1867. Commentators disagree about whether the Fourteenth Amendment formed a new constitutional baseline limiting the ability of Congress to "suspend" meaningful access to federal review of constitutional claims raised by state prisoners as well as federal prisoners. Compare Jordan Steiker, *Incorporating the Suspension Clause: Is There a Constitutional Right to Federal Habeas Corpus for State Prisoners?*, 92 Mich.L.Rev. 862 (1994) with Gerald L. Neuman, *The Habeas Corpus Suspension Clause After*

---

[a] Federal habeas corpus is examined in detail in Chapter 28 of Wayne R. LaFave, Jerold H. Israel, Nancy J. King & Orin S. Kerr, Criminal Procedure Treatise (4th ed. 2016) (available on WESTLAW at database name CRIMPROC, hereinafter cited as CRIMPROC). Postconviction remedies are also described as "collateral" because they require a petitioner to challenge his custody by filing a new civil case rather than an appeal of the criminal judgment.

INS v. St. Cyr, 33 Colum. Human Rts. L. Rev. 555 (2002) ("incorporation of the Suspension Clause in the Fourteenth Amendment could entitle state prisoners to state post-conviction procedures parallel to whatever the Suspension Clause requires for federal prisoners," but "would not create a right to federal habeas corpus for state prisoners"). When Congress restricted the availability of the writ for state prisoners in 1996 as part of the Antiterrorism and Effective Death Penalty Act (hereinafter AEDPA), claims that those restrictions violated the Suspension Clause were rejected.

3. ***The current statutory structure.*** The statutory provisions governing habeas corpus relief today are found in 28 U.S.C. §§ 2241–2266. They retain core of the Habeas Act of 1867 in which Congress first extended the writ to those in state custody, specifically to "cases where any person may be restrained of his or her liberty in violation of the Constitution, or of any treaty or law of the United States." The scope of this statutory remedy expanded dramatically after 1867, as Section 2, below, recounts. In more recent decades, the habeas remedy has been constricted. Consider the following summary of the development of the current statute (from Nancy J. King, Fred L. Cheesman, III & Brian J. Ostrom, *Final Report: Habeas Litigation In U.S. District Courts* (2007) (available at www.ncjrs.gov) (hereinafter King, et al., 2007 Habeas Study).

"The current habeas provisions are a legislative response to several decades of change in the federal oversight of state criminal proceedings. In the 1950s, 1960s, and early 1970s, the U.S. Supreme Court interpreted the Due Process Clause of the Fourteenth Amendment to guarantee to state criminal defendants many of the procedural protections that had previously been enjoyed only by defendants in federal criminal proceedings. At the same time, the Court expanded the scope of the writ, allowing more opportunities for state prisoners to obtain relief in federal court when actions of state police, prosecutors, and judges violated their constitutionally protected rights. In combination, these two trends produced an explosion in habeas filings.[b]

"By the 1980s, the Supreme Court's decisions began to narrow access to habeas relief for state prisoners. * * * For a majority of the members of Congress in the early 1990s, the Court's decisions did not adequately address growing concerns about federal court interference with the finality of state criminal judgments and about delay in the processing of habeas cases. After considering various legislative proposals for years, Congress passed the Antiterrorism and Effective Death Penalty Act ('AEDPA') in 1996, limiting federal habeas review. * * *

AEDPA narrowed habeas review for all prisoners by 1) establishing a 1-year statute of limitations for filing a federal habeas petition, * * * ; 2) authorizing federal judges to deny on the merits any claim that a petitioner failed to exhaust in state court; 3) prohibiting a federal court from holding an evidentiary hearing when the petitioner failed to develop the facts in state court, except in limited circumstances; 4) barring successive petitions, except in limited circumstances; and 5) mandating a new standard of review for evaluating state court determinations of fact and applications of constitutional law."

4. ***Habeas procedures.*** Procedures applicable in federal habeas proceedings are set forth in §§ 2242–2243 and in the Rules Governing Section 2254 Cases, a set of Rules separate from the Federal Rules of Criminal Procedure. The rules allow for pleading on forms designed to help a pro se petitioner present all critical information (e.g., state conviction, sentence, prior state proceedings, prior habeas proceedings). Ordinarily, each petition and any exhibits will be examined by a judge to determine whether the petition warrants further consideration. If it does not, the petition may be dismissed summarily. If the petition clears this preliminary review, the court will order the state to file a response. The state may raise the various defenses discussed in this Chapter, or answer the allegations on the merits, or both. Just under half of the petitions filed in non-capital cases are dismissed without reaching the merits of any claim. Evidentiary hearings

[b] See *Report to the Attorney General on Federal Habeas Corpus Review of State Judgments*, 22 U. MICH. J. L. REF. 901, 946–47 (1988–89) (number of state prisoner applications grew from about 1000 in 1961 to nearly 10,000 in 1987).

and discovery are rare in non-capital cases. King, et al., 2007 Habeas Study. See also Note 6, p. 1167 (on use of FOIA requests to discover proof for postconviction claims). If a federal court determines that the petitioner has met the requirements for relief under the statute, depending upon the constitutional error established, the order granting the petition typically permits the state a choice: conduct a new trial, sentencing, or appeal within a certain time, or else release the petitioner.

5. ***The exhaustion requirement.*** Section 2254 requires that a petitioner first present his constitutional claim to the state courts. This gives the state an opportunity to make its initial ruling on the prisoner's constitutional claim if it is willing to do so. "Exhaustion," as it is known, demands only that the state judiciary be given a single chance (through the highest available state court) to consider the substance of the petitioner's claim. See *O'Sullivan v. Boerckel*, 526 U.S. 838 (1999) (exhaustion requires state prisoners to file petitions for discretionary review when that review is part of the ordinary appellate review procedure in the state). When a petitioner files a "mixed petition" in federal court—including some claims that were adequately presented to the state courts and others that were not—the habeas court can deny, but cannot grant relief for any unexhausted claim. The petitioner must either (1) withdraw the petition, (2) proceed only on the exhausted claims, or (3) seek a "stay" of the exhausted claims that would allow him to return to state court to exhaust any unexhausted claims, then amend the petition to add the newly exhausted claims. See *Rhines v. Weber*, 544 U.S. 269 (2005). The exhaustion requirement is satisfied if the opportunity to present the issue to the state courts is no longer available.

6. ***Counsel in habeas proceedings.*** One of the most fundamental differences between appellate review and collateral review is that prisoners on appeal have the assistance of counsel, while prisoners seeking collateral review are usually on their own.

a. ***Constitutional entitlement to counsel?*** In *Bounds v. Smith*, 430 U.S. 817 (1977), per Marshall, J., the Court held that a state's constitutional duty to provide "meaningful access" to the courts "requires prison authorities to assist inmates in the preparation and filing of meaningful legal papers by [furnishing] adequate law libraries or adequate assistance from persons trained in the law." Dissenting, Justice Rehnquist, J., joined by Burger, C.J., protested that "if 'meaningful access' to the courts is to include law libraries, there is no convincing reason why it should not also include lawyers appointed at the expense of the State." Yet by 1989, the Court, in *Murray v. Giarratano,* 492 U.S. 1 (1989) (per Rehnquist, J.) rejected a constitutional right to the assistance of counsel on collateral review, even for death row inmates:

"[W]e held in *Ross v. Moffitt* [p. 95] that the right to counsel at [trial and on the first appeal] did not carry over to a discretionary appeal provided by [state] law from the intermediate appellate court to the [state supreme court]. We contrasted the trial stage of a criminal proceeding [with] the appellate stage of such a proceeding, where the defendant needs an attorney 'not as a shield to protect him against being "haled into court" by the State and stripped of his presumption of innocence, but rather as a sword to upset the prior determination of guilt.' We held in *Pennsylvania v. Finley*, 481 U.S. 551 (1987), that the logic of *Ross* required the conclusion that there was no federal constitutional right to counsel for indigent prisoners seeking state postconviction relief. [The] rule of *Finley* should apply no differently in capital cases than in noncapital cases. State collateral proceedings are not constitutionally required as an adjunct to the state criminal proceedings and serve a different and more limited purpose than either the trial or appeal. The additional safeguards imposed by the Eighth Amendment at the trial stage of a capital case are, we think, sufficient to assure the reliability of the process by which the death penalty is imposed."

The pivotal fifth vote in *Giarratano* was cast by Justice Kennedy, who concurred in the judgment and observed that "no prisoner on death row in Virginia has been unable to obtain counsel to represent him in postconviction proceedings" and that the state's prison system "is staffed with institutional lawyers to assist in preparing petitions for postconviction relief."

Justice Stevens, joined by Brennan, Marshall, and Blackmun, JJ., dissented, arguing that "even if it is permissible to leave an ordinary prisoner to his own resources in collateral proceedings, it is fundamentally unfair to require an indigent death row inmate to initiate collateral review without counsel's guiding hand." He noted that one study found the success rate for habeas challenges in capital cases ranged from 60% to 70%, demonstrating that "the meaningful appellate review necessary in a capital case extends beyond the direct appellate process"; that "unlike the ordinary inmate, who presumably has ample time to use and reuse the prison library and to seek guidance from other prisoners experienced in preparing *pro se* petitions, a grim deadline imposes a finite limit on the condemned person's capacity for useful research"; and that "this Court's death penalty jurisprudence unquestionably is difficult even for a trained lawyer to master."

b. Statutory rights to counsel in collateral proceedings. Although most (but not all) states provide a statutory right to appointed counsel for indigent death row inmates, only a small proportion of non-capital prisoners receive counsel in state collateral proceedings. For one recent empirical review, see Nancy J. King, *Enforcing Effective Assistance After Martinez*, 122 Yale L. J. 2428 (2013). The Court in *Martinez v. Ryan,* 566 U.S. 1 (2012), declined to address directly whether or not the Constitution required states to provide counsel in state collateral proceedings, but did hold that a state risks losing its ability to raise the defense of state procedural default to a later claim in federal habeas based on ineffective assistance of trial counsel, if the state fails to appoint counsel for a prisoner raising that claim for the first time in his first state post-conviction petition. See Note 1.d., p. 1439.

In federal habeas cases, Congress has required the appointment of counsel for indigent capital defendants, 18 U.S.C. § 3599, but not for indigent petitioners in noncapital cases. Only about 7% of federal habeas petitioners serving state noncapital sentences receive counsel.

7. ***Summary of barriers to relief.*** The most important barriers to habeas relief are examined in the Sections that follow. Section 2 examines why the writ is not available for certain categories of claims, namely claims that the state court failed to exclude evidence obtained in violation of the Fourth Amendment, and claims of factual innocence. Section 3 discusses the statute of limitations for filing and the ban against successive petitions. Section 4 details the defense of procedural default. Section 5 addresses limits on the retroactive application of rules announced after direct appeal of the prisoner's conviction and sentence. Even if a petitioner successfully negotiates these requirements and receives review of his claims on the merits, the federal court will not review all state court decisions de novo, and may simply find that an erroneous state decision was "reasonable" or "harmless." See Section 6.

Not surprisingly, of the small proportion of state prisoners serving non-capital sentences who are still in custody by the time they have exhausted state remedies and are able to seek habeas relief, few obtain it. District and circuit courts combined granted any relief in only 0.8 percent of a random sample of petitions filed in 2003 to 2004. Even fewer (0.6 percent) actually received earlier release; once back in state court, in multiple cases, "the petitioner's habeas victory landed him in a position that was the same as or worse than the position he was in before he sought habeas relief." Nancy J. King, *Non-Capital Habeas Cases after Appellate Review: An Empirical Analysis*, 24 Fed. Sent. Rep. 308 (2012). The success rate for petitions filed by prisoners sentenced to death is much higher than for petitions filed by prisoners sentenced to incarceration—closer to 15%. The most likely grounds for relief in capital cases are rules that are unique to capital cases, including retroactive application of new Eighth Amendment law and ineffective assistance of counsel during the sentencing phase of the capital trial. See Nancy J. King & Joseph L. Hoffmann, *Habeas for the 21st Century: Uses, Abuses, and the Future of the Great Writ* (2011), Chapter 7.

§ 2. ISSUES COGNIZABLE

1. ***From jurisdictional to constitutional error.*** Before the middle decades of the twentieth century when the Court expanded the constitutional obligations of state courts in criminal cases, federal habeas review was available only when a prisoner challenged the *jurisdiction* of the court of conviction. As the Court expanded the list of constitutional rules of criminal procedure that state courts must follow, it also expanded federal habeas review to reach claims that the new constitution rules had been violated. By 1963, the Court held that federal constitutional claims were cognizable on habeas review of state criminal judgments. *Fay v. Noia*, 372 U.S. 391 (1963). Speaking for a 6–3 majority in *Fay*, Justice Brennan noted: "Although in form the Great Writ is simply a mode of procedure, its history is inextricably intertwined with the growth of fundamental rights of personal liberty. For its function has been to provide a prompt and efficacious remedy for whatever society deems to be intolerable restraints. Its root principle is that in a civilized society, government must always be accountable to the judiciary for a man's imprisonment: if the imprisonment cannot be shown to conform with fundamental requirements of law, the individual is entitled to his immediate release. * * * Although the Act of 1867, like its English and American predecessors, nowhere defines habeas corpus, its expansive language and imperative tone, viewed against the background of post-Civil War efforts in Congress to deal severely with the States of the former Confederacy, would seem to make inescapable the conclusion that Congress was enlarging the habeas remedy as previously understood, not only in extending its coverage to state prisoners, but also in making its procedures more efficacious. In 1867, Congress was anticipating resistance to its Reconstruction measures and planning the implementation of the post-war constitutional Amendments. Debated and enacted at the very peak of the Radical Republicans' power * * *, the Act of 1867 seems plainly to have been designed to furnish a method additional to and independent of direct Supreme Court review of state court decisions for the vindication of the new constitutional guarantees." Through habeas review of state court application of constitutional rules of procedure, the lower federal courts were able to assist the Supreme Court in developing and enforcing those new rules.

2. ***Theories for restricting the scope of habeas review.*** Should the writ be available whenever a petitioner can show that a state court violated his constitutional rights? This broad view of habeas relief follows if the purpose of the writ is to enlist the lower federal courts to provide some federal review of state convictions, review that cannot possibly be provided in every case by the Supreme Court on direct appeal. See Barry Friedman, *A Tale of Two Habeas*, 73 Minn.L.Rev. 247 (1988).

A contrasting approach envisions habeas not as a device to correct all erroneous state court interpretations of federal law, but instead as a process guarantee, providing a federal forum to raise a constitutional claim only when the state fails to provide a "full and fair opportunity" to litigate that claim. See *Wright v. West*, 505 U.S. 277 (1992) (opinion of Thomas, J.).

Another theory is that the expansion of habeas review of state court judgments was needed to respond to an imbalance in federalism, serving as a stop-gap while states adjusted their own remedies to accommodate drastic changes in federal law. Under this view, routine federal habeas review of state non-capital criminal judgments is no longer appropriate once state courts develop mechanisms for reviewing compliance with new constitutional rules. King & Hoffmann, *supra*.

Alternatively, the purpose of habeas review could be to deter or correct only the very worst state court transgressions, cases in which state courts adopt unreasonable interpretations of existing federal law. This theory is reflected in the current habeas statute. As the Court explained in *Harrington v. Richter*, 562 U.S. 86 (2011), p. 1452, "Section 2254(d) reflects the view that habeas corpus is a 'guard against extreme malfunctions in the state criminal justice systems,' not a substitute for ordinary error correction through appeal." The statute, the Court explained, "is designed to confirm that state courts are the principal forum for asserting constitutional challenges to state convictions."

Still another theory of habeas review was championed in the opinions of Justice Powell. Concurring in *Schneckloth v. Bustamonte*, 412 U.S. 218 (1973), Justice Powell asserted that federal courts should review claims raised by state prisoners only when those claims relate to the determination of the defendant's *factual guilt*. The state in *Schneckloth* had argued that violations of *Mapp v. Ohio*, 367 U.S. 643 (1961), should not be cognizable in habeas corpus proceedings. The Court majority, finding that there had been no Fourth Amendment violation, did not reach that issue. But Justice Powell, joined by Chief Justice Burger and Justice Rehnquist, argued that limiting the habeas remedy to claims "relating to guilt or innocence" was supported by an examination of "the costs" of federal habeas review, as measured "in terms of [its] serious intrusions on other societal values." These values include "(i) the most effective utilization of limited judicial resources, (ii) the necessity of finality in criminal trials, (iii) the minimization of friction between our federal and state systems of justice, and (iv) the maintenance of the constitutional balance upon which the doctrine of federalism is founded." He concluded, "To the extent that every state criminal judgment is to be subject indefinitely to broad and repetitive federal oversight, we render the actions of state courts a serious disrespect in derogation of the constitutional balance between the two systems. The present expansive scope of federal habeas review has prompted no small friction between state and federal judiciaries." Quoting Judge Henry J. Friendly's influential article, *Is Innocence Irrelevant? Collateral Attack on Criminal Judgments,* 38 U. Chi. L. Rev. 142 (1970), Justice Powell argued that " 'convictions should be subject to collateral attack only when the prisoner supplements his constitution plea with a colorable claim of innocence.' " As is clear from the case that follows, Justice Powell's position gained ground.

STONE V. POWELL

428 U.S. 465, 96 S.Ct. 3037, 49 L.Ed.2d 1067 (1976).

JUSTICE POWELL delivered the opinion of the Court.

The question presented is whether a federal court should consider, in ruling on a petition for habeas corpus relief filed by a state prisoner, a claim that evidence obtained by an unconstitutional search or seizure was introduced at his trial, when he has previously been afforded an opportunity for full and fair litigation of his claim in the state courts. We hold * * * that where the State has provided an opportunity for full and fair litigation of a Fourth Amendment claim, the Constitution does not require that a state prisoner be granted federal habeas corpus relief on the ground that evidence obtained in an unconstitutional search or seizure was introduced at his trial. * * *

The exclusionary rule [is] a judicially created means of effectuating the rights secured by the Fourth Amendment. * * * The primary justification for the exclusionary rule * * * is the deterrence of police conduct that violates Fourth Amendment rights. Post-*Mapp* decisions have established that the rule is not a personal constitutional right. It is not calculated to redress the injury to the privacy of the victim of the search or seizure, for any "[r]eparation comes too late." * * *

The costs of applying the exclusionary rule even at trial and on direct review are well known * * *. [The Court here discussed those costs, which were said to include the "divert[ing] of attention from the ultimate question of guilt or innocence that should be the central concern in a criminal proceeding," the exclusion of "typically reliable" physical evidence, the "deflect[ion] of the truthfinding process" that "often frees the guilty," and, where the rule is applied "indiscriminately," without regard to the "disparity * * * between the error committed by the police and the windfall afforded a guilty defendant," the possibility of "generating disrespect for the law and the administration of justice."] These long-recognized costs of the rule persist when a criminal conviction is sought to be overturned on collateral review on the ground that a search-and-seizure claim was erroneously rejected by two or more tiers of state courts.

Evidence obtained by police officers in violation of the Fourth Amendment is excluded at trial in the hope that the frequency of future violations will decrease. Despite the absence of supportive empirical evidence, we have assumed that the immediate effect of exclusion will be to discourage law enforcement officials from violating the Fourth Amendment by removing the incentive to disregard it. More importantly, over the long term, this demonstration that our society attaches serious consequences to violation of constitutional rights is thought to encourage those who formulate law enforcement policies, and the officers who implement them, to incorporate Fourth Amendment ideals into their value system.

We adhere to the view that these considerations support the implementation of the exclusionary rule at trial and its enforcement on direct appeal of state court convictions. But the additional contribution, if any, of the consideration of search-and-seizure claims of state prisoners on collateral review is small in relation to the costs. To be sure, each case in which such claim is considered may add marginally to an awareness of the values protected by the Fourth Amendment. There is no reason to believe, however, that the overall educative effect of the exclusionary rule would be appreciably diminished if search-and-seizure claims could not be raised in federal habeas corpus review of state convictions. Nor is there reason to assume that any specific disincentive already created by the risk of exclusion of evidence at trial or the reversal of convictions on direct review would be enhanced if there were the further risk that a conviction obtained in state court and affirmed on direct review might be overturned in collateral proceedings often occurring years after the incarceration of the defendant. The view that the deterrence of Fourth Amendment violations would be furthered rests on the dubious assumption that law enforcement authorities would fear that federal habeas review might reveal flaws in a search or seizure that went undetected at trial and on appeal.[35] Even if one rationally could assume that some additional incremental deterrent effect would be present in isolated cases, the resulting advance of the legitimate goal of furthering Fourth Amendment rights would be outweighed by the acknowledged costs to other values vital to a rational system of criminal justice.

* * *

[Dissenting JUSTICE BRENNAN, joined by MARSHALL, J., argued that the Court was losing sight of the basic function of the habeas writ.] The Court* * * acknowledges that respondents had the right to obtain a reversal of their convictions on appeal in the state courts or on certiorari to this Court. * * * The Court, however, simply ignores the settled principle that for purposes of adjudicating constitutional claims Congress, which has the power to do so under Art. III of the Constitution, has effectively cast the district courts sitting in habeas in the role of surrogate Supreme Courts. * * * The procedural safeguards mandated in the Framers' Constitution are not admonitions to be tolerated only to the extent they serve functional purposes that ensure that the "guilty" are punished and the "innocent" freed; rather, every guarantee enshrined in the Constitution, our basic charter and the guarantor of our most precious liberties, is by it endowed with an independent vitality and value, and this Court is not free to curtail those constitutional guarantees even to punish the most obviously guilty. * * *"

[35] The policy arguments that respondents marshal in support of the view that federal habeas corpus review is necessary to effectuate the Fourth Amendment stem from a basic mistrust of the state courts as fair and competent forums for the adjudication of federal constitutional rights. The argument is that state courts cannot be trusted to effectuate Fourth Amendment values through fair application of the rule, and the oversight jurisdiction of this Court on certiorari is an inadequate safeguard. The principal rationale for this view emphasizes the broad differences in the respective institutional setting within which federal judges and state judges operate. Despite differences in institutional environment and the unsympathetic attitude to federal constitutional claims of some state judges in years past, we are unwilling to assume that there now exists a general lack of appropriate sensitivity to constitutional rights in the trial and appellate courts of the several States. * * *

NOTES AND QUESTIONS

1. ***The Court's refusal to extend* Stone.** In a series of subsequent cases, the Court declined to extend *Stone* to bar habeas review of other types of constitutional claims. Of the theories explaining habeas review listed in Note 2, p. 1429, which best support the Court's decision in *Stone?* Which explain *Withrow v. Williams,* 507 U.S. 680 (1993) (permitting review of *Miranda* violations, noting *Miranda* guards against unreliable statements at trial, protects a fundamental trial right, and that barring such claims would not lighten the burden courts bear, as they would easily be recast as involuntariness claims); *Rose v. Mitchell*, p. 954 (grand jury discrimination), or *Kimmelman v. Morrison*, p. 138 (ineffective assistance in failing to raise Fourth Amendment claim), both described in *Withrow*?

2. ***"Bare" or "freestanding" claims of innocence.*** It remains unclear whether a petitioner who presents persuasive new evidence of innocence but alleges no procedural error can establish a violation of the Constitution that would entitle him to federal habeas corpus relief. In *Herrera v. Collins,* 506 U.S. 390 (1993), two justices asserted that there "is no basis in text, tradition, or even contemporary practice (if that were enough), for finding in the Constitution a right to demand judicial consideration of newly discovered evidence of innocence brought forward after conviction." Three other justices concluded there was such a right, "at least in capital cases," so that on federal habeas corpus the petitioner would be entitled to relief if he showed that he "probably is innocent." But the other four justices did not reach that issue, for they concluded the petitioner had not made the "extraordinarily high" showing of actual innocence which would be required were there such a right. In *House v. Bell*, 547 U.S. 518 (2006) (also discussed at p. 1441), the Court again declined to decide whether federal courts have authority to review a freestanding claim of innocence as a basis for invalidating a state conviction or death sentence. Although House had managed to gather DNA and other forensic evidence that "cast considerable doubt on his guilt—doubt sufficient to satisfy [the] standard for obtaining federal review despite a state procedural default," [described in Section 4, *infra*] his was "not a case of conclusive exoneration." His showing fell "short of the threshold implied in *Herrera*." Later, in *In re Davis*, 557 U.S. 952 (2009), the Court took the remarkable step of transferring to the district court a claim of innocence raised by a capital petitioner in an original habeas petition filed in the Supreme Court under 28 U.S.C. § 2241, and ordered the district court to "receive testimony and make findings of fact as to whether evidence that could not have been obtained at the time of trial clearly establishes petitioner's innocence." After doing so, the district court concluded that "while executing an innocent person would violate the United States Constitution, Mr. Davis has failed to prove his innocence." The Court has yet to resolve "whether a prisoner may be entitled to habeas relief based on a freestanding claim of actual innocence." *McQuiggin v. Perkins*, 569 U.S. 383 (2013).

What are the potential costs and challenges of permitting the relitigation of factual guilt in collateral proceedings? For more on judicial review of innocence claims, see Brandon Garrett, *Convicting the Innocent: Where Criminal Prosecutions Go Wrong* (2011); Nancy J. King, *The Judicial System: Appeals and Post-conviction Review*, in Examining Wrongful Convictions: Stepping Back, Moving Forward (A. Redlich, et al., eds., 2014). For a different and promising approach for investigating cases of actual innocence, see Robert P. Mosteller, *N.C. Innocence Inquiry Commission's First Decade: Impressive Successes and Lessons Learned*, 94 N.C. L. Rev. 1725 (2016). On whether a plea of guilty inherently waives such a claim in state post-conviction, see Note 1, p. 1228.

§ 3. LATE OR SUCCESSIVE PETITIONS

1. ***Filing deadlines.*** To promote the finality of criminal judgments, Subsection (d) of § 2244 added a one-year time period in which a petitioner may file his habeas petition. This filing period ordinarily runs from the date on which the judgment being challenged becomes final on

direct review, but is tolled while a properly filed collateral attack is pending before the state courts. A later starting point is provided where: (1) state action in violation of the Constitution or other federal law impeded the timely filing of the habeas petition; (2) the petition relies on a constitutional right that was initially recognized by the Supreme Court after the date of finality and was also held to apply retroactively; or (3) the petition relies on a constitutional claim as to which the factual predicate could not have been discovered by the date of finality by the exercise of due diligence. An estimated 20% of the petitions filed by state prisoners in 2003 and 2004 were dismissed as time barred, as were 4% of petitions filed by death row petitioners between 2000 and 2002. King, et al., 2007 Habeas Study.

In *Holland v. Florida*, 560 U.S. 631 (2010), the Court held that a the limitations period may be "equitably tolled" if a petitioner shows "(1) that he has been pursuing his rights diligently, and (2) that some extraordinary circumstance stood in his way" and prevented timely filing. " '[A' garden variety claim of excusable neglect,' such as a simple 'miscalculation' that leads a lawyer to miss a filing deadline, does not warrant equitable tolling," the Court explained. But "the facts of this case present far more serious instances of attorney misconduct." Collins, the attorney appointed to represent Holland in his post-conviction challenges to his capital conviction and sentence, "failed to file Holland's federal petition on time despite Holland's many letters that repeatedly emphasized the importance of his doing so", "did not do the research necessary to find out the proper filing date, despite Holland's letters that went so far as to identify the applicable legal rules"; "failed to inform Holland in a timely manner about the crucial fact that the Florida Supreme Court had decided his case, again despite Holland's many pleas for that information" and "failed to communicate with his client over a period of years, despite various pleas from Holland that Collins respond to his letters." The Court stated "these various failures violated fundamental canons of professional responsibility," and "seriously prejudiced a client who thereby lost what was likely his single opportunity for federal habeas review of the lawfulness of his imprisonment and of his death sentence." Rather than hold that these circumstances constituted an extraordinary circumstance that entitled Holland to equitable tolling, the Court remanded the case for determination by the court of appeals. The Court did find Holland had established the "reasonable diligence," required for tolling. "Here, Holland not only wrote his attorney numerous letters seeking crucial information and providing direction; he also repeatedly contacted the state courts, their clerks, and the Florida State Bar Association in an effort to have Collins—the central impediment to the pursuit of his legal remedy—removed from his case. And, the *very day* that Holland discovered that his AEDPA clock had expired due to Collins' failings, Holland prepared his own habeas petition *pro se* and promptly filed it with the District Court."

Noting that "[s]ensitivity to the injustice of incarcerating an innocent individual should not abate when the impediment is AEDPA's statute of limitations," the Court later held in *McQuiggin v. Perkins*, 569 U.S. 383 (2013), that a petitioner who does not qualify for equitable tolling under *Holland* may nevertheless avoid the statutory time bar if he convinces "the district court that, in light of the new evidence, no juror, acting reasonably, would have voted to find him guilty beyond a reasonable doubt." The Court thought it reasonable to assume that "Congress would want a limitations period to yield when what is at stake is a State's incarceration of an individual for a crime, it has become clear, no reasonable person would find he committed." Four dissenting justices disagreed, calling the Court's ruling "a pure judicial override of the statute Congress enacted."

2. *Successive petitions.* Section 2244(b)(1) states: "A claim presented in a second or successive habeas corpus application under section 2254 that was presented in a prior application shall be dismissed." Another provision bars review of any claim not presented in a prior application unless a court of appeals first certifies that the claim 1) relies on a new rule of constitutional law made retroactively applicable by the Supreme Court, or 2) is based on facts—not previously discoverable through due diligence—that establish by clear and convincing evidence that but for the error, no reasonable factfinder would have found the applicant guilty of the underlying offense.

§ 4. CLAIMS FORECLOSED BY PROCEDURAL DEFAULT

1. ***Procedural default defined.*** In addition to restrictions on habeas review described above, a state's attorney responding to a prisoner's petition may raise "state procedural default" as a defense to habeas review. Developed by the Court over many decades, this defense is available when a habeas petitioner seeks to rely on a constitutional claim that was not presented in the state court in accordance with applicable state procedural requirements and therefore would be viewed under state law as "waived," "defaulted," or "forfeited," and dismissed.

2. ***Adequate and independent state ground.*** To establish the defense of procedural default, a state must first show that "the decision of [the state] court rests on a state law ground that is independent of the federal question" and is "adequate to support the judgment." *Coleman v. Thompson*, Note 1.b., p. 1438. A state rule is not inadequate just because it is discretionary rather than mandatory, *Beard v. Kindler*, 558 U.S. 53 (2009), or just because it is imprecise. *Walker v. Martin*, 562 U.S. 307 (2011). It might be inadequate, however, if (1) the state had not enforced its procedural rule consistently; (2) the petitioner had substantially complied with the rule's essential requirements; (3) the petitioner had no opportunity to comply with the rule; or (4) the rule required the petitioner to raise his objection repeatedly at trial, even when the judge had unambiguously ruled against him on the same objection. See *Lee v. Kemna*, 534 U.S. 362 (2002).

3. ***The development of the "cause-and-prejudice" standard.*** Assuming the state ruling dismissing the petitioner's claim before reaching its merits rested on an adequate and independent state procedural rule, is federal review always barred? At first, the defense of procedural default was limited to petitioners who fell within what came to be known as the "deliberate bypass" standard of *Fay v. Noia*, (Note 1, p. 1429). Speaking for a 6–3 majority, Justice Brennan concluded that a claim should be cognizable on a federal habeas petition *unless* the petitioner "understandingly and knowingly forewent the privilege of seeking to vindicate his federal claims in the state courts, whether for strategic, tactical, or any other reasons that can fairly be described as the deliberate bypassing of state procedures." As the Court became increasingly concerned about the costs of habeas review, however, it abandoned this standard in favor of a rule restricting review to only those petitioners who could show "cause" for and "prejudice" from the failure to comply with state procedure, firmly established by the case that follows.

WAINWRIGHT V. SYKES

433 U.S. 72, 97 S.Ct. 2497, 53 L.Ed.2d 594 (1977).

JUSTICE REHNQUIST delivered the opinion of the Court.

[At Sykes' trial for murder the prosecution introduced into evidence an incriminating statement that Sykes had given to the police after having been warned of his *Miranda* rights. Sykes claimed in his federal habeas petition that the statement was involuntary because he had not understood the *Miranda* warnings, but he had not raised that claim in the trial court, either before or during trial as required by the state's "contemporaneous-objection" rule (Fla.R.Crim.P. 3.190). Sykes also failed to raise his *Miranda* claim on appeal, but even if that had been done, the Florida appellate courts would not have considered the issue since Sykes had not complied with Rule 3.190. The federal Court of Appeals relied on *Fay v. Noia* to find that habeas review of the claim was not barred.]

* * * The simple legal question before the Court calls for a construction of the language of 28 U.S.C. § 2254(a), which provides that the federal courts shall entertain an application for a writ of habeas corpus "in behalf of a person in custody pursuant to the judgment of a state court only on the ground that he is in custody in violation of the Constitution or laws or treaties of the United States." But, to put it mildly, we do not write on a clean slate in construing this statutory provision. * * *

[The Court here discussed Supreme Court decisions dealing with several major issues relating to the scope of the writ, "illustrat[ing] this Court's historical willingness to overturn or modify its earlier views of the scope of the writ, even where the statutory language authorizing judicial action has remained unchanged." With this precedent in mind, the Court then turned to the issue before it—which it described as determining when "an adequate and independent state ground [will] bar consideration of otherwise cognizable federal issues on federal habeas review."]

[I]t is a well-established principle of federalism that a state decision resting on an adequate foundation of state substantive law is immune from review in the federal courts. * * * The area of controversy which has developed has concerned the reviewability of federal claims which the state court has declined to pass on because [they were] not presented in the manner prescribed by its *procedural* rules. The adequacy of such an independent state procedural ground to prevent federal habeas review of the underlying federal issue has been treated very differently than where the state-law ground is substantive. * * *

To the extent that the dicta of *Fay v. Noia* may be thought to have laid down an all-inclusive rule rendering state contemporaneous objection rules ineffective to bar review of underlying federal claims in federal habeas proceedings—absent a "knowing waiver" or a "deliberate bypass" of the right to so object—its effect was limited by *Francis,* which applied a different rule and barred a habeas challenge to the makeup of a grand jury. * * * Shall the rule of *Francis v. Henderson,* supra, barring federal habeas review absent a showing of "cause" and "prejudice" attendant to a state procedural waiver, be applied to a waived objection to the admission of a confession at trial? We answer that question in the affirmative.

* * * We leave open for resolution in future decisions the precise definition of the "cause"-and-"prejudice" standard, and note here only that it is narrower than the standard set forth in dicta in *Fay v. Noia,* which would make federal habeas review generally available to state convicts absent a knowing and deliberate waiver of the federal constitutional contention. It is the sweeping language of *Fay v. Noia,* going far beyond the facts of the case eliciting it, which we today reject.

The reasons for our rejection of it are several. The contemporaneous-objection rule itself is by no means peculiar to Florida, and deserves greater respect than *Fay* gives it, both for the fact that it is employed by a coordinate jurisdiction within the federal system and for the many interests which it serves in its own right. A contemporaneous objection enables the record to be made with respect to the constitutional claim when the recollections of witnesses are freshest, not years later in a federal habeas proceeding. It enables the judge who observed the demeanor of those witnesses to make the factual determinations necessary for properly deciding the federal constitutional question. While the [habeas statute] requires deference to be given to such determinations made by state courts, the determinations themselves are less apt to be made in the first instance if there is no contemporaneous objection to the admission of the evidence on federal constitutional grounds.

A contemporaneous-objection rule may lead to the exclusion of the evidence objected to, thereby making a major contribution to finality in criminal litigation. Without the evidence claimed to be vulnerable on federal constitutional grounds, the jury may acquit the defendant, and that will be the end of the case; or it may nonetheless convict the defendant, and he will have one less federal constitutional claim to assert in his federal habeas petition. If the state trial judge admits the evidence in question after a full hearing, the federal habeas court * * * will gain significant guidance from the state ruling in this regard. Subtler considerations as well militate in favor of honoring a state contemporaneous-objection rule. An objection on the spot may force the prosecution to take a hard look at its hole card, and even if the prosecutor thinks that the state trial judge will admit the evidence he must contemplate the possibility of reversal by the state appellate courts or the ultimate issuance of a federal writ of habeas corpus based on the impropriety of the state court's rejection of the federal constitutional claim.

We think that the rule of *Fay v. Noia,* broadly stated, may encourage "sandbagging" on the part of defense lawyers, who may take their chances on a verdict of not guilty in a state trial court with the intent to raise their constitutional claims in a federal habeas court if their initial gamble does not pay off. The refusal of federal habeas courts to honor contemporaneous-objection rules may also make state courts themselves less stringent in their enforcement. Under the rule of *Fay v. Noia,* state appellate courts know that a federal constitutional issue raised for the first time in the proceeding before them may well be decided in any event by a federal habeas tribunal. Thus, their choice is between addressing the issue notwithstanding the petitioner's failure to timely object, or else face the prospect that the federal habeas court will decide the questions without the benefit of their views.

The failure of the federal habeas courts generally to require compliance with a contemporaneous-objection rule tends to detract from the perception of the trial of a criminal case in state court as a decisive and portentous event. A defendant has been accused of a serious crime, and this is the time and place set for him to be tried by a jury of his peers and found either guilty or not guilty by that jury. To the greatest extent possible all issues which bear on this charge should be determined in this proceeding: the accused is in the courtroom, the jury is in the box, the judge is on the bench, and the witnesses, having been subpoenaed and duly sworn, await their turn to testify. Society's resources have been concentrated at that time and place in order to decide, within the limits of human fallibility, the question of guilt or innocence of one of its citizens. Any procedural rule which encourages the result that those proceedings be as free of error as possible is thoroughly desirable, and the contemporaneous-objection rule surely falls within this classification.

We believe the adoption of the *Francis* rule in this situation will have the salutary effect of making the state trial on the merits the "main event," so to speak, rather than a "tryout on the road" for what will later be the determinative federal habeas hearing. There is nothing in the Constitution or in the language of § 2254 which requires that the state trial on the issue of guilt or innocence be devoted largely to the testimony of fact witnesses directed to the elements of the state crime, while only later will there occur in a federal habeas hearing a full airing of the federal constitutional claims which were not raised in the state proceedings. If a criminal defendant thinks that an action of the state trial court is about to deprive him of a federal constitutional right there is every reason for his following state procedure in making known his objection.

The "cause"-and-"prejudice" exception of the *Francis* rule will afford an adequate guarantee, we think, that the rule will not prevent a federal habeas court from adjudicating for the first time the federal constitutional claim of a defendant who in the absence of such an adjudication will be the victim of a miscarriage of justice. Whatever precise content may be given those terms by later cases, we feel confident in holding without further elaboration that they do not exist here. Respondent has advanced no explanation whatever for his failure to object at trial, and, as the proceeding unfolded, the trial judge is certainly not to be faulted for failing to question the admission of the confession himself. The other evidence of guilt presented at trial, moreover, was substantial to a degree that would negate any possibility of actual prejudice resulting to the respondent from the admission of his inculpatory statement.

We accordingly conclude that the judgment of the Court of Appeals for the Fifth Circuit must be reversed, and the cause remanded * * * with instructions to dismiss respondent's petition for a writ of habeas corpus.

JUSTICE STEVENS, concurring.

* * * [C]ompetent trial counsel could well have made a deliberate decision not to object to the admission of the respondent's in-custody statement. That statement was consistent, in many respects, with the respondent's trial testimony. It even had some positive value, since it portrayed the respondent as having acted in response to provocation, which might have influenced the jury to return a verdict on a lesser charge. . . . it would have been admissible for impeachment in any event, *Harris v. New York* [p. 835]. Counsel may well have preferred to have the statement admitted without objection when it was first offered rather than making an objection which, at best, could have been only temporarily successful. * * *

[The concurring opinions of Justice White and Chief Justice Burger are omitted].

JUSTICE BRENNAN, with whom JUSTICE MARSHALL joins, dissenting.

* * *

[A]ny realistic system of federal habeas corpus jurisdiction must be premised on the reality that the ordinary procedural default is born of the inadvertence, negligence, inexperience, or incompetence of trial counsel. The case under consideration today is typical. The Court makes no effort to identify a tactical motive for the failure of Sykes' attorney to challenge the admissibility or reliability of a highly inculpatory statement. While my Brother Stevens finds a possible tactical advantage, I agree with the Court of Appeals that this reading is most implausible * * *

Punishing a lawyer's unintentional errors by closing the federal courthouse door to his client is both a senseless and misdirected method of deterring the slighting of state rules. It is senseless because unplanned and unintentional action of any kind generally is not subject to deterrence; and, to the extent that it is hoped that a threatened sanction addressed to the defense will induce greater care and caution on the part of trial lawyers, thereby forestalling negligent conduct or error, the potential loss of all valuable state remedies would be sufficient to this end. And it is a misdirected sanction because even if the penalization of incompetence or carelessness will encourage more thorough legal training and trial preparation, the habeas applicant, as opposed to his lawyer, hardly is the proper recipient of such a penalty. * * * This is especially true when so many indigent defendants are without any realistic choice in selecting who ultimately represents them at trial. Indeed, if responsibility for error must be apportioned between the parties, it is the State, through its attorney's admissions and certification policies, that is more fairly held to blame for the fact that practicing lawyers too often are ill-prepared or ill-equipped to act carefully and knowledgeably when faced with decisions governed by state procedural requirements. * * * In short, I believe that the demands of our criminal justice system warrant visiting the mistakes of a trial attorney on the head of a habeas corpus applicant only when we are convinced that the lawyer actually exercised his expertise and judgment in his client's service, and with his client's knowing and intelligent participation where possible. * * *

NOTES AND QUESTIONS

1. ***The meaning of cause.*** There are two primary ways to establish "cause" sufficient to excuse state procedural default: state interference and denial of constitutionally required effective assistance of counsel. In addition, the Court in 2012 recognized two additional narrow avenues for establishing "cause." All four types of "cause" are examined below.

a. ***"Cause" when default results from state interference with petitioner's opportunity to comply with state procedures.*** The Court in *Amadeo v. Zant,* 486 U.S. 214

(1988), found that "cause" excusing default is established by a showing that interference by state officials led to the petitioner's failure to comply with state procedures. In that case, interference was proven by evidence that a memorandum of the local prosecutor, noting a direction to the jury commissioners to limit the representation of blacks and women in the jury pool, had been concealed from the petitioner by local officials and therefore was "not reasonably discoverable" by petitioner's trial counsel, who had failed to object to the composition of the jury.

Similarly, a habeas petitioner's failure to pursue initially in state court a *Brady* claim (Ch. 21, Sec. 5) will be excused if the petitioner demonstrates: 1) that the state assured him in state court that it had furnished all *Brady* material; 2) that his reliance on that representation was reasonable; and 3) that the state had, contrary to its statements, withheld evidence favorable to the defense. See *Strickler v. Greene*, 527 U.S. 263 (1999); *Banks v. Dretke*, 540 U.S. 668 (2004). Explained the Court in *Banks*: "Our decisions lend no support to the notion that defendants must scavenge for hints of undisclosed *Brady* material when the prosecution represents that all such material has been disclosed." See also *Brown v. Allen*, 344 U.S. 443 (1953) (coerced confession claim cognizable in a case in which prison warden had suppressed a prisoner's timely appeal papers).

b. "Cause" when default results from state's failure to provide the effective assistance of constitutionally required counsel. The Court has recognized that the failure of defense counsel to raise a claim of constitutional error will constitute "cause" for default, when that failure amounts to a violation of the Sixth Amendment's right to the effective assistance of counsel. For example, a federal habeas court will consider the merits of a jury selection claim that a state court refused to reach because it was raised late, if the petitioner can show that his trial attorney's failure to raise the claim was itself a violation of *Strickland*, and that he pursued the *Strickland* violation in state court. See *Edwards v. Carpenter*, 529 U.S. 446 (2000). Not surprisingly, ineffective assistance claims are very common in habeas petitions, raised in approximately 81% of all capital habeas petitions, and just over half of all non-capital habeas petitions. King, et al., 2007 Habeas Study.

The scope and rationale for this rule was explained and applied by the Court in *Coleman v. Thompson*, 501 U.S. 722 (1991). Coleman's state post-conviction attorney missed the deadline for appealing his state post-conviction decision by three days. The state court then held the appeal was untimely and dismissed the claims. Coleman's procedural default, then, took place during the appeal from his state post-conviction proceeding. In rejecting Coleman's attempt to establish "cause and prejudice" for this default, the Supreme Court noted that " 'the existence of cause for a procedural default must ordinarily turn on whether the prisoner can show that some objective factor external to the defense impeded counsel's efforts to comply with the State's procedural rule.' For example, 'a showing that the factual or legal basis for a claim was not reasonably available to counsel, . . . or that 'some interference by officials' . . . made compliance impracticable, would constitute cause under this standard.' " Continued the Court, "Where a petitioner defaults a claim as a result of the denial of the right to effective assistance of counsel, the State, which is responsible for the denial as a constitutional matter, must bear the cost of any resulting default and the harm to state interests that federal habeas review entails. . . . In the absence of a constitutional violation, the petitioner bears the risk in federal habeas for all attorney errors made in the course of the representation." Because Coleman had no constitutional right to counsel for his state collateral appeal, his counsel's mistake, however egregious, did not itself amount to a violation of any constitutional right. Accordingly, there was no "cause" to excuse the default of his claims. Reiterated the Court in *Coleman*: "[C]ounsel's ineffectiveness will constitute cause only if it is an independent constitutional violation."

The Court has not interpreted the Constitution to mandate counsel during post-conviction proceedings. Yet most jurisdictions require that defendants wait until that stage, after direct appeal, to raise some constitutional claims—including ineffective assistance of counsel claims.[a] This means that under *Coleman,* if the absence or incompetence of state post-conviction counsel resulted in the petitioner's failure to comply with state procedural rules for raising his claim, he may receive no federal review unless he can show actual innocence, see Note 3, p. 1441.

c. "Cause" when default results from abandonment by legal representative. In *Maples v. Thomas*, 565 U.S. 266 (2012), Justice Ginsberg, writing for the Court, reiterated that cause for a procedural default "exists where 'something external to the petitioner, something that cannot fairly be attributed to him[,] . . . "impeded [his] efforts to comply with the State's procedural rule." ' *Coleman*. Negligence on the part of a prisoner's postconviction attorney does not qualify as 'cause.' That is so, we reasoned in *Coleman*, because the attorney is the prisoner's agent, and under 'well-settled principles of agency law,' the principal bears the risk of negligent conduct on the part of his agent. Thus, when a petitioner's postconviction attorney misses a filing deadline, the petitioner is bound by the oversight and cannot rely on it to establish cause. * * * A markedly different situation is presented, however, when an attorney abandons his client without notice, and there-by occasions the default. Having severed the principal-agent relationship, an attorney no longer acts, or fails to act, as the client's representative. His acts or omissions therefore 'cannot fairly be attributed to [the client].' *Coleman*. * * * [A] client cannot be charged with the acts or omissions of an attorney who has abandoned him. Nor can a client be faulted for failing to act on his own behalf when he lacks reason to believe his attorneys of record, in fact, are not representing him." Maples' attorneys had left their firm, "abandoned the case without leave of court, without informing Maples they could no longer represent him, and without securing any recorded substitution of counsel. * * * In these circumstances, no just system would lay the default at Maples' death-cell door. * * * He has shown ample cause, we hold, to excuse the procedural default into which he was trapped when counsel of record abandoned him without a word of warning."

d. Exception for substantial claims of ineffective assistance of trial counsel—"cause" when default results from state's failure to provide competent state post-conviction counsel. In *Martinez v. Ryan*, 566 U.S. 1 (2012), the Court carved out another narrow exception to the rule in *Coleman*. In *Martinez,* the Court held that the absence of effective assistance during initial review collateral proceedings may establish cause for a prisoner's default of one specific claim—the ineffective assistance of *trial* counsel—if state law required the prisoner to raise that claim in that collateral proceeding and not on direct appeal. Writing for the Court, Justice Kennedy explained that "where * * * the initial-review collateral proceeding is the first designated proceeding for a prisoner to raise a claim of ineffective assistance at trial, the collateral proceeding is in many ways the equivalent of a prisoner's direct appeal as to the ineffective-assistance claim." A prisoner presenting a claim of ineffective assistance at trial "likely needs an effective attorney," because these claims often require investigative work, an understanding of trial strategy, and information outside the trial record. "[W]hen a State requires a prisoner to raise an ineffective assistance of counsel claim in a collateral proceeding, a prisoner may establish cause for a default of an ineffective assistance claim in two circumstances. The first is where the state courts did not appoint counsel in the initial-review collateral proceeding for a claim of ineffective

[a] See also Note 4, pp. 124–125. In *Massaro v. United States*, 538 U.S. 500 (2003), the Court explained the justification for this approach: The trial court, in which collateral proceedings are filed, the Court reasoned, is "the forum best suited to developing the facts necessary to determining the adequacy of representation during an entire trial. The court may take testimony from witnesses * * * and from the counsel alleged to have rendered the deficient performance." When presented to the trial court in a post-conviction proceeding, rather than on appeal, the claim "often will be ruled upon by the same * * * judge who presided at trial, [who] should have an advantageous perspective for determining the effectiveness of counsel's conduct and whether any deficiencies were prejudicial." Were defendants required to raise ineffectiveness claims on direct appeal, the Court explained, "trial counsel [would] be unwilling to help appellate counsel familiarize himself with a record for the purpose of understanding how it reflects trial counsel's own incompetence," and "[a]ppellate courts would waste time and resources attempting to address some claims that were meritless and other claims that, though colorable, would be handled more efficiently if addressed in the first instance" by the trial court. See Note 4, p. 124.

assistance at trial. The second is where appointed counsel in the initial-review collateral proceeding, where the claim should have been raised, was ineffective under the standards of *Strickland*. To overcome the default, a prisoner must also demonstrate that the underlying ineffective-assistance-of-counsel claim is a substantial one, which is to say that the prisoner must demonstrate that the claim has some merit."

The *Martinez* Court was careful to note that this was an "equitable ruling" not a "constitutional" one, and "merely allows a federal court to consider the merits of a claim that otherwise would have been procedurally defaulted." The ruling "permits a State to elect between appointing counsel in initial-review collateral proceedings or not asserting a procedural default and raising a defense on the merits in federal habeas proceedings," and does not affect direct review of state collateral cases. The Court also stressed that its ruling affects only underlying claims of ineffective assistance of *trial* counsel,[b] and also does not concern defaults that occur in proceedings other than *initial* collateral review, including appeals from those proceedings, as was the case in *Coleman,* or successive collateral proceedings.

Justice Scalia, joined by Justice Thomas, dissented in *Martinez.* He criticized the Court's ruling as essentially forcing states to appoint counsel in post-conviction proceedings, ignoring "the very reason for a procedural-default rule: the comity and respect that federal courts must accord state-court judgments." He argued that the Court had abandoned the "North Star of our excuse-for-cause jurisprudence," namely that attorney error can be cause when it amounts to a factor "external to the petitioner." Lawyer errors are not external unless they amount to "constitutionally ineffective" assistance "imputed to the State (for the State has failed to comply with the constitutional requirement to provide effective counsel)," he reasoned. He also mocked the Court's effort to limit the ruling to ineffective assistance of trial counsel claims, predicting that it will be extended to other claims where a state post-conviction proceeding is the first opportunity to receive review, such as ineffective assistance of appellate counsel claims, *Brady* claims, and claims based on newly discovered evidence. By inviting litigation about the effectiveness of post-conviction and trial counsel in all federal habeas cases, he argued, the ruling will "squander[ ] state taxpayers' money" without making much difference in non-capital cases, and will defer execution in every capital case for several more years.

In *Trevino v. Thaler,* 569 U.S. 413 (2013), the Court explained that the *Martinez* holding applies where the state law does not actually "require" petitioners to wait until collateral review to claim ineffective assistance of trial counsel, but the "state procedural framework, by reason of its design and operation, makes it highly unlikely in a typical case that a defendant will have a meaningful opportunity to raise a claim of ineffective assistance of trial counsel on direct appeal." This phrase appears to describe the situation in the vast majority of states.

If you were a state legislator in one of these states, how would you evaluate the relative costs and benefits of the following: 1) amending state law to permit meaningful review of ineffective assistance of trial counsel claims on direct appeal, with remand for evidentiary hearings as necessary, 2) providing a statutory right to appointed counsel for petitioners in their initial state post-conviction proceedings; or 3) making no changes to state law and when petitioners raise defaulted ineffective assistance of trial counsel claims in federal habeas proceedings, defending those criminal judgments either by showing that that the claims are not "substantial" under *Martinez*, or by showing that the claims fail on the merits? For an empirically based argument

[b] The Court later declined "to extend *Martinez* to allow a federal court to hear a substantial, but procedurally defaulted, claim of ineffective assistance of appellate counsel when a prisoner's state postconviction counsel provides ineffective assistance by failing to raise that claim." Davila v. Davis, 137 S.Ct. 2058 (2017). It reasoned that such an extension is "not required to ensure that meritorious claims of trial error receive review by at least one state or federal court—the chief concern identified by this Court in *Martinez*" and "could ultimately knock down the procedural barriers to federal habeas review of nearly any defaulted claim of trial error," likely generating "high systemic costs and low systemic benefits."

that states will likely choose the third option, see Nancy J. King, *Enforcing Effective Assistance After* Martinez, 122 Yale L. J. 2428 (2013): "State judges know that strategies far less expensive than hearings and counsel are available to help deflect later attacks in federal habeas," such as "[i]ssuing an alternative ruling on the merits." Moreover, "[m]ost noncapital cases receiving federal habeas relief have been, and will continue to be, cheap to fix.". . . Even if state judges decided to safeguard their convictions against federal review by appointing counsel in postconviction cases, they could safely restrict this strategy to only those petitioners who are serving particularly lengthy sentences and challenging their *convictions* (not their sentences), after a trial (not a plea)." Compare Eve Brensike Primus, *Effective Trial Counsel after* Martinez v. Ryan: *Focusing on the Adequacy of State Procedures*, 122 Yale L. J. 2604 (2013) (arguing that to avoid the procedural default defense, petitioners should pursue arguments that state procedures for raising ineffectiveness claims are systematically inadequate, also stating "it is possible that refusing to give state prisoners reasonable opportunities to raise ineffective-assistance-of-trial-counsel claims will push the Supreme Court to recognize the constitutional right to postconviction counsel that it failed to recognize in [*Martinez*]. Alternatively, it might encourage the Court to look to other equitable doctrines to give states more of an incentive to provide defendants with a realistic chance to contend that their Sixth Amendment rights were violated.").

2. ***The meaning of prejudice.*** In *Kyles v. Whitley,* 514 U.S. 419 (1995), and *Strickler v. Greene*,527 U.S. 263 (1999), the Court explained that in order to establish prejudice under *Sykes*, a petitioner must demonstrate that there is a "reasonable probability that the result of the trial would have been different." A "reasonable probability" is described as a probability sufficient to "undermine confidence in the verdict." This is the same showing required for a claim of ineffective assistance of counsel under *Strickland.* See John Jeffries & William Stuntz, *Ineffective Assistance and Procedural Default in Federal Habeas Corpus,* 57 U. Chi. L. Rev. 679 (1990).

3. ***The miscarriage-of-justice or "actual-innocence" exception.*** In *Sykes,* the Court noted that the failure to establish cause and prejudice would not preclude habeas review "of the federal constitutional claim of a defendant who in the absence of such an adjudication will be the victim of a miscarriage of justice." Explaining the miscarriage-of-justice exception to the *Sykes* standard in *Murray v. Carrier,* 477 U.S. 478 (1986), Justice O'Connor stated: "[I]n an extraordinary case, where a constitutional violation has probably resulted in the conviction of one who is actually innocent, a federal habeas court may grant the writ even in the absence of a showing of cause for the procedural default." To establish the requisite probability, the Court explained later in *Schlup v. Delo*, 513 U.S. 298 (1995), the petitioner must show that it is more likely than not that no reasonable juror would have convicted him in the light of the new evidence. The petitioner thus is required to make a stronger showing than that needed to establish prejudice." In assessing the adequacy of petitioner's showing of actual innocence, "the district court is not bound by the rules of admissibility that would govern at trial. Instead, the emphasis on 'actual innocence' allows the reviewing tribunal also to consider the probative force of relevant evidence that was either excluded or unavailable at trial."

In *House v. Bell*, 547 U.S. 518 (2006), a majority of justices agreed the petitioner had met this stringent standard. Lower federal courts had rejected as procedurally defaulted House's claims that his murder conviction and death sentence should be invalidated due to alleged ineffective assistance of counsel and prosecutorial misconduct. The Supreme Court disagreed, finding that House's showing entitled him to pass through the *Schlup* "innocence gateway" and receive federal review of his defaulted claims. The Court emphasized that in evaluating whether a petitioner has demonstrated that "more likely than not any reasonable juror would have reasonable doubt," a habeas court must consider all the evidence, "old and new, incriminating and exculpatory, without regard to whether it would necessarily be admitted [at trial]."

At an evidentiary hearing before the federal trial judge, House had produced "new reliable evidence" of innocence, including (1) forensic evidence indicating that blood from the victim found on his pants was spilled on them from vials of blood taken from the victim at her autopsy; (2) DNA evidence demonstrating that the semen found on the victim's clothing was from her husband, not House; and (3) testimony by two different witnesses describing a confession to the killing by the victim's husband and the indifferent reception one of these witnesses encountered when reporting the confession to the Sheriff's Department, as well as testimony by other witnesses describing a history of abuse of the victim by her husband, and an attempt by the husband to construct a false alibi. A narrow five-justice majority disagreed with the district judge's assessment of this evidence and concluded that "the central forensic proof connecting House to the crime * * * has been called into question, and House has put forward substantial evidence pointing to a different suspect. * * * [A]lthough the issue is close, we conclude that this is the rare case where—had the jury heard all the conflicting testimony—it is more likely than not that no reasonable juror viewing the record as a whole would lack reasonable doubt."

House's success in casting doubt on his guilt did not mean he was entitled to habeas corpus relief from his capital conviction or sentence. Instead, his victory in the Supreme Court meant only that on remand he was entitled to federal review of the merits of his claims for ineffective assistance and prosecutorial misconduct. If either claim was established and habeas relief granted, nothing in the Constitution would bar the state from retrying House. This is because the *Schlup* "innocence gateway" is just that, a gateway to federal habeas review, not an independent determination that the petitioner is innocent or that the state's evidence of guilt was constitutionally insufficient. See Note 2, p. 1432 (discussing freestanding claims of actual innocence); *Jackson v. Virginia*, 443 U.S. 307 (1979), Note 3.a., p. 1412 (conviction is valid so long as federal court concludes, after viewing the evidence in the light most favorable to the prosecution, that any rational trier of fact could have found the essential elements beyond a reasonable doubt). On remand, the federal trial court did find that House had been denied the effective assistance of counsel and ordered the state to either release or retry him. Rather than retry the case, the prosecutor dropped the charges in May of 2009. House spent more than twenty years on death row.

4. ***Procedural default and guilty pleas.*** In *Bousley v. United States*, 523 U.S. 614 (1998), the Court applied the *Sykes* cause and prejudice standard to a petition seeking relief from a conviction following a plea of guilty. The issue in *Bousley* was whether the remedy under 28 U.S.C. § 2255 afforded any relief to a federal prisoner who pleaded guilty to an offense, the dimensions of which later were interpreted by the Court to be narrower than anyone at the prisoner's plea hearing had assumed. Claiming that his guilty plea was not intelligent, given his misunderstanding of the offense at the time of his plea, Bousley had sought collateral relief under § 2255.[c]

Writing for the Court, Chief Justice Rehnquist explained, "even the voluntariness and intelligence of a guilty plea can be attacked on collateral review only if first challenged on direct review. * * * Indeed, 'the concern with finality served by the limitation on collateral attack as special force with respect to convictions based on guilty pleas.'" The type of claims Bousely raised, he continued, "can be fully and completely addressed on direct review based on the record created at the plea colloquy. Where a defendant has procedurally defaulted a claim by failing to raise it on direct review, the claim may be raised in habeas only if the defendant can first demonstrate either 'cause' and actual 'prejudice,' * * * or that he is 'actually innocent.' * * * [Bousley's argument] that 'the legal basis for his claim was not reasonably available to counsel' at the time his plea was

[c] The Court's earlier ruling interpreting the scope of the federal statute applied retroactively to Bousley's conviction because that ruling "affected the reach of the underlying statute rather than the judicial procedures by which the statute is applied." See Note 1.c., p. 1449.

entered * * * is without merit. While we have held that a claim that 'is so novel that its legal basis is not reasonably available to counsel' may constitute cause for a procedural default, *Reed v. Ross*, 468 U.S. 1 (1984), petitioner's claim does not qualify as such. The argument that it was error for the District Court to misinform petitioner as to the statutory elements of [the offense] was most surely not a novel one." Also unavailing, concluded the Court, was Bousely's argument that raising his claim on direct appeal would have been futile. "[F]utility cannot constitute cause if it means simply that a claim was 'unacceptable to that particular court at that particular time.' "

Although unable to demonstrate "cause," Bousely deserved the opportunity on remand to "attempt to make a showing of actual innocence." The Court explained, "the Government is not limited to the existing record to rebut any showing that petitioner might make. Rather, on remand the Government should be permitted to present any admissible evidence of petitioner's guilt even if that evidence was not presented during petitioner's plea colloquy * * * . In cases where the Government has forgone more serious charges in the course of plea bargaining, petitioner's showing of actual innocence must also extend to those charges."

Justice Scalia, joined by Justice Thomas, criticized in his dissent the Court's requirement that the defendant show actual innocence of any more serious charge the Government has "forgone." "If, as is often the case, the bargaining occurred before the charge was filed * * * it will almost surely not be identifiable." Lower courts applying *Bousley* do not agree whether to measure "seriousness" using statutory or guidelines sentences. Should *equally* serious foregone charges be considered under *Bousley*'s analysis?

5. ***Failing to create a record in state court.*** A different kind of default occurs when petitioner raised his claim in state court, but failed to develop there the factual record supporting the claim. Section 2254(e)(2) now provides (emphasis added): "If the applicant has failed to develop the factual basis of a claim in State court proceedings, the court shall not hold an evidentiary hearing on the claim unless the applicant shows that—(A) the claim relies on—(i) a new rule of constitutional law, made retroactive to cases on collateral review by the Supreme Court, that was previously unavailable; or (ii) a factual predicate that could not have been previously discovered through the exercise of due diligence; *and* (B) the facts underlying the claim would be sufficient to establish by clear and convincing evidence that but for constitutional error, no reasonable fact-finder would have found the applicant guilty of the underlying offense."

The Court construed this provision in *Williams (Michael) v. Taylor*, 529 U.S. 420 (2000). A "fail[ure]" to develop the factual basis of a claim," is not established unless there is a lack of diligence, or some greater fault, attributable to the prisoner or the prisoner's counsel." Diligence "depends upon whether the prisoner made a reasonable attempt, in light of the information available at the time, to investigate and pursue claims in state court" and "in the usual case," will require "that the prisoner, at a minimum, seek an evidentiary hearing in state court in the manner prescribed by state law." Williams had not exercised the required diligence with respect to his *Brady* claim, the Court reasoned, because defense counsel had notice of the existence of the impeaching document at issue and failed to make an adequate effort to find it before filing the state petition. Williams was not barred from developing his claims of juror bias and prosecutorial misconduct in an evidentiary hearing, however, because it was only after an investigator helping with the federal petition stumbled upon a reason to check the County's marriage records that the petitioner learned that the woman who served as foreman of the jury was previously married to the lead police officer, and that she had been represented in the divorce by the prosecutor. Reasoning that defense counsel should not be expected to "check public records containing personal information pertaining to each and every juror," the Court held that Williams had made a reasonable effort to discover these claims.

If not barred by § 2254(e), an evidentiary hearing may be ordered or denied by the district court in the exercise of its discretion, after considering whether a hearing could enable an applicant to prove the petition's factual allegations. *Schriro v. Landrigan*, 550 U.S. 465 (2007). In in exercising that discretion, federal courts also look to factors noted in the pre-AEDPA case of *Townsend v. Sain*, 372 U.S. 293 (1963), cited in *Landrigan*. Those factors include whether the fact finding procedures in state court were adequate to afford a full and fair hearing.

§ 5. RETROACTIVITY—WHICH LAW APPLIES?

Assuming a petitioner's claim is not otherwise barred by the rules outlined above, it may fail if at the time that the state courts rejected it, the legal basis for the claim had not yet been established. The retroactive application of constitutional rules of criminal procedure in federal habeas proceedings was limited by the Court in the decision below.

TEAGUE V. LANE

489 U.S. 288, 109 S.Ct. 1060, 103 L.Ed.2d 334 (1989).

JUSTICE O'CONNOR announced the judgment of the Court and delivered the opinion of the Court with respects to Parts I, II, and III, and an opinion with respect to Parts IV and V, in which the CHIEF JUSTICE, JUSTICE SCALIA, and JUSTICE KENNEDY join.

[Teague, a black man, was convicted by an all-white Illinois jury of attempted murder, armed robbery, and aggravated battery. During jury selection, the prosecutor used all 10 of his peremptory challenges to exclude blacks, and Teague raised a fair cross section objection, which the trial judge denied. After failing to secure relief through direct appeal on his cross section claim, Teague filed a habeas corpus petition, adding a claim that the peremptory challenges violated *Swain v. Alabama*, p. 1251. After the Court of Appeals rejected both the equal protection and fair cross section claims, the Supreme Court granted certiorari.

The Court first held that Teague could not benefit from *Batson v. Kentucky*, p. 1250, because it was decided after his direct appeal was final, when his habeas petition was being considered by the Court of Appeals. A prior case, *Allen v. Hardy,* 478 U.S. 255 (1986), established that Batson did not apply retroactively. The Court then held that Teague's *Swain* claim was procedurally barred since it had not been properly raised before the state courts and petitioner made no showing of "cause and prejudice" under *Wainwright v. Sykes,* p. 1434. The Court's decision on Teague's properly preserved cross section claim appears below.]

IV

Petitioner's third and final contention is that the Sixth Amendment's fair cross-section requirement applies to the petit jury. As we noted at the outset, *Taylor* expressly stated that the fair cross section requirement does not apply to the petit jury. Petitioner nevertheless contends that the *ratio decidendi* of *Taylor* cannot be limited to the jury venire, and he urges adoption of a new rule. Because we hold that the rule urged by petitioner should not be applied retroactively to cases on collateral review, we decline to address petitioner's contention.

* * * In our view, the question "whether a decision [announcing a new rule should] be given prospective or retroactive effect should be faced at the time of [that] decision." * * * Retroactivity is properly treated as a threshold question, for, once a new rule is applied to the defendant in the case announcing the rule, even-handed justice requires that it be applied retroactively to all who are similarly situated. Thus, before deciding whether the fair cross section requirement should be extended to the petit jury, we should ask whether such a rule would be applied retroactively to the case at issue. * * *

It is admittedly often difficult to determine when a case announces a new rule, and we do not attempt to define the spectrum of what may or may not constitute a new rule for retroactivity purposes. In general, however, a case announces a new rule when it breaks new ground or imposes a new obligation on the States or the Federal Government. See, e.g., *Rock v. Arkansas* [Note 5, p. 1325] (*per se* rule excluding all hypnotically refreshed testimony infringes impermissibly on a criminal defendant's right to testify on his behalf). To put it differently, a case announces a new rule if the result was not *dictated* by precedent existing at the time the defendant's conviction became final. * * * Given the strong language in *Taylor* and our statement in *Akins v. Texas,* 325 U.S. 398 (1945), that "[f]airness in [jury] selection has never been held to require proportional representation of races upon a jury," application of the fair cross section requirement to the petit jury would be a new rule.

* * * Nearly a quarter of a century ago, in *Linkletter v. Walker*, 381 U.S. 618 (1965), the Court attempted to set some standards by which to determine the retroactivity of new rules. [Justice O'Connor here reviewed the development of the tripartite *Linkletter-Stovall* standard for determining the retroactive application of a new ruling on direct and collateral review.] Dissatisfied with the *Linkletter* standard, Justice Harlan advocated a different approach to retroactivity. He argued that new rules should always be applied retroactively to cases on direct review, but that generally they should not be applied retroactively to criminal cases on collateral review. See *Mackey v. United States,* 401 U.S. 667 (1971) (separate opinion of Harlan, J.); *Desist v. United States,* 394 U.S. 244 (1969) (Harlan, J., dissenting).

In *Griffith v. Kentucky*, 479 U.S. 314 (1987), we rejected as unprincipled and inequitable the *Linkletter* standard for cases pending on direct review at the time a new rule is announced, and adopted the first part of the retroactivity approach advocated by Justice Harlan. * * * [In part] because "selective application of new rules violates the principle of treating similarly situated defendants the same," we refused to continue to tolerate the inequity that resulted from not applying new rules retroactively to defendants whose cases had not yet become final. * * * [W]e held that "a new rule for the conduct of criminal prosecution is to be applied retroactively to all cases, state or federal pending on direct review or not yet final, with no exception for cases in which the new rule constitutes a 'clear break' with the past * * * ."

B.

Justice Harlan believed that new rules generally should not be applied retroactively to cases on collateral review. He argued that retroactivity for cases on collateral review could "be responsibly [determined] only by focusing, in the first instance, on the nature, function, and scope of the adjudicatory process in which such cases arise. * * * ." With regard to the nature of habeas corpus, Justice Harlan wrote:

> "Habeas corpus always has been a *collateral* remedy, providing an avenue for upsetting judgments that have become otherwise final. It is not designed as a substitute for direct review. The interest in leaving concluded litigation in a state of repose, that is, reducing the controversy to a final judgment not subject to further judicial revision, may quite legitimately be found by those responsible for defining the scope of the writ to outweigh in some, many, or most instances the competing interest in readjudicating convictions according to all legal standards in effect when a habeas petition is filed."

Given the "broad scope of constitutional issues cognizable on habeas," Justice Harlan argued that it is "sounder, in adjudicating habeas petitions, generally to apply the law prevailing at the time a conviction became final than it is to seek to dispose of [habeas] cases on the basis of intervening changes in constitutional interpretation." As he had explained in Desist, "the threat of habeas serves as a necessary incentive for trial and appellate judges throughout the land to conduct their proceedings in a manner consistent with established constitutional principles. In order to perform this deterrence function, . . . the habeas court need only apply the constitutional standards that prevailed at the time the original proceedings took place." * * *

Justice Harlan identified only two exceptions to his general rule of nonretroactivity for cases on collateral review. First, a new rule should be applied retroactively if it places "certain kinds of primary, private individual conduct beyond the power of the criminal law-making authority to proscribe." *Mackey*, 401 U.S., at 692 (Harlan, J.). Second, a new rule should be applied retroactively if it requires the observance of "those procedures that . . . are 'implicit in the concept of ordered liberty.'" Id. at 693 (quoting *Palko v. Connecticut*). * * *

We agree with Justice Harlan's description of the function of habeas corpus. "[T]he Court never has defined the scope of the writ simply by reference to a perceived need to assure that an individual accused of crime is afforded a trial free of constitutional error." * * * Rather, we have recognized that interests of comity and finality must also be considered in determining the proper scope of habeas review. Thus, if a defendant fails to comply with state procedural rules and is barred from litigating a particular constitutional claim in state court, the claim can be considered on federal habeas only if the defendant shows cause for the default and actual prejudice resulting therefrom. * * *

* * * Application of constitutional rules not in existence at the time a conviction became final seriously undermines the principle of finality which is essential to the operation of our criminal justice system. Without finality, the criminal law is deprived of much of its deterrent effect. The fact that life and liberty are at stake in criminal prosecutions "shows only that 'conventional notions of finality' should not have as *much* place in criminal as in civil litigation, not that they should have *none*." Friendly [Note 2, p. 1430]. * * * See also *Mackey* (Harlan, J.) ("No one, not criminal defendants, not the judicial system, not society as a whole is benefited by a judgment providing that a man shall tentatively go to jail today, but tomorrow and every day thereafter his continued incarceration shall be subject to fresh litigation."). * * *

The "costs imposed upon the State[s] by retroactive application of new rules of constitutional law on habeas corpus . . . generally far outweigh the benefits of this application." * * * In many ways the application of new rules to cases on collateral review may be more intrusive than the enjoining of criminal prosecutions, for it *continually* forces the States to marshal resources in order to keep in prison defendants whose trials and appeals conformed to then-existing constitutional standards. Furthermore, * * * "[s]tate courts are understandably frustrated when they faithfully apply existing constitutional law only to have a federal court discover, during a [habeas] proceeding, new constitutional commands."

We find these criticisms to be persuasive, and we now adopt Justice Harlan's view of retroactivity for cases on collateral review. Unless they fall within an exception to the general rule, new constitutional rules of criminal procedure will not be applicable to those cases which have become final before the new rules are announced.

V

Petitioner's conviction became final in 1983. As a result, the rule petitioner urges would not be applicable to this case, which is on collateral review, unless it would fall within an exception.

The first exception suggested by Justice Harlan—that a new rule should be applied retroactively if it places "certain kinds of primary, private individual conduct beyond the power of the criminal law-making authority to proscribe," *Mackey* (Harlan, J.)—is not relevant here. Application of the fair cross section requirement to the petit jury would not accord constitutional protection to any primary activity whatsoever.

The second exception suggested by Justice Harlan—that a new rule should be applied retroactively if it requires the observance of "those procedures that . . . are 'implicit in the concept of ordered liberty,'" *Mackey* (Harlan, J.)—we apply with a modification. The language used by Justice Harlan in *Mackey* leaves no doubt that he meant the second exception to be reserved for watershed rules of criminal procedure:

"Typically, it should be the case that any conviction free from federal constitutional error at the time it became final, will be found, upon reflection, to have been fundamentally fair and conducted under those procedures essential to the substance of a full hearing. However, in some situations it might be that time and growth in social capacity, as well as judicial perceptions of what we can rightly demand of the adjudicatory process, will properly alter our understanding of the *bedrock procedural elements* that must be found to vitiate the fairness of a particular conviction. For example, such, in my view, is the case with the right to counsel at trial now held a necessary condition precedent to any conviction for a serious crime."

In *Desist,* Justice Harlan had reasoned that one of the two principal functions of habeas corpus was "to assure that no man has been incarcerated under a procedure which creates an impermissibly large risk that the innocent will be convicted," and concluded "from this that all 'new' constitutional rules which significantly improve the pre-existing factfinding procedures are to be retroactively applied on habeas." * * *

We believe it desirable to combine the accuracy element of the *Desist* version of the second exception with the *Mackey* requirement that the procedure at issue must implicate the fundamental fairness of the trial. * * * [W]e believe that Justice Harlan's concerns about the difficulty in identifying both the existence and the value of accuracy-enhancing procedural rules can be addressed by limiting the scope of the second exception to those new procedures without which the likelihood of an accurate conviction is seriously diminished.

Because we operate from the premise that such procedures would be so central to an accurate determination of innocence or guilt, we believe it unlikely that many such components of basic due process have yet to emerge. We are also of the view that such rules are "best illustrated by recalling the classic grounds for the issuance of a writ of habeas corpus—that the proceeding was dominated by mob violence; that the prosecutor knowingly made use of perjured testimony; or that the conviction was based on a confession extorted from the defendant by brutal methods."

An examination of our decision in *Taylor* applying the fair cross section requirement to the jury venire leads inexorably to the conclusion that adoption of the rule petitioner urges would be a far cry from the kind of absolute prerequisite to fundamental fairness that is "implicit in the concept of ordered liberty." The requirement that the jury venire be composed of a fair cross section of the community is based on the role of the jury in our system. Because the purpose of the jury is to guard against arbitrary abuses of power by interposing the commonsense judgment of the community between the State and the defendant, the jury venire cannot be composed only of special segments of the population. * * * But as we stated in *Daniel v. Louisiana,* 420 U.S. 31 (1975), which held that *Taylor* was not to be given retroactive effect, the fair cross section requirement "[does] not rest on the premise that every criminal trial, or any particular trial, [is] necessarily unfair because it [is] not conducted in accordance with what we determined to be the requirements of the Sixth Amendment." Because the absence of a fair cross section on the jury venire does not undermine the fundamental fairness that must underlie a conviction or seriously diminish the likelihood of obtaining an accurate conviction, we conclude that a rule requiring that petit juries be composed of a fair cross section of the community would not be a "bedrock procedural element" that would be retroactively applied under the second exception we have articulated.

* * * [I]mplicit in the retroactivity approach we adopt today, is the principle that habeas corpus cannot be used as a vehicle to create new constitutional rules of criminal procedure unless those rules would be applied retroactively to all defendants on collateral review through one of the two exceptions we have articulated. Because a decision extending the fair cross section requirement to the petit jury would not be applied retroactively to cases on collateral review under the approach we adopt today, we do not address petitioner's claim.

[The concurring opinions of JUSTICES WHITE and BLACKMUN are omitted.]

JUSTICE STEVENS, with whom JUSTICE BLACKMUN joins as to Part I, concurring in part and concurring in the judgment.

* * * The plurality wrongly resuscitates Justice Harlan's early view, indicating that the only procedural errors deserving correction on collateral review are those that undermine "an accurate determination of innocence or guilt * * * ." * * * [A] touchstone of factual innocence would provide little guidance in certain important types of cases, such as those challenging the constitutionality of capital sentencing hearings. Even when assessing errors at the guilt phase of a trial, factual innocence is too capricious a factor by which to determine if a procedural change is sufficiently "bedrock" or "watershed" to justify application of the fundamental fairness exception. In contrast, given our century-old proclamation that the Constitution does not allow exclusion of jurors because of race, *Strauder v. West Virginia,* 100 U.S. 303 (1880), a rule promoting selection of juries free from racial bias clearly implicates concerns of fundamental fairness. * * * I would conclude that a guilty verdict delivered by a jury whose impartiality might have been eroded by racial prejudice is fundamentally unfair. Constraining that conclusion is the Court's holding in *Allen v. Hardy*—an opinion I did not join * * * [I]f there is no fundamental unfairness in denying retroactive relief to a petitioner denied his Fourteenth Amendment right to a fairly chosen jury, as the Court held in *Allen,* there cannot be fundamental unfairness in denying this petitioner relief for the violation of his Sixth Amendment right to an impartial jury. I therefore agree that the judgment of the Court of Appeals must be affirmed. * * *

JUSTICE BRENNAN, with whom JUSTICE MARSHALL joins, dissenting.

* * * [F]rom the plurality's exposition of its new rule, one might infer that its novel fabrication will work no great change in the availability of federal collateral review of state convictions. Nothing could be further from the truth. * * * Few decisions on appeal or collateral review are "*dictated*" by what came before. Most such cases involve a question of law that is at least debatable, permitting a rational judge to resolve the case in more than one way. Virtually no case that prompts a dissent on the relevant legal point, for example, could be said to be "*dictated*" by prior decisions. By the plurality's test, therefore, a great many cases could only be heard on habeas if the rule urged by the petitioner fell within one of the two exceptions the plurality has sketched. Those exceptions, however, are narrow. * * * The plurality's approach today can thus be expected to contract substantially the Great Writ's sweep.

Its impact is perhaps best illustrated by noting the abundance and variety of habeas cases we have decided in recent years that could never have been adjudicated had the plurality's new rule been in effect. * * * [Justice Brennan here listed several cases where the claim was novel and unlikely to have fit with the second exception, including *Moran v. Burbine*, 475 U.S. 412 (1986); *McKaskle v. Wiggins,* p. 104; *Estelle v. Smith,* p. 85; *Crist v. Bretz,* p. 1339; and *Barker v. Wingo,* p. 1071].

* * * Permitting the federal courts to decide novel habeas claims not substantially related to guilt or innocence has profited our society immensely. Congress has not seen fit to withdraw those benefits by amending the statute that provides for them. And although a favorable decision for a petitioner might not extend to another prisoner whose identical claim has become final, it is at least arguably better that the wrong done to one person be righted than that none of the injuries inflicted on those whose convictions have become final be redressed, despite the resulting inequality in treatment. * * *

NOTES AND QUESTIONS

1. ***The* Teague *three-step inquiry.*** Subsequent cases looked to the *Teague* plurality opinion as setting forth the Court's settled position on retroactivity. By 1997, the Court had distilled the "*Teague* inquiry" into three steps. See *O'Dell v. Netherland,* 521 U.S. 151 (1997).

a. ***Step 1: When did the petitioner's conviction become final?*** The first step involves the selection of the date on which the petitioner's conviction became final on direct appeal in the state system—that is, the expiration of defendant's opportunity to file a petition in the United States Supreme Court for a writ of certiorari, or the date that such a petition was denied. The Court in *Teague* refused to hold the state courts responsible for anticipating "new" developments in the law that occur after this date.

b. ***Step 2: Is the rule "new"?*** The second step is to determine whether the rule that the petitioner claims was violated was dictated by the law on the date determined in step one. If not, the rule is a "new" rule. Consider the conclusion of the majority in *Lambrix v. Singletary*, 520 U.S. 518 (1997). It was not enough that the rule of constitutional law that the habeas petitioner argued the state courts had violated was "a reasonable interpretation of prior law—perhaps even the most reasonable one." Instead, habeas review is limited to remedying violations of rules that were inescapable given prior law. In the Court's words, *Teague* asks "whether no other interpretation was reasonable." Even the Court's own declaration, in a case establishing a rule, that the rule was "compelled" by prior precedent will not remove that rule from the new rule category, if "a reasonable jurist * * * would not have felt compelled to adopt the rule." *O'Dell.*

The Court in *Beard v. Banks*, 542 U.S. 406 (2004), also suggested that if the United States Supreme Court decision announcing the rule that petitioner seeks to apply was closely divided on the merits, the rule is not likely to apply retroactively. *Banks* held that the rule in *Mills v. Maryland,* 486 U.S. 367 (1988) (invalidating capital sentencing schemes that require juries to disregard mitigating factors not found unanimously), was "new," because it "broke new ground" and was not "mandate[d]" by precedent. Pointing out that four justices dissented in *Mills,* at least one of whom protested that the decision was "stretching" precedent beyond proper bounds, the *Banks* majority concluded that "reasonable jurists differed" as to whether the rule the petitioner asked to be applied to him was "compel[led]" by existing precedent. Nevertheless, the Court observed later, quoting *Banks,* " 'the mere existence of a dissent,' like the existence of conflicting authority in state or lower federal courts, does not establish that a rule is new." *Chaidez v. United States*, 568 U.S. 342 (2013).

The Court in *Chaidez* explained that "when all we do is apply a general standard to the kind of factual circumstances it was meant to address, we will rarely state a new rule for *Teague* purposes." For example, "garden-variety applications of the test in *Strickland*," such as *Rompilla* p. 163, and *Wiggins,* p. 162, the Court stated, "do not produce new rules." But *Padilla v. Kentucky*, p. 1201, did not apply *Strickland*'s general standard to yet another factual situation, the Court concluded in *Chaidez. Padilla* decided the separate threshold question whether *Strickland* applied at all. "Before *Padilla*, we had declined to decide whether the Sixth Amendment had any relevance to a lawyer's advice about matters not part of a criminal proceeding," said the Court. *Padilla* announced a new rule because it held that advice about deportation was not "categorically removed" from the scope of the Sixth Amendment right to counsel just because it involved only a "collateral consequence" of a conviction.

c. ***Does an exception apply?*** Finally, even if the rule of criminal procedure that the petitioner raises was not compelled by precedent at the time, a habeas court must ask whether that new rule nonetheless falls within one of two narrow exceptions that would require retroactive application. The *Teague* exceptions are quite narrow.

The first exception requires retroactive application of "substantive" rulings. Substantive rulings "affect the reach of the underlying statute rather than the judicial procedures by which the statute is applied." They include decisions that "decriminalize a class of conduct" or that narrow the scope of a criminal statute, see *Bousley v. United States*, Note 4, p. 1442; *Welch v. United States,* 136 S.Ct. 1257 (2016) (applying retroactively earlier ruling that held a federal sentencing provision was void for vagueness), as well as decisions that prohibit "a certain category of punishment for a class of defendants because of their status or offense," such as the Court's rulings invalidating the mandatory application of life-without-parole sentences to juveniles. *Montgomery v. Louisiana,* 136 S.Ct. 718 (2016). Indeed, *Montgomery* held, "the Constitution requires state collateral review courts to give retroactive effect" to such decisions.

The second exception is for new "watershed rules of criminal procedure" necessary to the fundamental fairness of the criminal proceeding. The Court explained in *Sawyer v. Smith*, 497 U.S. 227 (1990), that any rule that qualifies under this exception must "not only improve accuracy, but also 'alter our understanding of the *bedrock procedural elements'* essential to the fairness of a proceeding." In *Beard v. Banks*, Note 2, above, the Court stated: "In providing guidance as to what might fall within this exception, we have repeatedly referred to the rule of *Gideon v. Wainwright* [p. 68] and only to this rule. * * * *Gideon*, it is fair to say, 'alter [ed] our understanding of the *bedrock procedural elements* essential to the fairness of a proceeding.' " And in *Tyler v. Cain*, 533 U.S. 656 (2001), the Court reasoned that it is not enough to find that a rule is "structural error" and not subject to harmless-error analysis, "classifying an error as structural does not necessarily alter our understanding of [the] bedrock procedural elements" essential to the fairness of the proceeding. "On the contrary, the second *Teague* exception is reserved only for truly 'watershed' rules" and "[a]s we have recognized, it is unlikely that any of these watershed rules ha[s] yet to emerge."

2. Teague *in practice.* The effects of the non-retroactivity principle appear the most stark in capital cases, where limits on retroactive application mean that execution may turn on what Justice Breyer has termed "an accident of timing." Consider *Schriro v. Summerlin*, 542 U.S. 348 (2004), a 5–4 decision in which the Court declined to characterize as falling within either exception the rule of *Ring v. Arizona*, Note 1, p. 1391, announced by the Court on direct appeal, which entitled a defendant to a jury determination of aggravating factors the government was required to establish before a death sentence may be imposed. Summerlin had been sentenced to death, after a judge found two facts that made him death-eligible—that he had been convicted before for a felony involving the use or threatened use of violence, and that he committed the offense in an especially heinous, cruel, or depraved manner. Summerlin sought habeas relief from his death sentence, arguing that his sentence suffered from the same constitutional infirmity as Ring's, and that he deserved the same relief that Ring received. The Court majority rejected arguments that a jury finding beyond a reasonable doubt was central to an accurate determination that death is a legally appropriate punishment. Instead, the Court noted that "for every argument why juries are more accurate factfinders, there is another why they are less accurate," and "when so many presumably reasonable minds continue to disagree over whether juries are better factfinders *at all*, we cannot confidently say that judicial factfinding *seriously* diminishes accuracy." Indeed, the Court reasoned, in its pre-*Teague* decision refusing retroactive application of *Duncan v. Louisiana*, p. 1230, which first applied the Sixth Amendment's jury trial right to the states, the Court had stopped short of asserting " 'that every criminal trial—or any particular trial—held before a judge alone is unfair or that a defendant may never be as fairly treated by a judge as he would be by a jury.' " Nor was the majority persuaded that the exception should apply because the reliance interest on the part of state courts was not strong, the rule implicated only about 110 prisoners on death row, and retroactive application of the rule would pose a limited burden on the administration of justice. These arguments, the *Summerlin* Court reasoned, were simply "irrelevant under *Teague*." Should they be? Interestingly, as of 2007, *Teague* was raised by states almost exclusively in capital habeas cases, where approximately one in four included at least one *Teague*-barred claim. Less than 1% of the non-capital cases included a *Teague* ruling. King, et al., 2007 Habeas Study.

3. ***Application of new rules of constitutional criminal procedure in state postconviction proceedings.*** As noted in Note 1.c. above, the Court in *Montgomery v. Louisiana*, 136 S.Ct. 718 (2016), stated that "the Constitution requires state collateral review courts to give retroactive effect" to decisions that fall within the first *Teague* exception. And although new rules that are *not* subject to retroactive application under the *Teague* doctrine need not be applied by state courts in their own post-conviction proceedings, state courts are free to apply that new rule if they choose. *Danforth v. Minnesota*, 552 U.S. 264 (2008) (reasoning *Teague* construed the scope of the federal habeas statute and "cannot be read as imposing a binding obligation on state courts"). Rejecting concerns about resulting nonuniformity if some states were allowed to apply a federal constitutional rule differently than other states, the Court argued, "Nonuniformity is, in fact, an unavoidable reality in a federalist system," and a state should be "free to give its citizens the benefit of our rule in any fashion that does not offend federal law."

§ 6. STANDARDS FOR REVIEWING STATE COURT INTERPRETATIONS AND APPLICATIONS OF FEDERAL LAW

This section examines the current standard for reviewing the state court's decision regarding the merits of a petitioner's constitutional claim, as well as the application of harmless error on habeas review, and the review of factual findings made by state courts.

The Court's decisions on the defense of procedural default and retroactivity, detailed above, together with the AEDPA statute, have narrowed the scope of habeas relief for state prisoners. A study of petitions filed in district courts after AEDPA found the rate at which habeas relief is granted to state prisoners has dropped. Far fewer capital defendants are receiving relief, down from about 40% before AEDPA. Most capital case petitions granted provide relief from the death sentence and not the conviction. As for non-capital habeas cases, only about 1 in 100 terminated in district court in the early 1990s received some sort of relief; today relief is even *less* likely, with roughly half of claims denied on the merits and the other dismissed or rejected for other reasons. See Note 7, p. 1428. Some federal judges may process non-capital habeas cases for years without ever granting a petition. The study also found that although a greater percentage of cases are dismissed or denied than before AEDPA, both the number of claims per petition and the time to resolve cases with multiple claims has increased. In light of these findings, consider the words of Justice Jackson, written well *before* Congress and the Court had put in place the many limits on habeas relief reviewed in the Sections above: "It must prejudice the occasional meritorious application to be buried in a flood of worthless ones. He who must search a haystack for a needle is likely to end up with the attitude that the needle is not worth the search." *Brown v. Allen*, 344 U.S. 443, 537 (1953) (Jackson, J., concurring in result).

A. CONTRARY DECISIONS AND UNREASONABLE APPLICATIONS

Section 2254(d) now provides: "An application for a writ of habeas corpus on behalf of a person in custody pursuant to the judgment of a State court shall not be granted with respect to any claim that was adjudicated on the merits in State court proceedings unless the adjudication of the claim—(1) resulted in a decision that was *contrary to, or involved an unreasonable application of, clearly established Federal law, as determined by the Supreme Court of the United States*; or (2) resulted in a decision that was based on an *unreasonable determination of the facts* in light of the evidence presented in the State court proceeding." (Emphasis added.)

As the Court explained in *Horn v. Banks*, 536 U.S. 266 (2002), this standard under § 2254(d) is "distinct" from the *Teague* inquiry. "[I]n addition to performing any analysis required by the AEDPA, a federal court considering a habeas petition must conduct a threshold *Teague* analysis when the issue is properly raised by the state." The analysis required by § 2254(d) is addressed in the decision below.

HARRINGTON V. RICHTER

562 U.S. 86, 131 S.Ct. 770, 178 L.Ed.2d 624 (2011).

[The details of Richter's ineffective assistance of counsel claim and the Court's discussion of that claim appear in Chapter 5, at p. 151. Briefly, Richter was charged with murder and other crimes after allegedly shooting Johnson, who became the state's main witness, and Klein, who did not survive. Johnson claimed he awoke to find defendant Richter and Branscombe in his bedroom, Branscombe shot him, then Johnson heard more gunfire in the living room and the sound of his assailants leaving. He got up, found Klein bleeding on the living room couch, and called 911. Items missing from Johnson's bedroom and ammunition (later tied to a bullet that struck Klein by a ballistics expert) were all found at Richter's residence. At trial defense counsel offered explanations for the circumstantial evidence, portrayed Johnson as a paranoid, trigger-happy drug dealer and gun fanatic who had drawn a pistol on Branscombe and Richter the last time he had seen them. She also pointed out inconsistencies in Johnson's story, such as his failure when calling 911 to identify Richter and Branscombe among the intruders. The defense theory, based on Richter's own testimony and that of other defense witnesses, was that Branscombe had fired on Johnson in self-defense and that Klein had been killed not on the living room couch but in the crossfire in the bedroom doorway. The prosecution called a blood pattern expert and a serologist to rebut the defense theory. Richter was convicted and sentenced to life without parole.

After his conviction was affirmed on appeal, Richter sought collateral relief in state court, asserting, among other grounds for relief, the ineffective assistance of trial counsel. He offered affidavits from experts that he claimed established the possibility that the blood in the doorway came from Klein, not Johnson, and argued his counsel should have presented such expert testimony at trial. The California Supreme Court denied Richter's petition in a one-sentence summary order. Richter then filed a petition for habeas corpus in federal court, reasserting the claims in his state petition. The court denied his petition, but the Ninth Circuit reversed, ordering that relief be granted because Richter's trial counsel had been constitutionally deficient.]

JUSTICE KENNEDY delivered the opinion of the Court.

The writ of habeas corpus stands as a safeguard against imprisonment of those held in violation of the law. Judges must be vigilant and independent in reviewing petitions for the writ, a commitment that entails substantial judicial resources. Those resources are diminished and misspent, however, and confidence in the writ and the law it vindicates undermined, if there is judicial disregard for the sound and established principles that inform its proper issuance. * * *

Under 28 U.S.C. § 2254(d), the availability of federal habeas relief is limited with respect to claims previously "adjudicated on the merits" in state-court proceedings. The first inquiry this case presents is whether that provision applies when state-court relief is denied without an accompanying statement of reasons. If it does, the question is whether the Court of Appeals adhered to the statute's terms, in this case as it relates to ineffective-assistance claims judged by the standard set forth in *Strickland*. * * *

II

The statutory authority of federal courts to issue habeas corpus relief for persons in state custody is provided by 28 U.S.C. § 2254, as amended by the Antiterrorism and Effective Death Penalty Act of 1996 (AEDPA). The text of § 2254(d) states:

> "An application for a writ of habeas corpus on behalf of a person in custody pursuant to the judgment of a State court shall not be granted with respect to any claim that was adjudicated on the merits in State court proceedings unless the adjudication of the claim—"
>
> "(1) resulted in a decision that was contrary to, or involved an unreasonable application of, clearly established Federal law, as determined by the Supreme Court of the United States"; or
>
> "(2) resulted in a decision that was based on an unreasonable determination of the facts in light of the evidence presented in the State court proceeding."

As an initial matter, it is necessary to decide whether § 2254(d) applies when a state court's order is unaccompanied by an opinion explaining the reasons relief has been denied.

By its terms § 2254(d) bars relitigation of any claim "adjudicated on the merits" in state court, subject only to the exceptions in §§ 2254(d)(1) and (d)(2). There is no text in the statute requiring a statement of reasons. The statute refers only to a "decision," which resulted from an "adjudication." As every Court of Appeals to consider the issue has recognized, determining whether a state court's decision resulted from an unreasonable legal or factual conclusion does not require that there be an opinion from the state court explaining the state court's reasoning. And as this Court has observed, a state court need not cite or even be aware of our cases under § 2254(d). Early v. Packer, 537 U.S. 3 (2002) (per curiam). Where a state court's decision is unaccompanied by an explanation, the habeas petitioner's burden still must be met by showing there was no reasonable basis for the state court to deny relief. * * *

There is no merit to the assertion that compliance with § 2254(d) should be excused when state courts issue summary rulings because applying § 2254(d) in those cases will encourage state courts to withhold explanations for their decisions. Opinion-writing practices in state courts are influenced by considerations other than avoiding scrutiny by collateral attack in federal court. At the same time, requiring a statement of reasons could undercut state practices designed to preserve the integrity of the case-law tradition. The issuance of summary dispositions in many collateral attack cases can enable a state judiciary to concentrate its resources on the cases where opinions are most needed. See Brief for California Attorneys for Criminal Justice et al. as Amici Curiae 8 (noting that the California Supreme Court disposes of close to 10,000 cases a year, including more than 3,400 original habeas corpus petitions). * * * Richter has failed to show that the California Supreme Court's decision did not involve a determination of the merits of his claim. Section 2254(d) applies to his petition.

III

Federal habeas relief may not be granted for claims subject to § 2254(d) unless it is shown that the earlier state court's decision "was contrary to" federal law then clearly established in the holdings of this Court, § 2254(d)(1); Williams v. Taylor, 529 U.S. 362 (2000); or that it "involved an unreasonable application of" such law, § 2254(d)(1); or that it "was based on an unreasonable determination of the facts" in light of the record before the state court, § 2254(d)(2).

* * * The pivotal question is whether the state court's application of the *Strickland* standard was unreasonable. This is different from asking whether defense counsel's performance fell below *Strickland*'s standard. Were that the inquiry, the analysis would be no different than if, for example, this Court were adjudicating a *Strickland* claim on direct review of a criminal conviction

in a United States district court. Under AEDPA, though, it is a necessary premise that the two questions are different. For purposes of § 2254(d)(1), "an unreasonable application of federal law is different from an incorrect application of federal law." * * *. A state court must be granted a deference and latitude that are not in operation when the case involves review under the *Strickland* standard itself.

A state court's determination that a claim lacks merit precludes federal habeas relief so long as "fairminded jurists could disagree" on the correctness of the state court's decision. Yarborough v. Alvarado, 541 U.S. 652, 664 (2004). And as this Court has explained, "[E]valuating whether a rule application was unreasonable requires considering the rule's specificity. The more general the rule, the more leeway courts have in reaching outcomes in case-by-case determinations." Ibid. "[I]t is not an unreasonable application of clearly established Federal law for a state court to decline to apply a specific legal rule that has not been squarely established by this Court." Knowles v. Mirzayance, 556 U.S. 111 (2009).

Here it is not apparent how the Court of Appeals' analysis would have been any different without AEDPA. * * * Under § 2254(d), a habeas court must determine what arguments or theories supported or, as here, could have supported, the state court's decision; and then it must ask whether it is possible fairminded jurists could disagree that those arguments or theories are inconsistent with the holding in a prior decision of this Court.

* * * Because the Court of Appeals had little doubt that Richter's *Strickland* claim had merit, the Court of Appeals concluded the state court must have been unreasonable in rejecting it. This analysis overlooks arguments that would otherwise justify the state court's result and ignores further limitations of § 2254(d), including its requirement that the state court's decision be evaluated according to the precedents of this Court. See Renico v. Lett, 559 U.S. 766 (2010) [p. 1341]. It bears repeating that even a strong case for relief does not mean the state court's contrary conclusion was unreasonable.

If this standard is difficult to meet, that is because it was meant to be. As amended by AEDPA, § 2254(d) stops short of imposing a complete bar on federal court relitigation of claims already rejected in state proceedings. Cf. Felker v. Turpin, 518 U.S. 651, 664 (1996) (discussing AEDPA's "modified res judicata rule" under § 2244). It preserves authority to issue the writ in cases where there is no possibility fairminded jurists could disagree that the state court's decision conflicts with this Court's precedents. It goes no farther. Section 2254(d) reflects the view that habeas corpus is a "guard against extreme malfunctions in the state criminal justice systems," not a substitute for ordinary error correction through appeal. *Jackson v. Virginia*, 443 U.S. 307, 332 (1979) (Stevens, J., concurring in judgment). As a condition for obtaining habeas corpus from a federal court, a state prisoner must show that the state court's ruling on the claim being presented in federal court was so lacking in justification that there was an error well understood and comprehended in existing law beyond any possibility for fairminded disagreement.

The reasons for this approach are familiar. "Federal habeas review of state convictions frustrates both the States' sovereign power to punish offenders and their good-faith attempts to honor constitutional rights." It "disturbs the State's significant interest in repose for concluded litigation, denies society the right to punish some admitted offenders, and intrudes on state sovereignty to a degree matched by few exercises of federal judicial authority."

Section 2254(d) is part of the basic structure of federal habeas jurisdiction, designed to confirm that state courts are the principal forum for asserting constitutional challenges to state convictions. Under the exhaustion requirement, a habeas petitioner challenging a state conviction must first attempt to present his claim in state court. 28 U.S.C. § 2254(b). If the state court rejects the claim on procedural grounds, the claim is barred in federal court unless one of the exceptions to the doctrine of Wainwright v. Sykes, [p. 1434], applies. And if the state court denies the claim on the merits, the claim is barred in federal court unless one of the exceptions to § 2254(d) set out in §§ 2254(d)(1) and (2) applies. Section 2254(d) thus complements the exhaustion requirement and the doctrine of procedural bar to ensure that state proceedings are the central process, not just a preliminary step for a later federal habeas proceeding.

Here, however, the Court of Appeals gave § 2254(d) no operation or function in its reasoning. Its analysis illustrates a lack of deference to the state court's determination and an improper intervention in state criminal processes, contrary to the purpose and mandate of AEDPA and to the now well-settled meaning and function of habeas corpus in the federal system.

IV

[The Court here turned to whether the Court of Appeals erred in finding the state court's rejection of Richter's ineffective assistance claim was unreasonable. (This portion of the opinion appears in Chapter 5, at p. 151). Noting that the *Strickland* standard is difficult to meet, the Court explained, "Establishing that a state court's application of Strickland was unreasonable under § 2254(d) is all the more difficult. The standards created by Strickland and § 2254(d) are both "highly deferential," and when the two apply in tandem, review is "doubly" so. The Strickland standard is a general one, so the range of reasonable applications is substantial. * * * When § 2254(d) applies, the question is not whether counsel's actions were reasonable. The question is whether there is any reasonable argument that counsel satisfied Strickland's deferential standard." The Court concluded that it was "well within the bounds of a reasonable judicial determination for the state court to conclude that defense counsel could follow a strategy that did not require the use of experts regarding the pool in the doorway to Johnson's bedroom." Klein's location and the blood's source were considered by the court of appeals to be "of central concern," but, the Court noted, this wasn't necessarily "evident at the time of the trial." "Reliance on "the harsh light of hindsight" to cast doubt on a trial that took place now more than 15 years ago is precisely what *Strickland* and AEDPA seek to prevent." Moreover, concluded the Court, it was reasonable for the state court to conclude that Richter had failed to establish prejudice. "There was ample basis for the California Supreme Court to think any real possibility of Richter's being acquitted was eclipsed by the remaining evidence pointing to guilt."]

* * *

The California Supreme Court's decision on the merits of Richter's Strickland claim required more deference than it received. Richter was not entitled to the relief ordered by the Court of Appeals. The judgment is reversed, and the case is remanded for further proceedings consistent with this opinion.

[JUSTICE KAGAN took no part; JUSTICE GINSBURG'S concurring opinion is omitted].

NOTES AND QUESTIONS

1. ***When is a claim adjudicated on the merits by the state court?*** As *Richter* notes, the deferential standard under § 2254(d) applies only when the state court decided a claim on its merits. A state court decision *dismissing* an application for relief because of the failure to comply with procedural requirements is not a decision on the merits. *Richter* establishes that a *denial,* even the most summary statement of denial, is presumed to be a merits decision.

The Court in *Johnson v. Williams*, 568 U.S. 289 (2013), held that the presumption that a federal claim was adjudicated on the merits should apply not only when a state court denies an application for relief without addressing any of the defendant's claims, as in *Richter*, but also when the state court addresses some but not all of a defendant's claims. The Court then went on to emphasize "while the *Richter* presumption is a strong one that may be rebutted only in unusual circumstances, it is not irrebuttable." If the state court denies the defendant's claim under a state standard that is either "quite different" or "less protective" than the federal constitutional standard, or "a provision of the Federal Constitution or a federal precedent was simply mentioned in passing in a footnote or was buried in a string cite," the Court explained, "the presumption that the federal claim was adjudicated on the merits may be rebutted—either by the habeas petitioner (for the purpose of showing that the claim should be considered by the federal court de novo) or by the State (for the purpose of showing that the federal claim should be regarded as procedurally defaulted)." The Court noted two circumstances that would constitute adequate rebuttal. First, "when a defendant does so little to raise his claim that he fails to ' "fairly present" ' it in 'each appropriate state court,' and second, "[w]hen the evidence leads very clearly to the conclusion that a federal claim was inadvertently overlooked in state court * * *." After reviewing the state court's opinion and Williams' litigation strategy, the Court found that he had not rebutted the presumption, and concluded it was "exceedingly unlikely that the California Court of Appeal overlooked Williams' federal claim."

As for determining the *rationale* of a summary decision by a state court, "the federal court should 'look through' an unexplained decision to the last related state-court decision that does provide a relevant rationale," and "presume that the unexplained decision adopted the same reasoning," explained the Court in *Wilson v. Sellers*, 138 S.Ct. 1188 (2018). The state "may rebut the presumption by showing that the unexplained affirmance relied or most likely did rely on different grounds than the lower state court's decision." Examples of evidence supporting such a showing include, "alternative grounds for affirmance that were briefed or argued to the state supreme court or obvious in the record it reviewed," and "the unreasonableness of the lower court's decision itself."

2. *"Unreasonable" applications vs. incorrect applications.* In *Renico v. Lett*, 559 U.S. 766 (2010), Chief Justice Roberts stated for the Court: 'a federal habeas court may not issue the writ simply because that court concludes in its independent judgment that the relevant state-court decision applied clearly established federal law erroneously or incorrectly.' Rather, that application must be 'objectively unreasonable.' This distinction creates 'a substantially higher threshold' for obtaining relief than *de novo* review. AEDPA thus imposes a 'highly deferential standard for evaluating state-court rulings,' and 'demands that state-court decisions be given the benefit of the doubt.' " * * * [T]he Michigan Supreme Court's decision upholding the trial judge's exercise of discretion—while not necessarily correct—was not objectively unreasonable." He noted that the question of whether the trial judge's declaration of a mistrial was right or wrong "is a close one," but is not the question a federal court must answer under the habeas statute. "Not only are there a number of plausible ways to interpret the record of Lett's trial, but the standard applied by the Michigan Supreme Court—whether the judge exercised sound discretion—is a general one, to which there is no 'plainly correct or incorrect' answer in this case. *Yarborough v. Alvarado*, 541 U.S. 652, 664 (2004). * * * AEDPA prevents defendants—and federal courts—from using federal habeas corpus review as a vehicle to second-guess the reasonable decisions of state courts. Whether or not the Michigan Supreme Court's opinion reinstating Lett's conviction in this case was *correct*, it was clearly *not unreasonable*."

Because of this difference, care must be taken not to conflate decisions applying § 2254(d) with decisions defining the scope of the Constitution. A decision by the Court that a state court's ruling is not "contrary to" or "an unreasonable application" of clearly established Supreme Court precedent is decidedly not the same as a decision by the Court that the ruling is constitutional. Instead, it means only that the Supreme Court had not settled the constitutional issue one way or the other by the time the state court handed down its ruling. In practice, when a habeas ruling under the § 2254(d) standard precedes the Court's later de novo resolution of an unsettled issue, the reasoning of the habeas ruling may foretell that later holding.

3. ***Refusing to "extend" a holding is not unreasonable.*** The Court rejected a so-called "unreasonable-refusal-to-extend rule," in *White v. Woodall*, 572 U.S. 415 (2014). "Section 2254(d)(1)," the Court explained, "provides a remedy for instances in which a state court unreasonably applies this Court's precedent; it does not require state courts to extend that precedent or license federal courts to treat the failure to do so as error. Thus, 'if a habeas court must extend a rationale before it can apply to the facts at hand,' then by definition the rationale was not "clearly established at the time of the state-court decision.' * * * This is not to say that § 2254(d)(1) requires an ' "identical factual pattern before a legal rule must be applied." ' To the contrary, state courts must reasonably apply the rules 'squarely established' by this Court's holdings to the facts of each case. * * * The critical point is that relief is available under § 2254(d)(1)'s unreasonable-application clause if, and only if, it is so obvious that a clearly established rule applies to a given set of facts that there could be no 'fairminded disagreement' on the question."

4. ***Which federal law?*** Under § 2254(d), the state court decision is to be measured against "clearly established Federal law, as determined by the Supreme Court." The cut-off date for which Supreme Court rulings count when reviewing a state court decision rejecting a constitutional claim on its merits under § 2254(d) is more restrictive than the test for which federal law will be applied retroactively under *Teague* when reviewing a non-merits decision by a state court. For example, if the state court rejected the petitioner's claim not on its merits but on a procedural ground, and the petitioner was able to demonstrate cause and prejudice sufficient to defeat procedural default, then § 2254(d) would not apply, but *Teague* would. Under *Teague,* the federal court could evaluate the petitioner's constitutional claim under the Supreme Court precedent that had been announced before the petitioner's judgment was "final," even if that date was *later* than the date of the state court's decision. See Note 1.a., p. 1449. Contrast that to the review of a state court decision rejecting a petitioner's claim on the merits, when the federal court must comply with § 2254(d), in addition to *Teague*. Under § 2254(d), the Court held in *Greene v. Fisher,* 565 U.S. 34 (2012), the federal court must evaluate the state decision "against this Court's precedents as of 'the time the state court renders its decision.' "

5. **Teague *exceptions under Section 2254(d)?*** Section 2254(d) contains no exceptions like those recognized under *Teague*. In *Greene v. Fisher,* the Court stated, "Whether § 2254(d)(1) would bar a federal habeas petitioner from relying on a decision that came after the last state-court adjudication on the merits, but fell within one of the exceptions recognized in *Teague*, 489 U.S., at 311, is a question we need not address." How should this question be resolved? Years after *Greene*, the Court in *Montgomery v. Louisiana,* Note 1.c., p. 1449, stated, "the Constitution requires state collateral review courts to give retroactive effect" to decisions that fall within the first *Teague* exception. Does that mean that federal habeas courts must read in such an exception to § 2254(d)? Consider Carlos M. Vázquez & Stephen I. Vladeck, *The Constitutional Right to Collateral Post-Conviction Review*, 103 Va. L. Rev. 905, 928–29 (2017), arguing if AEDPA does not recognize this exception, and states are free to "close their courts to collateral claims" generally, then "[e]ither AEDPA is unconstitutional in this regard or the state courts are constitutionally required to afford collateral relief to persons incarcerated in contravention of new substantive rules of federal constitutional law."

6. ***Reviewing and expanding the factual record.***

a. ***Merits decisions reviewed under 2254(d).*** Federal courts reviewing under § 2254(d) a state court decision rejecting a constitutional claim on its merits are limited to considering only those facts that the state court had before it when it rejected the petitioner's constitutional claim, held the Court in *Cullen v. Pinholster*, 563 U.S. 170 (2011). In state court, the petitioner Pinholster had alleged he was denied the effective assistance of counsel when his attorney failed to call an expert witness. When the state court denied the claim, he raised the same claim in federal habeas, but added allegations about additional failings of his attorney. The district court granted an evidentiary hearing, at which additional experts for both the petitioner and the state testified, then granted the writ. The Court of Appeals affirmed, but the Supreme Court reversed. It held that "[i]f a claim has been adjudicated on the merits by a state court, a federal habeas petition[er] must overcome the limitation of § 2254(d)(1) on the record that was before that state court." Section 2254 was intended "to channel prisoners' claims first to the state courts" and "[i]t would be contrary to that purpose to allow a petitioner to overcome an adverse state-court decision with new evidence introduced in a federal habeas court and reviewed by that court in the first instance effectively de novo." The majority found odd "the notion that a state court can be deemed to have unreasonably applied federal law to evidence it did not even know existed."

A habeas petitioner may also contest under § 2254(d)(2) a state court's finding of facts. For example, in *Brumfield v. Cain,* 135 S.Ct. 2269 (2015), the state court found that "Brumfield's IQ score was inconsistent with a diagnosis of intellectual disability," that he had presented "no evidence of adaptive impairment," and did not meet his burden of showing he deserved relief under *Atkins v. Virginia,* 536 U.S. 304 (2002), barring the death penalty for defendants with intellectual disability. The Court noted that a federal court reviewing a state court's factual findings in habeas may not characterize state-court factual determinations as unreasonable "merely because [it] would have reached a different conclusion in the first instance." But the state court record in this case "contained sufficient evidence to raise a question as to whether Brumfield met [the] criteria" for intellectual disability," such that the conclusion that his reported IQ score of 75 "somehow demonstrated that he could not possess subaverage intelligence * * * reflected an unreasonable determination of the facts."

b. Non-merits decisions. If a habeas court is reviewing a claim that the state courts had not decided on the merits, Section 2254(d) does not apply, and the ability of a petitioner to present new evidence at an evidentiary hearing or by other means may turn on the petitioner's earlier efforts to develop the facts in state court. See Note 5, p. 1443. Also, district courts may grant hearings to develop facts when needed to resolve a procedural question, such as whether there is cause and prejudice or a sufficient showing actual innocence to excuse a defaulted claim, or whether to toll the statute of limitations.

7. *When is a decision "contrary to" clearly established Supreme Court precedent?* Section 2254(d) also authorizes habeas relief for claims rejected on the merits in state court if the state court decision is "contrary to" clearly established Supreme Court precedent. In *Williams v. Taylor*, 529 U.S. 362 (2000), Justice O'Connor explained that to fall within the "contrary to" clause, "the state court's decision must be substantially different from the relevant precedent of this Court." "A state-court decision will certainly be contrary to our clearly established precedent if the state court applies a rule that contradicts the governing law set forth in our cases. Take, for example, our decision in *Strickland*. . . . If a state court were to reject a prisoner's claim of ineffective assistance of counsel on the grounds that the prisoner had not established by a preponderance of the evidence that the result of his criminal proceeding would have been different, that decision would be 'diametrically different,' 'opposite in character or nature,' and 'mutually opposed' to our clearly established precedent because we held in *Strickland* that the prisoner need only demonstrate a 'reasonable probability that . . . the result of the proceeding would have been different.' A state-court decision will also be contrary to this Court's clearly established precedent if the state court confronts a set of facts that are materially indistinguishable from a decision of this Court and nevertheless arrives at a result different from our precedent. Accordingly, in either of these two scenarios, a federal court will be unconstrained by § 2254(d)(1) because the state-court decision falls within that provision's 'contrary to' clause.

"On the other hand, a run-of-the-mill state-court decision applying the correct legal rule from our cases to the facts of a prisoner's case would not fit comfortably within § 2254(d)(1)'s 'contrary to' clause. Assume, for example, that a state-court decision on a prisoner's ineffective-assistance claim correctly identifies *Strickland* as the controlling legal authority and, applying that framework, rejects the prisoner's claim. Quite clearly, the state-court decision would be in accord with our decision in *Strickland* as to the legal prerequisites for establishing an ineffective-assistance claim, even assuming the federal court considering the prisoner's habeas application might reach a different result applying the *Strickland* framework itself. It is difficult, however, to describe such a run-of-the-mill state-court decision as 'diametrically different' from, 'opposite in character or nature' from, or 'mutually opposed' to *Strickland,* our clearly established precedent. Although the state-court decision may be contrary to the federal court's conception of how *Strickland* ought to be applied in that particular case, the decision is not 'mutually opposed' to *Strickland* itself."

The latest application of this standard came in *Lafler v. Cooper* [also discussed at p. 139 and 1192]. The state court decision rejecting Cooper's ineffective assistance of counsel claim read:

> "To establish ineffective assistance, the defendant must demonstrate that his counsel's performance fell below an objective standard of reasonableness and that counsel's representation so prejudiced the defendant that he was deprived of a fair trial. With respect to the prejudice aspect of the test, the defendant must demonstrate a reasonable probability that, but for counsel's errors, the result of the proceedings would have been different, and that the attendant proceedings were fundamentally unfair and unreliable.
>
> "Defendant challenges the trial court's finding after a . . . hearing that defense counsel provided effective assistance to defendant during the plea bargaining process. He contends that defense counsel failed to convey the benefits of the plea offer to him and ignored his desire to plead guilty, and that these failures led him to reject a plea offer that he now wishes to accept. However, the record shows that defendant knowingly and intelligently rejected two plea offers and chose to go to trial. The record fails to support defendant's contentions that defense counsel's representation was ineffective because he rejected a defense based on [a] claim of self-defense and because he did not obtain a more favorable plea bargain for defendant."

Writing for the five-justice majority in *Lafler v. Cooper*, Justice Kennedy did not consider whether this state court decision was an unreasonable application of clearly established federal law, but instead found that it was "contrary to" *Strickland*. He explained: "The Michigan Court of Appeals identified respondent's [ineffective assistance] claim but failed to apply *Strickland* to assess it. Rather than applying *Strickland*, the state court simply found that respondent's rejection of the plea was knowing and voluntary. . . . An inquiry into whether the rejection of a plea is knowing and voluntary, however, is not the correct means by which to address a claim of ineffective assistance of counsel. . . . After stating the incorrect standard, moreover, the state court then made an irrelevant observation about counsel's performance at trial and mischaracterized respondent's claim as a complaint that his attorney did not obtain a more favorable plea bargain. By failing to apply Strickland to assess the claim respondent raised, the state court's adjudication was contrary to clearly established federal law. And in that circumstance the federal courts in this habeas action can determine the principles necessary to grant relief."

The four dissenting justices in *Lafler v. Cooper* thought that the state court had indeed applied the *Strickland* test, and that relief must be denied because the state court's application was not unreasonable. The dissenters noted that the Supreme Court had never before held that a person could establish "prejudice" if plea negotiations ultimately resulted in a fair trial: "The first paragraph [of the state court's analysis], far from ignoring *Strickland*, recites its standard with a good deal more accuracy than the Court's opinion. The second paragraph, which is presumably an application of the standard recited in the first, says that 'defendant knowingly and intelligently rejected two plea offers and chose to go to trial.' This can be regarded as a denial that there was anything 'fundamentally unfair' about Cooper's conviction and sentence, so that no *Strickland* prejudice had been shown. On the other hand, the entire second paragraph can be regarded as a contention that Cooper's claims of inadequate representation were unsupported by the record. The state court's analysis was admittedly not a model of clarity, but federal habeas corpus is a 'guard against extreme malfunctions in the state criminal justice systems,' not a license to penalize a state court for its opinion-writing technique. * * * Since it is ambiguous whether the state court's holding was based on a lack of prejudice or rather the court's factual determination that there had been no deficient performance, to provide relief under AEDPA this Court must conclude that both holdings would have been unreasonable applications of clearly established law. The first is impossible of doing, since this Court has never held that a defendant in Cooper's position can establish Strickland prejudice. The Sixth Circuit thus violated AEDPA in granting habeas relief, and the Court now does the same."

Consider one author's reaction to the Court's decision: "*Lafler* appears to have loosened the 'contrary to' standard a notch for future cases, encouraging petitioners to argue that the state court never applied the correct federal precedent (even when that precedent is cited or described), instead of arguing than that the court's application of federal law was unreasonable. The combination of *Lafler* and *Richter* also suggests that when reviewing state court criminal opinions, 'less is more'—a summary state denial will not be disturbed unless all possible (hypothetical) applications would have been unreasonable, while a merits decision accompanied by an ambiguously phrased rationale that could be construed as failing to apply the correct rule is vulnerable to attack." Nancy J. King, *Lafler v. Cooper* and AEDPA, 122 Yale L.J. Online 35 (2012).

8. ***State court as the "principle forum" for constitutional challenges; the "parity" debate.*** The Court in *Burt v. Titlow*, 571 U.S. 12 (2013), unanimously reiterated: "AEDPA recognizes a foundational principle of our federal system: State courts are adequate forums for the vindication of federal rights. * * * 'state courts have the solemn responsibility equally with the federal courts to safeguard constitutional rights,' and this Court has refused to sanction any decision that would 'reflec[t] negatively upon [a] state court's ability to do so.' * * * Especially where a case involves such a common claim as ineffective assistance of counsel under *Strickland*—a claim state courts have now adjudicated in countless criminal cases for nearly 30 years—'there is no intrinsic reason why the fact that a man is a federal judge should make him more competent, or conscientious, or learned . . . than his neighbor in the state courthouse.'" [quoting *Stone v. Powell*, p. 1430].

A different view of state courts was expressed by Justice Brennan dissenting in *Stone v. Powell*: "State judges popularly elected may have difficulty resisting popular pressures not experienced by federal judges given lifetime tenure designed to immunize them from such influences," he wrote. Commentators continue to echo such concerns: Carol S. Steiker & Jordan M. Steiker, *Part II: Report to the ALI Concerning Capital Punishment*, 89 Tex. L. Rev. 367, 392 (2010): "Almost 90% of state judges face some kind of popular election. . . . Despite the fact that there is good reason to have confidence in the personal integrity of the individual men and women who comprise the elected judiciary, several statistical studies suggest that, in the aggregate, judicial behavior in criminal cases generally and capital cases in particular appears to be influenced by election cycles." See also Hon. Lynn Adelman & Jon Deitrich, *Why Habeas Review of State Court Convictions is More Important than Ever*, 24 Fed. Sent. R. 292, 294 (2012) ("habeas review by life-tenured federal judges remains the only viable means of protecting the constitutional rights of the criminally accused in states with an elected judiciary"); Burt Neuborne, *The Myth of Parity*, 90 Harv.L.Rev. 1105 (1977). Should federal habeas law vary depending upon whether a state's judiciary is appointed or elected?

B. HARMLESS ERROR ON COLLATERAL REVIEW

Constitutional claims are subject to harmless error analysis on collateral review, just as on direct appeal, but the standard is different. In *Brecht v. Abrahamson*, 507 U.S. 619 (1993), the Court held that the harmless error standard applicable on habeas to "trial-type" constitutional errors should be the *Kotteakos* standard, Note 2, p. 1416. That standard "is better tailored to the nature and purpose of collateral review than the *Chapman* standard, and application of a less onerous harmless-error standard on habeas promotes the considerations underlying our habeas jurisprudence." As support, the Court noted the "State's interest in the finality of convictions," concerns of "comity and federalism" and the recognition that the " 'liberal allowance of the writ * * * degrades the prominence of the trial itself,' and at the same time encourages habeas petitioners to relitigate their claims on collateral review." The Court rejected petitioner's argument that "application of the *Chapman* harmless-error standard on collateral review is necessary to deter state courts from relaxing their own guard in reviewing constitutional error and to discourage prosecutors from committing error in the first place. Absent affirmative evidence that state-court judges are ignoring their oath, we discount petitioner's argument that courts will respond to our ruling by violating their Article VI duty to uphold the Constitution. Federalism, comity, and the constitutional obligation of state and federal courts all counsel against any presumption that a decision of this Court will 'deter' lower federal or state courts from fully performing their sworn duty. * * * In any event, we think the costs of applying the *Chapman* standard on federal habeas outweigh the additional deterrent effect, if any, which would be derived from its application on collateral review."

In *Fry v. Pliler*, 551 U.S. 112 (2007), the Court held that *Brecht* is the appropriate standard for habeas review of error whether or not the state appellate court recognized the error or reviewed it for harmlessness under *Chapman*. Each of the primary reasons for adopting the less onerous standard in *Brecht*—strengthening finality, respecting state sovereignty over criminal matters, preserving the historic limitation of habeas to those "grievously wronged," and avoiding significant societal costs—applies with equal force whether or not the state court first considered the harmless error question, concluded the Court.

INDEX

References are to Pages

SEVERANCE

SPEEDY TRIAL AND SPEEDY OTHER DISPOSITIONS

STATE CONSTITUTIONS